W9-BAI-590

Date: 3/27/12

959.7043 HER
Hershberg, James G.
Marigold : the lost chance for
peace in Vietnam /

Marigold

THE LOST CHANCE FOR
PEACE IN VIETNAM

COLD WAR
INTERNATIONAL HISTORY
PROJECT SERIES

James G. Hershberg
series editor

(*continued on p. 891*)

Marigold

THE LOST CHANCE FOR
PEACE IN VIETNAM

JAMES G. HERSHBERG

Woodrow Wilson Center Press
Washington, D.C.

Stanford University Press
Stanford, California

EDITORIAL OFFICES
Woodrow Wilson Center Press
One Woodrow Wilson Plaza
1300 Pennsylvania Avenue, N.W.
Washington, DC 20004-3027
Telephone: 202-691-4029
www.wilsoncenter.org

ORDER FROM
Stanford University Press
Chicago Distribution Center
11030 South Langley Avenue
Chicago, Il 60628
Telephone: 1-800-621-2736

Library of Congress Cataloging-in-Publication Data

Hershberg, James G. (James Gordon), 1960–
Mairgold : the lost chance for peace in Vietnam / James G. Hershberg.
    p. cm. — (Cold War International History Project series)
  Includes bibliographical references and index.
  ISBN 978-0-8047-7884-8
  1. Vietnam War, 1961–1975—Peace. 2. Vietnam War, 1961–1975—Diplomatic
history. 3. United States—Foreign relations—1963–1969. I. Title. II. Series: Cold
War International History Project series.
  DS559.7.H48   2011
  959.704'31—dc23   2011034990

Woodrow Wilson International Center for Scholars

The Woodrow Wilson International Center for Scholars is the national, living U.S. memorial honoring President Woodrow Wilson. In providing an essential link between the worlds of ideas and public policy, the Center addresses current and emerging challenges confronting the United States and the world. The Center promotes policy-relevant research and dialogue to increase understanding and enhance the capabilities and knowledge of leaders, citizens, and institutions worldwide. Created by an act of Congress in 1968, the Center is a nonpartisan institution headquartered in Washington, D.C., and supported by both public and private funds.

Conclusions or opinions expressed in Center publications and programs are those of the authors and speakers and do not necessarily reflect the views of the Center staff, fellows, trustees, advisory groups, or any individuals or organizations that provide financial support to the Center.

The Center is the publisher of *The Wilson Quarterly* and home of Woodrow Wilson Center Press and *dialogue* television and radio. For more information about the Center's activities and publications, please visit us on the Web at www .wilsoncenter.org.

Jane Harman, Director, President, and CEO

The Cold War International History Project

The Cold War International History Project was established by the Woodrow Wilson International Center for Scholars in 1991. The project supports the full and prompt release of historical materials by governments on all sides of the Cold War and seeks to disseminate new information and perspectives on Cold War history emerging from previously inaccessible sources on "the other side"—the former Communist world—through publications, fellowships, and scholarly meetings and conferences. The project publishes the *Cold War International History Project Bulletin* and a working paper series and maintains a Web site at www.cwihp.org.

At the Woodrow Wilson Center, the project is part of the History and Public Policy Program, directed by Christian F. Ostermann. Previous directors include David Wolff (1997–98) and James G. Hershberg (1991–97). The project is overseen by an advisory committee chaired by William Taubman, Amherst College, and includes Michael Beschloss; James H. Billington, Librarian of Congress; Warren I. Cohen, University of Maryland at Baltimore; John Lewis Gaddis, Yale University; James G. Hershberg, George Washington University; Samuel F. Wells Jr., Woodrow Wilson Center; and Sharon Wolchik, George Washington University.

The Cold War International History Project has been supported by the Korea Foundation, Seoul; the Leon Levy Foundation, New York; the Henry Luce Foundation, New York; the John D. and Catherine T. MacArthur Foundation, Chicago; and the Smith Richardson Foundation, Westport, Conn.

For Annie, Gabriel, and Vera Hershberg
and for my parents, Arline and David Hershberg

Contents

Maps and Photographs

Introduction
Who Murdered "Marigold"?

Warsaw, December 6, 1966: a date that should live in diplomatic infamy. Five thousand miles away, the Vietnam War is raging, with the dead piling up and the escalating violence poisoning international affairs and American politics. Early that morning, the Pentagon informs President Lyndon B. Johnson at his Texas ranch that 6,250 U.S. military personnel have been killed in Vietnam (and Laos) since January 1961, when his predecessor, John F. Kennedy, took office[1]—but few imagine that 52,000 more Americans are still to die, along with millions of Vietnamese on both sides of the 17th Parallel. Outwardly, the bloodshed shows no sign of subsiding.

Yet, far from Southeast Asia's jungles and rice paddies, in this gray, frigid Central European city, a secret breakthrough for peace seems imminent. The United States and North Vietnam lack diplomatic relations and, relying on combat to resolve their clashing visions, appear stuck in a Catch-22 that precludes direct negotiations: Hanoi insists that it will not talk until Washington stops the bombing it began in early 1965, and Washington maintains just as stubbornly that it will not halt the raids until assured that Hanoi will pay a reasonable price, such as curbing its support for the Communist insurgency fighting to topple the U.S.-backed regime in Saigon.

But on that cloudy Tuesday, after months of furtive machinations by Polish and Italian intermediaries (with the Soviets lurking in the shadows), Washington and Hanoi have agreed that their ambassadors to Poland will meet to confirm a ten-point outline of a settlement, or at least a basis for direct talks. John A. Gronouski and Do Phat Quang are but a short stroll apart on the western banks of the Vistula River, the American huddling with Poland's foreign minister at his office, the North Vietnamese waiting at his embassy with a special emissary who has flown all the way from Hanoi to deliver guidance for the unprecedented encounter—a document so sensitive that his wife sewed it into his vest, and a senior North Vietnamese official ordered him to destroy it before dying if his plane crashed.

Yet the rendezvous between enemy diplomats does not occur that day . . . or the next . . . or the next, until, a week later, the whole business collapsed in a welter of mutual recriminations, hidden at first, but soon to explode into a scandal that would attract global headlines and widen President Johnson's "credibility gap"—and then vanish into history, unresolved, concealed by the thick fogs of war, diplomacy, and Cold War secrecy. To LBJ, it was all shadows and mirrors, a "dry creek," because the "simple truth" was that Hanoi was not ready to talk; his surrogates, from Dean Rusk to Walt Rostow to William Bundy to Averell Harriman to Robert McNamara to Henry Cabot Lodge, loyally parroted the party line (despite private doubts in some cases) that it was all a phony, a Polish "scam" or "sham" or "fraud" or "shell-game"—or even a KGB disinformation plot.

But to the junior Polish diplomat behind the "ten points," Janusz Lewandowski—the lone Communist ambassador in anticommunist Saigon—it was a squandered chance to stop the carnage, save uncounted lives, and dramatically alter history. At the time, the man at the center of what became known as the "Lewandowski Affair" remained shrouded in mystery, rebuffing reporters. For this book, four decades later, he has told his story for the first time. Sitting in a smoke-filled café in Warsaw, he recalled being pleased when Washington and Hanoi met in Paris and concluded the 1973 accords ending the war (or at least direct U.S. military involvement), "but I thought, my God, we could have done it better and seven years ago, you know, better because the solution also would be better for the United States than this havoc which happened."

Do you really believe the war could have been ended six or seven years earlier? I asked.

"Yes," he replied. "That was my feeling. And it still is."

Was Lewandowski right? Could America have escaped its disastrous involvement in Vietnam years earlier, and at far less cost, than it actually did? Was a real chance for peace tragically squandered? Or was LBJ right, that the "simple truth" was that no opportunity was missed? Was its failure predestined; accidental; or "death by murder," as a key participant (an American ally, no less) privately fumed, blaming Washington for its ill-timed bombing of Hanoi? What really happened? What went wrong?

Seeking answers to these haunting questions, this book explores one of the last great mysteries of the war that Henry Kissinger has retrospectively termed "the defining experience of the second half of the twentieth century" and "the black hole of American historical memory"[2]—the clandestine peace initiative, bearing the U.S. code name "Marigold," that in late 1966 sought to end the fighting, or at least open direct talks, between Washington and Hanoi. For some tantalizing days that December, this initiative seemed on the verge of success, but ultimately it failed and the war dragged on and even grew bloodier. The Marigold episode—which became an international scandal when it seeped into public view in early 1967, and was the focus of a brief yet intense "war of leaks"—sank into history as an unresolved controversy. Antiwar critics claimed that LBJ had botched (or, worse, deliberately sabotaged) a breakthrough for peace by bombing Hanoi on the eve of a planned historic secret encounter between American and North Vietnamese representatives in Warsaw. Conversely, the president and his top aides angrily insisted that there was no "missed opportunity," that Poland (the key mediator) likely never had the authority to arrange direct talks, and that Hanoi was not ready to negotiate. The conventional wisdom echoes this view, presuming that the combatants were then far too dug in and committed to chasing a military victory or advantage to enter into serious negotiations.

This book challenges this conventional wisdom. It establishes that Warsaw *was,* in fact, authorized by Hanoi to open direct contacts with Washington, and that North Vietnam's leaders *did* commit themselves to entering direct talks. It reveals LBJ's personal role in bombing Hanoi, at a pivotal moment, disregarding the pleas of both the Poles and his own senior aides. It argues not only that Marigold, far from a "nonevent," was truly a "missed opportunity" but also that the initiative's failure tilted Hanoi against negotiations and set it on the path toward the Tet Offensive in early 1968.

The book's historical implications are thus immense. It contends that Washington (and LBJ) could have entered into talks with Hanoi in late 1966 rather than in 1968, and in far more auspicious circumstances. Marigold might thus not only have considerably shortened the war (or at least the massive U.S. military involvement in it), but also drastically altered American political history, for LBJ's failure to open talks with Hanoi fostered the rise of an antiwar challenge that led him to abandon his quest for reelection. If his decisions (and contingent events) had varied only slightly, the book shows, the subsequent trajectory of events could have looked very different. (I conclude with a counterfactual analysis of what might have occurred if Marigold had succeeded.)

Beyond Marigold, the book offers a unique perspective on a crucial year during the Vietnam War, through the eyes of Janusz Lewandowski, a Polish Communist diplomat in South Vietnam (which no Communist country recognized) from April 1966 to May 1967, who dealt at top levels with Americans and both South and North Vietnamese, from William Westmoreland, Henry Cabot Lodge, and Nguyen Van Thieu to Ho Chi Minh, Pham Van Dong, and Vo Nguyen Giap. It presents Lewandowski's untold story on the basis of dozens of hours of tape-recorded interviews and thousands of declassified Polish *szyfrogramy* and other documents. (The perspective of Marigold's other driving force, Giovanni D'Orlandi, Italy's passionate ambassador in Saigon, is likewise evoked in deeply personal terms, from his intimate diary as well as his secret *telegramma.*)

When recounting the Vietnam War, historians often rush past the period between 1965 (when Washington spiked its military role) and 1968 (when the Tet Offensive forced LBJ to seek an exit), summing it up with a single word: escalation. Yet, as this book shows, this period bulged with fascinating events vital to understanding the conflict's later course and eventual outcome. Readers familiar with the war will encounter well-known U.S. officials (LBJ, Rusk, McNamara, the Bundys, Rostow, et al.), albeit often in unfamiliar situations, but lesser-known figures also seize the stage, ranging from the Polish and Italian envoys in Saigon and their foreign ministers in Warsaw and Rome to LBJ's own man in Poland, as do Soviet and Chinese leaders (Brezhnev, Kosygin, Gromyko, Mao Zedong, Zhou Enlai, et al.) and, most important of all, the secretive North Vietnamese. It is a tapestry of the international history of the Vietnam War that no one at the time, no matter how exalted his "vantage point" (as LBJ titled his memoirs), could have fathomed—or that prior accounts have constructed.

More broadly, this book explores once-obscure contours of the wider Cold War at a crucial juncture with the help of long-inaccessible Communist and other non-U.S. sources, including archives from and interviews in more than fifteen countries—Vietnam, Poland, Italy, England, Canada, Russia, China, Australia, India, Hungary, Albania, the Netherlands, and others. Moreover, this tangled tale of covert Vietnam diplomacy coincided with another mysterious, momentous story: the sharpening Sino-Soviet schism, as Moscow and Beijing entered an even more acrimonious phase of their confrontation. (For Americans who lived through the war, the fresh evidence of intracommunist mistrust, and even enmity, bears little resemblance to the simplistic Cold War rhetoric then often purveyed by politicians and some government officials implying a coordinated Communist menace.)

Even as this book provides fly-on-the-wall glimpses of this Sino-Soviet rivalry —when, for instance, at a cocktail party in Hanoi at the height of the war, a Chinese military attaché challenged a Soviet counterpart to a fistfight—it also goes behind the public protestations of solidarity within both the Warsaw Pact and NATO to reveal hidden tensions (between Soviets and Poles, among the Poles themselves, between Washington and allies such as Ottawa and London), and even instances of cooperation and commiseration across the "Iron Curtain." In so doing, it exemplifies a recent trend toward "pericentrism" in Cold War history, transcending a Washington-centric (or even U.S.- and Soviet-dominated) narrative to integrate more fully the motives and behavior of other important actors, which did not merely march in lockstep with and follow the orders of their superpower patrons.

How was Marigold transformed from an ultrasecret international diplomatic effort into a headline-grabbing global public scandal? This book presents a unique case study of national security leaking, still a perennial feature of Washington policymaking. By using both declassified files from various governments and reporters' private notes, it shows how U.S., Polish, and other officials competitively disclosed contradictory accounts of the failed peace bid (to the pope, the United Nations secretary-general, and other governments as well as to selected reporters) as they attempted to manipulate public and international opinion—and how the disputed tale became entangled with the internal politics of the *Washington Post, New York Times,* and *Los Angeles Times,* among other publications. This "war of leaks" brings into the mix some of the era's emblematic figures: Robert F. Kennedy, Henry Kissinger, Bill Moyers, Norman Cousins, William Fulbright, U Thant, Harrison Salisbury, Wilfred Burchett, and others.

This book also examines how Marigold has remained a matter of contested history, that "argument without end." From official perspectives emerging in the memoirs of LBJ and his associates (and in the declassified record in the Pentagon Papers' "negotiating volumes," which were *not* leaked to the *New York Times* by Daniel Ellsberg in 1971 but emerged only gradually), to later accounts by historians, the meaning of the tale—a missed chance for peace, or much ado about nothing, or very little?—has been hotly disputed, with more than a few analysts throwing up their hands in exasperation at Marigold's confusion and convolution. Though not pretending to be the endlessly elusive "last word" (which hardly exists on any complex event), this book does resolve mysteries than have lain for decades at the core of this tantalizing affair.

Unfortunately, the story of Marigold holds more than historical interest. The end of the Cold War, in whose name Washington waged the Vietnam War, hardly ended the United States' foreign military interventions or its involvement in crises that threaten to flare into war. From Serbia to Iraq to Afghanistan, from Iran to North Korea, from Cuba to China to Libya and beyond, the United States has continued to confront the challenge of comprehending and communicating with its actual or potential adversaries across cultural, linguistic, and ideological gulfs—with distinctly mixed results. Probing deeply into how the Johnson administration grappled with a tempting yet uncertain peace overture, trying to balance the hope of escaping a painful military predicament with entrenched skepticism and incomprehension toward the North Vietnamese enemy (and its Polish and Soviet backers), this book offers a case study pertinent to such issues as war termination, communication between belligerents, third-party mediation, "signaling," and coercive diplomacy.

At the book's heart, however, is the dramatic story—part mystery, part thriller, and ultimately Shakespearean tragedy with a few dashes of farce tossed in—of a few men who tried against long odds to change history for the better, and who in late 1966, at the height of the Vietnam War, came closer to succeeding than has previously been realized. "No episode in our history, I believe, will baffle our posterity more than the Indochina war," the historian Arthur Schlesinger wrote in 1971, as the fighting still ground on. "Many, perhaps most, Americans already find it incredible that we ever considered our national interest so vitally engaged in Vietnam as to justify the death of 50,000 Americans and God knows how many Vietnamese in the longest war Americans have ever fought."[3] The drama of Marigold's rise, fall, and disputed memory recounted in this book helps to explain how that conflict expanded, unnecessarily, far beyond any conceivable intrinsic importance in the global Cold War that dominated world affairs and American politics and foreign policy for nearly half a century after World War II.

But telling this tale requires first setting the stage and introducing the dramatis personae—and exhuming the buried tale of what happened in Washington, Warsaw, and Hanoi (among other locales) during LBJ's thirty-seven-day bombing "pause" that began on Christmas Eve 1965.

A Note on Names
and Terminology

In the text, the names of Vietnamese persons and locations have been rendered in common English usage, and the country name "Vietnam" has been standardized for consistency—rather than "Viet Nam" or "Viet-Nam"—except in titles of books and the like. (The same has been done with the name Lewandowski, which was occasionally rendered as "Lewandowsky.") Street and other locations in Saigon and Warsaw are given as they were at the time of the Vietnam War and the Cold War, in the 1960s, although they have in many cases changed since then along with shifts in the prevailing politics (in opposite directions, as it happens, toward Communism in one case, away from it in the other). Finally, in a few cases, to avoid distracting the reader, a variant spelling of a name in a quotation or the like has been made consistent with the predominant spelling.

One noteworthy exception is "135 Duong Pasteur"—the address of the secret three-way "Marigold" gatherings at the Italian Embassy in downtown Saigon. This address was already rare in 1966 for having retained its colonial name ("Rue Pasteur") a dozen years after the end of French rule. After North Vietnamese tanks crashed through the gates of the presidential palace a few blocks away in 1975, the triumphant Communist authorities marked the new era by avidly renaming landmarks ("Independence Palace" now became "Reunification Palace"), streets (the nearby U.S. Embassy building now found itself on an avenue named after Le Duan, the Vietnamese Communist Party leader), and of course the city itself (renamed to honor Ho Chi Minh). But they evidently respected the renowned French scientist and his apolitical struggle against disease, and "Duong Pasteur" remains to this day.

Abbreviations Used in the Text

ARVN	Army of the Republic of (South) Vietnam
CIA	Central Intelligence Agency (United States)
CPSU	Communist Party of the Soviet Union
DRV	Democratic Republic of Vietnam (North Vietnam)
ICC	International Control Commission
MACV	U.S. Military Assistance Command, Vietnam
MSW	Ministerstwa Spraw Wewnętrznych (Ministry of Internal Affairs, Poland)
MSZ	Ministerstwa Spraw Zagranicznych (Ministry of Foreign Affairs, Poland)
NLF	National Liberation Front (National Front for the Liberation of South Vietnam)
PAVN	People's Army of Vietnam (North Vietnamese Army)
PRC	People's Republic of China
PZPR	Polska Zjednoczona Partia Robotnicza (Polish United Workers' Party)
RVN	Republic of Vietnam (South Vietnam)
RT	Rolling Thunder
VWP	Vietnam Workers' Party; Lao Dong

Marigold

THE LOST CHANCE FOR
PEACE IN VIETNAM

Prologue
Mission Impossible? "Operation Lumbago" and LBJ's Thirty-Seven-Day Bombing Pause, December 1965–January 1966

You are behaving like bandits. But if you really want peace, then we are ready to help you!

> —*Władysław Gomułka to Averell Harriman, Warsaw, December 30, 1965*

Why must the Americans go sticking [their] nose in others' business? The American government has sent their military forces here and now they must stop the invasion. . . . The Americans must piss off! . . . We don't want to become the victors; we just want the Americans to piss off! Goodbye! *Gút bai!*

> —*Ho Chi Minh to Jerzy Michałowski, Hanoi, January 6, 1966*

God damn those Chinese!

> —*Michałowski, on returning to Warsaw, mid-January 1966*

The president does not want to be treated like a "fool."

> —*Norman Cousins to a Polish UN diplomat, conveying the White House's reaction to Polish arguments to prolong the bombing pause, January 30, 1966*

On a cold night in the Cold War, in the depths of a Warsaw winter, a phone rings after midnight. One clerk calls another—their names need not detain us; they are bit characters in our story, Rosencrantz and Guildenstern to the ensuing intrigues—what matters is that, at 1:40 a.m. on December 29, 1965, a U.S. Embassy officer awakens a Polish functionary on "a very important and urgent matter."[1] Their talk concerns a hot war in jungles and rice paddies half a world away. When he first took office, Vietnam had been a mere foreign policy migraine for Lyndon Baines Johnson. Anxious to block Communist gains yet pursue an ambitious domestic agenda (and secure election in his own right), he had kept the crisis on a back burner, despite upping military advisers by 10,000, to 25,000, in the year after John F. Kennedy's assassination. But by late 1965, he could not mask that America was now in a major ground war, with nearly 200,000 troops engaged and more en route. Despite his efforts to downplay the intervention's scale and gravity, and the usual rallying around the flag, a vocal, growing minority dissented. Vietnam, formerly a Cold War backwater, had vaulted atop the global agenda, and now some feared that it could shatter the superpower détente that had seemed to emerge in the final year of JFK's abbreviated presidency, or even be the Sarajevo that sparked a nuclear World War III.

The nocturnal call alerts the Poles to a surprise aerial invasion from the west. This time it is not the Luftwaffe, as it was twenty-six years before, still living memory for many Varsovians, but a single U.S. plane bearing a special presidential emissary—W. Averell Harriman, the grizzled seventy-four-year-old statesman and former financier known as "the Crocodile" for his habit of erupting from seeming slumber at meetings to snap off a speaker's limb. As World War II ended, Harriman had served as Franklin Roosevelt's envoy to Joseph Stalin; then, as the Cold War set in, he had been Harry Truman's commerce secretary; later, he had been elected New York State's Democratic governor when Dwight Eisenhower took the White House; still later, he had been a State Department aide to JFK; and now he was serving as LBJ's roving ambassador at large and self-styled oracle on the Communist world (to the annoyance of his nominal boss, Secretary of State Dean Rusk). His journey to Warsaw, one of a barrage of diplomatic forays in an LBJ "peace offensive," aims to open talks with North Vietnam—or to rally public support for a sharp escalation in the coming year once Hanoi, as expected, rejected them.

When the midlevel apparatchik in the Polish Foreign Ministry's Department III—all right, I will mention their names for the record—when Mieczyslaw Sieradzki groggily lifted the receiver, the voice he heard belonged to chargé d'affaires Albert W. "Bud" Sherer. Even as they spoke, Harriman's Boeing 707 left Andrews Air Force Base outside Washington. Having received a "flash" telegram from Foggy Bottom alerting him to the impending visit, Sherer told Sieradzki that Harriman wished to see Foreign Minister Adam Rapacki to explain Washington's latest peace terms; Rusk hoped the new U.S. ambassador, John A. Gronouski, could join them, but he was in Poznań attending a trade fair. Urgently requesting landing rights, Sherer supplied technical details about the flight and its anticipated arrival later Wednesday morning.

As Harriman sped over the Atlantic—to stop in Frankfurt, if needed, to await clearance to land at Warsaw's Okęcie Airport—the rude awakenings continued. Sherer phoned Gronouski at 2 a.m. to summon him back to the capital;

and Sieradzki rousted a deputy foreign minister, Józef Winiewicz, who reacted guardedly—it would be tough to consult the highest authority, given the late hour and absence of key figures on end-of-year vacations. Besides, as Sieradzki told Sherer, the talks' concrete aim seemed vague and their "overly spectacular" nature could attract publicity that might "hurt the cause."

But Sherer persisted and, using Washington's guidance, elaborated on the request's background. In the absence of a "major provocation," he explained, LBJ had privately resolved to indefinitely extend a brief Christmas "pause" in the bombing, whose unconditional halt Hanoi and the entire Communist world angrily demanded: "If the [North] Vietnamese side makes a serious contribution on behalf of peace, this will have a favorable effect on the future course of events. The U.S. government relays this message to the Polish government while being aware of its uneasiness and interest regarding the Vietnamese issue and expresses hope that the [Polish] government will make use of it as it sees fit." Analogous messages were being passed to Budapest and Moscow, Sherer added, implicitly prodding the Poles not to be left out of the action. He vowed that Washington would not publicize Harriman's trip and would do its best to limit the inevitable press notice.

Sherer's words had the desired effect. A Polish military counterintelligence officer awoke Foreign Ministry director-general Jerzy Michałowski, who in turn disturbed Rapacki and the man really in charge, Communist Party boss Władysław Gomułka, who decided to grant permission. Passing the news down the food chain, Winiewicz told Sieradzki that the responsible authorities had decided, given Sherer's clarifications, to let Harriman come. (Michałowski cabled Poland's ambassador in Hanoi: "We believed that our refusal could be exploited by the Americans in a predictable way."[2]) While it was still hours before sunrise, Sieradzki called back Sherer, who thanked him profusely; the paperwork was hastily completed. Harriman landed at 10:30 a.m., still the wee hours by his watch. After a shower and shave at the embassy, he raced to the Foreign Ministry.

Intense conversations would fill the rest of Harriman's day, evening, and next morning, first with Rapacki and then Gomułka, whom he had met in Stalin's Moscow. They inspired Warsaw, despite its firm support for Hanoi and harsh criticism of U.S. "aggression," to send an emissary on a secret odyssey through the discordant Communist world, via the USSR and China, to carry Washington's proposals to the North Vietnamese; he even, Communist archives reveal, strongly urged them to enter talks.

These exchanges foreshadowed a year of intense hidden maneuvering between Washington and Warsaw, and between Warsaw and Hanoi—with Moscow, Beijing, and other capitals lurking in the background—over peace in Vietnam.

LBJ and Vietnam: "That Bitch of a War"

Before plunging headfirst into the Vietnamese muck, Lyndon Johnson gingerly extended his toes. Having inherited a political, economic, and limited military commitment from JFK in November 1963, he at first hoped that the new Saigon junta that had ousted Ngo Dinh Diem and his brother in a United States–backed coup three weeks before Dallas would clean up the mess by establishing a popular, effective, and legitimate government and waging the anticommunist fight in earnest, letting the Americans remain in the background. Instead, the faction-ridden South Vietnamese military seemed more intent on staging coups, grasping for power and its spoils, than on fighting the guerrillas or setting up a rational state. The prognosis for preserving a noncommunist authority, which most U.S. officials judged a Cold War imperative, looked increasingly grim. In May 1964, after yet another Saigon shakeup, LBJ vented his doubts to his national security adviser, McGeorge Bundy:

> I just stayed awake last night thinking of this thing, and the more that I think of it I don't know what in the hell, it looks like to me that we're getting into another Korea. It just worries the hell out of me. I don't see what we can ever hope to get out of there with once we're committed. I believe the Chinese Communists are coming into it. I don't think that we can fight them 10,000 miles away from home and ever get anywhere in that area. I don't think it's worth fighting for and I don't think we can get out. And it's just the biggest damn mess that I ever saw.

Mentioning a military aide with "kids" being deployed to Southeast Asia, he wondered, "What in the hell am I ordering them out there for? What in the hell is Vietnam worth to me? What is Laos worth to me? What is it worth to this country?" He mused presciently: "It's damn easy to get into a war, but . . . it's going to be awful hard to ever extricate yourself if you get in."[3]

LBJ could hand-wring to Bundy or his old Senate crony Richard Russell, the conservative Georgia Democrat, but ultimately, he always reverted to Cold War orthodoxy, the antiappeasement axioms of Munich and the domino theory, and his innate terror—instilled during a hardscrabble Texas youth—of seeming "soft" or "unmanly." All these entrenched factors dictated standing firm: "Of course," he told Bundy, the ex-Harvard dean, "if you start running from the Communists, they may just chase you right into your own kitchen." ("If you let a bully come into your front yard one day," he said on another occasion, "the next day he'll be up on your porch, and the day after that he'll rape your wife in your own bed."[4])

Still, Johnson put off the tough decisions until after he defeated Barry Goldwater in November 1964; during the campaign, a quick air strike against North Vietnam in reply to alleged torpedo attacks against U.S. ships in the Tonkin Gulf in August served the dual purpose of showing measured toughness to voters and securing an open-ended congressional resolution endorsing the use of force. Even then, the Pentagon Papers later revealed, secret planning and covert operations were building momentum for deeper involvement. By winter, LBJ's top advisers had judged that without sterner actions, the present course was headed for "disastrous defeat"—the weak, inept, divided Saigon regime would crumble and the Communists would waltz in, handing Hanoi and its Chinese and Soviet patrons a dangerous triumph. In a famous "fork in the road" memo in January 1965, Bundy and LBJ's defense secretary, Robert S. McNamara, argued that the only alternative to failure was "to use our military power in the Far East and to force a change of Communist policy."[5]

It was the moment of reckoning LBJ dreaded. "I knew from the start that I was bound to be crucified either way I moved," he said after returning to Texas to lick his wounds. "If I left the woman I really loved—the Great Society—in order to get involved with that bitch of a war on the other side of the world, then I would lose everything at home. All my programs. All my hopes to feed the hungry and shelter the homeless. All my dreams to provide education and medical care to the browns and the blacks and the lame and the poor. But if I left that war and let the Communists take over South Vietnam, then I would be seen as a coward and my nation would be seen as an appeaser and we would both find it impossible to accomplish anything for anybody anywhere on the entire globe."

Recalling political shifts during previous wars, Johnson feared that right-wingers would exploit the Vietnam crisis to derail his domestic agenda. And he distrusted generals who "need battles and bombs and bullets in order to be heroic" and see "everything in military terms." Yes, he insisted, "I could see it coming. And I didn't like the smell of it." Above all, the squabbling in Saigon sapped his confidence in the ally for which he was to send American boys to risk their lives to defend:

> Yet everything I knew about history told me that if I got out of Vietnam and let Ho Chi Minh run through the streets of Saigon, then I'd be doing exactly what Chamberlain did in World War II. I'd be giving a big fat reward to aggression. And I knew that if we let Communist aggression succeed in taking over South Vietnam, there would follow in this country an endless national debate—a mean and destructive debate—that would shatter my Presidency, kill my administration, and damage our democracy. I knew that Harry Truman and Dean Acheson had lost their effectiveness from the day that the Communists took over in China. I believed that the loss of China had played a large role in the rise of Joe McCarthy. And I knew that all these problems, taken together, were chickenshit compared with what might happen if we lost Vietnam.
>
> For this time there would be Robert Kennedy out in front leading the fight against me, telling everyone that I had betrayed John Kennedy's commitment to South Vietnam. That I had let a democracy fall into the hands of the Communists. That I was a coward. An unmanly man. A man without a spine. Oh, I could see it coming all right. Every night when I fell asleep I would see myself tied to the ground in the middle of a long, open space. In the distance, I could hear the voices of thousands of people. They were all shouting at me and running toward me: "Coward! Traitor! Weakling!" They kept coming closer. They began throwing stones. At exactly that moment I would generally wake up, . . . terribly shaken. But there was more. You see, I was sure as any man could be that once we showed how

weak we were, Moscow and Peking would move in a flash to exploit our weakness. They might move independently or they might move together. But move they would—whether through nuclear blackmail, through subversion, with regular armed forces or in some other manner. As nearly as anyone can be certain of anything. I knew they couldn't resist the opportunity to expand their control over the vacuum of power we would leave behind us. And so would begin World War III. So you see, I was bound to be crucified either way I moved.[6]

Persuaded—or, in his self-pitying nightmares, trapped—Johnson opted to spike the U.S. role. In February came a suitable provocation: A Viet Cong attack on a barracks in Pleiku in South Vietnam's central highlands killed eight Americans and wounded more than a hundred, and coincided with a Bundy inspection tour, adding an emotional tint to his advice to hit back hard. Retaliatory strikes against the North ("Flaming Dart") soon became an ongoing campaign ("Rolling Thunder") of what Washington termed "sustained reprisal" raids—misleadingly, because they aimed as much to stiffen Saigon as to punish Hanoi for backing the Southern insurgency or to impede infiltration. Marines waded ashore in March to guard an airbase near Danang, and in July LBJ announced that he would raise the number of troops from 75,000 to 125,000 (actually nearly twice that, though he did not say so openly); the mission thus crept from protecting U.S. installations to "search-and-destroy" operations to wipe out the elusive Viet Cong (the National Front for the Liberation of South Vietnam, or the National Liberation Front, NLF, also commonly known as the Viet Cong).[7]

Washington felt weak on the ground and sensed only stubbornness from Hanoi, so diplomacy took a back seat to building up strength, retaking Communist-held territory, and bolstering Saigon—yet LBJ felt compelled to nod at least occasionally toward peace.

Washington and Hanoi

Communicating with Hanoi was hardly simple, however; the two sides had never established diplomatic relations. For a fleeting moment, prospects for friendly ties had seemed bright. During World War II, operatives of the U.S. Office of Strategic Services (the precursor of the postwar Central Intelligence Agency) and Ho Chi Minh's forces had collaborated against the Japanese, who seized direct control over Indochina from France in March 1945. The Viet Minh (Ho's national independence movement) helped rescue downed U.S. pilots, and the mutual warmth seemed in sync with Roosevelt's sympathy for granting Indochina independence after the war—the French had "milked" it for a century, he scorned—much as Washington had pledged self-rule for its own colony, the Philippines, once the Japanese were expelled.[8]

But FDR died in April, and Truman gave less priority to ending colonialism than building up postwar France, especially given strains with Moscow and the power vacuum on the continent left by Germany's defeat. On September 2, 1945, agents of the Office of Strategic Services sat on the dais as Ho proclaimed the Democratic Republic of Vietnam (quoting the Declaration of Independence), but Washington ignored his appeals for recognition and after vacillating backed French efforts to reassert control. Once Franco–Viet Minh fighting broke out in late 1946, U.S. aides debated Ho's ultimate aims; some, stressing his ties to international Communism, urged full support for France's bid to crush the revolt; others saw colonial rule as doomed and emphasized Ho's nationalism, envisioning a potential "Asian Tito" able to keep his land from Kremlin sway despite ideological affinity. Squeamish about embracing the old order, Washington urged Paris to grant the Vietnamese real autonomy (much as it advised The Hague to accept Sukarno's victory in the Dutch East Indies).

But by 1950, fears of a Communist tide overflowing East Asia swept such nuances aside—Mao Zedong's victory in China's civil war and forging of an alliance with Stalin, Ho's now open entrenchment in the Sino-Soviet camp, and North Korea's crossing of the 38th Parallel convinced U.S. policymakers to lump Indochina into the broad eastern front of the now global Cold War. Washington still gave lip service to eventual Vietnamese independence, but it now rendered Paris all-out political, economic, and military aid, short only of sending forces (which were otherwise occupied in Korea and also rushing to Western Europe, where a Soviet thrust was widely anticipated).[9]

Despite the U.S. help, the French faced defeat by early 1954, and the impending collapse of their besieged Dien Bien Phu garrison forced Eisenhower to grapple with the question he hoped never to face: Would Washington intervene directly to prevent a Communist takeover? With U.S. strategy geared to stemming Communist advances, a key Cold War ally in disarray and begging for help, a diplomatic showdown looming in Geneva, and politicians clamoring to confront the Red Menace, many Americans said yes; Pentagon planners even drew up "Operation Vulture" to use tactical nuclear weapons to obliterate the Communists in the jungle surrounding Dien Bien Phu.[10]

But Ike, having extricated troops from one Asian meat-grinder and fearing another once the flag was committed, said no.[11] Secretary of State John Foster Dulles grumpily managed the distasteful consequences; the French crumbled, and in July 1954, the Geneva Conference divided Vietnam at the 17th Parallel. In the North, the Communists set up the Democratic Republic of Vietnam (DRV) as a functioning state; and the noncommunists established the Republic of Vietnam (RVN) in the South. The Geneva Accords, a Cold War landmark, were signed by foreign ministers from both camps—Moscow's Vyacheslav Molotov and London's Anthony Eden, the cochairs; France and the DRV; and, in a dashing debut, China's Zhou Enlai. Washington stood ostentatiously aloof—Dulles famously shunned a handshake with Zhou—and refused to sign the accord. Instead, it focused on bolstering the RVN and drawing a new line to quarantine the contagion; hoping to replicate NATO, it herded its allies into a Southeast Asian Treaty Organization and vowed to stem further Communist expansion in the region (see map 1).

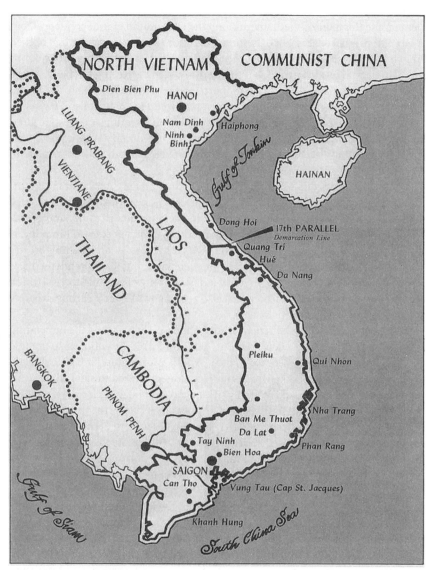

Map 1. Southeast Asia during the Vietnam War.
Source: *Tour 365,* Winter 1968.

In theory, the 17th Parallel was a temporary demarcation to separate rival armies pending national elections within two years to unify the country; in reality, Washington supplanted Paris as the outside power propping up Saigon, and had helped Ngo Dinh Diem—a Catholic in a mostly Buddhist country—consolidate control over sects and Viet Minh sympathizers. Eisenhower encouraged Diem to ignore Geneva's provision for elections, ostensibly because Communist strictures in the North precluded fair balloting, but also, he admitted in his memoirs, because Ho would have won 80 percent of the votes.[12]

As Washington tightened its embrace of Diem—hailing him as a Southeast Asian amalgam of George Washington and Winston Churchill—U.S.-DRV relations settled into a deep freeze; the acrimony sharpened during Ike's second term with crises over Laos and the onset of a Communist armed struggle in the RVN.[13] Kennedy kept the policy of boosting Saigon (increasing U.S. military advisers to 15,000 from 1,000) and shunning Hanoi, with one notable exception. In July 1962, a second Geneva Conference agreed to form a neutral coalition government in Laos, a rare moment of Cold War comity. (Nikita Khrushchev and JFK were willing to defuse the issue despite rifts over Berlin, Cuba, Congo, and other hot spots.) Unlike the earlier Geneva gathering, this time Washington participated fully; Kennedy named Harriman his chief negotiator. Unlike Dulles, "the Guv" had no qualms about fraternizing with "Commies"—he prided himself on being able to deal with them, enjoying the bracing mixture of chummy gossip and trash talk—and gained Kennedy's permission to see DRV foreign minister Ung Van Khiem privately even though Saigon would be infuriated if it found out. To elude reporters, he ducked through a back alley near the train station to reach the hotel where a Burmese diplomat hosted the talk. To break the ice, he harked back to the cooperation against Japan and asked after Ho's health. Khiem said his people fondly recalled Roosevelt and rued Truman's swinging behind the French; had he emulated FDR, much suffering could have been avoided.

After that promising start, the talk went downhill. Harriman warned Khiem against violating Lao neutrality, and they clashed over South Vietnam. Harriman insisted that the United States was merely helping a sovereign nation defend itself against outside interference; to his visible annoyance, Khiem called the conflict a popular "struggle" against foreign "aggression" and blamed Washington for violating the 1954 pact.[14]

There was no follow-up, no talk of setting up a communications channel, no further clarification of mutual perspectives or aims or probing a possible compromise deal. The furtive meeting turned out to be the *only* direct contact between high-ranking U.S. and North Vietnamese figures between the DRV's founding and the Paris talks nearly twenty-three years later. "Let us never negotiate out of fear," JFK had said at his inauguration. "But let us never fear to negotiate." In this case, however, he had no desire to risk Republican or South Vietnamese wrath by opening an ongoing dialogue with Hanoi.

Had the Geneva Laos accord worked, it might have enhanced Harriman's stature and prospects for extending the neutrality model to Vietnam or opening contacts with Ho—who voiced readiness to "negotiate with 'any' South Vietnamese regime that was 'willing to sit down with us at the same table and talk.'"[15] But it did not. Washington soon charged that Hanoi was consistently violating the pact (and had never intended to take it seriously), wrecking any slim chance that might have existed to consider the "neutral" solution that, most famously, France's Charles de Gaulle advocated.[16] The reflexive U.S. aversion to dealing with the North surfaced during the run-up to the November 1963 coup in Saigon. Besides the other grudges that JFK's aides nursed against Diem's regime—repression of Buddhists, corruption, resistance to reforms, diffidence in fighting Communists— they were alarmed by rumors that Ngo Dinh Nhu, his volatile brother, was secretly flirting with Hanoi.

To play footsy with Ho, Nhu allegedly conspired with a locally based Polish diplomat who periodically traveled to Hanoi to meet with DRV leaders: Mieczyslaw Maneli, Warsaw's ambassador to the International Control Commission (ICC). His presence was a unique Cold War anomaly: All Communist governments, including Poland, scorned South Vietnam as a U.S. puppet, and maintained embassies in Hanoi, not Saigon. So what was this senior Communist *doing* in South Vietnam's capital, and what was the ICC?

The 1954 Geneva Conference had created the ICC—formally, the International Commission for Supervision and Control—to monitor the Indochina pact, which set limits on military activities by both rival Vietnamese factions and foreign powers. In a delicate balancing act, the conference named as members Poland, Canada, and neutral India as chair—in the spirit of an earlier group (Switzerland, Poland, Czechoslovakia, Sweden) that made up the Neutral Nations Supervisory Commission overseeing the Korean armistice.

Washington never had much use for the ICC, which was supposed to observe the 1956 balloting, and its scant regard dwindled as the group proved unable to function effectively. "This Commission was considerably better than the one arranged for Korea, in that no member had an automatic veto," a State Department aide recalled, "but in practice, India's spinelessness, combined with the absence of real sanctions against North Vietnam's refusal to allow the Commission to travel freely, made it a paper tiger."[17] Nor did U.S. officials particularly appreciate Ottawa's performance; "to watching Americans," the historian Robert Bothwell has written of this period, "Canadians on the commission failed to act forcefully enough in combating Polish wiles."[18] Citing the North's limits on the ICC to back Diem's refusal to stage national elections, the Americans proposed that the UN monitor them, but Hanoi rejected this idea as too pro-West.

By the late 1950s, the Geneva pact was effectively dead, but no one wanted to pull the plug on the ICC. It kept staff in Phnom Penh, Vientiane, and Hanoi, but based commissioners and most personnel in Saigon, where logistics were easier. Because it was rarely able to reach unanimity except on minor procedural matters, it sank into a stalemate. Its meetings routinely degenerated into tabulating accusations from the warring sides and futile, if at times heated, squabbling. Occasionally, India voted with Canada or Poland, allowing a majority to slap one wrist or the other—for example, Washington's for topping Geneva limits by sending more than 1,000 military advisers to the South or (in an unusual 1962 majority report) Hanoi's for aiding the Communist uprising there. But New Delhi carefully rationed its alignments, alternately irking both Ottawa and Warsaw.[19] One reporter, calling the ICC's staff "the loneliest men in Vietnam," observed that both Saigon and Hanoi "tend to regard the International Control Commission with some embarrassment, but neither party apparently wants the commission to wind up its affairs."[20]

Amid rising tension between Kennedy and Diem, rumors that Nhu was using Maneli to dally with Hanoi evoked the prospect, abhorrent to Washington, of the two Vietnams plotting to move the South toward neutralism. They helped convince JFK's aides—including his new ambassador in Saigon, Henry Cabot Lodge, a senior Republican—that Diem must go. The gossip, spread by Nhu himself, was overblown, Polish sources now confirm: Maneli spoke to both sides but was not mediating and even got into hot water with Warsaw when his name appeared in the press.[21] (Of course, the Americans would have been lucky if Diem *had* cut a neutralist deal with Hanoi and requested them to leave, but that was not how it looked at the time.) The Maneli intrigue made no progress toward peace, yet it served as a reminder that the ICC delegates, though unable to fulfill their nominal mandate, might still serve as critical communications links.

The need for such channels remained cogent, because LBJ had inherited an aversion to dealing directly with "Ho Chi Minh"—as Washington tended to personify the DRV leadership. Now in his midseventies, Ho had in fact mostly relinquished day-to-day decisionmaking to others, especially Le Duan, the powerful first secretary of the Vietnamese Workers' Party (VWP; Lao Dong), and a militant Southerner who strongly backed the armed battle to unify the country—yet a figure unknown to most Americans.[22] In any case, U.S. officials believed, there was nothing to negotiate: Hanoi had no right to meddle in South Vietnam and thus should mind its own business. If it did not, it would suffer the consequences.

To transmit this blunt message, the inert ICC came in handy. In June and in mid-August 1964, after being briefed by U.S. aides, Canadian commissioner J. Blair Seaborn visited Hanoi, carrying a big stick (an implicit threat of force) and a hazy carrot (vague promises of economic aid should it desist). The formulation avoided the word "ultimatum," but the DRV got the message. Courteously receiving Seaborn, Premier Pham Van Dong nonetheless insisted on a full U.S. pullout from South Vietnam before any settlement (e.g., neutralization); and on his second visit, Dong, angry after Tonkin Gulf, declared that Hanoi could not be cowed by "aggression," rejected the de facto ultimatum, and forecast a Communist victory. As Washington expected, the rebuff set up a military showdown. Ottawa concluded sourly that it had been used to threaten Hanoi rather than seek negotiations (Seaborn felt queasy being Lodge's "messenger boy"). Seeing the whole exercise as futile, the Canadians flirted with ditching the ICC altogether, but in the end they gritted their teeth and awaited a more auspicious moment to reenter the diplomatic hurly-burly.[23] That autumn and winter, Washington also signaled a lack of interest in direct talks with Hanoi by responding diffidently to word from UN secretary-general U Thant that Ho had indicated he would approve face-to-face talks with the Americans. (We will return to this murky episode, which exploded into a public row, poisoning relations between LBJ and the Burmese statesman.[24])

In early 1965, as hostilities intensified, diplomacy took a back seat. Repeatedly, Ottawa asked whether Seaborn might aid in communicating with Hanoi, but Washington said no thanks.[25] Johnson's decisions to bomb the DRV and send more troops to the South alarmed U.K. prime minister Harold Wilson, who tried frantically to resuscitate the dormant Geneva process—to curb the violence, assure London a seat at the table, and dampen discontent in his own Labour Party. Moscow briefly seemed interested in reprising its cochair role, but Beijing and Hanoi shot the idea down and the effort collapsed. On April 7, LBJ publicly called for "unconditional discussions" with North Vietnam, but the next day, in a speech to the DRV's National Assembly, Dong insisted that Washington first stop the bombing and accept Four Points at the core of any settlement:

1. "Recognition of the basic national rights of the Vietnamese people—peace, independence, sovereignty, unity, and territorial integrity," which required the United States to withdraw all its forces from South Vietnam and cease all acts of war on North Vietnam.

2. Respecting the military provisions of the 1954 Geneva Accords, intended to ensure the country's neutrality as a prelude to unification, including, inter alia, tight restrictions on the presence of foreign military personnel which the United States had long since surpassed.

3. "The internal affairs of South Vietnam must be settled by the South Vietnamese people themselves in accordance with the program of the NFLSV [National Front for the Liberation of South Vietnam, or National Liberation Front], without any foreign interference."

4. Vietnam's "peaceful reunification" should "be settled by the Vietnamese people in both zones, without any foreign interference."[26]

Point three was the rub, because it implied scrapping South Vietnam's existing regime and substituting a coalition which the NLF—Hanoi's marionette, Washington felt—would dominate. Before talks, LBJ felt it essential to prop up Saigon, and in July 1965 he redoubled the U.S. troop commitment. Still, probing continued. In May, Johnson authorized a five-day bombing halt ("Mayflower") that Hanoi predictably ignored. That summer, quiet soundings transpired in Paris between a DRV diplomat, Mai Van Bo, and a retired yet authorized American official, Edmund Guillon; these intriguing "XYZ" talks covered key topics (e.g., what would actually happen if Washington accepted the Four Points), but Hanoi broke them off for unclear reasons.[27]

In the fall, as the violence intensified, LBJ came under mounting pressure to make—or at least seem to be making—a more strenuous bid for peace.

Parsing the Pause

What moved LBJ to OK an extended bombing "pause" in December 1965—the first real breather to explore diplomacy after nearly a year of escalation—despite acute private doubts that it would yield any progress and fear that Hanoi would see it as an admission of weakness? The influences on him merged issues, personalities, and arguments that would resurface repeatedly during the Marigold peace initiative, so it is worth pausing, so to speak, to disentangle them.

The heart of the matter, of course, remained the war itself, and to Washington it was not going so well. The Americanization of the conflict had accelerated, yet not only had Ho failed to "blink" (à la Khrushchev during the Cuban Missile Crisis), but the Communists seemed to fight harder than ever. By autumn, top officials lamented the slow progress, and military commanders elongated earlier optimistic timetables, seeking more resources with no promise of ultimate success—"a sobering picture," the U.S. assistant secretary of state for Far Eastern affairs, William P. Bundy (McGeorge's brother), later recalled.[28] In mid-November, the picture sobered up even more. In savage battles in the Ia Drang Valley, their first major clashes with the main units of the People's Army of Vietnam, U.S. forces on a search-and-destroy mission lost several hundred dead, pushing the year's toll near 2,000. Victory claims rang hollow; those Americans who had expected to cow the enemy with superior technology and firepower recoiled at this bloody show of tenacity and skill.

Yet, for most U.S. civilian and military figures running the war, the evidence of a tougher enemy just underlined the need to roll up their sleeves and get on with the job, send in more troops and weaponry, and keep at it until Hanoi caved. Amid louder grumbles about Vietnam at home and abroad, however, they worried about sustaining support for what they now realized was likely to be a prolonged, painful struggle. Americans still backed the war, polls said, overwhelmingly preferring escalation to withdrawal, yet a march on the Pentagon in early November dramatized dissenters' intensity, even if their numbers were modest. McNamara watched in horror as the Quaker activist Norman Morrison set himself afire not "40 feet away from my window"; another protester immolated himself a week later.[29] LBJ rapped critics as unpatriotic or even Communist dupes, but his aides warned that support on Vietnam might wane, especially with rising costs projected and midterm elections nearing. On Capitol Hill, Senate Majority leader Mike Mansfield and Senate Foreign Relations Committee chair

J. William Fulbright urged a bombing pause to test Hanoi before stepping up military action.

All that autumn, as concern about the war spread, LBJ secretly mulled a lengthy bombing break around the Christmas–New Year's holidays to convince skeptics that he really wanted peace and to either open talks on acceptable terms or else get even more serious about prosecuting the war. As he vacillated and Rusk also wavered on the fence, internal battle lines congealed. The debate pitted advocates of a long pause—led by McGeorge Bundy (if only to set the table for later escalation), McNamara (fast losing faith in the bombing), and Undersecretary of State George W. Ball (the house maverick), seconded by White House aides like Jack Valenti and Bill Moyers—against hawkish military figures and advisers (Clark Clifford, Abe Fortas, and Lodge, whom LBJ had sent back to Saigon for a second term as ambassador in August). The Joint Chiefs of Staff and the commander of U.S. forces in Vietnam, General William C. Westmoreland, decried anything beyond a token hiatus as a futile gesture that would gratuitously give the enemy a breathing spell and be hard to reverse. Hanoi would interpret any unilateral move as weakness, Lodge warned, and Saigon was too "fragile" to enter negotiations or even survive an open-ended bombing halt.[30]

Hints from the Soviet Bloc

Meanwhile, some diplomats from the Soviet Bloc hinted that Hanoi might respond to even a relatively brief bombing halt. Their claims fueled momentum for a pause among top LBJ aides—not that they really believed it would lure North Vietnam to the table, but because they perceived new side gains to a conciliatory gesture: Calling the bluff might prod the Kremlin to pressure Hanoi, exacerbating its already strained ties with the Chinese, who stridently opposed talks, and tugging it toward Moscow's more moderate stance.[31]

On October 7, in New York for the UN General Assembly, Hungarian foreign minister János Péter had told Rusk that if Washington ceased bombing, even for a few weeks, "conditions will improve, and negotiations leading to peace will be possible." Despite Rusk's probing, Péter cagily refused to say if he had recently visited Hanoi or reveal the basis for his "firm conviction" that the DRV was ready to talk.[32] "Everything that I have said to you I can state with the most complete responsibility," he insisted. "We are in intimate contact with Hanoi; we are completely familiar with the intentions of the government of the Democratic Republic of Vietnam."[33]

Rusk remained skeptical. But in late November and early December, Moscow's ambassador to Washington, Anatoly F. Dobrynin—to U.S. officials a much more reliable source—seemed to corroborate the Hungarian's claims. In a "candid and cordial" chat on November 24, the gregarious Soviet diplomat told McGeorge Bundy that to take a break of "only 12 to 21" days would produce "intense diplomatic effort," though he could not guarantee results.[34]

Impressed, the national security adviser told LBJ that he now felt assured of "quiet but strong Soviet diplomatic support in pushing Hanoi toward the conference table"—which should itself stir intracommunist discord even if it did not succeed in convincing the DRV to enter talks.[35] More skeptical than Bundy or McNamara, Johnson blurted out on December 7 that he "wouldn't give 4¢ for Dobrynin," but he did authorize a still-dubious Rusk to probe further.[36] After a long talk the next day with the Communist envoy, Rusk and his top Kremlinologist, Llewellyn E. "Tommy" Thompson Jr., predicted that Moscow "would make an effort to move things forward during the pause," as Bundy told LBJ.[37]

As Johnson pondered the pause proposition in November and into December, two controversies fueled charges that he had muffed chances to move the Vietnam conflict to the negotiating table—and amplified demands that he prove his desire for peace.

"The First Casualty": Thant and Stevenson

Nine months earlier, in mid-February 1965, as violence surged in Vietnam, U Thant had cast doubt on Washington's claim that Hanoi's intransigence blocked any move toward peace. At a press conference, the slight, soft-spoken UN leader declared that the "great American people, if only they know the true facts," would endorse his view that further bloodshed was unnecessary, and "discussions and negotiations" could permit the United States "to withdraw gracefully from that part of the world."

"As you know," he added cryptically, "in times of war and of hostilities, the first casualty is truth."[38]

The White House quickly countered that—despite "chit-chat" and "way-out feelers"—Hanoi had shown no interest in "authorized or meaningful negotiations" and that any discussion of direct contacts was solely "procedural."[39]

There the matter rested—until it roared back into the headlines in mid-November when a *Look* magazine article by the CBS commentator Eric Sevareid revealed off-the-record statements made by Adlai E. Stevenson, JFK's and LBJ's UN delegate, shortly before his death in July. Sevareid quoted Stevenson as saying that Washington had spurned a DRV offer, through Thant, to open direct talks. In his "final troubled hours," Stevenson related that in the autumn of 1964, Thant had told him that Hanoi—through the Soviets—had agreed to send an envoy to Rangoon to see a U.S. representative, but that when he reported this to higher-ups, "someone in Washington insisted that this attempt be postponed until after the presidential election." Thant tried again after Johnson's victory, saying that "Hanoi was still willing to send its man," but Stevenson again allegedly ran into a stone wall.[40]

In late January 1965, Thant checked anew with Stevenson, who, after conferring with Washington, reiterated official disinterest due to the risk that a U.S.-DRV meeting would leak and upset Saigon. The overture then lapsed, overtaken

by well-known events, and the affair had allegedly magnified Stevenson's disillusionment with LBJ. Thant "was furious over this failure of his patient efforts, but
said nothing publicly"—except, that is, his incendiary remark in February. U.S.
officials more than reciprocated his irritation; if truth had been the war's "first
casualty," his standing in the Johnson administration was its second. "With those
words," he later rued, "whatever utility I might have as a prospective go-between
came to an end, as far as Washington was concerned."[41]

With the war looming as a quagmire, Stevenson's posthumous revelations created new headaches for LBJ. His aides scrambled to dispel the impression that
Washington had blithely ignored a real overture for peace. From Rio de Janeiro,
Rusk cabled that Sevareid's piece had likely embellished the facts; Sevareid had
"probably received a very substantial fee," and Stevenson was a "scintillating conversationalist," especially off the record, with "a touch of Hamlet." To Johnson, he
acknowledged that behind the tepid response to Thant was the fear that if word
had leaked that "the U.S. was dickering for a settlement behind the backs of Saigon," it would have rattled the edgy regime.[42] Officials confirmed the story's outlines but denied that politics had interfered and insisted that there was no hard
evidence Hanoi wanted "serious" talks.[43]

However, newly available Russian archival evidence confirms that in August
1964, Hanoi *had* secretly agreed to a quiet rendezvous with a U.S. representative in
a neutral country.[44] Whether such contacts might have led anywhere is doubtful,
but in any case, Washington had no real desire to find out—Seaborn's vain missions
had already sated its curiosity. The incident poisoned dealings between Thant and
Johnson. For years, the UN head would retell the story to underline Washington's
incompetent or insincere peace seeking, and the memory darkened the lenses
through which he viewed its subsequent Vietnam diplomacy. For their part, U.S.
officials spoke privately of him "with the same disdain reserved for Charles de
Gaulle, Adam Rapacki and other world leaders and diplomats judged to be hostile
to America's Vietnam policies."[45] Thant and LBJ—who denied ever hearing about
Hanoi's purported offer to talk—lacquered later contacts with a veneer of cordiality,
but barely hid their underlying contempt. Looking back, Rusk asserted that "Thant
lied like a sailor. I never had much respect for U Thant's integrity."[46] This mutual
distrust would resurface at a key moment during the Marigold saga.

La Pira and Fanfani

The Thant-Stevenson furor had barely died down when, in mid-December 1965,
a new fracas broke out, dealing a fresh blow to the administration's credibility.
The new peace uproar concerned a visit to Hanoi the month before by the eccentric ex-mayor of Florence, Giorgio La Pira.[47] The Latin law professor, glib peace
activist, and Catholic mystic had gone with a fellow academic after being encouraged quietly by his old friend Amintore Fanfani, Italy's foreign minister. On his
return to Rome, La Pira claimed that DRV leaders had told him they were ready

to order a cease-fire and enter talks with Washington on the basis of the Geneva Accords (which they said boiled down, "in reality," to Hanoi's Four Points) and before U.S. forces withdrew from Vietnam (only a further buildup would be prohibited). "I am prepared to go anywhere; to meet anyone," he quoted Ho Chi Minh as saying. From New York—where he was presiding over the UN General Assembly—Fanfani wrote LBJ on November 20 to pass along these glad tidings and offer his services "for any step that you consider opportune in the matter."[48]

Washington was underwhelmed, to put it mildly. Forwarding Fanfani's letter to Johnson, a blasé Rusk called it "a simple restatement of the familiar . . . firm and inflexible Hanoi position," albeit "worded in the most palatable form possible." Like McNamara and Bundy, he advised a polite reply explaining why it was nothing new or exciting.[49] "This is not at all a real feeler for negotiations," Bundy agreed. The messengers hardly inspired confidence. Fanfani had not named his source, but a secret cable pegged La Pira as the Italian recently in Hanoi— and U.S. aides considered him an unreliable, egotistical clown—"a rather fuzzy-minded noncommunist leftist" was how Bundy put it to LBJ, while the embassy in Rome termed a recent La Pira interview "a typical conversation with the un-stable mayor, that is, a farrago of the insignificant, the irrelevant, and the ostentatious humility which is the stock and trade of the 'Holy ex-Mayor' of Florence."[50]

Fanfani was taken more seriously, but the "small, round" politician aroused ambivalence. The fifty-seven-year-old Christian Democrat, a former economics professor of humble Tuscan origins, had served centrist postwar Italian governments in various posts, including president and foreign minister, since 1947. The CIA judged him pro-Western and a "staunch advocate of close U.S.-Italian ties," and even detractors conceded that he was energetic, forceful, and indefatigable. Yet in his years of battle in Italy's no-holds-barred politics, the "bantam-size political fighter" had also earned a reputation as a mercurial, unpredictable, conniving, striving, and polarizing figure. His "sharp tongue and often sudden shifts in political direction have antagonized many of his former admirers and collaborators," the CIA noted.[51] Mincing few words, a British internal profile (which, unlike the American one, noted his prewar Fascist inclinations) termed him "brisk and efficient but tactless and ruthless":

> Fanfani is one of the outstanding figures in the Christian Democrat Party and in Italian politics. An intelligent, quick, tireless and restlessly ambitious man of great organising ability and oratorical skill. His lack of tact and patience, and his biting tongue are however severe handicaps and do not endear him to his colleagues (he is believed to have described himself "as the only cockerel in a farmyard of capons"). He does not inspire trust or affection and is indeed a man of few scruples where his ambition is concerned. His tiny physical stature perhaps contributes to his aggressiveness.[52]

As U.S. aides well knew, Fanfani had multiple incentives to be seen as a Vietnam peacemaker. Beyond the allure of personal and national glory, the role fit his domestic political interests; he was deeply engaged in an "opening to the left" to wean the Socialists from their alliance with the Communists and into an alignment with the Christian Democrats, and a peace breakthrough promised dividends for his center-left coalition.[53]

Rusk also recalled Fanfani's penchant for self-promotion as an East-West go-between. During the 1961 standoff over Berlin, then-president Fanfani had gone to Moscow and sought to interpose himself as a mediator between Khrushchev and JFK.[54] More recently, in late September, he had told Rusk that Hanoi was "somewhat more disposed to negotiate" than Washington believed, even without Beijing's approval, and sought his blessing to make "discreet" inquiries. Rusk reacted skeptically, but the lack of an explicit veto sufficed for Fanfani to approve La Pira's exploratory voyage.[55] (Fanfani had also derived some encouragement to wade into Vietnam peace diplomacy from his veteran ambassador in Saigon, Giovanni D'Orlandi, who in early September had visited Rome and assured his minister that "today an Italian initiative may have a lot of weight."[56])

On December 4, in a carefully hedged reply to Fanfani, Rusk expressed his doubt that Hanoi had really abandoned its "Four Points" and demanded harder evidence of its "real willingness for unconditional negotiations." Fanfani sent Ho a request for clarification two days later, but before he could reply, two events in mid-December effectively shut the channel. First, bombers struck a power plant near Haiphong—the first major DRV industrial target hit since the war began.[57] Then the *St. Louis-Post Dispatch* printed a garbled version of the Italian effort, suggesting that Washington had already rebuffed it. The administration, in response, promptly unveiled the secret exchanges with Fanfani to prove that it had, contrary to the story's insinuation, taken the feeler seriously; "in view of Stevenson/Sevareid episode," Rusk cabled Lodge, "we concluded we must release entire correspondence to make our full position clear and to maintain our peace-seeking posture."[58]

Hanoi, in turn, immediately blasted the American "peace hoax"—the "sheer, groundless fabrication" that it had initiated a "probe about negotiations" through La Pira. U.S. aides cited the comments as proof that the whole business was pointless, but critics called them a predictable DRV response to the new escalation and a reflection of sensitivity to Chinese criticism, and surmised that a real chance had been wasted ("in fact it is not a denial," Fanfani felt).[59]

✳ ✳ ✳

Were the critics right? Did Washington, by bombing Haiphong and divulging the secret correspondence, scupper a real chance to start negotiations? Probably not. The massive U.S. military intervention had disconcerted the North Vietnamese, some of whom recoiled at the rising cost of backing the Southern insurgency, but Hanoi's policy at this stage still dictated military victory or, at a minimum, U.S. acceptance of the Four Points and a full bombing halt before talks; it did not want to negotiate "from a position of inferiority."[60] New Vietnamese evidence seems to vindicate American suspicion that La Pira exaggerated Ho's ardor to talk. According to a Vietnamese record of the November 11 conversation, which was conducted in French, the Italian prodded his host, but the response was hardly so forthcoming as Fanfani implied.[61]

Unsure whether the Italian or even U.S. government had authorized La Pira's mission, after some banter, Ho asked: "So, on this visit you are carrying an olive branch to Vietnam? What did Fanfani ask you to say to us?"

"To say that we are ready," La Pira replied. "If Vietnam has peace, the world will have peace." Recounting how Fanfani had backed his trip, he urged Hanoi to enter talks to aid the U.S. peace movement, force Washington to stop bombing, and "rein in Johnson." At first, at least, Ho did not embrace the idea; when La Pira noted the antiwar students' "struggle," Ho acidly observed that the protesters who burned themselves "were very brave, but the ones who should have been immolated are Johnson and McNamara."

Peace required enemies to sit and sip tea together, the Italian persisted, but Ho and Pham Van Dong shot back that first the Americans, who had crossed the sea to "murder" Vietnamese, should go home.

The "technical problem" of the withdrawal could "be resolved while you drink tea together," La Pira countered.

"In order to talk," Dong said, "you must have someone to talk to. Do the Americans want to talk? No! They are still expanding the war in South Vietnam and bombing and attacking North Vietnam. They want to force us to accept an American-style peace. We can never agree to that. We sincerely want peace. At night we cannot sleep, and during the day we think a great deal about what we should do. Peace with justice is the four-point position that we put forward."

La Pira pressed: "In order to have peace, you must meet one another, you must talk to one another, and only then will the U.S. withdraw. On the Four Points, the U.S. has accepted almost all of them. If the U.S. did not talk about the Four Points, but talked instead about only one point, the Geneva Agreement, which encompasses all of problems covered in your four-point position, would you agree then? Would you accept that?"

According to the Vietnamese record, Ho did not answer clearly, but his ambiguous reply contained enough pacific phraseology to give his visitor something to latch onto:

We are prepared to roll out the red carpet and strew flowers in their path to let the Americans withdraw. But if the U.S. does not withdraw, then we have to drive them out. We and our people are ready to talk to the American authorities and the American people. But for Johnson and McNamara, it is either the red carpet or we kick their asses out the door. Naturally, we want peace, and we are ready to settle the Vietnam problem peacefully. We do not want children to be killed and houses to be burned down. We are ready to talk to the aggressors, but first they must stop their aggression. I want you to say to President Johnson and McNamara, or tell them through Mr. Fanfani, that Ho Chi Minh only wants peace. Who is the one who started the war? Who is the one who does not want to stop the war? It is the U.S.! The U.S. must withdraw from Vietnam, and then President Johnson can come here to talk, or he could invite me to come to Washington. I am ready! But first of all, the U.S. must leave us in peace. The U.S. must stop the bombing!

Ho seemed to leave unclear whether he was insisting on a military withdrawal ("first of all, the U.S. must leave us in peace") or merely a bombing halt before talks could start; and whether a mutual commitment to comply with the Geneva Accords, as opposed to Washington's explicit acceptance of the Four Points, would suffice.

"As long as the U.S. continues to commit aggression, we will continue to fight," Dong added. "The tea will come later."

"But you must have the tea brewed and ready," La Pira said.

"I agree," Dong conceded.

U.S. officials at this point had little desire to sip tea with the North Vietnamese, and there is scant evidence that either side truly desired to bargain at that point.[62] Yet Fanfani believed otherwise. Privately furious, he felt that Washington had sabotaged his diplomacy with first the Haiphong bombing and then the press leak, ruining a real chance for negotiations.[63] Compounding the debacle, in late December the foreign minister lost his job amid criticism stemming from his (and his wife's) ties to the irrepressible La Pira. "Unjust and unfounded suppositions and judgments" made it impossible to continue, Fanfani moaned in his resignation letter.[64] He would waste no time in plotting to return to power.

A "Hard-Line" Pause

Johnson also felt resentful, irritated at the outside pressures for a bombing pause as he tried to make up his mind. At a White House meeting after the La Pira probe leaked, he blasted "publicity seekers and amateurs" for meddling. Besides Fanfani, he was also fending off other allied leaders clamoring for a lull in the bombing; British prime minister Wilson, during a recent visit to Washington, had urged such a move to measure Hanoi's sincerity—and Rusk (just back from a NATO conclave in Paris) had sarcastically dubbed Wilson a "paragon of courage" next to other Europeans.[65]

Of course, besides burnishing his peace-seeking posture, a pause might also help Johnson determine whether talks were actually possible. Most aides, however, rated that prospect a long shot: Rusk put the odds at 1 in 20, Clifford at 1 in 20 or 1 in 50.[66] Moreover, that side benefit—confirming Hanoi's intransigence—hardly seemed to compensate, LBJ felt, for potential battlefield disadvantages. McNamara recalled that he and some other aides, despite being skeptical of immediate results, considered a bombing suspension "a step in a process that might ultimately bring about negotiated settlement."[67] But when he backed a prolonged break at the White House meeting on December 18, Johnson cited military concerns that "a month's pause would undo all we've done."

"That's baloney—and I can prove it," McNamara retorted.

"I don't think so," replied the president. "I disagree. I think it contains serious military risks."[68] Sympathetic to hawks' warnings that unilateral restraint simply encouraged Hanoi to fight harder, the commander in chief feared the proposed action "would make us look like a weak sister."[69]

LBJ ultimately came around, but his main aim in approving an extended pause was to prepare for war, not peace. By rebutting charges that he had not amply considered peace options, he hoped to do spadework (after Hanoi's rebuff) for looming escalation. Internal deliberations in late 1965 over "Phase II" deployments—Westmoreland's request for many more troops in 1966 than had been foreseen (first to 325,000 instead of 275,000, then beyond 400,000)—implied a "hard-line" pause that would be, as Johnson said, "preparatory to knocking Hell out of 'em."[70] Vietnam plans required, he noted just before OK'ing a halt, "budget increases of many billions of dollars which will become public in January, the deployment of large numbers of additional men during 1966 and the acceptance of stepped-up casualties associated with such increased deployments."[71]

In adopting this course, Johnson tilted toward those advisers who were confident in a mix of tougher military action against the North; building up morale, force levels, and "pacification" measures in the South; and readying the diplomatic terrain for *eventual* negotiations to ratify the existing status quo. From the State Department, an increasingly influential hawk urged him to "systematically bomb the oil refining and storage capacity and the electric power facilities in North Vietnam." Walt W. Rostow, director of the Policy Planning Council, also advised establishing a direct channel with Hanoi, because "our experience with third parties, however well meaning, suggests that they are not necessarily accurate; they leak; and they are too often bucking for a Nobel Peace Prize."[72]

"Fandangle" Diplomacy

When LBJ finally agreed to prolong the Christmas pause, at least for a few days, Rusk decided to take János Péter at his word on the intimacy of Hungarian-DRV ties and thus to use Budapest to inform Hanoi of Washington's plans to hold off (for an unspecified period) on bombing the North beyond the thirty-hour holiday cease-fire and hopes to begin talks toward a settlement based on the Geneva pact. "In this way," William Bundy later observed, "Rusk calculated, he could convey the clearest possible picture of the American position, avoid putting the Russians on the spot, and at the same time get whatever the combined resources of the Soviet Union and its close satellites (almost certainly acting in full concert) had to offer in the way of help or information."[73]

On December 23, Rusk summoned Budapest's top diplomat in Washington, chargé d'affaires János Radványi, to his seventh-floor office. After recalling that in

October he had invited Péter "to use a little '16th Century Hungarian diplomacy' with Hanoi," Rusk wondered if the foreign minister had made any progress, noted the imminent Christmas truce, and enumerated twelve points—soon enlarged to fourteen for public release[74]—to frame the U.S. stand. These included a readiness for peace on the basis of the 1954 and 1962 Geneva pacts (including free RVN elections and unification if "not imposed by force"), forswearing any long-term intent to keep military forces in South Vietnam or bases in Southeast Asia, a readiness for a bombing halt and unconditional talks that would include Dong's Four Points plus ones others might raise, and regional development aid. Rusk called it a basket containing everything but "Take Vietnam." He downplayed the thirty-hour bombing halt but said that if "the other side [were] responsive, we might find a way to move toward peace" by further steps.[75] Radványi agreed to relay the message, and after checking with Moscow, Budapest passed it to Hanoi.

As Washington awaited some response from Hanoi, maneuvers within the U.S. government—including a secret McNamara trip to the LBJ Ranch in Texas to urge a longer bombing pause, an act he later called a successful "end run around my colleagues"[76]—produced a presidential edict on December 27 to extend the halt indefinitely (with a presumption of resumption in the second half of January). Once Johnson finally decided that his Vietnam strategy required a more ambitious gesture to showcase his desire for peace, he dressed it up with as much razzmatazz as possible: "Down on the Texas range," wrote Stuart H. Loory and David Kraslow,

> they have a form of entertainment that is as big as life. They call it a "fandangle" and it has just about everything in it—barroom brawls, shoot-outs, singing, dancing, herds of cattle, fireworks. A fandangle is a sight to behold, as rancher Lyndon B. Johnson well knows. He has brought Texas fandangles to his LBJ Ranch, in sparse hill country forty-eight miles west of Austin, to entertain important guests. Even the most sophisticated come away impressed.[77]

Hoping to erase the doubts raised by the Thant and La Pira affairs, call Moscow's bluff and exacerbate intercommunist strains, probe Hanoi, and above all seed the ground for sterner military steps in 1966, LBJ embraced "fandangle diplomacy"—a free-for-all that included loud pronouncements, diplomatic safaris, and hidden contacts. From his ranch, he sent emissaries around the globe. Improvising his itinerary, Harriman would spend several weeks circumnavigating (flying, after Warsaw, to Belgrade, New Delhi, Peshawar, Tehran, Cairo, Bangkok, Tokyo, Canberra, Vientiane, Bangkok again, Saigon, and Manila before returning to Washington); McGeorge Bundy went to Ottawa; Vice President Hubert Humphrey jetted across the Pacific to brief the Japanese; UN ambassador Arthur J. Goldberg took the classic European tour (Paris, London, Rome; Johnson delighted at sending a Jew to see the pope[78]); one assistant secretary headed for Africa, and another to Mexico. LBJ also sent personal messages to world leaders to argue his case. More quietly, a U.S. diplomat in Rangoon, Henry Byroade, contacted a DRV counterpart to open a channel ("Pinta") to relay messages, though not for substantive dialogue.

＊ ＊ ＊

On Tuesday morning, December 28, LBJ called Harriman to alert him to his decision to launch a major peace campaign ("we ought to give it the old college try") and ask him to hit the road to engage in his favorite pastime: gabbing with Communists. He left it to Harriman to judge whom to visit—perhaps "your old friend Tito," the Poles, the Hungarians, the Russians, "just quietly, one of your general vacationing around, the elder statesman visiting around the world to see the state of the world, . . . any place you drop in or out." Then he could later say that he had stopped the bombing and "walked the last mile" for peace.[79] "Don't let Dean talk you out of it," LBJ warned—and sure enough, Rusk was taken aback when his State Department rival related that Johnson had ordered him to pack his bags for a Vietnam peace mission.[80]

Handed an open ticket (and LBJ's backup plane), Harriman skipped Moscow, to avoid exposing the Kremlin to Chinese charges of collusion with Washington; and he suspected, correctly, that the Hungarians preferred he stay away lest publicity endanger their quiet initiative already in progress. Instead, he set course for Poland, inciting the postmidnight hubbub in Warsaw.

Why the Poles?

Why did Harriman focus on the Poles? Among Soviet allies, Warsaw considered itself the most experienced in Southeast Asia. "Participation in the Commission brought with it considerable political, cadre, and financial obligations," recalled Jerzy Michałowski, Warsaw's delegate to the International Control Commission in the mid-1950s. "During the following years thousands of Polish diplomatic, administrative, translation and military personnel passed through Vietnam, occasioning substantial interest in the problems of that country and drawing us into its fate."[81]

To the extent feasible, Poles on the ICC projected reasonableness and collegiality, and even occasionally distanced themselves from Hanoi's harder-line stands.[82] But none doubted their mission—to defend North Vietnam's interests, in tune with Soviet policy, and counter Canada's pro–United States tilt. As the crisis heated up, a Polish leader explained his country's strategy to Pham Van Dong—to adopt a more moderate and "flexible" posture to "cushion" or "shield" aggressive DRV actions and assure that the Indian was not "thrown into the arms of the Canadian, to get him out of [his] clutches." "Naturally," Prime Minister Józef Cyrankiewicz went on, "we should carry this out after having consulted with you, because the tactics can and should be different, but it must be in accordance with your strategic goals. If our actions are satisfactory to you in this area, we are pleased." North Vietnam's premier effusively declared his satisfaction.[83]

Warsaw's sympathy for Hanoi, however, did not preclude promoting negotiations, especially when they suited Moscow's preference, in contrast to Beijing's ardor for armed struggle. Rapacki actively participated in the Geneva Conference on Laos, and afterward quietly advanced several peace bids to neutralize (literally and figuratively) the regional conflict by extending the Laotian formula's spirit to Vietnam.[84] Most histories mention the Maneli affair—to which, we have seen, there was less than met the eye—but Polish diplomacy in this early phase of the war also included more obscure episodes.

One episode involved an early 1963 approach to New Delhi, which championed nonalignment but edged closer to Washington due to its festering border spat with Beijing. Visiting New Delhi, Rapacki floated to Jawaharlal Nehru "the possibility of the neutrality of both Vietnams as well as organizing universal elections and reuniting the country." After Nehru said that Washington might accept a neutral Vietnam, Rapacki followed up the next day by having Michałowski speak with U.S. ambassador John Kenneth Galbraith.[85]

Because the Harvard economist Galbraith was one of a handful of Kennedy administration aides (along with Harriman) who was sympathetic to Vietnamese neutrality so as to avoid deeper U.S. involvement, he warmed to Rapacki's ideas, citing the Laos pact as evidence of JFK's eagerness to settle the conflict. Lacking instructions, reticence, or reverence for State Department procedure or hierarchy, Galbraith spontaneously advanced his own plan. It envisioned, Michałowski later wrote, gradual neutralization, the withdrawal of foreign forces, and replacing Diem's regime "with a more liberal administration, which would make it possible to establish talks between the North and the South."[86] In Galbraith's telling, it was the *Poles* who suggested a "liberal" Saigon government (i.e., sans Diem) and neutralization; "the North would then call off its help, the South would have a government it could accept, and the revolution would subside and we could withdraw." Galbraith cabled Washington that he had affirmed that America could not "turn our back" on Diem and proposed instead a six-month cease-fire to allow a cooling off and U.S. withdrawal. Intrigued, JFK directed him "to pursue the subject immediately," Galbraith recalled, but Rapacki had already left.[87]

Polish evidence supplies the denouement, to which Washington remained oblivious. After returning to Warsaw, Rapacki sent Michałowski to Moscow to see Andrei Gromyko, the Soviet foreign minister. Warily positive toward Galbraith's purported plan, Gromyko observed that "Vietnam constitutes a burden for the current USA administration and Kennedy's aim—similar to that in Laos—is to withdraw himself from excessive responsibility in this region of the world." However, Gromyko asked, how might neutralization, a troop withdrawal, and cease-fire "influence the evolution of Vietnamese democratic forces and the prospects for the further evolution of the situation in Southeast Asia"? Urging more consultation with Hanoi, he noted that "solving the Vietnamese knot will exert an influence on the reduction of international tensions, which suits our interests. Calm in this region surely also suits the USA. Here our interests are convergent."[88] (Yet, he added, "this solution must be in our favor and not in that of the Americans."[89])

Despite this mildly auspicious start, the initiative fizzled. As Michałowski recorded, "the Vietnamese leadership did not indicate greater interest in the matter, and the Americans did not return to it"[90]—probably because of Washington's dim view of neutralization, which was further discredited by problems already undermining the Geneva Accord on Laos. Nor did JFK's successor think much of neutrality: LBJ virtually spat it out, a dirty word, and de Gaulle's embrace of the concept hardly endeared it to him. "Your mission," he cabled Lodge, "is precisely for the purpose of knocking down the idea of neutralization wherever it rears its ugly head, and on this point I think that nothing is more important than to stop neutralist talk wherever we can by whatever means we can."[91]

To try to salvage the faltering Laos deal, and perhaps preserve it as a model for Vietnam, Poland in May 1964 advanced a new peace plan. This time, Warsaw suggested convening a new conference involving the Geneva Conference cochairs, the ICC members, and the rival Laotian factions—excluding North Vietnam, China, and the United States—a composition that some (but not all) U.S. officials could swallow. The Poles had run the idea by London and Moscow, and Washington seemed agreeable, largely for tactical reasons; it hoped to buy time to prop up Prince Souvanna Phouma, the country's beleaguered prime minister, a neutralist willing to wink at U.S. air strikes against Communist forces in his country. Hanoi and Beijing, followed by the Communist Pathet Lao, torpedoed the proposal, yet Michałowski credited it with stalling, at least for a few months, the Johnson administration's internal consideration of escalation in Vietnam.[92]

In December 1964, a late-night Rusk-Rapacki talk at Poland's UN mission illuminated how these key figures viewed the conflict and each other.[93] With only translators present, "speak[ing] freely and with complete frankness," Rusk bluntly warned that Hanoi risked obliteration if it kept backing the Southern revolt; I'm not threatening, he said, just "stating a fact." Invoking past Cold War showdowns ("Greece, Korea, the blockade of Berlin, the Philippines and Malaya"), he affirmed the United States' intent to defend South Vietnam and Laos from encroachment, and he urged Warsaw to have a "quiet talk with Hanoi," lest it fatally miscalculate.

Rapacki insisted that the situation was not so simple as Rusk ("a man whom he respects") put it. The RVN's rulers were hardly representative, and the violence sprouted not from foreign "intervention or subversion" but "expressions of the state of mind of the people." Hanoi certainly did not consider itself an aggressor, given that it felt entitled to pursue national unification against an illegitimate regime. Saigon governments changed so fast, the Pole quipped, that he did not even have time to memorize the names of prime ministers before they were overthrown.

If North Vietnam did not watch out, Rusk shot back, "it might very rapidly have no government either."

"Surely we're seeking a different kind of solution," Rapacki replied, one taking into account "the real situation in South Vietnam and . . . acceptable to the broad majority of the South Vietnamese people."

Rusk claimed to see "no difficulty about an unaligned position for Vietnam"— a bit disingenuously, given Washington's disdain for the notion. However, he countered, Rapacki wanted to alter Saigon's government to incorporate Communists yet said nothing about modifying Hanoi's—just another example of the old Communist dictum "What's mine is mine, and what's yours is negotiable."

The session was polite, but exposed mutual mistrust. Rusk bristled at Rapacki's allusions to the "fully justified" and "legitimate" U.S. "preoccupation" with "considerations of prestige." We do not want to save face, he retorted indignantly; we want to save South Vietnam. The Pole flinched at Rusk's bellicosity: "We shouldn't be talking about such things," he said when the American vowed that Hanoi would be "destroyed" if it persisted. Rusk voiced interest in learning if the DRV was "ready now to respect the 1962 Agreements and also to discuss the question of South Vietnam," but Rapacki doubted Washington's sincerity. "Unfortunately, when the United States feels strong in the area, it believes that talks are not necessary. When it feels weak in the area, it believes that talks are not possible." The exchange ended with mutual paeans to peace, but also with Rusk's ominous remark that it would be "a great pity" if Vietnam, where Warsaw had no real stake, hurt U.S.-Polish relations.

＊ ＊ ＊

As fighting escalated, the Soviets proclaimed solidarity with their Vietnamese comrades, yet they doubted the wisdom of taking on the Americans. Still, they were leery of incurring the harsh criticism from Beijing or Hanoi hard-liners that would invariably come if they openly urged moderation. After the Ninth Lao Dong Plenum in late 1963, Hanoi had assumed a more militant stand toward the armed struggle—hoping to "liberate" the South swiftly, before Washington intervened in force—and sidled closer to China in the Sino-Soviet split. In contrast to Beijing's enthusiasm for protracted war, Moscow had reacted cautiously to the Tonkin Gulf incident and even tried in the ensuing months, as we have seen, to broker U.S.-DRV direct contacts.

Khrushchev's October 1964 ouster altered the equation. Dashing initial hopes on both sides, the move failed to ease worsening Sino-Soviet strains; Zhou visited Moscow soon after, but he left in a huff after accusing USSR defense minister Rodion Malinovsky of insulting Mao at a reception. (Zhou rejected the excuse that he was tipsy, asserting that "drunk people speak the truth."[94]) However, the new troika—the first secretary of the Communist Party of the Soviet Union (CPSU), Leonid Brezhnev, Premier Alexei Kosygin, and President Nikolai Podgorny— moved to enhance ties with the DRV. In February 1965, as U.S. bombers struck after the Pleiku raid, Kosygin was in Hanoi pledging intensified military and economic aid. On his way home, he stopped in Beijing, where he had a testy exchange with Mao. Kosygin hoped to coordinate the Soviet Bloc's help to Hanoi, but the talk degenerated into mutual rebukes—the most the chairman of the Chinese Communist Party agreed to was to lop a thousand years off his forecast of "10,000 years" of Sino-Soviet polemics. Mao blocked a bid to cooperate on arms transfers, which instead became a new mutual irritant. Yet the Kremlin managed to restore a more balanced position with Hanoi, especially as Beijing's caution belied its shrill exhortations to smash the "imperialist aggressors." The Chinese blasted Moscow for betraying Vietnam by consorting with the Americans over negotiations, yet pragmatically signaled to Washington that they did not want to repeat their collision in Korea.[95]

Despite their improved standing in Hanoi, the Soviets tread warily when it came to advising it to negotiate, fearing charges that, as in 1954, they were selfishly sacrificing Vietnamese interests for their own. After backing off from hesitant support in early 1965 for reconvening the Geneva negotiations, they washed their hands of peace diplomacy, rebuffing repeated U.S. pleas for aid. At the same time, they told their Eastern European allies that they were welcome to urge Hanoi to enter into talks, given the unlikelihood of defeating America on the battlefield.

To the Poles, the Kremlin vowed "decisive" support for Hanoi yet also railed against the Chinese, who spouted "dogmatic and ultrashocking" rhetoric but impeded Moscow's efforts to coordinate military aid, egged on the Vietnamese to take actions liable to ruin their country, and even schemed to choreograph a clash between U.S. forces and Soviet Bloc ships. At a Byelorussian forest retreat in October, Brezhnev told Gomułka that he had bluntly counseled Pham Van Dong to face the prospect of all-out war against a superpower more realistically. "What is your future? Are you planning to fight until the last Vietnamese? Why don't you also take a political road in this fight?"[96]

Though resistant to Soviet advice that they negotiate sooner rather than later —before millions of Vietnamese perished as the Chinese cheered from the sidelines—Hanoi had pledged that, when the time was right, it would move toward a political-diplomatic track. Brezhnev even told Warsaw's leaders in April that a DRV official had said that the Poles, not the Soviets, should act as intermediaries regarding possible talks.[97] First, however (as noted above), the Hungarians auditioned for the part. During the summer, János Péter quietly probed on Hanoi's behalf during a visit to London, and in the fall he titillated Rusk with claims—allegedly based on intimate awareness of Hanoi's views—that a bombing halt would bring progress; as a result, Washington turned first to Budapest once the pause began in late December.[98]

Rapacki lurked in the background, awaiting the right moment to reenter the diplomatic fray. At Fanfani's urging, he had quietly greased La Pira's path to Hanoi; putting him in touch with the DRV ambassador in Warsaw, Do Phat Quang, who helped arrange his onward travel.[99] In mid-November, Rapacki indicated his readiness to more directly engage to a visiting U.S. senatorial delegation. When majority leader Mansfield cited LBJ's readiness to "go anywhere" for peace and solicited ideas to get "the other side" to a conference, the minister replied modestly that it would be presumptuous to offer advice because neither Washington nor Hanoi had sought it and Warsaw had no desire to mediate—yet pointedly added that as an ICC member, "both sides know our address and can rely on us to deliver any messages." Though "frankly and firmly" critical of U.S. actions, he vowed that "if any proposals are made through us, we will not shirk our duty."[100]

Setting Poland's Vietnam Policy: Gomułka, Rapacki, Michałowski

Who ran Poland's Vietnam policy—and in particular, who managed the secret peace diplomacy at the heart of our story? Of course, Moscow set the broad parameters of Polish international behavior. Constrained by the geopolitical realities that consigned it to the Soviet sphere after World War II, and bound by ideological fealty and a rigidly hierarchical "alliance," Poland, like other members of the Warsaw Pact, carefully followed the Kremlin's lead, aware defiance risked nasty consequences. Most Polish Communists knew (or even privately shared) the historical grievances toward Russia nursed by compatriots—the Nazi-Soviet pact, Katyń, Red Army apathy during the Warsaw uprising—but accepted the need to align with it. Complex motives, unique for each, drove them to serve a system that entrenched Poland within the USSR's empire: gratitude for liberation from the Nazis, aid in reconstruction, insurance against German revanchism; ideological affinity or idealism; opportunism and expediency; resigned realism; and, for some, patriotism, a desire to help their country even if it meant enlisting in a regime subservient to a foreign overlord.

Poland, in other words, was not Tito's Yugoslavia, able to defy Stalin and pursue a nonaligned course; and certainly was not barricaded Albania, whose quirky leader, Enver Hoxha, broke with Khrushchev and, alone in the Warsaw Pact, sided with China in the split; nor did the Poles emulate the maverick Romanians, staking out a more equidistant stance between Beijing and Moscow.

Yet, for almost a decade, Poland also could not be lumped with those nearby regimes (Bulgaria, Czechoslovakia, East Germany, and—after 1956—Hungary) that slavishly aped Soviet policies or took an even harder line. Under Stalin, Warsaw had fit that label, and though his death in 1953 began to unfreeze the international scene, Polish politics remained icebound—until the earthquake three years later rocked the Communist realm.

In the tumult after Khrushchev's February 1956 de-Stalinization speech at the Twentieth Congress of the CPSU—and the death soon after of Boleslaw Bierut, Stalin's hand-picked head of the Polish United Workers' Party (Polska Zjednoczona Partia Robotnicza, PZPR)—Poles sensed an opening for change. Protests and strikes erupted around the land, fueling a revolt in Poznań in June that was bloodily crushed. In October, the PZPR defied Moscow by evicting Soviet agents (including the defense minister, a Russian citizen) and choosing a new leader, Władysław Gomułka, a veteran party figure jailed on Stalin's orders for "rightist deviations."[101]

This "Polish October" sparked hope that "national Communism" could secure a freer existence, internally and in foreign policy, within Moscow's domain. Gomułka won popular support for his "Polish road to socialism," and for a time he promoted reformers and checked hard-liners, especially in the hated secret police. Yet, after riding a nationalist wave to power, he disillusioned Poles by remaining a staunch Soviet ally and, worse, curbing intellectual and political liberties after a burst of sunlight.[102] Poles "were optimists about internal change and liberalism in 1956," an observer wrote a decade later, "but those hopes are largely dead, leaving a spiritual jaundice in their wake."[103]

Eager to reassure Khrushchev he could be counted on, Gomułka endorsed his invasion of Hungary despite Poles' sympathy for their neighbor. Still, his regime tried to display a more appealing image to the wider world—and at least a smidgen of autonomy from Moscow—and to do so it had a fresh face: Foreign Minister Adam Rapacki, named in the spring of 1956, a backer, beneficiary, and personification of the reformist makeover.

Rapacki: A Colorful Communist

Finally escaping the shadow of his famous father, a mainstay of Poland's interwar cooperative movement, Rapacki reflected wide yearnings to push his nation in a more Westerly direction. Now in his late forties, he was born in Lwów—a Polish-oriented city later renamed Lvov in Soviet Ukraine (and known as L'viv to Ukranians)—but at ten went with his family to Warsaw. As a young man, he had traveled, studied, and worked in France, Italy, and Germany, imbibing their art, literature, food, and manner of thinking. Studying market economics at his father's institute, after graduating from the Warsaw School of Economics, he had leftist but not Communist ideas, and a taste for politics. "The son of a well-known theorist of the cooperative movement, partly educated abroad and with a good knowledge of foreign languages, Rapacki was characterized as pragmatic, liberal, and ambitious," one analyst wrote. An early leaning to the Polish Socialist Party (Polska Partia Socjalistyczna, PPS) reflected a slightly broader outlook, more open to work with West European Social Democrats, than that of hard-core activists (like Gomułka) in the Moscow-aligned Polish Communist Party (Komunistyczna Partia Polski, KPP).[104]

Fortuitously, Rapacki not only survived World War II but also expanded his political prospects. An army lieutenant, he spent five years in German prisoner of war (POW) camps, editing underground newspapers and befriending fellow officers, who were drawn disproportionately from the intelligentsia. Returning to Warsaw, he rose quickly in the postwar elite, chairing the executive board of Społem (the cooperative movement) and, in 1947, entering the government as a maritime minister. In 1948, he embraced the KPP's hostile takeover of the PPS, which became a junior partner in the new PZPR: "A facile political pamphleteer, he wrote extensively to rally wavering Socialists behind the merger demanded by the Communists." Having pledged allegiance to the new order, Rapacki won a Politburo seat and, in 1950, the post of higher education minister. His fortunes, like those of other ex-Socialists, ebbed in the late Stalin era—he was demoted to deputy Politburo member—but he regained full status in 1956 after becoming foreign minister.[105]

It did not take Rapacki long to make a splash: Exploiting a brief letup in East/West tensions, in October 1957 he advanced a scheme to denuclearize Central Europe, starting with Poland, Czechoslovakia, and the two Germanys. Washington shunned this Rapacki Plan, which it saw as aimed mainly at keeping Bonn's hand off the Bomb, yet many Westerners, from British Labor leader Hugh Gaitskell to George F. Kennan, praised it as a plausible way to soften Europe's division, push disarmament, and avoid a nuclear-armed Germany.[106] "Rapacki was not a utopian dreamer," a Polish analyst wrote. "True, he dreamed of a world without arms, but he was a full-blooded realist, aware of differences dividing the Communist and capitalist systems. . . . He wanted to create conditions under which these differences would be resolved via a competition of coexistence."[107]

Despite provoking global debate, Rapacki's vision of an atom-free Central Europe faded, doomed by the U.S.-Soviet arms race and crises in Berlin and elsewhere. "Adam Rapacki was shouting into the wind," one scholar wrote. "The West perceived a strong, Western-oriented [West Germany] as much more important than gains in disarmament."[108] Yet the plan burnished Poland's image as "more than an echoing board for the Kremlin" and Rapacki's panache, "gentler, old-world style," and relatively jargon-free utterances set him refreshingly apart from his dour, rigid Soviet Bloc colleagues. He "talked like a French diplomat rather than like a Communist functionary," recalled one Westerner.[109] The *New York Times,* twice bestowing a "Man in the News" profile, listed the words Poles used to sketch their foreign minister: "intelligent," "affable," "amusing," and, by women, "handsome"; credited him with restoring ésprit de corps to Poland's demoralized diplomats; and raised an eyebrow at his purported habit of curling up with Italian literature and history books. "With rare exceptions, the Communist system deliberately tends to color the individual in its own grayness," said the *Times.* "M. Rapacki is an exception."[110]

Rapacki's appearance suited an activist intellectual—"of medium height and stocky build, he has a leonine head topped by a shock of gray hair that always seems slightly awry"—but by the time Harriman came to see him, his workaholic habits had taken a severe toll. By 1958, the *Times* observed, his double duties as foreign minister and Politburo member had forced him to "give up music, sports and chess, the hobbies of his youth" and mired him in a "losing fight against a bulging waistline."[111] At about that time, he was stricken by a heart attack (hospitalized for "exhaustion," associates said), and later he suffered more cardiac flare-ups, most recently a coronary thrombosis that sidelined him for months; a British internal report termed his health "very poor."[112]

Still, stoked by caffeine and nicotine, Rapacki stayed at his post, a celebrity in a drab cohort of Communist foreign ministers (not exactly the Rat Pack). Americans thought him a wily sparring partner who *might* help on Vietnam—if Moscow nodded assent. His motives on the war reprised those behind his atomic plan. Within Kremlin-set limits, he felt, Polish "national interest required a lessening of international tensions—political and military—to provide greater room for domestic and international maneuver."[113] In 1962, before the Cuban Missile Crisis, he had quietly vied to dowse a Cold War hot spot by mediating between Washington and Havana (but had only irked both).[114] During the superpower thaw that followed that trip to the brink, he plumped vainly to revive his disarmament plan.[115] Now he set his sights on Vietnam, where more escalation—risking a direct U.S./Soviet clash—might kill hopes to ease relations between Europe's divided halves, or to improve Poland's political and economic ties to the West. Conversely, aiding peace might further those aims and win kudos for Warsaw (and Rapacki). So long as it did not unduly imperil ultimate Communist aims in Vietnam, such an achievement would also raise Poland's stature in Moscow, which wanted to counter China's claim that only armed struggle could advance world revolution.

Rapacki had considerable leeway to steer Poland's Vietnam course. The PZPR Politburo had to endorse key moves, yet Gomułka took only limited interest in foreign policy, aside from matters concerning Germany or Russia, and largely entrusted Rapacki with its conduct. That went for Vietnam, too, despite Gomułka's emotional views and delegation of interparty contacts with Vietnam's Communists to his old comrade Zenon Kliszko, like Rapacki a Politburo member, but more of a hard-liner. At the Ministerstwa Spraw Zagranicznych (MSZ, Ministry of Foreign Affairs), Rapacki could rely on a stable of trusted aides, led by deputy ministers Marian Naszkowski and Józef Winiewicz, ex-envoys, respectively, to Stalin's Moscow and Truman's Washington, who in turn dealt with ties to the Communist and Western worlds (and ran the shop during their boss's medical travails). However, on Vietnam, Rapacki turned to his old friend, MSZ director-general Jerzy Michałowski.

Michałowski: A "Cool Cynic"

The duo managing Poland's Vietnam policy had much in common. Like Rapacki, Michałowski was born in 1909 in Ukraine, and as a child he came with his family to Warsaw; worked in leftist social and housing groups in the 1930s; endured most of the war as a German prisoner; belonged to the Socialist Party until its involuntary merger with the Communists; and entered Poland's postwar government, where, despite fealty to the pro-Moscow regime, he remained a relative liberal oriented culturally toward the West. The "son of a Polish nobleman and a

Jewish mother"—listed in party files as having a family background in the intelligentsia—Michałowski earned a law degree from Warsaw University in 1934, but later did graduate studies in a rougher classroom: a POW camp whose denizens included Rapacki and other compatriots who would join the postwar elite. ("Polish politicians who shared prison camp experiences have seemed to form a sort of society in which the members are not permitted to fail in later life," his CIA profile noted.)[116]

Like so many Poles, Michałowski needed luck to survive the war. The reserve lieutenant's artillery unit was on the eastern front, facing the Red Army. Thanks to the Russian he learned as a kid in Kiev, he was named to a patrol into enemy-held territory. But his horse went missing, so he was ordered west to aid the last-ditch defense of Warsaw. His stand-in on the scouting mission was captured and ended up "on the first list" of Polish officers murdered at Katyń, while Michałowski surrendered to the Germans, who sent him to an officers' prison camp in Waldenburg. Though no picnic, it had a far higher survival rate than a stalag for ordinary foot soldiers; unlike the SS *Einsatzgruppen,* which preferred extermination, the Wehrmacht quaintly abided by the Geneva Convention. With their immediate physical existence thus assured, the camp inmates organized educational, cultural, and political diversions.[117]

After being liberated by the Soviets in January 1945, Michałowski briefly managed housing for the Warsaw city administration, and then joined the Foreign Ministry. Having learned English from a fellow POW, he served from 1946 to 1953 as ambassador to Britain and also regularly visited New York for UN General Assembly sessions. During one such voyage, the dark-haired diplomat—single again after a first marriage failed—met a vivacious Polish émigré named Mira, five years younger, whose escape from the Germans resembled Ingrid Bergman's in *Casablanca.* Before the war, the Łodz native had dabbled in radical politics and creative writing, and reportedly had wed a budding Communist activist, Zenon Kliszko (later Gomułka's close associate). When the war began, Mira was in Paris, married to a Polish nuclear physicist, Ignace Zlotowski, working at a research institute with Frédéric and Irène Joliot-Curie (he had earlier collaborated with Madame Curie); their investigations, using France's first cyclotron, included chain reactions involving uranium. In the spring of 1940, they fled the Nazis and escaped to French Morocco. The couple was interned by the Vichy authorities, but they somehow procured exit papers to Lisbon and onward passage on one of the last refugee boats sailing from neutral Portugal to not-yet-belligerent America.[118] There they split up. Mira, in New York, worked for a time for the Office of War Information and was a researcher for *Time* when she met Michałowski. Sparks flew. A whirlwind romance led to a Paris wedding, and the pair settled in London.[119]

As Cold War battle lines hardened, and Poland moved deeper into the Soviet camp amid persecution and hardship, the Michałowskis watched from a safe distance, immersing themselves in the local scene—hitting jazz clubs and pubs; hobnobbing with the literati; attending concerts, receptions, and dinner parties; Mira writing short stories under various pen names and a popular feuilleton for a Polish weekly. Their son, Piotr (born, like his brother Stefan, during the London posting), recalled that his parents loved America's (i.e., New York's) culture, and even admired its political system. "Make no mistake," he insisted, "my father was not a Communist, he woke up one day having been forced into the Communist Party when the parties merged."[120]

Yet that was no deal breaker: Michałowski still saluted MSZ instructions, even after his socialist faction vanished and his government grew more Stalinist; his talking out of school to Westerners seemed calculated, at least in part, to enhance the credibility of his formal views, which hewed to the party line. After Stalin died, he headed home to Warsaw, and in 1955—following a brief detour to the Education Ministry—returned to the MSZ and began a connection with Asian affairs as Poland's delegate to the newly formed ICC. While based in Hanoi, with side trips to Saigon, Phnom Penh, and Vientiane, he cultivated ties with the same Vietnamese Communist leaders who would still largely run the show a decade later. He was fluent in English, Russian, and French, and he became Polish UN ambassador in 1956, personifying his nation's more liberal image. But his first big task was not pleasant: backing Moscow's invasion of Hungary—though he proudly told his family how he abstained on a key vote, recounting with an "impy smile" that after getting in hot water, he invented a communications glitch to excuse his action.[121] The rest of his term went more smoothly. He lobbied for the Rapacki Plan, he needled the Americans openly and the Soviets and Chinese on the sly, and the "approachable and open-minded" (the CIA's words) couple socialized widely.

In 1960, Michałowski returned to Warsaw as MSZ director-general and overseer, variously, of dealings with "Communist Asia," Latin America, and international political and economic organizations. Befitting his new roost, chameleonlike, his conversational tone grew more anti-American, the CIA noted, yet he also displayed a less dogmatic side. Under the name "Stefan Wilkosz," he wrote for quasi-official journals such as *Polityka,* penning commentaries on John F. Kennedy that the U.S. Embassy judged "searching and frank" and "relatively objective and positive," including an admiring appraisal after JFK's assassination.[122] David Halberstam, who ran into him occasionally (as a *New York Times* reporter in Warsaw and vacationing on the Riviera), recalled him as ingratiating, "very smooth and very Western, . . . a very handsome looking man, . . . much tilted toward the West," whose wife wanted to hop "on the first plane to Paris and London."[123] Another reporter who saw him in France noted his "open-mindedness and sophistication," and his even recoiling in horror at the idea of a U.S. military withdrawal from Southeast Asia—which the Soviet Bloc loudly demanded—because Beijing would fill the resulting vacuum.[124]

Building on his UN and ICC experience, and already "stand[ing] in the front rank of Polish diplomats familiar with the West," Michałowski headed Warsaw's delegation to the Geneva Conference on Laos in 1961-62. You "Americans are backing the wrong horse" in Saigon, he warned a JFK aide, fretting that U.S.-Soviet friction over subsidiary matters (e.g., Cuba) helped China and diverted Washington and Moscow from the "main issue," disarmament, preferably a pact that blocked Beijing and Bonn from nuclear status.[125] He retained cordial ties to the North Vietnamese leaders—in July 1964, Pham Van Dong sent him a friendly card to mark the tenth anniversary of the Geneva Accords, jauntily predicting a "certain" victory and envisioning a reunion in a liberated Saigon.[126] By the time American involvement in Vietnam escalated, he was Rapacki's closest collaborator on Asia policy, recognized by U.S. officials as his "major adviser" on the war.[127]

Yet, despite enjoying his minister's confidence, Michałowski was rumored to be skating on thin ice. Noting his reputation as a "cool cynic," the CIA termed him "a political opportunist, who has skillfully adjusted to the changes of political climate in the past 20 years," yet "does not enjoy the trust of the present regime." Polish intelligence agents closely watched his (and Mira's) private and social activities, alert to any scintilla of disloyalty. U.S. intelligence did not fully trust him either, even if he made good company; "well liked by people generally, Michałowski is a man of considerable charm and self-confidence" but lacks "strong moral qualities."[128]

Harriman in Warsaw

When the Poles learned of Harriman's wish to drop in early on Wednesday, December 29, they were ready to cooperate, despite their vilification of U.S. policies in Vietnam. Landing at Okęcie Airport on a typically bleak winter morning, LBJ's emissary was greeted by Sherer (whose boss was still scrambling to get ready) and Michałowski before heading downtown. It was his first visit in nearly two decades, and outside the limo he could glimpse how Warsaw had sprouted pell-mell from wartime devastation, sacrificing form for function, beneath the jagged silhouette of the Pałac Kultury, the Stalinist behemoth foisted on the Poles by their liberator like a serrated stone dagger in the capital's heart. "To the newcomer, the sky over Warsaw seems to be gray all day," wrote Halberstam, who also arrived that winter. "The air is damp and there seems to be a constant layer of light slush on the streets." On sparsely trafficked avenues, "thoroughly bundled up" pedestrians displayed a "uniformity of dress that seems to match the sky."[129]

After a rest stop at the U.S. Embassy, where he joined Gronouski—who had sped back from Poznań on a predawn train—Harriman went a few blocks east to the Foreign Ministry, a reddish stone boxy vestige of prewar architecture that during the German occupation was in a closed zone controlled by the Gestapo (sparing it from destruction during the uprising), opposite a park on the Vistula River's west bank. The talks started shortly before noon—with Rapacki flanked by deputy minister Winiewicz, Michałowski, and another director-general; and

Harriman by Gronouski, Sherer, and a Foreign Service officer who had accompanied him.[130]

Cordiality initially prevailed. Harriman had seen Rapacki, Winiewicz, and other Poles in Geneva and New York, and despite jousting over various topics he found them "congenial and friendly and quite ready to talk frankly without rancor."[131] He got off on the wrong foot, however, by committing the diplomatic faux pas of uttering the truth. After listing the fourteen points, he said that if North Vietnam did not respond favorably (with an unspecified "sign of peace") to LBJ's bombing halt, he would be forced to "escalate" militarily: "The President has made the first move. If he is rebuffed, he will have no choice. . . . It is now Hanoi's decision if it wants to move toward peace or escalate."

More in sorrow than anger, Rapacki, seconded by Michałowski, objected that the U.S. proposal not only lacked new concrete elements but also constituted an "ultimatum" that the proud, suspicious Vietnamese would certainly reject. Because Hanoi definitely would not "knuckle under" to intimidation, the "chain reaction" of spiraling violence would only aid "those elements" opposed to peaceful coexistence (i.e., the Chinese) and boomerang against Washington. Harriman's words seemed especially ominous, Rapacki rued, after the "incomprehensible" release of the Fanfani correspondence, which had embarrassed the Italian and, that very day, compelled his resignation. Was LBJ taking a grievous wrong turn, he wondered, emulating John Foster Dulles's fetish of seeking "a position of strength" rather than peace? Warsaw would deliver Washington's stand to Hanoi as framed, if their esteemed guest insisted, but he hardly saw the point.

Harriman beat a hasty retreat. "You have put words into my mouth," he protested. He had not issued a threat, and thus the trouble was semantic, not substantive: the offending term—"Forget the word escalation"—merely alluded to the harsh "fact of war," the inevitable dynamic of intensifying carnage if hostilities continued. Though he could not promise that Washington would never resume the bombing, Hanoi should seize the opening for peace. "This is an opportunity, not an ultimatum."[132]

Rapacki found the reformulation "quite refreshing." Calling the bombing break a "positive step," he agreed to transmit the U.S. proposals after some editing to assure both accuracy and the greatest possible likelihood of their acceptance in Hanoi.

The air cleared, Rapacki and Harriman swapped banter about the Sino-Soviet split—good-natured yet "guarded" on the Pole's part, the American sensed—and adjourned to lunch at the neoclassical eighteenth-century Natolin Palace. As the atmosphere warmed, Harriman felt that the Poles now accepted the initiative as genuine and would do their best to persuade the DRV. "Rapacki said in very sincere and simple terms he would do what he could to present U.S. views to Hanoi," Harriman reported. "He concluded [by saying that the] ending of [the] Vietnam War was essential to the stability of the world."

Following his talks with Harriman, Rapacki described the exchanges to the members of the PZPR Politburo, who approved delivery of the proposals to their Vietnamese comrades, along with an oral message to the Lao Dong leadership— both to be delivered personally by a special emissary. The private interparty missive authoritatively endorsed entering direct peace talks, even while doubting U.S. motives. After the usual reiteration of support and recognition that the final decision was up to Hanoi, it stated:

> When it comes to the proposals for peace negotiations put forward presently by the USA and presented by Mr. Harriman, in our opinion, their value depends on the motives that drive the USA government, which are difficult at this moment to label definitively. It cannot be discounted that the USA government, faced with heavy losses sustained in Vietnam, faced with the pressure of public opinion and dissatisfaction in their own society, also faced with limited prospect of a military resolution, is beginning to come to terms with the fact that its military and aggressive policy in Vietnam has found itself in a blind alley, and is endeavoring to find a way out. In this case, in our opinion, it would be worthwhile from the DRV's perspective to undertake talks to gauge more closely the position of the USA government, and in particular to judge what kind of concession that government would be ready to make in the present state of affairs.

To a fellow Communist leader a few weeks later, with the "pause" still in effect, Gomułka summed up more pithily the Politburo's advice: Warsaw could not exclude that the U.S. proposals were framed "to create an alibi for the escalation of the war," but Hanoi needed "to kick back the peace ball which was thrown at it by the Americans." Contacts to "feel out" the enemy would impress world opinion, which was presently "confused because the Americans are talking about a peaceful solution and we are not seizing this opportunity."[133]

Wednesday evening, Michałowski joined Harriman at Gronouski's residence to review and soften the language that Warsaw could use to convey the U.S. stand; they hashed out a five-point summary the American could accept, and Rapacki promptly sent it to Hanoi. At the same time, Rusk endorsed Harriman's effort, telling the Poles that Washington had stopped bombing to enable "a period of relaxation and calm" that might facilitate peace contacts, and promising flexibility on the modalities of future talks, including the sticky topic of NLF participation.[134]

The next morning, in a rare audience with a Westerner, Gomułka hosted Harriman in his office.[135] The PZPR boss, now sixty, had met Harriman twice before, in Moscow during World War II and in New York during a 1960 UN session. A wary mutual respect existed between them, but the Communist had no illusions about the tycoon; Brezhnev had described him to Gomułka as "Johnson's scout," who, in seeking Soviet aid on Vietnam (i.e., to pressure Hanoi), had hid his cards and "wanted to swindle something out of us."[136]

Gomułka greeted Harriman as a "long-lost friend," but a "stormy two-hour argument" soon began. As Gronouski and Rapacki watched (the latter grinning at his boss's bons mots), Gomułka excoriated U.S. conduct, likening the Vietnamese resistance to Polish partisans who fought the Nazis. Harriman "sat up straight and with his finger jabbing continuously for about five minutes, each time within an eighth of an inch from Gomułka's nose," accused him of being a dictator and cynically warping U.S. actions. During one Gomułka tirade, Harriman's eyelids drooped—until the "crocodile" started from seeming repose to snarl a riposte, just as Gronouski prepared to elbow him awake.

Gomułka bragged later that in this verbal combat, he had kept his cool, even a smile, while Harriman, "an old and seasoned diplomat," had lost his temper.[137] But for the American, what mattered was the bottom line—Warsaw's readiness to deliver the goods to Hanoi—despite the Pole's vitriol, including a shot at U.S. "gangster-like methods" for bombing Vietnam without declaring war. As the fireworks subsided, with Harriman expressing thanks for the hasty hospitality, Gomułka shrewdly evaluated LBJ's motives:

> How am I to take this recent initiative of President Johnson's? I would like to think that it is a genuine effort (the pause in the bombing), but I have to say that I have some doubts. I am a politician, too, and I know how politicians sometimes act. It could be, and I cannot ignore this possibility, that President Johnson is simply setting the stage for a more vigorous prosecution of the war in Vietnam a short time later—that all this peace effort is simply a method of convincing the world that he did make every effort to arrive at peace in Vietnam before escalating war to much larger proportions. I don't know, but this could just be a means of satisfying world opinion. It could be a means to provide the President with the argument later on that he contacted the Poles, the Russians, and everywhere in an attempt to arrive at peace, but no one would listen and therefore he had no alternative but to escalate the war. Gomułka said the Poles will play their role, but would do so with some hesitation because they are not certain that this is a serious effort.[138]

"You are behaving like bandits," he admonished. "But if you really want peace, then we are ready to help you!"[139]

Gronouski: A "Rumpled" Rookie

John Austin Gronouski Jr. had only piped up occasionally during Harriman's talks with the Poles, but he savored the front-row seat. A political appointee, a "rumpled economics professor" whose Democratic Party activism (including an unsuccessful 1952 run against Joseph McCarthy for a U.S. Senate seat from Wisconsin) had helped win him an appointment as postmaster-general under JFK and then LBJ, did not let a dearth of diplomatic experience keep him from dreaming of using his new post to seek peace in Vietnam. The Wisconsin native's chief credential for the job was his Polish-American family ancestry, meant to appeal to a key Democratic constituency. Now forty-six, the "bulky, pipe-smoking extrovert" comfortably blended erudition—a University of Wisconsin–Madison PhD; teaching stints at universities in Maine, Chicago, and Detroit; expertise in arcane tax policy—with a pol's informal, populist style; and unabashed partisanship.[140]

Shaking their heads at this blatant identity politics, State Department insiders wondered how the genial Midwestern academic would fare opposite hardened Communists. As Herb Kaiser, then the political officer in Warsaw, recalled, "He was perceived widely by career people (I'm one myself) as an interloper," named due to his ethnicity and LBJ's desire "to get him out of the Cabinet" and make room for Democratic operative Larry O'Brien. Kaiser (later won over by Gronouski's intelligence and drive) said colleagues had "great suspicions" after hearing the neophyte envoy had Johnson's mandate to promote ties not only with his host country but the whole region: "What the hell is this; he's going out as ambassador to Poland and he's overseeing Eastern Europe?"[141]

Gronouski's rookie status loomed even larger when it came to Asia, yet one of his main tasks in Warsaw would be to continue conducting the fitful Sino-American ambassadorial dialogue started in the late 1950s. The periodic talks were mostly laborious exercises in futility, yet U.S. China watchers sifted the records for clues to Mao's inscrutable regime. Moreover, Warsaw's ICC membership ensured that Gronouski would deal at least occasionally with Vietnam issues, with which he also seemed to possess no particular competence. State Department pooh-bahs crossed their fingers that seasoned pros like Sherer would steer the new guy—stepping in for the ex-ambassador, the veteran diplomat John M. Cabot—clear of gaffes and report subtleties to which he might be oblivious. Finally, sensing skepticism from both Foggy Bottom and Warsaw, LBJ himself had asked Harriman to "build Gronouski up a little and pull him in on it," and he duly praised him to the Poles (a mite patronizingly) as the president's "favorite new ambassador."[142]

Gronouski himself had no lack of self-confidence, despite his lack of formal foreign policy training. Like many prominent Americans of his generation, he had served abroad during the war; as an Air Force navigator based in England, he flew twenty-four bombing missions and once bailed out over the English Channel (his parachute had been packed upside-down yet deployed correctly). He brushed up on Polish history, customs, and language—enough to parrot a few phrases and fool some reporters (though not Michałowski, who quipped that he "speaks Polish like I speak Chinese"[143]). In 1964, he stumped for LBJ among Polish-American groups and made a pilgrimage to his ancestral homeland to visit his paternal grandparents' grave, attend the Poznań trade fair, and inspect a few post offices to justify the junket. The trip, the first time he had set foot on to the Continent, highlighted his availability should Johnson consider tapping him as one of his "bridges" to Eastern Europe.[144] Serving as postmaster-general, then a high-profile post, left him feeling that he could operate at the highest level in Washington and had forged warm ties with the president.

For the moment, however, Gronouski was still finding his bearings as ambassador. Since reaching Warsaw in late November (to a rousing reception at the main railway station), he had thrown himself into introductory sessions with his staff and the Poles, moving in his family (wife and two young daughters), attending light public relations events (e.g., opening a hospital for orphans), and, in mid-December, having a first talk with his counterpart from the People's Republic of China (PRC) (leaving the heavy lifting to Sherer). Aside from brief interjections, he was content to leave the negotiating to Harriman and observe the exchanges, enhance his understanding of U.S. policy toward the war, get to know his eminent houseguest (Harriman) and the Polish personalities with whom he would deal in his post, and amass experience that he could use if he got to try his own hand at Vietnam diplomacy. He could scarcely imagine that, precisely a year later, events would place *him* at the center of an even more substantial and dramatic attempt to stop the war, and the incomparably more experienced Harriman on the periphery.

Operation Lumbago

Soon after Harriman flew from Warsaw on Thursday afternoon, December 30—after less than thirty hours in the city—he and Gronouski sent separate personal messages to LBJ and Rusk predicting that Warsaw would not only faithfully relay Washington's message but also add its own voice to prod Hanoi toward negotiations. Gronouski observed that the talks "reaffirmed my conviction that Poles are genuinely interested in helping to end Vietnam conflict." Because they needed "special channels" to communicate with the DRV leaders, who required "some time to ponder," he urged the White House against resuming the bombing "in near future unless there are other more important considerations of which I am unaware." Harriman did not explicitly urge a pause extension, but he also stressed the Poles' pleas for time and credited them with real concern that (as Rapacki put it) "everyone including U.S. may lose control of events."[145]

In fact, they were already moving quickly. Though Gomułka had only grudgingly conceded that Poland felt obliged by its ICC role to deliver the U.S. message, Rapacki warmed to the chance to display his wares as a go-between. He instructed Warsaw's ambassador to North Vietnam, Jerzy Siedlecki, to inform Pham Van Dong of Harriman's approach (and assure him that Warsaw had "emphatically rejected" its "ultimatum-like elements"), and inquire whether Hanoi would receive a special emissary to convey the U.S. proposals.[146] Finding the premier in a "lively and cheerful" mood on Thursday morning, Siedlecki related LBJ's readiness to extend the bombing halt, if it elicited a "sincere" response, and he added his "personal" view that the probe aimed mostly to impress public opinion. "The Americans want to feel us out," Dong agreed, attributing the peace campaign to Washington's growing international isolation. Still, while underlining that the U.S. stand "contained many problems," he cheerily agreed to receive a messenger.[147]

To handle the sensitive mission of carrying the Harriman and PZPR Polit-buro messages and negotiating with the DRV rulers, Rapacki passed over his two Vietnam-based envoys—Siedlecki, a stodgy hard-line apparatchik, and his Saigon-based ICC representative, Henryk Wendrowski, bored and nearing the end of his term. Instead, in a sign of seriousness, he designated the cosmopolitan Michałowski, his trusted aide, who was familiar with the key Hanoi personalities, and of course au courant on Harriman's visit; though excluded from the Ameri-can's talk with Gomułka, he could hear the party boss blasting U.S. policy while waiting in an anteroom to receive instructions for his impending journey.

Wasting no time, shortly after the testy conversation ended, Gomułka handed Michałowski the Politburo's "Note on the Verbal Declaration for the Vietnamese leadership." That same afternoon, Michałowski flew from Okęcie Airport shortly before Harriman left for Belgrade. (The Poles did not tell Harriman about the trip. Mira, who took Jerzy to the airport, thought the jig was up when she spotted his entourage and ducked into a women's restroom; but the Americans, if they noticed, did not make the connection.[148])

During the next seventeen days, Michałowski would make a secret Commu-nist grand tour, gathering insights into both the DRV leaders and the Sino-Soviet rift.[149] At this pivotal juncture of the war, his trek to Hanoi in early January—not the Hungarians' or Soviets' efforts, nor the fitful "Pinta" contacts in Burma—would confront North Vietnam most forcefully with arguments for seriously considering the U.S. proposals and moving toward negotiations. To preserve se-crecy, colleagues and friends—and even his son Piotr, who was at a university outside Warsaw, expecting his father's visit—were told that painful lower back spasms had suddenly afflicted Michałowski, requiring convalescence at a resort in Zakopane in the Tatra Mountains; hence Rapacki's code name for the voyage: Operation Lumbago.[150]

To Moscow and Beijing

Michałowski stopped in Moscow both before and after visiting Hanoi—first to run the plans by the Soviets, then brief them on the results. Late on December 30, 1965, he saw Gromyko, who promised to inform Brezhnev. Endorsing the Pole's mission, the foreign minister agreed "that the Americans have sunk themselves in Vietnam in a blind alley and judges that in fact they are ready for a political reso-lution with conditions that are possible for them to accept." Most likely, he fore-saw, they would look to preserve a military foothold, seek guarantees against co-erced unification, and "try to rescue the situation by appropriating large funds for South Vietnam." Revealing that Moscow soon would send its own emissary to Hanoi (Presidium member and ex-KGB chief Alexander Shelepin), Gromyko de-clined to predict the DRV's reaction to the U.S. proposals the Pole carried, and he worried (prophetically) that Chinese interference might doom his effort.[151]

Michałowski then tasted Beijing's attitude firsthand—but even before landing, he knew to expect a hostile welcome. A few days earlier, the PZPR had written the Chinese Communist Party to urge it to attend a high-level conference of Communist parties to coordinate aid for Hanoi against an expanding U.S. aggression enabled—it noted pointedly—by the "lack of unity and of coordinated actions of the socialist countries." The Poles had sent the letter despite knowing that Beijing firmly opposed such a meeting, correctly sensing a Kremlin power play to isolate it within the socialist camp.[152]

Cooperating with Harriman, they already had reason to believe, would further irk the Chinese. Told of the decision to relay his proposals, the PRC ambassador in Warsaw had declared them "lies" and said there was no point in talking to Americans.[153] From Hanoi, Siedlecki warned on December 31 that after he had seen Dong the night before, China's ambassador had gone to the premier's home shortly before midnight and the next morning, only eight hours later, suddenly flown to Beijing, taking the rare step of buying his ticket at the airport. "There is no confirmation, but it is hard to doubt that this is connected with your report," he cabled.[154] On New Year's Day, *Renmin Ribao*, the Chinese Communist Party's mouthpiece, set the tone by vilifying Washington's "debauched activities" as a patent disguise for plans "to widen its aggressive war in Vietnam."[155]

On Sunday, January 2, in the Great Hall of the People in Tiananmen Square, Michaowłski related the exchanges with Harriman to PRC deputy foreign minister Wang Bingnan, a former envoy to Poland and veteran of the Sino-U.S. ambassadorial talks in Warsaw, and also to ministry director-general Xu Deng. He stressed Harriman's retreat on the ultimatum-like language; the desirability of ascertaining whether America sought peace or a "pretext for new escalation"; the U.S. proposals' "flexibility"; and the Poles' belief that it was their "duty" to deliver them, because only their Vietnamese comrades were morally entitled to decide how to respond. But Wang was not buying. He launched into an "extensive lecture" claiming that Washington, facing defeat in Vietnam and internal contradictions at home, was plotting to expand the war; and he dismissed its peace proposals as "lies and deceits" and "blackmail." Rather than comprehend that the Vietnamese struggle could only be won on the battlefield, Wang added "with sorrow," Poland, a socialist "friend," had now fallen into the U.S. trap. Aghast that Michałowski would "transmit . . . the illusion of peace," Wang ridiculed the idea of advising Hanoi to enter talks before a decisive military victory, because "at the green [negotiating] table, nobody won."

Michałowski again stressed Poland's "duty" to relay the proposals, because only Hanoi could decide when to transfer the struggle from the armed to the political plane and needed the basis for doing so. No, Wang countered, Warsaw "should have immediately rejected and unmasked the lies and the fraud of the Fourteen Points" and only then reported the Harriman talks to Hanoi as information instead of fostering the impression "that the U.S. desires peace and we want war." The "venomous and personal" language stunned the Pole; Wang even called him a "horse's hoof," which he inferred was not a compliment. Irked at these "insulting" arguments, Michałowski observed that Poland and China clearly differed about an ICC member's responsibilities—"a big difference," Wang shot back. On this tart note, the formal conversation ended.[156]

The tense atmosphere had startled one Chinese diplomat present, Liu Yan-shun, who had previously been stationed at PRC missions in Gdansk and Warsaw. Translating the exchanges between men he thought were amicable old comrades, Liu was taken aback by the raised voices and abrasive language. He was equally surprised when, the formal talk over, Wang abruptly relaxed his tone and invited Michałowski to a Szechuan-style feast in his honor, and the two joshed about how the fiery cuisine suited their talk. At the twenty-four-course meal, they "returned to the relationship of old friends," swapping stories about the "good days in Warsaw as if the formal meeting conversation had never happened." When the puzzled translator asked Wang about the encounter; he replied that Foreign Minister Chen Yi had told him simply, "You are an old diplomat; you know what to do." With Beijing being belligerent about Vietnam, this meant taking tough yet retaining communications with the Kremlin ally, despite the deepening Sino-Soviet rift. Liu, who two decades later would become China's envoy to Poland, derived a valuable lesson in the "art of diplomacy"—rival diplomats could stridently argue yet remain friends.[157]

After the suddenly "charming hosts" had treated him to a "lavish Chinese banquet, with many cordial toasts and remarks," the mystified Michałowski spent the night at Warsaw's Embassy, where staff members supplied context for his sour-and-sweet reception by describing Mao's extremist turn.[158] The next morning, he may have felt a bit queasy about his hosts' hospitality when he read *Renmin Ribao* (*People's Daily*). "Lately," it warned,

> American imperialism is conducting suspicious operations on a large scale: so-called "searching for peace." . . . Puppets and go-betweens, a variety of satanic creatures, have spread everywhere from their cages to play or sing the same note, obligingly helping or acting like hired applauders. The noise and shouting about peace has reached its summit to the heavens. As a result of this, some people of goodwill began to doubt or even to reflect: Could it be that American imperialism is really considering hiding its butcher's knife and putting an end to aggression? But can it possibly deceive shortsighted people, this trick prepared by the Johnson administration? The Johnson government is trying to sell stale goods as fresh. . . . By selling its demagogic "peace negotiations," Johnson is staking particular hope on Khrushchevite revisionists and their lackeys.

Just in case the allusion was not explicit enough to suggest Chinese disdain for the "lackey" they had mao-tai'd and dined the night before, the newspaper noted incredulously that Harriman's visit to Warsaw had "disposed some Polish leaders to believe that the USA truly desires to extinguish the war in Vietnam."[159]

Beijing could do more than hurl invective to undermine Michałowski. That Monday, January 3, he planned to fly to Hanoi—but the Chinese authorities held up his plane the entire day in the southern city of Nanning, "under the pretext," the Pole later wrote, "that American raids were supposedly taking place in Vietnam." On reaching Hanoi the next morning, however, "I found out there were absolutely no raids that day, and the purpose of delaying my arrival was to allow a high-level functionary of the Chinese Foreign Ministry to get ahead of my mission to prepare the ground for its rejection."[160]

In Hanoi "at a Crossroads"

On January 4, 1966, Michałowski kicked off a week of talks with North Vietnam's leaders. His presence substituted, more concretely, for the distant Hungarians as a Soviet Bloc counsel of moderation, or at least a tactical willingness to engage Washington. A fellow Communist, he could make the case more credibly than the Americans or their Canadian surrogates; and Budapest mostly dealt with Hanoi during the pause at long range and via midlevel representatives. Moscow would soon send its own high-ranking emissary, but given its sensitivity to Chinese charges of collusion with Washington, Shelepin would be far warier than Michałowski about urging a political approach.

Ominously, even as the Pole arrived, the DRV Foreign Ministry issued a stern statement demanding anew that Washington accept the Four Points and stop the bombing "unconditionally and for good," and denouncing the pause as a transparent "trick" to hide aggressive plans for escalation.[161] Notably, however, in view of secret contacts already taking place in Rangoon (where a North Vietnamese diplomat had politely received a U.S. colleague delivering an aide-mémoire) and a somewhat more forthcoming message the Hungarians received the same day (indicating a readiness to "accept" conversations with Americans), the January 4 statement did not explicitly refer, positively or negatively, to the idea of direct encounters short of formal negotiations.[162]

As Michałowski could gather, Hanoi hardly welcomed being pushed toward the bargaining table. In private, the Vietnamese were firm on the matter: The party had just ratified a secret decision to press the military struggle, despite Washington's escalation from a "special" to a "limited" war. On December 27, 1965, Ho Chi Minh presided over the Twelfth VWP Central Committee Plenum, which approved "protracted warfare" and intensified guerrilla conflict while using the People's Army of Vietnam (PAVN) (regular DRV forces) as a "strategic reserve." Showing scant interest in negotiations, it affirmed its determination to vanquish Washington regardless of how many troops it sent. "Now the Americans have 200,000 troops in South Vietnam," Ho said a few weeks later. "They may increase this even more, to 300,000, 400,000, or 500,000 troops. We will still win. We are certain of victory."[163]

In a closed-door speech to the plenum, Le Duan elaborated Hanoi's approach to negotiations—a strategy blending violence and bargaining that had been successfully employed by Vietnamese resisters to Chinese invaders during the Ming Dynasty, and more recently by Mao against the "American–Chiang Kaishek clique" and by the North Koreans at Panmunjom.[164] Now the U.S. "imperialists" plotted escalation to avoid "defeat and stalemate," yet they also sought direct talks to coerce concessions. Hanoi would rebuff this effort, "fighting until we win and then talking"—after Saigon's "puppet army" had "essentially disintegrated" and Washington, once military setbacks "shattered" its "will to commit aggression," was "forced to recognize our conditions!" (A Lao-like compromise in South Vietnam was unacceptable due to a "completely different" balance of forces.)

Stressing the need for secrecy—Hanoi had not confided even in fraternal allies—Le Duan acknowledged that other nations had adopted stands on negotiations at variance with the DRV's. Whereas Washington favored "negotiating from a position of strength" and neutral nations (which also occasionally ventured futile mediation bids) ultimately acquiesced to U.S. imperialism, even "countries that sincerely supported us" had "their own specific diplomatic and domestic considerations." Lacking a "clear understanding of our situation," they "worried that in prolonged combat our side's losses and sacrifices will be too great. And then there are the concepts of a number of large nations in our camp whose strategic missions in the world are different than ours, and for that reason everything about their concepts, from the contents of their ideas to the tone of voice in which they couch them, is different from ours."

Le Duan politely refrained from naming these wobbly camp followers, but he was clearly alerting comrades to Soviet Bloc blandishments to curb the military struggle and accept a flawed settlement. Still, he conceded, using "weakness to fight strength," Hanoi must maintain tactical flexibility and could not exclude talking to the Americans even before achieving decisive military results. "In our situation," he explained,

> we may not have to wait until we have basically won before we agree to begin talks. Instead, at some point in time, under certain specific conditions, we may be able to fight and talk simultaneously with the objective of restricting our opponent's military actions, of winning broader sympathy and support throughout the world, and of concealing our own strategic intentions. The issue right now is the question of a favorable opportunity to employ this stratagem.

The secretive party leader's remarks recognized an inescapable fact: Hanoi was committed to attaining eventual total victory—unification under Communist rule—yet for diplomatic and propaganda reasons, it could not seem wholly uninterested in peace. It had to respond not only to U.S. probes but also pressure or insinuations from Moscow-aligned allies that it was time to go beyond a purely military approach. Heavily reliant on their support and delicately navigating a neutral course in the Sino-Soviet split in hopes of gaining maximum aid from both sides, the DRV had to deflect arguments from comrades who, unlike the Chinese, were less confident of beating Washington on the battlefield.

✳ ✳ ✳

In his first talk in Hanoi, with Foreign Minister Nguyen Duy Trinh, Michałowski recounted Harriman's visit, relayed the U.S. proposals, and emphasized the pluses of moving to the political plane. Trinh "warmly" thanked Poland for its fraternal help, but otherwise "rather stiff[ly]" echoed China's line: LBJ's peace offensive thinly disguised escalatory plans, and North Vietnam would fight until victory; eventually, triumphs comparable to Dien Bien Phu would reap political gains, but not yet. A second, dinner conversation with Trinh that Tuesday, lasting past midnight, was less formal, as was one the next morning, but equally futile. "He speaks in stereotypes and [one] cannot count on a real discussion," the Pole cabled Rapacki.[165]

Trying to shake Trinh, Michałowski spun out a series of contrary propositions whose flavor emerges from a Vietnamese transcript:

America has stopped the bombing of North Vietnam and sent Harriman to meet with Polish leaders and look into the problem. . . . If we don't respond to the Americans' act of peace, they will react by bombing harder than ever. Johnson is being is being pressured by his military circle to step up the war effort. The key to peace is in Hanoi. . . .

Poland [sees] two possibilities: Perhaps the Americans see that they are already losing and that now nothing would be gained from escalating the war effort and so are thinking that they must avoid stepping up the war at all costs. If it's like that then it's very important. And we should try to see if the Americans are ready to yield on anything else if they have no choice but to negotiate. [Second:] Perhaps the American bid for peace is a smokescreen to deceive the world. If that's the case, then we have no choice but to sit with the Americans and reveal their true face.

When we are in discussions, the Americans will put forward a price too high; . . . later, they will lower it. We will bargain with them and see how they sell their goods. We are afraid that the Americans are faced with an important decision; they will not stick with their war objectives as they do now, because if they do, they will lose. Therefore, the Americans will escalate the war. The Vietnamese losses will be even greater. The Americans plan to send 200,000 or 300,000 [more] troops to South Vietnam. It will be difficult for the Americans to step down the ladder and pull out their troops once they have started escalation. If we do not negotiate now, it will be very difficult later on. If the Americans increase their forces, then our struggle will not go as smoothly as it does now. America has stopped the bombings. There are indications that America may continue the cease-fire, but these are indications only. There is nothing there that will bind Vietnam to anything.

We believe that the Americans are sincere, and we believe that they are at a crossroads. The Americans have said that they are under pressure and that they want to see such indications [of Hanoi's readiness for peace]. If the Vietnamese show such indications, then they will be willing to relax the tension, and there will be a road ahead of us.[166]

The Pole made scant progress, however, and noted suspiciously that Trinh's reasoning, often even his phrasing, closely resembled what he had heard in Beijing, if in a friendlier tone ("the single difference"). Just before seeing him, Michałowski discovered, Trinh had received the special PRC envoy, who had leapfrogged him while he cooled his heels in Nanning. Relating Trinh's well-rehearsed "barrage" to Warsaw, he concluded that "everything points to the mobilized pressure of the neighbors."[167]

Withholding, for the moment, the special message from the PZPR Politburo, Michałowski had immediately requested a meeting with Pham Van Dong, with whom he had maintained "close and frequent contacts" a decade earlier, and kept up friendly ties. By the end of their three-hour exchange Wednesday morning, as Michałowski pressed the case for responding favorably to the Americans, Trinh seemed to bend. Becoming "notably more flexible and open to our arguments," the Pole sensed, "more and more [in a] defensive posture," he finally "took cover" by revealing that an appointment with the premier was set for that later that day so he could receive the government's official position.

That afternoon, January 5, 1966, Michałowski met with Dong for two and a half hours in an "exceptionally cordial atmosphere, with embraces, with grace, [and with] complimentary [expressions of] mutual friendship to our leadership from himself and Ho."[168] Besides the "Verbal Note" from Gomułka and the Politburo, he presented the premier with fresh hints of U.S. flexibility on the NLF's participation in talks (contained in a cable from Warsaw that had just reached him), and again laid out why Poland felt entering into talks now offered Hanoi real benefits (including an indefinite extension of the bombing halt and a "better appraisal of the opponent by probing"); conversely, a flat rejection would ensure more escalation and confusion and difficulties in world opinion. The Americans, under intense pressure, were "sincere" but "at a crossroads" between war and diplomacy, and "we can direct them in the direction of deescalating operations."

In contrast to Trinh, the Pole discerned in Dong a potentially forthcoming partner. He quickly relieved Michałowski's fears on at least one point. After hearing him explain Warsaw's motives for transmitting the U.S. proposals—"we cannot accept or reject anything; only those who are fighting and shedding blood"—and describe China's negative attitude, Dong "voiced his heartfelt thanks to Poland, strongly underlining the correctness of our conduct and repudiating the position taken in this matter by Beijing." The premier, "visibly angry" after being told that the PRC's foreign minister had blasted Warsaw for carrying the proposals to Hanoi instead of rejecting them outright, said that "it was not Chen Yi's business to make such an observation and added that he (Michałowski) was quite right in coming to Hanoi to convey Harriman's message."[169] In French, with no translator present, he thanked him for "a lot of material to think over" and, unlike the dogmatic Trinh, confessed to hesitations, uncertainties, and sleepless nights over the war.

However, for all his warmth, Dong also expressed grave doubts about Michałowski's recommendations. They concerned, after all, Vietnam's "fundamental survival," to be decided by an entire generation. The Americans sought to expand the war, and they had never accepted the Four Points—which, he added firmly, were "not for adjudication—they must be accepted or rejected." They spoke peace but would only negotiate from a position of strength. Yet they were "getting their butts kicked" in South Vietnam, unable to solve their military woes through air strikes, and in no position to dictate the terms for talks. "This we cannot accept, and because we are winning, consequently, it is we who will put forward conditions—just like it was with the French after Dien Bien Phu."

Michałowski did not give up after this initial, unpromising exchange. "I undertook an arduous discussion," he cabled Rapacki, "accepting the principles, but analyzing the tactical opportunities [and] benefits of accepting the peace initiative, [the] weight of the political struggle, of lessening the losses and taking a breath, unmasking the dishonest declaration of the enemy. [Pham Van Dong] agreed with the opportunities of our proposed tactic, though he harbored doubts about accommodating it in time." The Vietnamese record sheds light on how the Pole tried to lure Dong into agreeing to talks, framing pragmatic arguments and sometimes sharp criticisms that amounted to comradely tough love:

It really is pure strategy. I think that if you give information that you are looking into America's proposal then the duration of the cease-fire [i.e., bombing pause] will be extended and you won't be forced into anything. That is important. You will have time to consolidate your power, re-group, and do many other things.

You've said that the military and diplomacy must go hand in hand. The military struggle will receive the assistance and support of this political struggle.

We are afraid that if you blatantly reject these proposals then that will be a political failure on your part.

The public opinion among the world's progressives and Communists in the West will not be able to understand you. That is also something that the noncommunist Americans demanding peace will also be unable to understand. That would be a great opportunity for American propaganda. . . . When the public opinion cannot understand you, then that is a political failure on your part. I don't think we would be able to explain ourselves, and we won't be able to resist that kind of shift in public opinion.

We think that no matter what you must come up with concrete suggestions through actions that work closely with the Americans' proposals and diligently move toward discussions.

You have said that you have thought of discussions, but now they have not materialized and military victory has not yet been achieved. I am afraid that the Americans will choose to escalate the war and if that happens then it will be very difficult to have discussions. After there are many more troops, it will be very hard for a powerful nation like America to withdraw. They will lose face. . . . The situation will become more complicated. . . . As of now, America's possibility of withdrawal has not yet been cut off. . . . More important, more important than that possibility and this opportunity, will be what will happen after the war is escalated.

Now you need to look for a way to achieve peace. We will find a way to be strong and weaken the enemy. When their soldiers hear that there is news of possible peace, then they will not want to die anymore. That will give you time to consolidate your power. Then we will find a way to make America yield. They will have to pay a price for peace, withdrawing their troops, and saving face. Once they yield, it won't be long before you can bring up your principles. We think that that is possible. But perhaps first yielding on your part is necessary. We think that America's retreat after five years without war is better than their retreat after five years of war.

We think that talking with them and figuring them out will only be advantageous for us. We have nothing to lose from trying to feel them out, having direct or indirect talks with them, in whatever setting. And we will be able to think of going to the International Commission, the two chairmen of the Geneva Conference, and the participation of friendly nations.

We need to come up with a plan. We need to come up with proposals that prove that we want peace and after that you will take the world's public opinion. If you put forward such suggestions and the Americans reject [them], then they won't be able to look like friends of peace any more.[170]

Hanoi must respond to Washington's call for action, he urged, to avoid losing to this "foolish American game" by seeming to ignore "the suggestion to seek resolution through political measures."

In a long exchange, Dong generally held his ground. He stressed the risk of a U.S. trap and the imperative to remain "masters of our own strategy," but admitted the war's "terrible" and growing cost and that Michałowski had made some valid points. "In principle you are correct: Don't let the Americans be the ones to wave the banner of peace. It must be we who come up with a plan for peace. Public opinion will be with us and not the enemy. I promise you that I will carefully consider your suggestions."

Before leaving for a VWP Politburo session to review the proposals (and perhaps strategy for Shelepin, due soon), Dong "strongly and significantly" told Michałowski: "We are masters of our own fate and choose our own paths." The statement could only mean one thing: Hanoi, not Beijing, made the life-and-death decisions on the war, despite Soviet Bloc (and Western) suspicions to the contrary.

Michałowski left the premier's office slightly encouraged—the door seemingly still ajar, at least a crack. Despite the stern Foreign Ministry public statement the day before, Dong had not formally rejected the U.S. proposals, but asked him not to communicate with Washington while the leadership deliberated and vowed he would be informed once it made a decision. The Pole prepared to extend his Hanoi visit.

A Monologue with Ho

However, a de facto answer came the next day in a discussion—more a monologue, Michałowski rued—with Ho Chi Minh.[171] Revolutionary patriarch, vanquisher of France, DRV president, Communist Party chair, his wizened visage and reedy white beard now familiar around the globe, Ho was Vietnam's preeminent political figure and symbol, but for several years he had been more icon than leader, supplanted by Le Duan and others; in failing health, secretly visiting China for treatment, he had less than four years to live. Yet Ho still occasionally participated in or presided over Politburo meetings, and it was impossible to imagine the leadership opposing his wishes.[172]

But to the Pole's disappointment, chagrin, and even anger, Ho disdainfully rejected acceding to the U.S. proposals. Instead, he insisted, Hanoi must fight on until achieving inevitable victory on its terms. As a state-approved Vietnamese account acknowledged, the conversation "played out stressfully and there were tense moments."[173]

Michałowski once again deployed all the arguments at his disposal, further confirming that he more than anyone else during the pause made Washington's case for negotiations directly to the Vietnamese in the best possible light. His cable to Rapacki summarizing the talk with a "stubborn" (and, he believed, Chinese-influenced) Ho suggests the tenacity with which he argued and the resistance he faced:

(1) Talk with Ho. Deputy Premier and MFA Nguyen [Duy Trinh] and official recorder as well as Siedlecki present. Ho growing old, obstinate, sermonizing, unrealistic. Huge contrast with yesterday's talks with PVD [Pham Van Dong] and a complete change of argument and tone. He began with lavish praises of gratitude to our leadership and assurances of complete understanding of our motives. The party letter they will weigh and will give a reply through Siedlecki (that is, not quickly). As for the American proposals: [It is] too early to think about a peaceful

resolution. [It is] necessary to fight the enemy. Victory is certain, world opinion supports us, the camp is helping us. We want peace, but we are the victims of aggression, which we have to repulse militarily, just like we defeated France. There is today only one eventuality for peace: the complete withdrawal of America. On the peace offensive, they have only one reply: the declaration of 4 January. He has no doubts that the opinion of the whole world will appraise it as a peace gesture. He was completely informed by PVD and Nguyen of our information, opinions, and discussions. He is appreciative, thanks for trouble, kindness, and concern, but he believes he is absolutely correct and [has] all the opportunities to win the war and impose peace on the enemy.

I undertook an hour and a half of discussion, difficult because it was met with stubborn expressions. I unraveled all the possible arguments. Benefits of knowing intentions of the opponent ("we know them well"). Unmasking the pseudopeace slogans ("we don't need to, world opinion understands who is the aggressor"). Slowing the process of escalation ("they [the Americans] talk about peace and send reinforcements"). Possibility at the very least of prolonging the pause in the bombing ("they must completely stop"). Rise in losses to the Vietnamese nation ("no victory without sacrifice, if we die our children will be victorious"). Rejection occasions an increase in U.S. engagement, this makes their withdrawal difficult in the future ("we will talk when we decide it is appropriate"). Setting in motion great military potential of USA may change balance of forces in the South ("the same was said before Dien Bien Phu—now we are stronger and we have [the support of] the socialist family"). Unfortunately the family is not united ("on the matter of assistance to us there is cooperation").

Aim of taking advantage of the internal political situation in the USA and among allies ("nations will decide for themselves who is right"). Benefits of accepting peace proposals ("we will take it when the time comes"). Richness of unconditional forms of contacts ("we will undertake contacts with American nation when they leave Vietnam"), etc.[174]

The now-available secret Vietnamese record roughly squares with the Polish, but it includes earthier evidence of Ho's brusque dismissal of the U.S. proposals:

Michałowski:

I have been appointed by our leaders to come and try to understand your opinions on the matter. We will then speak of them to the American president. I want to know what I should say to him. I think that if the American president sees that you have rejected the possibility of negotiations, then America will only be able to follow the road to escalation.

We believe that in the present situation we need to feel out the situation [to see] if it is possible to have negotiations and according to what conditions, and if it is possible to force America to pay a price for negotiations. Perhaps the Americans will be forced to give in to your stance on the issues. If the Americans only emphasize their conniving goals in order to escalate the war, then in that situation we will have to do something in order to ensure that America fails. We have to make it clear to the people of the world that we wish to have peace. If the Americans refuse, then the Americans will lose politically. In Europe and Asia, there are many noncommunists who also want peace. We must make them understand us. If we refuse any attempt to communicate and contact them, then they will not be able to understand us. That would be a political failure—a huge failure. Even in our own country there are people who don't understand. America is a powerful nation; it will be hard for them to accept heavy failure. On the other hand, if we conduct negotiations, then I think that that would be a political victory for us.

Chairman Ho Chi Minh:

I would like to ask you just one question. "Do we not love peace?" There are many reasons and ways to prove that we do. Who are the invaders? Nobody would say that we are the invaders. At no time has anyone thought that way, including noncommunists. No one yearns for peace more than we do. So why is it that we must continue to fight this war? There is only one reason; we are forced to fight this war. We can only fight and raise our weapons.

Why must the Americans go sticking [their] nose in others' business? The American government has sent their military forces here and now they must stop the invasion. That's all they need to do to resolve the problem. The Americans must piss off [*cút đi*]! No matter what we may suffer, the Americans must piss off! They must stop the invasion. Johnson's mouth says "peace" but his hand gives the order to mobilize troops. We are not rejecting anything. But our people must have peace and stability. We don't want to become the victors; we just want the Americans to piss off! Goodbye! [*Gút bai!*]

We have already fought with the French; we have already suffered greatly. We didn't kick out the French so that we could succumb to the rule of the Americans. We will fight to the end. They have entered our home. They have killed our children. That is why they must piss off! Why must the Americans go knocking on everybody's door? If they fight with us, in the end they will have to roll up their bed sheets and go. Then everything will be settled.[175]

Siedlecki interjected, "If we are strong, then we will be able to talk to the thugs."

"But the thugs are not weak," Ho countered. "They still possess abundant strength. Our opportune moment has yet to arrive. It is not that we are deaf and mute!"

"But what should we say to the Americans?" Michałowski asked.

"You, comrades, can tell the Americans that they must leave Vietnam," answered Ho; "the American people" would "completely understand" Hanoi's stand, even if "Imperial America" did not.[176]

An admirer may commend Ho's grasp of Washington's masked escalatory plans and his heroic determination to fight for Vietnamese freedom, independence, and unity, regardless of the cost, but Michałowski found him not only intransigent but also "incoherent" and "a bit senile,"[177] mouthing "pompous vague phrases."[178] "Ho is an old man," he told a starry-eyed American who had lauded the revolutionary's supposedly open-minded and cosmopolitan outlook.[179] The encounter left Michałowski with a "hostile precipitation," a Soviet who spoke with him soon afterward recorded.[180] It was a sharp letdown from Dong, whom Michałowski would describe to Harriman as "one of the best statesmen he had ever met," the "leader of the doves" with a "humanistic approach."[181]

Though still awaiting a formal response, the Pole realized that the January 6 session with Ho had effectively ended his quest, leaving him empty-handed. While he was still in Hanoi, a Warsaw envoy in East Berlin crisply summed up his talks to a comrade from East Germany: Michałowski had concluded "that the Vietnamese comrades underestimate the enemy and overestimate the public opinion pressure of the world and the American population; they are still under the influence of the Dien Bien Phu military victory. The Vietnamese comrades proceed under the assumption that the DRV is not yet strong enough to be able to enter negotiations. To a conference, the Vietnamese comrades think, one can only come as a victor, and for this more military successes must be gained."[182]

Complications and Crumbs

Though bitterly disappointed, Michałowski found his visit eye opening. Mulling over the more forthcoming talks with Dong and even Trinh on January 5, 1966, he perceived varying approaches at the top of the DRV regime. Despite Dong's declaration of independence, he presumed that China had swayed Hanoi's ultimate decision—his own talks in Beijing, he believed, had "engendered a sharp reaction and pressure on the ruthlessly negative reply to Poland."[183] After hearing from Michałowski that Dong "inclined towards seeking some political solutions" but that a day later Ho "decisively rejected such suggestions," Gomułka also sensed "some difference of opinions within the Vietnamese leadership"—perhaps merely "shades." He also blamed China, telling Hungary's János Kádár that under its thumb, Hanoi could neither act freely nor "conduct independent talks with the Americans."[184]

Michałowski used his remaining days in Hanoi to probe the Vietnamese further and coordinate with Soviet Bloc diplomats. His stay overlapped Shelepin's, but he did not meet Moscow's emissary, instead tracking his progress via its ambassador, Ilya S. Shcherbakov (who seemed "very pessimistic" as Shelepin arrived, even before hearing of the Pole's dispiriting talk with Ho).[185] He gossiped with Hungary's representative on their nations' respective efforts and tried vainly at Warsaw's behest to dissuade East German and Bulgarian envoys from also urging the DRV to negotiate, for "this could create the impression of organized action and pressure with a tone expressly anti-Chinese in character."[186]

Michałowski had a "long and very sincere talk" with General Vo Nguyen Giap. The defense minister, famous for exploits against the French, evoked a "Polish cavalryman, full of fantasy, very brilliant, very temperamental and very enthusiastic." Though Giap seemed "in very gay spirits," even "relishing the fight with the Americans," Michałowski noted that he reputedly had had "several changes of heart," sometimes "certain of military victory," at others on "bad terms with the Chinese faction."[187]

The PAVN head predictably expressed "absolute confidence of victory," citing his success against France. "Acute Dien Bien Phu complex," the Pole cabled. "Constant comparison with 1954." But Giap also hinted at strains between Hanoi and the NLF—making the "very telling" remark that "the beginning of talks by the DRV with the USA could provoke objections within the NLF in the South and accusations of 'selling' their interests in return for the ending of the bombing in the North."[188]

A talk with "very militant" NLF figures, who were in "no mood to negotiate" (in contrast to "not so belligerent" DRV leaders), reinforced the sense of distinct perspectives, if not a "split." "When Michałowski told the NLF's representatives that if they persisted in fighting, it might even lead to World War III," Warsaw's UN delegate informed Thant, "they replied that they were aware of it but since they have been fighting for liberation of their country for twenty years, World War III would not make any difference to them. If their objective of complete independence is not achieved, they will continue to fight."[189] With some surprise, Gomułka told a fellow Communist that the NLF seemed to reflect "entirely a Chinese point of view," felt the "euphoria of victory and rejects all negotiations," planned to intensify military operations, and even accused Northern comrades of lacking zeal for combat with the Americans.[190] As Michałowski realized, the discovery that not only Beijing but also the NLF favored war until total victory further complicated Polish hopes of convincing Hanoi to accept negotiations short of a decisive military triumph.

However, Michałowski got a few crumbs in a farewell chat with Trinh on January 10. Besides "lots of thanks, compliments and honeyed words," the minister vowed that Hanoi would work on "improving the proportion between fighting and politics consistent with our suggestions" and "think about planning a transition to peace initiatives."[191] He also gave a warily positive reply to the Pole's earlier query to Ho, Dong, and himself: Would the DRV receive a private U.S. citizen who might serve as an informal channel to LBJ?

The American in question was Norman Cousins, the liberal editor of *Saturday Review* and prolific commentator, who considered himself no mere scribe but also a citizen-diplomat-activist, promoting world peace and nuclear disarmament through contacts with powerful statesmen. A few years before, he had gone to the USSR to see Khrushchev and convey messages from Pope John XXIII (seeking to ameliorate Soviet religious conditions and open a Vatican-Moscow dialogue) and JFK (Cousins believed that his efforts after the Cuban Missile Crisis had smoothed the way for a limited nuclear test-ban treaty).[192] Since the late 1950s, he had forged warm ties with Warsaw through his work bringing Polish women disfigured by Nazi medical experiments—so-called Guinea Pigs of

Ravensbrook—to the United States for treatment, complementing a project to aid Hiroshima radiation victims (*hibakusha*); the Poles had helped him arrange the talks with Khrushchev.

Now the restless *macher*, fifty, turned his energies to Vietnam, eager to reprise his earlier role. In mid-December 1965, after White House aide Jack Valenti briefed him on LBJ's views, Cousins had invited Polish UN ambassador Bohdan Lewandowski, familiar from earlier efforts, to dine at his Park Avenue apartment to attest to Johnson's sincere desire for peace and see if Warsaw could help. When the Pole said wistfully that he wished the North Vietnamese could hear so "convincing" a testimonial, Cousins offered to go to Hanoi if Warsaw set up a trip and Washington approved (after the La Pira affair burst a few days later, he contacted Rusk, and Bill Bundy called back to OK his going ahead).[193] Lewandowski agreed to explore the idea; Rapacki seemed amenable, and, after checking with Moscow, reported the notion to Hanoi; and Michałowski praised Cousins to Dong as "a good American with a certain degree of influence and position." "Vietnam will be able to use this person, and not only in the discussions," he said. "Poland is willing to help."[194]

Dong had asked Michałowski to "withhold the green light for the moment," and now Trinh flashed a yellow—a meeting was possible, but in a DRV diplomatic outpost abroad, not Hanoi; Cousins might also contact the NLF.[195] (A few days later, however, Hanoi sent word to delay conveying even this hedged willingness for contact.[196])

Michałowski also gathered views of figures he did not see, judging Le Duan "very rigid and definitely pro-Peking" in opposing negotiations and Politburo member Le Duc Tho as "reasonable, not a hawk." Despite a "shifting" "Chinese faction" favoring war over diplomacy, he later told Harriman, "all of the North Vietnamese are first of all Vietnamese nationalists."[197]

The Long Way Home

With little to show for his labors, Michałowski left Hanoi on Tuesday, January 11, 1966. Declining a second helping of Chinese abuse, he went west to Vientiane, on a predawn ICC flight from Gia Lam Airport just north of the capital—bombers had left it unscathed to allow the (usually twice-weekly) ICC traffic. In a talk with Souvanna Phouma, the Pole squirmed as the neutralist prince blamed North Vietnam for violating Lao sovereignty (and the Geneva pact). DRV forces, he said, used its land to send troops and supplies along the Ho Chi Minh Trail to insurgents in South Vietnam; had wrecked a coalition government; and "total[ly] dominat[ed]" the ostensibly indigenous Pathet Lao. When Michałowski listed aggressive U.S. acts, including hints of a possible intervention in Laos, Souvanna firmly vowed never to allow American troops in his country. The Pole "dodge[d]" probing on his talks in Hanoi, merely underlining the DRV's Four Points and the claim that LBJ's peace offer was really an "ultimatum."[198]

Then what Michałowski termed a "very amusing" circumstance intervened: That Thursday morning, in the somnolent town of palm trees, temples, diplomats, and spies on the Mekong River, he and Harriman nearly crossed paths again.

Hearing that the prince said the American, on the same voyage that had started in Warsaw and taken him to Yugoslavia, India, Iran, Pakistan, Egypt, Japan, and Australia, would soon be at the palace, Michałowski hastily exited. When Souvanna told Harriman that only a half-hour earlier the Pole had paid "a surprise visit," Washington had its first inkling of his secret mission. Souvanna was hazy about his unexpected guest's travels, but Harriman correctly surmised that he had been Rapacki's "unusual means" to deliver the proposals he had related a fortnight earlier. Contrary to speculation in Hanoi, the itinerant emissaries did not actually meet, but well-founded gossip spread that Michałowski had told Souvanna that the "North Vietnamese were in a most bellicose mood."[199]

From Vientiane, Michałowski went to Bangkok, New Delhi, and Moscow. He skipped Phnom Penh, despite a prompt from Warsaw to "get an idea what [Prince Norodom] Sihanouk is up to," especially after reports that he had asked the Geneva cochairs London and Moscow to probe violations of Cambodia's sovereignty along its Vietnamese border, perhaps with a beefed-up ICC. Such an inquest would please Washington, which saw Sihanouk's neutrality as a façade behind which Hanoi exploited his territory (both the Ho Chi Minh Trail and the port of Sihanoukville) to succor the Southern revolt. Hanoi, of course, vehemently opposed any steps that might imperil its infiltration routes. U.S. aides hoped, wanly, that the mercurial monarch—who had abruptly cut diplomatic ties with Washington the previous May to protest an attack on Communist forces using his land as a sanctuary—would muster the gumption to assert control over Cambodia's porous frontier, thereby boosting the ICC, and they urged London and Ottawa to push the idea.[200]

Michałowski begged off seeing Sihanouk, perhaps because not Rapacki but an underling, Romuald Spasowski, an ex-ICC delegate in Saigon, proposed it. A Phnom Penh stop was "not worth it," he cabled from Vientiane, especially because "terrible" flight connections would delay his journey for a week and local Polish officers could handle consultations. His substantive analysis exemplified his at times (as the CIA put it) coolly cynical attitude. Warsaw backed Cambodian neutrality in principle, but not at the cost of more vital aims. "I think that we must partly give in to Sihanouk, but not so much as to make the activity of the [NLF] on the borderlands difficult," he wrote. Moreover, it was "not unsafe" if a transfer of personnel to Cambodia weakened the ICC in South Vietnam; Hanoi preferred fewer monitors there anyway.[201] To Rapacki, he noted that new border controls could only impair the NLF's operations, so why not instead propose a new Geneva Conference on Cambodia? Sihanouk would probably favor the idea, so it would discomfit the Chinese, "tie the [Americans'] hands," and "open up the platform for wider talks."[202]

In Moscow, on January 15 Michałowski saw Deputy Foreign Minister Vasily V. Kuznetsov and the ideology secretary of the Central Committee of the CPSU, Leonid Ilyichev. Despite hitting a brick wall, the Pole insisted that his trip was "useful," noting in particular Vietnamese surprise at his candor. He heard an early report on Shelepin's visit, which appeared equally futile. Yet the Soviets put a positive spin on their collective attempts to coax the comrades. Sensing Hanoi's "stronger acceptance" of the need for "parallel political and military action" and concrete peace initiatives as "the result of our action," Kuznetsov predicted that their "necessary" work would eventually "yield results despite the presently hardened positions."[203] He distilled the Pole's findings:

1. The Vietnamese leaders see their situation in a rosy light, overestimate their military successes, do not realize the readiness of the USA for war on a broad scale, underestimate the military potential of the USA.

2. The Vietnamese comrades do not see that they lose on a political level, [by] turning down negotiations, do not take into consideration the changes in the correlation of forces in Asia and Africa (the events in Indonesia, the military revolutions in Africa), and overestimate the possibility of public opinion in the USA to speak out against the war in Vietnam.

3. The Vietnamese friends understand the serious character of their difficulties, but do not want peaceful negotiations at the present time. They fight a peace conference, as, in their views, the start of peace negotiations will be perceived in the whole world as capitulation of the DRV.

4. The impression emerges that relations of the DRV with the Front for the National Liberation of South Vietnam, whose leaders are under great influence of the Chinese, are highly complicated. In Hanoi, it is feared, that if the DRV goes for negotiations, then the NLF could perceive this as concessions from the side of their northern allies for the cessation of bombardments of the DRV. They observe a growth of giddiness from the successes [among] the leaders of the NLF. They think, that, winning light battles, they could go from victory to victory. They do not know other means of struggle, besides military action. . . .

5. It is felt that some figures of the DRV do not agree with the Chinese, however, the influence of the PRC on the Vietnamese friends remains great. This can namely be shown by the negative answer of the DRV to the Polish mediation. . . .

6. In the talks, the Vietnamese friends gave to understand the desirability that the socialist countries render great aid to the DRV. If they said earlier, that they do not want to drag the socialist countries into a world war, then now they do not stress the attention on that proposition. . . .

7. The Vietnamese comrades, using their channels of contacts with the Americans, will try in every way to delay the resumption of the bombardments of the DRV, strive to suspend the unfolding of the American military machine.

The Pole flew home to Warsaw that evening, ending Operation Lumbago—much to his wife's relief. Mira, an active socialite, finding the charade stressful, had gone "into seclusion rather than appear in public and risk giving her husband's secret away."[204]

Three days later, Rapacki updated Gronouski. Poland had "delivered [Harriman's message] loyally and precisely to the interested party," which listened "with due consideration and objectively." But Warsaw was not "yet" authorized to relay an official reply. Coyly, he insisted the "transmission of views was not unprofitable," but he admitted that the Hanoi situation remained "very complicated and may require persistent pressures calculated over the long term and without immediate results." Meanwhile, he pleaded against more escalation, claiming that the pause had not harmed U.S. interests.[205]

Rapacki neither mentioned Operation Lumbago nor explained the paltry result. But U.S. aides gradually pieced together a broadly accurate picture of the secret Hanoi trip—which seeped into public view in March through a leak to a *Washington Post* reporter, Daniel Schorr, who got the story from Michałowski, an old friend.[206] Gronouski's British colleague, George Clutton, reported a pithy remark that seemed to sum up why the Pole felt all his efforts to persuade Hanoi had been in vain. "Goddamn those Chinese," Michałowski was said to have muttered.[207]

Shelepin's Mission

Washington, being only dimly aware of Michałowski's peregrinations, paid far more attention to Shelepin and, to the extent they put any stock in the pre-pause talks with Dobrynin, presumed that his trip constituted the diplomatic reward for the bombing halt. The ambitious ex-KGB chief, evidently a wily politician (a Khrushchev protégé, he had jumped ship to join the plot against him), seemed an apt choice for a delicate mission.[208] By contrast, they viewed the efforts of Moscow's satellites mostly as sideshows.

But to U.S. irritation, the Soviets kept mum about Shelepin; officials then and historians since have disputed what he told the North Vietnamese. Some, citing military and economic pacts his delegation signed, argue that he did not truly urge moderation. In 1978, the Hungarian diplomatic defector János Radványi (of whom more later in the book) claimed that Michałowski had lost any hope for his own mission "when he learned from Shcherbakov that Shelepin had offered substantial new military aid to Hanoi and had refrained from recommending negotiations."[209] (In fact, Michałowski had already lost hope during his talk with Ho, before Shelepin reached Hanoi.) Besides Shelepin's firm public support for the DRV's hard line, Radványi wrote, he "made no attempt to modify" its antipathy to entering talks. Suggesting that Shelepin aimed to deepen military ties, his delegation included Dmitri Ustinov, the CPSU Central Committee secretary handling the military-industrial complex, and Colonel-General Vladimir Tolubko, the Soviet strategic missile corps' first deputy commander.[210] Yet the CIA judged that Shelepin likely "encouraged the North Vietnamese to give more serious consideration to recent U.S. moves toward a political solution" but "was unable to persuade them to modify their tactics," and the Russian historian Ilya Gaiduk later wrote that Shelepin prodded Hanoi toward negotiations, to its annoyance.[211]

New Communist sources suggest little divergence between Michałowski's and Shelepin's aims, but a substantial gap in how they pursued them. Gromyko told the Pole, when he transited Moscow en route to Hanoi, that Shelepin would "receive orders similar to ours only that they must be more cautious in the formulation of suggestions because of the Chinese position."[212] Later, Kuznetsov told him that Shelepin's "findings overlap with ours" and credited Warsaw with helping to push Hanoi toward a "stronger acceptance" of the need to blend military and political tactics and "to take up peace initiatives at the right moment." Yet, the Pole learned, "Shelepin had instructions not to exert pressure and not to condition assistance on uniformity of views on the matter of peace actions."[213] Like Michałowski, Shelepin got a Chinese cold shoulder when he passed through Beijing (though they did treat him to a puppet show); *Renmin Ribao* ripped Moscow for "actively peddl[ing] the peace talks swindle."[214] Brezhnev told the Czech party boss that Shelepin "spoke openly" to the Vietnamese about their "failure to take sufficient advantage of political forms of struggle against the U.S. aggression," but they insisted that "it is not the right time for any sort of negotiations with the Americans."[215] Yet he also acceded to requests for more military aid, and signed an "insipid and vague" joint communiqué.[216]

Shelepin's visit gave Moscow a glimpse of splits among the Vietnamese—evident even in arrangements for the trip and silences and absences of key figures. Shcherbakov told fraternal colleagues that a pro-PRC faction opposed receiving Shelepin at all, suspecting plots to press Hanoi "to capitulate to the USA imperialists" and "to pry the DRV away from China" before the Twenty-Third CPSU Congress in a few months. Senior Politburo member Truong Chinh, the ex-party chief demoted in 1956 for his part in implementing draconian Beijing-inspired land reforms and whose nom de révolution ("Long March") paid tribute to the Chinese Communist Party, reportedly led this group. Calling him especially "hard-knuckled" against the visit, Shcherbakov said that Chinh, as National Assembly head, had joined a welcome for Shelepin but had excused himself from the actual talks "for health reasons," as had veteran party figure Hoang van Hoan, said to be "taking the cure" in China (where he would later go into exile after losing a power struggle). Aside from Giap's military briefing, Dong ran the talks with Shelepin; Ho and Le Duan, a reputed hard-liner, were "reserved, making only interjections," and Le Duc Tho, a Le Duan ally, "said absolutely nothing."[217]

As they had to Michałowski, the DRV's rulers rejected negotiations as premature because the military prognosis remained favorable. Shelepin's team disagreed, Shcherbakov said, insisting that the Vietnamese had not "correctly evaluate[d] the situation" and were "seriously underestimating" U.S. power. It also doubted their claim that bombing caused "insignificant" losses—"this does not correspond to reality, according to the opinion of the Soviet comrades!"—though it is unlikely that Shelepin spoke so bluntly to his hosts. Still, he had strongly urged a transition to political and diplomatic steps. When the Vietnamese dismissed LBJ's proposals as a "bluff," he said they might be a real bid to escape a no-win situation, and "perhaps now the moment has come to take [the Americans] at their words and expose them. That would not be a capitulation but a struggle by other means." "Grab them by the hand. Don't wait, because you will lose," Shelepin later told Siedlecki.

Soothing Shelepin, as he had Michałowski, Dong insisted that the DRV "constantly" considered how to end the conflict politically and when to enter into peace talks. To the Soviets' pleasure, he distinguished Hanoi from Beijing in accepting "the necessity of the creation of a diplomatic and political front against the Americans," he commended Moscow's détente policies toward Washington, and he refused to criticize Polish (and Hungarian) peace efforts—even if ultimately rejecting them.

However, strains over China permeated the talks: Shelepin's group had "reproached the Vietnamese comrades for the harmful attitude of the Chinese" and had rebuffed a bid to "appreciate" the PRC's military aid in the final communiqué (Shcherbakov said that Ho privately admitted Beijing's military support was "insignificant"). The Soviets blasted China for impeding their efforts to coordinate military aid, colluding with the NLF to block negotiations, and scheming to lure Moscow into a clash with Washington by forcing it to use United States–patrolled Tonkin Gulf shipping lanes. To all these points, the Vietnamese had demurred, stressing they could not openly criticize their huge neighbor. Yet Shelepin's visit "improved relations and [was] a big step forward," Shcherbakov insisted.[218]

A Secret Rendezvous in Moscow

By mid-January 1966, though the pause went on, Hanoi had seemed to slam the door on any residual hopes of Warsaw, Moscow, or Budapest for making concrete progress. Yet, as Rapacki's equivocations to Gronouski implied, they were in no rush to relay this news to the increasingly impatient Americans, lest it hasten a resumption of the bombing.

To coordinate their respective futile initiatives and plot the way forward, the Poles, Soviets, and Hungarians engaged in intense secret consultations—a process then opaque to U.S. intelligence, but now illumined by long-hidden Communist sources. They confirm a conclusion that might have surprised Americans accustomed to Cold War rhetoric about a monolithic Communist Bloc: The Kremlin and its allies mostly blamed Hanoi's intransigence, and Beijing's, not Washington, for their diplomacy's failure.

The Poles and Hungarians conferred regularly. On January 7, with Michałowski already cabling bad news from Hanoi, Rapacki and Péter met in Warsaw and shared a "pessimistic evaluation of the Vietnamese position." Initially, Péter told Rapacki, the DRV leaders had seemed ready for contacts if the Americans took the initiative. But after Budapest delivered Rusk's "concrete proposal for a meeting by both sides in Rangoon," they had retreated, saying that they needed to consider their position. If Hanoi "continues to uphold its readiness to meet with the USA, but they do not want to take the initiative or Rangoon is not their preference," Péter and Rapacki resolved, Poland and Hungary would jointly organize a meeting in Warsaw, Budapest, Geneva, or elsewhere.[219]

On January 18 and 19, in Budapest, Polish and Hungarian leaders commiserated over their failure to shunt Hanoi onto a political track. Like the Hungarian Socialist Workers' Party first secretary János Kádár, Gomułka confessed uncertainty about future events, dark suspicions of Chinese meddling, and frustration at what he saw as the Vietnamese comrades' unrealistic approach—a myopia evident during a DRV figure's recent trip to Warsaw.

Le Thanh Nghi, Gomułka recounted, had implied the Communists won "only victories." ("It would be very good if it were like this in reality," Gomułka said wryly.) The Poles had tried to talk sense into their guest, stressing the war's unforeseeable course, risk of escalation, slim odds that Washington would accept military defeat (instead perhaps even resorting to tactical nuclear weapons), impact of socialist disunity (China's fault, of course), and need to use the "power of diplomacy" which LBJ effectively exploited. But the DRV vice minister had evaded a direct reply, merely affirming Hanoi's yen for peace and promising to relay the Poles' interesting remarks—plus "demanding" more economic and military aid, including "the most modern" matériel, in line with Warsaw's internationalist duty. "In a word, we do not know what to think of all this," Gomułka admitted; had Beijing and Hanoi conspiratorially divided their labor, with the latter, closer to Moscow's allies, fulfilling Chinese wish lists to gain otherwise off-limits Soviet technology?

Gomułka resented that Hanoi's obduracy had undermined Poland's high-profile diplomacy.[220] Yet, he sighed, there was "no choice but to be in solidarity with the Vietnamese party and to fully support its position, even if in reality this is a Chinese position"—but one could not blindly follow this path to "absurdity," a world war provoked by Beijing.

As for LBJ's intentions, Gomułka spoke less gruffly than to Harriman; perhaps when with comrades rather than a class enemy, he felt less compelled to parade his ideological colors. Discerning a high-level split in Washington over whether to pursue escalation or diplomacy, he placed Johnson in the latter group, which accepted the error of calculations that bombing could break Hanoi's will, grasped the war's "hopelessness," wanted to avoid a wider entanglement, and sought a face-saving exit; this faction could even accept a coalition government in Saigon leading to elections that the Communists might win ("One could say, 'Oh, well, the nation decided'—and this is how he could get out of the situation"). But, Gomułka admitted, no such solution lay on the horizon, and if one could believe intelligence reports of Chinese plans to support expanded "wars of liberation" beyond Indochina to Thailand, Malaysia, and South Korea, "then Johnson will be put up against a wall. And then the hawkish wing of the war adherents will win out."

In this unclear situation—the DRV stubborn, the Eastern European probes in tatters, yet the pause still in place, and Washington still uninformed about Hanoi's *no!*—Kádár and Gomułka agreed on a secret session of Soviet, Polish, and Hungarian foreign ministers, which occurred in Moscow on January 24 and 25.[221] Briefing Rapacki and Péter on Shelepin's just-returned mission, Gromyko said that it focused on a new "large-scale" aid pact but "drew attention to the need to reach a political solution." The Vietnamese had reiterated that talks should begin only after more military victories, "but in the interests of a political solution, they saw the need for improving diplomatic and propaganda work."[222]

In sum, "Comrade Gromyko assessed the situation as follows: The American proposals have honest elements to them, and they are looking for a way out, but for us the last word is with our Vietnamese comrades."[223] His remarks confirmed that Moscow had a relatively benign view of LBJ's stand but no appetite to lean on Hanoi or go out on a limb that would render it vulnerable to Chinese charges. In meetings during the pause, Gromyko noted—including Kosygin's recent encounter with Humphrey in New Delhi[224]—the Soviets had rebuffed "defensive and imploring" U.S. requests to deliver messages to Hanoi, insisting that they "would not take on any kind of postman's role."

With negotiations out of reach, at least for now, the foreign ministers reframed their primary task—"to put pressure on the United States in the interests of extending the suspension of bombing of the DRV"—and they agreed to coordinate actions to this end.[225] So, well after Hanoi privately made clear by mid-January that it was not seriously interested in talks, the Poles and Hungarians continued to string Washington along.

Warsaw already had reason to fear that Washington was fast losing patience. On January 20 and 24, Gronouski delivered demarches to Rapacki seeking word on Hanoi's reply to the U.S. proposals and stating ominously that despite the ongoing bombing halt, Viet Cong attacks in the South and infiltration from the North persisted at an alarming rate, exposing U.S. forces to harm.[226] Fiercely protesting the implicit ultimatum, Rapacki hinted that "something was moving on which he could not comment."[227] But Michałowski's mission impossible had given him precious little basis to claim that Hanoi had shown conciliatory tendencies meriting an extension of the suspension.

The Cousins Caper

Then, on Tuesday, January 25, a morsel arrived: Hanoi confirmed its earlier tentative willingness to talk with Norman Cousins, triggering frantic maneuvering in Warsaw, New York, and Washington in the final days of January to hold a meeting in the Polish capital. On Thursday, Michałowski cabled Poland's UN deputy envoy, Eugene Wyzner, instructing him urgently to contact Cousins with the news that a DRV representative would see him, not in Hanoi but "one of the capitals where they have their own [diplomatic] establishment, of his choice."[228]

Cousins, who had been hanging fire since Polish UN ambassador Bohdan Lewandowski had returned to Warsaw in mid-January, was thrilled to be back in play.[229] He dialed Valenti, who told him to hurry to Washington for talks and pack his bags for Warsaw; then he phoned Wyzner to say that after checking with the White House, he "accepts the proposition" with the proviso that Johnson still needed a "signal" of progress or else he would restart the bombing; there was "no time to lose."[230] At the White House Friday morning—January 28—Cousins saw Valenti and McGeorge Bundy, who implied that LBJ had already opted to resume the raids; the national security adviser conveyed the "strong feeling inside the government that 'the string had run out'" and his own view that DRV readiness to receive Cousins, a private citizen, "might be too little and too late." Valenti, also dubious, warned against letting the North Vietnamese feel that they could "vibrate the President" and get him to extend the pause "just by teasing us with negotiations." Cousins argued fervently that it might still be worth checking if Hanoi's consent to see him might be the "sign" Washington sought; after consulting LBJ, Valenti said he could tell Wyzner that he would leave that night for Poland.[231] Cousins duly alerted Wyzner that he would depart at 8:30 p.m., reach Warsaw Saturday afternoon, and have twenty-four hours to meet a North Vietnamese before returning to Washington.[232]

But a long talk Friday afternoon with Arthur Goldberg changed Cousins' mind. The UN ambassador agreed that "no sign should go unexplored" but argued that if Hanoi had been serious, it would have contacted one of LBJ's emissaries, and candidly told him a trip would likely be neither "propitious" nor "fruitful." He was free to go, but "personally, he would hate to see me placed in an awkward and untenable situation." Hearing Goldberg's dim view and assertion that "only specific word direct from Hanoi unmistakably indicating a desire to get into talks could change the present course," Cousins judged the bombing decision a fait accompli and his trip a fool's errand, and abruptly canceled his reservations.[233]

That evening, instead of flying to Warsaw, Cousins relayed to Wyzner word from the White House—"on the basis of the utmost authoritative reply"—that LBJ would restart bombing in forty-eight hours unless Hanoi authoritatively agreed to open a dialogue; a mere chat with Cousins would not do. If Poland had evidence of a real "signal," it could relay it through the U.S. Embassy over the weekend; otherwise, the pause's end was "inevitable." Observing (inaccurately, given the Rangoon contacts) that "Warsaw is at the moment the only single dip-lomatic channel at [U.S.] disposal," Cousins urgently requested a reply.[234]

Lost in Translation?

Suddenly overshadowing Cousins' fluctuating travel plans, on January 28 a Ho Chi Minh letter seemed to authoritatively rebuff LBJ's overture: "If the U.S. gov-ernment really wants a peaceful settlement, it must accept the four-point stand of the DRV government and prove this by actual deeds," it declared, as read over Radio Hanoi's English-language service. "It must end unconditionally and for good all bombing raids and other war acts against the DRV. Only in this way can a political solution to the Vietnamese problem be envisaged."[235] Ho's missive im-plied continued impasse: Washington had made clear that it could not "accept" the Four Points, especially point three endorsing the NLF program.

Rapacki, however, begged to differ: Having gotten mixed reports on Hanoi's interest in receiving Cousins, he switched gears. Early Saturday, he called in Sherer (Gronouski was out of town) to claim North Vietnam had given the positive "signal" Washington needed to prolong the bombing halt. Where? The same public letter from Ho that, in Washington, Rusk was describing to the NSC as the "hardest [DRV statement] yet," lacking even "a confusion ploy."[236] "Striving at all cost to prevent the resumption of bombing," as Michałowski later acknowledged, Rapacki claimed confusion in translation had blurred the required "signal." The English version said that Washington must "accept" the Four Points, but the French formulation ("*il doit reconnaître la position*") sug-gested it need only "recognize" them, he argued. Blending carrot and stick, he said Poland would gladly assist this "opportunity for more concrete exchanges and *precise* views," but a rash bombing restart would kill the chance and "open a new menacing situation entailing unforeseeable consequences on a global scale."[237]

In fact, Rapacki was improvising. He had no real basis from Hanoi for his claims, which he knew belied Michałowski's report that Dong had said firmly that the Four Points were "not for adjudication—they must be accepted or rejected."[238] Even as he claimed authority for a milder interpretation, he directed Sidelecki to ask the DRV Foreign Ministry if it were true—yet got no immediate answer to his plea for a "prompt reply."[239]

Down to the Wire

Nevertheless, in a further burst of activity that Saturday, Rapacki contacted Brit-ish and other diplomats to argue that Ho's letter should be seen more favorably.[240] Cabling the Polish UN mission again, he also indirectly told the White House through Cousins, quickly eliciting a response that Washington required Hanoi's confirmation of the softer interpretation "as well as a basis for belief that further contacts—including a contact with Cousins—do not limit themselves to listening to Ho Chi Minh's well-known position and already known conditions."[241] Sunday morning, Warsaw also had fresh grounds to spur a Cousins trip: North Vietnam's deputy foreign minister, Nguyen Co Thach, in a meeting with Siedlecki, had reiterated a readiness to receive him at a DRV mission of his choice; in Warsaw, Ambassador Do Phat Quang would welcome him "any time." Michałowski promptly cabled New York, hoping to restir the editor's wanderlust and defer the bombing renewal.[242] After getting the news and phoning Goldberg, Cousins told Wyzner late Sunday morning that, with LBJ at church, he had spoken to someone "in the know" who hinted that the decision to renew bombing had already been taken. White House skepticism had hardened, Cousins said, after it received, a week before, other supposedly "encouraging signals" that quickly faded out. "The President does not want to be treated like a 'fool,'" he said sharply.[243]

The response threw the ball back to Rapacki. Napping on couches in their offices Sunday night, Cousins and Wyzner anxiously awaited a sign from Hanoi, via Warsaw, that they could use to restrain LBJ, such as an authoritative confirmation that Ho had intended a more flexible interpretation, even if it took a middle-of-the-night call to awaken the president. "Every minute is crucial," Cousins implored. Yet no sign came.[244] Instead, Washington checked out Rapacki's claim through diplomatic channels, only to have DRV representatives in Moscow and Rangoon shoot it down.[245]

Near midnight, Cousins reached Goldberg and then McGeorge Bundy to reaffirm Poland's view that Hanoi remained ready to receive him "subject only to non-resumption of the bombing"—but now it really was too late. From the UN delegate, he heard the "shattering news" that bombing orders had already gone out; in fact, the strikes had already resumed, at 9 p.m. New York time (Monday morning in Vietnam).

On Monday, LBJ announced the pause's end, faulting Hanoi for failing to respond to his overture. After hearing the news on the radio, Cousins called Wyzner, who voiced "heartbreak and incomprehension";[246] in Warsaw, Michałowski fumed to Gronouski that Johnson should have waited a few days to get an authoritative DRV reaction from Dong or Ho (Gronouski privately agreed, even if "the Poles were grasping at straws, and there was no meaning to this");[247] and in Washington, Rapacki's last-minute machinations had squandered much of the credit he had earned by relaying Harriman's proposals to Hanoi.

Conclusion: "A Good Deal of Chaff"

Most accounts of the thirty-seven-day pause concentrate on the U.S.-DRV contacts in Rangoon, through which diplomats exchanged aides-mémoire but did not engage in substantive conversations; George Herring termed Pinta the "most important" of the many channels through which the Johnson administration relayed its interest in talks.[248] Far more vital, however, was Washington's attempt to communicate with Hanoi via Warsaw in a probe whose history was long obscured by Cold War secrecy but is now illumined by Communist records.[249] Harriman's trip and Michałowski's ensuing secret journey, Bill Bundy later recalled, amounted to "by far the most serious part" of LBJ's pause diplomacy. "The Poles at that time were close both to Hanoi and to Moscow, and Averell made a particular effort there . . . that to me was the real focus, and the rest was a good deal of chaff."[250]

Warsaw, and Michałowski in particular, made a good-faith effort to pass and even advocate to Hanoi LBJ's offer for talks; yet, like Péter, Rapacki was not beyond trying to mislead Washington regarding the DRV's position in order to prolong the pause—undermining his own credibility in ways that would later rebound against him.

Warsaw (like Budapest, in its own parallel initiative) acted not at Moscow's behest but in coordination with it and in a manner carefully designed to fit Kremlin policy and fill the more active role that the Soviets, due to Chinese criticism, preferred not to play themselves. Poland also had its own motives to try to curb the Vietnam violence. These included the desire to sustain the nascent détente in Central Europe (which would be imperiled by the sharper East/West tensions that escalation in Southeast Asia might cause) that gave them more room to maneuver and improve political-economic ties to the West; to reap the prestige awaiting whoever achieved peace (what LBJ derided as the Nobel Prize syndrome); and to undercut belligerent Beijing, pleasing Moscow.

There was no "missed opportunity" for peace during the pause. The preponderant forces on both sides still hoped to attain mutually incompatible aims through fighting, and thus they viewed any enemy tendencies toward compromise as signs of weakness justifying more military efforts rather than reciprocal concessions to promote peace. To Hanoi, the pause diplomacy had mostly been an annoyance, a distraction from the ongoing business of winning the war and achieving national unity under Communist control rather than a meaningful harbinger of peace or U.S. conciliation. Yet the Soviet Bloc's appeals to enter talks, especially the Michałowski and to a lesser extent Shelepin missions, were nagging reminders of Hanoi's need to better integrate diplomatic and military fronts—to alleviate outside pressure to scale back its aims and to prepare for the eventual negotiations that awaited, in its view, a sufficient ripening of the battlefield situation.

As for Washington, its dealings with Poland (and Hungary) during the pause had been a not very pleasant learning experience on the degree of cooperation that it might expect from Moscow's allies. U.S. officials were already divided as to whether the Kremlin preferred seeing its superpower rival mired in the Southeast Asian muck, or to the contrary would do its best to help extricate the Americans in order to concentrate on more important business (and limit the spread of Chinese influence—a shared, if unacknowledged, interest). They discerned mixed results from the experiment in using the Soviet Bloc's channels to communicate with the reclusive North Vietnamese. Some, like Harriman, were encouraged by the Eastern Europeans' seeming readiness to transmit messages to Hanoi and urge negotiations, despite harsh anti–United States rhetoric and exasperating opacity concerning purported contacts. "The Polish Government certainly did everything they agreed to do," Harriman wrote Gronouski in late January, "and I have no doubt that Shelepin was instructed to do what the Soviet Government felt they could under the circumstances."[251]

Others, however, including LBJ and Rusk, were left resentful, convinced that the Poles had strung them along regarding Hanoi's readiness to talk and lied in a last-ditch bid to lure them into extending the bombing pause—not to aid peace but to wring every last military advantage for their Vietnamese comrades. Though Cousins felt a valid opening for peace (his own) had been wasted, even Harriman (after he and Bill Bundy heard the editor relate the tale) was nonplussed at the "nebulous signal" that Poland had supposedly sent through him and convinced that the "highly intense" Cousins was "making a great deal out of very little." Bundy, stressing Hanoi's failure to make direct contact, suspected that the "desperately anxious" Poles had contrived the whole Cousins approach as a "last-minute attempt" to delay the bombing resumption.[252]

Not that Johnson ever had much hope that the pause would go anywhere. As Bill Moyers, then a close aide, said: "LBJ never believed after January '65 that there was a serious feather on the table, in terms of a dove." Instead, after the Bundy-McNamara "fork in the road" memo, a "suddenly morose" president vested his faith in military coercion, "that applying the tourniquet (as Walt [Rostow] kept saying) would cause the other side to bleed so much, and hurt so much, that they would cry for peace—peace being an independent South Vietnam."[253] The pause's failure soured LBJ on bombing halts to test prospects for peace talks. Hanoi's brusque refusal to play ball, in his eyes, undercut those aides (from Moyers to McGeorge Bundy to McNamara) who had cajoled him into a prolonged suspension and bolstered the hawks (e.g., Rostow) who had advised against one. All in all, Rusk recalled, the pause made "a lasting impression on Lyndon Johnson because from that time forward he was skeptical that bombing halts could accomplish anything."[254]

Washington's collective ambivalence—deeply distrusting the Eastern Europeans but viewing them as a perhaps necessary evil, a plausible route to reach an enemy with whom it would eventually have to negotiate—would linger, unresolved, until brought to the fore once again later that year when Marigold suddenly began to flower.

The Poles, too, had much to chew on. Despite Michałowski's failure to prod Hanoi into talks, Rapacki felt, his visit had deepened ties with the DRV and had initiated a dialogue, especially with Dong, which might yet pay off should conditions permit another peace attempt . The contacts had revealed a complex situation at the highest level, clouded by the preference for armed struggle of the Chinese and hard-line Vietnamese, yet perhaps evolving as the war wore on. As for Washington, though the translation flap had ruffled feelings, Warsaw had kept channels open and continued to feel that at least part of the U.S. administration, including LBJ, sincerely desired a reasonable solution in Vietnam that *might* eventually prove acceptable to Hanoi, once its confidence in total victory faded.

Sooner or later, it would be time to try again.

Đồng Chí Lewandowski's Secret Mission

The Players Take Their Places, February–June 1966

Touching on the current potential usefulness of the Commissioners individually as a link between Hanoi and Saigon he spoke with some enthusiasm of what an achievement it would be if any one of us could be instrumental in opening the door to a settlement.

—Canada's ICC commissioner on meeting Janusz Lewandowksi, April 1966

The Americans are not to be kicked in the balls.

—Lewandowski to Pham Van Dong, the spring of 1966

Do you think they are masochists?

—Lewandowski to Henry Cabot Lodge, June 1966

I hope you Americans are not escalating to a new peace offensive.

—Canadian ICC commissioner Victor C. Moore to Lodge, June 1966

Adam Rapacki was disappointed but not discouraged by the failure of his peace diplomacy during the thirty-seven-day pause. As Washington resumed bombing, the Polish foreign minister sought to position Warsaw to maneuver more effectively. Secretly sending Michałowski all the way to Hanoi had been an exceptional step, not easily repeated, and Rapacki wanted someone on the ground in Vietnam able to probe continuously to discern whether conditions were ripe to try again, and to seize any opportunity that might appear.

Coincidentally, he had before him a concrete opening to advance this objective. Poland's ambassador in Hanoi had only narrow room to maneuver, dealing with just one side of the conflict; he was also a rigid neo-Stalinist who instinctively exhorted the Vietnamese Communists on to total victory over the imperialist aggressors—not toward the kind of compromise settlement that would be the aim of any secret peace diplomacy.

However, Poland's delegate to the International Control Commission, who was also of ambassadorial rank, was another story. Henryk Wendrowski was deeply frustrated as he neared the end of his year-long term. Initially, he had imagined that the commissioners, uniquely able to shuttle between enemy capitals, might act to restrain the conflict. But by December 1965, he had concluded that neither Hanoi nor Washington was ready to compromise, and that negotiations could not start until both lost faith in military victory—maybe in a year or so. Originally slated to stay until June 1966, Wendrowski happily told a British diplomat that he would be "leaving here for good" in March. "He said he was personally glad because, contrary to the expectations which had been entertained when he was first appointed here, there was nothing in present circumstances which he or the Commission could usefully do."[1]

Nevertheless, Rapacki calculated that Hanoi's stridency would one day yield to a more sober approach—and then Poland's ICC delegate might again be eligible to conduct peace feelers. Gossip put a veteran diplomat in line to succeed Wendrowski, but the foreign minister opted to gamble on a less experienced but perhaps more energetic figure, the head of the United Nations desk at the Ministerstwa Spraw Zagranicznych (MSZ, Ministry of Foreign Affairs), Janusz Lewandowski, who was cosmopolitan despite his youth (he was not quite thirty-five years of age).

But first, in line with standard Communist procedure, Rapacki had to vet Lewandowski's appointment with the Ministerstwa Spraw Wewnętrznych (MSW, Ministry of Internal Affairs), the secret police overseer, keeper of the most sensitive files. So on February 3, the MSZ's human resources director informed the Interior Ministry's Foreign Operations Department that it wished to send "citizen Janusz Lewandowski" as the new ICC delegate but needed MSWs "opinion" before acting.[2]

* * *

In early February 1966, as the air attacks resumed, President Lyndon Baines Johnson fled Washington to confer in Honolulu with South Vietnam's two top military rulers: Prime Minister (and Air Force head) Marshal Nguyen Cao Ky and chief of state General Nguyen Van Thieu. The hastily arranged summit's ostensible goal was to stress political, economic, and social reforms aimed at expanding popular support for the Saigon regime. But it also afforded a chance to review plans for the war's escalation, ratifying the Johnson administration's secret intent to double the number of troops by the end of the year (from about 200,000 to more than 400,000) and step up offensive operations in South Vietnam and against infiltration routes in Laos.[3]

Even if most Americans still backed the war, LBJ knew the renewed bombing would provoke international and domestic censure. To blunt it, he resumed not "with a large and dramatic bang" but with less "noisy" strikes which he could then ratchet up far beyond the pre-pause level.[4] He also asked the UN Security Council to take up the war—a transparent public relations ploy, because with "Red" China and North Vietnam not even in the world body, and Moscow aloof, the UN could hardly act effectively; Hanoi blasted the proposal (Vietnam "falls within the competence" of the Geneva Conference, it said, not the UN), echoed by Communist allies, and it quickly perished.[5]

Poland and the rest of the Soviet Bloc predictably issued "harsh, sometimes violent" condemnations and forecast Hanoi's ultimate victory.[6] By arrogating to itself the right to bomb a small nation, Rapacki asserted, Washington "was creating a dangerous and deplorable precedent in international morality." Hinting at a sinister Chinese role, he told London's envoy that the war did not serve U.S., Soviet, British, or Polish interests, and "daily" exacerbated the risk of a broader conflict. U.K. ambassador George Clutton felt Rapacki's "highly emotional" views reflected his "Western liberalism," while Michałowski was "essentially a pragmatist and a realist and sees at once the American quandary," because an unconditional halt risked a domestic backlash if it exposed U.S. troops to intensified Communist infiltration.[7] Yet both Poles dismissed suggestions that the situation called for new peace efforts through the Geneva cochairs or the ICC. They reiterated the need to stop the bombing first and echoed Hanoi's line that the only item to negotiate was the modalities of a full U.S. withdrawal and Vietnamese reunification.[8]

To U.S. and U.K. diplomats, Rapacki and Michałowski lamented Washington's failure to use the Warsaw channel to resolve authoritatively the confusion over Ho Chi Minh's letter before restarting the air raids. Yet despite chagrin that its efforts during the pause had "shipwrecked," Warsaw remained poised to mediate when circumstances eventually compelled the combatants to seek peace. "Michałowski was far less pessimistic and bitter about the future than I had expected, and to my surprise there was no word of disengagement on the Polish side," Clutton reported.[9] Secretly, the Poles had not given up hope of acting as peacemakers. In early February, Wendrowski paid a farewell visit to Hanoi—and took a far more moderate line than Washington might have suspected.

Lunching with Pham Van Dong on February 4, Poland's ICC delegate gave an appraisal of the military and political situation that could hardly have comforted his host.[10] Citing "detailed information" from U.S., journalistic, and diplomatic circles in Saigon, Wendrowski told the premier that

1. The Americans are currently preparing very carefully to eliminate the NLF [National Liberation Front] (the building of the bases and the home front, doubling the number of planes, aspiring to cut the "Ho line" [Ho Chi Minh Trail] simultaneously from the side of Siam [Thailand] and [South] Vietnam).

2. The society of the South are against the governance of Ky, but at the same time they are anticommunist for the most part, and they do not always want to topple the military regime and facilitate the victory for the NLF.

3. Further development of the military situation in the South will not be easier for the DRV, it will only become harder.

4. Prolonging the conflict makes it easier for the "hawks" to transform the war in Vietnam into a wider dispute.

Dong, who "listened to the information with great interest," must have grasped that Wendrowski's analysis implied that Hanoi should negotiate with the Americans rather than rely solely on military means to vanquish them. Cautiously, he promised to relay his "assessments and fears" to the Politburo. However, he reassured him (as he had Michałowski and Alexander Shelepin) that the North Vietnamese would do their best to keep the war limited, could fight a long time because right was on their side ("They are prepared for the worst"), and even if Washington redoubled its troop strength in 1966, their "Marxist analysis of the situation" guaranteed eventual triumph.

Still, Dong sensed that his arguments were not wholly convincing. He stressed Hanoi's readiness to engage in contacts with Washington despite their futility as well as with fraternal Communist delegations to explain the DRV's stance, as "sometimes even the friends cannot understand it." Throwing a bone to Soviet Bloc criticism that the DRV's failure effectively to counter LBJ's peace diplomacy had cost support in what was then called the Third World, he also "finally" agreed to permit a visit by Ghana's Kwame Nkrumah, a leading figure in the Non-Aligned Movement, though Hanoi did not expect any significant results. Dong remained carefully neutral in the Sino-Soviet split, and thus he avoided mentioning China despite an acute awareness that Moscow put the onus on Beijing for egging Hanoi along the military path.

Two days later, General Giap invited Wendrowski for a de facto reply to the Pole's pessimistic statements to Dong.[11] Radiating confidence, the military commander argued that the Americans, like the French, were doomed. In a mirror image of Wendrowski's assessments, he cited successful past DRV and NLF military operations and predicted total failure for future U.S. attempts to subdue Communists in the South or intimidate the North. "We have losses," he admitted, "but they are significantly smaller than what the Americans are writing about. The bombings of the North are giving us difficulties, but they will not break our country. Even if all our cities are destroyed, our country will not fall. We cannot let the South become a great American prison." Giap put "great emphasis" on the socialist bloc's "unity and help," rather blithely, given its rampant discord. "There was no word uttered on the subject of China," Wendrowski noted.

Wendrowski's soundings in Hanoi reinforced his already-bleak assessment. Back in Saigon, he observed that despite alleged signs of "greater flexibility on the question of negotiations," Hanoi still felt it could win militarily, so peace appeared impossible, at least for now, "because the positions of the two sides were irreconcilable."[12] As Poland's commissioner prepared to make his escape, Rapacki confirmed the identity of his successor. On March 5, a senior Interior Ministry counterintelligence official notified the Foreign Ministry that he had no objection to appointing "citizen Lewandowski" to replace Wendrowski; an MSW official noted blandly that he had already worked at diplomatic posts abroad and received "a positive opinion," and recommended consent.[13]

Mystery Man: "A Very Serious Fellow"

The first word of Lewandowski's new job came out of the blue in early March. Lewandowski was working at his office when one of the deputy foreign ministers, Josef Winiewicz, poked his head in and said, "Rapacki wants to talk to you. . . . He wants you to go to Vietnam."[14]

The foreign minister had not plucked Lewandowski from the UN desk for the ICC job to engage in frivolous charades. The main reason no one had yet terminated the moribund ICC had been the slim hope that it might one day play a useful role in peace diplomacy—and the awareness that with its mixed composition and residual travel rights between Saigon and Hanoi, it constituted a unique potential communications link between the belligerents, who lacked direct normal relations.

Such calculations undergirded the secret mission Rapacki now gave the young diplomat. Recounting Poland's past efforts—Harriman's visit, Michałowski's odyssey, and so on—he instructed Lewandowski to probe aggressively for any opening toward peace, and to exploit to that end his unique status as a Saigon-based Communist diplomat shuttling to Hanoi, should the opportunity arise. "Look, we think that probably the time is now coming that something useful may happen on this Vietnamese question," he said, "so if you go to Saigon keep open your ears and your eyes and if any sort of possibility would exist there, do not overlook it." The briefing on prior contacts with Hanoi struck Lewandowski as "hopeless" regarding the DRV's obduracy toward peace talks. While offering no specific or concrete plan, Rapacki flashed him a "green light" to latch onto any chance, even a minuscule one, to ameliorate the conflict.[15]

The surprise ICC assignment excited Lewandowski. It put him in the midst of the globe's most acute international crisis, in a setting that promised intrigue, adventure, a possibility to contribute to peace, and the chance to explore a new part of the world after posts in Africa and the Middle East. It was a challenging and prestigious, if risky, plum for an ambitious junior diplomat. Though generally familiar with the conflict, he plunged into reading on Vietnamese history, culture, and politics. Besides reviewing cable traffic going back to the French colonial period, he received a "colorful" briefing from Michałowski, who, over coffee in his office, described Harriman's visit and his own "mission impossible" (Lewandowski's term) to Hanoi. He also got a military intelligence report—to acquaint him with espionage considerations running an outpost in a hostile capital, and the military setup he would oversee—and an appraisal of the military situation from the Polish general staff, which was doubtful that Hanoi could defeat the U.S. war machine. His predecessors filled him in; Romuald Spasowski, now a foreign ministry division chief, described the persons he would encounter, including Henry Cabot Lodge, and in East Berlin on his way to Paris to wrap up UN affairs, he had a short (and not especially illuminating, he felt) chat with Wendrowski.[16]

After these whirlwind preparations, Lewandowski headed for Southeast Asia in early April 1966. He was, he later recalled, newly "free." His marriage of nearly a decade—to an "attractive blonde," cultured, well-educated, and fluent in English—had recently dissolved, childless.[17] Alone, Lewandowski embarked on a new phase of his life and career. Bypassing Moscow, he flew Czechoslovak Airlines via New Delhi and Rangoon to Phnom Penh, where he checked in with Poland's small Cambodia-based ICC staff before boarding a rickety commission plane for the hop to Saigon.[18]

❋ ❋ ❋

Many years after the clandestine affair in which Lewandowski played the lead role, "an air of mystery" still surrounded him, a distinguished historian of the Vietnam War would write. "At the time," George C. Herring observed nearly two decades later, "Americans knew virtually nothing about him, and frequently confused him" with another Polish Foreign Ministry official with the same last name. Nor would time clarify his identity or motives. Lacking any better source, Herring quoted an ex-Hungarian diplomat, János Radványi, who had defected to the United States, as calling Lewandowski "a high-ranking officer in Polish intelligence and a hard-liner consistently hostile to the United States."[19] Subsequent accounts—until now—have failed to clarify his identity, motives, actions, or affiliations.

So who was this man who now, in April 1966, became the central figure in Poland's secret diplomacy in Vietnam? His titles reflected his dual identity. In Saigon, Poland's ICC delegate was known formally as "Monsieur L'Ambassadeur Janusz Lewandowski, Chef de la Délégation Polonaise CIC." (So read his black-leather-bound membership card at the Cercle Sportif Saigonnais, where, as a member d'honneur, he swam, played tennis, dined, drank, and schmoozed.) But when Monsieur L'Ambassadeur traveled to Hanoi, his Communist colleagues addressed him differently: "Đồng Chí (Comrade) Ambassador."

Slender, trim, of short to medium height, black-haired and blue-eyed, donning thick black-rimmed glasses (or sunglasses for sightseeing or tennis) and conservative dark suits, the Pole seemed as polite, earnest, and intelligent, even bookish, as a graduate student. But Lewandowski's youthful exterior, intellectual mien, and affable personality—surprisingly open, many felt, for the only Communist ambassador in Saigon—belied a lifetime already replete with hard experience.[20] Despite his taking a "predictable line" on the war, a British diplomat judged him "an agreeable and capable young man aged about thirty-five," and a U.S. analyst remembered him as "young, personable, intelligent, good looking, . . . often seen on the social circuit in Saigon." But a Polish colleague stressed that he was "a very serious fellow"—hardly a butterfly flitting between cocktail parties.[21]

Lewandowski also impressed a young Warsaw journalist who spent a few months in Saigon in 1966 under cover as a translator for the Polish ICC delegation. "He was for me a personality," remembered Daniel Passent, then a twenty-eight-year-old reporter for the magazine *Polityka* with a "frog's perspective" on his "unusually young" boss. "But very soon he had shown confidence in me and he was treating me very well, so I had the impression from the conversations also that he is very open-minded, not a type of Communist Foreign Service apparatchik. He never asked me to write something or to confirm something that was not true when I was reporting to him about some meeting that I participated in. . . . When I was discussing [matters with him], I did not feel any attempts to [pressure me], let us say, to color reality or to [use] any double-talk or any attempt to bear false witness." Passent became Lewandowski's friend, a tennis partner on the red clay courts of the Cercle Sportif after the afternoon rains. "It was a real pleasure to have him in Saigon," Lewandowski recalled. "Conversations with Daniel were not only a respite from a routine and worries but also useful exchanges of reflections and ideas." Passent thought Lewandowski a sharp, respected, hard-working, serious yet wry, "quite Westernized" figure, a far cry from the boorish party hacks and slick secret police agents who populated Soviet Bloc embassies. "You wouldn't tell any difference between him and an American or British diplomat. . . . In his vocabulary, his posture, his interests, he could be working in the foreign service of any Western country or even was superior."[22]

Despite his youth and polite, deferential demeanor, Lewandowski also struck U.S. officials favorably. Within a few months of his arrival in Saigon, a classified CIA sketch of Lewandowski, which a U.S. Embassy officer there shared with a Dutch colleague, noted that he spoke fluent English refreshingly free of Communist cant and added: "He is apparently a cultured and well educated person. . . . On first meeting he gives the impression of being quite shy and meek but on further acquaintance this impression dissolves as he is in reality both competent and intelligent."[23] Later, after Lewandowski returned to Warsaw, an American who saw him recorded that "the very first impression you get of Janusz is that he is poised, tough and humorless. He is the kind of man you always want on your side. He can do you great danger as an adversary."[24]

Like other Poles of his generation, Lewandowski had known firsthand the horrors of war. He was born in Warsaw on March 10, 1931, to a couple in their midtwenties—Józef Lewandowski, a career military officer, and his wife Zofia, a primary school teacher—two years after the arrival of his elder brother (and only sibling), Ryszard. Though raised in a modest Warsaw apartment—"social origins: working class," his Communist Party profile stated approvingly[25]—Lewandowski's childhood included intellectual, political, and patriotic influences, arising from diverse family roots swirling with nationalist, revolutionary, military, land-owning (he bristled at "aristocratic"), and even American connections. Until the early nineteenth century, the Lewandowskis resided on a small country estate. But the family "lost everything" in the aftermath of a failed 1830–31 insurrection against the tsar—nominally autonomous, Poland belonged to the Russian Empire throughout this "partition" era—when the authorities, cracking down on anyone suspected of nationalist activities, confiscated the Lewandowski family's property, forcing it to find shelter and work in the capital.[26] Nevertheless, a century later, Janusz entered a household in which patriotic sentiments and memories still ran strong.

"Our house was always full of books," he recalled, which the family "never dreamed we will sell," even when unable to pay heating bills. They were "books with a certain patriotic spirit," like *Pan Tadeusz* by the poet Adam Mickiewicz, imbuing the boys with an "optimistic view of Poland," which had only recently reemerged as an independent country. Cervantes' classic novel also left a strong impression on young Janusz, aptly enough because some would later scoff at his diplomacy as *quixotic*.

His mother helped instill a love of reading, and her own past deepened the clan's politically complex history. At the turn of the century, Zofia's father had belonged to a clandestine cell of Józef Piłsudski's nationalist movement. Typically, the nationalist forces split into bitter rival factions; the moderates favored collaboration with Russia to encourage reform or revolution there as a step toward Polish independence, while Piłsudski's so-called revolutionary faction of the illegal Polish Socialist Party (Polska Partia Socjalistyczna) advocated more aggressive actions at home, including terrorism. Discontent exploded into open resistance when Russia became embroiled in a war with Japan in 1904–5 and the nationalist activists, sensing an opportunity to hit their distracted overlord, staged attacks on Russian officials and in some cases made common cause with Tokyo.[27]

Amid this ferment, Zofia Jąderko was born in 1904 (a year before her eventual husband), and her father was arrested for involvement in an attempt to assassinate the tsar's governor of Warsaw (by bombing his carriage). Some conspirators were hanged and others were condemned to hard labor or banished to Siberia, but a few of the younger and stronger—including Zofia's father—were sentenced to twenty-five years' duty in the Russian fleet, a fate considered almost tantamount to Siberian exile and a virtual death sentence. But a port call in the New World stemming from Theodore Roosevelt's mediation of the Russo-Japanese War gave him a chance to jump ship. He landed a job as a dock worker in Baltimore, and his satisfied employer wrote Zofia's mother offering to assure a home and job if she and her children emigrated to America to join him. Yet the Russian authorities barred him from sending financial aid to his family in Poland and charged him with desertion. A few years later, he died in a work accident and was buried in Baltimore. Hearing this story, Janusz remembered, helped him develop empathy for nations divided by civil conflict, as well as nationalist pride in his own dealings with Moscow.

As for millions of Poles, World War II abruptly turned the Lewandowski family's struggle for subsistence into one for physical survival. In September 1939, Janusz was eight and half years old when the Germans invaded Poland and sent the Luftwaffe to punish the capital. The raids inflicted massive civilian casualties over large sections of the city, including the central neighborhoods on the west bank of the Vistula River. There, in the Śródmieście district, bombs leveled the Lewandowski home, trapping the family in the cellar beneath piles of debris. With his mother, elder brother, and grandmother (Józef, now an artillery officer, had gone to the front), Janusz spent six or seven terrifying hours. "We were almost dead because the air was running out," he remembered. In the darkness, amid whimpers and screams, they feared that trying to clear the rubble might cause a final, fatal collapse; so instead they banged on pipes and made as much noise as possible in hopes of being rescued. Finally, neighbors heard them and managed to dig them out.

Their house destroyed, their father missing (in a German POW, camp, it turned out), the Lewandowskis nevertheless survived the blitzkrieg—only to face life under occupation. As the Nazis tightened their grip, the boy witnessed death regularly and at close range. He saw bodies hanging from gallows and lying in the streets—"each week or twice a week there were public shootings of 10, 15, 50, 100 Poles made publicly in Warsaw by the Germans. . . . They close the street, they bring the people, and shot them."

For a time, after the city's Jews were herded into a walled-off ghetto, Janusz lived a few blocks away with his mother, now working in a factory. At first, while the barriers were still porous, Zofia used to leave out a pot of cooked potatoes for children who could sneak through small gaps to retrieve food for their starving families. But after five months, the Lewandowskis were kicked out of their residence so the Germans could install guards to tighten the noose. Once, Janusz glimpsed two Jewish childhood friends being led away by the Gestapo to be shot, a memory that more than six decades later still caused his eyes to well with tears. Twice, he heard the gunfire and explosions of street-to-street fighting—during the desperate ghetto uprising in 1943 and the sixty-three days of citywide battles of Polish partisans against the Germans in the summer of 1944.

When the Warsaw Uprising broke out, Janusz found himself caught in the center of the city on the way to visit friends. As street battles raged, the thirteen-year-old hid in a house, only to be seized by pro-German troops—actually members of the so-called Kamiński Brigade of collaborationist Russian émigrés—who lined him and about fifty other Poles up against a wall and pointed machine guns at them. Waiting to be shot, the crowd (old, young, "women with small dogs," et al.) shouted patriotic insults. Then an officer arrived and, instead of authorizing a massacre, ordered them to march through the burning capital to the city's western railway station. From there, they were herded onto a train headed toward Pruszków, about 20 kilometers west, to be put in a detention camp.

But along the way, Soviet planes (red stars on their wings) strafed the train, which halted. When their escorts fled, the passengers broke down the doors and he escaped into a cabbage patch next to the tracks. The train soon resumed its voyage, but Lewandowski had evaded capture, concealed in the late summer vegetation. Unable to return to Warsaw, which was swarming with German troops liable to shoot him as a "bandit," he lived for days off ripening cabbage—"I had nothing, absolutely nothing"—and contracted "some kind of dysentery." Wandering, wary of German patrols, he made his way to a nearby village, where a family fed him, nursed him back to health, and told the German police checking identities that he was their son. He stayed until the Red Army finally entered Warsaw in January 1945 (after politely allowing the Germans to crush the nationalist Polish Home Army, and much of the city in the process, by early October). He presumed that his family was dead, especially after finding their building a burned-out husk, but nevertheless he put up a scrap of paper listing their names and seeking information on the blasted walls of a local church. Two days later, he found a note saying that they had gone to the western suburb of Włochy (Italy), where he knew an uncle lived. He went there and, to their mutual astonishment, found that his mother and brother had survived (Ryszard, of an age to be shot on sight by the Germans or sent to a concentration camp, had hid in a tunnel under the house). "It was something, because they thought I was definitely killed, . . . and I, looking at the destroyed ruins, was inclined to believe the same [about them]."

Another miracle soon followed. Though Józef had escaped from a German POW camp early in the war, after a brief reunion with his family he had fled into hiding, fearing arrest; the family had no idea whether he was alive or dead.[28] "My mother probably believed he will never come back." But one day that winter, a few American trucks—Studebakers given to the Soviets under Lend-Lease—"came roaring up with Polish soldiers in them, and from one out jumped our father!" Amid Germany's chaotic retreat, Józef had joined Soviet-led Polish forces for the final thrust toward Berlin. Now, his family learned in a frantic few hours together, he was driving a tank; then, mirage-like, he vanished again, rumbling toward Pomerania to take part in the battle for the Baltic port of Szczecin. Only in the spring, after the final triumph, did he come home for good. Somehow, the Lewandowski family had made it through the war intact—and if his story seems implausible, so was that of every Pole who defied death during those years.

❋ ❋ ❋

Surrounded by the butchery of war, Janusz had also discovered a lifelong calling—as a result of a painful incident during the occupation that, in this case, could not be exclusively blamed on the Germans. Tromping around barefoot one day in late 1943, before the first winter frost came, he sustained a splinter, a "tree fragment," under the nail of one of his big toes. When it swelled up and Janusz grew feverish, his mother summoned a doctor. The elderly physician squeezed the inflamed digit, then announced that he would return the next day to treat it. "What I will do to you will be very painful," the doctor told Janusz—and he was not kidding: Without anesthetic (all medicines were in short supply), he used a knife and pincers to remove the entire toenail so he could clean out the wooden shards beneath to prevent further infection. To distract the boy, the doctor, noticing his precocious reading habits, handed Janusz a book, and asked him to look at it during the makeshift surgery. Of course, the twelve-year-old could hardly concentrate; nearly fainting, he fought desperately to control the pain until the doctor virtually ordered him to cry, at which point he screamed out.

A few days later, the doctor came back to change the bandage and asked Janusz if he had read the book yet. He sheepishly admitted that he had not, but now he inspected it more closely, and soon grew utterly absorbed. The volume presented a history of diplomacy from ancient times up to Versailles, describing Machiavelli, Napoleon, Metternich, Bismarck, Talleyrand, and other fascinating figures. As his new toenail began to grow, so did Janusz's determination to emulate the intelligent, clever, articulate envoys who handled relations among kingdoms, empires, and nations, carefully maneuvering to avoid, minimize, or regulate conflicts. "I learned from this book that diplomacy is a very precise thing," he remembered. "Your words may have a meaning." If he could survive the war, Janusz now had a consuming ambition.[29]

❋ ❋ ❋

As Lewandowski turned fourteen, in the spring of 1945, a new era in Polish history was starting. After the years of Nazi atrocities, he recalled, Warsaw residents greeted their new overlords as liberators. Unlike the residents of eastern Poland, who had already experienced a repressive Soviet occupation and widespread deportations, the capital's denizens knew less about their new rulers. "I mean we didn't experience any bad things yet coming from [Moscow.]" German charges that the Soviets had murdered thousands of Polish officers were widely dismissed as propaganda. "I remember people gathered at the posters, you know, . . . and they were walking around saying, 'Where is this Katyń, it is near Oświęcim [Auschwitz]?". . . So [there was] this distrust, you see, because what they have posted looked like normal behavior of the Germans. . . . We couldn't imagine that somebody [besides] the Nazis could do such things."

After the war, the Communist Party's stewardship of the huge effort to rebuild the devastated capital impressed the teenager. At seventeen, he joined a party-associated movement (the Union of Polish Youth, or ZMP) and went to the countryside to take part in a land reform and development effort that he considered idealistic and needed to avoid civil war. "It was a feeling we were doing something good for these people," he said, recalling grateful peasants who received land deeds, literacy tutoring, electricity, or sewerage for the first time. In 1953, he formally enrolled in the PZPR, which he credited with reshaping the country. Taking advantage of this "new social contract,"[30] which included free education ("you didn't have to pay a single zloty if you passed the examination"), he earned high grades at the Main School of Foreign Service and a state scholarship to study abroad.

Confirming his entry into the new elite, Lewandowski earned a master's degree in the history of international relations at the Taras Shevchenko State University of Kiev. While studying, he glimpsed the hardship of life in Stalin's final years. On a train excursion to the countryside for a picnic, he was startled to see militiamen assault poorly dressed villagers and seize sacks of bread. A fellow student sheepishly excused the action as an antismuggling measure, but it hinted at "devastation in rural areas." After Stalin's March 1953 death, he sensed around him the acute uncertainty over the future, along with early hints of a thaw in both personal and political spheres.

On graduation in 1955, newly married, he entered Poland's Ministry of Foreign Affairs, which was hungry for qualified Communist talent to replace the intelligentsia lost in the war or now deemed ideologically unsound. At this point, Poland was shackled to the Soviet Bloc—it was occupied by Red Army forces, with its military and secret police cobwebbed by Soviets—so it was hardly free to develop its own foreign policy. Symbolically, it had hosted the Warsaw Pact's creation that May to counter West Germany's entry into NATO.

And yet, Lewandowski fortuitously joined the MSZ just as Poland carved out a bit of autonomy from the Kremlin. After Khrushchev's de-Stalinization speech in February 1956, and the sudden death of Warsaw's neo-Stalinist leader, Boleslaw Bierut, Poles sensed a chance to challenge existing power structures. The "Polish October" ushered in a brief period of hope that "national Communism" could secure a freer existence within the Soviet Bloc. For the next few years, Lewandowski worked in the MSZ's International Organizations Department, specializing in UN affairs, even as he kept up his party credentials by serving as second secretary of the ministry's PZPR Committee. Each fall, he joined Poland's delegation to the UN General Assembly, using the opportunities to hone his English, explore New York City and America (including a trip to Baltimore to seek out his maternal grandfather's grave[31]), and amass experience dealing with varied issues and colleagues—Communists, Westerners , and nonaligned. A 1956 photo suggests his rising self-confidence: Dapper in a beige trench coat over a dark suit, he strides purposefully up First Avenue with colleagues toward the world body's headquarters on a crisp fall day, bareheaded, attaché case in hand, a jaunty smile on his face.[32]

Lewandowski rose quickly from the rank of "expert" (when he only had a seat when meetings were not crowded) to a full delegate entrusted to make important speeches (like one calling for seating Communist China rather than Taiwan). His UN successes—and occasional independent-mindedness, as when he deviated from Moscow on a decolonization vote[33]—"did not escape" the notice of the foreign minister, who assigned him to work on Poland's most prominent initiative of the entire Cold War: the Rapacki Plan. The nuclear arms race was revving up. Lewandowski recalled heady days for Communist diplomats when the USSR launched the first artificial satellite on October 4, 1957: the "hysterical" reaction in the United States, which feared the Kremlin was racing ahead in long-range missiles; the spring in the step of Soviet diplomats; the "Sputnik" cocktail in the UN bar (vodka with an egg yolk "swimming in it").

Two days before Moscow shocked the world, Rapacki unveiled his plan to create an "atom-free" zone in East and West Germany, Poland, and Czechoslovakia.[34] His motive was obvious: Poles feared that Bonn's rapid economic and military growth might herald its acquisition of nuclear capabilities—and were concerned by the growing nuclear arsenal NATO had already deployed in West Germany; sacrificing nuclear prerogatives in three Warsaw Pact member states seemed a reasonable price to preclude this peril. In retrospect, Lewandowski suspected that if Washington had accepted the plan, "Russia would say no." But given West Germany's centrality to Western defense strategy, there was little chance it would fly. "I don't think," he said, "that either party was really interested in having any kind of treaty which would really limit the nuclear armaments."

Although the "sharpened international situation limited our possibilities," Lewandowski worked on a team led by MSZ legal adviser Manfred Lachs to devise "plans, propositions, counterpropositions" stemming from Rapacki's idea. Lewandowski served as secretary for the discussions, which frequently included the foreign minister (as well as a junior military delegate, Wojiech Jaruzelski). Rising to the rank of senior counselor, Lewandowski also monitored East-West talks on nuclear and conventional weaponry at the UN and elsewhere. "It was my duty (among other problems) to keep a constantly updated catalogue of all disarmament proposals, to make critical analyses (what a nasty work) and to present periodical papers for the minister."[35]

Lewandowski then moved to the Middle East, going in early 1959 to Poland's embassy in Cairo as first secretary. Endorsing the assignment, an aide sent Rapacki a glowing appraisal: "Comrade Lewandowski, despite his young age, is showing a rapid and promising development given his many skills. The work he performed at three consecutive sessions of the UN showed that he is already a mature diplomat."[36]

Three years in Cairo offered him a chance to observe Gamal Abdel Nasser at the height of his powers as an Arab nationalist firebrand. Once, he met the Egyptian leader one to one, and received an impassioned history lesson.

"You are a very young diplomat," Nasser said. "Do you know the history of Egypt?"

"Well, concerning ancient Egypt, it was obligatory, . . ." he started.

No, Nasser interrupted, *modern* Egypt—detailing how his revolt had wrestled full independence from Britain, and his ambitions for rapid development to overcome primitive living habits.

"Look around you, see how much needs to be done," Nasser declared. Evoking the old empire, he stressed Egypt's need for more independence from the great powers and criticized Moscow's "preaching" to permit more political activity—a transparent bid, he felt, to help the Communist Party, which he had banned. Under King Farouk, he recalled, there were thirty-five parties, all controlled by foreign embassies. In 1952, as a young colonel, he had led a band of military officers to oust Farouk's pro-British government; four years later, he had defied London and Paris by nationalizing the Suez Canal. Why should he legalize a Communist Party so the Soviets could manipulate it? Besides, the advice seemed hypocritical—there was only one political party in Russia.

Ultimately, Lewandowski had a mixed view of Nasser, ruing his nationalist excesses yet believing that he had improved his compatriots' lot through workers' rights, land tenancy, and education reforms. Exploiting the embassy's accreditation, Lewandowski also visited Libya, Sudan, North and South Yemen, and Lebanon. A year after reaching Cairo, he assumed extra responsibility for embassy security matters; recommending him, an Interior Ministry agent (under MSZ cover) described him as an "active" party member, "very hardworking and energetic in his professional work," and a loner: "He does not maintain close relations with other employees of the post."[37] In one delicate task, he helped ethnic Poles lacking documents evade Nasser's xenophobic antiforeigner dragnet and escape the country.

Lewandowski received a Golden Cross of Merit and other honors befitting a successful first tour, and his assignment on the Nile propelled him toward deeper involvement in Africa. In late 1961, he was surprised to receive a cable from Julius Nyerere inviting him to ceremonies marking Tanganyika's independence from Britain. They had been friendly at the UN; the Pole liked the "quiet, reasonable, nondemagogic" lawyer lobbying for independence, now his new country's first leader. On Rapacki's instructions, he established formal ties and stayed in Dar es Salaam as Warsaw's envoy for two years beginning in May 1962, where he promoted Polish interests in a region—he also handled nearby countries, such as Uganda, Rhodesia, and newly independent Burundi and Rwanda—his compatriots knew, as he put it, "only from Tarzan." On some adventures, he joined another peripatetic young Pole who had survived wartime Warsaw—his "good friend" Ryszard Kapuściński, then a state news agency (PAP) correspondent based in Dar and later world-renowned for his lyrical journalism. On the front lines of the stirring drama of African decolonization, Lewandowski met a steady stream of high-level visitors who came to court Nyerere. When Israeli foreign minister Golda Meir—originally Golda Mabovitch, born in Kiev—passed through, she took him aside at a reception and the two chatted in Polish about their common Central and Eastern European heritage and wartime memories.

Lewandowski also had a front-row seat to an obscure Cold War struggle. Washington, Moscow, and even Beijing, among others, vied for influence as Nyerere gained international stature as a Pan-Africanist and nonaligned figure and a crisis flared in the offshore entrepôt of Zanzibar, which later merged with Tanganyika to form the new state of Tanzania. For a Soviet Bloc diplomat, and a junior one at that, Lewandowski had unusual freedom (or a lack of supervision) and high-level access. During the Cuban Missile Crisis, Nyerere sought his advice. "Look, Janusz," he asked, "tell me what is going on, because I had the American ambassador in here just an hour ago, and he told me that the Soviets had these rockets in Cuba, and then I have seen the Russian ambassador who denied everything and said it was an American lie." Rather than parrot the Kremlin line, Lewandowski pleaded ignorance. "What could I say to him? I myself knew nothing about it. I said, 'I don't know.' Nyerere was surprised I don't know, but really, what could I say?"

During Lewandowski's African stint, a classified U.S. intelligence profile noted, the young Pole "was often considered the unofficial leader in the bloc community," but "was never known to have 'spouted' the Communist line."[38] Read this description, Lewandowski guessed that one reason he earned this nondoctrinaire reputation was his skepticism about the large-scale industrial projects Moscow was pushing. These "stupid ideas," he advised Nyerere, did not suit an African country at a much earlier stage of development. "I really was trying to 'walk on the earth,'" he recalled.

In the spring of 1964, Warsaw recalled Lewandowski to run the MSZ's UN section, a post that gave him a well-placed vantage point on Poland's Vietnam diplomacy (and fostered confusion among intelligence services tracking Polish UN ambassador *Bohdan* Lewandowski[39]). Despite his lack of Asian expertise, he closely followed affairs there as two crises—the Sino-Soviet rift and Vietnam War—elbowed their way onto Poland's foreign policy agenda, which had been traditionally dominated by relations with its two troublesome neighbors.

And what of Radványi's charge that Lewandowski was also affiliated with Polish intelligence? "Never! Very firmly I tell you I was never any kind of officer of Polish intelligence; . . . neither I was any type of collaborator with the Ministry of the Interior." Of course, he said, he received military intelligence briefings, and his reports were sometimes distributed to intelligence agencies. But, he insisted, he never informed for or collaborated with intelligence services: "I worked for the minister of foreign affairs."[40]

Lewandowski's own claims, of course, could be discounted as self-serving—but I found no evidence to support Radványi's charge, and much to refute it. When the Hungarian diplomat defected in the spring of 1967 and was then debriefed at length by the U.S. assistant secretary of state for East Asian and Pacific affairs, William Bundy, he made no such accusation about Lewandowski and, indeed, gave no indication that he had direct knowledge concerning Marigold.[41] Nor did Radványi offer any evidence in *Delusion and Reality,* his 1978 exposé of "make-believe" Eastern European peace efforts in Vietnam, for his declaration that Lewandowski was "not a career diplomat" but a former high-ranking spy, a man consistently antagonistic to America, who was actually pleased by the eventual failure of his secret mediation effort.[42] By contrast, a U.S. intelligence "fiche" from mid-1966 noted that Lewandowski "is not known to have any intelligence ties."[43] Passent testified that his boss was hardly trusted by the Communist regime's espionage agencies. In fact, the reporter said, while he was in Saigon, a Polish civilian intelligence operative, visiting from Warsaw under diplomatic cover, asked him to spy on his boss. Taken aback, Passent said that he promptly warned Lewandowski, who brushed off the approach as if it was routine. But Passent suspected that the incident must have reinforced his awareness that he was "in a hostile environment in the double meaning of the word, hostile meaning South Vietnam under American domination and also surrounded by Polish military and other [Polish] people whose allegiance he was not sure of."[44]

Asked why Radványi would accuse him of being an intelligence officer, Lewandowski threw up his hands. He did not know the man and could only imagine that he had confused him with someone else of the same last name (hardly uncommon in Poland).

Lewandowski guessed correctly—and the proof that this was a case of mistaken identity comes (albeit unwittingly) from Radványi himself. In *Delusion and Reality,* he provided no footnote or citation to support his assertion, but he revealed the underlying foundation in a 1974 private letter to William Bundy. While working on the book, the Hungarian (who had gone on to an academic career) corresponded with the former U.S. official (then editor of *Foreign Affairs*). They exchanged observations on Warsaw's mediation efforts, in particular the episode in which Norman Cousins met with Polish diplomats at the UN during LBJ's thirty-seven-day bombing pause to discuss traveling abroad to see DRV representatives. Seconding Bundy's dim view of Poland's diplomacy, Radványi wrote:

> You are right; Cousins was completely misled by Lewandowski whom I knew very well and can tell you that he was even more sinister than Michałowski. Lewandowski started out as a Polish intelligence officer. From the Polish Ministry of the Interior he was transferred to the Foreign Ministry as a code officer. At the time Lewandowski had his conversation with Cousins, I asked [Polish Deputy Foreign

Minister] Winiewicz in New York whether he had heard anything new from Vietnam (Winiewicz knew of my involvement). He told me there was absolutely nothing new; Hanoi was not interested in talking. All in all I think I can and will clearly prove that Lewandowski's move had no substance whatsoever.[45]

Of course, in this context Radványi was alluding to Polish UN Ambassador *Bohdan* Lewandowski, but in his book, the Hungarian inserted into his discussion of Marigold his damning characterization of Rapacki's "ambassador at the ICC," who was, of course, *Janusz* (no relation).[46] Radványi got the wrong man, others repeated the canard, and the record should be corrected accordingly.

✳ ✳ ✳

If Lewandowski was definitely *not* the hard-line intelligence officer depicted by Radványi, what relationship *did* he have with Poland's powerful secret police apparatus—pervasive in all Soviet Bloc countries—as he left for Saigon? This shadowy link can now be at least partly illuminated with the aid of his Ministry of Internal Affairs personnel files, to which the author (helped by eminent Polish historian Andrzej Paczkowski) gained access in 2007–8 from the Institute of National Remembrance in Warsaw.

Though MSW records must be used with caution, they more plausibly depict a professional foreign service officer who knew he owed *some* cooperation to the intelligence services, particularly at his career's outset. Yet they also reveal a mutual wariness that corroborates Lewandowski's protest that he reserved primary loyalty to his own minister. This was not, of course, the first time the Interior Ministry had noticed his existence; it had tracked his ascent at the MSZ, the posts in Cairo and Dar es Salaam, and trips to New York. Nothing raised a red flag, and in early March 1966, a month after receiving his name for vetting, the MSW's Department I (concerned with foreign operations and intelligence gathering) officially informed the Foreign Ministry that it had no "reservations" regarding Lewandowski's proposed ICC appointment; internally, a senior officer had consented, given the "positive opinion" in the files concerning the young diplomat's work abroad.[47]

Signing off on the Saigon assignment hardly ended the intelligence service's interest, however. On March 8—a day before Rapacki formally handed him his signed nomination papers—a Department I officer, Lieutenant W. Kikitiuk, spoke with Lewandowski, who after all would oversee a substantial Polish military and civilian station in a Cold War setting rife with the espionage and counterespionage that the MSW handled.

"I asked whether our service could expect some assistance and cooperation on his part during his stay in Saigon," Kikitiuk recorded.[48]

Lewandowski "replied that he would, of course, always signal everything that he deems either interesting or important."

That didn't satisfy the MSW operative. The point, he (sharply?) clarified, was not whether the diplomat "deems something interesting or important, or his observations"—he should "seek out himself" information potentially useful for the intelligence apparatus.

Undoubtedly aware that Kikitiuk suspected him of insufficient zeal, Lewandowski affirmed that he was "ready to help us in gathering information." Trying to shift the burden, he requested that the MSW enumerate the specific topics or tasks it expected him to cover or fulfill; asked to see someone "familiar with the matters of South Vietnam" to discuss concrete details; and issued a reciprocal request for aid. "According to Lewandowski's words, he is not so much afraid of the work itself and the cooperation with the Indians and Canadians, the Vietnamese or Americans. He is most afraid of the difficulties with his own personnel inside the [Polish] mission, which, while having nothing to do, drinks, causes trouble, etc. [He said that] our assistance in this regard is very important to him." Kikitiuk promised that "such a meeting would materialize."

Summing up the conversation for his superiors, Kikitiuk noted that the MSW had already established "a contact, of operational nature" with Lewandowski before he attended, with Rapacki, the fall 1965 UN General Assembly session in New York; back in Warsaw, he had "relayed his observations to us" regarding fellow Polish delegates. "The present conversation is the next step toward binding Lewandowski operationally with our apparatus," he remarked.[49]

The lieutenant urged that an expert on Vietnam and a high-ranking MSW official ("someone from management") see Lewandowski before he left for Southeast Asia. (Lewandowski, meanwhile, consulted with a veteran deputy foreign minister, Marian Naszkowski, on how best to handle the potentially sticky situation.) Accordingly, on March 18, a deputy section chief (Captain Jan Bisztyga) and another officer met with him to hammer out an understanding regarding the mutual cooperation that could be expected once the diplomat reached the war zone. Lewandowski—according to Bisztyga—expressed a readiness to cooperate with the MSW in Saigon and, "while declaring his assistance, he also declared that he would not interfere with our work."

As Bisztyga recounted, Lewandowski accepted a three-part understanding of mutual obligations during his term: They would consult on the war as the situation warranted; swap "more interesting political information"; and the MSW vowed "assistance on our part in situations demanding swift intervention regarding members of the delegation when it is evident that they are threatening to the work of the delegation" (e.g., adopting a "harmful" "political stance"). Lewandowski "agreed to our postulates, while promising his help and noninterference in the work of our representative."[50]

On the surface, satisfactory terms of engagement had been worked out; Lewandowski promised to stay out of the spies' way, and hoped to do the minimum necessary so that they would stay out of his. But would the arrangement survive reality on the ground in Vietnam?

Lewandowski in Vietnam

Saigon in the mid-1960s was "a place to be" for a Foreign Service officer, "a place where a young diplomat might come face to face with intrigue, adventure, chaos."[51] On Easter Sunday, April 10, 1966, Lewandowski reached the South Vietnamese capital—a city scarred and rattled by war, swollen with refugees, overwhelmed by the metastasizing new foreign presence that had displaced the old colonial masters, filling the crowded, sweltering streets and sidewalks with the soldiers, money, goods (including a flourishing "open" black market in military supplies), businessmen, advisers, spies, contractors, and culture of the new overlord—"both literally and figuratively, Saigon has become an American brothel," a U.S. senator charged.[52] An observer who arrived around the same time as Lewandowski remarked upon the "profound impression" that the thousands of U.S. troops, with their "businesslike" sense of schedules and efficiency, had made upon the languid natives. "The stiff, square carriage of their shoulders set them apart from the limber Vietnamese," wrote Frances Fitzgerald. "Physically, Saigon seemed to change in their direction, the rectilinear shapes of the new American office buildings, billets, and hotels towering above the sloping red-tiled roofs of the French and Vietnamese city."[53] Hot, fetid, noisy, edgy, its verdant neighborhoods of villas and commercial core now surrounded and infiltrated by a mushrooming honeycomb of slums, the capital was no longer the "Paris of the East" (as colonial travel writers had rhapsodized). Violence still hit the city only rarely, yet the conflict's impact was visible in everything from the street urchins and beggars dislocated from peasant villages to the lumbering U.S. military vehicles interrupting the stuttering stream of taxis, pedicabs, motorbikes, and bicycles.[54]

But the Pole found the city transfixed, at least for the moment, by a political crisis that seemed even to supersede the war with the Communist insurrection. Challenging the Ky-Thieu military regime, a Buddhist-led "Struggle Movement" had sprouted to demand drastic changes in the government, including the elimination of corruption and of preferential treatment for Catholics, a transfer to civilian rule, and a sharp reduction in the U.S. presence. Compounding the image of disarray, a rebellious commander of the Northern I Corps joined the movement, defying efforts to fire him. Besides raising the prospect of violence between South Vietnamese army units, the military revolt linked the protests to the interminable squabbling among top generals that exasperated Washington. At its apex, the uprising controlled most of South Vietnam's northern provinces, including the cities of Hue and Danang, sidelining the anticommunist struggle. A showdown between Saigon and the Buddhists loomed, risking violence that might entangle the Americans in unpopular acts of repression or undermine central authority.

The threat appeared so grave that from March through May, U.S. officials worried that the protests—which they presumed were backed, infiltrated, and manipulated by Hanoi—might topple the Saigon government and doom the war.

Some in Washington flirted with installing an alternative to Ky to defuse Buddhist ire—or even, as in the case of McNamara aide John T. McNaughton, using the "semi-anarchy," the "all-out internecine strife," in South Vietnam as an "excuse" for "disengagement." (McNamara himself seemed to waver on whether to abandon the military commitment to Saigon as an anticommunist bastion.)[55] To the contrary, however, others favored a "sharp" escalation in bombing the North. (Military commanders and the Joint Chiefs of Staff; Lodge; and LBJ's new national security adviser, Walt W. Rostow—replacing McGeorge Bundy—were among those who urged the latter course, to bolster anticommunist forces in the South and coerce the leadership in the North.[56]) U.S. officials warily observed the machinations of the movement's enigmatic leader, Thich Tri Quang, and suspected his ultimate aim was to force the Americans out and allow neutralists, and then the Communists, to take power.[57]

On April 13, as Johnson administration officials secretly debated the risks of a crackdown on the Buddhists (and inevitable political backlash) versus the danger that Ky's regime might crumble, Lewandowski cabled his first impressions: "VC" (Viet Cong) actions in Saigon remained "small" despite "terroristic activities" on the city's outskirts (including an attack on the Tan Son Nhut Airport, where he had just landed), and the "local and organized demonstrations" against the regime were not interfering with daily life. Overall, however, uncertainty shadowed the internal political scene, with Ky seeking but failing to attain wider support and the Americans acutely worried.[58]

A First Trip to Hanoi: "Is It a Game, a Play?"

Rather than wading right into the active diplomatic and social life in the steamy South Vietnamese capital, Lewandowski followed ICC tradition by paying his first official calls on authorities in the Communist North before presenting himself to the pro-U.S. Southern regime (Canada's delegates did the reverse, and India's alternated). First, however, he spent a little over a week settling in. The ICC occupied a scattering of one-story buildings in the Camp des Mares, a poorly maintained (peeling paint, crooked signs, etc.) ex–French legionnaires barracks, enclosed by mustard-colored walls, the seedy colonial atmosphere accentuated by a lack of air-conditioning; old ceiling fans sliced the thick air. Lewandowski began taking charge of the ragged Polish military contingent of about a hundred—first impressions included the sight of soldiers lounging in their bunks guzzling beer[59]—and meeting his staff and counterparts: New Delhi's M. A. "Ishi" Rahman, who chaired the ICC's meetings, and Ottawa's Victor C. Moore.

The commissioners lived more comfortably about a mile to the west, toward the Chinese district of Cholon, in a compound known as the Cité Hui Bon Hoa. Lush grounds featuring "bougainvillea growing all over the place," exotic fruit trees, and bat-harboring stands of bamboo surrounded large colonial-style white stucco villas whose tropical accents (high ceilings, spacious dining rooms, marble trim, even noisy air-conditioners in some bedrooms) did not preclude grousing over ramshackle conditions (malfunctioning electricity, plumbing, and air-conditioning, etc.). Here the Indian, Canadian, and Polish ambassadors and their senior aides slept, ate, entertained, and relaxed (with strolls, drinks on the veranda, tennis, and badminton made "a bit tricky" by huge holes in the cement court) between chauffeur-driven trips in black Chevrolets bearing ICC and national flags to Camp des Mares.[60]

Though Lewandowski's relations with both Moore and Rahman would turn rocky at times, with moments of tension beneath outward civility, cordiality, and even camaraderie, the new commissioner did his best to start out on a positive note. In a courtesy call on Moore, a career diplomat previously posted to Pakistan, he praised a Canadian envoy he had known in Dar es Salaam and Warsaw, exaggerated Polish-Canadian harmony in foreign affairs, complimented Ottawa's recent ideas to improve ICC functioning ("our two governments are in full agreement"), and voiced "the hope that our work on the commission would be without acrimony."

An exchange on the Vietnamese military and political situation quickly revealed divergent views—the Pole predictably termed U.S. bombing the key bar to negotiations and a factor that "simply united the North Vietnamese to be more adamant and forced them into the arms of China." Still, he did not argue when Moore pooh-poohed his worries about a U.S. or South Vietnamese ground incursion into North Vietnam, a danger Lewandowski felt would push Hanoi to turn to Beijing as "a guarantor, a deterrent against ultimate escalation."

Only two days off the plane, the new arrival radiated optimism—and even hinted at his secret mandate from Rapacki: "Touching on the current potential usefulness of the Commissioners individually as a link between Hanoi and Saigon," Moore reported, Lewandowski "spoke with some enthusiasm of what an achievement it would be if any one of us could be instrumental in opening the door to a settlement."[61]

Then it was time to start testing his own usefulness as an individual link: On April 19, he flew to Hanoi, using a circuitous and dangerous route he would retrace repeatedly over the next thirteen months. The cash-starved ICC used a tiny, dilapidated fleet of Boeing 307 BI Stratoliners long since retired from stints with TWA and Aigle Azur, a French airline used to supply the metropole's military and colonial effort. Their fuselages painted white but for a horizontal blue stripe and the letters "CIC" (Commission Internationale de Controle), their wings, tail, and undercarriage left metallic silver, the four-engine prop planes were forlorn vestiges of Geneva's vision of an international machinery to "control and supervise" the accords so painfully hammered out in 1954.

Merely keeping these antiquated planes aloft required the small maintenance crew to improvise, cannibalizing parts and patching holes from ground-fire with materials on hand. "Ooh, *pas mal, pas mal* [not bad, not bad]," the hard-drinking, swearing French mechanic, "Fuokier," would mutter, inserting a wooden dipstick to check the oil. U.S. bombing and North Vietnamese antiaircraft fire precluded direct flights between Saigon and Hanoi. Instead, the Stratoliners would fly at dawn from Tan Son Nhut (if not delayed by military flights, which had priority) to Phnom Penh in neutral Cambodia; continue in the afternoon along a narrow air corridor north to Vientiane; and there refuel and await clearance from DRV authorities before a late-night, low-altitude (3,000 meters) hop to darkened Gia Lam Airport near Hanoi—a trip frequently canceled, interrupted, or diverted by combat (a recent flight had been downed over Laos, with all twelve aboard killed).[62]

"Flying at night, almost each flight was accompanied by shooting, you know," Lewandowski remembered decades later, laughing and shaking his head. "This is a special experience, you know. . . . You are sitting, and there is the window, eh? Dark night. And then you see, you know, the bright light going up to the plane, and the impression is further that it is going not only hitting the plane but hitting you directly in the eye!" Such dangers drove several pilots and stewardesses to quit or drink, and shattered nerves among those who remained. "Sometimes it was a dramatic situation because sometimes the flak was very strong and I remember the poor girl was squeezed on the chair and crying, you know; . . . some persons refused to fly on these flights." Even a routine Gia Lam landing, with the single light beam to indicate the runway, was "sometimes very rough, especially when a large amount of gin was consumed on the airplane." Having endured a one-way trip, the ICC passengers then steeled their nerves to reverse the journey to Saigon.[63]

Even before Lewandowski showed up, Hanoi had reason to anticipate more nagging to move toward a political process. A lull in diplomacy had followed the U.S. bombing resumption in early February, but the peace front was heating up again. After a still-smarting Rapacki deflected their bid for an ICC "good offices probing exercise," the Canadians took a turn. They were hardly strangers to this sort of activity, having sent their Saigon-based commissioner, J. Blair Seaborn, on several missions to Hanoi bearing U.S. warnings that the DRV faced dire consequences unless it stopped interfering in the South. They were also apprehensive over Washington's military escalation. During an April 1965 visit to the United States, Prime Minister Lester B. Pearson had set off Johnson's volcanic temper by criticizing the bombing of North Vietnam in a speech in Philadelphia. When he then went to Camp David, LBJ grabbed him by the lapels and subjected him to a tongue-lashing for behaving so rudely on U.S. soil.[64]

Despite these inauspicious antecedents, Ottawa wanted to try again, eager to exploit its access (unique for Westerners) to the DRV leadership. In an initiative cutely code-named "Operation Smallbridge," it sent Chester A. Ronning, an old Asia hand, to Hanoi on March 7–11, 1966. Ronning later told William Bundy that he had "traveled ten thousand miles to present a feather"—a U.S.-approved formula to trade a bombing halt for an end to infiltration of the South. The North Vietnamese were uninterested, confident that they were winning the war, "friendly in tone but completely obdurate in substance." Sensing a "team effort [aimed] at wearing him down," he "found his several hours of talks with Hanoi leaders very wearing and frustrating with conversations wandering down blind alleys and always returning to same intransigent dead end." Near the end of a long talk with Pham Van Dong, however, he discerned a nibble when the premier hinted at a willingness to talk with Washington if it halted attacks on North Vietnam "for good, and unconditionally"—instead of insisting on a prior agreement to withdraw its forces and recognize the NLF. But, to the Canadians' acute disappointment, U.S. officials dismissed this "possible glimmer of light" as no real departure from Hanoi's Four Points.[65]

In Moscow, however, Le Duan had a harder time deflecting comradely advice from Soviet leaders while attending the CPSU's Twenty-Third Congress. The Kremlin leaders publicly embraced him and Vietnam's heroic struggle, but Brezhnev urged the Lao Dong (Vietnam Workers' Party) first secretary to modify Hanoi's focus on waging war until victory:

> Perhaps it is necessary, along with military activity, to think over the intensification of political struggle in the international arena. We have talked about this with you and Com[rade] Pham Van Dong. We consider such a line correct. Political struggle is advantageous to our common interests. The Americans will not win the war in South Vietnam, and they know this. Maybe, it is necessary to help them leave South Vietnam. Let them preserve their prestige, but leave.

Le Duan assured Brezhnev "that Hanoi would maintain contacts with the Americans, either in Rangoon or in Moscow or in other places."[66]

During his initial encounters with the DRV's leaders, Lewandowski heard comparable predictions of ultimate victory but also discerned some hints of potential flexibility. After landing in Hanoi, he heard an extended analysis of the situation from the liaison of the People's Army of Vietnam (PAVN, the North Vietnamese Army) to the ICC Colonel Ha Van Lau, "a delicate-featured, slender, refined officer from Hue, of Mandarin ancestry."[67] Skeptical of U.S. plans to sharply raise troop levels, Lau laid out a three-stage process that he predicted would convince Washington to give up. Stages one and two appeared well advanced; Washington recognized that bombing the North (even during the dry season, which was nearing an end) had failed to force a DRV surrender, and would soon comprehend that "pacification" of the South was also doomed— and the wave of protests in Southern cities seemed to presage the final phase: the Saigon regime's collapse, leading to direct negotiations with the NLF (an idea Washington and Saigon resisted). While rejecting any permanent U.S. military role in Vietnam, Lau allowed that the manner and timetable for a withdrawal could be discussed, and he hinted that the ICC could help assure Vietnam's neutrality. The idea that talks with Washington might precede a decisive military blow raised Lewandowski's eyebrows ever so slightly—"thus," he observed, the prerequisite was "not Dien Bien Phu, or pushing the Americans toward the sea."[68]

Lewandowski's conversations with Lau inaugurated a relationship with the man who would be his closest DRV contact. Like the Pole, the older (almost fifty) Vietnamese colonel had a complex family history deeply entwined with his country's violent past. His father had been a provincial administrator in the French colonial regime who was executed by the revolutionary authorities when they briefly seized power after the Japanese surrender in 1945. He was born in the imperial capital of Hue in 1918, and he began his military career in the colonial army, adding to a résumé that hardly seemed auspicious for a trusted Communist functionary. Yet, Vietnamese sources relate, he assisted the revolution even while wearing the enemy's uniform, and after the war against the French broke out, he fought for the Viet Minh as an officer. His fluent French and higher education qualified him for sensitive tasks, and in 1954 he was tapped to join the Viet Minh delegation to Geneva; he then became a military liaison to the ICC, which also allowed him to monitor the situation in the South. Augmenting his international experience, he attended the second Geneva Conference, on Laos. Increasingly, his work put him in closer touch with the Foreign Ministry than the PAVN. By the mid-1960s, he was the ministry's top Americanist and, along with his ICC job, handled contacts with foreign organizations and visitors (a writer he escorted likened him to *War and Peace*'s Prince Andrei).[69]

The tall, thin Lau, code-named "Ludwik" or "Ludwig" in Polish documents for obscure reasons, would greet Lewandowski at Gia Lam after he caught a few hours' sleep at an airport villa for the early morning drive into the capital; accompany him on inspection tours to areas hit by U.S. bombs; see him off; and maintain regular contact with him in Saigon via a coded radio-telephone. The Pole respected and liked Lau, discussing European literature and bringing English-language cassettes and books purchased in Saigon.[70]

While on this first visit, Lewandowski met various senior DRV figures, including General Giap and Foreign Minister Nguyen Duy Trinh, though not the powerful party leader, Le Duan, or the revered but increasingly remote Ho. His most significant contact came on April 22, when Pham Van Dong received him. The premier always inspired the Pole's greatest hopes of progress. While Trinh and others proclaimed faith in an inevitable military triumph, Dong acknowledged the human suffering that such a struggle entailed, and he seemed to agree at least on the *desirability* of negotiations, even while remaining deeply skeptical of U.S. sincerity.

During this first conversation, Dong again expressed "deep confidence in victory," given Hanoi's "correct" political line, ideology, and (playing to his audience) aid from the socialist world. To explain more "concretely" his belief that the Communists were winning, Dong argued that America was "disappointed" by the results of its dry season operations—it was "easier," he claimed, "to beat a U.S. soldier than a French one"[71]—and he cited expanding fissures within the Saigon regime, the NLF's "enormous" increase in influence, and an unexpected intensification of fighting.[72]

Lewandowski did not want to quarrel, but in line with Warsaw's (and Moscow's) line, tried to inject a more realistic note. In replying to Dong's cocky statements, he expressed the polite wish—a contemporaneous cable from Poland's ambassador to Hanoi, Jerzy Siedlecki, related—that victory might be achieved "with minimal losses." The premier replied earnestly that the leadership felt the nation's burden, and thought "day and night" about reducing casualties, but was "determined to fight" to obtain "true peace and independence."[73]

Decades later, Lewandowski recalled a blunter exchange:

Lewandowski: "The Americans are a great power. They are not to be kicked in the balls."

Dong: "So, do you think we have to surrender to the Americans?"

Lewandowski: "No, but if there is a way to stop the suffering. . . ."

Dong: "Look, this is Vietnamese blood. . . ."

Lewandowski: "I am coming from a nation where every generation used to spill blood for the nation. . . . We will give you support—you decide."[74]

At times, the Pole felt that his hosts were testing him. "I was thinking, 'Is it a game, a play?' you know? They are trying to find out what I think about it, you know. In Asia, they are very much trying to find out what kind of personality you are. . . . [You have to] put a line between what you have to say and what you really think. . . . They are trying to find it out."[75] Hearing the North Vietnamese insist that they would vanquish the Americans as surely as they had the French, he wondered, "My God, what kind of people are they? Don't they realize what they have at hand? . . . I was sitting, listening, thinking, 'My God, this is a stone wall, . . . absolutely.'" Yet he carefully refused to let himself be provoked.[76]

Striving to strike a reasonable tone, Dong vowed—as the DRV's leaders had reassured other Soviet Bloc visitors—that Hanoi would not initiate any steps to spread the conflict or increase the chance of a world war (which would be more likely to erupt in Europe than Southeast Asia, he observed). Conversely, it would naturally respond if Washington escalated—for example, by launching military operations in Laos, Cambodia, or Thailand.

Disappointing if not surprising Lewandowski, Dong insisted that before talks could begin, Washington must accept the Four Points and completely halt military acts against the DRV and recognize the NLF as a negotiating partner—clear nonstarters. He also poured cold water on the ICC as a viable diplomatic actor, at least for now, though Lewandowski later reported that all the North Vietnamese with whom he spoke suggested that it might play a significant role "when conditions become suitable." For now, Dong told him, Hanoi made a "negative assessment" of Ronning's mission (though "tactful," Canada assumed a "pro-American" stance), and ties with India had "weakened"—Rahman had acted "with impudence" and had gotten "involved in dirty work" by urging the DRV to stop supporting the Southern insurgency.[77]

Though "very pessimistic" after this first visit, the Pole felt that his Vietnamese comrades had received him warmly and that he had established a good rapport with Dong. After their official meeting, the premier had invited him to a dinner at his residence, at which he was "much more open." Though interrupted by air-raid sirens, they covered topics that included Lewandowski's impressions of New York and the United States, his grandfather buried in Baltimore, Polish-Americans, the Warsaw Uprising, and U.S.-Vietnamese relations—Dong insisted that "no real antagonism" existed between the two peoples. Underlining the view that the North's backing for the Communists in the South was a civil war, not international aggression (as Washington maintained), he noted that South Vietnam's foreign minister, Tran Van Do, was a former colleague at Hanoi University. "We are not invaders," he stressed. "We are from the same land."[78]

Before leaving Hanoi, Lewandowski also met some of the capital's cloistered diplomatic corps. Naturally, his most important contacts would be Siedlecki and Moscow's ambassador, Ilya Shcherbakov, a veteran party functionary (ex-head of the CPSU's International Department section handling ties with other Communist parties) previously posted in Beijing.[79] On this occasion, Moscow's envoy was unavailable, so Lewandowski instead saw his deputy, P. I. Privalov, the chargé d'affaires. Warily, the Pole termed his initial talks with the Vietnamese comrades, both at formal meetings and receptions, "exceptionally warm but not always sincere." The DRV leaders—Dong, Trinh, Giap (twice), and Lau—had uniformly forecast victory by armed struggle over the Americans and their "Saigon puppets" (by inflicting not a "'big Dien Bien Phu'" but "many 'little Dien Bien Phus'"), and the Poles could not detect even the smallest discrepancy in their optimistic assessments. Lewandowski recounted that, in accord with the prevailing Soviet party line, he had urged his hosts to merge the military struggle with political and diplomatic approaches, but they had steadfastly insisted that the time for negotiations had not yet come. In a further sign of militancy, their arguments that Washington likely could not raise its troop levels to 400,000 without transferring forces from Europe had seemed to echo Chinese propaganda claims of U.S.-Soviet collusion "behind the backs of the Vietnamese people." Conversely, Lewandowski noted that the DRV leaders vowed not to do anything to expand the conflict beyond a "local war," and doubted the Americans would, either. Grasping at straws, he found in their statements about the NLF's potential role in eventual negotiations, and the ICC's possible usefulness in monitoring a neutrality deal, some basis for "bargaining" or at least a "pretext for discussion or exchange of opinions about ways of resolving the Vietnamese problem."[80]

Lewandowski's exchanges with the Kremlin diplomats were businesslike and cordial. But frictions would develop in his more intensive relationship with Warsaw's *other* ambassador in Vietnam, Siedlecki, who was almost a quarter century older than Lewandowski and had reached his Vietnamese diplomatic posting through a dramatically different route. He was born in 1907 in Piatyhozy, a Ukrainian town south of Kiev in the Russian Empire, and he grew up in a family whose social background was listed in internal PZPR résumés as "working intelligentsia" or "petit-bourgeoisie," though rumors of aristocratic blood earned him the nickname "the Red Count." Amid the chaos of the Great War, Bolshevik Revolution, and Civil War, the Siedleckis moved west to Lwów, which in 1918 came under Polish control. In his teens, Jerzy worked in a metal goods factory before studying chemistry at Lwów Polytechnic. In the interwar years, he was an "exceptionally devoted" activist in the Communist Party of Western Ukraine (Komunistycznej Partii Zachodniej Ukrainy, KPZU); for his underground work, he was jailed in 1932 by Piłsudski's military government, which closely watched the Polish Communist Party (Komunistyczna Partia Polski) under whose wing the KPZU operated. Though he was the secretary of a propaganda unit and an editorial board member of the KPZU's Central Committee, he was not a key party figure. In the late 1930s, he kicked through assorted odd jobs (forestry, construction, sales), and was at times unemployed. After Moscow seized Western Ukraine in September 1939 (under the Nazi-Soviet Pact's secret terms), he returned to L'vov Polytechnic as a "student and stipend recipient."[81]

But in June 1941, Germany invaded the USSR, and the Wehrmacht steamrolled through Lvov on its Drang nach Osten. Given his record, if captured, Siedlecki would have quickly ended up in a concentration camp or, more likely, a mass grave. So he decisively cast his lot with Stalin, joining other Polish Communist émigrés who put themselves under Moscow's protection and control. During the next few years, he helped organize combat units—the Union of Polish Patriots and the First Division of Tadeusz Kościuszko of the Polish People's Army (Ludowe Wojsko Polskie)—and attained the rank of private, second lieutenant. In comparison with the Red Army, such detachments contributed little to the struggle against the German war machine. Their significance was political, gathering "liberators" (the Lublin Poles) on whom the Kremlin could rely to run a pliant postwar regime to replace the wary London Poles who had fled into exile when the war started.

Once the Germans retreated from the ruins of Warsaw, the now battle-hardened Siedlecki, owing his existence to Stalin, launched a new career—as a cog in the postliberation Polish state's internal security machine, the Ministry of Public Security (Ministerstwo Bezpieczeństwa Publicznego, or MBP). The *bezpieki* targeted domestic enemies, primarily nationalist (and therefore anti-Soviet and anti-Russian) activists—above all the remnants of the Home Army and its alleged "imperialist" infiltrators as the Cold War heated up—but also ordinary citizens who did not show requisite loyalty toward the new order. As in other postwar Central and Eastern European "people's democracies," Poland's internal security apparatus extended throughout society, and it was 200,000 strong at its peak, stamping out dissent and sowing fear and terror; between 1944 and 1956, more than 20,000 Poles are estimated to have died in jails, detention, or labor camps, and in 1952 there were roughly 50,000 political prisoners in the country.[82] Siedlecki rose to head the swelling MBP's "functionaries" bureau, in charge of thousands of police officers.

Then Siedlecki's career took an unexpected swerve. Following the November 1953 defection in Berlin of Lieutenant-Colonel Jósef Światło, and his subsequent revelations of secret police abuses broadcast by Radio Free Europe, the MBP came under tougher scrutiny, and in 1954 it was subjected to a major reorganization and constriction. Perhaps not coincidentally, Siedlecki—a potential target of purges and inquiries—opted for new scenery. After the July 1953 armistice ending the Korean War, Poland had joined Czechoslovakia as Eastern Bloc surrogates (opposite Sweden and Switzerland) on a Neutral Nations Supervisory Commission (NNSC) set up to oversee the termination of hostilities, regulate relations between the Korean Peninsula's divided halves, and, in theory, pave the way toward elections and unification. In October 1954, Siedlecki went to Pyongyang in the dual roles of Poland's chief delegate to the NNSC and ambassador to North Korea.

Before leaving, Siedlecki had trained Korea-bound Polish personnel in espionage and counterespionage tactics in a secret "military unit 2000."[83] Once there, he displayed his trademark Stalinist tendencies, both in the NNSC (which deadlocked immediately and permanently) and in reports on Kim Il-sung's hermit kingdom, regurgitating official statistics and pronouncements and hailing its steadfastness against imperialist aggression. Being fluent in Russian, and eager to mimic Kremlin policy, he assiduously cultivated Moscow's envoy.[84]

From far-off Pyongyang, Siedlecki caught barely a whiff of the liberalizing winds, anti-Russian nationalism, and explosion of pent-up anger at the internal security service that blew through Poland in 1956.[85] Yet, despite his isolation, he felt some reverberations. Foreign Ministry higher-ups, nonplussed by his turgid, doctrinaire, and bland cables, pressed him to supply "not only official statements from the press, but also personal observations, information obtained in conversations with Koreans or with representatives of other embassies, and at the same time to identify the source of information, something which is often lacking in your reports, analysis and the assessment of presented facts"—oh, and while he was at it, to brush up on his grammar, style, and punctuation.[86] With the notion of a "personality cult" in vogue, Siedlecki grudgingly agreed with his Soviet colleague that one existed around Kim, but tended to sugarcoat Pyongyang's conduct, excusing its economic hardships (including those relative to South Korea) as a consequence of the war and continued capitalist threat.[87]

In late 1959, Siedlecki returned to Warsaw, to head MSZ Department (I), dealing mostly with Soviet affairs. But a few years later, Rapacki called on him to rush to another Asian hotspot—to replace Poland's ailing envoy in Hanoi. Siedlecki had been posted there since June 1963, stoutly supporting the North Vietnamese and also, as Lewandowski would discover, retaining his filial affection toward the USSR.

From the start, Siedlecki and Lewandowski did not hit it off. At first, their mutual aversion remained unspoken. The new commissioner saw himself as a proud Polish patriot, making adjustments dictated by geopolitical reality, but viewed Siedlecki as wholly devoted to Moscow: "He identified himself completely with the Russians and that probably his loyalty, his whole mind was believing that this is such a leading force, we are just the helpers."[88]

Lewandowski also schmoozed with other Hanoi-based diplomats, and he observed the social reverberations of the Sino-Soviet split at a welcoming reception in his honor thrown by Lau. Throughout the evening, a Canadian noted, the Chinese guests, "standing alone and wearing faded blue denims," stayed "aloof and uncommunicative." The PAVN hosts briefly shook their hands, but the Soviets, East Germans, Romanians, Egyptians, Cubans, and Poles present ignored them; Lewandowski "made no effort to speak with them" after they were pointed out.[89]

Summarizing this first trip to Hanoi, Lewandowski accentuated the positive. The comrades' anticipation of negotiations as the "final stage" of inevitable victory, he cabled, was "a new element which attests to the increasing realism in the North." Even if the DRV disdained the ICC, it viewed Poland's actions "very positively." Interestingly, the Pole noted that despite their bravado, the North Vietnamese "felt more painfully" the U.S. bombing, and had asked him to do his best in the ICC to limit or stop it.[90]

Firsthand observations of the impact of those raids informed Lewandowski's assessments, then and later, that they imposed enormous suffering. From Hanoi, he made inspection tours to recent targets—usually cities south of the capital such as Nam Dinh and Vinh. He vividly remembered nocturnal expeditions with Lau through lush jungles and cratered countryside on bumpy roads, headlights off, refueling from gasoline drums scattered in the grass rather than in vulnerable storage depots, crossing rivers and ditches over makeshift bridges (replacing destroyed ones), passing swarms of workers repairing bomb damage. Frequently, in Hanoi or on the road, he heard U.S. planes overhead or warnings that attack was imminent. But even as sirens sounded and bombs and antiaircraft fire thundered, Lewandowski exasperated the guards by rigidly refusing to go to underground shelters—a residue of his childhood trauma. Having almost perished once from suffocation beneath a blown-up building, and sensing his air running out, he preferred to stay "on the surface." "I have seen so many people dead and dying and witnessed the deaths of people. . . . But you know, I never believed it may happen to me, even flying this ICC plane, shooting, when the flak started, and I saw these horrible things coming up, but I never believed it can happen to us. . . . And if it happens, what is the reason to be afraid? . . . I developed in my life something that is close to the Islamic belief in fatalism, whatever is your fate will happen to you, it is in the hands of Allah to decide."

One night, soon after Lewandowski and his colleagues landed at Gia Lam, antiaircraft fire erupted and escorts steered the ICC guests down a stairwell to a dark shelter crawling with insects. "You know, I never again accepted to [go] into a kind of hole," he remembered. "I was afraid of this hole. . . . I was just sitting in the building, to the desperation of my Vietnamese guards." Once on his way to town from the airport, he was stuck in traffic on the Doumer Bridge over the Red

River when he heard aircraft and responding triple-A. "It was terrible, because we are in the middle of the bridge, . . . so if anything happened, you couldn't disperse"—the span was a prime target, but that time, the planes flew past. When an attack started during an ICC meeting at a Hanoi hotel, a "small Vietnamese girl" urgently requested he go underground. He refused. She insisted—then finally gave up, took a rife, put on a helmet, and grabbed a box of ammo. "I said, 'What are you doing?' She said, 'I am going on the roof and I will shoot at the planes'—and she did it! 'Boom, boom, boom!'" Eventually, Lewandowski's hosts built him an aboveground bomb shelter, small but "well-equipped, with a chair," at his villa in the old French quarter (the other ICC delegates stayed in a hotel).

Frequently leaving Hanoi to inspect bomb damage (far more often than the Canadians or Indians), the Pole occasionally got himself and others into trouble: In Nam Dinh, during a daylight attack, he spent twelve hours huddling with Lau in a ruined pagoda, and on a trip to Haiphong (described below), he had another scary run-in with U.S. planes. His readiness to accept risks put him in a privileged position in Saigon—he was able to testify personally to the civilian toll caused by the bombing as he lobbied for a halt.

Lewandowski in Saigon: Trading with the Enemy

Back in the South Vietnamese capital, after an inevitable case of indisposition, in late April Lewandowski called on Foreign Minister Tran Van Do, an experienced and respected figure, a relative moderate, and a civilized civilian in Ky's military junta. Their talk was far more stilted than Lewandowski's comradely exchanges with Dong. In a lengthy monologue, Do firmly and predictably blamed the fighting on North Vietnam, which was waging aggression against the South that required a (temporary) U.S. military presence. As for the NLF, it represented only Hanoi—units infiltrated from the North and a few coerced peasants. Saigon had "acknowledged" the ICC and the 1954 Geneva Accords, Do noted, though it did not sign them, and it accepted unification in principle, though this could not happen for at least fifteen to thirty years. His arguments, of course, wholly contradicted established Communist views. "The position of the current government totally lacks realism," Lewandowski reported. "It practically excludes any type of compromise."[91]

A Dutch diplomat who saw the Pole right after he saw Do found him deeply pessimistic. To the North Vietnamese, he had "defended the idea of direct contact between Hanoi and Saigon, and initially could not understand why this idea had been rejected out of hand." But listening to Do, he said—"strictly between you and me"—helped him understand the DRV rebuff. Compared with Saigon, he felt, Washington took a relatively flexible approach to negotiations.[92]

Nevertheless, what made the Do-Lewandowski meeting noteworthy is not that it produced an impasse but that it happened at all—a unique point of contact between the Communist world and a government it shunned. And this initial talk *did* lead somewhere. A week later, the Saigon leadership revealed a belief that this new Communist in town might serve a useful purpose—as a potential communications link to Hanoi. On May 6, Lewandowski had a remarkable secret encounter with Nguyen Van Thieu, chief of state and chair of the Saigon regime's military directorate.[93] The meeting came about almost comically. Periodically contacting Do in his office was a routine function of the Pole's ICC duties—Saigon's Foreign Ministry formally hosted the ICC—but on this occasion, in early May, Do suddenly said, "We shall go to another place," and invited him along without revealing where they were going. Soon, Lewandowski found himself in the back seat of a limousine being driven to—and through—the gates of the presidential palace. Stunned, he was led by a protocol officer down a hallway to the black-haired, smooth-faced Thieu, his hand extended, a friendly expression on his face.

"Well, I wanted to know you, Mr. Ambassador, I heard about you very good things, I am pleased to see you."

His mind racing, lacking authorization or instruction for a meeting with the head of, after all, an enemy state, Lewandowski felt like blurting out "Mr. President, there's been a mistake, I came to see the foreign minister!" "I was surprised and I really didn't know what to say," he recalled, laughing. "After all, you know, my God! There could be a havoc [scandal] possibly about it!?"

Instead, Lewandowski shook hands, smiled, and listened as Thieu softly and politely professed respect for Poland and Geneva, and said he had heard that Warsaw's new ICC delegate was already popular and wished the Vietnamese people well, innocuous statements that his startled guest did not bother to dispute. "We are having such a bad time but I think after all we will be able to become peaceful," Thieu remarked.

After pleasantries, Thieu shooed away an aide, so they were left "without any witnesses," as Lewandowski cabled. Saying that he "wished to speak in complete honesty" and asking the Pole to consider their talk confidential, he presented a strikingly moderate stance, without the usual angry accusations toward Hanoi. "The Vietnamese in the North and South are one people, brothers, who do not want to fight and destroy each other," the RVN leader began, as Lewandowski later told a Soviet diplomat.[94] Much later, he recalled that Thieu "said not a single word about these bad North Vietnamese, 'they are infiltrating,' etcetera, absolutely [not]." He not only stressed Saigon's desire for peace but also credited Hanoi's sincerity, speculating that it was hamstrung by Chinese pressure. Fear of Beijing, he noted, drove the countries in the region, which were too weak to protect themselves, to ally with Washington.

By underlining sinister Chinese aims, Thieu may have hoped to appeal to a Soviet ally at a time when Moscow was condemning Mao's excesses and ambitions. He may also have wanted to perk up Polish ears by, after lamenting the ICC's present moribund status and promising to support an expansion of its activities, "personally" forecasting an "important role" for the commission in any eventual solution to the conflict—a role that would obviously elevate Warsaw's prestige as well. (However, Thieu ripped a British proposal to have the ICC monitor the forthcoming Constituent Assembly elections, which he scorned as a blatant attempt by London to meddle in Saigon's internal affairs.[95])

At the key moment of the conversation, Thieu raised "a question from my end regarding the possibility of direct Hanoi-Saigon talks," offering Lewandowski a chance to convey any messages or impressions he might carry from his recent trip to the North, or ideas on how to promote contacts.

"You were in Hanoi, Sir," he prodded, "they are apparently not in a hurry as far as the talks with us [are concerned]."

Lewandowski declined to take the bait—"I did not comment," he reported home.

Nevertheless, Thieu pleasantly concluded, he hoped to see Lewandowski again. Afterward, walking through the palace's verdant grounds, Do reinforced the impression of reasonableness, recalling his acquaintance with Pham Van Dong during the 1954 Geneva Conference. Mulling over the episode, the Pole realized that Do had "tricked me, practically, to this meeting," fearing he might have declined a formal invitation.

In the context of the ongoing Buddhist crisis, he wondered whether Thieu had seen him to explore a possible overture to Hanoi as an alternative to continued reliance on Washington—much as, in September 1963, Nhu had met Maneli amid rumors of U.S. sympathy for coup plotting against Diem. "I think that the invitation for the talk and its course point to uncertainty which is taking place within the current group as to its future and fears that they will be sacrificed by the Americans," Lewandowski speculated.

The Pole's wary response to Thieu's broaching of a Saigon-Hanoi back channel may have been influenced by his awareness of the so-called Maneli Affair, whose records he had reviewed before leaving Warsaw. Despite speculation that the Polish ICC delegate mediated secretly between Saigon and Hanoi in autumn 1963, the MSZ had actually *not* authorized him to conduct any initiative, and had privately admonished him for seeing Nhu without prior approval; the affair had not enhanced his career prospects.[96]

This time, the press never discovered the encounter, yet Lewandowski reported that his talk with Thieu "stirred interest within the diplomatic corps." At a Foreign Ministry dinner that evening, a U.S. Embassy counselor "incessantly" pestered him for details. The next day, to the Italian ambassador, Lewandowski confessed surprise that Saigon's rulers—not only Thieu and Do but also Ky—had received him "with great courtesy and with great warmth" and observed that his "official visits have therefore become interesting conversations on the country's situation."[97]

Lewandowski had deflected Thieu's efforts to discuss a Saigon-Hanoi dialogue. Nevertheless, he relayed a full report on the conversation to the DRV—as he presumed Thieu had wanted—thereby becoming a de facto, if not formal, covert channel between the combatants. Less than a month after landing at Tan

Son Nhut, the Pole had already received his first bona fide peace feeler, seen his initial impressions jumbled and confounded, and become entangled in sensitive intrigues.

Making the Rounds: Getting to Know D'Orlandi

With his introductions to North and South Vietnamese leaders and his ICC colleagues complete—and the commission hopelessly stalemated[98]—Lewandowski began making the rounds of the local diplomatic corps, seeking intelligence on the political and military situation and to promote his (and Warsaw's) views. His first encounter proved portentous. Following the custom of calling on colleagues in order of seniority, on May 7 he visited Italy's ambassador, Giovanni D'Orlandi, who had been in his job since July 1962.[99]

A visitor described D'Orlandi as "short, thin, debonair dresser, dark-haired, well-groomed, wears highly polished black loafers and woolen anklets, speaks a colloquial English."[100] Soft-spoken, he walked gingerly, slightly stooped, looking older than his forty-nine years. A surviving photo of him sitting beside Lewandowski at a formal dinner indeed shows a dapper, white-jacketed man, with his black hair carefully combed, a thoughtful expression on a face with chiseled, even gaunt features—a reflection of the debilitating intestinal disease he likely contracted during years as a British prisoner in India during World War II. (The worsening condition still afflicted him in Saigon; after a recent flare-up, in January, he had needed to be hospitalized and medevaced to Rome.)[101]

D'Orlandi's heritage and family history nurtured a cosmopolitan outlook. He was born in 1917 in Alexandria to parents who embodied the eastern Mediterranean port's mélange of regional influences; his father was a well-known Italian pediatrician, and his mother was from the Greek island of Santorini. At the time, Egypt was a bastion of the British Empire, and Alexandria was a key transit hub near the Suez Canal. As a youth, D'Orlandi developed precocious linguistic skills, responding in whatever tongue he was addressed (Italian, Greek, Arabic, French, English, etc.), and easily associated with persons from diverse backgrounds—ideal training for a future diplomat.[102]

World War II detoured D'Orlandi's career shortly after he earned a degree in jurisprudence from the University of Rome La Sapienza in July 1939. In June 1940, he was en route from Alexandria to Rome to enter the Foreign Service when Italy attacked France. British ships seized his now-belligerent vessel, leading to his detention in India for the rest of the conflict—giving him an unplanned chance to perfect his English.[103]

After the war, in Western European posts dealing with continental and Cold War issues, D'Orlandi built a reputation as a calm, consummate professional and incisive analyst. A fellow envoy from the Farnesina (as the Italian Foreign Ministry is known, from its palace in Rome) dubbed him "very sedate, soft talking but hard inside. He was always known as a clever, intelligent guy, but he really came into his own in Saigon and people realized he was outstanding."[104] He exuded,

Lewandowski thought, sophistication hinting at generations of Machiavellian politics stretching back to the Renaissance. The Pole remembered a face evoking the Medicis, "a medieval Italian diplomat . . . rooted very deeply in the past."[105] "He always conveyed the impression that he was very involved in very important things," recalled a U.S. official who occasionally ran into him, conversing in French.[106]

The fresh arrival from Warsaw and the dean of Saigon's diplomatic corps hit it off, finding each other simpatico both personally and politically. "He was very open, and the conversation was very interesting," the Italian recorded after they first met.[107] "D'Orlandi and I spoke the same language," recalled Lewandowski, both literally (the Pole had learned Latin) and figuratively, trading ideas and experiences for hours, often over lengthy games of chess. They shared a deep fondness for Alexandria, which the Pole had discovered while posted to Cairo, making weekend excursions to stroll along the winding corniche and savor the vibrant café life and "joyful, international atmosphere" that was "more Greek than Arab" (he was saddened when Nasser uprooted the ancient Hellenic community that had thrived during D'Orlandi's childhood).[108] The two also had a bond of recent marital disappointment; D'Orlandi's first marriage, like Lewandowski's, had ended without children, and he was a bachelor in Saigon (he later married an embassy secretary, Colette, a young Vietnamese he had imported from Paris).[109] Lewandowski rapidly grew to admire his elder colleague as a man of real substance and experience from whom he could learn much, and D'Orlandi found the young Pole extremely able, intelligent, and convivial. Shedding formality, they became "Janusz" and "Giovanni" ("Nino" to Farnesina friends), and grew close despite their age gap. "He and Lodge are what made [my] assignment in Saigon so interesting and so much fun," the Italian later recalled.[110]

They also, of course, swapped political intelligence. Lewandowski described his surprise, shared by D'Orlandi, at the warm welcome the Saigon authorities had given him, and also related his impression that Hanoi, though strongly against plans for a South Vietnamese ballot in state-controlled territory, might accept a cease-fire if elections were staged countrywide and might even allow the ICC to monitor them—an idea the Italian found unlikely.[111] They agreed that Washington had underestimated the intensity of Vietnamese nationalism and needed to find a political formula to escape the quagmire.[112]

When D'Orlandi first assumed his post, he fully backed the United States' determination to preserve a noncommunist South Vietnam, if necessary by force.[113] Before going to Saigon, he had headed the Farnesina's Southeast Asian branch, but before that, from 1950 to 1957, he had been Italy's Paris-based representative to the Coordinating Committee for Multilateral Export Controls, also known as COCOM, the NATO watchdog panel guarding against the transfer of militarily sensitive materials or technologies to the Communist Bloc. Like U.S. officials, he at first not only firmly believed in "preserving South Vietnam for the free world" but also lacked "any tolerance for neutralism, which he consider[ed] to be dangerous."[114]

At the same time, this urbane diplomat, known for a suave sense of humor and refined tastes, acquired a reputation for courage in standing up to the Saigon regime. In August 1963, during Diem's raids on Buddhist pagodas, he responded sharply when it tried to censor diplomatic communications, barring the sending of coded cables by commercial carriers. Immediately (and without instructions from Rome), he threatened to move his embassy to Cambodia (to which, along with Laos, he was accredited) unless the government withdrew the order and apologized in writing within thirty-six hours—and it caved, earning D'Orlandi the diplomatic corps' respect and gratitude.[115]

Amid the intrigues leading up to Diem's overthrow, D'Orlandi sought a solution that would stabilize and bolster the regime to fight the Communists. Working with Vatican envoy Monsignor Salvatore Asta, he fashioned a plan for the Catholic ruler to jettison his controversial brother, Nhu (and his fiery wife, who had famously termed the Buddhist monks' immolations "barbeques"), and to broaden his government's makeup. After a coup plot fizzled in late August, JFK's new ambassador, Lodge, also swung behind the D'Orlandi-Asta scheme. However, in part due to opposition from Nhu and France's ambassador (in line with French president Charles de Gaulle's neutralist policy), Diem retreated from this "Diem without Nhu" concept, and momentum for a military coup again began to build.[116]

When U.S.-backed generals ousted Diem in November, D'Orlandi's behavior added to his stature. Some ministers, fearing for their safety, showed up at Italy's embassy pleading for sanctuary. Legally, he could not offer asylum, D'Orlandi replied, but nothing forbade him from inviting them to stay for lunch. And stay they did, for meal after meal (confiding valuable intelligence all the while), until the situation cooled. Ever after that, the losers in Saigon's coups ("government ministers, generals, police chiefs, etc.") often ended up dining at D'Orlandi's—some making advance reservations, just in case.[117]

Despite his (and Rome's) sympathy with U.S. aims in Vietnam, D'Orlandi watched the escalation of direct American military involvement with mounting unease. By 1966, he had grown skeptical of Washington's strategy; he was appalled at the human anguish caused by the war, and—in line with already-demonstrated Italian activism—was eager to promote a solution. His declining health intensified his desire to achieve progress before he had to leave. "There must be something which can be done," he would say, recalled Lewandowski, struck by the Italian's sensitivity to the suffering of Vietnamese children.[118] D'Orlandi felt growing disgust at the huge U.S. economic aid program's abject failure—due to corruption, inefficiency, and poor planning—to help ordinary South Vietnamese:

> If the American aid so far allocated had been distributed per capita, every Vietnamese family today would have a house, a fridge, a television and a garden. I'd like to know in what civilian sector a solid infrastructure has been created, or what economic problem has been solved. In this country, alongside shameless

profiteering, and shady dealing, everything proceeds without any preconceived plan. When the flood caused the exodus of hundreds of thousands of people, among them 200,000 Catholics, nothing was given them except a handful of rice and some blankets. The man in the street does not see any concrete help from the U.S. and is convinced that a large part of the money spent has returned to America, Switzerland or Hong Kong. How is it possible in the current politico-economic-military chaos to refute the arguments of those Vietnamese (and they are increasingly more numerous) who sustain that amid so much Vietnamese and foreign corruption the only honest ones are the Viet Cong? Much could have been done, and perhaps one could still try to do something to avoid this state of things, and very little has been done. . . . I must state with frankness to American friends everything that I've learned and everything that has worried me. When a thorough inquiry has to be opened, in the Senate and Congress, into the errors and faults that caused the Vietnamese situation to plummet, I wouldn't like to be in the shoes of the various administrators of American economic aid in Washington or in Vietnam.[119]

D'Orlandi's faith in the efficacy of Washington's military tactics also waned. "Who knows why the Americans persist so obstinately in continuing the bombing," he wrote in May 1966, "when the infiltrations of the North Vietnamese instead of diminishing have quadrupled? I learned from a trustworthy source that in the last month alone they haven't been less than 22,000 men."[120] An aide's account of D'Orlandi's gradual defection from full-fledged belief in the war helps explain his secret peace diplomacy activism and fondness for his young, in many respects like-minded, Polish colleague:

Progressively, however, his reports—which were always incisive, lucid, and of great intellectual honesty—began to call attention to other aspects of the complex Vietnamese situation, which did not coincide with the official version of the conflict circulating in Western chancelleries. Some of the aspects were, for example: the aura which the Communist guerrillas enjoyed with the Vietnamese nationalists by virtue of the fact that they personified the resistance against the foreigner and the admiration which they enjoyed with the people in the countryside because of their discipline and integrity (and, conversely, the reputation as oppressor which surrounded the Government Army due to the thievery, abuses, and indiscriminate violence with which it stained itself). Also: the dodging of military service by the sons of the Saigon bourgeoisie and the fact that the war was fought only by the poor; the consequences were low morale and a high level of desertion among Government forces. In addition: the fact that the guerrillas in the [NLF], in spite of a certain amount of resupplying of senior cadres and some materiel from the North, procured the basics for their weaponry by capturing it from Government forces; and as a consequence the inefficiency and uselessness of the bombings of the Ho Chi Minh Trail as well as the incredible corruption introduced into traditional Vietnamese society by the massive infusion of assistance and American personnel, and the ignorance or dishonesty of the latter.

In the various stages of the escalation subsequently carried out by the Americans in 1964 and 1965, . . . D'Orlandi saw not only, and not so much, a response to specific actions or Vietcong or North Vietnamese provocations (which was the Johnson Administration's hypothesis), as much as the intent to provide an indispensable support to the shaky Saigon regime (the Johnson critics' hypothesis).

Because of the combination of these elements, his view of the Vietnamese conflict could not but change appreciably. For D'Orlandi, little by little, the conviction took hold that it was somehow necessary to make the end of the war the first priority and the reestablishment of peace the primary aspiration and interest of the Vietnamese people. Not any peace, of course, but a peace based on an equilibrium which was to be reached among the Vietnamese, at the end of a process involving a minimum of self-determination and re-establishment of national normality, appeared to him at a certain point preferable to the continuation of a spiral of warfare which at times appeared to be almost an end in itself, armed with its own unstoppable dynamic.

Peace, therefore, was the concept which, years later, he would summarize his mission to Saigon.[121]

In avidly promoting peace prospects, however slim, D'Orlandi could now rely on strong backing from home: In late February 1966, less than two months after resigning, Fanfani had vaulted back into office as foreign minister, still hankering to star on the international stage, his ambitions suiting D'Orlandi's own inclination toward diplomatic activism.

Despite their mutual esteem, Lewandowski occasionally felt that D'Orlandi's fervent desire to see the war end might be clouding his judgment. In late May, after Lodge returned from a trip to Washington to consult on the Buddhist crisis, the Italian had "high hopes" that LBJ had given him "a binding instruction" to push for South Vietnamese elections by September that might speed a U.S. abandonment of Ky and "withdrawal from the Vietnamese quarrel," Lewandowski cabled. (Under Buddhist and U.S. pressure for political reforms toward restoring civilian rule, Ky had agreed to a Constituent Assembly vote as a prelude to a presidential contest a year later.) But the Pole disagreed, expecting that Ky would not back down. "I think that the opinion of the Italian is overly simplified and too optimistic," he concluded.[122]

Gradually, Lewandowski settled into his role as a unique, even exotic specimen on the Saigon diplomatic scene—a Communist ambassador, able to drop names from the Hanoi leadership and offer firsthand testimony from the other side of the "bamboo curtain" dividing Vietnam, fluent in English (and "weak" French), and socializing with a diverse mix. "They looked at me like I was from the moon," he remembered. Dissatisfied with his military advisers' reports on the battlefield situation, he also felt compelled to become his own intelligence officer. In his first month in Saigon, he reported talks with, besides his Indian and Canadian colleagues, the Italian, Australian, and Belgian ambassadors; the French consul; the Belgian, Dutch, and Malaysian chargés d'affaires; a U.S. Embassy first secretary; Agence France-Presse reporters; Buddhist movement figures; and the *Saigon Post*'s editor.[123] His most valued journalistic contact was the legendary *Newsweek* photojournalist François Sully, an ex–French Resistance fighter who came to Indochina as a soldier and stayed to record the war's finale and aftermath, and later earned the distinction of being expelled by Diem (though returning after his overthrow); every so often, the Pole dined with this "perfectly oriented" correspondent, who "had great feeling for the Vietnamese."[124]

Lewandowski excelled at forging relationships with diplomats from across the Iron Curtain. Meeting London's envoy, he discovered that the Briton had belonged to the doomed U.K. military mission in Poland in 1939. They swapped war stories, with Gordon Etherington-Smith apologizing for Britain's inability to help the Polish resistance. (The BBC had played inspirational music, Lewandowski later recalled, but that was about the extent of its aid.) The Briton gave the Pole the impression that, despite his government's "special relationship" with Washington, he was not very optimistic about the U.S. war in Vietnam, or thrilled by his office's proximity to the U.S. Embassy ("this bunker"), already a target of attacks.[125]

He became fairly friendly with the Dutch chargé d'affaires, Jacobus Jerome "Koos" Derksen. As with D'Orlandi, Lewandowski shared impressions from Hanoi visits and discussed current developments—and found a sort of kindred spirit. Lodge considered Derksen "intelligent, discreet, and dependable," yet he was increasingly skeptical of the U.S. war. Eager to gather gossip on secret peace probes, he was not averse to rueful commiseration with the Pole over the errors of their respective superpower patrons.[126]

At their first encounter, on April 27, 1966, they traded worries that the war would escalate further. Lewandowski sounded "somewhat optimistic" that "the last phase of the conflict would not be a military or a political phase," because Hanoi no longer seemed to count on a new Dien Bien Phu before negotiations, but he feared that the Americans did not grasp that "their 'very destructive bombings' in the North—bombings that would have brought Poland to its knees—are only hardening the North's resolve." Rather than cave, Hanoi would seek more Soviet and Chinese support, including troops if necessary; what would Washington do then? Pessimistically, Derksen guessed that LBJ had endorsed military demands to stick behind the Ky regime and apply more pressure to force Hanoi's collapse, overruling Lodge, who allegedly wanted to change the Saigon government and negotiate with the North. Having lost this policy battle, Lodge returned to Washington—not to consult (as announced) but to resign, Derksen speculated.[127] Later, the extent of Lewandowski's candor with Derksen would become a matter of angry dispute in the secret Marigold diplomacy.

And, of course, there were the Americans. In late May, Lewandowski ran into a U.S. Embassy official and held a "private and apparently deliberate conversation." The Pole professed to be "disturbed" by the apparent divergence on talks between Saigon hard-liners and Washington. "This did not augur well for the future," he said. "What kind of a peace conference could there be if USG [the U.S. government] wanted to negotiate and GVN [the South Vietnamese government] did not? There could be no agreement even between American and South Vietnamese delegation[s], much less with other members of conference." The U.S. aide insisted that the difference was not serious, and that if Hanoi entered into talks "in good faith," the two allies would cooperate.

After that unorthodox expression of concern about friction in the anticommunist camp, Lewandowski reverted to "standard" arguments that if Washington really wanted peace, it would stop bombing the North, escalating forces, building vast military facilities and logistical infrastructure, and so on. The embassy officer responded that such steps were necessary to frustrate aggression from the North, prompting the Pole to counter that this "dangerous course" might provoke deeper Chinese or even Soviet intervention.

Lodge had not yet met him, but cabled Washington that the conversation already fit a pattern: "Lewandowski spoke in sober thoughtful tones and expressed desire [to] discuss such matters at greater length another day. This interest in talking about negotiations has been consistent during Lewandowski's calls on GVN officials and diplomatic corps."[128]

Affable yet sober, articulate in plain English, not Communist cant, and well informed, the newcomer made an attractive ornament to a reception or dinner party and a valuable source for readers of Hanoi tea leaves. "There were a lot of parties given, and I was always invited," he chuckled, "because I was a little like a small star, the only one from the Communist camp. . . . I attended gladly."[129]

Lewandowski also sent Warsaw (which forwarded them to Hanoi and Moscow) regular, terse reports on the Buddhist uprising, which he blamed in large measure on the regime's refusal (backed by its U.S. ally) to deal with the NLF. By mid-May, he perceived a consensus that the internal crisis was the most serious since the Diem coup, a feeling that Washington had misplayed its hand by backing Ky over Buddhist compromise candidates, rising anti-Americanism, and a threat of internecine military combat. "The situation is tense," he concluded in a May 13 cable.[130]

Two days later, Ky moved firmly to crush the Struggle Movement, sending Marine and tank regiments to seize rebel strongholds in Danang and besiege pagodas. Washington reacted with alarm, but soon swung behind the bid to break the revolt's back. By late May, Ky was well on his way to quelling the crisis by using limited force and arresting, co-opting, or exiling movement leaders, partly with U.S. mediation. "I do not think that the action of the Buddhists, at its present intensification, would lead to toppling Ky or would force the U.S. to make concessions," Lewandowski reported. "This would require some disturbances within the military or spreading the demonstrations to other cities and their intensification."[131] Rifts between moderate and radical wings, which U.S. officials tried to exacerbate, helped doom the movement, he judged.[132]

Return to Hanoi: A Conversation with Pham Van Dong

On May 31, the ICC delegates boarded a Stratoliner at Tan Son Nhut and flew west, north, and then east to hold a rare session in Hanoi—the first there in eight months, after DRV officials hinted at objections to the prevailing custom of meeting in Saigon.

More important, the trip offered Lewandowski another chance to confer with North Vietnam's leaders.[133] He and a military aide gave Lau a full-fledged briefing on the political and military situation in the south. From the liaison's response, he gathered that his hosts' earlier hopes that the Buddhists might topple Ky had eroded. In April, Lau had felt the upheaval might prompt the military regime's collapse, hastening negotiations with the NLF. But now, after hearing the Pole, he said Hanoi, "far from overestimating the meaning of the current internal crisis," judged that Saigon, with U.S. support, could "control the situation." The crisis just might, he noted, prod Washington to "attempt a political solution." In the meantime, he foresaw "decisive" military successes in the coming dry season, and, offering details of U.S. bombing raids that had all but leveled two cities and inflicted many civilian casualties, requested maximal international support.

Far more significant—the event that launched the entire "Marigold" business, at least its first phase—was Lewandowski's conversation on Thursday, June 2, with Pham Van Dong. Receiving him warmly for more than two hours, the premier advanced "new elements" containing tantalizing morsels of flexibility and conciliation for the Pole's secret mission—even while sticking resolutely to stands Washington rejected at that time and stopping short of a specific or concrete peace plan or probe for him to relay. "They want to end the war as soon as possible," Lewandowski noted, headlining Dong's views. "It can happen if the USA wants honestly to come to a realistic level of a political solution."

Though the head of state, a key Politburo member, and a veteran revolutionary, Dong was not the most powerful figure in the leadership—most analysts believe at this time that title belonged to party boss Le Duan, a militant southerner, with Ho largely relegated to the status of avuncular figurehead and revered father of the nation and revolution. Moreover, as Michałowski and others had found, Dong presented the Hanoi regime's most humane face, sensitive to the suffering caused by the war, ardent in his desire for peace, and cosmopolitan and sincere to foreign and fraternal guests.

Nevertheless, Lewandowski had to be titillated as Dong laid out a scenario containing features he could try to sell to Washington. After noting that diplomacy had stalled, with U.S. efforts to intimidate the DRV and NLF frustrated, Dong asked the Pole to keep the North informed of any signs of a shift. Requesting secrecy, he revealed that Ottawa had again asked permission for Ronning to visit—and that he would arrive in two weeks, perhaps bearing a proposal to open direct U.S.-DRV talks. Repeating his earlier line to the Canadian, Dong said that Hanoi would "talk only if the USA stops the bombing unconditionally," and the aim of such exchanges would be solely to stop U.S. aggression against North Vietnam; Washington must talk to the NLF regarding the South, which it stoutly refused to do (despite hidden wavering during the Buddhist crisis). However, Dong sweetened the bitter pill he wanted the Americans to swallow:

> Many mistaken views exist abroad and in the South as to the policy of the NLF. It is thought that the NLF are the Communists and that they aspire to introduce socialism. Many Vietnamese in the South are afraid of land reform, hard work, and they worry about their private property. The government of the DRV and the NLF realizes this. The NLF groups the representatives of all social classes. It will currently conduct the policy of open arms in order to increase its scope even more. He expressed thanks for the information from the conversation with Thieu. They analyzed it at the Political Bureau. They do not have any doubts as far as T[hieu]. The NLF is prepared to receive everyone, even persons held in suspicion, so long as they are willing to change. One has to talk with them. After the victory, the policy of the NLF will be different from that of the DRV. The point here, at this current stage, is not to build socialism. Foreign relations will be different. He emphasized—the internal and foreign policy in the South will be different from that of the DRV, it is necessary that this is known.

Besides accepting the need to deal with Thieu and perhaps even Ky ("everyone"), Dong commented on the Buddhist movement's enigmatic leader. He recalled Thich Tri Quang as a leftist who grew up in the North (once meeting Ho in Hanoi) and assessed him favorably as now heading an anti-imperialist struggle—but also a "bourgeois" "afraid of socialism" (despite "contacts with the [NLF]") and influenced by France. Dong thought that the Buddhists could exert useful pressure on the Americans, but (like Lau) he had no faith that they might cause Ky's rule to implode—epitomizing what Lewandowski termed his "great realism, especially toward the troubles of the regime in the South."

While in Hanoi, the Pole also engaged in other business. At the ICC session, after the usual balanced reporting of alleged violations to both Saigon and Hanoi (Rahman breaking any ties), he deflected Moore's efforts to decide some pending issues (e.g., the Soviet-supplied MiGs and SAMs); the Canadian blamed "the general shellacking consistently taken by us on the result of obvious collusion by the Indians with the Poles."[134] The night before, a "very concerned" Lau had warned of "grave consequences" if the ICC criticized the DRV while meeting in Hanoi. "We promised that we would not let this happen," Lewandowski cabled. "They thanked us after the meeting."[135]

Outside the formal session, he joined fellow commissioners in a slew of meals —lunch at the Canadian's, dinners at the Indian's, Pole's, and the PAVN liaison mission. "Apart from over-indulgence in a rather standardized menu," Moore reported, the ceremonial events fostered conversation in a "cordial atmosphere," which peaked at Lewandowski's fete when a Canadian soldier swapped watches with the Soviet ambassador and was "not dampened by a storm which put out the lights at the Indian dinner with thunder and lightning that induced the 'Saigon jumps' among the visitors, to the vast amusement of those guests native to tranquil Hanoi."[136]

Lewandowski also conversed with Moscow's man in Hanoi in a more private setting. A vital contact for any Soviet Bloc diplomat, the gregarious Shcherbakov also welcomed capitalists, including, on this occasion, Canada's commissioner. After a "lively" and "cordial" three-hour talk—"on the physical side the going was a little heavy, as the quantity of cognac and beer pressed on us was not equaled by the amount of caviar available—and that at nine in the morning"—Moore hailed the "new wave of Soviet diplomats—practical, pragmatic, apparently free of the usual complexes and sensitivities. With a bowler and umbrella he would be undistinguishable in the City in London."[137]

When Shcherbakov received the very correct Lewandowski on June 1, the liquor flowed less freely, but with a comrade he could speak more candidly. The Pole updated his senior Soviet colleague on the "confusing" situation in Saigon, noting the "disorder" caused by the Buddhist movement, which he said had hampered both South Vietnamese and U.S. military operations. He detected increasing NLF influence on the movement, and rising anti-Americanism, including "frequent sabotage attacks and individual violence against careless Americans." Newly arrived U.S. troops, to the Pole's eyes, seemed "scared," "nervous," and trigger-happy amid the nearly "constant" machine-gun firing, and French nationals now seemed more comfortable moving about than Americans, freely visiting their plantations in "liberated areas" while paying taxes and other duties (i.e., protection money) to the NLF.

However, Lewandowski also paid tribute to the prowess of U.S. intelligence. In an exchange that U.S. officials might have enjoyed overhearing, the Pole acknowledged that Washington had clear proof of the PAVN's presence in South Vietnam, which Hanoi never acknowledged; besides prisoner and defector accounts, it had seized a trove of general staff documents. A U.S. Embassy first secretary had boasted, he related, that American intelligence "systematically" intercepted communications between the North's headquarters and field commands, and "easily decodes them and therefore knows a great deal." On another sensitive topic, Lewandowski described his surprise encounter with Thieu and Saigon's apparent interest in Polish mediation—the "one-to-one" talk was supposed to be confidential, he remarked wryly, yet "the next day the Americans let [him] know that they are aware of what's going on."[138] For his part, the Soviet related gossip on Ho's travels to Beijing and the performance of Soviet MiG-21s in a recent dogfight with U.S. planes. To the Pole's surprise, Shcherbakov groused about the Vietnamese comrades for various sins, from misusing generous Soviet military and economic aid, to failing to consult with Moscow on military strategy or share intelligence or captured weapons.[139] While in the North, Lewandowski also inspected damage from recent U.S. air strikes, and he joined an ICC tour of the War Museum, which featured a diorama of the Dien Bien Phu battle.

But all these activities and contacts were anticlimactic next to the forthcoming words Lewandowski had heard from Dong. He wrapped up an "eyes only" report to Warsaw: "The overall impression—the Vietnamese currently want to begin political talks, given their good starting position (the internal situation in the South and the rainy season). They realize that after several months, the military situation can be difficult." In sharp contrast to his pessimism after visiting Hanoi in April, the Pole came away this time feeling that he had something to work with.

Making the Rounds: Getting to Know Lodge

Lewandowski wasted no time spreading the word that an auspicious mood had arisen in Hanoi. On Monday afternoon, June 6, his first business day back in Saigon, he finally called on the city's most powerful diplomat, Henry Cabot Lodge, who was nine months into his second stint as ambassador.

The senior Republican, then sixty-four, was lending political cover to a second Democratic president. In the tumultuous summer of 1963, he had gone to Saigon for JFK (who in 1952 had unseated him as Massachusetts senator) and had played a key role in encouraging the Diem coup, which he saw as needed to implant a regime able to defeat the Communists. As the grandson and protégé of his famous namesake, the Senate Foreign Relations chair who in 1919 had derailed Woodrow Wilson's vision of a United States–led League of Nations, Lodge was also isolationist—until Pearl Harbor. But World War II changed everything. He resigned his Senate seat to join a tank regiment in North Africa, and he later accompanied General George Patton and General Dwight Eisenhower. Symbolically burying his isolationist pedigree, he represented Ike at the UN, dueling with Moscow's delegate and cementing an image as a tough Cold Warrior. After failed bids for national office—he was the vice presidential candidate on Richard Nixon's losing 1960 ticket, and had left his first Saigon posting to seek the 1964 Republican presidential nomination—the patrician answered LBJ's call in an act of noblesse oblige; he no longer had high political prospects, and the job was daunting. (LBJ appreciated Lodge's bipartisan spirit but not his efficiency: "He ain't worth a damn, he can't work with anybody [yet] won't let anybody else work."[140]).

This time around, persistent reports claimed, Lodge's wings were clipped and his profile was lowered ("very nearly an invisible man"). White House aides, if pleased with his loyalty and single-minded belief in his mission, were tired of his legendary imperiousness as "an independent force" answerable only to the president (if him) and mulled endless schemes to streamline the mammoth, sprawling civilian side of the war effort and integrate it with General William C. Westmoreland's military campaign. Itemizing his "outstanding qualities" and "equally real" weaknesses, McGeorge Bundy called Lodge a "determined, perceptive, and disinterested" public servant with "no axes left to grind," but said he had "little taste for the hard work" needed to translate a sense of purpose into a "concrete administrative achievement," lacked focus ("He can spend two days on a single cable, with time out for social activity and a daily swim and a couple of diplomatic visits"), underestimated the importance of economics, and "frets over trivia."[141] For his part, Lodge chafed at Foggy Bottom's micromanagement, and he rebuffed directives that he found unduly restrictive. "I do not think it is prudent to instruct me in such detail," he responded to a script for meeting Ky. "This has never been the practice before. To do so deprives the U.S. of the benefit of our local knowledge."[142] When "tired or irritated," he talks of resigning, Bundy reminded LBJ, so one had to coddle this proud, sensitive man and supply stronger staff to balance his shortcomings: "Since we have to accept the risk of bothering him on the big things, he should be humored on the little ones."[143]

Yet, even in his twilight, the "handsome, imperturbable Bostonian" assumed almost mythical proportions—a tall (six-foot-three), silver-haired, physically imposing figure, scion of Brahmin clans prominent since the Revolution, a Harvard graduate, fluent in French, a decorated war hero, already fictionalized (e.g., in Morris West's *The Ambassador*) as the personification of U.S. Cold War aspirations in Asia.[144] He embodied JFK's archetypical Free World diplomat: a "very rugged" "American-type" with *cojones,* not a soft, "languid" sort opposite a "hard and tough" dictator.[145] The *Washington Post*'s Ward Just wrote that despite grumbling over his performance, "our mandarin in Saigon" retained a direct "pipeline" to LBJ and radiated vigor. "At 64, he looks 50—tanned, ruddy, bothered a bit by arthritis but fit from slow crawls in the Olympic-sized swimming pool at the Cercle Sportif, which he visits at noon nearly every day."[146] "Charming and bland in an upper-class Bostonian way, he ignored the routine desperation of his staff" and studiously projected calm, wrote Frances Fitzgerald, attending Episcopal church services with his wife Emily each Sunday regardless of whatever crisis might be unfolding.[147]

Lewandowski had had a few words or clinked glasses with Lodge at the UN, but not serious contact—unsurprisingly given their disparate ranks. Before going to Saigon, he had heard dour appraisals from Wendrowski and Spasowski, who depicted an aloof snob. Spasowski told him: "You know, there [was] an American ambassador but I ha[d] no contact with him. . . . It was useless because people say that Mr. Lodge is talking only to Mr. Lodge"—a garbled allusion to the classic ode to Boston, "the home of the bean and the cod, where the Lowells speak only to Cabots, and the Cabots speak only to God."

But D'Orlandi, who came to like and respect Lodge during the Diem events, urged Lewandowski to keep an open mind: "You are talking about the Vietnamese, you know, all the time, but I must tell you the Americans are also not quite happy with their progress here and that they are, you know, business-like people. . . . Don't you think they would like to settle it, too? . . . to move to a reasonable solution?" "The Americans," he insisted, "are not as bad as you think."

Each time he spoke to the Italian, Lewandowski presumed (correctly) that D'Orlandi would pass on to Lodge his impressions of the only Communist ambassador in town. Even before meeting Lodge, the Pole had heard gossip that he might not be around for long—that his position was weakening, he was losing battles with the U.S. military command over war strategy and relations with Ky, his counsel cut little ice in Washington, and LBJ might seek his resignation when he went home for consultations in early May.[148] This speculation had some foundation. Close associates—for example, McGeorge Bundy, writing to his brother Bill—sensed that the president, despite lavishly praising Lodge, did not fully trust him.[149] Even Lodge's deputy, William J. Porter, whispered that the ambassador would quit that summer, suggesting that the White House "start thinking now about a replacement" because he lacked the "stomach for all the painful jockeying needed" to handle Saigon politics.[150]

Yet, Lewandowski also knew that whatever slim prospects he might have of fulfilling Rapacki's secret peace mission required good working relations with the top U.S. diplomat in Saigon, and so, notwithstanding his own comment that it was "routine" protocol, his first meeting with Lodge held special significance. To see him, the Pole had to navigate a cordon of military police, barbed wire, and white concrete barriers to enter the drab concrete American Embassy on Ham Nghi Street near the Saigon River—testimony to a Viet Cong car bombing a year before that had prompted Washington to order the building of a new, more secure embassy compound, which was now under construction. Once he had ascended to the ambassador's fifth-floor office, though constrained by secrecy and discretion from divulging the full details of his conversation with Dong, he nevertheless had an ideal chance to start seeding the ground for a peace probe.

"Coming quickly to the point," Lodge later recalled, Lewandowski made his pitch; the Pole confided that he had spent two hours talking with the DRV premier, and he hinted tantalizingly about enhanced North Vietnamese readiness for negotiations. "He says that he feels there is a definite will for conversations in Hanoi today," Lodge cabled. "I pressed him with questions, but could not get anything more concrete than that."[151]

"Do you think they want peace?" the Pole recalled Lodge bluntly asking him.

"Mr. Ambassador, do you think they enjoy being bombed and strafed?" Lewandowski responded. "Do you think they are masochists?"[152]

At another point, the Pole inquired whether Lodge had read the Vietnamese Communist Party's official history. When Lodge admitted that he had not, Lewandowski said that it showed Hanoi consistently opposed Chinese imperialism and could accept a solution that met national (as opposed to ideological) aims. "Do you think they are stooges?" he asked.[153]

In his memoirs, Lodge remembered that the unprecedented visit came "out of the fog" of murky, conflicting estimates, impressions, and interpretations to "cast a flickering light." The Pole's claim that "a definite desire" existed in Hanoi for talks "instantly made a deep impression on me and my hopes soared."[154] If so, Lodge effectively concealed those emotions in his contemporaneous report to Washington. He instead described an exchange in which the Pole no more than hinted vaguely at flexibility on the other side:

> I said we were, of course, willing to sit down and talk with anybody, but that ever since I had been connected with this problem, we were the ones who wanted peace and the other side wanted conquest. If there were a change in attitude, that would be good news indeed.
>
> I asked him whether he had detected any willingness to withdraw from South Vietnam, and he again said he could not be concrete—simply that he felt sure that there was now a willingness to talk and at least "make a list."
>
> I asked him whether he had any suggestions as to how such talks could be begun, and he again said he did not have any specific suggestions.[155]

Lewandowski sent a laconic, even blasé, cable: "The conversation was purely official. He talked about the desire of Americans to get out of Vietnam, but nothing concrete."[156]

In fact, the talk had been important, opening a fruitful personal connection between individuals from opposite sides of the Iron Curtain, of different generations and ideologies. They remained correct—"Mr. Ambassador" rather than first names—yet their dealings gradually induced not only mutual respect but also warmth. Politely professing to remember him from the UN, Lodge was surprised for two reasons when Lewandowski came to see him—first, that the Communist had shown up at all, to pay a courtesy call on his professed enemy; and second, that he was so young. "Oh, you remind me very much of my son," he would later say. Almost wistfully, the elder American, frequently described as stiff, would recall Lewandowski as "very sincere," short, wearing thick spectacles. "He was a nice chap. I liked him. He was young, about the age of my son."[157]

As their first encounter showed, they fundamentally diverged on the war's causes. Lodge stressed Hanoi's infiltration and aid to the insurgency, international Communist expansion, and the domino theory, in which he fully believed. (So convinced was Lodge of Vietnam's strategic significance that he once was quoted as telling McNamara, "We'd be there fighting for the place if it were populated by monkeys."[158] Shortly before meeting Lewandowski, he had told a journalist that failure to stop the Communists in Vietnam "would be the greatest defeat in American history and the immediate consequences would extend from Japan to Australia."[159]) Conversely, the Pole rooted the conflict in Vietnamese nationalism.

Nevertheless, deviating from his colleagues, Lewandowski was hardly convinced that further contact was pointless. Many U.S. observers shared the view that, as one put it, "Cabot has, I fear, very much the proconsul's attitude."[160] The Pole's relations with Lodge were "completely different" than his intimate friendship with D'Orlandi. Yet he would grow to respect Lodge as a patriot trying to do his best in an untenable position. Beset by intractable difficulties and opponents in Saigon and Washington, Lodge struck him as "very clever[ly]" following the U.S. "official line," rigidly concealing his personal opinion beneath authorized boilerplate—yet within those constraints, genuinely struggling to end the war even while wholeheartedly endorsing America's obligation to wage it:

> [To] somebody who met Mr. Lodge for conversation or official business, perhaps his impression of him would be, he is very strict, he is a difficult partner because you cannot involve him in any . . . conversation which would go out of [channels], . . . and he would say, I could read newspapers so I would have the same knowledge. . . . He would repeat the formulations, . . . but I think you know that he was—when we talked about the war as such, you know, casualties and so on, then of course you feel that he had the feelings inside, he had the feelings, that he really cared about that, not only because casualties produce political problems which they did but I think he was convinced that the United States had to do what it was doing there.

Surprisingly, given his and his government's solidarity with Hanoi, Lewandowski even came to feel, at least in retrospect, sympathy for Lodge's predicament. "Any American ambassador in Saigon had an almost impossible mission," he said, recalling the endless struggles to coordinate military and civilian efforts, and cajole Saigon into political, economic, and military reforms. "The fact is, all the effort which has been spent in different programs, and so on and so on, had not produced any sensible administration in South Vietnam, which was a tragedy. They really tried, you know, different agencies, economic, political, advisory, and so on, but . . . they have not been able really to produce any sensible administration or government. . . . So it was a frustration, and you know; sometimes Lodge used to give them quite harsh sessions, but it was to no avail."

On June 8, 1966, two days after hearing Lewandowski suggest an enhanced DRV readiness to parley, Lodge received another ICC visitor just back from Hanoi who reinforced that impression: Victor Moore.[161] Though almost never seeing Warsaw's delegate, and only occasionally New Delhi's, the American closely coordinated with Ottawa's. Besides going to the North for ICC business, Moore in March had accompanied Ronning to Hanoi, which had just agreed to a return visit in mid-June. Now, besides setting up an appointment to see Ronning when he passed through Saigon, Moore gave Lodge a readout on his own latest trip. The DRV leaders, he judged, under duress from the bombings (economic damage, dislocation, water shortages, power outages), plus heavy casualties and defections in the South, were considering negotiations with the Americans. "How can this war be ended?" was the question that had dominated long conversations with Ha Van Lau—the "honorary colonel and a professional French-trained civil servant" even contemplated a "fairly long interval" after fighting ceased, during which Vietnam would remain divided at the 17th Parallel. "After that, it would be possible to see whether there were changed ideas in Saigon and Hanoi," Lau said, though he never strayed from the idea that the NLF would *eventually* run South Vietnam.

While in Hanoi, Moore had heard rumors of Lewandowski's conversation with Dong—but when he asked the Pole directly whether he had seen the premier, he had, coyly, initially denied doing so, then brushed it off as a "routine courtesy call."[162] But on hearing from Lodge "that Lewandowski is pushing about his impression thus gained that 'they want to talk,'"[163] Moore endorsed this impression—as the American cabled Washington, the Canadian "agrees with his Polish colleague that there is a 'will to talk' in Hanoi and cited the receptiveness to the suggestion that Ronning could come as an illustration." Though the North Vietnamese bitterly resented U.S. bombing, Moore thought there existed "an incentive to find a way out without loss of face, providing you Americans swallow [a] pretty big pill." But, he warned emphatically, Hanoi's proud rulers could not be seen visibly as caving in to coercion, either through press leaks or new military pressures. "I hope you are Americans are not escalating to a new peace offensive," he said worriedly.[164]

Moore had grounds for his suspicions. Some Canadians, including Foreign Minister Paul Martin, feared that Washington was using Ottawa not so much to sincerely probe Hanoi for possibilities to move toward peace as to cynically build a diplomatic record to justify a subsequent preplanned escalation. "Obviously, the Americans did not want to negotiate," he concluded.[165] Ronning had also been unhappy with how U.S. officials handled his visit in March, believing that they had passed up an intriguing possibility to open negotiations in exchange for a complete and permanent bombing halt.

Top U.S. officials had, in fact, always scorned Ronning's efforts, regarding him as insufficiently pro-American and reflecting Martin's desire to display independence from Washington and to test the waters for an improvement of Canadian relations with "Red China." "Quite frankly, I attach no importance to his trip and expect nothing out of it," Rusk had telegraphed Lodge before the Canadian's March visit. Ronning sensed Washington's disdain. Before heading to Hanoi, he had stopped in Saigon and had seen Lodge, who sounded confident of military victory: "Nothing can stop us. We are chewing them up." And afterward, Washington had taken its good time to respond to his report, waiting more than a month (pleading the Buddhist Crisis to explain the delay) before dismissing Dong's "teasing suggestion" (as Bundy put it) and suggesting a hard-line follow-up oral message for Ronning to deliver if he wished to make another journey.[166]

In early June, just as it learned that Hanoi had OK'd Ronning's return visit, Ottawa was irritated by a U.S. press leak revealing that Washington had already delivered the same slender proposition it had given Ronning—a bombing halt in exchange for a verified halt to DRV infiltration—via the U.S.-Chinese ambassadorial talks in Warsaw.[167] Complaining that the Americans had sent Ronning on his mission with "an empty bag," Moore warned Ottawa that by carrying Washington's water in this fashion, it risked being viewed by Hanoi as a "mouthpiece to American propaganda." Noting widespread rumors of an impending spike in U.S. air raids, he observed caustically:

The Americans appear to be putting Hanoi behind the eight-ball and to be escalating what was allegedly a serious and practical cease-fire overture into a peace
offensive reminiscent of their campaign last Jan[uary]. You will recall that even
Cabot Lodge at that time pointed out the folly of driving Hanoi into a corner. . . .
I remain convinced that such pressure will be counter-productive. Further, if
these tactics raise doubts in even my mind about American sincerity, they will
surely convince [the North Vietnamese] leaders of the correctness of their earlier
suspicions. We can therefore expect them to withdraw into their corner and fool-
ishly, but doggedly and stubbornly, to continue the war.[168]

Shunning such pessimism, Lodge accentuated the positive in his ICC visitors'
reports that the DRV was hurting. Despite the "wispy and inconclusive" data, he
sensed "that in Hanoi today, there is a greater liking of the idea of talking than at
any time since I started following North Vietnamese matters in the autumn of
1963." The enemy, he cabled, was "genuinely disturbed by the vigor of our bombing, and genuinely would like to end the war." Reflecting Moore's advice, he
stressed that to help Hanoi "save face," Washington should avoid publicity about
negotiations, but let actions speak louder than words. "The situation calls for silence and action, the action to consist of steady bombing on the one hand, and a
discreet willingness to get into very secret talks on the other."[169]

Feeling Their Pain: New Plans for Escalation

LBJ's envoy, however, seeing intensified bombing and seeking negotiations as
wholly compatible, advocated precisely the tactics that Moore feared. In a cable to
Johnson the same day the Canadian visited, he prophesied that North Vietnam
might be preparing to end the war, by formal secret talks or "in a fuzzy way with
no dotting of i's or crossing of t's." To get Hanoi to the bargaining table, he advised
coercion, not compromise:

> If we are now going as hard and as fast as we can go in South Vietnam and can not
> get a decisive military result in a year, the question arises as to whether we should
> not intensify the air attack on North Vietnam—whether we cannot thus bring
> about strains which will neutralize their army in South Vietnam, in spite of our
> inability to do it in South Vietnam on the ground within a year.
>
> The reports I get are certainly consistent with the proposition that the Hanoi
> regime is feeling real pain because of our bombing. If there is this change in feel-
> ing in Hanoi—as seems likely—I believe the bombing has had a lot to do with it,
> although ground casualties, of course, play a part. This being true, an intensifica-
> tion of the bombing would be the most effective step we could take to get Hanoi
> to the negotiating table or—better still—to start "fading away."[170]

Far from considering escalation as "folly," as Moore urged, Lodge believed:
"Speak softly but carry—and use—a big stick." To hasten a potential North Vietnamese decision to "come to negotiations or to 'fade away' in the traditional Ori-

ental way," he advised on June 11: "We should continue our physical pressure on them, indeed increase it, while keeping a quiet door open if they choose to come into the room and sit at a table."[171]

Lodge's backing for sharper bombings strengthened a consensus at the top level of the Johnson administration in favor of the controversial plan to open a campaign against politically sensitive petroleum, oil, and lubricants (POL) sites, including gasoline storage facilities around Hanoi and Haiphong. For months, hawks like Rostow and the uniformed military (Westmoreland, the Joint Chiefs of Staff, and Lodge's predecessor, Retired General Maxwell Taylor, now a White House consultant) had strongly advocated a new round of "shock" attacks both to hamper Hanoi's support for the Southern insurgency and punish it for refusing to halt that effort. But now ex-skeptics like Rusk, McNamara, Humphrey, and Bill Bundy (who had previously opposed the proposed POL strikes, doubting their likely military impact and concerned about international political fallout) also swung behind them both for military reasons and to exert political pressure on Hanoi. Undersecretary of State George Ball, the in-house maverick, was ambivalent ("All things equal, this is a good thing to do, but it does not outweigh disadvantages"), but even he agreed that "if we are going to do it, do it now." Only Harriman and Goldberg remained holdouts, unconvinced by the optimistic Rostow that more force would tip Hanoi toward a white flag.[172]

Most important, LBJ himself was determined to go ahead, and he was exasperated by the repeated delays due to one or another peace feeler—delays he felt cost U.S. lives. Though he did not think that oil "plays a hell of a lot [of a role] in the life of the Viet Cong, or the Vietnamese rather," he sympathized far more with arguments that the new raids might reduce casualties than with warnings that they might spook peace probing or alarm foreign allies and domestic critics. "The military and the fellows out there, Westmoreland, just feel like that you're just lettin' 'em shoot our men unnecessarily," he told a dubious Mike Mansfield, the Senate majority leader. "That you ought to stop this—you ought to make it as difficult—we can't stop it, but make it as difficult for them to get supplies as possible or you oughtn't to be in there."[173]

To help the bitter medicine of controversial new strikes go down, Rusk prescribed a spoonful of diplomacy. After advance warning on June 2 that a bombing of POL sites near Hanoi and Haiphong might be imminent, British prime minister Harold Wilson alerted LBJ that he would have to publicly "dissociate" London from such actions.[174] While attending a NATO conference in Brussels a few days later, Rusk concluded that it would be a diplomatic disaster for Washington to launch the strikes right on the eve of Ronning's planned return trip to Hanoi carrying a U.S. proposal. On June 8, "deeply disturbed by general international revulsion, and perhaps a great deal at home, if it becomes known that we took an action which sabotaged the Ronning mission to which we had given our agreement," Rusk cabled Washington pleading for a delay in the start of the POL raids.[175] And this would not be the last time that Rusk would send an anguished cable from a NATO ministerial meeting in Europe warning that an ill-timed bombing of Hanoi risked international condemnation, even from U.S. allies, for sabotaging a secret peace effort.

Rusk won a temporary reprieve, long enough for him to beg Wilson in London (vainly) to back off from his "dissociation" threat and for Ronning to visit Hanoi. Like other U.S. officials, he did not anticipate that the Canadian's mission would actually prove fruitful, but he hoped it would provide a debating point to justify the already-prepared escalation. "If he has a negative report, as we expect," he argued in pleading to delay the POL attacks, "that provides a firmer base for the action we contemplate and would make a difference to people like Wilson and Pearson."[176]

Sure enough, the North Vietnamese were distinctly unimpressed with the message Ronning carried to Hanoi on June 14–18—if he had crossed the Pacific in March to deliver "a feather," this time his baggage was even lighter. He made the trip "with a heavy heart" and "against my better judgment" because he knew that the U.S. proposals would be unacceptable and, despite American assurances to the contrary, might well be designed for rejection in order to justify a new escalation. By the time he arrived, his hosts had been forewarned by the Chinese and the Washington press leak of the essence of the U.S. idea—you halt the infiltration to the South, we'll stop bombing the North—and made clear their disappointment. Unlike three months earlier, Dong failed to receive Ronning, leaving the task of rebuffing his overture to less senior officials (Lau, Deputy Foreign Minister Nguyen Co Thach, and Foreign Minister Trinh). Politely but firmly, they reiterated the Four Points and sent the Canadian packing.[177]

Back in Ottawa, Ronning reported the dismal outcome to Bill Bundy. Depressed and "markedly more sober and subdued" than after his March visit, he admitted that there had been no sign of flexibility in Hanoi, aside from a reaffirmation that it had not retracted its offer of talks in exchange for a complete and permanent bombing halt, which still failed to impress the Americans. Sending a "flash" cable to Rusk from dinner with Ronning and Martin, Bundy knew he was giving a green light for the delayed POL raids.[178]

At the same time, Lau sent a coded message to Lewandowski in Saigon offering a similarly negative appraisal of Ronning's mission. Besides rejecting the bombing-for-infiltration idea, Hanoi had scotched an overture to ease conditions for POWs, calling captured pilots war criminals who would "answer before a DRV court." In sum, "Ludwik" reported, Hanoi believed the Canadian's venture masked U.S. plans for more escalation, and it must "intensify even more its political, military, and diplomatic activities."[179] Lewandowski recalled that "Ronning made a very bad [impression] because he went just to say, 'If you will not give up they will bomb you to hell.'"[180]

The Poles Step Up Their Diplomacy

As rumors spread of the planned bombing intensification, including deliberate leaks of specific targets such as fuel containers and port facilities near Haiphong, and as the Saigon regime finished mopping up the remnants of the Buddhist revolt, the Poles quietly stepped up their own diplomatic activities.[181] One hidden episode involved an approach in Warsaw in mid-June by John Gronouski to Jerzy Michałowski. On instructions from Washington, LBJ's envoy dutifully if unenthusiastically proposed a (U.S.-financed) expansion of ICC activities in Cambodia to check North Vietnam's exploitation of that country's territory for its infiltration and supply routes. In line with Poland's steady refusal to let the commission interfere with Communist military operations, the director-general rebuffed the idea, on the pretext that it would require, in addition to a formal request from Phnom Penh, the consent of all participants in the 1954 Geneva Conference, an obvious impossibility.[182]

Exhausting his formal agenda, Gronouski moved to a more delicate question: Could Michałowski confirm that an "unconditional and final [bombing] halt" would really lead to negotiations (as Dong had hinted to Ronning)? Carefully, the Pole replied that he could not provide such an assurance, but talks would be impossible unless the bombing ended. At that, according to a declassified Polish record, Gronouski declared that "if the U.S. government received assurance that stopping of the bombing would cause, after a certain time, starting the talks, [then] the U.S. would go for such a solution."[183]

His reported statement—which Gronouski did not include in his own cable—went well beyond U.S. thinking at that time. Top Johnson administration officials viewed very skeptically the assurance that a bombing halt would produce talks that Ronning had brought from Dong two months earlier, and would be comparably unimpressed when he returned in June quoting Trinh as reaffirming the offer. Gronouski later admitted that on his own authority, without instructions, he promised the Poles that Washington would stop bombing North Vietnam within twenty-four hours if Warsaw provided a concrete indication that Hanoi would take a "significant" step toward peace in response.

"No, I didn't have any assurance of that in black and white; nobody ever said that to me," he said in a private 1969 interview. "But I am just as confident now saying it as I was then. I was confident enough that I was risking my reputation with a foreign power that I was assigned to." Gronouski explained that he "had talked to the President about it, not in specific terms but in general terms of what our objectives were," and to Rusk, Bill Bundy, and others. "I felt that I had a pretty good reading on what we would do, and I felt very clearly that if there were some definitive response in the offing and that the Poles would so assure us, that if I couldn't do it by telegram I would fly home and convince them to stop it. There's no question in my mind that I could have as I sit here today."[184]

This episode revealed more about Gronouski's eagerness for peace than the administration's actual position. Though able to see top officials during trips back to Washington (including LBJ), he was cut out of sensitive cable traffic on Vietnam topics, including the Ronning missions and senior officials' lack of interest in trading a bombing halt simply for the DRV's willingness to engage in talks. In a further sign that he had grown more dovish than the White House or State Department, over the summer he would repeatedly push ideas to probe Poland's ability to entice Hanoi into talks—for example, empowering Warsaw to transmit a reformulation of the Four Points—only to be shot down by Washington.

In this case, Gronouski reported, Michałowski had rejected any new Polish effort to influence Hanoi toward negotiations, because "under present conditions 'we have exhausted our possibilities.'" He promised to be more helpful if events permitted, but warned that Washington "had painted itself into [a] corner" and could not expect Hanoi to respond until the bombing ceased. On the bright side, Gronouski sensed a "deep and continuing interest and readiness to act, at least on [the] part of Western-oriented elements" within Poland's Foreign Ministry.[185] In fact, Warsaw secretly acted more helpfully than he realized: It immediately transmitted his proposal to the DRV's resident ambassador, Do Phat Quang, and to Siedlecki in Hanoi to relay to the leadership.[186]

In Saigon, meanwhile, Lewandowski continued to seed hints of enhanced prospects for negotiations, together with warnings that they could be wiped out by U.S. escalation. One opportunity came on June 16, when Derksen sought his version of his talk with Lodge earlier that month. The Dutch diplomat, aware that Washington's envoy had never met Wendrowski, the previous Polish ICC delegate, had "pricked up my ears" on hearing Lodge mention that he had seen Lewandowski as well as Moore after they returned from Hanoi. Asked to elaborate, the American said that he had told the Pole that Washington ardently desired talks but that the DRV took an "unaltered, hard-line position." Dissatisfied with this "simplistic" comment, Derksen wanted to hear the other side of the story.

As an opening gambit, he asked Lewandowski his opinion of a "fairly remarkable" just-published article citing alleged yearnings for peace in Hanoi. The Pole derided the "poetic author" who was "out to make a name for himself as quickly as possible," but he defended the basic message, saying it was significant that Hanoi's censors had allowed such a piece to appear. As evidence, he revealed that during his trip a couple of weeks earlier, Dong had summoned him and reiterated the DRV's essential willingness to talk with Washington about a solution envisioning a neutral Vietnam.

Warming to the theme, the Pole argued that it was "absolutely essential" to get talks between Washington and Hanoi going in the next three or four months, by the fall of 1966. Otherwise, Beijing—which vehemently backed the armed struggle and denounced the idea of negotiating with the "imperialist aggressors"—would take an "I told you so" position, strengthening Hanoi's hard-liners. Unfortunately, he said, it was difficult to rebut Beijing's claims of U.S. insincerity about being interested in peace talks, especially because he had already learned that Ronning had arrived in Hanoi "empty-handed."

Lewandowski told Derksen that his talk with Lodge only deepened his fear that Washington sought escalation rather than negotiations, despite evidence of Hanoi's relaxed stand. U.S. ideas evidently carried by Ronning for mutual "de-escalation" were hardly serious or feasible, especially at the start of the Southern fighting season.

With the Canadian mission obviously doomed, Lewandowski confided to Derksen that Poland might get into the game. He expected a recall to Warsaw in connection with "an imminent Polish attempt at mediation," whose main point— "but please keep this to yourself"—would be to convince Washington to soften its position in response to "unequivocal first steps by Hanoi." Remarking on "the cynicism of the great nations," specifically including Russia, Lewandowski observed that only a smaller country like Poland could accomplish this. "It can't be done by Canada, England is not an option, France is impossible, as is the Soviet Union."[187]

The summons to Warsaw did not materialize, but Lewandowski continued to promote the notion that an opening could appear sometime in 1966 for a smaller country—not necessarily Poland—to bring Washington and Hanoi to the table. On June 19, he phoned the Italian Embassy to set up a talk with D'Orlandi but was told that he was visiting Cambodia and would not return until the following week.[188] But two days later, he had a chance to push his agenda with a different U.S. ally: U.K. junior minister Lord Harry Walston, a special emissary of the Wilson government who was passing through.

The Pole jumped at the chance to see a representative of Washington's closest and most important foreign policy partner, yet one that had displayed open skepticism toward its Southeast Asian engagement. Testifying to the fresh evidence of realism in Hanoi, Lewandowski did not offer himself or Poland as mediators, but he projected the idea that conditions could ripen for negotiations toward a "compromise solution" that fall, as long as neither side disrupted the emerging military stalemate:

> The Polish Commissioner called on Lord Walston this afternoon at his own request. He said that he was acting without instructions on his own initiative. He believed that both Hanoi Government and the Liberation Front now realized that the Americans could not be defeated militarily in Vietnam. It was also his impression that in the last five months and particularly in the last two months willingness to negotiate had increased in Hanoi. On the other hand he believed that present regime in South Vietnam could not be maintained without American soldiers and he thought that United States would not want to keep their troops there indefinitely. There seemed therefore to be a possible basis for a compromise solution. But before any negotiations were begun he considered it important that all parties concerned should clear their minds as to the nature of the long-term

solution they wanted for South Vietnam. Moreover, he believed it was useless to expect the Americans, North Vietnamese, Saigon Government and Liberation Front to agree to sit down at a conference table together. It therefore seemed to him desirable that some suitable Government should mediate between these four parties. He did not consider the Canadian Government best qualified to fulfill this role. He also ruled out his own country and Yugoslavia, but considered India or Rumania possible candidates.

He agreed that timing of any negotiations would have to be carefully thought out. The present was not the right time. He expected this would come within the next three to six months, but he was insistent that during the intervening period the present equilibrium should be maintained. Any escalation on the part of the Americans might well make future talks impossible.[189]

Lewandowski's own report to Warsaw neatly fits Walston's impression that the Pole was "acting without instructions on his own initiative." In contrast to the Briton's assertion that Lewandowski had seen Walston "at his own request," the Pole cabled that the visitor "asked yesterday for a talk." He cited Walston as concluding that, because Ronning's mission had failed, hence, Hanoi was not ready for talks. He also told Warsaw that Walston had noted that some expected U.S. bombing increase might prod the DRV into negotiations, but he, himself, emphasized the danger of further escalation. Implying exactly the opposite impression of the British version of their exchange, the Pole omitted his own promotion of peace prospects or mediation, and cabled that he had refused comment when Walston suggested that the ICC stimulate contacts![190] Had Lewandowski become a peace activist, "on his own initiative," with or without explicit authorization from Warsaw?

On Thursday, June 23, 1966, two days after talking to Walston, Lewandowski visited Derksen for what the Pole termed a "routine contact"—but the information he provided was anything but routine. Offering purportedly comprehensive data on Ronning's talks in Hanoi, Lewandowski accurately related the sharp DRV rebuff of Washington's offer to trade a halt in bombing North Vietnam for a "clear reduction" in the Southern insurgency (both infiltration and attacks) and formal recognition of captured U.S. soldiers as POWs (permitting Red Cross visits and other steps to improve their conditions).

But the Pole stressed that the DRV leaders had told Ronning that they were ready to "cooperate in bringing about negotiations in order to reach a political solution to the problem."[191] Specifically, he said, they had pledged that Hanoi:

1. Did not seek immediate reunification of North and South.

2. Did not aim to force the implementation of the "socialist system" in the South.

3. Did not aim to break the ties between South Vietnam and other countries.

4. Did not seek the immediate departure of U.S. forces.

These became known as the Four Disavowals. Lewandowski also told Derksen that, when approached by Gronouski in mid-June, Warsaw had described Hanoi's forthcoming attitude on negotiations. Allegedly, it was open to various options as to who might take part in an initial phase, perhaps including "neutral" inter-mediaries who could deal with all parties to see who should be represented. Without comment ("the above speaks for itself"), Derksen cabled an account of his talk with Lewandowski to the Dutch Foreign Ministry.[192]

Lewandowski's remarks—assuming Derksen reported them correctly—seem puzzling. Nowhere in the record does it appear that Ronning heard such forth-coming statements (in particular, the Four Disavowals) in Hanoi. On the con-trary, a flat DRV rejection was reported to the Americans by the Canadians, who had every incentive to underline even the slightest scrap of DRV moderation, and by Lau to Lewandowski; nor did Gronouski hear such an alluring depiction of Hanoi's attitude from Michałowski.

One may infer, then, that Lewandowski creatively extrapolated these positions from his own conversation on June 2 with Dong, and decided to presume that Hanoi had made comparable statements to Ronning, and that his own Foreign Ministry chiefs in Warsaw (who had his report of the talk with Dong) had relayed their essence to Gronouski. Why would Lewandowski claim that such modera-tion existed in Hanoi? Obviously, he hoped to fan Dutch doubts about Washing-ton's escalatory plans, and perhaps even encourage The Hague to undertake its own mediation effort. Continuing his soundings, Lewandowski arranged to see D'Orlandi at the Italian's apartment on Monday morning, June 27.

"Go Ahead, Bob"—LBJ Approves the POL Strikes

In Washington, meanwhile, momentum gathered behind the decision to launch the POL strikes. At the White House, as soon as word arrived that Ronning's mis-sion had failed, LBJ extracted consent for the record from his top political and military aides. Last-minute weather problems and leaks delayed the strikes for a few days, but at 7:59 a.m. on June 28—Tuesday night in Vietnam—McNamara phoned LBJ to receive final authorization.[193] One last time, they went through the arguments. LBJ fretted about the risk of hitting a Soviet ship in Haiphong Harbor. The defense secretary warned against inflated expectations but called the bomb-ing necessary to sustain U.S. troop morale and reassured his president that the campaign, if bound to be controversial, was worthwhile.

"Things are going reasonably well in the South, aren't they?" Johnson asked.

"Yes, I think so," McNamara responded, even if the insurgents ("a relatively small enemy force" consisting of "a bunch of half-starved beggars") could fight "almost indefinitely"—unless, that is, America used its firepower to crush their will. He went on:

> That's the point. The only thing that will prevent it, Mr. President, is their morale breaking. And if we hurt them enough—it isn't so much that they don't have

enough men as it is that they can't get the men to fight because the men know that once they get assigned to that task their chances of living are small. I, myself, believe that's the only chance we have of winning this thing. And that's one reason I'm in favor of this POL [bombing], because there's no question but what the troops in the South—the VC and North Vietnamese troops in the South—ultimately become aware of what's going on in the North. We see this through the interrogation and the prisoner reports. I've been trying to watch those carefully to see what comes through those. And they know that we're bombing in the North. And they know we haven't destroyed the place, so that in a sense our bombing isn't fully effective, but they also know that nobody is protecting North Vietnam, and we just have a free rein. And when we bomb the POL, ultimately that will become known to the North Vietnamese soldiers and the Viet Cong in the South. And this is just one more foundation brick that's knocked away from their support. And when they see that the supplies are less likely to come down from the North, I think it'll just hurt their morale a little bit more. And, to me, that's the only way to win. Because we're not killing enough to destroy the morale of those people down there if they think this is gonna have to go on forever.

"Go ahead, Bob," replied LBJ.

The execute order went out, enciphered and cabled from the Pentagon across the continent and the ocean to the U.S. Pacific Command in Honolulu, and on to Southeast Asia, where military commanders alerted air pilots and crews at bases in Thailand and on carriers in the South China Sea to prepare for their missions. D'Orlandi, meanwhile, reacted so strongly to what he heard from Lewandowski that he telephoned Lodge to request an urgent meeting.

Diplomats and bombers converged on the stage as the curtain rose on Marigold.

"Could It Really Be Peace?"

Marigold's "Devious Channels"—Act One

July 1966

To my great surprise Lewandowski tells me that . . . his journey to Hanoi allowed him to ascertain the receptiveness of the North Vietnamese to a possible understanding with the Americans. . . . My heart is in my mouth with emotion, . . . Thus the most impassioned dialogue of my life began. . . . No siesta today: besides I'm still so excited I will have difficulty getting to sleep soon.

> —*Giovanni D'Orlandi, diary entry, June 27, 1966*

I don't put much credence in it, but before the day was over yesterday I had the most realistic, the most convincing, the most persuasive peace feeler I've had since I've been president.

> —*Lyndon B. Johnson, telephone conversation, June 30, 1966*

There might just be something in it. Poles and Italians might seem devious channels, but not all that implausible if Hanoi is having second thoughts.

> —*Dean Rusk, cable, June 30, 1966*

I'm sorry we can't have a glass of wine this time in celebration of a real result.

> —*Janusz Lewandowski to Henry Cabot Lodge, Saigon, July 24, 1966*

Marigold's Act I, at least so far as the Americans knew, opened in Saigon on Wednesday evening, June 29, 1966. Shortly before 7 p.m.—the time of day that often saw light showers in the steamy run-up to monsoon season—Henry Cabot Lodge strode to the Italian Embassy at 135 Duong

Pasteur, a thoroughfare near the presidential palace in a posh residential neighborhood, famous for its phở stalls and one of few streets to retain a colonial name (embassy stationery still read "Rue Pasteur"). The chancery occupied the first two floors of a five-story "ochre-colored stucco-and-glass building constructed during the French period"—once owned by a distillery—and Giovanni D'Orlandi lived in a rooftop apartment that opened onto a garden terrace.[1] Phoning Lodge that afternoon, Rome's envoy had said that he first had to attend a Catholic Mass honoring Pope Paul VI, but then the American should stop by (see map 2).

As they arranged their rendezvous, the long-planned, much-rumored, repeatedly delayed escalation in the air war finally began. After a week of strikes against petroleum, oil, and lubricant (POL) targets in the Red River "panhandle," Navy A-4 and A-6 jets struck fuel dumps and docks in Haiphong, and Air Force F-105 Thunderchiefs hit a "petroleum tank farm" on Hanoi's outskirts. Pilots reported clouds of black smoke rising more than 20,000 feet from the pyres in the cities below.[2]

This "dramatic new phase of air power application in the Vietnam conflict" (as a classified Air Force history put it[3]) generated screaming headlines and angry protests around the world. U Thant predictably expressed "deep regret," but even staunch allies grumbled; Britain's Wilson carried out his threat to "dissociate" London from the raids.[4] But U.S. officials, for whom the prospect of hitting the formerly off-limits POL sites was "the big apple in everybody's eye in the bombing campaign from a very early point in 1966," relied on them to boost Saigon's morale, punish Hanoi for aiding the Southern insurgency, and hamper Communist operations—especially traffic along the Ho Chi Minh Trail—by slashing the DRV's fuel capacity by more than half.[5] Elated Pentagon aides called the strikes on Hanoi and Haiphong "the most significant, most important of the war."[6]

All sides considered the action a major raising of the ante. Ho Chi Minh defiantly promised victory even as the "United States imperialists are frenziedly expanding their aggressive war in Vietnam and are perpetrating many crimes of the utmost barbarity in an attempt to subdue the Vietnamese people."[7] A half hour before the bombs began falling, the DRV deputy foreign minister summoned Soviet Bloc envoys to warn of a huge impending raid, which he termed a desperate gamble to compensate for political and military failures. Hoang Van Tien urged the embassies to cut their staffs to a bare minimum and evacuate dependents, but vowed that the government would "defend the capital and be there until the end"—and presumed fraternal diplomats would stay there as well.[8]

Washington mounted a robust defense of the controversial bombings. LBJ had stayed up late to await reports of the first attacks—and had made a nocturnal trip to a Catholic church to pray for the pilots' safe return[9]—but McNamara took the spotlight at a televised Pentagon briefing. "Crisp and alert" despite his own all-night vigil, the *New York Times* reported, he "looked as if a weight had been lifted from his shoulders," using a wooden pointer to denote "perishable" targets in Haiphong and Hanoi and reeling off statistics to argue that the raids were neces-

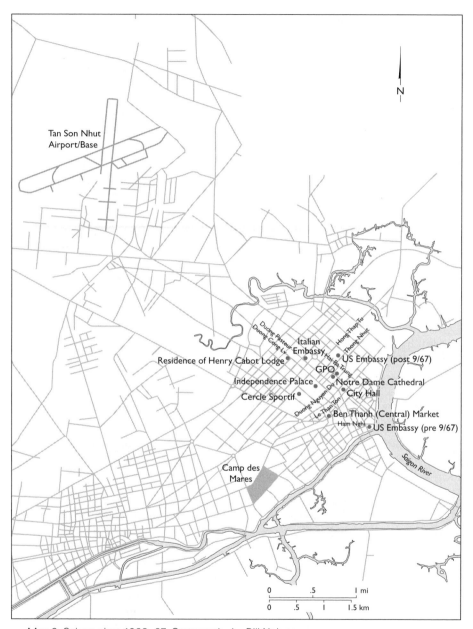

N

Tan Son Nhut
Airport/Base

Duong Pasteur
Duong Cong Ly
Residence of Henry Cabot Lodge
Italian
Embassy
Hong Thap Tu
Thong Nhut
Hai Ba Trung
US Embassy (post 9/67)
GPO
Independence Palace
Notre Dame Cathedral
Cercle Sportif
Duong Nguyen Du
City Hall
Le Thanh Ton
Ben Thanh (Central) Market
Ham Nghi
US Embassy (pre 9/67)
Saigon River
Camp des
Mares

0   .5   1 mi
0   .5   1   1.5 km

Map 2. Saigon circa 1966–67. Cartography by Bill Nelson.

sary, timely, and successful. The bombings, LBJ declared sternly, "will continue to impose a growing burden and a high price on those who wage war against the freedom of their neighbors."[10]

A less auspicious setting for a peace probe could scarcely be imagined. Yet, in an eerie premonition of Marigold's climax five months later, U.S. military actions that set off a global uproar—sudden, seemingly coincidental raids on sensitive DRV targets—precisely overlapped and perhaps undermined a secret diplomatic bid to stop the war.

When Lodge saw D'Orlandi that Wednesday evening, the Italian explained his urgent summons: Two days before, Janusz Lewandowski had come to see him bearing a "very specific peace offer" from Hanoi whose terms seemed surprisingly mild—enough to strike Lodge as almost incredibly forthcoming and briefly inspire LBJ to believe that they just *might* mark the beginning of the end of the war.[11]

D'Orlandi's talk with Lodge actually constituted half of a secret diplomatic two-step that Wednesday, choreographed by his foreign minister, Amintore Fanfani, who was then in Bonn. As Rome's envoy in Saigon laid out the peace proposals that he said the Pole had related, in Washington a special emissary from Fanfani told senior State Department officials the same story.

What provoked all this excitement? To this day, confusion lingers about Marigold's origin. It has been unclear how much reality, as opposed to invention or wishful thinking, lay behind the ideas that caused hearts to flutter in Saigon, Rome, and Washington, and it has been equally uncertain whether the impetus came from North Vietnam, Poland, or Italy. But now, newly available Polish and Italian archival sources, as well as declassified U.S. records, tell somewhat contradictory tales but resolve many of these mysteries.

Marigold Opens: The Italian-American Version

"My Heart Is in My Mouth . . ."
Thanks to the recent release of D'Orlandi's personal diary and formerly top secret coded telegrams, we can now learn from contemporaneous Italian sources—as opposed to Lodge's hearsay version two days later—not only what Rome's ambassador in Saigon recorded that Lewandowski told him on Monday morning, June 27, 1966, but also the intense emotions the conversation generated. The following account describes this encounter from D'Orlandi's perspective.[12]

Lewandowski rushed to see D'Orlandi at 11 a.m., a half hour after phoning to set up the meeting. Assuming that the Pole had come merely to gossip, D'Orlandi recounted his recent trip to Cambodia and talk with Prince Sihanouk, who doubted that Hanoi was set to compromise and hence dismissed immediate prospects for negotiations.[13]

Lewandowski disagreed sharply. "You'd be surprised how much my visit completely contradicts what Sihanouk says. I have been in Hanoi and can state a number of points." His talks with the DRV leaders, he said, let him gauge "the receptiveness of the North Vietnamese to a possible understanding with the Americans." His tone and precision left no doubt in D'Orlandi's mind that the Pole meant to imply that Hanoi was ready for peace. His heart pounding, he asked: "Are you the bearer of a proposal?"

Yes, Lewandowski replied. As the Italian took careful notes, he described what he said were Hanoi's terms. It was, he said, "ready to make substantial concessions to reach a political compromise with the Washington government in order to re-store peace to Vietnam." U.S. officials already knew this, the DRV believed, but had responded negatively, instead sending Ronning to demand de facto capitulation—that Hanoi cease infiltration and accept a prisoner swap in return for a bombing halt.

The North Vietnamese, Lewandowski said, had "expected more reasonable and above all, more political proposals"—not merely humanitarian gestures for prisoners of war but also "dialogue about peace arrangements for the area." Pri-vately, they would consider a far milder settlement than their belligerent public statements implied. Without explicitly identifying his sources, he said that Hanoi merely required the NLF's "participation" (not necessarily as South Vietnam's sole representative) and a bombing "suspension" (not a permanent halt) before nego-tiations could begin. Lewandowski also claimed, according to D'Orlandi, that to facilitate a "global" solution of the Vietnamese problem, Hanoi

1. Will not require immediate reunification ("either by elections or otherwise," D'Orlandi later told Lodge).

2. Will not require the imposition of a socialist system in South Vietnam.

3. Will not require a change in Saigon's foreign relations with the West (i.e., would not insist on neutralization).

4. Although it still demands the withdrawal of U.S. troops, Hanoi is prepared to discuss a timetable ("reasonable calendar").

(These "negative obligations," as D'Orlandi put them, matched the Four Disavow-als the Pole had described to Derksen four days before, except that instead of saying that the DRV leaders had stated these views to *Ronning*, he now *on his own authority* ascribed them to Hanoi.)

D'Orlandi read his notes back for confirmation—and did not need to change a word. So began what he called in his diary "the most impassioned dialogue of my life."

Hanoi insisted on "absolute secrecy" regarding these proposals, the Pole stressed, especially because it had not informed the Chinese, who hoped the war would go on "for the next several years." If they leaked, he warned, it would promptly disavow them.

Why, D'Orlandi asked, had the North Vietnamese chosen Lewandowski as a channel rather than Jean Sainteny, the former French high commissioner, to whom they were closer, and who would visit Hanoi in early July as de Gaulle's personal envoy? Because the United States does not want to work through Paris, replied the Pole, and the DRV preferred "actual secret negotiations" between Moscow and Washington.[14] The Italian prodded: Could Hanoi really exclude Beijing? Yes, provided preliminary contacts stayed secret.[15] Why had Lewandowski gone to him rather than directly to Lodge? Because LBJ gives little weight to Lodge's counsel, while Fanfani could push the initiative in Washington at the highest level. Still, D'Orlandi indicated that he would see Lodge about the proposals right after telling Rome, and Lewandowski agreed.

As the talk ended, Lewandowski reemphasized the need for secrecy and offered to go to Hanoi as soon as it might help or to any city in the region to arrange "preliminary meetings." Gloomily, he predicted that Washington would "intensify the bombing of North Vietnam with the objective of causing the collapse of the Viet Cong resistance"—hopes that were "pious illusions." This might be the "last possibility of receiving such reasonable proposals from Hanoi," he warned. If this effort failed, he added on a personal note, he would request to be transferred from Saigon. Finally, he implored D'Orlandi to lobby Washington to seek a "general and comprehensive" deal with Hanoi, not "fragmentary" agreements. "If possible, what is to be avoided is that after such great labor, the result is merely the exchange of packages or correspondence for the prisoners."

D'Orlandi was thrilled: "My heart is in my mouth with emotion." After escorting Lewandowski to the parking lot, he burst into the office of his young deputy, Mario Sica, his face so contorted that Sica feared he was suffering another seizure. Instead he blurted out: They are ready to negotiate![16] Regaining his composure, he drafted an urgent cable for Sica to encode to tell Rome that, according to the Pole, "Hanoi is willing to make substantial concessions in order to reach a political compromise with the U.S." Skipping lunch and his afternoon nap, he composed telegrams reporting and assessing the conversation and seeking guidance. "No siesta today," he wrote that night. "Besides, I'm still so excited that it would be difficult to go to sleep soon."

D'Orlandi indeed "did not shut an eye" Wednesday night, and he spent Thursday "on edge," awaiting Fanfani's response. Eager to convey Lewandowski's words to Lodge, he worried that the minister's absence from Rome might delay obtaining permission, or that he might not grasp his messages' "absolute urgency" and the "extraordinary opportunity" they contained. "Could it really be peace?" he wondered. "Sica is also on tenterhooks, but faced with my cold impassiveness, he attempts to imitate my inscrutable expression."[17]

Finally, that evening, the answer arrived.

D'Orlandi and Lodge

D'Orlandi need not have worried. On reading his cables, Fanfani decided to inform the Americans. After securing approval from Prime Minister Aldo Moro (a fellow Christian Democrat in the coalition government), he sent an envoy to

Washington and cabled D'Orlandi that he was free to tell Lodge, "as he would be inclined to do."[18]

D'Orlandi was also inclined to tell Lodge—they had been friends, collaborators, and even occasional coconspirators since the American's prior posting to Saigon during the John F. Kennedy and Diem years. During that tense period, Lodge grew close to the Italian and was instrumental in securing medical treatment for him (as during his trauma in January, arranging an emergency flight from Tan Son Nhut on a U.S. military aircraft[19]). They may have felt déjà vu over the idea of forming a covert channel to Hanoi via Poland's ICC delegate. During the fall 1963 intrigues, D'Orlandi reportedly convinced Nhu to see Warsaw's delegate to find out "what was in his stomach" and perhaps open a link to the North.[20] Shortly after the coup, the U.S. ambassador proposed a probe employing a relay from Lodge to D'Orlandi to Maneli to Pham Van Dong or Ho Chi Minh. "I have gotten to know d'Orlandi very well and believe he can be trusted," Lodge assured Harriman. "He is also an extremely precise man and well able to handle an idea in all its various refinements and shadings."[21] But the idea died, because Warsaw then had scant interest in mediating.

Now, on a June evening three years later, D'Orlandi informed Lodge of what seemed like a far more concrete Polish initiative, aimed at stopping a war that was consuming thousands of lives and had become a painful albatross for the United States.

As background, he praised Lewandowski as a "friendly and outspoken man" who was "not as stubborn as most Communists" and who, the Italian suspected, actually held a "rather high rank" and had been sent to Saigon on a "very special mission." He said that the Pole had previously called Hanoi "very obdurate and foolish" not to accept U.S. terms when Washington only had 30,000 advisers in South Vietnam (instead of 265,000 troops heading toward 400,000 to 500,000), and he noted that the two shared a desire to cut China out of the action.

But on Monday, D'Orlandi said, Lewandowski had asserted, based on his latest talks in Hanoi, that the DRV was "prepared to go 'quite a long way'" to make peace. He then recited roughly the same account of the Pole's presentation that he had sent Rome, adding some piquant details. For example, in a point sure to entice Washington, he quoted him as saying that the North Vietnamese preferred "someone other than Ky" but "do not want to interfere with the South Vietnamese Government."

D'Orlandi pleaded with Lodge to heed Lewandowski's warning to preserve strict secrecy. "It is useless of me to add," he quoted the Pole as saying, "that should there not be any kind of preliminary agreement, Hanoi will deny ever having made any offer." Lewandowski seemed "'proud of himself' for having brought these proposals about," the Italian noted. Flattering Rome (an "able debater") as the ideal intermediary to sway LBJ, he had offered Warsaw's aid in setting up a meeting, perhaps in Hong Kong or Singapore, between D'Orlandi and a suitable Polish envoy to push the effort. "We as Poles and you as Italians are missing a terrific opportunity for agreement between Moscow and Washington," he had said. "The sooner we settle it, the happier we will all be."

In sum, D'Orlandi gathered, "the Poles are desperately seeking a way out on Moscow's instructions" now that Hanoi, trying to "run out" on China, was "amenable to common sense," seeking a comprehensive accord, and ready to go far to end the war.[22]

Lodge took careful notes and listened intently but hid any emotions; D'Orlandi suspected that behind "the normal appearance that he wants to keep," his friend was "moved." After relating the purported proposal, the Italian fervently endorsed it in a peroration that revealed much about his mindset, philosophy, and modus operandi:

> And then I launch into an impassioned plea in support of this unexpected initiative. Washington cannot let it fall. It would not only be criminal, but also stupid. And we cannot allow the nitpicking to kill it all. The agreement should be comprehensive and resolve the problems of the conflict in their entirety. It is a very ambitious project, but far from unattainable. And, for purposes of methodology, I submit to [Lodge] the advisability of examining the future above everything else and not to get bogged down in the acrimonious details of the past and of the present as well. If you all agree on the least unpleasant solution (for each of you) for the future Vietnam, then you will be able or we will be able—if you want me as a partner—to find all the solutions to resolve the current problems. If, on the other hand, you should begin with a discussion of the present situation, then the imperatives of the North Vietnamese dialectic will clash with your dialectic and the situation cannot but worsen, causing you to acrimoniously reach a stalemate. "We shall not negotiate under bombing." "We will cease the bombings when you have stopped the infiltrations of the South." Instead of the sterile debate, why not face the problem with a working premise: "The war is over. What settlement can we give Vietnam?" Cabot Lodge appeared to me to be struck by my tumultuous arguments, and he immediately went to send a long telegram to Washington.[23]

Lodge reported the startling talk in a "literally eyes only" cable to Rusk (then in Australia), Acting Secretary of State Ball, and LBJ, and then added his own reaction. Warily, he admitted that it sounded too good to be true: "The proposals attributed to Hanoi, as a package, go far beyond anything we have heard mentioned before" and even "appear so forthcoming as to arouse suspicion concerning the credibility of the Polish intermediary."

But the talk had also piqued Lodge's interest. Consistent with his assessments a few weeks earlier, he guessed the overture stemmed from "the successes we are having militarily, politically, and economically." Echoing D'Orlandi, he judged that the North Vietnamese, fearing Chinese pressure, might logically reach out to the Soviets to extricate themselves from the war. "Unquestionably the Polish proposal would never have been made without specific Moscow approval," he presumed. Though cautious about Lewandowski, he heartily endorsed D'Orlandi as a mediator. Their "warm friendship" dated to 1963, and the Italian, fluent in English since childhood, was "a careful and accurate reporter."[24]

Lodge also found the new channel congenial for another reason. Like D'Orlandi and Lewandowski, he derided the parade of "special emissaries" sent to prod Hanoi to enter talks. Far from enhancing peace prospects, he believed, such efforts stiffened the Communists' will to fight. (He felt special disdain for Thant, who was reported to be sending an envoy to contact Beijing and what Lodge called the "so-called National Liberation Front.") Better to rely on quiet probing by Saigon-based pros like himself, who were well informed, authorized, and unlikely to attract publicity. "The conversations which I have been having here with D'Orlandi are a much more promising way to proceed," he advised.[25]

First Reactions in Washington

In Washington, the secret Italian descriptions of Lewandowski's approach immediately attracted attention at the very top of the Johnson administration. On June 29, Fanfani's emissary, Alessandro Farace di Villapresta, together with his ambassador in Washington, Sergio Fenoaltea, came to Foggy Bottom to relay the gist of Lewandowski's message to Ball and U. Alexis Johnson, the deputy undersecretary of state for political affairs. Ball reacted warily. Aside from the intriguing points on the NLF (hinting at participation in talks, but not necessarily as South Vietnam's sole representative) and bombing ("suspension" rather than "cessation"), he said, Hanoi's purported stand seemed "very similar to previous indications." Given how many hands through which it had passed, he doubted that its forthcoming aspects had "any significance." More clarification was needed.[26]

When LBJ heard of the Italian-Polish exchange in Saigon, he felt mixed emotions. Mingling euphoria and disbelief, he could not resist confiding the news. "I'm not going to tell anybody else this, Bill," he told an associate on the morning of June 30, "and I don't put much credence in it, but before the day was over yesterday I had the most realistic, the most convincing, the most persuasive peace feeler I've had since I've been president." But later in the same tape-recorded phone call, he stressed that he was "not a fellow like Adlai Stevenson that gets a drink in a bar and thinks that somebody buying for him means he wants to surrender. I'm too hard headed for that." He did not "think much of" the purported Hanoi proposals, "although the diplomats do," because "I don't think they've had enough yet."[27]

The top aides who were aware of the closely guarded Italian messages also felt unsure how seriously to take them. Ball swapped views with a "brooding" Rostow, who gave the proposition "a 50/50 chance it would 'blink.'"[28] They voiced confusion over Moscow's role and doubts about D'Orlandi: "Ball said he is fuzzle-headed, and it is hard to tell how much is his own reporting and how much is Pole's." Both favored shifting to direct contacts with Hanoi as quickly as possible, but if intermediaries were necessary, the national security adviser "would prefer the Soviets to the Italians."[29] Less ambivalent about the new channel, McNamara, grasping for any potential escape from the deepening conflict, advised LBJ to "pursue vigorously the Polish-Italian feeler"—as he told his dovishly inclined aide John T. McNaughton, who sensed that the North Vietnamese "may be getting ready to deal, partly because they see themselves being forced into the Chinese lap."[30] Likewise intrigued, Averell Harriman remarked to McNaughton on July 2 that he "should get on the move again," meaning, the Pentagon aide gathered, "to Moscow in connection with the recent overture by the Pole in Saigon."[31]

After heading to Texas the next day, LBJ received a memo from Ball warning against excessive excitement. "I think one must be very skeptical of the source," the State Department's number two man wrote, "since Lewandowski and D'Orlandi may both be indulging in wishful thinking, and they cannot be regarded as careful and precise reporters." Fearing leaks (from D'Orlandi, who was "known to be talkative," or from the Farnesina) and inaccuracies, he urged flipping channels at the first opportunity to a direct U.S.-DRV link.[32]

From Canberra, where he was attending ANZUS and SEATO meetings, Rusk also urged caution.[33] The NLF reference seemed "vague," and even if true would give the group "a major, and likely fatal, part in SVN [South Vietnamese] politics." A call for a bombing "suspension" would inevitably expand into a requirement for a permanent halt. And disclaimers of a desire for immediate unification or imposition of socialism "have a familiar ring from some past noises by DRV Reps trying to make themselves sound reasonable." Still, Washington had to play along, because a "refusal to follow up—even if message wholly phony—would expose us to recrimination from Fanfani and Rapacki alike." Besides, "there might just be something in it. Poles and Italians may seem devious channels, but not all that implausible if Hanoi is having second thoughts." (If the initiative were genuine, he admitted, the POL campaign might cause Hanoi to harden its terms, at least temporarily, for fear of seeming weak, but that was an argument to go slowly, not to cancel the attacks.)

Doubts about the diplomats involved—and confusion about the identity of one of them—magnified Rusk's skepticism. Prodded by Bill Bundy, who was traveling with him, he mistakenly believed that Warsaw's ICC delegate was not Janusz but *Bohdan* Lewandowski, whom he recalled from the contacts with Norman Cousins during the thirty-seven-day bombing pause. Perhaps, he surmised—consistent with his belief that Poland's foreign minister had used spurious means to try to delay the bombing resumption—Rapacki had sent the same Lewandowski to Saigon to make more such mischief. The Italian involved in the initiative likewise nonplussed Rusk. "D'Orlandi," he noted, "is a professional, although his opinions seem to go up and down in Saigon on [a] basis that seems to depend heavily on gossip."[34]

Responding from Saigon, Lodge did not clarify the confusion over the Pole's identity (or defend his credibility), but he vouched strongly for D'Orlandi. Yes, he had "a rather usual Italian love of making startling and paradoxical statements at dinner parties, . . . partly for his own amusement and also hoping it will startle and provoke other people into talking." And Lodge acknowledged disagreeing with him on some issues, such as his disdain for Ky (D'Orlandi scorned him as a "petit Hitler"[35]—for whom, incidentally, the mustachioed marshal had notoriously expressed admiration).

But more important, D'Orlandi—besides being a seasoned diplomat and an "extremely accurate reporter" who could "discern shadings and distinctions"—was pro-American "in the very core of his being," convinced "that the United States is carrying out a wonderful and indispensable role in this dangerous world for the benefit of all humanity. If, therefore, you were decided to work through him," Lodge concluded, "you could be guaranteed of devoted help actuated by the deepest feelings of friendship for the U.S. as well as absolutely accurate reporting with considerable insight into the implications of everything that is said."[36]

Despite this tiff over D'Orlandi's reliability and, more broadly, over the overture's significance, the few U.S. officials who were aware of the Saigon conversations and were considering Fanfani's request for guidance accepted that they were dealing with a *Polish* probe, perhaps sponsored by Moscow. Yet some doubted that Lewandowski had really been authorized to transmit a "very specific peace offer" from the *North Vietnamese,* as D'Orlandi had quoted him as claiming, and that he had accurately depicted Hanoi's views. They had no idea, in other words, how firm a basis existed for the Italian report and if it really signaled an opening for peace.

Historians, too, lacking hard evidence beyond U.S. archival records, which merely set down what the Italians relayed, have been stymied in trying to explain this surprising, sudden, provocative purported Hanoi peace probe—though they assumed that throughout Marigold, "Poland was the prime mover."[37]

Fresh evidence from Warsaw both illuminates and blurs the story.

The Polish Perspective

The Polish evidence, both contemporaneous documents and Lewandowski's recollections, offers a mixed picture of Marigold's opening scenes. Crucially, we can now establish that the initiative's alluring depiction of Hanoi's attitude did not simply materialize out of thin air or fertile Polish or Italian imaginations, as some Americans suspected. The most tantalizing elements in D'Orlandi's account of his June 27 conversation with Lewandowski may now be traced to the Pole's talk with Pham Van Dong on June 2. Echoes of the premier's remarks could be discerned in the "negative" points that the Italian quoted the Pole as attributing to Hanoi: Disavowing demands for immediate reunification, a "socialist" system in the South ("the point here, at this current stage, is not to build socialism"), or rapid shifts in Saigon's status ("the internal and foreign policy in the South will be different from that in the DRV, it is necessary that this be known"). Lewandowski equally could rely on that talk to assure D'Orlandi that Hanoi would accept a timetable for a U.S. troop withdrawal and deal with elements in the present Saigon regime (commenting on the Pole's conversation with Thieu, Dong had said that the NLF was "ready to receive anyone, even persons held in suspicion").[38]

Conversely, Lewandowski's cable reporting that talk in Hanoi nowhere mentions the two points that most intrigued Washington: the hints of flexibility about negotiations being possible after a "suspension" of the bombing, and acceptance that the NLF would "take part" in them. Dong had specifically authorized, and even encouraged, the Pole to correct "mistaken views" about the NLF's flexible and moderate aims, and to make "known" Hanoi's readiness to allow a separate RVN to exist with an independent foreign and domestic policy for an extended period, yet Lewandowski denied relaying to D'Orlandi a "very specific peace offer," as the Italian reported. "Giovanni went too far," he said decades later on seeing the Italian's cables about their June 27 conversation.

Contrary to Italian and U.S. records, Polish sources assign the "principal role" in setting Marigold in motion to *D'Orlandi*, the fervent peace advocate, perhaps prodded by Fanfani and Moro, who had political incentives to promote peace in Vietnam.[39] It appears that Lewandowski did not cable an account of his June 27 talk with D'Orlandi; none was found in the MSZ dossier of ciphergrams from Saigon, and Michałowski, who reviewed internal files in compiling a secret postmortem in the early 1980s, asserted that the ICC commissioner "did not report" relaying a "very specific peace offer" from Hanoi.[40] According to Lewandowski, the reason is simple: He did not mean to launch a diplomatic initiative when he visited the Italian that Monday morning, but D'Orlandi must have decided, due to his own passion to end to the war, to frame his description of Hanoi's views as a concrete peace offer. "D'Orlandi was feeling that to arrange some settlement will be his biggest life achievement," the Pole remembered. "He was absolutely obsessed. Sometimes he made some overinterpretation. . . . I never said 'the Vietnamese are going to accommodate,' or something like that. . . . D'Orlandi went too far, but I can understand him, he was very eager. . . . He really wanted to do something, he was pushing."[41]

While denying that he ever said a mere bombing suspension would suffice to start talks, Lewandowski acknowledged that D'Orlandi "might" have accurately reported his description of Hanoi's thinking; he would hardly have discouraged him from concluding that Washington was squandering a real chance to explore a settlement. "Probably, I said, 'Why do you believe the [North] Vietnamese are so unflexible, not ready to accommodate. . . . And here might come the question of the South, you know, I would say that, 'Look, they are more flexible than we believe, or than we know, on this matter.'"

Then, having heard enough to justify even a slim chance of progress, the Italian opted to treat the Pole's story as a full-fledged probe, he suspected. "We come here to the point, who initiated the meetings? Was it Lewandowski who asked Mr. Lodge to be received by him or to start talks in D'Orlandi's place or somewhere? Or was it Lodge who asked Lewandowski to come to D'Orlandi's . . . to have a talk with him? Now if we ask the direct question, who initiated these talks, it was D'Orlandi, it was certainly Giovanni!"[42]

Lewandowski's cables from Saigon confirm that Warsaw viewed the ensuing diplomacy as an *Italian,* not Polish or DRV, initiative, and also corroborate his claim that at the time he "never concluded there is any kind of opening."[43] In contrast to the hopes D'Orlandi's report inspired among some U.S. aides, Lewandowski's missives lacked any such optimism, especially once the bombing near Hanoi and Haiphong began on June 29.

At a party the next day hosted by Canada's ICC delegation, the air strikes aroused "serious concern" about a violent NLF reply or even a Soviet response, Lewandowski cabled. Saigon leaders felt "euphoria" over the raids,[44] but the Pole shared the gloom he sensed among foreign observers: "Pessimism and conviction exists among the diplomats and journalists that the American action obliterates the possibility of a peaceful resolution." He noted signs of panic—runs on gold and "attractive merchandise," hiding of goods, tightened security around the port and power plant, a hurried exit of foreign dependents.[45] (At the same party, he confided to Derksen that two days before, Fanfani had begun a new mediation bid with Washington and Moscow, hoping to restrain the former from escalation; he predicted his "path would be rocky, since the day after he began his endeavor the first bombs were dropped on Hanoi and Haiphong."[46])

The next morning, Friday, July 1, citing conversations with diplomats, journalists, and others, Lewandowski distilled his own nuanced yet pessimistic assessment: Hanoi's stand left room for direct talks to explore a neutralist compromise, but Washington was in no mood to explore this option and instead counted on military pressure:

1. I think that Hanoi would agree for political talks if the Americans were prepared to give up the dominating role in the South in the name of a progressive, neutral, albeit noncommunist, government. All the initiatives of deescalation, and the like, do not stand any chances, because they do not answer the key question: what will the South look like after military operations are stopped[?]

2. I have the impression that instead the U.S. is not prepared to undertake a similar solution. Their postulates, as a matter of fact, boil down to ending the [Communist military] operations and maintaining the status quo. Such a position does not constitute the basis for the talks. The American Embassy [i.e., Lodge] proposed lately "the self-ceasing of military operations." It is to be carried out through: increasing the bombings of the North, which is to cause diminishing the aid for the NLF. The weakening of the activity of the NLF is to, instead, lead to deescalation of the bombings of the North and a gradual withdrawal of the American troops. In the final phase, only Asian troops of the allies of the South would remain in South Vietnam.

3. I do not see any prospects for political negotiations in the near future in this situation.[47]

Soon after cabling this estimate, Lewandowski had a surprise guest: D'Orlandi, who had come in person after trying vainly to reach him by phone. Only then did the Pole learn that, as he reported, "Italy (specifically Fanfani) is examining the possibility of a new peace initiative in Vietnam." Ignoring his own role in stimulating this development, he told Warsaw that D'Orlandi thought an effort would be "timely" because Hanoi knew it could neither win militarily nor rely on a stronger commitment from Moscow or Beijing; because the battlefield situation seemed "balanced," at least temporarily; because Washington feared "further complications" in Saigon's volatile politics, because the lull in the struggle with the Buddhists had not solved "fundamental problems" (the promise of elections would have a "calming effect" only until they were held and "proven . . . brutally falsified"); and because the Americans faced increasing woes in conducting the war and no prospect of its ending. Even the Hanoi and Haiphong raids did not fully dampen the Italian's ardor.

"O," Lewandowski cabled, using his shorthand for D'Orlandi, "is optimistically disposed, although he is afraid that the last escalation of the air war on the North, should it appear not to be an isolated incident, might reflect unfavorably on peace prospects." Rome would "initiate very discreet probes" first in Washington and then—if initial soundings justified going ahead—in Moscow, for a solution resembling the "French conception" (i.e., South Vietnam's neutralization), though it could not be advertised as such due to the poor state of U.S.-French relations. Promising to keep him apprised, D'Orlandi requested the Pole's "utmost discretion."[48]

The Italian's accounts of this July 1 talk, however, deviated significantly from Lewandowski's.[49] In cables to Fanfani later that Friday and in conversation that evening with Lodge (after rushing to the U.S. Embassy to convey the news), he still described the unfolding initiative as a *Polish* "maneuver" and—in contrast to Lewandowski's messages—portrayed Warsaw's delegate as "more eager than ever" to pursue a probe, "sure that this was the right time to score against the Chinese," who were mired in an "internal political crisis." To Rome, D'Orlandi quoted Lewandowski's "reservations" about the latest raids. "Why did they bomb the fuel depots in Hanoi and Haiphong as soon as they learned of the peace proposals?" he asked reproachfully on greeting the Italian, who tried to calm him by noting that Washington had not yet digested the new proposals (true but irrelevant; Lodge's cable would not have sufficed to again defer the long-delayed POL attacks). Still, D'Orlandi assured Lodge, Lewandowski did not believe that the air strikes had "compromised" the initiative or—contrary to some U.S. senators' claims—hurt "the prospects for reaching a political settlement."

D'Orlandi quoted Lewandowski as offering tactical ideas to aid the peace probe—not just passively hearing a description of an Italian venture, as the Pole's cable implied. Responding to a U.S. plea for clarification, D'Orlandi had asked him if there were any significance to minor linguistic discrepancies in the descriptions that Italy passed on in Saigon and Washington of Hanoi's stand on a potential NLF role in talks and whether it insisted on a bombing "suspension" or a permanent halt.[50] Rome's envoy reassured Fanfani and Lodge: A mere suspension would do ("inasmuch as negotiation should succeed and therefore [a permanent] cessation is not requested"), and an NLF role would not exclude the present Saigon regime's participation (though it would help if Ky were "replaced with a less extremist nationalist political figure"). He told Lodge that he had vetted these points personally with Lewandowski, but his cable suggests that he spoke on his own authority.[51]

He also conveyed the Pole's irritation at what he saw as quibbles on issues far from the "heart of the matter"—South Vietnam's future. "In the doorway, Lewandowski repeated again to me that our attempt currently under way is particularly timely; he added that for the U.S. it is a case of accepting the broad outlines or of rejecting the proposal." Once both sides accepted the "broad overall outlines of a suggested compromise," the usual give-and-take of negotiations would ensue. In the meantime, why risk getting bogged down or sidetracked by mere procedural items? The Pole "evidently feels that we must get rid of the 'cease-fire mentality,' and think in terms of a political settlement of the whole Vietnam issue," Lodge cabled after seeing D'Orlandi.

Lewandowski was "particularly earnest" in warning that more efforts with limited aims (along the lines of the ill-fated Ronning missions) would be "most unfortunate," D'Orlandi told Lodge. Far from aiding peace, he felt, more bids by Thant, the ICC, or Ottawa (now discredited in Hanoi) would prompt Beijing to pressure Hanoi to immediately reject any such proposition, "and this would jeopardize the maneuver which he, Lewandowski[,] is trying to carry out." In D'Orlandi's telling, the Pole had reiterated that the crucial contacts would be between Washington and Moscow—the exact scenario Lewandowski was attributing to the Italians!

The Polish authorities were actually less enthusiastic about the initiative than D'Orlandi depicted Lewandowski to be. At a Warsaw Pact summit in Bucharest on July 5–7, Gomułka evinced no interest in negotiations and joined in vehement condemnations of U.S. "imperialism" and "aggression."[52] During this gathering, MSZ officials drafted a message for the Soviets:

> Lewandowski reports from Saigon that the Italian Ambassador over there informed him in confidence about the intention of Fanfani to sound out Moscow and Washington regarding the possibility of a peaceful conclusion of the war in Vietnam. The Italian probes are to be regarding a solution which is similar to the French conception. We do not predict that this initiative will have much of a chance.[53]

Who Started Marigold?

What really happened? What caused one, perhaps both, of these diplomats to distort the truth and mislead, by omission and shading if not outright lies, his foreign minister (and, by extension, his nation's superpower patron) about the genesis of a sensitive initiative in the world's most explosive flashpoint? Who really got Marigold rolling? A precise and conclusive answer may be elusive at this remove, but fresh evidence makes possible a more informed assessment.

It is now clear that Lewandowski lacked any special authorization from Warsaw or Hanoi to relay "a very specific peace offer" via the Italians to Washington. But he *did* have Rapacki's fishing license to chase even a tiny opening for peace, enticing statements from Dong to use in describing Hanoi's stance (without disclosing the source), and—with reports of an imminent step-up in U.S. bombing—abundant incentive to spread the word that peace talks were possible, in a last-ditch effort to stem the momentum for escalation.

D'Orlandi, too, had both motive and opportunity to gamble for peace, and the professional self-confidence to act on his own. "A good ambassador must be able to judge the reaction to one of his decisions," he later told *Los Angeles Times* reporter Stuart H. Loory, after it was all over and he had returned to Rome. "Americans are not given that authority and are not trained that way. They are only messengers who cannot act without cabling their government. They are very much like the Russians. A Russian cannot sneeze without asking Moscow how or when."[54]

When Loory probed for details of Marigold, D'Orlandi proudly claimed to have inspired it. "D'Orlandi obviously wants to be known as more than a middleman who simply pours the drinks," the reporter noted. "He takes credit for initiating the whole idea."[55] But four decades after the events, D'Orlandi's former aide bristled at the thought that, in speaking to Cabot Lodge, D'Orlandi might have embellished Lewandowski's approach. "No, no," insisted Mario Sica, "D'Orlandi was not a man who would indulge in . . . wishful thinking. . . . [He] had a sort of cult for truth [and always] described the situation as it was."[56] But others besides Lewandowski (and Rusk) questioned whether sentiment sometimes skewed his work; Derksen cabled that D'Orlandi had a reputation as "an emotional reporter."[57] On hearing rumors of his role in secret diplomacy, the Dutchman skeptically observed that, "during the course of his service here, this colorful Italian diplomat has become known for the fervor and drama with which he has defended and contradicted every conceivable course of events and desirable outcome of the conflict to members of the government and diplomats. Within these two circles, he does not have the authority that would most likely be required of anyone who was entrusted with a special assignment."[58]

Yet, D'Orlandi—despite his fervid desire to "do something"—could not have advanced a new initiative to Rome without *some* basis from Lewandowski, and this the Pole provided. Whether freelancing, fulfilling Rapacki's secret instructions, or both, his exchanges with Lodge, Walston, and Derksen since returning from Hanoi in early June suggested his zeal to spark some move toward peace that might constrain U.S. escalation. D'Orlandi's diary and Sica's vivid memory of his ecstatic reaction after seeing the Pole also testify that Lewandowski was far more than a passive witness to an Italian overture.

In sum, D'Orlandi and Lewandowski found in each other an eager coconspirator, and the initiative can best be considered a joint one.[59] Merging their understandings of Washington's and Hanoi's bottom lines, and peering into the crystal ball, they envisioned "the least disagreeable shape that postwar Vietnam would have."[60] The Pole—who was at a early point in his career, lacked specific authorization to launch an initiative (and did not wish to emulate Maneli, who had been penalized for excessive zeal in promoting mediation), and was skeptical of its odds of success given imminent U.S. escalation—perhaps found it politic, in his cables to Warsaw, to minimize his own role.[61] Conversely, in his own messages, D'Orlandi—a veteran diplomat who likely was facing early retirement due to failing health, was desperate to staunch the bloodshed, and had been watching in despair as the Americans intensified what he saw as a doomed quest for victory—had no qualms about boldfacing the Pole's presentation and availability as a covert channel to Hanoi to prod Rome into action. As for the statements that D'Orlandi attributed to Lewandowski explicitly claiming a Polish imprimatur for the initiative, it is impossible to say whether the Italian invented these out of whole cloth or, more likely, informally probed his hypothetical readiness for deeper involvement, and using his own judgment after many hours of conversation with his colleague, simply posited Warsaw's role as a given, confident that it would play the necessary part if the initiative took off.

The First Three-Way Meeting

Later, D'Orlandi would airily term this early peacemaking venture "an intellectual exercise" akin to those he had assigned international affairs graduate students while teaching at a Bologna center affiliated with Johns Hopkins University. A diplomat's job, he explained, is "completing a deal that will be good for both sides. If, as a businessman, I complete a deal that is good for me but puts you out of business, that is no good because when you go out of business our deal will collapse. Even if you are incompetent, I must look out for your interests as well as my own. Diplomacy is a framework on which good deals are built."[62]

At the time, however, D'Orlandi viewed the matter as one of life-and-death urgency. When he saw Lodge on Friday, July 1, he rued the difficulty of communicating with Lewandowski. He had, he explained, visited him that day after failing to reach him on the phone, and had arranged for the Pole to call twice daily, at 10 a.m. and 4 p.m., and to come to the Italian's apartment on Monday night.[63] D'Orlandi was also "perplexed" by the Americans' inquiries about minor discrepancies between the versions of the message that Italy had relayed in Saigon and Washington. "Do they really want to further develop the attempt, or rather through a great deal of nitpicking to discourage it?" he wondered.[64]

Over the weekend, as more technical queries reached him via Rome and Lodge, D'Orlandi grew even more exasperated at what he saw as U.S. dithering. Running into Lewandowski "by chance," he avoided mentioning "the petty, stupid and interlocutory telegrams."[65] Restraining himself from a more intemperate response, he cabled: "It appears to me that U.S. Government still does not realize the reasonableness and exceptionality of the proposal. The greater delay in responding to the broad overall outlines and the greater the risk of leaks which would kill the initiative."[66]

Irritated at such obtuseness, D'Orlandi welcomed Lodge's assurance that Ball and Alexis Johnson found the Pole's comments "very interesting" and would not let them "lapse," and above all that he himself would do his best. "Thus, now there are already three of us who passionately fight for the initiative: Lewandowski, Cabot Lodge, and myself," the Italian jotted in his diary. "May God help us."[67]

Washington mulled for a full week over how to respond to the Italian-Polish gambit. The few informed officials included, besides LBJ and some cipher clerks, Rusk (in Japan for trade talks), Ball, McNamara, Rostow, Thompson, and Alexis Johnson—and, to State Department and White House annoyance, Arthur Goldberg. The United States' UN ambassador, a holdout dissenter to the POL raids, had heard a garbled version of the Saigon diplomacy from Thant, who, swearing him to secrecy, revealed that Fanfani had informed him.[68]

Ball wired Goldberg, who was in Geneva on his way to Rome for a preplanned visit, not to mention the topic unless the *Italians* raised it—in which case he was to shut up, listen, and report. Meanwhile, Ball assured the lonesome dove that the seventh floor of the State Department took the matter seriously. "While we are skeptical of authenticity and inclined to believe it probably contains a large element of wishful thinking at least by Pole if not by Italians, we are following up in a very discreet manner to test its authenticity. Fanfani's propensity for gossip as indicated by his passing this on to U Thant points up difficulty of trying to carry on business through Italians. If he has told U Thant, he presumably has told others in spite of his stringent strictures of secrecy to us."[69]

Convinced that Rome was deliberately pressuring them, and irked by Goldberg's out-of-channels awareness, the State Department's inner circle now officially and secretly, "to establish more precise security control," gave the Italian-Polish initiative the code name "Marigold," the latest bloom in a classified bouquet of peace initiatives.[70]

Warily, State opted to move forward. Ball, backed by Alexis Johnson, proposed to have Lodge seek more information from Lewandowski and, through him, the North Vietnamese, by asking a series of procedural questions—specifically, "when, where, and with what parties Hanoi contemplates that negotiations would take place," how it might react to a bombing halt, and whether it was "realistic to keep negotiations secret if the United States suspends bombing with the inevitable speculation this would entail."

The probing exercise, Ball noted in a July 5 memo to LBJ, would help gauge the probe's bona fides and have added benefits: "Keeping the Italians in the act for the time being and, if nothing comes of it, satisfying them that it was through no fault of our own"; engaging the enthusiastic Lodge; and retaining an alternative ("XYZ," via the DRV's Paris representative, Mai Van Bo) to complement the new channel. "If anything positive comes from Lodge's talk with the Pole, we will have to decide whether or not to cut out the Italians." Ball recognized but deferred the hard substantive issues implicit in the Lewandowski proposals if they actually panned out: "What role we will give the NLF and how we can make that palatable to the [South Vietnamese government], what performance and degree of verification on cessation of infiltration we will require to suspend bombing, how we can best maintain our freedom to resume bombing if negotiations are unsuccessful, et cetera."[71] From Japan, Rusk cabled his OK, while McNamara and Rostow—who told Ball he did not "want to close down this line" until a better one opened—flew to Texas to secure LBJ's consent.[72]

On July 7, Ball cabled Rusk in Tokyo that LBJ had approved the scenario, which was to be implemented through guidance to Lodge and talks—including a scolding about leaking—with the Italians in Washington. "We are keeping our fingers crossed as to whether anything whatever will come of this," he added, "but it seems to me that there just may be an outside chance that, carefully nurtured, it just might develop into something."[73]

As Foggy Bottom instructed Lodge, Ball finally summoned Fanfani's ambassador and special envoy (who was still cooling his heels) to tell them that Washington was "interested in the possibilities that can emerge" from the Polish proposal. Could D'Orlandi arrange "a very informal meeting" with Lewandowski and Lodge to explore "how to go from here"?[74] (Ball also took Fenoaltea aside and, without mentioning Goldberg, complained about Fanfani's blabbing to Thant; the emissary, expressing "full understanding of problem of attempting to do business in this manner and much skepticism as to whether there was any real substance in approach," apologetically noted Fanfani's desire to "do something" about Vietnam, which hardly commended him to the Americans.[75])

On July 8, Lodge obliquely informed D'Orlandi that instructions for an encounter with Lewandowski had at last arrived, and he agreed to come by to discuss arrangements. The Italian promptly phoned the Pole to "offer him a return match at chess" and dinner late Friday evening—and to set up the first of what would become Marigold's hallmark: tripartite gatherings at the Italian's apartment.

"We were bubbling over with happiness like two boys," D'Orlandi recorded, when Lodge arrived at 6 p.m. to discuss the first three-way session. Noting the regime's vast intelligence apparatus, the Italian worried that the gatherings would be quickly detected: "Cabot Lodge's every move is tracked by a Vietnamese police jeep, Lewandowski is certainly shadowed and his offices must be bedecked with bugs in the most unimaginable places, so much so that he is forced to keep the radio on at a rather high volume." Urged to take all possible steps to preserve secrecy, Lodge agreed, but he was not as fearful as D'Orlandi that Saigon's government would fall if it learned of secret talks with Hanoi.[76]

The Italian Embassy's location afforded Lodge cover, because it was adjacent to the headquarters of the Military Assistance Command, Vietnam (MACV). He called often at the "three-story French villa with a forest of antennae and sandbagged bunkers," around the corner from Marie Curie Lycée, the elite girls preparatory school.[77] With evident glee, he later recalled his conspiratorial precautions to avoid being discovered cavorting with a Communist colleague:

> There was enough parking space for the occupants of both buildings. I could thus park in the common parking lot and then disappear into either building without being seen from the street. I knew I was always followed wherever I went in Saigon—by the Saigon government and by the Viet Cong. If it was necessary for me to be alone, I would use a beat-up old Japanese "Toyota" car, which is very common in Vietnam (American cars being too conspicuous) and, while still in the garage, would get my large frame down onto the car's rear floor. A Marine guard, in civilian clothes, would drive through the gates of the Embassy—apparently alone. Once we had passed the police guard I could sit up and be on my way. Thus the Italian ambassador's apartment at 135 Duong Pasteur was a good choice.[78]

Lacking a pretext to visit MACV, which already was an obvious counterespionage target, Lewandowski faced a more daunting challenge to shake snoopers. When he visited the Italian (after Lodge had left) Friday evening—"beaming" at the prospect of a three-way meeting the next day (Washington has some questions for you, D'Orlandi told him)—they hatched a creative scheme to maintain secrecy. The next afternoon, the Pole would take a taxi to the Cercle Sportif Saigonnais for tennis; after a half hour on court, at the door to the locker room, he would bump into the Italian military attaché, also still in his tennis shirt, and his wife. Colonel Cataldo would invite him to their apartment for tea. Once there, Lewandowski would walk to D'Orlandi's office; meanwhile, Lodge, after a postlunch siesta with his friend, would descend to join them by a different staircase.[79]

Over the course of Marigold, helped by his military aide, Colonel Ryszard Iwanciów (whom he did not fill in on the secret talks' substance), the Pole would vary and refine ever more elaborate ruses to evade surveillance on his way to and from sessions at the Italian's apartment, which were usually held in the late afternoon or early evening. Smiling, he recalled telling his chauffeur, a South Vietnamese police major and presumed informer known as "Peter," that he desired an afternoon swim at the Cercle Sportif. As "Piotruś" waited in the parking lot, Lewandowski would take a short dip before ducking into a cabana to doff his bathing trunks and don a dark business suit, despite the heat. Then he would crouch through a small hole in the rear wall, sneak through shrubbery to slip out a specially cut gap in the fence enclosing the pool, and get into an unmarked ICC car driven by a Polish military counterintelligence officer. Checking to ensure he was not being tailed, the driver would steer Lewandowski to a preset rendezvous with Sica, who would drive him to the meeting, the Polish car trailing to check for surveillance. And afterward, Lewandowski would reverse the process, dining at the sports club and strolling casually outside to the bored chauffeur.[80]

Sica also remembered the hijinks involved in ferrying the Pole to and from the assignations with Lodge at D'Orlandi's. A favored method was to meet at one of the many entrances to the sprawling, bustling Saigon central market; Lewandowski, he chuckled, suddenly developed a "great passion for Oriental cloth" as a pretext to visit the sprawling, mazelike complex built by the French. After leaving his car and entering through the building's front, the Pole would wander the stalls and then walk out a rear exit, finding the Italian waiting on the north side facing the presidential palace a few blocks away. Once inside Sica's Prussian blue Fiat 850, he, like Lodge, hid under a blanket on the floor of the back seat, bent over awkwardly due to the sporty coupe's cramped configuration. Transporting his concealed cargo, Sica sometimes used a trick straight out of a James Bond flick: Nearing an intersection, he would slow down, then race across an instant before oncoming traffic—a chaotic mass of cyclos, bicycles, pedestrians, motorcycles, rolling phở stalls, the odd car, truck, animal, or military vehicle—clogged the crossway, leaving any pursuer fuming in frustration.[81]

Sica's driving, tradecraft, and savoir-faire so impressed the Pole that he presumed D'Orlandi's aide was the embassy's professional intelligence agent. ("I was trained by Roman traffic," Sica laughed when told of his suspicion, denying any espionage link.[82]) As part of his own efforts to preserve secrecy, Lewandowski once directed one of his officers—without explaining why—to case the area outside the hole in the fence of Le Club Sportif to see if one could escape unobserved. While Lewandowski "was sitting at a table having a coffee," the officer strolled the surrounding lanes, spotting nothing suspicious. Yet, when caught in a sudden downpour, he entered a seemingly abandoned building—only to find a hidden police post, with a vantage point overlooking the club's perimeter! Lewandowski, alarmed, told Sica, but the Italian did not bat an eye. "You know, I think they are watching their own people," he said. "Nobody ever follows me."[83]

Such precautions may seem melodramatic in retrospect, but they were dead serious at the time: Sica recalled that Lewandowski, always "formal and serious," often seemed "very tense both coming and going"—whether from concern about being detected, the substantive circumstances of the secret conversations, or both.[84]

Beyond convivially hosting the clandestine diplomatic ménage à trois, D'Orlandi also carefully informed Fanfani about how he perceived his own role: "In the absence of specific instructions, I believe my assignment can be summed up as making every effort to facilitate agreement while carefully avoiding arbitrator-like behavior."[85]

Shortly after 4 p.m. on July 9, a cloudy, muggy Saturday, the first three-way meeting convened in D'Orlandi's modestly furnished, air-conditioned personal quarters, with the lights on because he had drawn heavy curtains.[86] His apartment, reached by elevator and entered through a large foyer, featured functional, austere décor, accented by thick Oriental carpets dating to an earlier marriage to a Turkish painter and bookshelves crammed with leather-bound classics of diplomacy, many French and monogrammed "GD'O" in gold.[87] The host, after welcoming his guests to this and later meetings, served refreshments (not always scotch, as D'Orlandi claimed, but usually coffee, tea, water, or juice), and the diplomats sat at a rectangular wooden table—the Pole and American facing each other, the Italian at a corner.[88] The trio spoke fluent English and presented a formidable ensemble, as sketched by journalists who met all three: D'Orlandi, "a soft-speaking, suave man of delicate style for whom the niceties of protocol were tools to be used with all the skill a great surgeon uses in performing an operation"; Lodge, "a tall, silver-haired, distinguished New England patrician"; and Lewandowski, "conservatively dressed, self-assured," a "quiet—even shy—cultured, undoctrinaire Pole," who, "with his slim and short figure, with his light beard and oversized thick glasses, . . . more closely resembled a college undergraduate than a carefully trained diplomat."[89]

After pleasantries, Lodge, saying that he spoke on LBJ's direct instructions, assured the Pole that the United States, too, wanted an "overall political settlement" in Vietnam. Reading slowly from the telegram to let the Pole and Italian take verbatim notes, he relayed Washington's three questions: When, where, and with what parties did Hanoi contemplate that negotiations would occur? How would it react to a bombing halt? Was it "realistic" to keep talks secret if the bombings were suspended?

Lewandowski vowed to use his "possibilities" to get quick answers, then began what Lodge termed a "systematic interrogation." The Pole's notes (though not Italian or U.S. cables) indicate that the American explicitly said the United States would accept the NLF as a party in negotiations, though not the sole one—Saigon, now in the dark, also had to participate. Lodge confirmed that Washington was ready for talks with Hanoi, and D'Orlandi interjected, when he hesitated, that it would surely be ready to negotiate on the basis implied in the latest proposals. Lewandowski cautioned that new contacts were needed to see if Hanoi still held the ideas it did before "the escalation of the bombing."

"This is a very, very delicate matter," he said, stressing the need for secrecy and that "special trips" (by Ronning, Sainteny, et al.) were useless (Lodge fully agreed). Lodge "absolutely" promised discretion and, while understanding that consulting Hanoi would take time, requested swift replies. "The matter is serious and urgent," Lewandowski quoted the American as saying, as "every day hundreds of young people are lost on both sides." (Lodge implied that *the Pole* said these words, that it was a "matter of 'utmost urgency'" to obtain quick answers.) After the daily cost in lives was mentioned, Lodge cabled, "there was then a pause with the three of us just sitting. And Lewandowski said with some feeling, 'I'm an optimist.'" (Of course, in his own reporting, the Pole studiously avoided any hint of optimism about the initiative.)

The conversation, at first stilted and even awkward, relaxed as the diplomats, their business done, reminisced. The Pole recalled UN visits overlapping Lodge's tenure as ambassador and lamented that the body was "not as valuable a place as it had been then." Lodge remembered nostalgically the days when he and Moscow's man could agree on a matter and it would automatically be endorsed unanimously. He apologized for having to meet "conspiratorially," given Saigon's sensitivity, but they all agreed on the need to preserve secrecy. The gathering broke up on a note of cordial, restrained optimism.

These exchanges convinced Lodge that the Pole "feels our word is good," and shared his desire for secrecy. He told Washington that he deliberately "did not ask [Lewandowski] when he thought he would have a reply because I thought it would seem overeager, and I believe that this whole démarche of his is due to the fact that we have 'played it cool.'" Instead, leaving first, on his way out he asked D'Orlandi to probe further. "I'm going to get that out of him now," his friend pledged.

D'Orlandi sounded upbeat in a cable to Rome that night: "My impression on the meeting is excellent, as are both the impressions of Cabot Lodge and Polish ambassador seen separately afterward. [Lewandowski] told me he believes he can provide answers within seven or ten days."[90] Privately, he was more fervent. "I am happy and full of hope," he recorded. "May God help us. Blessed are those who work for peace, because they will be the children of God. The meeting between the two was uncomfortable in the beginning, but cordial by the end."[91] That evening, after D'Orlandi had bade farewell to a hopeful Lodge, the Pole returned for a late supper and two games of chess and seemed guardedly optimistic. "Lord, I thank you," the Italian wrote in his diary.[92]

Lewandowski sent Warsaw a straightforward account, stressed secrecy and "precise accuracy," and requested guidance. In line with earlier cables, he attributed the unusual gathering to the "Italian initiative," which still (he confirmed from talking to D'Orlandi) envisioned a solution along French lines (neutralization).[93] Privately, the Pole left the meeting somewhat encouraged. The U.S. message struck him as "reasonable," because it omitted the standard formula of trading halts in bombing and infiltration, and included an "absolutely new" willingness to deal with the NLF. And, under the influence of his last visit, he believed that Hanoi was "more flexible" than its public statements suggested.[94]

On July 10, Lodge covered his tracks with the Saigon regime, just in case it discovered the secret meeting. On instructions, while seeing Ky on other matters, he vaguely, nonchalantly mentioned ("by the way") that he was checking "some rumors out of Hanoi indicating a desire to find a way out." The marshal, with a smile and nod, said "that he was sure that North Vietnam could not stand much more of what they were getting," but did not press for details.[95]

A Waiting Game—in Saigon, Hanoi, Washington, and Warsaw

At this point the U.S. chronology went blank for two weeks, until Lewandowski informed D'Orlandi on July 23 that he had a response to deliver and a second tripartite meeting was set for the next day. Polish sources now illuminate what happened in the interim on the Communist side.

Lewandowski was ready to carry the U.S. message to Hanoi himself, but Warsaw preferred otherwise, and the young diplomat was in no position to question its decision. On July 11, Poland's Foreign Ministry sent a cable containing the text of Lodge's message (as reported by Lewandowski) to its Hanoi ambassador, Jerzy Siedlecki, with instructions to convey it to the DRV Foreign Ministry, and to the minister himself if possible. The text said that the July 9 meeting had occurred at Lodge's initiative and had included, along with Washington's three questions, assurances that it sought "an overall political solution" and was ready for the NLF to join talks, plus a vow not to reveal the channel even if it did not achieve its goal. It also included Lodge's reported statement that the matter was "serious and urgent" because "every day hundreds of young people are dying on both sides."

Michałowski wanted to make sure that Hanoi understood that Warsaw was *communicating,* not *endorsing,* the U.S. overture. "Tell your interlocutor that we deemed [it] our duty to relay the above information," he instructed Siedlecki. "Do not comment on it. Inform about [their] reaction."[96]

At 6 p.m. Hanoi time on July 12, Siedlecki, stressing that Poland was fulfilling its "obligation," related Lodge's communication to Hoang Van Tien. Surprising the envoy, the DRV deputy foreign minister asked him how Lewandowski had reacted to Lodge's presentation. Admitting that he did not know, Siedlecki merely reiterated that Poland's view of the war was well known. Tien (who had sat in on Michałowski's talk with Trinh in January) praised Gomułka's angry attack on U.S. policy to Harriman in December, thanked Siedlecki for the information, and promised to pass it to the leadership. While avoiding any comment himself on the proposition, Tien "assumed a position of someone who was quite self-confident," Siedlecki thought.[97]

Then—for Siedlecki in Hanoi, and for Lewandowski and his cohort in Saigon —there was little to do but wait. At his day job, the Polish commissioner (at Ha Van Lau's urging) requested an emergency ICC meeting to deliver what Moore termed a "vitriolic and at times obscure" diatribe against the Hanoi and Haiphong bombings and demanding that the ICC condemn "those responsible for [this] escalation of aggression." The resolution, which was eventually watered down and deflected by the Indian and Canadian over the Pole's "half-hearted" objections, burnished Lewandowski's credentials in Hanoi as a hard-liner, even if it had no impact whatsoever on U.S. actions or international opinion.[98]

Washington, in the meantime, was left in the dark. Reading Lodge's report of his July 9 meeting with Lewandowski, Rostow, too, had felt guardedly optimistic—and had conceded grudgingly to Ball that the Communist diplomat's seeming concern about secrecy gave him a "certain credibility, at least he pretended he was operating professionally."[99] Lodge, determined to "play it cool," refrained from pressing D'Orlandi for news (let alone Lewandowski), but could not help but feel teased after seeing the Italian on July 13 at a diplomatic function. Earlier that Wednesday, D'Orlandi reported, he had received a phone call from Lewandowski. After they had exchanged routine inquiries about each other's health, the Pole had stated cryptically: "I am very, very much pleased by something that has happened and I look forward to seeing you soon to tell you about it." Probably, the Italian speculated, that meant a reply from Hanoi had been received and was being "phrased" for presentation, perhaps at another three-way meeting that weekend.[100]

That night, D'Orlandi hosted the Lodges for a late supper. After trading views of the latest Saigon cabinet shuffle—the American pleased, the Italian dubious given Ky's unpopularity ("While I think that I persuaded Emily, it is clear that I was not able to get through to Cabot")—conversation drifted to their clandestine diplomatic venture and absent Communist colleague:

> The latter part of the evening is set aside for speaking about Lewandowski, whose praises I [D'Orlandi] sing because I have deep confidence in him. To my great pleasure, Cabot Lodge agrees with this and describes himself as also admiring the ability and professional seriousness of our "partner." With respect to the basis of our initiative, Cabot Lodge has shown himself to be personally optimistic, but, I believe in order to avoid bad luck, maintains that possible developments go very slowly. By now, all our farewells end with "absolute secrecy." I go to bed happy.[101]

But then—nothing. Late Friday afternoon in Washington, July 15, Rusk (back from Asia) phoned Bundy to ask "if there was another date set for Lodge's next little party." Not to his knowledge, Bundy replied.[102]

Despite lingering doubts about these "devious channels," as Rusk termed them, the chance that an unexpected breakthrough might be near inspired hasty catch-up planning. Taking advantage of a previously scheduled trip to Saigon, Washington asked Harvard professor Henry Kissinger, a consultant, to explore confidentially with Lodge scenarios for the "contingency of finding ourselves with little notice involved in negotiation." U.S. aides especially worried about how to handle the volatile Ky regime, given its antipathy to concessions and other knotty issues linked to a move toward talks ("cease-fires and cessation of hostilities, standfasts, inspection by ICC or other body, etc.").[103] On July 19, as Lodge awaited news from Lewandowski, he and Kissinger reviewed negotiating aims and options for talks with both Hanoi and the NLF, including the roles of third parties and how to broach the topic delicately with Saigon to avoid "disarray in the [South Vietnamese government] and disunity as regards policies which we and they should support in common."[104]

At the White House, the eternally optimistic Rostow fed LBJ's hopes that Hanoi might soon throw in the towel. On July 16, interpreting no news as good news, he sent Johnson "the kind of memo a cautious aide who wanted to maintain his reputation would not write, because I could be proved wrong in a matter of hours." Assume, he urged, that Hanoi had opted before the POL strikes to enter talks, but now hesitated to do so "in a context where they have been weakened;

we have been relatively strengthened; but worst of all, we look to the world more confident than in the recent past and [are] operating from a position of increased strength." Looking on the bright side, as he usually did, Rostow suspected that recent hard-line noises from the Soviet Bloc (e.g., threats to send volunteers to Vietnam), and stern DRV statements announcing more mobilizations and threatening to try prisoners of war (POWs), aimed "to strengthen Hanoi's position in a negotiation" rather than "to strengthen Hanoi to face a further protracted period of conflict."

"Which it is we shall soon know," he wrote.[105]

That same Saturday evening, U.S.-Polish secret contacts about Vietnam briefly switched venues, to Warsaw, bringing together two figures who had dealt with each other during the futile "pause" diplomacy six months earlier and would tangle again, over Marigold, five months later.

Recent events had discouraged but not wholly soured John Gronouski on using his Polish contacts to promote peace in Vietnam. On June 30, the day after the POL raids began, a thousand protesters carrying banners ("Hands Off Hanoi") and shouting anti-American slogans had besieged the U.S. Embassy. A call for help brought a smattering of police to guard the building. But, as a state documentary unit filmed and secret police watched from their cars, a vanguard of demonstrators surged through the front gate, broke windows and lights, and scattered garbage. The ambassador decried the "well-organized demonstration which obviously had the encouragement of certain elements of Polish authority," though he thanked the police who did show and declared that "the destructive actions of this organized mob are not characteristic of the Polish people."[106]

Gronouski found a silver lining even in this nasty incident. Perhaps, he speculated, the Polish authorities had "considered it desirable to stage [a] public show [of] their support of North Vietnam." By orchestrating the rowdy protest, Warsaw could bolster its hard-line credentials in Hanoi and "offset" its more moderate diplomacy. "We find it significant that first protest demonstrations at our embassies in Eastern Europe were staged at Bucharest and Warsaw," he cabled. "Both Poland and Romania have intervened directly in attempts to lead North Vietnam to peace talks."[107]

Though oblivious to the furtive Saigon discussions, Gronouski soon had a chance to test his hypothesis of potential Polish helpfulness on Vietnam. After Hanoi called captured U.S. pilots "war criminals," Washington looked around the world seeking aid to intercede with the North Vietnamese to warn against trying POWs.[108] On July 16—even as Gomułka, in a speech opening a fertilizer plant, hinted at sending Polish volunteers to Vietnam[109]—Gronouski passed on Washington's request to Michałowski, arguing that the threatened trials, besides being illegal, would inflame American opinion and impede efforts toward a settlement. Michałowski initially demurred. This would be an unhelpful violation of the Geneva Convention, he agreed, but both sides were committing atrocities and the desire for vengeance was "bad but understandable."

Then, after hearing Gronouski's pleas, the man who had carried Washington's ideas to Hanoi six months before softened and confided another reason for his reluctance to be its messenger now. Poland was "currently actively working to find [a] peaceful solution"—specifically, Michałowski told Gronouski on a "strictly confidential" basis, its ICC ambassador was "carrying out" an unspecified request by Lodge—and "interceding on this issue now might lessen [Poland's] ability to play effective role as mediator in future." Still, he vowed, Warsaw would give the POW request "serious consideration."[110]

The next day, Rapacki sent a cable on the matter to Siedlecki that sheds light on how Warsaw prodded Hanoi on delicate issues, using pragmatic rather than moral or ideological arguments.[111] He instructed him to raise the matter with the DRV authorities but, if they confirmed their intention to try the pilots, to claim that he lacked instructions—thereby distancing Warsaw if Hanoi reacted angrily to what Siedlecki would then say was his personal opinion. He should first express solidarity by noting that the "Americans do not have any moral right to rely on international law, which they have been stamping on without any shame," and pledge that, just as Washington had rejected the ICC's right to interfere in current military operations, Warsaw would likewise block any U.S. attempt to get the commission to intercede on behalf of the captured fliers.[112]

Conversely, Siedlecki should urge the North Vietnamese to carefully consider the "political consequences of punishing the prisoners of war"—which would include a "serious and negative response" in the "not so small circles" in world opinion that have "opposed the American aggression," particularly after the latest bombings. The Communists would understand the matter differently, but trying prisoners would shock liberal and pacifist elements (e.g., those dovish U.S. senators who had publicly pleaded with Hanoi not to punish or execute the captives[113]) "and one could expect protests addressed against us from among many of those who are protesting against the American government today." Moreover, he should warn, LBJ and his hawkish inner circle would exploit such a step to "justify and strengthen its aggressive line."

In sum, Poland shared Hanoi's ire at the "murderous air raids" but felt it wiser to "strengthen and broaden" the international anti-U.S. front and leave war crimes accounting to another day. If pressed, Siedlecki could confirm that he spoke on instructions but say that these were logical conclusions that many friends of the DRV could draw.

On Monday evening, Michałowski took Gronouski aside at a British Embassy party and said "he wanted me to know, though he couldn't tell me officially," that the Poles were "being responsive to the request I made on Saturday." They acted despite concern about impairing Warsaw's diplomatic effectiveness "because they recognize seriousness of POW matter." Having done the Americans a favor, Michałowski offered some advice: Washington had no hope to get negotiations going unless it stopped bombing, though he lacked "any clue" as to Hanoi's likely reaction. Still, he insisted, if LBJ had stretched out his earlier bombing "pause" for two or three more weeks, North Vietnam would have responded favorably; and thus now it was up to Washington, even if it could not "flatly" accept the Four Points, to come up with something creative, perhaps accepting them "in principle, or as objectives, or in some other matter which might help to get negotiations question off dead center."[114]

A few days later, Sainteny relayed to Charles E. ("Chip") Bohlen, the U.S. ambassador in Paris, Pham Van Dong's secret assurance that "the American prisoners were being well treated and would continue to be well treated."[115] Since Sainteny had visited Hanoi in early July, before Gronouski's plea for help, Washington felt no special gratitude to Warsaw for influencing North Vietnam to drop its plans to try POWs (and, to Gronouski's irritation, it omitted Poland from an internal list of countries that had responded to Washington's request for help[116]); nor did Michałowski's arguments about the bombing impress U.S. aides who still resented Rapacki's machinations to extend the thirty-seven-day pause in January.

Michałowski succeeded in at least one respect: persuading Gronouski of Poland's genuine desire to seek peace in Vietnam. The U.S. ambassador in Warsaw had been excluded from Marigold cable traffic, but he would later become a key participant in the secret initiative at a vital moment, when Poland's motives would be the focus of intense controversy within the Johnson administration. Despite the harsh anti-American line in the Communist press and another unruly rally outside the embassy—Rusk ordered a "very gruff" protest[117]—Gronouski cabled on July 19 that the Poles "privately accept as sincere President's willingness to negotiate and are doing what they can to bring it about."

"Michałowski," he concluded, "seems to be groping to find means for Hanoi to enter negotiations without losing face."[118]

Hanoi's Response, and the Second Three-Way Talk

Hanoi, however, was not willing to take that step. At 10 a.m. on Monday, July 18, Tien gave Siedlecki the official DRV reply to the probing via Lewandowski. It was not the answer for which the diplomats in Saigon were hoping. He blasted Lodge's message as a deceitful "'peace' maneuver to cloak further intensification" of military actions and force Hanoi to negotiate on U.S. terms. Because they did not indicate any fundamental change in Washington's "aggressive" policy, the deputy foreign minister proposed that Poland reply to Lodge, in its own name, with a withering rebuff. Reading a prepared text, he scripted the remarks Lewandowski should make to Lodge:

> General assessment: the proposition submitted by L[odge], in the course of the intensification of the aggression in the South and the intensification of the bombings in the North, is characterized as a stratagem which aims at forcing the DRV to negotiations under the US conditions. The V[ietnamese] will not lay down their weapons so long as the U.S. carries out its aggressive policy.

The government of the PPR [Polish People's Republic] believes that the propositions of L, without stopping the bombings of the DRV, do not bring in any new content.

The U.S. government has no right to bomb the DRV, an independent and a sovereign country, and that is why it has no right to pose any conditions when it comes to stopping [the bombings].

The government of the PPR supports entirely the position of the DRV expressed in the Four Points and the position of the NLF in the Five.[119]

If the United States indeed desires a peaceful solution, it must adopt the Four Points and to prove it with its actions; [that is,] to stop the bombings and other military operations against the DRV. Only then can they count on a political solution.

Given the above, the government of the PPR cannot accept the proposition of relaying the views presented by L[odge] to the DRV.

After dictating this unyielding message, however, Tien added an oral postscript advising Poland that its representative should respond with a similar hard line to any comparable future proposals—but asking to be kept informed about the forthcoming discussion with Lodge "and other possible [talks] initiated by the U.S."[120]

Stung by the harsh response, Michałowski cabled Siedlecki a mollifying message for Tien affirming Poland's backing for the DRV but explaining that it felt obliged to relay all proposals so Hanoi could decide for itself and make a full assessment of the situation. To reassure the comrades about Lewandowski, Siedlecki should state that "during all conversations" Polish officials condemned U.S. aggression and stressed the need to stop bombing North Vietnam and accept the Four Points and Five Points. "However, we never thought that we could either reject or accept any propositions. In our opinion, only, and exclusively, the DRV and the NLF, which are carrying out the fight and spilling blood in Vietnam, have the right to such a decision in these matters."[121]

At the same time, Warsaw directed Lewandowski to arrange another meeting to pass Hanoi's hard-line message to Lodge. If he asked Lewandowski about the basis for the statement and whether his earlier questions had been relayed to Hanoi—as he surely would—the Pole should merely say that "we have reason to believe that," because the North Vietnamese had specifically requested that "the reply should come from us."[122]

Reading over the deciphered telegram containing Hanoi's answer, Lewandowski felt keen disappointment—tempered somewhat only when he reached its very end. Hanoi's expression of interest in receiving reports on the upcoming talk with Lodge as well as any further contacts with the Americans, combined with the lack of any evident intent to denounce the overture publicly, implicitly meant that the secret channel could be preserved for possible future use—leaving the door ever so slightly ajar. "This is very bad, . . . *but!*" he said after reading the cable decades later, recalling his reaction. At least it was not a complete, final rupture, and he could "keep eyes and ears open."[123]

Any reply promised to relieve his Italian friend, who throbbed with anticipation. "I do not feel well," he had jotted in his diary on Tuesday, July 19. "My physical discomfort is accompanied by the pounding worry caused by the failed arrival of the response from Hanoi." The Pole came to his door the next day, but he brought not the awaited reply, only worries that the latest U.S. raids near Hanoi and Haiphong were causing inordinate civilian casualties and spooking chances for progress. He also had nothing to report when the two dined on Thursday, leaving D'Orlandi even edgier, because he had received a summons from Fanfani to return to Rome by the end of the month for consultations.[124]

On Saturday morning, D'Orlandi again prodded the Pole. By a "strange coincidence," Lewandowski answered, the reply had just arrived and was being decoded, so he would be ready for another three-way session. D'Orlandi promptly phoned Lodge and, restraining his excitement, "in formal language" set a meeting for the next evening. Though mum on the message's contents, the Pole hinted that "quite lengthy discussions" might loom—a prospect that might influence the Italian's thoughts about retiring for health reasons. "In a friendly and very personal capacity," he added, "I believe that it would be useful if you found a way to stay here another six months."[125]

As for Lodge, after titillating Washington with his July 14 report of D'Orlandi's cryptic phone call from Lewandowski, he had heard nothing more—so had sent no further news. Finally, on Friday evening, July 22, Foggy Bottom had sent a polite, if impatient, one-sentence "MARIGOLD-NODIS" cable advising that State "would appreciate a report on developments since [his earlier telegram]."[126]

Lodge's response echoed his imperious treatment of Diem in 1963, when, after reaching Saigon, he had played hard to get to lure the South Vietnamese leader into making the first move to request a meeting. "There have been no developments at all since my [cable no.] 958," he wrote. "I have not thought it wise to make any inquiries. I believe that what got Lewandowski going in the first place was fear of the U.S. I did not want Lewandowski to think we were overly eager and thus give the impression to Hanoi via Warsaw that we were weakening." It made no sense to bug D'Orlandi, because he would get in touch as soon as he had news. Better to let Hanoi take the initiative "and for the U.S. to be 'playing it cool.' . . . the chances of getting peace are much greater if we maintain our maximum influence and appear strong. Should we give the impression of over eagerness, Hanoi would conclude we were weak. This would lessen the chance of peace."[127]

After dictating but before dispatching those words, Lodge received a call from D'Orlandi that promised to reward his cold-blooded patience. Burying the lead, he tacked on a sentence noting that the Italian had just told him that the Pole was ready to meet, and a rendezvous had been set for Sunday afternoon at 4:30 p.m.

Reaching Washington at midday Saturday, Lodge's cable aroused keen anticipation. Rostow drew LBJ's attention to the "punch line" at the end, revealing that a meeting had been set for Sunday (4:30 a.m. in Washington). The national security adviser also approvingly underlined Lodge's "rather wise observation on 'playing it cool.'"[128]

But his notion that the enemy would view the slightest sign of eagerness for peace as an indication of weakness was held by the North Vietnamese along with the Americans, and had ominous implications for Marigold.

D'Orlandi had gone to bed Saturday night nervously imagining the next day's events (and wondering if they would scuttle his plans to fly to Rome in a few days), but the next morning an inauspicious omen sharpened his fears: Hanoi had rebuffed efforts to strengthen the ICC in Cambodia, an action he found "strangely counterproductive" (though its military rationale, to protect the Ho Chi Minh Trail, seems self-evident). He worried it might presage a hard-line response in the secret channel that evening.[129]

It did. At 6 p.m. on Sunday afternoon, July 24, the three diplomats convened for the second time at D'Orlandi's residence.[130] Arriving for tea an hour beforehand, Lodge told him that while secrecy was imperative, the Italian must attend every meeting as a witness. Then Sica delivered Lewandowski, before retiring downstairs to await a long night of encrypting. Compared with their last meeting, the mood quickly grew strained ("a bad atmosphere," D'Orlandi noted). Lodge voiced concern over a recent spike in fighting, and then Lewandowski lowered the boom. In a "very matter of fact tone," he read aloud the stern statement that Warsaw had sent him. Demanding that Washington stop bombing the DRV and accept the Four Points and Five Points before talks could begin, it even claimed falsely (as instructed) that Poland had not even delivered the U.S. message.

By the time he finished, a deep gloom had descended. "All three of us are devastated," D'Orlandi wrote in his diary. "Pitiful silence. It is the collapse of our hope."

"D'Orlandi and Cabot Lodge were stupefied," Sica recalled, at this "pure and simple" recitation of Hanoi's unyielding public stance after two weeks of suspense.[131]

Breaking the funereal hush, Lodge observed that the message answered none of the three questions he had posed on July 9. The Pole silently nodded. When the American asked if Hanoi was really demanding a total halt to U.S. military actions while offering no return step, Lewandowski offered "my interpretation"—not explicitly commenting on its source—that the bombing was Hanoi's "most sensitive and important" concern. Noting the obvious, Lodge said the statement seemed to be a step backward: Washington was "being asked to give up a great deal" for nothing. Lewandowski replied sheepishly that someone has to take the first step; Lodge retorted that a simultaneous "give-and-take" procedure rather than "one-sided concessions" would be easier.

The three men agreed fully on only one thing: continued secrecy, so the channel might remain available.[132] Lodge bemoaned the constant police shadow, but the Pole surprised him by confidently declaring that he could attend future trysts unobserved.

D'Orlandi, until then reticent, said: "This is definitely a step backward. I had thought that the first meeting was rather encouraging. Both the opening and the American questions were encouraging. I felt something might come out and, as a matter of fact, I still feel this as a hunch. Accordingly, I hope the stiffness of your reply is due to prevailing circumstances, and that this channel may be kept open and resumed as soon as possible. We were expecting a reply. Now we have a statement. I understood what led to this statement. It is the circumstances of the moment."

Lodge asked what "circumstances" he meant, expecting a reference to the POL bombings, but to his surprise the Italian, backed by the Pole, cited the peace rumors and leaks as harming the climate for talks. Lodge then asked Lewandowski whether Hanoi had drafted the statement he had read, provoking a deflection rather than a flat denial.

After the Pole and American profusely thanked their crestfallen host for his hospitality ("nice but certainly no salve for my bitter disappointment"), the half-hour conversation ended. It was "cordial" and unpolemical, but depressing: Lodge was in "low spirits," Lewandowski reported; D'Orlandi thought Lewandowski "embarrassed and sad." As the meeting broke up, the Italian expressed "sorrowful regret" but also hope that the dialogue might resume later.

"I'm sorry we can't have a glass of wine this time in celebration of a real result," said Lewandowski with a smile as Lodge rose to leave.

Trying to pick up the pieces, D'Orlandi spoke with both men separately. Staying behind, Lewandowski paced back and forth and, "much distressed," worried that Washington was committing a "serious psychological error" by putting extra military pressure on Hanoi, which would only play into the hands of North Vietnamese and Chinese hawks and further erode chances for an "honorable compromise." He planned to go to the DRV capital in August to probe possibilities, but was not optimistic. Wishing him luck, D'Orlandi promised to get in touch after returning from Rome.

At nine o'clock, Lodge reappeared for a late dinner, a postmortem, and mutual bucking-up: "We try to give each other some hope," D'Orlandi recorded. He told Cabot he would leave for Rome immediately, because "there was now no reason to stay [in Saigon] if this was the kind of line that Lewandowski was going to expound." Outwardly more sanguine, Lodge seemed "not overly disappointed" and pleased that the Pole had agreed to preserve the secret channel for possible future use. Encouraged, D'Orlandi agreed that the abortive exchange perhaps was a mere preliminary skirmish and said he would prod Fanfani to "put the seized up motor back into gear." By the time Lodge left, around eleven, he felt a bit cheered up, writing in his diary that he "refuse[d] to consider the matter closed."[133]

Lodge's negative Marigold cables reached the White House Sunday morning as LBJ was attending church. Rostow left them for him to find when he returned, his prayers unanswered. Then he called Rusk, who had not yet seen them. Next time, the national security aide said, it might be "wiser" to try a "direct approach" to Hanoi instead of third parties. As an apostle of intensified bombing, rather than reflecting on whether the POL strikes had backfired, he speculated that leaks had dimmed Hanoi's interest in talking.[134]

What Happened?

But no one really knew for sure *what* had happened, and as the curtain fell on Marigold's first act, the tiny audience following the drama was somewhat non-plussed. Was it much ado about nothing? The tantalizing "North Vietnamese" proposals that D'Orlandi so breathlessly reported receiving from Lewandowski in late June had vanished, mirage-like, into the Saigon summer as abruptly and mysteriously as they had appeared. Why had Hanoi rebuffed Lodge's July 9 message so sharply after earlier seemingly hinting at a readiness for talks? Firm answers must await the opening of the relevant Hanoi archives, but new evidence lets us go much further than formerly possible.

Significantly, Lewandowski *did* have a basis for his claim of a relatively moderate DRV position: his June 2 talk with Pham Van Dong. But his assessment, which so enthralled D'Orlandi on June 27, was several weeks old. Rather than having just returned from Hanoi, as Washington (and later historians) believed, the Pole still relied on impressions he had gleaned at the start of the month. Subsequent events, including Ronning's visit and the pervasive rumors of an imminent major bombing escalation, had hardly made Hanoi more amenable to negotiations.

Newly opened Soviet Bloc records also finger another culprit for hardening the DRV's stand, even before Marigold began in late June: China. Of course, Beijing had long advocated achieving a glorious military victory over the Americans (as Michałowski had learned firsthand during his stopover in January). But Mao's—and hence China's—posture was about to grow even shriller. On June 2, even as Lewandowski and Dong spoke in Hanoi, *Renmin ribao* (*People's Daily*) hailed "big-character" posters on walls and dormitories at Peking University attacking university administrators, fueling outcries against "bourgeois" bureaucrats and "intellectuals"; the episode signaled Mao's behind-the-scenes support for an ultraleftist upheaval that would soon be known as the "Great Proletarian Cultural Revolution."[135] A week later, Ho secretly visited China and met in Hangzhou with Mao and Zhou Enlai, as well as Liu Shaoqi and Deng Xiaoping.[136]

During these talks—more than a month before Mao took his famous July 16 swim in the Yangtze River—the Vietnamese revolutionary heard the Chinese Communist Party chair explain his purges of four alleged "revisionists" ("all my friends," he cynically labeled them) that presaged the cataclysm.[137] Ho also got a full blast of his belligerence toward the war. According to Soviet Bloc envoys in Hanoi, Mao "rejected a political solution and stated that this problem can only be solved by the crossing of the 17th Parallel." In what Moscow saw as a blatant bid to ensnare the superpowers in a direct clash, he not only exhorted Ho to invade South Vietnam but also allegedly said the Soviets should use missiles to attack the

U.S. Seventh Fleet and military bases.[138] He reportedly extracted a pledge from Ho—after threatening that China would otherwise withdraw its "construction troops" from North Vietnam—not to enter into direct talks with Washington without first consulting Beijing; and in return, had lavished new aid and support, both economic and military.[139]

Hard Vietnamese or Chinese data on Ho's secret visit are sparse, but the Soviet Bloc accounts seem plausible. Moscow, by this point, had years of experience and a vested interest in emphasizing Beijing's irresponsible extremism, so it had every motive to embellish if not invent such reports. Yet, Mao *did* advocate an extremist course, fixed on the pursuit of military victory in Vietnam, deriding negotiations as an imperialist trick, championing world revolution, and denouncing the Soviets as "revisionists" and American lackeys. Chinese pressure on Ho to rebuff peace overtures would have been in character, even to the extent of threatening to remove support troops, although perhaps more subtly than the overt blackmail that Soviet Bloc diplomats depicted.[140]

Confirmation of Sino-Vietnamese strains at precisely this juncture comes from an unlikely source: the Albanian archives. In late June, soon after Ho's secret trip to China, Zhou Enlai visited Tirana. Albania had split with Moscow five years before at the time of the Sino-Soviet rift, essentially defected from the Warsaw Pact, and was now virtually the last country in the world to stand with Beijing. To its reclusive dictator, Enver Hoxha, the Chinese premier complained that the Vietnamese Communists, though "in reality" against U.S.-promoted "peace talks," were afraid to "raise their voice" openly against their "chief commander," the "revisionist" Soviets, who favored negotiations. Ruing a "decomposition" in Hanoi, Zhou reported that pro-Kremlin revisionists, who were "even more cunning than Khrushchev," had infiltrated the DRV leadership, producing a struggle between those who backed fighting until military victory over the U.S. imperialists (rapidly or gradually) and those who favored talks to end the war quickly. (Le Duan in particular had "changed course," he lamented—"until now he had been a leftist.")

Thanks to Soviet revisionism, Zhou acknowledged, Vietnamese "liberalization" had "quickened and that is exerting a great negative influence on the relations between Vietnam and China. It has caused the cooling of these relations despite the fact that comrade Ho Chi Minh does not accept this." Zhou hoped that the Vietnamese would seek final victory regardless of the risk or cost, but conceded that under Moscow's pressure—it was "scaring" Hanoi by predicting "that when the solemn meeting to celebrate the victory is called, Vietnam will not exist anymore, because all the Vietnamese will have perished," replaced by Chinese!—they might indeed succumb and enter negotiations. Moreover, "If there is some kind of compromise reached as a result of a betrayal by the [Soviet Union], the revisionists might denounce us saying that we did not help as much as we should have the war of the Vietnamese people." He insisted that "the war must go on," but admitted that Beijing had to prepare for these grim alternatives.[141]

These Sino-Vietnamese exchanges further suggest that China swayed Hanoi against peace contacts with Washington. Ho would have carried the hard-line advice he heard in Hangzhou back to his comrades in mid-June, around the time of Ronning's futile visit, and helped render Dong's comments to Lewandowski anachronistic. And reports of Mao's dip in the Yangtze and radicalization of the Cultural Revolution would have arrived just as the DRV gave Poland its negative reply on July 18 to Lodge's overture.

Of course, regardless of Chinese pressure, if North Vietnam's leaders had really believed that their nation's interests dictated talks with the Americans, they would have defied Beijing and entered into them (as indeed they did in April 1968). But in the summer of 1966, whatever willingness might have existed among DRV leaders to flirt with direct dealings with the Americans must have faded rapidly once they finally launched the POL raids in late June, including on Hanoi and Haiphong. Already deeply skeptical of U.S. sincerity (a view Ronning's visit did nothing to dispel), and presuming that only more battlefield struggles could determine the real balance of power, they could only have interpreted the new bombing campaign as confirming that Washington had no serious interest in talking on terms that Hanoi could consider, and instead counted on coercing it to the table through escalation. "The current stage of Johnson's 'Peace Campaign' is to aim at showing that the U.S. is forced to conduct the war since the DRV is not responding to any peace initiatives," a DRV vice premier told socialist diplomats in Hanoi on June 29 a half hour before the bombs began falling near the city and a few hours before D'Orlandi excitedly relayed Lewandowski's reputed proposals to Lodge in Saigon.[142]

To the extent that Dong's titillating comments to the Pole *ever* were anything more than forthcoming rhetoric to impress a fraternal visitor who urged a political track, then, their validity had shrunk drastically by late June, and the POL strikes then rendered them completely null and void—at least in their implication of a readiness for immediate, serious talks—by the time Lodge delivered the U.S. message for Hanoi at the first three-way session in Saigon on July 9, it appears. In Hanoi in early July, Sainteny found the DRV leaders "furious and determined, . . . they would not be treated like little boys getting a spanking. They were prepared to fight in the jungles and to see their cities razed."[143] After a trip to Hanoi in late August, Lewandowski also asserted that North Vietnam had stiffened its attitude on negotiations or concessions once the POL attacks began. "If Hanoi and Haiphong had not been bombed at the beginning of the first attempt [to initiate U.S.-DRV contacts] it perhaps would have been fruitful," the Pole told D'Orlandi.[144] Such post hoc arguments by Hanoi and its supporters were of course self-serving, because they laid full blame on Washington, but that does not necessarily make them false.[145]

✳ ✳ ✳

Dashing U.S. hopes that intensified bombing would coerce them to the table, the North Vietnamese felt compelled to prove they would not negotiate out of weakness, and could match any escalation, whatever the cost. A few dissented, but most U.S. military leaders and civilians like Rostow, Rusk, and Lodge had enthused that the POL campaign might tip Hanoi toward capitulation, and Washington's cautious willingness to explore the Marigold contacts reflected no diminution in determination to press forward with military pressure—quite the opposite, as they resolutely maintained faith that escalation and productive diplomacy were not only a compatible but an essential combination.

Of course, the Lodge-D'Orlandi June 29 conversation occurred too late for any reconsideration of the POL raids that day on Hanoi and Haiphong. But it hardly mattered: LBJ had already lost patience with delays to give diplomacy a chance, and the Italian-Polish approach did not look viable enough to make him hold back. Even after deciding to test Fanfani's probe, Washington felt no inclination to curb the strikes. On July 8—a day after Washington had OK'd Lodge's first "very informal meeting" with Lewandowski—McNamara told military chiefs in Honolulu that LBJ wanted them to focus on the North Vietnamese POL system's "complete 'strangulation,'" and he approved a schedule of intense attacks without sortie limits to do exactly that—Rolling Thunder–51, the latest tranche of missions in the sustained bombing campaign that Washington had launched in March 1965.[146]

As of late July, LBJ and his associates, despite intense international and growing domestic criticism, still clung to the hope that the POL campaign might prove decisive—disrupting operations to aid the Southern insurgency if Hanoi remained stubborn, or even convincing it to desist and enter peace talks. They could take comfort in the fact that all sides, even the Communists, had kept Marigold secret, protecting it for future use.

The Poles, too, were relieved that the channel was not blown—and that, despite their apprehensions, they remained in Hanoi's good graces. After the curt rejection of the U.S. message, Warsaw had to wonder whether it was now among those the DRV classed as Washington's "accomplices"—until, at a reception, Dong pointedly approached a Polish officer to relay "warm-hearted greetings" to Lewandowski in Saigon and "great praise and thanks for the hard and conscientious work of our delegation, which, as he stated, is on the front lines of the struggle with the American aggressor."

"If the Ambassador wants to come visit," he added, "he will always be welcome in Hanoi and warmly received by him."[147] Thrown a lifeline to continue his probing, Lewandowski had no intention of passing up the premier's renewed invitation.

3

Intermezzo
August to October 1966—A "Mosaic of Indiscretions and Rumors"

The fact is that either you and I are going to have these conversations or else nothing is going to happen at all anywhere concerning Vietnam.

> —*Giovanni D'Orlandi to Janusz Lewandowski, early September 1966*

We find Lewandowski's thinking as conveyed by D'Orlandi very interesting but not always lucid.

> —*Dean Rusk to Henry Cabot Lodge, September 12, 1966*

Our channel may disappear.

> —*D'Orlandi to Lodge, late September 1966*

You must not leave; there will be much to do after the fifteenth of November.

> —*Janusz Lewandowski to D'Orlandi, early October 1966*

Soon after Marigold's first act fizzled, an unforeseen event threatened to permanently shutter the whole production. On July 24, 1966, when Lewandowski read the stern statement closing the door on the initiative for the time being, at least there was universal accord on the need to preserve secrecy; even Hanoi, in its vitriolic statements, refrained from publicizing the Saigon channel. But in early August, an Italian magazine divulged precise details of Fanfani's clandestine diplomacy and the three-way conversations among D'Orlandi, Lodge, and Lewandowski.

Marigold Springs a Leak: "Buy the *Borghese* Immediately!"

In late July, D'Orlandi flew to Rome from Saigon for medical treatment, and within days, he and Fanfani were plotting how, despite the initial disappointment, they could revive the secret Vietnam peace collaboration with Poland, which the foreign minister had just visited. But on the morning of August 3, a Farnesina aide interrupted their scheming with an urgent imperative—"buy the *Borghese* immediately!"—and a doorman was dispatched to purchase a copy of the right-wing weekly.[1]

As the magazine hit newsstands across Italy, there was already widespread speculation that, during their recent talks in Warsaw, Fanfani and Rapacki had discussed secret Vietnam diplomacy. Joining the fray, the latest *Il Borghese* featured a scathing anti-Fanfani commentary. The foreign minister, wrote the editor, Mario Tedeschi, had connived to regain his office mainly to promote his contacts in the Communist world and had naively persisted despite his latest venture's failure. A few weeks earlier, Tedeschi disclosed, Fanfani had secretly sent Farace to Washington to seek a halt to the bombing of North Vietnam "while waiting for several proposals advanced in Saigon by our Ambassador D'Orlandi to come to fruition." Fanfani's Christian Democratic opponents, Tedeschi added, "make no effort to conceal their sarcasm, when saying that Americans decided to bomb Hanoi at the very time when Farace was there, just to show lack of esteem with which Fanfani's emissaries are received in Washington." Fanfani, the article accurately stated, had directed D'Orlandi to arrange a Lodge-Lewandowski meeting, but it proved "useless" because Hanoi still insisted on the Four Points, which had already been rejected by the United States. Even so, Fanfani had hailed his "old friend" Rapacki as a "man of peace," lending credibility to this Communist figure and the "fairy tale" of Hanoi's willingness to negotiate.[2]

Reading this exposé, D'Orlandi and his Farnesina colleagues were aghast—"completely lost" at what they immediately knew was an exceptionally grave matter. The *Borghese* bombshell, they grasped, must have reflected a leak from top-secret telegrams, and it could destroy the Saigon channel. "It is inconceivable that because of petty personal opposition, one can attempt to torpedo a peace attempt," the appalled ambassador wrote. "It is unheard of, and what is worse is that in Italy one can count on one's fingers the number of people who are aware of what happened in Saigon. One of them has talked."[3]

But, amazingly, nothing happened—at least in public. Later, D'Orlandi's aide, Mario Sica, would write, amusingly but not entirely accurately:

> Thanks to God, or perhaps thanks to the "dog days of summer," the *Borghese* article passed by completely unnoticed. It did not give rise to parliamentary questions or inquiries. There were no complaints from the North Vietnamese, the South Vietnamese, the Poles, nor from the Americans. It was not reported on by the news agencies, nor by the American media (despite being constantly unre-

strained on all the details of the Vietnamese issue). It is not even mentioned in the Pentagon [Papers] documents. It was, in short, as if it had never been written.[4]

Actually, the article *was* noticed, and it caused—as Lodge put it after talking with D'Orlandi—"considerable consternation." As soon as the article appeared, the U.S. Embassy in Rome sent Washington an extended summary and excerpt, highlighting the section alluding to the "secret" diplomacy. "*Il Borghese* is virulent rightist critic of center-left government," the embassy noted. "It is regarded as [a] 'scandal-sheet' not always remarkable for its accuracy and certainly less than objective." Yet, the embassy conceded, the magazine had been the first to disclose the details of the La Pira affair—running the incendiary interviews with the activist that had led to Fanfani's (temporary) downfall.[5]

Alarmed that the most sensitive diplomatic data had been compromised, Fanfani ordered an urgent internal inquest. Mulling possible culprits, he and D'Orlandi agreed that the leak had stemmed from a deliberate plot to sabotage the peace effort and speculated on its source: Farnesina, an intelligence service (perhaps in cahoots with the CIA), the Defense Ministry?[6] Rather than uncovering a convoluted political scheme, however, the inquiry fingered a young cipher clerk who apparently wanted to prove his importance (and that of Italy's diplomacy) to a journalist friend. On consulting the defense minister, Fanfani also discovered, to his chagrin, that the military, which had decrypted the coded radio telegrams, secretly kept its own files of classified embassy cable traffic. In the ensuing shakeup, Fanfani not only fired the clerk and cipher service chief but also ordered modern coding equipment be sent to the Saigon Embassy so only the Farnesina could read future telegrams. To guard against further embarrassment, he also decreed that the new cipher section chief must personally decode all subsequent D'Orlandi Marigold messages and immediately hand-deliver them to him or, in his absence, his chef de cabinet.[7] Rome, meanwhile, assured Washington that to prevent further leaks, D'Orlandi would send Marigold reports solely and only orally ("no papers") to Fanfani, who would tell "no one else."[8]

Fanfani also instructed D'Orlandi to see Warsaw's ambassador in Rome, Adam Willmann, who insisted that the Saigon talks "must go on," because the diplomats there were well informed, were unlikely to attract unwonted notice compared with "special" emissaries, and were able to exploit Lewandowski's unique ability to travel back and forth to Hanoi.[9]

So the show "must go on." But for the rest of the summer and into the fall, as the fighting dragged on, Marigold's dramatis personae puttered about the stage in a kind of extended intermezzo, seeking an opening to resume their diplomacy, studiously maintaining secrecy, and occasionally exchanging a few lines of dialogue.

"An Italian-Style Romantic Proposition"

Just as *Il Borghese* had insinuated, Marigold's initial setback hardly deterred Fanfani from continuing his active secret Vietnam diplomacy or collaborating with

Poland. During his July 25–28, 1966, visit to Warsaw, he told Rapacki that, through the Saigon channel, Italy could mediate with Washington just as the Poles worked with Hanoi, not only to stop the violence but also to outline an ultimate accord.[10] Ominously, however, Rapacki judged that not only were prospects for negotiations bleak, with Hanoi "unable to move without Chinese consent," but U.S. escalation, combined with Beijing's rising militancy, also hazarded a wider war.[11] As D'Orlandi told a colleague in Saigon a few weeks later,

> Minister Fanfani, during his recent visit to Warsaw, found that the Polish authorities were highly concerned about the threats of [expanded] war in Vietnam. According to [D'Orlandi], the Poles informed [Fanfani] that, in their opinion, if America were to cause the situation to escalate any further, Chinese intervention would be inevitable, and the Soviet Union would feel compelled to follow their example, which would bring about intervention by other "socialist" countries. According to [D'Orlandi], Fanfani was supposedly under the impression that the concern expressed by the Poles was genuine and not propaganda.
>
> *"Comme rien ne lui est plus cher que l'idée d'une médiation"* [Because nothing is more valuable to him than the idea of a mediation], according to D'Orlandi, Fanfani had called him to Rome to ask whether the ambassador had thoughts about the possibility of warding off the developments feared by the Poles. "As you will understand," D'Orlandi answered in the negative. As [D'Orlandi] told [Fanfani] when he summarized his recent report once again for him, the Americans were ignoring all the political aspects of the situation and moving ever closer to a purely military objective, which would cause much larger political problems than it would solve. And the most frightening aspect is, as he explained to his minister, that the Americans were pursuing this course in good faith.[12]

A verbatim record of the Fanfani-Rapacki conversations in Warsaw, with aides present, found in the Farnesina archives in Rome, illuminates the only personal encounter during Marigold between these two figures so crucial to our story.[13] Rapacki, who was cool toward Fanfani's peacemaking ardor, noted that given Poland's limited ability to influence events in Vietnam, he must for the first time express himself in "hopeless" terms. He assailed U.S. conduct, especially the "truly risky" bombing, and warned that the West did not appreciate the peril of a Chinese reaction. "For us the problem arises whether the world, and above all the Western world, will not be able—and I tell you frankly—to put pressure on the United States for them to stop or pull back. Whether one likes it or not, we will have to convince the United States that there must be a limit to the 'escalation' [English in the original]. If we do not, we head down a dangerous path."

As with other Western counterparts, Rapacki also seeded doubts about U.S. conduct by recounting Polish diplomacy during the thirty-seven-day bombing pause—and did not mind stretching the truth. Alluding to Michałowski's mission, he claimed that Hanoi's reaction to Washington's insistence on a concrete reply to the halt in air raids "was not at all negative," and spoke vaguely of positive "signals" it had ignored, including one, he added coyly, whose details he "cannot reveal and which was not noted by the press." In the last few "dramatic days" before LBJ resumed the bombing, Warsaw had relayed "a piece of news to Washington, which was defined as encouraging but unfortunately insufficient." Poland therefore knew this tactic of merging peace efforts with military acts that undercut them, even if the Americans preferred not to speak of it—"not even with their friends."

Fanfani nevertheless insisted that they could take "constructive action" together:

> Knowing that Poland, with a high sense of humanitarianism, did not fail to deal with the problems in this area [Vietnam] causes my pessimism to diminish. You refer to the allies of America; I refer to the friends and allies of Poland. Poland and Italy are not such large countries as to be able to impose a decision. If they were, they would find themselves in an even more delicate situation. Italy and Poland are disinterested enough to be able to carry out a useful action. We could refrain from taking into consideration the problem, but we are forbidden from doing so by our solidarity, the scale of the risks and the repercussions of the dangers. Solidarity, risks, and compassion for the suffering of Asiatic peoples ensure that we must continue to carry out our action even if we were to be convinced that it could be limited in success. But I am convinced that it can be useful. Every one of us knows what he can do through his contacts with his friends. It is necessary to try to make the points of view and the respective requirements [of the two sides] closer in order that something truly constructive can be undertaken.

Poland, Fanfani claimed, could "exercise a special role" in Vietnam diplomacy due to its ICC membership, and he pleaded for "common action" to show an expectant public that the "peace flame . . . has not been extinguished."

Outside the plenary sessions, the two spoke one to one about the Saigon channel (in Italian, which the Pole had learned as a laborer in his guest's homeland).[14] On July 26, after laying wreaths at a war memorial, they agreed in principle to "continue to probe" despite the recent disappointment, but they diverged on how best to do so: Rapacki put the onus on Washington to "signal" by stopping the bombing, while Fanfani stressed Washington's willingness to do so "if Hanoi also gives a sign." After dinner the next evening, Fanfani noted in his diary, Rapacki proposed continuing the dialogue by having Michałowski secretly meet D'Orlandi "at the Karlsbad [Karlovy Vary] Baths to see if it is possible to find a way out toward peace in Vietnam." The Italian recorded that he promised to see if Rome would approve, and he gained Prime Minister Aldo Moro's assent as soon as he returned home.[15] Conversely (and more plausibly), Polish sources say not Rapacki but *Fanfani* pushed for more Polish-Italian cooperation by urging the covert assignation between D'Orlandi and Michałowski (and possibly Rapacki as well) in the Czech spa town, which offered both a cover story and health facilities for the Italian.

Certainly, D'Orlandi's account of a three-hour talk on July 30 with Fanfani, just back from Warsaw, attests to the minister's zeal to revive the quest for a breakthrough. "He exudes energy from every pore and, he too does not at all consider the Saigon attempt to be finished," the ambassador wrote after hearing the scheme for him to "take the waters" in Karlsbad—and, more important, to see Rapacki and/or Michałowski and "lay out my opinions about the attempt, possible errors committed and opportunities for resumption, etc." Despite jet lag, D'Orlandi found his zest contagious.

> It is strange how after a meeting with Fanfani I feel full of energy and enthusiasm. I have the impression that we "pump" each other up; my optimism comes out of these meetings strengthened, and I have a great desire to get to work immediately for the success of the enterprise. Peter the Hermit must have had the same communicative enthusiasm as Fanfani. In this case, the crusade is for peace.[16]

D'Orlandi secured a Czech visa, but shortly before his planned departure—on August 3, the same dispiriting Wednesday as the *Borghese* piece appeared—word came that due to a "sudden indisposition," Michałowski could not attend.[17] "We declined, using my illness as an excuse," he later cabled Lewandowski.[18]

The Italians should have suspected that the ailment was diplomatic, but they refused to give up. Taking the demurral at face value, Fanfani had D'Orlandi see Willmann on August 4 to suggest deferring the rendezvous a few days. Proposing what Michałowski termed "an Italian-style romantic proposition," D'Orlandi said he would fly to Prague on August 8 tourist class on Alitalia (AZ 394), landing at 1:25 p.m. and holding "a green-colored diplomatic passport with the Italian weekly *Espresso.*" Michałowski would pick him up, then drive them in a Polish vehicle directly to Karlovy Vary, where the Italian would consult doctors, staying at a hotel chosen by the Poles—avoiding contact with Rome's embassy in the capital. He implored Willmann that the Poles not give up their Vietnam peace efforts, sensing, to his relief, he was "preaching to the choir." The talk also left Poland's envoy with a positive first impression of his colleague: "Serious and well-informed. A restrained optimist."[19]

However, aware of Hanoi's angry and unbending position, especially given the ongoing U.S. raids on Haiphong, the Poles saw "no basis" for special consultations with the Italians and declined the meeting.[20] Empty-handed, D'Orlandi returned to Saigon.

Putting the best face on the situation when he saw Lodge on August 12, D'Orlandi blamed the *Borghese* leak, not the Poles, for the failure to stage the talk in Czechoslovakia: Fearing exposure, Fanfani had rescinded his instruction to arrange it, the ambassador fibbed. Citing Willmann, he claimed that Warsaw still wanted him, Lodge, and Lewandowski to keep talking. As for the leak—which to his and Fanfani's surprise evidently originated with "extremely pro-American persons"—to D'Orlandi's relief, it "attracted no attention anywhere in the West or in the East," dismissed as "obvious journalistic speculation." Fanfani, he assured

Lodge, had taken stringent measures to prevent a recurrence, ordering him "in the future to send no telegrams whatever and no letters. If he felt the absolute need to communicate with Rome, he was to get on a plane and come back to Rome himself."[21] (The admonition presumably only applied until the embassy installed more modern encoding equipment.)

To "pick up the pieces" in Marigold, D'Orlandi suggested that they return to the "procedural questions" Washington had raised on July 9 and get Lewandowski to try anew to get answers from Hanoi. Coincidentally, the Pole was about to venture north for an ICC meeting that would afford another chance to prod the DRV leaders. Before flying from Tan Son Nhut on Monday, August 15, Lewandowski agreed to dine with D'Orlandi on his return to review the results.[22]

A few days later, in his absence, a cable from Michałowski arrived at Poland's ICC mission in Saigon describing Fanfani's desires to promote joint mediation in Vietnam and futile attempts to arrange a rendezvous between him and D'Orlandi. Rapacki's aide delivered Warsaw's disdainful bottom line and consequent instructions:

> We do not treat seriously these Italian ambitions. However, you can maintain contact to gain maximum information while representing the fundamental position, which has already been relayed to you. Maintain secrecy since one can take into account the Italian leaks.[23]

A Frustrating Trip to Hanoi

With their decrepit Stratoliner (only a matter of time before a wing fell off, Moore feared) already confined to a narrow corridor for the bumpy nighttime journey (which precluded maneuvering around bad weather), those aboard the August 16 ICC flight from Vientiane to Gia Lam got an extra jolt to their jangled nerves when they saw, outside the window, a surface-to-air missile being launched. It missed, but the incident (which left the French pilots "brave but understandably hysterical") prompted more complaints and (unheeded) demands to U.S. and DRV authorities to cease aerial activity and antiaircraft fire when ICC planes overflew North Vietnam.[24]

Formally, Lewandowski traveled to Hanoi for the stalemated ICC's 745th session, but his more serious aim was to touch base with the DRV leaders. He anticipated flying back to Saigon in time to sup with D'Orlandi the following Sunday (August 21), but Ha Van Lau invited him to remain after the predictably unproductive ICC meeting. He stayed an extra four days, meeting with North Vietnamese officials and foreign diplomats and making inspection trips to Haiphong and other targets of recent U.S. raids.[25]

However, the timing of his latest Hanoi sojourn was less than optimal. Hardline views favoring armed struggle until total victory were ascendant—the campaign against facilities for petroleum, oil, and lubricants had failed to cripple Communist operations or induce any inclination to negotiate, let alone surrender—and in China, more belligerent than ever, the Cultural Revolution had spawned paroxysms of violence as the Red Guards ran amok.

Also, to Lewandowski's great disappointment, his "two friends," Dong and Giap—"the only two in the whole place who talk sense and understand the real situation in the South," as he told D'Orlandi[26]—were out of town on secret trips to the USSR and China; he delayed his departure in hopes of seeing them, but to no avail. (To explain his remaining in Hanoi after the ICC wrapped up its business, the Pole complained that he felt ill. "So far as I know, this is genuine," the British consul judged warily.[27])

The visit did, however, offer an opportunity for what would be his only serious encounter with Ho Chi Minh—more a monologue from than a conversation with the legendary revolutionary, who was now seventy-six, he later told his Dutch colleague in Saigon. "According to Lewandowski, he did not speak during the meeting," Derksen cabled, "thin and old, but spry, Ho lectured him in passable English about the ins and outs of the Vietnamese struggle for independence over cigarettes and coffee." The Pole "made a point of" noting that Ho "emphasized" the complicated Sino-Vietnamese relationship; the countries were "traditional enemies, . . . seeking reconciliation under the current circumstances," but in 1946 "Vietnam had requested temporary assistance from the French, also an enemy, in order to prevent the annexation of the North by nationalist China."[28]

Lewandowski also sat through several hard-line "monologues" from Nguyen Duy Trinh. In contrast to his warm, lively exchanges with Dong and Giap, he found it depressing to endure tedious "rubbish" and "blah blah" from the "notoriously pro-Chinese" foreign minister, "a short, stocky man with a very stubborn face." The "cold" hard-liner stared intently into his eyes while sternly delivering tirades, as if scrutinizing for the slightest tic that might betray doubt. "He was a kind of a man who believed there is imperialism and imperialism is very bad, Americans are imperialists, and how can you make any kind of deal with imperialists? . . . They can only be dealt with by force, you have to fight them. . . . He was a man who could not understand how talks with imperialists could make any good, certainly a Chinese approach at the time. . . . 'If you really give them a good beating, you will [defeat] them.'"[29]

Unlike Dong, who lamented the war's human cost, Trinh spoke clinically about the destruction and suffering victory entailed. That U.S. forces had doubled to almost 400,000, for the dry season "great counteroffensive," merely meant that "their casualties will be proportionally bigger." As for the expected ramping up of air raids, Trinh used a chilling analogy: "[The Americans] will intensify the bombings of the North. They can destroy Hanoi, Haiphong, and other cities. The example of Warsaw shows that after the victory—the destruction will be rebuilt quickly. Also, the birthrate is quicker after each war. They also observed it in Vietnam after the victory over the French."[30]

Generally, the Pole did not bother arguing, keeping a poker face for hours despite inward boredom—hoping to amass credibility as a trustworthy comrade so DRV leaders might confide at least "a little bit." Occasionally, however, he felt compelled to rebut Trinh's digs. "Sometimes I was irritated [with] Nguyen Duy Trinh because . . . I felt he put me in a position that I had [become] an advocate of American imperialists, so I used to say, 'Listen, Nguyen Duy Trinh, I am just relating to you what our conversations in Saigon produced, it is up to you to make your judgment, but please don't [blame me.]'"[31]

The North Vietnamese never explicitly criticized Lewandowski for relaying Lodge's message, but put him on notice that Hanoi expected Poland to resist U.S. blandishments to ensnare it in further nefarious peace bids—especially through the ICC. While preparing broader military action aimed at decisive victories during the coming winter, Lau warned, "the Americans are getting ready for a new and wide peace offensive. They want to exploit all possible sources (the UN, the press, the neutral nations, the Commission) for this offensive. It will be strong, but in our opinion it should be unmasked since it serves the camouflaging of the American aggression."[32]

Under rigid instructions, the Pole opposed measures that might hamper the North Vietnamese, who implored him in particular to block any controls on operations in the Demilitarized Zone (DMZ) separating North and South Vietnam along the 17th Parallel. When the ICC met on August 19, Rahman proposed a letter (already informally endorsed by Moore) to both Hanoi and Saigon expressing concern over the deteriorating situation in the DMZ and requesting cooperation with inquiries. In a "violent exchange," Lewandowski, irked by the Indian's refusal to defer the matter despite his protest that he needed to consult with Warsaw, refused even to abstain in the vote, which he charged was illegal. That night, he conspicuously skipped a reception that he was formally cohosting with Rahman, leaving guests buzzing, the Indian "livid," and Moore unsure whether his absence stemmed from illness, "irrational pique following the meeting," or something more serious, like an imminent Polish exit from the ICC.[33] (Lewandowski recalls a more mundane reason: He really was sick—"miserable," "trying to survive," too weak even to lift the receiver.[34])

Lewandowski vented his exasperation in Hanoi to a Soviet diplomat. Besides expressing "uneasiness about the future existence of the Commission"—Canada and India might liquidate the ICC due to its ineffectiveness—he rued the North's unshakable military optimism. From his own, more pessimistic perspective, he sensed that the National Liberation Front confronted "great difficulties"—facing strengthened U.S. forces, who were able to anticipate Communist operations from "informants or aerial reconnaissance"—and that both the NLF and PAVN forces in the south were deserting and being taken prisoner in increasing numbers. "In Lewandowski's opinion, the leadership of the DRV may end up in the future in even more unfavorable conditions with regard to the resolution of the Vietnam question," P. I. Privalov cabled. "By delaying negotiations, it counts on choosing the most favorable moment for itself. However, the situation is getting more and more complicated, and it cannot be ruled out that the Vietnamese leadership will have to agree to negotiations on even more difficult conditions than what it was offered before."[35]

If Lewandowski had heard the secret discussions that Dong and Giap conducted with Kremlin brass in Moscow and at a Black Sea resort in Crimea, he might have felt even more pessimistic.[36] To Brezhnev and Kosygin, the DRV leaders seemed intent on "fighting against the Americans until the final victory." Only after "the new Dien Bien Phu arrives," Dong repeated, could they be chased from Vietnam, rejecting arguments that a "huge difference" existed between fading colonial France and present-day America. Discounting the latest U.S. escalation, the Vietnamese expressed sunny (and to Moscow deluded) optimism about the economic situation in the North and military prospects in the South, and concentrated on extracting maximal Soviet promises for military and economic aid. Dong conceded political shortcomings in countering Washington's peace rhetoric, but he deflected suggestions that Hanoi more seriously consider negotiations.

The DRV leaders' claims of interest in peace struck their listeners as half-hearted. "Symbolically—according to the Soviet comrades, for the very first time—Pham Van Dong was talking about the necessity to solve the problems flexibly," a Hungarian diplomat reported. "But from the answers given for the questions of the Soviet comrades, it was clear that the statement had no real practical background to it, and it remained a mystery what Dong meant by flexibility." (In the summary provided Polish comrades, Dong explained that "flexible tactics" meant a willingness to engage in contacts with foreign representatives— French, Canadian, even U.S.—but *not* any substantive softening or deviation from the Four Points.) Moscow found similarly unpersuasive Hanoi's rigid insistence on the Four Points as a basis for talks. Sounding not unlike Dean Rusk, a Soviet official briefing a Hungarian comrade called this demand "without any doubt an ultimatum." If the Americans accepted the Four Points and withdrew from Vietnam, he added sarcastically, "what would the Vietnamese talk about with them then?"[37]

The Soviets "frankly" told Dong that Hanoi had failed to fully or effectively utilize the "flexible and soft tactics" of which he spoke, and they urged more dramatic actions so the "banner of peaceful negotiations, which Johnson uses for the purpose of cheating [the people], is snatched from his hands." They suggested that it consider such steps as reinterpreting the Four Points and Five Points to let talks start, proposing to reconvene Geneva (although China would surely shun the idea), or "entrusting some third country to carry out a *sondazh*" (probe). The Vietnamese listened politely but only promised to report these views to the VWP Politburo and study them carefully.[38] (Outside the plenary sessions, a Soviet deputy foreign minister suggested that Hanoi at least "fog up" the Four Points for the sake of world opinion; his listener agreed that this would be wise.[39])

Sensing a more "stringent" DRV attitude, the Soviets were particularly disturbed that Dong, whom they (like Lewandowski) regarded as a relative moderate, "frequently (more frequently than in previous conversations) was using the

Chinese arguments." When the Soviets noted a recent reported Beijing statement denying the validity or relevance of Geneva or the 17th Parallel, he refused to make any criticism, remarking ambiguously that the Four Points were a "concentrated expression" of Geneva and the parallel was only a "temporary line of demarcation" that Washington should not be allowed to convert into an international border. While Dong repeatedly emphasized the closeness between the People's Republic of China and the DRV, likening it in classic Chinese fashion to that between "the mouth and the teeth," Moscow saw a different anatomical configuration: "Symbolically stated, the head is in Beijing, and Vietnam is only one of its limbs."[40]

Among other complaints, the Soviets groused that the Vietnamese had supplied misleading and false information (e.g., grossly underestimating damage and casualties, and inflating enemy losses); misused aid (e.g., SAM batteries); blocked access to captured U.S. equipment (e.g., downed aircraft) that might furnish useful intelligence; and fished for unneeded technical assistance, weapons, and materials (e.g., aluminum, used in constructing aircraft[41]), evidently to pass to China. Arousing special suspicion, a request to send thousands of Vietnamese to the USSR for technical training included specialists in cybernetics and "some areas of nuclear physics related to the production of nuclear weapons."[42]

The Soviets drew the line at helping Mao circumvent their cutoff of nuclear support but felt they had no choice but to satisfy most of the demands, lest the Chinese and Hanoi hard-liners accuse them of insufficient ideological solidarity and betraying a class ally. When reminded of the obstacles that Beijing had put in the way of delivering supplies by rail, the DRV visitors minimized the interference and suggested that Moscow send the supplies by ship—prompting the sarcastic reply that this would be practical once "South Vietnamese ports could be secured for the unloading."[43]

In fact, North Vietnam's ties with China were less than idyllic.[44] As Lewandowski lingered in Hanoi—where he found that the Cultural Revolution had generated "doleful astonishment" among Vietnamese leaders[45]—Dong went to Beijing, where his talks included some sharp moments. At one point, Zhou Enlai demanded that he explain why Hanoi newspapers had printed articles celebrating the heroic resistance of Vietnamese fighters to invaders from the north—in battles centuries earlier! Dong insisted that it was mere "research" on a "historical theme," but Zhou persisted: "But you are studying this issue while you are struggling against the US. What is the implication?"[46]

Still, there was no open Sino-Vietnamese discord, and Hanoi remained fully committed, it seemed, to Beijing's preferred path: military victory, not negotiations with "imperialist aggressors." Somewhat apologetically, a VWP official told a Soviet diplomat why the present "very difficult situation" was "unfavorable" for talks, even though the Vietnamese possessed the "tactical skills and sufficient political flexibility" for them. "What does it mean for us to join talks?" he asked. "This would be to lose everything. . . . If we agree to negotiations, this will cause a negative reaction in China, which will stop providing aid to us and, in addition, will cut the schedule of aid supplies from the Soviet Union and other socialist countries. In this case, our situation will become even more complicated because we would have lost aid and the USA . . . will have free hands."[47]

After eight frustrating days, Lewandowski left Hanoi at 4 a.m. on Thursday, August 25. Also on the ICC plane was the new DRV envoy to Cambodia, Nguyen Thuong, who was on his way to present his credentials to Prince Sihanouk and to greet Charles de Gaulle (who was to arrive shortly for a much-anticipated visit), and who would be a useful contact for the Pole in setting up meetings with NLF figures. Like Thuong, after disembarking that afternoon, Lewandowski never re-boarded the Stratoliner for the final leg to Saigon; he stayed in Phnom Penh for four days of consultations and sightseeing. Though rumored to be on the "wel-coming committee" for de Gaulle, he left shortly before the Frenchman landed for talks with Sihanouk and a speech promoting Southeast Asian neutralization and calling on the United States to remove its troops from Vietnam unilaterally on a fixed schedule—hardly propositions likely to entice Washington.[48]

Lewandowski returned to Saigon at the end of August "profoundly discour-aged." Hanoi, he told Derksen, exhibited "absolutely no willingness to negotiate" and seemed set on military struggle. He gave D'Orlandi a "particularly open and frank" account. After trying vainly to reason with the DRV leaders, who seemed swayed by the NLF's overoptimism, the Pole had "conclu[ded] that for the mo-ment there is nothing to be done in the direction of a possible negotiation," D'Orlandi cabled Fanfani.[49] Perhaps on Lewandowski's next trip north, then planned for late October, he could try again.

The Gronouski Initiative

In Warsaw, Gronouski—only dimly aware, if at all, of Marigold's initial failure or other machinations in Saigon—valiantly pursued his one-man campaign to enlist the Poles to bring Hanoi to the table. LBJ's ambassador later recalled that he and the Poles (especially Michałowski) "never ceased discussing Vietnam and try-ing—I was always trying to get from Hanoi some indication of some response. . . . I felt this was the [most] important thing I was doing in Poland—trying to find some key to solving the Vietnam War."[50] His summer 1966 initiative, previously absent from the record, could be written off as fruitless (and even somewhat quixotic). Yet the episode illuminates the passion and persistence of this ambas-sador who would play a central role in Marigold's climax, and the mindsets at this juncture of both the Johnson administration and Polish government.

The immediate catalyst for Gronouski's renewed activism was a conversation with Michałowski on July 25—hardly an auspicious moment, shortly after War-saw had learned of Hanoi's brusque rebuff to Lodge.[51] The State Department had sent its envoy on something of a fool's errand, to give the Poles a copy of a South Vietnamese complaint to the ICC about DRV military activities in the DMZ.

Leery of offending Hanoi, Michałowski wanted nothing to do with it. Refusing to accept this communication from a government Poland did not recognize, he pointed out that Saigon was perfectly capable of transmitting it directly to the commission (through which Warsaw would be informed). Following instructions, Gronouski insisted on expressing concern about the alleged North Vietnamese misdeeds. Michałowski promised to convey it to his government. "Just don't press me to take this note." The American relented, to their mutual relief.

On a more positive note, Michałowski then assured Gronouski that, after checking "seriously" in Hanoi in response to his request, Poland was now "reasonably sure" that the DRV would not try or punish U.S. prisoners of war. He advised Washington to "let sleeping dogs lie" rather than pushing its "worldwide high pressure campaign" to the point of provoking Hanoi to act rather than seem to give in. Thanking him, Gronouski steered the conversation in a more personal direction. While on vacation in Copenhagen, even riding a roller coaster in Tivoli Gardens with his children, he had pondered how to promote peace in Vietnam. Rather than swap speeches or polarize positions, he "seriously and genuinely" preferred "by nature" to seek a practical alternative. He invited ideas from Michałowski, "informal or otherwise," that might aid the search for peace.

Michałowski did have a suggestion, one he had raised informally before: Because Hanoi endlessly insisted on its Four Points, why could Washington not accept them "in principle" and offer "face-saving language" to get talks started? Together with a bombing halt and a pledge to withdraw eventually from Vietnam, the United States' readiness to accept the NLF as "one party" to negotiations might make progress possible. Gronouski noted that Hanoi had insisted that the NLF be accepted as South Vietnam's "sole" representative, but Michałowski "brushed this aside, noting that this was not part of the Four Points."[52]

Convinced that "ever since Harriman's visit [in] December 1965, [the] Poles have consistently demonstrated willingness to help resolve Vietnam conflict—to limited extent they can"—Gronouski mulled Michałowski's idea and, on August 6, proposed directly to Rusk and LBJ to call his (and by implication Hanoi's) bluff. Because the obstacle was the third point—accepting, or recognizing, the NLF's program as the basis for a South Vietnamese settlement—Gronouski called Washington's attention to relatively unobjectionable language in Ho's summary of the NLF's program in his January 24 letter ("To achieve independence, democracy, peace and neutrality for South Vietnam and to achieve peaceful unification of [the] fatherland") that could be creatively squared with Rusk's own public statements that the South Vietnamese people "should have [the] right and opportunity to determine their future in freedom without coercion or threat." Why not cite Ho to reframe point three in a more acceptable manner?

Gronouski also sought permission to tell Michałowski that the United States would accept the NLF as a party in talks and "end bombing in North Vietnam and cease buildup of our forces in South Vietnam as soon as we have assurances from Poles that Hanoi will respond by stopping its military movements from

North Vietnam to South Vietnam and is willing to negotiate [a] cease-fire in South Vietnam." Then it would be up to the Poles to reel Hanoi aboard. Offering his own suggested wording for a United States–approved version of the Four Points, to deal with the nettlesome third provision, Gronouski proposed incorporating Ho's description of the NLF's program in an endorsement of the principle that South Vietnam's "internal affairs . . . must be settled by [the] South Vietnamese people without outside interference, taking into account [the] program of their government and all organized groups in South Vietnam whose aims are independence, democracy, peace and neutrality." He conceded he could give "no guarantee that Michałowski was speaking with full authority and in good faith in making in his suggestions or that he will be able to follow through on them," but saw "nothing to lose and much to gain" from trying. After all, Warsaw presumably needed Moscow's concurrence before acting, which would draw the Kremlin further into peace efforts, and putting the question to Hanoi in this form could either elicit a positive reply or "demonstrate unequivocally who is guilty of not wanting to settle the Vietnam conflict by peaceful means."[53]

Washington balked at Gronouski's brainstorm. Passing a copy to LBJ, Rostow appended a disparaging cover note. Among other flaws, such as inadequate terms for a bombing halt, he said the envoy's plan could "do irreparable damage" to ties with Saigon, creating a "serious crisis of confidence with the South Vietnamese who could only read it as a sign of serious wavering on our part." It would "do more to boost Viet Cong and Liberation Front morale—which considerable evidence suggests is sagging—than almost anything I can think of." "In short," he concluded, "as formulated, this proposal is full of booby traps, and we will wish to give it the closest scrutiny before acting."[54]

Politely but firmly, the State Department said no. With a hint of condescension, Rusk commended Gronouski's enterprise and urged him "to encourage Poles and Michałowski in particular to continue to explore methods of initiating negotiations in one way or another." But he emphasized the "serious pitfalls" inherent in redefining the NLF's third point to hasten talks. Relying on a single phrase in Ho's letter, while ignoring unacceptable hard-line language elsewhere, would "be stretching matters too far for either credibility or sound negotiating position. We would be most reluctant to modify our stated negotiating position without much harder evidence of Hanoi's willingness to reciprocate." In the meantime, it would be "useful" for Gronouski to keep seeking clarity on where Hanoi stood, especially on the third point.[55]

Rusk shared the growing feeling in Foggy Bottom that the heretic in Warsaw needed to be reined in. "Someone should talk to our ambassador there," he told Rostow as the two discussed the possibility of Goldberg visiting Warsaw.[56] Helping to lay down the law, the secretary responded to what he considered Gronouski's dangerously naive policy advice to LBJ (after the two met in May). On Asia, this included the radical notion that Washington endorse China's admission to the UN General Assembly (rather than cling to its doomed policy of backing Taiwan) and take other steps to ease Beijing's "mistaken but nonetheless genuine and deep-seated fear" of U.S. aggression—for example, diminished high-altitude spy flights, considering a mutual nuclear non-first-use pact, increased sales of drugs and medical supplies, lifting the worldwide ban on casual U.S.-PRC diplomatic contacts, and even trying to raise the bilateral dialogue to a meeting of foreign ministers. Rusk derided the idea that Beijing could really fear Washington "in view of our record of restraint over the years" and doubted that blocking it at the UN was any tougher than usual. "The danger we must avoid," he lectured, "is losing Taiwan and all that means without gaining anything with respect to Communist China."[57]

Washington added insult to injury by also slapping down Gronouski's suggestion that he use his next talk with Michałowski on ICC matters to open a broader dialogue on the commission. After all, a cable reminded him, a key reason the body was so ineffective "has been Polish practice of hamstringing ICC by every possible procedural and substantive device, though they are not acting as free agents, but appear to be almost completely responsive to Soviet and Hanoi wishes." With Warsaw devoted to a "strict party line to protect Hanoi interests and to press one-sided condemnation of GVN [the South Vietnamese government] and U.S.," the State Department did not think such a dialogue would be "useful."[58]

But Gronouski was not so easily put off, viewing diktats from Rusk with less than complete reverence. He refused to take no for an answer, at least a final one—as Washington discovered after Gronouski saw Michałowski on August 18. Once again, he was sent to make a pitch relating to the ICC, this time to argue for an expanded ICC role in the DMZ and Cambodia. Michałowski politely sat through a briefing on Hanoi's sins, but again evinced little enthusiasm for Gronouski's pleas that the ICC could do more to constrain the war. Nor did he respond favorably when Gronouski transmitted a request to receive Goldberg; Rapacki would happily see him, he politely told the American, but given his crowded schedule, it would be sensible to defer such a talk until the UN General Assembly session in New York a month hence.[59]

As in earlier sessions, Gronouski only got down to brass tacks after the formal agenda. "When pressed," Michałowski acknowledged that the DRV's insistence on the NLF as the "only real" representative for South Vietnam was a barrier to talks, and he judged that "in last analysis" it would accept Saigon's participation in negotiations and less than the NLF demanded. But, he stressed, only if Hanoi were "really convinced that U.S. [is] sincerely interested in peaceful settlement" could Warsaw clarify its true stand. "You must make an overt act, and I know it might be difficult for you to do that out of fear that it might be construed as [a] sign of weakness."[60]

Though not authorized to offer his suggested revision of the Four Points, Gronouski probed Michałowski on how to deal with point three's "ambiguity." In response, the Pole described the NLF program as actually noncommunist, something "any liberal-minded person could accept." Once talks began, he conceded, Hanoi would "probably not exclude" ideas that were not part of the NLF's platform.

Encouraged, Gronouski argued to Washington that the best way to smoke out Hanoi was the idea he had floated—and the State Department had shot down—earlier that month. "I recognize that for us to modify our stated negotiating position requires hard evidence that Hanoi is willing to reciprocate," he admitted. "But somehow action must be taken which will cause Hanoi to do just this. My proposal (Warsaw 298) is designed to give Poles the job of convincing Hanoi to restate its position particularly on point three, in terms which would be acceptable to us."[61]

Gronouski's persistence did more to clarify U.S. and Polish thinking than North Vietnamese bottom lines. In Saigon, Lodge had read Gronouski's cables of his talks with Michałowski with growing unease. On August 23, he sent Rusk a personal message urging him to restrain the eager beaver in Warsaw. Dialogue with the Poles was all well and good, he allowed, recognizing the "need for discreet contact." But, he insisted, Gronouski had gone too far in implying that Washington would stop bombing in exchange for a "clarification" of the DRV's point three, and had also talked out of school in implying that South Vietnam's government was "sort of like the so-called Liberation Front, and that the Communists are doing us a favor if they do not block participation by the GVN in discussions." Lodge wondered, in sum, "whether in our anxiety to open a 'dialogue' with Hanoi, we don't tend to further the belief on the other side that we can dictate whatever role we may desire to the GVN."[62]

Lodge's caution deepened sentiment among top U.S. officials that Gronouski's talks with the Poles on Vietnam, while potentially useful, must be carefully overseen to prevent them from conveying an unduly dovish impression. Responding to Gronouski's latest message, the State Department termed Michałowski's comments "interesting" and again encouraged further probing. However, it rejected the idea that Washington unilaterally should take some "overt act" to entice Hanoi to the table, declaring that any tangible concession, such as a bombing halt, would come only if reciprocated. Echoing Lodge, it also spurned the notion that Saigon should be treated as just another "group" (like the NLF) in negotiations, insisting that its status be equal to that of the DRV.[63]

Despite the cold replies they elicited, Gronouski's repeated requests to rewrite the Four Points actually prompted Washington to consider that idea. Undertaking the job was the State Department's secret, newly formed "Negotiations Committee," which had materialized in the summer of 1966 at the impetus of LBJ's activist new "peace czar," Averell Harriman (formally named an ambassador at large). Though given a fuzzy mandate, and frequently at odds with Rostow and Rusk, Harriman leapt at the chance to deploy his Communist world expertise in battles for peace in Vietnam and against rivals at home. Starting in early August, he chaired the Negotiations Committee, which met weekly in his office to monitor, manage, and stimulate peace "feelers." The committee—a new policymaking nexus, at least in theory—assembled such senior officials as Alexis Johnson, Bill Bundy, Joe Sisco, and Tommy Thompson, plus insiders—who were powerful, yet less familiar to the public—like Leonard Unger, Ben Read, Leonard Meeker, Tom Hughes, and, keeping a leery eye on the proceedings for the White House, Rostow aide William J. Jorden.[64]

In late August, Harriman also added a ringer to the committee: his new aide-de-camp, Chester L. Cooper.[65] A blunt, opinionated veteran Southeast Asia hand, "Chet" Cooper was a street-smart product of a semiproper Bostonian upbringing and an education at the Massachusetts Institute of Technology. During World War II, while in Burma, he joined the Office of Strategic Services—he had no idea what the job entailed, but anything sounded better than the infantry. After a quick training course in India, the wartime intelligence agency sent him "over the hump" to southwestern China, where he trained anti-Japanese partisans and dealt with Jiang Jieshi's (Chiang Kai-shek's) Guomindang government. After the war, he joined the fledgling CIA, rising to head its Far East Analysis Branch (in which role he attended the 1954 Geneva Conference) and also doing a stint in London to liaise with British intelligence. During the Kennedy years, he was a CIA–National Security Council link, working first for the CIA's Board of National Estimates and then moving to McGeorge Bundy's staff at the White House. In 1961–62, he participated in the second Geneva Conference, on Laos; as an aide to Harriman, Cooper developed fond relations with the crusty, wealthy, and irascible politico more than two decades his senior, who became something of a mentor. "The Guv was a demanding, sometimes maddening, always interesting boss," Cooper recalled. "As time went by, I came to regard him almost as a favorite uncle; there were alternating periods of affection, anger, pride, and frustration."[66]

After JFK's assassination, Cooper stayed on with Bundy to work under LBJ. At first he was supportive of the increased Vietnam involvement, but he grew disenchanted; the last straw came in early 1966, when Walt Rostow replaced his boss. Personally and politically, Cooper had a low regard for Rostow, whom he thought delusionally overoptimistic that military force could succeed. The disdain was mutual. In April, Cooper quietly left the government to go to a think tank and write a "part history, part memoir, part cautionary tale" about how Washington became caught in a quagmire in Southeast Asia. But a few months later, he agreed to rejoin the administration—*provided* that he work for Harriman, not Rostow; and solely on negotiations, not other aspects of the war; and be free to leave if he felt his efforts were pointless. "My job," he explained, "is to dream up scenarios, dream up ideas, follow thru leads, check will of the wisps, push, cajole."[67]

One of the first will-o'-the-wisps that Harriman asked Cooper to chase was the notion of revising the Four Points to suit Hanoi *and* Washington, an idea that was percolating through the Negotiations Committee due to Gronouski. At the group's meeting on August 11—the same day Rusk's cable to Warsaw had shot down his first attempt to redraft the Four Points—Harriman, intrigued by the dialogue with Michałowski, sounded a contrarian note: Working with the Poles on an "acceptable" redraft, he remarked, seemed "worth exploring despite the rather negative reply we had sent to Gronouski."[68]

Rather than send the Americanized version of the Four Points to Warsaw, however, the Negotiations Committee opted to send it to Hanoi via U Thant, who in late July had visited Moscow. Kosygin and Brezhnev had rebuffed the UN chief's suggestion that they promote negotiations in Vietnam, saying that only those "who are doing the fighting" could take the initiative for peace. Yet a cordial chat with the DRV ambassador in the Soviet capital, who passed along greetings from Ho, had led him to believe that Hanoi might be responsive to a communication from him, and he sought something forthcoming from Washington to dangle in hopes of luring Ho into talks. With Thant unsure whether to seek a new term, the Johnson administration wanted to improve its often rocky ties with him. Meeting with the negotiations group on August 17, Goldberg pleaded for an appealing tidbit; Harriman surmised that the famous DRV Four Points, as safely redrafted by Cooper, just might do the trick. "The problem," Cooper recalled, "was to put forward something both robust and new and also something we could get people to stand behind in Washington." But this was an insurmountable problem: Unable to reach a consensus on new concessions, either linguistic or substantive, the negotiations group, after "considerable" argument, merely rehashed the language that Washington had already secretly given Hanoi in mid-February, in an aide-mémoire handed to a DRV diplomat in Rangoon.[69] On August 29, Harriman gave Rusk and LBJ such a "reformulated" Four Points as part of a package of proposals for "Establishing a Dialogue with Hanoi." The State Department dispatched the redraft to Goldberg to give to Thant to pass to Hanoi, which predictably failed to show any enthusiasm.[70]

Foggy Bottom communicated none of this to Gronouski, and had no intention of giving him such a sensitive assignment (though it agreed his channel "should be kept alive"). Instead, Rusk merely informed him that State "wished to give careful thought to how far and how fast we should move at this juncture in giving Poles as distinct from other potential channels 'the job of convincing Hanoi to restate its position.'"[71] Rusk's cable was sugarcoated with exhortations to continue "active exploration" with Michałowski, but Gronouski could tell he was getting a brush-off—told, gently but firmly, don't call us, we'll call you if we decide to use you in our Vietnam diplomacy. Yet, a few days later, on September 1, the Poles rewarded his tenacity with a new degree of candor.

Before and after a luncheon Gronouski hosted for the Polish ambassador to Washington, Edward Drozniak, deputy foreign minister Josef Winiewicz drew him aside for a long, avowedly heart-to-heart talk on various topics, especially Vietnam and China, "talking as Winiewicz to Gronouski, not as DEPFONMIN to AMB."[72] Of course, the American could not exclude that the official—like Michałowski a member of Rapacki's circle dating back to German POW camps and the old Socialist Party—might be putting a friendly face on a hard-line policy so as to cultivate him. But he sensed the candor was real, and in a cable for Rusk and LBJ called the exchange his "most extraordinary conversation" since reaching Warsaw a year before.

On the topic that preoccupied them all, Winiewicz "stressed repeatedly that Poles want to do all they can to end VN war, but that Hanoi is suspicious of Poles as result of such activity as role played by Poles after Harriman visit. Poles must be careful not to increase this suspicion. This is why they are so cautious with respect to ICC role in DMZ and Cambodia. If they are to be effective, they cannot act in any way which might undermine Hanoi's confidence in them."[73] Coming specifically to Gronouski's probing with Michałowski of the idea of revising the Four Points to let talks begin, Winiewicz assured him that the Poles were "working hard on [a] reformulation which both Hanoi and U.S. could live with" and in general were "doing all they can to find a solution." Gronouski—surprised that the Pole had failed to preface these remarks with the usual caveat that Warsaw was "powerless" to influence Hanoi until Washington first halted its attacks on North Vietnam—promised that "once we get hard news that Hanoi is genuinely interested in moving toward peace, we would have no difficulty in ending the bombing."

Winiewicz, flatly predicting that the war would end in 1967 unless "every leader in the world was out of his mind," also surprised Gronouski by seeing the Chinese chaos—due partly to Mao's "loss of faculties"—as opening up fresh opportunities for Poland to explore peace possibilities, at the UN and elsewhere. Drawing on several Polish direct encounters with Ho (including Michałowski's in January and Lewandowski's in late August), Winiewicz emphasized the Vietnamese leader's strong aversion to any Chinese occupation, even if allegedly to help resist U.S. aggression. "If you don't understand Ho's fear on this score," he told Gronouski, "you should visualize the reaction here if West Germans offered to send troops into Poland to protect the Poles."

Along with his unusually forthright vows to be helpful on Vietnam, Winiewicz delivered an emotional pledge to promote U.S.-Polish amity. When Gronouski noted that "breaking the windows" (as had happened at the embassy on July 19 as police watched passively) "does not help" bilateral relations, Winiewicz candidly admitted that others in power in Warsaw indeed wanted to sabotage those ties. "I tell you, Gronouski, nobody in the Foreign Office had any idea that was going to happen," he insisted, adding darkly, "We have some hard-liners above me who don't want coexistence. It would be suicide for me to buck them." MSZ moderates, he explained, had to gradually overcome their resistance. But at least—he declared "in a tone of determination and optimism," in a toast on Drozniak's behalf—"you can be sure that everyone at this table" (all Foreign Ministry officials) had "strong feelings of friendship" for America and would do "everything we can" to preserve and improve relations.

Winiewicz's "extremely friendly" and "unusually open and frank" comments infused Gronouski with hope that the conversation was a deliberate overture to convey Polish readiness to seek a Vietnam settlement in response to "some signal which leads them to believe that Soviets, Hanoi, or NLF, or all three, may be more receptive to peace moves than they have been in the past." It could also, he admitted, have been a sneaky attempt "simply to make us hesitant to 'rock the boat' by further escalation of the war." But he judged that the Chinese upheaval may have enhanced the prospects for peace talks by clouding the outlook for both Moscow and Hanoi—raising such unpalatable scenarios as a Sino-Soviet showdown, further impairment of Soviet Bloc supplies via China to North Vietnam, and a grimmer military outlook. "Given these alternatives, and if in fact Ho fears introduction of Chinese troops but knows he cannot call on Soviet and [Eastern European] troops without also accepting Chinese, Soviets may very well consider this [a] propitious time for its Polish ally to investigate peace climate."[74]

Washington responded warily to Gronouski's excited report. A terse cable to Warsaw over Ball's name judged the talk with Winiewicz "most illuminating on several important points, particularly Polish conception of role they can realistically play and Soviet caution in moves to improve its position re Hanoi." It also expressed continued interest "in any indications Poles may obtain of potentially significant shifts in NLF/Hanoi formulations."[75] But the State Department offered no concrete suggestions for further probing. The action in the Polish channel was shifting to New York, where foreign ministers would soon gather for the annual UN General Assembly session, and back to Saigon, where Lewandowski, D'Orlandi, and Lodge were engaging in a pas de trois in a search for a formula to sell to Hanoi and Washington.

A "Useful but Not Vigorous Facade"

Concurrent with his off-the-record chats, Lewandowski went about his formal mission—filling the Communist seat on the ineffectual ICC, and stoutly resisting Canadian (i.e., U.S.-backed) efforts to enlarge the ICC's role in spots where it might inconvenience the DRV's military plans. During the summer of 1966, Washington sought to reinvigorate the moribund commission in multiple areas: to institute patrols in the DMZ in an obvious attempt to reassert the 17th Parallel as a boundary between two independent countries; to monitor Cambodian frontiers, allegedly at Sihanouk's request, to impede North Vietnamese supply and infiltration routes; to establish a joint "mixed" commission including ARVN and PAVN representatives; and, in general, to acquire extra equipment to enable the ICC to expand operations.

While India's Rahman, the ostensibly neutral chair, maintained his careful balancing act, oscillating between stands favored by Polish and Canadian representatives and regularly infuriating both, Lewandowski studiously preserved an air of relaxed, cautious attentiveness, always producing legal arguments and precedents to oppose, deflect, dilute, and/or delay consideration of Canadian proposals. The Pole could, Moore reported, display "prickly propensities at formal meetings" or be quite "convivial."[76] (Moore and Rahman shared the impression that their Communist colleague was "socially very agreeable [but] clearly under instructions to watch his tongue."[77])

But reliably, regardless of his mood, Lewandowski displayed scant enthusiasm for any significant activation of the ICC's activities. Summing up the Pole's views, a fellow diplomat reported: "So long as the U.S. remained committed to the present hostilities there was virtually no serious work that the ICC could be expected to undertake, and he implied that, in these circumstances, he found the zeal of his colleagues, particularly the Canadian, excessive and rather tedious."[78] (The ICC's languor, incidentally, suited the monotonous lifestyle of the Polish military personnel in Saigon—"bored to death," waiting for their terms to expire, a delegation member recalls, they spent much of that summer wilting in the heat, gossiping, hoarding hard currency pay, leafing through old copes of *Life* and other American magazines, and scouring car catalogues plotting their purchases of a Volkswagen or Peugeot upon returning home.[79] A *Newsweek* article ("Policemen without Power") observed: "Around the swimming pool of Saigon's Cercle Sportif, Polish Communist officers chat casually with Americans just back from battling Vietnamese Communists in the boondocks. The Poles, like their Indian and Canadian colleagues, have, in fact, little else to do, for the labors of the ICC staff have actually diminished with the intensified fighting in Vietnam."[80])

The detailed private diary of Moore's senior military adviser—Brigadier A. G. Chubb, who joined "Candel" in September 1966—offers a wry, vivid, and intimate perspective on ICC personalities and ambience. Not long after reaching Camp des Mares, he walked over to the Polish villa to meet Lewandowski and recorded a first impression: "A slight, intense dedicated little man who hews extremely close to the party line. Obviously very able I would judge him to be not too easy to deal with and his reputation bears this out."

Chubb "tried him on for size" by soliciting Lewandowski's assessment of the recent September 11 Constituent Assembly elections, which generated a high turnout (coerced, said critics) and were touted by Lodge as a "first step toward stable, democratic government," despite limits that ensured Ky's regime a favorable outcome. Without missing a beat, the Pole "proved at least to his satisfaction that it had all been a complete failure and would undoubtedly result in another military coup in the future which in turn would fail to meet the needs and wishes of the people, etc. He did not volunteer a solution to the problem and time was running out on this first visit so I left it at that."[81]

While judiciously inscribing a positive view of his new boss—Moore "seems to be a very pleasant individual indeed, and I feel certain I will like working for him"[82]—Chubb reacted guardedly to Rahman and his military aide. "Both very, very charmin' but I gather very slippery indeed. Usual sort of general nattering that goes on on these occasions—the Ambassador is a keen hunter, and there was much worse talk of a joint flip to Cambodia for a tiger hunt. I do *not* plan to stand on one leg until it comes off."[83]

After meeting the whole trinational ICC crew and ARVN liaison, and touring the "pretty bloody basic" facilities, Chubb received his full-fledged initiation into how the three commissioners actually conducted business. Aghast, he wrote in his journal:

> Attended my first full Commission Meeting which started at 11 a.m. and went on until 5:30, with a break for lunch. Damdest [sic] thing you ever saw. H.E. Mr. Rahman, the Indian Chairman and Indian Delegation Head, flanked by half a dozen little men carrying masses of files in which they could seldom find what they were looking for. The Pole, H.E. Mr. Lewandowski, surrounded by masses of Poles, about eight in number—our side really quite modern with four on deck—and away we went. It is like an old-fashioned and very formal, stately dance and everyone knows for certain the next step and the one after and the one after that. A most infuriating procedure as far as I could judge of virtually no value to anyone of the three countries present. There are, no doubt, many wheels within wheels unappreciated by me at this stage, but no matter; a very urgent matter was talked over for five or six hours and not an iota of progress made. I thought Mr. Moore was excellent and the only one present who had any constructive ideas at all.[84]

Declassified Polish documents confirm what U.S. officials presumed: The Communist ICC commissioner's obstinacy flowed directly from Hanoi, which Warsaw sedulously informed and from which it sought guidance before making any important moves. And as Lewandowski quickly discovered (and Winiewicz told Gronouski), it made little sense to squander Poland's limited political capital with the North Vietnamese by pressing them to accede to an expansion of ICC capabilities. After weeks of resisting (on various pretexts) his schemes for a wider commission role in the DMZ, he explained to his Canadian colleague why Poland favored, in essence, just marking time.

> In private conversation with Moore, Lewandowski for first time intimated Polish motivations in keeping ICC functioning.
>
> Pole mentioned differences between Chicom [Chinese Communist] and Hanoi views on validity of 1954 agreements, and discussed Washington-Moscow-Hanoi and Washington-Peking-Hanoi communication channels, implying that ICC under present circumstances has no legal justification but is here under sufferance of two sides, both of which support 1954 agreements even though GVN was not signatory. If one side exploits ICC for propaganda purposes such as over present DMZ situation, this tends to erode ICC role even further. Poles, therefore, according to Lewandowski, have not pushed for strong actions (presumably by Hanoi) which would weaken ICC and, he implied, only push Hanoi toward Chicom view that 1954 accords are useless. Poland, therefore, wishes ICC to continue as kind of useful but not vigorous facade.[85]

Considering the Pole's "total quiescence," Moore found it apt when he pounced on "one of [Rahman's] 'let's get away from it all' proposals" for the commissioners to spend a few days in the relaxing hill country resort of Dalat with a light schedule of a meeting and perhaps a side trip for an inspection of a nearby team of ICC personnel. "It is indicative of Lewandowski's general attitude that he would like us to go into 'retreat' literally," the Canadian cabled Ottawa, quoting the Pole as saying: "There is in any case nothing for us to do in the Commission."[86]

Marigold in Limbo: "Quicken the Pace"

Behind his ICC mission's "useful but not vigorous facade," Lewandowski had plenty of spare time for potentially more rewarding extracurricular activities. In Saigon, the Marigold channel remained active, yet unproductive, throughout the late summer and early autumn. The maneuvering failed to produce any immediate progress, but it helped lay the groundwork for dramatic events to follow, deepened personal relationships among the diplomatic threesome, and fleshed out their thinking about the outlines of a settlement. For the time being, any prospect of peace talks remained dim due, among other factors, to escalating fighting (U.S. casualties reached a new monthly peak in September), political distractions (including the Constituent Assembly voting, the high-level UN consultations in New York, and upcoming midterm U.S. congressional elections), and the looming uncertainty created by the tumultuous, confusing events in China.

Nevertheless, Lewandowski and D'Orlandi—with Lodge and Foggy Bottom kibitzing from the sidelines—continued their secret search for a compromise settlement. Gradually, they developed a division of labor: The Pole would delicately nudge Hanoi toward negotiations, if and when the opportunity arose, while the Italian would work on Lodge. Though no new three-way meetings occurred at this stage, what ensued was a variant of the "proximity talks" concept that had proven useful in Middle Eastern diplomacy: With Arab representatives refusing to deal face to face with Israeli counterparts, mediators had shuttled between them, sometimes literally strolling between hotel rooms, to carry on conversations and bridge impasses. D'Orlandi acted as middleman, dining one evening with Lewandowski, then lunching a day or two later with Lodge, who in turn (after checking with Washington) would pass on comments and requests for clarifications for the Italian to deliver to the Pole—triggering another cycle of meals, drinks, and brainstorming. As Lodge reported after one bull session with D'Orlandi, they "had a wide-ranging, very informal discussion, trying to develop ideas which would mean some forward motion without at the same time having anybody lose face."[87]

Lewandowski, of course, had returned from Hanoi in late August to find Michałowski's instructions deriding "these Italian ambitions" yet authorizing him to continue contacts with D'Orlandi to extract "maximum information," as long as he represented Poland's "fundamental position" and preserved secrecy given Rome's propensity for leaks.[88] When he breakfasted with the Italian on September 3, Lewandowski radiated pessimism.[89] He had urged the North Vietnamese to resume the dialogue that had been interrupted in July, he recounted, but they seemed uninterested in negotiations (perhaps misled by Viet Cong reports that were "rosier than reality"). The Pole also lamented the upsurge in U.S. bombing, which he now "bitterly" blamed for destroying Marigold's first phase in July. In particular, he said, Washington was committing an act of "tragic foolishness" in pounding and paralyzing Haiphong. Having just visited, he lavishly praised the beauty of adjacent Halong Bay, but was less "dithyrambic" about the harbor itself.[90] The grimy port's backwardness and small capacity—"practically for fishing boats," only able to accommodate four medium-tonnage ships, and lacking cranes or mechanized unloading facilities—diminished its military significance, he insisted. Worse, by cutting off the only lifeline to Soviet support, the air raids were "delivering North Vietnam into the hands of the Chinese." "Why do a thing," he asked, "which would only throw Hanoi into Peking's lap and make it impossible for the Russians to have any influence?"

To make matters worse, Lewandowski agreed with D'Orlandi that time was not on their side, especially "because this negotiation is opposed by many people who, from different positions, put every bit of energy and guile into causing it to fail." The Italian's nagging ailments also compelled haste. Fanfani had instructed him, he told the Pole, to "quicken the pace" of peace efforts—or else retire to Rome to save his health.

Undaunted, D'Orlandi implored Lewandowski not to give up but, rather, to reconsider further initiatives. The fighting, he insisted, demanded all possible efforts to stop or at least limit the bloodshed and head off a direct Sino-U.S. collision. Among his "macabre visions," D'Orlandi worried that American hawks might deliberately contrive a clash with Beijing. He apparently did not confide this concern to Rome or, for obvious reasons, to Lodge, yet Lewandowski reported that the Italian feared intense Pentagon pressure for escalation might merge with LBJ's own desire to score a military success in 1967 to ensure his reelection. This alignment might yield, he speculated, a dramatic landing of U.S. forces just north of the DMZ to show Hanoi Washington's readiness to up the ante. Worse, it might aim to provoke a reaction that would justify "attacks on lines of communications in southern China and to threaten destruction of PRC economic objectives"—or, if Beijing backed off, to demonstrate to Hanoi its Communist patron's unreliability and impotence. Washington hoped, the Pole inferred, to exploit China's internal disarray and rift with Moscow to achieve a major advance in Southeast Asia.

"The Pentagon appears to be more and more convinced—and is informing Johnson of this—that without inflicting a blow to the Chinese or seriously threatening them, the Chinese will not allow an end to activities in Vietnam," D'Orlandi argued. "The military considers at the same time that the chances of serious engagement by the Chinese in the conflict is not great and that in the case of such an engagement the USSR will not grant the Chinese relief by assisting their military potential." Lewandowski suspected (incorrectly) that his friend had embellished this scenario so as to pressure him (and Warsaw) to focus on diplomacy, but he found plausible the report that Washington contemplated a "dramatic landing" to coerce Hanoi into concessions, which dovetailed with what he had heard from Danish and Japanese sources.[91]

In his own cable to Warsaw, sent that same Saturday, Lewandowski, as usual, stressed the Italian's desire to promote further talks. Requesting Michałowski's "urgent instructions," he quoted D'Orlandi as saying that Lodge, who felt "growing unease" over escalation, wanted a face-to-face meeting. But D'Orlandi told Lodge afterward that the Pole had fervently desired to continue their joint efforts: After hearing the Italian state that if there were "no forward motion at all from Lewandowski's side," he would start preparing to return to Rome and move on to other pursuits, "Lewandowski pleaded with him not to do this, citing his conviction that Saigon was the only place where the type of clandestine understanding, which is so indispensable, could be worked out."

D'Orlandi then suggested that, because Washington and Hanoi both demanded that the other move first before any progress were possible, "breaking new ground, we should try to lay the foundation of a broad overall agreement and then submit it to the two parties." Leaving open for the moment whether Lodge would join their "study" of a potential accord, or participate indirectly through D'Orlandi, Lewandowski agreed to consider this "interesting" notion, and the two agreed to dine a few days later, after the Italian ran the idea past Lodge.

Despite the bad news from Hanoi, D'Orlandi resolutely looked on the bright side. He drew hope from Lewandowski's seeming readiness to seek a way forward, and the Pole's earnestness and candor—"very frank and open as usual"—deepened his trust and affection: "Every day, I find greater confirmation of the esteem and faith that I have in him." Determined to see the glass as half full, D'Orlandi judged their talk "largely encouraging" and set about persuading Lodge (and Washington) to play along.[92]

At a Sunday lunch, D'Orlandi recorded, the American seemed cautiously interested, terming the notion of the Italian and Pole quietly hashing out a compromise pact "very useful and appreciated." When D'Orlandi observed that conducting such explorations without U.S. input would be an empty exercise, Lodge refused to make any promises but nevertheless urged him to go ahead.[93] In his own cable to Rusk, Lodge did not say that he had already suggested D'Orlandi proceed, but he forwarded—and warily endorsed—his proposal for a discreet joint study: "It could be that some ideas and clarification might come out of it, and that it would not, of course, commit us to anything. I doubt whether the Pole will be authorized."[94]

Even Lodge's hedged blessing to continue probing with Lewandowski sent D'Orlandi's hopes soaring. "Evidently, among the three of us a kind of harmony has been established as well as an identical burning desire to start the talks which would lead to peace," he exulted, noting the American's pleasure that the Pole had not "closed the door" on further exchanges. "The Good Lord has put the wind in our poor slack sail! . . . God forbid, but even if the attempt were to fail, the hours, days, weeks and months spent in exhilarating trepidation will remain impressed in my mind and heart as the most beautiful and worthy to-be-lived period of all my forty-eight years." (D'Orlandi's ardor infected his trusted confederate; when handed the report of the talk with Lodge to be encrypted, Sica "exudes trepidation and joy from every pore . . . happy solidarity.")[95]

Still awaiting a response from Warsaw, Lewandowski dined at D'Orlandi's on Monday and stayed for chess and conversation. Per Michałowski's earlier guidance, he warily agreed the two might secretly explore together, and through the Italian with Lodge, the elements of a peace formula to sell to the opposing sides.[96]

In the course of "exhaustively" discussing the matter, however, Lewandowski temporized by posing several preliminary reservations and queries for D'Orlandi to pass on to Lodge: He would not participate in a maneuver merely to ascertain "just how far the North Vietnamese would give in"; he sought assurances that Washington sought to resolve the Vietnamese problem "on its own" and not as a "piece of a general Chinese puzzle"; and he stressed again that rather than a limited, "partial 'de-escalation,'" the proposal must seek an "overall," "package," or "global" settlement covering the entire Vietnam dispute, not merely reinforce the "status quo" and leave the Thieu-Ky regime in power. The Pole did not aim to "inaugurate a 'socialist' regime in South Vietnam" but also rejected talks merely to formulate the terms of a "'cease-fire' and still less a 'standstill'" arrangement.

D'Orlandi found the Pole's doubts and equivocations reasonable, but told Lodge that he had responded heatedly: "I have very clear cut instructions as I have already told you, and they are: be useful or go home. Fanfani has instructions for me and Rapacki knows what they are. We may, of course, rule out an agreement confirming the status quo because this would be nothing more than the former approach. The fact is that either you and I are going to have these conversations or else nothing is going to happen at all anywhere concerning Vietnam. I was flatly told in Rome that you were to do something with me, and that it was you who wanted the conversation to go on with Ambassador Lodge."

At this, D'Orlandi recounted, the Pole softened, saying that he was "sure something could be done"—if only he could persuade the North Vietnamese (aside from the relatively realistic Dong and Giap) to stop viewing the war through the NLF's "distorted spectacles." "My job," he said, "is to explain to Hanoi that they have a wrong view."

Before embarking on the two-party talks with the Pole, D'Orlandi solicited Fanfani's stamp of approval. Characteristically, he dreamed up a dramatic method for him to reply swiftly (no coding necessary). To bar the proposed conversations, he should cable: "The hematologist cannot give an opinion prior to having examined you." To give a go-ahead, his message should read: "Professor Gigante requires an additional blood test from you." Predictably, news of the specialist's desire for more data soon arrived. "Green light," D'Orlandi jotted. "It is nice to work with a Foreign Minister like Fanfani."[97]

Within days, Washington and Warsaw also (independently) weighed in with wary, tepid OKs for their envoys to pursue the Marigold channel via their mutual

Italian friend. The State Department told Lodge that it saw "no objection to D'Orlandi's pursuing this with Pole if latter is so authorized."[98] Michałowski flashed Lewandowski a yellow light: "Do not decline a possible meeting with Lodge at D'Orlandi's, but do not seek out [to arrange it] yourself," he instructed. "Feel out Lodge as to the actual American intentions."

However, Warsaw put Lewandowski on a short leash. In any talk with Lodge, he must "present our fundamental position," which, Michałowski reminded, precluded negotiations so long as Washington kept bombing the North and dictated that they be based on the Four Points. As if that were not clear enough, Michałowski added: "Relay [Lodge's] remarks to the Headquarters, but [say] you do not think that under the current conditions one could talk about our engaging in any [diplomatic] activity. You are not allowed to directly mediate with Hanoi."[99]

One may imagine the reasons behind these firm constraints, which superseded the looser secret instructions to explore any opening for peace that Rapacki had given Lewandowski before he left for Saigon as well as Michałowski's guidance just a few weeks before. First, recent reports—both of Lewandowski's talks in Hanoi and from Dong's discussions with the Soviets—had clearly shown that the DRV leaders, consonant with Chinese desires, were taking an even harder line against negotiations, except on the two conditions (a bombing halt and prior acceptance of the Four Points) that Michałowski loyally echoed. Second, like the State Department's seventh floor, the MSZ top brass anticipated within a few weeks authoritative exchanges at the UN, including a Rusk-Rapacki encounter, and hardly wished to cede authority over such sensitive diplomacy to distant underlings.

The instructions gave Lewandowski a challenging assignment. Though forbidden to stray from Poland's official line, he was to elicit "maximal" data from Lodge and, if possible, discern the U.S. bottom line in negotiations. Yet he could hardly inspire candor simply by intoning demands to stop the bombing and accept the Four Points. So he had to get creative—drop vague but enticing hints about a readiness to help in Hanoi, play hard to get until conditions improved, complain about the Americans' intransigence and push them to make a more appealing offer, insist on an overall "package" that would allow the two sides to surmount standoffs over bombing and the modalities of talks—and, despite inevitable frustrations, keep the contacts alive, not let them collapse entirely.

Accurately reflecting the Pole's desires, D'Orlandi told Lodge that "Lewandowski absolutely does not want the conversations stopped." The Italian surmised that the "Communist intention" was to deny that they were talking with the imperialist aggressor even while wholly deniable "non-talks" between D'Orlandi and Lewandowski sought a settlement. "It is real 'double talk,' if not 'double think,'" Lodge observed.[100]

A flurry of conversations and cables in mid-September—between D'Orlandi and Lodge, Lodge and Foggy Bottom, D'Orlandi and Lewandowski—elicited and transmitted the Pole's desired assurances, although Lodge was left scratching his head over the claim that Washington sought to straighten out its China tangle in

Vietnam. "Perhaps Lewandowski has had this point impressed upon him in Hanoi or elsewhere," he guessed, unaware that D'Orlandi had helped coax this concern. "It is a curious angle, as I, of course, have never said or even implied anything to justify his admonition."[101]

Nonplussed State Department officials—"We find Lewandowski's thinking as conveyed by D'Orlandi very interesting but not always lucid"—authorized Lodge to deliver the requested assurances but expressed doubt as to "whether Hanoi and even Warsaw [were] likely to choose the Lewandowski-D'Orlandi channel for substantive negotiation." Foreshadowing future Marigold disputes, they sensed an oncoming Catch-22: "We suspect we will reach the point where we will not be able to be more concrete about our position unless we have better evidence Lewandowski [is] empowered to speak for Hanoi and that they are ready to go beyond standard positions." They promised to consider offering some token of "our earnest desire [to] move forward and smoke out Hanoi's intentions," such as a formula to halt bombing in exchange for a mutual pledge to halt subsequent infiltration, but told Lodge not to mention this "sweetener," at least for now.[102] On a key point, Lodge seemed to exceed instructions by assuring D'Orlandi that in accepting the goal of moving beyond the "status quo," as the Pole demanded, Washington did not exclude the concession, during negotiations, of Ky's removal from the Saigon government.[103]

Lodge doubted that Hanoi would take any positive action until after the U.S. elections on November 8, and Lewandowski questioned whether the Americans "really wish to talk," given what he viewed as the incompatibility of "military escalation grouped with political proposals." But D'Orlandi disputed such pessimistic appraisals. One could not "discard the possibility of discussions now," he told Lodge in mid-September, in light of the worsening turmoil in China, which might hasten an irreparable Sino-Soviet break and doubtless dominated Hanoi's thinking. But first, he felt, Lewandowski needed something concrete to tell the DRV leaders to convince them that "the Americans really mean business. If you don't take advantage of the opportunity now, you'll regret it."[104]

For the moment, however, no such step seemed likely. Dining at D'Orlandi's on September 16, Lewandowski groused that Washington seemed "hopeless," fixated on limited objectives, special missions (another Ronning trip was rumored), and escalation. Should a "reasonable proposition emerge, he would take the first plane to Hanoi and put it in the best possible way," the Pole declared, but that needed to be an overall settlement, perhaps one to make South Vietnam a "second Cambodia" with a neutral coalition government ultimately including both NLF and current regime figures.[105]

Lewandowski's ideas went well beyond thinking in Washington, where the ideas of coalition rule or neutralization were scorned; early Cold War experiences in Czechoslovakia and elsewhere had led U.S. officials to regard a negotiated withdrawal leading to a coalition government as "surrender on the installment plan" (as McGeorge Bundy put it[106]), and the collapse of the 1962 Geneva pact to neutralize Laos (which Washington blamed on Communist encroachment) further tainted the concept. U.S. officials did not exclude such an outcome in South Vietnam (or unification with the North, for that matter), as long as it resulted from "free" elections, but they still treated the war as the North's aggression against a sovereign Republic of Vietnam, not as a civil conflict.

Hence, when Goldberg unveiled the latest U.S. peace proposition in a UN General Assembly speech on September 22, he ignored neutralization or coalition schemes and simply stated that Washington was "prepared to order a cessation of all bombing of North Vietnam the moment we are assured, privately or otherwise, that this step will be answered promptly by a corresponding and appropriate de-escalation on the other side."[107] Privately, Johnson administration officials conceded Goldberg's reply to DRV demands for a bombing halt merely put a more forthcoming veneer on existing policy.[108] In Saigon, an unimpressed D'Orlandi refused even to present a "bombing-infiltration formula" to Lewandowski, who was only interested in brokering a final "package deal" rather than some "de-escalation" gimmick as an ice-breaker to start direct talks.[109]

By late September, tempers in Saigon were fraying to the point that the Marigold channel seemed near collapse. As D'Orlandi told Lodge afterward, during his back-and-forth with Lewandowski on September 16, both were so frustrated that they discussed cutting off their conversations. When Lewandowski floated the idea of a coalition that would include NLF ministers and current regime members "on the fringes," with "sensible South Vietnamese politicians" making up the bulk, the Italian retorted, "This is unthinkable. If this is what you want to talk about, it is better for us to stop the talks. . . . If [the ultimate goal] is to have the Viet Cong in the government of Vietnam, I won't even submit such a proposal to Ambassador Lodge."

Backing off, Lewandowski explained that what he had in mind was a "second Cambodia"—an idea worth talking about, D'Orlandi felt—but complained that U.S. obduracy made their efforts moot. "I don't believe the Americans really wish to talk. They are trying to do two things at once: military escalation grouped with political proposals. You can't do both. So long as they won't make up their minds, we can't do anything. We must wait until November."[110]

Cabling this reported statement to Washington, Lodge leapt to defend U.S. policy, loyally denouncing Lewandowski's criticisms as "thoroughly disingenuous" and citing D'Orlandi's feeling that the Pole undoubtedly "realizes that the only possible chance for significant talks is that our military success should grow."

Still, as the patience of both D'Orlandi and Lewandowski wore thin, even Lodge grew embarrassed by the measly offerings the State Department fed him, implying a lack of interest or confidence, or both, in the languishing Italian-Polish link. On September 26, when he relayed to D'Orlandi a limited suggestion that Lewandowski seek Hanoi's assent to an expansion of ICC activities in the DMZ to "test" the Pole's ability to influence, represent, and, ultimately, deliver the North Vietnamese, the Italian erupted.[111] The Pole, he reminded Lodge, had "stuck his neck out on the proposition of being against any form of barter such as 'we stop doing this and you stop doing this.'" There would be no point in asking him, because he was already "much too violent in his opposition to this proposition to make it profitable to take it up with him" and could hardly "disavow himself so blatantly." Lodge's "final tidbit"—that if Lewandowski succeeded, "we can widen the dialogue"—the Italian found "nothing short of offensive." As D'Orlandi's cable discloses, Lodge apologetically explained that "as a professional duty," he had related these ideas, but personally he asked him to say nothing of them to Lewandowski.

While Lodge insisted that LBJ and Rusk wanted their efforts to continue, perhaps awaiting more propitious conditions that fall after the U.S. elections and a decline in the Viet Cong's military prospects, D'Orlandi "did not fail to develop several pessimistic considerations on the eventual continuation of our work given the frame of mind in Washington." Lodge bluntly cabled Rusk: "D'Orlandi thinks that 'our channel may disappear.' He means by this that Lewandowski sees no sign that we are seriously interested in working through him and will, therefore, not remain in Saigon." A helpful signal, the Italian suggested, would be for Rusk to tell Fanfani that he hoped D'Orlandi would stay at his post, which might impress Warsaw as evidence of Washington's interest in the channel.[112]

In early October, the Italian ran into Lewandowski at a diplomatic reception and remarked that he intended to tell Fanfani that there no longer seemed to be any point in remaining in Saigon and further damage his health "when there was absolutely nothing to do." Much to his surprise, the Pole strongly disagreed. "You must not leave," he said "with great emphasis and earnestness"—and also cryptic precision. "There will be much to do after the fifteenth of November."[113]

The Pole refused to elaborate, but D'Orlandi presumed that he was alluding to plans to visit Hanoi after the U.S. elections, to which he "attaches special importance," because he felt they would clear the table for LBJ to bargain seriously.[114] Lewandowski cautioned him in mid-October, however, that if rumors that the Americans "are trying to feel out the Chinese" proved true, then "we are out"—he and Poland would cease trying to push the North Vietnamese toward negotiations.[115]

For the moment, however, he not only remained ready to carry new proposals to Hanoi, but he and D'Orlandi also seemed increasingly turf-conscious. When a Vatican official passed through Saigon on a peace mission in early October, D'Orlandi complained to Lodge that "we were never going to get anywhere if 'amateurs' were free to try to move in and out of Hanoi at will." Lewandowski advised the papal emissary to buzz off. It was necessary, he told Bishop Sergio Pignedoli, to use "our channel"—the Italo-Polish connection. Trying the Canadians (whom Pignedoli hoped might arrange a bishops' conference in the DRV that he could attend) was "wrong, . . . whipping a dead horse." (Ronning's missions had alienated Hanoi, he felt.) According to D'Orlandi, the Pole warned Pignedoli against returning to Saigon, which "disturbs everyone," saying, "If you want to try this again, try somewhere else."[116]

In another sign of Lewandowski's continued readiness to deal with the Americans—and in line with his secret instructions—he went out of his way to preserve a link to Lodge, even without further direct contacts. More than once, D'Orlandi reported that the Pole had made positive remarks about him, even while blasting U.S. conduct. Lodge, feeling a bit sheepish (but proud?) at being singled out for praise by his Communist colleague, had cabled Rusk in mid-September that Lewandowski had said (per D'Orlandi) that he was "convinced that I personally am very much in favor of ending the war. But he has doubts about Washington."[117] A month later, the Pole had told D'Orlandi, "I believe that it is a really good thing that we have here Ambassador Lodge." In relating this remark to the State Department, the recipient of this flattery commented:

> I am somewhat mystified by Lewandowski's references to me by name. While I do not doubt that he thin[k]s I am for peace—as indeed I am—I believe he must be doing this so as to promote this channel and make sure that he will be a participant in any activity. This seems to be part of his desire that we make it clear that he is "our channel."[118]

For the time being, however, Rusk and his top Vietnam advisers—Bundy, Harriman, Cooper, Thompson, Len Unger, Hey Isham—refused to designate the Pole as "their channel." Still temporizing, in mid-October the State Department cabled Lodge a set of questions aimed at clarifying Lewandowski's aims and authority, and at determining whether he could be used to probe Hanoi along Washington's preferred lines. (A first draft suggested asking him whether he might convey to Hanoi an interpretation of U.S. objectives so as "to begin an indirect dialogue conducted through him on matters of mutual interest," but an official crossed this out on the grounds that "we never wished to use Lewandowski as a general sounding board but for specific purposes.") On receiving the telegram, rather than seeing Lewandowski personally, Lodge sought out D'Orlandi to answer State's queries.[119]

Was the Pole's aversion to "any form of 'barter,' that is, 'we stop doing this and you stop doing that,'" based on his own or North Vietnamese thinking? It reflected the views of Dong and Giap, the Italian replied, though he could not tell how much power they actually held in the DRV leadership.

What about Goldberg's September 22 suggestion of a "bombing-infiltration" formula? Might Lewandowski square this reciprocal approach with Hanoi's rejection of concessions in response to U.S. pressure? No way, D'Orlandi replied, in line with Hanoi's preference that the Pole would only seek a final accord that "covers everything."

What might such a "package deal" contain? Channeling the Pole, D'Orlandi explained its key elements: internationally supervised elections in one to two years; a neutral Vietnam; U.S. troops would leave "eventually"; and probably a coalition government in Saigon containing a few "extremists" from both the present regime and NLF, but dominated by centrists. As to Washington's eternal quest for a satisfactory answer to the question "What would Hanoi do if we stop bombing North Vietnam?" D'Orlandi stressed again that this limited approach would yield no answer, but a "real package deal" would "immediately" get "very serious" consideration.

Looking to the future, D'Orlandi reported that Lewandowski, rather than going to Hanoi in late October as first planned, would return there soon after the U.S. elections, which he hoped would "clear the air, whatever the results might be." Less constrained by domestic politics, he calculated, Washington could "deal if it wants to" with painful compromises that would accompany any Vietnam settlement or serious negotiation.

But before the Pole went north, D'Orlandi would return to Italy in late October —both for medical treatment and to bring Fanfani up to speed on the exasperating contacts with Lewandowski, in hopes of generating fresh ideas for his friend to deliver to Hanoi.

"The Wild Card in the Deck"? Hints and Contacts in New York and Washington

As D'Orlandi and Lewandowski spun their wheels, U.S. officials dealing with Vietnam diplomacy concentrated their energies elsewhere. One reason that Washington was in no rush to pursue an overture through Marigold (or Gronouski) in September and October, aside from doubt about participants' authoritativeness or reliability, was the knowledge that Rusk and LBJ could soon probe for themselves the degree to which the Soviets and their allies might help end the war or communicate with Hanoi. Preferring to retain close control over policymaking, and suspicious that Italian or Polish diplomats (or even their own envoys in Saigon or Warsaw) might be too forthcoming, they viewed the meetings at the annual UN General Assembly session as a perfect chance for measuring peace prospects.

In fact, the Johnson administration's hopes were rising that the Soviets, who until then had carefully refrained from acting as mediators, might be edging closer to joining the game. Intriguing hints of diplomatic activism seemed to be cascading from Moscow's Warsaw Pact allies. Besides the Poles, the normally quiescent Czechs had gingerly stepped into the ring with a timid expression of interest in mediation, conveyed through Kissinger (in the Harvard professor's first exposure to secret Vietnam diplomacy), that flared in mid-September before dimming a few weeks later.[120] During the New York contacts, Hungary's foreign minister, not grasping the extent to which his diplomacy during the thirty-seven-day bombing pause had undercut his credibility in Washington, told Rusk that he was "absolutely sure" Hanoi would accept a deal based on the 17th Parallel—

though he coyly refused to disclose his basis for the startling claim.[121] The maverick Romanians also stepped in, predicting that if Washington announced a "permanent" bombing halt, "a concrete response from North Vietnam would not be lacking"[122] and, Foreign Minister Corneliu Mănescu told U.S. officials, "conditions for fruitful discussion would then exist."[123] Ruminating over this array of channels and initiatives at a negotiations panel session in late September, Bundy remarked that the Poles' role seemed less clear than that of the other Central and Eastern Europeans: "They might be the wild card in the deck."[124]

To varying degrees, these approaches intrigued U.S. officials, but they all took a back seat to dealings with the Communist kingpin. Despite Beijing's status as a military supplier for North Vietnam, Harriman judged, "I believe the only real chance now in sight to induce Hanoi to negotiate a settlement depends on the influence Moscow is willing and able to exert."[125] When Fanfani came to Rusk's Waldorf Towers suite on September 19, the two speculated that the time was right to probe the Soviet Bloc for signs Hanoi might finally come to the table. "This 'mosaic of indiscretions and rumors' gives rise to the thesis that Moscow would like to see the war settled and that October might be the month," the Italian suggested.[126] (Though they did not discuss Marigold at length, Rusk politely signaled continuing U.S. interest in the Saigon channel by expressing hope that D'Orlandi would stay at his post, health permitting; he would not be transferred, Fanfani duly promised a few weeks later.[127])

Before seeing Gromyko, Rusk had a much-anticipated encounter with Rapacki, preceded by distinctly mixed signals. When promising that Poland would do all it could to promote peace in Vietnam, Winiewicz had specifically told Gronouski that "useful discussions might be conducted in the halls of the UN."[128] Top U.S. Kremlinologist (and soon-to-be-named ambassador to the USSR) Tommy Thompson—suspecting that, in line with past practice, the Soviets might refuse even to seriously discuss negotiation prospects—urged that "we should keep open the option of discussing substantive points with Poles rather than Gromyko if Gromyko is not forthcoming."[129] Observing that Warsaw felt "fewer inhibitions" than Moscow about taking initiatives, Thompson even mused that Rapacki might have made hard-line statements to his Western counterparts as part of "a deliberate effort on the part of the Poles to create a smokescreen behind which they could operate."[130] In a pretalk memo approved by Harriman and obviously informed by an awareness of Marigold, officials urged Rusk to "ascertain seriousness of Polish interest in exploring basis for settlement, extent to which they are in active communication with Hanoi and are speaking with Hanoi's knowledge and consent, degree to which they are coordinating efforts along these lines with USSR." To highlight Washington's "strong interest in working out approach which would get talks started or otherwise to arrange mutual de-escalation," Rusk might note Gronouski's "useful conversations" with Polish officials, express thanks for the effort to reformulate the Four Points, and perhaps even pass along the U.S. restatement.[131]

However, considerable mutual ill will had accumulated between Rusk and Rapacki, largely dating from the thirty-seven-day bombing pause the previous winter. Irking the American, the Pole was not shy about spreading the claim that Washington had ignored a "positive" signal from Hanoi (whether an alleged response delivered by Michałowski, the purported mistranslation of Ho's letter, or the willingness to receive Norman Cousins) and had thus ruined a chance for peace by resuming air strikes—patent myths, felt U.S. officials, annoyed at having to repeatedly rebut his tales. Hours before Rusk saw him, the latest such report reached Foggy Bottom: Rapacki had told Belgium's foreign minister in Warsaw that Michałowski had gotten from Hanoi the "kind of response Harriman was looking for," but Washington still restarted the bombing. "Rapacki added that Poles had thereby lost credibility with Hanoi and stated very emphatically that Poles were in no position to play further intermediary role with Hanoi." Gronouski, after trying to set Brussels' ambassador straight, told Washington that the Poles were "likely to continue to peddle this line at UN session. We should nip it in the bud wherever it appears."[132]

When Rusk and Rapacki met at the U.S. UN mission on September 23, both felt somewhat nippy. The two veteran ministers—mild-mannered, professorial, formal, somewhat stodgy, in their midfifties (born the same year, 1909)—opened with kindly expressions of concern for the other's health, but the conversation did little to enhance mutual esteem or confidence. Summing up a prolonged exchange on Vietnam, the U.S. record assessed that Rapacki took "a relatively hard and uncooperative position," refusing to address Rusk's points and reiterating standard policy.[133] In his own terse cable to Warsaw, Rapacki judged: "A long discussion and perhaps futile. One thing is clear: They want to remain in South Vietnam alone, or through puppets."[134]

Rusk, claiming that U.S. readiness for a settlement based on the 1954 and 1962 Geneva pacts had been frustrated because Hanoi "keeps hanging up the phone," tried to lure Rapacki into discussing how to get talks going—but to no avail. Instead, he stressed that Poland was not authorized to negotiate for Hanoi and could not aid Washington's quest to open negotiations until it ceased bombing. Even then, he could not guarantee results, remarking, "I can only say for sure that there can be no negotiations while the bombing lasts." He accused the United States of escalating mechanically in Vietnam ("more than brinkmanship") and leading the world "halfway down the slope" to disaster.

Rusk, in turn, nixed a unilateral halt, but vowed that the bombing could "stop immediately if Hanoi indicated its readiness to take reciprocal steps" and ceased trying to conquer South Vietnam. His excursions into the history of failed accords and negotiating initiatives—including the ideas considered in the Gronouski channel, such as "revised language for point three" and beefing up the ICC—failed to stir Rapacki's interest. (When he suggested that a strengthened commission might patrol Cambodia's frontiers because Sihanouk was "nervous" over border violations—of course, both men knew well that Hanoi used Cambodian territory to supply Communist forces in the South—Rapacki replied airily that the ICC need not get involved in "old border issues" and that if Sihanouk was nervous, Washington "had every opportunity to 'calm him down.'")

According to Rapacki, the American tried to elicit some personal sympathy outside the formal meeting, taking him aside "in a 'traditional' elevator (without the note-taker)" to confide, with a sigh, that he, Rusk, was not responsible for the collapse of their joint efforts in 1964 regarding Laos or, more pertinently, "for the fact that our work in January 1966 was thwarted by the renewed bombing." Unimpressed, Rapacki told Warsaw: "Conclusion: He's either lying, or he was against the bombings, and since they had started, he did not see any other way."

Essentially, the meeting marked time. Comparing notes afterward on their respective conversations, Fanfani conjectured to Rusk that Rapacki and Mănescu were "under orders from Moscow not to get into this matter. They never talk about the role they could play in bringing about a settlement."[135] Still, the Rusk-Rapacki exchange had not disrupted the possibility of further U.S.-Polish cooperation. Even Rapacki admitted, in his report, that "according to the current tactics of the United States—they do not seek any quarrel with us." And the two conducted one positive piece of business concerning Marigold. In their formal talk, Rusk noted that Rapacki's hint that a bombing halt might create conditions for progress toward peace "could be clarified through diplomatic contacts," and privately he told the Pole—consistent with what he had told Fanfani about D'Orlandi—that Washington found Lewandowski's activities interesting and hoped he would stay at his post. Rapacki promised that there were no immediate plans to shift him.[136]

Rusk cabled the news to Lodge on September 29, the same day D'Orlandi expressed his worry to him that "our channel may disappear." Now they could be confident that it would not, but whether it would actually help end the war was another matter. For now, U.S. officials saw little help coming from Warsaw. In early October, McGeorge Bundy—still informally advising LBJ on Vietnam—saw Rapacki at Poland's UN Mission. As he had to Rusk, Rapacki urged an immediate bombing halt and warned that "mechanical" escalation risked a wider conflict, perhaps drawing in China and driving Hanoi into Beijing's arms—arguments that Bundy rebuffed. He assured Rapacki that LBJ "would respond instantly to any serious signal, public or private," along the lines of Goldberg's September 22 proposal, and suggested that it "would be more useful for the Poles to try to extract something of this sort from Hanoi than to press upon us such a hopelessly unrealistic and one-sided proposal as a complete halt to the bombing." But Rapacki "did not take the bait"; Poland could not negotiate for the DRV, he stressed.

Though Rapacki had toed the Communist line, Bundy sensed that he was going through the motions. "I had the impression that he was repeating an argument that he has made many times. I thought he did it skillfully but not passionately. He obviously felt it necessary to say nothing faintly disloyal to any established Communist position, but it was equally obvious that he was too sophisticated to peddle the Hanoi line as a whole with any enthusiasm."[137]

After Rapacki left New York, U.S. officials kept up Vietnam contacts with the Poles through Winiewicz, who remained behind. On October 18, Harriman hosted Warsaw's deputy foreign minister at his apartment for what the Pole acknowledged was an "exceptionally honest" two-hour conversation. The American stressed LBJ's desire to find a "political exit" from Vietnam once he received a concession from Hanoi, which did not have to be "big" but must satisfy U.S. public opinion. He also endorsed Gronouski as a "trusted man of Johnson" who would be informed of important Vietnam moves and be at Warsaw's disposal if it had an important message to communicate. And, while alluding to stepped-up efforts by other Eastern Europeans, he invited Poland "to take [an] initiative" to seek peace in Vietnam. Warily, Winiewicz expressed doubt that Washington had made any "fundamental changes" in its Vietnam policy that justified new initiatives but promised "that our government will not spare any efforts on behalf of peace and it will not shy away from any peaceful action once it is convinced about its purposefulness."[138]

By mid-October, however, those at the top of the U.S. administration, including LBJ and Rusk, had turned their attention to Moscow.

The Soviets had previously consistently rebuffed U.S. invitations to intercede with Hanoi, but two talks with Gromyko suggested a possible shift. Exchanging views with Rusk on September 24, he repeated the usual denunciations of U.S. aggression in Vietnam, especially the bombing, but he sparked interest by noting that such actions "had severely limited the Soviet Union's possibilities and had deprived it of opportunities to take some positive steps"—the implication being that the Kremlin might avail itself of another such opportunity.[139]

"Throughout the atmosphere was about as moderate and relaxed as [I have] ever seen in his five and a half years on an issue such as this," Rusk told Rostow the next morning, urging that LBJ read the detailed memorandum of the conversation. "The main point was [that] if we stop bombing in the North something might happen."[140] The Negotiations Committee was similarly heartened by Gromyko's "relatively relaxed attitude, his willingness to continue discussions and his emphasis on Soviet influence in Hanoi," all of which struck the group as "encouraging indications of a possible future Soviet initiative."[141]

LBJ did his best to sound forthcoming when he welcomed Gromyko to the Oval Office on October 10. Making many of the same points as Rusk had, but in classic Johnsonian style—vigorous, visceral, agitated, interrupting Gromyko's translator—the president stressed not only his personal commitment to peace but also his readiness to accept any result of a fair process that allowed the South Vietnamese people to make their own free choice, even unification with their Communist compatriots: "If South Vietnam wanted to vote to go with North Vietnam, that was their business." U.S. military actions belied such pacific statements, which in any case lacked precision, Gromyko responded. Though unable to say how Hanoi would react to a new bombing halt, he mentioned that it might be "of use" for the president to make a "more specific and concrete statement" regarding the United States' willingness to withdraw all its forces from South Vietnam in a final settlement, eschewing permanent bases. Johnson promised to consider the idea.[142]

American officials found Gromyko's posture "encouraging," and the Soviet left them in no doubt where to turn for help. When Rusk asked which Eastern European country had the most influence with Hanoi, he answered in one word: "Moscow."[143]

How did Gromyko assess his talks on Vietnam with U.S. leaders? Thanks to recently opened Communist archives, we can read his report to a secret Kremlin conclave.[144] On October 21, he recounted his trip to Brezhnev and other Warsaw Pact party bosses, dwelling on the talks with Rusk and LBJ. Terming LBJ the more flexible one, Gromyko underlined Washington's seeming acceptance of possible eventual South Vietnamese neutrality and unification with the North. Using far more positive words than were usually found in public Communist pronouncements, he concluded that the Americans "are looking for an exit and it would be a simplification, and even a primitivism, to say that they took the course of continuing the war. They are looking for an exit even to a greater degree than before." Gromyko noted LBJ's willingness in principle to withdraw all the United States' forces and close its military bases once the DRV stopped sending forces to the South. For him to halt the bombing, however, Hanoi had to "do something" in return.[145]

One by one, the heads of the Soviet satellites—Poland's Gomułka, Hungary's Kádár, Romania's Ceaușescu, Czechoslovak's Novotný, East Germany's Ulbricht, Bulgaria's Zhivkov, Mongolia's Tsedenbal—then spoke, followed by Brezhnev's summing-up. All hailed the "heroic" North Vietnamese military struggle, but also criticized their failure to devote equal attention to the political and diplomatic fronts and Beijing's malevolent behavior, including its constant pressure on Hanoi to avoid peace talks and interference with coordinated socialist bloc military aid. However, Brezhnev noted, unfortunately no one advanced any concrete ideas for how to prod Hanoi to move toward a political-diplomatic track. Gomułka added Poland's voice to the chorus of calls for Hanoi to broaden its approach beyond the purely military, but he made no mention of Warsaw's special diplomatic status or activities through its ICC man in Saigon.[146]

Gomułka had no special reason to; not only was Poland inactive on the peace front, after the brief burst of activity in July, but in a bilateral session beforehand with the Soviets, he had already secured their blessing for Poland to try to nudge Hanoi toward negotiations—and away from China. An exasperated, even resentful Brezhnev had recalled futile efforts to talk reason to the Vietnamese, most recently in August in the Crimea with Pham Van Dong: "We exerted pressure on them, and nothing." Worse, egged on by Beijing, the DRV had virtually extorted a "huge" influx of extra Soviet aid, implicitly threatening to condemn them for "not helping at all" if they refused, the general secretary of the Soviet Communist Party said: "We are convinced the Chinese are pitting the Vietnamese against the USSR in order to get as much out of us as possible. All this is based on this principle: The USSR is a rich country, so milk them as much as you can." Even before hearing Gromyko's report, he granted that LBJ truly wanted peace ("This is not purely propaganda") and would "ease conditions" for a settlement, as long as the war against Saigon ended. "We could play the game along these lines," he told Gomułka, implying a willingness to assume a more direct, active role in mediating between Washington and Hanoi. However, North Vietnam had refused to "let us in so we can cooperate," instead stubbornly resisting talks and insisting on prior acceptance of the Four Points—which Moscow and Warsaw recognized was tantamount to demanding Washington's surrender.

Frustrated by Hanoi's opacity or even dishonesty, the Soviets and Poles could not discern whether its hard-line stands were "bargaining chips" or "real" aims to gain at any cost. Gomułka felt enslaved ("dragged by the tail") by a bellicose Chinese policy that might spark World War III and—agreeing with Brezhnev that the Americans "would like to get out of this quagmire which they created for themselves"—suggested a Soviet Bloc effort to convince the Vietnamese to negotiate. If they felt constrained, "then we should work out a proposal on our own and present it to them." Brezhnev bandied a joint letter, but Kosygin that felt a coordinated approach would strike the Vietnamese as an ultimatum; conversely, informal, bilateral contacts, perhaps at an upcoming October Revolution gala or Bulgarian or Hungarian party congress, might work better. He urged caution, noting (in a mirror image of classic U.S. Cold War calculations) that the "socialist camp" must conduct Vietnam talks from a position of strength, because concessions might embolden Washington "to use force, for example, in Berlin." Yet, he agreed,

> It seems to me that, in fact, we are in favor of negotiations. But, what does it mean to conduct negotiations? . . . The point is for the Vietnamese and Americans not to feel defeated. Besides, we need to act in such a way so the Vietnamese could free themselves from the Chinese, and so that they are not afraid of them. After all, they do not respect them, but they are afraid of them. . . . We need to search for a formula, which would be acceptable to the Vietnamese. After all, we know what the Americans want, but we don't know what the Vietnamese want.

"We have done a lot to persuade the Vietnamese to sensible negotiations," Brezhnev said—and the Poles were welcome to try as well.[147]

Manila: LBJ Calls Gromyko's Bluff

Gromyko's challenge to LBJ to commit more firmly to a U.S. troop pullout from South Vietnam to lure Hanoi into negotiations came just as the faith of some leading Johnson administration figures in the war was faltering. The summer's escalation, above all the campaign against facilities for petroleum, oil, and lubricants (POL), launched with such fanfare, had manifestly failed to crush North Vietnam's ability or determination to carry on the fight. Military commanders, grumbling over continued restrictions on targets, began reporting in August that the strikes were producing diminishing returns. By mid-September, the CIA and the Defense Intelligence Agency jointly declared that they had detected no sign of POL shortages, serious transportation problems, weakened popular morale, or disruption of essential economic activities in the DRV.[148]

Perhaps most ominous, for U.S. officials who had hoped the stepped-up bombing might prove decisive, was a massive top secret CIA study, "The Vietnamese Communists' Will to Persist," which was commissioned by McNamara (who was dissatisfied with the Defense Intelligence Agency's reporting) and circulated in the late summer. This detailed study not only judged the POL raids indecisive—"the supply of petroleum for the essential military and economic functions will continue, and . . . the flow of supplies to the insurgent forces in South Vietnam can be sustained if not increased"—but observed, damningly, that the U.S. "aerial pressure" program had "not appreciably impeded North Vietnam's receipt of matériel support from abroad and its dispatch to South Vietnam." Despite "disruptions," Hanoi's "transport and logistic system is now functioning more effectively after almost eighteen months of bombing than it did when the Rolling Thunder program started."[149]

The CIA analysts forecast that a continuation of the war at present levels would not prevent Hanoi from effectively pursuing its military struggle, because its leadership considered the current punishment "a price it can afford, and one it probably considers acceptable in light of the political objectives it hopes to achieve."[150] A greatly expanded bombing campaign *might* produce "more meaningful" pressure, but even such an offensive "would not stop activities essential to support of the war."[151] After reading the vast report, McNamara received a briefing from a senior CIA Vietnam expert, who bluntly urged him to "stop the buildup of American forces, halt the bombing of the North, and negotiate a cease-fire with Hanoi." The analyst admitted that these steps might eventually result in a Communist takeover of South Vietnam, but suggested that, because a military victory was impossible (short of using nuclear weapons against North Vietnam), U.S. strategy could shift to a more regional and international approach aimed at keeping the region's other "dominoes" upright.[152]

The DRV's exceptional resiliency under attack demonstrated the value of a program it had launched the year before, at the onset of the U.S. bombing, to disperse and decentralize important industries, including oil storage[153]—as Lewandowski had observed during his bomb-damage inspection trips with Ha Van Lau, when they would refuel at numerous tiny camouflaged roadside depots, using a "primitive sucking device for gas," from barrels hidden in jungle overgrowth marked by flags poking out of the ground indicating a supply below. The Pole also marveled at the ingenuity of the North Vietnamese in replacing damaged or destroyed bridges ("not a single one not bombed"), departing from the practice during the anti-French war of building bamboo spans under water (visible to U.S. planes), and instead jury-rigging devices using ropes and tree trunks to separately deliver lorries and their wheels to a river's far banks, where they were reunited.[154]

The CIA's observations did not faze the perpetually optimistic Rostow. Summing up the huge study, he shamelessly spun it to reassure LBJ that U.S. military pressure was indeed straining North Vietnam's morale and capacity to wage war and would eventually force it to capitulate, and to stiffen his determination to take a hard line on negotiations. "There is no agreement in the intelligence community as to when"—not "if"!—the DRV's "morale may reach the breaking point," Rostow told him on September 19. "The intelligence community doubts that weakening morale will deprive the Hanoi leadership in the coming year of the freedom to pursue the conflict in any manner it chooses. My feeling is that the pressures on the regime may be greater than most of us realize.

"I make this point," he added, "not because I believe they are hurting enough to force them to negotiate now—or at any particular early date; but because debate about bombing in this town between crusaders and detractors has sometimes failed to make clear the important middle ground: that we are imposing a day-to-day cost on Hanoi; this cost is considerable, if not decisive; it is rising; and we shouldn't let them off the hook until the very day they make parallel de-escalatory moves."[155]

McNamara, by contrast, in a phone conversation with LBJ that day, expressed deepening concern over the bombing, troops levels, "and our whole position out there." In contrast to Rostow's belief that "we shouldn't let them off the hook" until "considerable" and "rising" North Vietnamese pain could be converted into concrete concessions, the defense secretary told LBJ that he was "more and more convinced that we ought definitely to plan on termination of the bombing in the North, but not until after the [November 1966] election, and I hate to even talk about it before then for fear of a leak." At the same time as he confessed that bombing was not the answer, he also indicated that more troops also could not guarantee success, and thus suggested a ceiling of 500,000 to 600,000, not "higher and higher and higher—600,000, 700,000, whatever it takes."[156]

Nor had political reform in South Vietnam, though hailed by Washington as evidence of progress toward democracy and civilian rule, been a panacea. Marred by charges of fraud, with neutralists barred from running, and with the new body widely perceived as powerless, the September Constituent Assembly voting generated little popularity, confidence, or legitimacy for the Ky-Thieu regime.[157]

This bad news led McNamara to secretly defect from the administration's policy of seeking military victory. On October 14, after a quick trip to Saigon, he sent LBJ a disconcertingly gloomy memorandum acknowledging that he saw "no reasonable way to bring the war to an end soon." "Enemy morale has not broken," he admitted, citing failures both in the "pacification" efforts in the South and the bombing in the North. Among his recommendations: Stabilize Rolling Thunder operations and consider a halt, and *"press for negotiations"* by, inter alia, taking concrete steps to enhance the "credibility" and "bona fides" of U.S. peace proposals and redoubling contacts with "North Vietnam, the Soviet Union, and other parties who might contribute toward a settlement."[158] (There is no sign that McNamara specifically recommended the Marigold channel to LBJ; yet at about this time he urged officials to "follow through with D'Orlandi and his Polish ICC contact" to open up communications channels with Hanoi.[159]) Not surprisingly, the Joint Chiefs of Staff and Rostow dissented from McNamara's advice, but the president could hardly ignore the fact that the official he relied on so heavily to run the war had lost faith in it.

Under increasing pressure both inside and outside his administration to bolster peace efforts, LBJ found something new to toss into the debate. Calling Gromyko's bluff, he decided to use an upcoming summit in Manila with Saigon and the United States' other Southeast Asian allies to put a firm timetable on a U.S. military withdrawal from South Vietnam after a settlement. At his insistence, the final communiqué, issued on October 25, included a vow that as North Vietnam withdrew its forces, ceased infiltration, "and the level of violence thus subsides," Washington would remove its troops and evacuate its military bases "not later than six months after the above conditions have been fulfilled."[160] Though carefully hedged and complemented by preparations for renewed military action, LBJ's pledge drew world headlines, effectively undercut charges that Washington sought a permanent military base in South Vietnam and would never tolerate its neutralization, and pumped new life into potential peace initiatives.

After the conference, as LBJ headed home from Manila via South Vietnam (where he famously exhorted the troops at Cam Ranh Bay to "come home with the coonskin on the wall"), Thailand, Malaysia, and South Korea, Harriman, LBJ's most prominent counselor on peace prospects, circled the globe to explain the administration's thinking. With Johnson's carte blanche blessing to pursue peace, and in particular to follow up on the Eastern European leads that he believed were "the most promising," Harriman flew from Manila to Indonesia, Ceylon, India, Pakistan, Iran, and eventually to Europe, visiting Italy, France, Germany, England, and then Morocco before returning to Washington.[161] Meanwhile, D'Orlandi, impatient at the slow pace and skimpy results of the months of fitful conversations with Lewandowski, flew home to Rome for consultations, medical treatment, and, he hoped, another bid to inject some life into the dormant Saigon channel.

In early November, their paths would intersect at a restored Renaissance-era Roman villa on a hillside overlooking the Tiber River—and set in motion Marigold's second act.

4

"A Nerve-Eating Business"
Marigold Blossoms—
Act Two, November 1966

You know, I'm convinced that it's about time you fellows stopped passing on to Lewandowski just questions or platitudes to bring up to Hanoi. Why don't you tell him something that the North Vietnamese can chew on? Something consequential?

—*Giovanni D'Orlandi to Chester Cooper, Rome, November 2, 1966*

Finally, we are at the beginning of the real work which should lead us to the end of this cruel war.

—*Janusz Lewandowski to Henry Cabot Lodge and D'Orlandi, Saigon, November 15, 1966*

What the devil can be happening to them in Hanoi?

—*D'Orlandi, in his diary, November 27, 1966*

Pham Van Dong asks to deliver to Gomułka assurances that if the United States takes a promising position then the DRV government will take a positive attitude. They are not apprehensive of talks if there is a basis for them. . . . I believe that the information arouses serious interest and there is a good chance for the beginning of progress.

—*Lewandowski, in Hanoi, to Adam Rapacki, November 28, 1966*

The curtain on Marigold's second act rose on Wednesday, November 2, 1966, in a rarefied setting far from Vietnam. On a chilly, cloudy afternoon in Rome, at the Villa Madama in the city's northwest hills, Fanfani hosted an intimate lunch for Harriman, who was entering the home stretch of his post-Manila 'round-the-world tour to explain Johnson's Vietnam policy.

The panorama from the *travertino* stone villa on Monte Mario overlooking the Tiber had long commanded admiration. Built from a Raphaelite design in the early sixteenth century, it was conceived by a Medici cardinal (later Pope Clement VII) who desired a place of relaxation, not work, and so, it was said, deliberately chose a vantage point from which one could *not* see Saint Peter's. It featured not religious but secular motifs (celestial bodies, animals, classical legends) and works by top artists (Romano paintings, Udine stuccoes, etc.) inspired by Roman ruins. Surrounded by sloping gardens, dramatically terraced, the "vineyard" expressed emerging Renaissance sensibilities, its celebration of pleasure, nature, and art reflecting "the new tastes of a society that had abandoned the Middle Ages and their dark dungeon-like palaces, imprisoned inside city walls, for long stays in charming country villas." In the 1780s, Goethe was said to visit often to contemplate sunsets falling on a nearby hill graced by a solitary pine.[1]

After the Villa Madama was restored in the early twentieth century by the aristocratic di Frasso family, which used it to stage "indescribably lavish parties" (Cary Grant recalled[2]), it attracted the notice of Mussolini's regime, which purchased it on the eve of World War II to wine and dine foreign big shots. Visitors ranged from an appeasement-minded Chamberlain to a rogue's gallery of Nazis, including Goering, Ribbentrop, and, on a "beautiful Sunday" in May 1938, Der Führer himself.[3] After Il Duce was strung up, and postwar Italy joined the Western alliance, the villa remained the Foreign Ministry's guest house, and NATO bigwigs slept amid Axis ghosts.

From the top-floor dining room in Countess Dentice di Frasso's old bedchamber —which was reached by a circular stone staircase widened so the *contessa* could ascend on horseback—one could see, in the distance, the city's oldest surviving cobblestoned footbridge spanning the Tiber at the Ponte Milvio; to the left, the boxy chalk-white Palazzo della Farnesina, which had originally been built under Mussolini to house Italy's National Fascist Party headquarters before being converted to host the Foreign Ministry, and the stadium built for the 1960 Summer Olympics; and, below, near the entry to the neo-imperial Foro Italico (the sports complex that Mussolini had crowed would put the Coliseum to shame), a phallic stone obelisk erected to honor "Dux" by acolytes in "Anno X" of his reign (1932), still standing more than two decades after his fall.[4]

But on this overcast afternoon in November 1966, Chet Cooper had little chance to savor the vista. Fanfani had deliberately seated him with his back to the window, next to a man he knew from classified documents but had never met: Giovanni D'Orlandi.

Cooper did not realize it, but the ambassador had done his best to prime the pump for the occasion. Soon after flying to Rome, he had lunched with Fanfani to ascertain whether he was still interested in the Polish channel. "With immense pleasure," D'Orlandi wrote afterward, "I received confirmation that he is not at all willing to give up on the attempt. However, a great deal of imagination is necessary in order to revitalize it and put some teeth back into it."[5] A few days later, he learned Harriman would transit Rome and discussed the Villa Madama lunch with the minister, who seemed deceptively nonchalant: "Fanfani does not appear to attribute any importance to the lunch, but in his eyes, I can clearly see the truth: the lunch will be important."[6]

The meal began around 1:30 p.m. with just a handful of officials from each side at the large table: Fanfani beside Harriman, of course, and D'Orlandi between Cooper and the U.S. Embassy's number two man. Cooper was still jet-lagged from "the longest day of my life" on Tuesday: breakfast in New Delhi, lunch in Rawalpindi, tea in Tehran, and dinner "someplace over North Africa" before landing at Rome's Ciampino Airport near midnight. After a few hours of sleep, he had already accompanied Harriman to a round of high-level meetings. He was poised to appreciate a fine meal and even finer wine; and after the cavalcade of foreign ministers, premiers, presidents, shahs, and popes, he also expected the conversation to be routine. But as the aide to his right pointedly turned away, D'Orlandi dispensed with small talk and got down to business. Cooper snapped to alertness, and regretfully slowed to a sip his intake of a "damn good" red, mentally preparing himself to compose afterward (taking no notes, not wanting to inhibit the exchange) a memo of conversation and, perhaps, an urgent cable for Harriman to sign.

The seating arrangement, he now grasped, was no accident: Fanfani knew that Cooper was Harriman's "action man," and he and his Saigon envoy wanted *action*. Of all the conversations on Harriman's whirlwind ten-nation tour, this would be far the most consequential.[7]

* * *

Fanfani had already hinted to the Americans that Vietnam would be the *piatto del giorno* at Villa Madama. That morning, "with considerable feeling," he revealed a deepening concern that the Southeast Asian mess was warping Washington's foreign policy, even as "particularly delicate and difficult" European matters— "unsettled" political situations in Germany and the Netherlands (and in Italy, too, he might have added), a "worrisome" British economy, an "especially difficult" France—needed full concentration. He did not fear that the war was draining U.S. military forces from the Continent, but he "worried that our preoccupation with Vietnam was drawing American attention away from European problems. For this reason, Italy was especially anxious to help the United States resolve the problem in Vietnam."

Fortuitously, Fanfani noted, Harriman's stop in Italy overlapped with D'Orlandi's home leave—and he invited the American to have a "private talk" at lunch with Rome's Saigon envoy, who "might have something of particular interest for the Governor."[8]

So it was that a few hours later at the Villa Madama, after a papal audience at the Vatican, D'Orlandi importuned Cooper about a chance that Washington should not miss.[9] They hit it off quickly: "Cooper and I immediately took a liking to, and trusted, each other." The Italian sensed that Cooper sympathized with his efforts and sought arguments to rebut skeptics. Answering detailed queries about Lewandowski—to the Americans, the biggest unknown in the equation besides Hanoi—D'Orlandi praised him as "a reliable channel and an accurate reporter": "I say all the good things possible emphasizing his very loyal conduct with respect to us negotiators."

"Even before dessert," they got down to brass tacks about how to reenergize the dormant initiative. Impressing the Italian as "very astute" and having deeply considered the matter, Cooper confided a new "negotiating twist" that D'Orlandi thought was a "brilliant" device to hurdle the enemies' seemingly irreconcilable conditions for starting talks. His innovation would emerge later as the famous "Phase A / Phase B" concept: Washington would stop bombing North Vietnam (seemingly unilaterally and unconditionally, as Hanoi demanded), and only after an interval (e.g., a few weeks) would mutual "agreed de-escalatory actions" occur, which would seem to the outside world to have emerged from subsequent talks but would have actually been negotiated beforehand.

In two days, D'Orlandi would head back to Saigon, where he would see Lewandowski before he left on November 11 for Hanoi. "The next few months may be critical," D'Orlandi told Cooper, explaining why he was returning despite ill health. Could not the Americans provide some fresh proposals, envisioning the outline of an eventual accord, to give the Pole to relay to the DRV leaders? Washington and Hanoi needed to "come to grips" with what they would settle for in a final deal; Lewandowski said Hanoi would accept a coalition government in Saigon comprising ten "noncommunist middle-of-the-road-types" plus two ministers each—"the least consequential ones"—from the "extreme right" and Viet Cong. What about Washington? It really could accept a "completely non-aligned Southeast Asia," Harriman had assured Fanfani that morning. Now D'Orlandi pressed the Americans to determine their true bottom line, to "face up to the kind of ultimate solution we wanted and then worry about moving toward it."

"You know, I'm convinced that it's about time you fellows stopped passing on to Lewandowski just questions or platitudes to bring up to Hanoi," he told Cooper. "Why don't you tell him something that the North Vietnamese can chew on—something consequential?" He added, "Why don't you think in terms of presenting Hanoi with your conception of a political settlement and then see if you can negotiate back from there?"

Cooper did not say so, but he agreed that Washington had to put up or shut up. Moreover, the Italian's professionalism, competence, and endorsement of Lewandowski convinced him that the proposition merited serious consideration.

When the meal ended, Cooper took D'Orlandi over to Harriman and asked him to repeat the gist of his presentation. At this point, Fanfani politely indicated to the other guests that "it would be opportune to leave . . . us alone." During a "long and fruitful conversation," D'Orlandi told Harriman that "all the elements are present" to resume the three-way talks in Saigon. Cooper aimed, of course, to enlist Harriman's full support, a prerequisite for getting Rusk and LBJ to approve something forthcoming. "I wanted him in on the act," he remembered.[10]

Impressed by D'Orlandi's "evident sincerity,"[11] Harriman urged him to ask the Pole to delay his travel plans for a few days to let Washington come up with "something meaningful." Encouraged, D'Orlandi promised to stall Lewandowski until at least November 13 or 14, to await news from Lodge, and predicted that he would cooperate. Flattering the Italians, the Americans termed the conversation the "most interesting" that they had had since leaving Manila, and Harriman implied to Fanfani that he might end up assuming a key role in getting negotiations started.[12]

Afterward, Harriman started to draft a personal plea to LBJ and Rusk: "It is time we should state our minimum (+ maximum) objectives + what we would settle for. Our military actions indicate [a] desire for unconditional surrender + so are statements by Sec State. 'All we want is for NVN to leave SVN.'"[13] Yet he gave up, aware that a cable would hardly suffice to convince the skeptics to be more flexible. He and Cooper sent a message reporting Fanfani's proposition, but they knew that extracting fresh terms would require face-to-face arguments. "Harriman thought there was some promise in it, especially because Fanfani went to such lengths," Cooper recalled wryly, "but William Bundy wasn't necessarily going to give up an afternoon of his busy life" to respond to the idea merely on the basis of an excited cable.[14]

Not until November 10 did they get to relate the Villa Madama lunch to their State Department colleagues and urge them to devise "something new and challenging," as Cooper recalled, "not just pull some [language] out of the file."[15] But they seemed more eager to signal Hanoi via another channel—Moscow, where U.K. foreign secretary George Brown would go in late November. To give him something to hurdle the deal-breaking DRV demand to halt bombing before talks, they opted to offer the face-saving Phase A/B concept that Cooper had concocted. He and Harriman did not dispute that Brown's trip had "better immediate possibilities," especially because Lewandowski might be freelancing. As Bundy put it, Moscow was "somewhat nearer the heart of things" than Saigon. And, noted Unger, the Pole had done zilch with the ideas to expand ICC activities in the Demilitarized Zone that the State Department had sent him via Lodge and D'Orlandi. Still, Harriman pressed for "morsels" to give the Italian; he was "personally impressed by D'Orlandi and believed that we should give him some encouragement."[16]

Rusk took the idea under advisement, though he was doubtful that Hanoi would bargain seriously and was leery of hints of moderation conveyed by third parties. Both traits were evident when he saw Swedish foreign minister Torsten Nilsson on November 11 to hear an update on secret contacts between Stockholm and Hanoi (given the U.S. code name "Aspen").[17] Nilsson had sought the session after an October 28 talk in Hanoi between Trinh and Stockholm's envoy to Beijing, Lennart Petri. The DRV foreign minister, Nilsson reported, had spoken in "a moderate tone," insisting that North Vietnam favored a political rather than military solution as long as certain conditions were met; notably, he did not insist on the Four Points, immediate U.S. withdrawal, or acceptance of the NLF as South Vietnam's sole representative, but he supported (in terms similar to those Lewandowski reported) the creation of a coalition government in Saigon "founded on a broad basis including all political and religious groupings as well as all social classes generally desiring to achieve national independence," with unification a goal for the indefinite future.[18] "We know what we will have to do," he said, if Washington stopped bombing unconditionally and "definitely" and recognized the NLF as "one" South Vietnamese party, "the most valid."[19]

Dismissing coalition rule or deferred unification as thin disguises for a Communist takeover, Rusk professed to find Trinh's supposed preference for a political path mildly interesting but remained fixed on a concrete question: What would Hanoi trade for a bombing halt? Teased by his remark that "we know what we will have to do," Rusk suggested that Nilsson ascertain more precisely whether Hanoi would withdraw its forces from South Vietnam if Washington stopped bombing; even if North Vietnam met U.S. conditions, he could not promise a permanent halt. A disappointed Nilsson sensed that Rusk "had throughout given the impression of wanting to demand more and more from his adversaries while not wanting to deliver anything himself."[20]

Fatefully, the military machine rumbled on. That Thursday and Friday, on November 10 and 11, after months of internal wrangling, LBJ authorized the next round of Rolling Thunder bombings, known as RT-52. During the intense discussions, in an ominous portent both for Marigold and the relations between the two men most responsible for the U.S. escalation in Vietnam, Johnson overruled McNamara and sided with the Joint Chiefs of Staff in approving four "controversial," previously off-limits targets—apparently the first time that had occurred, noted the defense secretary's close aide, John McNaughton—before later reversing himself. He deferred some targets in the Hanoi and Haiphong areas, but sites now eligible for strikes included a rail yard and truck depot within five or six miles of the capital's center. Aides delayed the execute order pending Brown's trip to Moscow and suitable weather, but they did nothing to coordinate the raids with other ongoing diplomacy.[21]

Though the talk with Nilsson was a reminder that he had other options to send messages to Hanoi, Rusk decided to give the Polish channel a try. On Sunday, November 13, he flashed Lodge a blinking yellow light to proceed. In a cable drafted by Unger, Rusk authorized him to meet Lewandowski (with D'Orlandi present) to see if this might produce a "useful mission in Hanoi by securing better understanding there of our position and bringing back to us some clarification, although past exchanges with Lewandowski, received through D'Orlandi filter, have not yet persuaded us Pole is in a position to provide effective line of communication."

Before sending any concrete new policy formulations, Rusk wanted Lodge to "get a better picture" of Lewandowski's motives and capabilities. What role did he envisage for himself? Did he seek to facilitate direct U.S.-DRV exchanges or to mediate himself? How did Hanoi view him? Had it given him specific messages? How did he imagine overcoming the bombing stalemate to achieve the "final" package deal, rather than a limited truce, that he so insistently advocated? "How does he propose to get from here to there?" Rusk went further than with Nilsson, sending "something new and shiny" (as Cooper wryly put it[22]) for Lodge to dangle before the Pole: the same Phase A/B notion Brown would carry to Moscow— perhaps this procedural trick would satisfy Hanoi's "considerations of face." Should Lodge's report justify further action, Rusk vowed to respond before Lewandowski left for Hanoi.[23]

Finally, after months of desultory maneuvers, Marigold was springing back to life. But was there any real reason to believe that this reincarnation stood any better chance of bearing fruit—that Hanoi and Washington might be more ready to deal the second time around?

Back to Saigon

Given the inevitable delay in hearing from Harriman, D'Orlandi took his time en route from Rome: a sentimental stop in Alexandria, a few days in Beirut. But on reaching Saigon on November 11, he promptly—even before learning the fate of his Villa Madama plea—sought out Lewandowski.[24] The Pole, he learned the next day, had recently taken a much shorter trip, to Phnom Penh. He enjoyed excursions to the sleepy city on the Mekong; its relaxed people and thriving markets were a welcome contrast to Saigon's chaos, poverty, and lurking violence. This visit also offered a pretext to avoid South Vietnam's National Day festivities, including a military parade on November 1 (the anniversary of the anti-Diem coup), to which diplomats were invited.[25]

Ostensibly, Lewandowski had gone to check on Polish ICC operations and confer with the Cambodians. He admired Sihanouk's ability to maintain his country as an "oasis of peace," even if this meant averting his glance when DRV forces used his land (i.e., the Ho Chi Minh trail and Sihanoukville port) for infiltration routes. To the Pole, the prince fretted at feeling trapped between Hanoi and Washington, which (lacking a Phnom Penh embassy) sent ominous threats through various channels to take unspecified action if he could not control his territory.[26] Trying to placate as many sides as possible, Sihanouk refused to alienate Hanoi by pushing too hard for the expanded ICC mission that Washington wanted; Warsaw deflected repeated proposals to this end.

But the visit's real import was Lewandowski's talks with Vietnamese Communists, who could operate fairly freely in the neutral capital. Meeting both the DRV ambassador and an NLF operative under journalistic cover, he came away "with a modicum of optimism," Derksen reported after seeing him in Saigon on November 8. The Vietnamese Communists, he said, had "painstakingly" dissected "every word" of the Manila communiqué, with its vow to remove U.S. forces from South Vietnam within six months of a settlement, and had discerned a hint of progress. "They had distilled from the text—and described as a streak of light on the horizon—that America, however obscurely, had not only admitted the existence of significant political opposition in South Vietnam but had also had Generals Thieu and Ky endorse that admission."[27]

Lewandowski, too, had pored over the Manila text. Despite the usual demand that Hanoi halt the insurgency before Washington stopped bombing, it struck him as a sign that America might be losing faith in escalation: "I mean on a practical basis that more or less it was the same: You stop it, we stop it, the status quo remain the same, . . . but even [so], it made an impression, it is a signal of a some sort of a beginning of thinking, in the United States, that maybe, maybe, that we should a little bit adapt ourselves to the situation."[28]

To his satisfaction, the Pole discerned a "moderated" approach from the Vietnamese Communists. Fearing China's influence, Warsaw and other Soviet Bloc allies had worried that the NLF would adhere to an even more militant stance than Hanoi in opposing negotiations and pursuing armed struggle until final victory. But Lewandowski sensed that both Hanoi and the NLF agreed on "the main issue": achieving unification in "at least two stages"—a negotiated U.S. exit and the preservation, at least for a time, of the 17th Parallel.

Lewandowski later recalled that this new, seemingly softer NLF view implied removing a major obstacle to talks and formed an important backdrop for the secret diplomacy about to occur. "Of course they would not interfere" with a real peace deal, he remembered NLF diplomats telling him. If the South Vietnamese were really free to choose their future, the NLF could "easily find [a common] language with people" in Thieu's regime. This attitude influenced his own thinking about a deal, because "if you were thinking about [an] honest solution, not tricking the Americans, [that] they will go and take it over, then you have to visualize the situation when you have a coalition government, temporarily or something, in South Vietnam which would replace the existing South Vietnamese administration in a friendly way, being friendly to Americans and to North Vietnamese . . . [and] would have to absorb moderate people from the NLF and moderate people from the Saigonese administration."[29]

Perhaps, Lewandowski speculated to Derksen, Moscow had "consistently overstated" China's influence on Hanoi—"demagoguery [was] a disease which affects 'socialist' countries, too," he admitted—and the DRV was finally "succumbing to pressure to moderate brought to bear by a virtually continuous series of delegations from Eastern Europe." When the Dutchman said the presence of 300,000

U.S. troops might have encouraged Hanoi's enhanced flexibility, the Pole did not demur, even while reporting that his Vietnamese interlocutors insisted that they remained optimistic about the military situation.[30]

When Lewandowski described his Cambodian contacts to D'Orlandi over dinner, the upshot was that he now felt, from "authorative" NLF sources, that the group (which he did not consider pro-Chinese) "will not cause problems" if negotiations opened; in an aside, D'Orlandi cabled Fanfani, they had also confirmed his own theory as to why the NLF had refrained from "seriously" bombing Saigon—it was an "important logistics base for the guerrillas."[31] "Saigon is, despite everything, a great lungful of air for them," the Pole observed.[32]

D'Orlandi filled in Lewandowski on the Villa Madama lunch and passed Harriman's request to delay leaving for Hanoi so the State Department could send Lodge new guidance.[33] He promptly agreed, deferring his departure for four more days, until November 15, so he could see Lodge.[34] The Pole relayed to Warsaw the Italian's hopeful view that the Americans "see the situation more realistically than before"—Harriman had confirmed that Washington sought an exit from the war. D'Orlandi informed Rome (and Lodge) that *Lewandowski* had asked to see Lodge, but the Pole told Warsaw he agreed to *Lodge's* wish for "a normal conversation and not negotiations."[35]

Of course, more than anyone, it was *D'Orlandi* who cajoled both men to join him for their first three-way meeting since the abrupt demise of Marigold's first phase in late July.

The Three-Way Meetings in Saigon Resume

Far more than a "normal conversation" ensued behind the drawn heavy curtains at D'Orlandi's fifth-floor apartment on November 14, a hot, cloudy Monday in the monsoon season's waning days.[36] The Italian first welcomed Lodge at three o'clock for a late lunch and was glad to hear that Harriman had kept his Villa Madama pledge to spur fresh instructions upon his return to Washington. Then, at exactly five, Lewandowski arrived for their first three-way meeting since July 24. It lasted an hour and a quarter, in a "relaxed and friendly" atmosphere. Adopting some of the Pole's terminology, Lodge said that Washington sought a "package deal" with Hanoi, not just limited measures; in emphasizing the United States' flexibility and sincerity, he also stressed what was and was *not* in the Manila communiqué, and he insisted that the Americans retained a "completely free hand"—implying they were not bound by the hawks in Saigon or at home.

Listening to him, Lewandowski felt "pleasantly surprised." He heard a new tune, not so much the lyrics but the music. "Lodge at this meeting was unusually outspoken," he recalled. "It was more or less nothing especially new, . . . but the *way* he put it, I mean, was different. And from this point of view, Manila *was* important. . . . My impression was, something is really changing."[37]

Despite the bonhomie, the two probed warily, as if inspecting a possible business partner. Each relayed four preformulated queries. Lodge asked Lewandowski how he saw his own role and Hanoi's likely behavior; the Pole wanted more detail about U.S. terms for a final settlement. Lodge needed to check with Washington, but Lewandowski replied promptly. "Both," in effect, he said when asked if he saw himself as "seeking merely to facilitate a better understanding on each side of the other's position in order to pave way for some kind of direct contact" or as an "intermediary" trying to "achieve agreement on specific issues." U.S. curiosity toward Hanoi prompted an appeal to Lodge's experience. "You have worked in Southeast Asia and you realize that diplomacy in Vietnam is different than what it is in Europe or the United States." Here, "clear-cut answers" were rare, and one had to be "very patient and look for indirect symptoms."

Lewandowski assured Lodge that he was not a DRV agent, yet Hanoi would use him to communicate with Washington. Calmly, he deflected as premature and theoretical a bid for specifics on negotiating procedure, but he welcomed the evolution in thinking behind Lodge's last query, whether a "package deal" might be forged starting with a delinkage of a bombing halt and subsequent, separate (but secretly preagreed) mutual concessions. The "Phase A / Phase B" concept, the Pole mused, "might be quite useful," but just "the beginnings of the alphabet. . . . We must go right through to Z, including everything that needs to be in the package deal."

But, D'Orlandi interjected, achieving a bombing halt through Phase A/B could be "an excellent point of departure" toward an overall accord, helping to "dispel reciprocal suspicions and distrust." With Lodge pledging a rapid turnaround to obtain answers for Lewandowski, the group dispersed, but not before a seemingly casual yet crucial exchange. As he readied to go, Lewandowski added, "very much as an afterthought and in an extraordinarily mild tone of voice," that he had forgotten one item he should have mentioned: There should be "no further escalation, because to do so would 'freeze the atmosphere.'" Equally casually, Lodge cabled, he had replied that this admonition certainly applied in both directions.

All three left feeling hopeful. As D'Orlandi escorted him out, a "very happy" Lodge murmured that he had been "struck" by the Pole's helpful and direct manner; the Italian agreed that he had displayed a "cordial" and "very cooperative spirit"; and Lewandowski stayed for dinner and spoke in "very glowing terms" of Lodge and the "much more open [U.S.] approach."

From the embassy, Lodge cabled Washington a detailed report—terming the atmosphere "much the best that it has ever been since we have met"—and pleaded for answers to the Pole's queries by nine the next morning so he could convey them before the ICC plane took off at eleven. At a Japanese Embassy reception that night, D'Orlandi signaled to Lewandowski that Lodge would want to see him again before he left.[38]

With rare speed, the State Department flashed Lodge a five-page telegram at 8:45 a.m. Saigon time Tuesday, November 15, replying to, if not fully answering,

Lewandowski's four questions.[39] Lodge immediately phoned D'Orlandi to set up another three-way meeting, hearing from the Italian that the Pole was "moving heaven and earth" to postpone his departure so he could see Lodge again. The three met at D'Orlandi's at ten.[40] At the start, Lodge said he wished to elaborate on his comments the day before on the U.S. stand, especially because Lewandowski seemed "convinced of the entire futility of all [peace] efforts."

Then, as the Pole and Italian listened closely and took "very careful notes," Lodge slowly read the cable, repeating it so they could "get everything exactly right." He affirmed Washington's "great interest" in Lewandowski's imminent journey, especially given the acute difficulty of learning Hanoi's views authoritatively despite the efforts of "literally scores of well-intentioned persons," and reassured him that it, too, wanted an overall accord but needed to learn first how Hanoi would respond before halting the bombing. America was, he stressed, prepared to remove its forces and accept a neutral and nonaligned *South* Vietnam (not insisting on the same for the North), as long as it occurred in the context of a settlement requiring a concurrent PAVN withdrawal (which could be done secretly to save Hanoi's face). "We are serious in expressing our willingness to remove our troops, to dismantle our bases, and accept a nonaligned South Vietnam so long as it is genuinely nonaligned," Lodge said. "We do not regard the genuine neutrality of South Vietnam as opposed to our interests."

In reply to Lewandowski's request for clarification as to whether Manila's vow of a U.S. pullout within six months of an accord "depends on control by the present South Vietnamese Government of territories not now under the control of Saigon," Lodge (i.e., Washington) fudged. Without identifying Gromyko, he said that the statement was carefully crafted in response to indications "from Eastern European sources" that this would help start peace talks, but the "mechanics of a phased withdrawal" would be up to negotiations. Asked if Washington would "interfere" with the creation of a new Saigon administration in the event of a cease-fire, or with "peaceful progress toward unification," Lodge reiterated the United States' readiness "to abide by the genuine manifestation" of the South Vietnamese will expressed through free elections to create "a responsive and representative government." Similarly, he declared, reunification should be settled freely by the North and South Vietnamese without outside interference once "peace and order" returned. Would Washington use the Geneva Accords machinery, including the ICC, to verify a deal? Lewandowski had asked. While accepting the 1954 and 1962 pacts as a basis for peace, Lodge said that events had revealed the need for "an effective and truly neutral mechanism of supervision and control," leaving unclear whether a beefed-up ICC might fill that bill.

As the Pentagon Papers analysts later noted, the "carefully worded and not fully responsive" U.S. replies contributed to a "not very clear" exchange: "Lewandowski seems to be asking if we would accept procedures (troop withdrawal, international inspection, etc.) that would allow changes in the SVN government favorable to the Communists. We seem to reply negatively."[41] D'Orlandi bluntly told Rome that Washington had evaded Lewandowski's cogent first question about the fate of South Vietnamese territory presently beyond Saigon's control.[42]

Still, almost four months after their first effort failed, the trio again felt the frisson of nearing a secret breakthrough. After Lodge relayed Washington's stands and warm interest in the Pole's impending Hanoi visit, D'Orlandi ebulliently recorded, "the euphoria seems to me to be universal, and I immediately declare myself happy about the atmosphere created between the three of us, which is one of trust, esteem and obvious optimism." Only slightly more restrained, Lodge cabled that the new U.S. stand "rather encouraged" his partners: "Never before" had the Pole's "attitude been so forthcoming, not to say eager."

"Finally," Lewandowski remarked as the hour-long meeting broke up, "we are at the beginning of the real work which should lead us to the end of this cruel war."[43]

After wishing his friend bon voyage, D'Orlandi, "beside myself with happiness," rushed to compose an urgent telegram to Fanfani.[44]

Lewandowski added his own observations in a cable to Michałowski that faithfully rendered the U.S. proposals.[45] Stating the obvious, he said that Lodge, despite employing the diplomatic convention of engaging in a "private exchange of views," fully expected Warsaw to report the contents to Hanoi; after all, when Lewandowski needled that other U.S. officials had recently made far more hawkish comments, Lodge had insisted that what he said had LBJ's total support. Yet, it remained unclear whether Washington was using the Poles as its sole channel or to check information exchanged through other intermediaries.

More profoundly, Lewandowski judged that the Americans' proposals stemmed from the realization that they had reached a crossroads—either they would find a diplomatic exit or feel obliged to launch a vastly expanded ground war. One basis for his view was a recent chat at a reception with General William C. Westmoreland. In a "very friendly" exchange, the jut-jawed U.S. commander frankly told the Communist diplomat that America could not win solely with modern weaponry and aerial attacks. It had to defeat the enemy on the ground—and because the ARVN was still not fighting effectively, this meant a huge troop buildup. The struggle reduced, he said, to "a man with a rifle on one side and a man and a rifle on the other side," and here the enemy had an edge, because the Viet Cong were "not afraid to die." To squelch the determined insurgency, he might need at least 200,000 more troops, on top of the more than 300,000 already in Vietnam.[46] The remarks fit the gossip that Lewandowski gathered in mid-October indicating that Westmoreland and McNamara had discussed the former's request for a "further, serious increase" in ground forces, significantly surpassing the half-million mark.[47]

Sensitive to signs of pessimism, Lewandowski interpreted the latest Lodge proposals as supporting the view that

> the U.S. is confronted with the necessity of making a new and important political and military decision regarding the war in Vietnam. The results of the means

used until now, however, do not promise a swift end to the conflict. If the escalation [occurred], then [it would have to be] very serious, at least [they would have to] double the number of troops, mainly the infantry. However, even this would not guarantee success, and it would threaten to expand the conflict.

His clear implication: Warsaw, and by extension Hanoi, should take these U.S. proposals seriously, because they might be the last chance to avert a far bloodier war.

❋ ❋ ❋

At this point, following the November 14–15 three-way meetings, the U.S. chronology of Marigold goes blank for the rest of the month, resuming only with Lewandowski's return to Saigon from Hanoi on November 30. New Polish and Vietnamese evidence fills in this void by describing a series of extraordinary Communist consultations triggered by the Pole's reports of his talks with Lodge.

"At a Crossroads"

As Lewandowski set to fly north, his cables describing the talks with Lodge "awakened great hopes" in Warsaw regarding possible direct U.S.-DRV exchanges and Poland's own role in getting them started.[48] Only recently, the MSZ brass had inclined to curb their ICC commissioner's activities even further. When Ottawa's foreign minister transited Warsaw earlier that month and suggested, during a discussion of how they might use the ICC to promote peace, that Canadian-Polish consideration of the topic continue in Saigon, Rapacki argued that "it would be better to consult on this at some distance from scene of events," preferring that Michałowski handle any discussions.[49] And only a couple of days before Lewandowski saw Lodge, the director-general had instructed him to limit the ICC to a "passive role" restricted to receiving complaints.[50]

But merely the report of the first exchange with Lodge, on November 14, inspired him and Rapacki to abruptly reverse their earlier admonition against mediation. They directed Lewandowski to deliver "the entirety of Lodge's arguments" to Pham Van Dong, report his reactions, and await instructions.[51] Lewandowski's telegram describing the November 15 conversation with Lodge aroused even more excitement.

Gone, now, were cracks about "Italian ambitions" or dismissals of LBJ's peace efforts. An internal analysis, prepared by Michałowski and approved by Rapacki, called the new U.S. ideas "interesting and worth serious consideration." It identified "new elements" representing progress from prior stands, including the "unconditional" bombing halt (i.e., the Phase A/B formula that removed the appearance of a quid pro quo); implicit recognition of the NLF as a party to talks; a backing off from an insistence on neutralizing all Vietnam (yet accepting it for the South); signs that Washington would not give the Saigon regime a veto in negotiations; no explicit requirement that Hanoi admit its forces were in the South or withdraw them; and the fact that negotiations would not only *not* weaken the North but permit a "continuation of the battles in the South under better conditions until securing profitable conditions in the package-deal." Lodge's clarifications in his second conversation with Lewandowski even effectively accepted the "main foundations" of the DRV's Four Points and NLF's Five Points—the bugaboos that so long had blocked progress.

This analysis attributed Washington's "much more flexible position" to its "sober estimation" of the military situation; concerns about the war's impact on the 1968 election and consequent desire to achieve peace before then; fear that the war might widen; worry over "hawkish" pressure for escalation (strengthened by Republican gains in the just-held midterm vote); belief that Hanoi might have more freedom from Chinese pressure due to the Cultural Revolution; and the "possib[ility] that the USA government wants to profit from a foreseen pause in the bombings during the holiday period to execute at the same time a deep probe of the possibilities for a peaceful resolution of the conflict."[52] Warsaw sent this analysis to Hanoi for Lewandowski to present it to DRV leaders together with Lodge's proposals.[53] At the same time, Rapacki may also have authorized Siedlecki, in Hanoi, to convey the gist of Lodge's propositions.[54]

While entrusting delivery of the U.S. proposals to his envoys in Vietnam, Rapacki acted to take personal charge of the matter. Though he was careful to secure broad authorization from Gomułka (whose foreign policy interest, in any case, centered on Russia and Germany) and the PZPR Politburo, he had a mostly free hand. From this moment on, Poland's Marigold diplomacy would follow two interwoven threads that did not always mesh: the actions of diplomats in Hanoi and Saigon, immersed in the war's intricacies but only dimly aware of what their chiefs at home were doing; and those of the increasingly assertive Rapacki and Michałowski, who felt themselves most qualified to handle delicate contacts, did not always feel bound to inform or consult their men in the field, and savored the prospect of scoring a diplomatic triumph that would raise Poland's (and their own) prestige, earning kudos from Washington and Moscow alike.

Inserting himself into the process, after reading Lewandowski's report of his second talk with Lodge (which reached Warsaw on November 17), Rapacki used the coincidental occasion of a Bulgarian Communist Party Congress to hold secret consultations with top Soviet and DRV figures. On Friday, November 18, he flew to Sofia by special plane and, with Michałowski, briefed Brezhnev on the Lodge-Lewandowski conversations.[55]

The Soviet leader gave the Polish effort Moscow's authoritative stamp of approval. "He shares our assessment of Lodge's propositions and our entire attitude towards the problem," Rapacki cabled. Forewarned by a secret letter from Rapacki of the reason for his abrupt visit to Sofia, the CPSU's general secretary said that he had already spoken with Nguyen Duy Trinh—also in town for the BCP Congress—"and found out that the [DRV] leadership had already examined

Lodge's proposals but not taken any decisions."[56] In what the Poles took as a sign of Hanoi's seriousness, Trinh had opted to cancel a stop in Budapest (where he had planned to attend a Hungarian Communist Party congress) and instead proceed to Moscow to rendezvous on November 25 with a VWP Politburo member—who turned out to be Le Duc Tho—"especially sent from Hanoi in order to jointly conduct consultations."[57] In addition, Brezhnev said, Le Duan had reportedly gone to Beijing. News of the secret diplomatic flurry, Rapacki felt, vindicated his hasty Bulgarian excursion. "Judging from this point of view, our arrival is just in time," he felt.

The next morning, November 19, Rapacki described Lodge's proposals to Trinh and praised them as showing flexibility and progress. "I do not think that [their] direct aim . . . is propaganda goals," he opined. "At least not for now." Because they implied a halt to bombing the North, Washington was seemingly ready to struggle with the NLF in the South, "backed up more effectively by the North that [was] now free of the bombings," because resuming after a suspension would be politically costly. Why would the Americans take this step? Rapacki noted four factors:

- Thanks to the heroic struggle of the NLF and the slogans of the DRV, they became convinced that they are not able to achieve their success by employing the present means and the present scale of operation, or they cannot achieve success quickly.
- In the face of upcoming presidential elections, Johnson cannot afford to prolong the current situation. Or he must achieve military or peaceful success.
- There is the possibility of intensifying the war. From all of the conversations in New York, however, it seems that the Americans are aware of the international consequences of this type of an action.
- There is also a fresh element here, namely the mid-term elections. It may be true that the foreign affairs, and especially the Vietnam issue, did not play a big role in these elections, but the fact remains that the peaceful forces became weaker. One cannot exclude the possibility that Johnson takes into consideration that once the new Congress convenes in January, then he will find himself under pressure of extreme elements and he may lose control in the future over these events. Perhaps this is why they picked this moment to [try] this new initiative.

Then he put forward an interpretation probably closest to the mark: "Perhaps the Americans want to sound out what they can achieve via peaceful negotiations in order to weigh the losses and gains of both possibilities, that is, further escalation and negotiations."

Trinh "listened very carefully" to Rapacki. Unable to "conceal his surprise at the content of the [U.S.] propositions," he questioned their accuracy. The Pole offered to have Lewandowski recheck with Lodge, but Trinh declined. Rapacki rejected his request for an aide-mémoire (which would more formally bind Warsaw) but agreed to furnish French translations of Lewandowski's cables.

(Michałowski slightly sanitized them, removing, for example, Lodge's reference to an "East European source" behind LBJ's six-month withdrawal offer.)

Trinh pledged to relay the information and Rapacki's assessments promptly to Hanoi (and asked to use the Polish Embassy's facilities to do so). Rather than argue, he acknowledged that the proposals merited careful study. When he stressed the need for total secrecy, the Pole agreed, noting that he had told no one besides Brezhnev, having explained to his Bulgarian hosts that he had come unexpectedly for ICC-related consultations. Rapacki praised the DRV's handling of the exchange of messages in July but stipulated that this time, Lewandowski could not deny communicating directly with Hanoi. "So, the question is whether the conditions are now ripe to move to the phase of combining the diplomatic struggle with the military one," Rapacki concluded—reviving the line that Michałowski had urged vainly upon Hanoi the previous January.

"He did not react as usual by giving me a whole bunch of clichés," the Pole acknowledged in his account to the PZPR leadership. Instead, the usually polemical Trinh only mildly protested that Hanoi had "already been conducting the diplomatic struggle" through the Canadians (i.e., the Ronning missions), and the talk turned to desultory ICC matters. As it ended, Trinh confirmed that he would skip Budapest and instead head "straight to Moscow" to "meet with the person from the leadership specially sent to the talks with Gromyko."[58]

Saturday evening, Rapacki saw Brezhnev again to relate the talk with Trinh and update him on the Saigon exchanges. Impressed, the Soviet acknowledged that the new ideas presented by Lodge seemed the "maximum" Washington could offer under the circumstances. In general, he sensed good conditions for progress. "While not exaggerating the results," Rapacki recorded, Brezhnev "thinks that the situation is favorable: The United States is at a crossroads, Vietnam is at a crossroads, and the PRC is busy with the 'Cultural Revolution.'" Yet his dealings with the North Vietnamese made him wary; one could "gain their understanding" speaking to them separately, but "the collective decisions turn out to be contradictory to those of individual people." They were under intense bellicose pressure, he noted, from both Beijing and the NLF.

Nevertheless, Brezhnev predicted that, thanks to sage Kremlin and bloc advice, Hanoi would see the light—repeating the old Moscow refrain that like "drops of water," such counsel would "gradually erode a path" for the comrades to reach the correct conclusion that negotiations rather than a myopic focus on military struggle was the best path forward. "To tell the truth, they should not be pressed more anyway," he told Rapacki, because they "know our arguments by heart." In parting, he sent regards to Gomułka and vowed to find some "free time when they can come for a hunting trip to Poland with the members of the [PZPR] Politburo."[59]

With Brezhnev abroad, they agreed, the Poles would tell Gromyko about the exchanges in Saigon and Sofia. Warsaw cabled a digest of the Lodge proposals to its Moscow embassy, but by the time Ambassador Edmund Pszczółkowski saw the Soviet foreign minister Monday morning, he had already discussed the matter with Brezhnev, who was back from Bulgaria.

Gromyko reacted guardedly. The new proposals "did not stray," he said, from what Johnson and Rusk had told him, and in one respect they were even "less flexible" than LBJ's remarks, because Lodge spoke only vaguely of a bombing halt, implying an unspecified DRV response, not an unconditional cessation. Still, he told Pszczółkowski, the fact that they were advanced "attests to the persistence of the desire of the Americans to get out of the situation in which they are bogged down in Vietnam." Perhaps LBJ had even used Manila to "prepare his partners toward this goal." Alluding to Trinh's expected arrival in Moscow for talks, Gromyko recalled "well-known difficulties" with Hanoi's policies and repeated "criticism of the Vietnamese position."[60]

Gromyko had ample evidence to feel pessimistic about luring Hanoi into peace contacts. At the start of the month, Dong had sternly told Moscow's ambassador that as Washington was escalating and lacked "the goodwill to begin talks," no progress could occur until it accepted the Four Points and "immediately and unconditionally" stopped bombing North Vietnam—which "would be a trial stone, a test of the USA's goodwill." The premier rejected Goldberg's formula, or any proposal demanding conditions or assurances in exchange for a bombing halt.[61] On November 12, when Trinh briefly stopped in Moscow en route to Eastern Europe, he told Gromyko that Hanoi had decided to "increase offensive activities—both military and political—against the American aggressors," and, insultingly, airily mentioned that the leadership was "still studying" Brezhnev's advice to Dong's delegation in August to devote more attention to possible negotiations. When Gromyko pressed Trinh to consider "the activation of the political struggle, about which was spoken in the Crimea," he put off a reply until after his trip to Bulgaria.[62] Gromyko also, as usual, rued China's influence on Hanoi; like Brezhnev, he noted that Le Duan was "recently going to be in Beijing" but confessed ignorance as to his visit's upshot.

What happened during the powerful VWP first secretary's secret trip to China at this key juncture? New Chinese and Polish evidence sheds light on these consultations, and, intriguingly, points in a very different direction than the Soviet-Vietnamese exchanges. On November 13, Siedlecki quoted an unnamed yet allegedly "quite reliable" Vietnamese source as saying that Le Duan had recently visited Beijing to inform the Chinese about the "need" to talk with the Americans.[63] In late December and early January, he would report, that Le Duan had told Zhou Enlai that "after arduous military effort," Hanoi intended "at present to accede to peace talks." When the premier riposted that the time was still "not ripe" for negotiations, Le Duan insisted that "the Vietnamese themselves know best." Mao received the delegation next, and in a "surprising" conversation, "disavowed" Zhou and agreed that Hanoi was best able to determine when to enter talks. "It is their war," he allegedly said, even vowing that China would "help the Vietnamese in these negotiations."[64] Siedlecki was not known for cultivating high-level DRV informants, but in this case, he was on the money; a Chinese record of the Mao–Le Duan talk relates that on November 8, after Le Duan described his exchange with Zhou, Mao told him: "I do not know what opinions he has presented to you, and whether or not they are suitable, or whether or not he has imposed them on you. Anything that you feel that you have been imposed upon, you do not need to accept. I have told President Ho that we follow your ideas. After all, it is you who are fighting on the front line. In addition, you have fought very well."[65]

In the dark about these Sino-Vietnamese contacts, Gromyko promised to keep the Poles informed on the results of the imminent Soviet-DRV talks; in response, he extracted a vow that Warsaw would likewise provide any further news on the Lodge-Lewandowski initiative.

Lewandowski in Hanoi

Lewandowski did not leave Saigon until November 18. Though he had previously been set to depart right after his second talk with Lodge, his flight was delayed by three days due to a recent incident in which an ICC plane approaching the Lao-DRV border was shot at, with flak exploding nearby. (The plane's French owner demanded a "guarantee" that this would not recur, a notion Lewandowski chuckled over decades later.) The situation regarding the ICC flights was dire, with complaints mounting not only of risky military activity but poor communications and failing equipment; the Pole endorsed Moore's use of the phrase "Russian Roulette" "as an accurate description of the game we are playing."[66] Pleading for modernized aircraft, the Canadian warned his government on November 15 that it did not grasp the issue's gravity: "It is a rather desperate and almost ludicrous situation that our international policy and the very useful contribution which both in Ottawa and here we are striving to make in this vital area of world tensions depend on the fate of an aged single aircraft which could be snuffed out through extreme metal fatigue, failing fuel pumps, stalling engines, by weather or, as was again last week demonstrated, by anti-aircraft fire."[67] With only one crew still willing to service and pilot the two Stratoliners—Rahman proposed a Polish crew, but Warsaw blanched—it took a few days to set a trip.[68]

The wait gave Lewandowski a chance to review his notes of the talks with Lodge and distill the U.S. position for presentation in Hanoi. Terming himself an editor or "redactor," Lewandowski recalled composing a summary in his office (his residence was not secure enough), writing it on ICC stationery, and checking some points with D'Orlandi. When he boarded the flight at Tan Son Nhut Friday morning, accompanied by his military aide, Colonel Ryszard Iwanciów, he dressed formally as always on business, and kept the notes in his suit pocket.[69]

The journey that night from Vientiane to Hanoi, frequently a nail-biter, was even worse than usual, Lewandowski remembered. As the plane neared Gia Lam, struggling to stay in the narrow approved low-altitude air corridor, the single light beam on which the pilot relied to guide him to the runway suddenly went out, and airport authorities radioed him to turn back because U.S. bombers were believed to be approaching and gunners were about to open up with triple-A. The Stratoliner, with limited fuel capacity, had to backtrack to the Lao capital, where passengers had to wait a full day before trying again. If that happened, the Pole spent Saturday at the ICC compound in Vientiane and did not reach Hanoi until late that night.

Waiting to greet Lewandowski at Gia Lam, as usual, was Ha Van Lau, who had a surprising question. "Look, what has happened?" the colonel asked. "For last few days, there is no bombing. Did you get the Americans to stop?"

"No," responded the Pole, who had no idea there had been any letup.[70]

On Sunday, November 20, Lewandowski reported receiving a "very good reception" in Hanoi, but no meeting with Dong was scheduled until Friday, just before he was supposed to leave. Hence, he thought it best to deliver Lodge's proposals immediately to Lau, who could relay them promptly to the premier.[71] Also present at the meeting at the Hoa Binh Hotel (where the ICC often met) were two midlevel DRV Foreign Ministry officials: Luu Van Loi, Lau's onetime deputy and a veteran of foreign negotiations since the anti-French war; and Nguyen Dinh Phuong, a senior English-language interpreter also aiding Lau on U.S. affairs.[72]

Taking out his notes, Lewandowski read them slowly so they could be copied sentence by sentence and read back without any chance of a discrepancy: Phuong translated his remarks from English into Vietnamese, and Loi transcribed them. Unusually, given the lack of access to Hanoi archives, we here can rely on a Vietnamese source: In 1990, Loi coauthored with Nguyen Anh Vu, a Foreign Ministry colleague, an internal study quoting contemporaneous records. Because these texts formed the basis of subsequent consideration by the DRV leadership, they are presented here in full. Regarding his November 14 conversation in Saigon with Lodge, which had featured the "Phase A / Phase B" concept, Lewandowski told the North Vietnamese:

> After an exchange of pleasantries, Cabot Lodge told me that he wanted to meet me in order to discuss Vietnam. I said that my primary official and sole responsibility was to be the representative of the Polish Government in the ICC in order to inspect the implementation of the Geneva Accords and other issues related to the implementation of those accords. Regarding the work related to that domain, I am ready to talk about.
>
> Cabot Lodge responded that he understood my duties. His objective was to make clear the American position to me as an individual.
>
> Cabot Lodge began by saying that the Manila Conference did not change the picture, nor did it divide the responsibility for the Vietnam problem among all the participants in the conference. The U.S. still had complete freedom to continue its efforts to find a solution for Vietnam. After reiterating that the U.S. had always sought to find a peaceful solution for the Vietnam problem, he stated the following issues:

—The U.S. has concluded that every effort it had made to deescalate without opposition has been fruitless. For that reason, the U.S. is now trying to find a more comprehensive solution.

—Washington is currently working to find such a solution, namely how to structure a cease-fire and all other remaining issues including even the withdrawal of U.S. troops from Vietnam.

—The U.S. does not necessarily think that a public declaration regarding such measures would be appropriate to the current situation and the conditions of its opponents. For this reason, the U.S. does not intend to make this document public or make any public statement about this plan.

—The U.S. problem now is that the U.S. does not know, whether a suggestion presented by the U.S. will be considered or not? Many people have said or indicated that they could be considered as representing the Democratic Republic of Vietnam or the National Liberation Front and they said that they had appropriate channels. However, now the U.S. realizes that these people in fact had no status whatsoever and were only acting for their own personal interests or for the publicity.

Cabot Lodge now wants to know whether, if such a suggestion as the one envisioned above was drafted, could it be transmitted to an appropriate person or not, and can comments on such a suggestion be transmitted back to the United States? The appropriate person would be someone with a clear understanding of the Democratic Republic of Vietnam and the National Liberation Front.

With these intentions, the United States is prepared to secretly consider and comment on any suggestion the Democratic Republic of Vietnam and the National Liberation Front wish to make, either jointly or separately.

Now the U.S. realizes that before any form of exchange can begin, it is essential that the bombing of the Democratic Republic of Vietnam first be stopped. The U.S. is now prepared to do this if such an action will have a direct effect. The U.S. does not expect that the effect will be immediate. The U.S. is not presenting any pre-conditions. The U.S. only wants a guarantee that this action will lead to practical efforts to hold talks aimed at finding a peaceful solution to the Vietnam problem.

The U.S. understands that the Democratic Republic of Vietnam will not agree to talks in exchange for a cessation of the bombing. The U.S. does not want to create the impression that the beginning of direct or indirect talks was the result of an American bombing halt. For that reason, the U.S. is prepared to take the following action:

—Phase A: The bombing of the Democratic Republic of Vietnam will be halted, and during this period no further action will be taken.

—Phase B: All other remaining matters, meaning direct or indirect exchanges of practical suggestions for all important problems.

Cabot Lodge asked for my comments on his message. I replied that I could not make any comment on his message, because anything I said would be only my

personal opinion. I continued, "If the U.S. truly needs to immediately and unconditionally stop the bombing and all other acts of war against the Democratic Republic of Vietnam, the U.S. should immediately end all hostile ground, sea, and air
actions against the people of South Vietnam. The U.S. must withdraw U.S. troops
from South Vietnam and eliminate all U.S. military bases. The U.S. must recognize the National Liberation Front as the sole and true representative of the people
of South Vietnam. The U.S. should acknowledge and do nothing to obstruct the
path of the people of Vietnam to the unification of the Vietnamese nation."

Cabot Lodge did not comment on my response.[73]

Describing the second three-way conversation, on November 15, Lewandowski
reported:

> Cabot Lodge said he wanted to meet me again because the previous day I had re-
> peated the official position of the Democratic Republic of Vietnam and of the
> National Liberation Front. He said that because of this, he thought that either I
> could not realize or refused to acknowledge the possibility of an exchange of ideas
> between the concerned parties. Lodge also felt that my refusal to comment on the
> contents of his message, in either an official or a personal capacity, meant that I
> believed that the position of the United States and the positions of the other con-
> cerned parties were completely opposed to one another.
>
> After further consideration, Lodge reached the conclusion that he needed to
> make it clear to me that my stated position did not eliminate the possibility that
> there still could be direct or indirect exchanges of ideas between the parties. He
> also wanted to make the following additional comments:
>
> 1—The U.S. is prepared to stop the bombing of the Democratic Republic of
> Vietnam if such an action could clear the way for a peaceful solution. The U.S.
> does not require any statement from the Democratic Republic of Vietnam about
> infiltration or any admission about the current or past presence of the People's
> Army of Vietnam in South Vietnam.
>
> 2—The U.S. has already declared its readiness to pull U.S. troops out of South
> Vietnam and to liquidate its military bases within 6 months ([as stated in] the
> Manila Declaration).
>
> 3—The U.S. is ready to accept a government in South Vietnam that is dem-
> ocratically elected with the participation of all citizens under international
> supervision.
>
> 4—The issue of unification is up to the Vietnamese people to resolve without
> any outside interference. For that reason, it is essential to restore peace and estab-
> lish a representative body to determine the true aspirations of the people. (These
> are my notes on Lodge's words, I did not inquire further.)
>
> 5—The U.S. wants to leave South Vietnam, but the U.S. cannot withdraw
> solely to turn the country over to the People's Army of Vietnam.
>
> 6—The U.S. is ready to accept fully and completely a neutral South Vietnam.

7—The U.S. is ready to exchange views directly or indirectly regarding all issues mentioned or not mentioned in this conversation.

The U.S. also needed to make it clear that it was not realistic to request the United States to announce that it simply accepted the Four Points or Five Points.

Lewandowski only listened and made no comments. Cabot Lodge further said that he had the authority to relay his opinions to Lewandowski, that they were the opinions of his superiors—U.S. decisionmakers.[74]

These Vietnamese sources resolve one key Marigold mystery at the time for U.S. officials (and later for journalistic and historical investigators): How fully or accurately did Lewandowski convey the American position to Hanoi? Did he correctly report Lodge's remarks, or did he, in the tradition of unscrupulous or overzealous mediators, sugarcoat or distort them in hopes of luring the recalcitrant North Vietnamese to the table?

The Vietnamese record suggests that Lewandowski fairly summarized Lodge's proposals, at least with regard to Washington's essential terms—even if he played down his own reactions at the three-way meetings (no mention of the friendly atmosphere or his own positive comments on the seemingly more flexible American stand). The Pole's language did no violence to official U.S. thinking, even if not necessarily phrased as, say, Rostow or Rusk might have preferred. As for "the beginnings of the alphabet," the Phase A/B proposition, that seems fuzzier, judging from the Vietnamese rendition, because it did not clarify that mutual agreement on measures in "Phase B" had to *precede* the bombing halt envisioned in "Phase A."

Lewandowski carefully refrained from endorsing the Lodge proposals when he first presented them but was glad to see that they impressed his listeners as new and noteworthy. After hearing him out, Ludwik cheerfully suggested dinner and seemed "excited" by the prospect of progress. Phuong also felt that the new U.S. stance was "good news," even "reasonable," and agreed with Lau that the proposals merited "serious consideration," in contrast to messages from other intermediaries (e.g., Ronning) that emphasized threats or pressure.[75]

On Monday, November 21, Lewandowski cabled Warsaw Lau's confirmation that the leadership had received and was considering the U.S. proposals, and Dong would give the Pole the response on Friday.[76] "We have to wait, we have to wait, they are talking," the "very tense" colonel reported.[77] His message delivered, Lewandowski had little to do besides, as Michałowski wrote, "waiting for the results of the long discussions inside the Politburo where, as we knew, opposing views clashed, in large measure" due to Chinese pressure.[78]

Lewandowski believed that the offer would tempt at least some in the Politburo. He expected Dong to argue forcefully for giving the U.S. proposition a chance, even at possible risk to his career, and hoped Giap would back him up.[79] But he also knew that the hard-liners would sternly resist sitting down with the enemy—a presumption bolstered by a talk with Nguyen Co Thach, who "declared himself categorically against accepting" the proposals. Using language that

Lewandowski felt echoed Trinh—who had presumably weighed in from Sofia or Moscow[80]—as well as the Chinese, the deputy foreign minister expressed blithe optimism about the situation on the battlefield and in international public opinion ("The support grows day by day"), dismissed the U.S. overture as a shopworn attempt to mask plans for further aggression, and, absurdly to the Pole's ears, even tried to explain away the United States' apparent willingness to stop bombing North Vietnam as stemming from a shortage of planes, which Washington could then divert to use against the "liberated territories" in the South. In any case, he added, because it was "well known" that the Vietnam War was a mere "prelude to the decisive fight with American imperialism," one could not imagine "a permanent and peaceful solution"—at most, perhaps, "an intermission to better prepare" for a final showdown. Declining to take the bait, Lewandowski merely observed "that the working masses in the world, including the USA, want peace and that they constitute a real force which binds the hands of the imperialists and which is able to thwart their plans."[81]

Decades later, Lewandowski, who presumed that Thach spoke at the behest of his harder-edged boss, angrily recalled how his stiff "indoctrination" on the evil imperialists—"this piece of, I don't know what you call it"—had disregarded the prospect of a bombing halt: "To take such a position when you have tons of bombs, strafings, victims, I mean, you must be either a fanatic or agent of somebody, because I tell [you] the main thing in such a situation that existed in Vietnam at that time, [is] all this suffering, not speaking [only] about South Vietnam, which is devastating people . . . if there is any perspective of avoiding [suffering] —and you say, 'even if they stop bombing, it means nothing'—'*nothing*'? When you stop killing the people, it means *nothing*?" Shaking his head incredulously, he emphasized that Dong never gave such a lecture.

"I wanted them to know what kind of people I had to deal with," he recalled when shown his telegram reporting the talk with Thach. "Otherwise, I probably wouldn't even send it."[82]

For the rest of the week, which seemed to stretch on endlessly, Lewandowski nervously imagined the decisive secret deliberations that would decide the initiative's fate. If the Politburo decided no, for any reason, he expected an "icy" reception from Dong and a "lesson" about "the nature of American imperialism and how to fight it" and the obligations of any honorable Communist. A rejection, he thought, would also end his usefulness as a peace-seeker in Vietnam or a Polish interlocutor with Hanoi. In that event, he planned to request an immediate recall: "I would only be an obstacle; I would be treated as a cryptosupporter of the U.S. imperialists."[83]

✳ ✳ ✳

Augmenting Lewandowski's tension that week in Hanoi was a sensitive incident that exposed the simmering disdain between him and Siedlecki. Lewandowski sensed that Poland's ambassador to North Vietnam saw him as an upstart, insufficiently respectful to his elder colleague (the young diplomat did not keep him adequately informed, he had already complained to Warsaw[84]) and ideologically suspect, too Westernized and eager to push talks with U.S. imperialists. In turn, Lewandowski thought that Siedlecki was a rigid, stodgy, *nekulturny* hack, a neo-Stalinist apparatchik lacking expertise or interest in Vietnam. "He was a relatively old man sitting in the embassy, and his hobby was to put [on the] tape recorder when the flak was started and American planes were coming, recording the boom-boom-boom-boom, boom-boom-boom-boom. He was very uncommunicative. He didn't really maintain contacts [with the Vietnamese leadership or] in the diplomatic corps, his only contact was the Soviet envoy. . . . He was a hardliner [with] very close links with the Soviet Union; as a matter of fact, he came to Poland in 1945 like a Soviet officer, . . . but he was Polish."[85]

Lewandowski had company in taking a dim view of Siedlecki. In a portrait of foreign diplomats in Hanoi, a Canadian ICC officer ranked him near the bottom of the barrel. Poland's ambassador was "extremely doctrinaire and has no flexibility in outlook," he reported, holding a "most unrealistic attitude toward negotiations": The Americans should leave and then "everything will be all right." "I am of the opinion," stated Lieutenant Colonel R. J. Kerfoot, who complimented other Soviet Bloc envoys (including the Czechoslovak and Hungarian), "that in the three years [Siedlecki] has been in Hanoi, he has not only become excessively sympathetic to the cause of the North Vietnamese, but believes a great deal of their propaganda."[86] "Doctrinaire and parrot-brained," Moore succinctly branded him.[87]

The matter that brought the friction between Lewandowski and Siedlecki to the surface involved their different approaches to both Marigold and Moscow. Intent on keeping the probe strictly secret, and acutely aware that an unauthorized leak could easily torpedo it, Lewandowski had no plans to brief Siedlecki on the U.S. proposals. Yet, on reaching Hanoi, he found that the ambassador had already learned of them from Warsaw. He quickly gathered that Siedlecki did not share his own ardor for the peace prospects they implied but presumed that he would at least abide by the need for discretion. As a November 19 cable describing the Rapacki-Trinh conversation in Sofia had stated that the contents of the talks with Lodge had already been "transmitted to Mikołaj"—code for the Russians—Lewandowski had no intention of bringing up the topic when he and Siedlecki went to the Soviet Embassy on Monday evening, November 21, to dine with Shcherbakov. After all, he felt, it was up to Warsaw to decide how to inform the Kremlin, and there was no need to spread the word among too many ambassadors, some more loose-lipped than others.[88]

Earlier that Monday—the same day that, in Moscow, Poland's ambassador filled in Gromyko—Shcherbakov had seen Dong, who had alluded cryptically to the exchanges in Bulgaria. As the irked envoy cabled Moscow, the premier told him that the VWP Politburo had directed Trinh and Le Duc Tho to rendezvous in the Soviet capital in a few days to meet the USSR's leaders "to inform them about the development of the situation in Vietnam and exchange opinions on questions of interest to both sides" but "evaded an explanation" when asked for their concrete instructions. Fanning rather than sating his curiosity, Dong merely said that Brezhnev already knew the visit's purpose, as Trinh had forewarned him in Sofia.[89]

Perhaps suspicious or tipped off that there might be a Polish connection, Shcherbakov invited Siedlecki and Lewandowski to sup with him—and apparently had more than a few words with Siedlecki beforehand, for when they sat down to eat, the Soviet raised the secret peace initiative in terms making it clear that he was fully informed; he even expressed regret that he was not told about it earlier, for he could have helped pressure Hanoi to cooperate. Lewandowski listened with rising alarm and consternation: "I did not make any remark but I was *crazy*. . . . I was furious."

As soon as they returned to the Polish Embassy, Lewandowski confronted Siedlecki.

"Have you informed him?" he demanded.

"How couldn't I, how couldn't I, you know?" Siedlecki replied sheepishly.

Did you tell him *everything*? Lewandowski pressed.

Yes, Siedlecki admitted.

Appalled—and convinced that Siedlecki was just currying favor with his Soviet buddy—Lewandowski now feared that Shcherbakov might return to Dong and raise the Lodge initiative, immediately casting doubt on his own (and Poland's) trustworthiness as a mediator who would carry out Hanoi's imperative to preserve total secrecy.[90]

The next morning, with Lewandowski on an excursion outside Hanoi, the ambassador tried to cover himself by obtaining post factum approval. In a message to Deputy Foreign Minister Naszkowski, Siedlecki, admitting that he might be "poking my nose into affairs [that are] not my business," mentioned a dispute with Lewandowski over whether to tell Shcherbakov about the Saigon talks and made the contrived case that the earlier cable's statement that Moscow *had been informed* should mean he *could inform* Shcherbakov of that fact so the Soviet did not need to rush to inform Moscow himself. He sought (retroactively, though he did not say so) permission to brief Shcherbakov, because this would be "beneficial for the tightening of cooperation in this area," and Moscow would surely inform him soon anyway.[91]

Naszkowski did not buy Siedlecki's pitch. "We would prefer that you limit yourself for the time being as not to include, unnecessarily, an additional channel of information for Moscow in order to avoid any misunderstandings of interpretation," he cabled. Sharply correcting his misreading of the prior instruction, Naszkowski said that if Siedlecki still wanted to say something to Shcherbakov, he might just assure him that Moscow already knows about the exchanges between Lewandowski and the Vietnamese comrades and would surely tell him about them soon.[92]

Squirming, Siedlecki tried to wriggle away. He obsequiously thanked Warsaw for its "objective" judgment on the need to "maintain even full secrecy on the spot, due to the delicate nature of the matter"—yet added that "a conversation [with Shcherbakov] about many issues with a full concealment even of the title of this topic could be understood as the expression of personal distrust and it could bring unnecessary artificiality in mutual relations."[93]

In the end, Shcherbakov did not interfere, as Lewandowski had feared, but the incident cast a permanent shadow over his relationship with Siedlecki—and illuminated a subterranean tension present, to one extent or another, in all Eastern and Central European chancelleries over the degree of obeisance they should show to their Soviet overlord.

* * *

Besides a few meetings at the embassy or Hoa Binh, Lewandowski spent much of the week at his villa in the French quarter, which was equipped with a small above-ground shelter especially built for him and a personal cook who prepared Vietnamese meals (he declined French cuisine). He also went with Lau to view bomb damage in Hung Yen Province southeast of the capital.[94]

Yet, much to his surprise, the bombing lull Lau had mentioned on his arrival persisted, despite good weather—in part due to Brown's presence in Moscow. Not wanting to embarrass Britain's foreign secretary (and showing that they could calibrate military and diplomatic actions if they felt like it), U.S. officials had put off the Rolling Thunder–52 program until after his November 22–25 visit.[95] Instead, they found a different way to humiliate him, though he did not know it then. They supplied the secret Phase A/B formula for the Soviets to pass to Hanoi, but not the proposals being sent via the Lodge-Lewandowski channel. But of course, Gromyko knew all about the Saigon talks from the Poles, and he fast surmised that Washington had left its ally out of the loop. When Brown related the Phase A/B idea, Gromyko and Kosygin curtly rejected transmitting it because it was not an unconditional bombing halt. With barely disguised scorn, Gromyko also rebuffed his bid to open a Soviet-British dialogue on Vietnam in the spirit of their Geneva partnership.[96]

Of course, because the Soviets lacked Hanoi's green light to mediate and were apprehensive about being branded American lackeys by the Chinese (and Vietnamese hard-liners), they hardly desired to act as deliverymen. But Brown's exclusion from full awareness of Washington's diplomacy rendered him doubly unfit as someone with whom to do business.

Bundy had earlier placed Brown and Moscow "somewhat nearer the heart of things" than Marigold. But it was Lewandowski who penetrated to the heart of the matter in Hanoi the very day that Brown wrapped up his disappointing visit.

* * *

After five days of excruciating suspense, Lewandowski was finally received by Dong at 10 a.m. on Friday, November 25.[97] It had been almost six months since they last met, and the Pole noticed more gray in the sixty-year-old revolutionary's neatly combed black hair.[98] As usual, they met in a large reception room in the prime minister's office building, sitting side by side in large plush chairs besides small tables bearing tea, snacks, and bouquets. Behind them stood two polished stone columns; above, a ceiling fan stirred the heavy air; and their shoes rested on a thick Chinese carpet. The Pole, dressed formally despite the "almost 100 percent" humidity, spoke English and Dong Vietnamese, with Luu Van Loi at his side, interpreting; Lau and a few other aides also attended.

At the outset of the two-and-a-half-hour conversation, Dong warmly greeted his visitor, expressed "complete uniformity of thought with the Polish comrades," and thanked them profusely for supporting Hanoi's struggle, in general and in the ICC in particular, asking Lewandowski to relay these friendly sentiments to Rapacki. Yet Dong did not immediately divulge the news that Lewandowski so anxiously anticipated, and prolonged the suspense by first subjecting him to an extended grilling. After observing that Hanoi judged that the "USA finds itself before a choice: seriously expand activities or search for peaceful resolutions," he interrogated Lewandowski about the situation in the South and "demanded" his appraisals of issues related to the initiative. Which tendency prevailed in Washington, toward peace or escalation? Did Lodge express his own views, or LBJ's? What topics would be hardest to resolve in any negotiations?

Listening to these questions, familiar with this tactic from his Middle Eastern experience, Lewandowski suspected that he was being tested. Had Warsaw (and he personally) conveyed the U.S. proposals due to a lack of confidence in Vietnam's cause or prospects? Were the Poles knuckling under to American pressure, trying to convince the DRV to soften its stand?

"Mr. Lewandowski"—he remembered being pressed—"you are a well-traveled man, you were in America, do you think it is serious? Do they really want to find a peaceful solution?"

"Well," he replied, "I think that they are, but . . . we can probe." Responding obliquely, he tried to evade explicitly giving his own evaluations. "I was trying to avoid direct, you know, replies, . . . because I knew what he is looking for," Lewandowski recalled, laughing. "I knew what he is looking for. . . . We knew each other fairly well."

Dong insisted, requesting his "personal observation."

So Lewandowski complied. The odds that Washington was serious, he ventured, were "pretty even"—much depended on the efforts of Hanoi and the "entire socialist camp" to promote peaceful tendencies. The Pole did not reveal that Lodge had showed him Rusk's cable, but assured Dong that the American reflected LBJ's views, as no ambassador would act independently in such an important matter. Looking ahead to possible talks, he judged that unification would pose the toughest problem, engaging U.S. interests and "prestige as a great power."

Dong agreed with Lewandowski that Washington "stands before important military and political decisions" and needed "a chance to direct their attention towards the search for peaceful resolutions," and accepted his judgment that Lodge "undoubtedly" spoke on LBJ's instructions. His Politburo comrades likewise expected unification to be the toughest issue in negotiations, but not necessarily insuperable. "They are patient," he said. "If the USA departs from South Vietnam, there is no reason to hurry. They are ready to wait."

"You may be sure that if the Americans decide to settle this problem in negotiations, we are ready to put a red carpet for them to walk from Vietnam," Dong told Lewandowski. "We are going to facilitate. We are not going to take over South Vietnam. . . . We are ready to be patient."

Evidently satisfied that Lewandowski had passed his exam, Dong finally came to the point. He asked him to schedule another meeting with Lodge and "deliver to him, without making reference to the Premier, the following declaration: 'If the USA is ready to confirm the views expressed in the talks between Ambassador Lodge and Ambassador Lewandowski, then it can do it through the Ambassador of the Democratic Republic of Vietnam in Warsaw.'"[99]

Lewandowski was elated to hear that the Politburo—after "animated" and "stormy" deliberations[100]—had approved going forward, authorizing a direct contact with U.S. officials that might quickly lead to negotiations, whether formal or de facto. But Dong's harsh strictures on secrecy tempered his excitement and relief: Not only must the Pole be "speaking for yourself only," rather than the premier, when telling Lodge about the DRV's assent to the Warsaw contact, but he should also warn that if *any* information about the prospective talks emerged publicly, Hanoi would instantly disavow them.

Lewandowski gulped. "Can you imagine my position?"

> I took a certain message to transmit to the Vietnamese. I have done it. And I have not done it like a postman, these practically were the results of many previous talks. . . . I made a meeting [in Hanoi], they decided to go ahead, to have a meeting [in Warsaw], but I was not free to characterize it [to Lodge] as being from Pham Van Dong. Only by implication; . . . but if anything is published, they will deny it. Can you imagine my position? (laughing) What would happen if a fool somewhere will publish something? Then, [it would be as if] nothing happened. If something changed, because they were under pressure from China. . . . They would deny it, . . . and I would become a simple, irresponsible liar. . . . I would have put also Rapacki in the same position, who went to Brezhnev, and then they [the Soviets] would say, "So, nothing happened, this is all an invention of Lewandowski."

Dong then raised another dicey subject: the bombing. Like Lau, he had noticed a seeming abrupt slackening in the air raids despite good weather, and he asked Lewandowski whether he could take credit for it, perhaps as a signal of support for the initiative; again, the Pole disclaimed any knowledge. Moving to the future, Dong called a bombing cessation "a self-evident matter, the minimum, before any kind of talks." But he did not term such a halt a precondition for the Warsaw contact. The premier asked Lewandowski to inform Rapacki, and agreed to see him again on Monday to answer any questions. As the meeting ended, Dong assured him that Hanoi viewed the potential impending talks seriously— not just as a propaganda gesture.

"The Vietnamese do not desire to humiliate the USA," he declared. "Their views are convergent with Polish ones. There is no need to dread the discussion with L[odge]. A better understanding of American views can only help at present and in the future."

Pleased but wary, Lewandowski returned to the Polish Embassy to draft an urgent cable reporting the conversation and requesting instructions, and shift his departure for Saigon until late Tuesday night so he could see Dong again Monday.

✳ ✳ ✳

Over the weekend, Warsaw secretly informed Moscow of the apparent break-through. Late Saturday afternoon, Pszczółkowski briefed Gromyko on Lewan-dowski's talk with Dong and relayed a copy of the analysis that Rapacki had given Trinh, adding that the DRV premier had said that Hanoi's assessment matched Warsaw's. Cautiously, Gromyko "evaded making any significant remarks"— perhaps slightly miffed that the Kremlin's subservient ally, rather than Moscow itself, seemed on the verge of such a major achievement, or else was too dubious about the likelihood of success to issue congratulations. Instead, he merely asked how Warsaw intended to inform the Americans (through Lewandowski, as Dong had desired, the Pole replied) and noted that Dong's demand that Lewandowski not use his name must reflect a Vietnamese desire to cover themselves—probably, he agreed with Pszczółkowski, from the Chinese.[101]

Gromyko then updated Warsaw's envoy on Soviet diplomacy. Recounting the brusque rejection of Brown's pleas for a bilateral dialogue on Vietnam, he derided the "pushiness" of the U.K. foreign secretary, who "ostentatiously" showed his disappointment.[102] But he had little to report regarding the covert consultations with senior DRV figures on the Polish probe that were supposed to be happening in Moscow. The afternoon before, the VWP Central Committee (CC) secretary, Le Duc Tho, had landed in the capital, joining Trinh (who had flown from Sofia via Bucharest[103]). Yet, Gromyko related with a hint of irritation, not only had Trinh not initiated talks but Tho had also begged off meetings, "saying he was tired and needed to rest"—perhaps he awaited new instructions from Hanoi.[104] The Soviets remained equally in the dark about Le Duan's visit to Beijing, he added, aside from "scant information" that a "heated fight" had occurred at a Plenum of the Chinese Communist Party. At this potentially decisive moment, Warsaw, not Moscow, was in closer touch with the DRV leadership, and Rapacki, not Gromyko, was calling the diplomatic shots.

✳ ✳ ✳

In Saigon, D'Orlandi's suspense neared fever pitch as his Polish friend repeatedly failed to alight from the ICC Stratoliners periodically puttering into Tan Son Nhut from up north. The Italian, already sensing mortality breathing down his neck, felt an even greater hurry to achieve something tangible from his clandestine diplomacy after breakfasting with Lodge on November 23. Besides speculating on the fortunes of their absent partner, they confided plans to finish their ambassadorial stints by March—D'Orlandi was convinced that his health could not stand another hot season, and Lodge was disgruntled with his mission. In the more immediate future, Lodge disclosed that Rusk would stop in Saigon for three days beginning December 9; afterward, Lodge would leave for a month-long vacation with his family in the United States. These plans could change, the Italian ruminated, depending on what, if anything, came of the secret sessions with the Pole.

"Men propose, then we shall see what God disposes," he reflected.[105]

As the Pole's absence lengthened, D'Orlandi grew less philosophical and more impatient. On November 26, he complained to his diary: "Still no news of Lewandowski." The next day: "What the devil can be happening to them in Hanoi?"[106]

✳ ✳ ✳

On Monday morning, November 28, Lewandowski returned to Dong's reception room for a second meeting.[107] Having received a cable from Rapacki containing instructions over the weekend, he began by relating his boss's message, which included greetings from Gomułka and the PZPR Politburo to the DRV comrades and Poland's analysis of the U.S. proposals.[108]

Dong returned Gomułka's fraternal regards and praised the Polish material, political, and diplomatic aid, and even more its nuanced comprehension of Hanoi's stand. "Not everyone from the socialist countries understands us as well as the Polish comrades," he said, an obvious dig at the Chinese (and perhaps also the Soviets) that must have heartened Warsaw. "What a pity that not all of the socialist states display the same propriety as the Polish comrades."

Moving to the U.S. proposals, he made explicit a crucial point—the Warsaw contact could occur even without a prior bombing halt: "Independent of everything, the USA should cease the bombing. It is not a necessary condition before a meeting in Warsaw. It is not known if the USA will realize a meeting. It is not known if they will confirm Lodge's expressions or if they will come out with something else. It is a plain matter that if they ceased the bombings, it would constitute a step forward."

On top of this statement—a startling deviation from almost two years of rigid insistence that a unilateral, unconditional bombing halt must precede direct talks —North Vietnam's premier asked Lewandowski to give Gomułka "assurances that if the United States takes a promising [*nadzieje*] position, then the DRV government will take a positive attitude. . . . They will prepare their positive position, and they will certainly consult with our [Polish] leadership." Though not binding, this was a politically significant commitment that Hanoi would do more than simply receive a U.S. confirmation in Warsaw that Lewandowski had correctly conveyed Washington's position—it would be willing to enter serious negotiations.

Dong insisted that the North Vietnamese were "not apprehensive of talks if there is a basis for them," but he also sounded a note of realism. Because the Johnson administration's "prowar wing" might yet prevail, "they do not want to construct an ice-castle." Much depended, he stated, on whether the Americans actually showed up for the Warsaw meeting and what they said there.

Dong also discussed practical aspects of the contacts. Thanking the Poles for offering to arrange the first meeting, he remarked that the level depended on whom the Americans nominated—if they came at all. If indeed "serious," he said, "then surely they will not delegate a minor official." The Vietnamese would return to the issue when the situation was clarified.

He asked Lewandowski, once back in Saigon, to sound out Lodge on Washington's positions, particularly toward the NLF, encouraging direct contacts with it if it truly desired peace. He also asked the Pole "to put pressure in the talks on the matter of bombings, indicating that demanding their cessation is a common postulate of all peace proposals put forward around the entire world." Finally, he again stressed "absolute secrecy"—Lewandowski must speak to Lodge only "in [his] own name," not Dong's.

When the conversation ended, Dong did something that he had not done before, and that left a strong mark on the Pole decades later: Bidding an emotional farewell, he stood, hugged, and kissed Lewandowski. "It was very, very unusual," he recalled. "He had almost tears in his eyes. He was deeply, deeply touched. Frankly speaking, I was a little bit surprised, you know, because, he was always polite, . . . making jokes, you know, but he never demonstrated such emotions. . . . There was a very strong feeling of warmth, of something very good."

Hearing Lewandowski recount this embrace, somewhat emotionally himself, in a smoky Warsaw hotel café in 2003, I asked: "Did you feel at that moment, in some way, that Pham Van Dong had joined your conspiracy?"

"I think so," he answered. "I was almost sure that this is, that, that I hoped that something very important is being born, you know, that maybe, you know, that something good for the Vietnamese people is going to happen."

"Moreover," he reflected, "the Vietnamese are very reluctant to show such a closeness, even with good friends, you find that when you are in Asia, even if they invite you to their home, it's something special, and to embrace you, [with] white skin you know, and kiss you, is something, you know, something special, something special. I believe it was a kind of recognition of my work in this business—but he did it."[109]

Underlying Dong's intensity, Lewandowski believed, were mingled emotions: hope that Vietnam might be verging on a historic turning point toward ending the war (at least its bloodiest phase), and an awareness that he had taken a huge risk that might backfire—for his nation, which he governed; for the cause for which he had fought; and for him personally. By arguing so strongly in the Politburo against strong opposition for taking a chance on the U.S. initiative, the Pole suspected, Dong had "crossed the Rubicon," staking his political reputation and career. Personally, he felt the moment sealed a bond between them: They were in this business together.

Driving Lewandowski back to his villa, the urbane, normally unflappable Lau was also "very shaken," moved by what he had witnessed and its potential implications.[110]

Quickly composing a cable for Rapacki, Lewandowski related Dong's remarks, noting the heartfelt and affectionate farewell. Then he added his own analysis:

> —The decision to undertake contact in Warsaw is a collective decision of the leadership taken, surely, not without discussion. This is indicated by my talk with the deputy minister of foreign affairs [Thach], which I will relate separately.
>
> —The Vietnamese comrades are awaiting something more than a simple confirmation of our information from the meeting in Warsaw. If this is confirmed, only then will they put forward the condition to cease the bombing. They are aware that stopping the bombing right now would not allow the fact of the contact to be kept secret and would engender massive pressure of public opinion on both sides.
>
> —It appears that the information has aroused serious interest and a certain chance has arisen for the initiation of progress.

Lewandowski tried to keep a cool, reserved tone, but he did not hide his belief that after so many fruitless efforts, a breakthrough had occurred—opening the door, finally, to direct talks between Washington and Hanoi on the basis of mutually acceptable terms for an eventual agreement.

✳ ✳ ✳

How significant were Pham Van Dong's statements? Lewandowski's cables relating his talks on November 25 and 28, 1966, reinforced by his vivid recollections and corroborated by Vietnamese sources, resolve conclusively what George Herring called Marigold's "central issue"—"whether Lewandowski was accurately representing the North Vietnamese position" when, on seeing Lodge back in Saigon, he conveyed Hanoi's willingness to meet with the Americans in Warsaw.[111] Indeed he was—and newly available archival evidence demolishes the extreme skepticism later displayed by U.S. officials, from LBJ down, about whether the Poles were *ever* in touch with authoritative DRV figures, received their approval for the Warsaw contact, or perhaps made up the whole thing to mislead Washington or probe its position. "The real enigma in the whole affair," observed a U.K. aide in 1967, after Marigold collapsed, "is the degree of North Vietnamese support for what the Poles were doing."[112]

The new evidence dispels this mystery. It shows that Dong, speaking for the DRV, authoritatively anointed Lewandowski to communicate its readiness to receive *even without a prior bombing halt* an official U.S. representative in Warsaw to confirm that Washington stood behind the Lodge proposals; moreover, he explicitly pledged to Poland's Communist leaders to adopt, on receiving said U.S. confirmation, a "positive attitude to a political resolution of the conflict" despite evident Chinese (and internal) opposition.

Yet the Poles could not discern the *degree* to which Hanoi had committed itself to *serious* peace talks (which implied painful compromise) or the meaning of its readiness to engage in direct contacts to confirm Lodge's proposals. Lewandowski had no way of knowing, for example, whether the outcome was a real victory for moderates, as he hoped, or a tactical compromise that might easily unravel. Though dimly aware of stormy Politburo debates, protocol and propriety precluded him from directly asking Dong about internal leadership deliberations. He and Lau could informally speculate on Politburo factions and disputes, but in this case, the colonel likewise lacked firsthand information. Lewandowski presumed that the comparatively moderate Dong, backed by Giap, had favored responding to the initiative, but that (as his talk with Thach showed) hard-liners pushed China's line of armed struggle until inevitable triumph, insisted Washington was weakening, and resolutely opposed any move toward negotiations. As for the stands of key figures such as Le Duan and Ho (who at least attended the session on November 23), one could only guess.[113]

Siedlecki supplies a contemporaneous scrap of evidence on the Politburo deliberations. In early December, he relayed to Warsaw some gossip of unclear reliability or origin, citing Shcherbakov as saying that two senior commanders of the struggle in the South, General Truong Chinh and General Nguyen Chi Thanh, both veteran revolutionaries, strongly opposed talks and urged "conducting the fight until final victory." They were said to be in the minority, overruled by a majority that backed negotiations, "but [only] after having taken advantage of military possibilities in the upcoming [southern] dry season," which was just starting and lasted until April or May. This did not mean, Siedlecki noted, that "negotiations, or rather preliminary talks, could begin only after the dry season was over —they could begin earlier, so [that] at the end of the dry season (of their final military effort) a decisive moment could take place"[114]—a scenario reminiscent of the decisive 1954 Dien Bien Phu battle on Geneva's eve.

Another Siedlecki cable, sent shortly before Lewandowski reached Hanoi, suggests that he fortuitously delivered more enticing U.S. proposals just as the DRV leaders were debating whether to move toward negotiations.[115] In a striking departure from his usual fervid endorsement of Hanoi's determined military focus, he reported that behind its firm front, troubles were mounting. His "quite reliable" Vietnamese informant described growing war-weariness—"People's tiredness can be seriously felt"—and rising rates (up to 17 percent) of desertion and nonreporting for duty in the PAVN; enforced drafts of older and younger men, leaving behind "mostly girls" in villages and factories; a "very difficult situation" in the South recently described by an NLF delegation to the VWP Politburo; Le Duan's above-mentioned secret trip to China "to present the need [for] talks with the U.S."; and a decidedly more pragmatic line purveyed by the first secretary to his propaganda department. Rejecting draft ideological statements, Le Duan was said to have emphasized expertise in handling advanced Soviet Bloc weaponry over "platitudes" exhorting soldiers to "combine new weapons with bamboo lances," and "patriotic feelings" over class hatred. "We are not fighting with imperialism in general, but with the U.S.," he was quoted as telling his propaganda chief, To Huu. "De Gaulle is a representative of French imperialism. Every imperialist, every bourgeois [who is] an enemy of the U.S. imperialism, is our ally." In sum, since mid-September, according to Siedlecki's Vietnamese source, the leadership had split into three groups: One advocated negotiations now; another urged a "maximum effort" during the upcoming dry season to strengthen battlefield positions before talks; and a hard-line group remained intent on military victory.

Of course, this report must be taken warily, but if Siedlecki's source proffered even broadly accurate data, it meant that the more appealing U.S. stand might have strengthened those in the leadership, such as Dong, who were willing to give peace a chance.[116] His informant was plugged in on at least one count: Le Duan's stress on mastering science and technology at home and welcoming broad support abroad (not solely from "class" allies). In December, he began urging these relatively moderate and pragmatic priorities—a seeming shift from his prior pro-Chinese tilt.[117]

The evidence, however tenuous, of Le Duan's move to a more flexible stance merits close scrutiny, because his position on negotiations at this point remains shrouded in secrecy. With Ho largely relegated to ceremonial duties and divorced from day-to-day decisionmaking, his powerful successor likely had the decisive voice in a divided Politburo; moreover, because Le Duan ultimately at least acquiesced in the approval of the direct contact in Warsaw (such a fateful step could hardly be taken over his strong opposition), he may have influenced his protégé, Le Duc Tho, usually seen as a hard-liner, to also endorse the idea.[118]

Alas, we still lack access to Vietnamese archives that might illuminate the internal Politburo debates and clarify the meaning of Dong's forthcoming statements to Lewandowski. Pertinent contemporaneous materials have, however, recently emerged in publications of documents from the VWP CC archives. Combined with the known record of Hanoi's later policy shifts, they offer strong circumstantial evidence to corroborate Lewandowski's and Siedlecki's sense that in late 1966, the Politburo was gripped by a strategic debate over how to blend military, political, and diplomatic struggles. This debate ultimately yielded a decision to move from a fight to beat the Americans and their Saigon "puppets" militarily to one that allowed *simultaneous* diplomatic combat through negotiations. That Hanoi had reached this conclusion became evident in late January 1967, when Trinh first stated openly that U.S.-DRV talks "could" begin once Washington "unconditionally" halted bombing and all other acts of war against North Vietnam.[119]

But Trinh's statement only exposed the tip of a long-submerged process comprising several months of internal policy debate, formulation, ratification, and coordination, extending back to the time when Marigold sprang back to life. In its Resolution 13, passed at its Thirteenth Plenum in late January 1967, the VWP CC would agree that "in coordination" and "in parallel with the military and political struggle in South Vietnam, we must *launch a diplomatic offensive against the enemy* . . . in order to gain even greater victories." "In the current international situation," it added, "because of the nature of the war between the enemy and ourselves, the diplomatic struggle will play an important, vigorous, and offensive role."[120]

But long before the VWP CC resolved to "step up the diplomatic struggle," the far smaller and more powerful Politburo had considered the role of diplomacy and negotiations in the war effort. A lengthy Politburo resolution ultimately ratified by the VWP CC in late January 1967—though considered by the Politburo in October and November 1966—more fully explains this "fighting while negotiating, negotiating while fighting" approach:

> In parallel with the military struggle and the political struggle inside our country, we need to attack the enemy on the diplomatic front by intensifying our international political and diplomatic struggle in order to more strongly denounce the brutal crimes committed by the American aggressors, to expose their scheme of conducting peace negotiations, to highlight the position of our government and the 5-point statement of the National Liberation Front, to illuminate the fact that our position is just, and to clearly state our resolve and the certainty of our victory. . . .
>
> To support the military and the political struggles and help them advance to score great victories, we need to take the initiative and actively create conditions that will enable us to employ our "fight-talk, talk-fight" stratagem in order to win broad support among the international public and to isolate the American imperialists and cause them further problems that will make them passive and confused and that will exacerbate their internal contradictions in order to contribute to the effort to bring about the disintegration of the puppet army and puppet government and to intensify our struggle movement in the cities.[121]

This resolution—larded with invective and jargon, bluster and bravado—hardly expressed confidence that negotiations were a plausible path to peace; instead, they were just another front in the war. It permitted direct talks with the American enemy, but subsidiary to the decisive ongoing military and political battles that remained the main path to victory. Yet the bellicose resolution was the end product of an elaborate, furtive policy process, and resolutions were commonly modified as they wound their way through Politburo debates and onward to the VWP CC.[122]

Did this belligerent "fight-talk, talk-fight" perspective prevail from the start—lurking behind (and vitiating the significance of) Hanoi's consent to the Warsaw contact? Or did the language and policy harden after Marigold collapsed, concealing a prior genuine willingness to explore a political settlement in direct exchanges (as implied by Dong's promise to Gomułka via Lewandowski to adopt a "positive attitude" if the Americans took a forthcoming position)?

Lewandowski believed then—and still believed, decades later—that North Vietnam was dead serious about exploring a package deal, in part because, as the Johnson administration dearly hoped and Hanoi bravely denied, it was suffering under the intense pressure of the U.S. war machine. After showing him the Politburo extract about "fighting while negotiating," which he dismissed as Communist cant, I asked Lewandowski if, in agreeing to the Warsaw contact, the DRV's leaders really hoped for a peaceful settlement or merely wanted to put the enemy on the defensive while continuing the war. He responded passionately:

No—peaceful settlement. I will tell you more about it. . . . It would be a great mistake to say that the Vietnamese were having all the military success. It was not. They were suffering horrible losses, both in South Vietnam and in North Vietnam, from the beginning. . . . In North Vietnam, you had both a horrible drainage of manpower, you know, very young people, I saw them training, boys with rifles running . . . in these rubber shoes, . . . teaching them, and then [they] disappeared in [the] jungle. Sometimes the rifles were just [crutches]. Population was starved, the rations were very limited, you know, the people gathered grass, herbs, finding the crickets. In the area of Haiphong, for example, where people used to live on the sea maybe, they couldn't fish because whatever went on the sea was bombed by Americans. They had . . . something like 150 grams of grease . . . a *month* for a family, and . . . it was a *very* difficult time. The transportation was very limited, . . . and military by having the predominant priority, even if you have goods, food, you couldn't send them—it was not swallowed by the transportation system, you see, bridges were broken. All transport movement was only by night. You have to move the population. What [have] they done? From the cities, they move them to the villages and still you could not find something. Those poor people, the children, at nights with the provisional bridges made of bamboo, nightly going on—it was not easy, it was not easy. They were suffering all the way, transporting this whole system, all ammunition had to be brought there, through the way which was bombed. . . . For every American, I think, there were [a] hundred Vietnamese killed. . . . When they tried to make something bigger, it was very difficult, because one of the questions was that, was transport dispersing the forces. . . . But if you want to make any attack, you have to gather them. So I mean—and I saw it when they tried Pleiku offensive [in August 1966], when they saw what the fire-power of U.S. Army is, [they had] horrible losses over there. They thought they would cut Vietnam in this narrow place, after they remembered the . . . divisions, having strong defeat, I think, Giap was criticized. . . .When they thought about the Tet Offensive, about offensive action, it was almost a desperate thing, the outcome of which nobody could foresee. And what I wanted to say for your background, were they interested or not? *Yes,* they were! Because the future was not only per-fect, or brilliant, the future was very doubtful. How long could they sustain things and what prospect? They made the offensive but—you give all forces you got. . . . After [all], what perspective have [they] got? Pham Van Dong [said,] "We cannot defeat the United States; we do not dream we can defeat the United States."

This did not mean, he stressed, that the DRV's leaders imagined relinquishing their national goal of eventual unification—but that at least some found alluring the idea of attaining it in stages, perhaps through neutralization to evict the Americans (along with Chinese and Soviet advisers, for whom they had no spe-cial love) and a perhaps extended South Vietnamese existence. "You may be sure that if Americans decide to settle this problem in negotiations, we are ready to put a red carpet for them to walk from Vietnam," Dong told him. "We are going to facilitate. We are not going to take over South Vietnam; . . . we are ready to be patient." He even jocularly supposed that Lewandowski might become Polish ambassador to South Vietnam—an Alice-in-Wonderland idea at a time when the Communist world shunned Saigon.

"Well," the startled Pole replied, "but Mr. Prime Minister, if you [are] one country, then there will not be two embassies."

"Don't worry, don't worry," Dong assured him, "there will be [a] place for rep-resentation, we are not rushing these things."[123]

Lewandowski also sensed that Hanoi preferred secret direct talks with Wash-ington to an international conference that Moscow or Beijing might attend. After the disastrous experience at Geneva in 1954, when they felt their Communist patrons had forced concessions to the French down their throat, squandering leverage won with Vietnamese blood, they trusted no one else to defend their interests. They also comprehended that the Americans—as Lodge emphasized— would never accept a formula that would allow them to waltz in and take over South Vietnam promptly after a U.S. withdrawal. Dong harkened back to their earlier conversations, in which the Pole had warned him that a great world power could not be kicked in the balls.[124]

Coincidentally, an authoritative secret CIA appraisal also concluded that North Vietnam, in part due to U.S. military pressure, might be edging toward a real interest in a direct dialogue with Washington. In a memo ("The View from Hanoi") to director Richard Helms, senior analyst Sherman Kent (for the Board of National Estimates) depicted Hanoi as increasingly pessimistic about its strat-egy of protracted war and torn between the alternatives of "procrastinating" until the dry season's end and "reconsidering its options"—either by adjusting its military tactics toward guerrilla operations (as opposed to large-unit attacks) or, perhaps, "a shift toward the political track, with all its hazards." Though unaware of Marigold, Kent felt a decisive moment had arrived: "For the first time in the last two years, there is a chance of a serious political move from the Communist side." This memorandum was dated November 30, 1966.[125]

✳ ✳ ✳

At 4 a.m. that same Wednesday morning, Hanoi time, Lewandowski took off from Gia Lam on one of the ICC's antiquated planes.[126] Before leaving, he reverted to his role as celebrity Communist informant from behind enemy lines. On Tuesday, he held forth on the military and political situation in the South to Soviet Bloc diplomats. He depicted a stalemate, with the Americans frustrating the NLF's plans in the dry season but the Communists enjoying an edge once the monsoons started. Politically, he judged that the September elections had failed to stabilize the Saigon regime, still suffering from pervasive corruption and intense if diffuse popular opposition. Yet, he acknowledged, the NLF's political influence had waned recently, in both government- and guerrilla-controlled regions. Keeping his tracks well concealed, he gave no hint of any progress toward peace, let alone of the secret effort in which he was so deeply engaged.[127]

His missions accomplished, Lewandowski headed for the airport. Despite his success in obtaining Hanoi's consent to deal directly with the Americans and even, implicitly, to negotiate peace on the basis of terms that he had personally crafted and delivered, he was not in a festive mood. During the wearying day-long voyage back to Saigon, he stayed tight-lipped. In the Stratoliner's VIP compartment, such as it was, he sat with Rahman, who was returning from a short visit to Hanoi before heading to New Delhi for consultations, but had—so the Indian told Moore—"as usual, nothing to say of any consequence."[128] Lewandowski indeed felt happy to be carrying positive, major news, but discretion kept his tongue firmly in check, just as anxiety and realism restrained any exultation. Though convinced that a plausible basis to begin negotiations now existed if both sides had the political will, he fully realized that they would be fraught with difficulties.

Lewandowski's immediate concern, however, was that something might sabotage the effort before direct talks even began. From what Dong had told him, he feared that everything could be ruined by one leak, one blabbermouth from any of the informed countries, eager to inform the world who deserved kudos for a stunning diplomatic achievement. From past experience, with the Italians but also the Americans, with their habit of passing scuttlebutt to favored reporters, he knew this was no idle concern; nor could he ignore the risk that his Canadian and Indian colleagues, aware that he had gone to Hanoi yet lacked any ICC excuse for his trip, might grow suspicious.

Even before he had left Saigon, the peace plotters feared their secrecy was compromised. Lodge confided to D'Orlandi that Moore had "gotten wind of" their gatherings, and probably even had the Pole tailed; worse, Ky "indirectly hinted" that he knew, perhaps having been tipped off by his police chief, which raised the peril that the South Vietnamese authorities could sink the enterprise with a leak if they feared that Washington might cut a deal they did not like behind their backs. When Lodge told D'Orlandi about this on November 16, with Hanoi's reaction to the U.S. proposals uncertain, the Italian found the news worrying but largely theoretical. "For now, all of this is not too serious, but in the long term, it could become embarrassing."[129]

Now the stakes had gotten much higher—not only for peace prospects but also for Lewandowski personally. If word slipped out, for any reason, the war would go on, and the hullabaloo would be written off to the fevered imagination, or worse, of a junior Polish diplomat.

"This whole operation," Lewandowski said intently, "was a nerve-eating business, a nerve-eating business."[130]

5

"Something Big Has Happened"
Toward the Warsaw Meeting, December 1–5, 1966

I am authorized to say that if the United States are really of the views which I have presented, it would be advisable to confirm them directly by conversation with the North Vietnamese Ambassador in Warsaw.

> —*Janusz Lewandowski to Henry Cabot Lodge, Saigon, December 1, 1966*

I am instructed to tell you that the United States Government is instructing the American Embassy in Warsaw to contact the North Vietnamese representative there on December 6. Our Embassy will be able to confirm that the ten points outlined by you broadly represent our position. We will have to say, however, that several specific points are subject to important differences of interpretation.

> —*Lodge to Lewandowski, Saigon, December 3, 1966*

I thought I had done something worthwhile in my life. We had a drink on it.

> —*Lodge, recalling his December 3, 1966, meeting with Lewandowski and Giovanni D'Orlandi*

Get ahead with it! Get ahead with it! . . . We've done all this diplomacy, now, let's get on with it. Let's do the job!

> —*President Lyndon Johnson on bombing North Vietnam, early December 1966*

Oh, shit!

> —*Undersecretary of State Nicholas deB. Katzenbach, December 3, 1966, on learning that U.S. planes had bombed Hanoi for the first time in more than five months*

L ewandowski's report that Hanoi had agreed to meet secretly with the Americans to confirm a specific set of terms to end the war set off a frenzy of activity among the handful of governments that were aware of the potential breakthrough. To track the complicated, at times confusing, sequence of overlapping diplomatic and military developments that ensued, it is necessary to reconstruct events on three continents—from Saigon and Hanoi to Moscow, Warsaw, and Rome to Washington and the LBJ Ranch in the Texas Hill Country —on virtually a day-by-day basis.

Thursday, December 1

Saigon: The "Ten Points"

Lewandowski was beaming when he showed up early Thursday morning at D'Orlandi's apartment; the Italian quickly motioned him inside and locked the door.[1]

"I have good news," the Pole told him.

"How good?"

"Very good."[2]

Lewandowski had phoned D'Orlandi Wednesday evening soon after arriving from Hanoi. Using cryptic language over the unsecure line, he nevertheless conveyed a sense of urgency, communicating that he had a vital message to transmit. D'Orlandi instantly understood this meant he needed to arrange another three-way meeting, but Lodge, who had asked his friend to notify him immediately of any news from Lewandowski, was out of town—up-country visiting Marines (III MAF) near Danang[3]—and unavailable until early Thursday evening, so the Italian first invited the Pole to see him alone. Suffering from colitis and fever besides anxiety, he exuded relief at finally hearing from his friend: "This afternoon he returned. We shall meet tomorrow. My God, I thank you."[4]

Once the door shut, Lewandowski explained that his trip had been "fruitful beyond measure." But it had not been easy. First, he had to convince his dubious superiors to "bet all their cards on the tripartite attempt." Then, in Hanoi, he endured tense days before learning that the Presidium had decided, after prolonged and stormy debate, to give him "a very secret mandate" to continue the negotiations. "This is a real triumph," he told D'Orlandi, one "could no longer object that this is a personal initiative born of the unrestrained fantasy of a Polish diplomat." North Vietnam placed only one condition on proceeding: absolute secrecy. Any "indiscretions," they warned, "whether accidental or willful," would provoke an immediate and total disavowal. "So that everything doesn't get torpedoed and fail at such a good point," he urged, the Saigon diplomats had to heighten secrecy to mask even better the three-way gatherings; D'Orlandi fully agreed.

Before leaving, however, the Pole said something that disturbed him: Once the foundations were laid for direct contacts, perhaps in the next few days, the North Vietnamese intended to negotiate directly with Washington. That struck the Italian as dangerous, given the risks that a clash between U.S. and DRV negotiators might rapidly rupture the contacts; it would be far better, he felt, to give the diplomats in Saigon time to smooth over sticking points. Lewandowski did not demur but pointed out that this, nevertheless, was Hanoi's present wish.

For the moment, Lewandowski withheld details of the proposals he carried, which he would divulge only when Lodge joined them that evening. But D'Orlandi had heard enough to send his hopes soaring; as soon as his visitor left, he exultantly telegraphed Fanfani.[5] Lewandowski's achievement, he stressed, meant that "we are no longer faced with a personal initiative, and we finally have the chance to have thoughts and binding answers from the Hanoi Government" rather than Dong's "personal thoughts." He alerted Fanfani to expect a "decisive telegram" after the talk with Lodge, and he noted that besides triangular ambassadorial chats, Rusk would visit Saigon on December 9, and soon thereafter, "Your Excellency will have the chance to exercise, if necessary, personal pressure" on him at a NATO ministerial conference in Paris.

In closing, D'Orlandi sang Lewandowski's praises, terming him "a valid interlocutor" in U.S. and DRV eyes, "and telling him all the good things I think of the Polish diplomat, who has shown himself to have insight, intelligence, sensitivity, loyalty and, something that does not hurt, . . . luck."

✳ ✳ ✳

The first inkling the Americans got of Lewandowski's success in Hanoi came at 6:15 p.m. Thursday, when D'Orlandi greeted Lodge in the vestibule outside his apartment and told him, "Something big has happened."[6] Escorting him inside for another rendezvous with the Pole, who was already waiting, the Italian emphasized again the "imperative" of total secrecy, lest a leak destroy everything; Lodge swore that Washington would "leave no stone unturned" to comply.[7]

After the three sat and exchanged pleasantries, the Pole began: "My trip to Hanoi was very important." His talks, he went on, had reached a possibly "decisive" moment, a judgment that Rapacki and Gomułka shared. He had presented in Hanoi his understanding of the U.S. stand, consisting of ten points—based on his talks with Lodge on November 14 and 15, but in his own language. Preserving deniability, he did not show or hand the text to Lodge, but read it aloud, slowly, twice, so the American could scribble verbatim notes:

1. I have insisted that the United States is interested in a peaceful solution through negotiations.
2. Negotiations should not be interpreted as a way to negotiated surrender by those opposing the United States in Vietnam. A political negotiation would be aimed at finding an acceptable solution to all the problems, having in mind that the present status quo in South Vietnam must [as noted below, prompted by Lodge, Lewandowski agreed to replace "must" with "would"] be changed in

order to take into account the interests of the parties presently opposing the United States in South Vietnam [as noted below, Lewandowski originally referred here to the NLF, but agreed to instead refer to "parties" opposing the United States when Lodge and D'Orlandi objected that the clause must also cover North Vietnam.], and that such a solution may be reached in an honorable and dignified way not detrimental to national pride and prestige.

3. That the United States is not interested from the point of view of its national interests in having a permanent or long-term military presence in South Vietnam once a peaceful solution to the conflict has been reached. [As noted below, Lewandowski agreed to insert this reference to a "peaceful solution" when Lodge noted the conditionality of the Manila statement that Washington would withdraw its military forces from South Vietnam within six months only in the context of an overall accord. The Polish version states that Washington would not "insist" on a "permanent or long-term" military presence in South Vietnam, rather than not being "interested" in it.] That is why the offer made in Manila regarding the withdrawal of U.S. troops and the liquidation of American bases [within six months of a settlement] should be considered in all seriousness.

4. The United States would be ready, should other parties show a constructive interest in a negotiated settlement, to work out and to discuss with them proposals of such a settlement covering all important problems from a cease-fire to a final solution and withdrawal of U.S. troops. [In his handwritten English text of his presentation, Lewandowski added here that "such a negotiation would be held in a secret way."]

5. That the United States, within a general solution, would not oppose the formation of a South Vietnamese government based on the true will of the Vietnamese people with participation of all through free democratic elections, and that the United States would be prepared to accept the necessary control machinery to secure the democratic and free character of such elections and to respect the results of such elections.

6. The United States held the view that unification of Vietnam must be decided by the Vietnamese themselves for which the restoration of peace and the formation of proper representative organs of the people in South Vietnam is a necessary condition.

7. The United States are ready to accept and respect a true and complete neutrality of South Vietnam.

8. The United States is prepared to stop the bombing of the territory of North Vietnam if this will facilitate such a peaceful solution. In doing so, the United States is ready to avoid any appearance that North Vietnam is forced to negotiate by bombings or that North Vietnam has negotiated in exchange for cessation of bombing. Stopping of bombings would not involve recognition or confirmation by North Vietnam that its armed forces are or were infiltrating into South Vietnam.

Lewandowski then interjected that this last point reflected the Phase A/B formula Lodge had given him in mid-November and which he had relayed to Hanoi. He continued:

9. I have informed the proper governmental sources [in Hanoi] that at the same time, the United States, while not excluding the unification of Vietnam, would not agree to unification under military pressure.

10. While the United States is seeking a peaceful solution to the conflict, it would be unrealistic to expect that the United States will declare now or in the future its acceptance of North Vietnam's Four [Points] or [the NLF's] Five Points.[8]

At that point, the Pole concluded his statement and formally—in what he considered classical diplomatic procedure—requested Lodge to confirm this recapitulation: "I ask you whether this is a correct statement of the United States point of view."

Lodge, according to his own account, responded "that obviously on a matter of such importance, I would have to refer to my government for a definitive reply, but I could say off hand that much of what he cited was in keeping with the spirit of our policy." He reported mentioning that "personally," he would prefer a "closer definition" of paragraph two's language, prompting Lewandowski to alter "must" to "would" in reference to changing the "present status quo in South Vietnam"; and that paragraph 8's first sentence—on a bombing halt—"might need some clarification." D'Orlandi's secret "office memo" to Fanfani largely comports with Lodge's cable; he recorded the American's general satisfaction but "slight reservation" on points two and eight—particularly regarding "the understandable difficulty of mentioning the North Vietnamese infiltrations"—and his prediction that the Pole's ten-point tablet "may be accepted [by Washington] with some requests for clarifications."[9] By contrast, Lewandowski's cable, though mostly consistent with Lodge's and D'Orlandi's, noted simply that the "pleasantly surprised" American gave a "positive" reply regarding confirmation of the ten points; "however, he will contact the President immediately."[10] In a follow-up cable, he also recalled that specific references to the NLF in points two and four were replaced with vaguer allusions to "parties opposing the United States" after Lodge and D'Orlandi insisted the language encompass the PAVN forces; he also accepted Lodge's insistence that point three's reference to a six-month U.S. withdrawal from South Vietnam should explicitly say that this would only occur in the context of an overall agreement.[11]

However, to Lewandowski, these modifications amounted to linguistic quibbles, not concrete objections or claims that he had misrepresented the U.S. stand Lodge had conveyed two weeks earlier. "Never came at this meeting any hint of hesitation regarding the substance of what they call [the] ten points," he recalled firmly. "There was not a single question that the substance of the [Lodge-Lewandowski talks] was not reproduced properly. . . . [It] never came to anybody's mind."[12] The question of whether Lodge hedged his approval of the ten points would later emerge as a sticking point between Washington and Warsaw.

After hearing Lodge's generally positive reaction to his restatement of the U.S. position, Lewandowski moved to the punch line, carefully using language crafted by Rapacki.[13] Asserting first—to "avoid any belief on your part that this was not a serious proposition"—that what he was about to say was "very firmly based on conversations with the most respectable government sources in Hanoi" and "vouched for by Mr. Rapacki," the Pole stated: "I am authorized to say that if the United States are really of the views which I have presented, it would be advisable to confirm them directly by conversation with the North Vietnamese ambassador in Warsaw."

He then reaffirmed the need for total secrecy—"of fundamental importance" and "an essential element of the whole proposition"—and stressed that "in case of any leak, a denial would be issued." Besides proclaiming readiness to deliver further messages to Warsaw and Hanoi, he also made a "personal" plea (actually inspired by Dong and seconded by Rapacki): "The United States should stop the bombing of North Vietnam apart from all other things."

Lewandowski cabled Rapacki that his presentation "equally pleasantly surprised" Lodge and D'Orlandi and the former welcomed the proposed U.S.-DRV contact pending confirmation from LBJ. However, he neglected to mention that Lodge had raised a very awkward question—precisely the one he had dreaded: Could he, "in friendship," identify the "most respectable government sources in Hanoi" who authorized his assertion that the DRV Embassy in Warsaw would receive a U.S. representative to confirm that the ten points were official policy?

Lewandowski hesitated. He had hoped that the coyly cryptic phrase would suffice, but now that Lodge had asked a direct question, his instinct told him that dodging it might imperil the initiative just when it seemed on the verge of a stunning success.

"I believe this is the absolutely critical moment," he remembered decades later. He was acutely conscious, of course, that Dong had specifically told him to give Lodge the statement proposing the Warsaw contact in his own name, without referring to the DRV premier, a request Rapacki endorsed. Yet, Lewandowski feared, if he failed to offer convincing evidence of Hanoi's authoritative backing, Lodge and Washington "would have the right" to treat his message like those of other self-styled mediators and peacemakers "who were running to Hanoi and bringing to America different ideas, you know, which came to nothing. So at this point, I really felt that I can not, you know, be very vague on this business." He continued:

> If I am saying that the Vietnamese will be waiting for them in Warsaw, then my God, you see, that unless I am [an] absolute, you know, fruit, that I am saying that somebody is waiting for them in Warsaw, without authorization, you know, I would make [a] fool of myself, you see. Because the partners [i.e., Lodge and

D'Orlandi] would be faced with two alternatives. Either they will know that this is coming from [the North] Vietnamese [leadership], from Van Dong, or that I am absolutely not serious, out of [my] senses, to say, to the representative of the United States that somebody will be waiting in Warsaw and that somebody accepted the base of the talks. . . . "From where you heard it?" you see, they [would] say. I would say, "Well, I heard it in the street"? [laughs]. . . . Secrecy was the basis [of the initiative, but] if I am evasive at this moment, I can really make a [reason] for them to say that maybe something is not really serious. That's why, I decided, I would stop to play the [game]. . . . I understood that Pham Van Dong [had told me not to] and so on and so on, but at this stage. . . . Frankly speaking, I was hoping that giving such a formulation about the meeting in Warsaw would be enough for them to understand, but once the question was asked, you see, [there was the implicit question,] "[Have] you invented it or not?" And then I felt that if I am really evasive on this issue, you know, I can make a real disservice, you know, to this thing, so in spite of any other matters, Rapacki or not, I felt I cannot be evasive at this moment. . . . I felt that any evasion might be very dangerous.[14]

Because Lewandowski was eager to give peace a chance even if it meant violating instructions and to aid Lodge ("so he can say he got it from the top leadership") with the skeptics in Washington, he divulged that his primary contact was Pham Van Dong, who had authorized his message after "collective debate among all the proper authorities." In other words, it had "the Presidium behind it," acting only, he related, "after several stormy sessions while poor Lewandowski, believing himself to be repudiated by the North Vietnamese, prepared to forward to Warsaw his request for recall."[15]

Besides concealing this step from Rapacki, Lewandowski never told Dong, but felt that he would have understood the defiance of his edict: "What would happen if Lodge and Orlandi would think it was really [authorized by] Ha Van Lau, hmn?, or deputy foreign minister [Thach], I mean, by somebody who did not have power of decision? So I have no remorse."[16]

Having revealed his interlocutor, Lewandowski told Lodge that they should soon hold another three-way talk "to clear up things of a practical character" about the upcoming Warsaw meeting (e.g., the identity of the U.S. representative); said the Poles had apprised Moscow of the latest developments; affirmed the "great importance" that Rapacki and Gòmułka put on Hanoi's consent for the direct contact; and urged Washington to "get at this as 'fast as possible'. The more delay, the greater the danger"—sabotage or a leak by "someone 'working against a solution'" (an ambiguous phrase that fit either side's hawks, the Chinese or the Joint Chiefs of Staff).

Finally, the Pole put in a plea to avoid alternative channels of communication to Hanoi, to minimize the risks of both leaks and of misinterpretation. Lodge did not contest this argument—which he surmised reflected Lewandowski's "belief, amounting almost to a phobia, that in the West . . . many want to take part"—nor did he or D'Orlandi mention the idea of a papal bid for a holiday truce that the American had hinted at shortly before they met.

Their business concluded, all three men felt satisfaction, restrained euphoria mingled with disbelief, at the prospect that their labors had yielded a breakthrough that might soon lead to direct peace talks, if not peace itself. Decades later, Lewandowski recalled the mood. "Everyone was very happy, you know, smiling. D'Orlandi said, 'Let's have a glass of wine for the success of the operation,' and went himself to the cabinet and opened it" to break out a bottle.[17]

After Lodge left, the Pole stayed behind to underline once more the imperatives of secrecy and haste, which he said that Gomułka and Rapacki fully endorsed. D'Orlandi—obviously recalling the fiasco in August that had nearly shut down their channel—assured him that the chief of the cipher service would personally decode his telegrams and hand them directly to Fanfani.[18]

Back at the U.S. Embassy, Lodge composed a "SECSTATE IMMEDIATE / TOP SECRET / NODIS / MARIGOLD" cable to Rusk. It was midnight in Saigon by the time it was encrypted and sent. Though withholding any summary judgment, the American clearly took Lewandowski's presentation seriously, and he called immediate attention to it at the highest levels, so he could give the Pole on Saturday what he hoped and expected would be a positive reply.

At his residence, D'Orlandi reflected that now the "ball is in Cabot Lodge's court." Taking heart from the prediction of a rapid response from Washington, he ended a diary entry on a note of suspenseful optimism: "So by the day after tomorrow we will have the happy result! May God assist us!"[19]

For the moment, all the omens for Marigold appeared auspicious—except for one: Above North Vietnam, for the first time in many days, the skies were clearing.

Washington and Texas: "By All Means"

Lodge's cable 12247 reached Washington—thirteen hours behind Saigon time—at 11:04 a.m. Thursday morning, December 1, and quickly drew Rusk's notice. After studying the "interesting" communication with Tommy Thompson, the secretary alerted McNamara and forwarded him a copy; in a midafternoon telephone conversation, Rusk said that he thought the message was "possibly important, but some things needed buttoning up," while the defense secretary cautiously noted "some language ambiguities."[20]

In a first effort to clarify matters, Rusk at 5:33 p.m. dispatched a telegram assuring Lodge that his cable was "receiving urgent highest level consideration with virtually no distribution," and seeking his guidance on several issues. Most important, were the ten points a basis for peace talks or merely a background for further North Vietnamese probing?[21]

Definitely the former, Lodge shot back. "It is clear to me," he declared in a reply sent Friday morning in Saigon (received late Thursday night in Washington), "that Hanoi is prepared to talk on the basis of Lewandowski's statement of the U.S. positions if confirmed by us."[22]

Rusk kept his cards close to his vest. Considering a response to the dramatic Marigold development, he initially consulted only a select few associates: Ben Read, Tommy Thompson, Bill Bundy, and one crucial newcomer: Undersecretary Nicholas Katzenbach, who two months earlier had replaced George Ball as the State Department's number two official. Katzenbach had piloted an Air Force bomber in Italy during World War II, and then become a high-octane, fast-track attorney and legal scholar (Yale Law School, Rhodes scholar, Yale and Chicago law professor). He had been a Kennedy man, and RFK's deputy at the Justice Department, where he served as frontline commander in tense civil rights confrontations. But when RFK left the Johnson administration in 1964 after his brother's assassination to run for the Senate from New York, Katzenbach had stayed, succeeding his mentor as attorney general and—at least in part—winning LBJ's trust by managing battles for civil rights and voting act legislation. On succeeding Ball in early October, he had immediately journeyed to Vietnam, accompanying McNamara, to make an on-the-spot inspection—and came away uneasy, despite predictably upbeat briefings.[23] In early December, he would assume a key role in handling Marigold as acting secretary of state once Rusk left town on a previously scheduled two-week trip.

Even as he consulted Read, Katzenbach, and Thompson, and checked with the White House (Rostow) and Pentagon (McNamara), Rusk conspicuously declined to have the hot Marigold news evaluated by a seemingly logical group, Harriman's secret negotiations panel, which held one of its weekly sessions in his office at 4 p.m. that same afternoon. Though nominally created "to develop, assess and follow up all leads to a peaceful settlement of the Vietnam conflict,"[24] and intimately involved in prior consideration of Marigold, even this inner sanctum did not satisfy Rusk's yen for secrecy or policy control.[25] The group assembled, therefore, without being collectively informed of the Lodge cable or the ten points, even as it debated a singularly cogent topic: the possible outline of "A Package Deal for Hanoi."[26]

The peripatetic Harriman himself was away, as he would be for the next fortnight, in Western Europe and North Africa for Vietnam-related consultations. (That day, he flew from London to Paris after hearing Brown recount his Moscow talks.[27]) Instead, his deputy, Chet Cooper, presided over a lengthy hashing-out of potential negotiating terms by nine men, six of whom were in the dark about the ten-point plan just received from Lewandowski. Of those around the table, only Thompson, Bundy, and Rostow's aide William Jorden were au courant, while Cooper, Unger, Sisco, Hughes, Daniel I. Davidson, and Monteagle Stearns had no idea that Marigold had gone beyond the mid-November Lodge-Lewandowski talks in Saigon.

The drastic shrinkage of the charmed circle entitled to read Marigold cables— evidently at Rusk's instigation (through Read) with LBJ's after-the-fact endorsement[28]—left several formerly involved officials out in the cold. It meant that fewer voices participated in pivotal deliberations over how to handle the suddenly lively initiative and coordinate it (if at all) with ongoing or planned military operations. In particular, Harriman's absence from Washington in the first half of December removed a voice that was more inclined to take Communist negotiating options seriously and question the efficacy of bombing North Vietnam. Of course, Rusk, Rostow, and LBJ might not have clued him in, anyway; Harriman's relations with the secretary and national security adviser were distinctly cool (Katzenbach: "Harriman drove Rusk crazy"[29]). Yet, had the elder statesman stayed home, they would have had a harder time excluding him, given his stature and personal role in jump-starting Marigold (not only had he plumped for the channel a few weeks before; along with Bundy and Unger, he had personally cleared the November 14 instructions to Lodge conveying U.S. terms to pass to the Pole[30]). Harriman's travels, conversely, gave Rusk a convenient pretext to scalpel him out of the action until he returned on the grounds of operational security—after all, cables can be intercepted—and to delay notifying his deputy, who had already earned a dovish reputation that hardly endeared him to the secretary.[31]

With his boss gone and his own position weakened, Cooper chaired the December 1 discussion (dissection, really) of his draft "Package Deal for Hanoi" despite being oblivious to the most relevant diplomatic development, one that he himself had helped bring about. Still, despite the lack of any explicit reference to the Polish channel, the deliberations were quite pertinent to Marigold. They exposed a basic truth: the lack of a clear consensus or understanding at the top of the Johnson administration regarding its "bottom line" for a settlement—even as it was being asked to, in effect, sign on the dotted line by endorsing the ten points to Hanoi's envoy in Warsaw.

That top U.S. officials mulled a package deal at all reflected Lewandowski's incessant pleas (echoed by D'Orlandi) since the summer that they focus on an "overall" arrangement rather than a limited mechanism for a bombing halt or cease-fire. Due to the Italian's prodding at Villa Madama, Cooper (with Harriman's blessing) had taken a crack at crafting Washington's minimal acceptable terms.[32] (Concurrently, Rostow tackled the issue from a harder-line perspective. In a November 17 memo to LBJ, he imagined "a secret negotiation of a total deal" followed by a "dramatic joint announcement," and mentioned the need to devise and inform the DRV of "*an end position which Hanoi and the Viet Cong could live with*" (emphasis in the original)—but the terms he envisioned were nonstarters, amounting to little more than the NLF's surrender and disarming and the PAVN's withdrawal from South Vietnam in exchange for a subsequent U.S. pullout.[33])

To the negotiations group, Cooper explained that he was working on the assumptions that, one, it would be useful to see if terms acceptable to both Hanoi and Washington could be fashioned and, two, that the "North Vietnamese would not negotiate until they had some notion of where the negotiations were going and what the final settlement might look like"[34]—Lewandowski's line exactly.

("Settle first, negotiate later," was how Cooper summed up this approach.[35]) But his draft ran into a hailstorm of hard-line objections from fellow State Department aides (e.g., Bundy thought it was too generous to the NLF in the terms for its participation in South Vietnamese elections). Bowing to prevailing skepticism, Cooper asked Jorden to supply a White House–approved outline. For the next few weeks, Rostow and Rusk would keep Harriman's shop sidetracked on this theoretical "package deal" exercise (which might suddenly become more relevant if talks with Hanoi actually began) while themselves controlling the conduct of the most sensitive and significant prospect for negotiations to arise since the negotiations group had come into being.

While his senior aides buzzed over the Lodge cable in Washington, LBJ was at his Texas ranch, still convalescing from surgery two weeks earlier to remove a nonmalignant growth in his throat and fix a small hernia. That Thursday, he engaged in routine duties and diversions—choppering to his boyhood home and the family cemetery, dropping in on his Austin office, relaxing with friends and cronies, chatting off the record with reporters.[36] Only late that night did the "Johnson green" trailer housing the "LBJ Ranch CommCen" receive Rostow's "literally eyes only for the president" message relaying Lodge's cable; in a cover note, the usually skeptical national security adviser admitted that it had to be taken seriously.[37]

Hanoi's seeming readiness for a direct meeting to confirm the ten points had impressed Rostow, who reported that Rusk and Thompson thought Lodge's cable was "a message of importance." There were, "of course, possible booby traps here we'll have to watch," he cautioned; yet he was struck by the insistence on secrecy and selection of Warsaw ("to keep Peiping and the NLF out of the act") and by Lodge's report that the Pole stressed that talks should begin "as 'fast as possible.'" Echoing the ideas he advanced two weeks before, Rostow added: "As you know, I have felt that if Hanoi was ever serious, they would want a quick complete deal, not a slow negotiation."[38]

Johnson's first reaction to the purported proposal for a direct U.S.-DRV contact was positive: "By all means confirm in both places [Saigon and Warsaw]," he told Rostow.[39]

Friday, December 2

North Vietnam: "Oh, Shit!"—RT-52 Hits Hanoi

As darkness fell over eastern and central North America Thursday evening, the sun rose over Southeast Asia on Friday morning. For more than a week, the weather conditions over most of North Vietnam had frustrated U.S. commanders. Impairing visibility, "thunderstorms, mist, fog and the low-hanging clouds of the northeasterly monsoon" had interfered with aerial reconnaissance and precluded accurate target location or bomb-damage assessment. Day after day—seven in all—pilots belonging to the Seventh Air Force specially selected for experience awoke primed to attack sensitive Rolling Thunder–52 targets in the Hanoi area, only to have their missions scrubbed. Consequently, besides a few isolated forays, the bulk of the strikes that LBJ had authorized on November 10 and 11 remained to be carried out, even after the lifting of political constraints imposed during Brown's visit to Moscow.[40]

But on the morning of December 2, "the clouds lifted" over North Vietnam. From bases in northern Thailand and aircraft carriers in the Tonkin Gulf, waves of Air Force F-4C Phantoms and Navy jet fighter-bombers, 194 in all, took off for targets in the Red River Delta that included the Ha Gia petroleum storage complex 14 miles north of Hanoi and the Van Dien truck depot 4 or 5 miles south of the city's center—a distance that the *Washington Post* helpfully likened the next day to that "between the Washington Monument and the Carter Barron Amphitheater" in Rock Creek Park. Dropping 500- and 750-pound bombs at midday "through holes in cloud cover," the pilots spotted numerous secondary explosions, fires, and columns of black smoke. Yet early reports confirmed only 9 of the 175 buildings in the truck complex as having been destroyed, leaving unfinished business.[41]

North Vietnam reacted angrily to the "piratical" and "savage" attacks. In state-run radio broadcasts and an official protest to the ICC, the authorities said that U.S. aircraft had "bombed and strafed" populated areas in the capital, causing many civilian casualties—Poland's military attaché claimed up to 600 victims, and a diplomatic rumor alleged a third that number—but also suffering a rebuff from antiaircraft fire from troops and the "people of Hanoi." This "extremely brazen act of aggression," Hanoi declared, constituted a new escalation.[42] Washington attributed the raids' timing to improved weather and denied they represented any policy shift. But the attack on Van Dien, reporters noted, carried out by fifteen or twenty Navy jets, was the closest to Hanoi since the campaign against petroleum, oil, and lubricant facilities opened on June 29—the same day, of course, that D'Orlandi told Lodge of the DRV's "very specific peace offer" via Lewandowski, in Marigold's first bloom.[43]

✳ ✳ ✳

Why did the United States bomb Hanoi on December 2, for the first time in more than five months, a day after learning that North Vietnam might finally be ready to enter direct peace contacts? Like so many aspects of Marigold, the answer is mired in controversy and confusion.

About the timing there is little mystery. After being approved by LBJ with some excisions and deferrals three weeks earlier, RT-52's implementation was delayed first by political factors related to Brown's visit to Moscow and then poor weather over North Vietnam. Regional commanders, authorization already in hand, merely had to wait for the clouds to disperse. The real question, though, was, why did not Lodge's December 1 cable describing the seeming Marigold breakthrough prompt a suspension of the bombing plans, at least in the Hanoi area?

From a technical and operational standpoint, it could have been done; a directive dispatched from Washington on Thursday afternoon, while Lodge's December 1 cable was under discussion, could have reached Southeast Asia in time to cancel the Friday morning RT-52 air strikes or limit them to exclude the most sensitive targets near Hanoi. "Jesus Christ," later commented an Air Force planning officer, "if you'd have told us about it, we could have stopped the bombings. If you want to work hard enough, you can stop the bombings in an hour."[44]

But no such order was sent. None of the handful of top officials cognizant of Lodge's cable and also informed of the RT-52 target list—not McNamara, Rusk, Read, Bundy, Thompson, Rostow, or LBJ himself—was moved to propose a restraining order against new attacks on Hanoi. Precisely why has been disputed. In the most intensive inquest, dependent on leaks rather than secret documents, Stuart Loory and David Kraslow would conclude the December 2 bombing stemmed from "poor organization," a failure to coordinate diplomatic and military tracks.[45] The journalists largely blamed two factors: first, excessive secrecy (e.g., besides the State Department aides cut out of Marigold traffic, those in the military chain of command—from Southeast Asia to the U.S. Pacific Command in Honolulu to the Pentagon—who knew of the impending raids had no idea of the secret initiative); and second, "a lack of vigilance" among those aware of Marigold and RT-52 who had simply "forgot they had approved the target." Dramatizing this view, Kraslow and Loory's book *The Secret Search for Peace in Vietnam* (see chapters 15 and 16) reported that a "senior official in the national security apparatus" in on Marigold was horrified to pick up a copy of the *Washington Post* as he sat down to breakfast on Saturday morning, December 3, and see, on the upper left corner of the front page, the following headline:

U.S. BOMBS
SITE 5 MILES
FROM HANOI

RAIDS ARE CLOSEST
TO REDS' CAPITAL
SINCE LAST JUNE

"Oh my God!" he reportedly exclaimed. "We lost control."[46]

"I'm sure my reaction was, 'Oh, shit!'" Katzenbach later recalled.[47] Though he was unsure whether Marigold was the real thing (he had imbibed some of the general State Department distrust of the Poles), the new undersecretary was taken aback. He was far more doubtful than Rusk of the air campaign's value— "Having bombed myself, I was always a little bit skeptical as to whether every bomb went on target with quite the same precision that gets claimed for it"[48]—he knew of no military consideration that justified hitting such a sensitive target at precisely that moment. Though he saw Thompson and Read on the afternoon of December 1, as they were drafting the first response to Lodge's cable, he does not believe that the imminent attacks on Hanoi came up.[49]

However, some officials later took umbrage at Kraslow and Loory's imputation of incompetence or absentmindedness, insisting that they had remained acutely conscious of which targets had been authorized in the Hanoi area (and which were vetoed or deferred) and had deliberately opted not to interfere. Rusk's executive assistant, Ben Read, stated in a private 1969 interview:

> One of the inaccuracies of their book is that we didn't put the military track and the political track together. From the day that the bombing program against North Vietnam began on a regular day-to-day basis, I had the military representatives in the Operation Center in the State Department prepare for me on a nightly basis a list of all "Op Ones," as they're called, which are the intended targets for the next twenty-four hour period. That list came up absolutely regularly, just like clockwork. And when there was a target on it of a nature to raise questions of possible political impact, and when it wasn't, we brought it to the attention of the Secretary and Under Secretary; it was just done with regularity and faithfulness. They are in error in the [alleged] fact that these facts weren't known to the top elements. They were! In the case of the particular bombings of early December which became the subject of this contention here, they too were brought to the attention of the top people.[50]

Read was certain that "the top people" included LBJ himself, "because he was personally reviewing all in-close targets at that period," and Rusk, whom he "would load . . . down . . . with very detailed memoranda of the volatile in-close targets with a discussion of pro and con of what the problems might be if they were struck and not struck precisely, as my Air Force friends always try to convince us will happen."[51] Yet Read never said explicitly whether senior officials reconsidered RT-52 targets near Hanoi on December 1 after Lodge's cable arrived.

Cooper later squared this circle by terming the December 2 bombing of Hanoi—in contrast to subsequent attacks—"accidental" in that the few people aware of both Lodge's cable and bombing plans "just didn't think about" any possible link between them.[52] Deflecting blame, McNamara advanced a similar claim (off the record) to a British journalist, Henry Brandon:

> There existed field orders and blanket authority with some restrictions for certain raids. Those who knew about the negotiations also knew about the field orders, but no one sensed how the action would be interpreted in Hanoi or elsewhere. It became a weapon to beat us with. Lodge, for instance, knew about the field orders, but did [not] say anything to warn us.[53]

Rusk denied the Hanoi attacks materially affected Marigold's fate, but in 1969 he privately conceded vaguely that "one could make the point" that a "lack of coordination" between military and diplomatic activities might have existed.[54]

Two decades later, he asserted unapologetically that Lodge's news simply did not merit a change in plans. "Personally, I wasn't surprised by the raids," he said. "We had discussed them at the Tuesday luncheons. I may have failed to report these discussions to my colleagues within the department, leading to some confusion. But the December raids on targets around Hanoi were planned, not accidental. The truth is, we simply doubted the authenticity of Marigold; after six months of talking with the Poles, we hadn't received any confirmation from the North Vietnamese that they wanted to talk."[55]

From the declassified record, it remains unclear whether anyone in a position to act on the afternoon of December 1 connected Marigold and the previously approved bombing plans—no concrete evidence anyone did so has emerged. Later, some officials defended the Hanoi raids as necessary to keep Marigold secret, arguing that they could not have suddenly eliminated the targets without tipping off the military that hush-hush peace diplomacy was afoot, risking a leak from an angry bombing enthusiast. However, critics countered plausibly, this would hardly have been the first time that targets were deleted or deferred for political reasons; the danger of sinking the initiative by provoking an angry North Vietnamese response outweighed the peril that irked commanders might sabotage it, and because Hanoi had not been hit for more than five months, omitting it while continuing to bomb other DRV sites would hardly have attracted notice.

In a deeper sense, it hardly mattered whether officials remembered the planned raid on Hanoi on December 1, or thought it feasible to alter plans without kindling military suspicions. Dismissing Lewandowski's warning against further bombing at such a delicate juncture, senior figures (certainly Rusk, Rostow, and LBJ, but perhaps not McNamara) presumed that inflicting more pain on Hanoi would enhance, not diminish, prospects for negotiations on U.S. terms. In urging LBJ to "lean more heavily on the North" by approving RT-52 a few weeks earlier, Rostow had confidently predicted the "increased burden may add to [Hanoi's] interest in a negotiated settlement."[56] LBJ himself had forecast to McNamara (who disagreed) that "limited, very quiet, expanded" bombing would "give Moscow a little leverage" on Hanoi to enter into talks, because it would do so only if "hurtin'."[57] LBJ ("not feeling very chipper through this period"), Bundy later recalled, was

set to step up the bombing program. And my recollection, which I haven't the files to confirm against, is that the Joint Chiefs came in with a very much stronger list of targets on his request on his return [from Manila], and he approved a very large number of them. And I was very much against some of them and said so to the Secretary of State and so on, and there was a back and forth. The President was by then down at the ranch and had had the operation [on November 16]. Eventually a number of the targets were removed, but several of them were left on and were authorized. These included the two targets five or six miles outside Hanoi that caused trouble in December. That's why it's of significance. The President was in

Texas and gave the impression just by the way he had acted on this that he—"Get ahead with it! Get ahead with it!" That was very, very strong. "We've done all this diplomacy, now, let's get on with it. Let's do the job!"[58]

Washington: "Important Differences of Interpretation"

Early reports of the air raids, though too late for the morning papers, reached Washington and the LBJ Ranch through classified military channels early Friday.[59] The news would have, however, little if any impact on that day's intense discussions over how to proceed in Marigold. Rostow phoned Rusk at 9:02 a.m. to tell him that LBJ had, indeed, approved going ahead, but before sending Lodge a confirmation to give Lewandowski, officials agonized over how to craft a response favorable in principle yet hedging Washington's bets—and covering its behind.[60] At the White House, Rostow assigned Jorden to redraft the ten points so they sidestepped "possible booby-traps" yet kept as much original language as possible.

Rostow's aide Jorden was an ex–*New York Times* reporter now harshly critical of much press coverage of the war (including his alma mater's), and his efforts suggest how close the ten points came to satisfying hawks and also how they might have fared had direct U.S.-DRV talks actually ensued. Preserving most of the original text, Jorden had only two serious caveats. The first raised an issue that now seems less of a problem than met the eye. Uncertain what exchanges had taken place between Lewandowski and Hanoi, officials were disconcerted by the lack of concrete reference to the Phase A/B proposal that Lodge had given the Pole in mid-November (and that Rusk had concurrently given Brown to pass to Moscow).[61] To remedy this omission, Jorden wanted the procedure explicitly written into the ten points—or even enshrined separately in an eleventh. However, Vietnamese sources establish, Lewandowski had already conveyed the idea's essence (albeit somewhat blurrily) in his memo describing the November 14 conversation with Lodge, as his December 1 statements to Lodge implied. Therefore, the DRV leaders seem to have implicitly accepted the procedure—though it was a bit absurd to expect them to accept a written document confirming their abandonment of a rigidly declared principle—or, perhaps more likely, regarded the issue mooted by their agreement to the Warsaw contact even without a prior bombing halt.

Jorden's second proposed amendment, however, portended graver trouble—an explicit requirement for a PAVN exit from South Vietnam. To point eight, Jorden advised adding, after the statement that Hanoi need not confirm its forces were in South Vietnam: "However, the withdrawal to North Vietnam of the personnel it has sent to the South must be part of any settlement and the United States would consider itself free to refer to that withdrawal."[62]

Only with these alterations, which "cannot be read as a major deviation," would the now eleven points be kosher to give Lewandowski to pass to Hanoi along with confirmation they were America's "considered views" and a valid basis for secret talks.

At the State Department, as they drafted messages to Lodge in Saigon and Gronouski in Warsaw, officials also registered qualms about Lewandowski's ten points and, indeed, the whole initiative. Hardly was heard an encouraging word when Thompson and Bundy sent Rusk some thoughts to prepare him for a meeting the next morning with LBJ for which "Marigold—Next Steps" topped the agenda.[63] (The secretary, along with Rostow and other top brass, would fly to Texas to join LBJ Saturday for festivities along the U.S.-Mexican border marking the opening of a new dam on the Rio Grande River.) Warily, Bundy and Thompson speculated that "our Polish friend in Saigon" had "embroidered his text in a rather free-wheeling fashion, either to us, to Hanoi, or both," and voiced a "strong suspicion of exaggeration," given his conduct in the Norman Cousins episode in the final days of the thirty-seven-day bombing pause (they *still* had him bollixed up with the Polish UN diplomat *Bohdan* Lewandowski). Warning that the ten points "contain quite a number of bugs," they agreed "we must for action purposes interpret [Lewandowski's message] as indicating a real interest in Hanoi (or some elements in Hanoi) in opening up the quietest kind of discussion," but stressed that they saw "no assurance" that talks would occur—Thompson "doubt[ed] it," seeing "just too much uncertainty in both the message and the channel." Urging caution even in the unlikely event that the initiative actually led to talks with Hanoi, they suggested that Rusk alert LBJ "to the possibility that it may just blow away next week."[64]

But despite their reservations about the ten points, the U.S. officials also saw an advantage in *not* proposing alternative wording.[65] After all, for the moment it remained a *Polish* document, which Washington could disavow—for example, in the awkward event that Saigon found out (a distinct possibility, given its broad intelligence apparatus). The RVN's leaders, especially Ky, would presumably be furious at Washington for making deals involving their country's fate over their heads, and advancing formal revisions would put an official U.S. stamp of approval on the text.

Another potential pitfall of editing Lewandowski's ten points or proffering a new version, the U.S. officials reasoned, was that they would undoubtedly harden them—as in Jorden's redraft—and thereby risk scaring Hanoi off what *might* be an authentic chance for peace. And despite stylistic carping, they recognized that the ten points basically did reflect U.S. views. Like a red-pen-wielding freshman English instructor, Bundy later gave Lewandowski poor grades for composition, calling his summary "ferociously tilted," a "rather bizarre concoction," and "a perfectly wretched draft, perfectly wretched!" The Pole, he sniffed, "would not win a Metternich prize" for the ten points. Katzenbach derided them as a "terrible mish-mash of language." But Cooper called his distillation of Washington's stands "very much in the same ballpark" as what the State Department had sent Lodge in mid-November. "It really was. He had reduced this long conversation to ten essential points."[66]

The trick, then, as the officials saw it, was to respond positively enough to the ten points to let the game proceed and see if Hanoi really came to the table, while at the same time waffling sufficiently to preserve wiggle room if they actually led to serious negotiations and deniability if the whole thing exploded prematurely into public view.

Aside from the ten points, U.S. officials were also apprehensive over Hanoi's choice of Warsaw as the venue, which raised the prospect of relying for this most delicate of diplomatic assignments on a man whom they neither fully respected nor trusted: Gronouski. Many State Department officials still regarded the ambassador to Poland as a political hack lacking diplomatic experience, expertise in Asian affairs (despite representing Washington in the ongoing Sino-American ambassadorial talks), and, in a word, gravitas—as a man whose principal qualifications for the job were his Polish-American ancestry and Democratic Party loyalty. Worse, he had repeatedly shown himself to be an eager beaver when it came to Vietnam peacemaking, as shown by his exchanges with Michałowski and repeated proposals to redraft the Four Points. Rusk, Rostow, Thompson, Bundy, and their associates prided themselves on being cold-eyed, hard-headed, steel-nerved, and infinitely suspicious in dealings with mortal Communist enemies, and the prospect of having an amateur *and* crypto-dove handle the vital exchanges with battle-toughened Vietnamese Communists provoked "agonized discussion," recalled one official (amid cracks about Gronouski's supposed inability to find Vietnam on a map).[67] At one point, Thompson drafted cables to Lodge and Gronouski stating flatly that the chargé d'affaires in Warsaw would handle the first talk with the DRV ambassador and return to Washington for a full briefing before further conversations.[68]

Finally, late Friday afternoon, the officials reached a consensus on less specific language as to who would make the first Warsaw contact and when. At 6:15 p.m., cables in Rusk's name—drafted by Thompson, cleared by Read for the secretary (off to Ohio for a speech), and OK'd by Katzenbach—went out to Saigon and Warsaw. One directed Lodge to tell his Polish contact that Washington was "instructing our Embassy in Warsaw to contact North Vietnamese representative there on December 6. (This date will give time for Hanoi to instruct their Ambassador if they have not already done so.)" The embassy officer, Lodge could say, "will be able to confirm that the ten points outlined by Lewandowski broadly represent our position." However, he would add "that several specific points are subject to important differences of interpretation." Were a DRV representative "prepared to engage in a discussion," the State Department would "brief appropriate officer in order that he may be able to explain directly our position."[69]

At exactly the same time, Foggy Bottom alerted Gronouski that Lewandowski had given Hanoi a ten-point "statement of our position on a possible Vietnam settlement" and suggested that Washington confirm its position directly to the

DRV ambassador in the Polish capital. "If talks should take place in Warsaw, we would wish you to guide them," Rusk grandly informed him, before itemizing instructions that hinted at State's actual misgivings. Given the risk of a leak, Gronouski was told, it would be "too conspicuous for you personally to contact North Vietnamese if in fact they agree to talk in Warsaw." Instead, the direct contacts might be handled after "appropriate briefing here" by his experienced deputy chief of mission, Walter E. Jenkins Jr. (a career foreign service officer and China specialist[70]) or "someone with [the] requisite background" sent from Washington. "In any event Jenkins or any officer you select should endeavor to see North Vietnamese Ambassador on December 6 or as soon thereafter as possible," the cable went on, and if received by him, state that the ten points conveyed by Lewandowski were "basically correct" yet "subject to important differences of interpretation." The American should then declare the United States' willingness to keep talking with the North Vietnamese "anywhere that is suitable to them." If they preferred Warsaw, a more authoritative representative would be dispatched.[71]

Washington's first Marigold-related State Department telegram to Warsaw that Friday evening conveyed just enough information to enable Gronouski to arrange the first contact with his DRV counterpart. The classified cable instructed him "broadly" to confirm the ten points' accuracy, yet it omitted the ten points themselves. For the time being, at least, Foggy Bottom expected Gronouski to "guide" the Warsaw talks to establish the U.S. position on the war without even knowing what it was!

Before heading home, Katzenbach joined Rusk in his office for a nightcap. With the secretary about to depart for a fortnight, they likely discussed Marigold. In after-hours informal chats, Katzenbach tried vainly to get the soft-spoken, round-faced Georgian with a bland Buddha-like expression to let his (figurative) hair down—especially on the war. Rusk always behaved courteously, despite occasional rifts (over Vietnam in particular), yet he resolutely refused to be drawn: "He was a wonderful gentleman, always extremely decent and friendly, but he told me what he told the press." Unlike his boss, Katzenbach sensed that Marigold might really be "going somewhere. . . . I felt it was the most promising [peace initiative] we had had."[72]

Warsaw: Swinging into Action

On a blustery, frosty Friday night in Warsaw—six hours behind Vietnam time—the Foreign Ministry hummed with top-level activity.[73] That afternoon, reports of the Hanoi raids had streamed in at about the same time that Lewandowski's cable describing his December 1 talk with Lodge at D'Orlandi's had arrived from Saigon and been decoded after delays in transmission.[74]

With the news in hand that the Americans had agreed in principle to a Warsaw meeting, Rapacki and Michałowski swung into action. They shot off a slew of cables aimed at keeping the initiative in motion—to Saigon, to instruct Lewandowski to make a stern protest over the Hanoi bombing the next time he saw

Lodge; to Moscow, to alert the Soviets; and to Hanoi, to send a report on the December 1 Lodge-Lewandowski conversation for Dong and also assure him that Poland would harshly protest the U.S. attacks.[75] In their message to Siedlecki, they also relayed concrete issues for him to raise for Dong concerning the prospective Warsaw talks—the likely level of contacts (presumably ambassadorial), the most convenient time frame for informing and instructing Do Phat Quang, the DRV ambassador in Warsaw, and whether there were any other ways in which Poland could aid Vietnam regarding the contact.[76] The MSZ officials also began to prepare to host secret U.S.-DRV peace talks—according to Michałowski, they even reserved a "pavilion" in Warsaw as a neutral site for private discussions.[77] Having swatted diplomatic balls back into several courts, Michałowski and Rapacki could retire into the sleety night.

Saturday, December 3

Hanoi: Informing Pham Van Dong

In Hanoi, Siedlecki received Rapacki's cable 12306 describing the December 1 Lodge-Lewandowski talk in Saigon before 7 a.m. Saturday. By 8:30 a.m., he was reading it in Russian translation to a "calm," "kind," and "very tired," but still acutely interested, Pham Van Dong. Listening intently, the premier asked him to repeat the entire text and interrupted several times to double-check—particularly passages reporting Lodge's consent in principle to Lewandowski's recapitulation of the U.S. stand and the proposed contact in Warsaw, and his lack of response to the suggestion that Washington, "regardless of everything," stop bombing North Vietnam.

On that topic, Dong thanked Rapacki for telling Lewandowski to scold Lodge "promptly and in a concrete manner" for the Hanoi raids the day before. Yet he gave no sign that the attacks had scotched prospects for the Warsaw meeting. Instead, he deflected Siedlecki's queries about arrangements, observing that "perhaps any further concrete steps on both sides were not topical until Lodge received instructions from Johnson." Then, after sending "kindhearted greetings" to Rapacki and Lewandowski, he excused himself, citing other business.[78]

Saigon: "I Thought I Had Done Something Worthwhile with My Life . . ."

A thousand miles to the south, at almost precisely that hour, Lodge received the directives to which Dong alluded: the taut, cryptic cable sent Friday evening from Washington. His voice thick with emotion, he telephoned D'Orlandi early Saturday morning to set a midafternoon rendezvous with Lewandowski. First, however, he went ahead with a previously scheduled meeting with Ky, raising issues ranging from corruption to relations with Cambodia—but not a word about Marigold, even though some U.S. officials feared that Hanoi might double-cross them by deliberately leaking it to the South Vietnamese leader.[79]

Then it was time for another secret encounter with Lewandowski, necessitating the usual precautions to evade surveillance on his way to the Italian's apartment.[80] The atmosphere was solemn when, shortly after 3 p.m., Lodge read to the Pole, with D'Orlandi present, the State Department text agreeing to a December 6 encounter in Warsaw:

> I am instructed to tell you that the United States Government is instructing the American Embassy in Warsaw to contact the North Vietnamese representative there on December 6. Our Embassy will be able to confirm that the ten points outlined by you broadly represent our position. We will have to say, however, that several specific points are subject to important differences of interpretation.[81]

His equivocation immediately prompted an objection from Lewandowski. ("I think that it was the case that this is first sign that something is going wrong," he remembered later.[82]) In his own report, Lodge mentioned blandly that the Pole merely "said he assumed from what I had said that some of the ten points in our opinion need clarification and that this interpretation will be done in Warsaw, to which I agreed." But Lewandowski's own cable (and memory) had him expressing sharp "disappointment" about the "important differences of interpretation" clause. (D'Orlandi quoted him as terming the clause his "main fear" only after Lodge left.) Lewandowski told Rapacki that during the meeting he had observed "in a very general way" that the reservation "must awaken doubts towards the actual intentions of the United States."

"What points arouse concerns of interpretation?" he pressed Lodge, insisting, with D'Orlandi's heated support, that he had adhered "strictly" to what the American said during their three-way meetings in mid-November.

Lodge sheepishly replied that he could not cite any "specific . . . important differences of interpretation," and had merely repeated verbatim what Washington cabled him. "Look, this is the dispatch I got from Johnson, and I don't know what are the reservations," Lewandowski recalled the "embarrassed" ambassador saying. "I just read it."[83] To save time, Lodge explained, he had not requested clarification before setting up their meeting.

Despite the contretemps over the interpretation clause, Lewandowski confirmed U.S. readiness to contact the DRV ambassador in Warsaw on December 6 and added, according to Lodge, "probably for the first meeting we will extend to you some help in getting in touch with the North Vietnamese. Someone from the [Polish Foreign] Ministry will be in touch with the Embassy and will effectuate a contact." In Lewandowski's version, Lodge *requested* MSZ aid in arranging the first contact and attributed Washington's failure to send a "big name" to Warsaw to its fear of arousing press interest.

Then, with "an increasingly worried expression," Lewandowski raised another complication: the Hanoi bombing the day before. Citing Rapacki's instructions, the Pole warned Lodge that "on the brink of such a delicate undertaking, it is wise to avoid anything which would create the impression that the United States interprets anything in Hanoi as a sign of weakness. To do this would be a most unhappy interpretation." Lewandowski himself reported telling Lodge "that all attempts to interpret the DRV agreement for Warsaw contact as a result of bombing or an expression of weakness could lead to a tragic mistake."

The notion that Washington might ruin the chance for peace through ill-timed military action cast a chill over the conversation—D'Orlandi noted in his diary that "the atmosphere, which at first was solemn, then happy, now has become tense."

Lodge flatly rejected the Pole's implication, stressing that bombings were planned long in advance, "awaiting only the right atmospheric conditions." (He did not say so, but more raids might have occurred Saturday but for bad weather over North Vietnam.[84]) So, he argued, the Hanoi strikes could not seen as a pressure tactic tied to the initiative; moreover, suspending them at the last minute might have alerted military officials that a secret peace bid was in motion.

As for D'Orlandi, Lewandowski vividly remembered (and Lodge neglected to mention in his own cable) that he "indignant[ly]" endorsed his criticisms of the Hanoi attack and warned against any further such provocations: "He was *furious,* he was furious, he said to me, 'Who did this bombing, who are these crazy people sending these bombers now, in such a situation?!'"

Puncturing the tension, Lodge vowed that he would report Lewandowski's concerns to Washington—and he did. The conversation, more relaxed, returned to details of the peace initiative.

In line with Warsaw's latest directive, which echoed Dong's request, Lewandowski halfheartedly reminded Lodge of the need to include the NLF in plans for talks, because "simple realism" dictated that sooner or later Washington would have to deal with its enemy on the ground to reach a modus vivendi. Politely, Lodge conceded the logic, but he deflected the request for future consideration, pleading a lack of concrete instructions. Considering the U.S.-DRV contact a far more urgent priority, Lewandowski did not press the point: "I was not insisting, this was my instruction, I had to do it, but I felt, again, don't try too much to squeeze. . . . Leave [it] to the Vietnamese and Americans . . . for the talks."[85]

Despite the snags and undercurrents of doubt already creeping into their conversation, the diplomats had reason to believe that they had achieved a breakthrough—that in a few days, direct contacts between the warring sides would commence in Warsaw and move quickly to serious negotiations because the general outlines of a settlement had already been "broadly" agreed upon. D'Orlandi proposed a champagne toast, "but to avoid tempting fate," he recorded in his diary, "we stuck to the usual whisky."[86]

"I thought I had done something worthwhile in my life," Lodge remembered. "We had a drink on it."[87]

With agreement on all sides for direct talks seemingly in hand, D'Orlandi was almost euphoric. He expressed "deep and moved satisfaction for the result obtained, notwithstanding the alternating pessimism" of the concerned governments. (Afterward, he thanked Fanfani for the "great faith" he had shown in him.) On his way out the door, a moved Lodge reminded him of their dark days together during the Diem coup upheaval three years earlier.

After Lodge left, Lewandowski expressed worry to D'Orlandi about the interpretation clause and "perplexity" about the first U.S.-DRV meeting. "I am left with the impression that the Americans want to withdraw," he said—a statement perhaps reflecting his real concern that the United States might be backing away from the prospective talks but also encouraging the Italian to exhort Fanfani to pressure Washington to cease any further bombings.

D'Orlandi strongly urged Lewandowski to fly to Warsaw to help arrange the first contact ("for a better presentation of the matter"), but the Pole balked—both because a sudden trip might draw attention to himself and spur a leak, and because it would be presumptuous, especially for a junior diplomat, to imply that the Foreign Ministry leadership required his help. ("Please do not understand it as my suggestion," he implored Rapacki.) D'Orlandi stressed secrecy and speed to secure the start of talks in Poland, but to Fanfani he also projected more tripartite meetings in Saigon, both to iron out any problems in Warsaw and to open a new channel to the NLF.

In his own cable relating the December 3 session, Lewandowski displayed mixed emotions: optimism that talks really could begin, mingled with concern that the hawks in the U.S. government and military might try to sabotage them. The fixed December 6 date that Lodge had given for the first Warsaw contact, he hoped, might mark the start of a planned bombing halt. Yet, he stressed, LBJ "dreads counter-action by the right," and despite Lodge's assurance that only LBJ and Rusk knew of the initiative, McNamara must also be informed, and it was "possible therefore to expect opposition" (of which, he guessed, the December 2 raids were a harbinger).[88] In fact, he had misread McNamara—who was already losing faith in a military victory and was privately sympathetic to a bombing halt to spur negotiations—but not the U.S. military, which stridently urged fiercer air strikes.[89]

* * *

D'Orlandi too had mixed feelings after the meeting, but for different reasons. Mingled with joy at the prospect of achieving a breakthrough toward peace was a wistful recognition that, as Washington and Hanoi entered into direct negotiations, his own role would rapidly fade. To his diary that night, he confessed "an empty feeling about the future, I would say like a father who has walked his daughter down the aisle." He went to bed exhausted, euphoric, and dreaming of leaving Saigon, his mission accomplished, for a healthier, more placid existence at a Farnesina desk job or at a "pleasant and peaceful embassy suitable for my convalescence."[90]

Warsaw: "It Would Be More Suitable for Me . . ."

Gronouski refused to take a hint. He was no career diplomat or old Asia hand, but he was not obtuse. He was fully capable of distinguishing between an *instruction* from Rusk—which he would salute and carry out, regardless of personal inclinations—and tactical *advice*, no matter how clearly worded. When the terse cable relating the Saigon news reached the Warsaw embassy shortly after midnight, it first went to his deputy chief of mission, who certainly felt up to conducting the contacts with the North Vietnamese himself and hoped his boss would agree.[91] On seeing the cable himself later Saturday morning, however, Gronouski had other ideas. He had no trouble discerning the snub behind the suggestion that the ambassador "guide" talks with Hanoi's envoy but leave the grubby job of handling the actual meetings to a seasoned professional like Jenkins.

This was, after all, the moment he had craved from the day he arrived in Warsaw almost exactly a year earlier; since then, he had yearned and schemed to use his post to promote peace in Vietnam—his most important endeavor, he felt, transcending the relatively mundane mission of improving bilateral U.S.-Polish ties. Despite his futile efforts over the summer, he had continued to scrutinize any sign that Poland might play a more active part in the search for a settlement.[92] To call him enthusiastic at the notion of a direct meeting with a DRV diplomat would be a gross understatement. If the State Department doubted his competence to handle so delicate a task, he reciprocated by considering departmental edicts less than sacrosanct. Rusk's *suggestion* to the contrary, no way would he leave to an underling the chance to participate personally in a historic breakthrough. "We'll both do it," he told Jenkins, who suspected that the Wisconsin Democrat envisioned a triumph that would not only silence guns in Vietnam but also grease his own "return to Washington to be involved with Johnson in the political world."[93]

So, although State had invited his "judgment" as to whether his deputy or someone sent from Washington would be most "suitable to carry on these important discussions," Gronouski replied with a firm preference for a third alternative: himself. In a polite "interpretation" of Rusk's cable, the ambassador argued that he—not Jenkins or anyone else—should make the first contact ("on Dec. 6 or ASAP thereafter"); after all, the peril of exposure would be no greater, and the DRV ambassador's counterpart would be a more "suitable" interlocutor.

Gronouski also proposed—given the "considerable risk of detection and publicity" in "an attempt by any officer this embassy to make direct contact with North Vietnam ambassador"—that he ask Rapacki "to serve as intermediary in arranging initial contact as well as any subsequent meetings," beginning with a first encounter in the foreign minister's conference room. To disguise this and perhaps subsequent sessions from the press, he suggested that the U.S. official (preferably himself) visit the Foreign Ministry building on Aleja I Armii Wojska Polskiego (still widely known by its precommunist name, Aleja Szucha) on an unrelated pretext a half hour before the DRV diplomat called on Rapacki, then proceed to his office at the time of the scheduled meeting. The Poles would then withdraw, leaving only the principals and interpreters to conduct their business in private (although presumably it would not have posed much of a challenge for the Poles to bug their own premises).

If the first contact yielded ongoing secret talks, Gronouski recognized that he would need to return to Washington for an "appropriate briefing," but he noted that such a trip could be masked as urgent consultations on the Polish debt crisis. A cover story "would be accepted by the press without question," because reporters were "well aware of my deep interest in the zloty use question" and also of an impending January 2 repayment deadline. Gronouski requested State's confirmation that he could proceed with the first contact and its reaction to his proposed arrangements.[94]

Washington: "We See No Objection . . ."
By the time Katzenbach, Thompson, and Read walked into the State Department early Saturday—the same cold morning that the *Washington Post* front-paged the Hanoi bombing and Rusk flew to Texas to join LBJ—the day's crucial Marigold cables had already been decoded. Lodge's report from Saigon (confirming delivery to Lewandowski of the hedged U.S. confirmation of its readiness to talk in Warsaw) required no immediate action, but Gronouski's defiant bid to take personal charge of the contacts with the North Vietnamese needed a reply.

After some hand-wringing, the de facto Marigold triumvirate caved. In the early afternoon, a cable went out accepting Gronouski's suggested arrangements and dropping the idea of having Jenkins handle the contacts. The message confirmed his understanding that "if security permits," he could "contact North Vietnamese ambassador on Dec. 6 or ASAP thereafter." Yet it also expressed doubt about "whether anyone on your level could carry on extended discussions without discovery" and reserved the right to reconsider the identity of the U.S. representative "pending the outcome of the first contact."[95]

Texas: "No Serious Effort . . . to Persuade Him"
A little before 10 a.m. Saturday, LBJ took off in his private Jetstar from the airstrip behind his ranch. After the short hop to Bergstrom Air Force Base near Austin, he crossed the tarmac to a waiting *Air Force One,* accompanied by Texas governor John Connally along with Rusk, Rostow, and other VIPs from Washington. Once airborne, at 10:18 a.m., LBJ and Rusk retired to a back cabin, where they spoke privately for most of the 45-minute flight to Laughlin Air Force Base in the frontier town of Del Rio, near the new Amistad ("Friendship") Dam.[96]

As mentioned above, "Marigold—Next Steps" topped their agenda, but precisely what transpired between them—their only face-to-face encounter during Marigold's climax in the first half of December—was not recorded. However, much may be surmised. Rusk fully shared the skepticism infusing the memo Bundy and Thompson had sent to prep him to brief LBJ regarding the Warsaw contacts. (Rusk "never believed in them," McNamara later told Lodge.[97]) Implicitly alluding to the ten points, Rusk observed later that the Poles "had the idea that their job was to find some face-saving formula by which we could save our face and get out of Vietnam; whereas, we were not trying to save face—we were trying to save South Vietnam."[98])

As for Johnson, despite his readiness to proceed with the Warsaw contact, he, like Rusk, had a jaundiced view of the Poles, reinforced by what he saw as their unscrupulous behavior in the waning days of the thirty-seven-day bombing pause. Both saw Rapacki's last-minute pleas to extend the pause in January, ten months earlier, as a patently mendacious ploy to extract maximum military advantage for a Communist ally at the cost of U.S. lives. Moreover, LBJ's ensuing actions would concretely reflect his view that, as he would tell Rusk, he "never thought it [Marigold] was anything but propaganda."[99]

It is highly likely, then, that besides relaying the latest Marigold news, Rusk accentuated a negative, skeptical, or at least exceedingly wary view of the Polish message and the likelihood that it really signified a DRV readiness for talks, let alone an imminent breakthrough. LBJ probably did not dispute such an assessment, yet he also remained keenly interested in probing further on the off chance that the initiative might develop into something realistic.

Lacking records, one cannot be sure what was said about Marigold in the skies above Texas that morning—but one thing *not* considered sympathetically, and perhaps not at all, was suspending the RT-52 raids on Hanoi that had started on Friday. Despite Polish warnings, Rusk had no qualms about continuing normal military operations, nor any inclination, at *this* point in Marigold, to urge LBJ to revoke or further whittle down the already-pared-down bombing plans, which they knew would have infuriated the military commanders, who hankered for harsher attacks. Bundy, who was traveling with Rusk but did not sit in on his talk with LBJ, recalled that over this weekend "no serious effort was made to persuade him that we should call off these authorizations because, among other things, it was quite clear on the face of this thing that no requirement with respect to bombing had been posed. And we didn't think the President would buy [a bombing suspension around Hanoi], but whether the thing was ever put to him, I do not know."[100]

Rome: Fanfani's Fury

If Rusk saw nothing untoward about hitting Hanoi on the verge of the proposed Warsaw contact, his Italian counterpart had a very different reaction: Fanfani was incensed. For the third time in a little over a year, Washington had escalated the war precisely as a delicate secret Italian peace maneuver neared fruition. His sentiments resembled those memorably attributed to John F. Kennedy in 1961 when he learned that Nikita Khrushchev had unilaterally resumed nuclear testing, breaking a three-year moratorium: *Fucked again!*[101] "Who in Washington wants to prevent the negotiation?" he wondered Friday evening on learning of the Hanoi bombing, just hours after cabling D'Orlandi to congratulate him on the apparent breakthrough.[102]

More than suspicion, Fanfani felt anger toward Italy's NATO ally, which he vented—in a stunning breach of Cold War etiquette—to the local envoy of the Warsaw Pact country with which he was collaborating. He had long cultivated close relations with Rapacki's man in Rome, Adam Willmann, even inviting the ambassador to join him for several days at his monastic summer retreat, and he felt comfortable enough to speak with him candidly. So, on Saturday, Willmann stopped by the Farnesina on a routine chore, to relay information about his country's gifts to Italian flood victims and discuss trade in potatoes. But after thanking Poland for the aid, Fanfani unburdened himself about the international situation —and above all the latest news from Vietnam.[103]

By bombing Hanoi, he fumed, Washington was, "for the third time, shattering the chances for negotiations"—after "repudiating his initiative" the previous November (the La Pira affair) and then ruining the Lewandowski-D'Orlandi contacts in June, just as the Pole signaled Hanoi's "allegedly modified position regarding the four points." Disgusted, he "emphasize[d] that one cannot count on the so-called Kennedy circles in the U.S. concerning the issue of Vietnam; they are only using the Vietnam issue for their games with Johnson and not peace in Asia."

For good measure, into this tirade against Washington, the agitated minister tossed some barbs at his own government. He denounced the decision by Premier Aldo Moro, a Christian Democrat (backed by Socialist vice premier Pietro Nenni), to deny Italian visas to the VWP delegation to the Hungarian Communist Party Congress taking place in Budapest, as a step that deprived him of a timely opportunity to personally commend the peace overture to senior DRV figures. But Fanfani had kind words for one character in this tangled mess, Willmann reported to Rapacki: He "highly assesses Lewandowski in Saigon."

Saigon: "Sniffing Around on This"

If the warnings over the Hanoi bombing and doubts about the interpretation clause were not enough to induce jitters among the three Saigon diplomats, an incident Saturday night further fanned Lewandowski's fears of a leak—which they all knew could wreck the whole effort. At the U.S. Embassy, Lodge had informed only two colleagues about Marigold: his deputy, William Porter, and senior political counselor Philip Habib.[104] Habib, a plainspoken Brooklynite of Lebanese-American ancestry, maintained contacts with a wide range of sources, including Canada's ICC delegate. Late Saturday night, Habib hosted Moore for a long conversation on the war's military and diplomatic prospects. They shared a fairly dim view of the commission, especially in view of what Moore termed India's "flaccid chairmanship," but mused various methods to expand its operations should peace prospects improve. The wide-ranging talk turned to ways in which the war might end. Spanning the gamut (and, incidentally, burying the actual Marigold scenario amid other possibilities), Habib listed eight alternatives ranging from a reprise of the 1954 Geneva Conference, to smaller gatherings of interested countries (Washington-Hanoi-Beijing?), to secret contacts between warring parties (Saigon-Hanoi? Saigon–Viet Cong?), to "notification by secret message resulting in a tacit reciprocal action leading to an eventual conference," to Lodge's favorite, a "fading away" of the insurgency once Hanoi grasped that it could not win. Habib acknowledged that the U.S. commanders dismissed optimists' claims that a current lull in attacks meant a "comprehensive scaling down" of Viet Cong units had already begun, but said Washington would gladly "match such de-escalation step by step, using the 'blue chips' of the bombing of North Vietnam" to reward such actions.[105]

At one point, Moore bluntly confronted Habib with suspicions that Lewandowski was covertly mediating arrangements for a Christmas–New Year bombing truce or cease-fire between Washington and Hanoi.[106] As evidence, the Canadian cited his "'peculiar' behavior and little hints dropped that he is doing important things." Moreover, Rahman was also "sniffing around on this," and both found the Pole's recent trip to Hanoi "strange" because he had no obvious business there and was in general "acting mysteriously."

"Rahman is a conniver," Habib snorted. Offering an innocent explanation of how the truce idea arose, he pooh-poohed the idea that Washington would use Lewandowski.

Moore did not dispute Habib's characterization of the Indian—and privately had initially considered Rahman's speculations "farfetched"—but added that he also had his own, more concrete grounds for suspecting the Pole was up to something: "I understand that Lewandowski met with Ambassador Lodge at D'Orlandi's before going to Hanoi, and when he returned D'Orlandi rushed to see him and another meeting was held with Ambassador Lodge."[107]

Habib demurred, doubting Lodge had ever met the Pole, "even socially." Still, Moore expressed confidence that Lodge had secretly met with Lewandowski at D'Orlandi's.

How did he know that? pressed the American.

"I would rather not say just now," Moore stonewalled.

Though the Canadian refused to disclose his source to Habib, Moore's own cable to the Department of External Affairs in Ottawa reveals that he was, in fact, tipped off by a South Vietnamese official to the Polish-American contacts in Saigon, implying D'Orlandi's role as a "go-between." Despite all the James Bond–like machinations, the diplomats' furtive gatherings had not escaped the eyes of the regime's intelligence apparatus.[108]

Habib lied like a trooper, "absolutely" denying the bombing truce story, and insisting that there was "nothing" to the rumor that Lewandowski was being used in secret peace probes. Moore, however, was not fully convinced. "Whether we should take the American denial at its face value," he cabled Ottawa, "is perhaps also open to question."

Sunday, December 4

Saigon: The Front "Answer[s]"

Sunday was not a day of rest in South Vietnam's capital—even before D'Orlandi was due to rise for morning Mass, explosions twice rattled his residence's doors and windows, the latter saved from shattering only by prophylactic taping.[109] As if to show that they could strike their enemy's heart on the ground as effectively as the Americans could from the air, Viet Cong guerrillas mounted a predawn assault on sprawling Tan Son Nhut Airport, symbol of the enormous U.S. military presence with more than 20,000 personnel and 300 planes (plus Ky's residence). In their first attack on the site in almost eight months, the insurgents shelled the complex with mortar fire for more than two hours beginning at 1:28 a.m., then penetrated the base perimeter from surrounding rice paddies, leading to fierce battles with U.S. helicopter gunships and Air Force C-47s.

Then, at about 5:30 a.m., "with flares still popping over the airport but with the shock of the attack there easing," a huge explosion tore through a heavily guarded U.S. military billet at the downtown Kinhdo Movie Theatre, which now housed a psychological warfare unit and other personnel after having been converted from an Americans-only cinema following an earlier bombing. The blast, later blamed on a Communist sapper who had climbed from an adjoining roof, wounded twelve Americans, four seriously enough to be hospitalized.

The NLF called the Sunday morning attacks against U.S. and "puppet" forces its "answer" to the Hanoi bombing on Friday and vowed that "the South Vietnamese [Communist] armed forces and people will hit back five or ten times harder." Washington doubted the claim, as they seemed too carefully planned to be in reprisal for actions only two days earlier.[110]

Hanoi: The Bombers Return

Nor was Sunday restful for Hanoi residents, who that afternoon endured U.S. air raids for the second time in three days, far heavier than Friday's and on two sections of town rather than one. Restriking the Van Dien truck depot, Air Force F-105 Thunderchiefs made twenty sorties and dropped ninety-six 750-pound bombs, the pilots reporting "that ordnance impacted throughout the target area causing secondary explosions resulting in a 30-foot fireball and a tall column of smoke" rising a thousand feet into the air. They also hit a second sensitive Hanoi-area target on RT-52's list, the Yen Vien railway yard 5 to 6 miles northeast of the city center, besides again striking the Ha Gia petroleum storage dump 14 miles north of the capital.[111] In all, the Pentagon Papers' analysts later noted, the December 2 and 4 raids deposited a combined total of almost 50 tons of ordnance on the Hanoi area—roughly twice the amount as the late June assaults on petroleum, oil, and lubricant facilities.[112]

For the second time in three days, the DRV authorities angrily protested the "barbarous" and "odious crimes" and reported numerous civilian casualties. "Many formations of piratical U.S. aircraft again launched frenzied attacks on a number of residential quarters in the northern suburb of Hanoi," Lau complained to the ICC.[113]

Saigon: "Lewandowski Is a Plausible Rogue"

As the Marigold action shifted to Warsaw, the Saigon diplomats had a chance to tidy up loose ends and ruminate on the increasingly dicey state of affairs in their channel. Lewandowski awoke Sunday to the sound of sporadic gunfire from the direction of Tan Son Nhut as U.S. forces tried to wipe out remaining pockets of resistance, and later that morning he cabled Rapacki the text of the "recapitulation" of the U.S. position that he had given Lodge on December 1—evidently the first time Poland's foreign minister saw the "ten points" that would become so famous; with allowance for differences in translation (as opposed to interpretation), they accorded with the versions earlier cabled by Lodge and D'Orlandi to their respective capitals.[114]

That afternoon, reports began to flow in of the second round of bombings of Hanoi in three days; not surprisingly, they inflamed Lewandowski's suspicions that forces within the U.S. government and/or military were backing away from, by deliberately sabotaging, the imminent peace contacts. "I was convinced, it's finished," he remembered; if the first air strikes on the Hanoi area were an "irritation," this second round—on the heels of the dodgy "interpretations clause"—was "decisive." Knowing how closely LBJ supervised the bombing, Lewandowski felt sure that "somebody in Washington decided it is not the time to negotiate" or wanted to "soften up" Hanoi. If Lodge's arguments about "pre-planned" raids merely awaiting suitable weather had previously strained credulity, swallowing them now, he felt, would be simply naive.[115]

That Sunday afternoon Lodge, too, was having second thoughts about the initiative—for very different reasons. Trudging in short sleeves through puddles left by firefighters, he inspected the Kinhdo Theatre's smoldering ruins and angrily denounced the "men dressed as civilians who come in and plant bombs." "There isn't any way to protect yourself against the hit-and-run terrorist," he observed. Only through a long, hard struggle entailing a reconstruction of "the whole political, social and economic structure in this country," he grimly told reporters, could the Viet Cong be defeated.[116]

The latest Saigon outrages reinforced Lodge's already-fervent belief that the Communists should not be rewarded for odious behavior. He underlined this view in a cable to Washington noting that as Marigold "enters a new phase," special attention should be paid to Lewandowski's "most important and difficult undefined point"—number two, which stated that the "present status quo in South Vietnam must [would] be changed to take into account the interests of the parties" opposing the United States.[117] Of course, this vague statement's concrete implications would be haggled over in negotiations between Washington and Hanoi. But out of conviction and probably a desire to assure Rusk that he had not turned soft and squishy, Lodge counseled firmly against any formula that would "put the NLF into the Government of Vietnam." Doing so would be not only impractical, because it would be completely unacceptable to the present Saigon leadership, but also immoral, as it would "in effect give official benediction to the vast criminal terrorist element which is at the bottom of this whole war. It would mean our defeat and the stultification of all who have made sacrifices here." On a practical military level, it would demoralize those fighting for the present government (and be "an individual death sentence" for many of the regime's members or supporters), legitimize Communist control of territory and population, and "give a hunting license to the Viet Cong to start the expansion of terrorism among the 80 percent presently not under 24 hours a day Viet Cong domination."

Rather than invite the NLF into a coalition government—the Pole's preference—Lodge urged merely allowing its candidates to compete in elections under the new constitution, which itself would be a significant concession. This would fit U.S. policy that the South Vietnamese must freely determine their fate—as enshrined in Lewandowski's fifth point—and also be a safer bet, because "it is, after all, not our fault that NLF appears to be highly unpopular."[118]

Explaining Marigold, Lodge attributed Hanoi's "change of attitude" to a recognition that "they cannot win and that we are sure to win," not only because of U.S. military success but also given South Vietnam's progress toward "constitutional democracy." The DRV probably acted to stop the latter, a "death knell for Communism," and it would be foolish to let the Communists switch gears by subverting Saigon's regime from within, and thus derailing its move toward democracy, when they had failed to topple it through brute force. "I believe we are plenty strong enough to maintain our position and really make it stick," he cabled. "Your instructions to me in this whole Marigold business have been magnificent. We've gotten as far as we have by 'playing it cool' and I think we ought to go on 'playing it cool.' Silence and action, with every consideration for their dignity, pride and prestige, should result in an end to the war and in the creation of a solid Republic of Vietnam that can stand by itself—and at maximum speed. Eagerness tends to harden Communist positions to a degree we can't accept, and this lengthens the war."

Lodge speculated that the day's attacks in Saigon might have a Marigold link. Was Hanoi "stepping up [terrorism] so as to make us eager to negotiate? Are they by terrorism seeking to get one more chip in Saigon area as they approach negotiations?" Hanoi's seeming new readiness for talks, he suspected, might aim at stemming Viet Cong defections, which U.S. officials crowed had reached record levels,[119] and undermining Saigon's "National Reconciliation Campaign."

Lodge also suggested that Washington consider protectively informing the Saigon leadership of at least Marigold's "broad outlines." It was bound to learn otherwise, probably sooner rather than later, and Hanoi might even maliciously and deliberately leak the matter to sow distrust between the United States and its ally.[120] At the same time, he wondered whether Westmoreland, still in the dark, ought also to be let in on the secret.[121]

✳ ✳ ✳

Lodge's concerns about an unauthorized Marigold disclosure were exacerbated by the report he received Sunday morning from Habib of his alarming talk with Moore the night before. The "quite interested" Canadian had only garbled information—far more than a holiday truce was at stake—but Lodge knew this meant trouble. Obviously, they were being watched, Lodge cabled Washington; someone was talking, and it might be a matter of time before word reached the press. He would alert D'Orlandi and suggest that he "inform Lewandowski discreetly that some of his Commission colleagues are speculating on his role as a mediator and there are rumors of his meeting with me, connecting it to truce arrangements."[122]

For the U.S., Italian, and Polish envoys involved in the delicate peace initiative, the fresh danger of premature exposure added yet another ominous item to a growing list of worries—and Moore, far from satisfied by Habib's denials, persisted in "sniffing about." That Sunday, he invited Lewandowski to a tête-à-tête lunch at the Canadian villa for the nominal purpose of updating him on various ICC matters (e.g., aircraft safety or replacement) in Rahman's absence. But Ottawa's nosy representative was also eager to glean intelligence on the Pole's recent Hanoi trip—and probe further the rumors linking him to secret peace contacts.[123] During the meal, however, as he had with Rahman during their long flight to Saigon, the Pole carefully hid his involvement in the initiative that had reached so delicate a stage.

Claiming, implausibly, that his trip's aim had been to check up on Polish ICC operations in Hanoi, Lewandowski sensed that Moore was itching to ask him bluntly whether he was up to something more intriguing and perhaps even knew somehow the real reason for his journey. "I was looking at him and thinking, 'Well, well, well?'" But the Canadian was too diplomatic to confront him directly, and when his various hints and overtures to elicit greater candor failed to pierce the cover story, he ended their conversation by cryptically yet earnestly wishing him all success in . . . whatever he was trying to accomplish.[124]

"The Pole's reaction to any approach on the question was as usual phlegmatic and non-committal," Moore cabled Ottawa of his attempts to raise the reported contacts with Lodge and D'Orlandi. As for his trip north, Lewandowski blandly "summed up the atmosphere and attitude [in] Hanoi as being unchanged."

Rather than be overtly uncommunicative, Lewandowski tried to allay Moore's suspicions by seeming forthcoming, freely (it seemed) dispensing observations. Hanoi's streets, he said, were far more crowded than on his previous visit—people had apparently concluded that the city was relatively safe from bombing, although leaders set a "good example" by keeping their families in the countryside. Having asked to travel more extensively to inspect bomb damage, he was allowed to go—chaperoned by Lau—as far as 200 kilometers (125 miles) from the city.

Describing his exchanges with DRV leaders, the Pole implied that nothing unusual arose during his calls on Dong ("in his usual 'good form,' the only noticeable change being an increased gray in his hair") and Giap ("his apparently unchanged sphinx-like self"), or his "quite rational discussions with the PAVN people, particularly on Viet Cong tactics." All displayed the same unwavering faith in ultimate victory—and here he neatly segued into a "rather interesting" digression over how seriously to treat these resolute statements. To Moore's remark that it was hard to tell in Hanoi "what is propaganda and what is genuine belief," he countered that the "protestations of determination and optimism reflect indeed a firm belief" but "did not demur at my interjection that this then is an indication of irrational thinking." Encouraging Moore's belief that he, too, viewed the North as intransigent, Lewandowski also did not dispute his charge that its recent violations of the Demilitarized Zone risked "changing the whole character and scope of the war"; instead, he merely stressed the danger of a "tragic miscalculation by either side." Most important, camouflaging the breakthrough he believed had in fact occurred, he declared that Hanoi's "different logic," so unfathomable to outsiders, "rules out any communication between them and 'white Europeans.' This was particularly so with respect to their making any gestures or reciprocal action when 'the skies are full of American planes and there are 300,000 American invaders—How can we North Vietnamese do anything but what we are doing?'"

Afterward, Moore seemed unsure what to make of Lewandowski's performance. The Pole, he told Ottawa, "is a plausible rogue and the foregoing is perhaps just a variation of the East European dodging of the issues to be taken with a grain of salt. I must, however, admit that it to a certain extent does coincide with my impression over the months of a blind and almost suicidal logical illogic which dominates at least the government offices in Hanoi itself."

Sunday evening, still "sniffing," the Canadian questioned D'Orlandi about peace efforts. The Italian confided that the Vatican initiative for a series of holiday truces was now a "dead horse." Perhaps already warned by Lodge of Moore's unhealthy curiosity, D'Orlandi kept mum about the Polish channel on which he pinned so many hopes; still, his comment about the pope's efforts reflected his worries about what was happening, or supposed to happen, in Warsaw.

"Everything is vague," he said unhappily.[125]

Washington: Rusk Departs

That Sunday, U.S. officials dealing with Marigold had little to do but read incoming cables. Having flown back from Texas the night before, Rusk stopped in at the office for an hour at midday to see Read and Katzenbach before heading to Andrews Air Force Base. At 2:23 p.m., with Bundy and a few other aides, he left for Tokyo—the first stop on a two-week journey to the Far East and across Eurasia to a NATO ministerial meeting in Paris.[126] Meanwhile, Katzenbach took over as acting secretary of state. At the White House, Rostow apprised LBJ of the latest news, relaying to Texas copies of Lodge's messages about ICC commissioners "sniffing about" and reflections on "how the NLF should and should not be brought into South Vietnamese politics."[127]

Warsaw: "Damned Little Material"

When it was all over, Gronouski would spread the impression that he spent that first December weekend in a bleary-eyed blur, preparing for impending encounters with Rapacki and, he earnestly hoped, the North Vietnamese ambassador by poring over long, highly classified cables that constantly clattered over the ciphered telegraph machine in the embassy's fourth-floor communications room (one floor beneath his own office) to reveal the entire Marigold story to date. A year later, he vividly recalled to visiting *Los Angeles Times* reporter Stuart Loory those first days after learning that the Saigon exchanges had yielded agreement for a contact in Warsaw. "From the time Gronouski received the first cable on Saturday night, Dec. 3 [*sic*—actually late *Friday* night / early Saturday morning], he spent 30 straight hours reading the Marigold record as he received it in toto on the embassy's ticker," Loory recorded. "A staff member says he did not leave the embassy until 5:30 a.m. Monday morning. G. says he received the complete file of Marigold—all the verbatim. . . . That weekend was the start of many sleepless nights for Gronouski. He could envision the Nobel Prize coming his way, and he wanted it and worked for it."[128] This was good stuff, straight from the horse's mouth; Loory and Kraslow incorporated the dramatic story into *The Secret Search for Peace in Vietnam,* and it thus entered history.[129]

The only problem is that it never happened—Gronouski told this story due to faulty memory, a desire to bury Washington's embarrassing lack of confidence in him, or both. In a private oral history interview with a member of the LBJ Library staff in early 1969, he started to retell the same tall tale, then caught himself in time to provide something closer to the truth: "And Sunday I got a whole raft of material that brought me up [to date]—no, I didn't get it Sunday. I got very damned little material Sunday, as I recall, pretty sketchy outlines, some of the details."[130]

In fact, from the surviving declassified documentary record, it seems that Gronouski got *nothing* further from Washington on Sunday, at least in writing, beyond the terse one-page cables he had already received. Most important, Washington still did not trust him with the ten points (already known, of course, to the Poles, Italians, and presumably North Vietnamese). To a considerable extent, he would have to wing it.

* * *

It is not clear whether Rapacki or Michałowski worked that Sunday. But at MSZ headquarters, the ciphergram section labored through the weekend, as usual. At

11:30 a.m., the clerks received the coded version of Lewandowski's cable describing his talk Saturday afternoon in Saigon with Lodge and containing the three-part official U.S. statement agreeing to the Warsaw contact "on December 6" but also hedging approval of the ten points. By 3:10 p.m. they finished the job, and could deliver the message ("Only in person," Lewandowski instructed) to the foreign minister.[131] When Rapacki and his chief Vietnam aide saw it—late Sunday or first thing Monday—they did not like what they read. Michałowski later recalled:

> In Warsaw the "interpretation clause" aroused serious unease. We did not understand how differences of interpretation could emerge when the talks had not yet begun. We considered that the White House already began to withdraw from the proposals contained in the Ten Points, which after all was the cause of the DRV agreement to begin talks. We therefore instructed Lewandowski to demand immediately from Lodge clarification of this clause. Furthermore, he was to protest again the bombing of 4 December.[132]

Monday, December 5

Saigon: "The Last Person We Would Use"

For a second night, the assault on Tan Son Nhut continued. U.S. spokesmen announced that another eleven Viet Cong had been killed trying to penetrate the airbase's western perimeter, bringing the total to thirty, and at 2 a.m. Monday gunners had opened fire on a transport plane approaching a runway, causing only minor damage.[133]

The Marigold ambassadors had no immediate business to conduct, waiting in suspense for news from Warsaw. To his irritation, Lewandowski got instructions to deliver a fresh protest to Lodge about the renewed Hanoi raids. Though incensed himself, he wondered why Rapacki was making such an issue of it, because Dong had not preconditioned the Warsaw contact on a prior bombing halt. "When I got from Rapacki this constant pushing to ask for this stopping of the bombing, incessantly, I was a little bit annoyed, because I felt that he want[ed] to be *plus catholic [que] le pape* [more Catholic than the Pope]––the [North] Vietnamese do not put such a stress to it, but Rapacki does, you know, and . . . because after [all] what Pham Van Dong said to me was a statement of principle, he didn't include it in his formal answer, he just said, 'Well, this [bombing halt] is [a] very important matter in any case.' . . . But it seems to be this beloved child of Michałowski and Rapacki and I had to do it."[134]

Nor was Lewandowski pleased by the directive "to demand immediately and categorically from Lodge an explanation" of the interpretation clause.[135] It seemed to him pointless, because Washington, not its ambassador, had lodged the reservation, and any "important differences in interpretation" would be debated in direct U.S.-DRV talks. Yet he knew he had to follow orders and arrange another three-way session with Lodge. "Rapacki is squeezing, squeezing, to ask him, so I do it," he remembered with a twinge of exasperation.[136]

* * *

Meanwhile, Lodge did his best to throw the Canadian bloodhound off the scent. At a reception at the Thai Embassy Monday evening, Deputy Ambassador Porter, obviously under instructions, made a point of seeking out Moore to ridicule the rumor that Washington was employing the Polish ICC commissioner as a go-between with Hanoi. Lewandowski, he harrumphed, would be "the last person we would use for anything like that."[137]

Warsaw: "A Question Mark on the Whole American Position"

If he did not hear from the Polish Foreign Ministry by the close of business Monday, Gronouski was instructed to contact Rapacki to discover what was up regarding the proposed U.S.-DRV contact.[138] But the eager envoy did not have to wait that long. In midmorning, he received a summons from Michałowski on an innocuous, ostensibly unrelated matter. To avoid alerting his staff, he went alone. Under cloudy skies, he drove in an unmarked car, sans ambassadorial emblem or stars and stripes, arrived by 11:30 a.m., and strode into the building via the less prominent entrance on Ul. Litewski. Inside, Michałowski greeted him and engaged in "a few minutes of unimportant conversation" on his "trivial pretext" for the meeting.[139]

Then, in spy novel fashion, he prompted the American to utter a secret passphrase.

"Do you have any idea why I might want you over here?" Michałowski asked.

Well, it might be "because of some conversations going on in Saigon," a relieved Gronouski responded.

"Then I can tell you that Mr. Rapacki wants to see you."[140]

Having ascertained that Gronouski was clued in, Michałowski escorted him to Rapacki's second-floor office for the first of what would be many secret talks between them in the coming weeks.[141] Rapacki proceeded to recount the events that had taken place in Saigon since mid-November, including Lodge's three-part statement to Lewandowski on December 3. He also complained about both the Hanoi bombings on Friday and Sunday and the "interpretation" clause, expressing "grave concern" at how the DRV would interpret this apparent "equivocation" about the ten points. Rapacki stated that the Poles were "holding up" transmitting Lodge's December 3 statement "in hopes of obtaining improved version, but observed that they have no right to delay too long conveying information to Hanoi." He urged Washington to delete or soften the interpretation clause, lest it (together with the bombings) cause North Vietnam to postpone or cancel the contact. "These formulations," he said, "put a question mark on the whole American position and will undoubtedly be read in Hanoi as a retraction by the USA. Therefore, it would be better if we could deliver the whole thing to Hanoi without these reservations."

Gronouski handled the meeting knowing only the barest outlines of the secret exchanges between Lodge and Lewandowski: "Rapacki told me more than I knew about what was going on in Saigon, and I kept a stiff upper lip and acted like I knew more than I knew."[142]

Rome: "I Extend My Congratulations"

When Fanfani read D'Orlandi's telegrams describing his three-way conversation on Saturday with Lodge and Lewandowski, including the U.S. consent for the first Warsaw contact, it put him in a far finer mood than he had been in while venting his frustrations to the Polish ambassador. Even though Washington had again bombed Hanoi the day before, on Monday evening he sent his ambassador in Saigon hearty congratulations "for the reaching of the first major objective owing to the perfect execution of the instructions given you" and declared proudly that Italy could "feel satisfied about the decisive contribution made defining the framework which permits the beginning of direct contacts from tomorrow among the principals involved."[143]

In praising D'Orlandi and directing him to express "satisfaction" to his Polish and U.S. "partners" and "thanks for the faith placed in us," Fanfani stressed that he did not "underestimate the present and future difficulties." Yet the religious politician closed his diary with an affirmation of faith and optimism: "Tomorrow may be the turning point. We can thank God."[144]

Fanfani had no idea that about eight hundred miles to the north, the plans for the next day's initial U.S.–North Vietnamese contact had already begun to go awry.

Washington: "Herewith the Poles Throw a Block . . ."

Gronouski's cable conveying Rapacki's request to delete the "important differences of interpretation" clause reached Washington at 10:43 a.m. Monday morning and quickly caused consternation. Passing the cable to LBJ in Texas, Rostow scribbled: "Herewith the Poles throw a block across the Warsaw contact."[145] That afternoon, sensing a probing maneuver by the Poles and/or North Vietnamese, Katzenbach drafted a reply to Warsaw instructing Gronouski to politely but firmly stand by the December 3 statement, despite Rapacki's objections. He should explain that Washington stood ready to accept the ten points "as the basis for direct discussions with the North Vietnamese if they are in fact interested in pursuing the matter," but failing to inform them clearly that there existed "a wide latitude for interpretation of the general language used by Lewandowski" might "expose ourselves to bad faith in any subsequent negotiations."

Before giving White House clearance to the message to Gronouski, Rostow checked with LBJ, sending him Katzenbach's draft instruction to Gronouski "in effort to clear Polish road-block" along with comments that reveal some of the thinking behind the U.S. determination to cling to the interpretation clause. "I believe this is as forthcoming as we can now be and protects our position for the record," Rostow told LBJ in urging his concurrence—a comment reflecting the preference of officials involved, especially Katzenbach and Thompson, for responding to the ten points with a catchall prophylactic clause rather than with official U.S. language that was "more precise and acceptable," but also impossible to disavow. Perhaps thinking of the cable from Lodge, Rostow explained that "our major concern right now is that Hanoi might use this exchange to damage our position with Ky, for we are dealing with matters that involve the sovereignty of his government." If direct contacts with Hanoi actually started, all agreed that "we cannot go very far without cutting in Ky on a personal basis." LBJ voiced no objection, and the cable to Gronouski went out at about 9 p.m. Washington time.[146]

For LBJ's bedtime reading, Rostow also sent along the CIA's "thoughtful, well-written" report, "The View from Hanoi," dated November 30, which postulated that the DRV was poised between choosing a "return to full-scale guerrilla war" or "opening . . . a negotiating track." In a cover note observing that the authors did not know of Marigold, Rostow added a remark that reflected his presumption that hitting Hanoi on the Warsaw contact's eve could only help prod the enemy to the bargaining table. The CIA analysis, he noted, "leaves out, curiously, the pressure of bombing in the North. This may be an item in the equation which could tip the balance toward negotiation; but we shall shortly see."[147]

They would indeed.

Janusz Lewandowski: A Very Serious Fellow

In December 1956, Janusz Lewandowski (in the light-colored trench coat) strides toward United Nations headquarters in New York City with members of the Polish delegation. As a junior diplomat, he accompanied the foreign minister, Adam Rapacki, to the annual UN General Assembly sessions from 1956 to 1959. *Courtesy of Janusz Lewandowski.*

French-trained Vietnamese *tirailleurs* (skirmishers) at Camp des Mares in colonial Saigon. After the French left, these barracks were used as the headquarters of the International Control Commission—consisting of Canada, Poland, and India—which was created by the 1954 Geneva Conference.

A young Lewandowski during his first posting at a Polish embassy, in Cairo. *From the Stuart H. Loory Papers; courtesy of American Heritage Center, Laramie, Wyoming.*

Lewandowski with Pham Van Dong and one of the Polish deputy foreign ministers, Zygfryd Wolniak, at the presidential palace in Hanoi. The Polish ICC commissioner frequently met here with the North Vietnamese premier, including the pivotal November 1966 encounters at which he discussed the U.S. proposals in Marigold. At the time of this visit, in March 1969, he headed the Asia section of the Polish Foreign Ministry. *Courtesy of Janusz Lewandowski.*

Lewandowski *(at the left, holding the child)* with his comrades in a village near Hanoi. Behind him stands Colonel Ha Van Lau, the liaison of the People's Army of Vietnam to the ICC, and Lewandowski's regular host in Hanoi; and smiling in the center is North Vietnam's deputy foreign minister, Nguyen Co Thach. Other Vietnamese in the photo include local residents and an army escort. In uniform at the rear is Poland's military attaché in Hanoi and at the right is a legal adviser to Warsaw's ICC delegation. *Courtesy of Janusz Lewandowski.*

In this ruined Buddhist temple near Nam Dinh, Lewandowski spent several hours shelter-
ing from a U.S. air raid together with Colonel Ha Van Lau. This occurred on one of Lewandowski's trips north, on which he made inspection tours outside Hanoi of damage caused
by American bombing, giving him evidence for eyewitness testimony back in Saigon to
argue that the raids were hitting civilians and residential areas, not only military targets.
Courtesy of Janusz Lewandowski.

Lewandowski sightseeing in the ruins at Angkor Wat in Cambodia. *Courtesy of Janusz Lewandowski.*

Lewandowski *(at the left)* with Colonel Ryszard Iwanciów; the two worked together closely until the senior military aide departed in early 1967. *Courtesy of Janusz Lewandowski.*

Lewandowski *(at the right, pointing the camera)* on the patio of his villa in Saigon in 1967 with Iwanciów's replacement as military adviser (at the left), and (in the center) his "political adviser"—and, he recalled, an Interior Ministry officer operating under diplomatic cover—Jerzy Kowalski. *Courtesy of Janusz Lewandowski.*

The Saigon Peace Plotters

Janusz Lewandowski *(in the center)*, flanked by the dapper Italian ambassador—and Marigold partner—Giovanni D'Orlandi *(at the left)*, and the Indian delegate to the International Control Commission, M. A. Rahman, at a reception in Saigon. *Courtesy of Janusz Lewandowski.*

D'Orlandi meeting in Phnom Penh with Prince Norodom Sihanouk, June 1966. When D'Orlandi returned to Saigon after this meeting, he met with Lewandowski and was thrilled to hear the Pole report that Hanoi was ready to negotiate—"the most impassioned dialogue of my life." And so Marigold began. *Courtesy of the Royal Household of Cambodia..*

Giovanni D'Orlandi and Henry Cabot Lodge in Saigon. *From the Henry Cabot Lodge Jr. Papers, Massachusetts Historical Society.*

Lodge shakes hands with the wife of the Italian military attaché as a dapper D'Orlandi looks on. *From the Henry Cabot Lodge Jr. Papers, Massachusetts Historical Society.*

Italian ambassador Giovanni D'Orlandi and South Vietnamese foreign minister Tran Van Do, a lonesome civilian in Saigon's military government. *Courtesy of Mario Sica.*

Lodge greets Mario Sica, the first secretary of the Italian Embassy in Saigon. Sica worked closely with his boss, Ambassador D'Orlandi, on Marigold, enciphering and decoding messages to and from Rome, and driving Lewandowski to and from secret meetings with Lodge while trying to evade the prying eyes of South Vietnamese intelligence. *Courtesy of Mario Sica.*

Lewandowski playing tennis on a court near his villa at the ICC compound in western Saigon. He also relaxed on the better-maintained grounds of the Cercle Sportif Saigonnais, where as a *membre d'honneur* he schmoozed with the city's elite—and also several times escaped his chauffeur to sneak away for a secret rendezvous with Henry Cabot Lodge at D'Orlandi's apartment. *Courtesy of Janusz Lewandowski.*

The building at 135 Duong Pasteur in central Saigon, which at the time was the Italian Embassy. Here, in his top-floor apartment, Ambassador Giovanni D'Orlandi hosted U.S. ambassador Henry Cabot Lodge and Poland's ambassador to the International Control Commission, Janusz Lewandowski, for secret three-way meetings in 1966. By 2005, when this photograph was taken, the building had been taken over by Vietnam's Ministry of Agriculture and Rural Development. *Courtesy of Malgorzata Gnoinska.*

Next door to the Italian Embassy, at 137 Duong Pasteur, was the U.S. Military Assistance Command, Vietnam, the headquarters of General William C. Westmoreland—which gave cover to Lodge to travel to that address and use the two facilities' shared parking lot. *Courtesy of the U.S. Army.*

Informing the North Vietnamese Ambassador in Warsaw

Nguyen Dinh Phuong's Marigold Mystery Tour

Even if the plane crashes and you are killed, before you die you must destroy this document.

> —*DRV deputy foreign minister Nguyen Co Thach to Nguyen Dinh Phuong, early December 1966*

Inside, I felt [the initiative] was important—if successful, it might change the situation, . . . may end the war, may open substantial negotiations.

> —*Nguyen Dinh Phuong, recalling his emotions while traveling from Hanoi to Warsaw in early December 1966*

The need to defer the USA-DRV meeting was also prompted by the fact that the DRV ambassador declared to me with astonishment that he had not received any instructions nor information.

> —*Jerzy Michałowski, recalling an exchange with Do Phat Quang, early December 1966*

As far as Washington knew, as of Monday afternoon, December 5, 1966, the Poles were holding up sending to Hanoi the U.S. statement agreeing to meet with North Vietnam's ambassador in Warsaw the next day due to dissatisfaction with the "important differences of interpretation" clause, whose removal Rapacki, through Gronouski, ardently sought. However, Michałowski's secret postmortem discloses that besides qualms about the "interpretation" equivocation, an entirely different reason lay behind Warsaw's failure to arrange an immediate contact: "*The need to defer the USA-DRV meeting was also prompted by the fact that the DRV ambassador [Do Phat Quang], called to see me in the same manner as Gronouski, declared to me with astonishment that he had not received any instructions nor information*" (emphasis added).[1]

Michałowski's revelation raises the curtain on a previously hidden aspect of Marigold: Hanoi's internal preparations for the proposed contact, and in particular the timing, form, and content of its instructions to the embassy in Warsaw. Besides yielding clues on how seriously the leadership treated the initiative, and what might have happened had direct talks actually started, probing this topic helps disentangle the mystery of *what went wrong* on December 6, 1966—when, it now appears, both U.S. and DRV diplomats were ready to stage their first, groundbreaking (and ice-breaking) encounter, yet somehow failed to meet.

Were Hanoi's representatives in fact ready to enter secret direct talks with U.S. officials in Warsaw on December 6? Did a communications lapse involving the DRV envoy expected to conduct those conversations spoil the crucial "bridge crossing" (as D'Orlandi put it[2])? Might Marigold have been foiled at a key moment, in other words, by "a very considerable two-way misunderstanding" (as Harold Wilson later estimated[3])—or, more accurately, a very considerable *three-way* misunderstanding—not doomed by an unbridgeable gap between the enemies, or the sinister machinations of one side or another, as most subsequent analysts have assumed?

Fresh evidence from both Polish and Vietnamese sources casts suggestive light on such questions, bringing into view perhaps the most dramatic new disclosure concerning Hanoi's secret diplomacy during the war. Yet, as will become clear, it also confronts the historian (and reader) with perplexing, convoluted, even exasperating puzzles and contradictions.

※ ※ ※

To explore Hanoi's internal preparations for the apparently impending Warsaw contact, the narrative must revisit the weekend of December 3 and 4. Recall that Saturday morning, a tired Pham Van Dong learned from Siedlecki of the U.S. consent *in principle,* given by Lodge to Lewandowski in Saigon two days earlier, to the proposal for a direct meeting. At this point, however, the North Vietnamese did *not* yet know that Washington had a specific date in mind: Only that afternoon in Saigon did Lodge tell Lewandowski that the U.S. Embassy in Warsaw would contact the DRV ambassador three days later, *on December 6,* to confirm that the ten points "broadly" represented U.S. policy despite their susceptibility to "important differences of interpretation." Lewandowski did *not* send this news directly to North Vietnam. Instead—leaving it to Rapacki to determine the modalities of informing Hanoi—he sent, at 11:30 p.m. Saturday night, Saigon time, a coded cable describing the talk with Lodge and containing the U.S. statement. This telegram did not reach Warsaw until shortly before noon Sunday (local time), and was only deciphered at 3:10 p.m.[4] We shall return presently to the matter of what the MSZ figures handling the initiative—Rapacki and Michałowski—did with this vital information.

For now, let us turn to how the DRV responded after learning Saturday morning that the Americans had accepted the invitation for the Warsaw contact. Vietnamese sources indicate that Hanoi used two separate, concurrent methods to alert and prepare its ambassador to Poland.

A Confusing Cable: "Be Ready to Receive" Gronouski

One comparatively routine step was apparently the Foreign Ministry's sending of a coded telegram. However, confusion surrounds the message's timing and substance. In their account of U.S.-DRV secret exchanges before the Paris talks, Luu Van Loi and Nguyen Anh Vu write, "After being informed that the U.S. would meet our ambassador in Warsaw *on December 6*, our Foreign Ministry instructed Ambassador Do Phat Quang to be ready to receive U.S. Ambassador Gronouski *on that date*" (emphasis added).[5] For this laconic assertion, the ex-officials offer no elaboration or source, contemporaneous or otherwise. The trouble here, of course, is that as of the weekend of December 3 and 4—when they imply that the instruction was sent—the North Vietnamese *had not yet seen* the U.S. statement, delivered by Lodge to Lewandowski in Saigon Saturday afternoon, which for the first time mentioned the December 6 date. Again, at that point, all they knew was that the Americans had consented *in principle* to the Warsaw contact.

So, when *did* DRV authorities learn of the December 6 date, enabling them to send a cable fitting the above description? That returns us to the murky business of what Rapacki and Michałowski did with the U.S. statement in Lewandowski's telegram that was only decoded in Warsaw on 3:10 p.m. on Sunday, December 4. When and how did they relay it to Hanoi? As will become clear, they did not *officially* transmit the text (with the offending clause) to the North Vietnamese until Wednesday morning (Hanoi time), December 7. Moreover, the earliest they *could* have sent word *simply of the proposed December 6 date for the contact* was late Sunday, December 4, Warsaw time, which—given the need to draft, encipher, and send a cable to Poland's embassy in Hanoi, where it had to be decrypted and delivered—would have meant Monday morning, December 5, in the DRV capital.[6]

This seems to leave only two plausible alternatives regarding the confusing DRV cable: *Either* the Foreign Ministry in Hanoi sent it to Quang in Warsaw on Saturday, December 3, or Sunday, December 4—but it did *not* contain the December 6 date; *or*, it *did* contain the proposed date for the contact, but *was not sent until Monday morning, December 5*, at the *earliest*, which means that it *might* conceivably have reached the DRV Embassy in Warsaw by that *evening*, in time to alert the ambassador to a meeting the next day.

One more thing about the cable seems clear: Whenever Hanoi might have sent it, the DRV Embassy in Warsaw did not receive, decipher, and pass it to

Quang *before* he saw Michałowski (most likely on Monday morning) and expressed ignorance of the whole affair.[7]

A Clandestine Courier to Warsaw: "Inside I Felt It Was Important"

The second method Hanoi employed to prepare Do Phat Quang for the talk with the American was far more dramatic. For such a momentous occasion, Hanoi decided that more than a terse telegram would be necessary: They chose to send a trusted messenger who could both hand-deliver secret instructions and also serve as a Vietnamese-English or Vietnamese-French interpreter. Unknown to either Washington or Warsaw, as news of the perhaps imminent contact between the warring parties wound its way to the Polish capital over the weekend of December 3 and 4, so too did a secret DRV emissary named Nguyen Dinh Phuong.

Who Was Nguyen Dinh Phuong?

The most tantalizing new piece of the Marigold puzzle concerns a man who in 1966 was a DRV Foreign Ministry official helping Hanoi to prepare for secret talks with Washington. Then in his early forties and working as a ministry English-language translator, Phuong later entered the annals of Vietnam War diplomacy as the interpreter for Le Duc Tho and Xuan Thuy in the Paris negotiations with Henry A. Kissinger that produced the January 1973 Peace Accords.[8] His face, if not his name, became familiar when the back channel leaked, and news photographers snapped pictures of Kissinger and Le Duc Tho strolling, with a bespectacled North Vietnamese interpreter between and just slightly behind them. In Kissinger's vast account of the Paris talks, Phuong rates exactly one reference, for his British pronunciation of the word "sched*yule*," although the White House aide, famous for his own Germanic inflection, hastened to add ("far be it from me to make fun of anyone's accent") that he was an "excellent interpreter."[9]

Like many DRV diplomats, Phuong emerged from the colonial class—his father was a functionary in the French administration—to join the revolutionary struggle against the fading overlords. A Northerner, he was born in Haiphong in, he said, 1924 (his identification documents gave the date September 20, 1925), and moved in childhood to Hanoi, where he studied and, during and immediately after World War II, attended university. Though Phuong dabbled in student activism, he seemed headed for a professional career, learning English (to supplement the French he already knew) and taking courses in law and veterinary science. However, he recalled, "as the revolution grew, I had no heart for study." When fighting broke out in 1946, he joined the Viet Minh, remaining with Ho's army (and serving as an instructor) for the duration of the war.[10]

After the 1954 Geneva Accords divided the country (supposedly temporarily) at the 17th Parallel, Phuong's linguistic skills qualified him to join the DRV's military liaison team to the newly created ICC. As assistant and interpreter to Ha Van

Lau—who besides dealing with the commission functioned as a leading expert on U.S. affairs—Phuong found his responsibilities shifting from military to diplomatic realms, and in 1960 he officially joined the Foreign Ministry. As the anti-U.S. war expanded, he belonged to a working group that handled foreign (especially Western) visitors and various peace initiatives. Gaining experience in sensitive diplomacy, he remained in Paris throughout the peace talks (1968–73), and later went on to become Hanoi's ambassador to Sweden before finishing his career as head of the ministry's European Division.[11]

Despite his later prominence as a diplomat, Phuong's secret Marigold role did not surface for several decades. The first reference to his covert mission to Warsaw appeared in Luu van Loi and Nguyen Anh Vu's 1990 Vietnamese-language book on DRV-U.S. exchanges before Paris. In a chapter on *"Me-ri-con"* (Marigold), it noted that besides instructing Quang to prepare to host Gronouski—an apparent allusion to a diplomatic cable, as noted above—the Foreign Ministry *"also"* (emphasis added) "urgently" or "immediately" sent Phuong to Poland with an "instructional plan" (*ke hoach huong dan*) to guide Quang in handling the talks.[12]

This Vietnamese version of the Marigold book, which was printed in small numbers with limited circulation, went unnoticed by Western scholars familiar with the record. Consequently, not until Phuong revealed a portion of his story at a 1997 conference in Hanoi involving Vietnamese and U.S. ex-officials (most prominently McNamara) did a non-Vietnamese historian—the present author—begin to investigate the possibility that a DRV emissary secretly visited Warsaw in early December 1966 in connection with the ill-fated peace initiative, and that *both* sides, not just the Americans, were ready to meet on December 6.[13] Amid the commotion at the Metropole Hotel, I had only a brief chance to introduce myself to Phuong, note the stark divergence between his story and existing historiography, and give him summaries of Michałowski's report and photocopied sections from the Pentagon Papers' negotiating volumes on Marigold. In the summer of 1998, I sent him more declassified U.S. and translated Polish documents so he could further see how differently from his own perspective these events looked from Washington and Warsaw.[14]

Then, a June 1999 visit to Hanoi for another conference offered a chance to question him more extensively. We spoke in a formal institute meeting room on a sweltering afternoon; tea and coffee were served but ignored; we were too intent on resurrecting the past. Now a frail, soft-spoken septuagenarian, clad neatly in gray suit and brown sandals, his black hair silvered, Phuong had given the matter considerable thought. As we began, he handed me a typewritten account of his activities in connection with Marigold. And over the next few hours, choosing his words carefully, he vividly and at times emotionally recalled his experiences, above all his journey to Warsaw, and responded to my requests for additional information and clarification.

By the time we finished, I believed that Phuong had told the truth as best as he could recall. His reactions seemed too human to be contrived, and he was willing to criticize his own and his compatriots' actions (or inactions), which he would hardly have done if he had been retailing a fabricated story meant to burnish North Vietnam's historical image. Moreover, I felt that his account constituted crucial evidence on the DRV's attitude toward Marigold. After all, if Hanoi had never agreed to or planned to attend the Warsaw meeting with a U.S. representative—as LBJ and his senior aides later fervidly argued—why would it hastily and secretly send a special emissary halfway around the world to deliver instructions to the official who was supposed to conduct the conversations?

Despite finding Phuong's account credible, I would be repeatedly frustrated in ensuing years in seeking more data, especially contemporaneous Vietnamese materials, to corroborate, amplify, or correct his story. Contradictions and discrepancies with other evidence require close scrutiny, which is undertaken below. But first, before parsing, let Phuong tell the tale his way.

Nguyen Dinh Phuong's Story

As Phuong recalled, he was urgently summoned late Saturday afternoon, December 3, 1966, from the DRV Foreign Ministry in Hanoi to the residence of Deputy Foreign Minister Nguyen Co Thach.[15] He reached Thach's villa in the Chon Fu district, near the ministry, at 4 or 5 p.m. There, in a drawing room, Thach told Phuong that as part of a "very secret initiative," he was to fly to Warsaw and deliver a one-and-a-half-page typed document to Ambassador Do Phat Quang, containing instructions for a proposed meeting with his U.S. counterpart.

"You must not let the contents of the document become known to anyone [else]," he implored—if his plane crashed, the courier must dispose of the paper before impact. The meeting lasted fifteen or twenty minutes. Thach betrayed no emotion and "appeared to be very indifferent." In "very cold and calm tones," he told Phuong: "You have to go to Warsaw. It is a very secret mission. You must take this document. Don't show it to anybody. If the plane crashes, you must destroy it before you die."

Thach did not reveal the precise contents of the formal instructions, which were in a sealed envelope, nor give a specific date for the proposed meeting, but he said that the DRV diplomats could decide on the spot whether to continue talking with their U.S. visitor if he acted in a "favorable" manner: "I think if his attitude, appearance, and tone were polite and not arrogant then . . . it is favorable," Phuong explained. "If he shows himself [to be] arrogant, then that would cut off the discussion."

This was not, of course, Phuong's first exposure to the Polish mediation effort. On November 20, he had translated the content of Lewandowski's meeting with Ha Van Lau when the Pole recounted the conversations with Lodge. Hearing Lewandowski describe the American stands, Phuong felt cautious optimism. "I think that is good news. The proposal of the U.S. side appears to be reasonable. . . . It is worth probing whether the intention of the U.S. is really good or a deception for propaganda." It would be too strong, he said, to term his initial reaction to the U.S. proposals excited or hopeful: He doubted they could bring a rapid end to the war, especially given that Washington considered troops and bombing its "trump cards" in any talks. Still, he viewed the ideas as "interesting enough to hear more about" and "worthwhile to consider."

Despite Thach's outward coolness, Phuong sensed the deputy foreign minister, too, was "persuaded" that the U.S. proposals merited exploration—"I think his reaction was . . . skeptical yet interested." After speaking with Thach, Phuong immediately returned to his home on Ba Trieu Street with the secret instructions, which his wife, Le Thi Yen, sewed into the vest of his coat for added security. That same Saturday evening, the Foreign Ministry secretariat arranged for him to be driven to Gia Long Airport, where, carrying a diplomatic passport, he boarded a regularly scheduled Aeroflot flight to Moscow. After "one or two stops"—he is not sure where, but definitely *not* in China, which he knew was not to be informed— his plane landed in the Soviet capital the next morning. Met on arrival by Vietnamese diplomats, he requested that they reserve a seat for him on the next flight to Warsaw. He then went to the DRV Embassy, where he rested until early afternoon. He was then driven back to Sheremetovo Airport for a LOT (Polish airlines) flight to Warsaw. While in Moscow, he neither discussed his mission with DRV diplomats nor had any contact with Soviet officials. Finally, more than twenty-four hours after leaving Hanoi late Saturday night, Phuong reached the Polish capital on Sunday evening December 4.

That same Sunday, for the second time in three days, U.S. warplanes had hit the Hanoi area, striking sites within the city and inflicting civilian casualties. The renewed Hanoi bombing, virtually on the eve of the scheduled direct contact in Warsaw, enraged those DRV, Polish, and Italian officials who were aware of Marigold.

But Phuong remained, for the moment, blissfully unaware of this new potential complication.[16] During the long solitary journey, pondering his scheduled meeting with a U.S. envoy, he could not stifle rising hope that his secret mission— his first covert assignment—might indeed help stop the fighting. He had met American journalists before, but this would be his first face-to-face encounter with an enemy official.

"I felt a little bit more optimism because the proposal at that time appeared more reasonable, but for the same reason I was disappointed when I heard about the [December 2] bombing [of Hanoi]," Phuong recalled. "I thought about how the meeting would happen, how I should behave, how I [would] talk to the American."

As a professional diplomat and a Vietnamese, Phuong was slow to feel or display excitement: "The humor of the Vietnamese is calm, or at least to show calmness. . . . We did not express our mood very easily." Yet he also believed the meeting might be a breakthrough: "Inside I felt it was important—if successful, it might change the situation, . . . may end the war, may open substantial negotiations. . . . It might lead to substantial negotiations, that was my personal thinking."

From Warsaw's Okęcie Airport, Phuong was driven to the DRV Embassy. Finally, he could rip open his vest, hand Quang the envelope Thach had given him containing the instructions, and read them himself. They directed the ambassador to tell the American that the best and most reasonable basis for a settlement would be Hanoi's Four Points. However—crucially—they also specified that only the first point (a halt to U.S. bombing and all other acts of war against North Vietnam) was a prerequisite to starting negotiations.[17] Of course, the diplomats were also expected to report to Hanoi the results of any talk and await further instructions. Whether they continued the immediate conversations depended on how the American behaved.

Phuong discussed the peace initiative with Quang, speaking in the embassy dining room "as two diplomats," from about 8 p.m. until almost midnight. The ambassador, a Southerner in his fifties, said nothing about any previous instructions, giving Phuong "the impression that with my arrival it was the first time he has heard about" the effort. Quang "received my explanation very calmly and took notes" and "studiously listened to my explanations and recommendations." He did not voice "any specific attitude" about the prospects for the initiative's success, but "agreed with me about the answer" they would give to Gronouski at the meeting: It would not take the form of a written statement—they would await a response to the report they would promptly send Hanoi before such a formal step—but the meetings could go on so long as the U.S. ambassador adopted a respectful attitude. They would not try to hash out the details of Lewandowski's ten points, but could "tackle the venue of the [subsequent U.S.-DRV] meeting [i.e., negotiations], the level of the participants, the issues to be debated, the procedures."

On Monday, December 5, after a Vietnamese breakfast, Phuong spent the morning conversing further with Quang and rested in the afternoon. All the while, he stayed within the embassy compound, making no contacts with Polish or any non-Vietnamese officials. Nor did Phuong recall Quang leaving the embassy on Monday.

After reaching Warsaw—Phuong was not sure exactly when—he learned (presumably from Quang) something that he had not known when he had left Hanoi: The meeting with the U.S. ambassador was set for Tuesday, December 6.[18] Accordingly, the Vietnamese went to bed Monday night anticipating that the next day—perhaps the next morning—they would receive Gronouski, who would come to the embassy to confirm the American position relayed by Lewandowski.

Evaluating Phuong's Story

So Nguyen Dinh Phuong remembered—but his chronology raises vexing questions. The first problem is relatively straightforward: Phuong recalled taking a scheduled flight from Hanoi to Moscow on Aeroflot, yet the Soviet airline did not inaugurate regular passenger service to Hanoi until nearly four years later.[19] Nor could he have hopped aboard one of the periodic ICC flights to catch a connecting Aeroflot departure to Moscow from Vientiane or Phnom Penh. In fact, the creaky Stratoliner *was* scheduled to lumber into the skies from Gia Lam on December 3, but before dawn that Saturday morning; in any case, Aeroflot then lacked service to either the Laotian or Cambodian capital.[20] Raising further doubts, a fellow ex-DRV diplomat, then posted in Beijing, observed that North Vietnamese on their way to Russia or Europe during that phase of the war usually transited China—and an American who visited Hanoi in December 1966 later asserted that the only civilian air link between Hanoi and the outside world was, aside from the ICC departures, an irregular Chinese airline flight to the southern city of Nanning.[21]

Informed of such discrepancies, Phuong held his ground: He insisted that he flew Aeroflot, on a plane filled with Russian and Eastern European passengers, on a route that avoided China.[22]

The apparent contradictions can be accounted for, however, by the fact that Aeroflot, as a fully state-controlled airline, routinely performed a wide range of functions for the USSR government, including nonscheduled flights to transport the rising number of Soviet and Soviet Bloc military and civilian advisers to and from Hanoi. Given the acrimony suffusing Sino-Soviet ties at the time, such flights would have skirted Chinese airspace and instead stopped for refueling en route to Moscow in politically more hospitable South Asian locales such as Rangoon, Calcutta, New Delhi, Karachi, and—in Soviet Central Asia—Tashkent.[23]

A comparable problem clouds Phuong's description of his onward journey from Moscow to Warsaw on LOT. According to the Polish airline's winter 1966–67 timetable (and the December 1966 international edition of the *Official Airline Guide, OAG*), LOT Flight 232 flew nonstop from the Sheremetovo to Okęcie on Sunday, using an Ilyushin-18 four-engine turboprop; however, its departure from Moscow is listed as 9:25 a.m. (landing in Warsaw at 10 a.m.) rather than in the late afternoon or early evening, as Phuong remembered.[24] Was the timetable in error, or did Phuong's memory, fuzzed by changing time zones, jet lag, the disorientation of a long voyage—and the possibility that he conflated this trip with later ones—blur this detail?

Why should the reader care about all this minutiae? What difference does it make whether Phuong took this flight or that, or arrived in Poland a few hours or even a day later than he recalled three decades later? The most problematic aspect of Phuong's story is his assertion that he reached Warsaw on the evening of Sunday, December 4. What is wrong with that? Recall Michałowski's assertion that Quang told him "with astonishment" that he lacked information or instructions about a scheduled meeting with a U.S. representative; the Pole's report omitted the time or date of this key conversation, but it clearly preceded his summons to Gronouski to the MSZ on December 5 (the American arrived at 11:30 a.m.), and *presumably* occurred earlier that same Monday morning. If so, then Quang's statement would have *made no sense* if Phuong had already arrived from Hanoi *the previous day* for that express purpose (or, for that matter, if Quang had already received a cable from Hanoi informing him of the expected contact).

So, what happened? Because it would have been absurd for Quang to express ignorance of the initiative after receiving a special emissary who had traveled halfway around the world to tell him about it, therefore, *if the North Vietnamese ambassador indeed saw Michałowski on the morning of December 5,* as it appears he did, *then Phuong must have reached the DRV Embassy in Warsaw only later that Monday, rather than on Sunday evening,* as he recalled.

There are several ways this might have occurred. Questioned closely on this point during our 1999 conversation, Phuong acknowledged that it was remotely possible Thach summoned him on Sunday afternoon, December 4 (rather than Saturday the 3rd), which would mean, of course, that he could not have reached Warsaw that same evening.[25] Then there is the LOT angle: If its Sunday flight from Moscow to Warsaw left at 9:25 a.m., Phuong would have missed the departure if he had left the previous evening from Hanoi and then had to wait until the next day. Again according to the airline's timetable and the December 1966 *OAG,* that Monday morning flight was scheduled to land in the Polish capital at 10 a.m. local time (an hour behind Moscow); and it would have taken at least a half-hour to disembark, clear customs and immigration, gather luggage, and be driven downtown—which would have brought Phuong to the DRV Embassy no earlier than, say, 10:30 a.m. If this scenario actually occurred, he might have neared and finally reached his destination just as the man he had come all this way to see, Quang, was a few blocks away telling Michałowski that he knew nothing about any proposed meeting with the Americans.

Hence, *unless and until told otherwise,* the Poles would have continued to believe that Quang lacked instructions for the meeting with Gronouski—and therefore they would have continued to believe that they needed to stall before bringing the enemy diplomats together.

How Did the North Vietnamese Know?

All this tangled circumstantial evidence bears on another major Marigold mystery, one not even apparent as long as historians only had access to the U.S. (as opposed to the Polish or Vietnamese) side of the story: Because the Poles did not officially transmit to the DRV government the U.S. statement agreeing to meet in Warsaw on *Tuesday,* December 6, until Siedlecki gave it to Dong in Hanoi on *Wednesday* morning, December 7, how did Phuong and Quang learn of the proposed date in time to go to bed *Monday* night, December 5, expecting Gronouski to appear the next day at the embassy gates—perhaps setting the stage for a tragic misunderstanding?

To delve into this mystery, we must sort through the evidence regarding what the Poles told the North Vietnamese, and when, about arrangements for the proposed contact with the Americans. Unfortunately, declassified Polish files regarding exchanges with DRV officials both in Hanoi and in Warsaw at this juncture—especially messages from the MSZ to Siedlecki in Hanoi, and records of communications with Quang in Warsaw—are spotty, and Michałowski's later statements on the precise timing and contents of Polish-DRV communications are at times infuriatingly ambiguous, contradictory, or even misleading. It is useful to briefly consider a few examples.

In April 1967, months after the initiative had collapsed, a British diplomat quoted Michałowski as saying that "the North Vietnamese had known from 3 December that the Americans had reservations about Lewandowski's ten points," yet, "knowing this, they had nonetheless instructed their Ambassador in Warsaw to prepare for talks with the United States Ambassador."[26] Such a claim about DRV knowledge of the "differences of interpretation" clause could not have been true, because Lewandowski's cable containing it did not even reach Warsaw until December 4; moreover, it also contradicted Rapacki's statements to Gronouski on December 5 (and 6, as we shall see) that Warsaw was holding up delivery to Hanoi of the U.S. statement, along with other evidence indicating that it did not reach Dong until December 7.[27]

Nearly two years later, in early 1969, Michałowski, now Poland's ambassador in Washington, reviewed Marigold with Harriman, who was no longer in office but was still intensely curious to hear the other side of the affair. As the U.S. record of the talk indicated, Michałowski said "that about the second or third of November [sic; December] the North Vietnamese ambassador to Warsaw was informed about the agreement on meetings in Warsaw and told that he would receive further instructions. The Poles began to discuss with the North Vietnamese such procedural details as where the meetings would be held, whether in the Ministry of Foreign Affairs or in a small palace, whether the Poles would make the introductions or let the North Vietnamese and U.S. introduce themselves, and so on. These procedural matters were also discussed with Gronouski."[28]

There are several problems here. First, Michałowski's quoted statement that the DRV ambassador was informed about "the agreement on meetings in Warsaw" does not specify *which* agreement—that is, it blurs the fact that as of December "second or third," the Poles in Warsaw knew only that Lodge had relayed a U.S. consent in principle to meet in Warsaw and not a precise date (information on *that* agreement reached Warsaw only in the afternoon of December 4). Second, the record does not indicate if Michałowski identified *by whom* Quang "was informed." Hanoi? Michałowski himself? Third, the record muddies whether Michałowski clarified exactly when or with whom the Poles "began to discuss . . . procedural details" of the impending contacts with the North Vietnamese— Quang in Warsaw? Dong in Hanoi? Both? If he meant the former, as implied, that would have to somehow square with Phuong's assertion that when he told Quang about the initiative (i.e., on December 4 or 5), he had no prior knowledge of it.

Of course, with secondhand records, it is impossible to tell whether Michałowski's comments were accurately or fully recorded. Yet, comparable imprecision mars Michałowski's *own* secret postmortem, which he prepared a decade and a half later, using internal MSZ records. In his report, he wrote that in early December 1966,

> we prepared ourselves in Warsaw to establish contact between the USA and DRV embassies. Upon informing Pham Van Dong that we are waiting for Ambassador Gronouski to turn to us on 6 December in this matter, we asked for a reply to a series of questions; namely, on what level will the contact be most likely. We judged that actually sending someone [on the U.S. side] to Warsaw would make it difficult to maintain secrecy. The best person, it would appear to us, is Gronouski, who is a person trusted by the President. Next, we asked what time-limit will be the most reliable for the DRV as well as when the DRV ambassador in Warsaw will be informed about the matter and receive the appropriate instructions. Finally, we asked in what manner we could assist the Vietnamese with regard to this contact.[29]

Though seemingly paraphrasing a contemporaneous document, Michałowski fails to provide the exact timing or content of this vital communication to Dong. By saying that the Poles informed him that Gronouski was expected to "turn to us on 6 December," Michałowski implies that this exchange with Dong *followed* receipt of Lewandowski's December 3 report of his talk with Lodge containing that date. The comments and queries he reports relaying to Dong also accord with Lodge's amplifications to Lewandowski on the U.S. statement—his explanation of the significance of December 6 date, suggestion that Gronouski (not a special emissary) would make the initial contact, and request for Polish aid in setting up the first meeting:

> L[odge] explained. Fixed date of 6 December indicates that from that date they [the Americans] will be ready to make contact. They do not want to send anyone with a "big name" to Warsaw because it will raise interest and might lead to breaking secrecy. They request making the contact possible through our MSZ. The United States Ambassador in Warsaw will, beginning on 6 December, be in possession of proper instructions.[30]

Michałowski's claim here, that the Poles informed Dong that they expected Gronouski to "turn to us on December 6," contradicts evidence that Warsaw delayed until December 7 delivering the U.S. statement containing the December 6 date and the "differences of interpretation" clause. Therefore, his summary only makes sense, and comports with statements by Rapacki and Michałowski to Gronouski that they were holding up communicating the statement to Hanoi—and with the claim by Luu Van Loi and Nguyen Anh Vu that Poland told the DRV that a U.S. representative "would meet our ambassador in Warsaw on December 6," prompting the Foreign Ministry to instruct Quang to be ready to receive Gronouski "on that date"—*if:*

1. After receiving Lewandowski's deciphered December 3 telegram on Sunday afternoon, December 4, in Warsaw (already late Sunday night in Hanoi), Michałowski or Rapacki sent a cable, most likely that evening (which would have arrived early Monday morning, December 5, in Hanoi) instructing Siedlecki to inform Dong that Washington had chosen Tuesday, December 6, as the date of the anticipated contact,

but

2. *Not* providing the full text of the U.S. statement containing the "interpretation" clause.

Michałowski indeed implies that the communication containing the December 6 date and asking the series of related preparatory queries was presented to Dong before December 5, because he goes on to say that "not waiting for Hanoi's reply," Rapacki "decided to take the initiative" and set a meeting with Gronouski for late Monday morning in Warsaw.[31]

So it would *seem* that we have a potential solution to the mystery, a case of a missing cable (or two) between Warsaw and Hanoi, inferable or deducible from circumstantial evidence, whose existence would dissolve much confusion—explaining how North Vietnam could have learned of the date of the proposed meeting before receiving the U.S. statement containing it, accounting for the delayed notification of Quang of the December 6 date until after Phuong's arrival in Warsaw on December 5, and helping to corroborate some of the unsupported assertions made both by Michałowski and by Luu Van Loi and Nguyen Anh Vu.

If only it were that simple. But there is a rub: There is absolutely no direct evidence that the Poles sent such a cable on the evening of December 4–5, and there is indirect evidence that they did not. One might brush off the absence of pertinent contemporaneous records in the MSZ archives dossier containing ciphered cable traffic between Warsaw and its embassy in Hanoi for December 1966—over several decades, documents can be lost, destroyed, misfiled, transferred, and so on. Yet it is less easy to account for the lack of any mention of such an exchange on December 4–5—a message from Warsaw, or a meeting in Hanoi to relay it—in a *contemporaneous* internal chronology of the secret initiative, using classified files, prepared within the Foreign Ministry *in December 1966.*[32] Nor, of course, does any mention appear in other Polish or Vietnamese sources, which refer to other meetings between Siedlecki and Dong (and other DRV figures).

It appears equally likely, in other words, that Michałowski (like Luu Van Loi and Nguyen Anh Vu) garbled the record—that the Poles actually relayed the queries regarding arrangements for the first meeting to Siedlecki to pass to Dong *without the December 6 date* after they received Lewandowski's December 2 cable relaying Lodge's general assent to a Warsaw contact. Alas, Rapacki's cable to Hanoi that Friday evening containing directions for the Polish ambassador's meeting with Dong has not been found. However, a hint that Siedlecki did in fact relay these questions to him on Saturday morning, December 3, appears in his cable on the meeting, when he notes that Dong, after hearing about the Lodge-Lewandowski conversation in Saigon two days earlier, commented that "perhaps any further concrete steps on both sides were not topical until Lodge received instructions from Johnson."[33] That remark *sounds* as if it were made to deflect exactly the kind of procedural inquiries that Michałowski reports were put to him.

So, *if* Michałowski's account is in error, and the Poles did *not* inform Dong in advance of their expectation that Gronouski would turn to them *on December 6,* this means, of course, that Hanoi could not have cabled that date to Quang for the upcoming meeting (and we already know that Phuong did not tell him). In that case, how *else* might Quang have learned this information on December 5 in time to expect a visit the next day from his U.S. counterpart?

One possibility emerges: If Quang indeed visited Michałowski that Monday morning and expressed astonished ignorance over any plans for a meeting with Gronouski, *Michałowski may well have informally shown him the American statement containing the December 6 date.* The MSZ director-general had, after all, a close working relationship with Hanoi's envoy in his capital; not only had he seen him regularly to coordinate Warsaw's policy on the ICC and the war, but Quang—a veteran Communist activist and diplomat who had served previously in DRV embassies in Pyongyang and Moscow[34]—had also become a key North Vietnamese point man in Europe (along with Mai Van Bo in Paris) for peace feelers (e.g., greasing La Pira's path to Hanoi, the "Aspen" contacts with the Swedes).[35] It would have been natural for Michałowski to share the statement with his experienced, trusted fraternal colleague, who in any case would soon get information and instructions from Hanoi; the Pole may also have wanted to alert him to a glitch in DRV communications, because Quang's government already *should* have informed him.

This scenario—and we are deep into circumstantial speculation—raises the possibility of a fateful misunderstanding that Monday morning between Quang and Michałowski concerning the devilish "procedural details" to which the latter later alluded. By this point, both the Poles and Americans understood that the MSZ, and perhaps Rapacki himself, would midwife the initial U.S.-DRV rendezvous. Lewandowski, for example, on December 3 had promised Lodge "some help in getting in touch with the North Vietnamese" and assured him that a ministry official would "be in touch with the [DRV] Embassy and will effectuate a contact." The two agreed on the advisability of "entrusting" to Rapacki the "practical solution" of "various technical details to be fine-tuned" regarding that first meeting.[36] Gronouski, in turn, having been informed by Washington of Lewandowski's promises, anticipated that Rapacki would introduce him to Hanoi's ambassador.[37]

Nevertheless, it appears that Quang somehow came away believing that Gronouski would *directly* contact him on December 6, by coming to the DRV Embassy, not the Polish Foreign Ministry, and for that matter without any further hands-on Polish involvement. In this regard, it is intriguing to note that the official U.S. statement delivered by Lodge to Lewandowski on December 3 stated that Washington would be "instructing the American Embassy in Warsaw to contact the North Vietnamese representative there *on* December 6" (emphasis added)—in contrast to the vaguer formulations used in virtually all other diplomatic communications referring to that date, such as the cable to Gronouski authorizing him or a representative "to see North Vietnamese Ambassador on December 6 *or as soon thereafter as possible*" (emphasis added).[38] Suppose, in other words, that on December 5 Michałowski *only* showed Quang the U.S. statement—but not, for example, Lewandowski's full cable, which included Lodge's clarification that Gronouski would possess "proper instructions" and be ready to meet "*beginning on*" December 6, and also his plea for Polish help in setting up the first meeting. Simply by reading the official statement, Quang might easily conclude that he merely had to wait and Gronouski would come.[39]

One may, then, imagine the following sequence. Quang awakens Monday, December 5, still oblivious to the secret plans for a contact with Gronouski on Tuesday, but he learns of them, informally, from Michałowski when he sees the Pole later that morning. Believing that Gronouski will be instructed to contact him, Quang returns to the DRV Embassy, where, in the course of the day, he finally receives guidance from Hanoi in the form of special emissary Phuong and, perhaps, a ciphered cable. By Monday night, then, Quang feels prepared: He expects Gronouski to show up the next day, and he holds guidance from the home office on how to handle the meeting.

The Bottom Line

Barring more definitive evidence from Vietnamese and Polish archives, we may never know exactly what transpired in and between Hanoi and Warsaw in the first week of December 1966 regarding the arrangements for the first U.S.-DRV contact. Phuong's and Michałowski's stories cannot be wholly reconciled—for example, each implies that *he* was the first to inform Quang of the secret initiative and plans for the contact with Gronouski, and both cannot be right. And history, in its infinite and sublime mystery, complexity, and perversity, undoubtedly transpired differently in important respects than what the author has been able to reconstruct.

Still, fuzziness on precise details should not obscure this chapter's most significant findings: that Hanoi, in line with Dong's assurances to Lewandowski in late November, *did* in fact in early December instruct its ambassador in Poland to receive his U.S. counterpart; that it considered the initiative serious enough to secretly send a special emissary all the way to Warsaw for the planned meetings;

and that Quang got his instructions and, one way or another, learned (most likely on Monday, December 5) the date of the planned encounter in time to anticipate a visit from Gronouski on Tuesday, December 6. The conclusion that Quang was instructed to receive Gronouski is not only consistent with recent, but retrospective, Vietnamese sources (i.e., Phuong's testimony and Luu Van Loi and Nguyen Anh Vu's account); it is also corroborated by *contemporaneous,* newly declassified Polish records. When Siedlecki saw Dong in Hanoi on Wednesday morning, December 7, and at last officially read him the text of the American statement, the premier alluded to Quang's willingness to receive his U.S. counterpart "in accordance with previously sent instructions to the DRV Embassy [in Warsaw]," as the Polish ambassador afterward cabled Rapacki.[40] And late in December, after things fell apart, Trinh gave Siedlecki an official secret DRV postmortem on the affair that explicitly mentioned Hanoi's initial consent for its ambassador in Warsaw to receive a U.S. representative to confirm Washington's position as a normal "diplomatic activity" (rather than formal negotiations) and declared that it had sent "proper instructions" along these lines to Quang.[41]

* * *

Before we may escape our tangled rat's nest of internal Vietnamese actions in the run-up to December 6, there remains one more snarl to untangle. I have established, or at least posited confidently, that some time on December 5, Quang finally received instructions from Hanoi regarding the impending meeting with Gronouski—via Phuong, a diplomatic cable, or both. However, Quang then *failed to tell Michałowski* that the anticipated communications from home had actually arrived (nor did he reveal, then or later, the presence in Warsaw of a special DRV emissary[42]) or that he was now ready to receive a U.S. official the next day. *Why not?* Did Quang regard such a notification as unnecessary, because he believed Gronouski would contact him whether the Poles knew or not? Was there a substantive reason, for example, a desire not to appear eager for the meeting? Had Hanoi directed him not to take any initiative, even if merely to correct Michałowski's now-inaccurate impression that he lacked instructions? Or was it something more mundane, like word arriving too late in the day or the Pole being unable to answer the phone?

Quang's reticence about updating the Poles remains inexplicable—and it would loom even larger as events unfolded. It led to yet another misunderstanding: As Monday ended, Quang and Phuong looked forward to receiving Gronouski the next day, while Michałowski and Rapacki had no idea that Hanoi's ambassador was now ready to receive him—and of course the Americans were even more in the dark, convinced that the Poles had "thrown a block across" the planned contact, as Rostow put it to LBJ, by refusing to deliver the U.S. statement to Hanoi.

So matters stood as the sun rose, first in Vietnam, then in Poland, on Tuesday, December 6, 1966.

"It Is Pity"
Waiting for Gronouski—
December 6, 1966

I wonder, why we did not call the U.S. Embassy and say, "Why don't you come to our embassy?" Why so? . . . They had promised to come. . . . We would have preferred if the Americans called us, apologized for not being able to come, rather than not to call. We were ready on the sixth.

—*Nguyen Dinh Phuong*

I was ready on the sixth, I can tell you, to sit down and have the first discussions. . . .

—*John Gronouski*

Warsaw: "We Were Just Waiting . . ."

Tuesday, December 6, 1966, dawned cloudy and gray in Warsaw, the temperature near freezing—the same as the day before, and the day before that, and the day before that—and the murk smothering the city was an apt metaphor for the mystery and confusion that would enshroud the day's events.[1]

Despite the gloomy weather, that morning a mood of subdued excitement animated the diplomats at the DRV Embassy at 18 Ulica Chocimska, a tree-lined side street off a traffic circle in the bustling Mokotów neighborhood south of the city center, on the Vistula's west bank. Phuong and Quang began the day in a state of curious, slightly nervous anticipation, awaiting word that the Americans were at the embassy's front door. That Tuesday, Phuong insists, the two were ready to receive Gronouski, and as time passed, they wondered where he was (see map 3).

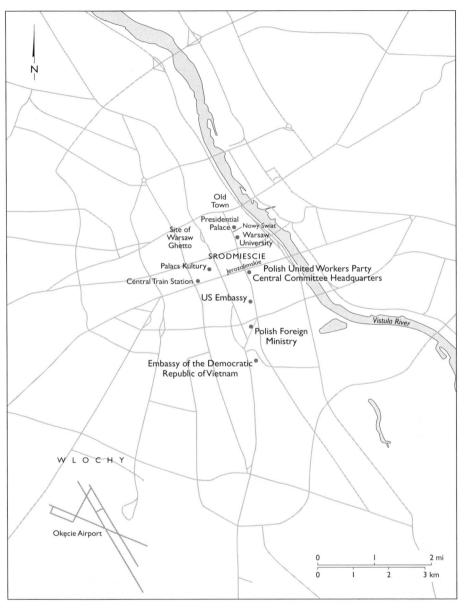

Old
Town

Presidential
Palace ● ‒ Nowy Świat

Site of
Warsaw
Ghetto

Warsaw
University

SRODMIESCIE

Pałac Kultury ●

Central Train Station ●

Jerozolimskie

Polish United Workers Party
Central Committee Headquarters

US Embassy ●

Polish Foreign
Ministry

Embassy of the Democratic ●
Republic of Vietnam

Vistula River

W L O C H Y

Okęcie Airport

0		I		2 mi
0	I	2		3 km

Map 3. Warsaw, December 1966. Cartography by Bill Nelson.

"We were just waiting at the embassy, Do Phat Quang and myself in the drawing room, talking about Vietnam, the world, Poland, work at the embassy, various subjects." They felt "a little impatient and a little anxious. . . . We had many questions." As the minutes, then hours passed they chatted aimlessly. Lunchtime arrived, but not the expected guest. Quang and Phuong rose to eat, after instructing a guard to notify them instantly should anyone appear at the gate.[2]

By now they were deeply perplexed: *Where were the Americans?*

Saigon: "Great God, *You* Help Us"

Lewandowski also wondered what the Americans were up to. Appalled by the Hanoi bombings of December 2 and 4, he feared that the peace effort he had helped engineer was already doomed. Far from persuaded by Lodge's excuses for the timing of the attacks or inadvisability of canceling them, he suspected that circles around LBJ, perhaps in the Pentagon, were deliberately sabotaging the initiative. Nevertheless, as long as even a slim chance of success existed, he sought to save the high-wire diplomacy from irreparable disaster—as shown by his reaction Tuesday morning upon receiving a coded radio-telegraph message from Ha Van Lau. In it, the PAVN colonel requested the Pole to disseminate a brief but "very angry" DRV pronouncement not only again condemning the Hanoi raids, but revealing that they had occurred on the eve of a planned direct contact—in effect, exposing and therefore terminating the covert peace attempt.

Even without consulting Warsaw, Lewandowski knew what he had to do. Immediately—a Pavlovian response—he composed and gave his cipher clerk a message to send Lau strongly advising against issuing the proposed statement. North Vietnam had every right to be furious and accuse Washington of betrayal, but now was not the moment to go public. Lau went along; Hanoi confined itself to angry protests to the ICC and a vitriolic broadcast charging more "savage" bombings of civilian districts.[3]

Having dowsed one flare-up, Lewandowski then had to deal with another: Rapacki's cable instructing him to pressure Lodge to withdraw the "interpretation" clause before the Poles conveyed the U.S. statement and to foreswear any further Hanoi bombing. While annoyed by this "squeezing"—which was pointless, he felt, because neither Gronouski nor Lodge could budge Washington, and it was better to let the Vietnamese and Americans hash such out issues—he dutifully signaled D'Orlandi "in encrypted language" to set up another three-way meeting.[4]

That Tuesday Lodge exuded his usual public confidence. Insisting that U.S. military and political efforts were slowly but surely succeeding, he told a television interviewer that fighting "just might fade out," because the enemy "cannot win" and "we cannot lose, we cannot be pushed out," even if "we haven't won yet."[5] Arriving early at 135 Duong Pasteur for an afternoon meeting with Lewandowski, he chatted briefly with D'Orlandi about the Polish request to drop the interpretation clause, which they agreed should be rebuffed. The Italian "seems to think," Lodge cabled, "that the fact that we snapped up their offer so fast has created an impression of eagerness which encouraged the Communists to make an extra demand of us." Did D'Orlandi really consider Washington's response to Hanoi's invitation for a direct contact in Warsaw to be excessively enthusiastic? That was unlikely—but regardless of whether he accurately quoted the Italian, Lodge appended his own view that "we were right to pick up the offer quickly."[6]

After taking the usual precautions, Lewandowski joined his fellow ambassadors.[7] Coming to the point, he said he had convened them to pass an urgent message from Rapacki. Reading his instructions aloud, he complained that the interpretation clause would drape a "big question mark" over the U.S. stand if Warsaw delivered it unchanged to Hanoi, thereby compromising the talks that were supposed to start that day. "At this point," D'Orlandi recalled, "Cabot Lodge and I looked at each other in a very eloquent and sad manner since the importance of the Ten Points, which are the basis for the negotiation to be initiated, weakened very significantly."

Ignoring their pained expressions, Lewandowski went on. Though privately unhappy with Rapacki's dilatory tactics, he requested U.S. understanding, stressing that "we, the Polish government, have reason to believe that this first contact is of extreme importance, and that every effort must be made not to kill it before it is started." He implored the Americans to drop the offending clause, which he termed gratuitous and unnecessary because the ten points were "not so sacred"— they lacked "the character of a diplomatic document" and were merely "a statement of intentions which may become a starting point for something much more precise." Moreover, he added ("rather as an afterthought," Lodge felt), the Hanoi raids had cast a shadow on the overture, exacerbating the DRV's distrust. Washington "should, therefore, avoid adding to the difficulties."[8]

Lodge, in turn, defended the hedge as aimed at avoiding later misunderstandings or recriminations, and, reading off the same sheet music the State Department had cabled Gronouski, noted that Hanoi had not budged from the Four Points, yet Washington had gone "quite far" in defining its position ("after all, it is us who have to go to their embassy"). As for the plea that Washington show restraint on bombing Hanoi, he tartly retorted that the Communists in recent days displayed no qualms about killing U.S. personnel in Saigon—not only hitting Ton San Nhut and Kinhdo but also nearly detonating a massive blast in the city's port that was only narrowly averted. Lightening the mood, he thanked Rapacki for his help, even as he rued the holdup in the Warsaw contact.

"Weighing in" on Lodge's side, D'Orlandi scolded Rapacki for the delay in transmitting the U.S. statement to Hanoi, and strongly urged that he go ahead and arrange the first U.S.-DRV meeting—"crossing the bridge"—and leave any further snags to be smoothed over afterward, either between the combatants directly or by the Saigon diplomats. "Lodge wants to avoid a misunderstanding," he told the Pole. "Your question [about the interpretation clause] should have been asked by North Vietnam and not by you. The United States has stuck its neck out. Hanoi has not stuck its neck out. It is not very fair to ask for a second statement by the United States."

Gamely, Lewandowski defended Rapacki, whom he insisted was doing everything possible so that "something important will happen, and turn the tide after all these years," and the North Vietnamese, maintaining that it was not fair to claim they had not done anything, because "to agree to meet with an American in a secret way is quite a lot."

Amid these troubling exchanges, at a little after 4:15 p.m., an aide interrupted to hand D'Orlandi the cable relaying Fanfani's congratulations on achieving the breakthrough for direct contacts ("owing to the perfect execution of the instructions given you"). D'Orlandi conveyed his minister's satisfaction to his "partners" for "the faith placed in us."[9]

But when the diplomats concluded their meeting—their third secret gathering at the Italian's apartment in six days—an atmosphere of uncertainty and discord, not satisfaction, prevailed. Nonplussed by Lewandowski's arguments, Lodge, in his report to Washington, judged the Polish objections to the interpretation clause "picayune." In his own cable to Rapacki, Lewandowski hinted at private sympathy for his colleagues' urgings to stop stalling. Of course, he observed, it would be preferable for the Americans to delete the interpretation clause, but if they refused to do so, further delay in passing the U.S. statement to Hanoi "would not be right." Regarding the Warsaw contact—which, of course, was supposed to have occurred that same Tuesday—Lewandowski tried to nudge his boss, noting that Rusk was coming to Saigon that Friday, and "it would be good if something were to be finalized in the meantime."

Filled with foreboding, the three diplomats felt that among themselves, they could settle minor problems or misunderstandings of the sort that had cropped up, but they worried that they were losing control of events—and that the chance for peace might be slipping away. Finishing his journal entry that night, D'Orlandi appealed for divine intervention: "Great God, *you* help us."[10]

Warsaw: A "Bridge" Too Far

Where were the Americans? Barely half a mile north of the DRV Embassy, not even a ten-minute walk, Gronouski was at the MSZ, wondering *Where were the Vietnamese?*

When he awoke that Tuesday, the ambassador had felt a mixture of anticipation, apprehension, and fatigue (because he had been staying up well past midnight in hopes of receiving the latest cable sent from Washington at the close of business there). Though his conversation with Rapacki on Monday had left in doubt the idea of meeting Quang (whom he had only glimpsed at cocktail parties) the next day, Gronouski later recalled that "I was ready on the sixth, I can tell you, to sit down and have the first discussions."[11]

At midday, at about the same time as the Vietnamese were sitting down to lunch, Gronouski left the U.S. Embassy on Aleje Ujazdowskie, a busy boulevard, and headed toward the Foreign Ministry, a nine-minute walk to the south. Leery of reporters, he avoided the glass front door and entered through a less conspicuous side entrance off Ulica Litewska.

At 1 p.m., Gronouski saw Rapacki again, using the host's interpreter, and conveyed the U.S. rejection of the Pole's appeal to retract or reformulate the interpretation clause.[12] In accord with the previous evening's cable, Gronouski explained that Washington had used the clause merely to preclude "charges of bad faith in any subsequent negotiations if we did not make clear that there is a wide latitude for interpretation of the general language used by Lewandowski," and reaffirmed that the ten-point plan "broadly reflects the position of the U.S. Government on the issues covered and we would be prepared to accept it as the basis for direct discussions with the North Vietnamese if they are in fact interested in pursuing the matter, and if they are informed that latitude for interpretation of such general language is inevitable."

In response, Rapacki again expressed "doubts and misgivings" about the clause (along with the Hanoi bombings) but said that the Poles would go ahead and transmit the U.S. statement to North Vietnam. Turning to the first U.S.-DRV meeting, "in the event it takes place," Rapacki said he expected that at that first encounter, the American would convey his government's "precise and official position" regarding the ten points, assuming that this would include a confirmation of U.S. readiness for an accord on that basis, and an explanation —which he assumed Gronouski already had "locked in [his] safe"—of precisely what points about which Washington believed "important differences of interpretation" existed.

Gronouski responded that his understanding was that the first meeting would be "more limited in scope," mostly concerned—aside from the qualified confirmation that the ten points "broadly represented" U.S. policy—with establishing a mutual desire to begin more serious negotiations, and discussion of where, when, and at what level such talks might begin. But he promised to convey Rapacki's understanding to Washington, and the two parted.

Soon afterward, the Poles finally cabled the three-point U.S. statement to their embassy in Hanoi—where it was already Tuesday night—to relay officially to the North Vietnamese.[13]

Austin: "No Intensification"

In Washington, the Hanoi raids had begun to generate suspicions of a new policy to ratchet up the bombing, although the public remained in the dark about their coincidence with the delicate diplomacy. "New Attacks Seen as Escalation of Air War in Vietnam," read a front-page headline in the *Washington Post* above a story citing "U.S. sources" as saying the attacks on sites so close to North Vietnam's capital "represented a political decision by the Johnson administration to destroy targets that have previously been exempted from the raids."[14]

Though he had fled Washington, LBJ could not escape reminders of the cost that the war continued to exact. Tuesday morning, the LBJ Ranch received a status report from the White House Situation Room informing the president that as of that day, 6,250 U.S. military personnel had been killed in Southeast Asia since January 1961[15]—a somber figure, but about 52,000 shy of the ultimate toll.

At 9:10 a.m., LBJ boarded a helicopter for the twenty-minute flight to the state capital to award a Medal of Honor (the first to a Marine since the Korean War) to a twenty-three-year-old Irish-American from New York City. On the chopper, LBJ checked by radio to see how his bulls and cattle had fared at auction the day before, and after reviewing his draft remarks for the ceremony, inserted a caustic sentence denouncing "draft-card burners."[16]

On landing at the Austin Civic Center, he ducked into a black Lincoln Continental sedan for the short drive to the Federal Office Building, where he met up with McNamara, Rostow, the Joint Chiefs of Staff (JCS), and other military and civilian advisers who had arrived a half hour earlier at nearby Bergstrom Air Force Base. For more than an hour, in LBJ's ninth-floor office, the group reviewed the Pentagon's budget plans for the coming year,[17] until it adjourned for the outdoors medal-pinning.

During the solemn ceremony, the dignitaries now augmented by Governor John Connally and Senator Ralph Yarborough, Johnson draped the blue-ribboned medal around the neck of the "smiling, stocky" Robert E. O'Malley, commended for heroism during an August 1965 firefight with Communist forces. In this sympathetic setting, LBJ could not resist a dig at antiwar critics. Earlier, he had scorned "nervous Nellies" who fretted about involvement in Vietnam. Now, in the added sentence, he observed acidly that U.S. soldiers' bravery "far outweighs the reluctance of men who exercise so well the right of dissent, but let others fight to protect them from those whose very philosophy is to do away with the right to dissent."[18]

After shaking hands with O'Malley's family and comrades in arms and kissing "many of the ladies," Johnson went back upstairs, peeking at the wire service news ticker outside his office before a working lunch with McNamara, the JCS, Rostow, and others to resume the budget review. A few hours later, after another scan of wire service reports to read accounts of the remarks he had just delivered, LBJ, with McNamara at his side, told reporters that they would request a $9 billion to $10 billion supplemental Pentagon appropriation from Congress to cover war-related expenses through June 1967—an admission that was the top story in newspapers around the country the next day.

The news conference offered reporters a chance to confront the president and defense secretary about reports of a decision to intensify the air war. But LBJ repeatedly deflected allegations that a stalemate in Vietnam was compelling harsher measures. When McNamara was asked whether the most recent Hanoi area bombing raids, including targets "that we had not bombed before," was an escalation or "new program that we decided upon," he denied any change. "These targets are part of the same target system that our military efforts have been directed against for over a year—the lines of communication and the supporting facilities supporting the flow of men and material from North Vietnam to South Vietnam." Any "apparent intensification," he claimed, was an illusion, caused by improved weather allowing previously delayed missions to go ahead. "There was no intensification," he insisted, once interrupting a reporter trying to refine a question on the bombings to assert, "I know what you meant."[19]

McNamara, flanked by a silently approving Johnson, was lying. The latest raids, he knew, stemmed directly from the Rolling Thunder–52 campaign approved the previous month. Though Rusk and McNamara had prevailed on LBJ to eliminate some targets that the JCS favored on the grounds that the risks (excessive civilian casualties, losses among attacking planes, third-country protests, etc.) outweighed their military value, he knew that the campaign's whole point was to up the pain on Hanoi to increase the likelihood that it would sue for peace. A "limited, very quiet, expanded program," the president had told McNamara on November 9, the day before authorizing RT-52, might "give Moscow a little leverage on 'em [to negotiate] if it weren't so damn violent that it forced 'em to react otherwise."

LBJ had stressed that he did not want raids "so dramatic that you have a headline every day that you're really changing your policy"—a wish belied by that day's *Post*—but, in Texas vernacular, voiced his conviction that more bombing made the enemy more pliable. "I think if we're causing 'em damage and they're hurtin' but we haven't got their children's hospitals afire and so forth, I think Moscow can say to Hanoi, 'Goddamit, this thing is gettin' awfully costly on you and on us and on everybody else. Let's try to find an answer here.' If it's not being costly, I don't think maybe they got any real desire to stop the bombing if it's not hurtin.'"[20]

On December 6, LBJ took no action to modify bombing plans he knew included more strikes in the Hanoi area.[21] That evening at dinner, back at the ranch, he marveled to friends "about how brilliant a man Secretary McNamara is and how he made some of the press look like fools in a very polite way as well as some of the Joint Chiefs."[22]

Warsaw: "Bullshit, or Words to That Effect"

At the DRV Embassy—around the same time that, at the MSZ, about an eight-minute stroll to the north, Gronouski saw Rapacki and felt somewhat let down that Hanoi's ambassador had failed to show—Quang and Phuong lunched, then resumed their vigil. As the day wore on, the clouds thinned, the sun emerged, and the weather cleared up—but not the diplomacy. The North Vietnamese waited, and waited—and by late afternoon, began to grow irritated, convinced that the Americans had stood *them* up. Having started the day filled with anticipation,

Phuong grew first puzzled and finally, by evening, "a little bit disappointed," even "angry."

"In view of these facts," Phuong wrote, "the Vietnamese side could only understand that the U.S. side did not want the meeting in Warsaw between the two ambassadors."[23]

* * *

That evening, Gronouski ran into Michałowski at a reception.[24] Calling the American aside, the Pole disclosed that "Rapacki had conveyed [the U.S. government's] position"—that is, the three-part statement containing the interpretation clause—"to Hanoi shortly after my [Gronouski's] meeting with him" that afternoon; he hoped to have some sort of response by the time the two lunched on Wednesday. Adopting a friendly, positive manner, Michałowski said that the Poles would do "everything possible" to bring about direct U.S.-DRV negotiations, deserved "faith" in their intermediary role, and could even be "very useful" in influencing the North Vietnamese once talks started; they were "in frequent contact with Hanoi and are hopeful that things are on track."

At the same time, in a gently critical rather than scolding tone, Michałowski noted that the "stepped-up bombing outside Hanoi" aroused suspicions not only there but "even" in Warsaw that "some [U.S.] elements" were "trying to undercut President's peace move." Calling Lodge's defense of the raids (planned long in advance, impossible to cancel without tipping off the military, etc.) unconvincing, he "expressed fervent hope that we can avoid future highly sensitive bombing raids in vicinity of Hanoi and Haiphong."

The two also discussed, apparently for the first time, the mechanics of the initial U.S.-DRV meeting. In contrast to the evident North Vietnamese impression that the contact would occur at their embassy, Gronouski and Michałowski informally agreed it would be a "good idea," in the interests of secrecy, to hold the session at the Polish Foreign Ministry building.

In his telegram describing the talk, which did not reach Washington until Wednesday morning, Gronouski observed that the Poles had evidently led the North Vietnamese to expect that at the first meeting he would present the ten points directly to the DRV ambassador, not merely affirm the validity of Lewandowski's presentation, "and are fearful that if we do not do so Poles will be discredited in the eyes of Hanoi."

Gronouski hardly needed to add (hint, hint) that this would be a difficult feat to pull off if he still had not seen them himself!

* * *

Polish suspicions toward Washington on December 6 may have been reinforced by a coincidental conversation that a midlevel MSZ official had that day with an ex-U.S. official who happened to be passing through. During JFK's administration, Roger N. Hilsman had headed the State Department's Bureau of Intelligence and Research and then served as assistant secretary for Far Eastern affairs, but he had resigned soon after Dallas, in part because of a rift over Asia policy. Now on leave from Columbia University, he had written, but not yet published, a memoir of the Kennedy years, and had embarked on an extended European tour.

Though in the dark about Marigold or other secret Vietnam diplomacy, Hilsman blasted LBJ's conduct of the war to Marian Dobrosielski of MSZ's policy planning staff.[25] The two had been friendly since the Kennedy years; as a Polish Embassy counselor in Washington, Dobrosielski had found Hilsman "much more flexible" on Southeast Asian issues than Rusk (whose chief Soviet adviser, in turn, considered Dobrosielski "one of the most frank and realistic officials of a Communist country with whom I have ever dealt"[26]). On December 6, Hilsman recounted that JFK had resisted "enormous" Pentagon and CIA pressure to escalate in Vietnam, clinging to hope for Laotian-style neutralization, but LBJ "bet on a military solution," swayed by the JCS and Rusk, whom Hilsman described as hidebound by "a whole bunch of prejudices and a highly rigid position" dating from his State Department work on Asia under Truman. Hilsman left the State Department in 1964, he explained, because he was loath to implement Rusk's Vietnam and China policies, which he disparaged yet could not alter—a predicament, he noted, that was also now Harriman's—and, having publicly criticized U.S. conduct in Vietnam, was now "cursed" by the White House. The current situation made him pessimistic. Not only were the Vietnamese Communists fanatically (and, to Hilsman, incomprehensibly) committed to military victory regardless of the cost, but Washington was also allergic to concessions that might allow an exit from the war, because LBJ, Rusk, and McNamara were "too deeply and personally involved" and any radical policy shift would vindicate antiwar critics; the best one could hope for was a "gradual de-escalation."[27]

While in Warsaw, Hilsman also saw Michałowski, from whom he got a whiff of Polish ire toward LBJ's handling of peace efforts, and especially the December 2 and 4 Hanoi bombings, to complement his own misgivings. Though not disclosing details of the Saigon channel, Michałowski was "madder 'n hell" over the raids, which he said had occurred just as Warsaw was making diplomatic headway. Hilsman later recalled that when he insisted that LBJ sought peace, Michałowski shot back: "Bullshit, or words to that effect."[28]

Washington: "Not Bad"

By late Tuesday afternoon, U.S. officials were getting antsy waiting for Gronouski: Though in fact he had already seen Rapacki in Warsaw, Washington had received no word from him, and from the LBJ Ranch in Texas, there were signs of mounting impatience. Read, who had stayed behind in Washington to assist Katzenbach when Rusk left for Asia, got "constant calls from Walt Rostow to see whether a cable we knew would be coming in, reporting an important conversation, had arrived, where it was—the President would want it, et cetera."[29] At 4:21 p.m. Katzenbach sent a "flash" telegram—actually drafted by aide John P. Walsh, now added to the circle with Marigold clearances—requesting "indication soonest" from Gronouski when he would see Rapacki to convey the message adhering to the interpretation clause.[30]

Finally, around dinnertime, came Gronouski's cable recounting his sparring with Rapacki.[31] Poring over the message, the officials managing the initiative in Rusk's absence—he was now in Tokyo, conferring with Japanese officials[32]—were grudgingly impressed by their envoy's handling of the exchanges despite his lack of Marigold data, diplomatic training, or Vietnam expertise. ("Not bad," Katzenbach grunted on rereading it almost four decades later.[33]) Into the night, the Marigold managers—Katzenbach, Thompson, and Read, checking periodically with Rostow—mulled the instructions for Gronouski's next moves.[34] Now more comfortable with his capabilities, and aware they had to take into account the Polish warning that at their first encounter the DRV ambassador would expect Gronouski to state the U.S. position, they decided the time had come to bring him more fully into their confidence.

This meant—finally!—sending Gronouski the text of the ten points. In a cable drafted by Read and cleared by Rostow, Katzenbach instructed him to "take no further initiative" with the Poles and await further guidance, to arrive shortly. However, in the "unlikely event" that before it reached him he was notified Wednesday morning that North Vietnam's envoy was "ready and available for talks with us," he was authorized—beyond prior instructions to say the ten points "broadly represent" U.S. policy but were liable to "important differences of interpretation"—to meet and read aloud the ten points, which the present cable included. He should also, "stressing that it is Lewandowski's formulation," inquire whether they matched "in all particulars" what the Pole had told Hanoi. Wary of relinquishing too much authority, the officials forbade Gronouski from "discussing the substantive problems" relating to the ten points and instead directed him to say they would "be the subject of actual negotiations." They did not expect the DRV diplomat to engage in such probing, presuming he would merely report the first contact.

Nevertheless, recognizing that the interpretation clause aroused uncertainty (in Warsaw and perhaps Hanoi), Katzenbach identified for Gronouski's own information as "obviously [the] most troublesome" of the ten points the reference in point two to changing the "status quo in South Vietnam . . . in order to take into account the interests of the parties presently opposing the United States," because it could mean anything from inserting the NLF "into government of South Vietnam forthwith" (as Hanoi might demand) or merely a "simple endorsement of election process under constitution now being drafted" (as the Americans naturally preferred). But the State Department did not want Gronouski to raise such a possible deal-breaker in his first talk—if he had to explain the clause, he should "allude to less contentious ambiguities elsewhere" in the ten points.

On the bombing, Katzenbach, keenly aware of White House sensitivities, gave him special instructions. Gronouski was to interrupt his recitation after point eight to note that Lewandowski had implied Hanoi's awareness of Washington's "phasing and timing" concept in which a halt to air raids would be followed "after some adequate period" by mutual and secretly preagreed "de-escalatory actions." If the North Vietnamese pushed, Gronouski should refer again to the Phase A/B idea and note that the topic could be taken up in later discussions.[35]

After Katzenbach and his aides went home for a late night's sleep, the instructions were enciphered and dispatched just after midnight, Washington time, reaching the embassy in the Polish capital before dawn Wednesday morning. So far as the State Department knew, as Tuesday ended, the proposed contact in Warsaw was still up in the air.

What Went Wrong? "The Choreography of How One Enters Negotiations . . ."

What happened on December 6, 1966, between Americans and Poles, both in Saigon and Warsaw, has long been known from declassified U.S. documents, now fortified by Polish accounts. That Tuesday, both countries' sources agree, Rapacki gave Gronouski (and Lodge garnered from Lewandowski) the clear impression that the prerequisites were still not met for the first encounter between U.S. and DRV ambassadors in Warsaw; that the Poles would continue to work with the North Vietnamese to facilitate it; but that further progress depended on Hanoi's response to the American statement, whose delivery the Poles had delayed.

In U.S. eyes, in other words, it appeared Hanoi was not yet ready to meet, or the Poles were not yet ready to arrange a meeting—and it was unclear whether Warsaw's gripes about the interpretation clause and latest bombings were good-faith efforts to hurdle real obstacles or cynical maneuvers to elicit a softening of U.S. terms and constraints on military actions.

Missing, until now, has been any word of what was happening on December 6 from the North Vietnamese perspective—and that is what Phuong's "Waiting for Godot" account provides. Unfortunately, I could not get access to Hanoi archives that might corroborate, correct, or amplify his version of that day's events—such as Quang's cables to the DRV Foreign Ministry or the postmortem on the failed contact Phuong believed Quang prepared.[36] However, his story gains currency from another Vietnamese source: Luu Van Loi and Nguyen Anh Vu support his basic contention that—contrary to the prevalent American presumption at the time and in later historiography—the conditions for a direct U.S.-DRV contact *did* exist on that day, because Hanoi's diplomats were prepared to receive Gronouski:

> Ambassador Do Phat Quang was ready on December 6 to meet Gronouski but the latter never showed. Later the Americans explained that [their] man was waiting for Do Phat Quang to show up to the American Embassy [*sic:* Clearly, this refers

to the expectation that Quang would appear at the Polish Foreign Ministry, as they never anticipated he would come to the U.S. Embassy]. Moreover, President Johnson also said [later in his memoirs] that the Poles promised [they] would organize the meeting, intimating that the failure of that meeting, then, lies with the Poles.

The American Ambassador refused to meet with the Vietnamese Ambassador on December 6 although they [the Americans] had agreed to it.[37]

In a book published in 2000, Loi affirmed that Gronouski "did not show up."[38]

We have examined, ad nauseam, how Quang might have mistakenly gathered by the end of Monday, December 5, perhaps from Michałowski, that he should expect a Gronouski visit the next day—contrary to U.S. and Polish understanding that the conditions for such an encounter had not yet been met, especially because Warsaw had not formally given Hanoi the U.S. statement agreeing to the contact on that date. Is it possible Quang was right, and Gronouski had erred by failing to appear at North Vietnam's embassy on December 6? Rather than a DRV-Polish miscommunication, could the miscue have occurred between *Gronouski* and the Poles?

At least one Communist who may have been in a position to know thought so. In mid-December 1966, Soviet ambassador to the United States Anatoly F. Dobrynin went home to Moscow for a short visit to attend a plenum of the CPSU's Central Committee. After returning to Washington, he saw Rusk in January 1967, and the two rehashed the initiative that had collapsed the previous month (the Poles had kept the Soviets closely informed). At one point, Rusk recorded, Dobrynin remarked that

> his information was that Rapacki had told us in Gronouski's first meeting [on December 5] that we should go ahead and establish our own direct contact with the North Vietnamese. This surprised me and I called in Ben Read to check the record carefully and could find no record of any such remark. Indeed, the record shows that the entire exercise was related to a Polish role in actually arranging the first meeting. Dobrynin seemed to accept this and said there might have been some misunderstanding.[39]

Was there? Actually, Gronouski's cabled account of his December 5 talk with Rapacki leaves slight room for (pardon the expression) differences of interpretation.[40] As noted above, the Pole indeed complained about the interpretation clause and indicated he was holding up relaying the U.S. position to Hanoi because the clause, as it stood, would undoubtedly prompt a "reexamination of the whole matter again" by Hanoi and "mean . . . that the contact in Warsaw would have to be postponed." Conversely, at that meeting, Rapacki read aloud Lodge's December 3 statement to Lewandowski, which included the assertion that LBJ would "instruct the U.S. Embassy in Warsaw to contact the North Vietnamese

Ambassador in Warsaw on December 6"[41]—language could be read as implying that the Americans were expected to take the initiative in contacting Hanoi's envoy directly, without a final go-ahead from the Poles.

Still, Rapacki's December 5 presentation suggested Hanoi was not yet ready for a face-to-face meeting, especially as it had not received Lodge's statement, and the Poles were not ready to arrange it. Consistent with Gronouski's cable, Michałowski's account of the same conversation has Rapacki reading Lodge's statement and warning that the interpretation clause would inspire Hanoi's distrust, but does not depict him either encouraging the American to go ahead on his own to initiate the contact, or discouraging him from doing so.[42]

Where and how Dobrynin got the impression he conveyed to Rusk—that Rapacki told the Americans to "go ahead and establish [their] own direct contact with the North Vietnamese"—remains unclear. Did the Poles deliberately mislead the Soviets? Was the Kremlin (in cahoots with Warsaw) maliciously seeking to foist blame for Marigold's failure onto Washington? Or was Moscow genuinely puzzled and confused as to what had gone awry?

Although it may be tempting to juxtapose Dobrynin's comments to Rusk with the fresh Vietnamese accounts claiming that Gronouski had stood up the DRV diplomats in Warsaw, the preponderance of evidence, both U.S. and Polish, militates *against* the hypothesis that the American misconstrued a suggestion from Rapacki to directly contact Quang. Not only does no suggestion to this effect appear in the U.S. or Polish accounts of Gronouski's talk with Rapacki on December 5, but there is also no indication that on the following day either Rapacki or Michałowski, both of whom had the opportunity, urged him to walk over to the DRV Embassy; moreover, Rapacki's subsequent behavior, as we shall see, indicates that despite *potential* openings to bring Gronouski and Quang together, the Pole preferred to play his cards to extract maximum concessions from Washington *before* arranging the first direct contact.

Regardless of whether or not Quang had a valid reason to expect Gronouski to appear at the DRV Embassy in Warsaw on December 6, 1966, one crucial lingering mystery which the Vietnamese accounts fail to resolve still stands out: *When the American failed to appear, why didn't Do Phat Quang contact the Americans, or at least the Poles, to find out why?*

This question haunted Phuong when we sat together in Hanoi in 1999 and reviewed that melancholy day. For more than three decades, he believed he understood this disappointing moment in his life: the United States, he assumed, simply did not want to meet and Gronouski deliberately (and rudely) missed his appointment. Only after reading declassified U.S. documents provided by the present author did he consider the possibility that Washington was in fact ready (and in Gronouski's case even eager) for the December 6 encounter.

And the possibility that a miscommunication or misunderstanding, not a deliberate U.S. decision, kept Gronouski from showing up at the DRV Embassy that day caused Phuong to wonder whether, in retrospect, he and Quang did all they could to achieve the contact. During our interview, after recalling the long hours of waiting on December 6, Phuong agonized over the Vietnamese failure to reach out. "I wonder," he stated with evident emotion, even agitation, "why we did not call the US Embassy and say, 'Why don't you come to our embassy?' Why so?"

Later, when the question arose of why the DRV diplomats failed to contact the Poles or Americans on December 6 when Gronouski failed to appear, Phuong elaborated: "I wonder how, why, we did not discuss this question. Possibly it is because of our pride"—that is, as a smaller, weaker power, Hanoi did not want to seem too eager for talks, especially when Washington had not ceased its bombing. "[We thought that] 'this showed that they are not willing to talk to us.'"

Crestfallen, Phuong shook his head and said softly, "It is pity, it is pity."

His explanation of why Quang failed to reach out to the Americans on December 6 rings true—the North Vietnamese were deeply proud and acutely conscious of the circumstances in which they might enter negotiations. This was a hard lesson they had taken from Geneva; the costly Dien Bien Phu victory on the conference's eve poised them to evict the French; yet, in their view, by following Soviet and Chinese advice, they had failed to attain on the "baize table" all they had won on the battlefield. A fierce determination not to seem weak nor negotiate under duress compelled Hanoi to take a firm, independent, and in its view principled stand against direct negotiations until Washington completely and unconditionally stopped bombing (and other "acts of aggression" against) North Vietnam—regardless of the enormous price it was paying against an enemy with utter technological and (despite Soviet-supplied SAMs) almost total aerial superiority. By secretly compromising on this endlessly repeated, seemingly rigid public stand, the North Vietnamese had reason to be even more sensitive to the danger of appearing weak once Washington began hitting Hanoi (where they lived, as the Poles kept reminding Gronouski), for the first time in months, precisely on the verge of possible direct negotiations.

Both sides were alert to this consideration—none more so than Lodge, who, as we have seen, repeatedly argued (and the White House had agreed) that the best strategy to lure Hanoi into talks and concessions was to "play it cool" rather than seem too interested in negotiations. Just such an attitude, Lodge believed, had produced progress in Marigold, both over the summer and in the fall. "Should we give the impression of over eagerness, Hanoi would conclude we were weak," he had warned Washington in July. "This would lessen the chance of peace."[43] Despite believing that it was correct to follow up quickly on the Lewandowski approach, just two days earlier he had reaffirmed the correctness of "playing it cool." "Eagerness tends to harden Communist positions to a degree we can't accept, and this lengthens the war."[44]

With neither side immune to fear of signaling weakness, Phuong's explanation of why Quang failed to reach out seems both credible and tragic. Perhaps under instructions not to take any initiative that might indicate eagerness, perhaps instinctively adopting such an approach, Quang took great pains to avoid giving

Washington or Warsaw—ideological comrades, yes, but, in tune with Moscow, consistently pressuring the North Vietnamese to enter talks—even a shred of evidence that Hanoi *needed* peace more than the Americans. At all costs, the DRV leaders wanted to avoid leaving the impression—in secret exchanges, or later, when the circumstances under which talks began inevitably became public—that they had been "bombed to the table."

Throughout the war, U.S. officials would retain confidence, or at least hope, that bombing would make Hanoi more pliable; Rostow, after all, had airily observed to LBJ on December 5 that the latest raids "might tip the balance toward negotiations."[45] Yet some informed observers feared that such tactics might backfire, eliciting a stiffer response. One such analyst, a Harvard academic and State Department consultant who had read the still-classified Marigold record and himself engaged in some fruitless Vietnam diplomacy, wrote in late 1968:

> The Vietnamese people have lived under foreign rule for approximately half of their history. They have maintained a remarkable cultural and social cohesion by being finely attuned to the realities of power. To survive, the Vietnamese have had to learn to calculate—almost instinctively—the real balance of forces. If negotiations give the impression of being a camouflaged surrender, there will be nothing left to negotiate. Support for the side which seems to be losing will collapse. Thus, all the parties are aware—Hanoi explicitly, for it does not view war and negotiation as separate processes; we in a more complicated bureaucratic manner—that *the way* negotiations are carried out is almost as important as *what* is negotiated. The choreography of how one enters negotiations, what is settled first and in what manner[,] is inseparable from the substance of the issues.[46]

The author—Henry A. Kissinger, about to enter the White House as Richard Nixon's national security adviser and soon to embark on a frustrating career as his secret Vietnam negotiator—was no Asia specialist and of course lacked knowledge of the DRV version of Marigold. Yet his observation that "Hanoi's margin for survival is so narrow that precise calculation has become a way of life; caution is almost an obsession" aptly fits Phuong's surmise that such considerations constrained Quang from taking the simple step, on December 6, of phoning the U.S. Embassy or, less dangerously, Michałowski, to ascertain what was going on.[47]

If he had . . . we will explore what *might* have happened later in this book. The evidence suggests that clearer communication, both Polish-Vietnamese and U.S.-Polish, might have yielded a different, better outcome far sooner than actually occurred—if not peace, at least ongoing direct contacts; if not ongoing direct contacts, then at least a step toward them, rather than a mutual belief that the other had acted in bad faith, making progress tougher than if the possibility of the Warsaw contact had never emerged in the first place. For now, let us end with Phuong's plaintive words as he wrestled with the possibility that, contrary to his presumption for more than thirty years, the Americans really were willing to speak with him and Quang that cold Tuesday in Warsaw and confirm Washington's general adherence to a mutually acceptable formula to end the war: "They had promised to come. . . . We would have preferred if the Americans called us, apologized for not being able to come, rather than not to call. We were ready on the sixth."

"It Looked as If We Could Move Forward"

Marigold in Suspense, December 7–13, 1966

The USA talks, talks, and then swallows their words. This is insolent and deceitful behavior, . . . unworthy behavior that does not engender trust. [But] if the USA ambassador knocks on the door of the DRV embassy in Warsaw then, . . . in accordance with previously sent instructions to the DRV embassy, he will be received.

—*Pham Van Dong to Jerzy Siedlecki, December 7, 1966*

All of us are skeptical as to exactly what Warsaw can and will produce, but there is still enough possibility to warrant serious action on our side. There is no better negotiating possibility currently in the works.

—*Nicholas Katzenbach (for Robert McNamara, Walt Rostow, and Llewellyn Thompson) to President Johnson, opposing more raids on Hanoi while Marigold remained alive, December 7, 1966*

It's clean as a whistle now.

—*Rostow to President Johnson, December 8, 1966, assuring him that instructions to John Gronouski contained no commitments to limit further bombing*

John Gronouski: It would be criminal if after having reached this point [your] efforts and ours to get the two parties together failed. . . .

Adam Rapacki: . . . It look[s] as if we could move forward. . . .

—*Conversation in Warsaw, December 9, 1966*

For a week, Marigold hung in the balance. December 6 had come and gone, with no direct U.S.-DRV contact, and despite Michałowski's hope that "things were on track," the peace effort had clearly gone awry. Yet, while wobbling, it had not completely run off the rails: Gronouski was still instructed to confirm the ten points "broadly represent" American policy; Hanoi had not withdrawn its consent to receive a U.S. representative; despite grave fears of leaks, the initiative remained hidden from public view; Phuong lingered in Warsaw, ready to interpret talks with Gronouski; for eight straight days, no further bombings of Hanoi occurred—and U.S. officials, hearing "the noise on the staircase," believed the breakthrough encounter might be only hours away.

Wednesday, December 7

Hanoi: "If the USA Ambassador Knocks on the Door"

Before 9 a.m. Wednesday, Siedlecki had in his hands Rapacki's telegram instructing him to deliver to Pham Van Dong—at last!—its report on the Saturday afternoon conversation in Saigon between Lodge and Lewandowski, including the three-part U.S. statement, and also a distillation of the exchanges to date with Gronouski in Warsaw; at 10 a.m., the premier received the ambassador.[1]

In "much better form" than when they last met, Dong seemed animated by anger as well as the later hour and listened intently as Siedlecki read aloud, through a Russian-language interpreter, the lengthy cable. Reacting in a "lively but in a controlled manner," he snickered at Lodge's remark to Lewandowski that the interpretation clause was simply meant to forestall charges of bad faith, and he radiated "suppressed indignation" at his effort to minimize the Hanoi raids as merely due to weather fluctuations. When Siedlecki invited the premier to assess the secret exchanges, he did not hold back:

> The USA talks, talks and then swallows their words. For example, Lodge first presented their position clearly enough. In the next talk it became more hazy and even hazier with Gronouski. Lodge's second talk with Lewandowski [on December 3] was conducted under conditions of intensive bombing of the DRV and Hanoi besides. This is insolent and deceitful behavior. We are not blind to it.

At one point, even Siedlecki, who shared Dong's contempt for U.S. conduct, thought he had gone too far. When the premier insinuated that, after Lodge started the initiative by advancing new proposals, Gronouski had tried to "turn the tables" and imply that Hanoi, not Washington, was seeking the contact, the Pole interrupted him to correct this misimpression; the statement he was delivering, he pointed out, explicitly stated that the U.S. ambassador in Warsaw would be instructed to contact his DRV counterpart. Sensing a "certain hastiness" in language conversion may have misled Dong, Siedlecki proposed that after their talk, Vietnamese and Polish interpreters jointly prepare an authoritative translation of Rapacki's cable, and the premier agreed.

Returning to the charge, Dong declared that "under these circumstances," the U.S. desire for contacts would "have the character of a probe"—he used the French term *sondage,* as in a nautical *sounding*—to ascertain "if we are ready to talk under the conditions (if also under the pressure) of intensive bombing. This is unworthy behavior and does not engender trust. All this induces us to examine again our position."

Yet, even as he said recent events compelled Hanoi to reassess the proposed contact, and again condemned Washington for acting "deceitfully and cynically," the premier offered a tantalizing hint that, literally, the door was not closed. "To my insistence about concrete circumstances," Siedlecki cabled Rapacki, Dong

> replied that if the USA ambassador knocks on the door of the DRV embassy in Warsaw then—about which Lewandowski spoke—in accordance with previously sent instructions to the DRV embassy—he will be received, but if the USA wants to establish contact of the nature [which is] currently being discussed, then, in the face of newly existing circumstances, the DRV must once again examine the matter.

Siedlecki's convoluted, herky-jerky rendition of Dong's comments provokes head-scratching in the original as well as in translation. When I showed Lewandowski this passage decades later, he shook his head and rued that at such a moment Poland lacked a more intelligent interlocutor. "Ah, frankly speaking, poor Rapacki! . . . My dear professor, this is a rubble, I have difficulty in reading it [even] in Polish"—he laughed—"to understand what Pham Van Dong, what Siedlecki, wanted to say. So, I think it was a puzzle which also [faced] Rapacki and Michałowski, what it really means."[2] Yet it is clear that Siedlecki had reported that Dong, for all his fury at Washington and insistence that Hanoi needed to reassess the entire matter, had explicitly stated that Gronouski would not be rebuffed if he came to the DRV Embassy.

If the Americans were to disclose the existence of the secret contacts to enhance their position, Dong sternly warned, the process would be ruptured, as "their fault, not ours," and Hanoi would be "obliged to unmask them and in our present attitude we must take into account such a possibility in order not to weaken our position in the future." Yet Dong also pledged that if Washington kept silent, the DRV would as well. After this conversation, Trinh later told Siedlecki, Hanoi sent "appropriate instructions" to Quang in Warsaw.[3]

Wednesday evening, when the air-raid danger had subsided until the next dawn, authorities escorted Siedlecki and his military attaché through darkened streets to inspect bomb damage. At one stop, he heard that on Friday more than ten bombs had hit the grounds of a "Polish-Vietnamese Friendship School" during a raid on a nearby auto-repair shop, collapsing roofs and injuring teachers and children. Urging Warsaw to exploit the incident's propaganda value, he cabled that embassy personnel had already helped by hauling away rubble and providing medicine, and he had donated 50 dong himself, but Poland should rebuild the facility: "The costs should not be too high, but the political effect would be surely greater than in any other more expensive endeavors."[4]

Saigon: "I Couldn't Do Anything"

Lewandowski, excluded from the latest exchanges with the Vietnamese and Americans, instead received from Michałowski a cable—obviously aimed at gathering information with which to tax Gronouski about the cryptic interpretation clause—asking for the precise wording of the recapitulation of the U.S. stand he had given Lodge. As requested, he clarified his minor modifications in reply to Lodge's and D'Orlandi's objections. A bit annoyed that his summary's accuracy was doubted, he insisted that no "fundamental divergences should exist" between the ten points as understood in Warsaw and Washington, and that in Hanoi he "was, of course, careful in formulations."[5]

After mediating between Lodge and Dong, and the exhilaration of a potential breakthrough to end the war (and boost his career and secure a spot in the history books), Lewandowski felt marginalized. He heard only muffled, delayed, even distorted echoes of events in Warsaw—he knew Gronouski was instructed to meet his DRV counterpart, vaguely sensed Rapacki's disappointment that Washington had not sent a bigger name, regretted the squabbling over the interpretation clause that impeded the first contact, and feared that the Hanoi attacks meant Washington was backing away in any case. Yet he was powerless to arrest the deteriorating course of events, and his isolation was accentuated by his exclusion from relevant cables; he never saw Siedlecki's ciphergrams from Hanoi, nor the detailed reports on the talks with Gronouski—at least, not until the present author showed them to him decades later. "I couldn't do anything in Saigon," he said sadly. "I couldn't do anything. . . . I was not in a position to make any comment."[6]

Washington: "More Fencing by the Poles"

Wednesday morning, Rostow sent LBJ a progress report at his ranch consisting of the latest exchange of cables. In a cover note, he termed Gronouski's latest talk with Rapacki "more fencing by the Poles to draw us out as much as possible before we meet the other fellow, if he, in fact, turns up" and the directive to Warsaw a "holding instruction" for the envoy, who had earned his spurs in dealing with the wily Communist despite being kept in the dark. "Nick, Tommy, and I agreed Gronouski should now know what the ten points are," Rostow wrote. "He has operated blind but skillfully thus far."[7]

Now that he deemed it safe to disclose the ten points to Gronouski, Katzenbach decided that others who had been evicted from Marigold's charmed circle a week before could, one by one, reenter it. On learning Wednesday morning from Gronouski that Warsaw had finally sent the U.S. statement to Hanoi, the State Department's top brass decided that he now needed (and deserved) far more information at his disposal. Katzenbach deputized Leonard Unger to draft messages to enlighten Gronouski on the channel's history and coach him on his script, even if he had to improvise a line or two, should he actually meet a DRV representative.[8]

Moscow: "We Could Have Helped"

Though the Soviet Union lurked offstage as the Marigold drama unfolded, it remained a presence that none of the major actors could ignore. Amid the intensive Polish-DRV and U.S.-Polish exchanges, both Warsaw and Washington, from very different perspectives, acted to ensure that Moscow heard its version of the story.

Both then and later, the USSR's role in Marigold mystified U.S. officials, who were unsure whether Warsaw acted independently, in coordination with its patron, or under its direct supervision. From the Soviets' failure to raise the affair with Washington until late in the game, the Pentagon Papers analysts—who conducted by far the deepest in-house postmortem—surmised they had "at most a passive role in Marigold," though it was "possible" they were its "principal sponsors."[9] Conversely, Rusk speculated at the time that Rapacki's tactics were "dictated from Moscow," and a Rostow aide dismissed the initiative as a "KGB operation," a "classic Communist agitprop" "set-up" choreographed by the Kremlin to bamboozle Washington into a bombing halt or other concessions.[10]

Polish and Russian archives resolve this uncertainty. The Soviets, they show, welcomed and endorsed (if unenthusiastically), but did not instigate or control, a Polish diplomatic foray. "The nature of the relationship between the Soviet Union and its Eastern European allies was such that the Europeans were unlikely to take any important step in the area of foreign policy without at least tacit approval from Moscow," noted the historian Ilya V. Gaiduk. "But they might propose such a step on their own initiative."[11]

In this case, Poland did so—and, Michałowski reports, informed the Kremlin "precisely about every stage of the Saigon talks" through its ambassador to the USSR, Pszczółkowski. That is a minor exaggeration, because these contacts were at times spotty or post factum rather than continuous, and the spat between Lewandowski and Siedlecki in Hanoi over what (if anything) to tell Shcherbakov illustrated the ambivalence that occasionally surfaced over the degree of consultation. Still, Polish sources confirm that once Rapacki secured Soviet leader Brezhnev's blessing to proceed in Sofia in mid-November, Pszczółkowski functioned as his main channel to Moscow, meeting with high-level Soviets to relate news and seek comment (and, implicitly, approval).

That Wednesday, the envoy reported to Rapacki the results of a talk with Brezhnev, who was busily preparing his secret report to the CPSU's Central Committee the following Monday on the international situation and the world Communist movement. With a new, perhaps more dangerous phase of the Sino-Soviet conflict at hand, the party boss set to put his personal imprint on policy. He had just returned from Budapest, where he had pressed his campaign for a world conference of Communist parties to "elaborate a common line for the future"—that is, to line up behind Moscow and against Beijing. Brezhnev's remarks to the Congress of the ruling Hungarian Socialist Workers' Party, in turn, echoed, a bit more strongly, his words in Sofia two weeks earlier. Meanwhile, *Pravda* launched a violent offensive against the Chinese, singling out Mao for "duplicity" and a personality cult and virtually urging his ouster.[12]

Vietnam featured prominently in Moscow's indictment. Alongside sins of "nationalism," the outrageous Cultural Revolution, and "slanderous" claims of Soviet collusion with imperialism stood the charge that Beijing had rejected joint aid to the heroic Vietnamese. Such broadsides left unstated, however, private Soviet Bloc complaints that the Chinese, blinded by revolutionary zeal, had consistently pressured Hanoi against entering negotiations—the topic on which Poland's envoy had called.

Per his minister's instructions, Pszczółkowski set up the talk with Brezhnev to report on Lewandowski's December 1 meeting with Lodge, and also the stern criticisms Rapacki had directed him to relay regarding the Hanoi raids; the envoy to Moscow also explained vaguely that "complications" had delayed the first U.S.-DRV contact.[13]

Brezhnev praised Poland's (and Lewandowski's) actions. Yet, with a hint of envy, he "expressed some regret that the Vietnamese did not turn to the USSR for help regarding the talks with the Americans, since they could significantly help in this matter given [that] they have greater capabilities to exert pressure on the Americans."[14]

Brezhnev's belief that Moscow could have been more persuasive than Warsaw in urging LBJ to curb bombing in exchange for an authoritative commitment that the DRV would enter serious, direct peace discussions was hardly far-fetched: Rusk, distrusting the Poles, would certainly have taken Gromyko's word more seriously; Brezhnev may also have resented being excluded from a prestigious diplomatic triumph.

Turning to Warsaw instead of Moscow was just the latest affront; North Vietnam's failure to confide or coordinate military, diplomatic, or intelligence actions, whether out of deference to China, their own innate stealth, or some combination, repeatedly irked the Kremlin. Most recently, in late November, top DRV figures had transited Moscow on their way to and from Eastern Europe, but, to their hosts' annoyance, were not candid about military or political strategy, contacts with Beijing, or secret peace probes; and in Hanoi, Dong conspicuously refused to discuss the Polish initiative with Shcherbakov (who flew home for medical treatment on December 5[15]). Even as they backed Hanoi to the hilt through gritted teeth, the Soviets had to rely on Rapacki's envoy for news.

Still—significantly—Brezhnev had high hopes that the Polish peace effort might bear fruit. Contrary to some U.S. suspicions, he saw it as far more than a propaganda gambit. The Hanoi raids amid the dicey diplomacy dumbfounded the Soviet, who confessed that he "did not understand what goals the Americans were making for themselves." "Overall," he calculated, recent moves "seemed to point to some change" in the two sides' postures, and "the end to the military activities in Vietnam would enable the Vietnamese to free themselves from the Chinese pressure and to assume a more independent position."

At the plenum, Brezhnev divulged, he would sharply criticize Mao and the Chinese Communist Party and fully describe Soviet aid to Hanoi, rebuffing Beijing's charges of miserliness (not to mention collusion in U.S. peace plots). He asked the Poles to keep him informed.

While Warsaw kept the Kremlin apprised, Washington sought its help. That Wednesday, Llewellyn Thompson (soon to replace Foy D. Kohler as ambassador to the USSR) handed Dobrynin a letter from LBJ to Premier Kosygin for the envoy, about to head home for the plenum, to deliver. Drafted by Rusk, it dwelt nonpolemically on the need for peace in Vietnam, stressing that Moscow and Washington, despite disputing the war's origins, shared an interest in rapidly ending it. Vowing to respect North Vietnam's security and sympathizing with its difficulty in entering talks due to Chinese pressure, LBJ voiced his readiness for contacts "either directly or through an intermediary" and solicited "any efforts you may be able to make to bring to an end this conflict."

The missive ended with a delicate allusion to Marigold, which had been added at the last minute after Lewandowski assured Lodge that the Soviets were witting. LBJ noted that he had received via the U.S. ambassador in Saigon "an important message from the Polish representative, Mr. Lewandowski, about which I am told you have been informed. We shall be giving this urgent consideration."[16] As Dobrynin read the letter, Thompson—in the spirit of Lodge's warning against seeming too eager—added that Moscow should not view the appeal for aid in opening talks as meaning that "we were desperate or that the situation was developing badly from our point of view."

Dobrynin asked about the Polish message—apparently the first the plugged-in Soviet diplomat had heard of the affair. Thompson warily described it "in very general terms" and did not elucidate the ten points. Instead, he said that Washington did not know exactly what Hanoi had heard (because Lewandowski's messages were oral, not written); yet it stood ready to confirm that the Pole's statement was "broadly in line with our position."[17] Dobrynin promised to hand the letter to Kosygin himself, but he cautioned against expecting a quick reply due to the press of plenum business.

Warsaw: "Policy Is More Important than Weather"
By midday Wednesday, reverberations of Siedlecki's talk that morning in Hanoi (the dead of night in Warsaw) were reaching Poland's capital. Quang received (by cable, presumably) what Trinh termed "appropriate instructions," and Michałowski called a directive that "he not begin the talks [with Gronouski] for the moment."[18]

Michałowski gave no source for this assertion; did he infer the sending of these instructions from what DRV officials told Siedlecki or have some other basis? A hint that he heard directly from Quang appears in a book by a Washington-based British reporter whose accuracy Michałowski lauded. In Warsaw that Wednesday, it asserts, Quang told the Poles that Hanoi was "reviewing the situation" after the latest bombings; he had instructions to see Gronouski but awaited further "guidance as to the substance of their discussions" and was "still uncertain whether, if there were talks, he would represent Hanoi or whether a special representative would be sent."[19] Subsequently available Polish and Vietnamese evidence renders this account puzzling: Quang's reported December 7 statement indicating that the U.S. raids had provoked a reconsideration fits Dong's words that morning to Siedlecki, yet his latter remarks make no sense if, in fact, Phuong had already arrived at least two days before, bearing more detailed guidance.[20]

✳ ✳ ✳

Just as Quang felt a restraining hand from Hanoi, Gronouski got a pat on the back from Washington. After flying "blind but skillfully" with Rapacki, he awoke Wednesday to find Katzenbach's telegram bearing the sacred ten points and examples of potential "differences of interpretation." During the day, more cables arrived, finally providing Marigold's background since the summer, including the instructions sent to Lodge in mid-November—the material later accounts mistakenly suggested that he had already read the preceding weekend. Having "made it pretty clear to Washington that I felt pretty much at a disadvantage," he recalled, he "started getting stuff by the reams, I mean to repeats of telegrams way back to June. And I was reading until I couldn't quit. So I got very well briefed."[21] To the neophyte diplomat's relief, he no longer had to bluff; finally, he held a playable hand that included far greater knowledge of the transactions in Saigon and a fuller degree of his own government's confidence.

Though Katzenbach told him to take no further initiative with the Poles, Gronouski figured that they should any time now get Hanoi's reply to the U.S. statement delivered the previous day and eagerly awaited the call heralding his next round with Rapacki—and, he hoped, his first meeting with North Vietnam's ambassador.

✳ ✳ ✳

In fact, the MSZ's cipher section decoded Siedlecki's telegram to Rapacki relating his talk with Dong at 2 p.m. Wednesday.[22] In response to this report—plus more accounts flowing in of the December 4 raid, and perhaps Quang's demarche—Rapacki summoned Gronouski at 6 p.m. for their third meeting in as many days, but now in a far fouler mood.

Echoing Dong's anger, though in his own name, Rapacki blasted the Hanoi bombings and warned that together with the interpretation clause they seemed a pressure tactic, perhaps a deliberate effort to scuttle the talks. "In these circumstances, I wouldn't see a possibility of fulfilling by Poland of its role in a fruitful way," he warned. Warsaw would cease trying to arrange the U.S.-DRV contact unless Washington stopped striking such sensitive targets and eliminated the risk that the interpretation clause would sap Hanoi's confidence in Lewandowski's description of the U.S. position. "It is necessary to gain clarity on these two points fairly early," he declared sharply. When Gronouski again argued that the raids were set earlier and delayed until the skies cleared, the Pole retorted: "Policy is more important than weather."

After Rapacki again implored Washington to desist from further provocations, above all more strikes on Hanoi, Gronouski asked if his remarks reflected the DRV's reaction. The minister "emphatically" denied this, but Gronouski shrewdly and correctly inferred that the Pole's summons "at an unusually late hour to express a much tougher position than he did yesterday could very well reflect Hanoi's response to the message transmitted by Rapacki to Hanoi yesterday."[23] Of course, one might attribute Rapacki's deceptive comments to protocol, because he could only take responsibility for himself and Poland rather than serve as a mouthpiece in a U.S.-DRV dialogue.

Harder to explain or justify, however, is his failure to relay, *in any form,* Dong's comment that if Gronouski "knocks at the door of our embassy . . . he will be received." Why did he not suggest or at least hint that the American do exactly that? Did he still hope to obtain a U.S. commitment to a bombing halt and/or retraction of the interpretation clause before a first direct contact? Did he believe, not unreasonably, that otherwise, given Hanoi's ire, a face-to-face U.S.-DRV meeting would be fruitless?

Perhaps. But Rapacki's delaying tactic proved a perhaps fatal miscalculation. It would have been far better for him to urge Gronouski to "cross the bridge" to Quang—to make contact, break the ice, and confirm that the ten points "broadly" reflected U.S. policy—before events foreclosed that possibility. Instead, the Wednesday evening talk ended with Gronouski believing that Hanoi still had not authorized any direct encounter. He cabled Rapacki's criticisms and request for "clarity" to Washington for reaction.

Washington: "Enough Possibility to Warrant Serious Action"

Washington's reaction was summed up by Rostow's comment to Johnson as he relayed Gronouski's cable—which reached Washington late Wednesday afternoon—to Texas shortly before 9 p.m.: "This is the latest from Warsaw. They are trying to get us to de-escalate bombing in order merely to see a North Vietnamese. We shall take counsel together and make recommendations to you."[24]

Reading over Gronouski's message, U.S. officials sensed that it was time to put up or shut up. As they pondered a response to Warsaw's demands to stop the intensified bombing and jettison the interpretation clause, the imperative to hang tough and evade a Polish trap mingled with concern about perhaps blowing the only chance for progress on the horizon and exposing Washington to international condemnation once the affair went public. Into the night, the State Department Marigold crew (Katzenbach, Unger, Thompson, and Read), checking periodically with McNamara and Rostow, hashed out two key documents embodying the next steps for Gronouski—and Washington—to take.

The first, a cable sent to Warsaw late Wednesday night, was a climb-down from the hotly contested interpretation clause.[25] Modifying earlier instructions, it directed Gronouski, if he met his DRV counterpart, first to stress that Lewandowski conducted his diplomacy "entirely orally"—"no pieces of paper have been exchanged which purport to state government positions"—then read aloud the ten points (interjecting the Phase A/B formula) and declare that this statement, though Lewandowski's phrasing, "presents a general statement of the U.S. position on the basis of which we would be prepared to enter into direct discussions." To edify Gronouski—in a passage whose editing hinted at U.S. uncertainty over the whole affair—Katzenbach explained that Washington preferred endorsing the Pole's language to advancing its own because doing so "would oblige us to take some harder positions than those put forward by Lewandowski which ~~possibly~~ apparently have gone far enough to make the North Vietnamese ready to ~~talk~~ consider talking with us"; a U.S. statement, moreover, could not be disavowed if Hanoi used it to "embarrass" Saigon or hurt U.S.-RVN relations. This strategy preserved "some room for maneuver at least until we know the discussions are really under way."

Without formally invoking the offending clause, Gronouski was prompted, after reciting the ten points, to "point out" to his DRV colleague that "some matters, because of their complexity and the danger of varying interpretations" (e.g., the mechanisms of a bombing halt), required "further elaboration" once substantive direct talks started. If Hanoi's man—U.S. documents rarely referred by name to Quang, and throughout Marigold he remained, to the Americans, more vague abstraction than flesh-and-blood individual—raised the clause, Gronouski should deny it signaled any retreat from the ten points and note the "normal" and "inevitable" process of clarifying "complex and controversial" matters during negotiations.

Katzenbach closed on an upbeat note. "We understand from your latest reports that the next step, if all goes well, will be the opening of the direct discussions with the North Vietnamese and if this in fact materializes you should avoid any further substantive discussions with the Poles." If Warsaw again reverted to the clause issue before any direct encounter occurred, Gronouski could say that he had "now consulted with Washington" and could confirm to Hanoi's ambassador that the U.S. stand would be "consistent with the discussions which Lewandowski has had with them and with us." No qualifications, hedges, reservations, or escape hatches need fetter this statement; those who devised the clause in the first place were now willing to abandon it, under Polish duress.

Rapacki's bombing demand, however, presented a thornier problem, partly because it meant revoking authorizations LBJ had OK'd after lengthy and contentious internal debate, but also because it stirred doubt about Polish motives. From his own perspective, Rapacki (echoing Lewandowski and Michałowski) merely pleaded to avoid *further* escalation (like hitting Hanoi again) at this sensitive juncture, not to reduce or (as Rostow put it) "de-escalate" bombing. Yet, the request hardened already acute American skepticism into suspicion that the whole initiative was a Communist plot to lure Washington into a bombing halt or other concrete concessions in exchange for the dangled, perhaps illusory, prospect of direct talks.

Nevertheless, seeing no other game in town, senior officials unanimously agreed that it was worth taking that gamble, and, in McNamara's word, "desperately" advised LBJ against further attacks on Hanoi so long as Marigold remained a live proposition.[26]

Katzenbach incorporated their views into a crucial memorandum to LBJ, drafted late Wednesday evening, proposing that Gronouski give Rapacki a mixed reply.[27] On one hand, he should "deny escalation and take steps to discourage further meddling" by Rapacki; yet on the other hand, Katzenbach recognized that additional raids on Hanoi would be seen as an escalation by the North Vietnamese, who "might get their backs up and refuse to negotiate at this time. Even if this were not true," he added, "it could be used by the Poles as an excuse for their failure to deliver the North Vietnamese for negotiations in Warsaw, thus leading to another U Thant–type 'revelation' at some future time." Moreover, he noted, Sweden's ambassador to China (involved in the "Aspen" feelers) would visit Hanoi from December 12 to 15, the pope would soon appeal for a holiday truce, and "similar peace exhortations" were emanating from other quarters.[28]

"For all of these reasons," Katzenbach asserted, "we believe there should be a review of current bombing schedules with a view to avoiding targets close in to Hanoi." Though advising against any explicit promises to the Poles about targeting, he gave LBJ several bombing options, from sticking to current plans to excluding Hanoi in the immediate future—which would please Rapacki "but could be interpreted by him or North Vietnam as a sign of weakness and whet their appetites for cessation or at least more concessions." Stating that McNamara, Rostow, and Thompson agreed, Katzenbach concluded that "all of us are skeptical as to exactly what Warsaw can and will produce, but there is still enough possibility to warrant serious action on our side. There is no better negotiating possibility currently in the works and a failure with respect to this possibility would probably prejudice other feelers in the near future."[29]

To put these conclusions into effect, Katzenbach enclosed with the memo to LBJ a draft cable to Gronouski containing instructions for his next meeting with the Pole.[30] It would direct him to "assure [Rapacki] that we had no intention in carrying out our bombing pattern to bring pressure on North Vietnam in relation to the projected talks with them." There had been, he could state, "no change in the types of targets which have been attacked—railway yards, missile sites and missile storage, POL [petroleum, oil, and lubricants] and vehicle depots"—and he should eschew any promises of a "radical change" in bombing plans, which were set well in advance and could not be modified without attracting notice.

However, the crux of the proposed instructions came in the next sentence, bracketed for LBJ's attention: "*[Nevertheless, we are reviewing our plans and will do what we can within the limits of maintaining the security of the projected talks to avoid what might appear as a further intensification.]*" Without explicitly saying so, the statement clearly implied a pledge to forswear further raids on Hanoi while the proposed Warsaw contact remained in play. Katzenbach informed LBJ that he, McNamara, and Thompson made a "strong recommendation" to keep the bracketed sentence—and Rostow, too, believed it "wise" to retain it as "essential to the linking of phases A and B."[31]

Omitting the interpretation clause, the proposed guidance would let Gronouski assure Rapacki that Washington was ready to negotiate Lewandowski's ten points "in the same terms which we affirmed to him." But it also warned sternly that U.S. patience was running out: "If Rapacki attempt[s] to nail us to anything on bombing beyond our first contact with the North Vietnamese, or again threatens to break off the operation, you should inform him in no uncertain terms that if he maintains this position he will have to accept the full responsibility for the breakdown of what appears to us to be a promising possibility for peace."

The White House communications center sent Katzenbach's memo and the draft cable to Gronouski to the LBJ Ranch at 1:22 a.m. on Thursday. Anticipating presidential concurrence, a copy of the proposed message to Warsaw was left overnight with a State Department watch officer who could await word from the White House Situation Room so it could be dispatched in time for Gronouski's next meeting with Rapacki.

Now it would be up to Lyndon Baines Johnson to make the final determination. Would he suspend raids on Hanoi while Marigold remained alive, as Rapacki demanded and his own senior national security advisers in Washington fervently urged? Or would the bombing plans go forward unaltered, despite Polish warnings (echoed by his own aides) that more such attacks would kill the chance of a direct contact with a DRV representative on a potential mutually acceptable deal to end the war?

Thursday, December 8

Taipei: Rusk Weighs In

Of course, the secret deliberations lacked the direct participation or approval of one key figure: Rusk, who was touring the Pacific Rim to rally support and if possible more troops for the war.[32] Since leaving for Asia on Sunday, he had flown to Tokyo—where the Japanese proposed their own peace feelers through the DRV Embassy in Moscow[33]—and Taiwan, monitoring Marigold via telegrams forwarding the Warsaw-Washington cable traffic. From the start, Rusk and Bundy (who came along) looked askance at the Polish effort, and Rapacki's behavior did not allay their skepticism. Warsaw's ire at the Hanoi raids, Bundy felt, seemed "rather phony as we read the cables on the trip," though had "enough plausibility to be of concern," and the carping over the interpretation clause impressed them even less.[34]

Satisfied with Katzenbach's and Gronouski's cautious approach, Rusk at first held back from intervening, perhaps not wanting to second-guess his stand-in, still fairly new to the job. But Thursday, knowing that Washington had to reply to Rapacki's demand that it forswear further raids on Hanoi, Rusk cabled from Taipei his antipathy (which Bundy shared) to any unilateral promises. Unlike Katzenbach, Rusk had gauged LBJ's comparably dubious perspective firsthand in the plane over Texas the previous Saturday. The United States should be "perfectly prepared" to talk with Hanoi about a bombing halt in the context of a mutual drawdown of fighting, he stated, but "I do not believe we should be drawn into commitments about our own military operations without some indication from the other side as to what they are going to do about their military operations."

Rusk's cable, contradicting the strong inclination of Katzenbach, McNamara, Thompson, and even Rostow to suspend bombing Hanoi for the moment, reached Washington at 1:32 a.m. Thursday morning—too late to sway their advice, but not too late to influence Johnson's response.[35]

Texas: "It's Clean as a Whistle Now"
Until now, LBJ was content to stay in the background. After his approval to move ahead in Saigon and Warsaw on learning of Lodge's report of his talk with Lewandowski on December 1, he had refrained from overt intervention in the decision-making process, letting the State Department, advised by McNamara and monitored by Rostow, handle the initiative.

His seeming hands-off approach, however, did not signal a lack of interest—quite the contrary. Johnson monitored Marigold "enormously closely" and "hovered over the cables," which Rostow religiously bounced from Washington to Texas. Rusk's (and then Katzenbach's) executive assistant recalled Rostow badgering him on the president's behalf to learn whether the latest report from Warsaw had arrived.[36]

LBJ's Marigold management was more "hidden hand" than "hands off."[37] Reading Katzenbach's memo and draft instructions to Gronouski Thursday morning, he opted for the first time in Marigold to overrule his senior aides. And to make his will known, rather than respond personally to Katzenbach, he turned to his trusted minion, Rostow. The night before, the hawkish national security adviser had, surprisingly, joined Katzenbach, McNamara, and Thompson in arguing that Marigold, and even the slippery Rapacki, deserved enough benefit of the doubt to shelve, at least temporarily, plans for more raids on Hanoi, both on the off chance the initiative might actually yield progress and to mitigate the risk of a "Thant-type 'revelation.'"

But when Johnson called Rostow Thursday morning, he quickly got the message that, as Bundy later put it, the president just "did not buy" the arguments in Katzenbach's memo. The 8:20 a.m. phone call was not recorded, but Bundy imagined LBJ's reaction to the counsel to cancel further Hanoi bombing: "'No, I'm not going to call it off.' And I can surmise as his reasons: that there was no condition about calling it off, 'These fellows are stalling, the thing looks like a phony, etcetera, etcetera.' . . . They had not made it a demand, but the Poles were raising all kinds of fuss about it. In effect, it was an almost added thing—added in—and the President did not like to do business that way."[38] One analyst plausibly suspects that Johnson was loath to offend the Joint Chiefs of Staff, who were "incensed" by McNamara's readiness to curtail air strikes to enhance peace prospects.[39] Contemporaneously corroborating this view in his private diary, John T. McNaughton, the assistant secretary of defense for international security affairs and McNamara's closest aide, astutely noticed a "diminution" in his boss's power and "less harmony" between him and the president as the latter tilted toward a tougher stance more congenial to the Joint Chiefs.[40] It was a harbinger of a deeper rift to come, one that would hasten McNamara's exit from the administration within a year.

In his memoirs, LBJ indicated that his doubts about Marigold had already crystallized: "I realized this channel was a dry creek when the North Vietnamese failed to show up for the critical meeting the Poles had promised to arrange in Warsaw on December 6, 1966. . . . The simple truth, I was convinced, was that the North Vietnamese were not ready to talk to us. The Poles had not only put the cart before the horse, when the time of reckoning came, they had no horse."[41] In cattleman vernacular, he thought the Poles were trying to hornswoggle him.

Johnson not only rejected but also bristled at the advice to tell Warsaw that no further raids on Hanoi were in the offing. "Soft" and "mushy," an aide penned atop the copy of the draft cable to Gronouski on State Department stationery (as opposed to the decoded copy LBJ read at his ranch).[42] Were those words scrawled by an official listening to the president when he phoned his reaction? They might as well have been. They evoked his visceral determination not to play along with Rapacki's games, which likely reminded him of the Pole's maneuvers in the waning hours of the thirty-seven-day bombing pause. After hearing the new line, Rostow dutifully called Katzenbach to relay his boss's directive to remove the bracketed sentence or any other reassurances on bombing from the cable to Gronouski.

The acting secretary did as he was told, and excised the vow to avoid "further intensification" of bombing and claim that there had been "no change" in targeting. "It's clean as a whistle now," Rostow assured LBJ after seeing the redraft before the considerably toughened cable was flashed to Warsaw at 2:29 p.m. Thursday afternoon.[43]

Decades later, Katzenbach seemed disappointed but unsurprised at Johnson's final decision—"I'm sure he was angry with the Poles and didn't want to do anything"—and bitterly bemused at Rostow's abrupt defection from the antibombing recommendation the instant he discerned where his boss stood. Smiling equably on a sunny spring afternoon in the book-lined study of his Princeton house, its wall crowded with signed portraits of JFK, RFK, LBJ, and MLK, Katzenbach recalled that Rostow was "as nice a person as ever lived" but that sometimes, in policy matters, "would stab us in the back."[44]

Saigon: "Anguished Considerations"

As more detailed accounts of the Hanoi bombings on December 2 and 4 streamed in, supplemented by (inflated or erroneous) reports of fresh raids, Lewandowski grew even more pessimistic and upset. Eager to show his Vietnamese comrades he was doing *something,* he sought and received permission to request an emergency ICC session to denounce the attacks[45]—a hopeless gesture, he knew, but better than total passivity. One had to be naive, he felt, to believe that the United States had hit Hanoi on December 2 and especially December 4 by coincidence rather than in a blatant attempt to coerce the DRV into concessions and, in so doing, sabotage the imminent contact; hence, the sole chance to salvage the effort was a recovery by pro-peace forces in Washington. "I was never a specialist on the United States," he recalled, "but I was in the United States, in New York, and I was not a novice, so, only, my hope was, maybe there are some fractions within the U.S. government fighting, one for the military solution, more bombing, [the other saying,] 'Let's try a peaceful solution,' you know, and I prayed that the fraction which is opting for the negotiations will win."[46] Rusk's impending arrival in Saigon, he thought, might offer a fortuitous opportunity to influence the struggle he presumed was ongoing within the Johnson administration.

Thursday evening, as Washington sent its stand to Warsaw, Lewandowski sought out D'Orlandi to deliver a message similar to the one Rapacki gave Gronouski, but more personal and fervent.[47] Citing eyewitness reports from Poland's military attaché in Hanoi, he ripped the December 2 raids—"indiscriminate and savage" strikes on southern suburbs and "cannon fire and strafing of the city center itself," leaving "over 600" dead and hurt (a gross exaggeration[48])—and used "blistering words" to rap those two days later.

The Pole found it incomprehensible and infuriating that Washington could launch this quantitative and qualitative escalation after a fortnight of relative decline just as the delicate secret effort neared fruition. "Everybody knows," he said heatedly, "that if negotiations are taking place reduction in the bombing is expected or at least not an increase in intensity; [but] in our case, [just as in late June,] serious escalation of the bombing has followed every significant agreement!" As for the claim that the attacks' timing stemmed from "meteorological conditions," that was unconvincing as well as banal, for Lewandowski was in Hanoi in late November and the city enjoyed "beautiful" weather. Sensing U.S. bad faith—not, he stressed, on the part of Lodge, presumably unaware of such machinations—the Pole charged that, as in earlier abortive overtures, America had dangled an interest in talks and pulled back when North Vietnam reacted positively. Only with great difficulty, he revealed, had he dissuaded Hanoi—"(of all days—on the 6th!)"—from issuing a public protest that would have scuttled a direct meeting once and for all; he feared the Warsaw contact was dying before it could even get born. Knowing that D'Orlandi would see Rusk the next evening, he implored him to persuade the American of "the insanity of such a provocation," because neither side could win an outright victory and the war could drag on indefinitely were the present chance squandered.

Aghast at Lewandowski's "frightening" report of "this infamous bombing" and sharing his fear that it could destroy the chance for peace, D'Orlandi pledged to relay his "anguished considerations" to Rusk. But having sympathetically heard out his friend's "diatribe," the Italian also had sharp words for Rapacki. His failure to arrange the first U.S.-DRV meeting also imperiled the initiative, he scolded, and his harping on the interpretation clause before relaying Washington's statement to Hanoi fanned suspicions that he was stalling to extort better terms—for example, a bombing halt, not part of the original deal.

We would both be better poised to make a request of the Americans, he said, if the first direct contact had already occurred. The Pole, unaware that Siedlecki had already given Dong the U.S. statement the morning before, conceded that he, too, felt Rapacki's refusal to immediately relay it inappropriate; he had urged him to do so as soon as possible and hoped within hours to confirm its delivery.

Lewandowski's words left D'Orlandi distraught yet clinging to hope. If only the first U.S.-DRV meeting could occur—even if consumed by an angry Vietnamese protest against the bombings—it would get the ball rolling, he felt. The time needed to surmount friction over the bombings might even allow the Saigon diplomats, united by common purpose and understanding, to remain engaged, smoothing out inevitable bumps in the road (e.g., disputes over the ten points). The other immediate imperative was to prevent further air raids from shattering the already-fragile situation. Almost miraculously, coincidental circumstances had given the Italian a "decisive" chance to confront Rusk face to face the very next evening with his "impassioned arguments," backed, he hoped, by an "authoritative appeal" from Fanfani. "My optimism," he wrote in his diary,

> is based above all on the relationships of trust, esteem and friendship among the three of us, and on the understanding which has derived from it. It is by now clear that the dinner with Rusk and Cabot Lodge on Friday will be decisive; it is absolutely necessary that these damned bombings cease. In addition, it is necessary that the U.S. note be delivered by Rapacki to the North Vietnamese. [D'Orlandi did not know that he had already done so.] As things now stand, the negotiation could not go worse. The three of us in Saigon no longer have any task or any authority, but no one has replaced us so far. May the contact in Warsaw be established and may God help them.[49]

Warsaw: Waiting Games

On a frigid, cloudy Thursday, with occasional flurries, Gronouski waited. For the first time since Sunday, no summons came from the MSZ; and only that evening did the State Department's "clean as a whistle" instructions arrive with marching orders for the next talk with Rapacki: Do not insist on the clause, deny variants in bombing related to the secret peace diplomacy, and talk tough if the Pole "attempts to nail us" on further concessions.

Also that night, the ambassador, after the previous day's confidence-boosting infusion of fresh information on Marigold, found himself chastised by Washington for seeking too much data. Wanting the latest, fullest reports to rebut Polish charges, he had cabled the Defense Intelligence Agency requesting "up-to-date information on our bombings of North Vietnam, . . . number and types of sorties, target location, estimated damage, and our losses." Instead, he got a slap on the wrist: Katzenbach gently edified the amateur diplomat on the ways of the world— that is, how to keep secrets within his own government's classified realms. His request, he was told, was widely distributed in the Pentagon and circulated to the State Department through "routine channels for such messages, thereby alerting many officers in both Departments to request." Considering the "overriding need for security of MARIGOLD exercise," it risked attracting "undesirable attention." Why should the envoy to Warsaw, of all places, suddenly make such a demand?

To alleviate this little headache, the seventh floor told Gronouski to expect "through identical channels a routine, bland denial to the request"—which he should show all embassy aides who had seen his earlier message. Then he would be supplied—*through this channel only!*—"information essential to effective handling of MARIGOLD."[50]

❋ ❋ ❋

Gronouski was not the only diplomat in Warsaw awaiting further developments in Marigold. Despite Tuesday's disappointment, Phuong remained in the capital —keeping mostly within the embassy grounds, venturing out occasionally (once to tour the old city, rebuilt after the war), but not making any contact with Polish officials. He asked Quang if he should leave, but the ambassador said no.[51] The initiative was trapped in limbo, but as long as Phuong stayed put, one prerequisite for a direct contact was still in place.

Rome: A Papal Plea

One perennial contestant in the Vietnam peace sweepstakes, shunned by Hanoi but courted by Washington, Warsaw, and Rome, was the Vatican. For years, the Roman Catholic Church had dabbled in Vietnam politics, trying to defend the tattered remnants of its once-strong presence in the North after the French exit, and in the South, watching and occasionally mixing in Saigon's turmoil. In line with its opposition to "godless Communism," the Vatican backed the West in the

Cold War. But as the U.S. military role in Vietnam grew, Pope Paul VI sometimes irritated Washington with pleas for truces and talks even as American officials doubted the efficacy of such tactics and preferred to use force. Hoping to keep the pope on the reservation during the thirty-seven-day pause in the bombing, LBJ took special glee (for reasons that remain obscure) in sending a Jew—Goldberg—to the pontiff to plead the administration's case.[52] Fanfani also took pains to avoid alienating the Vatican on Vietnam: His zealous pursuit of peace, U.S. aides guessed, stemmed in part from his attentiveness to the pope's "presumed or actual preoccupation" with that aim.[53]

Poland, meantime, was keen to enhance ties to the Vatican. Though a loyal Soviet ally and, hence, a natural adversary, Gomułka had a vested interest in better relations as part of Warsaw's strategy of co-opting Poland's Roman Catholic Church, which enjoyed some autonomy despite the state's official atheism and vast secret police network. Marking a millennium of Polish Catholicism in 1966, the PZPR regime wanted to show that communism and religion could coexist cordially.[54] With this aim in mind, it cultivated the pope on Vietnam, hoping to wean him away from Washington.

In this courtship, Fanfani typically tried to play matchmaker. Since his July trip to Warsaw, he had tried to set up a meeting with the pope during Polish president Edward Ochab's planned visit to Italy. Such contacts could be "historically monumental," he told Rapacki, not only "unblocking the impasse" in Polish-Vatican ties but also opening a dialogue on such mutual interests as Vietnam peace and détente.[55] In promoting this mutual sniffing, Fanfani had to maneuver warily, lest he alienate Vatican hard-liners, the cantankerously antiregime Polish Catholic Church, or both—just as he faced a challenge in simultaneously getting enmeshed in Polish and Vatican peace bids.

Pursuing his by now traditional holiday truce effort, on Thursday, Pope Paul VI urged a merger of already-set "noble and chivalrous" separate forty-eight-hour Christmas and New Year's armistices into a "single continuous" cessation of violence "so that new ways may be explored of bringing about an honorable understanding putting an end to the conflict." Favoring as long a break in fighting as possible, he also endorsed extending such a truce to cover Tet, the Vietnamese lunar new year (February 8–12, 1967).[56]

U.S. officials had vainly tried to head off the pope's proposal. From Texas came polite official word that LBJ would give it "sympathetic consideration," but few had any illusions he would heed the papal plea. Given his anger at the results of the thirty-seven-day pause, he was hardly likely to jump at a fifty-one-day sequel. Reporters were told, predictably, that any prolonged cease-fire would merely hand Hanoi a golden opportunity to ramp up support to the southern insurgents, and there was no chance Washington would go along.[57] What matters is not the papal appeal's fate but that the Americans, Italians, and Poles involved in Marigold knew that the Pontiff, once he learned of it, would take an active interest in the secret initiative—and, if it collapsed, in ascertaining who was to blame.

Friday, December 9

Saigon: Rusk at Tan Son Nhut

At 11:08 a.m., about two hours after leaving Taipei, the Air Force plane bearing Rusk landed at Tan Son Nhut, still scarred by the recent fighting. Amid tight security, RVN foreign minister Tran Van Do and a party that included Westmoreland and Lodge greeted him. To reporters, Rusk splashed cold water on the papal truce appeal and, indeed, any speculation of progress. "I have no information from the other side that they're interested in moving this problem to the conference table," he said. "We have told them many times that if they will tell us what they will stop doing we will consider stopping the bombing. We can't stop just half the war; they've got to stop their half of it."[58]

Intoning the administration mantra, Rusk professed optimism and determination: "We are in a much stronger position than two years ago. The North Vietnamese are not going to be able to seize this country by force." Peace would come, he declared, "because it must. [The Communists] will not be able to succeed here." His public message proclaimed, the secretary joined Lodge for the short ride to the embassy.

Rusk's three-day Saigon sojourn coincided with the secret Marigold crisis, and his dismissive comments puzzled some observers aware of the diplomatic context. Were his remarks deliberately couched to conceal the exchanges taking place? Probably not. More likely, they reflected his genuine belief, then and later, that because the Poles could not be trusted, there was no reason to credit their claim that Hanoi had agreed to the direct meeting in Warsaw or signed on to Lewandowski's rendition of the U.S. position.

Rusk's arrival also coincided—he later noted bitterly—with a spike in Communist attacks around Saigon. "One can hear constantly the sounds of air and artillery bombing," as well as machine-gun fire, Lewandowski cabled Warsaw the day he arrived, in a joint U.S.-South Vietnamese drive to expel the Viet Cong from the city and surrounding areas, an effort that included B-52 strikes that rumbled from 20 miles away.[59]

Rome: Il Motorino "Heartily Encourages" Contacts

Just a few days before, Fanfani had congratulated his Saigon envoy for achieving a breakthrough toward peace, and he could imagine the plaudits that would shower him once it became generally known. But as the Hanoi raids raised fresh doubts, and as news of the first U.S.-DRV meeting failed to arrive, the foreign minister's unease mounted.

Characteristically, this ambitious, energetic politician (known as Il Motorino —"the Little Engine"), labored mightily to jump-start the stalled effort. First he had a chance to prod the Poles. Friday morning, Willmann stopped by to deliver his minister's (slightly outdated) perspective on the confusing situation in Warsaw. Blaming Washington for erecting new roadblocks, Rapacki's "strong demarche" explained that "very serious difficulties in beginning contacts there" had arisen due to the "renewed bombings" plus "ambiguities" and "misunderstandings in terminology" (i.e., the interpretation clause). It implored Fanfani to help resolve both issues so that Rapacki, "without risks," could "convey the noted document" (the U.S. statement, which in fact Warsaw had already sent to Hanoi) and "begin the indispensable contacts."

Coveting Rapacki's trust,[60] Fanfani responded favorably. Italy's foreign minister sent thanks, Willmann cabled, for his "intervention in the matter of suppressing the provocative bombings" and promised that D'Orlandi would also seek their "immediate cessation." He also vowed to try to clarify "ambiguities" and "misunderstandings" through D'Orlandi, "so there would not be any grounds for differences of interpretations."

Yet, like his man in Saigon, Fanfani fervently wished that Rapacki would stop tarrying, and urged him to hurry up—even without awaiting a satisfactory U.S. reply on the clause and the bombings—and broker the first direct contact. "He heartily encourages initiating, still within the coming days, activities, which were to have begun on 6 December," the Pole cabled, "and he insists on this all the more so since Cabot Lodge is departing Saigon on the 12th of this month for approximately 4–5 weeks." Fanfani, unaware that the Poles had already decisively transferred the action to Warsaw, feared that Lodge's absence might undermine the Saigon channel, thereby cutting Italy out.[61]

Having pushed the Poles, Fanfani turned to pressing the Americans. He had a dinner date with Rusk in Paris at the NATO ministerial the following Tuesday, but did not want to wait so long to get word to him—and did not have to. Aware that D'Orlandi would see the secretary that night, Fanfani quickly drafted an "office memo" to Saigon describing the talk with Willmann. In line with his vow to Rapacki, he instructed his envoy to press Rusk to suspend the Hanoi raids and dispel the confusion clouding U.S. peace terms due to the interpretation clause so the direct contacts in Warsaw could begin. Fanfani dispatched the message at noon, Rome time, already after nightfall in Vietnam.[62]

Saigon: "Crushing Our Most Precious Hopes"

By the time Fanfani's cable reached 135 Duong Pasteur at 7:45 p.m. Friday, Saigon time, D'Orlandi had already left for a secret rendezvous with Rusk at Lodge's residence a few blocks away. The job of decoding the telegram in the locked downstairs communications room fell to the first secretary, Mario Sica. No longer dependent on old equipment requiring hours of painstaking labor, Sica used the faster, easier Swiss machine that arrived after the *Borghese* leak. Because he was cognizant of Marigold's predicament, he was thrilled by Fanfani's blunt call for Washington to suspend the Hanoi bombings and was eager to put the message in D'Orlandi's hands in time to aid his talk with Rusk. So as soon as his task was done, he bolted into the night, sprinting along the darkened streets.

✳ ✳ ✳

Meanwhile, Rusk was nearing the end of a long, crowded day—a working lunch with civilian and military aides; briefings from Lodge, Porter, and Habib on the political situation in the capital and "Revolutionary Development" reforms in the countryside; a call on Tran Van Do; and a dinner party in his honor attended by Constituent Assembly members and other notables devoted more to chatting than eating. Now, while devouring a late supper, the secretary heard an impassioned case for the defense of Marigold from its most ardent advocate. By prearrangement with Lodge, who urged Rusk to take him seriously, D'Orlandi was ushered in for an off-the-books appointment. Finally, the Italian was able to recount the whole affair face to face to this key skeptic and convey his own and Lewandowski's acute worries.[63]

After watching the hours drag by all day, D'Orlandi had arrived promptly at Lodge's shortly before eight and was quickly seated to dine with the ambassador, Rusk, and a handful of senior aides—Porter and Habib from the embassy, and Bundy and spokesman Robert McCloskey from the secretary's traveling road show.

D'Orlandi "reminisce[d]" about his "free-wheeling" talks with Lewandowski since the summer, but did not help his own cause when he said that the Pole's suggested compromise coalition in Saigon consisted of "14 cabinet positions with 2 each for present Ky group and [Viet Cong / NLF], and remaining 10 allotted to 'neutrals or whatever.'" Rusk and Bundy recognized the formula as identical to that "given by D'Orlandi to Harriman, as D'Orlandi's own, in Rome conversation in early November"—hardening their suspicion that the Italians had succumbed to Polish manipulation and their own wishful thinking.

D'Orlandi reviewed the overture's history, but he focused on convincing Rusk that the Hanoi raids must stop to give it a chance. In conveying his Polish friend's arguments, he supplied the Americans, he reported afterward to Fanfani, "many details for the purpose of shining light on the gravity of the situation, Lewandowski's good faith and his sincere anxiety." He related the Pole's fear, shared by DRV leaders, that Washington sent a "tacit signal of U.S. support" by easing bombing during his recent visit but hawkish elements in Washington now sought to block negotiations; and his warning that more strikes "could only threaten or destroy possibility of contact in Warsaw," as "Hanoi could not be expected to enter discussions in face of such escalation."

To D'Orlandi's dismay, the Americans were unmoved. "The atmosphere was not very positive," he admitted in his diary. When he related Lewandowski's "grave concern" at the Hanoi raids, dramatized by "lurid" Polish Embassy reports of civilian casualties, McCloskey interjected that U.S. damage assessments were far less "alarmist" and the Pole was undoubtedly exaggerating.

Rusk himself had a ready retort: If North Vietnam charged U.S. "bad faith" by hitting Hanoi at a sensitive juncture, he too could lodge such an accusation given recent Viet Cong attacks on Saigon, including the airport where he had just land-ed. If Hanoi wished, he said, a bombing halt could be item one on their mutual agenda. Pleasing the Americans, D'Orlandi reported telling Lewandowski that the U.S.-DRV meeting in Warsaw had failed to occur due not to the Hanoi bomb-ings but to Rapacki's "apparent refusal" to convey U.S. readiness for a first contact on December 6; the Italian said he also stressed that "his hope had been to make contact in any event." Even without seeing reports on Gronouski's talks in War-saw that week, Rusk cabled, D'Orlandi "surmised that Rapacki had 'tried to be clever' and get U.S. to withdraw all reservations before contact [was] made"— exactly what had occurred, the Americans felt.

D'Orlandi, however, did not slavishly fall in line behind Washington. He re-butted Rusk's contention that Rapacki's tactics were "dictated from Moscow" and his doubts that Lewandowski had ever really obtained Hanoi's consent to the ten points. "One had to have a little faith in Lewandowski," Rusk quoted the Italian as saying, "and he appeared to credit completely Lewandowski claim that he had fi-nally got Pham Van Dong to obtain Presidium agreement to Warsaw contact."

Even more alarming, D'Orlandi wholly shared his Polish colleague's convic-tion that the December 2 and 4 bombings had severely imperiled the initiative and that more such raids must be avoided. The Italian's argument had "a very emotional pitch; . . . he was very evangelical about it," Bundy later recalled. "He obviously felt a sense of mission."

"You've got to not do any [more] of this," D'Orlandi pleaded. "This is some-thing that counts." Hearing Rusk's explanations and justifications, he still be-seeched, "Don't let's do it again. Whatever may or may not have been done, let's not do it again."[64]

Lacking a verbatim record, we cannot tell exactly what D'Orlandi told Rusk to disparage U.S. conduct—but after seeing the Italian the next morning, Lewan-dowski gathered that it amounted to a clear pinning of blame. "On his own initia-tive," the Pole cabled, "O. let R[usk] understand that the Italians cannot avoid the conclusion that the Americans are sabotaging the possibility of a peaceful resolu-tion to the conflict." From D'Orlandi, he heard Lodge also urged Rusk to "do 'something'" about the bombing.[65]

If D'Orlandi's echoing of Polish scolding annoyed the Americans—it helped make such a negative impression on Bundy that he later strongly warned Rusk against using him in peace efforts[66]—they were appalled to learn that Fanfani felt the same. Midway through the conversation (they had already left the table for postprandial liqueurs and smokes) a uniformed Marine interrupted to tell D'Orlandi that a man outside claimed he had an urgent message to deliver im-mediately; the Italian quickly telephoned the guard post to admit the fuming visitor and agreed to come meet him.

It was, of course, Sica. On reaching the heavily guarded "airy stucco villa"[67]— always a prime Viet Cong target, but especially with Rusk inside—he had to nav-igate barriers, sandbags, barbed wire, and armed sentry posts. At the final checkpoint, in the tropical garden surrounding the colonial-style residence, the courier requested to hand an important communication to Italy's ambassador. The Marine on duty, however, refused to disturb the elite gathering for the sake of an agitated, unexpected young foreigner. Sica, his annoyance mounting, pleaded, cajoled, and begged to speak with a superior.

The irritated Marine, after checking inside, told Sica that he could not bother the VIPs while they were still at the table.

"Are they having the cheese?" Sica asked, fearing that the guests were consuming the *formaggio* and about to disperse.

"But sir," the Marine replied, misunderstanding the question, "this is a full dinner and is not limited to a cheese sandwich."

After what seemed an eternity to Sica—probably less than ten minutes, he later guessed—the guard wearily relented and summoned Italy's ambassador. Moments later, D'Orlandi stepped onto the porch, dapper as ever in a white tuxedo, puffing a cigar, calm outwardly though inwardly despairing. After reading Fanfani's telegram, he neatly folded it and tucked it in a suit pocket. I have already argued to Rusk against any further bombings, he quietly told Sica, but now I will do so in the foreign minister's name.[68]

Returning to the group, D'Orlandi read Fanfani's message aloud to Rusk:

> Rapacki informed me today of the very great difficulties in beginning contacts there, consisting of misunderstandings in terminology regarding several noted issues and renewed bombings. Consequently, he asks that ambiguities be clarified and bombings be halted to allow him, without risks, to convey the noted document and begin indispensable contacts there. While I share in the above two requests, I wish to inform you of my having advised Rapacki to immediately convey noted document, and commence contacts even while awaiting the effects of above requests. You should take steps there to press for clarifications of terms and suspension of bombings, in order to make the start of the contacts possible and efficacious—said contacts which I called for as non-deferrable.[69]

Rusk could derive comfort from hearing that his Italian counterpart had petitioned Rapacki to get direct talks going in Warsaw without further delay. But Fanfani's urgent request to suspend attacks on Hanoi underlined the embarrassing fact—which Lodge's detailed cable reporting the conversation omitted[70]—that a NATO ally had heretically sided with a Warsaw Pact enemy in this testy secret dispute over whether the U.S. raids might have derailed the peace effort.

D'Orlandi correctly feared that his animated performance, even with Fanfani's support, had failed to dent Rusk's skepticism, or persuade him or his retinue that the Polish initiative was credible enough to merit suspending bombing plans. Bundy recalled: "We didn't so recommend—the Secretary did not so recommend in so many words."[71] Instead, in his cable, Rusk pointedly refused to endorse Lewandowski's calls to limit raids, and, as noted, failed to mention comparable appeals by D'Orlandi or Fanfani (let alone Lodge). Having told D'Orlandi that he might have more to say to him before leaving Saigon pending developments in Warsaw, Rusk asked the State Department's advice as to what more, if anything, the Italian should be told.[72]

After taking leave of Lodge and Rusk, D'Orlandi returned to his embassy, where Sica and Sergio Emina, another consigliere in on the peace bid, anxiously waited. After commiserating, D'Orlandi drafted cables for Fanfani and, more emotionally, wrote in his diary. Hearing how the Saigon channel had been discarded in favor of the desultory talks in Warsaw left him "with a bad feeling," but the Americans' chilly response to his ardent pleas to stop the bombing depressed him far more. Rusk's placid assurance that a U.S. decision on further raids would come soon produced a "dreadful" impression, "because I sensed the obvious contradiction between the asserted fortuitousness of the bombings on the 2nd and the 4th—which were [according to the Americans] not known to the State Department nor to the President—and the reluctance to suspend them, and then because I got the impression that Rusk wants to negotiate the suspension which would take us back to the initial starting point of our tripartite attempt, thwarting the efforts of these last five months and crushing our most precious hopes."

Warsaw: "A Definite Change for the Better"
Meanwhile, in Poland's capital late Friday afternoon, the conversation between Gronouski and Rapacki, their fourth since Monday, went well.[73] Holding fresh guidance from Washington, this time the American requested they meet; following now-established custom, Michałowski and an MSZ interpreter sat in. Gronouski promised that at his first encounter with Hanoi's ambassador he could confirm that the U.S. stand was "consistent" with the ten points (abandoning the interpretation clause) and—while stoutly denying any connection between the current bombing and possible talks—noted that a "de-escalation" "package" could be considered once U.S.-DRV exchanges commenced.

Rapacki expressed disappointment that Washington still had not "achieved clarity" on its planned presentation at the first meeting with the DRV and had neglected political factors in bombing Hanoi at such a delicate moment. He would regret having to tell the North Vietnamese that the Americans were conducting "military business as usual," ignoring Warsaw's repeated pleas to avoid provocative actions "particularly when critical decisions are at stake" and effectively reneging on Lodge's mid-November pledge to Lewandowski that they would show good faith in approaching negotiations.

Gronouski replied with a fervid defense of U.S. sincerity, and he stressed the need for direct meetings to ease inevitable mutual distrust. Typically, he spoke in personal terms; never before during his time in Warsaw had prospects for a negotiated peace been so bright, he said. Sure, any U.S.-DRV exchanges would face daunting odds, but that did not excuse failing to "bend every effort to induce Hanoi to begin the Warsaw talks."

"No one knows whether these talks, once begun, will succeed or fail, but that is a risk worth taking," he said. "If they succeeded, nothing that [you] or I do in a lifetime would have been quite so important."

But, he stressed, it was "essential" to take the first step: "Nothing will be accomplished unless we begin the meetings. . . . It would be criminal if after having reached this point their efforts and ours to get the two parties together failed. I hoped and trusted that the Poles would do their best to bring about a commencement of negotiations."

Hearing this earnest appeal, Michałowski nodded affirmatively several times and Rapacki softened. The Americans, he acknowledged, evidently put great value on the first contact. "It looked as if we could move forward," he said. "You know the reasons for our concern: What basis do I have in our conversations to dispel suspicions of other side arising out of intensified bombing, bombing of Hanoi, the 'important differences of interpretation' clause? In such circumstances it is difficult for me to get a reply, to move the matter forward. There is not much material for this. It is not easy and we will have to wait and see what happens." He vowed to be in touch if news arrived, and the two parted.

The conversation encouraged both men. Though his readout to PZPR comrades accentuated the negative—Washington's refusal to eschew further "provocative" military acts—Rapacki interpreted the session as "a definite change for the better in behavior"[74] and immediately sent an account to Hanoi. In his own cable to Washington, Gronouski noted that Rapacki had taken a "much less intransigent" posture than two days before and found Michałowski's nonverbal communications an auspicious omen; because Rapacki did not repeat his earlier threat to cut off discussions, he left unsaid the menacing language he had received blaming Poland for ruining a "promising possibility for peace."

But as darkness and snow fell, neither Rapacki nor Gronouski knew that more raids on Hanoi would momentarily be under consideration in Washington.

Washington: "Carry Forward with What Was Necessary"

For the first time in weeks, Johnson returned from Texas to the nation's capital, enjoying a run of unseasonable, sunny warmth. After *Air Force One* landed at Andrews Air Force Base at 1:43 p.m., he helicoptered to the White House, where he greeted aides and dogs (Blanco, Freckles, and J. Edgar), then walked to the Oval Office; after a haircut, he met top civilian and military aides off the record to review Rolling Thunder–52 bombing plans.[75]

Having resolved *not* to forswear further attacks on Hanoi, LBJ saw the matter at hand to be whether to *expand* the approved target list, reinstating sites cut a month before due to political sensitivities, not shrink it. Joining him in the Cabinet Room from 4:35 to 5:02 p.m.—*after* Gronouski met Rapacki in Warsaw, but *before* his account reached Washington—were McNamara, Rostow, Katzenbach, Humphrey, Moyers, White House aide Robert Kintner, Army secretary Cyrus

Vance, and the chairman of the Joint Chiefs of Staff, General Earle "Bus" Wheeler. Johnson, Rostow noted, "considered the problem of next steps in hitting targets in North Vietnam" with his advisers, and decided to "carry forward with what was necessary but at this particular moment not to expand our targeting."[76] As a disappointed Wheeler cabled Sharp in Honolulu and Westmoreland in Saigon, the president "declined to make an affirmative decision" on withheld RT-52 targets "because of certain political problems" but indicated he might reconsider in a week or so.[77]

It is unlikely anyone explicitly raised the ongoing diplomacy in Warsaw, as several persons in the room were not cleared to know what was happening in Marigold. LBJ cryptically cited "certain political problems" in rejecting pleas from the Joint Chiefs of Staff to approve more targets, but there is no sign anyone objected to leaving the Hanoi sites on the RT-52 list, eligible for further strikes. That is not surprising, because Johnson had already clarified his own preference the day before, and underlings feared risking his volcanic ire by opposing an already-set course, especially in a group setting (Humphrey had learned this lesson the hard way after being banished to the doghouse after dissenting from the February 1965 decision to bomb Hanoi[78]). Rostow did not miss a beat somersaulting to back LBJ's refusal to forswear further attacks on Hanoi, and McNamara and Katzenbach, despite having "desperately" conveyed the "strong" belief that more raids might ruin the only live peace bid around, had no wish to alienate their volatile boss—they had made their peace with power, with Johnson, and at least for the time being, with the Vietnam War. But for one man in the Cabinet Room that afternoon, Johnson's decision factored into a more complex equation.

Moyers and Marigold

At the age of only thirty-two years, Bill Moyers was already seen as one of the most potent White House aides in memory and had endured a long, intense history with LBJ—a relationship so intimate he once said that to be effective, he needed "an umbilical cord right to his character, nature, and personality," and associates felt Johnson viewed him as "the son he never had."[79] Like LBJ also a product of modest rural Texan origins, Billy Don Moyers caught his future patron's eye as an undergraduate at humble North Texas State College, when he wrote the powerful Senate majority leader a long, earnest letter seeking a summer job. Impressed, LBJ took the honors student, class president, and journalism major under his wing; he hired Moyers to intern in his Washington office, helped him transfer to the University of Texas, and to defray expenses offered him a slot at his family-owned Austin television station.

After college, however, Moyers swerved away from journalism and politics and toward religion. Having been raised in a Baptist family that revered the ministry, he had long taken a strong interest in religious ethics and history. He pursued these topics in graduate studies on a fellowship in Scotland, and in 1957 entered Southwestern Baptist Theological Seminary at Fort Worth for a two-year program, during which he delivered biweekly sermons at a small Baptist church. However, more drawn to teaching than preaching, he signed up to lecture on Christian ethics at Baylor College in Waco. Then suddenly, in December 1959, LBJ called, and Moyers' life changed again.[80] The Texas senator, gearing up to seek the 1960 Democratic presidential nomination, convinced Moyers to help—and Moyers quickly climbed the campaign totem pole from "personal assistant" to top aide, and, once John F. Kennedy chose LBJ as his running mate, functioned as a liaison between their staffs.

When JFK entered the White House, Moyers joined the staff of the Peace Corps, a New Frontier job that tapped his idealism and offered valuable practical experience in foreign affairs and bureaucratic politics (he edged tough competition to become deputy director). LBJ's protégé came to love and admire his new patron, but on learning of JFK's assassination in November 1963, he immediately returned to his old boss: "I'm here if you need me," he scribbled in a note passed to LBJ on *Air Force One* at Love Field in Dallas, to which Moyers, sent to calm Democratic Party infighting in Texas before JFK's visit, had raced as soon as he heard the news.

Johnson did need him—and Moyers soon attained so exalted a status that LBJ called his wunderkind "my vice president in charge of everything" (nicer words than he ever bestowed on Hubert Humphrey). In 1964, Moyers won kudos as a political operative for helping manage the landslide over Goldwater. As chief of staff, he gained renown as an architect of the Great Society, overseeing task forces that designed the legislative program pushed through Congress in 1965. At the same time, he occasionally delved into realms far beyond his formal purview, including foreign policy. He was soon lionized as one of Washington's most influential and brilliant men, profoundly idealistic yet also a consummate pragmatist able to do hard jobs, a precocious reincarnation of Harry Hopkins, FDR's master fixer, whom LBJ explicitly advertised as Moyers' model.[81]

Then, in July 1965, beset by Vietnam, Johnson named his top "special assistant" to replace George Reedy as press secretary. "Moyers to the Rescue," the *New York Times* headlined, suspecting that LBJ had tapped him in the desperate hope that his Midas touch could reverse sliding polls.[82]

Yet even Moyers' magic, so potent in domestic policy, could not convert Vietnam dross into gold. The new spokesman put the escalation in the best light, but he could not stem rising doubts—and worse, to LBJ, he seemed to evade criticism himself, aided by whispers that he quietly pushed dovish views. Sturdy rumors circulated that he had urged a lengthy bombing pause in December 1965 to test the waters for talks with Hanoi. Its failure, consequently, reportedly undercut his standing with his mentor. Yet he continued to counsel against escalation—to defer strikes against petroleum, oil, and lubricant facilities in the spring of 1966, for example, "as far into the future as possible." "Here comes 'Mr. Stop-the-Bombing'" or "Here comes 'Stop the Bomb Bill,'" LBJ would crack. "He said it as if it were a jest," Moyers recalled, "but it was really a mocking comment." LBJ's irritation rose alongside public criticism of his policy; meanwhile, Moyers, after first backing the intervention, soured on it. Claims that he led an "underground conspiracy" to stop the war were inflated—LBJ *wanted* him to be a back channel to doves—but were grounded in real discontent.[83] Looking back, he wrote:

> I certainly can't claim to have been prophetic about the war and in fact I didn't have much to say about it in 1964 and early in '65 when my portfolio was politics and domestic policy. I regret that I did not anticipate the consequences of the escalation early enough to speak against it; like others, I trusted the judgment of the national security professionals and ultimately the President himself. My skepticism became acute when, at his request, I set up a back channel to young officers and analysts whose descriptions of what was happening on the ground in Vietnam were more realistic and pessimistic than those coming from official sources that were the basis of the President's decisions.[84]

Amid their creeping schism on the war, LBJ snubbed Moyers when two key national security posts opened up. In April 1966, he chose the hawkish Rostow to succeed McGeorge Bundy as national security adviser—Rusk had told Johnson that Moyers was too dovish, Moyers suspected—and that fall he moved Katzenbach from the Justice Department to the State Department to replace Ball as Rusk's number 2, telling his press secretary that he liked him right where he was.[85]

Policy rifts were not the only factors motivating Moyers to escape LBJ's pressure cooker. Working for him was never relaxing, but the stresses compounded when he was angry or, worse, distrusted you; a mutual associate confirms that LBJ "came to suspect that Bill Moyers disclosed information for his own benefit."[86] Besides strain over the president's worsening press relations ("at their lowest ebb ever," Moyers reported glumly in June 1966[87]), the job ravaged his health and psyche. By early 1966, he was suffering from "fatigue syndrome" and a thyroid condition; that summer, he was hospitalized for bleeding ulcers ("very sorry to have conked out on you at such a critical time," he apologized); and in September, personal tragedy struck: his older brother James, also a White House staffer, committed suicide, leaving Bill to help care for a sister-in-law and two young nieces besides his own three children.[88] The loss of James "shook him very deeply," a colleague recalled, and the workaholic, already running "on nerves" to a considerable degree, "was getting, I think, fairly near a snapping point."[89] Moyers himself recalled: "The real impact on me of his death, coming as it did when I was struggling with the other matters . . . was to rob me of any energy, stamina or will to continue the life I was—well, enduring, not living—and to think about my family's future in a way I never had. When you are young, as you know, you think yourself indomitable, and my brother was only 39 at the time; I felt precarious for the first time ever."[90]

The extra personal burdens magnified the allure of the invitation Moyers received from *Newsday* publisher Harry Guggenheim to come to Long Island to "help me run the paper." Enticed by his "luminous intelligence, integrity, smooth southern charm" and national stature, the conservative Guggenheim disregarded Moyers' liberal views and rumored private dissent on the war (which the mogul stoutly backed). In the summer of 1966, Moyers deflected an opening overture, but he found the publisher's offer of lavish compensation, enhanced independence, and a fresh career increasingly tempting. Accompanying LBJ to Southeast Asia in October—a trip marred by an episode that further soured his ties to the president[91]—the press secretary grilled reporters about *Newsday* and liked what he heard. "After my brother died," he later recalled, "in genuine remorse and reflection on 'Okay, what now,' in the realization I had about paid the price that one could pay for public life, and wanting to get out of the spotlight and wanting to concentrate on my family after four uproarious years," he decided to tell Guggenheim, "Captain, I think I'm changing my mind." Over lunch at the Metropolitan Club in mid-November, Moyers tentatively accepted a deal that seemed too good to refuse.[92]

But the decision was not final, and there was the minor matter of breaking the news to his patron, mentor, and boss. To do so, Moyers journeyed to Texas, where LBJ was recuperating from surgery at his ranch. LBJ did not accept his departure—to him tantamount to a betrayal—without a fight. The Saturday after Thanksgiving, on a warm afternoon, he drove Moyers for hours around his property's undulating hills in a new Thunderbird convertible, stopping at farms and his childhood home, just the two of them except for a short interlude when Lady Bird joined them.[93] He used all his vaunted persuasive powers to convince Moyers to stay on, or if not, to enter Texan politics. But Moyers, resisting the trademark hard sell, insisted that he wanted to enter the "newspaper business." He emphasized personal considerations, not policy differences, yet the war inevitably entered their rambling, at times sentimental, conversation. LBJ, Moyers recalled, waxed philosophical about how it would all look when they were gone:

> We sat for a long time as the sun was disappearing over the far horizon of the LBJ Ranch and we talked about . . . Vietnam. He said, "If history brings me out," . . . that is, if the Communists don't take over South Vietnam, "I will be considered by posterity a great man who took a great risk and won, and it'll all be all right." "If it doesn't come out," he said, "if the Communists wind up running South Vietnam, I will be considered an obscure footnote, a man who gambled all he had, and lost."[94]

Torn, and deferring a final decision, Moyers flew back to Washington to work on the State of the Union Address (leaving behind his successor, George Christian, to manage press affairs). In early December, he was at the White House drafting the address, still plugged in despite his prospective departure and hence poised to follow Marigold—including the debate over hitting Hanoi—via contacts with aides such as Katzenbach, who saw him as an ally in urging bombing curbs to aid peace prospects.[95]

The evidence on Moyers' influence on LBJ regarding Marigold is slim yet suggestive. On December 7, with the initiative in limbo, Moyers seemed to indirectly advise LBJ against more Hanoi attacks in a memo calling his attention to a *Saigon Post* editorial doubting the "wisdom" of air raids on North Vietnam, including on its capital; they were, said the paper (believed to be close to Ky), "not worth the candle" and, far from "shortening Hanoi's resistance to coming to the conference table," only made it "more intransigent."[96]

Whether Moyers also spoke personally with LBJ about Marigold is not clear. He had a chance to do so shortly before the December 9 Cabinet Room meeting, when he and other staff members greeted the president on his return to the White House.[97] Then, after LBJ had laid down his bombing edict, Moyers spent more than an hour and a half with him in a lounge outside the Oval Office. Afterward, he blandly told an aide that it was "just a social visit during which Pres. talked about the arguments for and against the tax increase, reminisced on a lot of Texas anecdotes," and displayed an Allen Drury novel (*Capable of Honor*) that he had autographed for Dwight Eisenhower.[98]

Yet this meeting was hardly so routine. When they discussed a bombing halt, which LBJ knew Moyers favored, the president "did not agree that 'softening' the attacks would persuade Ho Chi Minh to talk; he believed that force was the only instrument Hanoi would respect." Perhaps thinking of Rapacki, among others, he "went on for several minutes about the would-be 'Nobel Peace winners' who would like him to stop the bombing for Christmas as a signal to Hanoi. He repeated, with weariness and even despair in his voice, his belief that only force could prevail, and that he wasn't about to send a signal to Ho that could be misread as 'weakness on my part.' He talked about how he would be betraying the 'boys I've already sent there' if he was lured into a trap by Hanoi. Then he changed the subject."[99]

When he had left the ranch in late November, Moyers inclined strongly toward resigning but had not made a formal, irrevocable break; now his mind was made up. That day, most likely, he gave LBJ the following letter:

Dear Mr. President:

The contract [with *Newsday*] is almost in shape and I must now do what I have wanted to delay as long as possible: make the actual and final decision.

Ever since I came back from the Ranch following the helpful and understanding talks I had with you, I have suffered the hell of trying to decide whether I should do what is *best* for those who most depend on me . . . or what is *right* in terms of my obligation to you and my own personal desire to carve out a meaningful career in government. For a week I have been plagued by the fear that I will always feel I left when we were down and the going was toughest; no doubt some will write that, but their allegations bother me far less than the questions I will ask about myself.

I believe you know that I am not leaving because things are dark or because of any differences between you and me; I am leaving for the personal reasons you and I discussed, and as long as you know and believe that, I can endure myself. I wish honestly that the circumstances were different and that I could leave as others have when things were in better shape. They will get better—and I will do whatever I can on the outside to contribute to their getting better. Perhaps I can accomplish more than if I stay, particularly because there is a point in this job when one's effectiveness is diminished by its very nature and a change improves everything. At any rate, I intend to try to be of help to you—that I pledge.

Thank you for everything, above all for understanding.[100]

An aide drafted a warm reply, which Johnson subtly chilled before signing:

Dear Bill:

~~I appreciate the warmth of your letter, but I feel a little like the man in Lincoln's story who was ridden out of town on a rail. As you remember, he said, 'If it weren't for the honor, I'd just as soon walk.' So while I welcome your generosity, I had just as soon not receive it in a letter of resignation.~~

I do understand the personal considerations that compel you to leave. Often there is very little relation between the quality and importance of a man's work in government, and the monetary compensation he receives for it.

The spiritual compensation may be great—in your case, I know it is very great indeed—but it does not eliminate a family's financial needs.

Bill, you have been a tower of strength ~~to me, and to~~ to the work of the Presidency. ~~Wise far beyond your years, r~~Resourceful, efficient, capable in any work to which you turned your hand—you have been all these things and more. You leave a legacy of ~~trust and~~ deep respect behind you in Washington, as you end your ~~first~~ tour in government service.

You leave, too, a devoted friend in this House. ~~I treasure the past, and I look forward to a relationship just as rewarding—and counsel just as intelligent—in the years to come.~~ May God bless you and Judith in all you do. ~~I shall miss you very much.~~ *We will all need you and miss you.*

~~Faithfully,~~ *Sincerely*—[101]

A secretary left the revised letter in a desk drawer for LBJ over the weekend in case he needed it.[102] Moyers later said that an "understanding" LBJ had formally accepted his resignation (due to "overriding" "personal obligations") on Monday, December 12, two days before it was publicly announced.[103]

Was Marigold the last straw that reinforced Moyers' decision to leave, leading to a permanent rift between Johnson and his most famous aide? Did it confirm his sense that further efforts to move the president to a less extreme course on Vietnam were hopeless? Despite the widening gap between them, they never had an argument, "break," or "showdown" over the war. Yet LBJ's refusal on December 9 to alter bombing plans to enhance peace hopes confirmed to Moyers "what was pretty obvious to everyone": that he could not be diverted from the course to which he had committed himself—and the nation—in Vietnam. "The die had been cast," Moyers recalled. "And yes, it did cause me to believe that my earlier intuition—that he would not unilaterally moderate the policy—was right. In a state of utter exhaustion, and stunned by my brother's death, which I had had no time to grieve, I had already resolved to leave government." They did not spar openly over Marigold, but the episode symbolized the divergence on the war that helped drive apart these two men whose lives and careers were so entwined, and who only recently had shared great triumphs. "That gloom that descended over our relationship came, I think, from the realization on the part of both of us that the end no longer justified the means, and that I was leaving and he couldn't," Moyers recalled in 2010. "That was the impact of that long conversation, which [still] plays vividly in my head."[104]

Saturday-Sunday, December 10-11

Hanoi: "We Will Not Withdraw from the Contact If . . ."
Saturday afternoon, Siedlecki again called on Dong. The premier, "in a more cheerful mood than before," thanked the Poles for "very correctly" handling the talks with Gronouski and repeated almost verbatim his wary statements of three days before regarding what he termed the unforgivable December 2 bombings and the apparent U.S. retreat from Lodge's mid-November stands, which together suggested bad faith. Yet, he reiterated: "If the USA wants to confirm Lodge's words, then they can do this by the method of getting in touch with the DRV ambassador in Warsaw." The leadership needed to "rethink the matter once again," and he promised to get back to Siedlecki with a reply.

Dong repeatedly probed Siedlecki for a more detailed parsing of the Phase A/B proposition—an intriguing hint that Hanoi was still mulling over the implications of the idea, a key procedural component of the package deal that was supposed to be confirmed in Warsaw. "We will not withdraw from the contact if we see beneficial points for ourselves," he explained. "However, we cannot take a position which the USA might understand as a sign of weakness. We have to be very careful."[105]

Moscow: Informing the "Gray Cardinal"
Fulfilling his vow to keep the Kremlin informed, Rapacki sent Pszczółkowski a précis of the latest exchanges for Brezhnev, which arrived as snow carpeted the city. With the CPSU's boss preoccupied preparing his report to the plenum on Monday, the Pole instead relayed the message on Saturday to Mikhail Suslov. This Politburo member, dubbed the "gray cardinal" for his stern, authoritative doctrinal pronouncements, offered little substantive comment, mentioning only that

the news was useful to have in hand because the Soviets anticipated talks with VWP Central Committee's second secretary, Le Duc Tho, who was on his way to Moscow from Budapest after attending the Hungarian Socialist Workers' Party Congress.[106]

Saigon: "Things Are Going Less Badly"

Saturday morning found D'Orlandi shaken—troubled by his dismal meeting with Rusk, and jangled by the ongoing Viet Cong barrage. Friday night had been "the most turbulent and the loudest" he had experienced in Saigon in years, punctuated by bomb blasts at munitions dumps around the city. Then he learned that at dawn a "powerful plastic charge" had been found literally next door to the embassy and defused before it could "pulverize" the U.S. military complex next door. "It was only by a hair's breadth that I was not blown up," he reflected. Fearing still worse, especially near Christmas, he urged an aide with family in Saigon to send them to Phnom Penh, Singapore, or Hong Kong, "at least for a few days."[107]

At 11 a.m., Lewandowski appeared, and D'Orlandi tried to "attenuate" his pessimism.[108] Yet, had they known of it, LBJ's refusal to alter U.S. bombing plans would have amply fulfilled their worst fears and suspicions. But ignorance was hardly bliss, for they were already gloomy. Alarmed by (erroneous or exaggerated[109]) reports of heavy raids on Hanoi the day before, Lewandowski was "very discouraged" by the Italian's account of his talk with Rusk. According to the Pole, D'Orlandi relayed Rusk's desire to meet him, but Lewandowski declined to pursue the idea, figuring that the risk of exposure outweighed any likely gain and that the Italian was already making an ardent pitch to the same end. "Frankly speaking," he asked decades later, "was there any use for me to push Rusk?"[110]

Actually, there might have been. Because Rusk had so dim a view of Rapacki's mediation and no personal experience with Lewandowski, there was little to lose; a direct encounter *might* have enhanced his view of Poland's ICC commissioner (and clarified his identity—Janusz, not Bohdan), which *might* have altered his advice to Washington on bombing Hanoi. It would have still been unlikely, but it could not have hurt.

Instead, because D'Orlandi hoped to see Rusk again that night, Lewandowski urged him to again "implore" the American to suspend the air raids, which threatened to crush all hopes for talks, with U.S. responsibility "self-evident." Convinced of the situation's gravity—if the "escalation" continued, he agreed, "our attempt is dead"—the Italian "promised him that I would attempt the impossible with Rusk this evening."

As for the "fearful intensification of terrorism in the last few days" around Saigon about which Rusk complained, Lewandowski offered excuses. He blamed the South Korean troops that were "cleaning" the suburbs of Communist forces for provoking clashes, and the attempted blast at the MACV headquarters on the interrogation and torture of the NLF suspects there. Finally, he suggested that

D'Orlandi offer the Pole's services to Washington to contact the "Viet Cong leadership," unaware that the Italian had already done so but Lodge had rebuffed the idea.

Meanwhile, Rusk spent another day talking with the Americans and the South Vietnamese, attending military, economic, and political briefings; audiences with Ky and Thieu—divulging no hint of Marigold, and telling Thieu that he saw no sign Hanoi desired talks—and a dinner in his honor hosted by Tran Van Do.[111]

At precisely 8 p.m., D'Orlandi, too, made his way to the RVN foreign minister's. The same Americans he had seen the night before were there (Rusk, Lodge, and their aides), plus Westmoreland and the head of the U.S. Agency for International Development. Discovering that he was the only person there who was neither American nor Vietnamese, he presumed that Do had explained his presence as a protocol courtesy to the dean of the diplomatic corps. When the talk turned to the recent assassination of a politician ("poor Tran Van Van"), Lodge asked him to "share the reports you have collected with Secretary Rusk." D'Orlandi detected chagrin on Rusk's face, and pleasure on Do's, when he offered evidence pointing to Saigon intrigues, not Viet Cong terror.

Over coffee, the Italian again chatted privately about Marigold with Rusk. He conveyed Lewandowski's dire concerns, and his own, but Rusk remained upbeat: He had no news about bombing plans but brushed off the Pole's latest claims of Hanoi raids and—evidently thinking of Gronouski's cables on his talk with Rapacki Friday—said cryptically that "the news about the negotiation is better." Presuming that Rusk did not say this just to preempt more bombing criticism, D'Orlandi inferred correctly that "at Warsaw things are going less badly."[112]

But the Americans knew this might be the calm before another storm. Expecting a turn for the worse in Warsaw, Lodge and Rusk sent the State Department a list of recent "terroristic [Viet Cong] acts" that they thought might be potent ammunition in Gronouski's quarrels with Rapacki. Among other items, Lodge noted, D'Orlandi had told him that a "plastic explosive device" had been found in the "general area of the apartment house in which the Italian Embassy is situated." Rusk thought it a "useful debating point" to note that "at the very moment that Lewandowski was complaining about U.S. bombardment, the Communists were planning to blow [up] the building in which the conversations were taking place."[113]

Washington: "After All the Noise on the Staircase"

Shortly before 9 a.m. Saturday, Rostow composed a brief note to LBJ to cover Gronouski's account of his latest exchanges. "Rapacki has about exhausted his interim ploy," he judged. "I am confident in my bones that he has been in close touch with both Moscow and Hanoi. It is their move, and we shall soon see whether, after all the noise on the staircase, anyone comes into the room."

"In any case," he assured LBJ, Washington stood on firm diplomatic and public relations grounds: "If it fails, we have a straight story to tell, should they pull a U

Thant; and we have the virtue of the Italians on the record as backing us in urging that direct talks should begin, since we have taken what must be objectively judged a forthcoming position."[114]

Later that morning, however, the administration got a foretaste of the protests to come if it stuck to its bombing plans: Moscow belatedly seconded Poland's pleas to halt the attacks. A few days earlier, of course, Brezhnev had lamented Hanoi's failure to turn to the Soviets, because they had "greater capabilities" to pressure the Americans.[115] Deploying those capabilities, the Kremlin sent its chargé d'affaires in Washington (who was the acting ambassador until Dobrynin got back) a sharp, authoritative statement to convey to U.S. officials.

Early Saturday, a day after returning from Moscow, Alexander Zinchuk urgently requested to see the outgoing U.S. envoy to the USSR, Foy Kohler, to convey the oral message condemning the raids on the Hanoi suburbs, "including its populated areas," as "new aggressive acts" defying "elementary requirements of international law and human ethics" along with U.S. protestations of desires for peace. The escalation, it admonished, "inevitably complicates even more the already dangerous situation around Vietnam."

Kohler defended the bombing as solely aimed at military sites and, like Rusk, claimed that the real problem was that there was "no response from the other side, and so long as there is none there can be no cessation of bombing." Unaware of the latest Marigold news, he said there was no indication a bombing halt would be reciprocated in the South, and he invited DRV communication through any channel, including the Soviets.

Zinchuk then offered a "personal observation" alluding to, without explicitly mentioning, the Polish peace effort. The Soviet leaders, he said, "had been encouraged by the apparent earlier slackening off of air action over North Vietnam and had the feeling that perhaps this indicated a desire on the part of the U.S. to take the heat out of the situation. They were therefore surprised and disappointed" when this turned out not to be so. Kohler could only repeat that Washington stood ready to "de-escalate" if the other side did as well; if any increase in violence had actually occurred, he insisted, it was the Communists' "escalation of terrorism and other hostile activities" in South Vietnam.[116]

✳ ✳ ✳

Zinchuk's arguments had zero impact on U.S. decisions, but the officials handling Marigold braced themselves for the consequences of the explosions they knew would soon detonate near the DRV capital. Katzenbach cabled Saigon and Warsaw to alert Rusk and Gronouski of LBJ's refusal to forswear further attacks on Hanoi.

Reacting to Rusk's report of his Friday night conversation, Katzenbach judged D'Orlandi's analysis of the Polish foreign minister's tactics as "close to the mark"— "we can only hope that Rapacki has finished this clever game and is now making a real effort to get Hanoi aboard for direct U.S.–[North Vietnam] conversations"—but suggested that there was "nothing further to be said" to the Italian for a reason the next sentence made clear: "On the bombing point, you should know that RT-52 stands as it was at time of your departure from Washington and targets earlier set aside remain in suspense." "Please let me know if you feel we have left any stone unturned in this exercise," he added rather plaintively.[117]

Katzenbach's cable to Gronouski was even more ominous. The bombing plans were "unchanged," he warned, and "may well involve some targets which Rapacki will insist represent further escalation, just as in the past he took to be escalation certain variations in our bombing pattern which in fact represented no real departures in the pattern as a whole. . . . Present bombing pattern has been authorized for some time and we do not wish to withdraw this authorization at this time." Gronouski should not give the Poles "even any slight indications" that "we are escalating or de-escalating at present."[118] The acting secretary of state felt no compulsion to reveal to the ambassador or his boss that LBJ himself was the decisive factor; dismissing Polish warnings as a maneuver to extract concessions, the president had deliberately chosen *not* to avoid hitting Hanoi.

Warsaw: "You Should Be Aware"
A dreary Saturday dragged on: Temperatures crept above freezing, and the snow turned to sleet. At the embassy, the latest Marigold cable showed up in the evening. It praised Gronouski's "effective" handling of Rapacki's arguments, asked his estimate of Polish-DRV exchanges, affirmed earlier guidance in case a meeting with Hanoi's envoy suddenly eventuated—and after the sugarcoating, notified him that the present bombing plans remained in place, including targets liable to anger Rapacki.[119] The ambassador, so deeply committed to the initiative, could only have felt foreboding.

✳ ✳ ✳

Over the weekend, ignoring Fanfani's plea from Rome on Friday evening, Rapacki took no action to hasten the first U.S.-DRV contact. Siedlecki's cable from Hanoi relating his Saturday morning talk with Dong, when the premier had reiterated that the USA could "get in touch with" the DRV's Warsaw embassy to confirm Lodge's position, was deciphered early Sunday evening. And yet again, Rapacki failed to tell Gronouski.[120]

Saigon: "Targets . . . Remain in Suspense"
Early Sunday morning, Katzenbach's cable informing Rusk that RT-52 remained unaltered reached the Saigon embassy.[121] The secretary must have grasped instantly that the news would infuriate the Italians, not to mention the North Vietnamese and Poles. Earlier, he had promised to convey LBJ's ultimate decision to D'Orlandi, but now, as advised, he held back. At 8:37 a.m., without contacting or

leaving word for D'Orlandi, he departed Tan Son Nhut for Bangkok, the next leg on his circumnavigation to Paris.

Monday and Tuesday, December 12 and 13

Saigon/Beverly: Exit Lodge

Monday morning, after hosting Rusk, Lodge also left Tan Son Nhut, taking a U.S. Air Force jet to the United States for Washington consultations and more than a month of home leave amid whispers that he might not return. He landed Tuesday afternoon at Boston's Logan Airport, where dignitaries and family members waited in the blustery cold. In brief remarks to reporters, the ambassador—in suit and tie, as usual, and "tanned, trim, hatless and coatless" according to his hometown paper—deflected questions about Vietnam but spiked "rumors and daydreams" of his imminent retirement. Then he and his wife, Emily, decamped to Beverly on the North Shore, to the whitewashed Provençal brick house built after their marriage more than three decades before (modeled after a converted fourteenth-century monastery, the Côte d'Azur home of the novelist and Lodge family friend Edith Wharton). In the compound on a bluff overlooking Salem Bay, near their two sons, ten grandchildren, and assorted dogs, they could celebrate the holidays in relative peace.[122]

In the venerable New England harbor town, tromping in a black overcoat through evergreen woods in the December dusk, Lodge could hardly be farther from Vietnam's heat and carnage. Not privy to his inner thoughts—he was no diarist, unlike his friend, Giovanni—we do not know if he was tormented by the war, perhaps revolving in his mind the intrigues that days before had teased his hopes of a breakthrough for peace. Yet it seems that he had consigned them to the past. To him, Marigold was already dead; at least, he gave that impression in later accounts, abruptly ending his story once he left Saigon. Of course, the action had just shifted to Warsaw—and Washington and Hanoi.

※ ※ ※

Meanwhile, back in Saigon, Porter stepped in as acting ambassador and, along with Habib, took over any lingering Marigold business. Yet, for the moment, they had little to do.

Downcast and bedridden ("Colitis, polycythemia, or both?"), D'Orlandi rued that with his chum Cabot gone, he could only learn new developments from Lewandowski, or perhaps Fanfani after he saw Rusk in Paris and made his way back to Rome, from which he could send secure communications.[123]

The despondent, edgy Lewandowski—mindful of Hanoi's ire over the bombings, but still excluded from the Siedlecki-Dong or Gronouski-Rapacki exchanges—geared up to make his angriest protest yet at the emergency ICC meeting he had demanded to consider the December 2 and 4 raids on "populated areas of

Hanoi." Monday, he met informally with Moore and an Indian officer (chairing the ICC during Rahman's trip to New Delhi) to finalize plans for the emergency session, set for Wednesday morning.[124] He also groused, to the Canadian's sympathy, about the ICC's unsatisfactory, even embarrassing work conditions—shabby villas and office buildings, a paltry food budget, excessive red tape, and so on.[125] He tightly leashed his emotions and observed correct protocol, yet between the lines of Moore's cable, one senses Lewandowski's mounting frustration with his lot, compounded by the seeming collapse of his sideline secret peace venture.

Hanoi: "'Souplesse' in Our Tactics"

After seeing Dong on Saturday afternoon, Siedlecki heard nothing from the DRV leaders on Sunday, Monday, and into Tuesday. Their closed-door deliberations remain opaque. Was the VWP Politburo, which had agreed in late November on the Warsaw meeting only after stormy argument, again split? Had it, after the December 2 and 4 Hanoi raids and cryptic interpretation clause, now tilted toward reversing its earlier consent? Or was it edging toward a reaffirmation of its earlier readiness to go ahead?

Despite the dearth of hard Vietnamese data on internal decisionmaking as Marigold hung in the balance, some intriguing tidbits emerge from reports by "fraternal" observers in Hanoi. On Monday, Siedlecki cabled Warsaw more gossip from "quite a trusted source W," claiming that a VWP plenum the week before had ratified a decision to intensify military actions in the South during the coming dry season—a scenario that did not exclude opening negotiations. "The talks with the U.S. could be started even now," the informant explained, "but their realization could take place only after the [military] actions were over. Any breaks in the bombings or military actions (due to holiday or other reasons) in this period would be used to strengthen the forces in the South."[126]

Siedlecki's unnamed source previewed the "talk while fighting" strategy that Hanoi would later adopt. We can also inspect the evidence from another foreign source, thanks to the presence in Hanoi, from December 7 to 12, 1966, of an Italian Communist delegation led by ranking party figure Enrico Berlinguer. From a joint communiqué pledging solidarity against U.S. "aggression," from *L'Unità* articles filed by a correspondent in Hanoi, and from vaguely informed official Italian sources, Washington gathered that the Vietnamese had taken an intransigent line with their fraternal guests.[127] But one may now glean more revealing glimpses of those exchanges from the Partito Comunista Italiano group's secret trip report.[128]

In Hanoi, the delegation received closed briefings on the military, political, and international ideological situations from senior DRV figures, including at least two who were aware of the still-secret Polish peace initiative: a Politburo member, General Truong Chinh, and Xuan Thuy, head of the party's foreign relations department.

Despite Rome's role in Marigold, the Italian Communists did not know of it —and the North Vietnamese did not spill the beans, despite their fury at U.S.

conduct. Their overriding message was total confidence in ultimate victory: "We have won the first phase of the war and this demonstrates that the Viet people can defeat the USA!" Chinh boasted. Despite some difficulties (admitted only in private)—that is, discouragement among those Southern cadres with insufficient ideological grounding—he insisted that the protracted war strategy to wear down and outlast a technologically superior enemy would pay off.

Far more candidly than Hanoi did publicly, Chinh also decoded DRV political and diplomatic tactics, for example, the NLF's embrace of an "independent" and "neutral" South Vietnam rather than demanding immediate unification with the North. "We think that today it is useful to speak of a neutral South Vietnam, even if it is our opinion that Vietnam is one and must be reunified," he explained. "Fighting for a neutral South Vietnam today, however, allows for the isolation of the enemy by creating a wide front in the South such that it includes the national bourgeoisie as well. The reunification of the country, an objective which we do not abandon, shall be fulfilled at a later date."

The hard-liner spiced his résumé of the military situation with wildly inflated claims of U.S. losses and blood-curdling accounts of U.S. atrocities ("They have opened up the abdomens of victims and eaten the raw or fried livers"—such crimes must be publicized "to bring out the revolutionary spirit of the people"). Yet, he conceded, eventually, "either a cease-fire or negotiations will take place. Or else, negotiations together with combat. We believe that it is necessary to wait before entering into negotiations because these possibilities do not currently exist. We are not in a hurry—we have fought for nine years [against France] from '45 to '54 before having peace."

Chinh's statement that the time was not right for negotiations *could* have reflected knowledge that the Politburo had retracted consent to the Warsaw contact—and his own strong personal animus to talks[129]—but more likely derived from the same reflexive logic that underpinned Rusk's Saigon airport statement: In the absence of hard evidence to the contrary, it made sense to insist that the enemy lacked a sincere desire for peace. In the same spirit, Hanoi blasted (through its mouthpiece, *Nhan Dan*) Rusk's statements, and travels by Harriman and Humphrey, as "peace fallacies" that the "U.S. aggressors" had used "as a smokescreen to cover up their crimes against the Vietnamese people, which are piling up."[130]

The strict secrecy shrouding the Polish affair also militated against arousing suspicion that dramatic news might be near. Yet Xuan Thuy hinted at a hidden diplomatic context when he argued that Washington sought to coerce Hanoi into a one-sided deal. "It is not that we are against the negotiation," he told the Italians, "it is that on one hand, we are mistrustful because the U.S. says one thing and then does another and we have no illusions about its willingness for peace; on the other hand, we intend to negotiate when they will have accepted the Four Points and given concrete proof of their acceptance."

Xuan Thuy rated personalities engaged in various peace bids (not Lewandowski but Thant, de Gaulle, La Pira, et al.) and offered "critical observations" about those nations that professed to back Hanoi. He lumped them into three groups: first, those who "completely support us" in word and deed and were a "great help"; second, those who differed with Hanoi in some respects so not all their stands and actions conformed to its wishes; and third, "people who claim to support us but in practice behave in another manner. For example, they are happy with our struggle but [say] that the U.S. is strong and cannot be beaten. For this reason, they ask for a compromise with the U.S. Others deceive themselves about the U.S. believing that the U.S. wants peace and wants to make concessions. They think, therefore, that the U.S. tells the truth when actually it lies . . . [and takes] positions which are advantageous to the U.S." In this last category, Xuan Thuy alluded to Western and nonaligned states but might also have included Warsaw, given its avid (and, some in Hanoi believed, gullible) role in conveying American proposals.

While promising maximal material and political aid to Vietnam's struggle, the Italian Communists found Xuan Thuy's explanations somewhat unclear and asked him to further elucidate Hanoi's view on peace talks. So on Monday—before seeing the group off at Gia Lam—Thuy met them again. They spoke, it will be recalled, as the Politburo was still debating whether to approve the Warsaw contact that had been in suspense for almost a week. Perhaps indirectly signaling uncertainty as to the initiative's ultimate outcome, Thuy judiciously balanced a blast at "recent" U.S. behavior and an intent to "wait and negotiate only when the conditions are better" with an affirmation of tactical flexibility and a cautious acknowledgment that talks might start even as the fighting raged:

> With respect to negotiations, we are not closing the door to negotiations but we will participate when we want and when the conditions are better. Our objective is to fight for peace, independence and reunification. Everything which allows us to reach these objectives, we do not reject. But the U.S. does not want negotiations, they speak of negotiation but continue the war, they want victory in order to negotiate from positions that are more advantageous. In fact in recent times, they speak of peace but send other troops and bomb Hanoi. If they truly want peace and want to respect our rights, we are willing to negotiate. Our motto is the steadfastness of our principles and "*souplesse*" [French for "flexibility"] in our tactics. We negotiated several times with the French in Vietnam and with the Americans over Laos. We know therefore how deceitful the Americans are—for this reason we will wait and negotiate only when the conditions are better. . . . It is possible that the two sides continue to fight and that at the same time they begin to negotiate but in this case it is necessary to be very careful.

Moscow: "Certain Probing about Talks"

Monday morning, through heavy snow, the few hundred members and alternate members of the CPSU's Central Committee (CPSU CC) converged on the Kremlin Palace of Congresses, the boxy, gargantuan conference hall that Khrushchev had built amid onion-domed churches and other tsarist-era architecture. The party cadres got what they came for; after two years of relative restraint, Brezhnev was taking the gloves off. Since the Cultural Revolution had exploded the previous summer, Chinese conduct had entered a "new, dangerous stage," fanning fears that Mao was whipping up a prewar frenzy. The time had come, the CPSU leaders finally decided, to alert the Soviet populace, rally the Communist world, and abandon hope that their ex-ally would see reason—at least as long as Mao ran the show.[131] Brezhnev's report, the opening salvo of a new effort to isolate Beijing, presaged a public call for a world congress of Communist parties to condemn China—and a quiet redeployment of military forces closer to the PRC's frontier.[132]

The CPSU boss also addressed "the most urgent international problem," the Vietnam war.[133] A CPSU CC statement the next day routinely affirmed support for Hanoi "against the criminal aggression of United States imperialism." But behind closed doors, Brezhnev vented his frustration at the DRV's refusal to heed Moscow's advice—which had been dispensed "candidly," he noted, to Dong and Giap when they had visited in August and had been echoed by both Eastern European and Western Communist parties—to talk with Washington. Its failure to do so, he recalled arguing, had allowed LBJ to pose as a "martyr" for peace, while negotiating would let it gain time and either attain an acceptable settlement or "expose, in the clearest way possible, American lies." Yet such counsel always got the same reply: We want talks, but the time is not right; we first must score a big victory on the battlefield.

"We are having this conversation for two years now, and in the meantime the military situation is getting worse," Brezhnev complained. The Soviet leader now sensed a particularly "favorable atmosphere" for talks because the U.S. "ruling classes," despite enormous military resources, had reached a dead end in Vietnam and were genuinely "looking for a way out of it. It is not coincidental," he said— obliquely alluding to LBJ's private letter to Kosygin, which had not yet been answered[134]—"that both Johnson and Rusk approached us, as well as other countries, with the request that we mediate in Vietnam. We should not rule out the option that this is more than just a political ploy; that [they] sincerely want to find some sort of solution to the Vietnamese problem, especially in view of approaching presidential elections in the USA."

Fortuitously, a new factor had emerged to nudge Hanoi in the right direction: Beijing wanted to prolong the war to amass "leverage" to pressure Washington "to settle all outstanding questions of Sino-American relations"—but its internal distractions might open the door, at least a crack, to a political resolution. "People might ask: Don't the Vietnamese comrades see for themselves the complexity of the situation?" Brezhnev noted. "Of course, they see. The problem is, undoubtedly, the leadership of China, which puts the Vietnamese leadership under strong pressure, preventing it from giving an agreement to peace talks." Without getting specific, he hinted—in terms undoubtedly informed by his knowledge of Marigold—that the situation was changing for the better:

One should note, however, that in the recent weeks, the position of the Vietnamese comrades has been marked by some new points. Because of the turbulent events in China, connected with the so-called Cultural Revolution, the Chinese leadership has other things to worry about than the Vietnamese. This is what the Vietnamese comrades think, in any case, and they are beginning certain probing about talks.[135]

New Delhi: "Thoroughly Unsatisfactory"

En route to Paris, Rusk stopped Monday at Palam Airport near New Delhi and used the refueling break to see the Indian foreign minister, Mahommedali Currim ("M. C.") Chagla. The talk was tense, and to Rusk "thoroughly unsatisfactory." On the main issue clouding bilateral ties, New Delhi's request for more help to deal with a food crisis, Chagla said that Indians would resent and not understand an American failure to alleviate the situation. Rusk resented the remark, given what he considered massive U.S. aid. On Vietnam, he asked Chagla if India really wished Washington "to get out of Vietnam, at once," and was appalled to hear him reply—after "some embarrassed fumbling," noted U.S. ambassador Chester Bowles—"with a categoric 'yes.'"[136] "The foreign minister replied that this should be done and the South Vietnamese people left to decide their own future," the Indian record noted. "Mr. Rusk evidently did not like the answer." Despite a public statement terming the talks "frank" and "friendly," Chagla's foreign secretary, who sat in, sensed Rusk's "testiness" throughout and concluded that "Vietnam was weighing too heavily on his mind."[137] The exchange hardly enhanced Rusk's eagerness to involve India, the ICC chair, in Vietnam diplomacy.

Warsaw: "The Carrot-and-Stick Approach Does Not Work"

On Monday, Michałowski phoned Gronouski to say that "while there was nothing urgent," Rapacki would like to see him the following afternoon.[138] Tuesday at 2 p.m., Gronouski sat in the minister's office for the sixth time in nine days.[139] In a "relaxed and reflective mood," Rapacki said that the situation was "not urgent, but he felt it was good for us to meet frequently to transmit information and recapitulate attitudes."[140]

After informing Gronouski that Warsaw had, indeed, transmitted to Hanoi the latest U.S. stance, Rapacki reviewed events since mid-November. The Poles had been "generally hopeful" that direct talks could begin soon, but North Vietnam had "negatively assessed" the "new elements" that had arisen in early December: the interpretation clause and the Hanoi bombings. Consequently, a "reappraisal" was under way, as a result of which "we are faced with this postponement of Warsaw meetings." He then summed up Poland's role in Marigold and the impact of recent U.S. military actions:

Rapacki said he was not insensitive to USG's [the U.S. government's] expression of appreciation for role Poles were playing; however he was afraid U.S. does not understand nature of Poland's role. He said he feels we are assuming that all of his words come from Hanoi and everything we say to him goes to Hanoi. He said this is not the case; "True, we have our own views and we are friends of Hanoi, but our role is neither that of postman nor advocate; what we want is peace." He said that having knowledge of views of both sides, which neither of participants have, "we think we can play a contributing role."

Rapacki continued, saying that Poles are sincere and in this sincerity they must say that they are not sure what USG wants: talks, or to get soundings as to how far DRNVN [Democratic Republic of North Vietnam] is ready to yield under pressure. He added that Poles assume that prevailing intention of USG is to bring about talks. He said this is why they are engaged; they are acting on this working hypothesis.

He continued that if this working hypothesis reflects reality then he must say that USG did great harm to its own objectives in December. The USG cannot afford a repetition in future, especially at time when this matter is reassessed. He added that if we want peace then we must realize that the carrot-and-stick approach does not work with DRNVN.

Rapacki added that we should realize leadership of DRNVN does not want to and cannot yield under pressure; every step from our side that evokes impression that NVN is acting under pressure would be interpreted as sign of weakness and utilized by all those who have a different vision of this peace move than we have here in Warsaw. (Comment: Rapacki repeated this point with emphasis and was, I believe, making a clear reference to Communist China.)

Rapacki complained that recent public statements by U.S. officials had only exacerbated Hanoi's mistrust. A Navy spokesman who described plans to gradually intensify air pressure on North Vietnam might have been ignorant of the secret initiative, the Pole acknowledged, but the same excuse could not be made for Rusk and his Saigon airport arrival comments bemoaning the lack of "any indication which allows me to entertain hope" of DRV interest in peace and bragging that North Vietnam must eventually relinquish its aim of seizing the South and come to the table because "we are much stronger." Visualize how Hanoi must interpret such belligerent remarks, he urged. In sum, the Pole declared, Washington had "done a lot of harm in December, and it would be good if no more harm is done in future."

The other side was not showing much restraint either, Gronouski retorted. Freshly armed by Washington, he itemized recent Viet Cong attacks in Saigon: storming Tan Son Nhut, bombing the Kinhdo barracks, assassinating politicians, trying to blow up a bridge and even—the clincher, the "useful debating point" D'Orlandi gave Lodge—to set off a bomb near Italy's embassy, the site of the covert talks, a claim that caused Rapacki and Michałowski "to look at each other in surprise and then break out in broad smiles." It was, Gronouski concluded, precisely because neither side would relax its military actions before talks started that it was "so important to do everything we can to begin" them.

Rapacki did not disagree, but he insisted nevertheless that bombing North Vietnam was "the really sensitive point." With a smile, he concluded that this was what he had to say and he would await the U.S. response.

He did not have to wait long. Neither Rapacki nor Gronouski knew it, but halfway around the world, the events both men dreaded were already taking their course.

Conclusion: A Lost Week

For a week, the peace effort was a dead man walking. Rebuffing pleas from the Poles and some of his own top aides, LBJ had refused to issue a stay of execution in the form of a suspension or revocation of authorization to bomb RT-52 targets near Hanoi. Yet, fluctuating cloud patterns gave those involved in Marigold potentially precious days to close the deal and initiate direct U.S.-DRV contacts in Warsaw despite the snags that had spoiled the initially envisioned December 6 meeting. From December 5 to 12, when it was clear that any further raids on Hanoi would almost surely administer the coup de grâce to the wounded initiative, only "bad weather"—*not* political considerations—prevented further RT-52 strikes, according to a declassified Joint Chiefs of Staff history.[141]

North Vietnam, meanwhile, was hedging its bets. Dong had told Siedlecki on December 7 and 10 that U.S. actions had caused Hanoi to reassess the whole matter—*yet* explicitly affirmed that Washington's envoy in Warsaw would not be rebuffed should he appear at the DRV Embassy. Meanwhile, Phuong remained set to interpret any direct exchanges. "As long as I was in Warsaw," he recalled, "there was still the possibility [for Gronouski] to contact the Vietnamese ambassador."[142]

What use was made of this borrowed, accidental time? Too little. From the U.S. perspective, the Poles, and Rapacki in particular, were stalling, deepening suspicions that they were not really serious. "They fussed and they fiddled," Bundy recalled, "for several days in a row."[143] Scorning their complaints about the Hanoi bombings as a "pretext," Rusk said that the Poles were "simply unable to produce the North Vietnamese. . . . We had men all set to be in Warsaw, ready for the talks, but the Poles were unable to produce North Vietnamese warm bodies."[144] Slightly more cautiously, Ben Read noted, as LBJ left office—the initiative long dead, the fighting raging on—that despite the Poles' repeated assurances that Hanoi had authorized the contact, "we never saw the whites of their eyes in terms of the North Vietnamese. . . . And I don't think we'll know until war's end and considerably after whether this was really a tragically missed opportunity or not."[145] Of his week sparring with Rapacki, Gronouski later recalled his rising exasperation, which slowly overcame his sense that peace was nigh and his ardor to play a part in the breakthrough—emotions he ruefully blamed on wishful thinking:

> We had almost daily meetings. Each day I pressed [Rapacki] for the opportunity
> to sit down and talk to the Hanoi Ambassador, and each time the Hanoi ambas-

sador wasn't ready. Each time we would argue over some particular point in the American position, and each time I would in effect say, "Well, look, this is the sort of thing that first meeting is all about, to hash these things out. Let's get Hanoi—the Ambassador, let's sit down, and in one meeting we can probably solve some of these problems." But at any rate, it never happened, and we were obviously being stalled. I think we were being stalled because the Poles couldn't get the thing to happen.[146]

Gronouski, having already been prepared on December 6 to meet his DRV counterpart, insisted that he was "even more ready as time went on" during the ensuing week, "at any point, day or night," to enter "procedural" talks about the "ground rules" of ongoing negotiations, or immediately to "get into substance if the other side were ready to do so," particularly on the ten points.[147] With Marigold faltering, he tried his best to rescue the initiative within the limits of his instructions from Washington and the information at his disposal.

But that week, neither Gronouski nor those officials in Washington who also took Marigold seriously could convince the man whose opinion mattered the most to overcome his skepticism and take even a comparatively small gamble for peace. "The President would not be persuaded or diverted from his conviction that more pressure was the right prescription for Hanoi," Cooper later wrote.[148] It was not, he said bitterly, that the targets were militarily important; they "were fixed targets; it wasn't as if you didn't bomb them then, they would go away. They weren't troop concentrations massing to go down into South Vietnam. They weren't a covey of bombers that if you didn't hit would pick up and fly away the next day. . . . They weren't very consequential." Rather, it was "the principle of the thing"—"some people," notably Rusk and Rostow, felt that "the whole thing was a put-on in Warsaw, and that Hanoi was hurting badly, and they were going to do anything to stave off one more day of bombing. And that we were just being made suckers of and if they really wanted to talk, they'd talk anyway, bombing or no bombing. And this was a show of strength and our determination, and here we were ready to talk to them but we were not going to give up on this thing. So, okay. They bombed."[149]

If the primary blame for destroying Marigold's fading possibilities can be laid squarely on LBJ for rejecting warnings against more Hanoi bombings—now that we know that Dong really *did* authorize Poland to set up the Warsaw meeting—what about Rapacki? Did he squander a real opportunity to get the talks started during the week of December 7 to 13 by trying to be "clever" (as D'Orlandi surmised)? Did his fixation on perfection (i.e., a U.S. assurance against more attacks on Hanoi and an unqualified commitment to the ten points) lead him to blow a genuine chance to achieve what really mattered, getting Hanoi and Washington into direct contacts? Or did he do all that he could have done, given the circumstances?

New Polish archival sources, particularly Siedlecki's cables relating his December 7 and 10 talks with Dong, raise serious doubt as to whether Rapacki truly had to await a firm DRV recommitment to the Warsaw contact or, instead, could have taken the premier's explicit statement that the U.S. ambassador would be received if he appeared at Hanoi's embassy in Warsaw as a yellow (or pale green?) light to urge Gronouski to contact Quang. Of course, U.S. and Italian officials criticized Rapacki's dilatory tactics at the time. But now a critical view of Rapacki's conduct comes from a central *Polish* actor in the affair.

At the time, Janusz Lewandowski had little basis to judge his boss's performance and certainly could not have criticized him directly, though he confessed frustration to D'Orlandi over the delay in starting direct contacts and gently seconded the Italian's urging to get them going without further delay. After the initiative collapsed, he did not hear directly from the MSZ chiefs until he returned to Warsaw after his ICC assignment ended in June 1967; even then, he was not briefed on the exchanges with Gronouski, only told vaguely that the Americans were "not ready to negotiate peace."[150]

Only in 2003, when I showed him Siedlecki's cables from Hanoi and the U.S. records of the Gronouski-Rapacki talks, did Lewandowski gain a new understanding of what had happened. He felt some sympathy for Rapacki, faced with Siedlecki's circumlocutory messages and Dong's cryptic statements. But his strongest emotion was a belief that he and Michałowski had tragically botched the affair, pointlessly trying to wrangle American concessions—via Gronouski or Lodge—on the interpretation clause and bombing instead of leaving it to the parties themselves to resolve such issues:

> Of course, what I would have done if I was in Warsaw if I had Gronouski ready to meet the Vietnamese and I had the Vietnamese in Warsaw, I could have arranged the meeting, even if the Americans will say, we are backing [away from the ten points] or the Vietnamese will say, we are sticking to the Four Points, goodbye. But I would arrange the meeting, you know. I would not squeeze Gronouski any more, because it was useless. And after all, you know, is it difficult to show the Vietnamese and to say that he is here, and to call Gronouski to say that they are here? I would have done so. It may be that I don't know everything. . . . But maybe Rapacki had some reasons . . . to carry on how [he did]. . . . But after all what have [they gained]? . . . Nothing, you know. . . . The only thing [that could happen] could be that, let's say, Gronouski said, "No, this is not the position the Americans have." . . . Let them disavow me, and D'Orlandi. . . . It would appear that Lewandowski and D'Orlandi are liars, because they presented something which was not presented by the USA.

In retrospect, Lewandowski questioned the credentials (geared mostly toward Europe rather than Asia), judgment, and even professionalism of the MSZ managers. He could not fathom why they seemed to play games—seeking multiple objectives, "squeezing" Washington—instead of focusing all their efforts on achieving the first contact.

"Now when I am learning the details, I think that both Rapacki and Michałowski felt a little bit uneasy about the business, perhaps, because as I have said, what I would have done—if I had a Vietnamese in Warsaw and Gronouski ready to meet, *I would arrange the meeting*! . . . [not] waiting . . . for more communication[s]. . . . Can you not phone the Vietnamese, can you not send a dispatch to them, can you not invite them to the Foreign Ministry? I mean—it's, it's." He broke off, agitated, then added: "Frankly speaking, I don't understand what Rapacki and Michałowski had in mind. . . . I mean, for me, it is very easy what I have to do. . . . I don't know why [this] hocus-pocus, I would put these people together and say, 'All right.'"

A less "clever" effort by Rapacki that week, he felt, could have yielded ongoing U.S.-DRV contacts to clarify the ten points, which in turn would have generated pressure to limit the war: "I think, if the talks on this platform were going on, then concrete steps would be taken by both sides, you understand, because it is a different situation when you are talking and when you are fighting. But I really cannot understand why it was handled in this way; it was unprofessional. I think probably both Rapacki and Michałowski felt a little bit uneasy about that, because they never told me the whole truth about it."

9

"The Americans Have Gone Mad"
Bombing Hanoi Again, December 13/14–18, 1966

We must put an end to the talks that were started by the U.S. via the mediation of Ambassador Lewandowski. . . . [The raids on Hanoi] can be defined only as the highest cynicism and impudence. The actual activity of the U.S. sheds light on its true intentions.

—Pham Van Dong to Jerzy Siedlecki, December 14, 1966

The whole responsibility for wrecking this chance to resolve peacefully the Vietnam war rests on the USA.

—Adam Rapacki to John Gronouski, Warsaw, December 14, 1966

If we treat this turn of events as anything less than a crisis in our world leadership role then I believe we are making a tragic mistake. . . . I am concerned that while we may be able to develop a case which satisfies ourselves we will not be able to refute effectively to others the Polish line of reasoning.

—Gronouski to President Lyndon Johnson, December 14 and 15, 1966

By the time Rapacki warned Gronouski again Tuesday afternoon in Warsaw that more raids on Hanoi risked tilting North Vietnam against entering talks, the bombers had already struck again—dooming Marigold and setting the stage for a last-ditch U.S. bid to revive the peace effort, as well as an angry (if at first secret) battle over whom to blame for its demise.

Tuesday, December 13

Hanoi: The Bombers Return

Frustrating Rolling Thunder–52 managers, the weather over most of North Vietnam Tuesday was "cloudy and rainy with low ceilings," as it had been for much of the past week. But enough breaks opened to allow missions to restrike targets hit on December 2 and 4 (the Van Dien truck depot five miles south of Hanoi's center, the Yen Vien railroad yard 5 to 6 miles to the northeast) and new sites such as a Gia Lam petroleum depot (knocking out power and destroying a train shed at the airport). In coordinated midday raids, six waves of eighteen to twenty-four Navy fighters from the carrier *Kitty Hawk* in the Tonkin Gulf dropped 500-pound bombs on Van Dien, while Thai-based squadrons of speedy Air Force F-105-Ds surprised defenders by emerging from behind the "Thud" mountains northwest of the city and exploiting gaps in the overcast to swoop in on Yen Vien before racing for the sea.[1]

Communist news outlets called the attacks the first on Hanoi's civilian areas in the nearly two-year bombing campaign, Though the Seventh Air Force Thunderchiefs unloaded almost a hundred 750-pound bombs, most on or near intended targets, the explosions that caused the most civilian damage and set off the biggest uproar occurred in a workers' district along the southwestern embankment of the Red River near the Paul Doumer Bridge built in colonial times to connect the capital to the north (renamed Long Bien to avoid honoring a French functionary). (Continuing its custom of orienting readers by local landmarks, the *Washington Post* explained that Doumer "links Hanoi with Gia lam, much as the 14th Street Bridge connects Washington with Arlington."[2]) Agence France-Presse said a "small street" in the sloping approaches to the bridge was wiped out, with several civilians dead, and Soviet and East German agencies reported "numerous" residents killed and "scores of buildings . . . destroyed in the fire."[3]

The inferno near the Red River drew global censure. U.S. spokesmen would insistently deny planes released payloads on Hanoi or residential zones (except perhaps those near military targets). Yet an internal postmortem reached a less comforting conclusion more consistent with Communist claims. Of the seven flight crews that aimed at Yen Vien, one admitted during a "re-debriefing" that, "unable to acquire the target due to clouds and MiG attack," they dropped explosives despite being "uncertain of exact release coordinates" and "conceded that bomb trail distance might have caused ordnance to impact slightly southwest of the bridge located immediately south of the target."[4]

To the extent that the DRV's leaders still considered proceeding with Marigold —the evidence remains sketchy—the December 13 attacks dispelled any doubt as to U.S. intentions. Until then, the Poles had not received a firm reply to Siedlecki's report to Dong on December 10 of Washington's latest, seemingly more positive stand (dropping the clause). Now they would get it, for the new bombing decisively tipped the debate in favor of those who argued all along that they could not trust the Americans. Even if the longer-term Politburo decision to integrate the diplomatic, political, and military fronts remained in effect, awaiting approval from the Central Committee, it was time to wrap up the Polish affair.[5]

That night, DRV diplomats went into overdrive to make propaganda from the latest attack. Besides sending the ICC another complaint—"the U.S. imperialist again brazenly sent many formations of aircraft to bomb and strafe residential quarters in the city itself and its suburbs causing to the people losses in terms of human lives and property"[6]—the ministry drafted new instructions for embassies in Moscow and Warsaw and called in foreign envoys to denounce these "new crimes of the American imperialists," giving a tally of 12 civilians killed and 30 wounded in the capital and more than 20 dead in suburbs.[7] (The next day Siedlecki reported 55 dead and 136 injured.[8]) Meanwhile, Dong invited Siedlecki to see him at ten the next morning—a summons whose implications for the peace initiative the Pole could easily guess.[9]

Paris: Rusk Sees Fanfani

Finally reaching the object of his round-the-world tour, Rusk flew into Orly Airport from Tehran at noon Tuesday for the NATO conference opening the next morning and plunged into meetings with fellow foreign ministers and U.S. officials (including McNamara) converging on the American Embassy on the Champs-Élysées. At 6 p.m., he spoke privately with Fanfani. That morning, in Rome, the Italian had seen Willmann and on hearing Rapacki still had not arranged direct talks, again implored him "to not delay, even if the bombings continue, inasmuch as the only way to stop them is to establish contacts and then negotiate." When Rusk saw Fanfani, he praised Italy's role in Marigold, especially Fanfani's pressure on Rapacki, and urged him to keep D'Orlandi in Saigon; he also advised "silence" toward the pope. It is unclear whether Fanfani, then or at a black-tie dinner Rusk hosted that night for foreign ministers and NATO aides, seconded D'Orlandi's plea to avoid more Hanoi raids or, wary of irritating the American, politely refrained. (He later told Willmann that he had "exerted pressure" in this direction.)[10]

Of course, it was already too late. By Tuesday evening in Paris, the bombs had hit Hanoi hours earlier, but accounts were only beginning to trickle in.

Washington: "A Dirty Word"

As soon as the claim of civilian casualties in Hanoi clattered over newsroom teletype machines Tuesday afternoon, reporters sought an official U.S. response. At the Pentagon, such a contingency was anticipated. After LBJ OK'd the latest bombing plans a month earlier, Joint Chiefs of Staff chair General Earle Wheeler had secretly directed Westmoreland and other commanders to "instruct your public affairs officials and others who may be in contact with the press to refrain repeat refrain from depicting to the public the attacks authorized in Rolling Thunder–52 as being a substantial increase in the level of our air campaign against

North Vietnam. As you know," he cabled, "both domestically and internationally, any time we undertake a slightly different or increased initiative, it is characterized by those opposing U.S. policy as 'escalatory.' As you also know 'escalation' has become a dirty word; and such charges, true or false, impose further inhibitions here against moving ahead to win this war."[11]

So, when questioned about the reports from Hanoi, Pentagon spokesmen (and Saigon counterparts) affirmed that U.S. policy was solely "to attack military targets" and that there had been "no escalation whatsoever." Asked if inadvertent strikes on civilian targets might have occurred, they refused to budge from the script—although the State Department, more circumspectly, refused to exclude the possibility without further checking.[12]

For the moment it was a "he said, she said" dispute: a Communist news service (TASS), and a French one, versus the Pentagon. But the clamor was just starting.

Wednesday, December 14

Hanoi: "We Must Put an End to the Talks"
When Siedlecki saw Dong Wednesday morning, the DRV premier "smiled kindheartedly during the conversation, but he was serious and one could say also solemn."[13] His somber mien suited his message—the contacts with the Americans were *off*:

> We think that, under the conditions which have developed, we must put an end to the talks that were started by the U.S. via the mediation of Ambassador Lewandowski. The situation had significantly worsened in connection with the new escalation of the U.S. toward the North. Three air raids on the capital of the DRV took place within the first two weeks of December. Yesterday's, on the 13th of this month, was very serious from the point of view of the escalation. These actions by the U.S. during the time when contacts are being maintained by Lodge with Lewandowski in Saigon and by Gronouski in the Ministry of Foreign Affairs of the PPR [Polish People's Republic] can be defined only as the highest cynicism and impudence. The actual activity of the U.S. sheds light on its true intentions. That is why we are stating it clearly that we think it necessary to break all talks with the U.S. now and we are asking to relay this to the Ministry of Foreign Affairs of the PPR.

A sympathetic Siedlecki made no effort to dissuade Dong from breaking off the initiative.

While harshly criticizing Washington, the premier reassured the Poles that Hanoi did not blame Warsaw. He told Siedlecki to relay the party and government's thanks to Rapacki and Lewandowski for the "efforts carried out by them for the good of the DRV."

Yet, suggesting a bit of suspicion or uncertainty, Dong quizzed Siedlecki on two points. He requested that Warsaw "explain [D'Orlandi's] presence," implying that Lewandowski had blurred the Italian's role during his own talks with Dong, new doubts over Rome's involvement, or both. And the Russian-language text of a Polish summary of the Phase A/B concept that Siedlecki had provided at their prior talk so intrigued him that right after the meeting, he sent his translator to the Polish Embassy to get a fuller explanation.

Despite the inkling of interest in ascertaining the precise U.S. terms to stop the bombing, Dong's statements to Siedlecki Wednesday morning left no doubt that the strikes on Hanoi the day before had killed the already ailing Marigold initiative. That afternoon, even as the Pole transmitted his account of the conversation to Warsaw (at 3:15 p.m.), U.S. bombers returned to pound some nails into the coffin.[14]

Once more, now through clear skies, Navy and Air Force fighters bore in on Yen Vien, Van Dien, Gia Lam, and other targets—leaving the rail yard "ripped apart" by ninety-two 750-pound and twelve 1,000-pound bombs and the truck lot "moderate[ly]" damaged, pilots said. The two-hour raid, starting at 3:05 p.m., was the heaviest on the Hanoi area yet, involving more than a hundred and fifty planes, DRV officials and eyewitnesses said. The "air pirates were met with dense antiaircraft fire," a TASS correspondent wrote. "Numerous bursts clouded the clear sky. A rocket soared up, leaving a white trail behind. I saw a U.S. plane catch fire and a parachute detach from the plane." For a second day in a row, he reported, bombs struck the Red River embankment.[15] Again, the Communist claim, which Washington would publicly fiercely dispute, later gained validation from a secret U.S. government after-action report. The head of the State Department's Intelligence and Research Bureau, Thomas Hughes, noted: "U.S. planes jettisoned 23 bombs (750 lbs. each) in the vicinity [of Yen Vien] when MiGs were sighted on December 14; it seems quite possible that these were responsible for the damage to the homes near the end of the Doumer Bridge."[16]

This time, though, the damage that set off the greatest international furor was in the diplomatic district. Missiles allegedly blew out a wall and the roof of a Chinese Embassy building, leveled the Xinhua news agency office, and shattered windows at the Czech and Romanian chanceries; on his terrace at the Polish Embassy, about 200 meters from one explosion, the next day Siedlecki found "almost a whole rudder-blade in the shape of a right-angled triangle" that a military aide identified as a fragment of a Shrike missile designed to knock out antiaircraft radar.[17] (Debris even "holed" the roof of the Canadian ICC office, leading a wag in the delegation to courier a shard to American friends in Saigon with a note reading "Look here, chaps, this is going a bit far."[18])

Wednesday night, Deputy Foreign Minister Hoang Van Loi again gathered socialist envoys to detail the toll from the even "more brazen and insolent" raids and urge protests. Hearing that PRC grounds were hit, Siedlecki voiced "indignation" and sympathy to a Chinese colleague. Here, at least, even as Moscow blasted Mao and Beijing ripped the Kremlin, U.S. bombs had forged Sino-Soviet solidarity.[19]

Saigon: *"The Poles Have Broken the Truce"*

Wednesday morning at Camp des Mares, the ICC commissioners—an Indian general in the chair—gathered for the emergency meeting that Lewandowski had requested on the December 2 and 4 Hanoi attacks.[20] By then, he had seen reports of the new raids, stoking the anger behind his opening statement. Excoriating "acts of aggression" that "revealed the seriousness of the situation and made it necessary for the whole world to demand" their cessation, he insisted that the ICC was "morally bound" to deplore them. "The Americans were talking peace to deceive the world while in fact they were planning to continue their aggression," he declared—hinting at the secret effort he felt was bombed along with the sites in Hanoi.

Lewandowski presented two motions denouncing the United States and South Vietnam (as an accomplice) for the December 2 and 4 bombings, which Moore routinely shunted aside.[21] They required close study and Rahman's return to Saigon, he said, before formal consideration or vote. While acquiescing to the inevitable deferral, the Pole demanded urgency, especially given the latest attacks; but he had already accomplished his mission of placing a condemnation of the air raids "in the files of the Commission."[22]

Afterward, Moore cabled Ottawa that Lewandowski had seemingly deviated from Warsaw's stand that the ICC should shun controversy. "Now that the Poles have broken the truce so to speak," he proposed countering by raising Saigon complaints gathering dust (e.g., PAVN infiltration into South Vietnam and DRV possession of Soviet-made MiGs and SAMs). That would, as custom required, even the score.

Mystified at the Pole's behavior, the Canadian speculated on a motive. Was he fulfilling an obligation to Hanoi? Hoping to exploit an "excellent opportunity to make alarmist propaganda" about the "specter" of escalation? Or to put the Indians "in an awkward spot on the eve of their elections"? Yet, despite his prior suspicions, one theory Moore did *not* advance was that Lewandowski had been the point man of a secret peace effort that had collapsed, leaving Warsaw feeling burned and furious.

✳ ✳ ✳

The latest Hanoi bombing, the spike in violence, the "heavy" political atmosphere, and the silence from Warsaw left D'Orlandi feeling "especially downhearted," at the end of his rope. With his friend Cabot gone, he was reduced to "fruitlessly" contacting Porter and Habib "in the vain hope of any good news."[23]

Paris: *"I Hit George Brown Pretty Hard"*

On a cloudy Wednesday morning—as the *International Herald Tribune* and Paris papers front-paged stories of civilian casualties in Hanoi—Rusk breakfasted with George Brown. Even before reading the news, the U.K. foreign secretary was set to caution that the "emotive" December 2 and 4 raids, regardless of military rationale, were politically risky. Besides causing "civilian casualties in conditions which hand the Communists a propaganda advantage on a plate"—as an aide warned presciently on December 9—they undercut Brown's courtship of Gromyko and "also cause us much difficulty at home and make it less easy to reject the left-wing demands, which are still being made, for complete disavowal of American policy."

Fortunately for Washington, the early December attacks drew limited press in England due to bigger news elsewhere, but it might not be so lucky next time. In a two-pronged bid to restrain the Americans, after Brown admonished Rusk, an aide was to dine that night with Bundy in London and "take him strongly to task in similar terms."[24]

The new Hanoi strikes further jarred the already-jittery British: Brown asked Rusk point-blank if they heralded a new stage of the air campaign, only to hear him intone the party line. He knew of "no change in the pattern of the bombing" and disputed charges that U.S. planes caused civilian casualties or damage in the city. "We tend to be blamed for the explosions of anti-aircraft shells and SAM missiles, most of which fell to the ground and exploded there," he said, tossing up his own flak. Brown observed that the Americans "did not seem to be putting forward our side of the story effectively" and offered to help straighten out "slanted" BBC television coverage.[25]

Rusk thanked the Briton for the offer, but rolled eyes at his hand-wringing. "I hit George Brown pretty hard on the point that they have the same treaty commitment that we have to 'meet the common danger' in Vietnam," he cabled LBJ. "I intend to press them very hard for more participation, but they will probably act like scared rabbits in the face of their domestic political situation."[26]

Brown, of course, remained in the dark about Marigold, and Rusk did nothing to enlighten him. Unaware that the Soviets might have cold-shouldered him in Moscow because they knew Washington had used him to carry one message for Hanoi while not telling him it was simultaneously sending a more elaborate proposal to the same destination via Poland, Brown planned to press for peace with the Soviets, loath to relinquish his (and Wilson's) dream of capturing international acclaim and scoring a domestic political coup. Angling for an opening, he suggested extending the Christmas truce. Rusk refused to bite, predicting that Hanoi would exploit a cease-fire to rush supplies south. He said the Kremlin had not made any Vietnam moves since Brown's November trip, but did not shake the latter's dogged belief that London could both "preserve the link of confidence with Mr. Gromyko" and "deliver" Washington.[27]

Rusk also kept mum on Marigold when he spoke that morning with another disenchanted ally, Paul Martin. Hoping to return Ottawa to Vietnam diplomacy after the futile Ronning missions, the Canadian had visited Warsaw and Moscow in November. He tried to spark interest in activating the ICC, but Rapacki and Gromyko rebuffed him, insisting that if Canada wanted to promote peace, it should get Washington to stop bombing—though they could not say exactly what Hanoi would do in response.[28]

Nevertheless, when Martin had lunched with Rusk in Washington the day after Thanksgiving, reporting on his European journey, the secretary urged him to "start something going" with the ICC, perhaps a trilateral Canadian-Polish-Indian session in Geneva to brainstorm how to invigorate the commission. Martin thought Rusk sincere—"most anxious to find a way to initiate a move toward eventual negotiations and is exploring all possible avenues to this end"—yet had doubts; the American had advanced comparable schemes before, only to have them sunk by Soviet and Polish objections. Still, the Canadian promised to follow up "without delay."[29]

Coincidentally, Rusk's proposal came as Ottawa informally explored, with Indian and Polish representatives, a Harvard law professor's scheme for the ICC to entice Hanoi and Washington into curbing hostilities and entering talks.[30] Warsaw found that aim too lofty, but New Delhi, intrigued, in early December had offered to host a meeting of senior Canadians, Poles, and Indians to discuss improving the body's functioning.

Broaching the idea to Rusk in Paris, Martin acknowledged not yet knowing Poland's view and far preferring Geneva for a meeting—as Rusk had suggested—because in New Delhi Canada might come under extra Indian-Polish pressure to adopt anti–United States actions. Rusk said equably that he would be glad to see the ICC meet at a higher level and "find any handle which it could grasp" to act more effectively (e.g., strengthening Sihanouk's borders, actually demilitarizing the "Demilitarized Zone", exchanging prisoners, or "establishing discreet contacts" between the combatants); as for a venue, he preferred but would not insist on Geneva, and he even acknowledged a plus in a more quiet setting like New Delhi if the Poles accepted it.[31] Martin's formal plan, which he gave to Rusk the next day, termed a bombing halt "an indispensable element in any forward move if it is to stand a chance of being considered by the other side," yet reassuringly vowed that to bar Polish-Indian collusion, Canada would demand a balanced package deal and unanimity.[32]

Listening to Martin, Rusk silently wondered if the Polish channel in Saigon and the nascent ICC gambit might be "developing an interconnection."[33] But he made "no reference whatsoever" to Marigold, only alluding "vaguely to Poles doing something in North Vietnam and to their having a parliamentary delegation in Hanoi." When Martin remarked that this would be a strange way to conduct diplomacy, Rusk waved it off, saying there was "not necessarily any connection between the two."[34] Bestowing his blessing to go forward, Rusk gave Martin no clue that he might run right into a Polish buzz saw.

❋ ❋ ❋

That Wednesday afternoon in Paris, Rusk was uncertain whether or not North Vietnam had already pulled the plug on Marigold. After reading Gronouski's report of his talk with Rapacki the day before, when the Pole had mentioned "this postponement of Warsaw meetings," he cabled Katzenbach to ask "whether Rapacki was in fact giving us a negative reply from Hanoi. Could you give me a brief evaluation on this point?"[35]

In fact, Rapacki was not yet "closing the Marigold door," as Katzenbach clarified in a message Rusk received Wednesday night in Paris.[36] But had he craned his ears, the secretary might have heard the sound of slamming from about 850 miles to the east.

Warsaw: "The Last Drop That Spilled over the Cup"

Wednesday in the Polish capital began rainy, slushy, gray, dismal. At the U.S. Embassy, reading a cable reporting the new attacks on Hanoi, Gronouski felt "despair. He thought it should not have happened."[37] When the ministry summoned him to another meeting with Rapacki, at 6 p.m., he steeled himself for the worst.

Trying to avoid attracting attention, he went through his normal paces. Only at dusk, taking now customary precautions, did he make his way to MSZ's inconspicuous side entrance. The mood was far grimmer than the day before. Michałowski and the translator somberly received him.[38] Then "Rapacki entered the room unsmiling, and during entire meeting maintained a calm, serious and matter-of-fact attitude."

"You probably know what I have to tell you," he began. "I would still prefer to hear it," Gronouski replied.

Early that afternoon, Rapacki had received Siedlecki's report of the Wednesday morning talk with Dong.[39] Now, he told Gronouski that had he known the afternoon before that Hanoi had already been bombed again, "then our conversation of course would have had [a] different character than it did." He blasted Washington for launching, despite repeated Polish warnings (six, in Warsaw and Saigon), "a new and particularly brutal raid on the residential area in Hanoi precisely at the moment when the [U.S. government] knew that the matter of a Warsaw contact with Hanoi was being actively considered. This was the last drop that spilled over the cup." In fact, he said, from the time Poland conveyed the DRV's interest in talks—"more than a signal . . . a direct, positive response from Hanoi about the possibility of talks in Warsaw"—Washington hedged its position and, "worse, it entered a new phase of escalation." With U.S. intentions no longer in doubt, he said, Hanoi had ended consideration of the proposed contact. Rapacki, whom Gronouski sensed was "genuinely angry," stressed that Warsaw fully shared Hanoi's perspective.

"The Polish government states that the whole responsibility for wrecking this chance to resolve peacefully the Vietnam War rests on the USA," he said. "I am expressing more than regret because of your—I do not have you personally in mind—abuse of our goodwill. Once again it becomes clear how difficult it is to believe in your word. In the future only facts can be taken into consideration."

In a "tormented voice," Gronouski "expressed sadness" at the unfolding of events, and promised to deliver Rapacki's words to LBJ with suitable commentary. Asking to be able to communicate directly should the need arise, he professed faith that despite this setback, there were "no insurmountable difficulties."

Rapacki sensed Gronouski's anguish and, in words (that the American did not report) implying that he did not blame the ambassador personally, ended: "I understand your role and I understand you."[40]

Gronouski, "crushed,"[41] returned to the embassy and worked into the night on a long cable (Warsaw 1471) describing the chilly conversation. For the first time since becoming involved in Marigold, he sent the message personally to LBJ. Unwilling to give up on the peace effort, he appended an impassioned, desperate appeal to the man he saw as a "good czar" who would do the right thing if only he knew the truth. (He did not know, of course, that Johnson himself had overruled his aides to let the Hanoi raids go forward.) The United States faced "a crisis in our world leadership role," he warned, and must take "decisive and immediate action" to save Marigold:

Comment: If Moscow datelined account of latest Hanoi bombing published in Dec 14 Paris edition press reports of *New York Times* and *Herald Tribune* is true, then we are in an incredibly difficult position. I am convinced that if this represents the breakdown of the current peace initiative—and it surely does unless we take decisive and immediate action—then the Soviets, the Poles and the North Vietnamese will have no trouble convincing the leadership in every capital of the world that our stated desire for peace negotiations is insincere. If we treat this turn of events as anything less than a crisis in our world leadership role then I believe we are making a tragic mistake.

I am convinced that up till now the Poles, accepting the genuineness of our interest in negotiation, have used whatever influence they have in Hanoi (in all likelihood with Soviet backing) in an effort to initiate U.S.-NVN [North Vietnam] peace talks. I also am convinced that Rapacki was expressing genuine concern when he warned that the increase in bombing was destroying what appeared to him a good chance that NVN would overcome Chinese influence and engage in Warsaw talks.

We have no choice but to take immediate action to try to get discussions back on track. For any chance of success this would require, in my judgment, conveying to Poles that we are willing to accept Rapacki's Dec 13 reasoning (Warsaw 1458) and are prepared now to assure the Poles that we will take care not to create impression of bombing intensification in NVN during period of delicate negotiations over the holding of Warsaw U.S.-NVN peace talks. We would also assure the Poles that we do not intend to bomb in the immediate vicinity of Hanoi and Haiphong during this period. We would again express our deep desire for the initiation of talks and ask the Poles to continue their efforts.

I do not know whether this presentation will achieve its purpose, but I am deeply convinced it is imperative that we try. The alternative is not only to lose an opportunity for initiating negotiations, but also to do serious damage to the credibility of the U.S. government's stated objectives.[42]

Throughout his year of dabbling in Vietnam diplomacy, Gronouski trusted his ability to "deliver" LBJ (e.g., on a bombing halt) should the Poles convince Hanoi to play ball. Until now, he had never felt compelled to redeem this faith. But as Marigold wilted before his eyes, the distressed politician-turned-diplomat tried to vault over the heads of bureaucrats straight to the president. If only the czar knew.

Washington: "What Do You Mean by Hanoi?"

As Wednesday began, officials managing Marigold were still formulating a response to Gronouski's account, received the afternoon before, of his talk with Rapacki. The intervening Hanoi attacks, however, not only complicated the Warsaw channel but also generated a public crisis that threw the administration into disarray. Officials had grasped that going ahead with the Hanoi bombing risked Marigold's collapse along with a public flap once, as seemed likely, word leaked of the covert peace attempt's failure. Yet they hardly anticipated how fast the political repercussions would mushroom—even before the secret diplomatic context became known.

As State Department spokesman Robert McCloskey took the lectern for his daily noon press briefing, reports of the second consecutive day of Hanoi bombings were streaming in. Reporters, increasingly leery of administration denials, scented blood. At first McCloskey vehemently denied that sites within the capital could have been hit, but, "obviously flustered," eventually conceded that this might happened—an admission quickly hedged by quibbles over the city's official limits ("I don't know how they are defined").

"Have we bombed Hanoi?" a reporter asked outright.

"We have not. . . ." Pause. "What do you mean by Hanoi?"

The spokesman went on to explain, "I took the question to mean that these are civilian targets or population centers; people and the rest, which one generally associates when talking about a city."

Parsing questions, McCloskey disputed the meaning of "Hanoi"—wriggling over how far "suburbs" stretched, he noted, "I may live in one here, and you may live in another, and they may be distances apart. And I am not trying to be facetious at all here; I just don't know enough about the geography there to be of any specific help." Under fire, he clung to his mantra that America only bombs military or "militarily associated" targets, had not struck Hanoi itself (whatever that was), and above all, was not adding new targets or "escalating the war." His evasions elicited ridicule—newspapers took the unusual step of publishing excerpts from the official transcript[43]—and, worse, were unconvincing; the next day, the *New York Times* quoted unnamed officials as conceding that some targets "undoubtedly" were, by "normal man-in the street parlance," inside Hanoi, and a follow-up article, discounting denials of any escalation, linked the raids to a broader strategy of "slowly and quietly" ratcheting up pressure on North Vietnam.[44]

As in so many Washington ruckuses, the inept initial response to a charge magnified the damage, radiating the impression that the administration had something to hide. A British diplomat, describing the "furor" to London, sadly remarked: "The unfortunate State Department spokesman is clearly subjected to a merciless barrage of questions, and instead of admitting that he does not know the answers . . . has tried to talk his way out, but has only succeeded in becoming more deeply embedded in the mud."[45]

✳ ✳ ✳

December 14 was a tumultuous day for administration spokesmen. At the White House, Moyers made the surprise announcement of his resignation to run *Newsday,* effective February 1. He cited "personal family obligations," but observers linked his departure—he was the last to go of the original crew the Texan had brought to the Oval Office after JFK's assassination—not only to personal and financial reasons but also to strains over Vietnam. Fearing that a closet dove had fled the coop, many liberals regretted Moyers' exit. Arthur M. Schlesinger Jr., who had turned sharply against the war, called his friend after hearing the news to express "very mixed feelings over his departure: It was fine for him but sad for the country." "You know, Arthur," Moyers told the historian, "I would not be leaving if I thought I could do any good by staying."[46] An "imperious" president had lost his only aide "willing to say 'No' to him," the *New York Times* rued.[47]

Even on his way out, Moyers labored to close LBJ's widening "credibility gap" on Vietnam. Hoping to soften the belligerent image evoked by the Hanoi bombings, he told the press that Johnson would be "very glad" to discuss a prolonged cease-fire or any other reduction of hostilities in direct talks with the enemy. While seemingly responsive to the pope's plea for an extended holiday truce (and a modified version pushed by Mike Mansfield), the offer meant less than met the eye. Because hawks in Washington and Saigon strongly opposed a lengthy cease-fire without significant DRV concessions, the proposal was issued in full confidence that it would be rejected—the Viet Cong had already rebuffed the Vatican appeal, and Hanoi was certain to oppose a conditional approach that failed to incorporate the unconditional bombing halt that it publicly demanded.[48]

At the top of the administration, moreover, those who were aware of Marigold had extra reason to know that the North Vietnamese were unlikely to jump at the offer, given the latest strikes on Hanoi. Moyers was among them, yet he could hardly speak openly on this score. When asked if he had seen "any evidence at this point that the other side is interested in discussing" peace, he hedged judiciously: "I am not familiar with all the evidence that might be available. I can't answer that question."[49] It is not known, from the available record, whether, behind his black-rimmed glasses, Moyers—this unflappable "young man of intelligence, idealism and broad understanding" (as the *Times* hailed him), whose move to journalism was a "serious loss to President Johnson and to the Federal Government"—squirmed, batted an eye, hesitated, or otherwise felt or showed discomfiture in deflecting this query, or if he responded instantly, instinctively, having mastered the mouthpiece's craft of artfully composing (and delivering poker-faced) answers that were neither outright lies nor fully truthful.[50] In any case, he would later have a pivotal opportunity, after leaving office, to display greater candor regarding Vietnam—and Marigold.

* * *

How did the uproar over the Hanoi raids affect the officials handling Marigold? Mostly it annoyed them, and from that day forward, a more combative tone crept into U.S. statements, reflecting a rawer sensitivity to the peril that the administration might get blamed for ruining the most serious (indeed, the *only* serious) peace effort on the horizon. Far from warming to Polish arguments (or Gronouski's), senior officials, from LBJ down, dug in their heels, circled the wagons, and adopted the strategy that the best defense was a ferocious offense (choose your cliché).

But they plainly felt on the defense. Their attention was split between trying to get the dialogue with the DRV in Warsaw going (a fast-fading hope) and making a "record" of sincerely seeking talks. Wednesday afternoon, Rostow forwarded press items on civilian casualties in Hanoi to a perturbed LBJ as aides hastily cabled exculpatory data to Rusk and other officials abroad to help them justify the attacks.[51] Meanwhile, Leonard Unger drafted messages to Warsaw responding both to the previous day's talk with Rapacki and the tumult over the bombings. Katzenbach cabled Rusk in Paris: "Firm instructions are being prepared for Gronouski designed to keep the dialogue going, while at the same time making a clear record of the legitimacy of our participation in the MARIGOLD effort since its inception."[52] In taking a stiff, unapologetic stand, the acting secretary mirrored LBJ's desires; between conversations with aides drafting the messages for Gronouski, Katzenbach had ample opportunity to secure presidential guidance and approval, at White House meetings in the afternoon and over the phone that evening.[53]

The resulting cable to Warsaw, sent late Wednesday night, stoutly insisted that the Poles, not the Americans, were responsible for the delays and difficulties in opening the Warsaw contacts.[54] Terming Rapacki's remarks the day before "discouraging in terms of possibilities of our moving at an early date to direct talks with Hanoi," Katzenbach explicitly voiced the acute skepticism toward the entire effort felt by LBJ and his closest advisers. Just as they cast aspersions on Communist claims that U.S. ordnance had fallen inside Hanoi, officials began seeding comparable doubts about foreseeable charges that the bombings had blasted a real chance for peace.

"In light of Polish tactics," Katzenbach wrote, "we are now inclined to wonder whether they ever had any NVN commitment to a meeting in Warsaw or whether it is not more likely that they have been engaging in an effort to get us committed to something as close as possible to our maximum position and then see whether they could get Hanoi lined up to talk on that basis." He instructed Gronouski to, in exchanges with Rapacki, "keep the door open" for talks should a DRV rep actually show up, and ensure that the "record should clearly show our persistent efforts to move forward" and Polish assertions that U.S. actions put a "roadblock" in the initiative's path were "thoroughly refuted."

Katzenbach directed Gronouski to set up another session with Rapacki to review the affair since mid-November, stressing Washington's reasonableness, including its readiness for direct talks in Warsaw and "perfectly natural" interpretation clause. Refuting claims that the Hanoi raids constituted "escalation," he should stress that violence continued on both sides "before, during and after all this was taking place"; that the bombings' pace fluctuated depending on weather and technical factors; and that the "complications" blocking direct talks were introduced not by Washington, as Rapacki alleged, but by the Poles, who had diverged from what was agreed with Lewandowski by adding extraneous, one-sided conditions. Gronouski should leave Rapacki "in no doubt that we have done everything possible to open up the way to peaceful settlement, and we are very much disturbed at our having been unable to move forward at Warsaw as we had been led to expect from the earlier conversations in Saigon."

After setting the record straight, Gronouski would reaffirm his desire to speak with DRV representatives to agree on means to reduce the fighting, perhaps incorporating Phase A/B and upcoming holiday truces—and underline that Washington had "quite fully and frankly" discussed its stand, yet not heard one word directly from Hanoi.

This sternly worded cable left the State Department at 10:52 p.m. on Wednesday; however, due to a five-hour delay caused by "technical difficulties," Gronouski's own ciphered telegram from Warsaw, describing his gloomy conversation with Rapacki earlier that evening and imploring LBJ to take drastic steps to rescue the initiative, only reached Washington after midnight, at 12:32 a.m.[55] The crisscrossing missives dramatized the divergence between LBJ and the State Department, on the one hand, and their envoy in Warsaw. "Thus, just as Gronouski is ordered to launch a pre-emptive offensive," the Pentagon Papers' authors observed, "he is himself recommending retreat."[56]

※ ※ ※

When composing this cable, State Department officials had anticipated that Gronouski, promptly implementing fresh instructions, would see Rapacki on Thursday or Friday, then leave with his family for the West German resort of Garmisch in the Bavarian Alps for a long-planned ski excursion. After seeing Rapacki on

Tuesday, Gronouski had raised the question of what to do about the trip, which was supposed to last through New Year's Day. Due to Marigold, he felt it "most unwise" to be gone from Warsaw for two weeks "during this critical period," yet feared that "without a good cover," abruptly canceling the holiday plans, which were "well-known to embassy community," would arouse press speculation connecting the sudden move to Vietnam diplomacy. But, he noted, a potential excuse existed: On January 2, the Poles were due to make their first zloty repayment on a U.S. loan extended under LBJ's "bridge-building" policy to enhance ties with Eastern European nations, and hurried talks were already under way to grant Warsaw relief, provided it met certain conditions. Perhaps, he suggested, the department might invite him to Washington for Vietnam consultations, using the loan question as a pretext.[57] Hoping to minimize the risk of exposure, U.S. officials advised Gronouski to proceed with his vacation, while telling Rapacki that he could easily cancel or change plans if a meeting with the North Vietnamese were set up, if necessary rushing back to Warsaw under the guise of urgent debt relief consultations. However, they vetoed his idea of flying to Washington to discuss Marigold.

✳ ✳ ✳

A couple of hours before sending his instructions Wednesday night, Katzenbach tried to butter up the anxious envoy—perhaps anticipating his negative reaction to the new round of attacks on Hanoi and to the unyielding directive he would soon receive. The president, he cabled Gronouski, had been "most complimentary" of his handling of the secret exchanges with the Poles. "All of us in the Department heartily concur," he added. "Have a good vacation."[58]

Thursday, December 15

Hanoi: "We Would Have Talked with the USA . . ."

North Vietnam could tell that it had a good thing going with the international clamor over the Hanoi bombings, and—seeing Washington's clumsy efforts to counter charges that it had caused civilian casualties in the capital—avidly spread its side of the story. Thursday morning, Ha Van Lau summoned representatives of the tiny, isolated local ICC bureau and "repudiated the American denial, publicly made, of allegations that U.S. aircraft had attacked nonmilitary targets inside Hanoi on December 13 and 14." To bolster his case, a PAVN major escorted the Polish, Canadian, and Indian delegates, whose movements were usually strictly circumscribed, to inspect bomb damage in and around the city. The six locations they visited included the two at the heart of the flap: the diplomatic quarter and the shantytown near the Red River Bridge.[59] Afterward, the three ICC representatives agreed to meet the next morning to see if they could reach a consensus on the politically explosive question of whether, contrary to public U.S. denials, planes had bombed targets within Hanoi, causing civilian casualties.

✳ ✳ ✳

Even as it severed the Warsaw contacts and kindled an all-out campaign to pillory the United States, Hanoi sent a gentle but—Siedlecki thought—unmistakable signal that its interest in negotiations had not entirely dissipated. On Thursday, in the midst of a "rather active program of farewell visits" to DRV officials before his term ended, he received an unexpected invitation to see Xuan Thuy. The Pole naturally accepted and, he reported afterward to Michałowski, the influential head of the VWP Central Committee's Foreign Department "received me, and bid me farewell, very warm-heartedly." More significantly, the veteran revolutionary also "recalled in general the USA peace proposals" and several times repeated, almost verbatim, the following "thesis":

> Peace is the heartfelt desire of the Vietnamese nation. We would have talked with the USA on the subject of peace if they had taken an objective position on this matter. But we do not want to talk under pressure. In the face of the present conduct of the USA, we must be especially vigilant. To strength, to every attack, we will reply with strength and counter-attacks. We have the power for this.

Afterward, Siedlecki surmised that the last-minute meeting (on only two hours' notice) with such a senior personality, who repeatedly stressed the most important points, was "not accidental." "The objective could have been," he surmised, "to indicate—after PVD's last declaration—that the Vietnamese side does not want to lock completely the doors to talks."[60]

Warsaw: "Cards on the Table"
The first thing Thursday—another gray, wet, dreary morning—Gronouski read the hard-line State Department instructions. They appalled him. Though not a weatherman, he could tell which way the wind was blowing in Washington: diametrically opposite to his own intensely felt views. Rather than tamely submit, however, and promptly set up another session with Rapacki to rebuff the Pole's arguments, as ordered, Gronouski resolved to fight—and he found a pretext for doing so. Katzenbach's cable, he noticed, referred not to his most recent telegram from Warsaw reporting his Wednesday evening meeting with Rapacki and his appeal to LBJ, which had been delayed in transmission, but to earlier, now outdated, messages.

That gave the embattled ambassador a tiny opening to further plead his case—before Washington had a chance to decipher, digest, and, no doubt, decisively reject his earlier advice—and he gave it everything he had. All morning, constructing the most persuasive brief possible, Gronouski poured out his arguments in a second, even longer and more earnest, personal plea to the president.[61]

After explaining that he was holding off on contacting Rapacki pending receipt of updated instructions, he started with the unobjectionable observation that of the Pole's two key objections, the interpretation clause had faded to a "peripheral rather than a central issue" compared with the air attacks. Then he entered more dangerous waters by effectively taking sides in the rancorous argument over whether the United States had recently "escalated" its bombing of Hanoi:

> With respect to the increased tempo of bombing argument, the impression I have is that the level of bombing activity in the Hanoi vicinity has sharply increased since Dec. 2. Whatever the reasons are for this increase, assuming my impressions are accurate, one does not have to stretch his imagination to conclude that Hanoi might in fact be tying this in with the prospective Warsaw talks and thus interpreting it as pressure in the manner described by Rapacki.

After this heretical assertion, Gronouski conceded that the Pole might be "engaging in devious tactics" and in fact lacked the Hanoi commitment he claimed to possess; this was "a matter of judgment which must be deduced from the evidence available." But after two weeks of intense face-to-face encounters, Gronouski thought he knew better:

> My judgment is that Rapacki has had authority from Hanoi to attempt to arrange Warsaw meetings and that his efforts to persuade us on the interpretation and bombing questions is not only an attempt to get us committed to our maximum position, which I am sure the Poles as well as Hanoi would like to accomplish, but also reflects the intransigence of Hanoi on these points. My reading is that the Poles during the last few days de-emphasized the interpretation clause because they believed that they could convince Hanoi of the reasonableness of our position on this point, but felt that the intensification of bombing was too much to overcome in their efforts to bring Hanoi to the conference table.

Gronouski again argued that there was "much to gain and little cost" by assuring the Poles that no further intensification of the bombing would occur, especially around Hanoi or Haiphong, so long as the "delicate" discussions regarding possible U.S.-DRV contacts continued. Otherwise, he warned—in contrast to the resumption of air strikes at the end of the thirty-seven-day pause, after which Warsaw had claimed "on very shaky ground" that Hanoi had indicated its readiness for talks—Washington would "have a far more difficult time, if the peace efforts break down this time, in making a credible refutation of the arguments that the Poles, Soviets, North Vietnamese and their allies will inevitably make." They would "be able to point to what appears here to be clear evidence that at almost the precise time of the final phase of the move undertaken by the Poles to initiate talks in Warsaw, the U.S., despite repeated warnings by the Poles that intensification of bombing particularly in the vicinity of Hanoi was undermining promising attempts to bring Hanoi to the conference table," went ahead and bombed anyway. Regardless of whether the entire effort had in fact been an "exercise in Polish duplicity" (which he clearly doubted), Gronouski stressed that such arguments would be "very difficult to refute"—which is what he had meant by warning that the bombings put the United States in "an incredibly difficult situation." He continued:

> The Poles will be able to argue effectively that had we been sincere in our efforts to initiate negotiations, we certainly would not have aggravated the problem in the face of repeated warnings at the most critical stage of discussions leading up to the commencement of negotiations. They will be able to say that their request was reasonable; that they did not ask that we stop bombing North Vietnam but only that we refrain at this point from creating clear impression that we were stepping up our bombing tempo as a means of either bringing pressure on Hanoi or sabotaging our own peace effort. The Poles will also be able to point out that they made clear to us that the impression of intensification of bombing and the implications of pressure tactics played into the hands of Communist China and to disadvantage of Poles' attempt to induce Hanoi to overcome China's influence and engage in peace talks. I am concerned that while we may be able to develop a case which satisfies ourselves we will not be able to refute effectively to others the Polish line of reasoning.

Such considerations, Gronouski explained, had impelled him to warn that Washington faced "a crisis in our world leadership role," potentially exacerbating already grave doubts in Western capitals about the wisdom of bombing North Vietnam, unless rapid remedial action were taken—namely, the reassurances to the Poles against further air raids. If Washington were right, and Rapacki were simply stringing the Americans along in hopes of extracting concessions, then "we will have suffered no substantive loss and will have at the same time laid the basis for an eminently improved refutation" of eventual charges; but if Gronouski had correctly grasped the situation and the Poles were in fact "making a sincere effort," then this course "would improve the presently poor prospects for negotiations."

✳ ✳ ✳

Also on early Thursday morning, as Gronouski was crafting this cri de coeur a few blocks away, a crucial yet mysterious actor in the drama made an appearance at Rapacki's office—apparently his first since the affair had commenced. "The Vietnamese Ambassador turned up this morning," Rapacki began a *pilna notatka* (urgent note) on what he considered an eye-opening conversation.[62] Officially, Do Phat Quang came to deliver a formal DRV statement on the recent Hanoi bombings and to inquire about Warsaw's response—only to be told that he was "late" because a harsh draft official denunciation already lay "on [Gomułka's] desk" and would be broadcast later that day by Polish state radio and television— but the talk quickly broadened into a review of the secret diplomacy, including Washington's behavior and what it signified for the future.

Rapacki, probing, voiced surprise that the Americans had bombed Hanoi "precisely at this moment"—provoking Quang to, in the Pole's cryptic summary, "put [his] cards on the table. He was informed about everything." Rapacki then recorded, without elaborating, that he "familiarized [himself] with the extent of his [Quang's] knowledge" and "repeated part of some elements which were relayed to Hanoi"—indirectly confirming that neither he nor Michałowski (who would have automatically informed his boss of any contact) had previously clarified Quang's awareness, a potentially serious lapse in their handling of Polish-DRV communications during the exchanges with Gronouski.[63]

After Rapacki politely expressed "understanding and admiration for the concrete and flexible tactics of the DRV government," Quang, intriguingly, seemed primarily interested in "whether the Americans would take up our initiative." Had Hanoi's ambassador not yet received his government's firm rejection of any further contacts? Or, despite it, was he pursuing on his own the possibility of later renewing the peace probe? Whatever was behind this query, Rapacki responded vaguely that he had not considered the issue in detail, but that he suspected that an eventual resumption was "not excluded." Still, he observed that the U.S. conduct was "so insolent," offering Warsaw such good arguments for a possible "white book," that he had to wonder whether Washington already had some alternative diplomatic strategy in mind, perhaps exploiting a holiday truce or moratorium on further bombings of Hanoi, though it was unclear whether the Americans would return to the Lodge proposals and the Warsaw channel or put forward a different set of ideas, perhaps using a different contact point.

"We know how difficult it is to believe their words," he noted, repeating the formula he had used with Gronouski, so only facts should be taken "into account"—yet he acknowledged that one had to listen to them if they presented "something new." At one point, seemingly fishing for an optimistic sign, Quang noted that Johnson had stated that he was "ready to talk with the DRV on the theme of stopping the bombings."

✳ ✳ ✳

That day or the next, Quang informed Nguyen Dinh Phuong that, in light of the latest developments, his services would no longer be required in Warsaw. The December 13–14 raids had left Phuong "disappointed" and "angry." Even before Quang gave him the official word, he had already concluded that "we cannot continue to wait for contact. . . . [The Americans] will apply pressure, [and were conducting] a double-faced policy. . . . I knew their intention is to have the contact from a position of strength: 'If you do not agree to our position, we will intensify the bombing.'"[64]

Now the ambassador relayed Hanoi's instructions for Phuong to fly to Moscow to rendezvous with a DRV delegation on its way to Paris for a French Communist Party Congress.[65] He did so promptly, returning as he came, on a LOT Airlines flight to the Soviet capital. So ended Phuong's tantalizing, memorable, but ultimately dispiriting adventure in clandestine peace diplomacy.

✳ ✳ ✳

As Rapacki had forecast to Quang Thursday morning, an official Polish statement denouncing the "criminal," "brutal," "beastly," and "barbarous" U.S. actions was issued that evening. Gronouski, still gingerly awaiting a response to his earlier appeals, transmitted the text to Washington. He surmised that the acerbic statement, though disappointing, reflected the Poles' "feeling of need to quickly restore their credentials with Hanoi after a period of flirtation" with the U.S. government. It left him "no less convinced than before" of the need to take the actions he had recommended "to get talks back on track." It was, he insisted, "even more essential" to reassure Rapacki, and through him Hanoi, that the provocative air raids would cease. Still, Gronouski admitted he found it "hard to be optimistic at this point"—not only about the hardening stands of Hanoi and Warsaw but also, though he did not say so, that of his own government.[66]

Paris: "A Very Exposed Flank"

The disconsolate Gronouski might have been heartened if he had known that Rusk, following the cable traffic in Paris, had begun to share his deep concern about the latest Hanoi bombings' potentially devastating impact on world opinion and regard (especially in Eastern Europe) for the sincerity of U.S. interest in peace in Vietnam once the Polish negotiating initiative became public—even though the secretary of state remained dubious, to put it mildly, that any genuine chance for peace had been involved ("In my view, there was nothing to collapse"[67]). It was not that Rusk had a thin skin when it came to international criticism of the war, even from allies: He could shrug off the fretting of Brown or Martin or even de Gaulle's verdict, which he expressed when the American called on him late Wednesday, that the United States had allowed itself to become "bogged down in secondary and ridiculous considerations in Vietnam, particularly when we think of what could be done for world peace if this issue were settled."[68]

Indeed, behind closed doors Thursday afternoon, Rusk did his utmost to give the North Atlantic Council "some 'old-time religion' on Vietnam," as he told LBJ afterward.[69] To the nervous Europeans, he asserted that the Far East constituted a western "flank" of NATO, and anyone who expected the United States to abide faithfully by its treaty obligations in Europe while abandoning them in Vietnam "should be told to forget it." Far from contrite over the Hanoi bombings, Rusk noted the ongoing Communist violence against targets in South Vietnam and called for "a little dash of just old-fashioned fairness and reciprocity." Washington's sincerity and flexibility in seeking peace, he insisted, was unprecedented— some Asian friends even warned that it "tried too hard to find a solution"—and this had led Hanoi to overestimate Washington's eagerness for peace. Rebuffing those who were afraid that escalation in Vietnam endangered progress in East-West relations, he insisted, to the contrary, that détente would not be achieved by sacrificing little countries to "somebody who's got a big appetite." Concluding his pep talk, Rusk harkened back to the "dark days of the many crises since 1945" that had been overcome, and he voiced confidence that Vietnam would remain "a manageable problem."[70]

Rusk's sermon did little to convert his skeptical congregants. Some were aghast at his attempts to liken the East Asian clashes against Communism to the standoff in Europe, to claim that China was NATO's western flank, or to scold SEATO signatories for failing to line up alongside Washington in Vietnam. The last argument's "ingratiating disingenuousness," a British official privately carped to colleagues, "shows Mr. Rusk at his worst. He knows full well that we & the French do not believe that the [1954] Manila Treaty imposes any obligation on members of SEATO to help South Vietnam. The comparison is all the more ludicrous in the light of America's violations of the Geneva Agreements. The attempt to draw an implicit comparison between NATO + SEATO in these circumstances can, indeed, only be read as a calculated impertinence."[71]

While demanding stouter support, however, Rusk did not tell his fellow NATO ministers that even *he* felt uneasy over the latest bombings. Though he was an inveterate hawk who was deeply skeptical of prospects for negotiations, Rusk sensed how bad the record might look in light of Marigold's apparent collapse—and at this key juncture, he expressed his reservations, which have previously escaped historians' notice, directly and forcefully to the president. Early Thursday evening, he sent an "eyes only" cable from Paris to Washington (where it was early afternoon) for delivery straight to LBJ, cutting out Katzenbach—and, for that matter, everybody else in the national security bureaucracy who would ordinarily see even top secret, "nodis" messages:

EYES ONLY FOR THE PRESIDENT FROM THE SECRETARY
Decoding officer should ensure that this message is delivered only to the President without any other distribution whatever.

I feel obligated to express my concern that we are holding up a very exposed flank through the intensity of bombing in the immediate Hanoi-Haiphong areas in juxtaposition with the Marigold operation. Quite apart from the merits of the issues involved, we are in danger of being trapped into a situation where the Poles or the Soviets could cause us grievous harm by a charge that there was a serious effort by Hanoi toward peace and that we rejected it by intensified bombing. From a broader point of view our ability to hold Eastern Europe within certain limits on Vietnam is a matter of major political and military importance. It is possible that, given their ideological blinders and devious logic, we will be credited with unreliability through the most private contacts.

It is unfortunate that weather and other operational factors combined to concentrate actual strikes (which I had approved) in a short span of time just following Lewandowski's approach to Lodge.

I am reluctant to try to call the shots from here after a two-week absence from Washington but I am inclined to think that a temporary pause in the immediate

Hanoi-Haiphong area would be of advantage in terms of putting the responsibility up to Warsaw and Moscow to produce something. During the Christmas and New Year period we will be under considerable pressure for a general pause in North Vietnam but I would be opposed since infiltration continues and our hands should not be tied at this point in protecting our own forces. It does not seem to me, however, that there would be military disadvantage in staying outside of our traditional perimeters around Hanoi and Haiphong between now and, say, the first of the year. Obviously, my view is influenced by my own preoccupation with the international political aspects of the problem but these are not the only factors. Bob McNamara will be back tomorrow and I have not had a chance to discuss this with him. You may wish to do so. I have taken unusual means to limit this telegram to your own eyes because I did not wish to have any possibility that anyone outside of you, McNamara and myself could ever suppose that there is any difference among us. Your own decision on this will have my fullest support both inside and outside the government.
  —RUSK[72]

McNamara, too, was discomfited by the impact of the latest Hanoi raids, which were "getting a good ride in the Paris afternoon papers." In a background briefing for U.S. reporters at the Hotel Bristol before leaving the French capital Thursday evening, he "showed uncertainty and irritation—not at the questioner, but over the fact of the bombings," one correspondent present noted. While denying any policy change, and fencing over whether the North Vietnamese capital had actually been struck, McNamara seemed eager to change the subject. As the Pentagon delegation hurried to the airport, his spokesman, Arthur Sylvester, left "the impression that his Boss was not very happy about this one, and did not really know what had happened or what to make of it, but obviously it had not helped the U.S. with Rusk making yet another appeal for NATO understanding and support for the Vietnam War."[73]

To his closest collaborator at the Pentagon, John McNaughton, McNamara more candidly expressed his consternation. He would loyally "carry out" the president's will, but vowed that he would "fight hard" to curb the air strikes. The defense secretary "wants to tone down the bombing," McNaughton noted privately, convinced that it was "not worth the cost in men and equipment, that it is depriving us of international support, and it is frustrating negotiations—which he sees as the only way out of this war."[74]

Moscow: "A Picture of a Bazaar"

Meanwhile, also on Thursday, Hanoi officially informed the USSR of its decision to break off the Warsaw initiative; with Shcherbakov gone, it used the DRV Embassy in Moscow to relate the news to the Soviet Foreign Ministry.[75]

Like the Poles, the Soviets, closely following the secret diplomacy, were outraged and puzzled by the latest U.S. bombings. After returning to Washington later in December, Dobrynin would tell Llewellyn Thompson "completely off the record" that Kosygin's reply to Johnson's December 6 letter had "nearly been completed and that it was one we [Americans] would have liked" but that after news of the second round of attacks on Hanoi arrived in Moscow in the midst of the Plenum of the CPSU's Central Committee—particularly the vivid eyewitness reports—"this draft had been torn up and another one of quite a different character started."[76] Lunching with Rostow, he asserted that until the raids elicited an "emotional" reaction, Moscow was "hopeful" both about the Polish contacts and the correspondence with LBJ.[77] And to Harriman, Dobrynin stated flatly that "all of [the Soviet leaders] had believed that a meeting between the U.S. and [North Vietnam] was going to take place, and that this had not occurred only because of the bombing of Hanoi."[78]

Having helped spur the uproar with its reporting from Hanoi, Moscow led the international chorus of condemnation. On December 15, terming the latest attacks a "grave crime," the Soviets publicly denounced Washington for "fanning the flames of the aggressive war" and causing a "further aggravation of the international situation," and pledged to render utmost aid to the Vietnamese in their "heroic struggle against the criminal aggression of American imperialism."[79]

Significantly, however, newly declassified sources show that Moscow's consternation and, even more, its confusion at Washington's behavior extended beyond public propaganda or the private admonitions of U.S. officials to confidential intercommunist consultations. When the Polish ambassador saw Gromyko to report the latest developments, including Hanoi's decision to end the Warsaw exchanges, the Soviet confessed that he "could not understand the provocative conduct of the U.S."

"The policy of the U.S.," he told Pszczółkowski, "presents a picture of a bazaar, and not a policy of a great power."

Groping to explain how Washington could act so belligerently in the midst of such sensitive diplomacy, Gromyko, dourly assessing his opposite number, "emphasized the reactionary and extreme position toward Vietnam of Rusk, who represents the position of military victory." He stressed, however, that the United States should respond to the latest DRV statements, and asked the Pole to continue to keep him informed.[80]

* * *

Gromyko had reason to suspect that, despite the latest turn of events, Hanoi had not lost interest in diplomatic contacts with Washington. At precisely that moment, Communist sources disclose, Soviet leaders received firsthand, authoritative evidence that this was so. Earlier, as noted, Brezhnev had voiced "sorrow" that the North Vietnamese had not sought Soviet help in opening talks with Washington; now they did. In mid-December, Le Duc Tho stopped in Moscow for a few days of talks on his way back to Hanoi from Budapest. During his first meeting with the VWP Politburo member, on December 15, Brezhnev later recounted to Polish leaders, he "patiently" listened to a routine "lecture about the retreat of American imperialism and about the victory of the Vietnamese nation," then suggested that Tho "move to concrete matters." Then, according to Brezhnev, the Vietnamese Communist, stating that he was speaking on Politburo instructions, was practically "begging us" to take "an initiative in establishing contact with the USA in the matter of a peaceful settlement of the Vietnamese problem." Such contacts could take place, he explained in response to Soviet probing, through the DRV ambassador in Moscow or via Poland. Negotiations could accompany a continuing (military) "battle with American imperialism," he explained, terming Hanoi's new interest in them a "tactical move" because the Americans "still have not admitted . . . that they are losing [the war]." Meeting on December 17 with senior apparatchik Yuri Andropov (then head of the CPSU's department for liaison with Communist and workers' parties from socialist countries, but soon to become KGB chief), Tho—apparently after receiving new instructions related to the latest Hanoi raids—promised that additional messages would follow, but did not retract his earlier statements urging the Soviets to encourage contacts with Washington.[81]

Although fuzzy about exactly how Hanoi hoped Moscow would promote this aim, the new VWP Politburo stand reported by Brezhnev was a significant departure from prior flat statements that military conditions had not "ripened" enough to consider talks.

Washington: "We Are Counting on You in This Most Challenging Assignment"

The torrent of criticism over the Hanoi attacks, and even more over Washington's evasiveness regarding them, continued unabated on Thursday. Adding to the pressure (and to the administration's irritation with him), Thant denounced what he termed without qualification the "intensification" of U.S. bombing of North Vietnam and, fearing a "wider war," called for the air campaign to halt.[82]

At the State Department's daily press briefing, reporters again harangued McCloskey for a detailed response to the charges of civilian damage in Hanoi, and for the second day in a row the spokesman dug himself deeper in the mud; lacking concrete data, he could neither confirm nor deny that U.S. planes had struck residential areas within the capital, suggested that "no fixed geographical definition" of its municipal boundaries even existed, and repeated claims that only military targets (and perhaps some nearby houses) outside the city had been hit.[83]

Finally, late Thursday afternoon, the Pentagon tossed some meatier scraps. At a background briefing for reporters (who could only cite "U.S. officials") to relay the results of an internal inquiry, military sources "categorically denied" that American planes had hit Hanoi, and produced a detailed map of the DRV capital (which McCloskey lacked) to contend that the targets were outside official city limits (see map 4).[84]

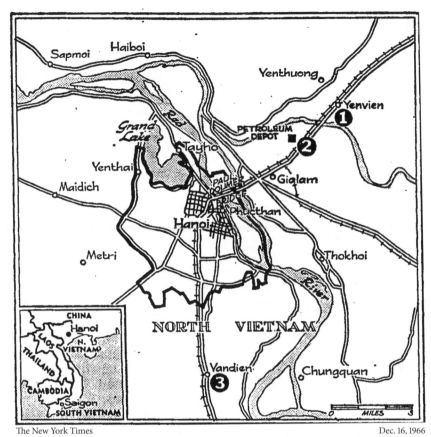

The New York Times   Dec. 16, 1966

The U.S. said American planes had bombed a railroad yard at Yenvien (1), a petroleum depot (2) and a truck yard at Vandien (3), but that no targets had been hit inside Hanoi, whose limits are shown by the heavy line.

Map 4. Pentagon map of Hanoi released during December 1966 and published in the *New York Times*.

Though the Pentagon argued that its delay in providing a sharper response merely reflected prudent checking, the administration was criticized for a hesitant, confused reaction that allowed the Communists "a romp" with their unchallenged charges. It seemed that the hapless McCloskey—the only official speaking on the record—had been hung out to dry, a "fall guy" left "in the lurch" by the Pentagon, White House, and his own bosses for two days without detailed or plausible information. But the real victim was Johnson himself; his eroding credibility on Vietnam had sustained yet another blow.[85]

* * *

Meanwhile, while around them officials dealing with Vietnam coped with the public bombing flap, the tiny State Department Marigold squad spent much of Thursday handling the secret crisis over the imploding peace diplomacy—and job one was getting their ambassador in Warsaw back in line. Shortly before 10 a.m., Rostow passed LBJ without comment Gronouski's cable (1471) reporting Rapacki's rebuff the previous evening and recommending an immediate bombing halt around Hanoi and Haiphong, and an hour or so later he relayed the diplomat's even more passionate follow-up personal message (1475), also received that morning.[86]

Johnson bristled at his envoy's ardent pleas to reverse course—his "rather heated tone," he later told Rusk, unpleasantly reminded him of Fulbright's fulminations[87]—and responded with guidance that strongly reinforced the prevailing line: acute skepticism toward both Rapacki's arguments and, more politely, Gronouski's virtual endorsement of them.[88] These presidential sentiments were incorporated by Unger, working on the draft cable, into an aggressive, unrepentant missive that amounted to a slap in the face both to its ultimate recipient, the Polish foreign minister, and the man charged with delivering its contents. At 5:25 p.m.—as LBJ, on the White House South Lawn, lit the National Christmas Tree—the State Department dispatched the six-page coded telegram to Warsaw. At its outset, Katzenbach assured Gronouski that his (first) message had been discussed with LBJ, who had approved the comments and instructions that he was now relaying.

Then Katzenbach lowered the boom. Washington saw no reason to modify its earlier edicts. Rejecting the Polish contention that the U.S. bombings had caused the prospects for talks to crumble, officials believed that Rapacki had "simply picked up lurid press reports and Communist accusations about recent bombing missions in Hanoi vicinity and decided to use them to the hilt in his tactic of getting maximum concessions out of us." Moreover, "we remain doubtful about how much part Hanoi has played in scenario which has unfolded in Warsaw over past two weeks."

Rather than take the conciliatory steps Gronouski so fervently urged, State ordered him to hold the line and even go on the attack. Rapacki should feel "the full force of our rejection of his arguments and our indignation at the Polish Government's changing the signals and then seeking to put the blame on us." To rebut the Pole's "apparent intent of pinning on us responsibility for possible breakdown of talks," Gronouski should "bear down hard" on Rapacki and argue that he, not Washington, bore primary culpability for the failure to begin direct talks. Complaints about the "reservation" clause and the bombings were spurious, he was to argue, especially given continued Communist infiltration and terrorism in South Vietnam, and the lack of any initial precondition related to the bombing for the Warsaw contact. Regarding Rapacki's "slur on the credibility of our word," Gronouski should retort that "we regretfully find ourselves being led to the conclusion that the Polish Government, whether on its own or in response to promptings from the North Vietnamese Government, is seeking to make a case which is based on false premises and does not relate to the facts as we know them." These actions could not only hurt prospects for peace talks but also damage U.S. officials' "attitude about our relations with the Polish Government."

On the hotly disputed issue of whether the Hanoi raids represented an "escalation" or effort to coerce the DRV government to the bargaining table, the message also took pains to straighten out Rapacki's thinking—and Gronouski's; the dangerously off-the-reservation ambassador's latest messages, of course, had expressed a view on the bombing that was now heresy, blasphemy, almost treason from the perspective of the besieged Johnson administration. There had been, Gronouski was firmly reminded, "neither escalation on our part, allegedly to put pressure on Hanoi, nor has there been any de-escalation in North Vietnam's infiltration nor in the terror in the South [which if anything had increased]. . . . The bombing of North Vietnam has proceeded on essentially the same pattern as before with no significant changes in intensity, proximity to Hanoi or type of targets." (In sensing an intensification, Gronouski had actually been far closer to the mark than his bosses conceded; as an internal Pentagon study later acknowledged, the December 13–14 raids collectively dumped more than a hundred tons of bombs, more than doubling the amount on December 2 and 4.[89])

As for the charges of attacks on civilian and diplomatic areas that had sparked worldwide outrage, the cable echoed the background Pentagon briefing that afternoon to reporters, some of whom, like Gronouski, seemed (in administration eyes) dangerously susceptible to Communist propaganda. Katzenbach's message directed him to advance to Rapacki the theory that antiaircraft fire or SAMs, rather than bombing errors, might have caused "such regrettable [civilian] damage as may have taken place"—and that in any case, "absolutely" no targets were inside Hanoi; the closest was more than 2 miles outside city limits, and more than 5 miles from the nearest claim of residential damage.

In a condescending section evidently intended to soothe the agitated envoy, Katzenbach also made clear that senior U.S. officials had concluded that Gronouski had, in essence, "gone native," failing to appreciate the "big picture" visible from Washington and perhaps afflicted by that ambassadorial disease known as "host-country-itis," which in this case implied something tantamount to becoming a Communist dupe:

> Your further interpretation and discussion contained Warsaw's 1475 is very much appreciated and I am sure you fully realize that all of us here profoundly share your concern over the turn events have taken in the last few days. Likewise I can well imagine that in the atmosphere of Warsaw and without full information available, particularly considering the bombing of North Vietnam, the Polish position may appear to be a strong one, whatever their motivation in presenting it as Rapacki has just done. We want to assure you, however, that on the basis of the overall picture as we can see it from Washington, the Polish case, except for some

fairly superficial and transitory matters, is a weak one and we wonder whether they will try to sell it to world opinion. We still believe that the Poles basically wish to work for a peaceful settlement and we think it more likely that Rapacki's present ploy is an opportunistic one, seizing the chance presented by the sensational publicity given to recent bombings in the Hanoi area (undoubtedly fed by the North Vietnamese) in order to extract one more ounce. . . .

Rapacki's last representations to you probably brings us to the crisis phase in our current efforts and we believe we will have the best chance of securing a resolution in our favor, i.e., by Hanoi's being ready to undertake talks on the basis worked out with Lewandowski, if we maintain and strongly defend our position and rebut and reject the line which Rapacki is trying to sell. We are counting on you in this most challenging assignment.[90]

Reversing its earlier advice, the State Department now urged Gronouski to cancel or postpone his vacation in order to promptly deliver his rebuttal to Rapacki. To arm him with debating points for his looming confrontation, Washington sent the envoy a detailed "résumé of [Viet Cong] terrorist activities directed against civilians in South Vietnam over recent weeks" and a lengthy justification of the bombings, fleshing out arguments that the Hanoi attacks were neither aimed at civilian targets, an escalation, nor an attempt to pressure the DRV in connection with Marigold.[91]

✳ ✳ ✳

None of these messages from Washington late Thursday, however, let Gronouski in on a vital bit of Marigold-related news he would have been overjoyed to receive. That afternoon or evening, LBJ made an unannounced decision to remove, at least for the time being, from the Rolling Thunder–52 target list the Yen Vien railroad yard and the Van Dien vehicle depot, which would otherwise be eligible to be rehit without further permission from Washington. Although a directive went out through military channels to "suspend further air strikes against these targets until further notice,"[92] Gronouski was not informed of this crucial decision to delete the two sites that had led to the controversial strikes; when reporters began inquiring why the raids near Hanoi had ceased, military spokesmen blamed bad weather, refusing to confirm that political considerations were involved.[93]

LBJ left no record to explain why, even as he approved a resolute defense of the Hanoi bombings to the Poles and the public, he secretly halted them. Besides the hemorrhaging of support the controversy was causing, undoubtedly the private entreaties he received that day from Rusk and, to a lesser extent, Gronouski, also swayed him. To some extent, the "good czar" may indeed have heard his subject's plaintive plea.

At the same time, however, Johnson adamantly refused to follow Gronouski's urging that he reassure Rapacki (and through him the North Vietnamese) that there would be no further bombing of Hanoi. Instead, at least for the time being, LBJ deliberately chose to foster the impression in Warsaw (and Hanoi) that Washington had absolutely no apologies, regrets, or second thoughts about the attacks that had raised so much ire.

New York City: "Uppick Visa Paris"

At 5:11 a.m. Thursday, a three-line telegram sent the previous day from Phnom Penh arrived in Times Square and quickly found its way to its addressee, Seymour Topping, the foreign editor of the nation's leading newspaper:

> NEW YORK TIMES TIMES SQUARE NEW YORK
> TOPPING INFORM HARRISON UPPICK VISA PARIS SUGGEST YOU PERSONALLY
> CABLE HERE REQUESTING GARRISON [sic] TRANSIT FACILITIES ASKING HIM
> CONTACT ME URGENTLY REGARDS
> BURPRESS[94]

Topping, an old Asia hand, himself coveted entry into isolated North Vietnam, but the wire delivered Thursday morning to his third-floor office signaled good news for a fellow *Times*man. He walked over to the assistant managing editor, Harrison E. Salisbury, and laid before him the terse, cryptic message. The former Moscow bureau chief and World War II correspondent was a dedicated maven on the Communist realm (proud of breaking the first intimations of the Sino-Soviet split in a dispatch from Mongolia), and had long—and until then, fruitlessly—cajoled, begged, harangued, and importuned the Hanoi leadership and its friends and sympathizers (from the Australian Communist journalist Wilfred Burchett to the widow of the antiwar activist Norman Morrison, who had immolated himself at a Pentagon protest in November 1965) for a chance to report from behind enemy lines on the world's top story. The previous June, on a trip to Southeast Asia, he had received a warm reception from the DRV consul in Phnom Penh, but then nothing, despite a continuing torrent of appeals, most recently a cable to Pham Van Dong in early December suggesting an invitation timed for the upcoming Christmas truce.[95]

Finally, it looked as though he had struck pay dirt—winning the race for a North Vietnamese visa not only with his own boss but also with other American reporters clamoring for entry. Who had sent the good news? "Burpress" stood for Wilfred Burchett, and both Salisbury and Topping had courted the Phnom Penh–based Australian correspondent, who enjoyed unique access within the Communist world, for aid regarding their pleas for entry into that realm.[96]

"Does this say what I think it does?" Topping asked Salisbury.

"Yes, I think it does."

"You're in."

"Well, let's wait and see. First let's send a cable for clarification and see if it really does mean to pick up the visa in Paris."[97]

Barely able to restrain his excitement, Salisbury quickly composed, in the same patois, a response to his helpful colleague:

> BURPRESS
> PHNOMPENH
> (CAMBODIA)
> WONDERFUL RE YOUR TELEGRAM TO TOPPING STOP DO EYE
> UNDERSTAND CORRECTLY UPPICK VISA PARIS AND TRANSIT VIA PHNOMPENH
> QUERY IF SO WILL PREPARE DEPART SOONEST AND ADVISE YOU TRAVEL PLANS
> STOP TOPPING MESSAGING PRINCE SIHANOUK REQUESTING TRANSIT VISA FOR
> UPPICK PARIS EMBASSY STOP ASSUME YOU INFORMING MINISTRY
> INFORMATION THERE STOP BEST REGARDS AND THANKS
> SALISBURY
> 11:00 A.M.-amg
> 12/15/66[98]

For the moment, Salisbury held his breath and his tongue—and awaited confirmation that the biggest scoop of his life, a bombshell in coverage of the war, might be only days away.

Friday, December 16

Hanoi: "Quite Stiff"

On Friday, a day after receiving a hint from Xuan Thuy of residual DRV interest in contacts with the Americans, Siedlecki got another blast of Hanoi's anger. The Polish envoy had requested a follow-up session with Dong to relate the contents of a cable he had received from Rapacki describing the latest exchange with Gronouski. Instead, Siedlecki was told that the premier was traveling and could not see him and shunted off to see Trinh. The hard-line foreign minister initially acted "quite stiff," apparently fearing—Siedlecki suspected—that Poland would try to convince the leadership to change its mind. But, hearing Rapacki's message and ascertaining that Warsaw fully endorsed Hanoi's decision to terminate the initiative, he became "more direct."

A more relaxed Trinh profusely thanked Siedlecki and Rapacki and hailed the uniformity of viewpoints of the two leaderships as "a valuable and most important point." Washington's conduct, he observed, had clarified its intentions for both Warsaw and Hanoi. Brezhnev, too, he added, had agreed that "responsibility for squandering the opportunity to establish contact falls on the U.S." Before the short conversation ended, the Pole noted the controversy over the U.S. denial that its planes had struck populated areas of Hanoi; Trinh responded that the DRV government was preparing "evidentiary and propaganda materials" to circulate abroad, and urged Poland to coordinate its own efforts in this campaign with Hanoi.[99]

✳ ✳ ✳

In fact, this campaign received a quiet boost from the outcome of a series of meetings elsewhere in Hanoi that Friday. Over the course of the day, the three ICC representatives who had taken the escorted tour of bomb damage—two of them, the Canadian and the Pole, military officers—hammered out an agreed "Statement of Factual Observations."[100] They reported seeing near the Doumer Bridge on the west bank of the Red River "an expanse of approximately 200 meters by 100 meters of scorched earth and charred debris" that had formerly been "the natural extension of a cluster of buildings" forming "a hamlet" consisting of "poor residential quarters for workers," many constructed from bamboo.[101] In a comment obviously responsive to the hullabaloo in Washington over where the city limits lay, they noted that "for all practical purposes this is part of Hanoi, lying as it does, close to sections of the city which are an integral part of it. If all areas on this side of the river are, technically, part of Hanoi then, technically, so is this hamlet." They also itemized the damage to the Chinese and Romanian embassies, noting that Bucharest's representatives had preserved remnants of a U.S. rocket as souvenirs. At one point, the ICC representatives cautiously eschewed rendering "either a conclusive or an expert military opinion" on precisely what had caused the damage they had seen. But they unanimously concluded, in the end,

> that there is prima facie evidence to show that on December 13th and 14th some places and structures which by DRVN definition lie inside the city of Hanoi, and which it appears reasonable to describe as non-military, were struck by bombs and/or projectiles; and furthermore, that in some instances there is reason to believe that the said bombs and/or projectiles issued, in whatever circumstances, from U.S. aircraft of which several were observed directly over all parts of the city of Hanoi proper on the two days the 13th and 14th of December 1966.

Their report constituted a devastating rejoinder to the Johnson administration's fervid efforts to refute Communist charges that the attacks on Hanoi had hit civilian targets within the city, not only because its descriptions concretely corroborated earlier accounts, but also because it came from credible observers in a rare, unanimous statement from the fatally divided ICC. Though the report remained officially secret—despite a suggestion from Ha Van Lau to leak it, which Warsaw rejected as a "dangerous" deviation from commission rules[102]—after it was transmitted to Saigon, Ottawa's delegates shared it with their British and U.S. colleagues, and probably others, leading to its wider dissemination to chancelleries around the world. With sensitive treatment (London's envoy noted that it "was received by Counsellor in strict confidence from Canadian delegation and must in no circumstances be quoted"), the damning report stayed out of the press, where it would have generated screaming headlines. Nevertheless, this gutting of Washington's claims by such an unimpeachable source further lowered its sagging credibility, even among allied governments.[103]

And what about the report's handling on the Communist side? Naturally, the report quickly made its way to Warsaw, where it was available for Rapcki to brandish should he need to rebut U.S. claims.

Saigon: "According to Those Who Were In on It"

Doing his bit to quell the bombing outcry, General Westmoreland issued a special MACV statement Friday unequivocally declaring that a "complete review of pilot reports and photographs" from the December 13–14 raids confirmed that "all ordnance expended by U.S. strike aircraft was in the military target areas. None fell in the city of Hanoi."[104]

However, as more detailed accounts of the damage flowed into Saigon (including from the ICC observers), the American denials did nothing to assuage the anger, mingled with disbelief and bewilderment, of the two Marigold diplomats still in the city. In a talk with Derksen, Lewandowski danced along, or perhaps a step over, the edge of propriety. While requesting "the utmost discretion," he disclosed much of the essence of what had occurred in the still-secret initiative—and he made quite clear which side was to blame for its failure. Recounting the conversation to The Hague, the Dutch chargé cabled (the italicized words are in English in the original):

> At the end of November, by order of President Johnson, personal contact was apparently established between Washington and Hanoi via a third party with the aim of reaching a compromise. According to Lewandowski, who very recently spent two weeks in Hanoi, this contact was received favorably at the highest level and *"according to those who were in on it"* it looked distinctly as though the parties would actually do business this time. The hope that had arisen has been thwarted by the American bombings in the urban area of Hanoi on the 13th and 14th of this month.
>
> Lewandowski described it as *"puzzling"* that the Americans would take such action while consultations initiated by the president were ongoing. One can imagine that the US would bomb Hanoi, or even that it would break off contact, with the announcement that the response it had received was unacceptable. However, since no such announcement has been made and bombings, which can only be regarded as escalatory, are being carried out, one can but wonder, according to Lewandowski, if "the American president is being fully obeyed." Lewandowski remarked that from telegrams he has received he surmises that this sequence of events has made a very painful impression on Moscow and others.[105]

Lewandowski, "unable to provide details (yet)," refrained from disclosing his own role, or otherwise specifying the third party who had made contact in Hanoi. But Derksen had little trouble filling in the blanks. Putting together Lewandowski's recent trip north and the "unusually harsh language" of Warsaw's denunciation of the most recent Hanoi bombings ("bestial escalation"), he speculated that it was, in fact, Poland that had "been involved in the ill-fated mediation."[106] In addition to sending off an urgent account of this revelatory conversation to his foreign minister, the Dutch diplomat also reported it to a CIA contact at the U.S. Embassy—where it would soon set off alarm bells.

As for D'Orlandi, who noted that the bombing had provoked "lively feeling in all sectors of Saigon," he carefully checked with friends intimately familiar with the North Vietnamese capital and found them "categorical" that the damaged sites were, contrary to Washington's denials, in central Hanoi. That night, the Italian began his diary entry with an historical allusion that few Americans would recognize—Friday marked the "20th anniversary of the insurrection of Hanoi (16/12/1946)"—and ended with an exclamation encapsulating his fury, despair, and confusion: "The Americans have gone mad!"[107]

Warsaw: "Very Shook"

The uncompromising State Department rebuff, which was decoded early Friday at the embassy, keenly disappointed Gronouski. The complete lack of responsiveness to his concerns left him "very shook," as did LBJ's failure to reply directly to his messages (he never did). He considered the instructions such "extraordinarily bad judgment" that he "almost resigned my ambassadorship at that point—. . . at least it went through my mind—because I felt this was such an egregious error on Washington's part."[108]

Instead, like numberless disgruntled officials before and since, Gronouski rationalized that he might have a greater impact on policy—and better preserve his future political viability and personal ties—by staying on. So far as is known, he never explicitly revealed to his associates that he considered resigning in protest.

Suppressing his emotions, the ambassador prepared to implement his instructions and sent off a dutiful response. I "appreciate very much" Katzenbach's cable, he replied. When he saw Rapacki the State Department could "rest assured that I will present our case with force and conviction."[109]

That presentation would have to wait, however. When Gronouski called Michałowski Friday to try to set up a meeting, that same day if possible, he discovered that the foreign minister was away, "in the provinces," until Monday. Presuming that he should deliver such an important statement personally to Rapacki, Gronouski declined Michałowski's offer to see him instead, and promised to call back Saturday to make further arrangements after checking with Washington.

As for the new instructions to cancel his trip to Garmisch, to minimize suspicions on his staff Gronouski requested that the State Department immediately send him via normal, non-Marigold channels a directive to stay in the capital in view of the possibility of urgent decisions on a zloty grant relief package. Though classified, the explanation would seep through the rumor mills and dampen alternative conspiracy theories, he hoped.[110]

Paris: *"A Kind of Combat Fatigue"*

While outwardly focused on NATO issues on Friday, Rusk privately pondered whether anything could be done to salvage Marigold. Acting on Katzenbach's suggestion to see whether Fanfani "might be able to help out with the Poles," the secretary sought his aid, assuring him of Washington's desire to pursue the Warsaw contacts; though irked at the Americans for the Hanoi attacks, Fanfani promised to "see what he could do."[111] Independently, Rusk devised a new concept to try to save the initiative while yet reaping some gain over the bombing fiasco; still fuming over the absence of comparable outrage over Viet Cong violence in Saigon, he hatched the idea of making both capitals "open cities" in line with the "traditional laws of war." Though conceding that the analogy was inexact—historical "open cities" were undefended, while Saigon and Hanoi each had a "substantial military presence"—Rusk cabled Katzenbach to suggest that he "get one or two brains," including the State Department's chief legal adviser, Leonard C. Meeker, working on the possibility of proposing a pact declaring "a certain radius" around the center of the two capitals "free from attacks by air, guerilla or otherwise." The North Vietnamese were unlikely to bite, in deference to more bellicose NLF sensibilities, he admitted, but "it might be an interesting suggestion to make to Rapacki."[112]

Before leaving Paris for Washington Friday night, a tired, cranky Rusk—like McNamara the night before—had an informal session with American reporters. One, Anthony Lewis of the *New York Times,* found his performance deeply "unnerving." Mystified by the lack of positive response to his exhortation to defend NATO's other "flank"—some ministers even laughed, he recalled in a "puzzled" way—the secretary of state "reacted snappishly" when reporters told him that the Europeans feared being "sucked into a Pacific war" by the Americans (just as de Gaulle had warned), and presumed he was alluding to Vietnam rather than "nuclear China," as Rusk insisted he had meant.

As such reactions were "totally predictable," Rusk seemed "remarkably insensitive to the European state of mind today"—further evidence of a broader disconnect between Washington and its allies that pervaded the NATO meeting. Lewis even diagnosed "a kind of combat fatigue—a compulsiveness over Vietnam that made it impossible to be sensitive on other issues."

The secretary of state certainly seemed "compulsive" when discussing the war, Lewis wrote a fellow *Times*man. He groused to the reporters about the "unfairness of the world" in criticizing the Hanoi bombings while ignoring Viet Cong assassinations and attacks on civilian targets in Saigon—"we haven't mined their harbor, but they have ours; we haven't bombed their embassies in Hanoi, but they have ours in Saigon." When someone mentioned the Agence France-Presse report that American bombs had hit the Chinese Embassy, Rusk merely smiled and noted that the report said no one there had been killed.

It was hardly surprising that, in this background press briefing, Rusk failed to disclose the secret goings-on in Marigold, which he had also concealed from his fellow NATO ministers. Instead, purveying the same line as in his Saigon airport press conference, that Hanoi had shown no interest whatsoever in peace, "he lectured us at length about the unwillingness of the other side to negotiate."

After the conversation broke up, and its participants were dispersing for dinner, Rusk suddenly turned around in a corridor to buttonhole Lewis (whom he did not know) to inquire, in a disbelieving tone, whether the Europeans *really* thought his "western flank" speech related to Vietnam rather than China. Yes they did, Lewis and a *Newsweek* correspondent standing nearby confirmed. Rusk asked a few more "puzzled questions along the same line," then "drifted off" into the Parisian night.[113]

New York: "Salisbury Understood Correctly"

A little after nine o'clock Friday morning, another telegram from "BURPRESS" in Phnom Penh reached Times Square: "SALISBURY UNDERSTOOD CORRECTLY AND NECESSARY INSTRUCTIONS GIVEN STOP CABLE SOONEST OF [IF] CAN REACH HERE BY TWENTY-SECOND REGARDS."[114]

With the news he yearned for in hand, Salisbury spent the rest of the day frenetically—yet quietly—making arrangements. As the early dusk fell, he walked briskly up Fifth Avenue through hordes of Christmas shoppers to the Air France ticket office, where he booked a Monday night flight to Orly so he could pick up the promised visas in Paris on Tuesday, as well as onward travel the next morning to reach Cambodia by Thursday per Burchett's instructions so he could catch the Friday ICC flight to Hanoi. Then he repaired to his home in "the tranquillity of the Connecticut hills" for a rustic weekend with his family, feeling guilty over his imminent departure (especially because one son would be getting married on New Year's Eve, and another was undergoing a college crisis) but unable to resist the opportunity.

Lyndon Johnson would dearly wish he had—for Salisbury's ensuing trip to Hanoi in late December and early January would be disastrous for the administration, yielding a spate of sensational front-page articles in the *Times* largely corroborating North Vietnamese charges that the American bombings had, in fact, caused the civilian damage and casualties in the capital that Washington so strenuously denied.[115]

Not unreasonably, administration officials would presume that the issuance of Salisbury's visa—so fortuitous for him and *The Times* journalistically, and for North Vietnam politically—was hardly coincidental. Hanoi, they figured, had opened the door to him in the midst of the uproar over the December 13–14 raids precisely to undercut Washington's stance on those attacks. In mid-1969, Lodge, by then handling the Paris peace talks with the North Vietnamese for the Nixon administration, would tell Salisbury that a "highly placed Communist" had confided that Hanoi had "broken off the Marigold thing because they decided to invite [Salisbury] to Hanoi and try publicity rather than peace negotiations."[116] Salisbury himself, ignorant of Marigold at the time, would later wonder whether his trip was connected to what he termed the "mirror-image dealings" of this "complex bit of hugger-mugger, the full outlines of which are not entirely known even today [1988]."[117]

Was the timing of Salisbury's visa in fact linked to the Hanoi authorities' simultaneous decisions to break off Marigold and launch a fresh propaganda blitz against the latest U.S. attacks? Not necessarily; though they certainly did not mind the result. As Salisbury pointed out, Lodge's tale "simply does not fit the timetable." A DRV Foreign Ministry official in Hanoi told him that an earlier cable letting him know that his visa had been approved was actually sent in late November but never elicited a response. The startled journalist, who had of course pined for months for an entry permit and responded promptly when he did get word on December 15, eventually ascertained that this prior invitation was sent to the newspaper's Paris business office and lost in the routine clutter of "advertisements and subscriptions" (it was never found)—and he had received a follow-up communication.

"We are delighted that you have come," the Foreign Ministry functionary told Salisbury over lunch. "We thought you had lost interest in Vietnam."[118]

A telegram in Salisbury's own papers at Columbia raises questions about his story, however. Sent by Burchett from Phnom Penh on December 13 to "AIR-EDITION PARIS," it stated: "HARRISON SALISBURY IDEA IN HIS CABLE DECEMBER FIFTH ACCEPTED WILL INFORM SOONEST WHERE VISA AVAILABLE BUT PROBABLY HERE STOP ASK HIM CABLE ME SOONEST."[119] (Stamped by Cambodian authorities, this was evidently Burchett's copy of the telegram, which Salisbury obtained from him because he never received it in New York.)

Was *this* the errant cable Salisbury stated had been sent to Paris in "late November" and lost? Or, in any case, did it reflect a decision by the North Vietnamese authorities *on December 13*, prompted by the latest U.S. bombing of Hanoi that afternoon, and then promptly communicated to Burchett? Possibly, although unusual bureaucratic efficiency would have been required. If so, this would indeed imply a link between Salisbury's visa and the DRV's international campaign to condemn the bombings—but not to the ensuing uproar over Washington's denials (which erupted days later), nor, necessarily, a connection with Hanoi's move to break off Marigold. As we have seen, the North Vietnamese were already vacillating on their earlier willingness to meet the Americans in Warsaw, and they had other reasons besides the prospect of a visit by Salisbury to sever the contact once the Americans resumed the attacks on their capital, despite repeated Polish warnings.

Washington: "No Sign of It at All, No"

When Johnson had approved Rolling Thunder–52, he had envisioned (as he told McNamara) that the new phase of bombings would put "steady but undramatic" pressure on North Vietnam rather than "something that is so dramatic that you would have a headline every day that you're really changing your policy."[120] Instead, that is exactly what he got—and on Friday the waves of censure over the Hanoi bombings kept on rolling. "The merry mood of Christmas," his wife Lady Bird rued, was "dissipating under the onslaught of hostile press articles."[121] Not only did front-page news stories still dissect the muddled U.S. accounts of the attacks, but the editorial reviews of the administration's performance also began to appear, and they were unsparing pans. In a pair of corrosive commentaries, the *New York Times* blasted both the attacks themselves and the administration's fumbling response ("confusion—if not deception"[122]). Like other critics both domestic and foreign, the newspaper contended that the raids not only undermined the credibility of the Johnson administration's repeated protestations that it desired a cease-fire and peace talks but also, contrary to official denials, constituted a significant escalation of the air war against North Vietnam. In a passage that would resonate uncannily when the still-secret Marigold context emerged, the *Times* declared that

> the manner in which this critical policy change has reached public awareness and the evasive statements that have accompanied it cannot but sap world confidence in Washington's intentions. For, along with military targets, what has been bombed on the fringes of Hanoi is any prospect of peace talks.[123]

Internationally, too, the administration could feel the heat, not only from Communist or neutral quarters (like Thant), but also, as Brown had warned Rusk in Paris, in Western European public opinion. That Friday morning in London, the same U.K. Foreign Office aide who had taken Bundy "strongly to task" warned a U.S. Embassy officer that the "head of steam over Hanoi bombing has become very serious indeed" and urgently requested supporting data to help Brown defend Britain's refusal to explicitly dissociate itself from the raids when he faced inevitable pressure to do so in Parliament on Monday.[124]

Desperate for a means to relieve the pressure, U.S. officials came up with the notion of having Goldberg write Thant requesting his intercession with Hanoi to achieve an extension of the upcoming Christmas truce and, if possible, the start of negotiations.[125] Though such a measure stood little chance of success, it might at least generate a peace-seeking headline or two.

✳ ✳ ✳

Back at the White House, where a kind of bunker mentality was enveloping the administration, Friday was reserved for Vietnam conferences. And in town for a top-level strategy session was Lodge, reporting to the president after a few days in Massachusetts with his family.

The Saigon ambassador was not the only globe-trotting State Department personality dealing with Vietnam who had returned to Washington bearing tidings from afar. Harriman, after two weeks in Europe and North Africa, was back in town—as, too, were William Bundy (although his boss would not arrive from Paris until Saturday) and McNamara. McNaughton, who had accompanied the defense secretary to the NATO ministerial, noticed the grimmer mood: "We returned to find that the bombing of North Vietnam is being construed by everyone as having escalated. The government is apparently trying to deny it, saying the targets are not new, etc. But the fact is that there has been noticeable escalation."[126]

On Friday afternoon, before joining the more rarefied White House audience, Harriman hosted the first meeting of the Negotiations Committee in more than two weeks, since December 1.[127] His and Bundy's trip reports consumed much of the session. Of his jaunt through England, France, Tunisia, Algeria, and Spain, Harriman found most noteworthy his conversations in Paris with Jean Sainteny —a good bet, he thought, to enlist in further probing in Hanoi—and in Algiers; though local DRV and NLF representatives had rebuffed his bid for a secret face-to-face meeting (citing the Hanoi bombings), the leaders of the nationalist, non-aligned Algerian government struck him as pragmatic and potentially cooperative in future peace efforts.[128] Bundy, reviewing the highlights of his own travels alongside Rusk (except for the detour to London), noted in particular Japanese officials' interest in trying their own hand at peacemaking, but apparently glossed over the intense encounters in Saigon with D'Orlandi when the Italian, in his own and his foreign minister's names, had importuned the Americans to avoid further Hanoi air strikes.

In fact, neither he nor Harriman nor anyone else, according to meeting notes, mentioned the elephant in the room: Marigold, and the possibility that the Hanoi bombings had killed it. Although, among the eight men present, Bundy and Unger were intimately familiar with the latest developments in the Polish channel, and Cooper and Harriman himself, albeit belatedly after his return, had been cut in on at least their outlines, several others were still not "cleared" to know or discuss them.[129]

Finally, however, an agitated Cooper indirectly raised the initiative's dire straits. As the hue and cry grew over the Hanoi bombings, Harriman's aide had steadfastly defended the administration in his contacts with reporters; when a *Washington Post* reporter, Chalmers M. Roberts, asked whether the attacks represented either a policy change or an escalation in the war, or at least a potential obstacle to peace talks, he had denied any such thing. "I told him that attempts to end the fighting in Vietnam were made in the context of bombing the North and a good case could be made that the bombing program would expedite rather than delay a negotiated settlement," he recorded in a memorandum couched to impress hard-liners.[130]

Privately, however, Cooper was greatly disturbed that the Hanoi raids had taken place at so delicate a moment in the secret diplomacy. Although it is not clear exactly how much he (or Harriman) knew about Marigold at this stage, Cooper had been working over the previous two weeks to draw up a plausible package deal for North Vietnamese consideration that would somehow be acceptable both to Hanoi and the White House, the idea that had been bandied about at the group's previous meeting.[131] Two key bombing targets had been set aside, he now observed, but what about the other "sensitive targets" that could be hit at any time? "If we were serious about trying to get a negotiating package to Hanoi during the Christmas-Tet period," the minutes of the December 16 meeting record him saying, "we ought to keep a tight rein on bombing operations." McNaughton interjected that the targets had been OK'd at the highest level and would be reviewed again that very afternoon; but Harriman, backing up his aide, remarked that regardless of their military justification, the attacks had "severely jarred world opinion."

This did not bother everyone in the administration, however. The tumult over the Hanoi attacks exacerbated existing internal rifts over the bombing policy; undaunted by the international criticism that so bothered Gronouski, Cooper, and Harriman, among others, some military and civilian hawks even derived satisfaction from what they read as welcome evidence that the bombing was in fact working. Urging Rostow that Friday to loosen, not tighten, restrictions on Rolling Thunder, an aide argued that "the very shrillness of Hanoi's propaganda campaign seems to me one of the strongest arguments for keeping the pressure on by continuing the bombing campaign (except for the agreed-upon holiday pauses). Now is precisely the time to obtain the attacks in depth which we have so far failed to achieve."[132]

Where did LBJ stand on this issue? As with so many other aspects of Vietnam policy, he tried to maneuver between doves and hawks, fully satisfying neither but tending strongly toward the latter. At the hour-long senior Cabinet Room session that began at 5:45 p.m.—attended by McNamara, Katzenbach, Lodge, Harriman, Goldberg, and Rostow—he offered few clues to his own thinking.[133] At one point, he asked the defense secretary (just back from Paris) for his assessment of the Hanoi bombings, and McNamara, burying any lingering qualms about the strikes (which of course he had opposed a week earlier), merely reported moderate damage to the two main targets and expressed "doubts that U.S. bombs fell within the city limits." Like his minions in their background press briefings, he advanced the hypothesis that SAMs and/or antiaircraft debris were culpable for the civilian and diplomatic damage, though he admitted it was "exceedingly difficult, however, to prove a negative."

There is no indication that McNamara or anyone else at the meeting, including Lodge, brought up the question of a possible link between the Hanoi bombings and Marigold's seeming collapse. Instead, after Johnson called on him at the meeting's outset for his views on the situation in Vietnam, Lodge—despite being the central American figure in the Polish initiative, reporting face to face to the president for the first time since it had aroused such high-level attention—ignored it entirely during a lengthy, mostly optimistic assessment of the war (overall going much better than a year before, both politically and militarily, and he anticipated "brilliant results in 1967"). Since leaving Saigon, Lodge had neither reviewed the subsequent Marigold cable traffic nor received a full briefing on the intensive Gronouski-Rapacki dialogue in Warsaw.[134] Still, after reaching Washington, Lodge obviously heard from officials that the initiative was essentially dead, that the Poles, as one cable put it, "may use Communist charges and allegations regarding U.S. bombing raids of December 13 and 14 as pretext for scuttling or at least post-poning indefinitely Warsaw talks."[135]

Harriman, too, when he finally learned of Marigold's sad fate, seems to have received a comparably jaundiced account of Rapacki's behavior. A year before, when Harriman had dropped in at the start of LBJ's thirty-seven-day bombing pause, he had been favorably impressed with Warsaw's seriousness and helpful-ness; despite Gomułka's vitriol during their encounter, and Washington's subse-quent irritation about Rapacki's last-minute machinations to extend the pause, Harriman had defended the Poles for making a good-faith effort (through Michałowski's secret journey) to transmit U.S. views to Hanoi.

Now, however, after being cut out of Marigold despite his Iron Curtain exper-tise (to his "immense annoyance" when he found out[136]), Harriman had caught a touch of the administration's rampant resentment and distrust toward Warsaw. Recounting "his probing of peace feelers" in Europe and North Africa, Harriman advised LBJ that "the Algerians or Sainteny would do [a] better job than East Europeans" to communicate with the "suspicious" Hanoi leaders, who felt they had been "fooled" in prior negotiations.[137]

At the United Nations, Goldberg, who had also been excluded until now from the Marigold maneuvering, was taking a battering for the Hanoi bombings, which he, like Harriman, thought ill advised. Washington, he pointed out, was put in a "bad light" by its failure to respond positively to the pope's call for an extended holiday truce, which aside from U Thant's endorsement had received wide public and congressional support. Though unable to persuade LBJ to back the lengthened seasonal cease-fire, Goldberg instead managed to gain presiden-tial assent for publicly soliciting the secretary-general's aid in getting negotiations started as a means "to bring back USA position into [the] limelight" before the General Assembly session adjourned. Not so incidentally, it might also serve as a means to bring back into play Goldberg himself; after trading in his Supreme Court seat for the UN post in order to aid in the diplomatic pursuit of peace in Vietnam, the former labor negotiator was growing increasingly frustrated and disillusioned with his inability to make any progress.[138]

As the meeting broke up, and Katzenbach accompanied Johnson to the Oval Office, Lodge walked to the West Wing lobby to speak to waiting reporters. Re-peating his sunny prognosis, he gave no indication whatsoever that only a couple of weeks earlier in Saigon, he had risen his glass with a Communist colleague to toast what he viewed as a breakthrough for peace and for direct talks with North Vietnam—and now already treated as forgotten footnote to (secret) history.

"Ambassador Lodge," he was asked, "do you feel that there is any likelihood that the North Vietnamese will want to talk peace some time in the next few months?"

When asked a comparable question two days before, Moyers had fudged judiciously. But Lodge had no qualms about crisply, flatly lying to preserve his government's image of an unrequited suitor in its quest to stop the bloodshed.

"I see no sign of it at all, no," he replied. "No, I see no sign of it at all. And I watch. I try to see people going to Hanoi and coming from Hanoi, of whom many come through Saigon. No, I see no sign of it at all."[139]

Like Rusk's dismissive Tan Son Nhut remarks about Hanoi's lack of interest in peace, Lodge's comments would not go unnoticed in Warsaw.

✳ ✳ ✳

After his press conference, Lodge went to the second floor of the White House, where he joined Johnson, Humphrey, McNamara, Harriman, and Goldberg for dinner. Perhaps the murky Polish peace diplomacy came up in the unrecorded table talk; perhaps not. Meanwhile, the State Department kept the Marigold ball rolling by sending Gronouski a brief assent to his plan to see Rapacki on Monday.[140]

And then LBJ fled the cold, contentious capital, flying through the night to the more hospitable ambience of his Texas ranch, where he would stay through the holidays.

Saturday, December 17, and Sunday, December 18

Saigon: "So Bitter He Planned to Write 'a Paper'"

On Saturday morning, D'Orlandi learned of the apparent breakdown of the Warsaw talks from an embittered Lewandowski, who relayed the substance of Dong's angry communication severing contacts and Rapacki's wholehearted endorsement of it. The Hanoi bombings, he said, had constituted a "decisive element" for both the DRV and Poland, clearly exposing America's "cynical" approach to peacemaking. "Now that the U.S. government has succeeded in wrecking any possibility of negotiation, there will no longer be such intense bombing of North Vietnam and especially of Hanoi," the Pole concluded scornfully.

While condemning Washington's conduct, Lewandowski praised Rome's. The Italian, he reported afterward, had a "strong reaction" to the turn of events. Though "convinced that Lodge conducted the talks sincerely and had Johnson's authorization for this," D'Orlandi "conjectured about the actual limitation of the president's freedom of action by the 'invisible government.'" D'Orlandi was so angry that, according to Lewandowski, he asked whether the Poles were "considering making the matter known to the public," adding that he favored such a course. (Lewandowski said he responded that he was "still obliged to secrecy and that Headquarters will decide.")

Morosely, the two Marigold coconspirators traded thoughts of leaving their jobs. The Pole cabled Warsaw that D'Orlandi, who had extended his stay in Saigon at U.S insistence, now "in fact feels ill" and was considering asking Fanfani to be reassigned; and D'Orlandi informed Rome that Lewandowski (who presumed that his credibility in Hanoi was now blown) had confided that he was requesting his own recall, prompting the Italian to despair that we would thereby "lose an able and heeded counselor to [Pham Van Dong] and [the] best 'channel' possible."[141]

✳ ✳ ✳

On Saturday, at the U.S. Embassy, there was a disturbing conversation. CIA station chief John Limond Hart informed Habib about Derksen's talk with Lewandowski, as described by the Dutchman to one of his agents; at the political officer's urgent request, Hart quickly secured a written summary. According to this version of the conversation—vaguely and erroneously dated as occurring sometime between November 30 and December 15 (actually Friday the 16th)—Lewandowski had disclosed that the latest bombings had wiped out a promising overture to Hanoi conducted by an unidentified "organization" or "group." Though not explicitly revealing his own or Poland's role, he had mentioned his own prolonged recent visit to the North Vietnamese capital, and purportedly stated that "he was so bitter that he planned to write 'a paper' on the subject." Sometimes it seemed to him that "the left hand of the United States Government doesn't know what the right hand is doing." From Lewandowski's remarks, Derksen had inferred that the Poles had been the frustrated mediators.

Habib gave the CIA report to Porter, who in turn instantly cabled it to Washington. It was not clear, the acting ambassador commented, whether the "obviously loose-tongued" Lewandowski was venting "frustration at being cut out of the picture by talking loosely and grandiosely" or firing the first shot in a calculated Polish "exposé." Either way, the potential implications were obvious—and ominous. Should he pass word to Lewandowski through D'Orlandi "that we find his behavior strange in view of his oft-repeated statements about need for secrecy?"[142]

London: "Not Materially Strengthen Our Case"
Saturday morning, responding to the petition for supporting evidence to bolster Brown's upcoming presentation to the House of Commons, a U.S. Embassy aide handed a British colleague an official defense of the Hanoi raids that, with a few extra details, hewed to the line being pushed publicly in Washington and privately to the Poles in Warsaw. But the document flopped. An analyst from the Foreign Office's South-East Asia Department, casting doubt on its assurances that

"no U.S. ordinance fell on" Hanoi, noted that press reports of planes "being seen to dive" near Red River Bridge suggested attacks on antiaircraft defenses; and though the message insisted there was "no basis for charging us with escalation of conflict over past few days, either in geographic terms or as to types of targets," it did nothing to alter the analyst's "impression" that "since July U.S. air attacks have centered nearer Hanoi and might therefore seem to the Vietnamese to amount to an intensification, if not escalation, of the American military effort."[143] In sum, the information provided by Washington "would not materially strengthen our case for not dissociating ourselves from the United States action," and contained nothing requiring modification of the already-prepared draft remarks for the foreign secretary to deliver to Parliament Monday.

Washington: "Most Unfortunate and Potentially Harmful"

On Saturday afternoon, the State Department's Marigold monitors responded to Porter's request for instructions on whether he should try to plug the potential leak in Saigon. Judging Lewandowski's "indiscretions" to be "indeed most unfortunate and potentially harmful to talks in Warsaw," Katzenbach approved Porter's idea of reminding the Pole of his past vows of secrecy, and at the same time suggested that he pass along to D'Orlandi, for his possible use with his colleague, the "rebuttal material" on the Hanoi bombings that Washington was circulating to diplomatic outposts. Despite mounting indications that Warsaw was exploiting the bombing controversy as a "pretext for scuttling" or indefinitely deferring the initiative, the Italian (and through him Lewandowski) should be assured of American intentions to "carry productive discussions forward as long as possible."

In view of the renewed danger of rumors reaching the Saigon government about Washington's secret peace diplomacy behind its back (and under its nose), Katzenbach also authorized Porter to tell Ky, if the premier confronted him, that the United States felt a "responsibility not to overlook any possible lead which might offer some promise," and that the Polish contact had, at least for while, seemed to fit that description. If any "real prospect of discussions with Hanoi" were to emerge, he would be kept informed.[144]

✳ ✳ ✳

As Rusk's plane touched down at Andrews Air Force Base outside Washington early Saturday afternoon, ending his two-week circumnavigation, his aides were, as instructed, sketching out his "open cities" brainstorm. Though Meeker, his legal adviser, indeed perceived major legal and practical obstacles in the way of declaring Saigon and Hanoi (and perhaps Haiphong) "open cities" as traditionally defined, both he and Joseph Sisco saw potential value in a modified approach. Averring that the "kernel of the notion which you suggested has great merit and should be explored further," the assistant secretary argued that advancing the idea of making each capital city an "attack-free zone" could help defang criticism over the Hanoi raids and blunt mounting pressure on Washington unilaterally to halt its bombing of all North Vietnam. Even better, the United States could preemptively stop attacking Hanoi within a defined radius that encompassed Yen Vien and Van Dien (of course, it had already secretly suspended raids on those targets), convey the decision "as clearly a unilateral step of de-escalation" through diplomatic channels to the North Vietnamese, and propose they take reciprocate around Saigon—putting the onus on them if, as expected, they refused. If they accepted the offer, "This would cost us much less militarily than a unilateral cessation of bombing of the entire North, yet give us very considerable political advantage." Either way, Washington gained.[145]

Sisco suggested using Thant to convey the idea to Hanoi, but it rapidly merged into thinking about how to proceed with Warsaw; Katzenbach jotted a note to Rusk that they should take up the Saigon-Hanoi linkage on his return to the seventh floor on Monday.[146]

Saigon: The "Thwarted Gambler Who Expected Make Profit"
On Sunday morning, with Washington's consent, Porter sent Habib to alert D'Orlandi to Lewandowski's "indiscreet remarks" to Derksen and to urge him to remind the Pole of the importance of continued secrecy. The acting ambassador assumed that the Italian would loyally carry out his assignment, but did not realize how the recent American actions had alienated him, especially now that Lewandowski had confirmed his worst fears. When Habib arrived, he got the full brunt of the Italian's resentment: D'Orlandi seemed to view the political officer as little more than an errand boy sent by a grocery clerk to collect a bill—and hardly bothered to conceal his disgust.[147]

Though visibly taken aback at the report of Lewandowski's talkativeness, D'Orlandi seemed far more perturbed by what the "bitter" Pole had told him the day before about the bad news from Warsaw, which he related to Habib along with the revelation that in view of the secret initiative's failure, both he and Lewandowski were considering giving up their Saigon posts. Worse, from the U.S. standpoint, D'Orlandi seemed sympathetic to Lewandowski's, and Poland's, apportionment of blame. D'Orlandi confessed that he, too, was "surprised" at the "absurd repetition of the bombings of Hanoi"—a "gross error" blithely disregarding his and Fanfani's warnings to Rusk—and even felt compelled to wonder "if there were not some people in the U.S. who had deliberately sought to create a problem."

This heretical expression of suspicion regarding U.S. conduct triggered a sharp exchange between these two occasionally hot-tempered diplomats. Habib, "with an expression of surprise that D'Orlandi would have such a thought," indignantly denied any possibility that the talks had been purposely sabotaged. As if trying to instill the catechism to a dull student, the American reiterated that "no connection" existed "between bombings and Lewandowski's proposals," and directed D'Orlandi's attention to the details of the confidential memorandum he had

brought along for his use in justifying the attacks if the Pole persisted in complaining about them. The Italian, however—by now aware of the ICC Hanoi bureau's confidential report—found it completely unpersuasive. Nor did he respond
appropriately, the Americans felt, when Habib heatedly tried to lay full blame on
Rapacki and his "procrastination" for the failure to arrange the Warsaw contact
with Hanoi's representative, and jogged D'Orlandi's memory about his comment
to Rusk that Rapacki was being "too clever."

Nevertheless, D'Orlandi replied, he was "disturbed at what had happened" and
feared that when the affair was exposed, as it inevitably would be, the story would
have a "profound effect on international public opinion." He and others might
"deny everything," he observed, "but people have suspicions, and denials and no
comments will have no effect as it appears prima facie a bad case"—a conclusion
closely resembling Gronouski's concern "that while we may be able to develop a
case which satisfies ourselves, we will not be able to refute effectively to others the
Polish line of reasoning."

Habib retorted that the Poles, not the Americans, had acted in "bad faith," and
Lewandowski's gabbing to Derksen "in itself called Polish good faith into question." Washington, he insisted, remained committed to the Warsaw talks, which
were still in progress—much to the surprise of the Italian, who considered them
dead.

Finally, D'Orlandi responded to Habib's requests. Having invited the Pole for
dinner on Tuesday, he promised to try to "calm Lewandowski down" and vowed
that regardless of his personal views he had just expressed, "my remarks to Lewandowski will not reflect anything of these impressions and I will do whatever I
can do to help."

Although doubtful that Warsaw had already abandoned its pledge of secrecy, D'Orlandi thought it possible—depending on whether the initiative could
be rescued—that it "would expose events to try and embarrass us," though he
sensibly refrained from endorsing such an action (as Lewandowski had quoted
him as doing). The "very serious" situation provoked by the latest Hanoi bombings, he stressed, made it all the more "incumbent upon Washington to take
those measures or make those steps necessary to show its desire to negotiate
and its own good faith."

"I do not think that whatever I can do will be of any avail if nothing is done in
Warsaw," he told Habib. "If the other chap [Rapacki] says so, Lewandowski will
talk. If Lewandowski is told by Rapacki to keep quiet he will. So something has to
be done [in] Warsaw quickly."

Before leaving, Habib asked if it was all right to quote his "strong remarks" on
the bombing to Washington, and the Italian, obviously feeling that he had nothing to lose, told him to go ahead. On a personal note, he added with a touch of
resentment that he had remained in Saigon despite poor health due to Rusk's
specific request to Fanfani, but thanks to the failure of the tripartite initiative, he
no longer felt obliged to stay on.

D'Orlandi's attitude, when conveyed by Habib, outraged Porter, who lacked Lodge's ardor for Marigold or regard for his Polish and Italian partners. When he had misled Moore a couple of weeks earlier by saying that Lewandowski was "the last person we would use" for secret diplomacy, he spoke something close to his real opinion, and now he put D'Orlandi in the same category: unreliable, untrustworthy, not someone who could be counted on to support U.S. interests. His own acerbic coda to a report to Washington of the Habib-D'Orlandi conversation dripped with disdain for the Saigon channel:

> Comment: Our judgment is that foregoing confirms correctness of changing venue to Warsaw. D'Orlandi is not only showing his personal pique at turn of events, but is displaying definite tendency to discard our explanations while endeavoring to induce us to do "something quickly in Warsaw." Instead of focusing on information provided by Habib, he launched into extended presentation of Lewandowski's latest animadversions, adding his own belief that there is "strong prima facie case against us" as well as [that secrecy was "still significant to Poles"].
>
> As for Lewandowski, we have always wondered what would induce [North Vietnam] to accept a Polish role in this most delicate business, and we have nothing but Polish assertions to the effect that they did. Lewandowski's reaction at present not unlike that of thwarted gambler who expected make profit playing with other people's money.
>
> Call on D'Orlandi was intended to call his attention to Lewandowski's leak, and pass on facts on bombing if Lewandowski raised the issue. It was then discovered that Lewandowski had already been to see D'Orlandi, allegedly on Rapacki's instructions. We do not doubt D'Orlandi account of his conversation with Lewandowski, although he may have embellished it somewhat. D'Orlandi's reaction in conversation with Habib was not good and could not be left completely unanswered. We do not, however, believe that D'Orlandi should now be used as a channel to Poles. That should remain in Warsaw. We suggest, therefore, that matter be left as is, unless Dept. desires anything further to be said to D'Orlandi. Any further reports by D'Orlandi of Lewandowski's views will be accepted without comment for transmission to Dept.[148]

With Lodge temporarily hors de combat, and not expected back in Saigon for another month, Porter had effectively yanked the U.S. Embassy out of the tripartite maneuvering. Happy to see the channel transferred to Warsaw, he doubted the whole affair was anything more than a diplomatic wild goose chase, a futile distraction from the business of running (and winning) a war, and he had no interest in emulating his absent boss's fondness for clandestine diplomacy with D'Orlandi and Lewandowski.

Texas: "Improving the Atmosphere"

At his ranch outside Austin, LBJ spent the weekend visiting friends, cultivating journalists in off-the-record settings, and relishing the more casual, less snarly atmosphere. Yet even while licking his wounds, he could hardly tear himself away from the latest news. Sunday he awoke at 4:30 a.m. to scan the *Times, Post, Baltimore Sun,* and *Wall Street Journal*—and around the clock, supplementing frequent phone calls to and from Rostow, Katzenbach, McNamara, and others, classified teletype messages arrived demanding his attention.

That Sunday afternoon, one such message relayed for Johnson's final imprimatur his newest Vietnam peace foray, the draft letter from Goldberg to U Thant. Framed as a response to the appeals from the pope and UN secretary-general to expand and extend the holiday truces, the letter turned to Thant "with the hope and the request that you will take whatever steps you consider necessary" to bring about talks leading to a mutual cease-fire, and promising Washington's full cooperation.

The proposed message, however, said nothing about a prior stop to U.S. bombing of North Vietnam—which Thant had urged as a first step toward negotiations —and was, as Rusk frankly acknowledged to Johnson in a cover note, "essentially a restatement of existing policy." That was why it gained quick endorsement from LBJ's senior aides; not only had Rusk, Katzenbach, and Harriman signed off, but even Rostow had agreed that it "might be a useful move at this time," despite the administration's often-rocky relations with Thant. Yet Washington had backed his reelection as secretary-general earlier that month (the alternatives had looked even worse), and—most important—the novelty of a conciliatory U.S. approach to a neutralist, internationally respected figure seemed a low-cost, low-risk tactic to stem the bombing uproar. Rusk would talk up the letter as more than a "mere gesture," insisting to London's ambassador that "the U.S. government meant business"—but the secretary signaled its aim more candidly when he explained to Johnson that Goldberg "believes it will be useful in improving the atmosphere in the aftermath of recent concern about the bombing near Hanoi."[149]

Johnson OK'd the letter's release for Monday, before the General Assembly wound up its session that night or the next day. Geared to make headlines, it would be circulated as a formal Security Council document.

By contrast, the drama in Warsaw remained hidden, albeit barely, U.S. officials feared, in light of Porter's disturbing report of Lewandowski's gabbing. LBJ would have to wait another day to hear how the next scene turned out: Gronouski's climactic talk with Rapacki.

Warsaw: Gronouski Makes a Date

A phone call to Michałowski confirmed a Monday appointment with Rapacki, so Gronouski, deferring the family ski vacation, had the weekend to ready his presentation.[150] Cutting and pasting from various cables, he fashioned an aide-mémoire articulating Washington's version of the affair, justifying its behavior, squarely blaming Warsaw for the failure to get talks started, and affirming American sincerity in still seeking negotiations. The cold set in, and a small blizzard hit the capital. But diplomatically, this was the calm before the real storm.

The Action in Warsaw—and Hanoi

Tajne
~~SPECJALNEGO ZNACZENIA~~

Czynienie odpisów wzbronione

Egz. Nr

Szyfrogram Nr 15023

z Hanoi .... nadany ...25.XI.g.17⁰⁰... przyjęty ...—...
Wpłynął do działu szyfrowego 25.XI.g.14⁰⁰

Tajne spec. znaczenia
Do rąk własnych
Natychmiast

M i c h a ł o w s k i

/-/ Michałowski

Rozmowa z Pham Van Dongiem o godzinie 10.

1. Niezwykle serdeczne przyjęcie. Bardzo ciepłe i serdeczne słowa o Polsce. Podkreślenie pełnej zgodności
myśli z towarzyszami polskimi. Prośba o przekazanie
towarzyszowi Rapackiemu podziękowania za postawę Polski
wobec DRW i postawę delegacji polskiej w Komisji.

2. Oceny sytuacji w USA i ich pozycji w Wietnamie dokony-
wane przez towarzyszy polskich pokrywają się z ocenami
wietnamskimi. USA znajdują się wobec wyboru: poważnie
zwiększyć działanie lub szukać rozwiązań pokojowych.
Pham Van Dong zadał dużo szczegółowych pytań o sytuacji
w Wietnamie Południowym.

v e r t e

Otrzymują:

Tow.Gomułka	Tow.Naszkowski
Tow.Cyrankiewicz	Tow.Winiewicz
Tow.Kliszko	Tow.Wierna
Tow.Ochab	Tow.Michałowski
Tow.Rapacki	
Tow.Czesak	

Wych. Nr ....676....

Rozszyfrowano ....25.XI.g.....

Rozszyfrował ....
podpis

Odbito w „............" egz.

egz. N 1...........

egz. N 2...........

egz. N 3...........

On November 25, 1966, in this coded cable from Hanoi to Warsaw (szyfrogram 15023), Lewandowski reported that Pham Van Dong had agreed to a direct U.S.–North Vietnamese meeting in Warsaw to confirm the American proposals that the Pole had relayed after meeting Henry Cabot Lodge in Saigon. *Courtesy of the Polish Foreign Ministry archives.*

Adam Rapacki, the Polish foreign minister, in an official photograph taken in his capacity as a PZPR Politburo member after the Fourth Party Congress, and published in *Trybuna Ludu* in 1964.

An official photograph of Jerzy Michałowski taken in Washington when he was Polish ambassador to the United States. *Courtesy of Stefan Michałowski.*

John Austin Gronouski, who was sent by Lyndon B. Johnson to Warsaw in November 1965 as U.S. ambassador to Poland. Gronouski had served as postmaster-general under presidents Kennedy and Johnson, and despite his lack of diplomatic experience, which drew scorn from State Department insiders, he would become a central figure in the Marigold drama opposite Polish foreign minister Adam Rapacki. *Courtesy of the U.S. National Archives.*

In February 1965, Gronouski was sworn in for a second term as postmaster-general, with his family and LBJ beside him at the White House. Attorney General Nicholas deB. Katzenbach (at right) administered the oath. Ten months later, LBJ would shift Gronouski to Warsaw as U.S. ambassador; and a year after that, he would move Katzenbach from the Department of Justice to the State Department to replace George Ball as deputy to Secretary Dean Rusk. The reshuffling put both men in crucial positions when Marigold climaxed in December 1966. *Courtesy of the Wisconsin Historical Society.*

The Polish Foreign Ministry in Warsaw, site of the December 1966 intense secret dialogue between U.S. ambassador Gronouski and Polish foreign minister Rapacki, shown in 2003, after its Communist-era insignia had been removed. The building was a rare example of pre–World War II architecture to survive the war and the 1944 Warsaw Uprising—thanks to its wartime location in a restricted Germans-only zone adjacent to Gestapo headquarters. *Author's photograph.*

Nguyen Dinh Phuong, the North Vietnamese interpreter, stands between Henry Kissinger and Le Duc Tho during a break in negotiations at a suburban Paris villa in November 1972. *United Press International photograph, courtesy of the U.S. National Archives.*

Hanoi on December 20, 1966. After U.S. bombers repeatedly struck the city, Ho Chi Minh inspected antiaircraft batteries surrounding it. *World Wide Photos photograph, courtesy of the U.S. National Archives.*

The Washington Policymakers

Ambassador Henry Cabot Lodge at a White House meeting in 1965. *This photograph was a gift from LBJ to Lodge, and is reproduced courtesy of Henry Sears Lodge.*

Saigon strategy session, January 15, 1966, during LBJ's thirty-seven-day bombing pause. *From the left:* W. Averell Harriman, South Vietnamese prime minister Nguyen Cao Ky, U.S. secretary of state Dean Rusk; and U.S. ambassador Henry Cabot Lodge. Harriman, on a round-the-world odyssey to explore peace prospects, had come from Vientiane, where he had nearly run into Polish emissary Jerzy Michałowski, who was returning from his secret mission to Hanoi. *United Press International photograph, courtesy of the U.S. National Archives.*

Chester L. Cooper, in a publicity photograph for *The Lost Crusade: America in Vietnam,* which was published in 1970. As an aide to Ambassador-at-Large W. Averell Harriman, Cooper helped get the Marigold ball rolling during a lunch with Italian officials in November 1966 at the Villa Madama in Rome. *Fabian Bachrach photograph, courtesy of Susan Cooper.*

Secretary of State Dean Rusk, President Johnson, and Defense Secretary Robert McNamara in a Cabinet Room meeting at the White House, January 1967. *LBJ Library photograph by Yoichi R. Okamoto.*

President Johnson crooning with his dog Yuki in February 1968, as his urbane ambassador to Great Britain, David Bruce, watches. The previous September, the dog had been at the center of a tense confrontation between LBJ and the new Polish ambassador to Washington, Jerzy Michałowski. *LBJ Library photograph by Yoichi R. Okamoto.*

LBJ confers at the White House in April 1968 with Averell Harriman and Llewellyn E. Thompson, two key State Department figures handling Vietnam diplomacy, on impending peace talks with North Vietnam. *White House photograph, courtesy of the U.S. National Archives.*

"The Christmas Present"
Marigold's Last Gasp, and First Leaks,
December 19–24, 1966

Stop! I will hear no more of this.

—*Adam Rapacki to John Gronouski, Warsaw, December 19, 1966*

I had in my pocket the means to get this thing going again. . . . I had high hopes.

—*Gronouski on getting Washington's approval, on December 23, 1966,*
of a unilateral 10-mile bombing halt around Hanoi's center

We were just starting to put some real pressure on Hanoi. . . . Let's roll up our sleeves and get on with this war. . . . The restrictions . . . should be removed. And then when Hanoi screams in anguish, we should hit them again.

—*Admiral Ulysses S. Grant Sharp, head of the U.S. Pacific Command,*
to General Earle G. Wheeler, chairman of the Joint Chiefs of Staff,
December 24, 1966

Saigon appears to me to be crazy with joy. . . . My God, my God, why does this cease-fire have to end?

—*Giovanni D'Orlandi, Christmas Eve, December 24, 1966*

An explosive encounter in Warsaw set Marigold on divergent paths: a desperate effort by Lyndon Johnson, prodded by Gronouski and secretly assisted by Poland, to salvage the initiative and lure Hanoi to the table; and, concurrently, Rapacki's opening salvos in the brewing war of leaks to inform world leaders of the failed secret peace bid and convince them why it had gone awry.

Monday, December 19

Warsaw: "Rapacki Absolutely Hit the Roof"

On a snowy Monday morning, Gronouski applied the finishing touches to the script he had crafted to read to Rapacki. Dreading his reaction, the ambivalent ambassador—carrying out instructions he thought misguided—made an eleventh-hour attempt to soften the blow. In a FLASH message to Washington, he requested permission to tell the Pole that the proposed talks "create delicate problems for us with other principals in this conflict who are not inclined to go nearly as far as [the U.S. government] to initiate peace negotiations"—an obvious reference to Saigon—and to propose linking direct U.S.-DRV discussions to an extension of the anticipated Christmas and Tet cease-fires. FLASHing its response to these "troublesome" suggestions, the State Department authorized "passing reference" to the first issue ("but don't imply we are backing away or in any sense qualifying what we have already said") and deflected the second, stressing that any "phased de-escalation" during the holiday season must be mutual.[1]

At 2 p.m., Gronouski went to the Foreign Ministry to see Rapacki for their eighth meeting in two weeks—and what would prove their most volatile.[2] Explaining at the outset that he would read an "unusually lengthy" statement to give the Polish government a full sense of the U.S. position, the American plunged into his eighteen-paragraph "oral presentation" of the path to Marigold's seeming cul-de-sac.[3] After recounting the initiative's genesis and Washington's prompt consent to the proposed Warsaw contact, he robustly defended the Hanoi bombings. They were not an "escalation," "intensification," or pressure tactic related to the impending talks, as the Poles charged. Instead, they were consistent with a pattern of attacks lasting since the summer (with fluctuations attributable to "weather factors"). Rather than indiscriminate assaults, as claimed by Communist propaganda, they were "tactical, precision" strikes on "military and military-related targets" (in "stark contrast" to Viet Cong "terrorist bombings, assassinations, kidnappings and so on" in South Vietnam). Insisting that "absolutely no target within Hanoi city limits was bombed," he rejected any U.S. culpability for casualties or destruction in residential areas of the capital. A "careful" internal review of "detailed follow-up reports" had failed to substantiate such claims, and "an objective observer" should consider "the possibility that stray [surface-to-air] missiles or anti-aircraft shells could have caused the damage cited."

Why, in fact, had the U.S.-DRV contact been delayed? Gronouski recalled Rapacki's allusion on December 13 to "complications having arisen" and threw the phrase back in his face: He, not Washington, had gratuitously "introduced" complications by trying to stiffen the terms of the deal with Lewandowski with "new terms and conditions"—quibbling about the "perfectly natural" interpretation clause, demanding one-sided constraints on U.S. military actions, complaining about public statements by U.S. officials even as Hanoi "monotonous[ly]" affirmed "its total unwillingness to take even the first minor steps toward opening up explorations for possible peaceful settlement."

Aside from one brief query, Rapacki held his tongue, restraining his mounting fury, until he heard Gronouski utter the first sentence of paragraph twelve: "We have been waiting now in Warsaw for almost two weeks to get started on discussions, and your government must bear the responsibility for the fact that these have yet to get under way."

Then thunder clapped.

"Rapacki banged his fist on the table vigorously and in great agitation said, 'Stop! I will hear no more of this.' In [an] angry tone, Rapacki said he categorically rejected this attempt to shift responsibility to Poles, that responsibility is squarely on us for destroying chance for peace talks, and that our attempt to shift responsibility is wholly unprecedented and unwarranted," Gronouski cabled Washington.

"As I could expect, as I anticipated," he reflected later, "Rapacki absolutely hit the roof."[4]

Michałowski, present, vividly recalled: "At this point Rapacki lost his temper and slammed his table with his glasses, such that the optical lenses became dislodged and flew straight into Gronouski's face. He attacked his interlocutor by declaring that the USA began the talks and torpedoed them themselves and was now attempting to throw the responsibility on others. He categorically rejected Gronouski's declaration [and] declared that he is able to listen further only if it contains something new on the matter."[5] (In another version, Michałowski told Harriman that "Rapacki threw his glasses at the floor and he feared that Rapacki was having another heart attack."[6] He was not exaggerating; Lewandowski confided to Lodge in early 1967 that Rapacki "had had three heart attacks and yet continues to be a chain smoker and drinks cups of black coffee all through the day," and consequently "cannot put in a hard day's work anymore."[7])

In the face of this outburst, Gronouski "started to fold my notes," thinking Rapacki had ended the meeting. But "the storm having receded," the Pole softened his tone. He was "keenly disappointed," for on learning that the American had sought an appointment, he anticipated news that would help overcome Hanoi's suspicions. Gronouski—trying to calm the Pole down, and jumping ahead in his presentation to the part he personally found most congenial—earnestly assured him that he was speaking out of an authentic desire to achieve the soonest possible opening of direct talks with Hanoi's representatives as the best way toward peace, . . . and, securing Rapacki's go-ahead, resumed his recitation.[8]

As Michałowski observantly spotted, however, Gronouski did not pick up where he left off; instead, he skipped a section of the aide-mémoire that would have riled the apoplectic Pole even more. "Inasmuch as Rapacki had gotten point on responsibility and given his reaction to the first sentence," Gronouski dryly informed Washington, "I thought it best to pass over remarks from second sentence para 12 through para 13." This was a smart snap decision, as it is hard to imagine the combustible foreign minister continuing his efforts in any form, let alone the immediate conversation, had he heard the ensuing passages (emphasis added):

> 12. We have been waiting now in Warsaw for almost two weeks to get started on discussions, and your govt must bear the responsibility for the fact that these have yet to get under way. [Gronouski broke off here.] *You well know that one important subject for such discussions would be to arrange for mutual de-escalation, including bombing of NVN [North Vietnam]. You also know that in all of the discussions leading up to the Polish proposal and our agreement to meet with the NVN in Warsaw, there was no condition relating to bombing. All of the increasingly indignant charges we have heard here, including the threat to terminate the conversations, are based on events subsequent to the agreement reached with the Polish Govt on Dec. 3, events which are extraneous to what was the basis of our agreement at that time.*
>
> 13. *We are deeply concerned over the gravity of Polish actions which serve the basic, long-run interests of neither of the parties whom you say you mean to be helping. We regretfully find ourselves being led to the conclusion that the Polish Govt, whether on its own or in response to promptings from the NVN Govt, is seeking to make a case which is based on false premises and does not relate to the facts as we know them. This gives us concern not only because of the damaging effect it could have on prospects for working out a peaceful settlement in Vietnam but because we would find it difficult not to have our attitude about our relations with the Polish Govt also affected.*

Gronouski devoted the rest of his presentation to the U.S. desire, despite recent setbacks, "to leave no stone unturned in our search for peace." Confessing confusion as to "what Hanoi has said and what represents the view of the Polish government," he lamented the lack of any direct message from or face-to-face contact with the North Vietnamese, despaired of progress toward resolving the "exceedingly complex and difficult" issues blocking peace absent a real exchange of views (as opposed to unilateral American statements), and reaffirmed his eagerness to sit down with DRV representatives "tomorrow"—or, if Hanoi preferred, to continue dealing indirectly. Washington stood ready to consider any DRV proposals, and could negotiate a limited initial mutual deescalation accord starting with a bombing halt (here Gronouski again advertised the Phase A/B formula) or, conversely, "proceed promptly to a total agreement" (à la the ten points). Summing up, Gronouski ventured that "the coming holidays and the truces associated with them offer an opportune occasion" to move toward negotiations and a "peaceful settlement."

So ended the American's formal statement. After hearing him out, the Pole responded less explosively than before, but no less acidly. When they last met,

Rapacki began, he had emphasized that in light of U.S. conduct—bombing Hanoi while privately passing moderate-sounding proposals through Lodge—he could only credit new "facts," not words. "Yet I find in your remarks, no facts." He had heard nothing to dispel his impression that Washington sought to employ "military pressure" to coerce Hanoi into negotiations. "The USA brought about the wrecking of the opportunity for a Warsaw contact and are presently ignoring everything that they did. A holiday pause is nothing new. There is no guarantee that even if some kind of talks were established the USA will not resume provocative acts."

Rapacki blasted Gronouski's disquisition on the Hanoi raids—already familiar from U.S. public statements—as "false and hypocritical." Echoing the theory of sinister Pentagon machinations entertained by Lewandowski and D'Orlandi, he noted that Washington's insistence that its bombs had not fallen on residential districts was so blatantly untrue as to provoke suspicion that it was being misinformed by its own military.

Then Rapacki played a trump card. Washington might cite aerial photographs and pilots' after-action reports to prop up claims of "precision bombing," but he had a better source: "our own people who were under the bombs." He then whipped out and, Gronouski reported, "read from what he referred to as [an] 'on the spot report from ICC in Hanoi'"—the same unanimous document hammered out a few days earlier, after their guided inspection tour, by Polish, Indian, and Canadian representatives in the capital. In the face of such credible eyewitness accounts, he went on, it was "hard to take seriously" U.S. denials.

Gronouski—who had no idea the ICC document existed, because no one in Washington had bothered to forewarn him—could only reiterate that "exhaustive" U.S. inquiries had turned up "not one shred of evidence" that its ordnance had hit residential areas. Sympathetically, he added, "I served as a bomber during World War II and I know it is inevitable that occasionally the target is missed and a bomb goes astray, but we found no evidence that this happened on December 13 and 14."

Rapacki cut him short. The United States had shown that at the precise moment of a potential breakthrough it considered bombing railroad yards "more important" than a chance for peace; presuming that Gronouski had correctly reported their conversations, he could only blame the U.S. government, not the ambassador, for disregarding his (and Lewandowski's) repeated warnings against such provocative actions.

If Washington's defense of the bombings left Rapacki cold, its "unprecedented and cynical" attempt to pin the onus on Poland for the entirely predictable (and predicted) result made his blood boil. "During our meetings," he told Gronouski,

> we brought up repeatedly that it was you who questioned your position through the "interpretation clause," and now you want to impute that we are introducing new conditions. We also warned repeatedly that intensifying the escalation at the

time when the matter of beginning the talks is being decided is extremely dangerous. The charge against us that we put forward new conditions when we insisted
on obvious matters in the interest of the talks is without precedent. Putting forward an argument about the weather is truly outrageous. Taking advantage of
a few hours of weather for air strikes, of which there were none for two years
[Rapacki seems here to allude to the Feb 1965 strikes on Hanoi, roughly twenty-
two months earlier], is more important to you than a chance for an agreement.
On 2 December, you resumed the bombing of Hanoi, which you had not carried
out for six months in spite of the good weather [actually, a little more than five
months, since the June 29 bombings of petroleum, oil, and lubricant facilities].
We did not lay down conditions. We merely advised: You want peace, do not intensify the bombing. You chose bombing, and now you want to deflect the blame
from yourselves and burden us.

His anger rising again—he had listened in silence and held back before exploding earlier—Rapacki added: "Your whole presentation today cannot be described except as confirmation of fears that [the U.S. government] has decided to
withdraw from [the] attitude expressed by Lodge, has chosen a brutal way to do
this, and is now trying to twist facts and shift responsibility. I reject categorically
as outright cynical the statement that we are responsible for postponement of the
Warsaw meetings. The Warsaw meetings were bombarded by you."

Worse, Washington hypocritically tried to mask its escalation with pious protestations that it desired peace and negotiations. "I am astonished that at the same
time you accuse us of stalling talks, you ask us to help you get them going again,"
the visibly "perturbed" foreign minister said, specifically assailing Lodge's White
House comment a few days before that Hanoi had shown no sign of interest in
peace as "an abuse of the fact that thanks to the secrecy of our talks the world has
not been informed of them."

Significantly, Rapacki expressly did *not* rule out further Polish peace efforts,
but stressed that Washington needed to give him something tangible to mitigate
Hanoi's hardening suspicions. "What was new to justify returning to North Vietnam on this matter?" he asked. "Your actions and their interpretations must
awaken distrust in Hanoi. . . . What must be done so that the Vietnamese regain
trust? In your declaration there is no foundation for this. It does not contain anything new. . . . I suspect that if we did approach Hanoi their response would be
that [the U.S. government] has proposed nothing new which would overcome the
reasons why Hanoi" cut off the Warsaw exchanges in the first place.

Lacking any fresh concessions to offer, Gronouski could only resort to generalities. "It wasn't a question of something new," he responded, "as much as it was
a question of bending every effort" to bring the warring governments together,
rather than simply let them fight it out. Warming to an argument he could make
far ardently than the defense of the bombings, he repeated his "firm knowledge
and personal conviction" of LBJ's desire for peace (and wished he felt confident of

Hanoi's). It would be nice, he mused, if "there was somebody making as strong a presentation and putting as much pressure on Hanoi to come to the negotiating table as the Poles were putting on us."

Rapacki replied that the problem for those trying to convince Hanoi to start talks was that "whenever they feel they are making progress the U.S. bombs their efforts."

By the end of the meeting, Gronouski cabled, Rapacki had "mellowed a bit," but his bottom line remained firm—if he reported to Hanoi the message he had just heard, "we will destroy any chance of their engaging in negotiations."

* * *

After this conversation, Gronouski rushed back to the embassy to compose an urgent cable. Despite privately sympathizing with many of Rapacki's criticisms, this time he did not bother adding his own commentary. Because Washington had so rudely rebuffed his earlier pleas, perhaps it made more sense to let the Pole's words speak for themselves.

Rapacki, meanwhile, still furious, moved briskly to follow up his tantrum with concrete diplomatic action: Having already gotten mad, he resolved to get even. So brazen was Washington's conduct, he rationalized—bombing Hanoi despite multiple Polish warnings, then foisting the blame on Warsaw for the initiative's collapse and piously bemoaning North Vietnam's supposed lack of interest in peace —and so palpable was the danger that it might peddle a skewed, self-serving version of events, that he felt justified in beating the Americans to the punch, even if it meant breaking the vow of secrecy to which Poland had sworn along with the United States and Italy. He directed Michałowski to draft a document enshrining Warsaw's version of events, suitable for presentation to third parties.[9]

Lewandowski's garbled gossip to Derksen had been a mere preliminary skirmish in the war of leaks: Now Rapacki would fire the real first shot.

Saigon: "An Exceptional Meaning"

Lewandowski, out of touch with the duel between Gronouski and Rapacki, had already shifted his focus away from the secret peace probe to the campaign to condemn the Hanoi bombings. On Monday, after receiving a radio-telegraph message from Ludwik, he transmitted to Warsaw the ICC Hanoi subcommission's unanimous conclusions that U.S. bombs had hit civilian areas within the capital, and Ha Van Lau's urging that the Pole call an emergency ICC session to seek a condemnation of the attacks and publication of the damning December 16 report—and, if unsuccessful, consider a "press indiscretion" to achieve the same aim. In relaying this advice, Lewandowski neither endorsed nor opposed the proposed leak, but stressed that he was pressing for the requested extraordinary meeting. He concluded by underlining the Hanoi ICC report's potential usefulness: "I think that the investigation regarding this issue has an exceptional meaning in face of the insolent denials of the Americans."[10] (Rapacki obviously agreed, brandishing the report to Gronouski that same day.)

London: The "Heat Seems to Be Going Out"

George Brown did his part to stay on Rusk's good side. As anticipated, he took a beating on the Hanoi bombings in the House of Commons on Monday, especially from Labour members of Parliament—but stoutly resisted demands to "dissociate" Britain from the American actions. All civilian casualties were of course deplorable, he observed, but "the U.S. assures me" it attacks only military targets. The Communists, too, had inflicted "horrors in their own way" on innocents. Blame must ultimately rest with "those who are prolonging the fighting": Hanoi and those who refused to use their influence to push it toward peace talks. The important thing now was to energetically pursue every opening to stop the violence.[11]

For Washington, it was just what the doctor ordered. "I believe there will be little further trouble and heat seems to be going out of issue," Ambassador David Bruce enthused; Rusk sent warm appreciation; and Brown said the remarks had quieted all but a few "habitual troublemakers" in his ranks.[12]

New York: "A Free Hand"

At 10:30 a.m. Monday morning, in the secretary-general's office on the thirty-eighth floor of the UN headquarters along the East River, Goldberg handed U Thant the letter that LBJ had approved over the weekend. After reading it aloud, Thant—according to his own record, though not Goldberg's—immediately expressed doubt that the other side would agree to start negotiations as long as the bombing continued. Nevertheless, he promised to study the letter carefully, relay it through diplomatic channels to both DRV and NLF representatives, and do "all I could to bring about the easing of tensions and cessation of hostilities." Leaving Thant "a free hand to make any suitable proposals," Goldberg mentioned that the U.S. mission would distribute the letter to the press. Though privately resentful that the Americans seemed more interested in making headlines than progress, Thant dutifully summoned the Soviet and Algerian delegates and asked them to relay the letter to the DRV and NLF representatives in their capitals; both agreed, though neither evinced any enthusiasm or optimism.[13]   ••

Goldberg's meeting with Thant was very brief and polite, but that was because he had already indirectly communicated the Johnson administration's expectations more frankly. Telephoning one of Thant's top aides—the illustrious Ralph Bunche, a Nobel laureate for his brokering of the armistice that ended the 1948–49 Arab-Israeli War—Goldberg had previewed the communication he would deliver and suggested that "it would be advisable for [Thant] not to respond by repeating his three point proposal for settlement of the Vietnam conflict, but merely to say that he would give the letter serious thought." Pushing his pet plan, which insisted on a bombing halt as a first step, would "impair [his] usefulness" as a mediator, Goldberg warned. Bunche, acutely aware of the friction between his boss and the Johnson administration, later told Goldberg that besides advising Thant to "forget" about his three points at this stage, he had also asked him "to cease rehashing the old Stevenson '64–'65 incidents and to concentrate on fresh efforts in the Vietnam conflict." Supposedly, Thant had agreed that this would be wise.[14]

Washington: "They Don't Miss by Five Miles"

For the moment, the State Department still stuck to its public line that no U.S. bombs had hit Hanoi, a stand that the beleaguered department spokesman, Robert McCloskey, reaffirmed (citing Pentagon data) at the noon briefing Monday. But this firm front concealed some hairline fractures. An aide advised Rusk that because eyewitness accounts might soon "bring a strong presumption that some American ordnance did in fact fall within the City of Hanoi," he would be wise to admit the possibility of an accident when he met reporters for a late-afternoon background briefing. "This hedge should, of course, be low key and casually expressed, the point being not to cast doubt at this point on the position we have taken thus far but simply to protect ourselves against any eventuality."[15]

Even before reading the record of the talk with Rapacki that day when the ICC report on the Hanoi bomb damage had made a surprise cameo—he had already left for the night by the time Gronouski's telegram arrived—Rusk was irked by the commission's inconvenient popping up. Upon learning shortly before the backgrounder that Bundy was seeing Canadian ambassador Albert Edgar Ritchie, the secretary asked him to ensure that Ottawa, "on this business of the ICC viewing of the bomb damage in Hanoi," also knew the full details of "the monkey business going on in Saigon"—the bombings, assassinations, and attempted sabotage that had also taken place in early December. Sympathetically, Bundy wondered how the Canadians justified signing the report, given their traditional stance that U.S. bombings of North Vietnam "were not within their purview."[16]

When Rusk met the press, the grilling over the Hanoi attacks annoyed him. "These things are happening in Saigon all the time and people don't get stirred up about them," he complained. "What we want is a little reciprocity in this business." Masking the fact that it had already secretly weighed in with a limited on-site inspection, Rusk nixed the idea of a commission inquest, explaining that "we've been under the impression that investigation of bombings is not part of the ICC function." And he was not a happy hedger. "As an infantryman, I'm aware that the Air Force can miss, but they don't miss by five miles," he averred, again pushing the theory that falling antiaircraft fire was to blame.[17]

Ottawa: "Narcissus"

Having secured Rusk's go-ahead in Paris, Paul Martin now acted to plug Canada back into the Vietnam peace equation. Eager to jump-start ICC collaboration but fearful of scaring off the Poles, he was glad to let the Indians take the lead in trying to organize the proposed three-way meeting in New Delhi. Before formally signing on, he had Ritchie check Monday afternoon in Washington with Bundy, who confirmed that Rusk remained "inherently sympathetic" to this "very imaginative proposal," even though U.S. officials understood that it implied a bombing halt (one step in a "pre-arranged sequence") and NLF participation in eventual talks (its status "fuzz[ed]," they hoped, by also inviting the Red Cross, Thant, et al.).[18]

Reassured, Martin dispatched a letter that evening to Indian foreign minister Chagla endorsing a secret "preliminary" trilateral gathering to deliberate how the ICC's "unique" capabilities might be "brought into play" to promote peace. As he had promised Rusk, Martin carefully reaffirmed the principle of unanimity to prevent Poland and India from ganging up, and presumed that any calls on parties to take particular steps—like a bombing halt—would be "balanced."[19] Now the trick would be to persuade Warsaw to go along.

So, just as Marigold veered off the tracks, another secret peace initiative involving Poland left the station. Bundy tagged it "Narcissus." Whether the code name merely perpetuated the floral motif or also implied an unflattering view of its chief promoter—not an entirely far-fetched notion; his own aide implied that the initiative's main purpose was "to canalize Martin's urge 'to do something about Vietnam'"—is not clear.[20]

Tuesday, December 20, and Wednesday, December 21

Rome: The First Shot

When a special message from Rapacki arrived late Tuesday afternoon, hand-delivered by courier for extra security, Adam Willmann already had an appointment with a Vatican aide to discuss Pope Paul IV's Vietnam holiday truce appeal. The new document, however, superseded his earlier mission: It contained the details of Marigold according to Warsaw, firmly blaming the Hanoi bombings for the bleak outcome, and instructions to place the materials in the pope's hands as quickly as possible.[21]

Swiftly fulfilling his assignment, the Polish ambassador handed the bombshell that same evening to Archbishop Franco Costa, the Vatican deputy secretary of state, who promised to deliver it to the pope immediately. After reading over the document, Costa expressed bewilderment at Washington's "errors and mistakes," which struck him as especially inexcusable in light of the apparently genuine chance for peace and the evident desire for it throughout American society.[22]

Tuesday night, Costa delivered the report to the pope, whose reaction he reported to Willmann the next day. Thanking Rapacki for the information, the Pontiff "very highly" praised Warsaw's peace efforts and urged it to continue them, though Costa did not convey any explicit papal criticisms of U.S. behavior comparable to his own.[23]

Pressing the campaign to curry favor with the Roman Catholic leadership, Willmann also spoke Wednesday to senior Vatican aide Agostino Cardinal Casaroli, whom the pope had already familiarized with Rapacki's document. Declaring that Poland "greatly appreciates" the Vatican's peace efforts, Willmann relayed Warsaw's agreement to transmit the latest papal truce plea to Hanoi (despite being privately convinced of its futility). Casaroli thanked Poland again for its labors on behalf of peace, and reiterated that the pope was "carefully studying" the provided information. Regarding the "wasted" chance to establish direct U.S.-DRV contacts, he noted that Costa had listened that morning—without revealing the Polish disclosure—to American ambassador Frederick G. Reinhardt's justifications of the Hanoi bombings, but that Vatican aides had found them unpersuasive. Now they were trying to discern Washington's motives in Goldberg's letter to Thant.[24]

The conversation ended cordially with a warm invitation from Casaroli to Willmann to attend a holiday party. In all, Rapacki's preemptive strike in the secret war of leaks—the first calculated, detailed, explicit indiscretion to a third party not already in the know—went just as he envisaged. Now he could swivel his guns to open a second front.

New York: "A Fish in an Unexpected Place"

As LBJ had hoped, Goldberg's letter to Thant purchased a breathing spell of positive news, bumping the bombing brouhaha off the front pages and impressing skeptics. Only a few days after skewering the administration, even the *Times* called it "a step in the right direction—not a giant step, but a good and useful one." Countering carps that the letter was a mere propaganda ploy, U.S. officials stayed studiously fuzzy about any greater willingness to consider a unilateral bombing halt—the first of Thant's three points to stop the violence—and Goldberg seized the rhetorical high ground by declaring Washington's "unconditional willingness" to engage in talks and to take "all appropriate steps" to realize peace.[25]

But if the Thant gambit succeeded in changing the subject after a week of relentless pounding, it also had some unintended consequences. Martin, in Ottawa, dismayed to see a fresh U.S. peace bid materialize out of the blue, feared that it might interfere with the ICC venture on which he had just embarked with Rusk's personal sanction. Wednesday morning, a cable from the Canadian high commissioner in New Delhi, Roland Michener, sharpened his concerns. It bore negative "flickerings" from Warsaw: Michener's Polish colleague in the Indian capital, Przemysław Ogrodziński, had suggested that the proposed three-way meeting made little sense because, due to Goldberg's letter, the UN chief "now occupied the stage." Though not quite a final Polish turndown—there was no word yet from Rapacki—Martin worried that Warsaw might scuttle the initiative before it left port, using Thant as a pretext.

Alarmed, Martin telephoned Rusk twice Wednesday seeking reassurance that the Americans did not intend their Thant overture to sideswipe the Canadian-Indian effort. When Rusk denied that the two were in any way "at cross purposes," Martin pleaded with him to tell Thant so his backing might be obtained for the

ICC plan even as he pursued his own peace bid. Agreeing, Rusk advised his Canadian counterpart to have Ottawa's UN delegate fill Thant in and solicit his aid in convincing the Poles to participate. But despite Martin's audible apprehension that overlapping approaches to Hanoi might trip each other up, Rusk still refrained from disclosing the hidden initiative that had far more bearing on Polish attitudes than the Goldberg letter, and only cryptically acknowledged that such a danger might exist. "The main problem," he remarked, "was that a multiplicity of channels may catch a fish in an unexpected place."[26]

* * *

Goldberg's letter disquieted another foreign minister engaged in secret Vietnam diplomacy, for a completely different reason. Washington had, of course, conspicuously turned to Thant for help in starting peace talks with Hanoi on the same Monday that, behind closed doors in Warsaw, Gronouski infuriated Rapacki by blaming Poland for the breakdown of the attempts made over the previous few weeks to attain that same objective. When Rapacki had retaliated by leaking Warsaw's side of the story to the pope, he had been motivated in part by the rationale that the Holy Father might receive a comparably warped U.S. version of events. Upon learning that the United States now sought to ensnare the UN leader in its diplomatic machinations, Rapacki leapt to the same conclusion: Before the Americans fed him a slanted account (if they had not already), Thant would get the *real* story from the Poles.

Washington/Texas: "Goodies to Give to the Man"

Gronouski's tense talk with Rapacki—what Rostow, forwarding the cables to LBJ in Texas, gingerly termed "this somewhat difficult session"[27]—prompted the administration to reassess its policy. Tuesday afternoon, Rusk, unsure whether the secret effort had reached a final dead-end or merely an unpredictable swerve, called the ambassador home for urgent consultations. Because Warsaw and Hanoi would doubtless take a while to figure out their next move, he cabled Gronouski, it appeared a "logical time to review Marigold with you and plan ahead." Reasserting himself after a two-week absence from Washington, the secretary desired a firsthand account of the dialogue with Rapacki—but also, in view of Gronouski's discomfiture with having to defend actions he opposed, wanted to smooth the envoy's ruffled feelings while also assuring that he now had a proper orientation. Sending the State Department's gratitude for the "time, attention and care" he had devoted to the matter and his "personal sacrifice of vacation plans," Rusk suggested Gronouski return at the "earliest feasible time" for a day or two of meetings. Could he dart back in the next week or so, leaving Walter Jenkins in charge, "without creating undesirable publicity and attention to your movements?"[28]

* * *

U.S. officials saw no reason to await Gronouski's reply or return, though, before responding to Rapacki's harsh criticisms—or to his challenge to produce "something new" to entice Hanoi. Though enjoying, thanks to the Goldberg letter, a respite from the barrage of bad publicity, they remained justifiably apprehensive about the danger of Marigold's public exposure, and Rapacki's pyrotechnics only fanned this concern. Still on the defensive, they now began to contemplate the concession of a pledge to forswear further raids on North Vietnam's capital—far short of Hanoi's long-demanded total halt to bombing and other acts of war against the DRV, but at least enough to call Rapacki's bluff and counter his claim that such raids undercut the chance for direct contacts.

Rusk, of course, had already secretly urged LBJ to suspend attacks around Hanoi from Paris some days earlier, and Bundy, though also dubious of Rapacki and Marigold, had concluded that attacks near North Vietnam's two major cities and delicate peace overtures just did not mix. "Whether the recent negotiating nibbles by third parties were authorized by Hanoi or not," the assistant secretary reasoned, they indicated a serious desire on the part of the Soviets and East Europeans (however "tough" and "slippery") to end the war more or less on the basis of the Geneva Accords. At the same time, recent intelligence indicated that for the first time since the U.S. escalation, Hanoi might be flirting with the idea of probing prospects for an acceptable settlement rather than relying solely on military means. Collectively, such developments implied that the time was ripe *now* to explore diplomatic alternatives. *But*, Bundy declared, "if we are to pursue a serious negotiating track on a 'package deal' basis, we must simply accept that we will not hit politically sensitive targets, and specifically the Hanoi and Haiphong areas, while we are pursuing such a track. Whether or not the nibbles of November and December 1966 were actually authorized, their present status has undoubtedly been communicated to Hanoi with the conclusion that the U.S. cannot be serious as long as it appears to escalate the bombing in this politically sensitive sense."[29]

Bundy also groped toward an understanding of *Washington's* real bottom line in any "package deal" (such as the ten points or Cooper's draft); if it wanted to go down the path of negotiations, it had to face up to the reality that any pact involving the departure of U.S. troops would inevitably entail "a certain irreducible minimum possibility" of an ultimate Communist takeover of South Vietnam. How great a risk would, or should, be acceptable?[30]

All these issues were on the table at 4 p.m. Wednesday when the Negotiations Committee assembled again in Harriman's office, with all present—Harriman, Thompson, Bundy, Unger, Cooper, Jorden, and Sisco—now cleared to consider, as the first item of business, the "state of play in Warsaw and where we go from here." However, with the outcome of the exchanges with Rapacki still unclear, Marigold discussion was desultory. Instead, much conversation revolved around the "package deal" idea, alternate channels to Hanoi if Warsaw were really dead, and how to relate the Polish situation to prospective diplomacy toward the Soviets with Thompson about to leave for Moscow to take up his ambassadorship. Harriman and Jorden, the White House watchdog, clashed over the potential utility of a direct secret appeal from LBJ to Ho Chi Minh; deriding Rostow's "sealed letter approach" as too ultimatum-like, Harriman favored continued use of intermediaries to feel out Hanoi, and suggested Sainteny for the next probe. Nor could the group agree on what Thompson should tell Kosygin; some felt that it would be "less confusing" to the Soviets—who presumably had been well briefed on Marigold—to simply reaffirm the ten points (perhaps slightly revised), but others felt "that we would be better off starting from scratch." As for Cooper's latest proposed package, the group judged it "a realistic position as background for negotiations" but still had "fundamental questions," and temporized by sending it to Rusk for reaction.[31]

* * *

That Wednesday, the real impetus to budge the U.S. posture on Marigold came not from Foggy Bottom but the White House—or, more precisely, its branch on the banks of the Pedernales. As LBJ, at his ranch, mulled over his response to Rapacki's blistering critique, he was visited by McNamara and Katzenbach, the two senior national security officials who had most fervently opposed further strikes in the Hanoi area as long as the Polish effort had a heartbeat. While Rostow stayed behind in Washington, the defense secretary flew to Texas Tuesday afternoon to spend several hours rambling, dining, and then breakfasting with the president; the deputy secretary followed Wednesday morning; and, at 10:25 a.m., the two saw him privately in the dining room and had a half hour to influence his thinking on Marigold.[32]

He did not need much pushing. As McNamara told Rusk, Johnson "was very much in the mood to get the conversations back on the track and his idea was to develop goodies to give to the man Gronouski talked to [i.e., Rapacki]."[33] The handiest "goody," of course, was the one that LBJ had already secretly ordered, but not divulged to the Poles, six days earlier: the suspension of further attacks on targets ringing Hanoi. But loath to give away anything for free, he wanted a quid pro quo for making the concession explicit. McNamara and Katzenbach cabled Rusk that the president "would approve" a message to Gronouski directing him to tell Rapacki that Washington was now "prepared to state that there will be no bombing within ten miles of Hanoi city center measured from" (precise geographical coordinates should be obtained from Deputy Defense Secretary Cyrus R. Vance) "for an indefinite period if talks with North Vietnamese can be gotten under way shortly"—with the proviso that "appropriate reciprocal action with respect to bombs, mortars and similar terroristic activities within ten miles of the center of Saigon would be anticipated by us as evidence of good faith."[34]

Besides instructing Gronouski to reaffirm the U.S. belief, based on "thorough" investigation, that its bombs had not struck Hanoi, the proposed message also tossed in a wild card: While the ambassador remained authorized to talk with DRV representatives, Washington could also, if North Vietnam preferred, send Goldberg to Warsaw "or any third country" empowered to conduct comparable negotiations. Most likely this suggestion reflected less a serious intent or desire to insert Goldberg into the diplomacy than a sop to the disgruntled UN envoy, who by now had been admitted to the widening circle aware of Marigold.[35]

Though conditional on receiving Rusk's OK before being dispatched to Warsaw, the hedged offer to halt bombing around Hanoi naturally appealed to the secretary of state—he had, after all, already privately urged LBJ on December 15 to stop attacks around the DRV capital, and the implicit reciprocal obligations regarding Saigon neatly fit the "open cities" concept he was toying with as a means to parlay a bombing concession into a mutual trade-off.

Rusk therefore left the bombing proposal unaltered, after checking with Vance to obtain the precise coordinates for the Saigon and Hanoi city centers. But by the time he cabled the final text to Warsaw at 4:46 p.m. Wednesday afternoon, he had inserted softer language to qualify the flat denials that any U.S. bombs had struck Hanoi—a claim that had, of course, aroused Rapacki's scorn. Now he authorized Gronouski to say that, though Washington had only attacked military targets more than 5 miles from the city center, "we cannot rule out completely the possibility of an accident," which might have been responsible for "any U.S. ordnance that may have fallen within the Hanoi city limits."[36]

Rusk left this rhetorical retreat unexplained, but one factor compelling U.S. officials to back off their earlier protestations of unalloyed innocence had been the ICC Hanoi bureau report. The previous morning, a Canadian diplomat had handed, on a "confidential basis," the text to a State Department official, who admitted, upon reading it, that Washington "might now have to abandon its sincerely held contention that no USA ordnance had fallen on city of Hanoi and to indicate that according to new info it was possible some damage within Hanoi might have been caused in error by USA action." Responding to Rusk's irritated query as to why the commission had poked its nose into the matter, the Canadian said that there had been "no opportunity" to consult either Martin in Ottawa or Moore in Saigon before the report was signed in Hanoi, and he added an explanation that would have delighted Lewandowski and Rapacki had they known of it: Once the Poles had made an official complaint (as they did at the December 14 emergency ICC meeting in Saigon), "it is difficult to put up effective legal argument against Commission involvement in issue."[37]

Though in no hurry to modify their public stand, the U.S. officials recognized that it now made little sense to cling to an absolutist position in the secret dialogue with Rapacki, who had access to the same information, and accordingly they altered the guidance to Gronouski. In view of his expected imminent trip home, and not wanting to attract press attention by a second change of travel plans, Rusk offered him the option of having Jenkins carry out the instructions.

Hanoi: I Told You So

Despite telling Gronouski on Monday that relaying the latest U.S. views to Hanoi would "destroy" any hopes for talks, Rapacki nevertheless directed his ambassador there to report the conversation to the North Vietnamese leadership. Unable to see Dong, Siedlecki instead passed the news from Warsaw to Trinh on Wednesday afternoon.[38]

Not surprisingly, the foreign minister reacted negatively, seeing the United States as out to pressure the DRV into talks "from a position of strength" and employing a "deceitful peace position" that "it was necessary to unmask." "Looking from hindsight," he observed, "it seems to us that the position of caution and reservation, which was assumed by us, was correct as was breaking off the contacts when they were using pressure." In other words—I told you so: Trinh had never been a fan of taking the initiative seriously in the first place.

Nevertheless, he assured Siedlecki that the leadership believed that "every proposition and every move of theirs must be scrupulously examined," seemingly leaving the door open to further efforts. Though unimpressed with the import of "the internal divergences within the U.S. governmental troughs"—mere tactical divergences about how best to combine force and diplomacy to coerce North Vietnam, he scoffed—Trinh derived satisfaction from British and French press criticism of the Hanoi bombings, and he cautiously expressed mixed feelings about the embryonic Thant initiative. Trinh praised his "supposedly subjective goodwill," but noted that Hanoi viewed the UN as incompetent to intervene in Vietnamese affairs and derided his "three points" as "objective[ly] harm[ful]" because they sought "mutual de-escalation by placing both the aggressor and the victim on the same level." Trinh added that it was "difficult to speak more precisely" about Thant's more recent activity, an atypically elliptical remark eliciting an unusually wary assessment from the Polish diplomat. "Unfortunately," Siedlecki confessed, "it is difficult for me to assess as to how honest [Trinh] was in saying [all of this]."[39]

Saigon: "Che Peccato!"

Lewandowski supped at D'Orlandi's Tuesday night, and the two downcast diplomats played Stratego and built a model ship. The Italian relayed Habib's remonstration against breaking secrecy (without identifying Derksen as the source of his concern), and the Pole "emphatically" denied leaking or that he was preparing a "paper" on the failed negotiations. D'Orlandi also mentioned Habib's hint that Washington would present "new proposals" in Warsaw aimed at reviving the dialogue, but after recent events, the notion failed to arouse any hope. Closing his melancholy diary entry, he mourned: "It really is over, and we will all three [he, Lewandowski, and Lodge] depart [Saigon] more or less together. What a shame! What a shame!" [Che peccato! Che peccato!][40]

＊ ＊ ＊

The Pole's protestations of innocence, when relayed by the Italian, failed to impress Porter. "Lewandowski is obviously lying to D'Orlandi," the acting ambassador cabled Washington, "but he is at least aware of our knowledge of his delinquency."[41]

Warsaw: After Midnight

Rusk's summons to Washington reached Gronouski early Wednesday. The secretary gave the ambassador a week to return for Marigold consultations, but the antsy envoy—convinced that the State Department had grievously misconstrued Rapacki's (and Poland's) behavior, and ardently wishing to persuade his superiors, and if possible LBJ himself, of a wiser course—saw no reason to delay. "I was told to come home at my convenience," he recalled, "and my convenience was to leave at nine o'clock the next morning."[42] (You go ahead, he told Mary, promising to join his family in Garmisch as soon as possible once he returned; they left with the Kaisers by train for their ski holiday.[43])

Before leaving for Washington early Thursday, Gronouski requested another session with Rapacki to review Marigold and, in particular, to try to ascertain to what extent the Poles had really been in contact with Hanoi and were able to represent its views authoritatively.[44] When Gronouski saw Rapacki at 6 p.m. Wednesday evening, the mood was less tense than two days before, but the basic deadlock remained. Hearing that the American planned to rush back to Washington for top-level consultations on Marigold (on the pretext, if there were inquiries, that he needed to discuss U.S.-Polish economic ties), Rapacki welcomed the news and expressed hope that in person he could convey more effectively the "nuances of positions and attitudes," including "Poland's dedication to solving the VN war." In response to this request to elucidate Hanoi's role, Rapacki assured him that Warsaw had reliably communicated with the DRV leadership on the basic decisions to agree to and then break off the proposed contact, and explained that warnings against trying to bomb Hanoi to the negotiating table had been Polish views that North Vietnam subsequently endorsed.

"Hanoi could never respond to pressure or give the impression that it was responding to pressure," Rapacki reiterated—that was why the bombing was so crucial, and why Washington's "main problem" now was restoring the DRV's "confidence" that the United States "genuinely" sought negotiations rather than merely to probe or pressure it militarily. Rapacki reacted tepidly to an apparent Gronouski trial balloon, mentioned only in the Pole's record, to extend the Christmas cease-fire through Tet in order to allow talks to begin against a calm backdrop; such an idea was impractical, Rapacki suggested, because it required the NLF's approval, and in any case was no substitute for a simple bombing halt.[45]

At 11 p.m., when Gronouski returned to the embassy, he discovered the State Department cable containing the new, albeit qualified, offer to eschew bombing within 10 miles of Hanoi's center indefinitely if talks could start soon, with the anticipation of reciprocal restraint around Saigon. Elated at this sign that Washington finally recognized the need to remedy the situation, Gronouski wanted to deliver the good news to Rapacki himself, discarding Rusk's option to let Jenkins handle the job in view of his imminent travel plans. He telephoned Michałowski and arranged a postmidnight rendezvous with the foreign minister.

At 1 a.m. Thursday morning, Gronouski and Rapacki met yet again.[46] The excited American apologized for the late hour, but explained that he had received a communication from Washington of such "exceptional importance" that he needed to discuss it with him before leaving—and hoped the Polish government would likewise "treat it as a very significant development." Intrigued, Rapacki had Gronouski read the statement twice and interrogated him closely to clarify whether the offer meant an unconditional bombing halt around Hanoi or was predicated on the opening of talks and reciprocal restraint around Saigon.

Gronouski urged him to see the step as "a breakthrough—a possibility to get off dead center," but Rapacki reacted warily. Though "appreciating" Washington's intentions and efforts to move forward, in particular the implicit recognition that hitting Hanoi could cause (accidental) civilian casualties and doom peace prospects, and again applauding Gronouski's own impending trip, "he could not share my enthusiasm regarding the substance of the communication." The key problems, as Rapacki saw them, were, first, that the proposition "appears to make U.S. action dependent on some signal that a contact will be established by Hanoi" and, second, despite Gronouski's denial of any "direct quid pro quo," the "indirect linking—or request—that an appropriate step (re Saigon) will be taken by the other side." Moreover, the tie to action in Saigon might imply to the DRV authorities that, even if talks started, Washington reserved the right to resume bombing Hanoi in response to events in the South. On this latter problem, Rapacki alluded to an additional complication: Any demands concerning activities in South Vietnam implied gaining the NLF's agreement, an unlikely prospect given the group's closeness to the bellicose Chinese.

One got the sense, the Pole observed, that Washington was "trying to 'kill too many birds with one stone.'" He would transmit the new proposal to DRV authorities if the Americans insisted, but he recommended strongly that they tweak the offer to eliminate the appearance of conditionality. Again, he stressed that North Vietnam, "a small, weak nation," could not afford to appear to be breaking under pressure. That being the case, in its present form the U.S. proposal "would not be well received in Hanoi." But its prospects might be enhanced if Gronouski used his trip home to give the proposal "better expression."

Impressed by Rapacki's arguments, Gronouski did not insist on the proposal's immediate transmittal to Hanoi, and he promised to try to improve it in Washington. At 2:30 a.m., the two parted on the understanding that Poland would defer any action until after Gronouski returned to Warsaw a couple of days later.

Thursday, December 22–Friday, December 23

London: "Every Tom, Dick, and Harry"
After Paris, Paul Martin had hopped across the Channel to England and had a cozy chat with George Brown. At Brown's country estate of Dorneywood west of London, surrounded by 1930s-style manicured gardens, the Canadian confided the same plan for a three-way ICC gathering he had related to Rusk a few days earlier, and received his British colleague's hearty encouragement. But when an aide summarized the state of play on the initiative on Thursday, Brown offered a more candid appraisal: "I am very skeptical. When Kosygin talked to me about 'every Tom Dick and Harry' having a plan—I've a feeling he had this in mind!"[47]

New Delhi: "I Propose That We Express Our Consent"
In the Indian capital, the proposal for an ICC powwow precipitated a flurry of behind-the-scenes activity. Hoping to overcome Polish reluctance, Canada's envoy informed Foreign Minister Chagla of his own boss's intent to convince Thant, with U.S. support, that the commission initiative would complement his own efforts. Meanwhile, Poland's ambassador, while conveying Warsaw's skepticism, actually thought it might be shrewd to cooperate. After seeing Chagla, he reported to Michałowski that the Indian had speculated that a three-way meeting might, "for example, come out with the demand for a total and definitive stopping of the bombings" and reassert the Geneva prohibition of foreign troops on Vietnamese soil—though he was uncertain whether Ottawa would endorse such moves and noted Martin's insistence that collective decisions be both "balanced" and unanimous. Insisting that it would help, not hinder, Thant's efforts, Chagla requested Warsaw's prompt agreement to attend a meeting of foreign ministry directors-general, or at least resident ambassadors, perhaps before the end of the month, to explore whether a basis existed for a gathering of foreign ministers.

Though the Polish ambassador, Ogrodziński, had immediately countered that a futile meeting could only prove harmful, privately he urged Michałowski to authorize him "to express our consent." Simply rebuffing the proposal would "strengthen the Rightist tendencies" in India's government, he argued, while accepting "could be played out to show that the rigidity of the Canadians makes it impossible to come to an understanding" and also "help to pacify unnecessary Indian initiatives within the Commission."[48]

Ogrodziński was an old Southeast Asia hand—a former delegate to the ICC and to the Geneva Conference on Laos—but his appeal would fall on deaf ears. Doubting that the timing of New Delhi's approach was coincidental, the MSZ leadership suspected that the Indians had learned that the U.S. effort had reached a dead end and decided to try their own hand. Had Washington put Chagla up to this new bid to ensnare Warsaw in Vietnam diplomacy, this time within the ICC's tight shackles? Their ardor for peace intrigues severely diminished by recent experience, neither Rapacki nor Michałowski would find their envoy's arguments persuasive.[49]

Moscow: Green Light

Before leaking the Polish version of Marigold to Thant, Rapacki judged it prudent to obtain Moscow's blessing. Thursday morning, Pszczółkowski called on Gromyko for that purpose. Like Trinh (and for that matter, like Rusk, though of course from an opposite ideological perspective), the Soviet foreign minister ambivalently appraised the UN chief's activities: sometimes "positive," sometimes "unbeneficial for the DRV," and sometimes he let himself be "used as a tool of U.S. policy"—an obvious peril in the case of Goldberg's letter. When the Polish ambassador mentioned that Rapacki feared that the Americans would mislead Thant and therefore proposed to "inform him about the correct" course of events, Gromyko fully endorsed the idea, agreeing that Washington was liable to distort what had transpired. Adding incentive, Gromyko speculated that the Burmese statesman, "feeling stronger and stronger in his position," planned to take a more energetic part in Vietnam diplomacy, perhaps visiting Asia himself in the near future.[50]

With Gromyko also confirming that Moscow had not yet taken any steps on its own to set Thant straight, Rapacki had a green light to let fly another salvo in his secret offensive.

Washington: "That Kind of Shut Up Walt Rostow"

Early Thursday morning—whether he caught any sleep after his nocturnal encounter with Rapacki is unknown—Gronouski headed to Okęcie Airport to catch the 9:10 a.m. LOT flight to Frankfurt; after missing his TWA connection, he continued to London and boarded a Pan Am jet to Washington.[51]

Meanwhile, telephone calls among Rusk, McNamara, and Rostow indicated divisions over whether Washington should further sweeten the pot by dropping the conditions attached to the offer to halt the bombing around Hanoi. Rostow was inclined merely to "quietly take stock now" and "consider very direct, covert, reliable secret communications" with Hanoi, bypassing Poland.[52] When McNamara hinted at a willingness to go further down the Warsaw route, telling Rusk Thursday morning of LBJ's desire "to get the conversations back on the track" by giving "goodies" to Rapacki, an unimpressed Rusk shot back, "We thought we gave him one yesterday"—the conditional 10-mile bombing halt around Hanoi's center.[53]

But Rusk's ingrained skepticism toward Marigold and the Poles eased slightly that afternoon after his comparably suspicious aide, Bundy, reported on a lunchtime conversation with Alexander Zinchuk.[54] In the first extensive direct U.S.-Soviet exchange on Marigold, the chargé d'affaires (acting ambassador, pending Dobrynin's return) had strongly vouched for the Polish effort and personally attested to "more than a general sense" of Hanoi's genuine interest in "starting something" as of late November, when the diplomat had been in Moscow. The subsequent Hanoi bombings on December 2 and 4, and then again on December 13 and 14, defying Polish and Soviet warnings against such actions, had puzzled the Kremlin leaders. They had thought they comprehended Washington's intentions and objectives reasonably well, but "this episode left them in real doubt whether there were military forces at work and whether they simply did not understand fully what we thought and meant to do." Bundy responded with the usual arguments denying any escalation related to the secret initiative and, while averring that the Saigon channel had been taken seriously, emphasized U.S. uncertainty as to whether the Poles had really spoken for Hanoi. This "'nuance' of doubt," he added, was exacerbated by Lewandowski's "'amateur' behavior" (e.g., leaking to third-country diplomats) and Rapacki's contrived attempts to prolong LBJ's thirty-seven-day bombing pause the previous winter and quibbling over the interpretation clause. Zinchuk only halfheartedly defended Warsaw's alleged indiscretions and "fuzzy" dealings with Hanoi, but he still insisted "most emphatically" that the Polish effort was real and Moscow fully backed it.

Zinchuk's affable yet serious mien enhanced his credibility with Bundy. He stated his criticisms "in a normal conversational tone and without vehemence or bitterness," and his argument that the Hanoi raids were ill timed resonated with the assistant secretary, who had already concluded that raids on "politically sensitive targets" and peace overtures did not blend. The two found they shared a common understanding on the distinction between stopping the bombing of North Vietnam altogether—which Washington steadfastly rejected—and avoiding "intensification." Though counseling greater sensitivity to Hanoi's allergic reaction to any perceived escalation, the Soviet would understand, Bundy noted approvingly, "if we continued to hit 'trails and other targets related to infiltration.' (He almost seemed to imply he thought this was justified!)"

This first concrete indication of Moscow's endorsement of Marigold induced Bundy and his boss to take the whole business more seriously and—though Washington's latest debate over a possible bombing limitation around Hanoi had not been explicitly discussed—to adopt a more flexible view toward additional U.S. concessions to test whether the Polish channel could produce something tangible.

For Gronouski, flying over the Atlantic, this modest attitudinal shift was exceedingly timely: It softened up the resistance he anticipated that evening in urging senior officials to heed Rapacki's call to remove the conditionality concerning the proposed 10-mile bombing halt around Hanoi and thereby give him "something new" for the DRV leaders. He was picked up at Dulles Airport at 6:30 p.m. by a State Department escort and was whisked to what he later termed a "very hush-hush meeting" in Rusk's seventh-floor office.[55] Those present—including, besides the secretary, McNamara, Katzenbach, and "one or two others"—reached agreement on a unilateral bombing halt around Hanoi. On the theory that he who writes the memo disproportionately influences its content, Gronouski stayed up until 1 a.m. with Unger to compose the text of the decision.

Friday morning, the exhausted ambassador reviewed the draft with McNamara and Rusk, who approved it with minor stylistic revisions. Then Gronouski and Rusk, accompanied by Bundy, joined a larger 10 a.m. meeting with the negotiations task force: Harriman, Katzenbach, Thompson, Read, Unger, and Walt Rostow and his brother Eugene, the undersecretary for political affairs. There, Gronouski recalls, "quite an argument" broke out. Rostow inveighed "very strongly" against any one-sided actions. "If you do this," he maintained, "then as we go down the line in peace negotiations they will expect unilateral concessions from us then; that we ought to make it clear right now that we aren't giving them unilateral concessions." To support his case, the hawkish national security adviser cited the Korean War peace talks, claiming that the Panmunjom negotiations had dragged on for another half year or so because of some U.S. concession. At that point, however, Rusk—who spoke with the authority of having been Truman's assistant secretary of state for Far Eastern affairs—brusquely rejected the analogy.

"I was there and this is not true," he said. "As a matter of fact, the reason the thing dragged on another six months is because of our mistake."

"And," Gronouski remembered, "that kind of shut up Walt Rostow at that point. And we carried the day."

By eleven, the group had agreed to advise LBJ to drop the two implicit conditions that had aroused Rapacki's objections. Rusk sent word to Texas that he, Rostow, and McNamara "strongly urged," without further haggling, an immediate cessation of bombing for 10 miles around Hanoi's center "for an indefinite period." Senior officials favored the move, he explained, to "test" Polish contentions that the December raids had been the main impediment to U.S.-DRV talks. Citing Rapacki's repeated statements that he requested not a total bombing halt but "merely that we do not escalate," Rusk added that if Hanoi really started talking in exchange for such a limited reduction, it "would be a major departure from the point which the Communist world has been insisting upon, namely, that there can be no move toward peace while the bombing of North Vietnam continues."[56]

What explains the senior officials' sudden conversion to sensitivity about bombing raids that might endanger Marigold? Some, of course, such as Katzenbach and McNamara, had already opposed further attacks on Hanoi, so they needed little convincing. But Zinchuk's vouching for the Polish effort's bona fides had influenced their recommendation—they might detest the Soviets as Cold War enemies, but they took them seriously, and their word meant far more than the Poles'.[57] Also, at Katzenbach's request, Rostow and Jorden had "systematically" reviewed the entire Marigold file and concluded, "somewhat to our surprise," that it was highly "likely that Hanoi wishes to end this war, but it doesn't know how." Though convinced that North Vietnam would respond more positively to a direct presidential appeal to Ho rather than messages through a "bewildering" array of intermediaries, the National Security Council aides now found less remote the possibility that the Poles were not just blowing smoke.[58]

Cooper later wrote: "For some it may have been a matter of prickly consciences; for others there was a genuine desire to salvage the talks, if only to test Hanoi's readiness to participate."[59]

The proposed concession abandoned language implying that the halt to raids on Hanoi depended on Communist abstinence from acts against South Vietnam's capital. It noted, however, "that in judging as to whether Hanoi is as interested in successful negotiations as we are, we would be impressed by similar restraint on their part"—for example, "a suspension of incidents" in the Saigon area, a "redisposition" of North Vietnamese forces near the Demilitarized Zone, a reduction in infiltration, or "perhaps other examples" that might "occur to the other side." Rusk explained that retaining "the idea of action on their part," even if not a quid pro quo, would "provide us a platform" for "the strongest comeback if they themselves escalate" and for insisting on reciprocity during eventual negotiations. Rostow added to LBJ that senior officials agreed that insisting on restraint around Saigon would "get us into lengthy negotiation with the Poles," while jettisoning it would permit a "quick test" of North Vietnam's willingness to enter into talks.[60] Strikingly, after reading Gronouski's report of his last talk with Rapacki, the usually skeptical Rostow had agreed with the Pole's argument that bringing the NLF into the picture by requiring reciprocal steps in Saigon might unduly complicate matters. "The single most persuasive message that has thus come far through the Marigold series," he told LBJ, "is Hanoi's requirement for secrecy at this stage with respect to [Beijing] and the NLF."[61]

At 1 p.m., a little more than an hour after receiving Rusk's message, Johnson approved the modifications to the 10-mile proposal in a telephone conversation with McNamara. After relating that he had secured Joint Chiefs of Staff chairman Wheeler's approval—"it would give him no pain to do what's said in there"—the defense secretary explained that the revised proposal served the dual purposes of testing the chances for talks and enhancing the administration's public relations posture if the initiative failed and erupted into a public dispute.

"Would it give you any problem, do you think, before the hawks later on in your [congressional] testimony?" Johnson asked.

"I don't think so," McNamara replied. "We wrote this first to try to get these things [talks] started but secondly, in the event they don't start and this thing all leaks, to have a reasonable position both with hawks and doves."

LBJ: "All right, it's OK with me."[62]

McNaughton, who was with McNamara when his call went through to the LBJ Ranch, reflected afterward: "The President went along with Bob's idea, but I sense that the President, like Dean Rusk, is a bit unyielding."[63]

At 4:08 p.m., Wheeler sent out formal secret orders to Admiral Ulysses S. Grant Sharp, head of the U.S. Pacific Command, notifying him that "until further notice from [the Joint Chiefs of Staff], you will not conduct air operations that involve attacks against targets within 10 [nautical miles] of the center of Hanoi."[64] The directive provoked an immediate, angry protest. "We were just starting to put some real pressure on Hanoi," Sharp groused. "Let's roll up our sleeves and get on with this war. We have the power. I would like authority to use it. We should be authorized to hit all [Rolling Thunder] 52 targets. The restrictions . . . should be removed. And then when Hanoi screams in anguish, we should hit them again." Unimpressed by the recent bombing uproar, which he saw as the product of a wildly successful North Vietnamese propaganda blitz, Sharp added that "if some civilians get killed in the course of these stepped-up air attacks, we should recognize it as part of the increased pressure. This war is a dirty business, like all wars. We need to get hardheaded about it. This is the only kind of action that these tough Communists will respect. That is the way to get this war over soonest."[65]

Epitomizing the chasm that had opened between the military and civilian leadership over the war's conduct, Sharp's frustration helps explain Rusk's concern, which he expressed to the president, that, although the holiday season should mask a covert bombing cutback, "Bob McNamara and I would have to take strenuous measures in our own shops to keep this point [the 10-mile exclusion zone around Hanoi] quiet."[66] It also exemplified the attitudes that fueled speculation by the Poles and others, such as Thant, that the military might have deliberately sabotaged Marigold by bombing Hanoi without LBJ's authorization.

Gronouski, by contrast—as he dashed from secret Vietnam meetings to routine consultations on Polish debt repayments[67] and the Sino-American ambassadorial talks—was "tremendously exhilarated" by the approval of the unilateral bombing halt and the relative ease with which it had happened. "I didn't have to sell anybody," he later recalled. "By that time, I think people were sold on it." Finally, Gronouski believed, "I had in my pocket the means to get this thing going again."[68]

After watching McNamara issue the order to cease bombing around Hanoi for an indefinite period, he telegraphed ahead to Jenkins to phone Michałowski and arrange an "urgent meeting for me with Rapacki tomorrow [Saturday] evening ASAP after my arrival" in Warsaw.[69] At the same time, the State Department cabled the proposal's text to the embassy "to obviate his carrying sensitive message on flight"[70]—a slightly higher-tech security measure than Nguyen Dinh Phuong's wife sewing secret instructions into his vest before he had flown to the city from the other direction a few weeks earlier.

During his brief stay in Washington, Gronouski had been the object of intense tutoring from Rusk on the realities of Marigold. Perturbed by his envoy's sympathy for Polish arguments and trust in Rapacki, which he most assuredly did not share, "I tried to give him some background or some sense on this while he was here," the secretary later told LBJ. "He responded all right here."[71]

But from Gronouski's standpoint, what mattered most is that his boss helped him attain his goal of a unilateral bombing halt around Hanoi that he could give Rapacki to test the North Vietnamese. Keen to deliver what State Department officials sardonically dubbed the "Christmas present," a groggy but euphoric

Gronouski departed for London with "high hopes" from Dulles at 7 p.m. Friday evening—barely twenty-four hours after landing there.[72]

New York: "A Kiss of Death"

Though partially mollified by Rusk's assurance that Washington "had no intention to cut across proposals," Paul Martin perceived "obvious pitfalls in [a] situation where USA appear to be pursuing parallel approaches through different channels" and feared that unless "brought into the picture promptly U Thant might once again be put in position where he would have good reason to have serious doubt in USA sincerity." On Thursday morning, accordingly, Canada's foreign minister directed his UN ambassador, George Ignatieff, to inform Thant "fully" regarding the Indian initiative and solicit his aid in persuading Warsaw to play ball. To emphasize Washington's backing, Martin suggested enlisting Goldberg to come along, but when he saw the American, Ignatieff did not push the idea. Though he reported to Ottawa that Goldberg had declined a joint approach for fear of press exposure, Goldberg informed Washington that the Canadian had worried that appearing together might give the wary UN leader the "impression U.S. has been in on or engineered ICC initiative from [the] beginning." Instead, they agreed that Goldberg would convey his sympathy for the initiative separately (which he did later in the day through Bunche).[73]

On his own, then, Ignatieff saw Thant at noon Thursday to disclose the ICC initiative and insist that "no contradiction" existed between it and the UN leader's own efforts. Though "guarded" at first—he often exasperated the Canadian, a self-described "emotional Slav," with his soft-spoken inscrutability[74]—Thant grew "more responsive" when Ignatieff explained that the Indian proposal required unanimity and Polish participation. His argument that the secret commission effort "had a chance of escaping too much public attention" struck a chord of "unhappiness" from Thant about the publicity surrounding Goldberg's letter, which he thought futile because "USA open association with any initiative in regard to Vietnam in present circumstances insofar as other side was concerned was regarded as a 'kiss of death.'"[75]

Ignatieff asked him to assure Warsaw that India's proposal did not "run counter" to his own efforts, but Thant warily refused to commit himself until he had spoken with New Delhi's representative. After ascertaining Friday morning that India had no objections, he was preparing to beckon Bogdan Tomorowicz—but the Polish ambassador called first.

When Tomorowicz showed up at noon, the real reason behind his preemptive request for an appointment emerged only after he had explained Warsaw's negative attitude toward the Indian ICC proposal.[76] As long as the U.S. bombing continued, he told Thant, "nothing positive could be achieved by such an action," and its inevitable leaking could seriously complicate Polish-DRV relations. Then Tomorowicz revealed some fresh background behind his cryptic remark that

Poland had experienced several "breakdowns" of negotiating initiatives despite initially favorable indications from Washington.

He showed Thant a long and "most interesting" memorandum and, despite "instructions not to leave it with me," let him take detailed notes after swearing him to secrecy. It was, of course, Warsaw's version of Marigold, from mid-November through Gronouski's talk with Rapacki on Monday; two days after sending it to the pope, Rapacki had transmitted the account to Tomorowicz to similarly edify Thant. Beguiled by this "first rate document," Thant embraced the Polish interpretation that hawks in the U.S. military had wrecked the effort. "In U Thant's opinion," Tomorowicz cabled, "the intensification of the bombing was initiated by the Pentagon, which sabotages in this manner all possibilities at establishing peace talks."

Shedding any inhibitions about criticizing Washington, Thant dismissed Goldberg's letter as "purely a propaganda move" containing nothing new. While transmitting it to Hanoi via the Algerians, he had "no illusion" that the letter would get a positive response, and he seemed "clearly upset" at being entrapped in a U.S. scheme to "throw responsibility" on him and the DRV for the predictable failure to start negotiations. "They passed this ball to me so they could next assert that one way out is to intensify military action, because even U Thant could not manage to persuade Hanoi to talks," he complained.

To "counteract" this scheme, Thant disclosed that he would shortly send Goldberg a public response reverting to his own three-point plan, which stressed the need for a U.S. bombing halt as a precondition for talks, and seeking an extension of the holiday cease-fire.

* * *

According to Tomorowicz, Thant shared Poland's "reservations" about the proposed ICC session in New Delhi, because "such a meeting, without an introductory foundation and preparations, could bring more harm than benefits." After seeing him, however, Thant had Bunche tell the Canadians that he had praised the Indian endeavor as "a good one" compatible with his own efforts, but Warsaw's UN ambassador was "sternly negative," primarily because the proposed three-way meeting "could not be kept secret and any publicity would evoke strong reaction from Peking which Poles consider inevitable and unacceptable." Bunche gave no indication that Tomorowicz had raised any subject besides the ICC initiative, but the Canadians smelled something fishy. "Interview had lasted nearly an hour, which U Thant had explained in terms of Tomorowicz's slowness in expressing himself in English (as latter has spent nearly seven years in England—in Polish air force during war and a subsequent posting to Polish Embassy in London this is not exactly credible, and we have always found him very fluent in English)."[77] As in Saigon, a whiff of Marigold now had Canadian diplomats "sniffing around."

Rome: Fanfani "Reacted Extraordinarily"

After the NATO meeting in Paris, Fanfani had meandered around northwestern Europe for several days, seeing de Gaulle and West German, Belgian, and Luxembourgian leaders, before returning to Rome late Wednesday night. Distracted by his travels, and separated from the special communications channel set up to receive D'Orlandi's ciphered telegrams, he had been unable to monitor Marigold's plunging fortunes.

His first day back at the Farnesina brought both good news and bad. Meeting with the Council of Ministers on Thursday afternoon, he was delighted to win D'Orlandi a promotion to first-class minister, "a well-deserved reward for what he has done and continues to do." It had not been easy to gain the approval of the top leaders, who were only dimly aware of the covert diplomacy. Prime Minister Moro had hesitated, on grounds that the proposed elevation skipped several steps and risked attracting undue notice, but Fanfani overcame resistance by declaring "that for reasons that I cannot now say—but which one day will be known—a timely reward for this courageous and loyal diplomat is required."[78]

But even as he celebrated D'Orlandi's advancement, Fanfani belatedly caught up on the envoy's grim messages, which had accumulated in his absence, and heard his gloomy telephone report from Saigon indicating that Rapacki had instructed Lewandowski to suspend his efforts. Only now did the foreign minister grasp the "difficulties" casting a pall over the initiative, and he was deeply distressed.[79] From visions of international and domestic acclaim, he had watched aghast as both his diplomatic dance partners, in Washington and Warsaw, committed what seemed to him egregious missteps. Seeking clarification of what had gone wrong and, if possible, to redress the situation, Fanfani on Friday morning welcomed Willmann to his office.

Poland's ambassador explained that he had come to deliver an urgent message from Rapacki that had actually arrived a week earlier but had awaited the Italian's return. He then read his foreign minister's rendition of how the U.S.-DRV contact had failed to occur, as the December 13–14 Hanoi bombings had caused the North Vietnamese to break off the initiative. Rapacki's words confirmed Fanfani's worst fears, and an allusion to Warsaw's having already given the Vatican a detailed account embittered him even more.

"He listened very attentively, after which he reacted extraordinarily," Willmann cabled afterward.

The agitated Italian minced few words in rebuking his counterpart. Not arranging the direct contact had been an "incalculable error, which ruined the fruits of long-term efforts"; unmoved by Polish arguments blaming U.S. "escalation," he insisted that the contacts should have been started anyway, which would then have immediately yielded a bombing halt. Calling Rapacki "wrong" to terminate the three-way channel in Saigon, Fanfani, above all, took offense at the disclosure to the pope. Not only did the leak imperil future use of the Saigon channel and blatantly violate the solemn tripartite vow of secrecy, Fanfani observed—and he had no idea a second calculated Polish indiscretion, to Thant in New York, was just hours away—but it also gravely embarrassed the Italian government, and him personally, to have the Vatican learn of the initiative from Warsaw rather than Rome. Willmann interjected that the Poles would have preferred that he, Fanfani, tell the pope, yet they had had to do so themselves because he was out of town, but the Italian was not buying; Rapacki could have waited, he retorted, or at least warned him through the Polish ambassador in Paris. Now the odds had multiplied of a public scandal that might trigger government or parliamentary inquests, which would force him—and perhaps the Americans—to tell their own side of the story.

Trying to sound constructive, Fanfani pledged to go on promoting peace and again beseeched Rapacki to "correct the situation" by orchestrating the Warsaw contact without delay, and authorizing Lewandowski to keep seeking progress in Saigon and Hanoi. But he conveyed an overriding impression of acute dismay at the Poles' behavior, combined with an ominous warning—as Willmann cabled, the Italian "even asserted that the moral responsibility for the further course of the conflict might be ascribed to us."[80]

After Willmann left, Fanfani sent an account of the quarrelsome session to D'Orlandi. Hoping to preserve the Saigon channel's primacy, rather than informing the U.S. Embassy in Rome about the conversation, he authorized D'Orlandi to inform his partners there and to emphasize that Italy still believed it necessary, "despite the errors made by all sides," to keep searching for peace, seizing "each and every minimal possibility." Having secured his envoy's promotion, Fanfani was disconcerted to read, in one cable, that D'Orlandi had told Habib that in view of the three-way attempt's failure, he should not "risk my poor health very much longer in Saigon." Imploring him to stay at his post if humanly possible, Fanfani—as yet unaware of the secret U.S. move that day to declare a 10-mile no-bombing zone around Hanoi—stressed that Rusk had assured him in Paris that Washington would try hard to revive the stalled contacts. D'Orlandi's presence was essential to preserve that chance. "Hoping that the New Year festivities bring you health and success," he signed off.[81]

Warsaw: "Lively Diplomatic Activity"

As his Pan Am Boeing 707 sped eastward toward Europe that Friday night, Gronouski's hopes might have soared even higher had he known that during his whirlwind visit to Washington, Polish Foreign Ministry officials were already also striving to break the logjam. Unbeknownst to the Americans, the Poles, according to Michałowski, "continued to hope for a victory by the pro-peace camp in Hanoi" and engaged in "lively diplomatic activity" aiming at "saving the whole initiative."[82] Although Rapacki had told Gronouski in their postmidnight conversation Thursday morning that he preferred to wait before transmitting the U.S. proposal to Hanoi until Gronouski had a chance to improve it, the Pole, sensing new American "tractability," acted immediately to mobilize pressure on the DRV finally to begin negotiations. Grasping at the "slight chance of saving the talks," Rapacki employed the "strongest, from the Vietnamese point of view," channel of communications: an official, secret message from the Polish Communist Politburo to its Lao Dong counterpart. Drafted "within a few hours" by Rapacki and Michałowski and then presented by the former to a hastily arranged rump session of the Polish United Workers' Party Politburo, the message analyzed events since Lewandowski had conveyed the Lodge proposals to Hanoi in late November. While reaffirming undying support for Vietnam's heroic struggle and fully endorsing the DRV leadership's refusal to start talks under duress, Poland's Communist rulers urged their Vietnamese comrades "to take full advantage of the opportunity for a political resolution to the conflict." Washington, they argued, presently faced a "difficult political situation" both domestically and internationally—including extra pressure due to the conjunction of the worldwide criticism of the Hanoi raids and the prospect of eventual blame for the failure of the secret peace initiative—along with the prospect of further "devastating and protracted war." Therefore, the present juncture was "particularly suitable and amenable" for political action, including "talks with the enemy."

Warsaw proposed this scenario: Washington extends its traditional Christmas Day bombing halt into the New Year; and Hanoi agrees that after ten days of nonbombing, during the first week of January, its ambassador in Warsaw will have a contact with the U.S. ambassador, "and then examine and take a position on the matter of the USA proposals and put forward its own." Promising full coordination, the Poles argued such a course would, per Washington's own Phase A/B proposals, constrain the United States from further attacks on the North and compel it to consider a "package deal" conforming to DRV and NLF interests.

Even before hearing the results of Gronouski's trip to Washington, Warsaw dispatched the interparty message "through the Politburo's own channels" to Hanoi.[83]

* * *

Rapacki and Michałowski, now firmly controlling Poland's diplomacy, felt no obligation to apprise Lewandowski promptly or fully of their latest exchanges with either Gronouski or the DRV leadership, or their calculated leaks to the pope and Thant. Instead, Warsaw merely instructed its Saigon representative, who believed that the peace initiative was already dead, to intensify his efforts within the ICC to disseminate more widely the Hanoi subcommission's still-secret report indicting the Americans for bomb damage to civilian neighborhoods in the capital. While rejecting Ha Van Lau's suggestion to leak the report as a "dangerous" and potentially counterproductive deviation from procedure, the MSZ's Asia Department chief directed Lewandowski to cite the document extensively so it appeared in the official ICC record, to propose collectively transmitting it to the Geneva cochairs (Britain and the Soviet Union), and—once the Canadian and Indian commissioners predictably voted down the idea—to declare his intent to submit it to the cochairs unilaterally.[84]

As they urged North Vietnam's leaders to swallow their doubts and enter talks, the Poles, sensitive to Hanoi's wariness toward them, wanted to establish a clear record to show they had done their utmost to promote the propaganda campaign against the bombings and undermine the U.S. position.

Ottawa: Luring Rapacki

Assured of Thant's backing for the Indian-Canadian initiative, however tepid, and reasoning that Tomorowicz's "sternly negative" stand did not necessarily or authoritatively reflect his foreign minister's views, Martin tried to entice the Poles. In a letter cast as a natural follow-up to his Warsaw visit the previous month, the Canadian wrote Rapacki to encourage him to accept Chagla's invite to a meeting of ICC powers in New Delhi—"preliminary, exploratory and certainly at this stage without any kind of commitment"—to discuss the stalemated body's predicament and, inevitably, "broader aspects of the Vietnam problem."[85]

Saigon: Head to Hanoi?

On Friday morning, Lewandowski conferred informally with his fellow commissioners and, as coordinated beforehand with Ludwik, ventured his ploy to elevate the ICC's profile in the bombing controversy. Why not fly to Hanoi the following week to stage their already planned upcoming emergency session to consider the U.S. attacks? He justified the trip as a chance for on-the-spot inquiries, but the idea struck Moore as a transparent publicity stunt—and indeed, Lewandowski explained to his superiors that a Hanoi meeting would serve the dual aims of spotlighting the ICC's inquest (and already-reached conclusions) and forestalling further raids while the international body convened in the DRV capital.

The Canadian predictably opposed Lewandowski's brainstorm, and Rahman failed to endorse it; instead, the three agreed to gather at their usual site five days hence to take up the matter at the ICC's 753rd formal meeting. Anticipating that his motions to condemn the bombings would fail, the Polish commissioner urged Warsaw to, as a fallback position, support sending the ICC Hanoi bureau's report on bomb damage to the British and the Soviets, because the latter would certainly publish it—and if not, "we should cause a press indiscretion," as Ha Van Lau urged.[86]

Hanoi: "Mis-ter Har-ri-son?"

Awaiting the next diplomatic move, Siedlecki sought clues to what was happening behind the bellicose public facade concealing the secret debates he presumed were taking place among the DRV's leaders over whether to enter talks with the Americans. On Thursday, he discussed peace prospects with Tran Chi Hien, a deputy to Xuan Thuy, the party's international relations chief. Like Trinh, Hien scorned Goldberg's letter and, while complimenting U Thant's "positive personal intentions," denounced the Burmese statesman's "three points" for failing to distinguish between aggressor and victim—contrasting his reticence with de Gaulle's forthright condemnation of U.S. conduct. Cautiously, Siedlecki cabled Warsaw that Hien, whom he knew better than the stolid foreign minister, *seemed* candid; at least he did not seem to be hiding "anything special" about Thant.[87]

Siedlecki also gathered North Vietnamese impressions of the international reaction to the Hanoi bombings. A midlevel Foreign Ministry aide had complained that the response seemed weaker than to the raids on petroleum, oil, and lubricant facilities five months earlier. Yet Hien equably observed that, while the Lao Dong Central Committee had not yet rigorously compared the two, he personally believed that the recent protests organized by socialist countries had been "swifter and stronger" than in late June, and he also expressed satisfaction at the general worldwide reaction.[88]

Their assessments were premature. Even as the Polish Embassy transmitted Siedlecki's ciphered telegram early Friday evening, an American was about to reach Hanoi who would prove a far more effective weapon than socialist propaganda in exploiting the bombings to undermine the Johnson administration's standing both at home and abroad.

✳ ✳ ✳

After taking off from Vientiane at dusk, the regular-irregular ICC plane, the silver-bottomed, four-engine Constellation, rumbled in the dim light of a crescent moon along the narrow air corridor to Hanoi, and touched down at Gia Lam at about 7:30 p.m. In addition to the usual smattering of commission personnel, diplomats (Eastern Bloc, Indian, and French), couriers, and activists, it bore special cargo for the holiday festivities—a plump live goose, desperately straining to wriggle free of the red canvas diplomatic pouch in which it had been confined by a Canadian staff sergeant, destined for the Christmas Eve party hosted by Ottawa's isolated ICC contingent—and also one tall, mustachioed, tired but exhilarated American journalist. Since Monday, his odyssey that had taken him, first, from New York to Paris for a harried Tuesday of rushing to retrieve the promised DRV visa and vainly seeking a Cambodian transit visa; then onward Wednesday on Air France via Tirana (where the edgy Albanian authorities had barred passengers from leaving the plane), Cairo, Teheran, and Karachi, to sweltering Phnom Penh. There, after finessing the transit pass at the airport, he ventured to the Hotel Le Royale, finding "the same mildewed Graham Greene atmosphere" he had found the previous summer. But before collapsing into his room's "big brass bed," the tired but wired correspondent hobnobbed with the hotel's assortment of "pleasant Poles, jolly Canadians, and mysterious individuals of unknown nationality," all of whom seemed to presume (despite ardent denials) that he was on some sort of official peace mission, on which they congratulated him and wished him well. "'Wait till you get to Hanoi,' one of the Poles told me, eyes sparkling (a good Pole, he loved diplomatic intrigue)."

The next morning, he bid farewell to his wife, Charlotte, and around noon Friday, accompanied by Burchett, took off on the ICC plane that had arrived from Saigon earlier in the morning. Reaching the sleepy Laotian capital at 2:30 p.m., he happily accepted an invitation from one of the Poles to stop by his embassy for drinks and snacks during the refueling stop before returning to the airport for the final hop to Hanoi.

At Gia Lam, after the plane taxied to a halt and cut the propellers in front of the concrete hut that served as a terminal building, flashlight-toting North Vietnamese police entered to check passengers' passports against a "dog-eared list of typewritten names" before waving them past. Gingerly, they descended an aluminum ladder at the rear of the ancient aircraft and onto the puddle-spattered tarmac of the blacked-out airport.

Two men walked up to the assistant managing editor of the *New York Times,* who clutched a manual typewriter and a camera as he peered at the unfamiliar, shadowy surroundings.

"Mis-ter Har-ri-son?" one asked tentatively.

"Yes."

"Welcome to Hanoi."[89]

Saturday, December 24

Hanoi: Message Delivered

The latest missive from Warsaw—presumably the Polish United Workers' Party Politburo analysis urging North Vietnam's Communist leaders to enter talks[90]—reached Siedlecki early Saturday. Once again, he tried to see Pham Van Dong, but the premier's office steered him to Nguyen Duy Trinh to receive the message on his behalf. For much of the day, Foreign Ministry aides put off the meeting, first saying that Trinh was too busy, and then using the excuse of difficulty in locating a Russian-language translator. Were these delays a signal of the DRV's displeasure with the Poles? Siedlecki and Rapacki could only guess.

Finally, at 8:45 p.m. on a misty Christmas Eve, Siedlecki saw Trinh, finding him "greatly tired" but in a "quite kind mood" and "less stiff" than when they had spoken a few days before. Relaying his message, the ambassador noted that the last time the foreign minister had immediately taken a position on the material he received, but this time he should first obtain the leadership's official response. Agreeing to do so, Trinh "kindly" promised to see the Pole again on the matter, though he could not resist observing that continued "provocative" U.S. raids by both land and sea seemed to "supersede" the latest Polish communication.[91]

✳ ✳ ✳

Salisbury had awoken before dawn—he would soon learn that this was the custom in the city—to a cock-crowing cacophony outside the window of his room at the Thong Nhat (Reunification Hotel), the French-built landmark formerly (and later again) known as the Metropole, which was centrally located across the from the ornate old colonial governor's mansion and a few hundred meters from historic Hoan Kiem Lake. Shivering, the *New York Times* reporter soon discovered that in the excitement of arrival, he had left his topcoat on the ICC plane (it would shuttle back and forth between Hanoi and Saigon for ten days before being returned).

But the chill did not stop Salisbury from his appointed rounds. His sightseeing started at 6 a.m. after a gulp of Nescafé, with a de rigeur tour of the "Museum of the Revolution" (formerly attached to the École Française d'Extrême Orient), a "chamber of horrors" that besides propaganda offered clues to two thousand years of Vietnamese resistance to northern (predominantly Chinese) invaders. Then, escorted by government minders, he devoted the rest of the day to inspecting damage in various sectors of the city allegedly caused by the U.S. air raids, especially on December 13 and 14, and interviewing witnesses through an interpreter. After darkness fell, he took in Christmas Eve services at a cathedral and church before being driven back to the Thong Nhat in his Russian-made Volga.

Taking advantage of the time difference—it was still Saturday morning on the East Coast, and there was thus plenty of time to make the Sunday papers—Salisbury banged out his story and, inevitably, endured "agonies of bureaucratic negotiation to get it transmitted to Paris for relay to New York" (along with a photograph he had taken of bomb damage on Pho Nguyen Thiep Street). His long day's work done, he descended the hotel's elegant curved marble staircase to round out the evening at a small Christmas fête put on by the Vietnamese Journalists' Association for the few, mostly Communist, foreign scribes present—the Australian (Burchett) and Italian reporters, a Hungarian writer, a Cuban poet. One of those present limned the mystery guest from New York: "in his mid-fifties, a mixture of English lord and German principal: posture very erect, carefully trimmed gray-blonde moustache, serious and cool, inquiring eyes behind rimless glasses." Amid roast turkey, ersatz French pastry, bibulous toasts ensued —including a harsh one from the North Vietnamese host, who, after decrying the "barbarous crimes of the American aggressors," lifted his glass to the day "when the American invaders leave our country."

As all eyes turned to Salisbury to see how he reacted, the Vietnamese politely added: "On the other hand, the Americans who visit our country without weapons are welcome."

"Be careful, he's got a typewriter!" Burchett shouted jovially, breaking the tension.

Salisbury, still quiet, rose to his feet, raised his own glass, and solemnly but with "a trace of a smile," drank earnestly to "true friendship" between the Vietnamese and American peoples.

Around midnight, Salisbury called it a night, emotions churning. At one extreme, he felt depression at the imbecility and human cost of war—having reported on far more extensive devastation during World War II in cities ranging from London to Leningrad, he was "nauseated . . . to witness again this banal newsreel which history had played over and over in my lifetime now being put into reruns by men who did not understand the meaning of its banality or did not care." But there was also the thrill of scooping the competition to grab a dateline and a story that, only hours later, would command worldwide attention.

"I hope you see Santa in your dreams," a Vietnamese minder told him as he started up the stairs. "Good night."[92]

Saigon: "Crazy with Joy"

D'Orlandi was putting up a small Christmas tree in his apartment late Saturday afternoon when Emina, his first secretary, called up from the downstairs chancellery to alert him that important ciphered telegrams from Fanfani were coming in over the daily 4:30 p.m. communications link. The first, informal message contained "a nice Christmas present": news of his promotion, along with affectionate Yuletide greetings. Soon more official word arrived—"By Order of the Council of Ministers, upon my recommendation, Your Excellency was nominated Minister, First Class, on this date"—followed by a long cable relating the tart talk with Willmann on Friday and requesting that D'Orlandi postpone any plans to leave Saigon.[93] D'Orlandi was more than willing to linger in Saigon to pursue peace on Fanfani's behalf, and he warmly reassured his boss to that effect, but he also grimly warned that such labors would be pointless wheel spinning without progress (i.e., the delayed first U.S.-DRV contact) in the Polish capital: "In the meantime if something doesn't get done in Warsaw, [the] three-party effort may be considered to be a failure and this failure will gravely damage every other [Vietnam peace] effort."[94]

Having been instructed to tell his diplomatic partners about Fanfani's conversation with the Polish ambassador, D'Orlandi could not reach Lewandowski but was able to contact Habib, to whom he read the foreign minister's account of the talk, including his scolding of Rapacki's conduct, so the American could report it to Washington. Though Habib cabled Rusk that he had not reacted substantively, D'Orlandi recorded that the political officer seemed "alarmed" at the news that Warsaw had divulged "all details" of the secret diplomacy to the pope and voiced general support for preserving the tripartite channel while cautioning that one could only "wait for developments" to see if it could yet serve any useful purpose.[95]

His assignment half-accomplished, D'Orlandi then joined the embassy staff to make his way to Saigon's red brick cathedral, styled after Notre Dame, for Midnight Mass. The temporary halt in fighting for the holiest day in his calendar teased his emotions. "The Christmas truce began this morning at 7," he recorded in his diary. "A Child is born!" That night, the war-weary diplomat witnessed an explosive yearning for peace made even more poignant by his private conviction that a recent opportunity to stop the carnage had been squandered:

Saigon appears to me to be crazy with joy. Pedestrians and motorists crowded the streets where traffic was crawling along. Confetti, masks, and candy. Tonight there is peace and everyone is shouting it out happily. In the cathedral, packed with the faithful, there was a shortage of consecrated hosts, such was the crowd to receive communion. The procession lasted a good twenty minutes. For the first time the peace of the night was not lit up by flares, the aircraft did not take off, the cannons were quiet. The only explosions were those of the firecrackers (prohibited but tolerated) and of popped balloons. My God, my God, why does this cease-fire have to end?[96]

Warsaw: "On the Track"

Delayed by blizzards, Gronouski transited London and Vienna before finally reaching Okęcie Airport late Saturday afternoon.[97] Before racing to the Foreign Ministry to see Rapacki (Jenkins had made a 7 p.m. appointment), the jet-lagged diplomat, who had barely slept in thirty-six hours, first stopped by the embassy to change clothes. While in his office, he was unpleasantly surprised by an urgent phone call from an Associated Press reporter, Gene Kramer, who suspected that the ambassador's mysterious travels were linked to secret Vietnam diplomacy. Asked point-blank if his hasty return meant that "something unusually important" related to the war was happening, Gronouski—still religiously abiding by the Marigold secrecy pact, unaware that the Poles had already violated it—did his best to sidetrack the inquisitive journalist. He had hurried back merely to try to spend at least part of his Christmas holiday with his family, and thanks to a "good and tight" schedule, had squeezed into twenty-four hours in Washington meetings with all the State Department and White House people he needed to see: Rusk, Katzenbach, Eugene Rostow, and others regarding the zloty crisis and U.S.-Polish ties, and, more briefly, William Bundy and Paul Kreisberg on the Sino-American ambassadorial talks—though he had not spoken to LBJ, off at his Texas ranch. Had Vietnam entered the China consultations? Naturally, he dodged, the topic was "on everybody's mind," but it had cropped up only in a general way.[98]

Hoping that he had deflated Kramer's curiosity, the ambassador then rushed to the Foreign Ministry. Accompanied by Jenkins and Michałowski, Gronouski and Rapacki briefly exchanged Christmas Eve greetings before getting down to business. Gronouski then read aloud the four-paragraph text of the decision to suspend indefinitely bombing within a 10-mile radius of Hanoi's center. By taking this step, he emphasized, Washington had removed what Rapacki had termed the "major impediment" to direct U.S.-DRV talks. While still denying any intention to pressure Hanoi with its earlier bombing, the statement declared that the United States' action reflected its desire to "leave no stone unturned to get negotiations started," a wish that the American authorities "are assuming" the Poles shared.[99]

Rapacki rued that this action had not come on December 4 or earlier—"Had that been the case, we might already have the first [U.S.-DRV] meeting behind us and have good results by now." But he acknowledged that, compared with two days earlier, Gronouski had now delivered a "concrete proposal," which he would immediately transmit to North Vietnamese authorities, even though he could not predict their reaction.[100] Still wary, Rapacki said he hoped this latest step represented "more than simply a gambit to get negotiations started" that might be undermined by escalatory actions elsewhere, perhaps by those who opposed talks, and fretted that the reference to desirable responses might still be viewed as implying conditions.

Gronouski, for his part, stressed the action's "very positive" nature. Having personally witnessed McNamara's order, he could now attest to the fact that the action was not "contingent" or conditional—in effect, he argued, "Phase A" had already been implemented, at least around Hanoi. In any case, the important thing was to overcome the obstacles that had blocked contacts thus far. "The quicker we get talks going, the better the opportunity to avoid such problems in the future," he argued, prompting Michałowski to again nod in agreement. Despite Rapacki's usual reticence, Gronouski sensed that he, too, was "quite overjoyed" by the U.S. action and now "clearly had what he wanted" to get Marigold moving again.

His mission accomplished, Gronouski bade farewell to the Poles. Walking into the darkness after the "very good" hour-and-a-half discussion, he thought to himself: "We are [back] on the track." Finally, the "drained" yet exultant ambassador could catch a night's sleep before leaving Sunday morning to join his wife and daughters in Garmisch for at least an abbreviated family holiday together, leaving Jenkins authorized to handle any Marigold communications in his absence.[101]

※ ※ ※

The "Christmas present" had been delivered, and it was up to the Poles to gift wrap it and give it to the North Vietnamese. For the moment, in Warsaw and Washington, there was little to do but wait and wonder: How would Hanoi respond?

11

"The Ultimate Reply"

The End of the Affair,
December 25–31, 1966

We reject these piratical proposals. . . . The talks are over, but the USA continues to be stubborn and insolent. The matter is not ripe for political settlement.

—*Nguyen Duy Trinh to Jerzy Siedlecki, Hanoi, December 28, 1966*

In this moment of frustration, it would be easy to conclude that the Poles have led us down the primrose path. But I think this would be an unfortunate misinterpretation of events.

—*John Gronouski to Washington, December 30, 1966*

It was propaganda all the time, wasn't it? . . . Too much.

—*President Lyndon Baines Johnson, at the LBJ Ranch, December 30, 1966*

In the final days of 1966, as the bombing controversy reignited, both on the front page of the *New York Times* and behind the closed doors of the International Control Commission in Saigon, Hanoi responded decisively to the last-ditch attempt to save Marigold—even as convoluted intrigues uncoiled in cities around the globe aimed at reviving the stalled peace effort and positioning Washington and Warsaw for the looming public and diplomatic scandal over its demise.

Sunday, December 25

Saigon–Vung Tau: A Drive to the Coast

On Christmas morning, D'Orlandi strolled through central Saigon, observing the "completely different" expressions on people's faces as they savored the rare peaceful interlude. Still unable to locate his Polish friend to deliver Fanfani's message, the Italian lunched with an aide, then accompanied his military attaché's family on an afternoon drive in the countryside north of the city. Outwardly, it was a relaxing holiday, but the fleeting tranquillity tormented the Italian. "It is still the last few hours of peace," he wrote in his diary. "Tomorrow at 7 [a.m.] this dreadful, exhausting war will restart."[1]

✳ ✳ ✳

Where was Lewandowski? Though also raised as a Roman Catholic, like most Poles (and also D'Orlandi), Warsaw's ICC representative had skipped Midnight Mass. Since shortly after surviving World War II, he had stopped attending church and confessional, repelled by the hypocrisy of organized religion and resisting sectarian classification, despite a residual agnosticism over how the universe had come into existence and a willingness to partake in the trappings of seasonal cheer.[2]

Over Christmas weekend, Lewandowski instead honored a less reverent ritual practiced most devotedly by American college students—a road trip! With his military and legal advisers, Warsaw's commissioner and a few dozen other Canadians, Indians, and Poles piled with Vietnamese drivers into official vehicles flying the ICC flag. The caravan headed north on Highway 1 past the sprawling Bien Hoa Air Base, then veered to the southeast on Route 15 toward the South China Sea resort of Vung Tau, a favorite colonial retreat (still widely known by its French-era name, Cap Saint Jacques), at the tip of a peninsula jutting into the mouth of the Saigon River. Nowadays, few dared to make the 80-mile (128-kilometer) trip, because the route traversed territory controlled or at least infested by Communist guerrillas since the Viet Minh struggle against the French, but the forty-eight-hour truce offered a perfect window for a safe getaway, and checking on a small "fixed team" of inspectors in the port provided a perfect pretext.[3]

Escaping the teeming capital in his big black Chevrolet, racing past the verdant tropical landscape of rice paddies and rain forests, Lewandowski felt upbeat. Though he still simmered over the stalemated peace initiative—bitter at the Americans for bombing Hanoi, irked at Rapacki and Michałowski for shutting him out—a bundle from Hanoi had boosted his spirits. A pouch carried by courier on the most recent ICC flight had brought a personally signed card "with warmest wishes for 1967" from Ho Chi Minh, friendly holiday greetings from Dong and Giap, and a special present from Ha Van Lau: two jars of wild bee honey, which the Vietnamese treasured as a curative for rheumatism and other ailments. The gift evoked a shared memory: driving through the jungle outside Hanoi to inspect bomb damage during one of the Pole's visits, their party had spotted a hive and stopped so the soldiers escorting them could steal some of the sticky nectar.

Lewandowski had feared that the disastrous events since his last trip to Hanoi had rendered him persona non grata there, exposing him as naive or worse for encouraging the North Vietnamese to deal with the Americans just before they proved their bad faith. But now he had reason to believe he was not "finished" in Hanoi after all, and might even still be considered an acceptable diplomatic channel. "I feel that there is no grudge against me, otherwise they would not make these gestures. It was absolutely not necessary for them to do so."[4]

On their excursion to the coast, the Poles jotted observations to relay to Warsaw and to Lau and the Russians in Hanoi. Every bridge and checkpoint they encountered was smashed, with U.S. troops guarding provisional replacements and, in some cases, building fortifications. Driving by Bien Hoa, they saw helicopter landing pads, ammo dumps, barracks, repair shops, and assorted military vehicles, and about 40 kilometers (25 miles) from the capital, they spotted huge weapons stockpiles. Though they passed through larger towns such as Long Thanh and Ba Ria (which hosted a newly arrived Australian contingent), the smaller villages had been converted into "strategic hamlets," enclosed compounds of peasants and small garrisons of the Army of the Republic of (South) Vietnam (ARVN) set up since Diem's time in a scheme to isolate the population from the Viet Cong. Once, they shared the highway with an armored personnel carrier column transporting a mechanized infantry brigade, and in the back country they noted intensified U.S. jeep and chopper patrols and roadside minefields— marked but not cleared.[5]

During the relaxing, if brief, respite in Vung Tau, Lewandowski stayed near the white sand beach, swam, and ate fresh crabs. With the guns silent, the vacationers' closest brush with mortality came when a Canadian rescued an inebriated American cavorting in the surf. By late Sunday afternoon, the ICC contingent was packing its bags, preparing to scurry back to Saigon before the shooting resumed.

Lewandowski had other ideas. He wanted to spend the night in Vung Tau and return Monday—after the truce ended—to check U.S. assertions that, thanks to operations by its own soldiers and the Australians, the strategically vital road linking the port and Saigon (as well as the Bien Hoa Air Base) was now secure for military and civilian traffic. "I wanted to see what really is the situation," he recalled. "There were conflicting reports."

Lacking Lewandowski's zeal for onsite verification, his associates pleaded with him to reconsider. They were free to join the ICC convoy that evening, he replied, as would two other carloads of Poles, but he would stay. Colonel Ryszard Iwanciów, an older man who had fought (and was twice wounded) in World War II, contended that the route was too hazardous, contrary to U.S. claims. (Normally, the Poles had learned, ground travel to the capital was restricted to one weekly heavily armed convoy; most went by air.) When his pleas failed, the military adviser threatened to report the incident to Warsaw.

Do it, Lewandowski dared.

His bluff called, Iwanciów relented ("if you must"). He and the legal adviser resigned themselves to remaining at Lewandowski's side for the extra night by the sea and potentially risky ride home on Monday.

Shaking his head over the escapade decades later, Lewandowski sympathized with Iwanciów, whom he respected; in trying to hurry him back to Saigon, the colonel was only "trying to protect me, doing his duty. . . . I certainly shouldn't have done it."

"I was a little young, you know."

Hanoi: "Open: Discussed"

On Christmas Sunday, Siedlecki delivered the latest U.S. proposition along with an earnest endorsement, passing to Dong reports of Rapacki's most recent talks with Gronouski, as well as the foreign minister's advice "to take full advantage of the opportunity for a political resolution to the conflict." Echoing the Politburo message, Rapacki praised Hanoi's stand to date, but stressed the benefits of now entering negotiations. "We consider that the present moment is particularly suitable for a move to determined political action by undertaking direct talks with the enemy," he judged. "Refusal from our side would not be understood and it would hand to the Americans all the arguments. Taking up the contact, conversely, would tie their hands or would also unmask them for good." Whatever Hanoi decided, Poland promised firm support.[6]

While receiving no immediate reply to this new U.S. proposal, Siedlecki sent Warsaw an assessment of the DRV leadership based on inside dope from an unidentified "rather authoritative" Vietnamese source. Meeting almost daily, the source related, the Politburo agreed on the need to inflict maximum casualties on ARVN forces to weaken Saigon's position during possible upcoming negotiations and formation of a coalition government; it also resolved to send as much military equipment as possible to the Communist forces in the South, for which a lengthy holiday bombing pause, ideally extending from New Year's to Tet, would be helpful. At the same time, the Politburo deliberations were reportedly marked by "hesitation and controversy" over whether to enter negotiations with the Americans now or only after a "decisive" dry season offensive.

"The matter is open: discussed," Siedlecki cabled.[7]

❋ ❋ ❋

Like residents in Saigon, some Hanoi denizens took advantage of the Christmas truce to enjoy a Sunday afternoon stroll or bicycle ride, able to ignore the ubiquitous cylindrical individual concrete manhole shelters along sidewalks and streets.

But at 2:45 p.m., the "quiet was shattered" by the buzzing of overhead planes, wailing of air-raid sirens, and firing of antiaircraft guns. It turned out to be a false alarm, set off by unarmed, unmanned reconnaissance drones. Hanoi and Beijing radio, reporting one plane shot down, castigated the Americans' intrusion into DRV airspace "in complete disregard for their proclaimed Christmas 'truce'" and "while U.S. imperialism and its lackeys were propagandizing a halt in air raids on North Vietnam." Washington, naturally, saw the noncombat missions as consistent with both the cease-fire and the secret 10-mile no-bombing pledge. Nevertheless, they served as a blunt reminder that it could resume bombing any time it chose, and blared dissonant mood music just as the Hanoi leadership began considering its enemy's latest peace proposition.[8]

New York: "On-the-Spot Inspection Indicates"

Among LBJ's surprise Christmas gifts, the lead article at the top of the front page of Sunday morning's *New York Times* resembled a lump of coal. Salisbury's first report from North Vietnam's capital opened quaintly: "Late in the afternoon of a drizzly Christmas Eve the bicycle throngs on the roads into Hanoi increased. Riding sidesaddle behind husbands were hundreds of slender young Hanoi wives returning to the city from evacuation" in the countryside, including mothers with "small children perched on the backs of bicycles." Noël observations, he noted, ranged from solemn masses in Catholic churches still functioning after most practitioners fled south after 1954, to more spirited celebrations among small clutches of foreigners, such as the goose-fed Canadian ICC officers and the correspondents and activists at the "rambling, old high-ceilinged" Thong Nhat. The American "unexpected observer" contrasted the outsiders' cozy festivities with the mood of the wartime city outside, "a bit like a mixture of the Moscow and Algiers of World War II," its khaki-clad, uniformed residents and camouflaged vehicles moving about "briskly, energetically, purposefully."

Finally, in the article's jump, Salisbury got to the point: His initial checks flatly contradicted U.S. claims that its attacks had hit only military targets outside Hanoi's municipal boundaries. Though admittedly "no ballistics specialist," the reporter noted that residents at several damaged sites—from Pho Nguyen Thiep Street in the downtown Hoan Kiem district, to the "thatch-and-brick houses" along the Red River near the Doumer Bridge, to the embassies in the Ba Dinh diplomatic quarter—"certainly believe they were bombed by United States planes, that they certainly observed United States planes overhead and that damage certainly occurred right in the center of town." Chipping away further at Washington's case, Salisbury testified that the city's "built-up, densely populated urban areas" extended well beyond the heavy black outlines of the city limits on a map officially released by the State Department and encompassed the raids' ostensible military targets—the Yen Vien rail yard and Van Dien truck park as well as the oil tanks between Yen Vien and Gia Lam. "Contrary to the impression of given by United States communiqués," he concluded, "on-the-spot inspection indicates that American bombing has been inflicting considerable civilian casualties in Hanoi and its environs for some time past."[9]

Salisbury's damning dispatch, the first by an American reporter from Hanoi since the war had escalated, created a worldwide sensation. Caught flat-footed—a warning from the U.S. Embassy in Vientiane that the correspondent had transited the Laotian capital on the way to Hanoi had reached Washington at 1:18 a.m. Saturday morning but had gone unnoticed[10]—the Johnson administration again found itself on the defensive. But the onslaught was only beginning.

Texas: "A Separate Hand"

On Christmas Day, Rostow passed a trio of cables from Warsaw and Saigon to LBJ in Texas: "(1) John delivered and Hanoi will be told. Good. (2) The Poles have told the Pope [Paul VI] and Fanfani has made exactly the right noises to the Poles. Bad. (3) An AP man in Warsaw smells a dove. Bad."[11] While Rapacki's willingness to transmit the latest message to Hanoi pleased senior officials, the news that he had already broken secrecy to the Vatican deepened their distrust—as Johnson and Rusk made amply clear during a tape-recorded telephone conversation Sunday evening in which they also swapped disparaging assessments of their own man in Warsaw.

After exchanging holiday pleasantries and political scuttlebutt, LBJ abruptly switched gears and asked his secretary of state what he thought about Marigold. A bit startled, Rusk allowed as he was disturbed that "they'd been talking."

"Yes, I think you'll probably be hearing that from the Pope at any day now," Johnson responded with a rueful chuckle.

"So," Rusk continued—in double-talk even over this supposedly secure line—"I think in the first place we ought to go back to this fellow [Rapacki] and say that you oughta tell us when you tell people 'cause you said you wanted to keep everything secret and then secondly we've gotta go to this other fellow [the pope] and give him the straight story because I suspect he's gotten a very one-sided story on this."

Prodded as to who would tell the Holy Father, Rusk identified the U.S. ambassador in Rome, Frederick Reinhardt, as the man for the job, perhaps as soon as the next day.

Before hanging up, Johnson asked if Rusk saw any need for him to return urgently to Washington. No, the secretary answered, because "if anything gets hot on this Marigold thing, I can run down [to Texas] and see you and . . . I think it'll be two or three days before we get the slightest reaction from the other side."

The president observed: "I've never thought it was anything but propaganda, but maybe we're wrong. I gather you are more hopeful."

"Only marginally," Rusk replied, "because I don't think the intermediary is very good on this." (Hmm-hmm, LBJ assented.) "I think he's playing a separate hand there and he's been—I don't like the way he's handled it very much."

LBJ then let off steam about "our friend that came over for a visit"—Gronouski. Misconstruing his latest telegram from Warsaw as suggesting that he had disloyally confided doubts about Washington's bombing policy to Rapacki, LBJ told Rusk that he did not "want to lose him overboard and act like he did this last message." After fishing around, he found and then recited the offending passage aloud to Rusk.[12] He soon realized that he had misread it, but that failed to salve his consternation at Gronouski's earlier "heated," Fulbright-ish cables after the December 13–14 Hanoi bombings urging immediate action to get Marigold back on track.

"I was a little bit disappointed," Johnson said, "that we better watch, we better watch his handling of things like that if he's gonna get emotional about 'em."

Rusk interjected that he had tried to impart "some background or some sense" to Gronouski in Washington and he seemed to respond well, but seconded LBJ's sentiments by cracking, "Everybody wants to make a Nobel Peace Prize these days."

"Incidentally," he added, Gronouski had "more faith in the fella that he's dealing with [Rapacki] than I do. . . . I've dealt with him for six years and I don't have much."

"Well," Johnson responded, "I think everybody's got more [faith] in him than I have."[13]

Monday, December 26, and Tuesday, December 27

Hanoi: "Pretty Waitresses with Rifles"
On Monday afternoon in the DRV capital, air-raid sirens blared again to warn of approaching U.S. planes, three large explosions shook the downtown area, and a cacophony of small arms fire rat-a-tatted into the sky. Like Lewandowski during his own visits, Salisbury observed rifle-toting hotel staff, "little waitresses in their black sateen trousers and white blouses," racing toward battle stations, as he and other foreign guests at the Thong Nhat darted from their rooms and "hurried down the great marble staircase, through the long lounge with its slightly bedraggled Christmas tree, its bar with a remarkable collection of liquors of all lands—including Stolichnaya vodka from Moscow, rice wine from Peking and Gordon's gin from London—and out across the interior courtyard" to take cover in the hotel's "sturdy concrete bunker."[14]

Like the day before, all the excitement—a novelty for the foreigners but "deadly serious business" for the locals, Salisbury noted—turned out to be superfluous. The planes were again drones, not fighters; the thundering detonations not bombs but launches of antiaircraft missiles. It is not known whether the ruckus interrupted the Lao Dong Politburo's consideration of a reply to the U.S. pledge of a 10-mile no-bombing zone around central Hanoi.

Washington: Waiting Games
After the long holiday weekend, as the capital dug out from a surprise blizzard, officials trudged back to their offices. Those aware of Marigold's parlous state and

trying to fathom Hanoi's and Warsaw's next moves found scant cause for optimism. Rostow sensed, and Rusk agreed, that the North Vietnamese saw U.S. demands for concessions in exchange for a bombing halt as demanding "initial unconditional surrender" and therefore sought the outlines of a satisfactory final settlement at the start of negotiations. (Once the DRV leaders "decided to deescalate," Rostow reasoned, "they were in effect cutting the throats of the Viet Cong and the whole situation might go sour on them.") Disconcerted by the leak to the pope—and still oblivious to the one to Thant—Rusk wondered why Rapacki was "broadcasting [Marigold] around." Probably, Rostow guessed, because he was "getting ready for propaganda rather than negotiating."[15]

On Tuesday afternoon, still awaiting further news, Rusk and Bundy cooked up instructions to Rome, Saigon, and Warsaw. In response to the report of Fanfani's conversation with Willmann that D'Orlandi had given Habib, the secretary requested Reinhardt to, on his behalf, thank Fanfani for reproving Rapacki for failing to start the direct U.S.-DRV contacts; inform him of the 10-mile zone; and—per his phone call with LBJ—solicit his advice on whether Washington should straighten out the pope; while chary of endangering Fanfani's own "sources and channels," Rusk wanted to counter the biased version he presumed the Poles had given the Holy Father.

Though Rusk also sent appreciation to Fanfani for keeping D'Orlandi at his post, he simultaneously directed Porter to "take no action" concerning Marigold with his Italian colleague—an edict that suited the acting ambassador, who had low regard for the whole exercise. "For security reasons alone," Rusk explained, "we are trying to get this operation out of Saigon to maximum extent possible."

Rusk and Bundy also decided to play it coy with the Poles. Not wanting to tip off Rapacki, they directed Gronouski, in his next talk, to "again stress need for total discretion and security in strongest terms," and to state that U.S. officials "assume" the Poles were not informing any third party about the secret diplomacy (other than the Soviets, of course) and would be "gravely concerned" otherwise. He was to give no hint, however, that Washington *already* knew that Warsaw had spilled the beans to the pope; were Rapacki or Michałowski to confess voluntarily, he should declare that he would promptly "report this to Washington and [would] have no doubt it will have a disturbing effect on security grounds alone."[16]

Finally, Bundy checked in with Alexander Zinchuk again Tuesday to inform him of the bombing abstention around Hanoi, a step intended to allay the concerns the Soviet had stated at their lunch five days earlier. *Now* would he, and Moscow, believe Washington was really serious about wanting negotiations?[17]

Warsaw: "Strangers in the Night"

Gronouski did not have much of a vacation. While he raced back and forth across the Atlantic, his family was having a ball in Garmisch—schussing down the slopes, sleeping and dining in the officers' residence of a nearby U.S. military base (and nightly hearing an Army sergeant croon "Strangers in the Night," the Sinatra throwback that had zoomed past the Beatles' "Paperback Writer" to the top of the charts), the two Gronouski girls playing happily with the three Kaiser kids. From the hastily improvised departure plans and the furtive long-distance phone calls Mary Gronouski had received from Washington, the Kaisers sensed that "something definitely out of the ordinary" was afoot, maybe even tied to Vietnam—but etiquette precluded direct questions.[18] (She would not have been able to say much, because Gronouski did not confide in her about Marigold.[19])

They waited for the missing father and husband to arrive . . . but he never did. On Christmas morning, Gronouski had gone to Okęcie Airport, only to find it closed for the holiday. Schlepping his bags to the central railway station, he boarded a train to Vienna, hoping to book a flight from there to Munich, only to discover that the airport there was closed the day *after* Christmas—for the second day in a row, he was left holding tickets or reservations for a phantom flight. Giving up, the disappointed diplomat trekked back to Warsaw.[20]

"The skiing was great!" Joy Kaiser remembered, but "John never saw the snow in Garmisch." Oh well, the Kaisers recalled affectionately, John was not much of a skier anyway, and they sang "Strangers in the Night"—*scooby dooby doo*—for him back in Warsaw.

✳ ✳ ✳

Having sent the U.S. proposal to Hanoi along with their own arguments, the Poles also had little to do but wait. Anticipating an answer only after intense Politburo debates, they tried to keep Washington from taking any actions that might spook the North Vietnamese again. On Tuesday, when Jenkins called to tell Michałowski that Gronouski had just returned to Warsaw, he asked the deputy chief of mission "for the record" whether the 10-mile zone around Hanoi referred to nautical or statute miles—especially as wire service reports that day had spoken of raids against targets only 12 miles from the capital.[21] As Michałowski later candidly explained, his inquiry aimed to "interfere with an overly hasty USA decision to resume bombing and to stretch out the matter."[22]

The nibble of interest "buoyed" the exhausted Gronouski, who relayed Michałowski's question to Washington together with his own entreaty to avoid unwise military actions that might snuff out whatever chances remained to save Marigold. "I am most concerned if we are choosing targets so close to the margin that even a slight error could put us in technical violation of our commitment," he cabled. "Such a violation could seriously dissipate the positive impact of our commitment and, for little gain, retard movement toward direct negotiations."[23]

Within hours, Rusk shot back a reply specifying that the exclusion zone referred to nautical miles—but from Hanoi's center, not its outer limits—and cautioning Gronouski that it was "very important" that he and the Poles "not . . . be diverted from the main effort by niggling and haggling about whether a particular bomb fell on this side or that side of this or that circle." Washington had promised not to hit "314 square nautical miles," and it was time for "Hanoi to sit down and talk business. The next move is up to them and we can not let them play games with a side issue in view of the major concessions we have made to clear the way for talks."[24] Gronouski, anxiously awaiting word of Hanoi's response, telephoned Michałowski with the information.[25]

Saigon–Vung Tau–Saigon: "How Is It Possible to Be So Blasphemous . . .?"

"War again," D'Orlandi recorded glumly after the truce ended at 7 a.m. Monday. Adding to his frustration, he read in the morning papers of a hawkish Christmas Eve homily by Francis Cardinal Spellman, the archbishop of New York, who served as "military vicar of the armed forces for the Roman Catholic Church in the United States" and was making his twenty-first annual holiday visit to U.S. armed forces stationed abroad.

The previous year, Cardinal Spellman had celebrated Midnight Mass before thousands of troops (after warm-up acts featuring Bob Hope) from a wooden platform on a soccer field at Tan Son Nhut Airport. This December, Spellman again transited Saigon (staying, along with evangelist Billy Graham, as General Westmoreland's house guest), and Hope again played Tan Son Nhut, receiving a medal from the commander of MACV. But the recent Viet Cong raids led the jittery security authorities to conclude that, truce or no truce, such a huge congregation of U.S. military personnel on Christmas Eve might prove an irresistible target, and so Spellman staged the climactic event of his visit at the less vulnerable Cam Ranh Bay Naval Base 200 miles to the north.

The cardinal, garbed in white vestments with gold and scarlet trim, and sermonizing beneath "a canopy made of camouflage parachute cloth" to an estimated 5,000 personnel on a sandy hillside under a moonlit sky, had prayed for triumph in what he termed their "war for civilization" that "tyranny" "thrust upon us." Any outcome "less than victory is inconceivable," he declared, adding that it was "common knowledge" that Washington had many times offered Hanoi "the path to negotiations but these offers were rejected with contempt!"

"Who told him these things?" D'Orlandi seethed. "How is it possible to be so blasphemous on the night of Christmas?"[26]

However exasperated, the Italian remained resolved to track any scent of peace, no matter how faint. Monday, he telegraphed Fanfani that his remark to Habib about leaving due to poor health had been "merely rhetorical" and his doctors had assured him that, "all things considered," he could remain in Saigon "without *appreciable* prejudice" until the hotter season began in March. "I will not leave the field," he vowed, for "as long as it will be necessary to carry out Your Excellency's instructions and policies."

D'Orlandi reported that he had seen Habib to relay the account of the Italian foreign minister's conversation with Willmann, but not yet his Polish partner, still out of town and unavailable for another twenty-four hours.[27]

* * *

Lewandowski had inclined to accept at face value U.S. claims that it ruled the road between Saigon (i.e., Bien Hoa) and the coast, but he started to wonder shortly after leaving Vung Tau a few hours after the cease-fire expired Monday morning. When his car approached a makeshift American checkpoint (an armored personnel carrier, some trenches) on the edge of town, a soldier tried to wave them back. The Poles kept going, but any doubts that they were driving through a war zone that the Americans did *not* fully control evaporated around 1 p.m. about 20 kilometers from Vung Tau. To their *left,* they saw a large U.S. military complex, apparently a logistics base, ablaze from a daylight mortar assault. As more shells landed, causing fresh explosions, counterattacking helicopter gunships flew overhead in front of them, followed by infantry and armored personnel carriers, firing on positions in jungle-covered hills about a mile off to their *right.*[28]

Caught in the cross fire, Lewandowski flashed back to his childhood, the savage fighting in Warsaw, the narrow escapes. Having cheated death before, he trusted his instincts.

Telling the story decades later, he remembered taking charge of the situation upon realizing that his fellow passengers seemed paralyzed—in the back seat, Iwanciów and the legal adviser were "sitting like two dead men"—and beside him the Vietnamese chauffeur was "shaking with fear."

"I said, the worst thing we can do is to stop," because their vehicle would be a sitting duck. Seizing the wheel from the terrified driver, he floored it and raced head-on through the combat. From then on, fearing land mines or a sneak assault, Lewandowski drove at top speed—past rice paddies and villages, and the rubber plantations of Long Thanh "straddling the highway in sinister orderliness, their corridors of trees stretched off into the distance, convenient pathways for Viet Cong guerrillas who sometimes swooped down on the road, their guns blazing in bloody ambush."[29] Intensifying their foreboding, the Poles did not spot another civilian vehicle on the deserted road for the next 60 kilometers, until safely reaching the outskirts of Saigon. As the shaken passengers emerged from the Chevy at Camp des Mares, Lewandowski declared, "Gentlemen, you are here. I invite you for a drink."

As the legal adviser rushed to the nearest bathroom to vomit, Iwanciów, with formal military bearing, stated: "Mr. Ambassador, with all due respect, you are crazy."

Laughing, Lewandowski replied, "You are right."

Then they stepped into the commissioner's villa for a glass of Cognac to calm their nerves and celebrate their survival.[30]

* * *

When Lewandowski came to D'Orlandi's Tuesday morning at 11, the mood during their lengthy review of the situation was "much lighter" than when they last met. The Pole seemed "particularly euphoric," the Italian observed, as a result of his holiday tidings from Hanoi, which suggested that he might still do business there. Lewandowski was disturbed, however, to hear D'Orlandi relate Fanfani's account of his conversation with Willmann—"surprised" by Warsaw's disclosure to the pope and disapproving of its violation of the trilateral secrecy accord. He reassured the Italian that his own instructions spoke of "freezing" rather than terminating their three-way channel, although further progress would depend on Hanoi.[31]

D'Orlandi found Lewandowski "very reluctant" to see Porter—and Lodge's stand-in clearly reciprocated the sentiment—but was delighted to hear that, despite everything, his friend retained his standing in Hanoi and their channel remained potentially operational. "Therefore," he effused to Fanfani, "nothing will prevent resuming the talks if, in my humble opinion, it will be possible to discern a decrease in the bombings of North Vietnam in general, and the cessation of those of Hanoi." The Pole, though less optimistic, agreed to join D'Orlandi for dinner a couple of nights hence to plot further tripartite meetings once Lodge returned to Saigon in mid-January.[32]

Rome: "Free from the Spell of Rusk"

Encouraged by D'Orlandi's report that Lewandowski had described the three-way initiative as frozen but not necessarily dead, Fanfani sent word to Willmann Tuesday, once more "earnestly asking Minister Rapacki for his positive and prompt actions in the name of carrying out the initiation of the contacts in Warsaw."[33] That evening, the Polish envoy visited Fanfani, and the atmosphere was far less tense than their conversation four days earlier. Willmann "comes to rectify what he said on the 23rd," the foreign minister recorded. The Pole had relayed a message from Rapacki explaining that Warsaw had informed the pope of the secret diplomacy because on December 15 the Pontiff had requested information on Poland's Vietnam peace efforts (a lame excuse that Fanfani politely declined to challenge). Once again, the Italian stressed that it was vital "not to waste time" in getting the Warsaw talks under way, because a direct meeting could clear up "ambiguities" over the ten-point formula—thereby easing Washington's fear of being subjected to Hanoi's "subtle game" of exploiting hazy terms—"and so one thing leads to another."[34]

Willmann approvingly reported that Fanfani—"evidently free from the spell of Rusk" and recoiling at Spellman's bellicose remarks—"returned to a more sensible language." The Italian viewed the Vatican's peace efforts as hopeless, but he expressed confidence in Rapacki and a desire to continue cooperation. "No one else but Poland is capable of doing this," he insisted, repeating the mantra he had intoned during his visit to Warsaw in July. He urged Rapacki to let the Saigon channel remain in place (preserving Italian involvement), noting that Lodge might expedite his return in order to resume the three-way exchanges. Regarding the bombing, he emphasized that achieving the first direct contact would undercut U.S. arguments and remove "any shade of an alibi"—and he would "insist" that Washington stop the air raids so the direct discussions could advance. To overcome the DRV's hesitation, he suggested that Rapacki order Lewandowski to make another trip to Hanoi to obtain renewed consent for the preliminary contact in Warsaw that was supposed to have occurred exactly three weeks before.[35]

New York: "Little Connection with the Reality"

In Tuesday's *New York Times,* Salisbury followed up his Christmas surprise with two more front-page reports. One elaborated on his earlier account of bomb damage in and around Hanoi, describing one target supposedly beyond the city limits, the Van Dien depot, as a "large, open area with light buildings and compounds that may or may not have been a truck park" situated in a "continuous part of the urban center." The other piece detailed hitherto unreported destruction and death in Nam Dinh, 50 miles south of the capital, despite a paucity of evident military installations. Without attribution, he cited a figure of 89 civilians killed and 405 wounded in more than 50 (apparently unannounced) raids on the city, which had reduced the center of North Vietnam's third-most-populated urban area to "block after block of utter desolation."

"Whatever the explanation, one can see that United States planes are dropping an enormous weight of explosives on purely civilian targets," Salisbury concluded. "Whatever else there may be or might have been in Namdinh, it is the civilians who have taken the punishment. . . . President Johnson's announced policy that American targets in North Vietnam are steel and concrete rather than human lives seems to have little connection with the reality of attacks carried out by United States planes." Salisbury pinpointed a "basic flaw in the bombing policy from a military viewpoint" by recounting the astonishingly rapid and effective repair activities along Route 1, the north-south highway, to keep supplies flowing despite the relentless air raids. Another front-page *Times* article, by Neil Sheehan, featured U.S. admissions that, inevitably, "American pilots had accidentally struck civilian areas in North Vietnam while attempting to bomb military targets."[36]

These stories added fuel to the firestorm of criticism, at home and abroad, engulfing Washington's bombing campaign.

Wednesday, December 28–Thursday, December 29

Hanoi: "We Reject These Piratical Proposals"

On Wednesday, the Poles received Hanoi's final answer, and it was not the one for which they or the Americans had hoped. Trinh called Siedlecki to his office and read aloud a formal note reviewing events since November 20, when Hanoi received Lodge's proposals from Lewandowski. The statement presented the DRV government's acerbic analysis of Washington's conduct, resolute rejection of its proposals, and firm refusal to consider further communications from Gronouski. Trinh handed the ambassador a Vietnamese-language text, and later, in midafternoon, couriered a Russian version to the embassy. As North Vietnam's definitive secret pronouncement on the affair, at least to the Poles (an internal postmortem has not yet surfaced), it merits close attention.

We may have high confidence in its authenticity, as both Polish and Vietnamese contemporaneous versions have surfaced—Siedlecki's ciphered telegram and a lengthy excerpt in the 1990 study of pre-Paris U.S.-DRV interactions by former North Vietnamese diplomats Luu Van Loi and Nguyen Anh Vu—and are compatible (aside from translation idiosyncrasies).[37] The text used here (unless otherwise indicated) was cabled by Siedlecki and found in the MSZ archives.[38] The statement opened straightforwardly:

> We carefully studied your views. Today, we would like to present our opinion. On November 20, Cde. Lewandowski informed us about the statements of Lodge. We contemplated those views. On [November] 25, Cde. Pham Van Dong suggested that L[ewandowski] tell Lodge: "if the American side deems it necessary to confirm in front of us what Lodge had told L[ewandowski], then the USA can do so via the DRV ambassador in Warsaw." These words were supposed to be the view of Lewandowski and not our views.

But it then minimized the significance of this consent for direct contact between U.S. and DRV representatives, in language implying that Hanoi wanted to shrug off the entire episode as routine:

> It is understandable that if the USA is asking for a meeting and if we accept their representative, then this will be clearly a demarche (a diplomatic activity), and not simply a meeting from which a discussion and negotiations begin. Our representatives abroad usually receive those, including the Americans, who visit our embassies in order to explain their views or to familiarize themselves with our position regarding the Vietnamese problem.

It then blamed Washington for the encounter's failure to materialize:

> However, the Americans turned white into black. They are inconsistent in their statements.

(The translation directly from Vietnamese reads, "The Americans, however, have double-crossed us, saying one thing one time and another thing at a different time." According to Phuong, Trinh told the Pole—and this remark if actually uttered corroborates the impression of a genuine gap in perceptions of the fateful nonmeeting of December 6—"*The U.S. swallowed its words and did not keep its appointment.*"[39])

Continuing its recapitulation, the statement observed that the Americans

> are impudently intensifying the bombings of North Vietnam. Even more seriously, they have bombed Hanoi. They have conducted 4 air raids on the interior

parts of Hanoi within only 2 weeks. Given these conditions, we told Siedlecki on December 7 that we had to reconsider the issue of receiving the USA [ambassador] by our ambassador in Warsaw, in case the USA side were to ask for it.

We also gave proper instructions to our ambassador in Warsaw. However, until now the USA has been pretending that it did not understand and it continues to ask you to convey its views [to us]. Their insidious plan is designed to lead to negotiations without any conditions. Instead, the USA demands of us to undertake concrete steps in stage B, while they are carrying out [the steps] from stage A. The plan of the USA is designed for [them] to climb the steps of escalation. In order to exert pressure, every time they raise the escalation by one degree they demand payment from us.

In the Vietnamese-language version, but not the Polish, there is a more explicit, derisive allusion to the 10-mile bombing-free zone around the DRV capital, for which the Americans' anticipated a comparable gesture toward Saigon: "They even bargain about the cessation of the bombing of Hanoi." The reference to the Phase A / Phase B formula shows that the North Vietnamese failed to buy Gronouski's claim to Rapacki on Christmas Eve that by suspending bombing around Hanoi, LBJ had already implemented Phase A, at least in part. Instead, they pounced on the proposition's implication that the Communists should restrain themselves around Saigon as evidence that Washington was scheming to extort Phase B concessions even before extending the bombing halt to the rest of North Vietnam, as Phase A mandated.

Nothing the Americans had said or done since December 14 had altered the DRV authorities' sharply negative view which Dong had relayed to Siedlecki two weeks earlier, after Hanoi had been hit again despite repeated Polish warnings. Nor had Warsaw's arguments persuaded them. From the North Vietnamese syllogism—that Washington was acting in bad faith—the harsh corollary flowed naturally:

> We are decisively rejecting such piratical propositions of the USA. The leadership of the Polish comrade-leaders agreed with our conduct. We express our appreciation towards the fact that you, Comrades, criticized the USA. In our opinion, we cannot allow for the USA to carry out its intention of 'direct or indirect contacts' under the current situation when they continue to bomb North Vietnam. That is why we will not consider the words of Gronouski if he proposes to relay them to us. The talks are already over.[40]

Having made its point, the statement devolved into polemics, partly boilerplate but also offering a sneak preview of a new strategy already secretly approved by the Lao Dong Politburo: a diplomatic offensive to parallel the military track:

> The U.S. continues to be stubborn and insolent. It is clear that the issue has not yet matured to [the level of] a political solution. We think that we must adhere to the

line which relies on a military fight and which is firmly tied to a political and diplomatic struggle in order to break the will of the aggression of the U.S. Life has shown that such a course is correct.

We attach great importance to the renewal of a diplomatic struggle. Thanks to the support of fraternal socialist countries we have been garnering more and more sympathy from the nations of the world and from the American people; we are unmasking the aggressive intentions of the U.S. government which is conducting double-faced negotiations; we are raising high our banner of justice. While increasing our vigilance, we always take into consideration that the American intentions are taking on a more and more deceitful and insidious character with each day. They can be playing new mockery in secret, or announce publicly new "propositions" in order to feel out the public opinion and to position it toward the direction that suits them.

We are categorically decided to unmask these intentions and to make it happen so the U.S. is condemned with an even more indignation by the public opinion of the nations of the world, and that it sinks into further isolation.

Politely, the statement concluded with gratitude for Warsaw's efforts, though the Poles had to wonder about the sincerity of those honeyed words:

We thank, once more, the Polish comrades for the interest that they showed regarding the Vietnamese problem. We thank for the fraternal support and aid which the party and the government of Poland have shown for the fight of the Vietnamese people against the aggression of the American imperialism in defense of their motherland. On the occasion of the New Year, we would like to wish health and successes to the comrades-members of the Polish leadership.

The statement left no doubt that, as Phuong later wrote, the peace initiative had "come to an end."[41] Siedlecki sent Rapacki the text without comment.

Saigon: "A Dialogue of the Deaf"

As Marigold staggered through its death throes, Lewandowski and D'Orlandi remained, for the moment, unaware that Hanoi had already rebuffed a last-gasp U.S. (and Polish) attempt to salvage the mortally wounded initiative. Yet their prognosis was already grave. Left offstage during the drama's closing act, neither diplomat expected a deus ex machina or entertained much hope of a revival any time soon.

An encounter with Porter Wednesday morning—a "long and animated discussion which left me with a very dreadful feeling"—deepened D'Orlandi's despair. Porter dismissed the entire Polish diplomatic "action" as a "bluff"— Lewandowski, he believed, had never received any mandate from Hanoi, which explained Rapacki's "grand refusal" to arrange the contact in Warsaw. "All my attempts to make him change his opinion proved to be useless," the Italian lamented, now even more morose because he sensed that Porter's skepticism reflected State Department sentiment.[42]

That afternoon, D'Orlandi received a message from Fanfani reporting the latest exchange with Willmann—including the puzzling Polish hint that the Vatican somehow had prior knowledge of the secret diplomacy ("For our part, we can assure: no leak," Fanfani declared). Citing Rapacki's claim that the Hanoi bombing remained the "insurmountable" hurdle to arranging the direct contacts, Fanfani (not yet clued in on the 10-mile exclusion zone) directed D'Orlandi to seek this obstacle's "removal" by appealing to Lodge's stand-in.[43]

Dutifully, D'Orlandi summoned Habib. Seemingly more sympathetic than Porter, he promised to relay the bombing halt appeal to Washington, and he speculated that the Vatican's cognizance originated in Lewandowski's indiscretions— one reason why U.S. officials were shying away from the Saigon channel.[44]

The next afternoon, D'Orlandi received another Fanfani cable, containing allegedly encouraging news: Rusk's message, delivered by the U.S. chargé d'affaires in Rome, Francis E. Meloy Jr. thanking him for pressing Rapacki and revealing the order to cease bombing within 10 miles of Hanoi's center.

Combined with the marginally more positive noises from Rapacki relayed by Willmann the night before and Lewandowski's earlier comments to D'Orlandi suggesting that he could still do business in Hanoi, Rusk's message had sent Fanfani's emotional roller coaster skyward again. "I infer a strengthened resolve to renew contacts and proceed with the search for a beginning to a negotiation," he cabled, urging D'Orlandi to persuade his Polish partner to convince Hanoi to approve the opening of direct contacts and to reduce infiltration of the South and "terrorism" around Saigon, not as a precondition for negotiations but as a token of "good faith."[45]

Far from sharing his boss's buoyancy, D'Orlandi thought that Fanfani had succumbed to wishful thinking. "We are in the middle of a dialogue of the deaf," he wrote in his diary, noting that he had quickly responded with a more pessimistic (and realistic) message to Rome indicating that the situation in Saigon was "deteriorating appreciably." He felt even more reluctant than his Polish friend to chase the chimerical prospect of three-way negotiations, "which have a definite smell of failure." Should unexpected events warrant resuming them, he would summon Lodge back to Saigon earlier than his planned January 17 return date. Like Lewandowski, he had no wish to deal with Porter and his sneering disdain.[46]

⁂ ⁂ ⁂

The final days of 1966 also climaxed Lewandowski's campaign to persuade his fellow ICC commissioners to condemn the Hanoi bombings, and offered a textbook case of the hardball tactics and tit-for-tat fencing that paralyzed the body. Foiled in his bid to hold a special session in Hanoi, the Pole sat with Moore and

Rahman Wednesday morning seeking votes on the resolutions he had advanced on December 14 condemning the December 2 and 4 raids, plus new ones to cover the later attacks.[47] Lewandowski sought censure of the bombings or at least the widest possible circulation of the Hanoi bomb damage report, but he also had to deal with the Canadian's sly counterstroke. After the prior meeting, when Lewandowski had "broken the truce" by deviating from Poland's passive posture, Moore sought and received Ottawa's permission to toss his own chips into the pot. Accordingly, he persuaded Rahman to expand the December 28 agenda to include two items that had long lain fallow: well-documented charges that, contrary to Geneva stipulations, Hanoi had accepted Soviet MiGs and SAMs, and infiltrated regular troops (the PAVN's 325th Division) into South Vietnam. For months, the Canadian had politely refrained from pursuing the matter, even though North Vietnam had failed to respond to the allegations. But if Lewandowski insisted on upbraiding Washington for the Hanoi raids, Moore served notice, he could press for equal and opposite action and worse, publicity, on topics embarrassing to the Communist side.

In his opening statement, Moore declared that he would vote against the Pole's sharper resolution criticizing the December 2 and 4 raids as "a further escalation of war in Vietnam" and a "clear violation of [the Geneva Accords'] provisions, spirit, and letter," yet demurely refrained from showing his cards on Lewandowski's second, softer motion chiding *Saigon* for violating Geneva's edict against entering into a military alliance with a foreign power or allowing its territory to be used "to further an aggressive policy." Rahman, in turn, joined the Canadian in opposing (largely on legalistic grounds) the harsher Polish resolution, then advanced his own milder substitute noting simply that the Hanoi bombings were a "further expression" of the "de facto" U.S.-RVN military alliance, which the ICC had already cited as contravening Geneva.

The Pole and Indian introduced similar resolutions on the December 13–14 raids, with the important exception that Rahman's, while not enumerating the damaged civilian sites listed in Lewandowski's, attached the Hanoi bureau report as an appendix—an idea welcomed by the Pole, who offered to follow the same practice in his own resolutions.

Because Moore had been authorized to vote on only two of the six resolutions on the table—against the two more sharply anti-American Polish motions—he requested time to obtain instructions from Ottawa. Rahman grumbled, but to the Canadian's surprise, Lewandowski agreed that all six resolutions should be voted on at the same meeting. Rather than insist on an immediate poll, Lewandowski remembered the testy session in Hanoi four months earlier, when *he* had pleaded vainly to defer balloting for lack of instructions, only to be overruled by Rahman. Making "gleeful reference" to his standing complaint about that procedure, Moore reported, the Pole "rather shrewdly came to our support" and magnanimously accepted a delay.[48]

For lack of time, the group put off debate on the Canadian resolutions until the next morning. Summarizing the meeting for Warsaw, Lewandowski admitted discomfort at Moore's riposte. It would be, he cabled, "inconvenient" to consider the Hanoi bombings together with the anti-DRV allegations, because his fellow commissioners "could demand that all [passed] resolutions were handed over to the [British and Soviet] co-chairmen, which would imply a connection between the bombings and infiltration."[49]

Lewandowski's dilatory strategy dictated his tactics when deliberations resumed Thursday. After Moore urged the group to reproach Hanoi for multiple Geneva violations stemming both from the PAVN's infiltration (based on testimony by prisoners of war and deserters interviewed by an ICC control group in Saigon) and the SAMs and MiGs (both hailed openly in Hanoi media), the Pole indignantly rejected consideration of the topics as inappropriate, given the DRV's right to defend itself against U.S. aggression, and demanded that they be stricken from the agenda.[50]

To his annoyance, however, Rahman pronounced both issues fit for consideration. On infiltration, the Indian introduced his own draft, softer than Moore's but still rapping Hanoi's wrist for breaching Geneva; and concerning the SAMs and MiGs, he adopted what Lewandowski considered a "formalistic" stand: Regardless of context or justification, the only relevant question "was whether there was any doubt that the MiGs and SAMs were present in North Vietnam."

Lewandowski managed to forestall an immediate vote, but once the session adjourned, he cornered Rahman to convey his displeasure. "I warned the Indian after the meeting against supporting the resolutions of the Canadian given the situation in Vietnam," he told Warsaw. "After a while, the Indian informed me that he would try to consult with the Canadian to postpone both issues for 2 to 3 weeks." Lewandowski may well have hinted that India's formal endorsement of the Canadian complaints would imperil Poland's continued cooperation with the ICC, which of course threatened the final dissolution of the group as a whole.

Whatever Lewandowski's precise arguments, however undiplomatically expressed, Rahman got the message: Further action on the Canadian resolution was deferred, at least for several weeks, but balloting on the Hanoi bombing resolutions was set for as early as Saturday, pending Moore's receipt of updated guidance from Ottawa.

Rome: "Everything They Knew"

When Meloy (in Reinhardt's absence) saw Fanfani Wednesday evening to deliver Rusk's urgent message disclosing the 10-mile zone around Hanoi and thanking the Italian for pressing Rapacki, the Italian foreign minister, in turn, elaborated on his recent exchanges with Willmann.[51] On the bright side, from Washington's perspective, Fanfani had been "very severe" in criticizing Rapacki's delay in arranging the direct talks in Warsaw and his "great mistake" of informing the pope, to whom the Poles admitted telling the "whole story" of Marigold, "everything they knew." Per Rusk's phone call with LBJ, Meloy asked Fanfani whether the Americans should set the pope straight. Not yet, he replied. If Washington leapt in, "a three-cornered discussion might develop which could be very confusing." Perhaps Fanfani wanted a chance to act first—rather than see his embarrassment compounded by the Vatican's learning details of Italy's most sensitive Vietnam diplomatic venture from Rome only after *both* Warsaw and Washington had revealed them.

* * *

Though they heeded Fanfani's advice to hold off on contacting him, Washington had fresh reason to fret about the pope. Wednesday, the authoritative Vatican newspaper *L'Osservatore* praised Salisbury's reporting as "a service to truth"—an encomium resembling that lavished by the Communist daily *L'Unità*, whose Hanoi correspondent, after encountering him at the Thong Nhat Christmas Eve bash, wrote that he seemed to be "a man sincerely devoted to the search for truth." Moreover, far from echoing Cardinal Spellman's call for victory in Vietnam, the "visibly embarrassed" Vatican repudiated his remarks as inconsistent with a negotiated settlement. Roman Catholics "owed 'unconditional loyalty' to Pope Paul's efforts for peace 'without any possible partiality or reticence,'" *L'Osservatore* reminded.[52] (Privately, Casaroli told Willmann the pope had already given up on a positive reply to his appeal for an extended holiday truce—the post-Christmas resumption of fighting was a "dolorous epilogue" to the holiday—and rather desperately sought Rapacki's aid in urging Hanoi to "signal" the Vatican to send humanitarian aid to the North Vietnamese people, a gesture he hoped would impress international and especially U.S. public opinion. Willmann politely agreed to transmit the request, but it had no chance of success.[53])

Moscow: Never Mind the Bullocks . . .

Following custom, Rapacki continued to update Gromyko via his ambassador in Moscow. Wednesday, Pszczółkowski relayed Rapacki's latest précis describing the renewed U.S. attempt to get the Warsaw talks going—presumably featuring the 10-mile zone around Hanoi—as well as the rumblings about a possible ICC gathering in New Delhi, which the Pole dismissed as pointless. The Soviet, who had also received Zinchuk's report of Washington's latest step, agreed with Rapacki's envoy that the Americans' most recent actions could be read as a return to their "initial propositions" in the Lodge-Lewandowski channel, but again confessed confusion regarding LBJ's inconsistent Vietnam policy. Johnson, he remarked, "succumbs to different pressures" and seems "more concerned with taking care of the bullocks on his ranch."[54]

New York: The Secret Sharer

For five days, ever since Tomorowicz confided it to him, the incendiary secret had burned inside Thant. In disclosing the details of the failed peace initiative, and how the ill-timed Hanoi raids had doomed it, Poland's UN delegate had cautioned him not to reveal the tale to anyone, even his closest advisers. But as he pondered his response to Goldberg's letter, and Salisbury's dispatches incited fresh uproar, Thant felt an irresistible compulsion to share this fresh evidence of U.S. perfidy—just as Rapacki undoubtedly hoped.

The unsuspecting beneficiary of Thant's loose lips turned out to be Canada. At noon on Wednesday, George Ignatieff called on him to report on the progress, or lack thereof, of Ottawa's efforts to persuade Warsaw to accede to the Indian scheme for a three-way gathering of ICC powers in New Delhi.[55] The idea still seemed alive, he related, as Martin awaited an answer to his letter to Rapacki urging favorable consideration of the proposition. (Ignatieff did not know yet that in Warsaw, Michałowski had just delivered Rapacki's essentially negative reply to the Canadian ambassador, and New Delhi's enthusiasm was already fading due to the lack of Polish interest.[56])

The UN chief then described his meeting with Tomorowicz the previous Friday. Confirming the word he had relayed through Bunche, Thant told Ignatieff that he had assured the Pole that the ICC proposal did not conflict with his own efforts and he wished it well.[57] But he quickly moved to what was really on his mind: Tomorowicz had actually requested the appointment, he disclosed, not to discuss the ICC matter but to convey "very secret" information about his government's efforts to arrange direct US-DRV talks.

"U Thant then said," Ignatieff reported, "that although he had undertaken not to divulge info Tomorowicz had given him and had not discussed it with any of his advisers, he felt he should tell someone and that in particular Mr. Martin should be aware of what Tomorowicz had told him."

Thant then proceeded to relate the story he had heard, first from memory and then allowing Ignatieff to transcribe the memorandum Tomorowicz had shown him. It was the first *secondary* leak stemming from Rapacki's campaign, and Thant's comments suggested the Polish account had exactly the intended effect. Thant agreed with Rapacki that as a consequence of its Hanoi bombings, Washington "must accept full responsibility for this negative result," and added that "his own impression was that there seemed to be a lack of direction coordination and control in USA Govt with Pentagon going in one direction CIA in another and State Dept in a third."

Reinforcing Thant's doubts about U.S. conduct, the Polish j'accuse seemed to validate retrospectively his own earlier charge, indignantly denied by the Johnson administration, that Washington had ignored a UN-mediated DRV overture for peace talks two years earlier and had then misled the public about it. It was "unfortunate," Ignatieff expressed with worry, "that U Thant has been given only Polish side of this story which confirms his own impression derived from his effort beginning in Aug/64 to arrange through Stevenson for direct USA–North Vietnamese discussions of USA unwillingness or inability effectively to coordinate whatever efforts they make or are made on their behalf to bring about a negotiated settlement in Vietnam." (On this episode, see the prologue above.)

In transmitting to Ottawa his top secret account of this revelatory conversation, Ignatieff noted that it put recent events in an entirely new light. Recalling Moore's cables from Saigon in early December, he speculated that D'Orlandi's comment that "everything is vague" and Lewandowski's allusion to Hanoi's "different logic" actually related to the secret initiative. It also raised questions for Martin about Washington's (and particularly Rusk's) recent dealings with him with respect to his own Vietnam peace diplomacy; Ignatieff, in his own bailiwick, wondered whether Thant's reaction portended an even more pronounced anti–United States tilt to his views and behavior, and the inevitable problems for Canada that would result. One way or another, he thought, the Americans needed to balance the very effective Polish presentation with their own version of what had gone wrong.

✳ ✳ ✳

Meanwhile, Salisbury kept stirring the pot. On Wednesday and Thursday, the *New York Times* front-paged articles from Hanoi describing the atmosphere during an air-raid scare and the authorities' steely determination not to let their capital's anticipated annihilation impede eventual victory—they were already planning a replacement. While flush with his journalistic coup, Salisbury also got a whiff of the controversy roaring at home when a telegram from his managing editor reached him Wednesday warning him to carefully attribute his sources for any "controversial" claims and to "avoid expressions that readers might consider editorial." Forewarned, in his next piece Salisbury noted in passing that while his descriptions of bomb damage were based "wholly on visual inspection," readers should know, "incidentally, that all casualty estimates and statistics in these dispatches are those of North Vietnamese officials."[58]

Warsaw: "Inaccurate and Demagogic Assertions"
A little after noon on Wednesday, Siedlecki's cable conveying the unyielding DRV statement given him by Trinh reached the MSZ decoding room. But even before clerks deciphered what Michałowski later termed "the ultimate reply to all our efforts,"[59] Warsaw anticipated a negative answer. Hanoi's determination to fight on rather than enter talks, at least for the time being, seemed clear when the secret peace diplomacy briefly arose that morning during a conversation between Gomułka and two senior visiting Soviet figures responsible for relations with other Communist parties, Yuri Andropov and Boris Ponomarev.

"Not long ago we had a talk with the ambassador of the USA, Gronouski, who came back from Washington," the Polish United Workers' Party (PZPR) first secretary related. "He told us that they will not bomb certain parts of Hanoi. They still want to establish contact with North Vietnam. We conveyed this to Hanoi. However, they still do not agree to establishing contact."

This view accorded with the Soviets' sense, based on their reading of Le Duc Tho and other DRV officials who had recently visited Moscow. "The Vietnamese told us that they still need two dry seasons," Andropov said. "They want to achieve some kind of victory. They are getting ready for this. They asked for additional assistance and support. This is a difficult matter."[60]

Later Wednesday, Rapacki updated the PZPR Politburo on his efforts to convince Hanoi to open talks with the Americans, although, from the laconic protocol, it is impossible to tell whether the foreign minister offered a correspondingly bleak appraisal.[61] His deputy certainly oozed pessimism to the Canadian ambassador that day. Gently conveying Rapacki's rebuff to Martin's appeal to accept the Indian invitation to attend a three-way ICC meeting in New Delhi, Michałowski partly blamed the Indians and their inflated, unrealistic ideas, such as initially proposing foreign ministers meet with a "very ambitious agenda." Despite a hasty Indian retreat—clarifying that foreign ministry directors-general or even resident ambassadors would suffice—Ottawa's envoy judged that the original invitation "scared off" the Poles.

Yet Michałowski underlined that the real problem was not procedural but political—the recent Hanoi bombings were such an escalation that it was "difficult to envisage even a limited preliminary meeting of representatives of commission countries at this moment." Only after Washington showed it was "seriously interested in deescalation" might Warsaw reconsider. "American declarations about wanting peace," he added sternly, "were not enough when they were accompanied by signs of increasing military activity, which even extended to bombing residential areas."[62]

Though not especially surprised, then, by Hanoi's spurning of talks, Michałowski and Rapacki were taken aback by the North Vietnamese statement's ferocity and defensiveness. In some respects, they felt, it distorted the reality of what had happened. They must have resented the implication that the Polish leaders had engaged in intense high-level exchanges merely for the sake of ho-hum, quotidian diplomatic business rather than a potential breakthrough to arrange serious negotiations (as Dong had explicitly assured Gomułka in late November). Hesitating before informing either Washington or Moscow, the Polish authorities mulled over options for more than a day before opting against sending a rebuttal to Hanoi or taking any other extraordinary measures to resurrect the initiative.

"We decided not to respond to the DRV note . . . in order not to carry on a polemic with the DRV about their inaccurate and demagogic assertions— undoubtedly formulated with the Chinese in mind," Michałowski remembered. "We could not publish the DRV arguments, both for reasons of secrecy, which still bound us [*sic!*], and because its assertions would not have facilitated our position towards the USA."[63]

❋ ❋ ❋

Thursday morning, an apprehensive Gronouski, left in the dark by the Poles, received a personal message from Rusk couched to fan the ambassador's suspicions toward his diplomatic partners. Making clear his own wariness, the secretary speculated that Warsaw "never had any intention of pressing Hanoi for talks without an unconditional and unreciprocal cessation of bombing," and claimed that a surge of North Vietnamese shipping to southern areas of the country during the Christmas truce called into question the "good faith and the intentions of the other side." Most of all, he was "deeply disturbed" by Rapacki's leak to the pope "without any indication to us" after long insisting on the "greatest secrecy." Passing along Meloy's account of his conversation with Fanfani, Rusk observed that Washington now faced the likelihood that the pope had a "very one-sided view of recent transactions from the Poles and the question as to whether we should not correct that account by direct discussions with the Pope."[64]

By Thursday afternoon, Gronouski was growing fidgety. It had been five days since he had delivered a "more than satisfactory" proposition, and he still had heard nothing. Waiting for the phone to ring, he seriously considered popping over to the Foreign Ministry to accost Michałowski or Rapacki, but restrained himself. Perhaps the Poles needed a bit more time to persuade a recalcitrant Hanoi.

But Gronouski did not want to spend the weekend on tenterhooks, and he cabled Rusk late Thursday seeking permission to see Rapacki the next afternoon "to express disappointment" at the lack of a response and to request his evaluation of the situation. "I would also tell Rapacki that I am beginning to wonder whether Hanoi actually wants negotiations," he suggested, mimicking his boss's skepticism. Dismayed by the Italian report of the leak to the pope, whom he thought needed to be enlightened on how far Washington had gone to clear the path for talks, he also proposed asking Rapacki to confirm his "assumption" that the Poles had discussed Marigold with Fanfani and the Soviets but "no other party or government." He might even allude to Lewandowski's reported indiscretion in Saigon.[65]

Hold your horses, Rusk shot back. Pressing Rapacki now would be "premature," implying an "overeagerness" that might whet Hanoi's appetite for further concessions. Backstopped by Bundy and Katzenbach, the secretary even expressed understanding for the North Vietnamese, pointing out they had had only four days "to reach governmental position on matter of utmost importance." The Poles, he reassured Gronouski, would surely pass on Hanoi's answer "without delay once received."[66]

Ottawa: Limits to Loyalty

It seemed an ideal moment to flee the icy, sleepy Canadian capital, so Paul Martin did just that. Leaving aides to mind the store, the foreign minister jetted off to Barbados.

Ottawa's deep freeze and holiday lassitude, however, did not ensure diplomatic inactivity. On Wednesday, classified cables from Warsaw, New Delhi, and New York abruptly put the kibosh on Martin's latest Vietnam peace foray—and (thanks to Thant's blabbing) parted the curtain concealing Marigold from Canadian eyes. Besides the report of Rapacki's rejection of Martin's pleas to attend the proposed trilateral ICC gathering in New Delhi, a message from the Indian foreign minister, M. C. Chagla, arrived stating that due to Polish disfavor, India, "for the time being" at least, would drop the idea.[67] When Ignatieff's news of Thant's revelations arrived, the Canadians needed little imagination to connect the dots— and to surmise that Rapacki's ire at U.S. behavior in the secret initiative had underlain his rebuff to Martin. Had Washington's secretiveness and belligerence, they could not help but wonder, not only sunk Martin's efforts but a far more substantial peace chance with the Poles?

To bring his vacationing boss into the picture, the undersecretary of state for external affairs, Marcel Cadieux, prepared a detailed analysis to be carried to the Caribbean along with Ignatieff's messages, which appeared, he noted drolly, "to open a window on another phase in the pursuit of a Vietnam settlement of which, so far as I know, we have had no previous knowledge." A lawyer by training (and later Canada's ambassador to Washington), Cadieux judiciously cautioned that they had only received one, perhaps slanted, version of the affair and should quickly approach Rusk to get the U.S. perspective and alert him to Thant's awareness of the defamatory Polish account.

Nevertheless, perplexity and dismay at American conduct permeated his analysis. Should the Polish account prove even "substantially accurate," he found it incomprehensible that Rusk would repeatedly (both in Washington in late November and Paris in mid-December) encourage Martin to pursue his own Vietnam peace initiative involving the Poles while keeping him in the dark on a simultaneous U.S. approach to Hanoi via Warsaw. Nor could he understand Washington's rationale for "pursuing at least three separate and simultaneous approaches to a Vietnam settlement (this would include the Goldberg appeal to U Thant), which could not readily be reconciled with one another" and risked crossing wires. Still worse, if the Poles gave Thant "anything like an accurate reflection of what happened," it was "hard to explain how the United States would have been prepared to prejudice the results of this initiative" by the Hanoi bombings on December 2 and 4, and again on December 13 and 14 —especially when Ottawa understood that each such bombing required LBJ's personal approval.[68]

Lacking secure communications to send ciphered telegrams to Barbados, the Canadians decided to dispatch Klaus Goldschlag, head of the ministry's far eastern division, to Barbados to personally hand Martin copies of Ignatieff's cables and Cadieux's analysis, and secure his approval for draft instructions to send to Washington to brief the Canadian ambassador for an audience with Rusk to discover what he had been up to behind Ottawa's back.

* * *

In the midst of these disturbed considerations landed Moore's cable from Saigon requesting "flash" final instructions for the Hanoi bombing balloting. Nearing the end of his tour, he wanted to dispose of the matter on Saturday, December 31, so it did not carry over into the new year and interfere with his impending farewell trip to Hanoi. Going by past experience, including Ottawa's handling of Polish protests of the bombings of targets near Hanoi and Haiphong over the summer, Moore assumed he would be directed to vote against all Lewandowski's motions, while abstaining on Rahman's gentler resolutions terming the raids an extension of a U.S.-RVN military alliance and, in the case of the December 13–14 attacks, appending the Hanoi subcommission's unanimous report.[69] However, those were not the instructions CDEA officials, freshly miffed at the Americans and perhaps feeling less obliged to display lockstep loyalty, dispatched on Thursday to Moore.[70]

Texas: "No Reaction as Such"

LBJ had hoped to spend a quiet week convalescing (politically and physically) at his ranch between the Christmas and New Year's holidays. The uproar produced by Salisbury's articles scotched those plans, but the Texas White House—like the Pentagon in the midst of a transition of press secretaries—reacted sluggishly. Only on Wednesday, three days after the Hanoi-datelined reports began appearing, did acting spokesman George Christian take questions on the subject. (Moyers was back in Washington laboring away on the State of the Union Address.) While leaving more detailed rebuttals to the Pentagon, he insisted that Johnson (who purportedly had "no reaction as such" to the articles) had never authorized attacks on civilian targets and was confident that the military had followed his instructions to confine its raids to solely military objectives.[71]

Friday, December 30

Saigon: "Reweave the Fibers"

During his day off from commission combat, Lewandowski visited D'Orlandi for a long, inconclusive conversation about the stalled negotiating channel. Even before the Pole arrived for an early supper, the Italian alerted Fanfani to his partner's reluctance to deal with any Americans aside from Lodge—an aversion mirroring D'Orlandi's own and, for that matter, fully reciprocated by Porter and Habib. If "favorable conditions" suddenly developed, D'Orlandi explained, he would ask his absent friend to expedite his return to Saigon so the three-way sessions could resume.[72]

When D'Orlandi and Lewandowski rehashed the situation, however, the Pole discouraged any idea of summoning their colleague. The "current lull," he insisted, was "not harmful." Were U.S. officials "serious" about restarting the three-way talks, they would cut short Lodge's home leave themselves without outside prompting. In any case, before a renewed effort could make any progress he would have to journey to Hanoi again "to reweave the fibers of the attempt."

Confiding that he anticipated new instructions from Warsaw "any time now," the Pole was merely temporizing, doubtful circumstances would justify any new initiative. The two resolved to talk again the next evening, when the Italian hosted a New Year's Eve party.[73]

* * *

Friday evening, at a Foreign Ministry reception hosted by Tran Van Do for the departing RVN ambassador to Washington (Bui Diem), Lewandowski engaged Moore in a "bantering but leading talk" about ICC business. Asked his view of the proposed three-way meeting in New Delhi, the Canadian cautiously mouthed his government's view: Ottawa believed the idea very useful—it could not do any harm and might at least demonstrate that the ICC countries grasped and sought to ameliorate the problems stalemating the group.

I thought so, too, Lewandowski replied, but on further reflection (and probably on receiving guidance from Warsaw), he expressed his fear that such a gathering might be "the last straw," doomed to a deadlock and a "meaningless communiqué" that would expose the ICC to "international public ridicule to an extent that would kill it." Moore countered that the public hardly expected miracles but would welcome a trilateral session in New Delhi as "itself action of a sort" and at least a token of good intentions. We could all just as well meet in Saigon, Lewandowski responded, "but what is proposed is a conference" that would raise unrealistic hopes.

Reverting to immediate ICC affairs, Moore needled Lewandowski about his supposed desire for the ICC to remain "quiescent" (it had to work both ways, he pointed out, eliciting a grin) and his failure to emulate Canada's noble example by occasionally condemning Hanoi as Ottawa had frequently criticized Saigon. Would not Lewandowski's "only honest and objective course" be to vote alongside him in chiding the DRV for harboring SAMs and MiGs, because he admitted they were there?

Lewandowski laughed: "Try me: Put your resolution to the vote."

"That remains to be seen," Moore remarked in reporting the exchange, "but I would rate the remark simply as one of the better jokes of the evening."[74]

* * *

When Lewandowski returned to his villa Friday night, he found a cable from Michałowski purporting, finally, to apprise him of recent developments in the dialogue with Gronouski. Judging from Lewandowski's brief yet revealing reply —alas, like most other Marigold-related messages from Warsaw, the outgoing ciphergram is missing from the MSZ archives—Michałowski informed him only now of the 10-mile zone around Hanoi,[75] yet provided not only a belated but an incomplete and even distorted summary of the situation.

Michałowski evidently neglected to note that Warsaw had already sent Washington's proposal to Hanoi, because Lewandowski replied that "passing on [Rusk's] new proposition would not be right." (Peeved at the tardy notice, he could not resist noting, with a hint of asperity, that D'Orlandi had already told him about the U.S. move.) From Lewandowski's later comments to the Italian, Michałowski may also have unfairly characterized the unilateral U.S. step as conditional, requiring (rather than urging) reciprocal restraint around Saigon. At any rate, the reported new offer failed to impress Lewandowski, whose attitude toward Washington had hardened considerably. Bitter at what he saw as the Americans' sabotage of the peace breakthrough, he exhorted Michałowski to hold them firmly to the stands Lodge stated in mid-November—he did not know that they had dropped the "important differences of interpretation" clause and no longer contested the ten points—and conspiratorially speculated that in view of the latest maneuver, "the goal of the bombings on the 2nd, 4th, 13th, and 14th of this month, becomes clear."

Lewandowski also calculated that despite the deployment of almost 400,000 troops to Vietnam as the year ended, Washington had neither achieved a decisive military advantage nor had any prospect of doing so even with more forces, and that the insurgency against the Saigon regime continued to gather momentum. "The situation in South Vietnam," he concluded firmly, "does not justify, in my opinion, any further concessions."[76]

Warsaw: "A Tragic Development"

Gronouski dreaded enduring the New Year's weekend without hearing an answer from Hanoi, but a phone call from Michałowski at noon on Friday to arrange a meeting with Rapacki for 2:30 p.m. finally promised to end the suspense.[77] During the past four weeks, he and the Polish foreign minister had met eleven times. Though Marigold's tribulations had occasioned moments of discord, anger, and tension as the two men argued, sometimes passionately, on behalf of their respective governments, they had developed a mutual trust that both, as individuals, sincerely sought a breakthrough for peace. This conversation would be their most melancholy.[78]

Coming right to the point, Rapacki told Gronouski that Warsaw had acted on the Christmas Eve proposal, the 10-mile zone around Hanoi, but it proved inadequate to overcome the "damage done by previous actions." Now "we have to consider our role at this stage as terminated."

"We regret very much that [the] matter took such a turn," he added, insisting that the Poles had done "everything they could have" to get talks started. Rapacki voiced appreciation for Gronouski's personal efforts and sorrow that his Christmas vacation had been ruined. "It has been said that work done in a good cause sooner or later will yield results," he consoled. "I don't know if this is always the case, but we hope."

The "horribly crestfallen" American responded that it was "not the holiday that matters," but the collapse of prospects for peace that had risen again during his trip to Washington. "I had high hopes," he said. "I know there is a point where one gives up but I do not like to." The main question now, he added bleakly, was "where we go from here." The latest development, he admitted, "leaves me feeling that maybe we have been kidded from the very beginning."

Rapacki empathized with Gronouski's exasperation, but assured him that "authoritative" North Vietnamese had not been kidding when they acquiesced to the Warsaw meeting. "I don't make such an accusation against Lodge or anyone else," he added, "but how the bombing could start at just that moment is something which evades me." Had the latest U.S. step been taken earlier, say on December 4, or even between the first two Hanoi raids and the December 13–14 attacks, he maintained, the first contact would already have taken place. But this was water under the bridge. Someday, he hinted, "we may talk about it in a different capacity. . . . We share common misgivings and concerns; but our views on a solution differ."

Unwilling to accept Rapacki's insistence that the affair was over, Gronouski insisted that Washington had taken a big step forward: "I am reluctant to give up this opportunity; slowly the conditions for negotiations were being created. To recapture this, we would have to go way back to recreate the conditions we now have. This is a tragic development."

Perhaps moved by his evident anguish, Rapacki commiserated. For the first time, he said clearly that his reaction to the latest U.S. proposal, "while mixed, was not negative." Arguments as to which side had shown more willingness to start talks could be made either way, he acknowledged. Yet, he insisted, the United States, as "a great power," had the "key" to remedy the situation—clearly, though he did not have to say so, by stopping all bombing of the North.

Clutching at straws, Gronouski suggested that Poland consent to the proposal for ICC consultations with Canada and India in New Delhi in order to "pick up a few of the pieces." The idea failed to rouse Rapacki's enthusiasm. The ICC's labors over the years, he noted dryly, had failed to produce "any brilliant achievement," and a futile meeting could only be destructive. Moreover, because the other two nations were ignorant of what had occurred in Marigold—he did not know Thant had already dished to Ignatieff—any three-way discussions "might be divorced from the realities of the situation."

Then, as instructed, Gronouski bearded Rapacki on secrecy. He affirmed that Washington remained bound by its vow to maintain "absolute silence" on the initiative (aside from interested parties such as Fanfani and Moscow), and presumed Poland had done and would continue to do the same. Sheepishly, Rapacki agreed in principle but allowed that "probably the Pope is informed."

"By whom?" asked Gronouski, knowing full well the answer.

"Possibly Fanfani," Rapacki equivocated (according to the American), "but I don't know, I am not saying it was Fanfani, I don't know, but the Pope probably is informed." He pledged, not very credibly, to abide by mutual promises of secrecy unless jointly agreed. (Contradicting Gronouski's contemporaneous account, Michałowski later stated that Rapacki had acknowledged that "the Pope was informed by us."[79] But, barring confusion in translation, this seems implausible:

Gronouski had no motive to conceal a forthright admission by Rapacki and knew his dissembling would further undermine his credibility in Washington.)

Cabling his account of the conversation, Gronouski gamely defended Warsaw's good faith:

> In this moment of frustration it would be easy to conclude that Poles have led us down the primrose path. But I think this would be an unfortunate misinterpretation of events. If the Poles had been playing this kind of game they would have come in today asking us to sweeten the pot. Instead, they threw up their hands and bowed out.
>
> The posture of both Rapacki and Michałowski today was one of regret. I am convinced that Poles have had at least limited authority from Hanoi to investigate negotiation and Warsaw meeting terms, that they felt that our December 24 position was a satisfactory one, and that since December 24 they did what they could to induce Hanoi to enter negotiations. Failing this, they recognized Hanoi's intransigence and bowed out.

With the Poles exiting the scene, Gronouski urged Washington to turn promptly to Moscow to take up the initiative, and to prolong the 10-mile bombing moratorium until the Soviets failed or rejected the U.S. appeal. Adopting less emotional, more pragmatic language to promote his aim of retrieving *something* tangible from Marigold's wreckage, he concluded: "I believe we now have the initiative and should exploit it with the Soviets, the Pope and U Thant with the alternative objectives of either moving along the path toward negotiations or, if this fails, leaving us in a strong public relations position. Hasty withdrawal of our December 24 position would, I believe, seriously compromise either objective."

✳ ✳ ✳

As the MSZ chiefs informed Gronouski of Hanoi's rebuff, they also sent word to Pszczółkowski in Moscow (for Gromyko) and to Lewandowski. In their cable to Saigon, Rapacki and Michałowski opined that the DRV statement's "accusatory manner clearly shows that it was written with the PRC in mind." They also took a couple of jabs at the Americans. The United States' refusal to order a bombing halt despite the initial positive DRV step "did not make our common position easier," and the limited no-bombing zone around Hanoi was an obvious attempt "to obliterate the impression" that the earlier air strikes had undermined the initiative. (It is unclear whether they clarified that Washington had, in the end, taken that step without insisting on a prior Communist pledge to forswear attacks on Saigon.) Trinh's message "closes the whole affair," they concluded, but if D'Orlandi or Lodge approached Lewandowski to make further efforts, "he was not to back away from talks but not to accept any obligations to deliver anything to Hanoi."[80]

London: "I Must Tell You Quite Frankly"

When the Canadians passed along word to the British that the proposed three-way New Delhi conclave had fallen through, they blamed the Indians for frightening off the Poles by proposing a high-visibility foreign ministers' gathering and prematurely going into too much detail. Ottawa was "deeply disappointed and cross" with the Indians, and its envoy in London "in a somewhat typical Canadian fashion" also blamed Washington for undercutting the discreet initiative with its letter to Thant, a Foreign Office aide reported; rather smugly, the Briton noted that the news vindicated his own foreign secretary's skepticism toward the "Martin Plan" from the get-go.[81]

But George Brown also felt intense pressure to make a visible, even if equally futile, Vietnam peace gesture to stem the tide of anti-American opinion rising throughout his country (and especially in his own Labour Party) as a result of the *New York Times* dispatches from Hanoi.[82] "I must tell you quite frankly and as an old friend that these articles have worried me," he wrote Rusk on Friday. "It is not only that Salisbury is producing circumstantial detail that seems to be new to the Western world—and some of it is new to me. What causes me concern is the fact that Salisbury and other Western journalists who may get to Hanoi are going to be totally believed by much of the public they serve. Moreover"—he added, anticipating Rusk's usual rejoinder—"there seems little doubt now that American bombs have caused civilian casualties in North Vietnam, even if other casualties have been caused by North Vietnamese antiaircraft shells and missiles."

If earlier the heat seemed to going out of the issue, Salisbury's eyewitness accounts of civilian damage had stoked the furor, generating "a lot of political steam," Brown wrote Rusk, including likely renewed calls for "dissociation" once the House of Commons reconvened after New Year's. Hoping to vent the building pressure, Brown felt he had to act immediately—whether or not Washington approved (or Moscow joined in, as Brown and Prime Minister Wilson ardently desired). Though the foreign secretary was at pains Friday to give Rusk advance notice and explanation—by telephone, letter, and consultations with London's ambassador—he explained, as one statesman-cum-politician to another, that the situation required him "to be seen to be taking some action on my own responsibility and not in the wake of anything which is done on your side of the Atlantic."

While promising to "do my best to damp everything down" and steadfastly resist intensified demands to "dissociate," Brown warned that he might soon feel obliged to condemn civilian casualties "more bluntly" than in the past (to balance the score-sheet, Rusk should keep stressing Viet Cong atrocities, he urged). And late Friday night, London publicly called on the United States and North Vietnam and South Vietnam to meet immediately to "arrange a cessation of hostilities," and grandly offered British territory in Hong Kong or elsewhere for their representatives to parley.[83]

Facing an inevitable rebuff from Hanoi, this "Brown Plan" had no more chance than Martin's of stopping the fighting or starting talks, but it served its author's aim of appearing to do *something,* though skeptical British quickly divined its true purpose (as did the Soviets, who promptly denounced it).[84] From Washington's perspective, it usefully reminded the public that the Communists had rejected unconditional negotiations even as the story of Marigold's collapse, still buried in classified crypts, crept toward the sunlight.

New York: "Lock, Stock, and Barrel"

Friday morning, Ignatieff updated Thant on the matters they had discussed two days earlier. The Canadian informed the secretary-general of Rapacki's snub of Martin's appeal to attend the proposed New Delhi meeting and, more sensitively, assured him that the Polish report of the failed secret peace initiative he had divulged was being carried, even as they spoke, to Martin in the Caribbean by the "safe hand" of the Far East Division chief (Goldschlag).[85]

* * *

When Thant had gossiped to Ignatieff about Marigold on Wednesday, he rationalized the indiscretion on the grounds that Canada, pursuing its ICC gambit, needed to know about the secret diplomatic context for its exchanges with Warsaw. However, the UN head now trumped that leak with one explicable only by uncontrollable garrulousness, or a desire to ingratiate himself with a nation that shared his skepticism toward Washington. France was not then involved in any particular initiative to end the war, but its deep interest in Southeast Asia was well established—as was de Gaulle's animus toward the U.S. project in Vietnam and his rocky relations with the Johnson administration. Like a *tarte aux fruits* in the window of a Parisian patisserie, the temptation to confide simply proved too delectable for Thant to resist.

Accordingly, in the course of a general discussion on Friday with French UN ambassador Roger Seydoux, Thant volunteered on a "very personal and confidential" basis the beguiling tale he had heard a week before from Tomorowicz. Like the Pole, Thant blamed the attempt's collapse on the Americans—in particular Pentagon opposition to any negotiations, and the faith of hawks around LBJ that squeezing Hanoi would undermine its will to resist. Seydoux promptly sent a report to his foreign minister, Couve de Murville, marking it "*diffusion très restreinte*" to curb circulation.[86]

* * *

Thant had hoped the Indian-Canadian ICC initiative, now apparently dead, might complement his own efforts by calling for a bombing halt, even if such an appeal exceeded its formal terms of reference.[87] Regardless, he was determined to press Washington in that direction. In his own response to Goldberg—which Bunche transmitted Friday evening in draft form to an official at the American mission as a courtesy before its public release the next day—Thant promised to exert all his energies to promote peace, as requested. However, pointedly disregarding the advice Goldberg and, supposedly, Bunche had given him, he reiterated his three-step plan to stop the fighting: a unilateral cessation of U.S. bombing of the North, followed by a mutual stand-down of violence in the South and direct discussions between "those who are actually fighting" (i.e., including the NLF). With equally remote odds of success, he also called on Washington to embrace the prolonged holiday truce urged by the pope and other religious figures. However polite, the letter made clear that Thant still sharply diverged from LBJ on the bombing issue.[88]

* * *

Even as the *New York Times* spotlighted another exclusive dispatch from Hanoi, the newspaper backpedaled and, under heavy pressure from the administration, made an obvious attempt to "balance" its coverage. Friday's front page juxtaposed Salisbury's latest—a cultural review of musical, dance, and theatrical dimensions of DRV internal propaganda—with a lengthy "news analysis" by the paper's military correspondent Hanson Baldwin, articulating the Pentagon's insistence that the bombing of North Vietnam had "proved effective, restrained, and essential," saving the lives of "an awful lot of soldiers and marines on the ground in South Vietnam." Some civilian casualties were inevitable in any air campaign, military officials acknowledged, but residential areas were never deliberately hit, and the figures Salisbury quoted appeared to be "grossly exaggerated."[89]

Late Friday night, Rusk kept the heat on the *Times* by telephoning publisher Arthur Ochs "Punch" Sulzberger. Was Salisbury was ever going to ask the North Vietnamese any "serious questions" (as opposed to just swallowing propaganda)? "[Rusk] said it boiled down to whether Salisbury's reporting was prolonging war"—a blatant bid to guilt-trip the young publisher.[90] Trying to soothe the agitated secretary, Sulzberger had the managing editor, Clifton Daniel, call him back a few minutes later and assure him that of course Salisbury would be asking Hanoi's leaders tough questions, "That was why he was sent over there." Perhaps, Rusk acerbically suggested, he should inquire "how their regiments and divisions were getting along in South Vietnam—something like that and to point out that Hanoi is still there which was a clear indication we were not trying to bomb civilian centers."[91]

The administration's damage-control campaign would produce mixed results. A belated, frantic Pentagon effort had produced Baldwin's article, along with others in subsequent days critical of Salisbury's reporting, particularly his reliance on official DRV figures for civilian casualties from U.S. bombing. With few exceptions, mainstream media outlets generally recoiled from the heretical critique of orthodox tenets of Washington's war implicit in his articles—not only regarding the bombing's impact (on both civilians and Hanoi's military machine) but also in his depiction of the North Vietnamese as dedicated nationalist individuals rather than mindless, fanatical Communist automatons, the NLF as an authentic Southern guerrilla movement (not simply a Northern puppet), and the DRV leadership as ready to negotiate once the bombing stopped.

Some, out of both jingoism and more than a bit of professional jealousy, would take pot shots at Salisbury and the *Times*—as the Pentagon spokesman Arthur Sylvester mocked, "Harrison Appalsbury" of the "*New Hanoi Times*" had fallen "lock, stock, and barrel" for "Communist propagandists." "To American eyes, it read like the line from Tass or Hsinhua," scorned *Newsweek*. "But the copy carried the byline of one of the U.S.'s best-known journalists." Ho had let Salisbury into Hanoi as a military tactic, wrote the *Washington Post*'s Chalmers Roberts ("the very embodiment of an establishment reporter," in the words of David Halberstam), "one as clearly conceived as the poison-tipped bamboo spikes his men emplanted underfoot for the unwary enemy." Ultimately, Salisbury would be denied a Pulitzer Prize when the hawkish publishers responsible for the final award overruled the recommendation of a jury of editors, in a decision some attributed to administration pressure. But it was too little, too late— the *Times* series leveled the most "traumatic" blow yet to the administration's credibility on the war, both at home and abroad, a wound a Pentagon spokesman termed a "national disaster."[92]

Washington: "We Must Ruminate on That One"

When State Department officials tracking Marigold came to work a cold Friday morning, they found a cable from Gronouski stating that Michałowski had called to set up an appointment with Rapacki later in the day—so it would be just a few hours before they found out whether Hanoi had chomped, nibbled, or ignored the lure tossed out by Washington a week before.[93] Before receiving Gronouski's report, however, Rusk and his top aides were reminded of their vulnerable position in the secret diplomacy when Dobrynin, back from Moscow, saw Llewellyn Thompson. Asked if he had brought Kosygin's response to LBJ letter's (which he had carried to the Kremlin more than three weeks earlier), the Soviet diplomat responded that speaking "completely off the record he could tell me that a reply had nearly been completed and that it was one we would have liked but then the [December 13–14] bombing of Hanoi had occurred and this draft had been torn up and another one of quite a different character started."

Dobrynin had advised the Soviet leaders to wait until tempers cooled before sending LBJ a formal response, he reported, though they were plenty angry after reading their Hanoi embassy's cables and had no doubts whatsoever that U.S. bombs had indeed fallen on civilian neighborhoods, notwithstanding Washington's vehement denials. When Thompson recited the now-familiar refrain that fallen SAMs might have been culpable, Dobrynin retorted that they could not have caused the kind of crater that had been seen. Then, well informed of the state of play on Marigold, he asked whether anything new had developed from the

Poles; Thompson mentioned that Gronouski was to see Rapacki that day (he already had, in fact), but the outcome was not known.

Moscow's ambassador then reiterated, more sharply and authoritatively, the message his deputy had given Bundy eight days before: The Soviets had invested "considerable hope" in the Polish effort, viewing it as a serious bid to open peace talks, but the untimely Hanoi raids "spoiled everything." Scorning the claim that the attacks were set far in advance and only by "pure coincidence" overlapped with the secret diplomacy, Dobrynin said U.S. actions had "frankly baffled" his government, which "did not know how to judge our policy." He and many other Soviets even "wondered whether some of our military were deliberately trying to frustrate a policy of moving toward negotiations or whether our policy was really one of military victory." Thompson assured him that Washington genuinely desired talks; while hawks indeed favored stronger actions, in this case it was "not a question of military officers disobeying orders."[94]

A little after noon, Thompson escorted Dobrynin in to see Rusk. The Soviet again related how the Hanoi bombings had "turned upside down" the Kremlin's draft response to LBJ and aroused his government's "genuine concern" in "appraising our policy." Rusk, in turn, trotted out the usual arguments to explain and justify the strikes (advance planning, weather shifts, terrorism around Saigon including the Tan Son Nhut attack "the day before he arrived there and the bombing of the main bridge during his stay there"). Rusk suggested that with visitors waiting outside, they "talk this matter out" late the following week.[95]

* * *

At 1:36 p.m., after ushering out a *Time* magazine delegation, Rusk fielded a call from a "very anxious" George Brown, who had phoned to reinforce his earlier warning that due to Salisbury's articles, he faced mounting demands to more forcefully condemn civilian casualties—though he promised again to resist calls to "dissociate." To ease this stress, he was thinking of issuing a public appeal to the foreign ministers of Washington, Hanoi, and Saigon to gather for cease-fire negotiations.

Rusk pleaded that he "needed time to turn around on this one," but Brown insisted that he and Wilson must go ahead that very night, "if we are to reduce the pressure which I know will be building up this weekend." At 2 p.m., London's ambassador in Washington, Sir Patrick Dean, joined Rusk in his office and stayed for most of the afternoon to coordinate on the language of the proposed British initiative, which, aside from a couple of minor wording changes, was something the Americans could live with.[96] Dean had fresh impetus to keep U.K. criticism within careful limits; during the last few days, he had canvassed Rusk, Rostow, and Harriman to gauge their current thinking on the war, and had received fresh warnings—implicitly from Rusk, explicitly from Harriman—that any further "dissociation" would infuriate LBJ and eliminate any hope that Wilson might retain to influence U.S. actions in Vietnam. Dean counseled London accordingly.[97]

Rusk also had Bundy gather some material for Dean to send home to rebut Salisbury's articles, but he refrained from passing along a more self-critical spot analysis of the reporter's charges he received that Friday from Tom Hughes. While conceding considerable uncertainty, the Intelligence and Research Bureau director acknowledged, on the basis of Pentagon poststrike photography, that "considerable damage to civilian installations has been done in areas surrounding selected military targets," including in Nam Dinh, where Salisbury's reporting had aroused the loudest furor, and greater Hanoi in the first half of December.[98]

* * *

As Rusk conferred with Dean on the seventh floor, downstairs Gronouski's report of the conversation that spelled Marigold's doom was arriving. After it was brought upstairs, the secretary rang the president to inform him and directed that the text, like other urgent messages on the initiative over the preceding month, be transmitted to LBJ at his ranch. At 5:10 p.m., Rostow called to review various Vietnam matters, including how to deal with the war in the State of the Union Address and the building pressure in England from what Rusk called "the Harrison Salisbury business." Only in passing did he and Rostow note Gronouski's latest, grimmest cable. "We must ruminate on that one," Rusk concluded.[99]

Texas: "The End of the Line"
Extinguishing his last embers of hope, the news Johnson expected, yet still dreaded, reached him at the ranch little after 3 p.m. Friday afternoon, when Rusk telephoned to say that "the Marigold series apparently has come to an end."

"It was propaganda all the time, wasn't it?" the president asked, as if seeking absolution, reassurance that he had not squandered a genuine opportunity for peace.

"Well," Rusk answered, cautiously yet supportively, "it begins to sound that way, as though they didn't have anybody on the hook much on the other side, but we'll see."[100]

Relaying Gronouski's report of his terminal conversation with Rapacki to LBJ on Friday evening, even the optimistic Rostow admitted: "We are at the end of a phase if not at the end of the line with Marigold. We shall now have to pause and consider next steps."[101] An aide handed it to LBJ in his office a little before 7:30 p.m.

"I will have to answer this later," Johnson told a secretary, after scanning the depressing message. "Read it."

"Too much," he added.[102]

Saturday, December 31, 1966

Saigon: "Such an Exciting Year"
At 10 a.m. on a sultry Saturday morning, Lewandowski, Rahman, and Moore gathered at Camp des Mares for their showdown over the Hanoi bombings. Pre-

dictably, the Canadian and Indian teamed up to sink the Pole's resolutions blasting the attacks as "a further escalation of war in Vietnam" and "a clear violation of the provisions, spirit and letter" of the Geneva Accords. But a procedural kerfuffle erupted over his less strongly worded motions affirming that Saigon had contravened Geneva because it was "acting in a factual military alliance" with Washington when the latter "bombed and strafed" residential areas of Hanoi, causing, as the ICC's bureau there confirmed, civilian damage and casualties. Lewandowski voted in favor, of course, but when Moore abstained instead of voting no, contrary to Warsaw's expectations (and Moore's own, before he received Ottawa's instructions), Rahman "after some hesitation" did the same.[103]

With a tally of one for, none against, and two abstaining, Lewandowski triumphantly declared that the resolutions had passed, sparking confusion over whether a "majority" meant of all present or only those voting aye or nay. Taken aback, Rahman asked to annul the vote and take a new one, but the Pole refused. Supported by Moore, Rahman asserted that the dispute over the definition of a majority required further study, effectively tabling Lewandowski's resolution. Then he put forward his own delicately balanced alternative, which, while retaining pro forma criticism of Saigon for its military alliance with Washington, deleted explicit references to bomb damage in "residential" or "civilian" areas "in the Hanoi area" yet tacked on the onsite inspection report as an appendix. Moore favored the Indian proposal, and Lewandowski—after first objecting that because his own resolution had passed, it was improper to consider Rahman's—made it unanimous. Then he inaugurated a fresh quarrel by requesting that the Indian resolution, with the Hanoi report appended, be officially transmitted to the ICC cochairs, the British and the Soviets.

Brushing aside the Pole's contention that this was a mere "procedural matter" that could be decided instantly, Rahman postponed the issue for later consideration and the group adjourned its 755th formal sitting. Moore resolved to thwart Lewandowski's maneuver, if necessary by pressing for an analogous message to Moscow and London admonishing Hanoi for its own Geneva transgressions. "Last night the Pole had spoken to me jokingly (but not in retrospect it would seem seriously) about a unanimous vote emerging today," he cabled. "This he made sure of by throwing in his vote with ours at the last moment on the second Indian resolution, having lost out on his resolutions. I believe you would wish us to resist his current efforts to project this into what would amount to a one-sided report to the cochairmen for propaganda purposes."[104]

✳ ✳ ✳

On the final day of 1966, all the Saigon-based diplomats mired in Marigold—save Lodge, cocooning with his family in New England—converged on one atmospheric setting for drinks, gossip, and intrigues: the new Independence Palace. Officially inaugurated two months earlier, though not quite finished, the vast presidential headquarters had been erected on the site of the demolished French-built colonial governor-general's building, damaged by bombs dropped by rebel pilots during a 1962 coup attempt against Diem. The unpopular dictator had ordered the old palace torn down and commanded a lavish replacement, and reportedly rejected ten plans before settling on a design intended to blend modernist and traditional themes. After ousting him the following year, his successors gradually built Diem's "dream house" for their own use. The symmetrical, starkly angular, five-story, T-shaped edifice, configured to evoke traditional Chinese characters for luck, fidelity, intelligence, prosperity, and other virtues, was plunked in a 21-acre downtown park, its gates surrounding gardens, fountains, tennis courts, and more, and inside its concrete walls featured a hundred rooms and working spaces (from rooftop helipad to offices and living rooms to basement bunker suitable for monitoring battles and coups). To contrast with the Western exterior, public reception areas employed Vietnamese and Oriental materials, motifs, and decor, from ornate carpets over teak floors to stone floral curtains to Bien Hoa ceramic tiles to Chinese-style red lacquered cabinets and pearl inlaid screens.

Like so much else ventured by the Saigon government, the expensive stab at splendor in the grass failed to inspire the admiration and respect it so desperately craved. Critics, including some Americans, tagged the gargantuan structure a white elephant, queried its funding, mocked design accents (e.g., bamboo wall joints resembled "dog bones set end on end"), and sniffed that instead of harmoniously merging East and West, it pompously mingled dystopian Brasília and fascist Italy, down to a second-floor balcony ideal for a caudillo.[105]

Straining to project an image of dignity, permanence, and legitimacy, the embattled Saigon rulers invited the diplomatic corps, including the ICC commissioners, to the palace Saturday morning for a year-end soirée. Dressed "in high uniform," the ambassadors and the senior members of the military regime assembled beneath imported chandeliers in the cavernous, high-ceilinged ground-floor reception chamber fringed by half-moon-shaped ponds planted with lotus and water lily to induce memories of ancient temples and pagodas.

As dean of the diplomatic corps, D'Orlandi delivered formal greetings to the head of state, General Thieu (who had just moved his offices into the palace), and good wishes for 1967. The suave Italian thrived on such occasions, and his statements mingled standard boilerplate Cold War rhetoric ("the countries of the Free World stand by the Vietnamese people") with heartfelt pleas for the Vietnamese people to escape "the horror of war and from such evils as destruction, famine, and hatred, that obstruct the path of peaceful national development."[106]

A little before noon, having driven straight to the palace from their sparring session, the three ICC delegates, "each with a retinue of officers," were received, separately from the diplomatic corps, by Thieu and a bevy of RVN dignitaries, including two vice premiers, War Minister General Nguyen Huu Co and ARVN chief of staff General Cao Van Vien, the secretary-general of the leadership committee Lieutenant General Pham Xuan Chieu, and the lone civilian, Foreign Minister Tran Van Do. (Despite having greeted the diplomats in an adjoining room a few minutes before, Premier Ky skipped the ICC ceremony, arousing speculation that the air vice marshal's absence reflected his contempt for the group.[107])

The gathering's conviviality accentuated anew the incongruity of the smiling young Communist ambassador chatting cordially with those fighting to the death against his ideological brethren. Eyebrow slightly raised, Moore reported afterward that the Pole had "for a change" joined him and Rahman in calling on Thieu. On behalf of all three commissioners, the Indian transmitted "felicitations and good wishes" for 1967 and pledged that they would "rededicate" themselves to the ICC's mission, "based on total impartiality in the supervision of the Geneva Agreement, on which so many throughout the world place their hopes of peace." Vowing "unreservedly" their "fullest cooperation" and soliciting the same from Thieu and his government, Rahman warmly yet innocuously affirmed that, "however dark and dangerous the situation may appear, we believe that the genius of the Vietnamese people will emerge superior, just as we are convinced that justice, honor and independence are integral to the ancient traditions and history of the Vietnamese nations." In a "very cordial" reply, Thieu alluded to Communist truce violations as indicative of the difficulties ahead, but Lewandowski cabled Warsaw merely that the general had avoided "touchy questions" and "strongly emphasized his desire for peace." "It was a very pleasant occasion with all the above mixing with the representatives of all [ICC] delegations over a glass of champagne," Moore recorded.[108]

Lewandowski's fraternization with the anticommunist Saigon government was hardly spontaneous. He had carefully requested Warsaw's permission to participate in what he described as an "old custom," and received its approval with the proviso that he emphasize that he was there "only to underscore the unity of the ICC"[109]—a forlorn sentiment in view of the pervasive discord that stalemated the ICC in general and that very week had derailed the Indian-Canadian effort for even a low-key three-way meeting in New Delhi. Like Moore, Lewandowski had also carefully reviewed and approved Rahman's remarks.

Lewandowski's conspicuous cordiality did not pass unnoticed among the South Vietnamese authorities, some of whom, at least, were aware of his extracurricular diplomatic activities. During the reception, Do took him aside and, in effect, sought to open Saigon's own Polish back channel to Hanoi. The RVN, he insisted, sincerely desired "national reconciliation" (using the English phrase) and recognized that this, not military victory, would truly end the war. The foreign minister recalled that he personally knew Pham Van Dong, and had a friendly talk with him at his villa in Geneva in 1954. Though they failed to reach an understanding then,[110] now everyone was twelve years older and wiser. "Presently," he continued, "he would again be ready to talk sincerely with PVD. He has no doubt that PVD and other leaders are patriots, although their political views are different."[111] On a personal note evocative of Vietnam's tortured history—and which the Pole omitted from his reporting telegram—he also asked Lewandowski to see if Dong might check on the health of his elderly mother in the North, whom he could no longer see.[112]

Having alluded politely to his government's bitter enemies, Do used singularly conciliatory language—and a striking historical analogy—to commend a compromise peace that would keep a divided Vietnam for the indefinite future: "Further conflict will lead to still greater destruction of the country and human losses, equally in the South as in the North. Internal considerations as well as external serve to make the immediate unification of the country impossible. This will have to wait. It should not, however, lead to the devastation of the country. Poland was divided into three parts for over a hundred years. Presently, it is an independent and united country."

Responding to this unusual advance, Lewandowski thanked Do and asked permission to make a number of observations that might strike his listener as "not altogether pleasant." The foreign minister's conciliatory words, he went on, sharply diverged in tone from the expressions of military members of the Saigon leadership, and many wondered whether the South Vietnamese government could make independent decisions, given the preponderant U.S. military and political presence. Poland sympathized with "the tragedy of the Vietnamese nation," but it could not help but note that Southern "politicians" were responsible for inviting the massive war machine that had inflicted the largest losses upon the economy and population.

"Under these conditions, it is difficult to believe in the sincerity of assurances about aspirations to unite the nation," Lewandowski concluded. As for Poland, he added that his nation "throughout those hundred years did not stop fighting even for a moment against foreign intervention."

Do responded "very calmly" to Lewandowski's blunt criticisms. Even if not everyone in his government agreed with his views, he explained, they were shared by a majority. Moreover, he assured the Pole, he "did not at all desire for the Americans to arrange their affairs," and their presence was a "sad necessity." In line with the Manila declaration, Saigon was ready to give solemn, written undertakings that within six months of an end to fighting it would itself "demand" the Americans' "unconditional and complete withdrawal." He was not irate at Lewandowski's "frank observations," but anxious to convince the Pole that for him, "who has dedicated his entire life to the service of his country," Vietnam's fate weighed on his heart.

Lewandowski suspected Do's approach was instigated by Thieu (who himself accosted Moore to reaffirm his desire to "make contact" with Hanoi[113]) along with key military associates (e.g., ARVN chief of staff General Vien and former IV Corps commander lieutenant colonel Dang Van Quang), out of anxiety that "the USA might undertake some kind of commitments" behind Saigon's back—fears fanned by (well-founded!) rumors that Washington was engaged in secret peace initiatives not coordinated with its ally. The attempt to create an independent channel to the North might also reflect "ferment within the ruling group."

Officially, Lewandowski reacted coolly to Do's overture, both in his immediate response and in his subsequent report to Warsaw. "In different circumstances it would be interesting to play out," he cabled, because it might produce direct contacts or even bargaining ("conditions for an auction") not between Saigon and Hanoi but between the South Vietnamese regime and its enemies in the NLF. However, in an obvious allusion to Marigold's collapse, he observed that presently the information was moot ("useful only as a contribution to a political examination") and added, "I did not transmit this to Hanoi for fear that it will be understood as a suggestion."[114]

Privately, Lewandowski found the conversation both intriguing and encouraging. He was not entirely surprised by Do's remarks—he had previously chatted cordially with the foreign minister, whom he respected as a venerable, moderate civilian in the military regime. Moreover, he believed there were other nationalists in Saigon official circles who only grudgingly accepted military dependence on the Americans as a necessary evil and were eager to evict them as soon as Vietnamese could settle affairs themselves. What whetted his interest was not the substance but the context of the obviously premeditated conversation—"that he said it to me, and, my God, not in a dinner party, but in the . . . presidential palace!"

Lewandowski presumed it could hardly be coincidental that the unprecedented bid to use him as a conduit to the DRV leadership came immediately after the collapse of the three-way effort, and suspected that it was prompted by knowledge of his secret dealings with Lodge and D'Orlandi (either through RVN intelligence or a U.S. leak). Perhaps, he calculated warily, with the failure of the earlier attempt, Do was "trying to drag me into" an alternative second channel which Poland, after getting burned once, would be foolish to promote to Hanoi.

Yet he also recognized a potential bright side: Saigon might not, after all, dogmatically oppose the kind of negotiations with the Communists (the NLF as well as Hanoi) envisioned in the ten points. While diehard anticommunists like Ky might blanch, he now felt the ten points, including the Phase A/B formula, were "quite realistic," even if they required South Vietnamese consent to some sort of temporary transitional coalition government that included the NLF.

So, he remembered thinking, it was "*not* true that the Americans have such a wall from the South Vietnamese. . . . There *are* forces also in the Saigonese set-up, which would be willing to go to a settlement. . . . They want to be in! They don't want to be left behind."[115]

✳ ✳ ✳

As waiters offered champagne, D'Orlandi too was sequestered by Do, who steered him to a quiet corner. The South Vietnamese foreign minister sought the Italian's unvarnished assessment of Brown's proposal for U.S., DRV, and RVN representatives to gather to discuss cease-fire arrangements. He was not sure what to make of it: Had London sent the invitation for "purely internal political purposes," to soothe British public opinion? Or was it a serious initiative, preceded by an approach to Hanoi assuring a positive response? Probably the former, D'Orlandi responded, without disclosing the sad story underlying his pessimistic appraisal.

Brown's brainstorm also arose when D'Orlandi bumped into the U.K. ambassador, who knew little beyond the formal text, and Porter, who candidly belittled it. "The initiative will obtain the result of showing the world at New Year's that Hanoi does not want to hear talk of peace," the American wisecracked "half-jokingly" when D'Orlandi asked his evaluation.[116]

* * *

After their earlier exchanges, Porter did not need to remind D'Orlandi that he viewed the Polish channel, in which the Italian invested such hope, equally disdainfully. But just in case Washington wondered how Lodge's temporary replacement felt about Marigold, after reading the latest cables from Warsaw, he shot off a scathing telegram denouncing the "unsatisfactory" Poles and strongly advising that they be replaced or at least supplemented by more "trustworthy" intermediaries, such as the Canadians.[117]

Unlike Gronouski, Porter had no doubt that the Poles were, indeed, leading the Americans down the "primrose path." "We have been watching with increasing puzzlement the Polish minuet danced by Rapacki," he began (implying that he also spoke for Habib). "We still do not know with any clarity to what extent he, or Lewandowski in the past, reflected Hanoi's views." Warsaw may have indeed had "some detailed discussion" with Hanoi, but Rapacki's "suspicious" conduct raised the possibility that the Poles for their own purposes had "constantly manipulated [the] terms of understanding." All claims regarding Hanoi's alleged part in the affair, he noted, rested wholly on the word of the Poles, "whom we have reason to distrust."

Facing the breakdown of the Polish channel, or at best "further procrastination by Rapacki," Porter suggested "a better way of smoking Hanoi out in this matter." Dismissing Gronouski's idea of turning to Moscow to pick up the pieces, he urged Washington to find a noncommunist mediator. Moore's upcoming visit to Hanoi offered a "natural occasion" to switch communications channels; though a "pedantic rather precise type," the Canadian was "always ready to try a move," comparably reliable, and able to gain access to high DRV officials, perhaps even Dong. Though Porter observed that the Poles' leaks released Washington from any strictures of secrecy, he advised against divulging Marigold in its entirety to Ottawa, particularly given Martin's activism and attitudes. However, a "carefully constructed scenario" for Moore might allow him to "define the reality of Hanoi's willingness to pursue the Marigold concepts and procedures." Such, at any rate, were the Saigon Embassy's "tentative thoughts for clarifying what has become a confused channel of communication with Hanoi."

* * *

Late Saturday afternoon, after leaving the palace, the devout D'Orlandi stopped at a church to say a prayer of gratitude. Having started 1966 virtually on his death-bed—he had been evacuated from Saigon on a military aircraft to obtain emergency treatment in Rome—and having ended it with a crescendo of high-stakes secret diplomacy, he did not let the Lord's failure to answer his pleas for peace diminish his faith. "I went to thank the good God for such an exciting year," he recorded. "Who would have ever thought [this would happen] in January and February when I was in the hospital and appeared to be done for!"[118]

Then he hosted about fifty guests at 135 Duong Pasteur for a New Year's Eve gala. In the midst of the party, Lewandowski took his friend aside to tell him the latest news from Warsaw, the garbled exchanges with Gronouski. Though Rapacki's cable related that the American had made a hasty trip to Washington and returned with a revised proposal, it erroneously stated—at least according to what Lewandowski told D'Orlandi—that the U.S. 10-mile bombing restriction around Hanoi remained conditional on a cessation of "terrorism" in Saigon and that Rapacki had "refused to convey it to Hanoi."

Because Rapacki's cable has not been found, the provenance of this misconception remains unclear. Did Rapacki deliberately mislead his envoy in Saigon—perhaps to conceal Poland's role in transmitting and commending a U.S. proposal that Hanoi by now had vehemently rebuffed, or to prod him to keep pressing for a total bombing halt? Or—less likely—was Lewandowski for some reason misinforming his friend?

In keeping with Warsaw's mandate to string the Italian along and not break off their conversations, Lewandowski also told D'Orlandi that Rapacki had complimented Italy's role in the initiative and instructed him to stay in close touch and remain available for any eventual three-way meetings once Lodge returned. But his distorted description of Washington's stance confused and further discouraged D'Orlandi. The Pole's version of the conditional U.S. bombing limitation, he cabled Fanfani, contradicted both what he had heard from Cooper and Harriman at Villa Madama (i.e., the Phase A/B sequence) and also Fanfani's own report of Rusk's message delivered a couple of days earlier by Meloy.

"Therefore," he added, "I do not feel I should push Lewandowski for now to go to Hanoi because he would be compromised and we would lose the only worth-while intermediary. Allow me to repeat that if there is no attenuation in the bombings generally or suspension of those of Hanoi, without requiring any quid pro quo, it will not be possible to pick up the thread of the dialogue again with Hanoi."[119]

Moscow: The Vietnamese "Must Have Had Their Own Plans"

When Pszczółkowski handed Gromyko the note from Rapacki relating Hanoi's severance of the Warsaw contacts, the Soviet did not despair about prospects for negotiations, despite the now-undeniable demise of the Polish enterprise, and did not even exclude "more concrete" fresh peace efforts. The Vietnamese, he observed cryptically, "must have had their own plans," and one could "count on some kind of a positive reaction" from them if the Americans were to cease bombing for two or three weeks. Noting the controversy over Salisbury's articles (*Pravda* had printed excerpts), Gromyko observed optimistically that "American society" seemed to be turning against the bombing. But he also agreed with the Polish envoy that the diplomatic failure could strengthen U.S. hawks, foreshadowing a further sharp escalation in the level of violence.[120]

Rome: "Exactly What . . . We Would Have Already Done"

Remaining in the capital while his family left for a New Year's holiday, Fanfani reacted wearily to London's proposal for direct negotiations between the Vietnam combatants. "It is exactly what we have been trying to do for months," he fumed, "and which, without the bombings, we would have already done."[121]

New York: "The Desire of Dictating Peace"

On Saturday morning, Salisbury swung back at his Pentagon critics. In twin pieces, tucked inside the *New York Times* instead of on the front page, he presented additional details of alleged civilian damage in Nam Dinh—likening its bombed-out areas to "blitzed London, devastated Berlin and Warsaw, or smashed Soviet cities like Stalingrad and Kharkov"—and offered some context for his reporting, recounting his long and winding road to a visa and acknowledging that North Vietnam, like other Communist states, sharply circumscribed journalists' access and activities. Nevertheless, he argued, there was a special value to observations "behind enemy lines" and so far, at any rate, authorities had not censored any of his writing or photographs. Describing the tiny Western colony, he observed jauntily that "Hanoi is not exactly a swinging town, but there is more bounce to it than one American at least had foreseen."[122]

✳ ✳ ✳

Thant had no illusion that the Johnson administration would welcome his entreaty to take the "first and essential step" toward peace by unilaterally ceasing its bombing of North Vietnam, and it did not. After reading an advance copy of Thant's "very poor" letter Friday night, an irritated Rusk called Goldberg in an eleventh-hour effort to get the UN chief to pull back—requiring one-sided action without recompense from Hanoi was "outrageous," and referring to a dovish statement by the National Council of Churches constituted an "intrusion" into domestic affairs that "could ruin him" with the U.S. government. Through Bunche,

Goldberg persuaded Thant to drop the reference to the religious group, but he otherwise stood his ground.[123]

On Saturday afternoon, after his office released his letter, a worried Thant received Tomorowicz at his Bronx home, where he was staying to escape the press. After hearing the Pole pass along news from Rapacki (presumably of Marigold's final failure), he voiced pessimism that his own efforts would make any headway, either. Johnson and Rusk would quickly rebuff his appeal, perhaps even that day, he anticipated (correctly), just as Goldberg had told him that they had rejected his own pleas. It was, Thant complained, impossible to deal "rationally" with Washington when it insisted that before stopping the air campaign, Hanoi must first privately agree to enter into talks, a demand he regarded as a diplomatic nonstarter. "In his opinion," Tomorowicz cabled, "the actions of the U.S. can be interpreted in two ways: either as [seeking] a final victory, the Pentagon line, for the solution of the conflict by way of the military escalation, or as an intention of expediting peaceful negotiations by a periodic intensification of the bombings and military actions. In both cases, it boils down to the desire of dictating peace from the position of force and, of course, this cannot lead to negotiations with the DRV and the NLF."[124] Thant's disdain for Washington's tactics suggested that, as Rapacki had hoped, Poland could rely on him in the looming controversy over the failed peace effort.

✳ ✳ ✳

Within hours, Goldberg's formal reply was released to reporters, ensuring, as intended, same-day coverage with Thant's own letter. While profusely thanking the secretary-general for his readiness to seek peace, it rejected clearly his case for an unconditional halt to the air campaign, specifying that Washington would only take such an action after receiving "assurance, private or otherwise, that there would be a reciprocal response toward peace from North Vietnam."[125]

Paris: An "Unjust [and] Detestable War"

Seydoux's telegrams from New York relating Thant's Polish-inspired version of Margiold reached the Quai D'Orsay before dawn Saturday morning, allowing plenty of time to be deciphered and passed to General de Gaulle before he delivered a televised New Year's Eve address to his country. Perhaps not coincidentally, the seventy-six-year-old statesman—speaking without notes "in strong, clear tones, seated behind the desk in an ornate room of the Elysée Palace," periodically waving an arm or raising "his bushy eyebrows to emphasize a point"—used the message to denounce the U.S. intervention in Vietnam more harshly than ever. While Europe "takes the road to peace," he declared, "war rages in Southeast Asia. Unjust war, for it results, in fact, from the armed intervention of the United States upon the territory of Vietnam. Detestable war, since it leads a great nation to ravage a small one." Calling on Washington to withdraw its troops forthwith, he omitted any countervailing criticisms of Communist conduct. Previously, he had chided "foreign intervention" in Vietnam without naming the offender, but "the gloves are now off," a commentator observed.[126] (The next day, at a reception for the diplomatic corps, he would again blast Washington on Vietnam; the war, he said, was being "cruelly prolonged"—leaving no doubt who he held responsible for the prolongation.[127])

Texas: "They Just Cannot Make a Budge"

Speaking with Goldberg on the phone Saturday morning, Johnson sounded confident that the whole Polish affair had been much ado about nothing. He had little patience for his UN man's arguments that the Soviets ("bad fellows" but "responsible people") were in fact "awfully anxious" to help end the war and ready to prod Hanoi toward peace if only Washington stopped bombing.

They told us that before, LBJ countered skeptically, in an obvious allusion to Moscow's assurances before the thirty-seven-day bombing pause a year earlier. "I just think that Hanoi is not ready," he continued. "Everybody thinks that Hanoi is ready; the Pope, the Poles, the Russians, but when you really get down to it, they just cannot make a budge there with this situation as it is."

Implicitly discounting the indication in early December that North Vietnam *had* been ready for the direct contact in Warsaw to confirm the ten points, even without a complete bombing halt, he complained that despite holding back from attacks on sensitive targets for long stretches, "we didn't get one movement, we haven't got one response"—and then, "when the weather cleared up and we hit some targets, railroad yards and truck concentration center they tried to shoot at us."

His voice tinged with indignation, even self-pity, LBJ blasted Hanoi for not responding to his restraint, and faulted himself for not bombing harshly *enough* to save the lives of U.S. troops.

> So I say OK, tell you [North Vietnam] what I'll do. You will not see a plane fly over Hanoi, and you won't see a plane fly over Haiphong. And we got a [10-mile] circle here, and we won't do anything. Now you give me some reciprocate action. And by God, they just shoot down one of my patrols [drones] immediately. They don't do one damn thing and they don't acknowledge it. And you can't hear from them and you ask the Russians why they can't deliver something and they say, well, they're not quite ready yet. Now I haven't been over Hanoi in days. I haven't been over Haiphong in weeks. And I'm just sitting here urging them. But I've got all the weight of the world saying for God's sake quit letting these trucks assemble there and come down and just kill our people. I think I'm going to be tried not by Bertrand Russell but by Mrs. Goldberg for killing her boy without giving him the weapons to protect himself.

Goldberg interjected that the British philosopher, who was organizing an international "war crimes tribunal" to investigate American actions in Vietnam, had "become a nut."

"No but do you heed my point, sir?" Johnson stressed. "I think my great danger is, how can a commander in chief stop his men from fighting unless the other side is just willing to do something?"[128]

Shortly after hanging up with Goldberg, Johnson strolled to the ranch's auditorium to meet reporters. Vietnam dominated the year-in-review press conference from the start, beginning with the latest peace proposals floated by London and Thant. Flanked by an American flag and with his admiring wife Lady Bird seated a few feet away, LBJ pronounced himself "delighted" by Brown's idea of unconditional talks toward a cease-fire, but he effectively rejected Thant's appeal to stop the bombing as a first step. While benignly remarking that he would be "very glad to do more than our part in meeting Hanoi halfway in any possible cease-fire, truce or peace conference negotiations," he ruled out unilateral concessions. "I have said on a number of occasions that we're ready to talk any time, anywhere," he insisted. "But up to this moment, we have heard nothing from the other side. And you can't just have a one-side peace conference, or a one-side cessation of hostilities. Or ask our own boys not to defend themselves, or to tie their hands behind them, unless the other side is willing to reciprocate. Now, I assure you that we're willing to meet them more than halfway if there's any indication of movement on their part."

Johnson also attempted to strike a moderate tone when asked about Salisbury's articles; insisting that he had authorized only military targets, he acknowledged and regretted the inevitable civilian casualties. Still, reporters detected "some sharpness in his voice" as he recalled innocent victims of Communist atrocities and wondered why they did not deserve comparable attention.[129]

Not a word of LBJ's betrayed the slightest belief that Marigold had signified a scintilla of progress toward talks with Hanoi, let alone a real opportunity for peace. Porter's caustic cable, which had arrived that morning from Saigon, fully accorded with LBJ's and his top aides' prevailing skepticism toward the Poles, and their determination to try other methods to communicate with Hanoi (Rostow, for instance, now fixated on a direct presidential letter to Ho).

So far as the Johnson administration was concerned, it was time to consign the failed initiative to history. Kraslow and Loory would note: "The bookkeeping operation was all very tidy. Ben Read was able to take Gronouski's last Marigold cable and close out the Marigold file with the old year."[130]

Conclusion: An Invisible Bridge

It was all over except for the shouting, of which there would be plenty. Yet the definitive DRV rejection of the initiative Trinh conveyed to Siedlecki on December 28 (whose essence Rapacki related to Gronouski two days later) left many questions unanswered. After Dong's withering rebuff to Siedlecki on December 14, had there ever really been a chance to salvage Marigold? Did the 10-mile exclusion zone around Hanoi, the "Christmas present" Gronouski relayed to Rapacki on December 24, have any real prospect of enticing the North Vietnamese back to their earlier willingness to sit at the table in Warsaw?

Most likely not. Unwilling to fault their own actions for the initiative's downfall, U.S. officials, convinced that it was all a Polish scam, would claim that their proposals never received serious consideration in Hanoi, or else seek a scapegoat to explain its ultimate rejection of the Warsaw contact despite the 10-mile offer. Rusk, for instance, in early January 1967 eagerly pounced on a secret report that Tokyo's ambassador in Moscow had imprecisely told his North Vietnamese counterpart on December 23 that Washington was "ready to stop bombing if there were clear prospect of peace conference or reduction in DRV military actions." Because it had never explicitly offered a bombing halt in exchange for a mere promise to talk, the secretary reasoned, perhaps the diplomat's loose talk had led Hanoi astray. Rostow was happy to pass the exculpatory conjecture to LBJ: "Herewith the Japanese-DRV conversation which led Sec. Rusk to think [the North Vietnamese] may have cut off Warsaw gambit to see if they couldn't play for unconditional cessation of bombing in return for general promises to talk."[131]

Blaming Japanese diplomatic incompetence rather than American blunders for Marigold's final failure was comforting, creative, and transparently self-serving, but also highly implausible. Even Bundy confessed the department's "overall impression that DRV is not really treating [the Japanese] channel seriously but simply using it to see if they can get indications of change in [the U.S. government's] position."[132] Even if the DRV ambassador in Moscow actually promptly cabled a compatible account of the talk to Hanoi (which one can hardly take for granted), it defies belief to postulate that the Lao Dong Politburo would base so fateful a decision on so slender, peripheral, and unauthoritative a reading of Washington's bottom line.

After the initiative's collapse turned into a public scandal, and he had returned home, Lodge would peddle the theory that Salisbury was responsible for North Vietnam's definitive slamming of the door on the Warsaw channel. In late 1967, in Washington between assignments, he confided to reporters "on deep background" what he claimed was the State Department's "latest thinking"—that "Hanoi really wanted to talk" in early December 1966, but once Salisbury's stories started appearing, the DRV leaders "copped out, realizing they had a pretty good thing going and could use American public opinion to get a better deal." The rumpus, in other words, "made Hanoi think they did not hold such bad cards after all and had better keep fighting. . . . 'They thought they were something pretty special' after the coverage in the largest newspaper in the United States and thus changed their minds."[133]

To Rusk, Lodge conceded that this "explanation"—which he later privately attributed to Gronouski[134]—was "nothing more than rumors." It was also, of course, a blatant attempt to shift the onus for destroying a chance for peace from Washington and its ill-timed bombings to one of the administration's most despised critics.

But did that necessarily make the theory *wrong*? It actually meshed fairly well with the chronology of Marigold's denouement. Salisbury's first dispatch from Hanoi, the reader will recall, led the *New York Times* on December 25, the same Christmas Sunday that Siedlecki delivered the 10-mile zone proposition, and the clamor over his accounts reverberated around the world precisely as the DRV leadership approved the resounding rebuff that Trinh gave the Poles (and, through them, the Americans) three days later. Hanoi, moreover, hardly shied away from exploiting the controversy for maximum propaganda benefit, claiming that Washington's "acknowledgment" that its bombs sometimes hit civilians "exposed the U.S. imperialists' cruel, aggressive nature and insolent, despicable and deceitful attitude," and unmasked their leaders as "wild, cannibalistic beasts."[135]

Yet the palpable evidence of the Johnson administration's growing discomfort could also have been easily read as bolstering the Polish arguments—relayed in the inter-Politburo message from the PUWP to the VWP—that because Washington faced a "difficult political situation" over the bombings, the moment was "particularly suitable and amenable" for Hanoi to enter into direct talks.[136] More important, there is no indication that Hanoi had ever deviated from its earlier severance of the initiative that Dong conveyed on December 14 to Siedlecki (even before additional bombing that day). While hinting that they did not want to "lock completely the door to talks," DRV officials in Hanoi and Warsaw gave no hint of residual interest in contacts between Quang and Gronouski. No mere tactical device or bargaining position, this hardened position reflected a strategy approved by the Lao Dong Politburo to give greater emphasis to the international diplomatic struggle, but only in the context of fighting while negotiating, in the expectation that decisive military victories would be required before the Americans could be evicted on satisfactory terms; only *then* could *serious* negotiations commence. As the Politburo declared sharply in a resolution debated in late 1966 and unanimously approved by the VWP's Central Committee in January 1967, "On the diplomatic front, the American authorities are using the trick of 'peace negotiations' to deceive world opinion, to hide their plot of stepping up their war of aggression, and to pressure us into negotiations on terms favorable to them with the goal of using talks to win things that they have not been able to win on the battlefield."[137]

In sum, for the DRV to have reversed its earlier decision to break off the Warsaw exchanges on the basis of what it viewed as the belated, grudging, hedged, minuscule, and even insulting U.S. concession of curtailing raids within a limited radius around central Hanoi would have been precisely the sort of confession of weakness or eagerness for talks that had become anathema to the grizzled veteran revolutionary fighters, who believed they had already learned from past mistakes against the French and were determined not to repeat that history. The 10-mile-zone proposition in late December had no chance of reviving Marigold, even with Polish support, whether or not Salisbury unexpectedly and coincidentally showed up in Hanoi.

Yet the chance to move forward had been real. In the fall of 1966, Washington had ever so slightly softened its tune—and perhaps lowered its expectations. In late October in Manila, hoping to impress Gromyko, LBJ had promised a full U.S. military withdrawal from South Vietnam within six months of peace; and in mid-November, nagged by the Italians to come up with "something new" to give Lewandowski to carry to Hanoi, the administration had authorized Lodge to convey terms, including a recognition of the possibility of a neutral South Vietnam, that struck some key Communists who heard them—whether Poles, Soviets, or North Vietnamese—as surprisingly reasonable.

In response, at least some in the DRV leadership, notably Pham Van Dong, were warily willing to explore whether the Lodge proposals might offer an acceptable deal, that is, one assuring a U.S. departure and *eventual* Vietnamese unification under Communist leadership, even if after a potentially lengthy interregnum of a "neutral" South Vietnam. This view prevailed in the VWP's Politburo, albeit narrowly, to authorize the Warsaw contact to confirm the outlines of a plausible interim settlement that might allow the fighting to subside, or at least the opening of serious talks.

The relevant metaphor was a bridge. At about this time, in late 1966, LBJ had launched with much fanfare an initiative to "build bridges" to Eastern European countries, treating them individually rather than lumping them together as Soviet satellites. Yet, quietly, behind the scenes, the most important "bridge-building" effort in Washington's dealings with Moscow's Warsaw Pact allies involved the U.S.–Italian–Polish–North Vietnamese exchanges aimed at coaxing Hanoi into negotiations. In January 1967, Chet Cooper, without explicitly mentioning Marigold, would tell a Canadian diplomat that a formal accord to end the Vietnam War would require erecting an "invisible bridge" between public U.S. and North Vietnamese positions so that both sides could quietly indicate flexibility on a few key points and "come down a few notches." With the intercession of a helpful third party, perhaps an ICC power such as Poland or Canada, such a mutual understanding in advance of formal talks might allow the two enemies' bargaining positions to "gradually come together, even if each side claimed that the other side was in fact meeting its own terms."[138]

Janusz Lewandowski had himself functioned as a kind of "invisible bridge"—hidden from public view, concealing his actions from diplomatic colleagues in the ICC, able to transit between the Communist and capitalist worlds and open a unique communications channel between bitter enemies—and, more important, he had tried to fashion an ethereal span between Washington and Hanoi of the sort Cooper imagined.

For a few fleeting moments, a few men—in Saigon and Warsaw, in Washington, and even in Hanoi—had glimpsed that "invisible bridge," and these leaders on opposite banks of the chasm had even authorized their representatives to approach each other cautiously. Through the fog of war and diplomacy, across barriers of enmity and distrust, in the Polish capital half a world from the fighting,

John Gronouski and Do Phat Quang (and Nguyen Dinh Phuong) came tantaliz-ingly close to meeting, to crossing the bridge, to breaking the taboo on direct, official U.S.-DRV conversations, and to confirming at least provisionally a set of principles for subsequent, higher-level negotiations. Then contingent events had intervened—the preplanned bombings of Hanoi and LBJ's refusal to suspend them; the haggling over the "important differences of interpretation" clause; meteorological vicissitudes; Rapacki's failure to close the deal, despite Pham Van Dong's openings; and, perhaps most fatefully, one or more misunderstandings over what was supposed to have happened on December 6, 1966—and the pre-existing patterns based on achieving basic ends through military struggle reac-quired primacy on both sides.

The invisible bridge had collapsed.

Secret Spats
Talking and Fighting, January 1967

The Americans have not behaved well.

—British diplomat Michael Stewart, January 4, 1967

It is clear that our negotiation is dead, and it was death by murder.
May God forgive those who took such a crushing responsibility
upon themselves!

—Giovanni D'Orlandi, diary entry, January 21, 1967

[The North Vietnamese] haven't thrown us a baseball; . . . it's only
a marshmallow, but it's the first marshmallow they've thrown.

—A U.S. official quoted in the Washington Post, January 31, 1967

Happy New Year? Streets without Joy

As 1967 began, Vietnam was at peace—well, a peace only of the most evanescent sort, another forty-eight-hour truce to mark the turning of the Western calendar. On the first morning of the new year, Giovanni D'Orlandi again meandered through central Saigon, as he had the previous Sunday during the Christmas cease-fire. This time, however, the faces of the people strolling by wore more subdued expressions.

"There is less joy in the streets," he sensed—evoking, perhaps subconsciously, the title of Bernard Fall's epic narrative of the doomed French struggle in Indochina, *Street without Joy*—"very little light-heartedness, greater worries about the future" and especially concerning the fate of the planned cease-fire during the

Vietnamese lunar new year observances little more than a month away. Earlier, hopes had flourished for a "long holiday of peace," an agglomeration of Christmas, New Year's, and Tet truces into one extended calm that might enhance the atmosphere for negotiations. Not only had that idea died, but Ky also cast doubt on future breaks in fighting by angrily denouncing Viet Cong cease-fire violations (more than a hundred in the first twenty-four hours of the latest one, he charged). In other ominous portents, the Italian noted rumors of "looming" government and U.S. ground offensives in the Mekong Delta, and the presence offshore of shiploads of American soldiers waiting to disembark at Vung Tau once the truce expired at seven the next morning.[1]

The Vietnamese, and D'Orlandi, had solid grounds for their apprehensions; 1967 would prove by far the bloodiest year of the war yet. The troop carriers bobbing in the South China Sea helped to lift the number of U.S. forces in Vietnam above 400,000, twice as many as a year before (with others based elsewhere in the region also involved), and the number in the country would approach, then surpass, the original ceiling of 470,000 and hurdle the half-million mark, reaching 525,000 by 1968.[2] Fueled by a belief in both Washington and Hanoi that decisive military struggles were still necessary before negotiations could consolidate an acceptable outcome, clashes in the South (including massive U.S. "search and destroy" missions to root out entrenched Communist strongholds) would intensify, exacting a rising toll in Vietnamese and American lives (virtually doubling the U.S. casualty rate and killing, wounding, dislocating—and alienating—civilians at a steeply rising tempo); and the bombing of the North would likewise expand as the White House loosened targeting restrictions.[3] The grim Vietnam news put LBJ in a funk. "Now is indeed 'the Valley of the Black Pig,'" his wife wrote in her diary. "A miasma of trouble hangs over everything."[4] Yet, for the moment, despite pockets of resistance, most Americans still supported or at least tolerated the war, and notwithstanding internal doubts in some quarters, the Johnson administration exuded confidence that tightening the screws could coerce the Communists into submission: Before returning to Saigon in mid-January, Lodge publicly forecast "very sensational" military gains and substantial political progress for 1967.[5]

As the year began, the White House and Pentagon salivated at a diverse menu of escalatory options, but unresolved diplomatic questions also lingered. A grudging acknowledgement that stepping up military pressure required first making yet another stab at negotiations coexisted with a residual uncertainty about the meaning of the misfired Polish peace bid. Though Marigold seemed defunct, numerous mysteries endured, not merely of recondite historical interest but also with cogent operational implications. Had the Poles and their initiative ever been serious? Should Washington continue to try to communicate with Hanoi through Warsaw, or even—because all three principals remained at their posts, for now—give the Saigon channel another go? Should it look to Moscow, or outside the Soviet Bloc, to fill the job of mediator? Were the North Vietnamese really willing to engage in face-to-face discussions, perhaps even without a prior bombing halt?

Were they even, conceivably—as Rostow, who favored a *direct* secret overture to Ho Chi Minh, speculated to LBJ in early January—"trying to get out of the war, but don't know how"?[6] Or was even more ferocious fighting required before talks could start (or, as Lodge preferred to believe, before Hanoi conceded that the "jig was up" and the insurgency simply melted away)? More immediately, who would get blamed for Marigold's failure, both in diplomatic circles and (once it inevitably leaked) in public opinion, both at home and abroad?

The Empire Strikes Back: Rapacki "Lied Like a Sailor"

On Sunday morning, January 1, 1967—an ocean away from the conflagration that cast a thickening miasma over their national life—millions of bleary-eyed Americans slept, nursed hangovers, attended church, geared up for a strenuous afternoon of televised playoff football (for the right to compete in the first-ever Super Bowl), or otherwise took advantage of the day off. In San Francisco, the groovy epicenter of an emerging "counterculture," concertgoers' ears still rang with the raspy howls of Janis Joplin and the wry chords of Country Joe and the Fish (and their antiwar anthem, "I-Feel-Like-I'm-Fixin'-to-Die Rag": "For it's one, two, three, what are we fightin' for? Don't ask me I don't give a damn, my next stop is Vietnam"). As Haight-Ashbury hippies anticipated the first "Human Be-In" (presaging a "Summer of Love"), a hundred miles to their east, and far to their right, in Sacramento, their sworn enemy Ronald Reagan prepared to take the oath of office at midnight to become California's governor.[7]

Meanwhile, in the contentious establishment capital, Washington, snow covered and momentarily quiescent, Dean Rusk forsook a day of rest. From his Foggy Bottom headquarters, the secretary of state worked the phones, diligently chiseling away at his in-box. (Critics accused Rusk of myriad sins, from execrable judgment to hubris to complicity in war crimes, but not sloth.) At 11:25 a.m.—he had, coincidentally, just roused an aide to get a handle on Gronouski's zloty deal with the Poles[8]—he heard an unexpected voice on the line.

It was Paul Martin, calling from Barbados. The Canadian explained that his ambassador to Washington, Albert Edgar Ritchie, would be requesting an appointment that evening or perhaps the next morning, on a topic so sensitive he could not mention it over the long-distance connection. He hoped Rusk could see him as soon as possible.

Fine, I'll ring him up, Rusk agreed.

Not yet, Martin cautioned, he had not received the pertinent materials but would later in the day.

All right, then, I'll see him first thing in the morning, replied Rusk.

Martin "was most appreciative and was calling to give emphasis to the importance of the message he was sending."[9]

The topic that dared not speak its name was, of course, Marigold. Martin had read the materials that Klaus Goldschlag had delivered from Ottawa to his Caribbean resort—George Ignatieff's telegrams relating U Thant's indiscretion, Marcel Cadieux's analysis, draft instructions for Ritchie—and, foreshadowing his British counterpart's reaction, was "fit to be tied." On a personal note, he felt bitter that in Washington and Paris in late November and mid-December, Rusk had encouraged him to go forward with peace probes but had neglected to mention that Washington was pursuing a separate Polish initiative—or, once that effort collapsed, had not conveyed the slightest hint that Warsaw might not be in the best frame of mind to be enlisted in a new peace effort. And in policy terms, Martin found it "almost impossible to understand" Washington's bombing of Hanoi just as delicate contacts were nearing fruition. Sending these considerations, he instructed Ritchie to get Rusk's side of the story (and urge him to set Thant straight if the Polish version was wrong), and to seek enlightenment on what, if anything, Ottawa should do now in its Vietnam diplomacy.[10]

Monday morning at 10 a.m., Rusk received Ritchie, who laid Ignatieff's revelatory telegrams in front of him and solicited a response. Diplomatically hinting at his boss's displeasure, the ambassador indicated that Martin "had been somewhat surprised not to have had more direct info on talks with Poles, particularly since Poles themselves had probably assumed, in interpreting our own approaches to them, that we were already aware of USA-Polish contacts."[11]

This was Rusk's first intimation that the Poles had leaked not only to the pope but also to the UN secretary-general, and he was not pleased. He insisted that Tomorowicz's account was slanted, inaccurate, and (because it ended in mid-December) incomplete. Remembering Rapacki's fudge a few days before when Gronouski asked him whether the pope had been informed, Rusk added that the Polish foreign minister, supposedly "so fanatically insistent" on secrecy, had "lied to us" twice—"lied like a sailor," according to the Canadian record—"directly as to whether he himself had informed any governments or parties." Rusk firmly denied that the December 13–14 Hanoi bombings had quashed the proposed Warsaw talks and noted acidly that the Polish account omitted the December 7 mortar strike on Tan Son Nhut, "where he himself was just about to land" (two days later), as well as other guerrilla assaults on Saigon during this period.

To Rusk's annoyance, however, Ritchie "did not appear convinced by such arguments." Such attacks in the South were commonplace, the Canadian noted, and perhaps not subject to North Vietnamese supervision. By contrast, the Hanoi raids, obviously approved by Washington, "could create [an] unfortunate impression not only on SecGen but also on many others when contacts with Poles became known." That view, Rusk responded sharply, reflected the double standard that decried U.S. bombing while excusing "what the North Vietnamese and Viet Cong were doing in the South." By the conversation's end, Rusk had the distasteful impression that not only Thant—unreliable in any case—but also Ottawa blamed the Hanoi attacks for ruining a chance for peace and even suspected Washington of contriving support for a new ICC initiative to blur its sabotage of the Polish effort. Even worse, Ritchie indicated that Ottawa considered neither the Poles "mischievous" for letting Thant in on Marigold nor the UN leader "indiscreet" for telling the Canadians.

Rusk had had enough. The next day, he told the president that due to Warsaw's "disturbing" leaks, the "danger is now acute that the pope, U Thant, and the Canadians all believe we were badly in the wrong," and there was a comparably serious peril "that the widening of the circle may lead at any moment to a public disclosure in some fashion highly unfavorable to us." At the weekly senior-level Tuesday lunch, LBJ approved retaliating with a spate of counterbriefings. U.S. officials would give Thant, the pope, the Canadians, and also the British a description of Marigold designed to rebut the Polish claim, still hidden from public view, that the Hanoi bombings and waffling about the ten-point agreement had wrecked a promising peace overture. (Unaware that the UN boss had also leaked to Roger Seydoux, they left the French off the list—leaving uncontested the Polish-crafted version that had reached Paris a few days earlier.)

Not surprisingly, this secret American account emphasized Washington's "totally forthcoming" posture (its good faith and ongoing readiness for secret negotiations or contacts); Warsaw's suspicious conduct (Rapacki's "haggling" over the interpretation clause and "extraordinarily vague" references to Hanoi's role); and the lack of any direct communication from the North Vietnamese. To counter the inevitable charges that the Hanoi bombings had ruined the venture, it stressed the "abnormal wave of special and major" Communist assaults on Saigon during the same period; and it insinuated that the December 13–14 attacks were irrelevant because, according to Rapacki, the North Vietnamese had already (on the 13th) withdrawn the offer to meet in Warsaw.[12] To underline Washington's sincerity, the U.S. summary—unlike the Polish account—extended to the end of December to cover its erection, to no avail, of the 10-mile bombing exclusion zone around Hanoi (in effect "for an indefinite period," at least through the upcoming Tet cease-fire).[13]

Rusk wasted no time putting Thant in the picture, cabling this account to Goldberg to use in briefing him that same afternoon—though, distrusting the UN chief, he asked the ambassador to "read a good deal of the material" but not leave any paper behind. Thant listened to his "recital with close interest." It largely overlapped with the Polish version, he noted, except for Rapacki's view that the U.S. "escalation" by bombing Hanoi in mid-December had spoiled the effort. Using Washington's script, Goldberg heatedly rebutted the charge. Another emerging discrepancy concerned the provenance of the "ten points": Thant recalled that Tomorowicz had emphasized that they reflected Lodge's presentations in mid-November, but Goldberg stressed that they were a Polish formulation. Hoping to undercut Warsaw's credibility, the American noted that the Poles had broken their word by leaking both to the pope and to Derksen in Saigon ("Ambassador Lewandowski is not a discreet diplomat"). Masking his own reaction, Thant promised that he would keep the U.S. disclosure private ("absent any additional dramatic events," he would probably do so, Goldberg predicted), and the two agreed to consult about how they might cooperate to promote negotiations.[14] Informing the pope, too, was relatively straightforward—Reinhardt did the honors in Rome[15]—but handling the Canadians and British entailed complications that were both political and, considering the bruised egos, personal.

Canadian Considerations: "Shades of . . . 1914!"

Ottawa presented the more immediate operational dilemmas. Martin required ongoing input regarding his sputtering ICC initiative with New Delhi; and, more significantly, Victor Moore's imminent farewell visit to Hanoi raised the questions of what, if anything, the Canadian ICC commissioner should be told about Marigold (now that his government knew), and what, if any, U.S. message he might carry.

While Rusk had reaffirmed to Ritchie his general support for the ICC initiative, he and Bundy were more ambivalent about entrusting Moore with full knowledge of Marigold or a mission directly connected to the now-inactive Polish channel. Though they, like Porter in Saigon, trusted Martin and Ottawa more than Rapacki and Warsaw (which was not saying much), they did not want to risk confusing Hanoi by conflating confidential communications.

On the evening of January 4—a few hours after Goldberg, "reading rapidly from a voluminous file," had edified Ignatieff on Marigold[16]—Bundy handed Ritchie the official U.S. account. (The Canadians, unlike Thant, were deemed trustworthy enough to receive the actual document.) Reading it, Ritchie registered one serious reservation: He found neither persuasive nor reassuring the contention that a possible leak precluded canceling the December 13–14 Hanoi bombings. "How was it going to be possible," he asked, "for the USA ever to carry through a secret negotiation of the kind that was going to be needed if there was always a risk that such negotiation might be upset by preordained military operations?" Though not "serious," the leak danger "had to be weighed," Bundy insisted—but he admitted that "this was a very unsatisfactory situation" and that "steps were being taken to permit at least somewhat more timely control."

Bundy gently suggested that Moore, to leave for Hanoi in just a couple of days, "not be fully informed on Marigold"—though of course it was up to Ottawa to decide—so as to avoid divulging to the North Vietnamese a wider awareness of the channel and nixing any slender chance it might be revived. However, he proposed that Moore remind the DRV leaders of Washington's Phase A/B proposal and continued readiness for direct discussions; and, if they complained of "escalation," that there had been no bombing of Hanoi "or any exceptional attacks in general" since December 14.[17]

Martin, however, was fed up with serving as an errand boy for Rusk and Bundy. Already "bitten twice" by their treatment of the Seaborn and Ronning missions, he declined the invitation to once again carry limited and, he judged, not particularly forthcoming U.S. proposals to Hanoi.[18] Instead, Ottawa relayed the gist of Bundy's message to Moore in Hanoi merely for his information. "After careful consideration," Martin explained, "we judged that no useful purpose would be served by a [Canadian] presentation along these lines which would contain nothing that has not already been put to North Vietnamese by others, but would in fact be something substantially less than full basis of USA–[North Vietnam] exchanges through Poles of which as far as North Vietnamese are concerned, we are presumed to be unaware." Sourly, he recalled past experience when Canada had carried a "message" that was "really only carbon copy of what the USA had said earlier to Chinese in Warsaw to be passed to Hanoi," yielding "unproductive" exchanges and a damaged channel. "We did not wish to repeat this experience, especially in present circumstances when it may be possible to develop something useful through commission medium."[19]

Moore's presence in Hanoi amid whispers of peace progress (most prominently a Salisbury interview with Dong in which the premier had allegedly softened the terms for negotiations) generated considerable speculation in both public and diplomatic circles, though U.S. and Canadian officials minimized the trip's significance.[20] In London, Foreign Office aides now aware of Marigold's collapse pondered a report from the British consul-general in Hanoi that Moore was "engaged in clandestine discussions over negotiations"—contrary to Ottawa's private assurances that the timing of his farewell trip ("a piece of routine business") was mere "happenstance." (One Foreign Office aide suspected that the Canadians were resolutely propping up "a cover plan which has been half blown!")[21]

The buzz concealed a more prosaic reality. From Hanoi, Moore reported a "very cordial" yet unremittingly hard-line atmosphere, and he poured cold water on any hopes raised by Salisbury's interview with Dong by noting the still "insoluble question" of Communist participation in a Saigon government between a cease-fire and eventual unification.[22] Moore had hoped to see the premier (to whom he could convey personally Do's regards and desire for a Saigon-Hanoi dialogue) but instead saw Trinh; the Canadian hinted at the Phase A/B formula, but the taciturn foreign minister failed to bite.[23] Similarly, when he related impressions of the Saigon government—Trinh's "Buddha-like silence being for him a warm indication of receptiveness"—its interest in contact only elicited his blasé reply that "we have been in a position to hear what you have said from Rusk, Johnson, and other Americans."[24]

"My impression from all my conversations with the Vietnamese," Moore concluded, "is that Hanoi is standing pat for the time being and indeed that the estimate reported earlier that the [North] will continue its efforts against the South for another six to twelve months may well be the case."[25]

Back in Saigon, Moore dined with Habib, who apologized for the false denials he and Porter had given him in early December about Lewandowski's role in secret peace diplomacy—just following "strict orders," he explained. When the American mentioned that he felt freer to talk now that the State Department had "briefed" the Canadians, Moore could not resist interjecting that actually "it had been the other way around, but did not elaborate."

However, the Canadian had no hard feelings, and he sympathized with Rusk's "doubts as to whether the Poles for their part had dealt frankly with the North Vietnamese." Without explicitly badmouthing his fellow ICC commissioner, he expressed his suspicion "that the Poles were more interested in the exercise for its own sake in order to build up their image but without going to the extent of achieving anything practical because of their wish not to 'offend' Hanoi."[26]

Moore's Foreign Ministry colleagues, however, doubted Washington's explanations. Martin found Bundy's plea that long-planned military operations could not be canceled "just too much to bear," evoking "shades of the Kaiser's mobilization orders in 1914!"[27] Though Ottawa refrained from public criticism (leaking was another story, as discussed below), the episode further soured the foreign minister on LBJ's war. Martin had yearned to succeed Lester Pearson both as Liberal Party boss and prime minister, and the possibility of bringing peace to Vietnam kindled visions of matching the Nobel Peace Prize his rival had won a decade earlier for brokering Middle East peace talks after the Suez Crisis. Now, however, Martin was coming to believe that Washington neither seriously desired negotiations nor took Canada seriously. Later in 1967, he would openly break ranks by backing a unilateral bombing halt as "the starting point in the process of solving the Vietnam problem."[28]

Placating the British: "But Apologize for Nothing!"

Washington had a comparatively easy time assuaging Ottawa's hurt feelings compared with what it took to mollify London and limit harm to the Anglo-American "special relationship," which was already strained over Vietnam. In Ottawa, Pearson, after his lapel-yanking April 1965 run-in with LBJ, had largely left Vietnam diplomatic activism to Martin, but in London, there were *two* sulking statesmen with ruffled sensitivities to smooth.

On Tuesday evening, January 3, 1967—just as, across the Atlantic, LBJ authorized Rusk to begin quietly disseminating the U.S. version of Marigold—Brown happened to be in Rome, dining with Fanfani at—where else?—the Villa Madama, the setting exactly two months earlier of the lunch that had set the affair in motion. Swapping views on the war, the Italian foreign minister flattered his British counterpart on his recent peacemaking labors ("a series of 'hammer blows' at a situation which had so far proved unyielding") but, disputing Brown's contention that "developments favourable to a cease fire were now perhaps beginning in Hanoi," assessed North Vietnam as "completely intransigent" on the basis of the Italian Communist Party's delegation's recent visit. However, despite frustration with their mutual superpower patron, Fanfani did not confide the secret exchanges involving his Saigon ambassador.[29]

A few hours later, however, Rusk began lifting the veil. A suitable occasion to come clean with London presented itself that Tuesday evening, when word arrived that the *New York Times'* Harrison Salisbury had the day before interviewed Dong, contents unknown. Though refusing to disclose details to the isolated British consul, John Colvin, Salisbury conveyed the impression from other "ministerial-level" contacts that Hanoi "urgently" sought negotiations and was ready to exchange "military concessions" for a bombing halt and troop freeze. Always eager to be helpful (and relevant), Brown flashed this tidbit to Washington for Rusk—if true, it closely resembled the package he had taken to Moscow, and must be taken "extremely seriously"—along with an offer to facilitate secure communications between the State Department and Salisbury while the latter remained in Hanoi.[30]

Though skeptical, Rusk affably told the embassy's number two man, Sir Michael Stewart, that London should notify Salisbury that the U.S. government would welcome his full account of any "ministerial" conversations, and that he (or the North Vietnamese, for that matter) could employ the British to send any confidential messages to Washington. Having dispensed with the nominal agenda, he dropped his Marigold bombshell. Handing Stewart the secret account, Rusk—"a good deal embarrassed," the Briton thought—said he "deeply regretted" not informing Brown when the two had met, but his hands had been tied by the insistence of the Poles and North Vietnamese on total secrecy. Trying to contain the swelling chatter, Rusk expressed his hope that Brown would not mention the Polish business to "Signor Fanfani," although he could hardly expect him to profess ignorance if the Italian brought it up.[31]

This post hoc disclosure of Marigold bashed open a beehive of British resentment. Harold Wilson and George Brown envisioned themselves both as peacemakers and the Americans' "special" confidants, and thus, in their eyes, this belated revelation meant that Washington had left them in the lurch by allowing Brown to carry the "Phase A / Phase B" formula to the Kremlin in late November while oblivious to the Polish channel to Hanoi. Justifiably concerned at how the hot-tempered foreign secretary would react, Bundy called in Stewart to ply him with arguments to "cool [Brown] off."[32] Stewart, himself a former foreign secretary, heard him out but was not impressed. "The Americans have not behaved well," he wrote London after warning Rusk's aide that Brown would undoubtedly feel "pretty sore about being treated this way."[33] Indeed he did: "I was furious, and so was the Prime Minister, to discover that instead of bringing a bright new plan to the Russians, we were being used to peddle ideas that had been put to them already."[34]

Forwarding Stewart's telegrams, an aide lamented to Brown that Washington had "put you in a false position" when speaking with the Russians—and now it seemed clear why they had been so obdurate.[35] From Rome, Brown flashed Rusk a bitter (by reserved British standards) personal note: "Thank you for this information. But, though I realise your difficulties, I must say I wish you had told me this before I went to Moscow. To put it mildly, a very valuable opportunity may have been lost. It is not surprising that the Russians were so puzzled." Keeping a stiff upper lip, he expressed confidence that Rusk would keep him "fully in the picture" in the event of any "further opportunity."[36]

At 10 Downing Street, dismay also ran deep. Reading the "disheartening" telegrams, a top aide fumed to Wilson at the Americans' "disconcerting lack of frankness with us." Unmoved by Rusk's protestation that secrecy precluded more timely candor, and unaware that it was actually Warsaw's leaking that had prompted Washington finally to open up, Michael Palliser (and later Wilson) erroneously inferred that "Rusk's hand . . . had been forced" due to the fact that Salisbury had "talked to our man in Hanoi"—otherwise London would still be in the dark. From the U.S. version, the British also gathered that Lewandowski had imprecisely relayed Washington's stand to Hanoi, particularly the Phase A/B proposition, sowing confusion and crossing Brown's wires in Moscow. "All in all, a rather gloomy story of muddle, lack of [U.S.] confidence [in us] and incompetence (either by the Pole or by Ambassador Lodge in explaining the American position to him)," Palliser minuted the prime minister. "I think the Foreign Secretary will have good reason to feel pretty aggrieved at the way he has been treated by Rusk."[37]

Wilson also felt pretty aggrieved at what he termed "the farce of the Lewandowski affair," but he hesitated before protesting directly to LBJ—like Pearson, he had learned a painful lesson about detonating "an outburst of Texan temper." Almost two years before, when Washington had started bombing North Vietnam, Wilson had telephoned LBJ to suggest flying over to consult (as Clement Attlee had rushed to see Truman after the Chinese intervened in Korea); the U.S. president not only ridiculed the notion of "jump[ing] across the Atlantic every time there is a critical situation" but had also told Wilson to mind his own business: "I won't tell you how to run Malaysia, and you don't tell us how to run Vietnam."[38]

This time, rather than risk provoking LBJ's wrath, Wilson waited to huddle with Brown upon his return from Rome, and then summoned U.S. ambassador David K. E. Bruce to let off steam. Washington had treated him "like a second-class citizen," he groused to the urbane diplomat, who had not seen him so angry "in a long time." Venturing a baseball metaphor, Wilson complained that the Americans had "put [Brown] in to bat" in Moscow in an "impossible" position, "and it was even more unacceptable that the Italians—and even the Italian foreign minister, who had no 'need to know'—knew the facts, whereas the foreign secretary, who had to deal with 'some of the toughest eggs in the business[,]' did not." Brown's "relatively temperate message" to Rusk had, if anything, understated the gravity of the situation: The "intolerable" U.S. behavior had "raised a major issue of confidence in relations between the foreign secretary and himself and the president and Mr. Rusk." To restore Anglo-American trust, he insisted that Washington update him fully before Kosygin visited London in the second week of February, coincident with the Tet truce. Perhaps, Wilson suggested, Chet Cooper, a shadows man familiar since his stint in London in the late 1950s as a CIA liaison to British intelligence, could come over—but preferably *not* Rostow, whom the premier's restive public might perceive as carrying White House orders to a branch office before the big boy came to town.[39] Determined to let LBJ know directly of his displeasure, yet gingerly discarding more discursive drafts, Wilson laconically wired: "I want you to know that, as I have told David Bruce privately, I am seriously concerned at a matter which is, I think, pretty fundamental to our relationship."[40]

Brown also stewed, unappeased by Rusk's "disappointingly disingenuous" response (there was "nothing" to tell him before he went to Moscow, because Lewandowski had not yet returned from Hanoi) to his own note. Baloney, Brown thought, but instead of riposting frontally, he had an aide, Murray MacLehose, fill in his ambassador in Washington, Sir Patrick Dean, on the background: The perfidious Americans had not only misled a supposedly trusted partner ("this is what really hurts him") but had also perhaps garbled a crucial communication to the DRV. Rusk's blithe excuse simply would not do, because "it could have made all the difference" if Brown had known of the parallel Polish channel, permitting him to prove his bona fides to Kosygin and the Kremlin as the authentic and authoritative bearer of U.S. proposals; instead, the Soviets were left "needlessly puzzled" and convinced that the Americans had failed to take Brown into their confidence. As MacLehose put it,

> In the long run, and after they had time to check it all up (and no doubt to grill Lewandowski), they have probably got it all straight now, and realized that Lewandowski muffed it, and [Brown] got it right. Perhaps as a result of this belated realization, his stock may even have risen rather than the reverse in Moscow, and the extent of the generous U.S. concession which he conveyed may have now got through. But the risk which the Americans ran, both to their own interests and to his reputation, by their lack of frankness, strikes us as amazing.

"We do not want an argument," MacLehose further explained, "but the State Department must not be allowed to pass off the impropriety of this action in this way."[41]

After Dean conveyed how "deeply hurt" and "offended" Brown was by Rusk's lack of candor, the American secretary of state tried to pacify him by claiming that Brown's message, not Lewandowski's, "was the clear and solid one we were sure would get through" to Hanoi, and thanking him for a job well done. The United States, he insisted, "recognized [an] absolute obligation never to put [the] British in [a] false position and hence to provide them with all information they needed for any contacts they had." (Actually, Rusk doubted Brown's discretion if he *were* told of the Lewandowski matter but preferred not to debate the point.)[42]

The White House was even less keen to coddle London, but Rostow wearily admitted that it had to be done. "I do not believe that we owe it to the British to keep them fully informed on every move in this game when 500,000 U.S. men are under arms and the British fighting contribution is zero," he wrote LBJ. "Nevertheless, keeping the British tolerably happy is part of the job."[43] Because he regarded all but an embryonic contact with the DRV Embassy in Moscow "as pretty thin stuff" anyway, he recommended that the president authorize Cooper to enlighten and placate Wilson and Brown in order to patch up relations and put them in the know before Kosygin showed up; LBJ approved grudgingly, scrawling next to his check marks "But apologize for nothing!"[44]

Accordingly, on January 18, en route to Paris,[45] Harriman's aide-de-camp stopped in London. "Friends or not," Cooper recalled, "the temperature inside 10 Downing Street when I arrived . . . was as chilly as it was in St. James Park outside." In his full-day "stroking exercise," he briefed Brown and Wilson on the rise and fall of Marigold (now "dormant, if not dead") and other ongoing peace moves, earnestly reassured them that Washington would apprise them in the future to the maximum extent possible, and promised close coordination concerning the Kosygin summit. Cooper found Brown—known for his acute allergy to "any real or imagined slight," along with his hard drinking—"somewhat tense and very sober (i.e., serious)" and "still troubled" by Rusk's treatment, but eventually he settled down. To soothe an outwardly "relaxed and cordial" Wilson, Cooper stressed the "total 'clampdown' on security" surrounding the Polish matter—even Harriman and most U.S. ambassadors had been cut out, so the British had good company—and termed LBJ "in a 'psychotic' state about leaks not only in regard to top secret matters such as these but over anything that he wished to keep confidential." Cooper contrasted Washington's esteem for London's competence in handling sensitive Vietnam exchanges with its dim regard for Warsaw—"no doubt" Lewandowski "had mishandled the affair," leaving Rusk scrambling "to correct the mistakes in the ten points." Deriving the sad story's moral, Wilson concluded that Vietnam peacemaking "was not a task to be entrusted to amateurs." To assure seamless consultation with Washington during Kosygin's visit, when he hoped to retest the waters for cooperation with his Geneva cochair, Wilson requested that Cooper return to London before the Soviet arrived and remain on call throughout his stay.[46]

All this tea and sympathy, camaraderie, and inside dope seemed to work wonders, at least for the moment. "All is well," Cooper cabled. "No apologies from me. No abuse from Brown. No whining from PM."[47]

＊ ＊ ＊

With respect to Saigon, in contrast, Washington felt no compulsion to circulate its Marigold account, but judged it prudent to tell Ky just enough to "mitigate" any leak. Keeping the exchange "low key," Porter sent Habib to tell Tran Van Do that Washington was "receiving a number of third-country messages sometimes based on conversations with DRV representatives," apparently part of a campaign to stop the bombing rather than genuinely seek peace. The foreign minister agreed that

North Vietnam was simply probing and praised U.S. steadfastness. "It was still premature to expect a change of attitude in Hanoi," he judged, "but sooner or later this would happen."[48] Habib did not explicitly mention the Polish connection, nor did Do let slip that he, too, was trafficking with the enemy via Lewandowski.

Marigold Sidelined: "Not Yet a 'Dead Duck'"?

Was the Warsaw contact (and with it, the Lewandowski-Lodge-D'Orlandi channel) really dead? Yes and good riddance, felt Rusk and Bundy, who found dealing with the Poles (and Italians) exasperating and futile, who correctly sensed that the president shared these sentiments, and who would shed no tears at seeing the whole business consigned to the morgue of departmental archives.

But one coroner refused to sign the death certificate. Just to be on the safe side, Rusk cautioned Johnson on January 3 that, "even though Rapacki assumes Marigold is dead, it is possible that Soviet intervention could bring about some forward motion."[49] Right on cue, hints appeared to substantiate this possibility. That day, Zinchuk affirmed to a top McNamara aide that the Polish endeavor was "serious" and had "real promise" before the bombings wrecked it. Over lunch at the Federal City Club near the White House, the Soviet chargé d'affaires told Assistant Secretary of Defense John T. McNaughton that "after a little time things might resume again"—the proper "environment" (i.e., "if we don't escalate and if we lay off Hanoi") might tilt the balance in the North Vietnamese leadership back toward moderates who favored negotiations. "I asked him whether he thought the Poles had, by the recent exercise, destroyed themselves as middlemen. He said no." In sum, Zinchuk implied that "Poland may be back in the act and that the Soviets themselves may play a role."[50] The next afternoon, in a lengthy rehash of Marigold, Dobrynin conveyed a similar impression to Rusk.[51] Teased, Bundy told Ritchie on January 7 that the "whole project was not yet a 'dead duck'"[52]

The Soviets' seemingly forthcoming attitude encouraged Washington to imagine Moscow as a channel to Hanoi—both to relay communications via the North Vietnamese Embassy in the USSR capital and, perhaps, to test Kremlin mediation, especially with Thompson about to arrive as ambassador. Moscow's endorsement of Marigold's authenticity did not, however, revive Washington's appetite to reengage with the Poles—as the frustrated but still eager Gronouski and the engagé Italians in Rome and Saigon would soon discover.

✳ ✳ ✳

On January 4, Gronouski—appalled by Porter's scornful New Year's Eve cable from Saigon advising Washington to ditch the Warsaw channel—fired off a fervent rebuttal: References to "Rapacki's Polish minuet" and "procrastination" were "understandable in light of frustrations we all feel," but the view they implied was inaccurate, insupportable, and unacceptable, and the recommendation to switch to a different mediator was misguided. Gronouski attributed Marigold's ultimate demise not to Polish deceit but to Hanoi's rejection of the revised U.S. position that he had presented on December 24 (the 10-mile zone), which he believed Warsaw found satisfactory: "I submit that the Poles had no reason on their own initiative to delay that agreement ten minutes."

Despite firmly supporting Hanoi, the Poles saw stopping the fighting to be in their own interests, Gronouski argued. Why? Their plausible motives ranged from superpower distraction from European security issues; to the drain on the Polish economy of aid to North Vietnam; to fear that the Sino-Soviet split, exacerbated by the violence, could prompt Moscow to sign a Soviet–West German security deal detrimental to Poland; to the Southeast Asian conflict's potential to spark a broader East/West clash. For these reasons, plus his own "subjective judgment that Rapacki personally is genuinely desirous of bringing this war to an end," Gronouski rejected Porter's claim that the Poles had acted in an obstructionist or "unsatisfactory" manner.

Moreover, Gronouski maintained, Porter's preference for a noncommunist mediator missed the point. It was true that Canada or another U.S. ally or friend might be "more trustworthy from our point of view. But for this very reason, they would also be even less effective than Poles were in convincing Hanoi." Persuaded that Warsaw had tried earnestly but failed to reel Hanoi in, Gronouski suggested that Washington consider Moscow, because the "best hope" of locating a capable interlocutor lay in the "Communist world (although I would not completely exclude from consideration de Gaulle and U Thant)."[53]

The next day Gronouski called on Michałowski for an "informal chat" to review, at times emotionally, recent events. Told frankly that some U.S. officials doubted the "sincerity of Polish effort," particularly given the failure to produce a DRV representative, Michałowski stressed "with some feeling" that Warsaw had "put heavy pressure on Hanoi and in fact put [its] prestige . . . on [the] line." "Believe me," he insisted, even after the early December raids, "we talked to them several times a day to keep pressure on them and convince them." But the December 13–14 bombings had "undercut our whole argument, destroyed that little bit of confidence that existed in Hanoi about intentions of [the United States], and left us wide open to charges of being completely naïve." The 10-mile zone failed to compensate for the earlier actions, which he would never understand—but, the Pole added, "this is past history, I guess."

For his own part, Michałowski prodded Gronouski to discover why the fatal Hanoi bombings had occurred, despite Warsaw's repeated warnings and his "emphatic and personal assurances" of LBJ's desire for talks. Unaware of the true story, and still fervently convinced of LBJ's sincerity, the American unwittingly led the Pole astray, fostering a legend that would later cloud the record:

> Gronouski dodged the question by hiding behind state secrets. However, in the course of a lengthy discussion, during which I would return to the issue, I could

figure out from various and out-of-context sentences that the bombings on 13 and 14 December took place against the instructions of both Johnson and McNamara. Gronouski talked with McNamara many times on 23 December. He [McNamara] got angry at the American military command in Saigon, which although was not formally informed about the ongoing talks, knew about them from the intelligence and continued to carry out its work in the framework of overall right to do the [military] operations. McNamara did not inform Saigon, because he was afraid that (General Nguyen Cao) Ky would find out about the negotiations.

Still grasping for a way to move forward despite the inevitable "peaks and valleys," Gronouski floated a new idea, his own: that, in the absence of direct U.S.-DRV talks, the Poles themselves propose "specific, verifiable" measures Hanoi might take in response to a total bombing halt along the lines of the Phase A/B package that Washington had been dangling since November. Though dubious, Michałowski promised to consider it over a cup of coffee with Rapacki, and Gronouski—disregarding the Pole's skepticism—asked the State Department to supply "de-escalation alternatives" that the Poles could transmit to North Vietnam.[54]

The Italians, too, labored to reanimate the inert initiative. From Rome, Fanfani again pressed Rapacki to urge Hanoi to produce some "sign of goodwill" in response to a bombing halt, to "overcome the wall of mistrust that still blocks the beginning of direct contacts." Mirroring Gronouski's hopes, Rome's foreign minister groped for some magic formula that could rouse Marigold—perhaps, he ventured to D'Orlandi, Lewandowski might be empowered on his next trip to Hanoi to negotiate "a double series of events to prepare direct contacts, and namely on the part of the United States, an increasing reduction of the bombed areas to the north of the 17th Parallel and on the part of Hanoi an increasing intensity of goodwill gestures proportional to the importance and times of the reduction of the bombed areas."[55]

D'Orlandi dutifully purveyed these suggestions when Habib visited him in the hospital (for a checkup) on January 5, but the Americans were distinctly diffident. No doubt the Italian wants to get back in the act, but we did nothing to encourage him, Porter assured Washington, terming Fanfani's scheme "curiously naive." More politely, Habib advised D'Orlandi to await Lodge's return to Saigon in a couple of weeks before making any moves with the Pole, and he added "confidentially" that "without [Fanfani's] intervention, the initiative would already be dead and buried."[56]

D'Orlandi had no better luck pitching his boss's concept the next day to Lewandowski over lunch. After the Italian offered to telegraph Lodge to accelerate his return if the Pole agreed to press Hanoi, Lewandowski unleashed a "lengthy diatribe."[57]

"In a very sorrowful manner," Lewandowski explained that there was no point in summoning Lodge back early because Washington's conduct indicated either "bad faith" or deep divisions; either way, he would lack useful instructions. More-over, the latest ideas had completely destroyed the basic premise of their conver-sations during the past six months, which envisioned a "comprehensive" deal rather than "little limited agreements." And the Pole listed fresh reasons for doubt: Belying Lodge's repeated assurances that the tripartite Saigon conversations con-stituted the primary conduit to Hanoi, "it appears that we were one of many channels"—Harriman in Algiers, Goldberg at the UN, overtures toward the Sovi-ets and even, he added resentfully, the NLF and Beijing. Lewandowski seemed rattled, D'Orlandi sensed, by hints that Washington was edging closer to Beijing (Moscow's worst nightmare, given renewed credence by news that U.S. and People's Republic of China authorities had amicably arranged for the U.S. Navy to repatriate a boatload of Chinese fishermen it had rescued during a storm in the Tonkin Gulf). The Pole also seemed miffed that after Lodge had declined his re-peated offers to put him in touch with the NLF, the CIA had evidently gone ahead and established such contacts (achieving the release of two American civilian contractors captured on the road between Saigon and Vung Tau the previous May).[58]

To Lewandowski, all this activity buttressed his impression that "the U.S. gov-ernment wants to make a show of its desire to negotiate, but as soon as an agree-ment is within view, it torpedoes it." In such circumstances, he "absolutely does not feel like going to Hanoi with proposals of this type (that of the 10 miles)." After all, Washington could technically abide by its commitment and simultane-ously hit Haiphong. Only a complete bombing halt, he maintained, could foster suitable conditions to try again.

D'Orlandi tried to rebut his friend's arguments, but his heart was not really in it; the Pole was probably right, he reflected. "The more I think over the mat-ter, the clearer it is that we were one of the many channels through which the Americans had wanted to test their opponent without a real desire to negotiate. The little agreements concluded either with the NLF or with the Chinese are very much indicative of this mentality of theirs which has not yet understood that at this point one must negotiate in earnest. In any case, it is a big dis-appointment!"[59]

Dead duck or not, even as Gronouski and the Italians tried to resuscitate Mari-gold, Washington effectively lowered it into the grave. At a January 5 meeting, the secret negotiations group—including Harriman, Bundy, Cooper, and Lodge—"generally agreed that, in the Marigold operation, Hanoi was trying to see how far it could go in getting U.S. concessions before being confronted with the necessity of talking to us." Though Lodge exempted Lewandowski from censure (he prob-ably felt "let down" by Warsaw), officials suspected that "Rapacki himself may have been less than forthright in his handling of the talks."[60]

The next day, the State Department brusquely shot down Gronouski's trial balloon and instructed him to avoid any new initiatives via the Poles.[61] "I . . . got slapped down pretty hard," he later rued.[62] More gently, stressing thanks for past labors and undiminished ardor for "substantive discussions" with Hanoi, Rusk also (via Frederick Reinhardt) requested that Fanfani lay off the Polish channel.[63]

The Italians, however, were not ready to call it quits. A day after receiving word from Rome that the Americans wanted to shelve the channel, at least pending Lodge's return to Saigon, D'Orlandi hosted Lewandowski for dinner and their weekly chess match. To his surprise, the Pole expressed renewed, albeit wary, interest in reprising his earlier role. On his next visit to Hanoi in a few weeks, he could survey prospects for "eventually picking up the conversation which was interrupted" and carry any new ideas Lodge brought from Washington to test whether the chaos in Beijing had made the DRV leaders "even more receptive to the idea of negotiations." Unlike American officials, however, who considered the 10-mile zone a gesture that was more than sufficient, the Pole pressed for a further "manifestation of U.S. goodwill."

A prime reason for believing that action might be timely was Lewandowski's view, based on MSZ experts, that China's turmoil was growing ever more serious, perhaps even presaging "the real and actual break-up of the state, party and armed forces apparatus." Still, Lewandowski worried that Washington might try to exploit the upheaval to make common cause with Beijing against Moscow, rather than focus on a settlement with Hanoi. In that case, he told the Italian, "then the two of us would not have anything left to do," and the Japanese could inherit the secret mediation portfolio.[64]

The Pole, it appears, was just following orders to keep his contact alive rather than expressing authentic faith in the feasibility of progress in Hanoi. Nevertheless, his words nourished both Fanfani's and D'Orlandi's wan hopes that, despite Washington's reticence, they could perform an encore of the three-way Saigon drama once the missing lead actor—Lodge—retook the stage.

* * *

Shortly after this conversation, Lewandowski found support from a singularly eminent authority for his hypothesis that the Chinese situation was tempting Washington to ratchet up the military pressure on Hanoi. Upon being named ICC commissioner, the Pole, a voracious reader, had started consuming the relevant literature, and in Saigon he devoured Bernard Fall's acclaimed accounts of the Viet Minh's triumph over its European colonizers—especially *Hell in a Very Small Place* (about the siege of Dien Bien Phu) and *Street without Joy*. The French-born, United States–based analyst's military expertise, informed by experience as a teenage Resistance fighter during World War II, garnered widespread respect, and his bitter dissections of French mistakes profoundly impressed Lewandowski. Some U.S. officials, however, distrusted Fall, particularly since his prescient warnings in 1962 (after interviewing Ho in Hanoi) against the dangers of seeking a military rather than a political solution in Vietnam; nor did his trenchant criticism as U.S. involvement grew endear him to hawks.[65]

In December 1966, despite persistent health woes and his own and his wife's "sense of foreboding," Fall, on sabbatical from his post as a professor at Howard University in Washington, returned to Vietnam to conduct additional hazardous onsite field research.[66] In Saigon, he stayed with a fellow French expatriate expert (and veteran), the *Newsweek* photojournalist François Sully, who had stayed behind after most of his compatriots fled Indochina and had established himself as perhaps the most seasoned member of the resident press corps; new arrivals sought him out to ingest the conflict's flavor and history, catch a "fill" before deadline, or sample the latest gossip.

So did Lewandowski: Sully quickly became his most valuable source among local journalists. (It was he who tipped the Pole off to clandestine Saigon-NLF contacts, authorized by Thieu and approved by the Americans, regarding the holiday truces.[67]) Lewandowski remembered the *Newsweek* correspondent, with whom he would dine every month or two, as not only "perfectly oriented . . . (he knew all people)" but also, like D'Orlandi (who sometimes joined them), intensely sympathetic to the suffering of ordinary Vietnamese.[68]

Sully told Lewandowski about his houseguest, and one evening in mid-January, the Pole visited his "wonderful flat" in central Saigon, near the bustling Le Loi traffic circle and convenient to the popular Givral Coffee Shop, which sometimes supplied pastries for his gatherings. During an off-the-record dinner party, the Pole reported, Fall attributed to the Chinese events the emergence of "a new, significant stiffening" in the U.S. posture toward the war. The internal chaos induced by the Cultural Revolution, he reported, had spurred Washington's hopes that a paralyzed, distracted Beijing would passively accept North Vietnam's evisceration; and this belief, in turn, "took the wind out of the sails of those critics within the administration who pointed to the danger of getting embroiled in [a] land war with the PRC." In Fall's view, popular antiwar sentiment in American society was insufficient to curb the escalatory tendencies that Rusk and McNamara were "decisively" urging on LBJ ("until the entire area becomes occupied"), but he predicted that the conflict's financial costs would soon "cause some serious troubles for Johnson."

So Lewandowski cabled Warsaw on January 17.[69] A month later, Fall was dead, the victim of a land mine while recording observations during a foot patrol with a platoon of Marines on the "street without joy" in northern South Vietnam. In 1971, Sully, too, would perish covering the war, killed in a helicopter crash.

* * *

Washington had firmly relegated Marigold to the sidelines, but, like wispy subatomic particles, two other Vietnam peace initiatives involving Poland unexpectedly flickered to life.

The Death of Narcissus:
"Our Hopes Are . . . Completely Deflated"

First came a seeming reversal of fortune in the Narcissus channel, the proposal for a mini-ICC gathering in New Delhi, which had been left for dead in late December after Rapacki had cold-shouldered Indian and Canadian entreaties to attend. "In light of what we now know"—that is, Marigold—"it is not at all surprising that the Poles backed away," judged a British Foreign Office aide in a secret obituary for the "Martin Plan."[70]

Yet, mysteriously, the corpse suddenly developed a pulse. On January 4 at the UN, Ignatieff speculated to Goldberg that the Poles might yet attend a tripartite session in New Delhi, though only in conditions of "absolute secrecy and on understanding unanimity rule prevails," and probably not until February or March, after a new ambassador settled in.[71] That same evening in the Indian capital, however, at a farewell dinner thrown by his Yugoslav colleague, Przemysław Ogrodziński spoke favorably to his Canadian counterpart, Roland Michener, about the idea of a quiet three-way ICC gathering at the Indian Foreign Ministry, and said that he had postponed his impending departure by a week or so in order to participate.[72] A few days later, at another going-away party, the Indian Foreign Ministry's director-general, T. N. Kaul, "informally" invited Michener to join him together with Ogrodziński, who was said to have already agreed on January 10 "for discussion of possible commission initiatives as recently proposed by Indians."[73]

Kaul had extra reason to hope that India was, suddenly, seizing center stage in secret Vietnam diplomacy. On January 4, the DRV consul-general in New Delhi had told him that "if America stops bombing of North Vietnam unconditionally and indefinitely, this would lead to cessation of hostilities and other steps." Passing the exchange to Washington, the Indians insisted that the consul's comments —warmly endorsed by Moscow—amounted to "more than a whisper" and urged a positive reply; Bundy puckishly code-named the channel Nirvana, but the State Department took no immediate action.[74] At the same time, DRV officials hinted publicly at more flexibility; besides Dong's interview with Salisbury, Hanoi's Paris-based representative, Mai Van Bo, a diplomatic focal point, declared that if the United States "definitively and unconditionally" stopped the bombing, his government would "examine and study" its proposals.[75]

Connecting the apparent positive Polish shift on the New Delhi meeting to the recent DRV public statements, Michener tasted the delectable emotions that Gronouski had savored a month earlier. Keen to play his part in a move toward peace, the diplomat—soon to be named Canada's governor-general—cabled Martin seeking "your guidance as soon as possible for what might be the beginning of unanimous and constructive action by the Commission countries."[76]

Convinced that the consultation might really occur, the Canadians notified Washington, which was markedly less euphoric. Downgrading the recent DRV utterances (nice mood music, but nothing new), Cooper warned that any ICC call for a bombing halt as a first step toward negotiations—as Thant had urged and New Delhi favored—would destroy the body's credibility (such as it was) among U.S. officials: "Unless some new formula could be devised which neither he nor anyone else has yet been able to think of, a mere rehash of previous appeals would be most unhelpful and might impede ability of Commission powers to play [a] constructive role."[77]

Washington did not fully trust *any* of the three participants in the proposed New Delhi meeting, but it need not have worried. From Warsaw—after hearing Quang "decisively" condemn the Indian-Canadian proposition and endorse Poland's reservations—Michałowski had cabled Ogrodziński on January 6 to eschew any "talks of the 'three' even at the ambassadorial level."[78] On learning that the envoy had already told Kaul that he would attend[79]—the messages crossed in the ether—Warsaw ordered him to stay away ("cover yourself with lack of instructions"). "Trilateral talks in Delhi do not suit us," Naszkowski explained. "We assess the initiative as a dishonest attempt to pull us into a situation advantageous to the partners [Canada and India] to achieve their own aims."[80]

The deputy foreign minister mentioned the danger that Ottawa and New Delhi would exploit the meeting for propaganda purposes, but fear of irking Hanoi undoubtedly dictated Warsaw's refusal to take part. After Marigold's failure, DRV officials had politely refrained from criticizing or second-guessing the Poles to their faces. Trinh even seemed "relaxed" in early January when Siedlecki called on him to deliver Rapacki's cable relating his delivery of the final rejection of the 10-mile zone to the U.S. ambassador. ("How did Gronouski react?" was his first question.)[81] Nevertheless, acutely aware of their vulnerability to charges of naïveté or worse for promoting talks with the imperialist aggressors, the Poles considered their status in Hanoi shaky and hardly wanted to add offense.

Ogrodziński put up a bit of a struggle. At a trilateral session, he would gladly relate any arguments that Warsaw provided to decline participation in an ongoing dialogue, and in any case his impending departure would "interrupt the issue." But, he cabled, simply refusing to see the Canadian at Kaul's would insult New Delhi's Foreign Ministry, and leaving town without some kind of conversation with the senior Indian official would be "indecent."[82]

Naszkowski offered the chagrined ambassador a modest fig leaf to cover his embarrassment: He could tell Kaul that the "three" could keep their appointment, but only so he could convey Warsaw's stand. The Poles were glad to consult bilaterally with their ICC partners, but special collective meetings were out.[83]

When Ogrodziński saw Kaul to tell him the news, the Indian tried to change his mind, stressing that "pressures must be multiplied" so the Tet holiday marked the onset of peace and displaying (but not handing over) a draft three-way appeal to Washington to stop the bombing of North Vietnam that the ICC countries might issue if they met. But instructions were instructions, so the Pole broke the date with Michener.[84] After hearing from Kaul that the rendezvous was off again, the jilted Canadian sought out the Pole at his home for an explanation. Though unaware of Marigold's details, Ogrodziński gave the reply that suited Warsaw's (and Hanoi's) stiffer stand: As long as the Americans kept bombing (despite knowing "quite well" that a halt would elicit a positive response), the Poles would not press North Vietnam, and saw no point in raising unrealistic expectations.[85]

"Our hopes for some unanimous action here are completely deflated," Michener dejectedly telegraphed.[86] In Ottawa, a Foreign Ministry official concluded that Ogrodziński "has had [his] fingers burned."[87] And in Washington, Bundy framed the episode as another footnote to undergird his thesis that the Poles were scheming to extract a bombing halt from the Americans, not seeking peace.[88] When New Delhi proved unable to resist trying to convert the diplomatic flop into a peacemaking coup—a Foreign Ministry spokesman "went out of his way to tell reporters" that Indian, Canadian, and Polish representatives, after active consultations, had agreed to meet "at a suitable place and a mutually convenient time"—the self-serving and distorted leak not only put a nail in Narcissus' coffin but also undercut "Nirvana" and accomplished the singular feat of uniting the two other ICC members, along with Washington and Hanoi, in annoyance.[89]

Down the Primrose Path?
"See the Marketplace in Old Algiers . . ."

Around this time, Chet Cooper, who had a penchant for vivid phrases, mused that Washington and Hanoi might need to work out "some very quiet and private deal 'under a palm tree'" before they could negotiate a more formal pact to end the war.[90] And as an exotic tropical setting for such stealthy conversations, it was hard to beat the ancient, intrigue-laden, bullet-scarred, sun-dappled port city of Algiers on the southern shores of the Mediterranean. Though Algeria's leaders were barely four years removed from their own triumph over French colonialism after a savage eight-year war, and though they were still apostles of revolutionary nationalism, proclaiming solidarity with the Vietnamese struggle against American "imperialism," they had turned in a more pragmatic direction following the June 1965 bloodless military coup that had toppled Ben Bella, the first post-independence ruler, and installed defense minister Houari Boumediène as the new president. Even as it continued to radiate radical rhetoric, Boumediène's government began quietly staking out a more equidistant position between East and West (befitting a champion of the Non-Aligned Movement), and signaling a readiness for greater cooperation with Washington.

In early December 1966, Harriman had tested those waters by adding an Algiers stop to his tour of Western Europe and North Africa to promote Vietnam peace prospects. Beijing, Hanoi, and the NLF, as well as the United States, all maintained diplomatic outposts in the city, augmenting its allure, and before leaving Washington, Harriman had obtained sanction from Rusk and LBJ to arrange clandestine meetings with local DRV and/or NLF representatives, separately or together, if the Algerians were willing to mediate and the Vietnamese agreed. A direct contact with an official NLF representative would be particularly dicey, for it would violate the prevailing orthodoxy of both the Johnson administration and Saigon dismissing the NLF as Hanoi's creation and puppet and viewing as anathema any step that might accord it greater legitimacy (or bolster its claims to a substantial chunk of any coalition government). Because Harriman was more attuned than most U.S. officials to internecine Communist strains, he credited claims that the NLF in fact enjoyed some autonomy from Hanoi, and that the chaos engulfing China (a major NLF backer) might also give the Southern Communists some breathing room. Though he was nominally authorized only to discuss prisoner exchanges, he saw value in opening a covert channel to the NLF for purposes ranging from intelligence gathering and message sending to mutual probing concerning South Vietnam's political destiny.[91]

At the United States' behest, the Algerians contacted the Vietnamese Communist envoys before Harriman arrived to see if one or both might see him—but they rebuffed the invitation, on the grounds that direct talks were impossible "at time when [the U.S. government] had renewed and intensified bombings of Hanoi" and seemed intent on escalation. Nevertheless, in two days of talks with Harriman, both Boumediène and his foreign minister, Abdelaziz Bouteflika, though still criticizing U.S. policy, vowed to do their best to arrange secret talks. Harriman felt ambivalent about the Algerians personally—"unimpressed" by Boumediène (weak, perhaps a figurehead) but enjoying the repartee with Bouteflika ("a forceful personality, young, confident"[92])—but found them "worth cultivating" and credible potential intermediaries. On returning to Washington (where he learned, of course, of Marigold and its apparent collapse), he advised LBJ that the Algerians (or Sainteny) could do a "better job than Eastern Europeans."[93]

Then, out of nowhere, the Poles entered the picture. The catalytic conversation in Algiers happened neither "under a palm tree" nor, for that matter, in the claustrophobic labyrinth of the Qasbah, but a few miles to the south, in a comfortable suburb. On December 21, Warsaw's new ambassador, Edward Wychowaniec, came to the whitewashed U.S. Embassy on Chemin Cheikh Bachir Brahimi to pay a courtesy call on his counterpart, John D. Jernegan (who had, coincidentally, succeeded Porter, now Lodge's deputy).[94] Neither envoy knew much, if anything, about the secret peace effort in which their governments had been so deeply enmeshed—and yet their conversation, inevitably, turned immediately to the war and the possibility, however slim, that their present posting might facilitate hidden U.S.-Vietnamese contacts. Though both agreed that the Algerians wanted to lend a hand (though they were also, Jernegan thought, "a little gun shy" from Vietnamese and Chinese brush-offs), Wychowaniec proffered his own services. He had spoken recently with the local DRV and NLF representatives, and though both displayed "great rigidity," the NLF man seemed ready to "sit around a table," at least to discuss prisoners of war and a cease-fire before tackling broader issues.

The American—who had vainly tried to arrange Harriman's contacts with the Vietnamese—found the Pole's last remark particularly intriguing; it fit Algerian gossip that the local "Viet Cong representative was somewhat more disposed to accept idea of talks than his Northern colleague," even preferring to meet separately with an American, without the North Vietnamese present, if an encounter actually took place.[95] When Jernegan questioned whether the NLF could act independently of Hanoi, Wychowaniec agreed that they would have to reach some sort of "understanding." At least, he observed hopefully, China's internal tumult meant that the Vietnamese would not need to worry too much about Beijing peering over their shoulder. Stressing that he was "personally very anxious" to be of service and knew how to keep his mouth shut (and be "especially discreet" with "socialist colleagues"), Wychowaniec volunteered to inform Jernegan "if anything interesting transpired" when he next saw the NLF representative, Tran Noi Nam.

All in all, the new Pole in town made a good first impression. Jernegan cabled Washington that Wychowaniec seemed "friendly, agreeable and reasonably frank," and noted that, according to the CIA station chief, he had an intelligence background but was not a professional agent.

In this case, however, the Pole seems to have been running a rogue, if benign, operation. His ciphergram to Warsaw after seeing Jernegan hinted at Vietnamese willingness to engage in "initial" contacts, and quoted the U.S. ambassador as confirming Boumediène's willingness to serve as an intermediary (and unsuccessful past efforts to sound out Hanoi)—but it made no mention whatsoever of his own eager offer to help bring the Americans and the local NLF representative together (or, for that matter, any reference to implementing instructions).[96]

Jernegan did not know this, of course, and he left it to those "more steeped in Communist operations" to judge whether Warsaw's diplomat (who modestly admitted that he was not "an important name") had acted on his own. Having already been deputized by Harriman to keep probing for opportunities to meet local Vietnamese, he suggested to Washington that the probe opened up "a possible avenue for secret exchanges with our opponents if [the State] Department wished to attempt it."[97]

Did it? In fact, U.S. officials remained torn over whether it made sense to approach the NLF—and if so, over the form, content, and ambit of any such contacts. These divergent perspectives clashed during a prolonged and, it seems, contentious discussion during the January 5 meeting of the Negotiations Committee (plus Lodge) in Harriman's office.[98] The ambassador, soon to head back to Saigon, disdained contacts with the NLF, because, he felt, Hanoi controlled both Viet Cong military operations and the NLF leadership (if necessary through the "power of assassination"). Eventually, though probably not until at least another year of fighting had passed, the South Vietnamese government might determine "when the time was right" to talk to the NLF—but it was necessary, first, to wipe out its "hard core terrorist apparatus" and preferable in any case "to wait until the Viet Cong or Hanoi takes the initiative to seek us out."

By contrast, Harriman, Lodge's fellow elder statesman (and old political rival), contended that NLF-Hanoi frictions were "probably greater than intelligence analysts tended to believe." Harriman had never been shy about flashing his own credentials dealing with Communists, and now this former ambassador to Moscow under Roosevelt and Truman cited alleged "differences within the Politburo even under Stalin." "From my own experience," Harriman wrote LBJ and Rusk the next day, "I am satisfied there must be some differences between Hanoi and the NLF, even though both are controlled by the Vietnamese Communist Party. It is important that we attempt to understand and exploit these differences."

Splitting the difference between Lodge and Harriman, the negotiations panel (including Bundy and Read as Rusk's stand-ins) agreed that the issue needed more study (assigning the job to Cooper), and for the time being only "secret and deniable" NLF contacts should be authorized. No one had bothered to restrain Jernegan, however, and when the ambassador paid a return call on Wychowaniec in early January, he asked the Pole to check whether the local NLF delegate would be willing to meet, perhaps to inaugurate an ongoing dialogue to consider a cease-fire and other matters. Wychowaniec cautiously cabled Michałowski that the American had spoken "convincingly," but he could not judge his sincerity. "It appears to me that this is an attempt to drive a wedge between the NLF and Hanoi," the envoy ventured. "I replied evasively. Should I get involved?"[99]

Of course, Wychowaniec had *already* gotten involved—and his disingenuous message to Warsaw reinforces the impression that the junior diplomat had acted independently, confident that he remained within the general contours of Polish policy and perhaps emboldened by a pre-Christmas conversation with the Soviet ambassador in Algiers, who told him that Moscow "definitely" favored negotiations and wanted the war over by the end of 1967.[100]

Despite Poland's anger over Marigold, merely relaying to the NLF a U.S. interest in talking conformed to its policy that only those "shedding blood" had the moral right to accept or reject overtures for negotiations. So, even as Warsaw reined in its envoy in New Delhi, Rapacki flashed a green light to Algiers. (At precisely this juncture, without divulging details, Michałowski consoled Gronouski with the vague news that "something is going on right now in Algeria" and "maybe this offers some possibility."[101]) On January 7, Wychowaniec relayed Jernegan's proposal for a secret meeting to Tram Noi Nam, who promised to consult his superiors. Three days later—just as, four thousand miles or so to the east, Ogrodziński stood up Michener and the air whooshed out of Narcissus—the NLF representative replied: No, not until Washington first stopped the bombing and declared a cease-fire, he told the Pole. "They cannot accept any talks from the position of force. They want to see an act of goodwill on the U.S. side." To his fellow Communist, Nam confided that he had rejected an appeal to see Harriman (Bouteflika was "disappointed, he insisted, and even offered a discreet venue") and that the Algerians still hoped that the NLF would change its mind. When Wyochowaniec sounded Nam out regarding China, his words and tone implied pleasure that Beijing's distractions meant that the Vietnamese "were being less controlled."[102]

The next day, Wychowaniec relayed the NLF's refusal to enter covert "*pourparlers*" in Algiers to Jernegan, who reacted "calmly." As the Pole reported, talks now were impossible, but if Washington "would cease bombardments and declare a general cease-fire on all fronts, NLF would accept truce and be willing to enter into secret discussions." (This meant that Hanoi would also go along, he presumed.) Wychowaniec quoted Nam as saying—in a distant echo of Communist claims regarding Marigold—that his "superiors" had been willing to authorize conversations in early December, but then the Hanoi bombings "forced" them to "take a negative stand." Implying a degree of independence from the NLF's powerful patrons, Nam said that he had not coordinated his actions with the DRV ambassador, and he asked the Pole to likewise refrain from discussing the matter with him or the Soviets; he seemed more concerned with excluding Beijing than Saigon in any eventual talks. Nervously, Wychowaniec implored Jernegan to maintain "complete discretion," because "from his experience in the Polish Foreign Ministry"—memories of the Maneli affair?—"he knew that if he undertook something of this kind and it leaked out, his career would be finished."[103]

Washington's response, hammered out at a meeting of the negotiations group in Harriman's office a few days later, merged interest in pursuing a channel to the NLF in Algiers through "a covert deniable contact" with a determination to cut out the Poles, "as it seems wiser to deal directly than to do so through them."[104] As Rusk (in a cable drafted by Bundy) explained to Jernegan, "at worst," the reported NLF demarche "represents a Polish ploy to get major U.S. concessions on cessation of bombing and some form of recognition of NLF; at best, it indicates willingness of NLF (and possibly Hanoi) to sit down with us for serious discussion of general cease-fire." Either way, he should shunt the Poles aside "in such a manner that they cannot interpret our action as closing channel which they could maintain they have opened with the NLF," nor indicating "any change of [the U.S. government] position on question of NLF status or on reported NLF 'conditions' for talks, which Poles could later exploit." As the embassy fulfilled this delicate, somewhat contradictory task, Washington would dispatch a "special emissary"—under the noses and behind the backs of the Algerians, the Poles, the Chinese, the Soviets, and perhaps even Hanoi—to engage in "discreet, deniable talks to probe NLF views on cease fire, question of participants in future discussions necessary to effectuate end of hostilities, etc."

Bundy code-named the new initiative Primrose—evidently a nod to Gronouski's rejection of the view that, in Marigold, the Poles had "led us down the primrose path."[105]

With Jernegan out of town (meeting other U.S. ambassadors in Tangiers), his deputy dutifully trooped to the Polish Embassy to tell Wychowaniec, in effect, thanks very much but don't call us, we'll call you. The Pole seemed less insulted by the brush-off than disappointed at the intransigence of both the NLF representative and the "more hard-headed" DRV ambassador (who had complained to him at a reception a few days earlier, "If [the Americans] want peace, why don't they let us alone?").[106]

Rather than rely on Polish aid, the State Department hatched a scheme lifted straight out of a cheesy airport novel. In late January, a retired U.S. diplomat (a veteran of the "XYZ" effort in late 1965 to probe Hanoi's views through Mai Van Bo), described in classified cables as a "white-haired gentleman" or "Y," flew to Paris and on to Algiers, gaining a visa on the pretext of visiting the son of an old friend and staying with a nonofficial "cut-out" arranged by the CIA station chief. Then, masquerading as a commentator preparing a piece for *Foreign Affairs* on the shape of a postsettlement South Vietnam, he inveigled an appointment with Tran Noi Nam, who received him politely and responded with boilerplate. "Y" hoped that "Roger" (as he labeled the NLF envoy in cables) would grease his path to see more authoritative figures to gather further "background material" and was authorized to proceed to Phnom Penh to do so, but Nam failed to take the bait when the American mentioned the desirability of higher-level secret contacts between the NLF and someone who knew Washington's thinking.[107]

After this cordial but unproductive meeting, during which the American revealed neither his true identity nor his mission, Jernegan suggested reverting to Wychowaniec. Perhaps he should ask Warsaw's ambassador to tell Nam outright that Washington would send a special emissary for secret conversations if he were willing to talk. "Realize this runs counter to Department's desire to keep Poles out," he cabled Rusk, "but it might be considered as last resort if there is no repeat no sign of change of [on] Roger's part."[108] No, came the response, discouraging Jernegan from any further efforts, because "we wish keep contacts as invisible and deniable as possible, which makes your participation very difficult."[109]

"Y" returned to Algiers in March, but his efforts to lure "Roger" into greenlighting a trip to Phnom Penh to see more senior NLF figures again proved futile, and he left empty-handed. In Washington and Saigon, the desirability of establishing a direct link to the NLF remained hotly contested. Poland's part in stimulating the Algerian wild goose chase remained a hazy Marigold sidebar; after ignoring Lewandowski's repeated offers in Saigon to put U.S. officials in touch with the NLF in Phnom Penh, Washington had likewise looked a Polish gift horse (of unclear value) in the mouth in Algiers and had instead concocted a convoluted scenario to wangle an invitation to exchange views—deniably, unofficially, "under a palm tree"—with the Front leadership. But the spy thriller's pages went blank well short of the climax, and the Primrose path indeed led nowhere.[110]

"Mr. X" in America: "Apparently the Opening Shots"

In mid-January 1967—against a confusing backdrop of diplomatic whispers, feelers, and dead ends—Michałowski journeyed to Minnesota to speak at Carleton College. Was it a mere coincidence that Rapacki's right-hand man visited the

United States just as secret recriminations over Marigold were spreading? Not entirely. More than two months earlier, in early November, before the Lewandowski channel sprang to life, Carleton's president, John W. Nason, a former diplomat who had become friendly with Michałowski at the UN in the late 1950s, had invited him to participate in a panel discussion on "The United States in Foreign Eyes," part of the college's centennial celebrations.

At first the Pole temporized, pleading his uncertain work schedule; on December 16, after the Hanoi bombings mortally wounded Marigold, he apologized for the delay ("due to many complications") but expressed optimism that he could attend ("would be truly delighted and already preparing address"); and two weeks later, after the DRV's final rejection of direct contacts in Warsaw, he telegraphed a belated acceptance: "Happy able to come."[111] Besides a chance to see an old friend, the invitation offered a fortuitous pretext to conduct some secret diplomacy—and spread Poland's perspective on the recent events—in New York, which he would transit and where he could see Tomorowicz and Thant at the UN, and perhaps others, even U.S. officials if they were interested.

But they were not. After getting wind of the upcoming trip, Gronouski urged Rusk to "consider arranging meeting between Michałowski and, hopefully, Katzenbach," in order to "impress Poles with seriousness of our interest and provide opportunity for Undersecretary to gain firsthand impression of Polish interest and attitude."[112] When the Canadian ambassador, Edgar Ritchie, raised the topic of the Pole's imminent arrival with Cooper, Harriman's aide assured him that Michałowski "would be discussing Vietnam with senior Washington personalities during his forthcoming visit to USA."[113]

Disgruntled with the Poles, however, the State Department ignored Gronouski's suggestion (though Katzenbach and Michałowski would later get their chance to testily swap Marigold impressions) along with Ottawa's hints that the Pole might be worth seeing.[114] Washington hardly lacked plausible interlocutors. Besides Goldberg in New York, the speakers in Minnesota included Carleton alumnus Thomas L. Hughes, '47, head of State's Intelligence and Research Bureau and a member of Harriman's secret negotiations group. Though a suitable contact, Hughes received no instructions from Rusk or anyone else to broach Marigold with Michałowski, and he merely exchanged pleasantries with the Pole, whose "perspicacity" on Vietnam impressed him.[115] In his public remarks at Carleton—on a panel that included, besides Hughes, his old ICC colleague, the retired Indian diplomat M. J. Desai—Michałowski acknowledged America's achievements and virtues (and its popularity in Poland) but blasted its conduct in Vietnam, which was undermining its mostly positive image in his native country and continent. "What is it that worries us most in Europe?" he asked:

> It is, first of all, the messianic doctrine of exclusive righteousness. The danger stems from the fact that American policy regards other ideologies and political systems as evils that must be opposed by force. The force is there and is being ap-

plied. It is a missionary attitude of conversion by force, pressure, and invasion. If allies prove to be weak and unstable, America claims the right to support them militarily. When intervention proves to be unrealistic and ineffective, the U.S. government does not know how to withdraw and seems to think that withdrawal would indicate weakness. This is the case in Vietnam. The image of America abroad is being formed today mainly in the light of the conflict in Vietnam.[116]

Michałowski castigated the United States for "unlimited escalation" in a conflict it did not comprehend, and he emphasized that only a bombing halt could "open the way to a peaceful solution," because Hanoi could not be expected to negotiate while under assault. He stressed the need to "remove the dangerous shades of Vietnam hanging over the world and poisoning the international atmosphere," yet he demurely refrained from mentioning the still-secret recent peace initiative for whose failure he fully blamed Washington.

Instead, he exploited his New York City stopovers to disseminate Poland's version of events. Lacking an invitation from Washington to establish contact, he did the next best thing, seeding Poland's message via influential insiders. On landing at Kennedy Airport, he telephoned his former contact with the U.S. UN delegation, Kenneth T. Young, a specialist on Far Eastern affairs. After serving as ambassador to Laos, Young now ran the Asia Society, a philanthropy founded by David Rockefeller to promote U.S. relations with Asia, and known to enjoy close government ties.

When the two met at 6 p.m. on Tuesday evening, January 10, over cocktails at the Century Club, the elite midtown Manhattan gentlemen's watering hole, Michałowski vented his frustrations with Washington's Vietnam policy, especially juxtaposed with a radicalizing, increasingly menacing Communist China. Young had never seen his friend so downcast, even by Slavic standards for "despondency and exaggerated gloominess." A decade earlier, the Pole had seemed "understanding or even accepting" of America's efforts to establish a "progressive" nationalist regime in Saigon under Diem, but now he spewed vitriol on U.S. actions.

It is unclear whether Michałowski revealed to Young the *Polish* role in the recent failed secret peace diplomacy.[117] However, he did not hide his fury at the "incredible" bombing, which was not only militarily ineffective (though that did not bother him particularly) and rallied the North Vietnamese (including anticommunists, and even Catholics) behind the Hanoi government, but—most explosively—"had destroyed the probability of negotiations just as they were about to be arranged." Michałowski darkly intimated that "some Americans, although not the President, had deliberately sabotaged diplomatic efforts by particular bombing attacks at certain times." Yet, he insisted, a chance to start talks still existed, if only Washington halted the bombing "indefinitely but not necessarily unconditionally."

Michałowski left Young convinced that their conversation had been purely personal and confidential, that he had no intent whatsoever of his words reaching government ears or Young acting as a sort of "emissary or go-between." Regardless, the well-connected ex-diplomat would circulate the Pole's observations to key officials, including Bundy, Cooper, and Jorden, undoubtedly exacerbating their resentment at Warsaw.[118]

By the time Michałowski and Young finished catching up at the Century Club, two hours had passed. It was dark and freezing on 43rd Street outside—and well after midnight by the Pole's internal clock—but Rapacki's chief aide had not completed his appointed rounds, even though he had to fly to Minneapolis the next morning. Instead, he went ten blocks south to visit someone he had not seen in seven or eight years, since his days as UN ambassador, but who had become a familiar, friendly face to the Polish delegation in New York: Norman Cousins.

The two greeted each other warmly at the door, and Michałowski settled in for another carefully calculated Marigold leak—Warsaw's first, it appears, to a journalist, or in this case, more of a commentator-activist. Cluing in the passionate, plugged-in, prolific, and somewhat egotistical *Saturday Review* editor, and ideally stimulating his moral outrage, could serve dual purposes: He could spread Poland's version of events in elite circles, and he could also amplify its arguments through his magazine. Aware that Cousins sympathized with Polish claims that LBJ's rash resumption of bombing at the end of January 1966 had scuttled a significant Hanoi overture (i.e., its consent to receive him at its Warsaw embassy), Michałowski counted on a receptive audience—and that is what he got, as shown by his host's own private account of the late-evening visit to his 10 Park Avenue apartment by a man identified only as "Mr. X."[119]

Michałowski began by nostalgically, and ingratiatingly, recalling the "flurry that almost culminated in the negotiations" a year earlier—when he had secretly traveled to Hanoi, and Cousins, in New York, his bags packed, had vainly urged the White House to hold off—before revealing "that he had just been through another round with the North Vietnamese, in many ways, as eventful and promising as the one in which we were both engaged a year ago."

Michałowski then described the recent overture's ascent and collapse, stressing Poland's earnest efforts to persuade Hanoi of the United States' sincerity and success in attaining its consent to direct talks before a full bombing halt, contrary to its public stand; and Washington's subsequent demolition of the initiative by bombing Hanoi in the face of repeated Polish warnings. Although "incredulous" at and "stunned" by this behavior, Michałowski disclaimed any desire to "embarrass" the United States by "premature disclosures" (nor, for that matter, did he want to discomfort Hanoi's "nationalist" and anti-Chinese faction favoring negotiation). He also, apparently deliberately, fuzzed some details—for example, inflating the role of Pope Paul VI and the Vatican in an apparent attempt to conceal the actual Italian actors.

Nevertheless, Michałowski confided more than enough to set Cousins beavering away. In subsequent weeks, Cousins would compare notes with Thant, buttonhole administration officials, including the vice president (after hearing his story, Humphrey held his stomach and muttered, "It makes me sick at my gut"), and stoke the ire of the country's leading antiwar critic, J. William Fulbright, the Senate Foreign Relations Committee chair, hardening his belief that the adminis- tration was not serious in seeking peace ("I'm absolutely certain that the Presi- dent doesn't want negotiation," the Arkansas Democrat responded. "There have been too many documented opportunities. Secretary Rusk just isn't telling the truth"). And soon, Cousins' mounting skepticism toward administration peace claims (and allusions to, though not *yet* details of, the Polish episode) would per- colate into the *Saturday Review,* alarming the White House. At one point, LBJ personally authorized an aide to show Cousins classified records (on Nirvana, not Marigold) in an effort to convince him that the administration had tried its best, but the crusading editor-activist was unconvinced.[120]

* * *

After speaking in Minnesota, Michałowski again exploited a New York stop to promote Warsaw's perspective. On Sunday morning, January 15, he ventured north to Thant's stately Riverdale residence overlooking the Hudson River and, in effect, trumped Goldberg's earlier briefing.[121] Besides taking a historical excursion to review his trip to Hanoi the previous January as well as the more recent affair, Michałowski (as he cabled Rapacki) "straightened out" the secretary-general's understanding of the ten points' provenance, disputing Washington's implication that they were a Polish invention rather than a faithful summary of the U.S. posi- tion that Lodge had related to Lewandowski. Agreeing that the Hanoi bombings had killed a real chance to start talks, the two speculated as to who carried them out and why. Convinced that LBJ, strongly backed by Goldberg, had genuinely sought negotiations, Thant blamed the "pressure tactics" of Rusk and the "mili- tary cohort," Michałowski reported to Rapacki; the UN chief, in turn, recorded that the Pole, thinking along similar lines, presumed that Westmoreland and the military, perhaps via "very efficient" U.S. Army intelligence in Saigon, had moni- tored the Lodge-Lewandowski talks and sabotaged them as they neared frui- tion—an interpretation reflecting his inferences from the conversation with Gro- nouski ten days earlier. Neither suspected the truth: that on December 8, LBJ had personally overruled his top advisers' recommendation to suspend raids near Hanoi, a decision in which the uniformed military played no part. Promis- ing to keep each other informed, agreeing Washington had to stop bombing as a precondition for progress or successful mediation, Thant and the Poles parted cordially.[122]

The next morning, it was Canada's turn. Though the Americans yawned at the prospect of a face-to-face conversation with Rapacki's top aide, the Canadians were chomping at the bit. Repeatedly, through Ignatieff, Martin invited Micha- łowski to take a side trip to Ottawa, even offering to retrieve him in a private jet and, if necessary, fly him back to Warsaw; the Poles declined the detour, but the

Canadians insisted so earnestly that Tomorowicz feared offending them with a flat refusal.[123]

Finally, Michałowski agreed to receive a Canadian delegation at the Polish UN mission for consultations on Vietnam before flying back to Europe Monday evening. He had, after all, already seen New Delhi's UN representative for a brief chat mostly devoted to the aborted trilateral ICC meeting, and he had discovered that the Indian (like his colleague in Warsaw) had a "general" inkling of the Polish involvement in secret diplomacy outside ICC confines.[124]

Frustrated in his efforts to lure Michałowski to Ottawa, Martin dispatched two aides (Goldschlag and Ralph Collins) to New York to join Ignatieff for the meeting, while summoning the Polish ambassador to stress his zeal for Vietnam peacemaking (offering to meet Rapacki secretly).[125] On sitting down with Michałowski, the Canadians initially maintained the polite fiction that they were merely following up on their minister's early November conversations in Warsaw. Then one mentioned "recent Polish mediatory activities" as one of the "potentially interesting developments" they might discuss. You were not supposed to know about those, Michałowski "wryly" responded.

Once the cat was out of the bag—rather than disclose Thant's leak, the Canadians said that the Americans had informed them—an extended discussion of Marigold and its demise ensued. Repeating the same case that he and Rapacki had made to Gronouski, the Pole asserted that a genuine prospect of direct exchanges in Warsaw had collapsed when Washington bombed Hanoi on December 13 and 14, despite "about fourteen" Polish warnings:

> As Michałowski put it, this was a "stupid and irresponsible act." It was a blow struck against Warsaw as much as against Hanoi. It put Poland in impossible position vis-à-vis the North Vietnamese. It also put "certain people in Hanoi" in equally impossible situation. Michałowski said he could not believe that responsibility for these bombings lay with military commanders. He could not conceive that in most democratic state on earth [sic!] president did not have means of stopping this operation. And if he could not believe that, how could anyone expect Hanoi to do so?

If only Washington had given its Christmas Eve undertaking to eschew bombing within a 10-mile radius of Hanoi two or three weeks earlier, the story might have had a happier ending. Instead, the "North Vietnamese had even less confidence in USA intentions than they had before this recent experience," and "we were now much further back than we had been on December 1." Consequently, Michałowski saw no hope or point in renewed peace efforts until Washington unilaterally halted the bombing.[126]

The Canadians prodded—suppose Washington coupled the 10-mile limit with a no-escalation pledge or other "good faith" measures?—but the Pole remained doubtful; there was now a huge "credibility gap" in Hanoi, and the U.S. "requirement for reciprocity in terms of de-escalation" raised "very delicate" questions in

Hanoi's relations with the NLF. Michałowski's insistence that the DRV leaders firmly believed in a battlefield victory nonplussed the Canadians, who wondered "why, in those circumstances, Hanoi was allegedly willing to go further in recent exchanges than previous North Vietnamese pronouncements had led any of us, including Poles, to believe." Such nagging inconsistencies aside, Michałowski succeeded in conveying his main point: Peace efforts were doomed until an "unrequited" bombing halt (even an unannounced one) convinced Hanoi that the "climate of negotiations was likely to be productive." Politely, Michałowski agreed with his guests that their conversation was "useful" and promised to stay in touch "as matters developed"—but afterward he cabled Rapacki that the Canadians, incapable of restraining Washington, had presented neither convincing arguments nor new or concrete considerations, and seemed mostly interested in "securing some kind of a role for themselves if possibilities were to open."[127]

When a Canadian official passed the detailed memorandum of conversation to the State Department a week later, terming Michałowski's comments "largely a 'rehash' of previous Polish statements," Bundy observed resignedly that the "Poles were expressing sort of recriminations that might be expected under circumstances. . . . [He] doubted whether further progress would be achieved via Poles in near future, although this channel might come back to life at some stage."[128]

After seeing the Canadians, Michałowski had jetted to London, another former posting—but the sentimental journey ended sadly when he learned of his mother's death. "As you know, it was not unexpected," he wrote Nason, "but I hardly was able to think about anything else for some time."[129]

✳ ✳ ✳

These secret arguments were starting to resemble a tennis match in the dark; reinforcing doubts about U.S. conduct and sincerity in seeking peace, Michałowski had crisply volleyed the American briefings for Thant and the Canadians, and his talks with Young and Cousins—and others?—had propagated a Polish spin on the spreading scuttlebutt. In their reconstruction of the affair, the journalists David Kraslow and Stuart Loory would later describe Michałowski's New York conversations as "apparently the opening shots in a quiet propaganda war fought in diplomatic circles to assign blame for the failure of Marigold."[130]

But of course, Rapacki had fired the opening barrage in late December, and Washington had already begun retaliating earlier in January. The combat was only intensifying.

Lodge Returns to Saigon: "Was Cabot Able to Convince Them?"

Shortly after noon on Tuesday, January 17, 1967, after a thirty-six-day absence, Henry Cabot Lodge returned to Saigon. Before heading back, he had spent several days in Washington in early January interspersing classified consultations—including an Oval Office chat with LBJ—and highly optimistic public pronouncements.[131] Then, after bidding farewell to his children and grandchildren in Beverly, he boarded a C-135 military transport plane at Andrews Air Force Base, accompanied by Emily, Deputy Secretary Leonard Unger, and a retinue of Marine guards. Instead of backtracking across the Pacific, Lodge flew via Rome, in order, he wired Reinhardt, to break up the journey with a night's sleep and, perhaps, pay courtesy calls on the pope and Fanfani, the latter to "express appreciation for D'Orlandi's tireless efforts."[132]

But the Italian foreign minister had grander ambitions for his encounter with Lodge. When they met on January 15, he spoke "prudently in very vague terms" due to the presence of people "not conversant" with the secret diplomacy. Nevertheless, armed with D'Orlandi's marginally more auspicious report of his latest talk with Lewandowski, "Il Motorino" tried to reignite his visitors' interest in Marigold. Afterward, Lodge and Unger nonchalantly informed Washington that "nothing new of significance emerged" from the "useful exchange of views," but Fanfani believed otherwise. He cabled D'Orlandi that Lodge had seconded his suggestion that Lewandowski return to Hanoi and, this time, obtain Ho Chi Minh's "authoritative" blessing "in order to guarantee the activation and respect for the eventual conclusions." Fanfani also reported relaying Lewandowski's concerns regarding China, and in response obtaining from both Lodge and Unger assurances that Washington was not conducting or contemplating secret negotiations with Beijing, aside from routine contacts regarding prisoners.

Newly flush, Fanfani directed D'Orlandi to arrange new three-way talks as soon as Lodge (who needed "a complete update") reached Saigon, in order to take full advantage of the Pole's next trip to Hanoi. Ideally, any new exchanges could remain under the wing of the diplomatic trio, "to avoid running up against other hesitations in Warsaw."[133]

After a Vatican audience Monday—Marigold did not come up, but Pope Paul VI fretted at "how badly our case was being presented in the world" (Salisbury's articles were "a disaster") and asked Washington to consider a "noble and generous" gesture (e.g., a unilateral bombing halt[134])—Lodge flew to Bangkok and, after depositing Emily at the Oriental, on to Tan Son Nhut. A flock of VIPs (Westmoreland, Porter, Habib, et al.) clustered there to greet him—none more ardently than D'Orlandi, eager to resume their collaboration. "Was Cabot able to convince them?" he had wondered since Habib had told him the previous day that his friend would shortly arrive.[135] As the dignitaries idled, the political counselor took the Italian aside to lower his expectations. "Habib is categorical; according to him the attempt has been ditched and we can do nothing about it. Is he right?" In the reception's hubbub after the military plane touched down, D'Orlandi secured a lunch date with Lodge for two days hence to assess Marigold's health. Having awoken in a state of nervous anticipation, he returned to his embassy in a downcast mood; but his fading hopes rose again that evening on receiving Fanfani's message indicating that Lodge had agreed on the desirability of exploiting Lewandowski's next trip north.

"The telegram returns me to a state of grace," he recorded. "I responded with thanks."[136]

But D'Orlandi soon fell back into despair. Lunching with Lodge on Thursday, he learned that the American not only carried no new instructions for three-way talks but also seemed oblivious to developments since his departure from Vietnam; no one in Washington had briefed him on what had happened since December 12, either in Saigon or Warsaw. "I am very disappointed and Cabot Lodge does not hide his embarrassment from me," the Italian recorded. "What the devil will I say to Lewandowski? The only thing to do is to tell him that I have not been able to speak to Cabot Lodge alone yet"—otherwise, he would have to admit that Washington had entirely given up on the channel.[137]

With a few days to spare before he would next see the Pole—who was making a short side trip to Cambodia—D'Orlandi stressed to Lodge the importance of not wasting his upcoming visit to Hanoi, especially given the Chinese developments' potentially favorable implications. And, the Italian insisted, Lewandowski—despite condemning recent U.S. behavior, both the Hanoi raids and the "tit-for-tat" bargaining—was "eager" to try again. "If Washington truly wants a negotiation, I believe that it will not be very difficult to set it up on a reasonable foundation, given that Hanoi appears to me to be more receptive today than in the past." Perhaps humoring his friend, Lodge claimed that he "personally" favored resuming their activities, and he vowed to seek immediate and precise instructions from Washington.

D'Orlandi's report of his repast with Lodge discouraged even Fanfani, for, he replied to his ambassador, it fit the fragmentary information from other sources that Washington had discarded the Polish-Italian channel and had adopted other intermediaries to probe Hanoi, such as Sainteny, and was flirting with direct contacts with the NLF. Though that very day, January 20, the U.S. undersecretary of state for political affairs, Eugene Rostow, had effusively conveyed LBJ's gratitude for Italy's peace efforts, Fanfani correctly sensed that Rome was being eased aside.[138]

Fanfani's communication confirmed D'Orlandi's worst fears regarding the United States' "abandonment" of the channel, which had mounted since Habib's "categorical" remarks, and his discovery that Washington had not bothered to give Lodge ("already so clearly cut out by his government") any new proposals. Worse, D'Orlandi believed the Chinese turmoil offered a valid opening to probe Hanoi's willingness to talk peace, and that, despite the "current undeniable escalation of the war," if Washington "truly" sought negotiations, then the three-way Saigon conduit had "already proven its effectiveness and was far from having exhausted its potential."

However, D'Orlandi, so pro-American in his basic orientation, had lost faith in the United States' sincerity and motives. Though he was ready to continue friendly contacts with both his partners (to avoid "contentious aftereffects"), he privately shared his Polish friend's bitter conviction that LBJ and his advisers had chosen a quest for military victory over a search for a compromise settlement:

> Our perseverance is born of despair, but it is clear that our negotiation is dead and it was death by murder. May God forgive those who took such a crushing responsibility upon themselves! It appears obvious to me that Washington wants to take advantage of the Chinese situation. If they had wanted to take advantage of it for the purposes of peace, the conditions would have been extremely reasonable. But they want to be triumphant.[139]

* * *

Despite D'Orlandi's desolation, Fanfani—in a move he hid from his man in Saigon—had something else up his sleeve. He told Rostow that a DRV interlocutor in Rome whom he declined to name (but not an Eastern European, he stressed) had approached him with an interest in starting talks with U.S. representatives. The foreign minister had replied that a suitable channel already existed (Marigold), but perhaps Washington wanted to follow up on this new potential avenue to Hanoi. Intrigued, Rostow stressed the importance of coordinating with the State Department, which sought more details from Fanfani while informing Lodge but telling him not to mention the matter to D'Orlandi and to defer any further action on Marigold until the Fanfani business was clarified.[140]

It never was. On the evening of January 23, Fanfani politely rebuffed Reinhardt's probing for the identity of the mysterious DRV emissary, only saying that the person "was not Vietnamese and had simply informed him [on January 20] that Hanoi was prepared to send him a representative, if agreeable." In "vigorous" terms, he assured the American that the contact had nothing to do with the La Pira gang that had caused so much trouble (for both LBJ and Fanfani) in late 1965. Unimpressed, Reinhardt replied that if Fanfani "considered this contact potentially productive," he could pursue the matter on a "personal basis," leaving "both Washington and he himself . . . uncommitted [*senza impegno*]."[141]

Who was Fanfani's mystery man? His handwritten diaries, opened more than four decades later, identify his hidden collaborator—and why he was so reluctant to divulge his identity to the Americans. On January 16, 1967, Rome's foreign minister saw a senior figure of the Partido Comunista Italiano (PCI), Carlo Alberto Galluzzi, expecting to hear his impressions as a member of the PCI delegation that had recently visited North Vietnam and other Asian Communist capitals. To his surprise, Galluzzi proposed that Fanfani himself "meet with a representative from Hanoi for more conclusive talks on Vietnam." Fanfani responded cautiously that a channel already existed for such exchanges (Marigold), but he had to "ascertain" whether it was still a valid method of communications.[142] The next night, he dined with Adam Willmann, who was finishing his eventful term as Poland's envoy in Rome. Regarding the "tripartite talks in Saigon," Warsaw's diplomat politely told Fanfani that he was "still hopeful that they may be resumed," but said nothing to indicate that that was a concrete possibility any time in the foreseeable future.[143] On January 20 Fanfani spoke with Rostow, offering himself as a potential new channel to supplement those Washington was already exploring—only to be pressed a few days later by Reinhardt (on Rusk's behalf) to reveal more information on the DRV emissary before authorizing any overture. "My deduction is that Washington still needs other channels, not being satisfied with those it says it is using after abandoning the tripartite talks," the Italian concluded.[144]

Yet Fanfani declined to name Galluzzi, and it is not hard to guess why: He knew that U.S. officials deeply distrusted the Italian Communists, and had they learned that Fanfani was collaborating with the PCI on such a sensitive matter, this would also have cast aspersions on him. After deflecting Reinhardt's bid to get him to reveal the interlocutor, Fanfani saw Galluzzi again and sought details on the Hanoi representative's "personality, mandate, powers, before I can decide whether to meet him."[145]

From Fanfani's diaries, it is evident that he did not know with whom (if anyone) he was indirectly dealing on the DRV side—and that Galluzzi did not immediately follow up on this initiative. Yet this murky episode foreshadowed a sequel to Marigold that would only begin to germinate half a year later, in the summer of 1967. By then D'Orlandi had returned from Saigon to Rome, and this new peace effort, known as "Killy" (see chapter 16), would finally bring the ailing, ardent ambassador, along with his energetic minister, into direct contacts with the elusive North Vietnamese.

* * *

But all that was many months off. Unaware of his foreign minister's latest gambit, D'Orlandi reported sadly that Lodge, evidently "in the dark" about alternate channels, had received orders "not to advance any initiative and to wait." Even worse, Habib had confided that the Johnson administration foresaw waiting another year before "undertaking serious negotiations," and Lodge had sensed in Washington that the hawks had the upper hand.[146] Lodge sensed right, and one symptom of this hardening had been the decision to give up on the Poles—a move that reflected a variety of considerations: a new focus on Moscow as the most likely venue for direct contacts; mounting irritation at Rapacki's leaking; and senior State Department suspicions that neither the Poles nor, for that matter, the eager U.S. envoys in both Saigon and Warsaw fully shared their own strategy or sentiments regarding peace talks.

"Quite a Garden of Flowers"

As Marigold languished, other efforts to bring the enemies to the negotiating table, or at least pass messages or signals between them, moved forward. Like LBJ's thirty-seven-day bombing pause a year before, the period from December 1966 through mid-February 1967 marked one of the war's most intense phases of diplomatic activity before the opening of direct United States–DRV talks in the spring of 1968. Signaling an approaching crossroads, the feverish efforts to ascertain possibilities to open peace talks paralleled a private White House determination to prepare for an intensification of the war. "The problem," Rostow wrote LBJ on January 19, "is this: If we do not get a diplomatic breakthrough in the next three weeks or so, it probably means that they plan to sweat us out down to the election of 1968. As you know, I share your view that we would then have to think hard about how to apply our military power against the North with maximum effort and minimum risk of enlarging the war as a whole."[147]

By late January, U.S. officials were hard-pressed to keep track of the mushrooming initiatives—from secret messages to public appeals or cryptic statements, third-party mediation efforts by governments, private organizations, and individuals (including a veritable parade of Western activists, sympathizers, and do-gooders to Hanoi in Salisbury's wake) to quiet direct United States–DRV contacts, serious overtures to half-baked stunts or cynical ploys, schemes hatched in both Western and Eastern camps as well as in nonaligned countries. You have got "quite a garden of flowers to fix up today," Rusk cracked to Bundy one morning.[148]

From Washington's perspective, the most serious contender for the title of Marigold's successor was the Soviet channel, code-named "Sunflower." Washington's inclination to turn to the Kremlin had been prompted by increasingly explicit diplomatic hints: Thompson, about to leave to take up his new post, was told by Dobrynin "that perhaps during my stay in Moscow I would be able to have contact with a certain ambassador, obviously meaning the North Vietnamese."[149] To this was added Dong's seemingly forthcoming approach to talks ("we would know what to do" if the United States unconditionally halted bombing) in his interview with Salisbury, which he conveyed personally to Rusk in mid-January after returning to the United States.[150]

Johnson administration officials experimented with other ideas at this stage to probe DRV thinking. As Fanfani had learned, one, favored by Harriman, was to employ Sainteny; after Rusk and LBJ approved, Cooper went to Paris to encourage his return to Hanoi, and found him willing, even eager, to do so, but de Gaulle vetoed the proposed trip, considering French cooperation "premature" because he doubted Washington's readiness for peace.[151] Amid the proliferation of would-be mediators, Rostow pushed his pet notion of a direct LBJ-Ho message ("I have the strong feeling that these fellows in Hanoi may want to talk to us without Poles, Italians, Canadians, British or even Russians in the act"[152]).

But Washington increasingly viewed the Soviet channel as central. On January 6, 10, and 20, the U.S. chargé d'affaires in Moscow, John Guthrie, was able to hand messages proposing secret direct talks to his DRV counterpart, Le Chang—in marked contrast to May 1965, when the North Vietnamese had refused communications during a brief bombing pause ("Mayflower"). Hanoi's seeming readiness to deal quietly and directly, at least on the technical level, offered modest encouragement, as did the hint of growing tacit Soviet cooperation, particularly given Kosygin's impending trip to Britain. "We have less difficulty in communicating with the Russians than with the Canadians or U Thant," Rostow told a reporter off the record (and he undoubtedly would have added the British if he had not been speaking to a *London Sunday Times* correspondent).[153] But was Moscow really prepared to help—or Hanoi to talk?

Communist Convolutions:
The "First Round in Oriental Rug Trading"

On January 17 and 18, in the midst of these machinations, the Soviet leaders Brezhnev, Kosygin, and Podgorny visited the northern Polish town of Lansk to consult with Gomułka and other Politburo figures (and perhaps shoot some game, as Brezhnev had suggested in Sofia). The records of these secret talks help piece together one of Marigold's lingering puzzles: the nature and extent of Soviet involvement.[154] As U.S. officials presumed, the Kremlin knew and approved of Marigold, but—contrary to the belief of some, including Rusk—did not instigate or micromanage the Polish diplomacy. Still unanswered, however, were other questions later raised by the Pentagon Papers' analysts: What lay behind Moscow's willingness to take a more active role in encouraging U.S.-DRV peace contacts in early 1967, even after Marigold had collapsed? "Did the Russians receive encouragement to try further?" they asked. Or did the Hanoi bombings provoke Moscow to take its own initiative in an effort to head off further escalation?[155]

Brezhnev's remarks to Gomułka indicate that in directly promoting talks, Moscow was indeed responding to DRV prodding. The Soviet party boss related Le Duc Tho's plea in mid-December, in the name of the VWP Politburo, to aid Hanoi in "establishing contact with the USA in the matter of a peaceful settlement," either through the local U.S. Embassy or through Poland, and his suggestion of direct Polish-Soviet consultations on the subject. "In continuing the battle with American imperialism," he quoted Tho as saying, "it is possible simultaneously to begin negotiations with them," at least as "a tactical move." Later, Brezhnev reported, the Soviets received an unspecified "lecture by Pham Van Dong" that "contained hints regarding negotiations." Then—silence. Not hearing any retraction from the North Vietnamese, the Soviets had decided to "proceed as if their request was still up to date." (Confused, Rapacki openly wondered why, then, Hanoi had rejected direct contacts with the Americans in Warsaw in late December despite their bombing halt around the DRV capital.) Concerning Sino-Vietnamese ties, Gomułka and Rapacki noted recent reports that Chinese pressure against entering talks had recently lessened,[156] and Brezhnev confirmed that "similar information" had reached Moscow, adding that the Chinese were trying to foster discord between the VWP and the more militant NLF. Trading gossip, Brezhnev discounted Polish reports that India and Burma were involved in mediation efforts, and Gomułka assessed that in Washington, the hawks now had the upper hand and there was "no possibility" of forcibly evicting the Americans from Vietnam. Brezhnev's bottom line: Moscow must act cautiously and "show the Americans that we are not bent on unleashing a great war. But what the imperialists in the depth of their souls are planning—the devil knows."[157]

Though the Soviets would not have acted without Hanoi's blessing, ultimately, of course, they acted in their own interests. A few days before the leadership left for Lansk, the Politburo of the Communist Party in the Soviet Union had secretly approved a broad analysis of Moscow's dealings with Washington. This document, drafted by Gromyko, urged continued and, if need be, intensified military help to Hanoi but also noted that "putting an end to the Vietnam conflict would undoubtedly have a positive effect on Soviet-American relations and open up new possibilities for solving certain international problems" (e.g., a nuclear nonproliferation treaty, which both superpowers favored). "We should not avoid agreements with the United States on questions of our interest," the foreign minister counseled, "if such agreements do not contradict our position of principle in regard to Vietnam." Above all, Moscow must "avoid a situation where we have to fight on two fronts—that is, against China and the United States."[158]

※ ※ ※

However, by late January 1967, fighting between the Russians and Chinese had become more than a remote contingency.[159] Moving past polemics to actual violence—though not yet full-scale war, or even a formal rupture of diplomatic relations—the hostility between the Communist powers sharpened following a melee on the cold cobblestones of Red Square between Chinese students (who had been summoned home from Europe to partake in the Cultural Revolution and were transiting the USSR capital) and Russians in line to enter Lenin's tomb. The scuffle erupted, according to the Soviet authorities, after the students blocked the entrance to the mausoleum and, when asked to move aside, "hysterically" chanted anti-Soviet slogans, waved Mao's "Little Red Book" of quotations, and engaged in "other childish stunts." Such "provocative conduct," on "this site, which is holy for all Soviet people," aroused the "just indignation of Soviet men and women who were in Red Square at the time." The police joined in, and injuries were sustained on both sides (the Chinese ostentatiously touted bandages to foreign reporters before boarding the Trans-Siberian Express the next day, but most removed them after the train departed, sparking Soviet charges that the PRC Embassy had staged a "real masquerade").[160]

A paroxysm of anger ensued in Beijing. Inflamed by shrill newspaper reports of the "barbarous suppression" of the students—who, it was claimed, had merely wanted to lay wreaths at Lenin's mausoleum and Stalin's grave but had been surrounded and cruelly pummeled by the Soviet police and militia—and, of course, by Mao's minions, throngs of slogan-shouting Chinese, estimated at more than a million, paraded past the snow-covered grounds of the USSR Embassy for days on end, virtually imprisoning its inhabitants. In a round-the-clock siege, protesters egged on by the Red Guard frenziedly hurled amplified invective, lynched effigies of Kremlin leaders, lit bonfires, and threw paint, glue, and flaming torches over the compound's gates, which they topped with "antiparty" dunce caps and festooned with posters demanding "Fry Kosygin!" and "Shoot Brezhnev!" The *People's Daily* likened the Moscow authorities (the "most reactionary and most savage fascist dictatorship") to the tsar, Hitler, and the Ku Klux Klan. "Listen, you handful of filthy Soviet revisionist swine!" the Chinese Communist Party mouthpiece scowled. "The Chinese people, who are armed with Mao Tse-tung's thought, are not to be bullied! The blood debt you owe must be paid! We will hit back resolutely at your provocations!"[161]

Not to be outdone—but of course they were, because the Chinese were past masters at this sort of pageant—the Soviets organized protests around the PRC's Embassy on Druzhba (Friendship) Street, to heap "shame on the clique of Mao Tse-tung!" Compared to the "hostile bacchanalia" (as Kosygin wrote Zhou) or "Witches' Sabbath" (as TASS put it) outside the their Beijing embassy, these were fairly tiny and tame affairs; order broke down only briefly when a door of the diplomatic mission opened and protesters surged inside—only to be promptly yanked out by Soviet, not Chinese, security personnel. Heavy-handedly offering Beijing another propaganda windfall, the Moscow police ripped down cases on a wall outside the embassy displaying photographs of the Red Square brawl and, allegedly, beat up embassy staff members who rushed to their defense; a Western correspondent was duly escorted in to see the chargé d'affaires, "lying in bed, his face covered with what appeared to be bruises," and the PRC officials fulminated against the "violation of diplomatic immunity."[162]

This intercommunist food fight gladdened U.S. officials' hearts, especially when the Kremlin accused the Chinese of interfering with the sacred cause of aiding North Vietnam; in a "disgusting provocation," *Izvestia* charged, the Red Guard had harassed, threatened, and delayed a planeload of military technicians and specialists during a refueling stop at an airport outside Beijing.[163] Such reports could only fan Washington's hopes that the deepening Sino-Soviet discord would render the DRV more pliable to military pressure, amenable to negotiations, or both. But contrary to the beliefs or presumptions of some Americans, what ultimately mattered was not the rhetoric or wishes of figures in Moscow or Beijing but the internal considerations and deliberations of the secretive Communist leadership in Hanoi.

✴ ✴ ✴

On January 28, 1967, after months of speculation, North Vietnam authoritatively declared its revised position on negotiations: If the United States "really wants talks, it must first halt unconditionally the bombing raids and all other acts of war against the DRV," Nguyen Duy Trinh told Wilfred Burchett. Only then, he continued, "could" talks between U.S. and North Vietnamese representatives begin. To underline their significance, Hanoi Radio and *Nhan Dan,* the party newspaper, prominently featured Trinh's comments.[164]

Hanoi's revised stance aroused intense interest and debate in U.S. government and intelligence circles as to whether it was a mere propaganda nuance or a real hint of interest in negotiations. "They haven't thrown us a baseball," an official told the *Washington Post,* "it's only a marshmallow, but it's the first marshmallow they've thrown."[165] Varying the metaphor, Unger told an allied diplomat that Washington indeed took the signals seriously, but it sought more substantial concessions than an offer to talk if it were to halt the bombing: "The United States is not willing to exchange a horse for a rabbit; . . . but it is not slamming the door either."[166] To Thompson, now in Moscow, this meant that Hanoi had unlocked the bazaar, opening the "first round in oriental rug trading." North Vietnamese "concern over escalation may indicate they are hurting," he surmised, "and also may be effort to exploit experience of Warsaw talks to hold down our bombing activity."[167] Hoping to preempt pressure to halt the air campaign, LBJ and his spokesmen dismissed Trinh's remarks as not "serious," novel, or sufficient. "We have heard their signal," an aide acknowledged, "but it isn't the right one. We'd welcome another."[168]

Yet most analysts, both then and later, considered Trinh's interview a milestone in the evolution of Hanoi's attitude toward negotiations. Though still labeling the famous Four Points the "most correct political solution to the Vietnam problem," it no longer demanded their prior acceptance before talks could start.[169]

New evidence, from both Vietnamese and Polish sources, helps to explain how, when, and why this shift occurred—and its possible link to Marigold. For several months, since October, the VWP Politburo had debated how to integrate a diplomatic front into its military and political strategy; the Lodge-Lewandowski proposals had reached Hanoi in late November in the midst of these deliberations and had produced, after intense debate, a tenuous willingness to probe the U.S. position through direct contacts in Warsaw, even before a complete bombing halt, and to advance to more serious exchanges if Washington confirmed the stands Lewandowski had relayed. Yet subsequent events, climaxed by the December 13–14 raids, had bolstered those stressing the primacy of the battlefield and U.S. bad faith, resulting in a retraction of the offer to meet in Warsaw and the onset of a full-tilt propaganda blitz to exploit the bombings.

Nevertheless, the Politburo still agreed that *something* must be done to upgrade DRV diplomacy—to respond to international public opinion and political pressure (from both friends and neutrals), to compel Washington to stop the bombing, to exacerbate strains between the Johnson administration and reluctant allies, and to lay the groundwork for eventual negotiations once the military situation had "ripened" sufficiently. According to Siedlecki's Vietnamese source,

even after Marigold collapsed, the Politburo, meeting "non-stop," favored opening direct contacts with Washington, perhaps not in Warsaw (which was vulnerable to Chinese "diversion and sabotage") but in Rangoon, where Thant (as an
Asian statesman rather than UN leader) might play a role.[170]

As noted above, Brezhnev reported that Tho—clearly reflecting the Politburo's
wishes—had spoken of the desirability of opening negotiations with the Americans as "a tactical move" in his mid-December conversations in Moscow, and by
the end of that month, according to Siedlecki's informant, intimations of an impending "serious change" in Hanoi's position had begun to permeate the Communist Party's hierarchy. In one instance, Nhan Dan's editor in chief ("Le Duan's
man") briefed newspaper editors. After first ascertaining the absence of a representative of a Chinese-language periodical serving the minority ethnic community—"that's good, I will be able to speak with you honestly"—and swearing the
members of his audience to secrecy, he warned them to be ready to tackle a very
difficult task: explaining the opening of talks with the American enemy. He assured them, however, that the "unchanged and strategic purpose remains the liberation of the South, and the negotiations are a tactical element." Senior VWP
Central Committee (CC) official To Huu and his deputy purportedly gave a similar though somewhat vaguer heads-up to cadres in the propaganda apparatus—
alerting them to a coming "difficult change," though not specifically negotiations.[171]

By January, party wordsmiths had converted the Politburo's decision to launch
a new diplomatic offensive into a portion of a long resolution suitable for orienting high-level cadres, plus a shorter version ("On Intensifying the Diplomatic
Struggle and Taking the Offensive against the Enemy in Support of Our People's
Resistance War against the Americans to Save the Nation") fit for ratification by
the Thirteenth VWP CC Plenum, which met January 23–26, 1967, and for wider
distribution. Both underlined the need to intensify military and political struggles in South Vietnam, while at the same time opening a "flexible and skillful"
diplomatic offensive; whether or not talks actually began, the military and political arenas would remain primary.[172] As Trinh candidly elaborated, the "fighting
while talking, talking while fighting" strategy provided for direct negotiations
with the U.S. government (at the ambassadorial level) once Washington had
stopped bombing North Vietnam—"not to solve the Vietnam problem," but
merely as a probing exercise to "clarify each side's views while the fighting continues in South Vietnam."[173]

Trinh's speech on the first day of the closed-door plenum—along with a secret
cable the Politburo sent to military commanders in the South (i.e., the Central
Office for South Vietnam, or COSVN, then headed by Nguyen Chi Thanh) to
notify them of the policy shift[174]—stressed the need to seize the diplomatic initiative from the "crafty and stubborn" Americans and their deceitful "peace offensives" and "duplicitous" secret peace feelers, to exploit the propaganda opening
created by the uproar over the Hanoi bombings and Salisbury articles, to encourage domestic opposition to the Johnson administration (because the U.S. govern-

ment knew of Hanoi's willingness for talks, but not the American people), and to preempt a new escalation.

Neither Trinh nor the Politburo explicitly mentioned the still-secret Polish initiative, but both alluded to Washington's efforts to ensnare socialist countries, among others, in its nefarious plots. Like Goldilocks, the leadership chose a middle path—neither warmly embracing negotiations nor coldly rejecting them—before its Soviet Bloc patrons applied more pressure either to enter or abstain from serious talks. "Our friends," the Politburo delicately explained to the Central Office for South Vietnam, "may take actions that stray off course, in one direction or the other, thereby making it more complicated and difficult for us to employ our strategy."[175] Trinh came closer to revealing the hidden context behind recent events. The Americans, he explained, had proffered "a package deal" (using the English expression so redolent of Marigold), seeking to swap a bombing halt in the North for a resolution of their problems in the South. They were "lobbying for the support of a number of socialist Eastern European countries and have sent people to make feelers to us directly. During these 'peace offensives,' the U.S. has made maximum use of their 'bombing' and 'cessation of bombing' cards, and their recent attacks against a number of locations in Hanoi were aimed at placing further pressure on us."[176]

Now Hanoi hoped to turn the tables and squeeze the Americans—stepping up the military and political struggle, even as it edged toward an open-ended negotiating *process* that might constrain the Pentagon. Describing LBJ as "very hesitant," vacillating between hawkish and dovish advisers, Trinh predicted that he would reject the most extreme escalatory options that would risk war with China, yet strive to achieve military successes and a favorable political settlement before the 1968 elections, thereby assuring four more years in the White House.

The upcoming presidential vote now loomed as a crucial factor in DRV—and White House—calculations. Dispelling any illusion of rapid progress toward peace, even in the (unlikely) event of a bombing halt and the beginning of talks, the CC resolution warned that with "the American leadership clique" desperately building up forces in hopes of inflicting crippling military blows and achieving a rapid victory, "*the years 1967–68 and especially 1968, will see extremely fierce and savage combat between the enemy and ourselves.*" North Vietnam needed, therefore, to prepare a devastating preemptive counterstrike to convince Washington that it had arrived not at the threshold of success but at the precipice of a "strategic impasse" from which it must retreat. Though still formally adhering to a "protracted war" strategy—Trinh spoke of "secur[ing] victory one step at a time"—the party resolved "*to mobilize and concentrate the resources of the entire nation to make a maximum effort to crush the schemes of the enemy and secure a decisive victory in a relatively short period of time*" (emphasis in the original).[177]

As Trinh explained the Politburo's "vision," subject to modification depending on circumstances, the "fighting while talking, talking while fighting" phase, of indeterminate duration, would be followed by the second, "most important" phase: a "decisive victory on the battlefield" that compelled Washington, still straitjacketed from bombing the North, to negotiate with the NLF and withdraw its forces. That would clear the path to the "settlement of the problem of South Vietnam"—that is, the North's de facto takeover and, in due course, unification under Communist auspices. Phase three would be a diplomatic mopping-up operation, securing international recognition and confirmation of the final result.[178]

The recently released Vietnamese records, long hidden in Lao Dong CC archives, combined with the Polish evidence of the unmentioned diplomatic context, prompt a novel reinterpretation of the January 1967 developments in Hanoi. In this view, Marigold's breakdown sharply stiffened Hanoi's positions, reinforcing both the already-deep distrust of U.S. intentions and preconceptions about the preeminence of the military and political struggles; whereas the VWP Politburo, or at least a tenuous majority, was willing to explore serious exchanges with the Americans in late November and early December 1966, hardening attitudes had then relegated diplomacy's purposes to propaganda, coercion, limited probing, and at most "fighting while talking, talking while fighting." Only when battlefield victories could be translated into attainable, acceptable results might negotiations become serious—and that meant preparing for climactic clashes with the Americans. Though nodding to the importance of better diplomacy, the VWP CC resolution prescribed a "spontaneous uprising [in South Vietnam] in order to win a decisive victory in the shortest possible time."[179]

This calculation would, exactly a year later, underpin one of the Vietnam War's most pivotal events: the Tet Offensive, Hanoi's carefully prepared surprise guerrilla assaults on Saigon and other South Vietnamese cities, at the end of January 1968. Although this revolt failed to spark a general revolt or the disintegration of the Thieu-Ky regime, as its sponsors had hoped, it traumatized U.S. politics just as the quadrennial campaign season opened, turning mainstream America against the war, forcing LBJ to drop his reelection bid, and finally causing his administration to reject further escalation and reluctantly begin the long, hard process of withdrawal from Vietnam. The planning for Tet, which is still incompletely understood, accelerated in the summer and fall of 1967—but the idea's seeds may have germinated during the previous winter, in Marigold's rubble.[180]

* * *

DRV officials carefully choreographed Trinh's interview, flanking it with private contacts with foreign diplomats for maximum effect. On January 27, Le Chang privately conveyed the new stand to Guthrie in Moscow, and envoys in New Delhi, Cairo, Paris, and other capitals underlined Trinh's statements to host governments.[181] In Hanoi, senior officials briefed the diplomats of socialist countries on whose understanding and support they relied. In a preview for the Polish Embassy, a vice minister outlined the strategy contained in the secret party resolutions, and requested intensified aid in the international campaign against the bombing—and, without impugning Warsaw's own recent efforts, in discouraging aspiring mediators who would merely "complicate things even further." Poland's acting ambassador (Siedlecki had gone home) also reported that Trinh had frankly told Burchett, over dinner, that Hanoi's new willingness for negotiations was merely "tactical," though Shcherbakov, reflecting Moscow's priorities, optimistically appraised the interview as a step toward an eventual political settlement that the Chinese had been unable to block.[182] Ha Van Lau sent a confidential message to Lewandowski, explaining the shift and asking him to observe its reception in Saigon.[183]

More Maneuvers in Saigon: "Far Too Busy Spying"

After a short side trip to Cambodia, the Pole was back in the South Vietnamese capital, where he faced difficult situations on both the Marigold and Commission fronts. On Thursday morning, January 26, he saw D'Orlandi, who dreaded telling him about the dispiriting lunch with Lodge but felt compelled to do so. Dashing hopes of a renewed push to communicate with Hanoi via Lewandowski, the American had been evasive about further three-way meetings, the Italian related. Only when prodded had he commented vaguely that the volatile, rapidly shifting Asian situation precluded serious planning. Relating Lodge's view that China's internal "paralysis" might so interfere with its aid for North Vietnam that Hanoi's own supply stream to the NLF might dry up, crippling Communist operations in the South, D'Orlandi inferred that Washington now sought a better deal than the one available in early December through the Saigon channel.

Hearing this, Lewandowski also discerned a "regression" in the U.S. position since the fall—encouraged by the Communist disarray, the Johnson administration appeared "deluded by the mirage of military victory," perhaps even hoping to salvage its bases in the South (contrary to its Manila promise). Retreating further from the ten points, Washington had narrowed its negotiating interest to secondary matters (a bombing halt, prisoner swaps) "without taking up conversations on the fundamental matter" of South Vietnam's political fate.

Though Lewandowski reaffirmed Rapacki's commitment to continued secrecy to preserve the channel's viability, neither had many illusions. With "nothing left to save here," D'Orlandi observed that he needed to start thinking again of his health and returning home. His friend also mulled escaping his post. "Melancholy leave-taking," the Italian recorded.[184]

D'Orlandi's pain leapt across the decades when I showed Lewandowski his *szyfrogram* relating this late January 1967 conversation. By then, the Pole felt certain that the three-way channel was a "dead horse; . . . I try not to mix my hopes with reality." Yet, against the odds, his friend (in part reflecting Fanfani's wishes) clung desperately to the idea of raising this "Frankenstein" from the dead: D'Orlandi "believe[d] it was the most important thing in his life," and so he kept trying to resuscitate Marigold "as if your own child is dropped into the sea, . . . and you are trying to revive him."[185]

* * *

By mid-January, Hanoi, justifiably content with its global propaganda campaign against the bombings, had lost interest in fighting for the release of the still-secret ICC report concluding unanimously that U.S. planes had indeed caused civilian damage within the city limits. During Moore's farewell visit, Ha Van Lau needled the Canadian that the ICC had blown a golden opportunity to grab the spotlight. Its report, the PAVN colonel said, had aroused "a ray of hope" that the body might play a more active and positive part, but instead it had tarried and allowed Salisbury to seize the stage. "One should not confuse the role of the ICC with that of a newspaper correspondent," Moore countered. True, Lau allowed, but if the ICC had published first, "its role would have been enhanced."[186]

Having made his debating point, Ludwig secretly radioed Lewandowski, advising him to stop pushing for the ICC to send the bombing report to the Geneva cochairs. Otherwise, the Canadian and Indian might gang up to "exploit the next opportunity to submit other uncomfortable" (i.e., critical of the DRV) "matters" to London and Moscow. Besides, "public opinion has been sufficiently moved, and even if the report were published, this would not make a great impression." Instead of trying to publicize the report, the Pole should "tactically exploit" the issue to "paralyze" any negative Canadian or Indian activities.

However, Lewandowski disregarded this prescient warning. "I think, however, that we should continue to exert pressure, so the report is submitted," he cabled Warsaw. "The dangers of which L[udwig] is talking about exist. However, it seems that the advantages would be greater."[187] Nor did he change his mind when his MSZ overseer, Spasowski, endorsed Ha Van Lau's "apprehensions," also urging Lewandowski to use the report as leverage "in a further game with the partner[s]" rather than trying to push it through.[188]

The Pole's strategy backfired. Just as the PAVN liaison feared, at the next ICC meeting, on January 27, the Indian and Canadian joined forces to pass resolutions admonishing Hanoi for accepting Soviet SAMs and MiGs (with Rahman voting for Moore's motion) and for sending PAVN's 325th Division to the South (with the chair abstaining on Moore's sterner motion on infiltration but gaining his support for a milder version).[189] In both cases, the Indo-Canadian majority easily hurdled Lewandowski's objections that the items should be stricken from the agenda because North Vietnam had acted in legitimate self-defense. "It was not the commission's business to make political or military judgments on the Vietnam War" but only to note violations of Geneva, Rahman and Moore retorted. At the same time, the Indian rejected Lewandowski's request to put first on the agenda his plea to transmit the unanimous Hanoi bombings report to the Soviets and British, and instead shunted it to the limbo of a drafting committee, ominously signaling sympathy with Moore's argument that any message to the cochairs must be a "balanced document, and not only about one aspect of the Vietnamese problem." He similarly dismissed Lewandowski's contention that his anti-Washington bombing resolution had passed on December 31 by a vote of one for and two abstaining, consigning the issue to a legal committee for further study. On virtually every issue, Lewandowski grimly reported to Warsaw, the Indian had "fully supported" the Canadian. (Ottawa presumed Rahman's aid was "obviously" a quid pro quo for Moore's backing for the chairman's December 31 resolution on the Hanoi bombings.[190])

The 756th ICC meeting ended cordially, with warm regards from Lewandowski and Rahman to Moore on his last session and joshing threats to call a final emergency meeting at Tan Son Nhut before he flew off on Monday.

Lewandowski also revealed some dry wit that Friday evening, when he joined his fellow commissioners again (plus other guests such as Westmoreland in civvies), for a farewell supper for Moore at Rahman's villa. Awaiting the meal, the Canadian's senior military adviser "was pulling [Lewandowski's] leg a little and asked him why he no longer turned out for tennis. With a straight face, he replied that he was far too busy spying and could not spare the time! I giggled my way through a rather dull dinner on this remark, which I found most amusing."[191]

But no bon mot could disguise that the Pole had suffered a stinging defeat. As Chubb giggled, Lewandowski whispered to D'Orlandi that Rahman's unexpected pro-Canadian (i.e., pro–United States) tilt had not only sidetracked the Hanoi bombing report but had also yielded anti-DRV resolutions. This put him and his government "in a position of great embarrassment" vis-à-vis the North Vietnamese, who even in the best of times complained of ICC partiality toward Washington. D'Orlandi wondered how Warsaw would "swallow the toad"—and worried that this "incredible" development might close the door to mediation efforts by the commission or its member countries. "Without a doubt," he rued, "the situation has been radicalized!"[192]

Indeed, Lewandowski had a bitter pill to digest. "At that time I was really upset, I must tell you," he remembered.[193] Thanks to his promotion of a report to the cochairs on the Hanoi bombings, the Canadians had successfully parried by resuscitating and then, with Indian help, ramming though resolutions awkward for the North Vietnamese. Though Moore's military aide grumbled privately that Rahman was "once again pretty shifty and all in all a pretty frustrating morning the more so as the primary subject started just over one year ago," Ottawa congratulated the commissioner as he ended his term: "Thanks to your perseverance," the commission had criticized the North for the first time in four and a half years, since mid-1962, finding Hanoi in "substantive violation" of Geneva for only the eighth and ninth time since its creation. "The 756th meeting is therefore something of a landmark in the troubled history of the ICC."[194]

Lewandowski tried to get to Hanoi as quickly as possible so he could explain the situation personally to his North Vietnamese comrades. He had planned a trip for weeks, timing it to allow delivery of a message from Lodge (before Washington scotched the idea) and also to gauge the impact of the dramatic Chinese events, but the ICC setback supplied fresh impetus. The Pole requested a special flight to Hanoi on January 31, but the ICC in Laos refused to clear the final leg due to safety considerations, so he had to await the next scheduled departure three days later.[195] Meanwhile, Warsaw's reaction to his cable describing the January 27 meeting probably left him squirming: Though his report was "sufficient for us," Spasowski, in a cable approved by Michałowski, requested that Lewandowski do a better job of keeping Hanoi informed, and also coordinate more closely with the new Polish ambassador in Hanoi, Bogdan Wasilewski, when he arrived. It was an unmistakable clipping of Lewandowski's wings.[196] Stymied both in peacemaking and commission maneuvering, Lewandowski set to depart for Hanoi in a far dourer mood than when he embarked on his far more auspicious journey ten weeks earlier.

13

"A Sunburst of Recriminations"
Riders on the Storm, February–June 1967

The Americans bungled it.

—*"An informed source,"* Washington Post, *February 2, 1967*

It is as though we are all riding in a boat with the current and there is nothing for us to do at present time.

—*Janusz Lewandowski to Victor Moore, February 16, 1967*

I was the greatest wishful thinker in the world. The hope was father to my thoughts. I thought that maybe we had it.

—*John Gronouski, private remarks to the Senate Foreign Relations Committee, May 15, 1967*

To sum it all up, thus far, no one has been able to produce . . . the warm body of a North Vietnamese anywhere, at any time, with whom I can talk. [Laughter] . . . There are hundreds of candidates for the Nobel Prize wandering around the world, and . . . some of them visit Hanoi, some of them have contacts with Hanoi's representatives in one or another capital. Most of them don't understand what it is they are hearing. And so they come away eight months pregnant. They are just about to deliver peace. [Laughter]

—*Dean Rusk, off-the-record comments to a conference of editors and broadcasters, May 22, 1967*

The Phở Hits the Fan: Marigold Goes Public

It was only a matter of time before the phở hit the fan. In early February 1967, the emissions from what Salisbury would dub "a sunburst of recriminations" finally became visible to the naked eye.[1]

By late January, gossip about the failed peace bid was caroming around the United Nations and a growing number of chancelleries, and the versions of the tale seeping through diplomatic, political, and, inevitably, journalistic circles hardly flattered Washington. Of course, the Hanoi bombings were already a global cause célèbre. But for those in the know, and who were furious about what had happened or were just looking to dump on a U.S. policy they opposed, it was hard to resist the temptation to spread the charge that the air raids had also wrecked a promising chance for peace.

Rapacki and Fanfani were resentful enough to loosen their tongues—and launch well-calculated indiscretions aimed at causing maximum discomfort for LBJ. Visiting Paris in late January, the Polish foreign minister "confidentially" volunteered the story of the aborted peace attempt to the French foreign minister, Maurice Couve de Murville, suggesting that the effort's failure had stemmed from Washington's attempt to "blackmail" Hanoi into concessions. Then, during an audience at the Palais de l'Elysée, Rapacki—declaring Polish and French views on Vietnam "very close if not identical"—discussed the affair with President de Gaulle. Having just vetoed Sainteny's trip to Hanoi on the grounds that Washington was insincere about peace, Le Général found in Rapacki's recitation further corroboration of his views (which already, of course, had been informed by the account Thant had given Roger Seydoux).

"This is very interesting, very striking," de Gaulle observed. "The United States give[s] the impression that they are looking for doors, but don't want to cross any of them. They are ready to open doors, but not to go through them. They cannot because of their internal situation, of the military, of the mechanism in which they got involved and from which they cannot escape. It is going to take a long time."[2]

Another visitor to Western Europe in late January and early February was the New York senator Robert F. Kennedy, who was restless and unhappy over the administration's conduct of the war but was not yet ready to break openly with LBJ's strategy, let alone to challenge him for the Democratic presidential nomination. Having become increasingly persuaded that the administration was mishandling chances for peace, however slim—for example, in the La Pira affair, when he believed Johnson's precipitous bombing of Haiphong had undermined Fanfani's efforts to clarify Hanoi's position[3]—RFK dabbled on the fringes of secret Vietnam diplomacy. In early 1966, he had vainly sought to contact the NLF to achieve the release of an official of the U.S. Agency for International Development; after seeing him, the Czech ambassador in Washington reported that RFK, deviating from official U.S. orthodoxy, "agree[d] that it is necessary to recognize the National Liberation Front, and he even hinted at an interest in personal contact."[4] Though RFK had loyally declared to the Communist envoy that despite reservations "in principle he will always support the President of the United States," his hesitant calls to move away from bombing and toward negotiations increasingly irked Johnson.[5]

RFK's voyage to Europe would not enhance the mutual regard between him and LBJ. Passing through London and Paris, "combining youthful good looks with the solemn posture of a statesman," the charismatic Kennedy grabbed public attention—as when he expressed "grave reservations" about U.S. policy to the Oxford Union.[6] Privately, he reviewed peace prospects with British and French officials, some of whom knew about the failed Polish effort. Wilson and Brown held their tongues regarding Marigold, but not de Gaulle, who briefly mentioned the failed Polish mediation attempt in December while criticizing the Johnson administration's approach to peace negotiations.[7] In Rome, RFK's next stop, Fanfani showed even less restraint. Two months earlier, in a private conversation with the Polish ambassador, the Italian had scorned "Kennedy circles" as unreliable, more eager to score points against Johnson than promote peace.[8] But when the senator's itinerary brought him to town, Fanfani candidly vented his frustration to the leading keeper of John F. Kennedy's flame—and the incumbent president's bête noire. Without divulging Poland's role, the Italian claimed that his "very good contacts" with North Vietnam had in early December led to "essential agreement on all major points" of a peace settlement, only to have hopes dashed by the ill-timed Hanoi bombings. According to a record kept by a Kennedy aide, "Fanfani said that he had asked the United States to cease activity around Hanoi, but in reply we had said that the military was planning and executing the bombing and that their plans had been formulated for months and could not be interfered with." Though Fanfani suggested that perhaps the Soviets had also sidetracked the overture, his tale could only have reinforced RFK's doubts about Washington's competence and sincerity in seeking negotiations.[9]

These indiscretions remained, for the moment, private—but the coup de grâce to any immediate prospect of reviving Marigold was administered when newspaper accounts of the secret initiative's failure began appearing. On February 2, in a short, sketchy inside story, a *Washington Post* UN correspondent, Robert H. Estabrook, citing unspecified "excellent authority," revealed a "Polish initiative to establish peace discussions" that had allegedly foundered due to the U.S. "bombing of the Hanoi area" in mid-December. Though Estabrook described the Poles as "extremely frustrated, not merely over the effect of the bombing, but more particularly with the uncooperative attitude of Hanoi," his story prominently displayed an anonymous quotation that put the blame squarely on Washington: "The Americans bungled it," an "informed source" concluded.[10]

Estabrook was not the only journalist chasing the story. Two weeks earlier, Drew Pearson had told Arthur Goldberg that an unnamed "Communist source" had claimed that a "substantial peace initiative was aborted" due to the December 13–14 Hanoi bombings; after the UN ambassador, who guessed Dobrynin had fed the columnist the tip, warned him that the reality was more complex and he "would fall victim to a Communist ploy" if he ran the story, Pearson held back.[11] In Saigon, a *New York Daily News* reporter told Lodge in late January that he "knew" Gronouski had been "having conversations" with the Polish government "about settling the war in Vietnam" but had failed to file the story.[12] The same day Estabrook broke his exclusive, the *Boston Globe* bannered a vaguer account by its own UN correspondent claiming that Hanoi had "bowed to third-party efforts" by an unnamed "neutral government" to "meet with USA at a conference table" but had then been "rebuffed." Draius Jhabvala's piece faulted the mid-December raids for the initiative's collapse and for Hanoi's "more intransigent and less responsive" position ever since.[13] Beaten into print, the *St. Louis Post-Dispatch's* Donald Grant told U.S. officials that he had sat on the Polish story for ten days because he "feared repercussions on peace talks."[14]

Attentive readers could infer that Estabrook had picked up the scent in Ottawa, which he had visited on a reporting trip two weeks earlier. In a story from the frigid capital datelined January 20, he quoted "high Canadian officials" as disclosing that the "accidental U.S. bombings of Hanoi in mid-December" had "disrupted" unidentified "private soundings then under way" to start peace talks, causing North Vietnam to harden its terms.[15] His February 2 piece, moreover, linked the "Polish initiative" to Martin's stimulation—betraying Canadian self-promotion, because no one else had a motive to leak such a nuance (particularly because it was untrue).

That Estabrook—or any *Post* correspondent—was even reporting from Ottawa and the UN in the winter of 1966–67 was an accident of newsroom politics. A decade earlier, Estabrook, an Ohio native with journalism in his blood (he had even started up a local paper as a teenager) had been something of a wunderkind at the *Post.* Joining the paper right after World War II, he had ascended its ranks with alacrity, and publisher Phil Graham had named him editorial page editor in 1953 at the age of thirty-four. But his precocious elevation engendered staff resentment, and his ties with Graham grew strained, exacerbated by the publisher's increasingly erratic behavior, symptoms of the manic depression that would drive him over the edge. In 1961, after opining for more than a decade on topics ranging from McCarthyism to civil rights to the Cold War to the domestic and foreign policies of the Truman, Eisenhower, and Kennedy administrations, Estabrook left the editorial page to become the *Post's* London correspondent. His departure was hardly voluntary. "Phil's and Bob's personalities were not in harmony," Phil's widow and successor as publisher, Katharine Graham, later remembered, "and they had developed various differences on issues over the years." In fact, Graham had "turned on" Estabrook (in one quarrel, pulling an editorial he had written critical of the Bay of Pigs invasion without telling him) and wanted to fire him, but the publisher was talked into instead offering him a plum foreign slot by a powerful Estabrook ally and mentor—the executive editor, James Russell Wiggins, the former managing editor who now added his colleague's duties to an already bulging portfolio.[16]

Although Estabrook was disconcerted by his transfer, and was unsure whether he would return to stewardship of the editorial page (which the masthead still listed him as running), he plunged into reporting from London and around the Continent. Encountering the era's giants—Khrushchev, de Gaulle, Adenauer, Macmillan, Monnet, and others—he gradually came to appreciate the shift, which Graham confirmed by naming him chief foreign correspondent, free to travel and devise his own assignments ("a magnificent opportunity. Go, go, go!"). Making trips to South Asia, the Middle East, and Africa as well as the Balkans, the USSR, and the Kremlin domain in Central and Eastern Europe, he developed a feel for East-West and North-South interactions, and he cultivated contacts on both sides of the increasingly permeable Iron Curtain; on a late 1964 visit to Warsaw, he conveyed a Polish warning that time was running out to negotiate a Vietnam settlement with Ho.[17]

Naturally, Estabrook also covered U.S.-European relations, getting into hot water with Rusk over a story from London (based on a background briefing) that the secretary of state denounced as inaccurate. Estabrook believed he'd gotten his facts straight, but on checking, he discovered that the copy desk in Washington had distorted his language. To calm the irate reporter, foreign editor Philip Foisie promised to explain the circumstances to Rusk (who, in an illustration of Washington's incestuous nature, also happened to be his brother-in-law). Nevertheless, Estabrook recalled, "Rusk never trusted me again, as he made clear on several occasions."[18]

When the now-worldly Midwesterner returned to Washington in 1965, he anticipated landing a senior slot in either the news or editorial department. The *Post,* however, was in flux following Phil Graham's suicide and succession by his wife, Katherine (known as Kay), and senior management looked to transform the paper into a higher-grade operation by luring some outside ringers. Estabrook found news side advancement blocked by the rise of a new star, Ben Bradlee, who had been snagged from *Newsweek* to become managing editor, and instead was assigned to the editorial page—not as editor, to his chagrin, but merely as Wiggins' deputy. After a year or so of feeling "like a fifth wheel," Estabrook heard Wiggins inform him that he was being sent back to the foreign desk, to inaugurate a new UN bureau. Estabrook was "flabbergasted" at his second expulsion from headquarters, which he later attributed to Graham's and Bradlee's desire to bring in the *Wall Street Journal*'s Philip Geyelin as editorial page editor ahead of him, and their belief that his proximity would be awkward. He also blanched at the hefty (29.4 percent) pay cut, "a real jolt," that came with the job. But Estabrook, now in his midforties, needed to pay the bills, especially with three kids to put through college, so he gulped and moved to New York in October 1966.[19]

Though aware that his position had been "invented to get me out of Washington," Estabrook determined to make the best of the opportunity. Leaning on the foreign expertise and diplomatic sources he had acquired during his four years in London, he began filing copy on an assortment of international stories, though inevitably, Vietnam dominated the scene. Besides forging friendly ties with Goldberg and Thant, Estabrook took particular care to recruit Central and Eastern European informants capable of kibitzing on the confused Communist realm. The reporter, in turn, shared tidbits gleaned from Eastern Bloc sources with officers attached to the United States' UN Mission, angling for reciprocal garrulousness. "Estabrook is a serious, capable journalist with good contacts among Communist delegations," one remarked approvingly.[20] Almost as an afterthought, Wiggins had suggested enlarging Estabrook's UN beat to include Canada, to be covered though occasional drop-ins. This side job was what had led him to book a room at Ottawa's venerable Château Laurier hotel, adjacent to the Parliament building, for January 16 to 18, 1967, and to the background interview with Paul Martin that would set him on Marigold's trail.[21]

Estabrook's February 2 story, the first into print with the Polish angle, caused immediate ripples atop the Johnson administration. That Thursday morning, Rusk phoned Goldberg in New York to solicit his guess on who had spilled the beans.[22] Probably the Poles, "swinging this all around the UN," were the "initiators," and the Canadians had confirmed it, hazarded the ambassador (who had noted rumors that Estabrook and Jhabvala were seen chatting with the Polish and Indian "permreps" at a party hosted by the latter the day before[23]). The secretary suggested that he might call Russ Wiggins, an entrenched Vietnam hawk still in charge of the *Post*'s editorial page in addition to overseeing news coverage. Perhaps Wiggins could send Estabrook back to his sources to say "You did not tell me the whole story." Goldberg demurred, citing a prior attempt to prod the paper via Bradlee that had "got a bad reaction."

So for the moment, Rusk held off on contacting the *Post*'s chief editor. Hoping to avoid fanning the flames, he cautioned White House spokesman George Christian to "slide away from" any comment on the item.[24]

At a press conference on Thursday, LBJ did his best to downgrade the speculation generated by Trinh's interview and Estabrook's story. Washington had not received, he insisted, any "serious indications" of North Vietnamese interest "to either go to a conference table or to bring the war to an end." Reinforcing the message, Rostow discounted peace-feeler claims in backgrounders with *Time,* the *Post,* the Associated Press, and other news outlets, and a State Department spokesman scoffed at the notion that the Hanoi bombings had impeded concrete peace soundings.[25]

Though Estabrook had not named any sources, Goldberg expressed "great annoyance" at Warsaw for leaking so slanted a story. "Poles have read themselves out of act" as a potential channel, he told Ignatieff, vowing to scold Tomorowicz "firmly and frankly."[26] He got his chance Friday evening in a "chance encounter" with the Polish UN delegate at a dinner party hosted by Soviet ambassador Nikolai T. Fedorenko. According to Tomorowicz, Goldberg "pulled me to the side by stating that he wished to talk to me without any witnesses." Though not explicitly charging him with leaking, he admonished him that intermediaries must "preserve absolute secrecy" if they wished to be effective. The Pole admitted nothing, but Goldberg discerned a guilty conscience: "Tomorowicz seemed very embarrassed, and his attitude served to confirm my own impression that Poles [were] responsible for leaks," he cabled Rusk.[27]

On Saturday morning, Estabrook struck again in the *Post*—and far more spectacularly. Beneath a screaming front-page headline, he reported that the North Vietnamese had "definitely agreed" to direct talks with the Americans in early December before the Hanoi bombings caused them to back off, accusing Washington of "bad faith." In making this confident declaration, Estabrook cited a "highly authoritative Western source" apparently annoyed by Johnson's dismissive press conference comments. Going much deeper than in his first piece, Estabrook revealed that before being scuttled, the effort had gone so far as to specify Warsaw as the site for conversations, and, citing Communist sources, that Hanoi had agreed to talk without insisting on a prior bombing halt, contrary to its endlessly repeated public demand—a disclosure obviously meant to underline North Vietnam's reasonableness in the affair.[28]

Now Rusk decided to discreetly pull the *Post* into line. On Saturday afternoon, he phoned Wiggins, and, politely but firmly, warned the paper's powerful executive (the last to lead the editorial and news operations simultaneously[29]) to beware of the story that his protégé had broken:

> Sec. just wanted to have a very, very private word with W. not aimed at any action but thought W. might be entitled to a little evaluation on Sec's part. Before W. lets it get tangled up in editorial attitudes, W. should know that the Estabrook business is highly fragmentary and only excerpts from something that is quite a different story in its total story. This is basically Polish propaganda distortion. The Poles, Canadians and U Thant know a lot more about it than is in the Estabrook story. His sources are with people who are not coming clean with him. Sec. said there is a lot more to it, and wanted W. to know that in regard to his editorials. W. said he was worried about the whole posture. W. said they become in between with all the peace rumors. Sec. said the trouble is if we clarify them then we get in the way of things that we are trying to do. W. understood. Sec. will tell W. very privately and ask that he not circulate it around that Sec. thinks the chances are 50/50 that Hanoi will deny that story quite categorically. Sec. wanted W. to know that Bob got hold of distorted fragments. Sec. said the Poles have been campaigning on this and they know better. W. thanked Sec. very much.[30]

Although rumors about the affair had been circulating for weeks, U.S. officials believed they had a solid basis for blaming Warsaw.[31] Estabrook's information "could only have come from the Poles in New York," Bundy told a British diplomat, and their leaking "must be regarded as a depressing indication of real intentions on the Communist side."[32] At a February 8 National Security Council meeting, responding to LBJ's request for a recapitulation of "our peace probes," Rusk said flatly that the "Poles have put out fragmentary and false accounts of a probe which is called 'Marigold.'"[33]

Though the U.S. UN Mission collected contradictory reports regarding the *Post* stories' origins—Estabrook told one officer that he "had it from high Polish source he would not identify," corroborated by other Eastern Europeans, Martin, and Thant; but to another, he cited only Martin and Thant—Goldberg firmly fingered the Poles (abetted in confirmatory roles by the Canadians and Thant), and derived clear implications from such villainous behavior. Recalling their spreading of a "tendentious" version of the thirty-seven-day bombing pause, which he had "only with great difficulty" persuaded Cousins not to publish, he stressed that Warsaw's political interests regarding Vietnam differed significantly from Washington's and motivated it to "put [the] worst possible light on each development." He advised sternly "that we should no longer use Poland or any other bloc country as [a] channel to Hanoi."[34]

Reading the cable traffic in Warsaw, Gronouski strongly challenged Goldberg's "inferences and conclusions." Circumstantial evidence, the beleaguered envoy argued, primarily implicated Martin and his aides as the sources behind Estabrook's stories. Perhaps the Poles and Thant had helped, but only to confirm an earlier tip from the Canadians rather than the other way around, as Goldberg insisted. Not only had Estabrook's Ottawa story clearly foreshadowed what was to come, Gronouski argued, but his February 2 revelation had linked the Polish peace effort to the Rapacki-Martin conversations, "which is not true, but it does not hurt Martin's image to be cast in this role"—and Canada's envoy in Warsaw had supplied a motive for an anti-Washington leak: Martin felt "miffed" at Rusk for not informing him of Marigold during their mid-December conversations in Paris. Quite reasonably, Gronouski also pointed out that from both U.S. and Polish briefings (and secondary leaks), diplomats from an expanding circle of countries knew of the affair, enabling any of them to aid an inquisitive reporter. And once again—as after Porter's blistering indictment a month earlier—he gamely defended Poland's efforts to intercede with Hanoi. Though he had hoped Moscow might rise to the occasion,

> to my knowledge experience has been that Poles are only Communist country willing to take on this chore. Fact that they are allies of Hanoi and have different political interests than we do was known to us long ago. But . . . Poles have vested interest in ending VN war; . . . Poles (I am convinced) tried to persuade Hanoi to enter talks after our Dec. 24 action; they have good contacts in Hanoi; and there appears to be no one in the wings to replace them. That they do not love us does not mean they cannot be useful in situation where their interests parallel ours. I submit that with respect to the single question of getting negotiations started (in contrast to condition for negotiations or their results), their interests and ours do parallel.[35]

Not surprisingly, Gronouski's arguments—both on the *Post* pieces' provenance and their implications for Poland's suitability as a mediator—fell on deaf
ears in Washington. Where, then, had Estabrook gotten his scoop? Were Goldberg, Bundy, and Rusk justified in maligning the Poles? Or was Gronouski justified in dissenting?

Certainly Rapacki and the Poles were guilty of the first diplomatic leaks, and
Michałowski had stirred the pot when he passed through New York in mid-
January. But with gossip rampant, Estabrook hardly needed to get the story *directly* from Polish sources. Moreover, in his own secret cables home to Warsaw
(where he might have proudly owned up to leaking a story so damaging to Washington), the Polish ambassador to the UN proclaimed his innocence. After Estabrook's first scoop naming Poland, Tomorowicz speculated that he had gotten the
story from "American sources" and declared that "nobody from our side" had
spoken to him (and he personally was "trying to avoid the press").[36] Two days
later, after the front-page *Post* exposé, the Pole guessed that Estabrook's "first
source" had been Martin, in view of his recent Ottawa sojourn.[37] Ignatieff confirmed to him that the Canadians had supplied Estabrook with "full information"
even before he left for Ottawa, Tomorowicz later claimed.[38]

Estabrook himself gets the last word. Decades after these events, he identified
neither Martin nor Tomorowicz but *Denmark*'s UN ambassador, Hans Tabor, as
the key source who disclosed the "blighted arrangement for peace talks" and
judged that Washington had "bungled it." When the *Post* reporter took the gregarious diplomat to lunch at a midtown French restaurant in late January, "he
dropped this in passing, knowing full well what he was doing. . . . He felt the
United States was not telling the truth about the general negotiating climate."[39]

How did the *Danes* know? Possibly from the Poles. A few weeks before, in
early January, Danish prime minister Jens Otto Krag had visited Warsaw, where
the Polish leaders emphasized Hanoi's willingness to talk if the bombing stopped.
Although Gronouski speculated that they also told their guests about Marigold,
the confidential Danish record suggests that Rapacki held his tongue about the
affair, merely reiterating the familiar lament that Washington had squandered a
chance to open a dialogue during the bombing pause a year earlier. Reticence
during formal bilateral sessions, however, did not exclude more candid disclosures at some point during Krag's five-day stay—and the Polish summary indicates that Rapacki told the Dane that three times, Hanoi had signaled a willingness to talk, only to be rebuffed by U.S. escalation and bombardment.[40] Later in
January, Denmark's deputy foreign minister, Hans Sølvhøj, passed through
Washington and New York, where he divulged knowledge of Marigold to Goldberg and, according to the American, "attributed it to the Poles." Presumably, he
also passed the tale along to Tabor—who, of course, might also have heard it from
the loquacious Thant or others in the know.[41]

Though Estabrook seemed somewhat fuzzy about the story's origins, both in
guarded comments at the time and when interviewed decades later, two contem-

poraneous memoranda found in his papers at the Wisconsin Historical Society help clarify how he got that story. They confirm, first, that Martin at least hinted to Estabrook at the Polish dimension of the unidentified "soundings" that were disrupted by the mid-December Hanoi bombings—but only off the record, because the reporter did not mention a Polish angle in his January 20 story from Ottawa. Though no record of his talk with the Canadian foreign minister (or any of his UN representatives) has been located, and in his memoirs and interviews Estabrook did not recall Martin's naming the Poles, in a contemporaneous memo of an off-the-record conversation with a different source who divulged the basic story, the reporter noted that Martin had "told me the same thing two weeks ago in Canada."[42] The timing of Estabrook's first reporting expedition to Ottawa worked out perfectly; Martin had just received a report of Michałowski's talk in New York with Canadian diplomats, and was able to tip him off to the Pole's quiet UN transit. After going to Montreal, where he produced a long preview of the upcoming world's fair, Expo '67, Estabrook returned to New York in late January, where he was evidently able to augment Martin's off-the-record information with Tabor's slightly more usable snippets.

In search of confirmation and detail, the reporter then secured an off-the-record interview on January 30 with Thant (through his helpful spokesman, Ramses Nassif, an Egyptian civil servant[43]), and this time he *did* memorialize the conversation. By then, Estabrook had a good rapport with Thant, whom he later remembered as "impassive appearing until you got to know him—then he was a very warm person who would talk about his days as a newspaper man." Estabrook had met him once years before, when he was editorial page editor and Thant was the Burmese ambassador, but their talk on the thirty-eighth floor of the UN headquarters building was his first private interview with him.[44] Having heard the Polish tale from, first, Tomorowicz, then Goldberg, and most recently Michałowski, Thant made clear to Estabrook whose version he found more credible:

> Private off-the-record session with United Nations Secretary General U Thant. His stipulation is that this cannot be written about.
>
> American bombing of Hanoi in December badly fouled up the possibility of peace talks. Until then Thant had been quite hopeful. Some of these negotiations had been going on through Poland. But the utility of what the Poles had been doing diminished after the bombing.
>
> Nevertheless, something is now transpiring. Thant would not say what it was, but gave the impression that talks about talks are proceeding somewhere other than in Warsaw. He confirmed that the locale had been Warsaw last month and that Jerzy Michałowski, former Polish Ambassador to the UN (who made a trip to Hanoi last year after Harriman's visit to Warsaw) had made an unannounced visit to New York and the U.S. recently. Paul Martin told me the same thing two weeks ago in Canada.

. . . On several occasions Hanoi told him it was interested in talks with the U.S. The last was in December—but then the bombing delayed matters. Thant seemed discouraged on this point. I asked him how badly the bombing had set things back—a month, two months, etc. He declined to say, but said it was serious.

One consideration here, he emphasized, is the feeling in Hanoi that every time it has expressed willingness to talk, there has been an intensification of the bombing or other U.S. military activity.[45]

Although Thant's words were explosive, they were still off limits for publication, so Estabrook sought other sources to get the story into print. On February 1, he lunched with deputy Yugoslav ambassador Antun Duhaček (who was actually an intelligence agent), whom he had known in London and considered reliable.[46] "The Polish initiative is dead," Duhaček confirmed, on a not-for-quotation—but otherwise unrestricted—basis. "The Poles have now abandoned it in disgust, partly at the effect of the American bombing in December, but also in frustration at the hard attitude of the North Vietnamese government," which had subsequently adopted "a very much harder attitude."[47]

Now Estabrook had enough for his first piece, which bore traces of the conversations with Martin, Tabor, Thant, and Duhaček. Then, after LBJ publicly denied that Hanoi had shown any "serious" interest in peace talks, he went back to Tabor (the "highly authoritative Western source") for the more detailed account that ran two days later.[48] Contrary to the surmise of Goldberg, Bundy, and others, and vindicating Gronouski's forlorn plea, he had written without direct aid from a single Polish source (though he admitted to a fellow journalist that he had spoken with Tomorowicz at the Indian ambassador's reception, he insisted that the Pole "gave me no help" on his two major stories, despite later confirming some details).[49] Yet, undeniably, Rapacki's campaign—and Warsaw's wooing of Thant, in particular—had paid off handsomely.

✳ ✳ ✳

These *Washington Post* stories prompted a flurry of secret U.S. diplomacy toward both friends and enemies. Rusk sent instructions to the U.S. Embassy in Moscow to get word to the local DRV representative that Warsaw was responsible for the leakage—a move calculated to preserve whatever (negligible) credit Washington retained in Hanoi and, perhaps, maliciously exacerbate Polish-DRV ties (the State Department had heard fourth-hand rumors that the North Vietnamese were "furious" over the disclosure).[50] Le Chang had no reaction when the U.S. chargé d'affaires in Moscow, John Guthrie, told him that the Estabrook story "had come from Polish sources and that U.S. Govt will maintain complete silence and avoid comment on it."[51] Thompson also raised the leak with Poland's ambassador in Moscow, who, well aware of Warsaw's calculated indiscretion vis-à-vis Thant, speculated that it had emanated from the UN Secretariat; but the American (evidently uninformed of Goldberg's detailed report to the secretary-general) countered that this was impossible, given strict U.S. limitations on knowledge of the affair, "unless of course someone else had informed UN officials." Regardless of who caused the leak, both agreed that Washington and Warsaw should now keep silent.[52]

Now that a fragmentary version of the affair had publicly emerged, in a not-so-flattering form, Rusk also authorized a second round of Marigold briefings for U.S. allies—starting with Ky in Saigon and the troop-contributing countries, especially Australia and New Zealand—adopting the line that the leaks had proved that Warsaw could not be trusted. "We were never sure whether the Poles were speaking for Hanoi or entirely for themselves," Rusk cabled Lodge, "and we concluded ultimately that the exercise had been primarily a fishing expedition by the Poles in order to get us to change our position with respect to bombing of North Vietnam." When he saw Ky, Lodge duly derided the "quite incomplete and misleading" *Post* stories, assuring him that the fruitless contacts had not led to any change in U.S. position and that Washington would apprise Saigon of "any substantive developments."[53]

Ky "seemed to accept all of this in good spirit," and U.S. allies like Taiwan, South Korea, and Japan received the news politely, but not all were so understanding. The Australians, who were fielding close to 5,000 troops in South Vietnam, already resented having initiatives like Goldberg's letter to Thant sprung on them. In response, Canberra's envoy in Washington, John Keith Waller, had extracted Bundy's regrets for not first consulting with his country and his denial that the U.S. officials were "opening any new channels" or anticipated any significant "new developments" on the peace front.[54]

The diplomats from Down Under were all the more peeved, then, to learn about the Polish channel from the Canadians rather than the Americans. Cooper vividly recalled an Australian Embassy official, Robert Furlonger, "normally a placid and understanding man," "storm[ing] angrily into the State Department early in January" to demand information on talks (which he had just heard about from Ignatieff) that the Poles had revealed to Thant.[55] In mid-January, Rusk indicated to Bundy that Australia and New Zealand could be told more about Marigold—they were contributing troops and, besides, "now that London knows more, [the British] may talk." (They "certainly should not," Bundy replied, but one could hardly take that for granted.)[56] Bundy promised to fill in Canberra's and Wellington's envoys but did not get around to doing so until February 4—*after* the *Post* stories (which he blamed on Polish sources, perhaps confirmed by "other Europeans to whom the Poles had talked").[57] In view of Washington's spotty record—even Bundy's belated Marigold briefing had been "vague" on key points—Waller pondered how far his country ought to press its demand to be consulted. Apprehensive of the "obvious danger" that the Americans may make "irreversible concessions" to entice Hanoi into talks, he warned his foreign minister that "we could thus find ourselves presented with faits accomplis."[58]

Like George Brown and Paul Martin, the Australian foreign minister, Paul Hasluck (a member of the Liberal Party), felt affronted at discovering what had gone on behind his back, even more so because his country had men on the battlefield. Australia had reason to fear being bound by secret U.S. undertakings, he agreed, and he also found Washington's treatment humiliating. Though appreciating the "delicacy of the enquiries," he believed that Australia should insist on a "right to American confidence" if a peace feeler led to substantive exchanges "or when 'third' or 'fourth' governments become involved whose discretion cannot necessarily be relied upon."

"The history of the Polish initiative has shown that exploratory contacts can be pursued over periods of six months or more before being brought to our knowledge, even though countries like Italy whose interest in the problem is peripheral may have been privy to them from the outset," Hasluck cabled Waller. "It is insufferable in Australian politics that others should be given higher measure of confidence than ourselves."[59]

✳ ✳ ✳

Far more than appeasing antipodean allies, of course, the Johnson administration worried about the Marigold revelation's impact on the American public. Hoping to dampen speculation aroused by Estabrook's stories, the administration went into damage-control mode. As the State Department hunkered down in a formal no-comment posture, Rostow, briefing White House reporters, refused to be drawn into the specifics of what he cryptically termed "an extremely interesting and delicate phase of what is or what might turn out to be a negotiating process," but he nevertheless insisted—in line with LBJ's press conference—that "nothing has yet happened that would justify us in saying we have a serious offer to negotiate."[60]

In Saigon, too, Lodge and D'Orlandi—Lewandowski was out of town—did their best to fog reporters' inquiries. The day Estabrook's February 4 exposé appeared, coincidentally, the Italian lunched with Lodge and his wife, bitterly reviewing recent events and anticipating their respective impending departures.[61] The next morning, an Agence France-Presse reporter startled D'Orlandi with a phone call requesting comment on the *Washington Post*'s claim that he had hosted Lodge and Lewandowski at a dinner on December 2 to arrange direct U.S.-DRV talks in Warsaw. D'Orlandi wearily dismissed this story as unfounded speculation and sensed that the French correspondent, carrying out his editor's instruction, agreed. But privately, Rome's envoy feared that a barrage of calls from U.S. reporters to the Marigold trio would destroy the channel.[62]

The next evening, on the eve of the Tet cease-fire, D'Orlandi briefly stopped by Lodge's residence, where he bumped into Chalmers M. Roberts, the senior *Wash-*

ington Post national security correspondent, who was visiting Saigon. Roberts solicited his reaction to Estabrook's story, and the disconcerted Italian "vague[ly]" protested that he did not recall hosting the meeting it described. Lodge came to the rescue, however, checking his desk calendar and triumphantly naming different dinner companions on December 2; he could do so honestly, of course, because the tripartite gatherings had occurred the day before and after, and not during dinner. (Out of the reporter's earshot, Lodge told D'Orlandi that he suspected Thant was behind the leak.)[63] The Agence France-Presse reporter independently verified that Lodge and Lewandowski had dined separately on December 2—and the fleeting interest of the frazzled Saigon press corps petered out.[64]

Then an unwelcome arrow punctured the administration's firm no-comment front. On February 7, just as he plunged into the summit with Kosygin, Harold Wilson told Parliament that the Polish initiative mentioned in the press ("of which, of course, I have all the details") had failed due to "a very considerable two-way misunderstanding."[65] Merely by authoritatively confirming that "the Polish discussions" in December had in fact occurred, the British prime minister undercut LBJ's public insistence that Hanoi had shown no interest in talking and would—as a friendly European embassy observed—"nurture the ongoing debate" over the president's "credibility gap."[66] Even worse, Wilson's implication that *both* sides bore some onus outraged Johnson; on his orders, Rostow shot 10 Downing Street a private wire insisting that there was no "misunderstanding" and that "other explanations better fit the facts as we know them."[67] Wilson's comments encouraged others to pipe up. Thant now authorized Estabrook to put on the record that he had been "aware" of the Polish discussions as they had occurred (a stretch, because he did not know until December 23) and was deeply disappointed by their collapse.[68]

As the administration grappled with the Polish flap, a far juicier controversy over Vietnam peace prospects suddenly blew up, this one pitting LBJ against RFK. The brouhaha broke out over a conversation the senator had conducted in Paris during his just-concluded European trip. In addition to seeing de Gaulle, Couve, Jean Monnet, the writer-politician André Malraux (the author of *Man's Fate* and other novels), and Jean Sainteny (at the suggestion of Henry Kissinger, who was also in the French capital), Kennedy met Étienne Manac'h, the Quai D'Orsay's top Asianist. Through an interpreter, Manac'h assessed Hanoi's current position, underlining indications that a bombing halt would bring it to the negotiating table. An embassy official (John Gunther Dean) accompanying RFK, who did not understand French, piped up that this "seems very new and very interesting to me, and I am taking the liberty of calling Senator Kennedy's attention to it."[69]

To the president's fury, a *Newsweek* "Periscope" item hailed the talk as a "significant" North Vietnamese peace "feeler," funneled through Mai Van Bo to Manac'h and "unveiled for the benefit of Robert F. Kennedy for reasons best known to the enemy." LBJ predictably went ballistic, smelling an RFK conspiracy to humiliate the president while raising his own profile as a prospective Vietnam peacemaker. A face-to-face Oval Office meeting between the two men on February 6 degenerated into a shouting match. When Kennedy denied leaking the story and suggested that it had emanated from "someone in your State Department," LBJ spat back: "It's not *my* State Department, it's your goddamn State Department!"

"I'll destroy you and every one of your dove friends," Johnson reportedly snarled. "You'll be dead politically in six months." At one point, RFK noted Fanfani's (Marigold-induced) complaints about the Hanoi bombings, only to hear LBJ disparage the Italian foreign minister. After Kennedy urged him to consider a unilateral bombing halt and other conciliatory gestures to get negotiations started, the president not only peremptorily rejected his advice ("not the slightest chance") but also accused him and others recommending concessions of prolonging the war and yelled, "You have blood on your hands." Kennedy, "pale with repressed anger," turned to leave, muttering, "Look, I don't have to take that from you." Katzenbach and Rostow calmed the two down, and a few minutes later, through gritted teeth, Kennedy dutifully verified to waiting reporters the White House's assertions that he "did not bring home any feelers."

Nevertheless, tales of the confrontation churned through the gossip mill. "Well, that wasn't a very pleasant meeting," Kennedy told aides, describing Johnson as "very abusive. . . . He was shouting and seemed very unstable. I kept thinking that if he exploded like that with me, how could he ever negotiate with Hanoi?" Johnson vented to Rostow about RFK's "belly-aching to me" and "whoring around" with his "God-damn State Department." Nourishing his boss's paranoia, Rostow fed LBJ gossip that RFK himself had been *Newsweek*'s source, perhaps in cahoots with Manac'h ("anti-U.S. and very much tied up with the left"), even as Katzenbach (who investigated the leak at LBJ's request) exonerated Kennedy and instead blamed State.[70]

At the seething president's behest, Rostow redoubled behind-the-scenes press contacts to "get the party line across on peace feelers."[71] To a reliably sympathetic *Time* correspondent, Hugh Sidey, he insisted that no direct communications had been received from Hanoi, which was mounting the "most systematic and purposeful Communist psychological warfare operation since 1945" to get Washington to stop bombing unilaterally.[72] Rostow also discouraged the influential columnist Joe Alsop from pursuing Marigold, counseling him that the December 13–14 Hanoi bombings "had nothing to do" with the Warsaw contact's collapse; Alsop obligingly sneered in print at "the groundless whispers of the Polish Foreign Office."[73]

Rusk, too, could proudly claim a victory on the public relations front: his telephone counsel to Wiggins hit pay dirt. Though some younger *Washington Post* editorial page staff members increasingly chafed at his hawkish views, and even Kay Graham's doubts grew, for the time being, the pillar of the Washington journalistic establishment still steered a stubbornly ("obsequiously," Fulbright charged) proadministration course; LBJ, who enthused that "one of Wiggins' editorials was worth as much to him as a division in Vietnam," would reward his friend by naming him UN ambassador in late 1968, when he retired from the *Post* after twenty-one years.[74]

On this occasion, Wiggins eschewed Rusk's suggestion to spur Estabrook to go back to his Polish sources, but he did use the editorial page to, in effect, warn readers to take with a grain of salt the stories splashed across the front page. On February 8, the *Post* commented that "some of the recent peace rumors have been less serious omens of peace than significant as a part of a worldwide propaganda effort to coerce the United States into suspending the bombing of North Vietnam unconditionally." Without specifying to which category the Polish affair belonged, Wiggins' editorial declared that if some peace "rumors" did not stem from calculated propaganda, they perhaps reflected "plain misunderstanding" or "mere wishful thinking."[75]

At the White House, LBJ summoned Sidey to pop the RFK peace bubble and pooh-pooh other such claims, insisting that every "whisper" of Hanoi's alleged interest in peace had proven illusory. "We've had maybe 200 flickers and Harriman tracks down every probe," he told the pliable *Time* scribe, "but so far there has been nothing."[76] Johnson's aides, however, worried that stonewalling and cautions to friendly journalists might not contain magnifying doubts about the president's attitude toward negotiations. Concerned about his credibility, one recommended conducting "counter psychological warfare" by releasing more data on the secret diplomacy:

> While I realize Secretary Rusk could not detail the reasons for the break-up of talks, including the specific question on Warsaw, unless there are overriding diplomatic or military reasons, it would be helpful from a public viewpoint, if a definitive explanation of the contacts tried by the United States with Hanoi were made.
>
> From an opinion standpoint, forgetting other considerations, I think over the next couple of weeks the Administration will be at the point that unless they detail attempts of peace and avenues of peace to which Hanoi refused to respond, there will be a recurrence of the claim that while outwardly the United State says it wants peace, actually it is not trying too hard.
>
> While this is inaccurate, I believe this viewpoint is going to spread as a result of psychological warfare by Hanoi all over the world. If it is diplomatically or militarily feasible, obviously counter-psychological warfare is important to the Administration in national and world opinion.[77]

Anticipating the need to mount a more dynamic defense of peace-seeking efforts, Rostow quietly commissioned Bill Jorden, his negotiations watchdog, to prepare detailed classified chronologies of the most crucial initiatives, including Marigold, Sunflower, and the whole Phase A / Phase B proposal, to have them handy for any contingency—for example, secret dialogues with other governments, internal reference when future negotiating possibilities cropped up, an official "white paper" (whether issued by the White House or Rusk), backup for a presidential speech, or a detailed leak to a trusted reporter.[78]

Lewandowski Returns to Hanoi:
"Until Now, the Most Concrete"

In early February, Lewandowski flew back to Hanoi for the first time since Marigold's rise and fall, the bombing controversy, and the closed-door ICC developments. There was much to discuss. From the moment the Stratoliner landed at Gia Lam Airport, the North Vietnamese showed their displeasure over recent commission actions by ostentatiously snubbing the Canadian officers who met the plane (Colonel Ha Van Lau and his PAVN comrades "observed the barest greetings and then pointedly turned their backs"). These rebukes would continue not only toward the Canadians but also the Indians, both the consul-general and M. A. Rahman (who was also visiting Hanoi).[79]

Though spared such slights, Lewandowski could not help but sense his hosts' unhappiness. Greeted, as usual, by Ludwig, he then saw Trinh, who threw a welcoming dinner. They discussed the recent ICC maneuvering, especially what the "very anxious and perturbed" Vietnamese complained was New Delhi's, and Rahman's, increasingly blatant pro-U.S. tilt. Promising to make the Indians and Canadians feel their wrath for taking such "outstandingly hostile and harmful" positions, they warned Lewandowski that if the resolutions criticizing the North were published, Hanoi would not only openly condemn Canada and India but also reevaluate its entire stand toward the commission. The Poles should act urgently to prevent this from happening, even if it required top-level intercessions in Ottawa and New Delhi.[80]

Lewandowski had a far broader exchange with Dong.[81] The premier greeted the Pole warmly, with hugs and kisses, before grilling him on the internal political and military situation in the South, as well as within the ICC, and above all on the U.S. "position and intentions." Citing informants in Saigon, including Bernard Fall, Lewandowski noted the clear "hardening" of the U.S. position, which he linked to the sharpening Chinese turmoil and Sino-Soviet hostility, evidence of Communist disarray, which Washington was counting on to eventually wear down Hanoi.

Turning to the diplomatic front, Dong expressed confidence that the DRV propaganda campaign had put the Johnson administration on the defensive both internationally and at home. Endorsing Lewandowski's analysis, he surmised that the Americans wagered—vainly—on some "miracle," not on the battlefield but externally, to rescue their position. Hanoi would never surrender, and if Washington failed to escape its predicament through talks, it would slowly be defeated through military losses and political pressure, even if it ravaged Vietnam in the process. Signaling a toughening of Hanoi's stand since Lewandowski's last visit, Dong affirmed—in line with Trinh's interview—that North Vietnam would now enter into negotiations only *after* a bombing halt. "The point here," he stressed, "is not to give the Americans an opportunity to create the [false] impression that important talks are talking place and to deceive public opinion."

As for the failed peace effort in which the Polish commissioner had played such a pivotal role, Dong prodded him to endorse the conclusions of the DRV leadership. "He asked me, 'Do you see how the Americans are behaving themselves?'" the Pole recalled. "'We believed that something positive is coming, you believed it was so.' I said I did, and he said, 'What do we have to do now, except fight to the end, do you agree with us?'" Feeling guilty for perhaps misleading the premier earlier, Lewandowski did not challenge his analysis.[82]

Despite the channel's ultimate failure, however, Dong did dispense some compliments. He thanked Warsaw for its efforts, asked Lewandowski not to break contact with D'Orlandi—"some interesting signs may come out of there"—and remarked that, despite the multiple conduits opened up in Hanoi's diplomatic offensive to signal or communicate with the American enemy, the leadership considered the Polish-Italian channel in Saigon as, "until now, the most concrete." (In a conversation with D'Orlandi after returning to Saigon, Lewandowski quoted Dong as praising it as "the most serious and most concrete attempt carried out thus far," and as remarking that the "preliminary accord" it produced "did bring, and will bring, results."[83]) "It was very beneficial to them, and it may come in handy again," Lewandowski summarized to Warsaw. And with regard to the ICC, Dong echoed Trinh's bid for Polish aid in countering "the slipping of the Indian delegation to the pro-American side" and vowed that Hanoi would also press New Delhi.

Dong also took more than passing interest in Saigon's "mini-Marigold," displaying acute curiosity regarding the Pole's conversation with the man he had met in Geneva in 1954. In late January, before Lewandowski left Saigon, Ha Van Lau had radiotelegraphed him a brusque rebuff to the message that Tran Van Do had passed at the New Year's Eve reception at the palace. The PAVN liaison snidely dismissed the overture as a mere bit part in the U.S. peace offensive, a pretentious gesture by the Saigon "puppet administration" implying an independence it in fact did not possess, despite potential differences with Washington that merited observation. As for Do personally, Ludwik had radioed ominously that Lewandowski did not need to initiate another meeting, but if he ran into the foreign minister, the Pole could relate that "the DRV government does not believe in his honesty and it must continue to observe his behavior."[84]

In contrast to the colonel's harsh tone, Dong spoke mildly of Do, smiling broadly as he promised to look after his relatives and asking Lewandowski to maintain and even intensify contact with him: "Yes, he was my colleague in Hanoi. . . . Tell him we take good care of his mother." After hearing the Pole convey rumors of clandestine conversations between Saigon and the NLF, he acknowledged that the RVN's ruling circles contained disparate elements and noted that Do himself had already had covert contact with the NLF—"interesting, especially if Thieu were behind this"—that was interrupted due to U.S. pressure. While gently ignoring Do's interest in an ongoing dialogue, Dong gave the Pole a pithy message to relay to him the next time they met:

You bet on the wrong horse. If you understand the most vital interests of Vietnam, then it is about time that you change the horse. The first step is to establish
direct contact with the [NLF]. He [Tran Van Do] believes that the Americans are
interfering. However, he should show independence. Otherwise, sooner or later,
the Americans will do the same to him as they did to Diem. There is no other way
for them. The only way is to do something good for the motherland. It is never too
late. And as far as doing things, there is a lot to do and there are many possibilities
in Saigon as well.[85]

(Lewandowski delivered Dong's message to Do after returning to Saigon, huddling in a corner of a dinner party to accomplish the mission; the foreign minister
smiled at the horse-changing analogy but had no special reaction, and so far as is
known the two never continued the dialogue.[86])

Summing up the conversation, which lasted several hours, Lewandowski was
more impressed than ever by Dong's "realism," especially his tactful comments
regarding Beijing and tactical "flexibility" toward Saigon.

Yet the plunging peace prospects left the Pole in a grim mood. Calling on
France's representative in Hanoi, he did little to hide his pessimism that peace
talks could start any time soon, though he did not divulge details of his own futile
diplomacy. Asked about rumors that ICC members dabbled in clandestine mediation efforts, he noted pointedly that neither Canada nor India was suitable to
undertake such a mission, given their political and/or economic ties to the United
States—leaving unsaid what an implicitly better-positioned Poland had recently
tried to accomplish. In any case, he added, the ICC should not unrealistically attempt an initiative that might "pointlessly" squander its credit, "which it needs to
protect for the time where it would be needed once again." Lewandowski also
suspected that some Americans in Washington and Saigon preferred to test
whether the sharpening Sino-Soviet rift and internal Chinese chaos offered an
opening to step up the military pressure on Hanoi, or even cut a deal with Beijing
behind Moscow's back, to achieve a more favorable outcome in Southeast Asia.[87]

Before leaving Hanoi, Lewandowski got a vivid glimpse of the Sino-Soviet acrimony at a party he threw to mark the departure of his military aide, Colonel
Ryszard Iwanciów, and his replacement's arrival. Though the PRC's ambassador
did not show up, his deputy military attaché, Yuan Yun Lou, did appear and, spotting the Soviet military attaché, General Alexei Lebedev, accosted the "revisionist
swine" and shrilly upbraided him for the "fascist treatment" of the Chinese students in Moscow. The "big, bearish" Russian, his face and hands reddening from
the effort at self-restraint, contemptuously turned his back, but the shorter man
circled around and continued haranguing him.

"You social imperialist!" Yuan Yun Lou shouted as he orbited. When the pug-
nacious Chinese officer "threatened with his fists," the nervous Vietnamese hosts
interposed themselves between the antagonistic comrades like linesmen trying to
separate would-be hockey pugilists.

To Lewandowski's immense relief, General Lebedev "abstemiously" declined to put up his dukes. Decades later, the Pole chuckled at the memory of the Red Army officer fleeing across the hotel ballroom to avoid a diplomatic incident, which the Soviet Bloc diplomats present presumed had been the Chinese officer's aim all along.[88]

Lewandowski's reception also offered another venue for the DRV to flaunt its grievances toward Poland's ICC partners. PAVN officers treated the Canadians "with calculated coolness," but the Indians felt the brunt of their bitterness. Perhaps also irked by New Delhi press leaks claming a warming tend in ties with Hanoi, an "extremely bitter" Nguyen Co Thach warned the Indian consul-general that the recent ICC resolution criticizing Northern infiltration would, if known, "lower Indian prestige in world opinion." The vice foreign minister "spoke in scathing terms of Rahman personally," calling him "more American than the Americans."[89]

Shaken by his hosts' insults (including the return of his traditional Tet gift), Rahman concluded with "some annoyance" that Lewandowski had rushed to Hanoi to tell the DRV leaders about the adverse resolutions and encourage their brusqueness toward the Indians—in effect, deliberately to set him up.[90] The irritation was mutual; though they were civil face to face, Lewandowski had tired of Rahman's balancing act, viewing his latest maneuver—joining in criticism of the DRV when it was under U.S. assault—as a cynical move by a careerist "not really very much interested in the whole business."[91] Though the Indian later tried to palliate the Pole ("he was a little bit ashamed"), tensions inside the ICC were climbing as its plane carrying Lewandowski rose from Gia Lam into the predawn darkness on February 8, hours before the Tet truce came into force.

A Tet Diplomatic Offensive: "Hope Is Born Again"

The four-day Tet cease-fire (February 8–12, 1967) was widely seen as a last chance to achieve diplomatic progress before military escalation again seized center stage. Thus it set off a new rush of Vietnam peace efforts. Some were predictable, like appeals from Pope Paul VI and U Thant to prolong the truce and begin negotiations.[92] More surprisingly, Kosygin came to London ready to do business.[93] Climaxing weeks of hints that Moscow might play a more active role as a mediator—the Soviets told U.S. officials that they knew and approved of the Le Chang–Guthrie contacts[94]—the premier elated Harold Wilson from the day his Ilyushin-18 landed at Heathrow Airport on February 6 by avidly seeking a formula to open direct U.S.-DRV negotiations in exchange for a permanent bombing halt; at the American Embassy, Ambassador David Bruce and Chester Cooper, back in town for the summit, also found their hopes rising. What prompted the Russian's unprecedented flexibility? Not only did he carry Hanoi's general proxy, as described above—and Dobrynin recalls a special DRV request to "use" Wilson's government "to put pressure on Washington to reach a peaceful solution in Vietnam"[95]—but Beijing's anti-Soviet venom also inspired Moscow to edge westward, closing cultural and even racial ranks; Kosygin "seemed obsessed" with the Chinese, Wilson told Cooper, talking about them "the way Pakistanis talk about Indians."[96]

On learning of Kosygin's seeming readiness to cooperate, Washington started fencing to obtain better terms, insisting on a concrete military quid pro quo for an indefinite extension of the Tet bombing hiatus rather than a mere promise to enter talks. To aid in bargaining, the White House began plying Wilson and Brown with arguments and data (e.g., evidence of intensified infiltration during the stand-down).

At the same time, without cluing in the British (or the Americans advising them), Rostow convinced LBJ to send a direct secret letter to Ho Chi Minh.[97] Though he had fancied the idea for weeks, Estabrook's *Post* stories had put extra pressure on the administration to take a more dramatic peace step. From New York, Goldberg had suggested curtailing the bombing of North Vietnam to targets directly linked to infiltration in order to test whether Hanoi seriously sought negotiations or only a propaganda advantage. "Our public record on this score will need bolstering," he advised LBJ and Rusk, "for it now appears the record is being rather badly clouded by Polish version of how our mid-December bombings interfered with what they conceive to be a very promising chance of talks with Hanoi."[98] Goldberg's idea of a unilateral limit on air attacks appealed to neither man, but Rostow thought, and Johnson agreed, that a personal appeal to Ho—initially secret, but sooner or later to be made public—offered a powerful riposte to the accusation that Washington was not making the extra effort to open a dialogue with Hanoi. Bringing the president into a personal exchange with the Vietnamese Communist icon might be risky, Rostow admitted, but "with the Marigold leaks and all the rest, we need to clear the record."[99]

In his letter, transmitted on February 8 via the DRV Embassy in Moscow, Johnson alluded obliquely to Marigold by noting the danger that "our thoughts and yours, our attitudes and yours, have been distorted or misinterpreted as they passed through" various third parties. He proposed, instead, "direct talks between trusted representatives in a secure setting and away from the glare of publicity." Rejecting Trinh's demand for an unconditional advance bombing halt before talks, LBJ declared his readiness to "order a cessation of bombing against your country and the stopping of augmentation of U.S. forces in South Vietnam as soon as I am assured that infiltration into South Vietnam by land and by sea *has stopped*" (emphasis added).[100]

By now insisting on DRV action *before* a bombing halt, LBJ had effectively *reversed* the sequence envisioned for the past three months in the Phase A/ Phase B formula. But Johnson did not inform Wilson of the letter to Ho; instead, he sent for his guidance a sequentially ambiguous paraphrase of the new U.S. stand: If Hanoi "will agree to an assured stoppage of infiltration into South Vietnam, we will stop the bombing of North Vietnam and stop further augmentation of U.S. forces in South Vietnam."[101] Nor did he tell the Americans at the London Embassy. In the confusion, relying on earlier data from Cooper, the British prime minister still used the Phase A/B language in explaining Washington's position to Kosygin on February 7—setting the stage for another huge Anglo-American snafu.

In Saigon, distant from these intrigues, the Marigold diplomatic ensemble nevertheless was swept up, at least peripherally, in the frantic efforts to transform the ninety-six-hour truce into something more lasting. For some of the officials who had recently been involved in Marigold and Narcissus, Tet offered an irresistible pretext to excavate these expired initiatives.

On the cease-fire's eve, in Ottawa, Martin summoned Warsaw's ambassador in a bid to reinvigorate Rapacki's interest in some sort of collaboration, proposing an immediate secret meeting between the two; but the Canadian failed to evoke any enthusiasm because he envisioned reciprocal U.S. and DRV concessions rather than a unilateral bombing halt. Despite opposing the American air strikes, he told the Pole, Canada could not join a collective condemnation due to neighborly, alliance, and internal considerations.[102] Instead, Martin had his ambassador in Washington propose that the ICC appeal for an indefinite extension of the Tet truce, "whether de facto or by agreement," to facilitate potential negotiations. Though unenthusiastic about an open-ended cease-fire that would permit continued infiltration, U.S. officials (confident that Hanoi would reject it anyway) told Canadian ambassador Edgar Ritchie that they "would surely have no objection."[103]

India floated a similar idea. As the truce went into effect, the Indian foreign minister, M. C. Chagla, called in DRV and U.S. diplomats to propose that the cease-fire continue indefinitely in order to allow negotiations to start.[104] At the same time, the Indian Foreign Ministry's director-general, T. N. Kaul, summoned Poland's acting ambassador (Spasowski had not yet arrived) to inform him of the foreign minister's action and raise anew the notion of a three-way ICC gathering in New Delhi (he apologized for the earlier press leak). Kaul, who obviously had been the recipient of some alarmed messages from Saigon, also complained that Lewandowski "unjustly does not trust" Rahman; far from dragging its heels regarding the Hanoi bombing letter, he insisted, India favored distributing it to the cochairs and earnestly desired good relations with Warsaw.[105]

As Warsaw mulled over these propositions, and the Wilson-Kosygin discussions intensified, New Delhi opted to promote a joint ICC statement—to be issued from Saigon to surmount Polish objections to an extraregional session—calling on Washington and Hanoi to extend the Tet cease-fire in order to enhance the atmosphere for diplomacy. Rahman then convened an informal commissioners' meeting, at which he read the draft statement aloud on Sunday morning, February 12, just as the truce was ending. Lewandowski dourly observed that it was already outdated—if he had heard the suggestion a couple of days earlier, he might have immediately consented, but because the radio had already announced that hostilities had resumed, he first needed to consult Warsaw.[106] So he unenthusiastically forwarded the text of the statement to Spasowski, underlining that the Indian formulation essentially mirrored the U.S. call for "unconditional discussions" under the implicit threat of renewed attacks, and that therefore the North Vietnamese would likely see it as an unpalatable ultimatum.[107] Warsaw predictably agreed, and the matter was mooted when Washington restarted bombing North Vietnam less than two days later.[108]

From Rome, Fanfani had also gotten into the Tet action. His mystery DRV interlocutor had faded away, so he reverted to the dormant Saigon channel. On February 9, with his competitive juices having been stirred by hints of other peace efforts (including the pope's appeal and Kosygin's comparatively moderate public statements in London), he prodded D'Orlandi to undertake "all measures for the purpose of resumption and continuation of contacts."[109] The message raised the ambassador's flagging spirits: "Hope is born again as well as a certain happy excitement," he gushed. "When Tet is over, we must reconnect."[110] D'Orlandi promised to "make every effort" upon the return of his Polish friend (who had stopped in Phnom Penh on his way back from Hanoi). Nevertheless, he cautioned his eager foreign minister that although Lodge had recently reaffirmed "his esteem for Lewandowski's fairness," Washington seemed cold to any additional gatherings of the three diplomats (all of whose postings would soon end), and thus for there to be any real chance of progress, Fanfani should first intercede with Rapacki and Rusk.[111]

The Italians sensed an opening to act on Sunday, February 12, as news streamed in that, with Kosygin still in England, Washington had refrained, for the moment, from resuming attacks on North Vietnam as the Tet truce ended. Getting into the spirit, D'Orlandi advised Fanfani that if the halt continued, he should "put all possible pressure" on U.S. and Polish officials to start direct contacts in Warsaw and resume the clandestine gatherings with Lodge and Lewandowski. "Allow me to insist on the advisability that the tripartite channel in Saigon not be circumvented for a second time, also because beyond the reciprocal esteem and trust between the three of us, the contacts with Hanoi are much easier from Saigon with Lewandowski."[112] Seizing the moment, Fanfani dispatched identical messages to Rapacki and Rusk hailing the bombing nonresumption for "fulfill[ing] one of the important conditions identified in the noted three-way meetings of Saigon last November and December" and advertising Italy's availability to collaborate in any and all diplomatic dealings. "Hoping for a felicitous result of today's decision," he signed off to the American.[113]

When the Italian's bubbly message reached Washington that Sunday afternoon in the midst of intense discussions about when to resume the air strikes, it nonplussed senior U.S. officials, probably reinforcing their impression of him as an unrealistic, Nobel Peace Prize–driven pest. A bit puzzled, Rusk suggested that Bundy draft a reply thanking Fanfani but clarifying that "we haven't announced any suspension of bombing. The matter will be clarified tomorrow." When the assistant secretary mused about whether to clue the Italian in "confidentially" about "what we are doing," Rusk rejected the idea because, he admitted, "we didn't know" ourselves.[114]

In fact, Johnson had only approved a brief extension of the Tet pause in bombing the DRV—not out of any belief that Wilson had a real chance of achieving progress through Kosygin, but because he feared an even worse public relations backlash atop the emerging story of the Polish initiative's collapse. Wilson, already appalled at the tense-flipping in the Phase A/B formula, told LBJ that he was in a "hell of a situation" with Kosygin because of having to substitute the harder-line language, and he pleaded for more time before the bombing resumed in order to persuade the Soviet to transmit a workable proposal to Hanoi. With the White House digging in its heels, Rusk had warned Johnson that if Washington restarted the strikes before Kosygin left London, "we shall inevitably be charged with having broken up a major possibility of peace," and this precipitate action "would be taken as confirmation of the December charges and would multiply the effect of those charges very greatly." Moreover, exploding the British-Soviet summit would seriously harm U.S. relations with both countries, and "unlike the December case with the Poles, we are dealing with two key and generally responsible nations."[115]

LBJ grudgingly agreed to hold off until after Kosygin's scheduled departure on Monday morning, February 13, to see if Hanoi would accept the U.S. insistence on a prior infiltration halt—and then, after more anguished cries from London, wearily added another six hours, but no more. Despite his flattery of Wilson's "gallant last minute effort," Johnson's rigidity exasperated the British (as well as Cooper and Bruce), who unlike Washington believed that a breakthrough might be attainable, but that days, not hours, were required merely for communications and even bare-bones DRV deliberations. Surprisingly, the Soviet premier agreed to transmit the de facto U.S. ultimatum to Hanoi, where Dong promptly and scornfully rejected it. Though British intelligence had intercepted a phone conversation from Kosygin to Brezhnev referring to "a great possibility of achieving the aim," the Soviet premier told Thompson a few days later that "he knew it was hopeless the minute he had read" Washington's take-it-or-leave-it proposition.[116]

The resumption of U.S. bombing of North Vietnam early on February 14, Vietnam time, made clear to all that negotiations would not be in the offing any time soon. Rusk had delayed responding to Fanfani until events had overtaken his cheerful appeal. In a reply drafted by Bundy, he politely dismissed the Italian's implication that a bombing halt was needed to start talks—after all, two months earlier, the DRV had agreed to the Warsaw meeting without that precondition— yet he admitted that he was "a little at a loss to interpret Hanoi's attitude at the present time."[117]

In Saigon, lunching that Tuesday at D'Orlandi's, Lodge was "very pessimistic." Washington, he confided, had placed its chips on military success through stepped-up counterinsurgency operations, and it would be at least six months before another stab at talks made sense: "Only then will Hanoi understand that it is no longer able to win and will be willing to negotiate." D'Orlandi argued the time was right now to reopen their channel, but Lodge reacted tepidly—and afterward advised Washington against reviving Marigold. Doing so would be "premature," he judged, because "overeagerness tends to defeat its own purpose and actually tends to prolong the war," and it remained doubtful that Warsaw could speak for Hanoi.[118] In reply, the State Department (i.e., Bundy), noting that Rusk had given Fanfani "no encouragement in this direction," not only agreed fully but instructed Lodge to stop rehashing the bombing issue with D'Orlandi.[119]

Wednesday evening, after checking in again with Lodge—who dismissed the short-lived add-on to the Tet bombing pause as merely "a courtesy" to Wilson and Kosygin[120]—the Italian caught up with his old chess partner. During "a comprehensive, particularly frank exchange of views," Lewandowski and D'Orlandi commiserated over their common readiness to promote peace talks but inability to act without U.S. help (i.e., a permanent bombing halt). Once again, the Pole worried that Washington was not interested in talks with Hanoi because it secretly sought a breakthrough with Beijing—a visceral Soviet fear that Kosygin had made plain to Wilson. But the evening's main fare was Lewandowski's account of his Hanoi trip (which he requested D'Orlandi to communicate only to Fanfani personally) and especially his lengthy talk with Dong. While relating the premier's flattery toward the Polish-Italian channel (and lack of interest in a French alternative), he rejected, in response to D'Orlandi's questions, any inference that a prospect therefore existed to reopen the initiative—that depended on Washington.

In an atmosphere of "affectionate sincerity," the two turned to personal matters. Noting his own likely departure in April, Lewandowski urged D'Orlandi not to imperil his health by delaying his return to Italy—he could go on leave rather than officially end his term, in case events justified a return for more three-way discussions. After his friend left, Rome's envoy updated Fanfani, on the whole expressing pessimism but stressing the Pole's continued availability if only the Americans could be budged. "I believe that at this time the success of efforts through other channels to be difficult and Lewandowski's position is very strong in Hanoi," D'Orlandi reported. "Additionally, I confirm my judgment on the competence and total loyalty of Lewandowski."[121]

Such judgments had lost their relevance, however. That day in Moscow, Le Chang had handed Guthrie the text of Ho's response to LBJ's letter. After a polite salutation ("Your Excellency"), Ho vituperatively indicted U.S. "war crimes, crimes against peace and against mankind"; vowed to defeat Washington's "war of aggression"; and flatly rejected negotiations unless and until it "unconditionally" ceased its attacks on North Vietnam—in effect, the Trinh formula. "The Vietnamese people will never submit to force," he declared. "They will never accept talks under the threat of bombs."[122]

On the heels of the Wilson-Kosygin summit's failure, Ho's negative reply effectively ended the two months of intense diplomacy (though peace efforts of course muddled on). It confirmed, Rostow told LBJ, that Hanoi had "decided to sweat us out to the 1968 election," and the need for a broad "stocktaking of Vietnam policy."[123] Independently, Lodge reported a spate of Viet Cong attacks within 10 miles of Saigon and suggested that Washington inform Hanoi, via the Poles, that it no longer considered itself bound by the self-imposed limit on bombing within a comparable radius of the DRV capital.[124] Though U.S. officials held back, momentarily, from endorsing his advice, their attention was refocusing on new steps to sharpen military pressure.

Saigon Blues: "More Vietnamese than the Vietnamese"

Neither hopeful nor happy, Lewandowski found his Vietnam assignment increasingly burdensome. Several factors contributed to the Polish ICC member's mounting desire to end his stay. Most important, he was no longer experiencing the thrill of conspiring to bring about peace to compensate for the dreary business of waging desultory battles in the ICC; Marigold's flameout and the consequent hardening and escalatory momentum on both sides made it all too obvious that his odds of achieving any progress for the remainder of his term were essentially nil.

The Hanoi trip had exacerbated Lewandowski's malaise. Flying over the devastation—the cratered landscape, the smoking villages, the ruined bridges—he wondered how long North Vietnam could "sustain this bloody business." Unable to share his comrades' bravado, he sensed "no clear victory ahead," and he regretted having succumbed to the "illusion" the previous fall that the Americans were really ready to make peace. Thus feeling depressed, he foresaw only intensified fighting. And even though his politics tilted him in one direction, he insisted, when interviewed decades later, that the sight of battle-weary U.S. soldiers—"these poor boys," some wounded and bandaged, being driven through Saigon streets or dumped behind barbed-wire enclosed compounds, protected by steel netting to block hand grenades—evoked not ideological contempt but human compassion. "Understand one thing," he told me:

> Watching this whole thing, being engaged in this business, my motivations were at that time, not that I wanted to, let's say, to do something against the United States, or something very much in favor of Vietnam. You must remember, I was a child of the war, in 1939 when my country was overrun by the Germans, [causing] horrible slaughter. [I lived] in Warsaw surrounded [by] this horror of occupation, so when I had behind me an experience of people suffering from the war business, and all that it was connected [with], when I watched in Saigon the cars with wounded GIs, you know, with young boys, exhausted, I was feeling the same way when I saw the North Vietnamese wounded. I thought, "My God, for what are these people are fighting, for this crazy business, . . . this napalm dropping and all these things." My motivations were not just political but moral. . . . I sympathized

with the North Vietnamese because they were the weaker side but I felt very strongly about victims [on both sides].[125]

The responsibilities of managing the Polish delegation may also have taken a toll on Lewandowski. Overseeing hundreds of military officers—along with Communist Party activists and secret police agents eager to enforce discipline, security, and ideological orthodoxy—in a hostile war zone thousands of miles from home, surrounded by suspicious South Vietnamese and U.S. forces, presented a serious challenge in the best of circumstances, especially for a junior diplomat. But these were not the best of circumstances; there is evidence that behind the bland facade it assiduously maintained, the Polish delegation seethed with intrigues and turmoil. As Lewandowski feared, some of his toughest trials involved dealing with bored or unruly personnel who drank, brawled, loafed, or otherwise defied regulations. Pushing soldiers to shape up (and stow the vodka) inevitably incurred grumbling, some of which evidently led to grievances voiced in the "basic party organization" within the delegation, which filtered back to apparatchiks in Warsaw.

More gravely, acute mutual resentment and animosity had developed between Lewandowski and the undercover intelligence agents who had infiltrated his delegation. Despite the arrangement he and the Interior Ministry had ostensibly hashed out before he left for Saigon, tension had flared between the new commissioner and the secret police agency soon after his arrival in Vietnam in April 1966. As noted above, Lewandowski had (at least on the surface) reacted nonchalantly when Daniel Passent (the young *Polityka* reporter working as an interpreter for the delegation that spring and summer) confided that a visiting "courier" had tried to recruit him to inform on his boss (see chapter 1). But he hit the roof when his personal secretary, who was the widow of a Spanish Civil War veteran, came to him in tears to report that she, too, had been pressured by the "courier" to spy on him. After comforting the distraught woman and promising that no one would harm her, he went directly to Jerzy Kowalski, the "senior political adviser" that the Ministerstwa Spraw Wewnętrznych (Ministry of Internal Affairs) had told him was actually its top officer in the delegation, the man to approach in case of any problems. Enraged, Lewandowski demanded that the "courier"—this "hit man"—immediately cease his activities and leave Saigon within a week, rather than the several months he was supposed to stay. If the "son of a bitch" was not gone in seven days, Lewandowski threatened, he would make a stink, complaining directly to the ministerial level.[126]

"What kind of a bordello [do] you have here?" Lewandowski recalled railing.

The "political adviser" duly dispatched the "courier" back to Warsaw, and Lewandowski actually maintained decent relations with Kowalski for the remainder of his term in Saigon (and beyond). Yet the incident left scars. It deepened Lewandowski's suspicions toward the MSW—he later came to suspect that, despite what he had been told, even Kowalski was not really the MSW's top figure in

Saigon[127]—and it appears that, together with his senior military aide (a genuine professional whom he *did* trust), he warily began to scour his delegation for other undercover operatives. At least, so believed an MSW agent in the delegation who in the spring of 1967 filed a detailed, bitter report on Lewandowski's conduct since assuming his post. The ICC commissioner, he charged, abetted by his senior military advisers (including Colonel Iwanciów), had led a "notorious" witch hunt to ascertain the identities of those under his command who were working for the intelligence apparatus. Once rooted out, they fell under an "aura of suspicion," and Lewandowski, driven by "hatred," did all he could to "literally make their lives hell." His "perfidious" actions and attitudes fostered "very harmful relations and a tense atmosphere" within the delegation, "pitting the employees against one another" and paralyzing its military functioning, the MSW source reported. He accused Lewandowski of pulling strings to evict critics, and misleading Warsaw in order to stay in the good graces of the Foreign and Interior ministries and the PZPR's Central Committee. It appears that troubles within the Polish delegation strained Lewandowski's nerves far more than his routine ICC duties.[128]

Even within the deadlocked ICC—a "dead body," a "stupid business"—things were not going well. The North Vietnamese, who were still trying to persuade the Indians and Canadians to annul the anti-DRV resolutions approved in late January, had bluntly told Lewandowski that at all costs, he must prevent their distribution or publication. Accordingly, it was time to admit the defeat of his strategy of pushing for an official report to the cochairs on the December attacks. The Canadians were aiming to circulate no resolutions at all or else all three—an outcome Washington saw as a "net gain," because "citation of U.S. for de facto alliance with [the government of South Vietnam] is old hat, but the ICC has never before noted the presence of North Vietnamese regulars in [South Vietnam]"—and seemed likely to garner Indian support. On February 14, Lewandowski officially threw in the towel, withdrawing his request to transmit the Hanoi bombing resolution to the cochairs.[129]

Lewandowski's fellow commissioners sensed that he had been taken down a notch. "Rahman believes—and it is indeed self-evident—that Lewandowski rushed up to Hanoi with news of resolutions and of his efforts to have bombing resolution publicized and promptly had a strip torn off him by PAVN," Moore cabled. Pleased at the Canadian strategy's success, he surmised that it "may have dawned on Lewandowski after event, or have been pointed out to him in Hanoi, that his initiative was a very dicey one since it was clear we would not agree to a message containing only bombing resolution and might at very best agree only to a balanced message containing at least the two resolutions condemning the North."[130]

Although the North Vietnamese had directed their displeasure primarily against the Indians and (less stridently, because they expected no better) the Canadians, the Poles sustained at least a bit of collateral damage. Rahman had based his gossip partly on "off-the-record info volunteered by a Polish interpreter"[131] and—coincidentally or not—Ha Van Lau insisted to a Polish officer at precisely this juncture that henceforth all conversations with Vietnamese comrades be translated by a DRV translator, "since they do not trust our current interpreter in Hanoi." Not only had Warsaw's translator maintained suspicious contacts with Westerners and other foreigners, the PAVN liaison asserted, but even worse, he had made appointments using the Indian delegation's telephone, implying that he was hiding something from his own compatriots.

Obviously exasperated, Lewandowski did not really know what to make of his interpreter's actions—except that they were, at a minimum, extremely foolish: "One must not do such things in the DRV." Regardless of whether the accusations carried any weight, he concluded that the interpreter must go; otherwise, his presence would impair Poland's dealings with the hypersensitive North Vietnamese, shrinking their already slender conversational candor and access to authoritative sources. He saw no other way to dispel Hanoi's mistrust, so Warsaw's "far more important interests" dictated a recall.[132]

Outwardly, Lewandowski remained "in a generally relaxed mood," thought Moore (who had returned to Saigon only a couple of weeks after leaving due to a delay in his replacement's arrival).[133] In a wide-ranging, "very cordial" conversation on February 16, the Pole made "deadpan comments" on a variety of matters connected to the ICC and Hanoi. But he also spoke "with well-calculated emotion of his feelings of frustration and satisfaction with prospect of leaving" Vietnam come April. "It is as though we are all riding in a boat with the current and there is nothing for us to do at present time," Lewandowski lamented—neither Washington nor Hanoi seemed seriously interested in either a cease-fire or negotiations.

When Moore asked how long this "present state of suspension" might last, Lewandowski refused to name a specific date but guessed that Washington, hoping to exploit Communist chaos, would press its military campaign at least for the next year, "and then come round finally to negotiations" by the time of the 1968 presidential elections. "In the meantime," he said, "there is nothing anyone can do—neither Brit[ish], French, the Commission, etc. There was no question of there being a lack of wisdom in finding a solution: the solution is at hand, only the will to peace is lacking. As it is, with all possibilities being discussed openly and peace proposals being urged publicly, nothing can happen."[134]

To Moore's surprise, Lewandowski conceded that the Americans were "achieving military success," an "inevitable" development, given their immense firepower, manpower, and technical prowess. Though he hastened to add that "winning militarily does not mean winning in a broader sense," and discounted claims of progress in the "pacification" and political spheres, the Canadian found his comments on the military situation "significant and encouraging, since it is the first such admission I recall from the Communist side either here or in Hanoi."

Moore also broached delicate ICC matters—in part at the behest of Rahman, who, the Canadian believed, was "running scared" after the snubs in Hanoi and feared that North Vietnamese ire might presage the commission's eviction, severance of diplomatic ties with New Delhi, or other nasty actions that might rebound against India and him personally. The ICC chair flinched at the idea of sounding the Pole out himself, but Moore had no such inhibitions. Playing dumb, Lewandowski "pretended that he was quite unaware of any change in atmosphere surrounding commission or its delegations in Hanoi," and claimed that he had devoted his recent visit to handling Polish Embassy business in the interim between accredited ambassadors. When Moore mentioned that the DRV authorities obviously knew of the (supposedly confidential) resolutions criticizing them and seemed to be reacting unusually violently, Lewandowski "quickly said with a straight face that they had not had it from him."[135]

This was somewhere between a fib and a lie. Though not reporting the outcome of the ostensibly confidential ICC session of January 27 directly to Hanoi, at the top of his cabled summary to Warsaw, he had routinely written "FYI—Hanoi—Ludwig—Mikołaj" to indicate that the MSZ should forward it to Ha Van Lau and the Soviets. The Canadians played the same game. Ottawa routinely shared internal cables on ICC business with the Americans (as well as its Commonwealth partners Britain and Australia), and on February 6, a Canadian diplomat in Washington furnished the text of the recently approved anti-DRV resolutions to the State Department, and Rostow later informed LBJ of the resolutions' content and Hanoi's angry reaction.[136]

Regardless of how it learned of the resolutions, Hanoi's reported reaction was "par for the course," Lewandowski reasoned, given the tense atmosphere and the well-worn DRV dictum that if the ICC could not do anything good, it should not do anything bad. He discounted fears that the North Vietnamese might formally sever cooperation with the commission. Even if the Geneva Accords were a "dead letter," as the Chinese claimed, he added, North Vietnam still clung to their legality and would make its own decision regardless of Beijing's attitude. When Moore belittled Hanoi's tantrum, remarking that both sides had reason to be "fed up" with the ICC (Saigon even more so because it was not a Geneva signatory), Lewandowski observed that if not for the Americans, the South Vietnamese would have already kicked it out.[137]

Eventually, the conversation veered into pure gossip. Arguing that the political process could not succeed due to frequent assassinations, Lewandowski claimed "with a straight face" that the killer of a South Vietnamese politician gunned down in early December was not a Viet Cong (as widely assumed and reported) but an ARVN lieutenant acting on Ky's orders. When Moore, unimpressed, remarked that he had already heard that rumor months ago, the Pole offered his "other hot tip for the day": The prime minister was a drug addict! "At this," the Canadian reported, "I congratulated him on his imminent posting home, telling him he had reached the advanced state of being more Vietnamese than the Vietnamese in his rumour-mongering."[138]

By late February—exhausted, worn down, but more important, convinced that his presence no longer mattered—Lewandowski was eager to head home. To prod Warsaw, he meekly indicated that he "did not want to make difficulties," but he asked the Foreign Ministry to promptly set a "concrete date" for his departure from Saigon, preferably by April 22, "or even earlier"—leaving adequate time, but no more, to prepare a final report and make farewell calls, including a final trip to Hanoi. The young diplomat was a proud, ambitious man at an early stage in a promising career, so it must have taken real distress to compel him to admit to his superiors: "I am somewhat tired both physically and psychologically."[139]

"Poles Apart": A Time for War

Inadvertently, Lewandowski in his own small way contributed to the confidence in Washington that ratcheting up military pressure, rather than cutting back bombing and pushing for negotiations, constituted the best hope of achieving an acceptable outcome in Vietnam. A day after the Pole surprised Moore by acknowledging U.S. battlefield successes, the Canadian gleefully reported his remarks to Lodge, who in turn—going further than Moore's own report to Ottawa—cabled Washington that Lewandowski had admitted "that the military war in Vietnam was going very well for our side and there was no doubt in his mind that we would win it. He stressed poor performance in pacification, however, while grudgingly admitting some success for our side in the political field. Moore says this is the first time Lewandowski has ever made a statement to him so different from the usual Communist line." At the White House, the perpetually optimistic Rostow forwarded Lodge's cable directly to LBJ to buttress his broader case that the Soviets and Eastern Europeans now believed that "we are winning the war in Vietnam."[140]

The much-appreciated news of the Communist's faltering confidence reached LBJ in the midst of the "stock taking" Rostow had advised after the failure of the Tet peace efforts. To the delight of frustrated military commanders, Johnson indicated that he would now approve "rougher" tactics to squeeze the North Vietnamese. He was reportedly "swayed" by a confluence of factors: a hawkish, impatient public; Ho's "hard-nosed" letter; Communist infiltration during Tet; and—as Lewandowski and D'Orlandi suspected—optimism bred by the Chinese events that Hanoi might be vulnerable to coercion. As their "coach," LBJ asked his aides to devise a program to achieve results by the end of 1967, "with maximum efficiency and with everything we have. We have probed for talks and found nothing substantial. Now we must act strongly."

Although LBJ rejected or deferred some measures pushed by the Joint Chiefs of Staff and Westmoreland, on February 22 he approved both more aggressive ground operations and an accelerated force buildup in the South and stronger actions in the North, including an expansion of Rolling Thunder to hit previously off-limits industrial targets near Hanoi and Haiphong—several within the temporarily untouchable 10-mile radius prompted by Marigold.[141] For weeks, Mc-Namara had sensed that LBJ was "getting itchy" to "act more decisively," and now, despite the defense secretary's conviction that stepping up strikes was "insane" amid hints "in the wind" of Communist interest in talking, the president was determined to scratch that itch.[142] To enhance civilian-military coordination, overall management, and dealings with Ky and Thieu, Johnson also OK'd a shake-up of the Saigon Embassy. To replace Lodge (who quietly sent a note of resignation on February 19), he at first leaned toward adding ambassador to Westmoreland's titles, formalizing his status as a MacArthur-like proconsul. But after pleas (from Katzenbach, among others) that appointing the general would convey an unseemly implication of military occupation, LBJ instead settled on a career diplomat, Ellsworth Bunker (whose calm efficiency as envoy in Santo Domingo during the spring 1965 crisis there had impressed senior officials); also sent a gruff White House aide, Robert Komer, to bolster the "pacification" effort; and shifted Porter to South Korea.[143]

✳ ✳ ✳

As these escalatory plans churned ahead, Thant's fitful peace efforts climaxed with a meeting in his native Burma in early March with a DRV delegation led by Ha Van Lau. Thant had solicited the Poles' (as well as French) help to set up this talk, and despite the distaste of the North Vietnamese for the organization he headed, they agreed to see him, allegedly out of respect for him as an Asian statesman (Trinh was impressed by his "very resolute" response to Goldberg's letter).[144] More important, Hanoi hoped to seem forthcoming, in line with its private move to beef up the "diplomatic front." Yet the encounter failed to produce progress. The Communists showed scant interest in Thant's new proposal (which superseded his earlier three-point program) for a cease-fire in place in South Vietnam followed by negotiations, and they soon sent a formal rejection.[145]

On his way back to New York, Thant stopped in Rome, huddling for a half hour with Fanfani. His discouraging report on the just-concluded conversations confirmed the Italian's belief that the Saigon channel's effort "remained the most advanced to date." Reviewing the Polish affair, Fanfani corroborated Goldberg's assertion that Lewandowski, not Lodge, had formulated the ten points.[146] Perhaps Thant still had Marigold on his mind when he landed at Kennedy Airport later that day and met reporters, for the UN leader—a careful speaker with an understated sense of humor—chose the term "poles apart" to describe the gap between the U.S. and North Vietnamese viewpoints.[147] Asked about the comment, Goldberg responded that the "best way to eliminate misunderstanding—poles apart or shorter than poles apart—in my experience, is dialogue. The opening for such a dialogue is present."[148]

While Thant and Lau palavered in Rangoon, Robert Kennedy made his own move in Washington. On March 2, appalled by LBJ's behavior during their last meeting and evident determination to ramp up the war rather than scale back military operations and seek negotiations, RFK issued his most dovish and, in Democratic Party terms, insubordinate pronouncement yet. In a much-anticipated speech on the Senate floor, he urged Johnson to stop bombing and announce his readiness to start negotiations "within a week," accept a mutual limit on fighting or reinforcement if talks actually began, and permit the NLF to participate in elections. Admitting his own part in the decisions that had led to the present quagmire, he asked: "Can anyone believe this Nation, with all its fantastic power and resources, will be endangered by a wise and magnanimous action toward a small and difficult adversary?"[149]

Though actually mirroring U.S. policy during the bombing pause a year before—when Hanoi's agreement to enter negotiations would have sufficed to elicit a bombing halt—RFK's challenge to the revised shibboleth of requiring a reciprocal military concession not only heartened antiwar critics but also paralleled the doubts privately harbored by several key Johnson administration officials. Goldberg, despite prosecuting the Poles for leaking and distorting the aborted peace bid, had complained bitterly to Rusk and Rostow about the mid-December Hanoi bombing and their failure to consult him in a timely manner regarding both Marigold and the Wilson-Kosygin summit. "All this cuts pretty deep," the national security adviser told LBJ.[150] And in early March, Rusk told Johnson flatly that Goldberg was determined to resign—and identified the principal cause: "It is quite clear to me that he is motivated by disagreement on Vietnam and feels that we have not done enough to probe for peace. He was especially critical of the two bombing strikes in the Hanoi area on December 13 and 14."[151]

When Johnson solicited comments on RFK's proposal from senior aides, Mc-Namara—a more crucial figure—used the occasion to imply, heretically, that he had sympathy for the view that Washington had blown a real opportunity in Marigold. While Rostow and Rusk routinely dismissed RFK's plan, McNamara—a regular guest at the senator's Hickory Hill estate in the Virginia countryside—did not endorse his friend's proposal but went partway in his direction and, strikingly, diverged from the party line on the Polish initiative. Estimating the correlation of forces in Hanoi, the defense secretary saw a DRV leadership split into "two groups, one group favoring a negotiated settlement now, and the other group favoring a continuation of the war, presumably until after the U.S. election in 1968." The pronegotiations group, he judged, "was in the ascendancy during the latter part of last year and was prepared to start negotiations in December but was deterred from doing so by our bombing attacks of December 13 and 14." Now, he advised LBJ, "because of their experience in December and for other reasons, the political leaders of North Vietnam distrust both our statements and our motives." Though unwilling to endorse a full-scale bombing halt unless talks started and moved "at a satisfactory pace toward an acceptable settlement," McNamara advocated another push toward negotiations and a unilateral bombing limit (e.g., to below the 20th Parallel) to encourage Moscow to prod Hanoi to the table.[152]

Rostow acted fast to cushion LBJ from this sacrilege. Terming McNamara frustrated, "in a great hurry—as are we all," and "thrashing about for a short cut," he took issue with the defense secretary's readiness to consider unilateral bombing cutbacks to induce negotiations, and disputed his implication that the air campaign in northern North Vietnam was counterproductive, with "positive" effects outweighed by the impact on domestic and international public opinion and on Hanoi's attitude toward talks. "He honestly believes—without independent evidence—that our bombing around Hanoi stiffens the resistance of the people in authority there and makes it harder for them to negotiate an end to the war. As his memorandum suggests, he tends to accept the theory that our bombing attacks of December 13–14 were damaging to negotiations."[153]

McNamara decorously confined his heresy to secret memoranda—just as he had fallen into line after LBJ had rejected his advice on December 8 to suspend further Hanoi raids so long as the Polish effort remained alive—and Goldberg, despite his unhappiness, would soldier on at the UN for another year, sparing the White House embarrassment. Nevertheless, the public criticism regarding his peace efforts rattled LBJ. Convinced that the classified record refuted the charges of insincerity and/or incompetence, he chafed at secrecy restrictions that precluded a full airing of the covert diplomacy. "[I'm] sick and tired of being afraid to blow a contact," he blurted at a Tuesday lunch on March 7, requesting the preparation of "orderly public accounts" of various U.S. peace bids.[154]

Drawing on Bill Jorden's chronologies, Rostow plied Johnson with potential statements partly divulging the history of secret contacts, with options ranging from a special presidential message to Congress to a Rusk press release, offering alternative drafts with more or less "blowing of channels."[155] Ultimately, LBJ decided to take a relatively low-key route. Selective leaking produced a few favorable stories about Hanoi's intransigence, and Jorden quietly passed around a lengthy compendium of overtures—sans Marigold—meant to show that for years, Washington had said yes but "Ho Keeps Saying No," as a favorable *U.S. News & World Report* piece headlined.[156] At the same time, Rostow circulated Jorden's classified chronologies to George Christian so that he could coach reporters probing the shadowy diplomacy.[157]

※ ※ ※

As the Johnson administration moved to portray its actions more convincingly, the Poles, too, assiduously disseminated their side of the story. To fellow Communist leaders, Gomułka recounted the events, with a predictably damning anti–United States spin, explaining that Warsaw had wanted to disclose the matter publicly and fully but had been restrained by Hanoi.[158] And in meetings with

Westerners, Polish officials added the December 1966 tale to their repertoire of belligerent U.S. behavior ruining chances for negotiations. Alongside the end of the December 1965–January 1966 bombing pause, this latest episode showed "Hanoi's readiness to have war stopped," Winiewicz told the Danes during a trip to Copenhagen.[159] In Rome, Prime Minister Edward Ochab pointedly reminded the Italians what had happened the previous fall to crush his country's peace efforts and urged them to curb their ally's "warmongering and aggressive tendencies."[160] (As the Poles would doubtless have been pleased to know, U.S. NATO officials unaware of Marigold were thrown on the defensive when the Danes and Italians relayed these remarks and sought illumination.[161])

When Rapacki finally saw Martin—not at a secret rendezvous to collaborate on urgent peace measures, as the Canadian envisioned, but at a special UN conclave in New York to discuss the June 1967 Middle East war—Warsaw's foreign minister, "in a tone of resigned despondency," recited the sad tale to explain why in current circumstances he "dare [not] urge" Hanoi to cooperate in a renewed push for negotiations.[162] Most visibly, in mid-April, a "key East European ambassador" at the UN—almost certainly Tomorowicz—gave Estabrook a detailed rendition of Marigold's failure, to support his contention that Washington sought military victory rather than peace talks. The ensuing *Post* piece stoked U.S. officials' irritation toward Warsaw and hardened their determination to rebut the Poles' account.[163]

Preliminary Postmortems: "We Simply Had a Clear Misunderstanding"

In the late winter and into the spring of 1967, as the war intensified after "months of initiatives, high expectations, and soul-destroying frustrations,"[164] arguments festered over Marigold's collapse (and then exposure), along with the failed Wilson-Kosygin effort.

For various reasons—the press of other Vietnam and peace "feeler" controversies, the firm "no comment" stance of U.S. officials in Washington and the diplomatic trio in Saigon—the mainstream media had failed to follow up on the early February *Post* stories unveiling the Polish initiative. And most important, the "paper of record," the *New York Times,* did not bother to dig deeper. After Estabrook's scoops, Tomorowicz found it "peculiar" that the *Times'* UN reporter, Drew Middleton, "who is known for making up 'all sorts of information' upon request, this time is entirely silent."[165] Nor did the *Times'* Washington Bureau display any gusto to more than dutifully recapitulate its rival's scoop. One *Times*man who did pursue the matter was Harrison Salisbury. Back from his tumultuous Hanoi tour, he wrote Wilfred Burchett seeking a Communist perspective on the Polish affair. But Burchett—though dropping cryptic public hints that the "first contacts for talks" were "foiled" by the same Hanoi raids that Salisbury had so famously investigated[166]—was not (yet) authorized to retail details. "On the question of 'quiet clandestine exploring,' I think U Thant would be able to enlighten you on what happened just prior to the December 13 and 14 bombings and the relation of the lighter [latter] to various moves already on foot," he advised— though he added that "it is in no one's interests to reveal the details at this time."[167] Salisbury planned to approach the UN head, who had not disclosed the Polish angle when they spoke in mid-January, but by the time they met again in mid-March, other events had taken precedence, most notably Thant's recent encounter with the North Vietnamese in Burma.[168]

Instead, the most detailed early journalistic inquiry into the affair came from a comparatively obscure source: the *War/Peace Report,* a small-circulation newsletter put out by the Center for War/Peace Studies, a left-leaning New York foreign policy educational group. Its editor, Richard Hudson, had gathered tales of the Polish initiative from "very well-informed sources in and around" the UN to produce, in late February, a more detailed account than Estabrook (e.g., revealing Dong's approval of the Warsaw contact) but making the same basic point: The December 13–14 Hanoi bombings "did derail" mutually agreed-on U.S.–North Vietnamese conversations set for the Polish capital. Seeking comment, Hudson approached Bundy in Washington, but after getting a "very 'cool reception,'" he provided a draft to the U.S. UN Mission.[169]

Alarmed, Rusk tried to spike the story. "Proposed Hudson article would of course be extremely damaging and would tend to revive controversy over December events and put President and [the U.S. government] in bad light," he cabled Goldberg. To convince Hudson to desist, he supplied various arguments: It was misleading, inaccurate, omitted some details while containing others "falsified by Polish informants," and if printed could endanger future cooperation both from Warsaw and "whatever elements in Hanoi may in fact desire some form of talks."[170]

With Goldberg already off on a trip to East Asia, his deputy, William Buffum, called in Hudson and counseled sternly against publication. Initially, the editor seemed "somewhat taken aback," insisting that "he was first a man of peace, secondly a journalist," but then he recalled being "scooped" several times after holding back on stories that were allegedly injurious to negotiations; insisted that "not all" of his story came from Polish sources, contrary to Washington's implications; and—"gain[ing] conviction as he continued"—candidly stated that the "more important consideration is to lay out story so as 'to put pressure on Washington to change its policy.'" Ultimately, Hudson "believed his judgment on [whether the story would damage peace prospects was] as good as ours," and would likely go ahead, Buffum reported.[171]

Faced with Hudson's determination, Rusk backed off. At Bundy's prompting, he had considered issuing an official clarification if the story appeared— expressing "grave doubts" whether the U.S. government had ever received any "authoritative message" from Hanoi—but he appeared to buy Buffum's argument that this would merely attract greater notice. "[I don't] think we ought to get mixed up in it—let him go ahead," he told Bundy, who after hesitation granted that the article should "not cause much trouble."[172]

Hudson's reconstruction of the secret diplomacy ran in the *War/Peace Report* in early March, attributed to unnamed sources, "both Communist and noncommunist, who were privy to the negotiations involved." Though indeed marred by errors and gaps, which were mostly minor, it spotlighted an essential mystery: Why was Hanoi bombed on December 13–14 when direct negotiations, so long desired, finally seemed imminent? Hudson posited four hypotheses, in ascending order of plausibility. The explanation that the raids were set long in advance and not coordinated with diplomacy he found "incredible" (given the time available to modify plans) but could not rule out; "more conceivable" was deliberate sabotage, by military or civilian officials opposing negotiations; a "real" possibility was that LBJ wanted to pressure Hanoi into accepting "certain 'clarifications'— perhaps preconditions—to talks" (i.e., the interpretation clause fracas); and "most likely," "President Johnson personally approved the bombings in order to disrupt the talks, which he decided were premature." Yet, Hudson admitted, this last scenario begged the question of why Washington, through Lodge, had initiated the overture in the first place in mid-November, only to squelch it a few weeks later; perhaps intervening developments, such as optimistic military reports or the Chinese turbulence, had compelled Johnson to change course.[173]

Before publishing his account, Hudson circulated an advance draft to gin up interest—generating wire service reports that, in Rome, prompted Italian Communist Party leader Luigi Longo to ask Fanfani in Parliament about Italy's role. Calling for discretion, the foreign minister said that premature revelations had "not helped the cause of peace" but, without disclosing details, he praised D'Orlandi for helping to achieve, under instructions, the "best results so far" in Vietnam diplomacy.[174]

Yet the *Times* took a pass: Hudson dangled a peek to the foreign desk, but he got nary a nibble.[175] Salisbury, who was out of town at the time and thus unable to lobby for coverage, found Hudson's tale enlightening but puzzling. "I cannot for the life of me understand why this began and was then, as it seems, deliberately torpedoed," he wrote Burchett (who had confirmed that the *War/Peace Report* addressed the matter that had prompted his earlier suggestion to see Thant). "But I would like to get all this material on the record in the *Times*."[176]

He did not. Neither Burchett nor Dong, who politely rebuffed Salisbury's cabled queries, supplied any usable illumination, and the newspaper left the story fallow. Nor, though it received close attention from specialists, did Hudson's account inspire any other serious media inquests.

✳ ✳ ✳

In fact, more governments than journalists launched special probes to discover what had gone wrong and why. The subject repeatedly came up in U.S.-Soviet exchanges, with Moscow's diplomats insisting that the initiative was real. During "a long specific discussion of the December events" on February 17, Zinchuk told Bundy (who claimed that "the original message from the Poles had been exceedingly vague") that Hanoi had been "definitely willing to talk, in the sense of exchanging views." Zinchuk "had gone back over this with Hanoi and had ascertained firmly that this was the Hanoi position at that time." If so, Bundy conceded, "we had simply had a clear misunderstanding as to what Zinchuk now described as Hanoi's intent at that time."[177]

Despite the ill will generated by the leaking, U.S. and Polish officials also sporadically tried to reexamine events dispassionately. Aside from the exchanges between Gronouski and Michałowski, Goldberg, at the UN and, during a visit in early March, in Saigon, pursued his own quixotic inquiry in hopes of rebutting the account that Warsaw had given Thant and, he believed, Estabrook. Accompanied by Lodge, he held an "entirely private and off record meeting" with D'Orlandi on March 3 in order, as he put it, "to secure firsthand confirmation from entirely independent source of inaccuracy of Polish version," especially the claim that Lodge had approved the ten points only to renege later through the "interpretation clause." On that point, the Italian corroborated the U.S. view, offering valuable testimony to "set the record straight" with Thant and others, "including some journalists." (Fanfani also backed Goldberg's version when he saw the UN leader outside Rome a couple of days later.[178]) But Goldberg also had to admit that D'Orlandi expressed "great confidence" in Lewandowski's "integrity," "loyalty," and "cooperation" and shared the Pole's view that the December 13–14 bombings had "derailed the Warsaw talks." D'Orlandi also recalled "vigorously" conveying to Rusk, when he passed through Saigon, Fanfani's urgent warning against further raids on Hanoi.[179]

Under instructions, Lewandowski avoided Goldberg, but he received a report from D'Orlandi, who sensed that Lodge did not "particularly like" the meddlesome visitor ("who assumed a position of 'special investigator'"). D'Orlandi relayed Goldberg's interest in the ten points' provenance and evasion when asked if they still represented U.S. policy, Lewandowski reported, and his suspicion that Poland's UN delegation had leaked the matter (the commissioner assured Warsaw that despite "great pressure," he was rebuffing all journalistic inquiries).[180]

The day after seeing D'Orlandi, Goldberg checked in with Ormond Wilson Dier, Moore's replacement as Ottawa's ICC commissioner. They lunched at the U.S. ambassador's residence, joined by Lodge, minutes after Goldberg returned from a "helicopter tour (no flak jackets) to [a Viet Cong] stronghold immediately south of Saigon." A couple of weeks earlier, when they met in New York, Goldberg had confided to Dier that he was a "dove" on the war, but now—as they adjourned to the study for further discussion—Goldberg not only failed to repeat this self-description but also adopted the hard-line view favored by Bundy and Lodge that only heightened military pressure would convince Hanoi to relent. "Perhaps helicopter trips over enemy territory constituted a nice refinement of high-level brain washing," the Canadian quipped in his report on the talk. LBJ's disgruntled UN envoy soft-pedaled his Marigold inquest, but Dier sensed the affair's reverberations, finding him "particularly bitter against the Poles for the manner in which they had inaccurately publicized peace feelers recently."

Though fresh off the plane, Dier, 48, had a finely honed wariness toward his U.S. colleagues, which likely had been reinforced by Martin before he left Ottawa.[181] He was unimpressed by Lodge's disquisition (which he presumed was largely for Goldberg's benefit) on the pertinence of the Asian concept of "face" to hopes for negotiations—"that Oriental mind has a peculiar logic not fully comprehensible to most Occidentals, and therefore a high degree of flexibility was an essential"—and his "set lecture" on the ICC. And, especially after hearing Bundy downgrade any likely role for the commission when he passed through Washington, he was hardly bowled over when the Americans suggested that Canada might "carry the ball for the USA" in future contacts with the North Vietnamese. "It is perhaps not too cynical to conclude," Dier mused, "that having tried unsuccessfully to utilize the Poles and having written off the Indians as channels to Hanoi, the USA has now decided to call on the third team."[182]

Back in New York, Goldberg found that Tomorowicz now largely accepted his understanding of the ten points' authorship. However, new divergences had cropped up: The Polish record (unlike Lodge's cables) did not mention any hedging on the ten points by Lodge on December 1, and also indicated that the Poles had warned repeatedly, starting that day, that any bombing "intensification" could endanger the proposed talks (as did the U.S. record from December 3 on, after the first attack on Hanoi, although only implicitly in Lodge's December 1 cable). Goldberg urged the skeptical Pole—who found the December bombings on the eve of the proposed contacts too coincidental to be unrelated—to clarify these matters when he returned to Warsaw, but the short-lived U.S.-Polish joint investigation faded away.[183]

✳ ✳ ✳

The most intriguing postmortem involved the British and the Poles, who were on opposite sides of the Iron Curtain but felt considerable empathy—aspirant Vietnam mediators sharing a sense of having had the rug pulled out from under them by Washington. Thus, Cooper's late January and early February briefings in London were meant to heal wounded British feelings, but Anglo-American frictions over Marigold persisted. The even more mortifying mix-up over the Wilson-Kosygin summit left the frustrated British leader broadly hinting in public that peace "was almost within our grasp," convinced that Washington had tragically botched a "historic opportunity"—and wondering privately to Cooper and Bruce "where the responsibility really lay for the confusion in the Lewandowski affair."[184]

The still-fuming British leader soon had a chance to pry further when Rapacki came to town. On February 24, over lunch at 10 Downing Street, Wilson pressed his guest to explain the "nature and cause of the misunderstandings" that had wrecked Marigold. The Briton, as he had to Parliament, suggested that mistakes on both sides, "some lack of precision" and "a failure in human communications" involving Lodge and Lewandowski, must have been responsible. Not so, Rapacki replied. He faulted the Hanoi bombings, and perhaps "deliberate sabotage" by "Saigon hawks." Wilson proposed, and Rapacki agreed, that the British and Polish experts should "compare notes" on why the initiative had collapsed. Rapacki gave the British "the strong impression that he felt he had taken a personal risk in the December project, had gotten burned, and was very disillusioned about the experience"—and therefore was "not disposed to get burned again."[185]

Coincidentally, that same Friday afternoon, Wilson hosted Rostow—whom he largely blamed for the reversal of tenses during the Kosygin summit—for another discussion about how recent events had turned so sour. Hours after agreeing with Rapacki on a British-Polish postmortem, Wilson proposed a U.S.-British "detailed inquiry" into the recent "major failure of communication" between Washington and London, both in November and February. Wilson thought this exercise might resemble Harvard professor Richard Neustadt's classified analysis of the 1962 "Skybolt Affair," which roiled Anglo-American relations during the Kennedy administration. However, Rostow was "noncommittal." The joint inquest never took place, and London instead embarked on its own autopsy.[186]

Although comparably annoyed at American behavior, the U.K. Foreign Office saw little benefit, and some risk, in following up on Wilson's inquisitiveness with both Warsaw and Washington. As Sir Patrick Dean, at the premier's behest, reviewed with LBJ the foul-ups during the Kosygin visit,[187] the Foreign Office, with a sigh of resignation, pursued the "Lewandowski Affair" with Warsaw after it relayed word that Michałowski was ready for a "thoroughgoing" review of the December events with British ambassador Thomas Brimelow, and gave the impression that it was "determined to get as much information out of us" as possible. One aide feared "considerable dangers in this exchange of information with a Communist power," because the Poles might try to extract data that they could use to exacerbate the already-evident Anglo-American discord, and for general anti-U.S. propaganda.[188]

Washington, too, was wary after learning of the talks with Poland's foreign minister.[189] It discerned "further evidence of Rapacki's continuing vindictiveness" and presumed that "his feelings [would] badly discolor the Polish contribution to a 'more detailed postmortem' between the British and the Poles." Unable to stop it, however, the State Department gave London a rebuttal to Polish arguments—denying that Lodge had "reneged after giving firm agreement" to the ten points, or that stopping the bombing had been a precondition for direct talks—along with Washington's own chronology.[190] Aware that "Wilson and Brown still do a lot of churning over the Kosygin visit and may still have some scars from our having given the Phase A / Phase B formula to the Poles in November without telling Brown," U.S. officials fretted that the U.K.-Polish review might deepen British doubts about Washington's interest in peace.[191] "It was a mistake for Wilson to rehash the Marigold exercise with the Poles," Cooper told Dean. "This was pretty much a dead issue, and I could no see useful purpose that Wilson could serve by raising the matter again."[192]

Cooper correctly suspected that neither Dean nor Brown shared Wilson's ardor for the joint inquiry. Foreseeing "pitfalls" in the encounter with Michałowski, Foreign Office aides agreed that Brimelow should "go through the motions" and remain "as uncommunicative as possible." They briefed him with the secret U.S. account and warned him to stay on guard, because the Poles "will exploit anything you may say," and would likely claim that "the Americans have lied to us" and were never serious about the proposed Warsaw meeting in December. While probing "the real enigma" of the affair, the actual degree of Hanoi's backing for Warsaw's diplomacy—did the Poles have a "clear mandate" from the North Vietnamese, or were they acting as an intermediary, despite not having fully "'sold'" them on the idea of making the attempt?—Brimelow should "avoid being drawn into any discussion which could impugn American veracity or which could lead, in your judgment, to Polish wedge-driving between the United Kingdom and the United States or to the danger of Polish propaganda about the 'perfidious Americans.'"[193]

In the event, British and U.S. fears proved overblown. When Michałowski saw Brimelow on April 4, he did not pump for inside dope on Anglo-American exchanges (though he expressed interest in Britain's efforts during the Kosygin-Wilson summit). Instead, predictably, the Pole laid out the case that the Hanoi bombings had been primarily liable for the initiative's failure to get peace talks started. In what he agreed was "purely a historical exercise," Michałowski termed the effort a "Polish initiative" rather than a DRV one. "It was," he added, perhaps significantly (in light of Quang's reluctance to advertise his readiness to receive Gronouski), "very difficult indeed for the North Vietnamese to make any move themselves. They were afraid that if they were to make any move, it would be interpreted as a sign of weakness." Yet, he insisted, Warsaw had remained "in regular contact, . . . and not only by telegram," with DRV authorities, alluding vaguely (for the first time, so far as the British knew) to "talks with the North Vietnamese Foreign Minister in a third country," that is, Bulgaria. Those contacts left no doubt that Hanoi was serious and had been ready for direct talks if the ill-advised bombings had not ruined the best opportunity yet to stop the war—either before or since—and "confirmed the North Vietnamese in all their suspicions that the Americans do not really want to start talks." While noting the gratuitous confusion, delay, and suspicion caused by the "interpretation clause," Michałowski emphasized that both Warsaw and Hanoi blamed the effort's downfall on the bombings (throwing cold water on Wilson's theory that diplomatic errors had doomed it). Rejecting Washington's denial that the air attacks were culpable, Michałowski conceded that Hanoi had not insisted on a complete halt before a Warsaw meeting, but he argued that it nonetheless perceived the December raids as an "obvious" pressure tactic that provoked first a "reconsidering" and then a decision to "terminate the conversations on the possibility of direct talks."

In other words, not the bombing's *continuation* but its *intensification* had done the damage. Though the Poles "did not think this was double play by Washington" but rather a "deliberate action by the U.S. military authorities in Saigon," the DRV leadership interpreted the attacks as a conscious, top-level American ploy synchronized with the imminent talks. In the end, Hanoi judged that the Poles had been "naive and that they, the Vietnamese, had been correct in doubting whether any good could come out of these talks." The outcome "had been a great setback. . . . It would be harder to get talks started in future. He saw no early prospect of further talks."[194]

Michałowski's account—which is roughly consistent with internal Polish documents[195]—nonplussed London. "My own view is that the record [of the Brimelow-Michałowski exchange] confirms our earlier suspicions that the Poles probably never had a sufficiently clear mandate from the North Vietnamese to the point of arranging a meeting between the United States and North Vietnamese ambassadors on December 6, as the Americans had proposed," observed the U.K. South-East Asia Department's D. F. Murray. "In other words, the Poles were trying an initiative on their own; they may have made a certain amount of progress with it because they had good contacts with the North Vietnamese; but they were never in the position of being able to 'deliver' their friends."[196] After colleagues seconded this assessment,[197] the South-East Asia Department passed Wilson its verdict: Brimelow's interrogation had yielded some new evidence of DRV-Polish contacts, but the "most important point of all" had been Michałowski's "failure to give any clear indication that the Poles really had a proper mandate from Hanoi." Judging his claims of consultation with Hanoi "not sufficiently precise," and sensing other indications "that the Polish efforts were possibly more in the nature of an intermediary attempt which may not have been effectively 'sold' in Hanoi," it deduced that "the Poles were simply not in a position" to arrange the direct U.S.-DRV meeting in Warsaw or to provide "good offices in arranging the contact," and no meeting would have occurred even if the Americans had not bombed Hanoi.[198]

Having reached a conclusion likely to please Washington, Murray passed a record of the Brimelow-Michałowski conversation (minus a reference to the Pole's inquiry about the Wilson-Kosygin talks[199]) to Cooper, who "expressed gratitude but added that he devoutly hoped that this was the last we would all hear of this particular exercise."[200] Harriman's aide "indicated that all concerned in Washington were taking this very much as a historical episode to which they hoped they could write finis," MacLehose informed Wilson.[201] The Foreign Office likewise saw "very little point or value" in further rehashing Marigold, but they were compelled to produce further analysis after the prime minister pressed them to "sit down and reconcile or identify the points where things went wrong, if possible saying why the misunderstanding occurred and who was responsible."[202]

Though exasperated by this "depressing" and "entirely profitless" exercise, the South-East Asia Department submissively expectorated a further dissection of "the Lewandowski Affair." While judiciously hedging that it remained "difficult to apportion blame"—and some belonged to Washington—Brown stressed to Wilson "the essential point," that "the Poles were probably never really in the position of being able to 'deliver' their friends, and consequently misled the Americans."[203] A top Wilson aide chimed in: "I think it is true that neither this nor any other postmortems are likely to clarify this unhappy business any further. And I think we should accept Chet Cooper's view as X."[204] To the relief of his associates, to say nothing of the Americans, the prime minister, by then engrossed in new peace efforts, finally agreed to stop harping on the matter with Washington.[205]

A "War of White Books"? "Sec. Maybe Could Tidy It Up"

"4-MONTH U.S. BID IGNORED BY HANOI," blared the front page of the *New York Times* on Tuesday, May 9, 1967. After three months playing defense against charges that its December bombings had sideswiped a genuine chance for peace, the Johnson administration finally turned the tables when the Associated Press ran—and the *Times* prominently featured—a lengthy, sympathetic account of the secret diplomacy. The story, by senior AP reporter John M. Hightower, purveyed Washington's view that the disputed December 13–14 Hanoi bombings, contrary to Polish contentions that they "wrecked one of the most hopeful approaches to peace in the recent history of the war," instead "might have presented Hanoi or Warsaw a convenient pretext" to evade the proposed direct U.S.-DRV contact. It described unnamed U.S. "high officials" as doubtful that Rapacki "was in fact relaying United States views and making known Washington's readiness for talks to Hanoi" and as "skeptical that Warsaw ever had a firm commitment or Hanoi a serious intention to open secret talks." As the *Times'* headline indicated, the article highlighted Washington's secret late-December pledge to abjure from bombing within a 10-mile radius around Hanoi and North Vietnam's failure to respond, prompting the lifting of the self-denying ordnance in late April.

Careful readers had no trouble discerning that Hightower's story reflected U.S. officials' views—but they may not have suspected that it bore the fingerprints of Rusk himself. The secretary of state frequently spoke off the record with Hightower, who at his own initiative "had been nibbling at the story" for some weeks or even months and had spoken on background to Lodge, among others.[206] On Friday afternoon, May 5, a few days after a half-hour session with Rusk, Hightower had telephoned to ask him whether "it was possible to go ahead on the Hanoi peace story."[207] Rusk invited the reporter to bring a draft by his office the next afternoon: "Sec. thought if H. wished to pull it together Sec. maybe could tidy it up for H." Rusk might point out "a number of facts which could be deduced from what is available from public sources"—presumably including, for instance, the assaults on Tan Son Nhut and other Saigon locales in early December, relevant context for Rusk's lack of enthusiasm for withdrawing authorization for planned strikes near Hanoi. Spurring the sympathetic reporter to hurry up, Rusk noted that there were "one or two others who, without any encouragement from [him,] are sniffing around on this." (He was not whistling "Dixie"; an hour later, he would receive *Washington Post* reporters Murrey Marder and Chalmers Roberts, who were chatting up officials for a report on high-level Vietnam decision-making and paying special attention to the controversial December 13–14 bombings, on which they reputedly hoped to "peg" the piece. "Is it possible," Roberts challenged one official, "that decisions are being taken at the upper levels of a military character and precisely timed to kill off certain steps being taken to achieve a peaceful solution?"[208])

When Hightower opined that he had a "pretty good" story, Rusk counseled him on how to proceed: "Sec. told H. to write the story that takes into account some of the things Sec. has said privately and then Sec. will go over certain points with H." Hedging at this blatant guidance, Hightower cautioned that he could not actually submit a story for "clearance." Rusk assured that he fully understood and respected this. With the ground rules clarified, the symbiotic relationship between authoritative source and friendly reporter resumed.

Hightower got the authoritative green light on Saturday afternoon. Meeting with the trusted AP reporter, Rusk telephoned Rostow to warn that a fuller version of the "Marigold exercise" was about to leak, confirmed that the White House had no objection, and raised the possibility of accompanying the piece with an "authenticated" release; instead, the national security adviser suggested a background briefing, a course Rusk adopted.[209] Rostow's reaction reflected LBJ's urgent desire to counter the slew of negative press about the administration's peace efforts. "Day in, day out we get clobbered about who said what to whom in Rangoon in 1964, etc., etc.," one aide had lamented to him. "While third parties concerned would have to be protected, it would be in the national interest (as I see it) to give a responsible journalist . . . access to the 'peace files' and at least get our side on the record."[210] It is not clear whether LBJ personally approved the leak to Hightower, but Bundy—who had also funneled information—explained to a diplomat that the reporter "had ferreted out about two-thirds of story on his own (based on earlier leaks, e.g., via Estabrook) and that someone in authority had decided that he should be given rest of story in interests of accuracy."[211]

Rusk was pleased by the AP article, which he found "essentially accurate and reasonably favorable from our point of view," and State Department spokesman McCloskey told reporters on background that he "would have no quarrel with it."[212] It was, of course, a delayed rejoinder to the *Post* stories in early February, as Rusk could not resist gloating to Estabrook as Hightower's opus hit the wires. "[Why don't you] go back to the Poles and make them tell you the rest of the story?" he needled. "They certainly victimized you."[213] Best of all, from the administration's perspective, was the lofty perch it received in the *Times*, which normally was not prone to so prestigiously showcase a bylined wire service story at the top of the front page, with its unseemly implication that its own staff had failed to produce something "fit to print" on such a newsworthy topic.

The result was a paradox in Vietnam press coverage in the nation's two leading newspapers. The *Washington Post,* still editorially hawkish, had given the public its first glimpse of Marigold, with a vivid hint that Washington had "bungled" a chance to open negotiations. Yet the more dovish *New York Times* had allowed its hallowed front page to trumpet a Rusk-approved account casting stones at the Poles, and reinforcing the administration's line that a stubborn Hanoi had blocked peace talks.[214]

* * *

Hightower's article aroused grumbles from those who had already written about the Polish affair. The *War/Peace* editor, Hudson, called the AP man "to suggest rather strongly that he had been had" and wrote the *Times* to complain that the story had, significantly, neglected to mention the December 2 and 4 Hanoi raids, despite Polish warnings against escalation, which had already complicated the initiative. In his letter, Hudson speculated that the December 13–14 bombing "was carried out deliberately to disrupt the talks or to bring pressure on North Vietnam to accept some precondition to the talks."[215] Estabrook, for his part, retaliated with a piece arguing that excessive secrecy had hampered U.S. officials' attempts to explain the American position on the war to foreign diplomats, undercutting Washington's credibility. Exhibit A for this thesis was the administration's refusal to disseminate, until now, its version of the controversy over the aborted December meeting. "The Poles, incidentally, were not the source of my published report," Estabrook noted, contrary to the insinuations of the "high State Department official" who had needled him.[216]

Besides appearing in papers across America, Hightower's piece also quickly attracted attention in international diplomatic circles. UN corridor gossip presumed that officials inspired it to "correct" the impression left by Estabrook's articles in February, and Thant's blurry response to press inquiries as to whether he believed Washington or Warsaw fanned speculation that he leaned toward the Communist rather than the "Hightower–State Department version of events."[217]

The AP story's quasi-official imprimatur aroused speculation that it foreshadowed a more formal release of information, fed by rumors that Rusk had said over the previous weekend that the administration planned a public accounting of the secret diplomacy.[218] In Rome, some Italians who were aware of what had transpired rushed to get their own version on the record. On May 9, *L'Unità* bannered its own exposé, without naming sources but clearly informed by D'Orlandi or someone intimately familiar with his thinking (Fanfani had briefed some Parliament members, so there were other suspects). The famous "Lewandowski Affair," the Partito Comunista Italiano mouthpiece claimed, emerged from months of quiet chats between the Italian ambassador in Saigon and his Polish partner "to try to get down on paper, if only for an exercise in diplomatic style, a few points on which there would be a sufficient possibility of obtaining the agreement of the parties concerned." In December, *L'Unità* declared, this "mere exercise in diplomatic style" had turned into "a concrete platform for peace," the ten points, only to be undermined by the Hanoi bombings. "Who ordered a barbaric action whose effect could only be the destruction of all the work that had been accomplished?" the paper asked, the same question that haunted D'Orlandi. "An explanation has never been given."[219]

The sudden burst of attention to Italy's secret diplomacy triggered a minor political rumpus in Rome. Having privately confided his displeasure to many foreign visitors—from Poland's ambassador to RFK to Libya's foreign minister—Fanfani uttered his most candid public criticism to date of U.S. Vietnam policy, especially the ill-timed military actions he said had repeatedly disrupted diplomatic soundings: "Every observer attentive to the different attempts that have been made to set in motion a peaceful solution to the Vietnam conflict notes that the resumption of bombings did not favor the success of those attempts," he told the *Senato,* calling for a full halt to retest Hanoi's sincerity. Lamenting Fanfani's open breach with Italy's superpower patron, Rome's ambassador in Washington, Sergio Fenoaltea (who eleven months before had helped deliver the message that launched Marigold) resigned in protest.[220]

Of course, no foreigners followed the published reports more intently than the Poles, who immediately suspected the Hightower article's provenance. "The author is Rusk even though his name was not disclosed," Poland's UN ambassador cabled Rapacki. The "tendentiously" skewed account, he judged, aimed both at rebutting prior criticism and justifying recent escalation. Tomorowicz found "especially outrageous" the accusation that Warsaw had failed to inform Hanoi of Washington's readiness for talks, and thought that its claim that diplomats at the UN "made public informally" the "Polish version" of the initiative's collapse was "entirely groundless"—only in late February and March, after Washington had begun depicting Poland's role in a "tendentious light," had he started leaking. Now, however, because U.S. officials felt uninhibited about disclosing the details of an episode they considered "closed," should not Poland retaliate with a "proper commentary" in its own press?[221]

Such thoughts were not far from the minds of top MSZ officials on the morning of May 9 as wire service digests of the Hightower and *L'Unità* articles reached Warsaw (Tomorowicz's cable had not yet arrived). Coincidentally, that Tuesday, Gronouski made calls on Michałowski and Winiewicz before departing on a previously arranged trip to Washington for consultations. Both Poles, he discovered, were rankled about the implicit questioning of Rapacki's integrity along with rumors that the release of an official U.S. "white paper" on the affair might be imminent. This would not be "fair play," the "perplexed and irritated" deputy foreign minister warned. Expressing "worry," Michałowski cautioned that if Washington unilaterally put out an account, Warsaw "would be obliged to enter the war of white books and publish its own version."

Conveniently forgetting Rapacki's own early role in leaking, Michałowski regretfully remarked that exploiting the affair for "propaganda" purposes would "close the Polish channel" in Vietnam diplomacy. Rapacki's right-hand man had an additional, personal motive to contain the damage: The foreign minister had recently tapped him to become Poland's next ambassador in Washington, a sensitive post he would occupy come fall. "I know Vietnam will hang like a cloud over our bilateral relations," he told Gronouski, "but let us try to separate ourselves as much as possible from Vietnam problem."

The American, ignorant of Washington's intentions in the matter, was predictably receptive to Michałowski's pleas. Still convinced that Warsaw might yet come in handy in Vietnam diplomacy, he cabled Rusk to advise against releasing an authorized Marigold version, lest it "destroy thin thread of hope that Poles might in future serve a useful intermediary role."[222]

No problem. Hightower's article had already done the trick, easing the pressure to produce a full-blown official account. "We consider news stories filed yesterday on December peace probes to be essentially accurate and reasonably favorable from our point of view," Rusk cabled back. "We would prefer to let matter rest there avoiding to extent feasible public exchange of interpretations with the Polish Government." The embassy should reassure Michałowski that U.S. officials, loath to "exacerbate" bilateral ties, had "no present intentions [to] publish 'white book' on this subject," and, of course, remained "ardent" in their quest for peace and ready for unconditional talks with Hanoi.[223]

By Wednesday, when the embassy's political officer, Herb Kaiser, came to the Foreign Ministry to mouth these soothing words (Gronouski had left for Washington), Michałowski was incensed. He had not yet read the full text of Hightower's article, but having seen Tomorowicz's cable, he responded tartly to Kaiser's reassurance that no American "white book" would be forthcoming: "U.S. officials had apparently chosen another way to put out the story." Blasting the "disturbing distortions, errors and innuendoes challenging the integrity of Rapacki," he indignantly insisted that the Poles "had of course delivered [U.S.] messages [to Hanoi]." While accepting Kaiser's assurance that Gronouski retained full confidence in Rapacki, Michałowski deduced correctly from Hightower's report that other U.S. officials did not share this stance—"a very disquieting and harmful phenomenon" that boded ill for potential future Polish-American cooperation on Vietnam. Warsaw had not yet decided whether to formally rebut the Hightower story, he concluded, but in the meantime, the State Department should disavow it.[224]

This request was dead on arrival. State did not necessarily exclude resorting to the Poles on Vietnam at some future date, but it was hardly willing to undercut this carefully nurtured propaganda boon to preserve that remote possibility. Besides, huffed Bundy when the Canadian ambassador inquired about whether

Hightower's piece implied that Washington had ditched Warsaw as a potential mediator, "if anyone had loused up that channel, it was the Poles themselves."[225]

Inevitably, news of the Hightower exposé also fluttered to Hanoi, irritating the North Vietnamese much as it had the Poles.[226] On May 15, Deputy Foreign Minister Nguyen Co Thach called in Lewandowski—who was about to wrap up his farewell visit to the DRV capital—to discuss how the Communists should react. He noted that the leadership was considering whether to disseminate a response to the distorted U.S. account, either an official statement or a "leakage" via Burchett. Lewandowski advised caution—Warsaw was undoubtedly also conducting its own review, and the two allies should act in tandem—and Thach agreed to consult before acting.[227]

A few days later, Ambassador Bogdan Wasilewski updated Thach on Warsaw's tentative decision to refrain from immediate public response to the Hightower article; Trinh's deputy seemed less sanguine. If the Poles wanted to stay silent, that was their business, but because readers around the world may "mistakenly assess the 'goodwill' of the U.S.," he suggested that "instead the Vietnamese side could unofficially straighten things out through the press ('leakage') without involving anyone directly."[228]

Warsaw sent back strong counsel to let the matter rest. "We assess that even though the leakages, which caused the well-known articles regarding the conversations, contained many false and biased data, it nevertheless became clear to the public that, in the end, it was the American bombings of December 13–14 which were the precise reason for breaking off the initial talks," Wasilewski was instructed to tell Thach. "Given the above, we do not see as necessary to publish any explanations or corrections."[229]

Hardly eager to publicize that it had agreed to talk with the Americans without a total bombing halt, the North Vietnamese accordingly resisted the impulse to participate in a public dispute. And though Michałowski privately compiled detailed chronologies for possible use in a "white paper," the Poles likewise held back.[230] Nevertheless, in the leaking competition to convince "the public" who was culpable for Marigold's failure, the Johnson administration had at least momentarily evened the score.

* * *

Returning to Washington for the first time in almost six months—since his pre-Christmas dash to argue for a unilateral bombing halt around Hanoi—Gronouski hoped to see LBJ for at least "a few minutes" to convey face to face "the atmospherics of our discussions with the Poles on Vietnam." As Rostow explained, "Gronouski believes the Poles can play a useful role, and wants to discuss whether we should make them a channel in the future. He has some comments on the Hightower story."[231] On May 18, Gronouski saw the president in the Oval Office for thirty-five minutes but failed to ameliorate LBJ's visceral antagonism toward Warsaw.[232]

Instead, Gronouski's May 1967 trip to Washington yielded an entirely different twist in the Marigold saga—the neutralization, on this issue at least, of one of Johnson's most trenchant critics: J. William Fulbright. The irascible Arkansas Democrat and chair of the Senate Foreign Relations Committee (SFRC) had initially backed his old friend's Vietnam policy and voted ("hoodwinked and taken in," he said later) for the August 1964 Tonkin Gulf resolution. But as U.S. involvement grew, so did Fulbright's doubts; the war, he judged, had become both immoral (because the enemy was primarily indigenous nationalism rather than international Communism) and a self-defeating distraction from vital foreign policy priorities. By staging televised hearings in early 1966 that spotlighted prominent skeptics such as George F. Kennan and James M. Gavin, and repeatedly questioning the administration's judgment and competence, Fulbright emerged as the sharpest congressional thorn in Johnson's side, and their personal relationship, dating back to the president's days as Senate majority leader, eroded. "It's easier to satisfy Ho Chi Minh than Bill Fulbright," spat out LBJ, who in a fit of paranoia even ordered the FBI to investigate whether the senator was a Kremlin dupe. Articulating the belief of a growing number of intellectuals, Fulbright popularized a phrase encapsulating the view that Washington had badly overreached politically and militarily: "the arrogance of power."[233]

Still, in the spring of 1967, doves remained a vocal minority in the Senate, and Fulbright had refrained from putting on an encore performance of his klieglighted hearings on the war; behind closed doors, he told his SFRC colleagues that he "wanted to guard against an accusation that he was starting another vendetta against the administration."[234] Though suspicious of Johnson's handling of peace efforts, he yielded to his pleas that a formal inquest might endanger quiet attempts that might soon bear fruit. "Will Fulbright and [Senator Bourke B.] Hickenlooper [R.-Iowa] give us this little chance?" LBJ cajoled Senate leaders in mid-January. "Public hearings can do us no good at all at this moment, only harm. Can the Senate hold off?"[235] Still for the moment on speaking terms, he telephoned Fulbright: "If we can hold out just a little while longer, I think we will get somewhere. . . . We've just got to hold a stiff upper lip and be careful and don't rock the boat."[236]

Though his "caustic carping" continued to irk LBJ, Fulbright eschewed inquests into specific negotiating options and worked behind the scenes to prod the president toward a bombing halt to get Hanoi talking.[237] The morning the *Washington Post* broke the Polish story—which Fulbright found eerily reminiscent of the Stevenson-Thant affair—the SFRC chair, coincidentally, was at the State Department complaining about Johnson's refusal to receive two private Americans (Harry S. Ashmore and William C. Baggs) recently returned from Hanoi purportedly bearing a conciliatory message from its leader. ("You know, Bill, I can't see everybody that goes over there and talks to Ho Chi Minh," he had deflected, as if such requests crowded his schedule.) "All you guys are committed to a military settlement," the senator, in a "foul mood," told the State Department welcoming committee (Katzenbach, Harriman, and Bundy, but not Rusk). "You don't want to negotiate; you're not going to negotiate. You're bombing that little piss-ant country up there, and you think you can blow them up. You've been doing this all the time. It's a bunch of crap about wanting to negotiate."[238] Sending Rusk a copy of the "disturbing" Estabrook article, Fulbright requested an accounting of this and other "formal and informal" peace overtures over the past two years—but the secretary refused to OK a detailed briefing, only a personal chat with Katzenbach.[239]

Three months later, however, Hightower's piece offered Fulbright's SFRC an excuse to scrutinize the administration's handling of the controversial episode, at least behind closed doors: Gronouski happened to be in Washington, anticipating one of his routine chats on Polish-American relations with the SFRC subcommittee on European affairs. The panel summoned Gronouski to a closed-door hearing on the first floor of the Capitol on Monday morning, May 15, 1967, but after gaveling the executive session to order, the subcommittee chair, Senator John J. Sparkman (D-Ala.), emphasized that besides the usual topics, the group wanted to cover the recent story on the *New York Times'* front page, greeting the witness thus: "I am sure that all of us will be particularly interested in your views in connection with the much advertised, but futile efforts last December to arrange contacts with the North Vietnamese through the Warsaw mechanism. We would welcome any clarification of this episode which you might be able to provide for us."

Gronouski had expected a grilling on Marigold, of course, and before heading to the Hill had checked with Bundy to ascertain the State Department's desires. Bundy punted to Rusk, calling to say that Gronouski "could testify as blandly as possible from his personal knowledge or buck it all to Sec; which would Sec prefer?" Rusk told Bundy to bring him to his office immediately.[240]

What exactly transpired during the six minutes in the secretary's office, from 9:48 to 9:54 a.m., was not recorded but easy to imagine: Rusk likely reinstilled the seventh-floor Marigold catechism, deriding Rapacki's conduct, doubting his claims that the North Vietnamese were ready to talk, and dismissing the whole business as a Communist fishing expedition. He hardly needed to spell out to Gronouski that if he wished to stay on the team, wringing his hands to Fulbright about the Hanoi bombings—as he had done contemporaneously in his cables to LBJ—would be verboten.[241]

Gronouski got the message. In his two hours of closed-door testimony, about half of which was devoted to the failed initiative, he parroted the party line: There was no missed opportunity, the Hanoi bombings were not to blame, and he himself had engaged in "wishful thinking" at the time.[242] Nine senators listened and interrogated him from the elevated horseshoe dais in Room S-116, an eclectic aviary of Vietnam hawks, doves, and fence-sitters that included such notables as Fulbright (along with trusted aide and SFRC chief of staff Carl Marcy), Minnesota Democrat Eugene McCarthy (the future insurgent antiwar presidential candidate), and Vermont Republican George D. Aiken (who had famously declared that Washington ought to declare victory in Vietnam and get out).[243]

After Gronouski reviewed U.S.-Polish ties and the quiet ferment in the Central European country, which he described as moving gingerly toward a looser economy and a more westward (or at least Yugoslav) social orientation, Sparkman and Fulbright steered him to the Hightower story. Though quibbling with a few details, Gronouski pronounced it "fairly accurate" and began his own recapitulation of the December events. Recounting the intensive exchanges with Rapacki, he was not quite willing to dismiss the Pole as completely dishonest but confessed exasperation at his "circumlocution" and inability to "produce the [North Vietnamese] body" in the week before the December 13–14 bombings, despite the "tremendously appealing" Phase A/B proposition, "a magnificent out for Hanoi." Pressed by Missouri Democrat Stuart Symington for his current judgment as to whether North Vietnam's approach was sincere or a "charade," Gronouski reflected that the Poles "probably had a very thin thread to rely on in their talks with Hanoi"—lacking its authority to arrange a meeting but angling for the best possible package to then sell to their comrades.

"I was the greatest wishful thinker in the world," he admitted. "The hope was father to my thoughts. I thought that maybe we had it."

For this "informal session," the State Department did not furnish the SFRC with any of its voluminous classified Marigold files, and Gronouski alluded only vaguely to the passionate cables he had sent to LBJ six months earlier (imploring immediate action to salvage the initiative), which he now discounted as, essentially, much ado about nothing. "So despite all of my wishes and hopes—and I will have to admit that some of my telegrams were wishful thinking—I have to come to the conclusion that I really do not think that there was a lot of sincerity from Hanoi's side. I think there was less from Hanoi's side than the Poles hoped there was."

Fulbright, for his part, seemed to accept Gronouski's verdict that in the final analysis, Hanoi's intransigence had doomed the December diplomacy. Further "rehashing" appeared pointless, he commented, "unless you can read their minds." While raising his eyebrow at Gronouski's straight-faced insistence that the disputed December 13–14 bombings were unrelated to the secret diplomacy—"That may or may not be hard to take"—the president's chief critic had only compliments for the ambassador and did not contest his basic argument. "Thank you very much for coming here. I think that you have done a good job with the Poles. It is too bad that we cannot do something about Hanoi. Maybe we can."

Rusk could not have scripted Gronouski's testimony better himself. Fulbright and the SFRC had expected a chance to ask some follow-up questions when the secretary of state appeared in executive session the next day, but Rusk (perhaps happy to leave well enough alone) canceled at the last moment, citing a scheduling conflict, to the consternation of the chairman and some of his colleagues. By the time he showed up a week later, a Middle East crisis had displaced even Vietnam on the international scene, and dominated his testimony.[244] Fulbright would take no further serious formal action to get to the bottom of the Polish business.[245]

In its quiet but determined quest to defuse the Marigold controversy, the Johnson administration was on a roll—not only had Gronouski dampened Fulbright's dangerously roaming curiosity, but the wayward ambassador himself, though hardly happy over how Washington had handled Marigold, had swallowed his doubts and edged back into line. Rusk had a chance to ensure that conformity when the ambassador visited his office late on Wednesday afternoon, May 17, 1967.[246] In more leisurely fashion than their rushed exchange on Monday morning, Rusk could review the Warsaw events, and assure that Gronouski had placed the disappointing experience into the proper context in advance of his Oval Office audience the following day.[247] And just in case Gronouski still had any lingering doubt regarding Eastern European double-dealing on Vietnam, Rusk had in his hand a shiny new trump card to play that he lacked two days earlier.

✳ ✳ ✳

The Johnson administration caught yet another break that week. Katzenbach lived on a quiet side street in affluent Upper Northwest Washington. Normally the house near Connecticut Avenue was reserved for family, not business, but on the evening of May 16 it hosted a bit of Vietnam—and Cold War—diplomatic intrigue. Late that Tuesday afternoon, Rusk had fielded, via an underling, a telephone call from János Radványi, the Hungarian chargé d'affaires since 1962. Formerly posted to Ankara, Paris, Bern, and Damascus, the forty-four-year-old career diplomat ranked as one of the senior Soviet Bloc diplomats in Washington (Budapest had no resident ambassador since the 1956 invasion, so Radványi was acting ambassador, due for elevation once normal diplomatic ties resumed). He had dealt from time to time with Rusk on Vietnam peace possibilities, especially during the thirty-seven-day pause, and the past two autumns he had sat in on meetings in New York during UN General Assembly sessions between the U.S. secretary of state and Hungary's foreign minister, János Péter, during which the latter had hinted at Hanoi's readiness to accept the 17th Parallel as a legitimate border.

This time, however, Radványi was calling not to relay a communication from his government but to request a face-to-face meeting with Rusk—and only him— on "an urgent private matter," and preferably not in his office at the closely observed State Department headquarters. Rusk arranged a rendezvous at a less conspicuous location, and at 6 p.m. surreptitiously left Foggy Bottom for his deputy's residence.

He surmised two possibilities: either some news regarding Moscow that Radványi deemed too sensitive to relate to an official of lesser stature, or, more likely, a defection. It only took a few moments after sitting down with the "extremely agitated" Hungarian before the latter suspicion proved correct. "With a voice shaken by emotion," Radványi poured out a tale of fear and loathing. He felt entrapped by a tightening web of secret police informers (who included all his embassy staff, and even the family maid, whom his wife suspected of trying to poison her; she had attempted suicide two days earlier), and his insecurity had reached the point where—he pointed to his pocket—he was carrying a gun. Turning to political matters, he heaped contempt on his foreign minister, a "con artist" who had repeatedly lied to the Americans regarding Hanoi's alleged willingness to make peace (and also at times treated him "like a dog"). Because a look at the internal ministry files during a recent visit home had exposed the truth—that Péter's claims had been pure inventions, designed to extract U.S. military concessions rather than promote peace—Radványi deeply regretted his unwitting role in promoting a dishonest policy, he explained. (Don't worry, Rusk assured him, he didn't take Péter's "peace feelers" so seriously in the first place.) "Slowly regaining my composure," Radványi declared that he could no longer serve his government, which appeared to be veering in a more hard-line direction, and the former underground member of Hungary's Communist Party (as a young auto worker on the eve of World War II) formally requested asylum in the United States.

Rusk recognized an intelligence and propaganda windfall when it landed in his lap. After obtaining LBJ's approval, he worked with CIA officials to devise a suitable "scenario." The next afternoon—after the Radványis' son had been whisked from his class at Gordon Junior High School and the family had been sequestered at an undisclosed location—the State Department announced the first-ever defection of the head of a Communist mission in Washington.[248]

It all happened just in time for Rusk to relate the defector's private revelations of "make-believe" peace diplomacy, if he desired, when Gronouski showed up at 5:40 p.m. Wednesday for his half-hour appointment. The next day at the White House, the ambassador to Warsaw decorously refrained from rocking any boats, earning a public pat on the back from the president. "He is diligent and dedicated," LBJ told reporters. "We believe that he is doing a good job."[249]

Radványi's defection supplied the administration with welcome reserve ammunition for its campaign to persuade both the public and other governments—and itself—that only further military pressure, not phony Communist "peace feelers," could produce negotiations and an acceptable settlement. Though the public was told that Radványi had resigned from Hungary's Foreign Service and taken up residence in the United States "for personal reasons," Radványi freely vented years of resentments and insider knowledge regarding his Communist experiences to U.S. officials, and, in particular, submitted to a thorough debriefing from Bundy on Eastern European and Soviet peace diplomacy. He claimed personal knowledge that Péter had embellished peace prospects during the thirty-seven-day bombing pause and again in the fall of 1966, but he lacked first-hand awareness of Marigold; in his debriefing report, Bundy wrote that he "does not have much light to throw on this episode," and he knew nothing at all about the Polish initiative while it was in progress.[250]

Nevertheless, that Radványi's data on Marigold was admittedly "second-hand" did not stop Bundy from crowing to Rusk that it "tends strongly to indicate that we missed nothing, . . . as indeed we had believed"[251]—or from citing the Hungarian to persuade some (in or out of the administration) who had doubted Washington's handling of the affair that the skeptics had been right all along. To Canadian ambassador Edgar Ritchie, who had so irritated Rusk in disclosing Ottawa's awareness of Marigold, he noted that despite "only indirect knowledge of Lewandowski operation," Radványi had detected the "same lack of response" from Hanoi as in the cases he knew firsthand; and he told an Australian diplomat that the defector had unmasked the Poles as "shysters" who had "deliberately tried (but failed) to mislead the Americans about North Vietnamese intentions."[252]

Bundy later told another Canadian that Radványi's evidence, allegedly based on a close perusal of Hungarian Foreign Ministry files during his last trip to Budapest before his defection, "was the most conclusive they had to support their suspicion that the Poles had got themselves out on a limb over their offer to mediate" and in fact lacked the Hanoi commitment they claimed to possess.[253] "I start with the assumption that the Polish episode of early December was a fraud on the part of the Poles," Bundy wrote McNamara, citing Radványi's statement that "Hanoi was dug in as of late November, as well as pretty clear evidence that Hanoi did not authorize the Poles to do anything."[254] Even Harriman, who questioned Bundy's claim that the episode was a Polish "fraud," loyally told foreign diplomats that "we had some doubts at the time and had become convinced since then that Lewandowski had no commitments from Hanoi."[255]

Radványi stiffened Johnson's conviction that Soviet Bloc diplomacy could not be trusted. When Wilson visited the White House in early June, LBJ cited his testimony as evidence that Budapest's initiative had been "completely phony—the Hungarians had never been remotely in touch with Hanoi." Hastening to agree, the British prime minister asked with scorn: "Did the President really think that any of the East Europeans had a separate existence [from Moscow] in this matter or a direct line to Hanoi?"[256]

The administration, which was generally tight-lipped about defectors and defections, even while debriefing and citing Radványi in classified realms, kept him under wraps—in strategic reserve to augment its public diplomacy when the time was right.

✳ ✳ ✳

The good news triple play on the Marigold public relations front boosted the Johnson administration's confidence that it could ride out criticism of its so far unsuccessful peace efforts. Speaking on background to an audience of editors and broadcasters in late May, Rusk ridiculed claims that Washington had missed any authentic chances to start negotiations:

Peace moves? There have been literally hundreds of efforts by individuals, by governments, by groups of governments, distinguished world personalities, to try to engage the other side into sort of—or the two sides—into sort of discussion, which would lead toward a peaceful solution of this problem in Southeast Asia.

To sum it all up, thus far, no one has been able to produce; and I hope that if anyone who reports this on a background basis—you do not use this particular expression: No one has been able to produce the warm body of a North Vietnamese anywhere, at any time, with whom I can talk. [Laughter]

Now, if somebody can do that—if somebody can do that, I will be there. I will be there. But Hanoi is the ghost in all of these propositions.

And when rumors go about that somehow, you know, Hanoi took an initiative which we rejected, little by little the full facts come out, and the picture looks rather different than what it was rumored about. . . .

Now, there are hundreds of initiatives by all sorts of people. And let me make this remark *off the record,* because even for me it sounds too cynical if I put it on background.

There are hundreds of candidates for the Nobel Prize wandering around the world, and they wander around, some of them visit Hanoi some of them have contacts with Hanoi's representatives in one or another capital. Most of them don't understand what it is they are hearing. And so they come away eight months pregnant. They are just about to deliver peace. [Laughter]

And then when we check it out through our own established channels, directly with the other side, their impressions prove not to mean very much and have nothing in them.[257]

Though Rusk did not explicitly mention the Polish initiative that had recently flashed across the front pages, he did not need to. Even before Hightower's article appeared, antiwar critics, even some with impeccable anticommunist credentials who had initially backed U.S. policy in Vietnam, suspected a lack of seriousness in the administration's pursuit of peace talks. In March, the historian Arthur M. Schlesinger Jr. had charged that the administration "has made it clear, I would judge, that, while negotiation remains its ultimate objective, it does not consider negotiation advantageous at this time." Why else had Washington "considerably stiffened its position" just as Hanoi appeared willing to enter talks in exchange for a bombing halt?[258] ("LBJ has evidently decided on a quick and brutal escalation of the war," Schlesinger elaborated in his diary in late April. "It was clear in February that he did not wish negotiation until the existing military balance could be turned considerably in our favor; and his clear intention now is to bomb North Vietnam until Hanoi is prepared to sue for peace on terms which will meet Rusk's idea of a satisfactory settlement."[259]) A political commentator, Theodore Draper, scrutinizing the administration's recent Vietnam actions—particularly its attempts, largely successful in domestic political terms, to blame Hanoi for the failure to move toward peace—wrote in early May: "The main thing that has been achieved by the recent diplomatic maneuvers is what Washington considers to be a more favorable public relations ambience for making the war bigger, bloodier, and beastlier. This is the transcendent triumph of Johnsonian diplomacy which the American press has recently been celebrating."[260]

But Schlesinger had spoken on behalf of the liberal Americans for Democratic Action, and Draper made his case (in which the Polish affair figured prominently) in the *New York Review of Books*—and at least for the moment, Johnson saw little to fear from sniper fire on his left flank; the polls still showed that despite creeping discontent and noisy street protests, a plurality of Americans favored a "total military victory" in Vietnam rather than disengagement at any price, with seven out of ten still backing LBJ's handling of the war, and even college students were more hawkish than dovish.[261] With the White House exploring even more belligerent options, Rusk's remarks to the media bigwigs bespoke cocky self-assurance that the Hightower story, together with Gronouski's deflection of Fulbright and Radványi's secret testimony, had defused the Marigold land mine, helping to buy time for military pressure to succeed in Vietnam before the public lost patience.

14

The Long Year Wanes
D'Orlandi, Lodge, and Lewandowski
Leave Vietnam, March–June 1967

Well, anyway, no one can ever say it was either your fault or my fault
that conversations did not start.

— *Janusz Lewandowski to Henry Cabot Lodge at Giovanni D'Orlandi's*
farewell party, March 1967

One could live here so well were it not for this war. This war, which
no one seems to be able to stop anymore.

— *D'Orlandi on his last night in Saigon, March 15, 1967*

When I wished him good luck on his next assignment he replied that
the luckiest thing that had ever happened to him was to be leaving
Vietnam.

— *Canadian ICC commissioner on Lewandowski's farewell call,*
May 25, 1967

My God! Am I again in Saigon?

— *Lewandowski's first thought on being woken up by explosions in*
Beirut, June 5, 1967

In mid-March 1967, with his health deteriorating and peace prospects dismal,
D'Orlandi finally prepared to leave the post he had taken nearly five years
before and repeatedly prolonged in hopes of ending the carnage around him.
During his last weeks in Saigon, he laughed off speculation about his role in secret

603

peacemaking efforts. When Derksen broached the subject in mid-February, he cabled the Dutch foreign minister, Rome's ambassador

> showed me several clippings from the Italian press with titles such as "D'Orlandi mediatore" and, as he commonly does, ridiculed these speculations, which apparently arise from time to time in Italy. He also noted that his minister probably welcomed these reports because Fanfani had not given up hope of playing a role in the situation at some point. Needless to say, according to D'Orlandi the speculations were groundless. A diplomat in Saigon is the last person who should be harboring illusions of mediation.
>
> D'Orlandi's remarks could be considered a smokescreen. Objectively speaking, though, the diplomats here have made it perfectly clear that they, and the three delegates to the ICC, are the last people who would be picked for the special assignment in question while they are serving in their normal capacities in Saigon. In addition, it is worth mentioning the belief generally held in diplomatic circles here that neither side's Vietnam policy is determined in Hanoi or in Saigon.
>
> Speculation regarding D'Orlandi may have stemmed in part from the fact that the ambassador whose transfer has been talked of as certain for months is still here. This is all the more remarkable considering D'Orlandi's health has taken a turn for the worse and he is barely capable of performing his regular duties. In this respect, too, it is difficult to accept that he would be given a special assignment. Finally, it should be mentioned that, during the course of his term of service here, this colorful Italian diplomat has become known for the fervor and drama with which he has defended and contradicted every conceivable course of events and desirable outcome of the conflict to members of the government and diplomats. Within these two circles, he lacks the authority that would most likely be required of anyone who was entrusted with a special assignment.

On hearing that Fanfani had claimed D'Orlandi had achieved the "best results" yet in Vietnam peace diplomacy, Derksen wrote it off to his thirst for international acclaim.[1] Even after stories detailing the secret contacts appeared, Britain's envoy dismissed his Italian colleague as a "notorious intriguer."[2] Marigold rumors briefly excited the Saigon press corps, but Lewandowski assured Warsaw that despite "great pressure," he was resolutely rebuffing all inquiries.[3]

Early March found the Italian and Polish Marigold participants feeling gloomy. Reporting to the Pole on his talk with Goldberg, D'Orlandi strained "to highlight a few reasons to be optimistic" but without success. "We are both downhearted and close to our departure dates. The only news which would have roused Lewandowski would have been the postponement sine die of my departure and the news of 'concrete' proposals by Goldberg."[4] Nevertheless, D'Orlandi continued to take soundings. As Fanfani instructed, he relayed to his partners Thant's "flattering assessment" of their channel, and his minister's exhortation that if Hanoi could be persuaded to identify "goodwill gestures" it would make if the United States stopped bombing (the present "bottleneck"), tripartite efforts might bear fruit the second time around. Lewandowski scoffed, "If we were to resume our attempt, I am sure that Hanoi or Haiphong would be bombed just as they were on the two previous occasions (July and December)." D'Orlandi got no further with Habib (Lodge was away for a few days), who again doused any optimism; Washington "is definitely playing the military card," the Italian surmised.[5]

Then, in a final tease, days before he was to leave, D'Orlandi's hopes perked up one more time. Hosting Lewandowski for lunch on March 8, D'Orlandi sensed a faint chance that the three-way production might stage a revival—or even go on tour. The Pole still saw Washington as uninterested in negotiations, but he thought that posture might soften once the rainy season began in a few months. By then, of course, both diplomats would be gone—and Lewandowski noted with "regret" newspaper rumors of Lodge's impending replacement, further excluding talks in Saigon. Yet, he hinted, more three-way conversations might convene in Rome or Warsaw, given that the trio had proven more effective than any other channel. D'Orlandi also derived the "reassuring" sense that Hanoi still considered the ten points valid, and he reminded Fanfani that Hanoi's demand for a unilateral, unconditional bombing cessation might be finessed with the Phase A/B device.[6]

Four days later, after seeing Lewandowski again, he cabled Fanfani that the Pole thought Hanoi would talk if Washington halted the bombing for three weeks and reconfirmed the ten points: "The duration of the suspension could remain secret and it would not be difficult to establish [a] substantial quid pro quo that Hanoi would perform in exchange for purely formal concessions on the part of the U.S." Lewandowski doubted that Washington would seriously probe these possibilities until it had exhausted military options, but he felt it might reconsider when the June rains arrived, because the Chinese situation was stabilizing and decisive battles before then were unlikely. D'Orlandi also reported that Lewandowski planned to pass through Rome on his way back to Warsaw in May so they could jointly review the situation, and, if events warranted, vowed to summon him back to Saigon even earlier—more signs that Poland had not given up entirely on the channel.[7]

Going back to the well, Fanfani wrote Rusk again, more soberly than during Tet: "I would feel remiss in my duty if I failed to inform you" of D'Orlandi's view, per Lewandowski, that Hanoi would enter into negotiations after a three-week bombing pause and reconfirmation of the ten points, in a sequence consistent with Phase A/B.[8] Intrigued, though still averse to dealing the Poles, Rusk asked Lodge to clarify this new Marigold peep personally with D'Orlandi—but the instruction reached Saigon shortly after the Italian had departed.[9]

By then, the Marigold plotters had assembled for the last time, at a farewell party for the ailing D'Orlandi. Lodge seemed wistful, judging by Lewandowski's report:

> I spoke briefly with Lodge at D'Orlandi's farewell dinner (he is flying out from Saigon on the 16th this month). He said that he was also getting ready to leave. I

expressed regret that we were not able to finalize this great matter, that [at the time] seemed quite plausible. I reiterated that we did everything possible. And [that it] was not the Vietnamese who made such steps that made further action impossible. L[odge] stated that he wished to assure D'Orlandi and me that he personally did everything he could for the talks to be successful.[10]

Lodge reported that Lewandowski had come up to him "with none of his usual rather formal and stiff manner, but with a very cordial and friendly expression on his face," and said: "Well, anyway, no one can ever say it was either your fault or my fault that conversations did not start"—a remark that mystified his Marigold partners, who were not sure whom he meant to blame: Washington's bombings, Rapacki's "deplorable tactics," or Hanoi? (When shown Lodge's cable, Lewandowski said he mostly meant Washington, though he also had qualms about Warsaw's conduct.)[11]

D'Orlandi felt even more pensive, convinced that his life's most intense experience was ending. Formally he was only going on home leave, and he passed up the customary round of farewell calls. But given his health, he and his friends suspected that he would never return. Friday evening, March 10, he hosted a de facto goodbye party, a "cold buffet" for about sixty people (including Lewandowski, the Lodges, Do, and Westmoreland), on the margins of which he checked Marigold's pulse again.[12] Two mornings later, his last Sunday in Saigon, he attended Mass at the cathedral. That night, Do threw a dinner in his honor and made a "short, stirring and affectionate speech" in tribute. In his reply, D'Orlandi alluded briefly to Fanfani's statements praising his clandestine peace promotion. These "less well-known and necessarily secret efforts associated with my work in Saigon," he stressed, were also in Vietnam's best interests.[13]

His final full day in Saigon—Wednesday, March 15—stirred melancholy reflections. "In the afternoon, the last meetings," he wrote. "The dismantled residence causes me great sadness. It has witnessed five years of very interesting activity. I remember my impressions when I arrived, then the unfolding of the sometimes happy and sometimes sad events during the many years, and finally, the five months of tripartite negotiations: the hopes and the disappointments. The library and the books are no longer there, along with the magnificent and rich collection of beloved tin soldiers; all have been boxed and will be shipped in a few days."

For his last supper in Saigon, D'Orlandi joined Lodge, who had earlier confided his own impending exit.[14] The Italian sensed the once imperious ambassador's clout ebbing; Ky, whom he detested, felt "haughty" after seeing LBJ on Guam and no longer took Lodge's advice too seriously. But Lodge and Do remained warm friends, and the foreign minister and his wife joined Cabot and Emily—and the columnist Joe Alsop—for the meal, which grew mistily sentimental. "When the glasses are raised for a toast," D'Orlandi recorded,

Cabot Lodge gives a short speech which is as affectionate as it is informal. He calls upon me to respond, and at first I do so with difficulty, but then, ever more passionately, I allow my heart to speak about this beautiful, unforgettable and so-unlucky country. How could I ever forget it, or the friends made here, first of all Cabot Lodge and Tran Van Do. I finish with Yvette Guibert's words: "Je garderai toujours Saigon en tête et rien, jamais rien ne pourra l'en effacer" I've always keep Saigon in the forefront of my thoughts and nothing, nothing will ever be able to erase it]. We are all moved, and so I do not need to explain that in the famous song, Yvette Guibert sings "Robinson" and not Saigon.

Afterward, D'Orlandi

returned home in sadness. I sit in the armchair, looking at the bedroom. The re-corder is still on, yet I turned on the radio: first Radio Vietnam, then that of American armed forces—again playing "I Want to Go Home"; I have never been able to understand why this song is played so often. I, who am leaving tomorrow morning and must absolutely do so for urgent medical reasons, would like not to leave—but to remain here longer with these people who are so kind, so civilized, and so unfortunate. It is a country which has been blessed by God, rich and full of the sweetness of living, and one could live here so well were it not for this war. This war, which no one seems to be able to stop anymore.[15]

Thursday at Tan Son Nhut, the VIP lounge bulged with diplomats; Do, the ministers of education and industry, and other dignitaries; the ICC commissioners; and friends, mostly French and Vietnamese. D'Orlandi hugged Father Mario of the Apostolic Delegation, the only one there who had also been present to greet him on his arrival in Saigon five years before. On the tarmac, a band struck up "The March of the Bersaglieri"—the Italian sharpshooter corps' anthem—and 400 children from the orphanage D'Orlandi had founded waved beside a banner reading "Farwell to Our Benefactor."

After final embraces, Lodge escorted a "very moved" D'Orlandi to the Pan Am 707. At 11:30 a.m., it rose and arced south, toward Singapore, where he would connect to Rome. "From the airplane, I see for the last time the golf course, the river, the city and as if it were my own, I leave my city."[16] He left Saigon clinging to the frail prospect of returning if Lewandowski summoned him—conspicuously declining to accept a silver plate, the traditional gift for a departing ambassador, and leaving his name atop the Italian Embassy's roster. He would also spend the rest of his life accompanied by a tangible reminder of his adopted homeland: Colette, the young Vietnamese woman he had met in Paris and recruited to work in Saigon, accompanied him to Italy.

✳ ✳ ✳

The war's escalation rendered the stalemated ICC, and Lewandowski's work in it, more pointless than ever. Still, seeing the end in sight, he played out the string. An awkward moment arose on April 6, when Rahman sternly denounced the "unauthorized communication" beyond the ICC of the two resolutions critical of the DRV—a scolding that Ormond Wilson Dier promptly endorsed.

Are you accusing any particular delegation? Lewandowski challenged.

No, Rahman backed off, and the Pole "let the matter drop."

More charges and countercharges followed, leading nowhere.[17] "The blasted meeting in the afternoon was the usual travesty, and virtually nothing of any value accomplished," Chubb summarized. "Delay, delay and stagnation following the maneuvering of one side or other; this time on the part of Canada."[18] Two weeks later, he wrote in exasperation:

> A full meeting of the Commission in the morning with the usual maneuvering to score off one side or another. Masses of paper flowing from one side of the table to the other and the inevitable final results that add up to virtually nothing. Mr. Lewandowski really quite amenable this morning with no tirades. Today it was the turn of the Canadians to indulge in a little relatively mild shouting and waving of arms. Several matters of no import came to the vote and the record solemnly taken—no hits, no runs, no errors. We continue the nonsense tomorrow afternoon![19]

To Chubb's relief, the next session was "probably the shortest and least useful Commission meeting on record," consuming only fifteen minutes from "start to finish, including a farewell oration by Mr. Rahman."[20]

Besides cabling periodic situation reports, Lewandowski also occupied himself with a bit more socializing, for Poland's honor. At a farewell dinner for Rahman, he received barbs from the Canadian military adviser for the Poles' lack of fraternization outside formal functions. The next day at the tennis court, Chubb noted with pleasure, "Lewandowski and one of his minions appeared on schedule directly as a result of my needling the Pole at dinner last night!"[21] Before Rahman left in late April, Lewandowski threw an extravagant bash, replete with national delicacies flown in for the occasion. Chubb showed up "bang on time" but was first to appear:

> I was received by Mr. Lewandowski, Mr. Kowalski and three very reserved little guys whose names never came up. On my cold's account I had a Polish vodka and some 15 or 20 minutes later the Rahmans, Kawalskis and Adris arrived complete with ladies. We sat down about 10 p.m. to a very nice table, very elegantly set and started in on what turned out to be quite a dinner. Masses of hors d'ouvres, Polish ham and sausage, eggs, sardines, etc., followed by very good Polish soup; next an enormous artichoke, next dozens of clams in the shell; the main course of chicken and three vegetables, followed by ice cream and finally fruit washed down by vodka, one red and one white wine, ending with champagne. By the time these goodies had come and gone, it was midnight, and conversation, never very good, had pretty well dried up. We swept into the room next to the dining room, stood about for a couple of minutes, and as the coffee arrived, the Rahmans swept out

followed by their little group, which included me, I might add. It was really a tremendous effort, but much too elaborate for the time and situation.[22]

In his last days as chair, Rahman—still worried about Hanoi's attitude toward him and New Delhi, and pushed by Lewandowski—edged away from the resolutions that had so alienated the North Vietnamese (and Poles): He evaded a British diplomat's inquiry on them by declaring that the war was "not a suitable subject for discussion between two gentlemen, and [so he] continued to interrogate me about big-game hunting in Malaya."[23] When the Indian in early March proposed citing Washington for its "escalation and intensification of war" by shelling the northern Demilitarized Zone and mining nearby river mouths, the Canadians suspected that he had latched onto an idea of Lewandowski's "to mend his fences with Hanoi."[24] Similarly, later that month, Ottawa's delegate expected Rahman to give the Pole "a lot of leeway" to "rant and rave" at an upcoming meeting; "I smell a little collusion here between [the Polish and Indian delegations], and I think both Rahman and Lewandowski want to leave in the good graces of the DRVN."[25]

However, Rahman rejected angry and repeated DRV demands to annul the offending resolutions and endured a "very frosty reception" on a farewell visit to Hanoi in early April.[26] A few weeks later, he departed Tan Son Nhut, to be replaced by a junior diplomat whose lesser stature seemed to mirror the commission's decline.[27] Rahman's plane took off late, as well-wishers "stood about drinking lukewarm Cokes," a witness recorded. "Poor Rahman looked almost embarrassed as he was laden down with masses of very heavy leis of roses, etc. He kept taking them off and new ones were put on; I am certain that he was mighty glad to finally get aboard. The whole business is really overdone and verges on being a farce."[28]

✳ ✳ ✳

Even in Rome, D'Orlandi refused to give up on Marigold. On April 7, Reinhardt lunched with him to pose the "purely clarifying" queries, stimulated by Fanfani's message to Rusk, which reached Lodge just after the Italian left Saigon. It still made sense to attempt to achieve results via Lewandowski, D'Orlandi argued, dispensing tips to learn from December's sad experience to succeed the second time around—such as nailing down key details in advance, coordinating a bombing halt with the Pole's visit to Hanoi, and confirming U.S. readiness to talk on the basis of the (still-secret) ten points. This time, he stressed, it was "essential" that any contacts, once begun, not pass "*sic et simpliciter*" (thus and simply) to other negotiators: Instead, he and Lewandowski might form a "working group" to help interpret the ten points and smooth inevitable frictions between U.S. and DRV negotiators. Predicting that Hanoi might show surprising "reasonableness" (e.g., on a timetable for a U.S. military pullout), he urged Washington to move fast, because the Pole would leave Saigon in mid-May. Reinhardt tempered D'Orlandi's hopes by stressing that his probing did not reflect any U.S. desire to revive the three-way channel.[29]

The next day in Saigon, at a party hosted by Derksen, Lodge and Lewandowski had a long and fairly candid talk. The Pole "made a real effort to come over and sit down next to me," Lodge reported. He gossiped about Rapacki's three heart attacks, addictions to cigarettes and black coffee, and inability to put in a "hard day's work anymore," and said he planned to stop in Rome to see D'Orlandi on his way home before taking his next job, perhaps at the UN in New York. "Evidently Lewandowski wants to keep in touch with me, but it is hard to see why he told me about Rapacki's health," Lodge opined. An "exceptionally talkative" Lodge seemed "depressed about the intensification of the conflict and the losses 'on both sides'" and "considers his return to Vietnam as a serious mistake," the Pole cabled. He expected to work on the war in the State Department after returning to Washington and eagerly anticipated advising LBJ directly, because he suspected that his cables from Saigon were being "'processed'" and "distorted" before reaching him.[30]

Lodge's digest of this conversation intrigued Washington sufficiently for Rusk to suggest he meet formally with the Pole to "make him feel we will still be interested" in staying in touch and see if he had "any new ideas on possible approaches to Hanoi either by Poles in Saigon or elsewhere, or others." The State Department also authorized Reinhardt to set up a quiet meeting with D'Orlandi and Lewandowski when he transited Rome—not for a "postmortem on Marigold but [for an] analysis of main elements in North Vietnamese calculations and discussion of possible new approaches to issues of settlement." The session could also probe Fanfani's claim that a three-week bombing halt would produce talks. "Apart from anything else, this might be useful in distinguishing where Lewandowski ends and D'Orlandi begins, a problem inherent in Marigold from outset."[31]

Even before Reinhardt broached the idea, the Italians were trying to entice Lewandowski into a Rome stopover to refresh the dormant Italo-Polish collaboration. On April 10, Sica—now acting ambassador—"showed up" at Camp des Mares on D'Orlandi's behalf to ask urgently about Lewandowski's travel plans and request again that he consider an Italian detour; he might even meet with the pope, it was hinted. Because he was amenable, he made suitable flight arrangements for mid-May, but naturally he also sought the MSZ's approval.[32]

Warsaw at first responded diffidently yet indecisively—"We do not deem this meeting as necessary"—but when Lewandowski persisted, Michałowski put his foot down. "We prefer"—he began, then crossed out the words and eliminated any wiggle room: "We do not want you to meet with O. in Rome." Instead, he directed him to revise his itinerary to meet en route with his successor, Janusz Zablocki, who would already be on his way to Saigon. Lewandowski suspected that lingering ruffled feelings between Rapacki and Fanfani had prompted Warsaw's curt rebuff of the proposed reunion with D'Orlandi. Their tense exchanges, both over the postponed U.S.-DRV contact and leak to the pope, had irritated

Poland's foreign minister (who presumed that D'Orlandi would "drag" Lewandowski to see Fanfani), and the U.S. focus on squeezing Hanoi militarily hardly encouraged him to dive back into diplomacy.[33]

* * *

On Saturday, April 22, Lodge and Lewandowski met privately for a final time in Saigon. The mood was friendly, even nostalgic, as their unlikely partnership ended. Lodge had invited the Pole in a somewhat clandestine manner, sending an aide to show him, but not hand over, a card requesting his company. Lewandowski gladly accepted, determined to part on good terms, and happy to agree to stay in touch, especially if he went to the UN. Personalizing the occasion, Lodge introduced the Pole to his wife. Aware of Emily's love for classical music, Lewandowski brought as a gift a recording of the annual international Chopin Festival in Poland. Cabot spoke of George Lodge, then in his late thirties, an economist who consulted for the U.S. Agency for International Development in Vietnam, and told Lewandowski, "Oh, you remind me very much of my son, you know."[34]

Bitterness about Marigold remained, though not between the two personally. To Lodge's avowal that "we were wholeheartedly in favor of leaving no stone unturned for a just peace," the Pole wearily repeated that no solution was possible if U.S. officials kept chasing a bombing-versus-infiltration formula instead of a broader pact. When Lodge said that Washington could accept a neutral South Vietnam, Lewandowski replied, "I am sure you really believe this, but I don't believe the United States Government thinks this." As instructed, Lodge raised the Canadian foreign minister's latest nonstarter peace plan—a mutual pullback from the Demilitarized Zone, verified by the ICC—prompting the Pole to exclaim: "Ten miles here, ten miles there, cease-fire here, standstill there, what does it matter? You are never going to do it that way. I suspect that this is all internal politics and that Paul Martin wants to be prime minister."

After recalling their mutual vow of secrecy the previous fall, Lodge wondered about the "strange" amount of leaking during Marigold by "doubtless well-intentioned" people who did "great harm"—without saying so, he was airing U.S. suspicions toward Lewandowski himself. The Pole refused to rise to the bait, merely agreeing that this was odd. Instead, he grew "very eloquent on the importance of the Soviet Union and the United States working together"—only Vietnam blocked these powers, "the greatest on the face of the Earth," from collaborating. He even voiced understanding for U.S. interests in the Western Pacific (which he likened to the Soviets' in Hungary!), while wishing that they could be secured by means other than war in Vietnam.

Sending the conversation "eyes only" to Rusk, Lodge said that the Pole was "more warm and forthcoming than I have ever seen him. He has always been very stiff and formal. He obviously wants to keep in touch. . . . For almost eight years, I saw the Iron Curtain diplomats at the United Nations. I rank Lewandowski pretty much up at the top. It is, of course, utterly vital, that knowledge of this talk be held to absolute minimum."[35]

Three days later, at noon on April 25, after the customary full-dress sendoff (from the diplomatic corps; the government sent only a protocol officer), Lodge left Tan Son Nhut, ending his second term as ambassador after less than two years. Fed up with "the way in which the military was being used," he had flirted with a public protest—then, characteristically, avoided any bridge burning.[36] He went quietly, proclaiming confidence in eventual victory (most likely a "fade-out" rather than "an Occidental-type, formal negotiation with written undertakings and all that"), privately convinced it had been a mistake to accept LBJ's request to return to Saigon. His deepest frustration was almost certainly Marigold's failure, but that, too, he concealed.

"What disappointments or regrets do you carry with you?" a reporter asked.

"Oh, my!" Lodge answered, seemingly startled. "Well I don't know. I don't think that way. There are lots of things that you try to do that don't work out, but I can't. . . . You keep on trying, you know; you don't give up. I think. . . . No, I can't think of anything offhand."[37]

✳ ✳ ✳

Pham Van Dong closely monitored Lodge's exit—as Dier soon found out. Before his first trip to Hanoi, the new commissioner had stopped in to see the departing U.S. ambassador, who gave him a personal message to take North. The Canadian feared a cold reception, and his concern seemed justified when "stony faced" PAVN liaison officers at Gia Lam rapped Ottawa's conduct. But after a few days of low-level meetings and hints to Communist envoys that he carried a communication from Lodge, an invitation arrived to see the premier.

On April 28, Dong—in a "light gray Chinese type suit similar to the one he wore in the recent photo in *Life* magazine and expensive looking Chukka type boots," "smiling, courteous, and intent on creating a relaxed and informal atmosphere," "healthy, relaxed and confident"—cheerily welcomed the Canadian. As they sipped beer, Dier passed Lodge's message: Hanoi would have been better off entering talks six months ago than it is now, and would be smarter to enter them now than in six months, when its negotiating position would be worse.

"Au contraire," Dong shot back: The Americans would be wise to leave Vietnam sooner rather than later, when they would be defeated. "As for Cabot Lodge, he must be a disappointed man. He had failed to achieve his objectives. He was leaving Saigon 'with bowed head.'"[38]

Parting Shots: A Last Trip to Hanoi

In early May, Lewandowski flew to Hanoi for the last time as commissioner, a trip "to say good-bye" that lasted longer and covered more substance than he expected. Warsaw actually sent last-minute instructions to postpone the visit and delay his final departure from Vietnam planned for later in the month—for unspecified "important reasons"—but he had already flown the coop by the time they were deciphered at Camp des Mares and only caught up to him in Hanoi.[39]

Lewandowski's final Hanoi sojourn coincided with a surge in U.S. attacks— recent weeks had seen bombing of previously off-limit targets. In late April, planes hit sites in Haiphong, including a cement factory, ammunition dump, and thermal power plant, and formerly untouched DRV airbases (though Gia Lam remained sacrosanct, at least for now). The Pole arrived amid raids near Hanoi; after inspecting the industrial outskirts of the city targeted on May 4 and 5, he reported little direct damage but many civilian casualties when a bomb had hit a shelter near a factory.[40]

Yet, it was a secret peace gesture that initially occupied the Pole. Colonel Nguyen Anh Vu handed him a copy of a confidential letter from LBJ to Ho—a sequel to their unproductive secret correspondence in February that Hanoi had, in late March, unilaterally publicly revealed. In a somber, weary tone, LBJ affirmed his readiness for secret talks and quoted Ho favorite Abraham Lincoln as arguing (on the eve of the Civil War) that eventually the combatants would have to stop fighting, "after much loss on both sides, and no gain on either," and negotiate a settlement of "the identical old questions." Inevitably, he insisted, a settlement would rest on the 1954 and 1962 Geneva Accords, with the South Vietnamese people determining "in peace" their future governance, all Vietnamese resolving "peacefully whether and how they should unite," and regional economic development replacing warfare. "You and I will be judged in history by whether we worked to bring about this result sooner rather than later," he warned.[41]

On April 6, a U.S. official in Moscow had tried to deliver LBJ's letter to Hanoi's embassy, but the envelope came back with "Non conforme! Retour a l'expediteur" [Not accepted! Return to sender] written on it.[42] Before returning it, however, the North Vietnamese had pragmatically copied the letter (Washington quietly circulated the text to various governments to reap credit for reasonableness) and now, Vu explained, Dong desired Lewandowski's analysis when the two met in a couple of days.[43] The Pole had already considered the missive, having received advance excerpts from Lau before leaving Saigon along with word that the DRV dismissed it as propaganda and was mulling whether to publish it as well.[44]

Nevertheless, Lewandowski urgently sought Warsaw's guidance, and Michałowski shot it back with a tight leash: He should stress, as his own "personal opinion," that the letter was just "another"—he crossed out "skillful"—"maneuver" to display LBJ's "so-called peaceful and humanitarian will." He should advise Dong not to reveal it, because this would only play into the hands of hawks (including LBJ himself) who claimed dialogue with Hanoi was impossible. The DRV should use "flexible" diplomacy and psychological warfare and "even more intensive exploitation" of political struggle to complement military operations "in order to influence world and U.S. public opinion" and paralyze Washington.[45]

"I got the impression that [Pham Van Dong] expected something more," Lewandowski dryly cabled Michałowski after seeing Dong on May 6. (The Pole implicitly rebuked his boss's shallowness by stressing that he had assessed LBJ's letter "exactly according to instructions.")

Implying a belief in Marigold's residual relevance, Dong pressed Lewandowski on whether he linked the letter to the November–December talks with Lodge. This was unlikely, the Pole responded, because LBJ could have "referred to them at any time" but had failed to do so.[46]

Despite this pessimism, however, a secret Vietnamese record indicates rather mysteriously that the Pole relayed a more forthcoming evaluation of Washington's stand:

> The U.S. is prepared to give a proposal to develop and exchange views with representatives of the sides who are fighting against the Americans in South Vietnam in order to resolve entirely the Vietnam problem including the cease-fire issue and U.S. withdrawal from South Vietnam. Then talks will proceed secretly.
>
> In the scope of the resolution, Americans won't object to the establishment of one government in South Vietnam in accordance with the will of the people and with the participation of the sides that are fighting Americans in South Vietnam, though a free and democratic election.
>
> Americans are ready to accept appropriate international control regarding the aforementioned elections.
>
> Americans will fully respect the results of that election.[47]

No other evidence suggests that Lewandowski gave Dong a formal U.S. message, but the formulation fit Washington's views, including the fudging of the NLF's status in future talks and a willingness to accept the outcome of a "free and democratic election" with "appropriate" safeguards in South Vietnam. However, the spring of 1967 was a season for war, not peace. "In the current situation," Dong emphasized, diplomacy could not replace and must not impede the military struggle. "Americans are still not ready to accept a just political solution," he said. "They continue escalation of the war, and their position since November–December has hardened. They are still hoping that they can achieve military victory. Therefore, [North Vietnam] must continue the fight."[48]

At this final formal talk with the premier, Lewandowski counseled him against precipitous action against the ICC out of pique at India and Canada, and he urged the PAVN liaison mission to resume sending formal complaints about the U.S. bombing, a practice that had recently lapsed, so commission files "contain possibly full documentation of the U.S. aggression." Dong agreed to reconsider Hanoi's posture—and indeed, it soon curbed hints of draconian steps against the ICC.

After this relatively short, ceremonial session, Dong more visibly showed his esteem for Lewandowski. The next evening, at the Hoa Binh Hotel, the Pole threw a farewell party for his hosts and the diplomatic corps. More than a hundred attended the reception, which was lavish by Hanoi standards ("a splendid buffet including a few treats from Saigon"). "The most interesting event of the evening," a guest wrote, "was the appearance of the Prime Minister Pham Van Dong, who proceeded slowly around the room with Mr. Lewandowski and stopped to talk with various groups including mainly [Egyptian], Indian and Polish." His attendance provoked "a big surprise" and considerable comment, Lewandowski (proudly) cabled Michałowski. The atmosphere was far lighter than at his last Hanoi bash. Beijing's chargé d'affaires came but did not cause any commotion. Dong wagged his finger at an Indian diplomat—New Delhi "should faithfully uphold the Geneva agreements," he scolded—but refrained from name-calling or threats.[49]

To underline his regard, Dong also breakfasted privately with the Pole. More candidly than at their formal meeting, he elaborated Hanoi's strategy for "combining military struggle with political and diplomatic struggles" but regretted the disunity in the Communist camp, whose help was needed more than ever. "Unfortunately," he said, "some socialist countries do not trust them." Moscow's views "fundamentally differed from that of the Vietnamese." The Soviets relied on traditional military analysis and did not grasp the political situation in the South, where Hanoi had a "more realistic" understanding. Yet Dong exempted Lewandowski from such barbs and urged him to relate his own impressions of the South to other socialist diplomats.[50] Jocularly, he even invited him to stay and join the leadership: "Đồng Chí Lewandowski, be in my government, we could work very well together, . . . because we understand each other so well."[51]

He also presented what passed for, in wartime, a sentimental farewell gift. A few weeks earlier, at an MACV dinner in Saigon, Westmoreland had presented Lodge a memento to recall his second term as ambassador: a 9-millimeter Browning pistol in a leather case with a bronze plate naming him "Honorary Field Marshal," plus a shoulder holster made of elephant hide and a heavy-handed gibe that when visiting Harvard for his fiftieth reunion he would "probably be well advised to wear this sidearm and shoulder holster for his own protection against the Vietniks on the campus."[52] Now Dong handed Lewandowski a .38 "Chief's Special" Smith & Wesson revolver taken from a U.S. pilot whose plane had recently been downed north of Hanoi and who had ejected, parachuted at low altitude, and broken his legs. The diplomat gingerly accepted the trophy, but after returning to Poland, grew leery of it and eventually donated it to the Polish Army Museum. "I was afraid to carry it, I was afraid to leave it at home, in case of any burglary, someone will take it and shoot the people. . . . It had bullets, it was ready to use. . . . So I decided I will ask the army people to immobilize it, so that it could not be used, but when I went to them, they saw this revolver, and said, how nice this weapon is. . . . It would be such a waste to destroy this thing, better to leave it in deposit with us. . . . They say [it is] in military museum in Warsaw, and now I don't know what happened to it."[53]

* * *

Besides Dong, Lewandowski also paid farewell calls on Trinh and Giap. They reinforced his belief that much more intense fighting lay ahead.

In a virtual monologue, Giap assured him that Hanoi would not neglect political or diplomatic fronts (echoing Dong) but stressed the military struggle—and ardently urged maximum material help from the socialist camp. The Pole did not know it, but the legendary mastermind of Dien Bien Phu, who favored protracted warfare, was losing influence to more hawkish figures, such as Le Duan and Nguyen Chi Thanh, who urged a shattering blow against Washington and its "puppets" to attain a rapid victory. This "general offensive, general uprising" idea would gain momentum in the summer and fall of 1967 and culminate in the Tet Offensive in January 1968. As plans for the massive surprise attack advanced (despite Thanh's death in July), Giap would be quietly sent to Hungary, allegedly for medical reasons, and his associates would be brutally purged.[54]

Avoiding explicit reference to the internal rift over military strategy, Giap outlined to Lewandowski the path to victory. "Vietnam does not aspire to break the American war machine" (nor could it), but instead to "break the will of the aggressor," a goal it could readily achieve with adequate socialist support. Some military experts failed to notice that the Vietnam War was "of a new type"—if it had simply followed a "classical model" based on troops, planes, and firepower, the Communists would have lost long ago, but guerrilla tactics permitted active defense to minimize casualties during the dry season and a shift to a more aggressive posture during the rainy months. Washington, too, had "learned much," but suffered from "weak" leadership. The fighting cost it, he claimed, "significantly more" than the more than two thousand soldiers per week it admitted losing. Westmoreland might get a hundred thousand troops more, but they would not alter the outcome—though U.S. escalation would require correspondingly greater socialist aid.[55]

When Lewandowski saw Trinh, the normally cold foreign minister was "very warmhearted, warmer than during our previous meetings."[56] Why so mellow? A recent chat with Gomułka in East Berlin at the Seventh Congress of the Sozialistische Einheitspartei Deutschlands (SED; Socialist Unity Party of Germany) had left him "very happy"; the PZPR boss had pledged undying support for Hanoi's fight.[57] Trinh praised Poland's ICC labors, thereby reassuring Lewandowski that he was ending his term still in good graces. (Perhaps the hard-liner was also relieved that the pesky Pole and his irksome peace notions would soon be gone.)

Echoing Dong and Giap, Trinh stressed the socialist bloc's "valuable and indispensable" aid and vowed that Hanoi would blend military, political, and diplomatic struggles, because Washington had "weak points on all three fronts and one needs to exploit them actively." More strikingly, he conceded shortcomings in the DRV's candor and pledged to explain thinking and actions "in more detail and more concretely." Like Dong's breakfast remarks, Trinh's admission hinted at schisms behind the facade of socialist solidarity. On the ICC, Trinh relayed decisions—per Lewandowski's advice—to resume sending formal complaints and eschew "repressions" against New Delhi and Ottawa; yet Hanoi would tighten the screws by pressing India's Consulate to cut its current level of seventy by firing "personal hairdressers, cooks, and shoeshine boys."

* * *

Lewandowski intended to zip in and out of Hanoi in less than a week, but when the ICC courier plane failed to show at Gia Lam on May 9, he cabled Michałowski that he would take the next flight back to Saigon (on May 12) and await there the promised "important" instructions, which still had not arrived. In reply, Rapacki's aide ordered him to stay put to join a parliamentary delegation headed by Zenon Kliszko, which was slated to reach Hanoi on May 18.[58]

Lewandowski used the extra time to brief Soviet Bloc diplomats on the situation in the South, emphasizing the strong NLF position and troubles marring the U.S.-Saigon "pacification" campaign.[59] Then, industriously, he decided to dart to Haiphong to inspect bomb damage and greet the crews of two Polish ships docked there, the *Kraszewski* and *Kościuszko*. Usually, due to the risk of American marauders, transportation between the capital and port left after sunset to travel under cover of darkness. However, Lewandowski fretted, that meant that his car would constantly have to yield to military traffic, stretching the journey out for as long as six or seven hours. To avoid the congestion, he opted to brave a daylight drive, hoping to do it within two hours.

At first, the morning departure seemed to pay off nicely. Speeding along in their green Soviet-built Pabieda (Victory), a Stalin-era luxury sedan, Lewandowski and Ha Van Lau made excellent time. Trailing them in their three-vehicle caravan, one car bore his military aide and the military attaché of Poland's Hanoi embassy, the other PAVN escorts.

They were driving on National Highway 5 through flat countryside when Lewandowski's driver suddenly shouted "*My bay!*" (American plane!) and slammed on the brakes. Everyone leapt out. Lewandowski saw the Vietnamese soldiers dive headfirst into roadside rice paddies, but instead of emulating them, he lay down on the road beneath the car ("What is the use of it?" he felt). Pressed to the asphalt, he heard antiaircraft fire crackle and rockets explode as the jets shot at a nearby artillery post, then zoomed overhead at low altitude and disappeared on the horizon.

As the Vietnamese soldiers arose, muddy and soaking, and Lewandowski dusted himself off, he was puzzled when the Polish military attaché stood up and "started to dance." But it was not a jig of joy. Wearing his ceremonial uniform, the attaché had shunned the plunge into mucky, stagnant water and had nestled face down into the grass of one of the crisscrossing dykes that peasants used to traverse the rice paddies. There, he learned the hard way why the Vietnamese had acted as they did: He was crawling with huge fiery red ants, many already stuck to his skin and avidly burrowing inside. (Thus did Lewandowski refine his local expertise: "In such cases, jump into water, not on green. Ants do not like water."[60])

On reaching Haiphong, the caravan drove straight to a hospital so doctors could extract ant heads from the hapless attaché. "On the way back," Lewandowski recalled sheepishly, "we went at night."[61]

Back in Hanoi, Lewandowski found a Rapacki cable telling him never mind, Kliszko's visit was postponed again and he could revert to his original itinerary. Yet by then he had missed the May 12 flight and had to reserve a seat on the next one four days hence.[62]

The spare time allowed Lewandowski to deal with the latest mini-crisis— calming Hanoi over two unfavorable international press leaks, both concerning his own activities. In one, *Newsweek* revealed ("Diplomatic Defeat for Ho") the ICC resolution approved over Poland's objection three months earlier admonishing the DRV for infiltrating PAVN units to the South. The Vietnamese were furious, but Lewandowski persuaded them not to evict the Indians and Canadians nor organize "massive demonstrations" in front of their offices, and instead agreed to help disseminate denials both in Hanoi and Saigon.[63]

The second leak presented tougher dilemmas for both Warsaw and Hanoi: Hightower's story on Marigold, blazoned across the *New York Times*' front page. On May 15, Lewandowski conferred on a possible response with Deputy Foreign Minister Thach, counseling caution, before heading back to Saigon and leaving the matter in Ambassador Bogdan Wasilewski's hands.

Farewell, Vietnam: "The Luckiest Thing That Had Ever Happened to Him . . ."

As far as Lewandowski was concerned, his last days in Saigon could not fly by fast enough. With the war bloodier than ever, neither side showing any flexibility, the ICC moribund, and his closest colleagues gone along with his own now distant hopes of achieving a secret breakthrough, his posting's novelty had long faded. After returning from Hanoi, with no formal ICC meetings scheduled, he had little to do besides pack and prepare to head for home.

First came the inevitable farewell calls—their grandeur diminished by the earlier exits of Moore and Rahman, who would have been more likely to have organized a substantial sendoff. The new Indian chair ("very young and nervous as a cat," Chubb felt) had arrived only a week before Lewandowski himself left at the end of May, and Dier opted against any serious festivities to mark his exit (surprising Chubb, who "had the impression that protocol would have demanded some effort").[64]

Nevertheless, formal goodbyes crowded the Pole's last days. Testifying anew to his surreal status, the ARVN liaison mission threw him a fancy "stag dinner."[65] That is, the representative of the fiercely anticommunist South Vietnamese Army cordially honored the Communist delegate to a body established by the Geneva Accords, which Saigon had never signed, representing a state that militantly backed Hanoi's battle to oust Saigon's "puppet" regime.

Paying a formal farewell call on Dier, Lewandowski was deeply pessimistic. He termed Hanoi "grim and determined," a posture reflected in people's "calmness and discipline under air attack." He felt "depressed" by U.S. "intransigence," worried that escalation might prompt Chinese intervention and a great-power confrontation: Hanoi would not ask Beijing to intervene unless desperate, but if asked, it would respond "immed[iately] and effectively, with consequences for all others concerned." Nasser's recent bellicose moves, threatening a Middle East war, struck him as an ominous sign that Vietnam was "distorting international relations to a dangerous degree."[66]

On the basis of his "brief acquaintance" with Lewandowski, Dier dashed off a parting sketch of his colleague: "a shrewd competent operator who, outside commission meetings, is personable but as aloof as the rest of [the Polish delegation]."[67] But Dier's military aide discerned a bit more. On first encountering Lewandowski the autumn before, Brigadier Chubb had sized him up as a tough-as-nails doctrinaire Communist. In the eight months since, he had watched him doggedly promote the party line. Yet, on his departure's eve, the Canadian limned a more complex, sympathetic personality:

> I went to a reception put on by Lewandowski, the Pole, who leaves on 30 May. I truly think that he is or could be a very reasonable little guy. Lord knows he is very intelligent and does his job in a very able manner, but it is quite clear that sometimes his heart is not in the tripe he has to dish out. For certain he leaves here with no regrets at all and has no hesitation in saying so now that he is virtually on the plane out of here. I suspect that he has had a very lonely 14-month tour here.[68]

Two days before his departure, Dier and his wife hosted a buffet supper for the Pole at their villa. "The usual crop of Indians, Poles and Canadians and frankly I found it somewhat dull," Chubb recorded grouchily. Most guests scattered by 10 p.m. but not before Lewandowski had dispensed some valedictory observations. Sounding the same note that he had sung to D'Orlandi and Lodge, he said Hanoi would never stop fighting until it had in hand "some advance indication of political settlement which would result from negotiations particularly as it applied to the South." Yet, there remained one hope: If Moscow and Washington worked together, the Chinese could not block them. "The implication of his remarks," Dier cabled, "was that while USSR would not wish to put pressure on Hanoi to agree to talks without knowing where talks would lead USSR still had reserves of influence which could be brought to bear to persuade Hanoi to accept a specific and reasonable situation if one could ever be agreed upon."[69]

Lewandowski had already unburdened to his Canadian colleague his glee at escaping his soul-deadening task of fiddling while Vietnam burned. "With respect to the ICC, Lewandowski said he was frankly pleased to be relieved of his responsibilities on such [a] frustrating and ineffective organization." Again he complained that U.S. and RVN use of the commission for "propaganda purposes" was "an affront to his own and his country's dignity," to which Dier, naturally, riposted that "this complaint cuts both ways." Briefly fueling the halfhearted final debate, Lewandowski retorted with "a brief but vehement attack on USA policies along the usual lines" before, more calmly, reiterating Warsaw's desire to preserve the ICC despite its present futility "because of its potential if at the moment nebulous future usefulness." Poland and Canada, he affirmed, shared an identical desire to attain peace, "but both were powerless to alter the present course of events." Dier wished Lewandowski "good luck on his next assignment."

The "luckiest thing that had ever happened to him," he replied, "was to be leaving Vietnam."[70]

❋ ❋ ❋

Lewandowski was not the only Pole in Saigon pleased that he would soon depart. Earlier that spring, as noted above, an intelligence agent in Poland's ICC delegation had composed a damning indictment of his hostility, even "hatred," toward and persecution of MSW employees and party activists. The agent and his "comrades" had found his attitude "deeply baffling and outrageous" and wondered why Warsaw had tolerated "this scandalous situation." In making these "serious accusations," the agent demanded a "deeper investigation" of Lewandowski's conduct and offered to present evidence in a "confrontation."[71]

Responding to this denunciation, the Interior Ministry in Warsaw accordingly made plans for a "confrontation" when Lewandowski returned, but it seemed ambivalent about following through. An MSW officer—apparently the same Captain Bisztyga who had interviewed him before he left—requested "facts which could be used as an argument proving to him that he did not adhere to his promises." Yet, alluding obliquely to the conduct of ministry personnel in Saigon, he conceded that Lewandowski could raise inconvenient facts "which we must admit" and would be hard to rebut because the MSW itself had "condemned this at some point in the past." Sounding reluctant to take on the diplomat—the "confrontation" never occurred or did nothing to derail his career—he also asked for a summary of "the facts with no comments on the relations with Lewandowski."[72]

The Long Way Home: "My God! Am I Again in Saigon?"

With the Rome stopover dead and Kliszko's trip off until mid-June, Lewandowski was instructed to fly as soon as possible to Beirut to brief his Vietnam-bound successor, then rush home no later than June 12 to brief the powerful Politburo member before he left for Hanoi.[73]

Early Wednesday morning, May 31, he flew from Tan Son Nhut on an ICC Stratoliner for Phnom Penh.[74] After a few days in the sleepy city on the Mekong, he boarded a Czechoslovak Airlines Tupolev-104. Landing in the Lebanese capital on Sunday night—June 4, 1967—the exhausted diplomat went right to the Polish Embassy to dine with the ambassador and Zablocki before collapsing in a guest bedroom. His itinerary called for him to brief Zablocki formally Monday morning and leave Beirut Wednesday on Air France for Paris. There he would connect to Vienna before catching a LOT Airlines flight to Warsaw in time to brief Kliszko.[75]

But history had other plans.

"After long flight I went to bed and at 5 in morning, boom! Boom! And I opened my eyes and thought, 'My God! Am I again in Saigon?'"[76]

After weeks of rising tension, war had exploded in the Middle East—as the (literally) disoriented Pole learned when he knocked at the ambassador's door. Shortly after dawn, Israel had launched a preemptive strike on Egyptian air bases. What Lewandowski heard outside his window is not clear; he recalled later being told of an explosion at a petroleum depot near the airport, but the record does not show any Israeli raids on Beirut targets that morning.

The violence stranded Lewandowski; not only was the airport shut indefinitely, but Israel had also blockaded ports to prevent arms shipments, cutting ferry service, and fighting in and over Syria ruled out the Beirut-Damascus highway. Nevertheless, cables to the embassy ordered him to leave immediately, war or no war, authorizing any means necessary to reach Warsaw on time.[77]

Amid the chaos, he briefed Zablocki, who was supposed to fly Tuesday to Phnom Penh but now also had to forage for an alternative. Lewandowski had adjusted to the familiar sound of gunfire, but as he described the Vietnam fighting his successor seemed more concerned at his immediate surroundings. "We were rather distracted by the situation," he recalled, laughing.

Desperate, Lewandowski investigated means of escape. He tried to charter a boat to Cyprus but could not find any takers ("nobody wanted to, no [amount of] money was enough").[78] He enlisted a Lebanese army colonel—appropriately named Nasser—who had aided LOT when the airline ran into jams and earned a reputation as a master fixer ("he could do anything," Lewandowski heard; "people could arrive without a visa, he'd escort them through, he had such wings there"). Refusing payment, Colonel Nasser agreed to help: "I'm your friend—I will try to do something."

After a few days, the enterprising colonel found a potential solution: He had wangled seats for Lewandowski and Zablocki on a U.S.-sponsored evacuation flight for American nationals, which was leaving the next morning. The Poles would receive boarding passes and should not say anything to give away their identities: "I will take you to the airport, don't ask any questions."

One problem: The evacuation flight would land in Athens—and anticommunist colonels had overthrown the Greek government in late April and were busily rounding up left-wingers. Might the junta arrest Lewandowski, too, if he showed up, especially without a visa? Hoping to avoid this predicament, late at night, after business hours, he sought out the Greek ambassador in Beirut to relate his story of woe and seek a transit visa. The fellow diplomat sympathetically told him that normally he would provide the visa immediately—but these were not normal times, and he needed to cable Athens for authorization, which might take days, more than a week, or maybe not come at all. Lewandowski pleaded, not as a Polish Communist but as a colleague. Finally, the Greek "softened" and issued a provisional visa after securing a promise to leave Athens on the first flight available; I do not know what the reaction will be, he cautioned.

The next morning—Saturday, June 10—Lewandowski and Zablocki left the embassy to catch the evacuation flight. Even the ride to the seaside Beirut airport held hazards. Their taxi ran into pro-Nasser protesters who blocked their way, but a second attempt succeeded when the vehicle conspicuously displayed portraits of the Egyptian leader.[79]

His boarding pass worked, and the jet flew uneventfully over the Mediterranean. But in Athens, his apprehensions rose. Peering out the window as the plane taxied toward the terminal, he saw military vehicles pull up—and on stepping down the stairwell, he was taken aside. To his relief, an officer greeted him politely ("Mr. Lewandowski, very happy to see you here, how long would you like to stay?") and offered a hotel room and even a city tour. He explained that he had urgent business at home and must catch the next flight out—and the hospitable hosts helped him nab a seat to Vienna. On landing there, he never left the airport, catching the next flight to Warsaw after phoning the Polish Embassy to request that it flash Rapacki to warn of his impending arrival.

When his plane touched down at Okęoie Airport, a Central Committee car was waiting to whisk him downtown. Please, we must hurry, there is no time to change clothes, a PZPR apparatchik told him brusquely. Kliszko is expecting you; in two hours he will be taking the train to Moscow, the first leg of the journey to Hanoi. On reaching the squat concrete building known as the "White House," Lewandowski was led to the second floor to see the Politburo heavyweight. Mentally, he had thoroughly prepared himself to distill thirteen months in Vietnam for the benefit of one of the Communist elite's most powerful figures, Gomułka's associate since before his elevation to the party leadership in 1956 and now his "right-hand man," who was far closer personally and ideologically than Rapacki.[80]

But before Lewandowski could open his mouth, Kliszko lit into him. "I don't understand today you young people," he blurted, denouncing his briefer's gallivanting. "I have very important business, I wanted to see you, you cannot be on time, this is unacceptable, etc., etc.," Lewandowski recalled hearing. "He was giving me a lesson, putting to me my behavior, that I am taking lightly my obligations. . . . Kliszko was interested to give me a lecture, and he did so."

The diplomat meekly pointed out that there was a war on, but when Kliszko waved that aside ("If somebody wants to come, he will find a way to come"), he felt constrained from arguing. By the time the senior Communist had finished hectoring, Lewandowski had barely begun relating experiences before Kliszko cut him off and left in a huff. "All right, I must go."

Now it was really over.

Looking Back

Amintore Fanfani meets with visiting Senator Robert F. Kennedy at the Italian Foreign Ministry in Rome, on February 3, 1967. When away from the photographers, the foreign minister complained bitterly that the recent American bombing of Hanoi had sabotaged a promising peace effort. *Bettmann Archive / Corbis.*

Stuart H. Loory with LBJ, May 1, 1967. Shortly after taking the White House beat at the *Los Angeles Times*, the young reporter Loory had an off-the-record interview with LBJ. And soon afterward, he launched a skeptical inquiry into LBJ's Vietnam peacemaking efforts—together with his *Times* editor, David Kraslow—that led in 1968 to their book *The Secret Search for Peace in Vietnam. Courtesy of Stuart Loory.*

In 1968, the Los Angeles Times journalists Kraslow *(on the left)* and Loory coauthored *The Secret Search for Peace in Vietnam,* which included a dramatic reconstruction of Marigold based on background interviews with American, Polish, Italian, and other officials. *From the Stuart H. Loory Papers; courtesy of American Heritage Center, Laramie, Wyoming.*

Former North Vietnamese diplomats Nguyen Dinh Phuong (at the left) and Luu doan Huynh in Hanoi in June 1997, at an international conference that brought together former Vietnamese and American officials—including Robert McNamara—to discuss the war. At this gathering, Phuong publicly revealed for the first time his clandestine mission from Hanoi to Warsaw during Marigold. *Photograph by Monica Church.*

After Janusz Lewandowski married Wanda Brzozowska in 1970, they started a family during his ambassadorship in Cairo. Here Wanda holds Krzysztof, who was born in 1973, and Janusz carries Joanna, who was born two years earlier. *Courtesy of Janusz Lewandowski.*

Janusz Lewandowski reviewing documents in Warsaw, June 2003. *Author's photograph.*

Janusz Lewandowski in Warsaw, June 2003. *Author's photograph.*

Lewandowski with the author in Warsaw, June 2003. *Author's photograph.*

Janusz Lewandowski reading his personal handwritten copy of the "Ten Points" in his Warsaw apartment, 2011. *Photograph by Mikołaj Morzycki-Markowski..*

15

"You Will Never Get the Inside Story"

The Secret Search for *The Secret Search for Peace in Vietnam*, May 1967–March 1968

When [I] asked at close of session if the name M[arigold] meant anything to him he flushed a deep red.

—Los Angeles Times *reporter David Kraslow, in his notes of his interview with Henry Kissinger, October 2, 1967*

I know what you're doing. Everybody and his brother knows what you're doing. You remind me of Laurel and Hardy trying to play sleuths.

—*Walt Rostow to Kraslow, December 18, 1967*

Change swept through almost every sector of American life in the late 1960s, including journalism—even that bedrock Republican bastion the *Los Angeles Times*. For decades, under the iron grip of the Chandler family dynasty and fueled by Southern California's explosive economic boom, the newspaper had reliably championed probusiness, conservative values and politicians. In the post–World War II era, it had fervently espoused hard-line Cold War views and promoted rising Republicans, most notably an ambitious young veteran by the name of Richard M. Nixon. Unabashedly using its news and editorial pages to make friends and break enemies, the paper grew into a dominant political, economic, and social force in Los Angles—but did little to enhance its journalistic reputation, especially on the East Coast, where the *New York Times* and, a bit behind it, at least in political circles, the *Washington Post* reigned supreme.[1]

By the late 1950s, Norman Chandler had signaled the dawn of a more balanced era by naming the well-regarded Nick B. Williams as editor of the *Los Angeles Times,* bypassing ideological stalwarts, and telling him to "do what is right." In 1960, Otis Chandler, barely thirty, succeeded his father and speeded the shakeup. The paper still routinely endorsed Republicans but became less predictably right wing—shocking its readers, for example, with an exposé of the John Birch Society, and leaning toward the moderate Nelson Rockefeller, not the archconservative Barry Goldwater, for the 1964 Republican nomination. Coveting their more professional status, the newspaper's new guard began to fill its posts on the basis of talent instead of loyalty. Their choices raised eyebrows, included a hard-driving *Time* reporter, Frank McCulloch, as managing editor; the irreverent Pete Conrad as political cartoonist; and, in 1962, a new Washington bureau chief, Robert J. Donovan. By the end of the decade, a liberal analyst judged that the *Los Angeles Times* "probably has fewer bastards in authority on the news side than do most papers."[2]

Installing Donovan, a veteran White House correspondent, "purchased instant respectability" for the *Times.* He had been lured from the faltering *New York Herald-Tribune* with a lavish salary and budget, and he beefed up the staff by recruiting ambitious young reporters from other papers instead of mechanically advancing ancien régime holdovers. The firmly anticommunist *Times* backed LBJ's buildup in Vietnam, yet its relations with the president cooled. LBJ invited Otis Chandler to his ranch to apply back-country Texas charm, but the visit backfired; the publisher abhorred the host's hunting technique—driving in an air-conditioned Lincoln and "shooting at terrified deer from the car, while Secret Service agents ran back to collect the dead carcasses."[3] Donovan and LBJ also grated on each other. Covering a trip to Australia in 1966, the urbane bureau chief abhorred the president's crudeness. After he joined LBJ and the Aussie prime minister, Harold Holt, in the back of *Air Force One* for an interview, the Texan demanded three "rut beers," then upbraided (humiliated, Donovan thought) a Filipino steward who could not find the beverage—causing Donovan to imagine cases of root beer being shipped, at taxpayer expense, to "every other air base around the globe where Johnson might land." At a boisterous barbeque at a ranch near Brisbane, the free world's leader, in a ten-gallon hat, nominated Donovan to engage, involuntarily, in a local pastime: kangaroo boxing. He claimed to enjoy the bout with his marsupial foe, whose style resembled "Lyndon Johnson's famous 'treatment' of shoving his nose toward another man's as a way to dominate him."[4] Still, their mutual disdain hardened. In February 1967, a White House aide suggested helping this "excellent reporter." LBJ checked "no" and scrawled: "I don't trust him or the *Times.*"[5]

The *Los Angeles Times* Washington bureau's latest addition only deepened the animus. Donovan snatched Stuart H. Loory, another *Herald-Tribune* alumnus, from the *New York Times,* where he had gone briefly when he sensed the *Herald-Tribune* was on its last legs. The New Jersey native and Cornell and Columbia Journalism School graduate had honed his street smarts doing gritty urban stories for the *Newark News*. At the *Herald Tribune*, he had covered domestic beats (civil rights, space flights, etc.) and then, fluent in Russian, had been its last Moscow reporter.[6] His stint at the *New York Times* would last only three months. Having been championed by Harrison Salisbury, he was hired in late 1966 to cover science, but soon chafed at office politics—"I would suggest a piece and . . . the national editor . . . would say no, that's a Washington story, not a New York story. And so on." When Donovan called to offer a slot in Washington to cover the White House, the unhappy reporter was sorely tempted. Bob, how can I do that? Loory recalled protesting. I know nothing about the White House. Nonsense, the bureau chief replied. Anyone who can solve the Kremlin can solve the White House.[7]

Lured to Washington, Loory began covering LBJ for the *Los Angeles Times* in early 1967, and it did not take long for his press operation to tag the new arrival an irritant, no "team player" but a zealous believer in the fourth estate's adversarial relationship to power. "He is a little cynical, but is still in the impressionable stage," White House press secretary George Christian wrote the president, urging him to see Loory in April 1967, a few months after he took the White House beat and began pining for a one-on-one interview ("George, I want to be the president's friend," Loory said after Christian told him that LBJ did not grant interviews to reporters but occasionally chatted with "friends" like Hugh Sidey of *Time* and Max Frankel of the *New York Times*). Johnson consented to a background chat, but their relations only got rockier: Loory published a piece that the press secretary protested was a "thinly veiled interview, which is the very thing I told you we could not schedule" and "flatly violated the off-the-record basis of your appointment." Called to the woodshed, Loory "finally agreed that he had circumvented" the ground rules and endured Christian's lecture on "the problems that such things cause." (At least, so Christian informed his boss; "I don't think I admitted to violating ground rules or that I was contrite in the wood shed," an unrepentant Loory insisted decades later.)[8]

Hightower's spoon-fed article (see chapter 13) piqued the suspicions of Donovan's deputy and Loory's boss, *Times* news editor David Kraslow, an experienced Washington hand who had been recruited from Knight-Ridder. He had won kudos as "a marvelous investigative reporter" (Loory) for scoops on the Bay of Pigs invasion (which his paper, the *Miami Herald*, had allegedly spiked under pressure) and a corruption scandal involving LBJ aide Bobby Baker. Uneasy at the official manipulation of press coverage, he had cowritten a vaguely roman à clef novel about a Washington-based correspondent for a Miami newspaper who resists co-optation by State Department bureaucrats (and cavorts with a source's blond daughter on a volatile Caribbean island, but that's another story). "The complex and controversial relationships that have developed between the national government and the press under Cold War conditions present serious conditions that warrant explorations," the journalist coauthors earnestly told readers. "We do not suggest any easy answers, but hope this fictional treatment of real problems will be enlightening as well as entertaining."[9]

His bullshit detector tripped, Kraslow prodded his new White House blood-hound to sniff around. "Kraslow is a worrier," Loory later wrote. "He does not read news reports; he gnaws at them. He chews over the facts carefully, noting discrepancies, relating recent stories to earlier ones, driving reporters in the *Times* bureau to distraction with his constant questions aimed at explaining the unexplainable."[10] (Another target of his trenchant and persistent interrogatives, JFK, considered Kraslow one of the two most "consistently ornery" reporters at presidential press conferences.[11])

Loory, his competitive juices stirred, assembled a second opinion on Hightower. At first, he only dimly grasped the contours of what a newsroom memo termed "the curious case of the wops-poles-yanks-hanois late 66."[12] A crash course yielded a more nuanced understanding. The resultant story—under Loory's byline, in "a cooperative effort" with Kraslow and two bureau staff members—ran on the *Los Angeles Times*' front page on May 21, 1967.[13] With a headline and lead alluding to "a botched peace effort," it took a tougher tone and implied harsher conclusions than Hightower, closer to Estabrook's implicit bottom line four months before. It broke new ground by quoting a "knowledgeable official" as admitting that Washington erred by hitting Hanoi at a "particularly sensitive" moment (and later conceded the point to Moscow); alleging that, "contrary to what the administration has been saying," the Poles *and* Italians had "complained that their efforts were being undermined" *before* the December 13–14 bombings; and (aided by Loory's colleague on the Pentagon beat[14]) probing targeting procedures and whether the strikes had stemmed from poor coordination or a deliberate decision not to "interfere" with existing plans. "I'd rather be hung for a knave than a fool," said an unnamed aide who insisted on the latter.

The article admitted that the "full story" of the effort's collapse "has not been told" and "may not be known for years," yet insisted that it was acutely relevant to ongoing moves in Vietnam, because any new peace bid had to hurdle the wrecked one's legacy. Kraslow felt Loory had only scratched the surface of a buried tale engaging vital questions: Was peace possible? Was Washington ruining real chances for talks due to belligerence or incompetence? Was it leveling with the American people? "Throughout the spring and summer of 1967," Loory recalled, "Kraslow was on my back to explain the discrepancies between the Hightower account and the cocktail party rumors."

The brash, intense thirty-five-year-old, who could not care less about his paper's hawkish tilt ("Very frankly, I never read the *LA Times* editorial page"), relished the prospect of exploding dubious administration claims but at first made little progress. While filing stories on his White House beat on various domestic and foreign topics, he asked aides about the Polish affair but ran into a stone wall. "You're beating a dead horse," Rostow told him. "Hightower had that whole story." Sheepishly relating vain efforts to Kraslow, who always "shot back" nagging questions, left Loory "with deep feelings of inadequacy." Then—one day in July or, more likely, August—there was a breakthrough.

"A Marigold Is an Orange Flower"

Bill Moyers was still getting his feet wet as a budding journalistic mogul at *Newsday*. Before leaving the White House the previous winter, he had witnessed the Polish affair's sad denouement, having been present at the decisive December 9 session at which LBJ affirmed his refusal to alter the bombing authorizations that included targets near Hanoi. The initiative's collapse left him "heartbroken," he later recalled, and confirmed his belief that, as he told Arthur Schlesinger, he could "no longer do any good by staying."[15]

Since his strained exit, Moyers had tried vainly to keep friendly ties to Johnson, who resented his protégé's leaving and was furious at any hint of disloyalty (LBJ even wrongly suspected that Robert F. Kennedy had interceded with Harry Guggenheim to get him the job, Moyers learned[16]). Justifiably insecure about their relations, he sent Johnson supportive notes and *Newsday* clips, fed gossip about Boston and New York intellectuals, and publicly only gingerly implied dissent on Vietnam policy.[17] Torn by clashing emotions, disillusioned over the war yet still beholden to his ex-benefactor, he held back from telling all he knew about the secret diplomacy, yet let slip enough to whet the *Los Angeles Times* reporters' curiosity.

From a person identified in typed notes as "~~bill moyers~~ source M," Kraslow first heard the code name "Marigold" and got some discouraging, yet tantalizing, advice. There were, Moyers related, "no more than 10 people in government who knew of M. We would not get story because none would talk to us."

"You will never get the inside story," the reporters would quote this anonymous "close associate of the President" as saying.

Why not?

"Because it makes our government look so bad."[18]

Pressed on whether the Hanoi bombings deliberately or accidentally coincided with the secret diplomacy, Moyers said that "it was purely and simply a lack of coordination."

Afterward, an excited Kraslow called Loory "at home one Sunday" and asked: "Do you know what Marigold is?"

"A marigold is an orange flower. My wife grows them in front of our house."

No, said Kraslow, "Marigold was the code name for the Polish peace initiative. All of the peace initiatives were named after flowers."[19]

The next day at the *Los Angeles Times* Washington bureau, at 1700 Pennsylvania Avenue, NW, a block from the White House, the two conceived a far deeper investigation into Marigold and other peace efforts than daily journalism allowed —"a massive test of the private record on Vietnam negotiations against what Johnson, Rusk, Robert S. McNamara and Rostow were saying publicly." "Loory, there is a book in this," Kraslow encouraged. After a week compiling information about murky peace bids gone awry, a compendium replete with contradictions and gaps, they approached Donovan with an unusual proposition. Could they

628 **"You Will Never Get the Inside Story," May 1967–March 1968**

ditch their normal duties for a special inquest, which would be likely to consume many months and a vast budget, with no guarantee of publishable results, to get to the bottom of the secret diplomacy?[20]

Donovan was sympathetic but needed management's approval. And that was problematic, because—like the *Washington Post*'s rift between the hawkish Wiggins and dovish staff members—a Kulturkampf simmered in the *Los Angeles Times* between the Washington bureau and Norman Chandler–era conservatives in the home office. Still, Donovan and Kraslow obtained a green light from the *Times* editor, who had signaled a willingness to approve risky investigative projects. "Williams took the gamble," Loory recalled. "Go anywhere, talk to anyone, take all the time you want, he said. If we did not get a story, that would be all right."[21] By late summer, they had assembled a lengthy outline, found a potential publisher (Random House), and begun identifying interview targets. "We started with the presumption that we weren't being told the truth," Loory recalled.[22]

. At first, they were not being told much of anything. In late August, one informed official confessed lingering uncertainty over the Polish business, citing the "vagaries" of those claiming to be in touch with Hanoi, and implicitly contradicted the claim of a "lack of coordination," asserting instead that a high-level debate had taken place over whether to hit Hanoi and that a "go decision" had been made.[23] Then, in mid-September, the pendulum on that issue seemed to swing in the opposite direction, when a high-level source on "deep background" confessed feeling a shocked sense of lost control ("Oh my God!") on picking up the December 3 *Washington Post* and seeing that targets near Hanoi had been hit. "Not entirely," the source (Katchenback) had said when asked if steps taken since then precluded a recurrence of such wire-crossing between military and diplomatic efforts.[24]

The reporters still felt stymied on the Polish angle, but on September 19 they got a key tip from a key source: Robert F. Kennedy. Since RFK's March Senate speech, following their testy Oval Office exchange about alleged peace feelers, he had avoided taking on LBJ directly about Vietnam and had vacillated when antiwar activists urged him to mount a challenge for the 1968 Democratic presidential nomination. Yet he remained aghast at the war and the president's handling of it. "How can we possibly survive five more years of Lyndon Johnson?" he asked a friend. "Five more years of a crazy man?"[25]

LBJ still confounded RFK when he was visited by Loory and Kraslow, who had cultivated him since he had been a Hill staff member probing organized crime. "You know what he's like," Kennedy said. "How can you figure him out?" LBJ "wants to get out of this mess," he presumed, but he seemed driven by "a serious psychological problem," perhaps rooted in unresolved maternal conflict. Also, Rostow "keeps telling president he will win war, that he's like Abe Lincoln, does not have to listen to critics."

Desperate for help, the reporters shared their tentative outline of secret peace contacts. Though "very tender about discussing this thing," RFK named two people worth quizzing: Norman Cousins ("quite active in this sort of thing up until about 9 months ago") and Henry Kissinger ("used for some time, and still is being used, primarily to work with French channels to Hanoi")—whom, as noted above, RFK had met in Paris during his European jaunt the previous winter.[26]

The two reporters set trips to New York and Boston but first saw Rostow to check RFK's hint that LBJ had sent a still-secret letter to Kosygin or Ho Chi Minh in February with terms different from the correspondence that Hanoi had released. Like Christian, Rostow denied the story or any inconsistency. Yet, surprisingly, he admitted "that North Viets *wanted* to negotiate last winter." Now, however, they seemed to prefer watching the "U.S. being ripped asunder and torn apart" until the "domestic situation compels us to pull out." "'We've been waiting to see if they want to pee a little,' he repeated at least three times. But they don't want to pee now."[27]

In late September, the reporters visited Manhattan and reeled in a Marigold chronology from Cousins, who was privately sparring with the administration over the affair. Since "Mr. X" (Michałowski) had visited in January, the *Saturday Review* editor had refrained from printing an exposé, but his criticism of U.S. conduct had intensified. A recent editorial cited the failed Warsaw effort to rap Washington's hypocrisy—claiming to want talks, yet when chances arose, they were "privately spurned or allowed to die." Cousins did not name the culprit behind the December 1966 Hanoi raids that had allegedly sabotaged the chance for peace, stating only that he "had scored a square hit on his main target."[28]

Bundy had phoned—tracking him down in San Francisco—to correct him. Politely (he believed that Cousins had "no deliberate intent to mislead") yet firmly, he said that the Polish affair (instigated by Lewandowski, not Lodge) was "far less pat" and "far more indefinite" than the editorial implied. No direct discussions were "scheduled," the air raids would not have blocked Hanoi from talking if it was truly ready, and "we had a clear postmortem from Communist sources" —János Radványi, though he did not say so—"that the Poles never had anything firm from Hanoi at any time."[29] Cousins duly noted the caveats in a later editorial, but he reiterated that the bombings had killed the Warsaw contact.[30]

Bundy's failure to persuade Cousins was clear when the *Los Angeles Times* duo called on the "short, [thin], bow-tie wearer with demeanor part deeply serious, part quizzical and smiling, dressed in tweed jacket." He was friendly but at first wary, saying that a White House contact had warned him that his cozy Madison Avenue office was bugged; only after they moved to a conference room in his publisher's Park Avenue building did he relax.

Contrary to Washington's leaks, Cousins termed the probe a U.S., not Polish, initiative, and related a fairly detailed account—mostly based on what he had heard from Michałowski, whose name he hid. But Cousins, like his main source, was fuzzy on why the Hanoi raids had ruined Lewandowski's "major breakthrough." Admitting that he might know only a small part of the truth, Cousins concluded that the "U.S. has not been honorable. He refuses to blame the president, he sees possibilities (1) president not always informed, (2) his hands are tied (by military?), and (3) other possibilities that are vague."[31]

While in New York, Loory also met with Paul Martin, who insisted that "no country has done more than Canada to bring about peace." On Marigold, he had a mixed message: He "saw nothing" in the Polish effort but felt that Washington "should have taken a chance" on it. The reporters also spoke to a French diplomat who doubted that the Pentagon had intentionally undercut LBJ with the Hanoi strikes. "He does not think military mind is subtle enough, smart enough to go around deliberately sabotaging peace efforts with precise bombings on a schedule as last December. Those things just happen."[32]

A few days later, Kraslow—who had taken his defense policy seminar as a Nieman fellow—visited Kissinger in his Harvard office. Famous for his writings on nuclear weapons and foreign policy, the historian had supplemented his scholarship with government consulting. In the JFK years, he had analyzed Berlin and nuclear issues for McGeorge Bundy until a press flap broke the link; under LBJ, he was advising on Vietnam, cultivating officials like Lodge and Harriman, and had traveled several times to Saigon. Though not directly involved in the Polish affair, he had also participated in several Vietnam diplomatic ventures, all futile, among them a Czechoslovak effort in autumn 1966; pushing Sainteny as an intermediary that winter; and finally, in the summer and autumn of 1967, serving as the "Pennsylvania" channel to Hanoi via two French scientists, Raymond Aubrac and Herbert Marcovich, who in turn worked through Paris-based DRV representative Mai Van Bo.[33]

Championed by McNamara, "Pennsylvania" was spurred by the Frenchmen's cordial conversation in Hanoi in late July with Dong, and this led to intense exchanges in August and September as the intermediaries ferried messages between Bo and Kissinger over the terms of a bombing halt and the start of direct negotiations. By October, however, the probe had foundered. To Kissinger's acute disappointment, Bo had rejected direct contact. More important, the two sides could not bridge the gap between the DRV's insistence on an "unconditional" end to the air attacks and a U.S. request for prior assurance that a bombing halt would "lead promptly to productive discussions," during which Hanoi would not seek military "advantage." This failure to make headway exasperated LBJ, and on September 29, he issued the "San Antonio formula" publicizing the secret terms. A few days later—as Kissinger received Kraslow at Harvard's Center for International Affairs—Marcovitch told Bo of rising U.S. impatience, and Hanoi formally rebuffed LBJ's latest offer.[34]

While Kissinger was an unofficial yet authorized U.S. liaison, he sought access to the highly classified record of prior initiatives. He was aware that McNamara had commissioned a secret study of Vietnam policymaking, and so he sought and got permission from his old grad student, Leslie H. Gelb, the study's coordinator, to read the materials compiled for the volumes on the negotiations. He spent two or three days in Gelb's Pentagon Papers office across the hall from McNamara's, poring over the Marigold saga. "This is fascinating," he muttered.[35]

Yet Kissinger refused to tell Kraslow what he knew, suggesting instead that he "talk to Washington" before divulging any information. If Kissinger asked Rusk for permission, the reporter suggested, he would surely say no. Kissinger agreed, so he pledged to check with Harriman, with whom he was lunching the next day; his OK would do (even though, he added proudly, neither "the Governor" nor Cooper had read the "complete peace file" he had).

Kraslow pressed him on the "Lewandowski affair," but Kissinger refused to be drawn. He claimed to have known contemporaneously about the initiative "until the denouement" (and to have learned that a week later), and he denied that "a date had been set for talks with Hanoi"—maybe "talks about talks," he qualified vaguely—but rebuffed specific inquiries. When Kraslow provocatively said that officials' explanations of the Hanoi bombings in the midst of the delicate diplomacy "impressed us as defying common sense" and implied a "disturbing pattern," Kissinger cautioned "not to underestimate stupidity, lack of judgment, and lack of coordination as factors in foreign policy, that what appears to be a pattern may not be a pattern at all—that things simply happen that are not supposed to happen." Asked if the Polish peace effort had been "the most promising" thus far, Kissinger "hesitated for quite a bit" and then refused to answer; warily, he promised to render an opinion later, but not to supply more information "until he gets an OK."

Exasperated with the fencing, as the interview ended, Kraslow tossed a wild card. Does the name "Marigold" mean anything to you? he asked—the first time the taboo code name had been uttered.

Kissinger "flushed a deep red," the reporter recorded, "then grinned a bit sheepishly and said he would not comment on any names. Said I was a clever questioner, but said he would not put himself in the position of saying yes to one code name no to another, and so on."[36]

Decades later, Kraslow happily remembered the moment. "We were chatting and chatting, and he was being very coy and very tight-lipped. I said, 'Henry, what do you know about Marigold?' He turned beet-red and said, '*How* do you know about Marigold?' And that told me everything I needed to know."[37]

Kissinger did not say another word about the affair, but Kraslow felt that he had "hit pay dirt."[38] *Now* the reporters felt sure they had a book in the making.

Michałowski in Washington

As Kraslow and Loory rooted about, Michałowski arrived in Washington as Warsaw's new ambassador and promptly demonstrated that Vietnam and Marigold still rattled U.S. officials and shadowed Polish-American ties. Before taking up his post, he had told Gronouski that he knew the war would "hang like a cloud over our bilateral relations, but let us try to separate ourselves as much as possible from [this] problem."[39]

Yet this hope faded fast, largely due to Michałowski's own strong feelings. The dispute reignited from the day (September 12) the Pole (accompanied by Jamaican and Ecuadorean colleagues) presented his credentials to LBJ in the Oval Office, normally a purely ceremonial occasion.[40] Even during the photo opportunity, there was an omen of trouble. After Michałowski handed LBJ a letter from Polish president Edward Ochab thanking him for a picture of the moon taken by a recent lunar probe, the president praised "the wonderful achievements and possibilities for cooperation in this field."

Perhaps we could start by bringing cooperation down to Earth? the Pole replied.

Once the journalists and photographers had been shooed away, talk resumed. To LBJ's pleasantries about Polish-Americans' contributions to the nation's "growth and freedom" and hopes for warmer bilateral ties, Michałowski responded that they could improve even faster if not for Vietnam. Citing the Pole's call for earthbound cooperation "and ignoring [his] colleagues," LBJ launched into "a rather long exposé on Vietnam according to a well-known pattern," blaming Hanoi for aggression and rejecting negotiations.

Hearing him proclaim that he remained "anxious" for talks, Michałowski could not resist a dig: Washington "had resumed bombing too quickly last December," ruining the Poles' and Gronouski's labors. LBJ disagreed; DRV claims that air strikes blocked talks were "a broken record which they have used over and over again," despite six pauses. The essential thing was for Hanoi to stop trying to take over the South. "They are bombing us all the time in South Vietnam," he said.

"I don't see any North Vietnamese planes bombing Washington," the Pole replied.

"That's not the point," Johnson shot back. Terrorist explosions in South Vietnam killed more people than U.S. bombs in the North.

Washington and Warsaw saw the issue differently, Michałowski said, haughtily adding that "Poland, because of its special position in Vietnam, probably knew more about the situation there than any other country." What was occurring was "civil war and not aggression."

Jamaica's envoy chimed in that "seven is thought to be a lucky number," so perhaps LBJ should try another pause. Maybe we are already doing so, he said, Hanoi had not been hit for "a long time." After the Pole said that any new pauses or probes should be carried out quietly, LBJ veered away from Vietnam, raising Latin American issues with Quito's representative. Even then, the talk twisted back to the war, though no further blowups ensued.

This encounter enraged LBJ, who shunned contact with foreigners critical of his Vietnam policies, the anger compounded by the chorus of small-country diplomats. But what *really* riled him was an incident, absent from either the U.S. or Polish official records, involving his dog. During their "violent clash of arguments," Michałowski later reminisced, LBJ's dog Yuki—a small, whitish stray mutt found by his daughter Luci Bird at a Texas gas station and recently adopted by the president—jumped on the Pole's knee, and "I had the impudence to scratch him behind the ears. LBJ did not like this ~~intimacy~~ at all, so he reached out ~~with his hand~~ to interrupt it. ~~The hand was met with His~~ The dog reacted by showing dozens of white and sharp teeth. You could imagine how LBJ reacted. I am afraid it was [a] serious impediment to my diplomatic [career] in Washington."[41]

"As you can see from the [memo of the conversation], Michałowski is off to a flying start," an aide wrote Rostow.[42] LBJ's fury emerged at his weekly lunch right afterward with Rostow, Rusk, and McNamara. Poland's new envoy, he said sarcastically, was "quite vehement" that peace had been about to blossom in December until the bombing had ruined everything. "If his Foreign Minister had not tried to play tricks when we sent messages, he would not feel that way," retorted Rusk, who vowed to review the matter with Rapacki's man.[43]

During the next month, the State Department's irritation grew as Michałowski, at introductory sessions with U.S. officials, continued to blame the bombing for scotching peace prospects. (Harriman, however, seemed merely curious. Hosting him for lunch in lieu of a formal courtesy call, he heard the Pole recount Marigold and his January 1966 trip to Hanoi—in Moscow, he learned "that the Russians would not take too much initiative for fear of Peking's accusation that they were working for the Americans," the Chinese were "most disagreeable," and the North Vietnamese considered talks "very seriously" but, having "been burned twice on negotiations," were "fearful of undertaking another discussion for fear they would be 'sold out' again."[44])

Michałowski also spread Poland's views among fellow diplomats. Irked by a Goldberg UN General Assembly speech asserting that no third party had ever delivered a firm message from Hanoi that a bombing halt would yield direct talks, he forcefully reminded a Canadian colleague that the December events, which Goldberg "personally knows very well," contradicted that claim.[45] Relating a similar tale to France's ambassador, he insisted that Washington had understated Hanoi's interest during the previous winter's effort, noting that the Poles had even reserved accommodation for expected U.S.-DRV sessions.[46]

Nor did Michałowski shy away from reporters, at least at first. In April, the head of the State Department's Intelligence and Research Bureau, Tom Hughes, who had been on the Carleton panel alongside the Pole (see chapter 12), described him to Rusk as a "very clever and disarming performer."[47] Now officials feared that these skills could be a dangerous weapon in the battle over Marigold—especially as pressure for a bombing halt built. In early October, a Columbia University political scientist, Zbigniew Brzezinski, then working for State's Policy Planning Council (and acutely skeptical that Moscow or its allies were "really trying to help" Washington escape its Vietnam predicament), wrote Rostow:

> I understand from some of my journalist friends that the new Polish Ambassador, Mr. Michałowski, is extremely effective in presenting the Polish version of the breakdown of the allegedly developing negotiations, and he is assiduously disseminating his version among Washington newsmen.

He is an effective and engaging person, and his efforts could have some impact.

Although—as I recall—at the time a semi-official version was put out, it might be useful to prepare a more complete U.S. account of what actually took place and make it available to some reliable journalist for purpose of publication. Otherwise, I have no doubt that within a few weeks Michałowski's version will become the generally accepted one.[48]

By the time Michałowski stopped by on October 11 to see Katzenbach, officials were seething. Prepping the undersecretary, Habib noted the Pole's talks with officials and journalists about Marigold since taking his post, which evidently were aimed "not to clarify the events of this period in the interests of serious new explorations with Hanoi but rather to cast doubt on U.S. good faith and generate additional pressures for an unconditional bombing cessation on Hanoi's terms." Raising "such a complicated and contentious issue" during courtesy calls violated protocol. Katzenbach could tell Michałowski that "we question the propriety of discussing such complicated and sensitive matters with individuals in Washington, both in and out of government, who may not be in possession of the facts or otherwise prepared to discuss the issue."[49]

The two did not take long to move to jousting and recriminations over the affair.[50] Katzenbach insisted that America "wanted peace in Vietnam" and "could get on with it" if only a negotiating partner could be found; this "shouldn't be too difficult," the Pole remarked. When Katzenbach said that "we never received one message from Hanoi"; Michałowski cited the one that Poland had delivered in December 1966. That was only a willingness to listen, not talk, Katzenbach volleyed, and Washington had faithfully observed the only stated condition for the contact, secrecy. Unfortunately, "Others have not done so, including the Ambassador. Mr. Katzenbach said he was aware that the Ambassador had been discussing this with columnists, which was not the right way to go about it, nor helpful in our mutual relations." He "only discussed these matters privately," Michałowski replied, and in any case a genuine "opportunity" was missed. Katzenbach "demurred," stressing that "the Poles had failed to produce a single living North Vietnamese," whereupon Michałowski blamed the Hanoi bombings despite repeated Polish warnings. Katzenbach rebutted that "Gronouski had been ready every day from December 3 to December 12, and not one live North Vietnamese had been produced by the Poles."

On it went, with Katzenbach and Michałowski hashing out in person the events they had lived through in Washington and Warsaw ten months before, echoing Rapacki and Gronouski's arguments then, only now venting accumulated ill will:

> M: Hanoi was truly interested in talks—it was "touch and go" in the VWP Politburo—until the December 13–14 raids. Why, despite warnings, did Washing-

ton hit Hanoi "while delicate exchanges were going on"? Why hadn't it insti-
tuted the 10-mile zone earlier?

K: The proposed Warsaw meeting was never conditional on such a restriction;
Hanoi "evident[ly]" just "did not wish to make the contact" and used the attacks as an "excuse."

M: No, they destroyed something fragile yet vital, "namely a certain confidence
on the part of Hanoi that the U.S. was looking for a political solution."

K: Washington did what it had to—no bombing halt was required.

M: But was secrecy an adequate excuse not to limit air strikes? Were weather
changes sufficient reason to risk a chance for peace? "The Poles could understand the bombings of December 3 [*sic;* 2] and 4, but not the 13th and 14th."

K: That was plenty of time to produce a North Vietnamese.

M: ("As a friend") The probe's failure made starting talks even tougher due to the
DRV's "deep feeling about the lack of U.S. sincerity."

K: Washington had its own doubts about Hanoi's "sincerity" and Warsaw's as
well, including whether North Vietnam was ever really ready to meet in December 1966.

"What the Ambassador said nine times did not make it true," said Katzenbach
—who failed to note that he himself had "strongly" urged LBJ against more Hanoi
bombing during Marigold. Further contacts with columnists, he warned, could
endanger both peace prospects and bilateral ties (a message Bundy sternly reaffirmed[51]). The journalists, the Pole said defensively, were "well informed" and often knew more than he did; he only confirmed "in general that opportunities for
peace talks had been possible but that the bombing of December 13 and 14 had
destroyed them. These were the facts."

"I don't call my opinions facts," said the exasperated Katzenbach. "The fact was
that the North Vietnamese did not appear in Warsaw."

Michałowski tried to change the subject, but more testy go-rounds ensued.
They finally unclenched after Katzenbach cautioned the Pole not to "misunder-
stand" U.S. politics: Despite grumbles about the war (and rumors of an antiwar challenge to LBJ's renomination), criticism would not induce a premature
withdrawal.

Though unapologetic about his views, Michałowski felt chastened, fearing
(with good reason) that he had impaired his effectiveness. By the spring, he would
confide, "somewhat ruefully, that he had made a real mistake in talking about
Vietnam as much as he had when he first came to Washington," and "now realizes his error."[52]

Rise Weeping Marigolds

Into the fall, Kraslow and Loory picked up the tempo of their interviewing, trying
to reconstruct the complex hidden history of Vietnam overtures. They talked at

length with travelers to Hanoi, such as Ashmore and Baggs, who had begun going public about their interview with Ho and unsatisfactory exchanges with the administration.[53] In early October—as Loory followed up on his talk with Martin in New York with written inquiries—Kraslow visited Ottawa to see Ronning and Seaborn.[54] Ronning, though "very skittish" about divulging details that might identify him as a source, recounted his futile missions to Hanoi in March and June 1966—which had been doomed, he felt, by both sides' "hard-headed" confidence in victory and, in the latter case, U.S. "sabotage" by leaking the terms he would carry beforehand to the Chinese and the press.

Seaborn, the ex-ICC commissioner, now heading the Foreign Ministry's far east branch, preferred a less cynical explanation for "a number of unfortunate occurrences" that interfered with peace soundings. Doubtful that LBJ had deliberately undercut them, he blamed Washington's "monster bureaucracy." He reacted warily to Kraslow's bid for still-secret data, put on guard when the reporter, in describing his project with Loory,

> admitted frankly that their purpose was to determine whether it was true, as it had not infrequently been alleged, that a number of potentially helpful peace initiatives had in fact been spoiled (deliberately or inadvertently) by the Johnson administration. He referred in particular to the Polish initiative of late 1966 and the bombing of the city of Hanoi in December. He said that the evidence which his paper had accumulated to date seemed to be pointing in the direction of the conclusion that the actions of the United States administration had spoiled a number of peace prospects, but this was not yet certain.[55]

Seaborn feared that revealing too much might irk Washington (or other diplomatic partners), but a flat refusal might prompt the *Los Angeles Times* pair to castigate the Canadians in print for noncooperation "—and that in itself could cause the minister problems." The best path, he suggested, would be to supply Loory with limited information and tell Kraslow that that was all they would get; Martin followed this advice.[56]

Back in Washington, chasing details of peace bids and bombing decisions, the reporters sought out midlevel Pentagon and State Department officials. Gradually, they filled out chronologies of Marigold and other probes, answering some questions, raising new ones, confirming some theories, deflating or modifying others. Most denied intimate knowledge of Marigold or stuck firmly to the party line, but some confessed regrets: Isham doubted that Warsaw would ever have delivered Hanoi, yet rued not canceling the December 13–14 raids, which "would have shown once and for all there was nothing going."[57] One aide pressed on the air strikes told Habib that "these two gents, Kraslow in particular, have the manner of a prosecuting attorney cross-examining a witness. They are obviously trying to build a case that the right hand doesn't know what the left hand is doing within the U.S. government, especially in regard to peace negotiations."[58]

The two gents also chatted up senior State Department figures, with mixed results. A "source R," who "came on duty in wash oct. 3 66"—the day Katzenbach succeeded Ball as undersecretary—related further Marigold tidbits, including memories of Gronouski's hasty pre-Christmas visit to Washington and the post-collapse "autopsy report," and confirmed internal schisms over whether the Hanoi strikes should have gone forward.[59] Loory visited Harriman's opulent Georgetown residence, adorned with Van Gogh and Cezanne paintings and memorabilia attesting to the great man's peers: busts of Harriman and FDR in the front hall, walls hung with a signed Churchill painting and inscribed photos of Harriman with King George VI and Queen Mary, Stalin, and every Democratic president since World War II. However, the conversation yielded mostly atmospherics. "Averell likes to talk about Averell's career," the reporter noted, but he clammed up about classified matters. The "crocodile" gladly discoursed on Sino-Soviet and NLF-Hanoi relations and recalled the logistics and ambience of his December 1965 trip to Warsaw, but when Loory asked what he and the Poles actually discussed, "he snapped 'that's none of your goddam business and I'm not going to tell you.'"[60]

The mood was less snappish and more wistful when Loory saw Lodge. Since returning from Saigon, the ex-envoy had labored, to little effect, at the State Department as a Vietnam adviser with the title ambassador at large. In shirtsleeves, sitting at a desk in a "bare" office with one wall dominated by a signed photo of LBJ, he reminisced ("on deep background") about Marigold. He fondly recalled sneaking to D'Orlandi's on the floor of the back seat of a "beat-up Toyota," the drink the three diplomats shared to toast their success ("I thought I had done something worthwhile in my life"), and his "very sincere" Polish partner: "He was a nice chap. I liked him. He was young, about the age of my son."

Yet—as he assured Rusk afterward—Lodge firmly denied that the December 13–14 bombings (which he blamed on a lack of coordination) had wrecked the initiative, and he dispensed theories ("nothing more than rumors," he later admitted to Rusk) that Warsaw had not cleared the ten points with the DRV and was rebuffed when it tried; or that Hanoi wanted to talk but backed out after Salisbury's articles started appearing, hoping that the pressure on Washington might yield a better deal. "We never did for Hitler's Germany what we did for Hanoi," he said of Salisbury's exploits.[61] Bundy also denied blowing any real peace chances: "I've tossed in my bed at 4 in the morning on that question, but honestly I can't think of a situation where we missed the boat."[62]

In the fall, the reporters nailed down a contract with Random House for their book, tentatively titled *Rise Weeping Marigold*, after an apt Shakespeare quotation:

> Here's flowers for you;
> Hot lavender, mints, savory, marjoram:
> The marigold, that goes to bed wi' the sun,
> And with him rises weeping. . . .
> —Shakespeare, *The Winter's Tale* (IV, iii, 103)

Convergence: "Their Book Will Spell Trouble"

In November 1967, like tangled tributaries in a delta, multiple narratives entwined: Washington and Hanoi's soundings, against the backdrop of the looming presidential race and (though only the North Vietnamese knew of them) the intensifying preparations for the Tet Offensive; Michałowski's tempestuous early ambassadorship in Washington and Warsaw's continuing interest in mediation; and the Kraslow-Loory inquest, gaining momentum and alarming the administration at the highest levels.

✳ ✳ ✳

As they interviewed present and former U.S. officials, sometimes several a day, in person and by phone, Kraslow and Loory also set their sights on obtaining foreign perspectives, especially on Marigold. They had already plucked the lowest-hanging fruit, the Canadians, but seriously probing Marigold from a non-U.S. perspective required stalking more exotic prey. Bagging a candid, credible, and informed DRV view posed a daunting challenge. Yet seeking out the Poles and Italians who had been involved in the affair—above all Lewandowski and D'Orlandi—seemed plausible. In early November, they began laying the groundwork by approaching Warsaw's and Rome's envoys in Washington. Italy's reacted positively; Egidio "Eddie" Ortona knew only "bits and pieces" of Marigold, but he agreed to write to D'Orlandi and Fanfani to seek their aid in arranging interviews in Rome.[63]

The Poles proved more elusive. The reporters first spoke to First Secretary Stanislaw Pawlak, formerly deputy head of Warsaw's ICC delegation in Saigon.[64] He had wrapped up a year-long stint in the South Vietnamese capital in April 1966, just as Lewandowski had arrived, but he had a working knowledge of Marigold, which he shared, along with his government's views. Pawlak urged the journalists to consider the inscrutable "Asian mind"—a "yes" meant "maybe," a "no" sometimes "yes," and "Lewandowski got a 'yes' [from Dong] and took it as a 'maybe'"—but insisted that the ill-timed Hanoi bombings had ruined a real opportunity, leaving Poland "furious, it felt like it had been had." He continued: "We were so close to peace, I think. It really looked very good—you could just feel something was happening, as if it were on your fingertips. I think if those talks had begun, we would have peace in Vietnam today."

Pawlak termed Michałowski the "man managing the crisis (if that's the word)" for Rapacki, and the next day the reporters buttonholed the ambassador to see if he would talk. "I am sworn to secrecy on this matter," he replied, gun-shy after the lectures from Katzenbach and Bundy. "I will not say anything. I will not be a source." When one of the reporters asked if he could get Poland's side of the story if he went to Warsaw, the envoy said "someone" would "talk to us," but not necessarily Lewandowski. Michałowski agreed to "hear us out on our story" yet refused to promise to say anything.

"Maybe you can say yes or no as we repeat it?"

"Well, I can smile or not smile," the diplomat responded.[65]

* * *

While Kraslow and Loory made their rounds, the United States and DRV pursued their secret mutual probing. With the collapse of the "Pennsylvania" channel—the Kissinger exercise via the two French scholars—Washington opened a new channel in November to ascertain what price Hanoi might pay for a full bombing halt. This channel involved the maverick Communist government of Romania, another Eastern European country with interparty links with the Lao Dong and motives (both political and economic) to improve its ties with the West and Washington. In November, the Romanian attempt picked up pace as Harriman went to Bucharest to hear officials' impressions and explain American thinking. With Moscow passive after the Glassboro summit's failure, and U.S. officials disdainful of Hungarian and Polish efforts, Romania was establishing itself as Washington's Eastern Bloc country of choice for peace feelers, earning the code name Packers, after the Super Bowl champions.[66]

But the Poles had not yet left the peacemaking gridiron—and this time Hanoi took the initiative rather than Warsaw, in an episode that has heretofore escaped notice. On November 6, as leaders from the discordant Communist world (aside from Beijing and its tiny ally, Tirana) gathered in Moscow to mark the fiftieth anniversary of the Bolshevik Revolution, Le Duan and Gomułka met. After they agreed on the usefulness of preserving the dormant ICC, the Polish party boss invited his counterpart to present his views on negotiations—particularly because Michałowski, in Washington, would soon see Rusk and, a few days later, LBJ himself. "I am bringing up this matter," he explained, "because if you had any suggestions, we are ready to convey them to Johnson, that is, if he really brings up the problem of the war in Vietnam and puts forward any initiatives."

Le Duan had a ready and, by North Vietnamese standards, concrete response:

We know that the U.S. comes out strong in words, but in reality they are looking for possibilities of carrying out negotiations with us. Therefore, on one hand, we are getting ready for stubborn fights with the American army for the period of the next few years, but on the other hand, if the U.S. wants to talk with us, we are prepared to negotiate with them. I already told Com. Kliszko that on one hand we are ready to carry out a long lasting war, but if there were a possibility of ending it even by one day early, we are prepared to do so.

That is why we are currently prepared to be explicit about our position. The Politburo of our party decided that if the United States stops bombing North Vietnam, then after three weeks pass, we are ready to enter into negotiations. During the negotiations, we will only demand that the U.S. recognizes the independence of South Vietnam and stand on the grounds of the Geneva Accords. We do not intend for the United States to lose face and influence. We know that the U.S. is a great imperialist power, and we do not intend for it to lose its face and prestige.

In form, at least, Le Duan proposed a return to Marigold, to even bilateral ambassadorial contacts in Warsaw as a first stage. Hanoi was informing only the Soviets and the Poles of the decision to enter into talks three weeks after the bombing ended, he said, "due to the complexity of the diplomatic struggle" and "also because you are often helping us in the diplomatic work." Gomułka could best determine how to use this knowledge "in your negotiations with the U.S.," he added, implicitly encouraging him to inform Washington.

Publicly, Le Duan would repeat the usual boilerplate, but to the Poles, he pledged that Hanoi would take a more moderate stand. He never mentioned the once-sacrosanct Four Points, acknowledged that Washington genuinely sought talks, and implied that the sticky subject of NLF participation could be finessed, as a side issue to be handled by the Saigon and the NLF: "As far as our official policy is concerned, what we will state publicly is included in my speech for the ceremonial session on the occasion of the fiftieth anniversary of the revolution. But I tell you here that three weeks after the bombings stop, we will be ready to enter into negotiations in Warsaw."[67]

Sensing that Poland had been given an important task, Gomułka sent Rapacki a report of Le Duan's remarks.[68] A few days before, the foreign minister had puzzled over how to instruct Michałowski for his upcoming talks with Rusk and LBJ, whom he guessed might have a new "peace" move up their sleeves to mask planned escalation. Frustrated as he crossed out and redrafted, he admitted: "We do not have a ready position as to sounding out [the Americans], and all the more to [be putting forward] suggestions." Michałowski might have to throw "old cards on the table" unless he could propose better ideas.[69]

Now, however, armed with Le Duan's private vow, Rapacki had something concrete to send Michałowski. No session with LBJ transpired, but he secured a date to see Rusk later in November—offering a chance to pass along Hanoi's firmest commitment yet to come to the table by a date certain if the air campaign halted.

❊ ❊ ❊

Among the observers who failed to detect anything new or noteworthy from Le Duan's attendance at the USSR's fiftieth-birthday bash was CIA director Richard Helms—as one of the *Los Angeles Times* reporters (probably Kraslow) learned a few days later.[70] They spoke over lunch in a quiet dining room at CIA headquarters ("the service, including the black double-breasted uniform of the tall, heavy-set Negro waiter, could match that of top grade restaurants. And so could the filet mignon."). As they ate off plates with CIA insignias, the career intelligence officer—"a meticulous man, wears garters, button down shirts, conservative ties, drinks sherries, dislikes dirty glasses, polishes the rim before he drinks. Hard features but softened by smiles time and again, very frank, crooked teeth"—edified his guest on how the White House functioned. Helms warned the reporters against "institutionalizing" their narrative, because LBJ was "the most uninstitutionalized man around." "The only place decisions are made here in Washington in this year 1967 is in the mind of Lyndon Johnson, and that could happen at anytime—at 4 o'clock in the morning, at lunch, while he's sitting on the can—anywhere."[71]

Helms groused that LBJ, who could cut individuals or agencies out of the information "grid" on the slightest whim, had not consulted him on peace efforts in advance, and he had learned about Marigold only "in its dying stages." (Gronouski had likewise failed to inform the Warsaw CIA station chief of his talks with Rapacki.[72]) Had anyone asked Helms, "which they didn't," he could have warned them about the pitfalls of dealing with the Italians and the untrustworthy, leak-prone Poles. "Maybe next time," he said, LBJ and his aides "will think differently when they get a little bit of a sparkler."

The CIA director's bottom line, however, resembled the president's: He discerned "no give at all" in Hanoi's position, as evidenced most recently by Le Duan's speech in Moscow. "Go back over previous statements and [you] find nothing really different—maybe some semantic differences, but that's about all."

The reporters had better luck in early November interviewing other officials, notably Cooper and Katzenbach. These key figures shared background on Marigold, Sunflower (they concealed the code name), and other secret peace efforts, but they evaded some of the most sensitive questions (e.g., the lineups pro and con bombing Hanoi in December) and tried to punch holes in the argument that any serious opportunity had been missed or botched. Reporting the contacts internally, both insisted that they said nothing that contradicted administration interests, and the reporters' notes largely bear this out.

While consenting (with the State Department's approval) to discuss Marigold with the *Los Angeles Times* pair, who visited his home "for several hours" on the evening of November 6, Cooper defended the party line that Washington had competently handled the initiative. He firmly rejected the reporters' sense that bombing Hanoi during the Warsaw talks reflected "either gross negligence or a great gap in communications and orchestration." The administration, he insisted, had taken "great care" in selecting targets and coordinating them with the State Department. In his memo of the talk for superiors, he claimed to have boasted: "Never before in the history of war has such close attention [been] paid to day-to-day military operations by the highest levels of government."[73]

A week later, Kraslow and Loory called on Katzenbach (whose note-taker was Richard Holbrooke, formerly stationed at the Saigon Embassy[74]). Like Cooper, he balanced candor and caution, harboring private dissent toward some Vietnam moves (e.g., the Hanoi strikes during Marigold), yet keenly aware that he worked for a keenly suspicious president who would harshly punish any underling (especially a JFK holdover and RFK friend) he thought was guilty of unauthorized leaks.[75]

Katzenbach tried to be more helpful than indicated by his "memorandum for the record" for internal consumption, which, like Cooper's, stressed his stiff-arming of Kraslow and Loory's hunt for dirty laundry. "[I] thought marigold was a flower," it quoted him as saying blandly when they raised the topic.

Consenting to discuss it, he insisted that "the whole thing was a phony on the part of the Poles to begin with." Washington regarded the Poles suspiciously from the outset because they seemed "funny choices" for authentic DRV communications. Cryptically, he said that he was "surer of this now than I was then" due to something he had learned about Warsaw's role, not Hanoi's, that he could not discuss (another clear allusion to Radványi). He had snide asides for several Marigold principals: Lewandowski's ten points were "a terrible mishmash of language"; D'Orlandi, "that idiot in Saigon—the Italian—who was going around telling everybody what's going on"; and the Nobel-driven Gronouski "was climbing the walls—he was happy to be remembered."

Kraslow and Loory "pressed extremely hard" on the Hanoi bombings, but Katzenbach held firm. After Rusk's deputy noted the argument that suspending authorization for the attacks would have tipped off the military, they prodded him to confirm that he had nevertheless urged LBJ against more strikes near Hanoi during Marigold. "I'm not going to tell you," Katzenbach replied, refusing to discuss his advice to LBJ and insisting that he "concurred in" the raids. Even if they had not occurred, he suggested, the Poles would have devised some other pretext: "You do get into the position of saying, Jesus Christ, this is an excuse—how do you cut off all possible excuses? . . . And that's hard to do." Even when the highly classified record eventually opened, he cautioned, those trying to piece the affair together should not rely overly on the "huge paper record":

> People feel compelled to answer cables showing they've read something or reacted to it or had an opinion on it. I don't know what's happening to all that paper—who's going to read it? Maybe the historians but when they do, they'll have a very distorted picture of just what's happened—because all the important decisions are made as a result of unreported phone calls and talks without anything put in writing. If the president tells me he wants something done, I'm not going to tell the guy who drafts the cable that the president wants it—there's no need to. The more I see of this government, the more I realize no one knows all of what goes into a decision—literally no one.[76]

In talking to the reporters while also filing memorandums likely to be read by Rusk and LBJ, Cooper and Katzenbach knew they were walking a tightrope. After the conversation with his boss, Holbrooke implored Kraslow and Loory: "Don't be too good to him and don't be too bad to him. Either way can hurt him."[77]

✻ ✻ ✻

On November 18, two prime Marigold antagonists finally had a chance to argue face to face.[78] Michałowski had seen Rusk when he first came to Washington in late August, but that was mere protocol.[79] Now they had a "tour d'horizon" that, predictably, dwelled longest and most contentiously on Vietnam.

Rusk wondered why Hanoi had not embraced the San Antonio formula, sparking contention over whether it would really enter into negotiations in return for a bombing halt. If Washington "wished to have assurances of talks from Hanoi," Michałowski declared—without specifying Le Duan as the source of his prophecy—it "would receive these assurances three weeks after a bombing suspension."

Why not three days? Rusk shot back.

Because Hanoi "would not negotiate under duress," the Pole countered. It was "a fact" that the North Vietnamese would come to the table, but they "now need assurances that there would be no repetition of their experience last December, when Hanoi had been bombed during a period of difficult and delicate efforts to arrange contact."

That got the Marigold ball rolling. Already well aware of Michałowski's prior conversations about the affair since reaching Washington, Rusk had fresh grounds for annoyance—a report from Oslo of Rapacki telling his Norwegian counterpart "in great detail about the Polish effort 'on U.S. behalf' to open contact in December 1966."[80] Resentfully, Rusk charged that Poles at the UN had leaked "a limited and incomplete version of this episode." They "only provided confirming and amplifying details when confronted by the knowledge of others," Michałowski retorted. Familiar spats ensued over the ten points, the Hanoi bombings (and Saigon assaults, Rusk "cried out," including an "assassination attempt"), and the DRV's failure to show up in Warsaw. Explaining why the December raids had provoked North Vietnam to end the overture, Michałowski alluded to its original "difficult" decision over "much internal opposition," only to hear Rusk reply unsympathetically that internal opposition was Hanoi's problem and the 10-mile zone should have eased its concern. When the Pole insisted that if that step had been implemented a few weeks earlier, "we would have been sitting at a negotiating table in Warsaw," Rusk stressed anew that Washington never heard anything directly from Hanoi.

With the subject of Marigold momentarily exhausted, Rusk confided "something of a very private nature," that Washington "had been in contact with Hanoi from mid-August until late October"—a clear allusion to the "Pennsylvania" exercise. (Warsaw knew this, Michałowski "murmured.") But, Rusk said, North Vietnam had effectively replied, "Go to hell." Despite the restraint around Hanoi, it launched "the largest offensive of the war" in the Demilitarized Zone, and Washington had "determined from captured documents that the North Vietnamese are prepared for a strategy of 'fight and talk.'" To this (accurate) claim, Michałowski weakly responded that "some captured documents are those which Hanoi wishes us to capture."

The ambassador tried to steer the conversation back to the signal he was trying to convey, stressing Poland's belief that "negotiations could be conducted on the basis of Geneva for a settlement which would be honorable and politically sound for the United States." After Rusk agreed, "Michałowski repeated that three weeks and one day from a cessation of bombing, talks could begin." If the secretary had probed his basis for this assertion, he might have discovered that it reflected not mere speculation but Le Duan's authoritative commitment to Gomułka —just as, a year earlier in Saigon, Lewandowski, when prodded by Lodge, had audaciously exceeded his instructions by identifying Dong as the DRV figure who had authorized the Warsaw contact. Instead, Rusk asked Michałowski what Hanoi would do during this three-week period. When the Pole supposed that both sides would send "troops and munitions" to reinforce their positions, Rusk stressed that the Americans would bomb North Vietnam if it attempted to do so—and the conversation lapsed into recriminations over the Hanoi raids, ICC ineffectiveness, U.S. claims that SEATO obligations compelled South Vietnam's defense, NLF legitimacy and autonomy (or lack thereof), the collapse of the Geneva Accord on Laos, and other matters.

Where do we go from here? Rusk asked plaintively.

Stop the bombing, Michałowski predictably replied.

Eventually, they recognized the debate's futility. Trying to end on a positive note, Michałowski asked Rusk "to believe that when the Poles talk to the North Vietnamese, they attempt to be as persuasive in explaining the U.S. point of view as they are in explaining Hanoi's point of view to the United States"—a plausible claim for himself and Lewandowski, though certainly *not* Siedlecki—and Rusk reciprocated by wishing bilateral relations "could be improved in spite of differences over Vietnam."

Still, Michałowski cabled Rapacki, the encounter ended somberly. "Rusk fell into a long silence, which lasted a few minutes. He suddenly got up and said: 'Oh well, despite everything, one will most likely have to fight for a while,' and then he bid farewell, thanking me for the conversation."

❊ ❊ ❊

Even before seeing Michałowski, the arguments raging over blame for the failure of past peace efforts had made Rusk touchy. A day earlier, he had asked Bundy to draft a detailed statement on secret Vietnam diplomacy to show the public that Hanoi, not Washington, had blocked bids to end the war. He felt heat from multiple sources; dovish senators, irksome journalists and commentators, even ostensibly supportive foreigners spread doubts about LBJ's handling of peace feelers (Brown had "slipped up" at a recent Council on Foreign Relations lunch by mentioning the "hiccough" and "joker in the pack" when Washington hardened terms during the Kosygin summit[81]). Supporters urged a strong rebuttal: Joe Alsop privately badgered the White House to issue a report on failed peace efforts using captured documents to prove Hanoi's intransigence and insincerity.[82]

Bundy soon turned in the outline ("The Search for Peace in Southeast Asia") of a "major publication" and sought reactions from Rusk and others "intimately familiar with the problem." About Marigold, it concluded: "In all probability, an over-zealous intermediary who in fact had no message from Hanoi."[83]

✳ ✳ ✳

Rusk and Bundy would not have quarreled with applying the adjective "overzealous" to Kraslow and Loory. After seeing Katzenbach, in short order they spoke with, among others, Fulbright; Bunker, back from Saigon for consultations; and, "strictly for the deepest background," Clark Clifford, the dapper presidential counsel soon to succeed McNamara. The contacts yielded mixed results. Clifford—"tall, wavy gray haired, he talks and looks like Ralph Bellamy playing FDR in Sunrise at Campobello," "smooth, quiet, unruffled, solicitous"—airily and erroneously speculated that Hanoi was bombed only after Washington "already knew nothing would come of" the Warsaw contacts.[84]

But their courting of the crusty Senate Foreign Relations Committee chair paid off. At lunch in the Senate dining room on November 16, the Arkansas Democrat (a "natty, diet conscious, southern gentleman who talks of the weightiest foreign affairs problem while keeping an eye on the political situation back home") repeated that LBJ sought not a negotiated peace but Hanoi's "surrender so that this country can keep a base in Southeast Asia until China becomes an ally."[85] He did not detail secret diplomacy himself, but let his staff member Carl Marcy show the reporters the transcript of Gronouski's May 15, 1967, executive session testimony. Four days later, Loory typed a dozen pages of single-spaced verbatim notes of Marigold-related passages. The transcript lacked a formal Executive Branch classification, but the *Los Angeles Times* duo now had a detailed secret account of the exchanges in Warsaw.[86]

✳ ✳ ✳

Fortified by their coup, the reporters met Michałowski on November 22, hoping to secure his version of Marigold and aid in greasing the way for Loory to visit Warsaw and interview Lewandowski. Perhaps freshly irritated by his conversation with Rusk, the Pole had shed some of his inhibitions. In the postmortem of the affair that he prepared for possible publication more than a decade later, he would praise Kraslow and Loory's "excellent professional research" but coyly neglected to say if he had spoken to them, instead noting that it was "easy to presume" that Cooper had been their primary source on Marigold.[87]

However, the reporters' notes show that Michałowski did more than smile, discussing the December 1966 flap and the thirty-seven-day bombing pause. He left Kraslow and Loory in no doubt of Poland's view that the Hanoi raids (carried out despite Warsaw's warnings) had doomed Marigold, and he vigorously disputed insinuations that the Poles acted without DRV authorization. He also supplied anecdotes from the Rapacki-Gronouski talks, such as the need for a translator to compensate for the American's pigeon Polish.[88]

Equally important, Michałowski agreed to help in other ways. In a cable to Rapacki, he minimized his own loquacity—"using discretion as an excuse," he had resisted Kraslow and Loory's inquiries, though he "incidentally straightened out some harmful errors"—but urged cooperation with the reporters. Besides amassing "significantly greater" information than prior leaks, they were headed in a "positive" direction, because "they are placing responsibility on the Administration for bombarding the talks." Describing their planned research trips to Europe, he endorsed Loory's visa plea and suggested that Rapacki find some method, perhaps indirect, "to influence" him—though he said nothing about making Lewandowski available.[89]

Warsaw approved the visit, informing Michałowski that he could tell Loory an "appropriate" figure would speak to him. But the MSZ cautioned against promising anything more explicit and requested further data on the reporters—especially their prior affiliations and prospective book's "angle"—before determining how cooperative to be: "Our attitude toward them will depend on the information we get." Michałowski, in reply, again vouched for Kraslow and Loory: Their investigation would undoubtedly undercut official U.S. claims, they had gained approval for their project from Otis Chandler himself, and their book would "strengthen the anti-war movement."[90]

Before leaving for Europe, the reporters got a chilly reception from McNamara. On November 24, they saw the defense secretary in his Pentagon office ("in shirt sleeves behind a huge desk—the largest executive desk in Washington, easily twice the size of Lyndon Johnson's, . . . covered with purple felt and a glass top over that") and found him "not at all in sympathy with our project." Though he, like Katzenbach, had in December 1966 strongly urged LBJ to suspend raids near Hanoi during Marigold—and more recently had privately counseled him to stop the bombing unilaterally before 1967 ended to hasten negotiations, advice that instead hastened his exit from the administration[91]—McNamara also hid internal disagreements. He insisted that he and Rusk had "properly adjusted" military and peace moves, yet he ostentatiously embraced culpability for any errors: "Anything that has gone wrong, any mistakes that have been made, I take full responsibility for," he said. "Don't blame them on the state department, blame them on me."

But he refused to discuss Marigold's details, discounted claims of Hanoi's readiness for peace (which he likened to reports before the 1962 Cuban Missile Crisis—"out of the 20,000 Cuban missiles rumors, only a half dozen or so were really good ones"), and gruffly blasted the reporters: "'You're dealing with the most delicate subject confronting the United States government today. Nobody should talk to you except the president and the secretary of state. Anybody else who talks to you should have his goddam head cut off.' Then he promises to cut off the heads of any one in [the Department of Defense] who talks to us."[92]

* * *

McNamara was not the only top official Kraslow and Loory disconcerted; alarm reached the highest levels of the State Department and White House. On November 20—the day the reporters scored their biggest advance yet by securing Gronouski's secret testimony—Ben Read, Rusk's executive aide, summarized the peril for Rostow. Having found enough data "to show that our past diplomatic efforts had not been coordinated with our bombing program," Kraslow and Loory planned to write not only a series of newspaper articles, to appear in the spring, but also a book. Noting the many officials with whom they had spoken, Read credited their "industrious and impressive job collecting information, piecing together the public record and filling in the gaps through personal interviews." On Marigold, they already "have the code name and most of the sequence. They are pressing hard to find out who authorized strikes of December 2–3 and 13–14, 1966. Nick told them that the strikes had been part of a bombing package for that period of time and that this had been agreed upon without dissent by all the concerned officials. They have obviously talked to the Poles and the Canadians and perhaps the Italians on this one."

"Their book will spell trouble for the Administration," Read warned. To counter them, he had advised State Department officials to "duck appointments with these reporters without stating that they have been instructed to do so, so that any contacts can be limited to those on a political level."[93] But Rostow and Rusk thought that more measures were warranted, and so did McNamara. Their fears pushed the Kraslow-Loory project onto the agenda of the November 28 gathering of the administration's most elite (and secretive) Vietnam policy group: the "Tuesday Lunch."

LBJ, McNamara, Rostow, Helms, Wheeler, Christian, and note-taker Tom Johnson listened as Rusk said the *Los Angeles Times* reporters were "about to publish a book" on peace probes that would include code names. To preempt their unsympathetic account, he suggested that Bundy make a speech rather than issue a formal white paper. "This would take a lot out of the book, particularly if Bundy used the code names," he asserted.

LBJ suggested that Bundy go on *Issues and Answers,* the ABC Sunday television talk show.

McNamara complained that "the Canadians, the Italians and the Poles have 'spilled their guts'" to Kraslow and Loory; "executive branch people" had also blabbed. The reporters, he discovered, had collected a surprising amount of data "on Warsaw and on the connection between some of the peace offensives and the bombing."

Like Rusk, the defense secretary—whose departure to head the World Bank would be announced the next day—also proposed undercutting the reporters. He suggested that "we take some of the juice out of the story by using the code names prior to publication. We could torpedo them since the code names are not important except to people who have never heard them." Nevertheless, he admitted, their book would contain "a lot of material which could prove to be embarrassing."[94]

As a conduit for leaking the Marigold code name who could be relied on to put the revelation in a sympathetic context, officials had just the man. LBJ had grumbled at the meeting that the gist of a secret letter from Kosygin, just delivered by Dobrynin, had already been revealed that morning by *Washington Post* national security correspondent Chalmers Roberts. "Chal" Roberts occasionally irked LBJ, yet the president's aides considered him a team player (as Rusk saw Hightower): Halberstam would peg him as "the epitome of the establishment reporter, . . . a journalistic extension of the national security complex, he judged dangers and enemies on the same scale as the people he covered, and he had almost unconsciously over a career accepted the limitations that his sources had wanted to accept. He was the kind of reporters that high officials judged to be sound."[95]

As the administration plotted to yank the rug out from under them, Kraslow and Loory fanned out to Europe in hopes of making an end run around the Maginot Line they encountered in Washington.

Stuart and David's (and Wilfred's) European Adventure

While Kraslow went to London in search of insider accounts of the Wilson-Kosygin summit, Loory flew to Rome. As promised, Ortona had relayed his interview requests to D'Orlandi, endorsing his "utmost professional responsibility." Unsure how to proceed, the ex-Saigon envoy huddled with Fanfani—who opted not to see Loory himself but asked D'Orlandi to receive him and, while parrying his queries, ascertain the scope of his knowledge and, if possible, identity of his sources. Fanfani advised him "not to be too guarded" but to avoid direct replies by handling questions by the bunch.[96]

On Friday morning, December 1, Loory came to the Palazzo della Farnesina, the Foreign Ministry's imposing white travertine headquarters in northern Rome. Afterward, he distilled his first impressions of the Italian lead actor in the Marigold drama:

> D'Orlandi is short, thin, debonair dresser, dark-haired, well-groomed, wears highly polished black loafers and woolen anklets, speaks a colloquial English—"I'll see you around elevenish," he said in the phone conversation in which our appointment was arranged. He works in [the] Foreign Ministry building—a huge, Fascist modern marble block next door to the Olympic Stadium complex Mussolini built prior to World War II. When you cross the Tiber at the bridge closest to the building, a huge

needle of marble rises on the other side, on which is written "Mussolini Dux" and a stylized Fascist symbol is carved. It is the only place in Rome where Mussolini's name survives, it is said. You wonder whether the determination of the Fanfani-D'Orlandi group to carve a name for itself as peacemakers arises from the same desire to be recognized that made Il Duce a man of war.

In the margins he penned: "He looks sickly, bleeds easily from his diseases."[97]

D'Orlandi took a shine to his "very likable and intelligent" visitor. He explained at the start that he could not violate the negotiators' vows of confidentiality, and intended to play "the 'hot' and 'cold' game" to see if he could guide Loory without volunteering much. But the journalist's first "salvo" of detailed queries—the precise timing of specific meetings, the libations at celebratory toasts (whiskey or champagne?), "and so on and so forth"—bowled him over. Obviously, the reporters had already horded a vast store of secret information from highly placed sources. So D'Orlandi too began to open up; the Americans were talking, so why shouldn't he? "Giving him a bit of background information and some notes of color cannot cause harm nor betray any secret," he rationalized, "but rather can help to find out how far his information goes." Explaining the affair's origin, he immodestly emphasized his own (and Italy's) role by describing the "intellectual exercise" of imagining the "least disagreeable" postwar setup and working backward to devise a mutually acceptable package deal before formal negotiations. He also furnished vivid glimpses of the clandestine diplomacy, from the mood ("all three of us felt pretty good about what we had accomplished") to the beverage ("scotch was poured at all the meetings") to his coded phone calls to "Cabot" to arrange meetings.

Both men staked out limits to their candor, however; Loory categorically refused to name his sources, and D'Orlandi—who came away convinced the *Los Angeles Times* pair's forthcoming book would usefully sway public opinion—withheld substance. Nor did he breath a word to Loory, then or later, to reveal that, a year after Marigold's rise and fall, he and Italy were again engaged in intense secret efforts to forge a breakthrough between Washington and Hanoi.[98] They agreed to resume their conversation on Monday.

Over the weekend, Loory made a side trip to Florence to interview its voluble, eccentric ex-mayor, Giorgio La Pira, about his 1965 trip to Hanoi and talk with Ho Chi Minh.[99] Then, a little before noon Monday, he sat down again with D'Orlandi.[100]

Picking up where they left off, D'Orlandi elucidated the "Italian philosophy" behind the initiative, seeking broad principles to serve as bases for an overall accord rather than narrow "Phase A, Phase B type" mechanisms. He also gave Loory the sense that Rome had hoped to stay at or near the table even after direct talks started, serving as "kind of a second to the United States while Warsaw acted as North Vietnam's second."

Amused by Loory's tale of confusion in Washington between Lewandowskis (at the UN and in Saigon), D'Orlandi continued to be impressed by his detailed knowledge of Marigold—but only through early December, after which it blurred. In the midst of the conversation, "apropos of nothing," the Italian said, "You haven't mentioned it yet but I'm sure you're aware that on Dec. 8 Secretary Rusk arrived in Saigon."

"After flushing several colors," the flustered reporter admitted that no, he had not known, but was sure he would have run across the visit in his research.

"Well, now you don't have to come across it," D'Orlandi teased.

Having simultaneously enlightened and embarrassed Loory, he then exasperated him by refusing to discuss the substance of his exchanges with Rusk. When pressed, he did not dispute the inference that if Fanfani had urged Rusk to forgo further Hanoi raids as long as the delicate peace initiative lived (as the reporter already gathered), he too would surely have issued a comparable warning. The Farnesina, he added, would not confirm or deny anything—and if Rusk denied speaking with him, he could say nothing.

Probing, D'Orlandi ascertained that the reporters' sources were "much more reticent, if not untruthful" regarding Marigold's origins—minimizing Fanfani's role and trumpeting their own—and also withheld the ten points' content, as did he, hoping that they might still prove useful.

After some desultory discussion of La Pira and a D'Orlandi disquisition on diplomacy—real ambassadors needed decades to learn how to independently craft mutually beneficial compromises, in contrast to Soviet or U.S. envoys implementing detailed cabled instructions—the two parted ways. D'Orlandi rushed to brief Fanfani, though he later told a U.S. aide that he had refrained from telling him "how many specific details were known [to Loory] for fear of upsetting him."[101]

Bowdlerized or not, D'Orlandi's account left Il Motorino worried that he and Italy were lagging behind in the war of leaks—and, as a result, would reap insufficient credit. Did D'Orlandi retain an "accurate memory" or, better, a written record of the episode? Fanfani wondered. D'Orlandi assured him that he had kept his Vietnam journal "very much up to date." "If these indiscretions multiply it might be necessary to publish your diary," the minister observed. "In any case, for now we shall see."[102]

* * *

On his way to Warsaw, Loory stopped for a few days in Prague, where he had scant success chasing Vietnamese perspectives on secret diplomacy or a visa to Hanoi to pursue the matter with higher-ranking figures. He spoke with the DRV cultural attaché (failing to get an appointment with the ambassador) and an unofficial NLF representative, but he made little headway piercing standard rhetoric and was politely rebuffed in seeking a coveted pass to the enemy capital (too much bombing at the moment, even though, in principle, "we welcome every genuine American—every genuine peace loving person").[103]

His additional contacts in Prague, with U.S. ambassador Jacob Beam and a Czech journalist formerly posted to Moscow, seemed to confirm that the picturesque city with whispers of change in the air—Alexander Dubček would take over the Communist Party the following month, presaging the reformist Prague Spring the Soviets would brutally crush—remained a backwater in clandestine peace diplomacy.[104] Assured by Beam (who did not suspect otherwise) that there were "no peace feelers in Prague," Loory caught not a whiff of the secret contacts in progress there involving the man he had just interviewed in Rome and the DRV envoy he had vainly tried to see.

✹ ✹ ✹

As Loory approached Warsaw, his partner pestered U.S. and local officials in London and Paris. In the U.K. capital, Kraslow inquired about the Polish affair, but mostly delved into the still-mysterious Wilson-Kosygin summit in February. Of special interest, of course, were the rumors of Anglo-American rancor over a communications breakdown between 10 Downing Street and the White House caused by Washington's hardening of terms, and Wilson's tantalizing hint that peace was "almost within our grasp."

Kraslow's detailed knowledge of those events "astonished" David Bruce, who of course had experienced firsthand the summit's excitement and consternation. But the ambassador also discerned key gaps in his awareness and had little trouble deflecting his efforts to dig deeper—or so he cabled Washington. Kraslow's notes suggest Bruce, "a very cool customer, flushed for a moment" under questioning, when he reversed himself and blamed Wilson for "misunderstanding" the U.S. position—and once during their two talks, when he "flared" and objected to being pressed for details of Anglo-American exchanges.[105]

At the Foreign Office, midlevel aide Donald Murray ("audited" by the press office head) politely stiff-armed Kraslow, offering platitudes. Besides rejecting his request to interview Brown, the British assured Bruce that they "were a stone wall on passing out any information and told him that whatever views Kraslow might have about what took place in February, Fonoff attention was centered on present and future prospects for further talks."[106] "Zilch," Kraslow disgustedly began his notes.[107] He had a bit more luck siphoning background on Marigold and Sunflower from a midlevel U.S. official, Wilson's press secretary, and local Polish and Soviet diplomats.[108]

Then Kraslow set off across the English Channel to focus on French angles, especially RFK's controversial interview with Manac'h in February, and the more recent murkiness over the summer said to involve Kissinger and two leftist French academics. Though the (mostly) imperturbable Bruce and the tight-lipped British had nonchalantly swatted Kraslow away like a pesky fly, in Paris he ruffled feathers right and left. His aggressive questioning and unapologetic snooping into classified matters prompted one U.S. diplomat to complain to Washington that he was "pursuing his inquiries here with more assiduity than tact."[109] Invited by resident *Los Angeles Times* reporter Don Cook to dine at the Hôtel de Crillon with a visiting colleague, embassy first secretary John Gunther Dean anticipated a sumptuous meal bestowing diplomatic wisdom in the elegant mansion on the Place de la Concorde. Kraslow, however, subjected the embassy's Vietnam expert to "what can only be described as interrogation, giving 'third degree'" (as he later huffed). Kraslow sensed his source's mounting wariness (and host's discomfort), but he plowed ahead on topics ranging from the RFK-Manac'h interview to Marigold to various "flower messages" to Kissinger and, finally, the "XYZ" affair (the furtive Parisian exchanges in 1965 between Mai Van Bo and a retired State Department aide). The career diplomat ("tall, a bit stocky, snub-nosed, thinning hair") could no longer contain himself:

> At this point I interrupted Kraslow and told him very bluntly that he was asking questions about subjects which I felt were none of his business. He disagreed sharply, stating that there are a number of people back home who feel that the President and Secretary Rusk were misleading the American public on Vietnam and that his questions are designed to document that the North Vietnamese had been receptive to U.S. efforts to enter into negotiations with us, something the Administration denies. I replied that what he was saying sounded seditious to me, that what he was doing amounted to undermining the national interest of the U.S. by prying into business which only concerns the Executive Branch and that his action might even jeopardize future efforts to find a peaceful solution to the conflict. Furthermore, it is not a Foreign Service Officer's task to pass on sensitive information to anybody outside the Government. Under these circumstances, I said I felt there was no further need to continue the discussion. I apologized to Don Cook for this outburst, explaining that I had not expected to be submitted to a third degree when I accepted the invitation for dinner, but that I did not consider Mr. Kraslow's questions to be of any concern to a newspaperman.[110]

The two had a civil "quickie" chat over coffee at the Crillon a couple of days later, but Dean remained evasive (XYZ? "just letters in the alphabet").[111]

Kraslow also rattled cages by digging into Kissinger's French connections. Aided by the local CIA station chief, he unearthed the dates of their July visit to Hanoi (from ICC records) and their identities: Raymond Aubrac, a Communist functionary and old friend of Ho Chi Minh (his son's godfather), now with the UN Food and Agriculture Organization in Rome; and Herbert Marcovich, a molecular biologist at a research laboratory in a nearby suburb.[112] Kraslow immediately phoned Marcovich, who reacted edgily ("how did you get my name? repeats this several times, as if alarmed") but agreed to see him. The next morning, he cordially discussed his past but resisted Kraslow's efforts to unravel his secret peace activities: "Please understand that I just cannot help you."[113]

After getting a worried letter from Marcovich about Kraslow's unwelcome visit, Kissinger called Read to convey the biologist's urgent warning that the *Los*

Angeles Times man seemed "au courant" with "Pennsylvania." Aghast that Kraslow had insinuated to Marcovich that he had gotten his information from him, Kissinger insisted that he had "not seen either Kraslow or Loory"—a blatant lie, if Read's record is accurate—"and had refused four specific requests by them for appointments." Rusk's aide advised urging Marcovich to avoid further contact with Kraslow, who "feigned more knowledge than he possessed."[114]

✳ ✳ ✳

Like Loory in Prague, Kraslow worked in Paris to obtain Hanoi's views, but he did not get far. He spoke to a DRV first secretary, who insisted that Hanoi had no trouble communicating with Washington when needed, yet declined to provide details, but he failed to get an audience with Mai Van Bo.[115] Coincidentally, however, his stay in the city overlapped with that of a garrulous, well-informed source on Hanoi's thinking: Burchett.

In early December, Burchett engaged in quiet Parisian contacts with Westerners centering on secret peace diplomacy, including Marigold. Washington publicly disparaged Burchett for his leftist leanings, yet U.S. aides occasionally sought him out to decipher the Vietnamese Communists. They did so now at the prompting of an old Asia hand, the *New Yorker* correspondent Robert Shaplen, who had recently seen him in Phnom Penh while accompanying Jacqueline Kennedy on a visit to Cambodia.

A trip to Europe to testify to the Bertrand Russell War Crimes Tribunal in Denmark offered a convenient contact, and a few days after alleging U.S. atrocities, Burchett privately met officials of the government he said had committed them. On December 5—between his talks with Kraslow—John Gunther Dean hosted Burchett at his apartment for a three-hour whiskey and lunch together with State Department aide Isham, "a tall professorial-type" specially sent to Paris to waltz with the Australian in an operation code-named "Matilda."[116] Burchett, last in Hanoi in October, now discerned a "distinctly harder" DRV line on negotiations than the previous winter. Explaining their belief in U.S. perfidy ("talking peace while intensifying war"), he asserted that the "North Vietnamese had agreed to talk at Warsaw last December and even had official en route when U.S. resumed bombing Hanoi."[117] Was he alluding to Nguyen Dinh Phuong's secret mission? Perhaps, but the Americans evidently did not ask him to elaborate. Instead, Burchett told Harrison Salisbury a few days later, they said that the bombings were "a mistake and a blunder and it will not happen again."[118] Isham verified Washington's continued adherence to the "ten points" and interest in preliminary, ambassadorial-level contacts with Hanoi. Dean, still smarting from Kraslow's "third degree," warned that reporters "were running around" Paris seeking dirt on peace contacts, and Burchett—"cheered" by the contact, which he considered the most serious effort since the Trinh interview to find a basis for talks—promised discretion.[119]

Burchett also raised Marigold with London's envoy, who afterward grumbled that taking "the Australian renegade and fellow-traveling journalist" to lunch was "rather a waste of entertainment allowance, since he had nothing new to say, and took far too much to drink." Again, Burchett claimed that Washington had missed "a great opportunity" with Poland in December 1966. U.S. military commanders, he suspected, had sabotaged the initiative, convincing North Vietnam of Washington's insincerity.[120]

Though Burchett confided in Salisbury—who was seeking a return visa to Hanoi—in Paris, he and Kraslow never crossed paths. For all their derring-do, the *Los Angeles Times* duo came no closer to locating an authentic or informed Communist Vietnamese perspective.

✳ ✳ ✳

On December 8, Roberts' story revealing Marigold's code name appeared in the *Washington Post*—and a day later, in Europe, it graced the *International Herald-Tribune*. For the most part, it innocuously rehashed prior leaks; Burchett told the British diplomat it was, "to his personal knowledge, substantially correct."[121]

But the leak LBJ hoped would undercut Kraslow and Loory boomeranged in one respect: Michałowski shrewdly read between the lines and urged retaliation. "The version is false on many points, but not caustic," he cabled Rapacki. "Despite the anniversary pretext, the point perhaps is to take away the wind from the sails of the California journalists. I think that in this situation, we especially need to leak out information to them, and I would not exclude a meeting with Lewandowski."[122]

In Rome, D'Orlandi likewise inferred from Roberts' article that matters had reached "the point of the State Department leaking, or allowing to leak, a good deal of information regarding Marigold." Discussing the story with Fanfani— whom he now judged a model of discretion compared with his U.S. and Polish counterparts—he was told to organize his diary to be ready for a potential official Italian disclosure.[123]

The *International Herald-Tribune* story also caught the eye of Herbert Marcovich, who felt that it cast new light on his own efforts. Kissinger's Parisian contact now viewed as "much more significant" the DRV's readiness to engage in the indirect contacts he had facilitated with Washington, despite what Mai Van Bo referred to as U.S. "double dealing." He also concluded that a hawkish faction in the administration, led by LBJ himself, was ascendant, with its triumph capped by McNamara's exit. Pursuing the "Pennsylvania" channel "under such conditions," he wrote Kissinger, "has completely ruined it on both sides," and if he had known earlier about Marigold, "he would probably have refused to continue as early as the end of August. I can only admire all the more," he added, "your effort and the persistence you have demonstrated at the cost of conflicts that were, I imagine, very sharp."[124]

Of course, Kraslow and Loory also noticed their rival's mini-scoop on the story that obsessed them. Read played coy when Kraslow called after returning from Europe.

Where did Roberts' piece originate? Maybe the Poles, suggested Rusk's aide (who knew better). How would *they* have known the *American* code name? he pushed; they did not get it from us. Read dodged the question, puzzling Kraslow—unaware that the leak to Roberts was a shot across his and Loory's bow that LBJ had personally approved.[125]

* * *

Gronouski was not sure what to expect when Loory, who had cold-called for an interview after reaching Warsaw, showed up at the embassy on December 11. But he was soon blown away by the reporter's "fantastic" inside knowledge of his exchanges with the Poles in December 1966. Using the same tactic as with D'Orlandi, the journalist quickly threw his source off-balance with ultraspecific queries to drive home that adhering to official secrecy was hopeless, they already knew too much, others had talked, so he might as well get across his own side of the story. Loory, the stupefied diplomat cabled, was "exceptionally well informed on Marigold exercise, having specific details with names, dates, ten points including A and B stages, etc. He asked, for example, 'On what day, between your meetings with Rapacki at 1900 on Dec. 24 and on Dec. 30, did Michałowski call to ask whether 10-mile limit was in statute or nautical miles?'"

During three days of conversations, Loory's meticulous questioning left Gronouski convinced not only that the *Los Angeles Times* reporters had gotten "all kinds of inside help" but also access to a highly classified, detailed State Department chronology of Marigold. "If Loory didn't get a copy of that I'll eat my hat," he later recalled, "because he had me seeing Rapacki at 7:00 p.m. on Christmas Eve; he had me leaving on a certain plane. . . . I mean, I sat there with my jaw dropped open, he had such detail." He never suspected that Loory actually had a different joker up his sleeve—the bootleg edition of his own closed-door testimony in May, leaked by a Fulbright aide a few weeks earlier.

Convinced that the reporters already had "the whole story," Gronouski related his own version, though he insisted to the State Department that he divulged nothing they did not already know and loyally pushed the administration's line. The Hanoi raids were "unfortunate" or "stupid," he conceded—not because they destroyed a real opportunity, but because they enabled a Communist propaganda blitz. Most likely, Warsaw had only a "hunting license" to probe Washington's terms, not an authentic imprimatur to arrange direct U.S.-DRV exchanges. If Hanoi had really been set to talk, it would not have let a few air raids derail a major policy shift.[126]

Loory also spoke with Thomas Brimelow, the British ambassador, who seemed less sure that no opportunity was missed. Before a glowing fireplace, the hospitable Briton, "the picture of the proper diplomat—erect, immaculate, using carefully chosen words, always pursuing precision, saying only what he can and no more"—equivocated when asked if he felt Washington had sincerely sought negotiations. Regarding Marigold (which he had reviewed with Michałowski in April), he demurred at Gronouski's contention that the Hanoi raids would not have dissuaded the DRV from talking, had it really wanted to.[127]

But the high point of Loory's Warsaw visit—indeed, of his entire Marigold quest—was meeting the man at the heart of the story. On December 12, Gronouski received an emissary from Rapacki to discuss Loory's visit. The American expressed shock at the reporter's bountiful knowledge of the secret diplomacy, evidently derived from "hundreds of conversations in the UN and in Washington, among others, with the Poles." The MSZ aide hotly denied responsibility for any leaks, only to elicit Gronouski's dubious, "We are not so sure about this." Asked if he had an official position on whether Warsaw should cooperate with Loory, the envoy agnostically "left it up to our discretion."[128] With Gronouski declining to flash a red light, Rapacki followed Michałowski's advice. He refused to see Loory himself—much like Fanfani—but sanctioned a background talk with Janusz Lewandowski.

Since returning from Saigon, the ex–ICC commissioner had remained closely engaged with policy toward the war, as deputy chief of the MSZ Department V handling Asia. Neither Rapacki nor Michałowski had asked him to pen a postmortem of his Marigold role or briefed him on "the Gronouski business and the way it was handled" (a failure perhaps due to uneasy consciences, he speculated decades later).[129] Still officially treating the matter as highly secret, Rapacki kept Lewandowski away from journalists, working anonymously at his desk job—until Loory came to town.

While making this exception, however, Rapacki put Lewandowski on a tight leash. Aside from biographical data, he told him, he could not volunteer information or respond to questions, only confirm or correct what Loory already knew (or claimed to know). "You are only free to [speak] if he says something that doesn't correspond to the truth. You can reject it, say, 'No, it's not true.'" For his protection against suspicion of unauthorized disclosures—Michałowski had told him that the MSZ had investigated charges that he had leaked information in Saigon—and to obviate the need to take notes, Lewandowski asked that the interview be "registered" (secretly recorded), and Rapacki agreed.[130]

On Wednesday, December 13, "a cold wintry morning with the small, dry northern European snow flakes flying"—exactly a year after the Hanoi raid that mortally wounded Marigold—Loory strolled down Aleje Ujazdowski to the Foreign Ministry. He noted the weather, traffic, atmospherics, Gestapo ghosts, and, after entering the reddish stone box, the scant security, architecture, and décor. This was his chance, he knew, to record the setting for the book's climactic scenes —and to take the measure of its mysterious protagonist.

At 11 a.m., a handler escorted him up a green-carpeted stairway and down a "more magnificent hallway" past Rapacki's handsome office ("oriental rug, . . . traditional Flemish tapestry"), and into Deputy Minister Naszkowski's modern one. As the minder backed off and closed the door, Loory saw a compact, well-dressed young man rise from a desk and motion him to a chair ("Danish modern covered with black leather") as he sat on a couch.

Happy to meet you, the American said. I feel as if I've known you for a long time.

I didn't realize I was so famous, Lewandowski replied. Would you like coffee?

Loory's first impression: "Poised, tough, and humorless, . . . the kind of man you always want on your side. He can do you great danger as an adversary."

As coffee arrived promptly, the Pole opened a pack of cigarettes, offered his guest one, and smoked only a few drags himself, leaving the impression that he had lit up for show. Loory captured his appearance and essence:

> He sits straight against the back of his chair with his right leg crossed over his left. If he changed that position at all during the 1½ hours, I was not aware of it. He is a small man, easily an inch and a half shorter than me, thin and well groomed. I wouldn't be surprised if he got himself a haircut for the occasion. His hands were lily white and his nails were clean and well trimmed. His black shoes were shined. His gray suit was without a wrinkle, his shirt was detergent bright, and his blue tie was done in a Windsor knot. His glasses are his most distinctive feature. They are large for a small face, and they have an odd kind of rectangular shape. The eyes are dark. The mouth is small. The smile, when it comes, is thin. Somehow I don't get the impression that Janusz Lewandowski allows himself the pleasure of a good belly laugh.[131]

Lewandowski struck Loory as the "perfect counterpart" for William Bundy—the intense, precise, erudite State Department fixture who managed a comparable portfolio and whom a colleague once described as "nervous, but also prudent, a banker's banker, a lawyer's lawyer, a bureaucrat's bureaucrat, . . . a tight-assed professional."[132]

At the outset, Lewandowski made clear that he considered the conversation a "distasteful" obligation compelled by the unfortunate actions of others who had leaked confidential information. He would not violate his pledge of secrecy, only comment on the facts the reporter already knew, "and not on all of these."

That said, he explained his general attitude toward the affair, and his philosophy toward peace efforts—conveying accurately his (and, Loory now knew, D'Orlandi's) "strong belief" that negotiations could only succeed if both sides understood beforehand the ultimate destination. He was harder to pin down on operational details. For example, he minimized his exchanges with Lodge and D'Orlandi (and falsely denied any three-way meetings) before mid-November, when he acknowledged their gatherings before he left for Hanoi. His drafting of the ten points was a mere "technical operation" to sum up the U.S. stand, even incorporating some of Lodge's language. When Loory pressed—had he told Lodge on returning from Hanoi that the DRV had confirmed the ten points as a "basis for negotiation"?—he became "really ruffled for the first time."

No, he insisted, this was not so: "Either you do not know what you are talking about and are trying to get me to say something or you have been given wrong information. Now tell me everything you know about this point." Loory denied holding anything back, and Lewandowski offered a more measured explanation. "You cannot expect to have a plan for peace in Vietnam worked out in two meetings," he said. "If you know that a bridge can be built between the two parties, you can start something."

Loory's persistence, particularly on the ten points, made Lewandowski uneasy—and his suspicions spiked when the subject of money arose. He recalled rebuffing Loory's invitation to write a personal account of Marigold for the *Los Angeles Times,* for the then-lavish fee of several thousand dollars, and Rapacki joking afterward that the MSZ could have used the money in its budget.[133] Told this, Loory indignantly denied that he ever broached the topic of money.[134] It was likely a misunderstanding—the reporter, frustrated by the Pole's reticence, suggesting he pen a more candid piece for the paper, for which he would of course be compensated, and Lewandowski, already wary, construing this as a bribe.

As the clock ticked past noon, Lewandowski began to fidget. Loory got in some final queries.

"Can you say categorically that the American bombing attacks spoiled the initiative?"

"Yes," he shot back emphatically. And after a pause, on his own, he added "and it was done on purpose."

Why? Due to "a change in the American position on talks" between mid-November and early December. Asked if he had warned Lodge against attacks on Hanoi, Lewandowski initially refused comment—then said that he would not deny such a statement if the reporters printed it, and elaborated that Loory "will not be wrong in writing [Lodge] was warned" before the December 2 raid. "The American government had no doubt about the effect bombing would have on the whole process. I can assure you of that."

At 12:30 p.m., ignoring a ringing phone, Lewandowski stood up, and the talk ended.

Afterward, the Pole sensed Loory's disappointment that he had not said more; he and Rapacki, too, were chagrined when they discovered that their bugging gear ("magnetophone") had malfunctioned.[135] Lewandowski was less impressed than Gronouski or D'Orlandi with the reporter's grasp of Marigold, and thus he told associates that his knowledge went no further than prior accounts. Warsaw cabled Michałowski that he had revealed "some serious gaps" in awareness of "the most important issues," and Lewandowski did not fill them. Instead, as instructed, he had confined himself to "debunking" errors of fact or interpretation derived from other sources, and Gronouski seemed satisfied by the Poles' limited cooperation.[136]

✳ ✳ ✳

On his way home, Loory backtracked through Rome, where he bounced some of Lewandowski's comments off D'Orlandi—who was puzzled that the Pole would imply that no Marigold meetings had been held until November, but who confirmed his claim that he had warned Lodge against bombing escalation before the December 2 and 4 Hanoi raids. But the Italian remained cagey, refusing to say if he agreed that the attacks spoiled the effort or to reveal the ten points. Inventing a convenient pretext to evade further inquiries, he said that his notes were "locked up in Suez"—on a ship stranded when war erupted in June—"and cannot be freed until the canal opens." Maybe then he could help more, at least on dates.[137]

The reporter also used his Rome stop to track down Aubrac, Kissinger's other French contact; his "face went white when I confronted him," and he was cordial but wary, like Marcovich.[138] Loory then flew home, hoping to start writing in a month or so.

Winter of Discontent: "Operation Poppycock"?

In Washington, classified cables, letters, and memorandums on the reporters' European exploits piled up, adding to officials' fears that they faced a leak of potentially devastating proportions—perhaps damaging secret Vietnam diplomacy, but definitely hurting administration credibility. "I've been hearing about you from Ottawa, London, Paris, who knows where else," Read told Kraslow, rejecting a "leisurely interview" because he foresaw "nothing but trouble ahead" from their inquest.[139] "I had an amusing time with them because they pestered my secretary for weeks on end to see me," he recalled later. "And finally I got on the phone with one of them and said, 'I know all about what you're doing and I haven't any desire to see you, and won't see you until after your book is written so I can have a completely free hand at torpedoing it.'"[140] A call to Rostow found him fuming. "I know what you're doing," he snapped. "Everybody and his brother knows what you're doing. You remind me of Laurel and Hardy trying to play sleuths." Asked if officials referred to the *Los Angeles Times* project as "Operation Poppycock," Rostow denied that it had a classified moniker and accused the reporters of contravening the "public interest," harassing devoted public servants "going up every alley" in search of peace.[141]

Undaunted, Kraslow and Loory redoubled their efforts, but they often found sources—even some who had seen them before—clamming up, as word of their aggressive tactics circulated and the White House circled the wagons. Isham "brood[ed]" about seeing Kraslow again in view of signs that he was acting as "sort of a prosecuting attorney" with "preconceived ideas."[142] "I have no time for you," Habib said.[143] Contacts grew tenser. Cooper informed Rusk that Kraslow, phoning him at home one Saturday afternoon,

> expressed a great deal of urgency and, indeed, shrillness, in his request to see me. He talked about having uncovered a great deal of material which "troubled" him and which he felt needed straightening out. He mentioned "hatchet jobs" being performed, and implied that my neck was one of those being severed. He said when he analyzed the people who were being "hatched," it seemed "to fit a pattern."

When Cooper confessed "deep reservations" about agreeing to another talk, the reporter shot back: Why not, if he had nothing to conceal? "I didn't think there was a question of having anything to hide, in the sense Kraslow was implying," he replied, "but there were certain aspects of the whole negotiation picture that I thought should remain secret or, in any case, should be left to historians rather than reporters."[144] Kissinger also put off Kraslow. Asked how he would feel if the reporters "surfaced" the link with "your friend in Paris and your friend in Rome," he warned that it would hurt the national interest. "I thought you were just looking into the Warsaw matter," he protested.[145]

As legends of their Perry Mason–like cross-examinations spread, some mid-level officials quivered. Anthony Lake feared a kind of Spanish Inquisition when Kraslow and Loory visited, and he exhaled with relief when they refrained from Torquemada tactics. "The conversation was quite friendly, contrary to my expectations," he reported. "I think they decided fairly quickly not to fry such a small fish."[146]

In late December, Kraslow's interview request reached Rusk, the reporters' top potential victim aside from LBJ. The secretary of state had read the classified accounts of their European travels, including Dean's indignant report that Kraslow mentioned a "feeling" that he and Johnson were "misleading the public on Vietnam." Buzzing his deputy for advice, Rusk was inclined not to see the *Los Angeles Times* pair. Katzenbach agreed, and Rusk resolved to "stay out of it."[147] Read likewise "steered him away from them."[148]

Though averse to a grilling himself, Rusk was still eager to influence Kraslow and Loory's inquest, so he deputized his closest Vietnam aide to talk with them—the man he trusted most to articulate his own thinking on the war and spin the tangled negotiations stories, revealing just enough and no more. On the second day of 1968, Bundy welcomed the pair to his office, "a corner suite with [the] usual array of LBJ pictures on the wall and . . . a little etching of JFK in a sterling silver frame on an end table" cluttered with classified files. Still made up from a TV appearance, in a "dark blue shirt—perhaps custom made—under gray checked suit," the "tall, lean and youthful looking" bureaucrat seemed friendly yet edgy: "He smiles easily but talks tightly."[149]

Predictably, Bundy blamed DRV intransigence for ruining all the peace efforts. He "denigrate[d] all intermediaries" other than the Soviets and British but reserved special disdain for the Poles—who were "shell game artists" and "bad reporters and diplomats" promoting "the other side," not peace. He turned up his nose at the ten points (they "would not win a Metternich prize"), insinuating, falsely, that Lewandowski had composed them without first hearing Lodge's formal presentation of the U.S. stand. And he pushed his and Rusk's pet theory that Rapacki's "bizarre" performance reflected a lack of authority from Hanoi.

Not surprisingly, LBJ also refused to see Kraslow and Loory—and, like Rusk, let a surrogate talk for him. Rostow had tracked their activities with mounting dismay, and at a meeting in the White House basement in early January, he shrilly expressed his (and likely his boss's) ire. "What you guys are doing is worse than the *Chicago Tribune* writing a story that we had broken the Japanese code!" the "very flushed" national security adviser yelled. "It's as bad as giving away war secrets. . . . Never have I seen the efforts of two experienced reporters misdirected in [such] an unproductive and dangerous way."

"He accused us of treason," Kraslow recalled.

Despite rebuffing the reporters' appeal for help in checking their accuracy and "launching instead into a violent anti-Loory-Kraslow diatribe," Rostow believed that his persuasive powers might steer them onto a more patriotic course. If they wanted "to help their country," they could expose Hanoi's propaganda campaign to press Washington into a unilateral bombing halt, "the biggest PSI [psychological] war I've ever seen the Communists conduct." He refused to go into Marigold's details, repeating the catchphrase (which he attributed to JFK) that "there has been a lot of talk on the staircase but still no one has come into the room," and warning them "not to believe everything [the Poles] say."[150]

Not all their sources were so hostile. Ex-officials turned antiwar critics Richard Goodwin and James C. Thomson Jr. freely discussed personalities and events, such as the Stevenson-Thant affair.[151] Burma's UN ambassador offered background on U.S.-DRV contacts in Rangoon.[152] In late December, Katzenbach elaborated on Marigold and other initiatives.[153] In early January, in what Loory recalled as a eureka moment, he located Thant (visiting a granddaughter), who, after being first taken aback ("how did you get my number?"), agreed to receive the reporters in his office. The UN chief, whom Loory found "charming" and "delightful," furnished his side of the Stevenson brouhaha.[154] Hightower told the story behind his story, and he seemed "fascinated" by what his rivals had learned.[155]

Their research largely done, the reporters began churning out their manuscript. In January, Kraslow returned to the *Los Angeles Times* news desk, leaving Loory to type away at his house in the Chevy Chase neighborhood of Northwest Washington, trying to cram 150,000 words of typed interview notes, plus "a file drawer" of research materials, into a dramatic narrative. In the next few months, he would draft fifteen chapters, posting them piecemeal to Random House editor Bob Loomis in New York and handing chunks to his coauthor for hole poking. "Each time I finished one, Kraslow would stop by, take it home to read and then come back with comments and questions—always those nagging questions."[156]

✳ ✳ ✳

In the winter of 1967–68, Bundy started but failed to finish the draft white paper on futile peace overtures that Rusk had assigned him in November. He dictated a quarter of it or so—noting that Marigold "raised serious questions about Hanoi's actual willingness to talk in a serious way without demanding unreciprocated preconditions affecting military operations" and that it "was never entirely clear then or afterward how firm a mandate the Poles actually had from Hanoi to arrange a meeting"—but repeatedly got distracted. First came an LBJ trip to Asia ("my Christmas vacation was knocked to bits"); then a Trinh statement just before New Year's seemed to open up the prospect of imminent talks with Hanoi. At a Mongolian Embassy party on December 29, the DRV foreign minister altered "could" to "would" in describing North Vietnam's stand on entering into talks if Washington halted the bombing—prompting an intense U.S. effort, via Romania, to discern his statement's significance. The stepped-up diplomatic activity and ongoing fighting meant that Bundy had to focus on more pressing Vietnam business, as did the two aides helping him on the project, Isham and Daniel I. Davidson, who had replaced Cooper as Harriman's chief Vietnam aide.[157] (Davidson drafted a brief summary of peace bids, the kernel of a possible white paper, for his boss. Before sharing it with LBJ, Harriman hardened its already wary view of Marigold, altering Davidson's formulation that "it is not at all clear to us" that North Vietnamese ever intended to show up in December 1966 to the flat claim that, contrary to Polish assurances, "in retrospect, it seems evident that they never intended to do so short of further United States concessions to be made in Warsaw well beyond what the United States originally understood to be the terms of a meeting."[158])

As Bundy's chronicle remained an "unfinished edifice," the administration sought a different means to rebut charges its peace diplomacy was lacking—and to steal Kraslow and Loory's thunder. For this purpose, an ideal ringer waited in the wings: Radványi. Since his defection the previous spring, the Hungarian ex-diplomat had stayed under wraps, hoping to embark on an academic career in his new homeland. With quiet State Department support, he obtained a two-year scholarship at Stanford to write a study on Communist decisionmaking, but U.S. officials encouraged him to unveil his basic argument—that Eastern European peace efforts in Vietnam were fraudulent—in a splashier, less scholarly fashion. As officials hoped, he distilled the information and views he had revealed in private debriefings (and a lengthy secret manuscript) into a dramatic exposé that highlighted Hanoi's obstinacy and the Hungarian foreign minister's deception. "I commend it for your bedtime reading, and perhaps you would find that [your wife] Elspeth had an outsider's view," Rusk wrote Rostow in circulating a mid-December draft. "To me it reads like a detective story, and all to the good. Let's see what you think."[159]

To the administration's delight, in February *Life* magazine—like *Time* a hawkish flagship of Henry Luce's publishing empire—not only accepted Radványi's piece but also paired it with a detailed exegesis of prior U.S. bids for peace in

Vietnam. *Life's* decision to prepare a "lead article" on the past history of negotiating initiatives, Bundy told Rusk, was a "golden opportunity to get before the public, in responsible and detached hands, the extent of the effort we have made and the total lack of response from Hanoi at any point." A *Life* article "might have all the advantages and none of the disadvantages" of putting out a white paper—liable to offend foreign governments or spook Hanoi, and impossible to deny—of the sort Bundy had worked on but "shelved" after Trinh's statement. "Secondarily, but far from inconsequential, an advantage is that it may to some degree preempt the job being done by Kraslow and Loory."

Bundy was also pleased with *Life's* choice to write the piece: Frank McCulloch, "an old Asian and Vietnam hand of unusual reliability and acumen." The balding ex-Marine, who covered the war for *Time* after Luce lured him back from the *Los Angeles Times* in 1963, had recently returned from Saigon to take over the magazine's Washington bureau. With Rusk's OK, and "enthusiastic" White House backing from Rostow and Christian, Bundy fed McCulloch background, both public materials "and filling in gaps necessary for clear understanding, but of course without blowing any channels or specific episodes, [other than those] known at least to Kraslow and Loory."[160] Beating the *Los Angeles Times* duo to the punch, just as officials hoped, the *Life* package on futile Vietnam diplomacy, bearing a pronounced proadministration tilt, hit newsstands in mid-March.[161]

✳ ✳ ✳

By then, Vietnam's turmoil had engulfed Washington. In early January, when he had tried to entice Kraslow and Loory to write about the DRV's strategy, Rostow specifically said that "captured documents" prove "they are tooling up for one more big push" on the battlefield "to show the American people they are winning," akin to how the Viet Minh jolted the French at Dien Bien Phu.[162]

But accurate strategic intelligence in U.S. hands did not preclude the Vietnamese Communists from achieving a tactical surprise—and on January 30 and 31, 1968, the Lunar New Year, they did exactly that. In a long-planned offensive, they staged audacious attacks throughout South Vietnam, most dramatically in Saigon itself, where commandos penetrated the U.S. Embassy compound before being repelled. Intense battles raged for weeks in major cities, especially Hue, inflicting a grievous toll on both sides; civilians suffered even more. Historians would argue about the Tet Offensive's military impact, and some, both U.S. and Vietnamese, judged it in that sense a Communist failure. Throwing vast resources into the gamble, Hanoi hoped that the coordinated strikes would spark a national revolt that would oust the Thieu-Ky regime. Not only did that not happen, but the fighting also eviscerated southern Communist forces (leaving the bulk of later fighting to PAVN regulars).

Yet the assaults inflicted a mortal political wound to the credibility of the Johnson administration, which for months had told Americans that the war was being won, and they thus undermined LBJ's bid for reelection. Even if the bold offensive did not yield a rapid triumph, Hanoi calculated that it would cripple Washington's will to continue the fight and force it to the negotiating table at a disadvantageous moment. To a considerable extent it did—dealing a decisive blow on the U.S., if not Vietnamese, battlefield. Abandoning visions of total victory, America's political mainstream began seeking an exit strategy, and fractures in the political establishment multiplied. Walter Cronkite left his CBS anchorman's desk to go to Vietnam and returned declaring the war unwinnable; the long-shot antiwar presidential candidate Eugene McCarthy nearly defeated LBJ in the New Hampshire Democratic primary on March 12, prompting RFK to end his hand-wringing and finally enter the race; reversing earlier advice, the "Wise Men," the gang of ex-officials on whom LBJ had relied for bipartisan support, in late March urged a bombing halt, negotiations, and troop withdrawals; and the administration engaged in a ferocious internal fracas over whether to respond to the Tet Offensive with a new buildup of ground forces: Westmoreland requested another 206,000 troops, but key figures, including McNamara's replacement, Clark Clifford, instead counseled LBJ to scale back the war and make a new push for peace.

Normally, Loory would have been at full throttle covering the upheaval in the White House and the country. That was where he wanted to be. Instead, he was typing away on the manuscript on failed peace bids, hoping that it would sway the national debate yet eager to return to the trenches. "It was not a good time," he recalled, "to be stuck home in one's attic writing history while the world seemed to be crashing down outside the window."[163]

16

Sequels, Revivals, Regrets
Marigold's Echoes during LBJ's Last Year, February 1968–January 1969

To have gotten so close to peace and now abandon all hope is something to which Fanfani cannot reconcile himself.

> —*Giovanni D'Orlandi to a North Vietnamese diplomat, Prague,*
> *August 1967*

But the Poles are crooks.

> —*Dean Rusk to Averell Harriman, late December 1967*

I have no regrets. Except for one thing—that in 1966 we did not take advantage of the opportunities and your role as go-between.

> —*Rusk to Polish ambassador Jerzy Michałowski, January 1969*
> *(according to the latter)*

The surge in Vietnam violence did not stop diplomacy—quite the contrary. Even during Tet's fierce fighting, the enemies intensified indirect soundings on starting negotiations. Since the Pennsylvania peace initiative's collapse, by October 1967, Washington had mainly turned to Bucharest to probe Hanoi, seeking a commitment to prompt, productive talks and no military advantage (i.e., the San Antonio formula announced by LBJ in late September 1967, publicizing Pennsylvania's secret terms). But by mid-January 1968, the Bucharest channel had also run dry. When Tet exploded, U.S. officials concluded that the DRV had thumbed its nose at their recent restraint (no raids on Hanoi or Haiphong) and had chosen to fight, not talk.

Yet a few days later, word arrived that the enemy had opened a new, if still indirect, link: a Marigold spin-off starring the lead Italian cast members of the original production. On Saturday morning, February 3—amid carnage in Saigon, Hue, and other South Vietnamese cities, along with fears of an imminent storming of the besieged U.S. base at Khe Sanh—Rome's envoy in Washington handed Rusk a message from Fanfani stating that a "qualified Hanoi representative" had requested an "urgent meeting." The foreign minister, backed by President Aldo Moro, felt this was an offer they could not refuse. What did the Americans want him to tell his guest?[1]

Rusk was skeptical. Hanoi already knew Washington's views, he told Egidio Ortona bitterly, and unleashing Tet hardly implied a desire to negotiate: "We are not fools; we can read signs and signals." Fanfani was welcome to see the DRV's representative, but the Americans had "nothing to say. We are 'all ears and no tongue.'"[2]

Fanfani's terse note neglected to mention that this ostensibly out-of-the-blue overture had actually sprouted from delicate, secret Italian-DRV contacts dating back to the previous summer and centrally involving his old Marigold sidekick, D'Orlandi. Since returning from Saigon in March 1967, despite worsening health, he had remained deeply engaged in Italy's diplomacy toward the war (despite his formal title as the Farnesina's inspector general). That summer, he had revisited Saigon for several weeks on a quiet mission to prod Ky and Thieu to switch positions on the upcoming presidential ballot; he went in response to an "urgent personal request" from Foreign Minister Tran Van Do, who thought the strutting air marshal's election would be disastrous.[3] D'Orlandi, who agreed, claimed a part in the intrigues that led Ky and Thieu to trade slots. Having flown back to Rome in early July, he briefed Fanfani and declared "Mission accomplished." Then, after they had shaken hands and D'Orlandi was heading for the door, he asked cheekily what his next task would be.

Fanfani, "with his unmistakable half-joking look," responded: "Would you go to Prague to make direct contact with the North Vietnamese?"

"Without delay, Mr. Prime Minister!" a "startled" D'Orlandi replied jocularly (using his patron's old title)—not sure how seriously to take him.

"Good, then go get some rest now and we will speak about it again later."[4]

After catching up on sleep, D'Orlandi again saw his boss to review the situation. Given the United States' suspicion and disdain toward the "suspect" Poles and Lewandowski ("just 'one of many candidates for the Nobel Peace Prize,'" with "no serious contact" in the DRV government), they concluded that any new mediation bid should be solely via the Italians.[5] D'Orlandi saw huge difficulties, but agreed with Fanfani that "having advanced so far in his peace attempt [in Marigold], it would be unjustifiable for our consciences not to try again."[6]

To replace Rapacki, Fanfani had a new middleman: Carlo Alberto Galluzzi, the senior Italian Communist who, like the Poles, could relate fraternally to his Vietnamese comrades. Fanfani had dealt with him in connection with the December 1966 trip to Hanoi by a Partito Comunista Italiano (PCI) delegation, of which Galluzzi had been a member; despite the failure of Galluzzi's abortive attempt in January 1967 to broker a contact between Fanfani and a North Vietnamese representative, the foreign minister still hoped the PCI could set up direct Italian-DRV talks. A conversation in early June 1967 rekindled those hopes; Galluzzi told Fanfani that he had just returned from Prague, where he had met with the DRV ambassador about the possibility of setting up a new point of contacts between the Italian and North Vietnamese governments.[7] From his contacts with DRV representatives in Europe, Galluzzi ascertained that Hanoi would receive an Italian emissary at its embassy in Moscow or Prague; Fanfani chose the latter for convenience and because the envoy there was said to rank higher.[8] Acutely aware that Washington trusted the PCI no more than it did Poland, he would assiduously shroud his collusion with the party.

At the end of July, D'Orlandi finally met Fanfani's "mysterious" collaborator. As the two put "cards on the table," he found Galluzzi simpatico—with "a nice open manner," about his own age, equally committed to peace and to secrecy, agreeing that any leaks would be "deadly." After a few long talks, D'Orlandi sensed "reciprocal trust, esteem, and warmth" and felt confident, despite periodic PCI sniping at Fanfani, that his new partner was "too honest" to "exploit this attempt of ours for party purposes."[9]

For the first time since Marigold, the ex-ambassador felt renewed hope that he might help end the war he hated. "D'Orlandi was as enthused as if on his first assignment," Galluzzi recalled.[10] After Galluzzi said that the North Vietnamese had opted to work with Italy because they admired its handling of the Lewandowski contacts, D'Orlandi was "beside myself with emotion," and Fanfani, too, was "very happy but hardly shows it," because what counted was the new undertaking.[11]

Logistical and procedural snags delayed the first meeting in Prague until later in the summer, leaving D'Orlandi edgy with anticipation during a stay in the medieval mountain village of Rocca di Mezzo east of Rome. After hearing on August 16 from a Farnesina operator that the "fateful appointment" was set for eight days hence, he fretted to his diary at how slowly time was passing.[12]

As with the aborted bid to rendezvous with Michałowski a year before, the tryst with a DRV diplomat offered an excuse for spy-novel trappings. At the Prague airport, which he would reach on an Alitalia plane via Milan, D'Orlandi was to hold an *Il Messaggero* (a centrist daily) in his right hand and find a man gripping a *Settimana enigmistica* (a weekly compendium of brainteasers) in his left; after "a few words with the crossword puzzle solver just to see him clearly in the face," he would learn more about his date. "And to think that I go to see James Bond at the movies for 1,600 lire!" he mused.[13]

The day before he left for Prague, D'Orlandi heard Fanfani explain his approach. The overriding priority was secrecy: "No one at the ministry must suspect anything," nor would he tell the rest of the government or the embassy in Prague; Galluzzi had pledged silence to the Czech authorities. For the "dreadful eventuality" of his trip being leaked, D'Orlandi devised a flimsy cover story: He had gone to confer with DRV diplomats about visas for a "rather large labor union delegation" to visit Italy. Washington, too, would be "kept in the dark" until the exchanges elicited a "minimum response." Ideally, word from Prague would reach Rome before Fanfani left for New York on September 11 to attend the annual session of the United Nations General Assembly, so he could decide whether to reveal the contact to Rusk "or wait for it to continue gaining strength and look out upon a more welcoming environment."[14]

After a sleepless night, the next afternoon D'Orlandi flew to Prague, where the elaborate arrangements went off without a hitch. Clutching his assigned newspaper—"a bit wrinkled because of my frequent handling"—he quickly spotted in the crowd beyond passport control "a young, elegant man with an intelligent expression" holding the correct magazine in his left hand. Their eyes met. A few minutes later, as he looked for a taxi, D'Orlandi was approached and told quickly to be exactly 100 meters to the left of his hotel, the Alcron, at 7 p.m. Too nervous to read, the Italian killed the hours by bathing in his stately hotel ("very Central European, very comfortable, but from a half a century ago"), ordering tea ("also very Central European"), and ambling to the Charles Bridge, "with its imposing statues over the magnificent green color of the Vltava [River] with a few couples in romantic little boats [and] the riot of baroque on the other side."

At 7 p.m. sharp, a car pulled up to D'Orlandi as he loitered on the sidewalk and window-shopped. He got in, and "Bianchi" instructed him to be 50 meters away at 9 the next morning. D'Orlandi then resumed playing the innocuous tourist. He took "a long walk trying to read the film titles and price lists of the restaurants and beer halls," ate a late supper at the Alcron, and before retiring strolled nearby streets, "where the prostitutes have a touching petit bourgeois respectability, in addition to the blessing of the assembled authorities. And what about tomorrow?"[15]

Promptly at 9 the next morning—August 25—"Bianchi" and a driver retrieved D'Orlandi outside the Alcron. Taking a convoluted route though residential areas ("we slowly prowl around the houses with their tree-covered gardens"), they "discreetly scan[ned] the cars around us with a professional eye." Finally, convinced they were not being tailed, they deposited their charge at the DRV Embassy. Ambassador Phan Van Su was waiting in the foyer. After he ushered his guest inside, an aide brought "a tray with coffee, tea, beer, vodka, appetizers, water, etc., after which he disappears."

Su knew how to break the ice: Flattering D'Orlandi, he said with a smile that Hanoi, having closely watched the Lewandowski affair, "very much appreciated my work in Saigon in the tripartite attempt, and he recognizes my perfect good faith and my keen desire to bring an end to the horrendous slaughter." Despite deep skepticism induced by U.S. actions, he went on, Hanoi could not ignore Fanfani's wish for a dialogue "to pick up the threads of the possible attempt." Yet, he was purely in a listening mode, authorized only to report, and could not even express a personal opinion.

D'Orlandi stressed Rome's commitment to secrecy, noting his cover story. Substantively, he implied that he and Fanfani envisioned a sort of Marigold redux. His minister, beyond a desire to promote a "peaceful, reasonable, and acceptable solution" in Vietnam, was driven by the "nagging thought of not having succeeded in the tripartite attempt, . . . which brought us very close to the hoped-for conclusion" and produced "great and concrete possibilities." "To have gotten so close to peace and now abandon all hope is something to which Fanfani cannot reconcile himself," he said.

Italy did not seek to debate that failure's causes—for example, too quickly moving talks from Saigon to Warsaw—but Fanfani wished to know if Hanoi still considered the ten points "valid." If so, he could sound out Washington with the goal of confirming both parties' readiness to negotiate on this basis, before initiating formal talks to ratify the solution. According to Fanfani's calculus, D'Orlandi reaffirmed the probe's "indispensable condition"—total secrecy (pointedly recalling that key Marigold leaks sprang from Poles and Americans, not Italians). The prior experience could be exploited, he added, to avoid repeating errors and profit from the expositions of opposing viewpoints. D'Orlandi specifically asked for a date certain by which Hanoi would enter talks in reply to a bombing halt, noting that Fanfani would be in an ideal position to press Washington to accept such a timetable.

The DRV diplomat listened closely and took careful notes, but all he could do was promise to refer the Italian's views and questions back to Hanoi.[16]

Personally, D'Orlandi liked Su, a Southerner who mixed "extreme courtesy" with "a very human affability." After their substantive exchanges, the Vietnamese asked about people and places he recalled from Saigon ("not without a spot of nostalgia"), eliciting extended reminiscences from the Italian, who had to hold back his own "unforgettable memories." By their talk's end, D'Orlandi judged Su a sincere "dove" who sympathized with what he and Fanfani were trying to do. Su promised to relay Hanoi's response as soon as it arrived, if possible in time for Fanfani's impending journey.

D'Orlandi was exultant. He had opened a direct channel to North Vietnam and had established, he thought, a friendly rapport. In an expansive mood, he bought lunch for "Bianchi" (who considerately refrained from asking about the meeting) at a restaurant with a "breathtaking view," spent the afternoon soaking in the castles and the old town, and in the evening savored "a comfortable dinner and a magnificent Havana cigar" (beyond the U.S. embargo's reach, the Cubans sold "at very reasonable prices").[17]

Back in Rome, D'Orlandi rushed to see Fanfani and enthusiastically described the encounter; Galluzzi also seemed "very satisfied," evidently reflecting his Vietnamese comrades' view.[18] But the Italians' excitement hardly guaranteed results— and their concern rose as days, and then weeks, passed with no further word from Su. When Fanfani went to the United States in mid-September, he thus had little to report beyond a cordial, inconclusive chat against a backdrop of intensified fighting. He spoke with LBJ in Washington during a summit with Italian president Giuseppe Saragat, but the American had insisted that contacts with Hanoi were ongoing (a clear allusion to the not-yet-dead Pennsylvania channel), and that the United States hence had "no need of other intermediaries." Yet Johnson had seemed at a loss, Fanfani recorded: "Hanoi however does not give in, so that J. doesn't know what to do. He cannot withdraw, cannot conclude, and cannot negotiate either."[19] Given no encouragement, Fanfani stayed mum on the Prague channel when he then met Rusk (whom he found "evasive if not cold," he later told D'Orlandi) in New York.[20]

While Fanfani accompanied Saragat to Australia before returning to Rome in early October, D'Orlandi received dismaying news from Galluzzi: Hanoi had instructed Su to drop the Fanfani initiative, apparently in response to a step-up in American air attacks. "Will these damn bombings ever stop?" the frustrated Italian diplomat wondered.[21]

This did not mean, however, that the Italians had given up. In mid-October, D'Orlandi even offered to return to Saigon "to promote the start of a negotiation"—it is not clear how—but Rusk politely declined the offer.[22] Fanfani refused to take no for an answer from Hanoi, so through Galluzzi and the PCI (which agreed to relay an urgent, official interparty démarche to the VWP), he pressed Su in late October for "an unsolicited follow-up" meeting with D'Orlandi to communicate the "very important" results of his contacts with the Americans.[23] Finally, to the Italians' joy—D'Orlandi had "never seen [Fanfani] so radiant" and "even Galluzzi" was out of his skin with happiness[24]—Su consented to receive D'Orlandi again.

Accordingly, the two met again in Prague on the evening of November 6, after parades marking the Bolshevik Revolution's fiftieth anniversary—the same day Le Duan relayed a more authoritative DRV stand to Gomułka in Moscow. The Italian found the DRV ambassador "particularly cordial and very affable," perhaps, he surmised, to compensate for Hanoi's earlier stern message, which Su attributed to "the escalation of indiscriminate [and] always more deadly [U.S.] bombardments," which precluded even secret peace exchanges. Arguing that North Vietnam had nothing to lose from hearing privately conveyed proposals, D'Orlandi sought something more explicit than a general pledge to negotiate in reply to a bombing halt, and he again pitched the Marigold-like idea of hammering out an accord's outline before formal talks began. Going out on a long limb—for it is unlikely that Fanfani received any such assurance from Rusk or Johnson—he claimed that Washington would "consider suspending the bombings" if assured, through Fanfani, that on a "fixed" date soon thereafter Hanoi would enter secret negotiations. To his frustration, however, Su decried the United States' "bad faith" yet offered nothing, saying that he still lacked hard instructions; he vowed to travel home to get them; he also denied LBJ's claim to Fanfani that U.S.-

DRV contacts were ongoing (of course, the Pennsylvania channel had expired in the interim).[25]

Given its paltry results, Fanfani also did not tell Washington of this session; nor of course did D'Orlandi breathe a word of the channel to Loory in December. But on January 19 came news of a sudden breakthrough: a "radiant," smiling Galluzzi told D'Orlandi that Su would receive him in Prague and was even ready, in principle, to come to Rome to confer with Fanfani. After making hasty arrangements, the excited D'Orlandi visited Su in the Czechoslovak capital four days later. The affable DRV diplomat declined to accompany his guest back to Rome, saying that he had to check with Hanoi before fixing a precise date, yet confirmed that the impending visit (tentatively set for February 4–6) would not simply be "an end in itself" but a concrete bid to achieve progress toward a bombing halt and peace talks with the Americans. After the intense evening meeting with Su (and a late dinner with his faithful driver and escort), D'Orlandi was "deadly tired but intensely happy" as he went to sleep. "During the long years in prison in India I waited impatiently for the night with dreams as an escape," he reflected. "Today, I can't wait to wake up tomorrow and find myself again in Rome."[26]

A week later, Tet exploded. Su's unusual plea to see Italy's foreign minister—after a recent trip to Hanoi—was likely not a coincidence but an effort to meld military and political offensives. As George Herring speculated, the DRV probably timed the overture "to exploit the anticipated political backlash in the United States and to open negotiations under favorable military conditions."[27]

Before their North Vietnamese guests arrived, D'Orlandi and Fanfani huddled to plot strategy for the secret visit—logistics, bargaining strategy, preventing a premature ("fatal") leak, and the delicate question of informing the Americans. Rejecting the option of immediately relating the whole story to their perhaps dubious allies, Fanfani opted to wait until he had something firmer in hand. "Better to know what will result from the Roman conversations and then hook Washington with concrete points and no longer with only desires or burning hopes," D'Orlandi summarized their calculus. Having already been "scalded" by Washington during peace overtures—"Fanfani two times [La Pira and Marigold], myself once"—the Italians did not want to get burned again.[28]

To whet Washington's appetite, however, Fanfani now deemed it appropriate to tell Rusk about the impending meeting with Hanoi's representatives. On receiving the American's lukewarm approval, he gave final clearance to Su's visit.[29] The day before he landed, the two Italians spent hours going over the "score" they would use in their conversations. Late Sunday afternoon, February 4, D'Orlandi—after a sleepless night and prayers of thanks at morning Mass—greeted the DRV envoy and an aide at Fiumicino Airport, escorted them past puzzled customs and security officers, and drove them to town. As a hospitable gesture that also enhanced operational security, he vacated his comfortable apartment in Rome's central Avventino district, leaving a governess behind to help the guests but sending Colette to Capri for the weekend. That night, after checking in with Galluzzi and the PCI, Su met Fanfani for a get-acquainted meal and conversation (in French), at which the foreign minister ingratiatingly "showed friendly comprehension of the sufferings and the legitimate aspirations of the Vietnamese people." When the Italians rose to leave shortly before midnight, they felt buoyed. "The ice has melted more than expected," D'Orlandi recorded before taking a sleeping pill to prepare for a day that he hoped might be a capstone to his career.[30]

Monday dawned "nice and sunny." Breakfasting with D'Orlandi, the Vietnamese praised the climate, which was so much milder than Prague's. Then their host drove them past tourist sights (the Colosseum, Foro Romano, Saint Peter's, etc.) to the Farnesina, where they used a concealed rear entrance. Fanfani showed them to his private study, and they got down to business. Su stressed the DRV's readiness for "serious conversations" with U.S. officials in reply to an unconditional bombing halt—yet he refused to clarify a point critical to Washington: how soon thereafter Hanoi would talk. "What kind of delay have you in mind?" Fanfani asked; "18, 2, 3, 4, or how many days after the cessation of bombing?" Vaguely, Su insisted that his country first had "to be sure" that the raids had really ended, but he pledged to consult Hanoi so he could "establish the date" when they next met; for now, Fanfani could assure Rusk that Hanoi had already decided to sit down "X" days after the bombing stopped.[31]

Marigold's ghost hovered over the talks; the Italians still believed that the fall 1966 formula might undergird a peace pact. Yet when Fanfani interjected allusions to the "ten points" or "tripartite agreement of Saigon"—"dragged in from deep left field," snorted a U.S. aide when he saw the Italian record[32]—Su reacted tepidly: "The ten points have been perhaps bypassed by events. We can refer to them in broad outline." When Fanfani cited Phase A/B, "a device adopted during the tripartite Saigon conversations to overcome the obstacle of reciprocity," Su warned that he was "not authorized today to discuss the tripartite contacts of Saigon, nor can I express an opinion on the present validity of the ten points. I shall not fail, nevertheless, to submit the questions to my government."[33]

To further lure Washington, Su said that Hanoi accepted South Vietnam's continued separate existence (pending voluntary unification), but Fanfani and D'Orlandi sensed that his remark was too ambiguous to elicit a positive U.S. response, let alone a bombing halt.

In the afternoon, the Italians took their guests to the coast. In the private room of a restaurant near the port of Civitavecchia, they enjoyed fresh fish and a panoramic view of the Mediterranean: "A nice warm sun and a vivid sea of intense colors." Seeing the ocean "visibly moved" Su after years in his landlocked post, D'Orlandi thought. The group had a "very relaxed and pleasant conversation" before returning to Rome, yet D'Orlandi felt that the visit was not going so well. Driving the Vietnamese back to the Farnesina after a siesta at his residence, he pleaded for more flexibility. "In the car, I did not fail to point out to Ambassador Su that in my modest opinion, we did not conclude much in the morning and that perhaps it was necessary to venture more in the direction of peace. It seemed to me, I told them, that in Prague they showed themselves to be more explicitly favorable to our attempt."[34] But that evening, over tea, Su stood firm: Hanoi had given enough, and "we are not here on our knees imploring for contacts or for negotiations."[35]

Afterward, Fanfani cabled Rusk about the visit of a figure he described only as a "qualified Hanoi representative." Putting the best face on the "calm" yet "intense" talks, he stressed Su's readiness to accept "peace in liberty" for South Vietnam, with Vietnam as a whole to stay divided until a "freely chosen" Saigon government negotiated the terms of future unification. But the bottom line remained blurry and inauspicious: Hanoi would enter into "a serious negotiation" an unspecified number of days after Washington had ceased air attacks, but it rejected any "reciprocity" (e.g., the San Antonio formula's no-advantage provision).[36]

Anticipating further word from Washington and Hanoi, Su had indicated that he was ready for further conversations, and the Italians expected a rapid response from Rusk so they could set up another meeting. But for a week, Fanfani heard nothing, and he grew increasingly impatient. Finally—at least according to one secondhand yet contemporary Polish source—he resorted to a devious tactic (though one hardly unknown to his Marigold counterparts) to grab the American's attention. On February 14, the Communist paper *Paese Sera* detonated a bombshell in the form of screaming, eight-column, front-page headlines: Italy had received a Hanoi peace feeler, which had been personally delivered by official representatives! Predictably, the story caused a sensation, and two hours later Fanfani hastily drafted a terse communiqué for the Farnesina to issue confirming talks with "qualified" DRV delegates "about possible hypotheses of a start of negotiations to settle" the war.[37]

Why would the PCI blare the covert contacts when its own foreign policy manager, Galluzzi, who had repeatedly sworn himself to secrecy, helped set them up? Because, the party boss Pietro Longo told Poland's ambassador, Fanfani himself had quietly requested the "veiled leak" to compel Washington to respond.[38]

Rusk—already sitting on a hedged draft reply—now had to act; reporters demanded comment on the *furore*, eliciting a caustic dismissal of DRV "propaganda gestures whose purpose it is to mislead and confuse."[39] The State Department spokesman's statement appalled D'Orlandi, who considered it a "true cold shower" but "we hope that [U.S. officials] are only putting up a façade."[40] They were not. Privately, Rusk sent word to Fanfani, listing factors besides the ongoing "savage—but unsuccessful—offensive" to doubt the probe's sincerity. He also requested more details, unable to judge the North Vietnamese representative's statements without knowing his identity and exact language.[41] Privately, U.S. officials suspected that Hanoi had shrewdly crafted its approach to "whet the known Italian appetite for playing a peacemaking role" and spur Rome to harangue Washington about a bombing halt; they also noted D'Orlandi's "questionable" role.[42]

Eager to please Rusk (and convince him that the new initiative was not "devoid of possibilities"), Fanfani promptly named Su as the DRV's interlocutor and offered to share records of the talks if the State Department sent an emissary. Rusk told Ortona that he would "think over" the idea, but he and his aides were ambivalent.[43] Because they were oblivious to Galluzzi's deep involvement in the affair, they did not suspect that Fanfani had stage-managed the *Paese* leak— Bundy guessed the *Paese Sera* leak had been "artfully" orchestrated by "interested Communist elements"[44]—but the episode further soured them on Rome's ability (or desire) to keep secrets. And even worse, the *Washington Post* quoted a "well-informed Italian source" as saying that the conversations with Su examined broad ideas for a pact modeled after Marigold's "ten points or steps"; supposedly "less crude and limited" than a mere bombing halt, this approach covered tough political topics, such as "the possible makeup of a coalition government to be formed in Saigon." The comments doubly irked U.S. officials, because they implied that Fanfani had failed to mention key topics discussed with the North Vietnamese to Rusk and reeked of D'Orlandi's baneful influence.[45]

Yet, the Americans could not simply blow off Rome. Besides the usual desire to avoid alienating a NATO ally, they desperately desired insight into Hanoi's thinking. And even though they distrusted the Italians' overeagerness, this time it seemed that North Vietnam was really trying to open a channel to them. Plus, Washington lacked any better alternatives.

Killy

So, warily, the Americans went ahead with the "Italian track." Puckishly, Bundy chose an auspicious code name—in the spirit of "Packers," he used a sports rather than floral motif, naming it "Killy" after the French alpine skier Jean-Claude Killy, who had just nabbed a third gold medal at the Winter Olympics in Grenoble. Yet Rusk's February 17, 1968, cable to Reinhardt containing a reply to Fanfani's message hardly meant that Washington thought the new venture was a winner. The envoy could tell Fanfani that, as he had proposed, the State Department would send an expert "solely to get full and accurate account of all that has been said by North Vietnamese representatives, as well as full background that led to their visit to Rome."

Yet Rusk also itemized Washington's worries, especially the *Post* story's indication that the Italians' talks with Su had ranged broadly over political matters that skillful mediators (i.e., themselves) might tackle before U.S.-DRV negotiations began. "All this has the strong ring of D'Orlandi's hand," he wrote, as did the "vague and tendentious nature of [Fanfani's] original report." Moreover, the recent publicity and knowledge of the Italian operative's role in Marigold could nourish Saigon's "suspicion that we are lending ourselves to another gambit like that one. The plain fact is that we approach this particular one not only with reserve, but with the most acute doubts whether D'Orlandi can be trusted even to be minimally accurate."[46]

D'Orlandi was expected in Prague to see Su again, but the Italians delayed his trip to consult with Washington's special emissary.[47] That turned out to be Dan Davidson, the young New York lawyer whom Harriman had recruited to replace Cooper. Having been previously immersed in the Romanian channel, Davidson had anticipated being sent to Europe for a different Vietnam-related secret rendezvous—with the shah of Iran at the Winter Olympics—when the Italian job cropped up instead. Before crossing the Atlantic, he got a full dose of U.S. skepticism toward Killy.[48]

Sensing Washington's chill, Fanfani, at his first meeting with Davidson (and U.S. embassy minister Francis Meloy) on February 21, opened by vigorously defending his efforts to maintain secrecy, explaining that the unfortunate *Paese* leak had forced his hand. "Then, getting in his licks"—and following the axiom that the best defense is a strong offense—he complained that Goldberg had gabbed to Italy's UN envoy, an especially gauche indiscretion because Rome had told him nothing. Replying to Davidson's request for more details on the exchanges with Su, the Italians supplied verbatim notes of the February 5 talks (except for a few off-the-record exchanges). As D'Orlandi converted his scribbling into English, he put Davidson on guard when "he consistently (ten or fifteen times) made North Vietnamese statements somewhat more positive than were warranted by the Italian, and each time when Meloy (who was looking over his shoulder at the notes) suggested a different translation, D'Orlandi, occasionally with reluctance, accepted the change."[49]

Nonetheless, several grueling "marathon" conversations convinced Davidson that the Italians had come clean; Fanfani and D'Orlandi, he cabled Harriman on February 24, had displayed "seriousness, earnestness, and openness," and had "succeeded in conveying the impression that they are being as open and frank about these recent contacts as it is humanly possible to be." He also became a believer in their "balance" and judgment, contrary to U.S. fears that they had made concessions or distorted the American or DRV stands to promote their venture.[50] Flattered that Fanfani was "willing to work hour after hour with someone as junior as me," the American (who was not yet thirty) started to imagine that the Italian bid, with his aid, might actually work. He too had caught Nobel Peace Prize fever, Davidson acknowledged decades later, with a laugh; "they were pitching me and had some success."[51]

Fanfani asked bluntly if he should pursue his exchanges with Su, and Davidson urged Washington to reply *yes.* The DRV envoy had said "nothing substantively new," yet Hanoi genuinely seemed to view Italy "as a preferred channel," and Fanfani and D'Orlandi, whatever their faults, had acted in a "responsible and professional manner during the current episode (as well as Marigold)." To Su, he noted approvingly, they accurately represented Washington's views while not claiming to speak for it. And—unaware of the collusion with the PCI—Davidson applauded their labors to keep the matter secret. The next steps had risks, including the "danger" that "we might face prospect of negotiations at time when the political-military situation makes negotiations undesirable." Yet rupturing the contact might anger Hanoi, and Fanfani would "be miffed by being told either that he must permanently disconnect Prague channel" or could not pass along any substantive U.S. reaction. As with Marigold, irritation could spur damaging leaks, implying that again American "recalcitrance" had "foiled" a promising peace attempt; conversely, if Su refused to commit to talks promptly after a privately conveyed bombing halt, "then the propaganda shoe could be on the other side's foot"—D'Orlandi even suggested that Washington might then advantageously spread the story.

With such considerations in mind, Davidson urged letting D'Orlandi return to Prague with carefully calibrated guidance. He might tell Su that Washington saw his remarks as no more "forthcoming" than what Hanoi had said publicly, but assure him that the bombing would stop if North Vietnam were to "flatly state" that it would join, within a day, "serious negotiations" at which both sides could raise any issue. D'Orlandi should end the contact if Su said no, but if he agreed, he could seek assurance that Hanoi would not exploit a bombing halt militarily, perhaps by forswearing "bad faith" actions (e.g., major new attacks on U.S. forces or South Vietnamese civilians). Rather than take D'Orlandi's word for it, Washington would require direct confirmation by Hanoi to an American official (as with Marigold, when Hanoi had sought Washington's confirmation of Lewandowski's summary).[52]

As Rusk read Davidson's reports, his animosity toward Killy softened—to the alarm of his top Vietnam aide. As Bundy drafted (with Harriman and Isham) new instructions for Rome, he and Rusk agreed that Washington should green-light further meetings with Su, but they disagreed on what they should authorize the Italians to say. Rejecting Davidson's suggestion that D'Orlandi be given modified U.S. terms for opening talks to use with Su, Bundy preferred only "very general guidelines" seeking further clarification.[53]

Yet Rusk saw no harm—and some possible gain—in letting the Italians probe Su on a potential settlement, and discerned merit in their case that efforts should be made to achieve as much progress as possible before initiating direct U.S.-DRV talks, given that mutual distrust and hostility might cause them to collapse quickly; the idea seemed "worth thinking about."

Bundy blanched. D'Orlandi was "the man behind the 10 points," he reminded the secretary, "a ferociously tilted document," and they did not want to revisit that.

Rusk persisted. Indirect exchanges before formal direct talks might not be so bad. It would be better to come to a "clutch" with Hanoi sooner, not later. He was "a little inclined to encourage the Italians to see how far they can get on this."

Seeing his boss wobble, Bundy insisted. During Marigold, D'Orlandi spread "wrong impressions" and manipulated Lewandowski. Washington should not entrust its most sensitive communications with Hanoi to someone who would be liable to distort them: "B. would not play through this channel!"

OK, Rusk relented.[54]

The new guidance Rusk sent to Rome the next day, February 27, reflected his aide's coolness. Davidson should thank the Italians for their reports and "certainly" not give "the impression we are being negative on following up any possible exchange." Yet Rusk rejected any "new formulation" of the U.S. stand or "weakening" of the San Antonio formula, and mandated a low-key approach. "It would seem well to keep the Italian channel open for possible future use rather than to pursue it actively at the present time," he cabled.[55]

Davidson could not hide his chagrin when he carried out the instructions; he was "visibly embarrassed," D'Orlandi sensed. Still, the Italian grimly resolved to go to Prague "to see what I can do."[56] The next afternoon at the Farnesina, when Davidson formally conveyed the U.S. response, Fanfani was likewise underwhelmed. D'Orlandi, he said, would need to maneuver "skillfully to avoid a break" and to convince Su that he was not being strung along. What was the risk, he pleaded, in taking a less negative, more constructive approach than ritually intoning the San Antonio formula?[57] "I complain that they are not giving us a greater negotiating latitude," the irritated minister jotted in his journal.[58]

On March 1, D'Orlandi flew to Prague to do what he could with Su. Greeting him "very cordially," the DRV envoy voiced surprise that he had not shown up a week earlier, a failure that, together with Rome's and Washington's public statements, had led him to presume that the channel had lapsed. Eager to dispel this notion, D'Orlandi explained that he had delayed his trip to confer with a U.S. special envoy, who was in Rome awaiting the results of their present conversation. Su was "very encouraged" to hear this, but—to D'Orlandi's sharp disappointment—said that he still had not obtained his government's reply to the question posed at their prior meeting: How long after a bombing halt would Hanoi enter into direct talks? Su insisted that setting a date would be "no problem," but the main hurdle remained the San Antonio formula, which Hanoi viewed as posing unacceptable conditions. Straining for something positive, D'Orlandi teased out Su's "personal" assent that once direct talks began, any spectacular escalation that would "sink the whole thing"—such as an assault on Khe Sanh, a large-scale invasion across the Demilitarized Zone, an effort to detach South Vietnamese provinces from Saigon's control, or a "second wave of attacks" on cities—would be "absolutely out of the question." Su vowed again to get hard answers from Hanoi and to set up another meeting as soon as they arrived; he did not reply when D'Orlandi mused that he himself might need to go to Hanoi "to receive assurances directly from the top."[59]

Back in Rome the next day, D'Orlandi and Fanfani agreed: Despite the session's meager results—an Italian analyst later harshly dismissed it as "pointless"—the attempt was still alive, and therefore hope still existed.[60] To the Americans, they accentuated the positive. Though Su had not clarified how quickly a bombing halt would yield talks, D'Orlandi argued that his "personal" acceptance of the inadmissibility of military action during talks that might provoke renewed bombing suggested that the North Vietnamese were trying to finesse the San Antonio formula without formally accepting it. Davidson privately found this plausible—but not Meloy, who summed up D'Orlandi's account "by saying that the atmospherics were excellent but that there was nothing substantively new from Hanoi." The Italian meekly agreed.[61]

Testifying to Italian fears not only that the peacemaking bid might flop but also that its failure might prove harmful domestically—especially with elections coming—D'Orlandi asked Meloy to whisper a kind word regarding Fanfani's diplomacy to conservative, pro–American editors. If their publications kept lambasting the minister for his peace efforts (which allegedly alienated Washington and weakened its position), he might have to abandon Killy. Meloy deflected this awkward request, saying that even the most discreet approach would inevitably be seen as an intolerable intervention in Italy's internal affairs.[62]

At a goodbye session with Davidson on March 5, Fanfani predicted that the next visit with Su would be "decisive." But because that would not happen until Hanoi finally supplied firm instructions, the moment seemed right for Davidson to go home to give Rusk and company his personal impressions. He left the next day. En route to Fiumicino, he paused at D'Orlandi's for a "very cordial" off-the-record chat, which made clear his own support for Rome's peace efforts, even if Washington's attitude was "more than cold, even icy." D'Orlandi hoped that Davidson would erode the "potent barriers of skepticism and hostility erected in Washington. He has faith; let's hope that he can move mountains!"[63]

Davidson tried, on his return to Washington, to rouse enthusiasm for Killy. He easily convinced Harriman that Su's assurances constituted a de facto acceptance of the San Antonio formula that was worth testing, which could be expected (and discounted) from the State Department's in-house peace zealot.[64] But Bundy proved immovable; everyone was focused on the Tet fighting, he said, and LBJ did not think it was a good time to take chances or make concessions to hasten talks.[65]

As Davidson exited the stage, a familiar figure strode in: Lodge, now LBJ's ambassador at large for Vietnam, who had largely been excluded from high-level policy decisions since returning from Saigon and now restlessly foraged for a meaningful role. Thus he was eager to refresh Italian and Vatican ties, and he set a trip to Rome for mid-March, during which he could inform himself about Killy; almost certainly he calculated that, as D'Orlandi's friend, he might be able to insinuate himself into the action by serving as a liaison to the Italians.

But before Lodge left for Rome, aware that officials had divergent views of Killy, he sought orientation from LBJ. The White House, he found, shared Foggy Bottom's skepticism; passing LBJ the cable reporting the March 1 talk with Su in Prague, Rostow snidely alluded to the "eternally optimistic Italians—especially D'Orlandi."[66] LBJ instructed him "*not* to use the channel"—"He said I could talk to him, but not to go ahead," recalled Lodge, who considered this directive a blunder.[67]

The first post-Saigon reunion between the Marigold veterans occurred as both Killy and D'Orlandi were in precarious shape. After Davidson left, Fanfani received word from Ortona that Rusk and Bundy had been "reticent" with him, despite supposedly believing that the Italian channel was the best currently available.[68] As Lodge arrived in Rome, Meloy told Washington that Fanfani's key Vietnam aide may appear "deceptively healthy" but was an "ill man." His doctors, who had already removed his enlarged spleen, were "unable to identify or treat effectively" his condition, though they said he did not have leukemia or cancer. He was prone to, "among other discomforts, almost constant nose bleeds," and he believed he had the same degenerative disease that had killed war correspondent Marguerite Higgins, who succumbed in January 1966 to a tropical malady (leishmaniasis) contracted while visiting Vietnam. His doctors urged him to promptly begin a two-week regimen of daily blood transfusions and roentgen radiation exposures, but, "convinced of the potential importance of Killy and being a dedicated and courageous man, D'Orlandi has refused to submit to treatment until after his next trip to Prague."[69]

Friday evening, March 15, Lodge saw his friend for the first time in a year; then he, too, reported grimly on his health. His blood sickness ("which almost killed him in Saigon") had worsened, and he had "'bad days' from time to time when his gums and nose bleed a great deal." Lodge confided to D'Orlandi that opinions at home were "split" on Killy, with some unnamed officials (among them Rusk, the Italian presumed) griping about Nobel Peace Prize aspirants. In his own cable, Lodge stressed that, as instructed, he had focused on "asking questions and trying to elicit as much information from [D'Orlandi] as possible," confining himself to declarations that "we did not consider ourselves limited in any way to using the Italian channel" and Saigon could not be ignored. D'Orlandi, however, effusively describing the talks with Su, stressed "North Vietnamese 'readiness' with respect to the negotiation, their seriousness and substantial reasonableness." He outlined ideas for "guarantees" to assure a pact's implementation, and in a burst of optimism that Lodge had wisely omitted from his cable, predicted that with U.S. flexibility and a desire to reach peace, and adequate prior preparation (by, he implied, a qualified mediator such as himself), talks could achieve a "happy conclusion" in a few weeks, surely by the summer.

Naturally, the two reminisced about Marigold and its possible bearing on current diplomacy. D'Orlandi flattered Lodge by citing Su's supposed interest in his views and hints that Hanoi fondly recalled their Saigon channel: "He believes that Lewandowski gave them a very good report of what we did and that they feel that I was truthful, precise and kept my word. He says they are an extremely suspicious people and the reason that they came to D'Orlandi this time was because they felt they had not been tricked or double-crossed at any time during the Marigold meetings." Lodge thought this fit his theory that Marigold "broke down because Hanoi changed its mind and not because of trickery by Rapacki." As he had speculated to Loory, he opined that the prospect of a propaganda windfall from Salisbury's visit had prompted the DRV—perhaps on Soviet advice—to ditch quiet talks and launch a noisy campaign to exploit the bombings.

Near the end of the long conversation, Fanfani joined the diplomats for a late supper. Hearing from the American of Rusk's skepticism and Johnson's ambivalence, he seconded D'Orlandi's impression of the Prague contact's importance and gossiped with Lodge about the war's political impact in the United States—where LBJ reeled from his poor showing in the New Hampshire primary against antiwar candidate Eugene McCarthy, and Robert F. Kennedy was poised to enter the race—and in Italy. After Lodge left at about 10:15, the Italians reviewed the "particularly useful" talk and concluded that they had won a "powerful ally in Washington who will fight for our attempt."[70]

Lodge had indeed become an ally, but the Italians overestimated his impact. Cabling home, he noted D'Orlandi's beliefs that Washington should use only one reliable channel to communicate with Hanoi, that it was "absolutely clear" that "if the president wants talks he can have them," and that "a decent self-respecting agreement is possible." Though well aware of LBJ's lack of sympathy with these views and aversion to Killy, he gamely contended that his "close friend" deserved sympathetic consideration.

Striving to seem objective, Lodge acknowledged that he "seldom" endorsed D'Orlandi's substantive ideas (e.g., his disdain for Diem and Ky and—though he did not mention it—his belief that the National Liberation Front would win a fair vote), dubbing him a "well-known type of Latin conservative." And, in a nod to the Nobel sneers, he conceded D'Orlandi's egotistical incentives—while also crediting him for "being actuated by the highest motives of service to the United States and the cause of peace, and for wanting to do something selfless with his life before he dies." Then Lodge made his case:

> [D'Orlandi] is convinced—and I believe rightly—that the Vietnamese question is tremendously complicated, with a very long and intricate history, and that only individuals who have firsthand familiarity with Vietnam can hope to get results—and it is difficult even for them. In this I frankly think he is right. In any case it is surely not a bad thing to have an intelligent, well-disposed man actively trying to promote a settlement. Indeed, in this situation it is hard to see how peace talks will ever come about if the initiative is placed exclusively upon either the North Vietnamese or the United States while they are in combat.
>
> On the positive side it must be set down that, although D'Orlandi has his defects, they are all on the surface where anyone can see them and that he is a highly intelligent and thoughtful man. He is also accurate and precise and I cannot recall that he has ever told me anything which was not true concerning dealing with the enemy. He is also most discreet and bends over backwards not to cause us embarrassment. He has a large store of information on this question such as few Westerners possess. Finally, he is both by conviction and emotion strongly pro-American.

In sum, Lodge concluded, the Italian "believes that day of working through the Poles is over and that the North Vietnamese now wish to deal with the United States sometimes directly and sometimes using D'Orlandi as a channel."[71]

Lodge and Davidson were not the only U.S. officials urging a kinder view of Killy. In late March, Tom Hughes, the head of the State Department's Intelligence and Research Bureau, gave a thumbs-up to the Italian effort. Fanfani's careful supervision and Davidson's presence, he felt, offset D'Orlandi's "reputed penchant for presenting the Hanoi position in the most favorable light." Moreover, Su's statements fit other clues, and the "distortion factor" was probably less than in most contacts. In stark contrast to Bundy, State's top intelligence analyst wrote:

> From our view point the Italians look about as good as any channel we have had. They have been relatively discreet, even under pressure. D'Orlandi is more familiar with the issues than most intermediaries. Fanfani did not just listen obsequiously to Su's remarks in the same fascinated manner which seems to grip many Western officials when Hanoi representatives hold forth. He challenged Su several times and even backed him into a corner once on the timing of talks. Though he obviously cannot negotiate on our behalf, this performance suggests that with a careful briefing on the U.S. position he and D'Orlandi can get more information from—and perhaps have a greater constructive impact on—Hanoi representatives than most of our other intermediaries. Of course, like some others, he has a tendency to ask us for refinements which we may not want to make at the time.[72]

In the Pentagon, too, there was sympathy for Davidson's arguments that Su's comments offered an authentic opportunity. On March 12, Paul Warnke, the assistant secretary of defense for international security affairs, advised his boss, Clark Clifford, that Hanoi, in its contacts with the Italians, had indicated "acceptance of the operative portion of the San Antonio formula." He urged a prompt test to see if the DRV would endorse Su's assurances.[73]

But the pro-Italian arguments fell on deaf ears. Lodge made a pitch to Rusk on returning to Washington, but Rusk only showed interest in D'Orlandi's belief that Hanoi would accept a pledge not to take military advantage of a bombing halt during talks, and concern at his parlous health.[74] Meanwhile, the Italians—optimistic that Lodge would be able to sway Rusk and LBJ—hoped to get a "positive and detailed" reformulation of the U.S. stand in time for their next conversation with Su. But to their immense frustration, day after day passed without further word—from Washington, Prague, or Hanoi.[75] Neither Fanfani nor D'Orlandi wanted to admit it, but "Killy had clearly come to a dead end."[76]

Down the Homestretch:
"Let Loory Stew in His Own Juices"

During February and March 1968, as the reporters sprinted down the homestretch, Loory occasionally broke from writing to investigate Kraslow's "nagging questions." On Marigold, their most glaring missing link remained the "ten points" that they knew Lewandowski had given Lodge on December 1, 1966. "We still don't know to what degree [the United States] had to subscribe to the language of the ten points, whether they were topic headings, points of departure or whether we had to accept them as written as blood," Loory confessed to Isham in early February. Seeking guidance as to their relative accuracy, if not exact language, he passed State Department sources a paraphrased guestimate of the ten points, but found them unsympathetic. Aware that the ten points popped up periodically in Killy, Isham claimed that they "still might prove 'useful in some fashion'" and Loory "grudgingly conceded the point." Looking over the reporters' version, officials happily found them "wide of the mark . . . clever speculation combined with a grain of verisimilitude," but were in no mood to correct them. "I suggest we decline comment and let Loory stew in his own juices," Davidson advised Bundy, noting that Isham and Read agreed. Probably after checking with Rusk, Bundy assented. Accordingly, Isham refused to elaborate when he saw Loory, but kindly warned that the reporters' ten points were "'not authentic' but a mish-mash," and they should not "put too much stock in them."[77]

In desperation, Loory wrote D'Orlandi, only to get a cryptic reply: "The ten points you quote are far from their real version as drafted by the three. I am very sorry not to be free to expand on the subject." The handwritten note—penned as the Italian tensely awaited word from Prague and Washington—was cordial ("Very best wishes of success for your book") but unhelpful and even misleading; of course, Lewandowski, not "the three," had drafted the ten points, albeit based on Lodge's presentation.[78]

In late March, the *Los Angeles Times* reporters—probably Kraslow[79]—checked in again with Katzenbach. The deputy secretary seemed taut, confining most replies to "yes or no or nodding responses," but he tried to help. The *Life* peace package had just appeared, and he corroborated the journalists' sense that Mc-Culloch was fed warped information. He clarified Pennsylvania's failure and "spoke very highly" of Kissinger, but "tore Walt Rostow to little bits and pieces. Very dangerous man. His nickname for him is WW III." Katzenbach said he had vainly urged Rusk against leaking Marigold to Hightower—"poor Dean, because he was doing it from memory and skimpy notes got a few things wrong"—and opposed issuing a white paper, because an incomplete account would only make matters worse. "A guy like Kraslow who knows a lot," he said, flatteringly, "will point out omissions, and then the issue will become credibility rather than substance."[80]

As the month ended, the reporters applied the finishing touches to their draft manuscript, which was now suitable to submit to Random House and to the *Los Angeles Times* editors for chopping into a series. Their narrative of diplomatic futility spanned three years, from the Stevenson/Thant affair to Pennsylvania, but Marigold remained the centerpiece. A haggard Loory finished the final chapter on Sunday afternoon, March 31, then rushed to Kraslow's, "where he hurried

through it because both us wanted to watch a speech that Lyndon Johnson announced he was going to make that night. We thought he might announce a
bombing [halt]. I was wearing an old sweater, torn khakis and beat-up shoes. I
hadn't shaved in days."[81]

As LBJ's somber visage appeared, the reporters had every reason to believe
that their forthcoming stories would be blockbusters, able to affect the ongoing
debate over a pressing national issue: Why was the president, seeking four more
years in office, with more than half a million troops in the field, unable to move
the Vietnam War toward peace?

To the ~~Warsaw~~ Paris Peace Talks: "I Almost Blew My Stack"

From the Oval Office that night, LBJ announced that he would unilaterally curb
the bombing of North Vietnam to just north of the Demilitarized Zone—and then
shocked viewers by declaring that in order to search for peace full time he would
not seek reelection. Kraslow and Loory "raced" to the *Los Angeles Times* bureau,
which bustled with excitement. Loory then walked to the White House and—
disheveled and underdressed—soon joined a bunch of reporters in the upstairs
living quarters, sitting on a couch beside an unburdened LBJ, "carrying a Fresca
and dressed in a turtleneck sweater, . . . look[ing] almost as casual as I did."[82]

Three days later, Hanoi publicly proposed "contact" with Washington on ending the bombing "and all other acts of war" against North Vietnam, "so that talks
may start." The step finally moved the conflict toward a formal diplomatic track
and was a surprise because LBJ's bombing limit hardly met the venerable DRV
demand for a full halt.[83] (It also instantly mooted Killy and other probes in progress.[84]) On April 4, 1968, as the country digested these headlines, it reeled from a
fresh trauma: Martin Luther King's murder.

That morning, Kraslow and Loory began to unveil their findings. In a series of
Los Angeles Times articles, they revealed the Pennsylvania channel, reconsidered
the Wilson-Kosygin summit, then dwelled on the Poles and Marigold, blaming
the Hanoi bombings on inadvertence and a "loss of control."[85] For a week, the
stories jumped off the front page, but inevitably, the timing dulled their impact.
Suddenly—with LBJ a lame duck, peace talks finally imminent, and the nation
shaken by violence and absorbed in a wide-open presidential race—exposés of
misfired secret peace bids a year or two earlier seemed passé. Marcy prodded
Fulbright to reprint the series in the *Congressional Record*, along with praise for a
"classic example of contemporary history" that posed "embarrassing questions"
about the administration's handling of sensitive diplomacy.[86] Yet few cared to ask
these questions. Interest in the reporters' inquest had "evaporated," Rostow gloat-
ed, and their book "would now be a total flop"; Wilson agreed "that the latest
developments over Vietnam will have knocked the publicity bottom out of the
Kraslow-Loory story."[87]

Though inopportune journalistically, the *Los Angeles Times* articles were timely in another sense: They reminded LBJ of his unpleasant dealings with the Poles on Vietnam, just as Hanoi proposed Warsaw as the venue for direct contacts. If not for his bitter memories of Polish behavior, in fact, both during the thirty-seven-day bombing pause and during Marigold, the negotiations and eventual accords might have been hosted by Warsaw—not Paris.

Communicating via the U.S. Embassy in Vientiane, the DRV first suggested Phnom Penh as the venue for talks. After Washington rejected that city on the grounds that it lacked an American mission, and offered instead four Asian alternatives (Jakarta, New Delhi, Rangoon, and Vientiane), Hanoi responded with the idea of Warsaw, to which they offered to send Ha Van Lau.[88] Some U.S. aides considered Poland's capital "an acceptable 'fallback position.'"[89] Harriman, who was likely to head a delegation to the talks—hence the secret code name for the maneuvering over their site, "Crocodile"—called LBJ on April 11 with a warm endorsement.

"Mr. President," he began, "I wanted you to know I feel very strongly that Warsaw has a number of advantages over any other place."

"I have rejected it outright, flat, all the way," LBJ shot back. "I saw where the State Department said it was excellent. But as long as I am President we are not going to Warsaw where we have been once before and negotiate in that kind of atmosphere." He preferred a neutral country, perhaps in Asia.

Harriman: "The people in Eastern Europe want to end this conflict and have a reasonable settlement. It doesn't bother me to negotiate in an Iron Curtain country."

Johnson cut him off. "It does bother me," he said. "I don't want any part of Warsaw, Czechoslovakia, or any of these other Eastern European countries."[90]

In his memoirs, LBJ explained his veto of Warsaw. "I was opposed to public meetings with the North Vietnamese in an openly pro-Hanoi capital. The deck would be stacked against us, just as it had been in the early peace talks in Korea. The South Vietnamese and our other allies had no relations with Poland, no representation in Warsaw. The Communists would control all facilities and arrangements and would have the local press 100 percent on their side. Poland was supplying arms and other support to the North Vietnamese and could not pretend to neutrality."[91] Yet LBJ's rejection of an Eastern European venue was not rigid; he secretly OK'd Bucharest, despite Romania's equally fervent support for Hanoi, tight Communist control, and lack of relations with Saigon.[92] In Poland's case, however, bad memories had triggered a viscerally negative reaction.

✳ ✳ ✳

LBJ had reason to recoil from Warsaw beyond scorn for Rapacki's conduct in Marigold and the thirty-seven-day pause: "Poland was then conducting an anti-Jewish campaign, and I refused to meet in a place where some members of our delegation or press corps might be refused entrance or be unwelcome."[93] For those urging Washington to accept the city as the venue for peace talks, the timing could not have been worse; militant Polish nationalists, led by Interior Minister Mieczysław Moczar, had cracked down on students, intellectuals, and other "cosmopolitan" and liberal forces. The campaign, reflecting a murky internal power struggle, had an ugly anti-Semitic tint that spurred much of the tiny residual Jewish community to flee. It vented pressures that had been rising since the June 1967 war, when some Poles had cheered Israel's victory (contrary to the official pro-Arab line), alarming hard-liners; evoking the Nazi occupation, Gomułka called those Poles who backed Israel a "fifth column" and warned gravely that "every Polish citizen should have only one Homeland—People's Poland."[94]

Fanned by press hysteria, the xenophobic movement grew into a hunt for alleged "Zionists." At a rancorous MSZ caucus, Moczar's shock troops called for the heads of Naszkowski and other "politically unreliable" officials and turned their wrath on Rapacki when he rejected their "order" to fire them. In what the CIA termed "a sustained vituperative attack," they charged Rapacki with "sponsoring and nurturing the careers of alleged pro-Zionists still holding positions of great influence," shouted him down when he tried to defend himself, and howled for his resignation.[95]

Rapacki's refusal to knuckle under to the rabble effectively ended his career. By early April, the fifty-eight-year-old minister had gone on leave, ostensibly for health reasons, and in December he would make his resignation official; he died in October 1970. Yet his refusal to preside over an anti-Semitic cleansing cemented "a reputation for loyalty and personal integrity even among his political opponents."[96] It was said that "Rapacki, an honorable man, was so offended by the purge that when he was handed a list of names of Jewish officials under him whom he was to fire, he added his own to the top and walked out the door."[97] Despite the minister's defiance, Naszkowski was "literally hounded out of his office. First his secretary stopped reporting for work, then his telephone was cut off, and finally he gave up and stayed away from the ministry."[98]

One day that surly spring, leaving the MSZ, Naszkowski ran into Lewandowski. They strolled to a nearby park. Though aware of the deputy minister's reputation as a "cold man" who brusquely implemented personnel decisions, Lewandowski had decent relations with him. He did not know or care whether Naszkowski was Jewish, as "partisans" claimed, but had heard (from his mentor, Manfred Lachs) that at a ministry colloquium during the 1967 war, only Naszkowski had opposed Moscow's edict that Poland cut diplomatic ties with Israel (which all Warsaw Pact satellites save Romania promptly obeyed). Poland, he argued, was not formally allied with the Arabs, nor had Israel harmed it. Lachs told Lewandowski that he had agreed but stayed silent, lacking Naszkowski's guts.[99]

Sitting on a park bench, Naszkowski, who was fifty-five years old, ruminated on what had befallen him after decades as a Communist stalwart—prewar activist and political prisoner in Western Ukraine, wartime editor and Polish Army officer, ambassador to Moscow, senior posts in the postwar Polish Defense and Foreign ministries. "Do you see what is going on?" he asked. Finally, he said wryly, his son and daughter, who had been raised as secular Poles, were learning "what it is to be a Jew." He minimized his fate, sounding resigned and even accepting, like Rubashov, the old Bolshevik caught up in Stalin's purges, falsely accused and ultimately shot, in Arthur Koestler's *Darkness at Noon*. "We revolutionaries are the manure of history," Naszkowski mused, fertilizing flowers that would blossom for future generations.[100]

During the 1967 war, of course, Lewandowski was stranded in Beirut on his way home from Saigon, and after reaching Warsaw, he managed to stay "a little bit outside these events." When the knives came out, he was in some respects a logical target. Though not Jewish, he was a Rapacki protégé and, moreover, his behavior in Vietnam had irked the Interior Ministry; some MSZ colleagues thought he was aloof, and they tried (vainly) to link him to sinister cliques. However, Lewandowski said he evaded the brutal office politics, perhaps because he was a specialist, often abroad, not a high-ranking figure with political ambitions: "I was doing my job, not . . . trying to get a bigger job, I didn't need it." His voice dripping with disgust, he called Moczar "a dreadful man, a real bandit" and the episode "revolting."[101] The hard-line swerve in Polish politics and foreign policy troubled him. In mid-July 1968, he attended a convocation of Soviet Bloc leaders (minus Czechoslovakia's) in Warsaw and was appalled to hear Gomułka harshly condemn the "Prague Spring" and its reformist Communist leader, Alexander Dubček. Not only did he decry the "counterrevolutionary" and "reactionary" forces that were taking over, but he also implied the need for stern action by the rest of the Warsaw Pact ("Our countries are the fist of the socialist system") to arrest the drift to "neo-capitalism." Hearing Gomułka's words, which foreshadowed Poland's participation in the Warsaw Pact's invasion of Czechoslovakia the following month, completed Lewandowski's disillusionment with the man who a dozen years before had led his own country's thrust for greater autonomy from Moscow, defying the threat of Soviet tanks during the "Polish October" of 1956. "I was thinking, 'What happened to him?'"[102]

Yet Lewandowski, who was no dissident, kept such misgivings private. A U.S. aide tracking the struggle between the "Boors and the Jews" even lumped the "mild-mannered, apparently liberal-minded" Lewandowski with other, younger aides who were "thirst[y] for advancement" and eager to exploit the purge of senior figures; "none of them were dismissed without very good reason," he was quoted as saying, though he felt that the real causes dated back "to an earlier period."[103] Whatever his personal view, Lewandowski gained from the shakeup. In September 1968, he was named to head the Asia Section (Department II), replacing a purge victim.[104]

If he had still been in Warsaw, Michałowski—one of Rapacki's closest associates, fond of life in the West, and half Jewish to boot—would have been red meat for Moczar's mob. Even at a distance, he was among the "principal targets of

'Young Turks' who pressed for a purge in the ministry." Yet he was allowed to carry on as ambassador in far-off Washington. As a good soldier, he tried to mitigate the upheaval's impact on bilateral ties, minimizing its anti-Semitic nature; the affair, he claimed, was "unpleasant but not serious," and a "great deal of fuss" was being made because sixty or seventy people, many not Jewish, had lost their jobs. He even blamed "Jewish interests" in America for waging an "anti-Polish campaign" to punish Warsaw for its pro-Arab policies.[105]

However, Michałowski admitted that Poland was undergoing "a period of struggle, anguish, and turmoil," and that the atmosphere there was "very bad indeed." The chaos paralyzed the Foreign Ministry, leaving it unable to make even minor decisions; urging an American to wait before officially raising any issues, Michałowski even despaired of asking Warsaw for $500 to fix the embassy's roof.[106]

The bad news from home further dispirited the diplomat, who already was ruing his earlier run-ins over Vietnam. As sinking bilateral ties restricted his official efforts to damage control, he was also troubled by attacks from Polish émigrés, including threatening letters and articles denouncing him and Mira as "Communist spies" (a Republican representative echoed the charge, sparking a protest from Naszkowski to Gronouski). The couple tried to maintain a "pose of amused tolerance," but their patience wore thin, and Jerzy lodged protests with the State Department (which said it could do nothing to stop the harassment).[107]

As reports of the purge flowed in, U.S. aides sensed that the ambassador "considers himself in political trouble." In mid-April, they heard that a defector who had asked at the embassy if Michałowski might intervene on behalf of his aged mother in Poland had been told that "the only person for whom the Ambassador is in a position to intervene right now is himself."[108] Shortly before going home for "consultations" in late spring, Michałowski reviewed the sorry state of affairs with U.S. officials. Gronouski, just ending his own ambassadorial term, stopped by and said that, given the "ferment" in Warsaw, he had heard the Pole might not return from his trip home. "Ambassador Michałowski shrugged and said that would be all right with him, since his time here had not been particularly happy."[109] Conversely, Davidson, who spoke with Michałowski during an excursion to the Delaware shore over Memorial Day weekend, sensed that recent events had so depressed Michałowski that he was mulling defection.[110] However, when the U.S. Embassy threw a luncheon for him in Warsaw, he seemed "grayer" but "spoke with customary assurance," giving no sign that anything was awry; the only personal help he sought was a visa so his son Piotr could begin graduate studies at Yale (his other son, Stefan, was attending Carleton).[111]

So Michałowski stayed in his post, but he later told an American that his fate had hung by a thread. "You can imagine what it was like for me in the Polish Embassy in Washington, not to know your future from one hour to the next," he said, noting that Gomułka was nearly forced to replace his closest aides with "those lice and fleas."[112] At some embassies, militants called party cell meetings to malign the ambassador, but Michałowski preempted this peril by convening a staff meeting himself; acknowledging that Poland was passing through difficult times, he urged all to act in a dignified manner—and warned that troublemakers would be instantly sent home (ending their treasured access to Western goods).[113] Nevertheless, the atmosphere grew so toxic that Michałowski felt "really at war with the embassy," his son recalled, and thus isolated except perhaps from his deputy, Pawlak, who had also served with the International Control Commission in Saigon.[114]

The regime gradually curbed the hard-line surge, but U.S.-Polish ties deteriorated severely again in August when Warsaw joined Moscow's invasion of Czechoslovakia. The beleaguered ambassador pleaded with U.S. officials to confine Washington's retaliation to political steps rather than curtail cultural and economic ties; maybe they should just expel him because, after all, "his mission had been one tragedy and disappointment after another. If he had known what was in store, he would never have come."[115]

＊ ＊ ＊

The "March events," as the Polish crackdown became known, reinforced LBJ's resolve to reject Warsaw. But the story did not end there. In late April 1968, during more jousting over a venue for the peace talks, Hanoi reintroduced the city—if only to host preliminary discussions to determine the locale where the actual negotiations could take place.

In the Polish capital, the DRV's efforts to entice the Americans into direct contact took several forms. Though aware of White House reservations, Gronouski had, predictably, sought to participate in the renewed peace process. On learning that Hanoi had proposed Warsaw as the venue for the talks, he warned Washington that an outright rebuff—after LBJ's offer to meet "any time, any place"—would hand the enemy an "ideal propaganda instrument to blame" the U.S. government that would resonate "both in Western Europe and among some elements in U.S.A." The State Department promptly sent him a stern message reminding him of Warsaw's serious drawbacks, but a few days later a new overture arose. A visiting Swedish emissary who had just seen Do Phat Quang invited Gronouski to an informal private talk with the DRV envoy, perhaps lunch at Stockholm's embassy —no commitments, just a chat to "take the temperature" and encourage a "climate of confidence." Gronouski, who was out of town for a few days, would have loved to finally sit down with the man he had yearned to meet during Marigold, but U.S. officials promptly nixed the idea—a channel already existed in Vientiane, and it would not be "helpful" to open another one.[116] In view of Washington's evident distaste for Warsaw, the Poles tried to turn up the heat by appealing to third parties with "an honest interest in bringing peace to Vietnam" (Britain, Canada, Italy, Holland, France, Sweden, India, U Thant, et al.) to pressure the Americans to allow at least a preliminary contact there.[117]

Michałowski, who had vainly sung Warsaw's praises, resumed plumping for the city. The Poles might not be "neutral," he conceded, but the "'confidence [of the North Vietnamese] in their Polish friends' could be a great asset." Regarding White House concerns, he said that all reporters could be welcome, "bugging" could happen anywhere (the Americans could always retreat to their secure embassy), and, in sum, Washington "would really find a better atmosphere in Warsaw for talks than in Paris," an emerging alternative.[118] (In another faint Marigold echo, Fanfani and D'Orlandi offered Rome, but Hanoi did not express interest when Washington included it on a list of acceptable host cities.[119])

Rusk, who was sensitive to LBJ's animus to Warsaw and anxious to keep Gronouski in line, sent a firm personal message to disabuse him—and through him the Poles, and through them Hanoi—of any notion that Washington would accept direct talks in the city ("definitely out of the picture"), given Poland's pro-DRV tilt. Yet, as during Marigold, Gronouski refused to take no for an answer. Though professing to concur with Rusk's objections, Gronouski made the case to him and the president for permitting initial contacts in Warsaw (solely to agree on a site for formal negotiations) to show that Washington had gone "that extra mile" for peace; otherwise, it risked a serious propaganda setback.[120] Some officials (notably Clifford) agreed, but Gronouski's appeal fell on deaf ears where it mattered; Rusk did not respond, and an unmoved LBJ groused that North Vietnam was "still trying to drag us in kicking and screaming to a place where clearly we don't want to go."[121]

Yet Gronouski had one more frisson of excitement left. A few days later, as Washington and Hanoi continued to fence over a site for talks, Poland's vice foreign minister urgently summoned him. Flanked by a mostly silent Lewandowski, Zygfryd Wolniak repeated the case for Warsaw as host, noting that Washington had not minded that possibility in December 1966. Poland, he insisted, was not trying "to get you in a hot place" but to promote peace. Then he sprang a surprise: That morning, Quang had called on him and expressed a desire to see Gronouski "privately" at the DRV Embassy or "any other place mutually acceptable" as soon as possible, even the next day, to settle the dispute over a venue. This was real, a démarche, not a vague hint or informal feeler. This news "elated" the American because "at that point we didn't know whether talks were going to get started, and this was what we had fought so hard to happen." He sent a "flash" cable, the highest priority, seeking guidance. Seventeen months after Marigold's collapse had dashed his dream of a historic conversation with Quang, it finally seemed imminent. Despite Rusk's admonition that Washington viewed Warsaw unfavorably, Gronouski foresaw a quick positive reply. Instead, he "waited interminably"— only a day, but it felt longer—before a "prosaic wire" explained that Washington had already vetoed this idea and refused to authorize him to engage in contacts with Hanoi's representative.

"I almost blew my stack," he recalled.[122] But that was that. Gronouski never did meet Do Phat Quang. In early May, Washington and Hanoi settled on Paris for "talks about talks," which began later that month and quickly degenerated into haggling over the shape of the table and other procedural wrangles before formal "negotiations."

✳ ✳ ✳

After frantic last-minute updating to include LBJ's speech and the fencing over a site for talks, Loory and Kraslow finished the preface to their book on May 5, 1968, and sent in the final manuscript. Random House published *The Secret Search for Peace in Vietnam* a few months later. With America rocked by violence in Vietnam and at home—riots in some inner cities after King was gunned down, RFK's murder in June, and televised police rampages in the streets of Chicago at the chaotic Democratic convention in August—it won admiring reviews. The *Washington Post's* Chal Roberts gave Kraslow and Loory "the highest marks for their ferreting efforts" and rated their book "a prime source for the ultimate volume, years hence, on what really happened and why."[123] In the *New York Times,* David Schoenbrun praised the "indefatigable" authors for making "a valuable contribution" to democracy with a riveting "case history of grievous error in the highest levels of government," and Eliot Fremont-Smith termed the book "profoundly embarrassing" for Americans, "a record of almost continual snafu and miscalculation, fuzzy and contradictory aims, deliberate obfuscations, muffled antennas and obsessive, self-defeating secrecy, all practiced under the apparent illusion of hard-nosed realism, efficiency, carefully calibrated response and other fine-sounding notions of sophisticated diplomacy."[124] Kraslow and Loory were edged out for the Pulitzer Prize for international reporting—an omission that Nick Williams told Kraslow would cause him to rate the prize "somewhere along with the 'Miss Personality Cup' at Atlantic City"—but they snagged a prestigious Polk Award for journalism in the public interest.[125]

Politically, however, *Secret Search* created only a minor stir. "The book seems to have aroused little interest in the United States and so far none here," a British aide told Wilson. "Its main theme, that potential peace moves were stultified by an intensification of American bombing, has lost something of its sting now that peace talks have started and American bombing has been dramatically cut back."[126]

Yet *Secret Search* had a seminal impact on the historical debate over Vietnam peace diplomacy. Kraslow and Loory revealed many details behind the collapse of Marigold and other floral miscues, presenting a damning picture of bungling and incompetence at the highest levels. The Johnson administration, they wrote, "missed opportunities over the years to secure, if not peace, at least negotiations; if not negotiations, at least talks; and if not talks, at least a propaganda advantage over the enemy that would have improved the nation's standing in the world community and the President's credibility at home."[127]

Second Thoughts? "You Know, John, You Were Right . . ."

Marigold had become a matter of public controversy, informed by leaks of unknown reliability. But the voluminous U.S. government record remained sealed—which did not prevent classified internal reviews of the affair and its meaning.

Going beyond the State Department and White House chronologies compiled to prepare (or leak) a public defense of U.S. conduct, the most detailed secret postmortem of Marigold during the Johnson administration was undertaken as part of the Pentagon Papers inquest into Vietnam decisionmaking commissioned by McNamara in June 1967 and extensively using State Department and Pentagon (but not White House) files. The Marigold case study, one of a series on Vietnam diplomacy, was overseen by a RAND Corporation analyst, Richard Moorsteen, in close cooperation with the study coordinator, Leslie H. Gelb, who shared his conclusions.[128] In stark contrast to Rusk, Rostow, Bundy, and of course LBJ himself, the study concluded that North Vietnam most likely "did in fact agree to a meeting in Warsaw," and it was "highly improbable" that the Poles would have "gone far out on a limb" in their dealings with Americans, Italians, "and, apparently, the Russians," without Hanoi's commitment, given the consequences that would have ensued from "the revelation that the whole venture was built on air."[129]

Some other internal inquests hewed closer to orthodoxy. A CIA study of Hanoi's attitudes completed in early 1968—using "relevant classified materials" but probably less informed on Marigold than Kraslow and Loory—noted skeptically that "Bloc sources" claimed the December 1966 raids destroyed "whatever hope there may have been—not very much"—to rescue the Poles' already stalled effort based on "a 10-point statement (drafted by themselves) which in their view held promise as a basis for talks and negotiations."[130] A Pentagon staff review judged the affair not an earnest effort to end the war but a probing maneuver intended to stop the bombing of North Vietnam and, when that did not work, to blame Washington for its collapse. Ideology ran thicker than blood, the study implied: "What the United States had to keep in mind was, that regardless of the color of their skins, the Polish officials were Communists and therefore on the side of the [North Vietnamese] and would do whatever they could get away with to promote Hanoi's interests."[131]

✳ ✳ ✳

As the talking and fighting dragged on and LBJ's presidency staggered through its lame-duck final stretch, Marigold's memory lingered uneasily for some senior aides.

In late May 1968, disappointed at the administration's tepid peace approach, Gronouski resigned and rushed home to campaign for Hubert Humphrey for the Democratic presidential nomination.[132] During his State Department farewells, Bundy—an inveterate Marigold skeptic—told him, "You know, John, you were right in December of 1966." Gronouski did not ask what he meant, and Bundy did not elaborate; it is unclear whether he was being polite or contrite.[133]

In July 1968, McNamara (now head of the World Bank) passed through Bonn and discussed the war with Lodge, now ambassador to West Germany. In a reflective mood, McNamara (who had of course initiated the then-secret Pentagon

Papers) remarked that "there should some day be a critique on Vietnam—to see what had been accomplished and what had gone wrong." He recalled in late 1966 having "had high hopes" for the Lodge-Lewandowski talks and retrospectively expressed a belief that they "might have shortened the war by two years," and "wondered why Rapacki had backed away so fast." Lodge again suggested that Salisbury's articles in the *New York Times* had caused Hanoi to back out, anticipating "really good play," but McNamara stuck to his belief—which he had voiced to LBJ in early 1967—that "the American bombing had caused the change in Hanoi's attitudes."[134]

Shortly before LBJ left office, a balm for troubled consciences regarding Marigold came from an unlikely source: Burchett. Earlier, the Australian had insisted that Washington had ruined a real peace chance with its ill-timed Hanoi bombings. However, when interviewed by Estabrook at the UN in December 1968, he now said that the initiative "had been concocted by 'well-meaning friends' of North Vietnam" (i.e., the Poles) and "indicated that the sale had been less than successful." In December 1966, he stressed, "North Vietnam did not then waver from its previous insistence that there could be no talks without a cessation of American bombing. He added that he had misunderstood the North Vietnamese position at the time." As Estabrook chivalrously noted, the "State Department has long given a similar explanation for the failure of the effort, but this was the first time doubt has been cast on the Polish initiative from the Communist side."[135]

Burchett's remarks gladdened U.S. officials (we told you so!), but they could also be attributed to Hanoi's desire to burnish the record retroactively to buttress its claim that it had never retreated from its demand for a bombing halt before direct talks—at a time when both sides were underlining toughness in the stalemated Paris talks.

Burchett's revised story did not alter Isham's private view, confessed to British journalist Henry Brandon, that the "one great mistake the U.S. did was in 1966 to kill the Polish initiative for negotiation" by its Hanoi bombings. "Even if the Poles did not have a mandate, it will always be on the record as a question mark."[136]

In the Johnson administration's waning days, a far more surprising, and senior, figure also appears to have admitted having second thoughts, and even regrets. Dean Rusk was a confirmed skeptic, to put it mildly, about the Poles and Marigold. In late December 1967, Harriman discovered the intensity of his residual sore feelings when he mentioned Michałowski's understanding of U.S. conditions for a bombing halt.

"But the Poles are crooks," the secretary bristled.

Harriman begged to differ. Poland had done more than any other country to bring about talks, he contended, recalling Michałowski's trip to Hanoi during the thirty-seven-day bombing pause to transmit the stands he had carried to Warsaw.

"But, oh they were crooks in their talks of November–December 1966," Rusk specified. Asked why, he mentioned their failure to tell Washington that a DRV emissary was "on the way" to Warsaw—Burchett had just made this claim—or clarify their exchanges with Hanoi about the ten points or the interpretation clause. Harriman defended the Poles, attributing their conduct to a middleman's understandable efforts to bring enemies together, and said they had "every right to be upset" by the Hanoi raids.[137]

Rusk gave no sign of being moved by such arguments, and after leaving office he would consistently scorn the Polish efforts, both in private interviews and in his 1988 memoirs. However, he adopted an entirely different tone a few days before his term ended. The occasion was a farewell party, attended by the diplomatic corps, in the State Department's elegant seventh-floor reception room overlooking the Potomac River.

After toasts and "sentimental speeches" at the "sad, but formal, ceremony," Rusk's secretary informed Michałowski that her boss would like a private word with him. After ruminating about plans for retirement and future academic work, a "subdued" Rusk, speaking in a "ceremonial and emotional tone," told him:

> During my long tenure as Secretary of State, I'm sure I made many erroneous judgments and bad decisions. But my intentions were always pure, and I acted according to the dictates of my conscience. Thus, I have no regrets. Except for one thing—that in 1966 we did not take advantage of the opportunities and your role as go-between. We should have begun a negotiating process that, with your help, could have ended a conflict that has cost us so much blood and treasure, and that now has cost us the election. I wanted to say this to you today, and to ask that you convey my words to Minister Rapacki.[138]

Epilogue
"A Lot More Dead Young Soldiers"— Last Words, and the Battle for History

When he became president in January 1969, Richard Nixon named Henry Cabot Lodge to replace Averell Harriman as head of the U.S. delegation in Paris. "I am the most hopeful man you have ever known in your life," the senior Republican, seemingly chipper, said when reporters asked his outlook for an accord. In the outgoing administration's final days, the talks surmounted one hurdle, "the shape of the table," choosing a circle, not a rectangle, to finesse a rift over the status of the rival South Vietnamese parties. But as fighting dragged on, the formal sessions in the Paris International Conference Center on the Avenue Kléber—in the old Hotel Majestic, around a green baize tablecloth beneath three large crystal chandeliers, before TV cameras and the "rich Gobelin tapestries showing Diane the Huntress"—remained in a dismal stalemate.[1] Mired in polemics, frustrated by slow or opaque guidance from Washington, Lodge soon despaired of achieving progress.

Janusz Lewandowski glimpsed his old partner's discontent when he saw him in March while transiting Paris en route to the Far East (chaperoning a deputy minister). Asked by Adam Rapacki's successor, Stefan Jędrychowski, to chat up his American contact to see how the talks were going, the Asia section chief phoned Lodge, who invited him over. To reach the U.S. Embassy that foggy afternoon, he ran a gauntlet of antiwar protesters on the Champs-Élysées. Inside, Cabot greeted Janusz "very warmly" and insisted that he was getting used to the trials of dealing with the North Vietnamese.[2] Putting up a brave front, he stressed Nixon's intent "to find a political solution to the conflict in spite of delays and difficulties" and blamed the "present impasse" in part on the new president's need to review the negotiating history and prepare new proposals. He confidently prophesied that Nixon would "not get himself into the situation which the escalation got Johnson into."

Yet, Lewandowski reported, the American looked back with deep resentment: "Lodge said bitterly that they are making him responsible for being the author of the engagement in Vietnam—he was only the executor and he was no authority for the former president who had his own advisers who 'either did not see Vietnam [at all] or only saw it from inside the bombers.'"

They sparred—according to Lewandowski's cable; it would have been unseemly not to chide the imperialists—over the Pole's charge that Nixon's "Vietnamization" strategy belied his professed desire to end the war through negotiations. Lodge "lightly" brushed this off, insisting this would not be an obstacle, because the Pole knew that the ARVN could be "disassembled" in a few months.

Lodge remembered Marigold wistfully. Echoing their farewell conversation in Saigon two years before, he said that "it was not his fault that the initiative, in which Poland was involved, was broken off, something that he felt sorry about. He now considers it his greatest ambition to play a positive role in bringing peace to Vietnam."[3] Walking the Pole to the elevator, he called returning to Saigon for a second term "my biggest mistake."[4]

In his own cable, Lodge conceded no such regrets. He depicted Lewandowski as upset the Paris talks were going "much 'too slowly'" and fearing the rivals had missed the boat—the "best time" for negotiations was when China was "still in the throes of the revolution of the Red Guards," that is, during Marigold. (Lodge agreed that circumstances were far more auspicious when they were both in Saigon, though he did not say so in his cable.) The Pole stressed that he had come on a "purely personal call," not to deliver a démarche, but relayed his sense of Hanoi's stand. A strong faction still opposed sitting down with the Americans, he reminded Lodge, blaming a recent Communist offensive on North Vietnamese concerns that while the Paris talks dragged on, their forces in the South were "exposed and being badly hurt and [the South Vietnamese government] is getting stronger." Yet, he was "absolutely sure" that they wanted to staunch the bloodshed and move toward national reconstruction; in 1965, they confidently expected to "kick the U.S. out of Southeast Asia," but they were "realistic now" and not ready to enlist in "worldwide Communist crusades."

Yet the hawks in Hanoi and Washington still dreamed of victory, and both sides had to abandon illusions that they could achieve in Paris what they had failed to win on the battlefield, Lewandowski implored—otherwise, "they will simply end up where they started with this difference: a lot more dead young soldiers."

Lewandowski also passed along grisly gossip on another Cold War flare-up— the recent fighting along the frigid Sino-Soviet frontier. The confused reports of clashes on a disputed Ussuri River island between the nuclear-armed Communist giants had aroused global apprehension. Would their rift, having moved from polemics to violence, escalate to full-scale war? What would that mean for the world? From the MSZ's Asia section, the Pole closely tracked the confrontation. Making no attempt to sugarcoat Kremlin fears when "every fourth man in the world is Chinese, and pretty soon every third man will be," he again pushed the idea (favored by many in Moscow) that the conflict impelled U.S.-Soviet cooperation. For the clashes, for which both sides accused each other, he fully blamed the Chinese. In a premeditated ambush, they had shelled Daimanskii/Zhenbao Island, stormed ashore, and "literally 'slit the throats' of every single Russian there," he said—dramatizing by "the gesture of putting his finger under one ear and then bringing it around until it met the other ear." Mao Zedong did not seek all-out war, he guessed, but to force the USSR to mobilize its military along the 5,000-mile border at huge extra expense.

Lodge closed his report for Washington with words that hinted at the trust and regard he had come to feel for his Communist colleague: "I know Lewandowski well and believe he is telling me the truth as he sees it."[5]

They never met again.

Despite his nostalgia, Lodge apparently never probed Marigold's fate with the DRV officials he faced across the conference table—some of whom had been deeply involved in Hanoi's handling of the Polish initiative, including Ha Van Lau and Nguyen Dinh Phuong, although the odds of their talking out of school were nil. Lodge's overtures for an informal dialogue went nowhere. Shortly after seeing Lewandowski, he finally held a "first substantive private meeting" with his counterpart—but there he found Xuan Thuy no less truculent than in the formal sessions, demanding an unconditional U.S. withdrawal and "dismantling" of the Saigon government.[6] More such talks followed, including one at the end of May with Le Duc Tho, but they proved similarly barren.

Lodge, Kissinger, and Marigold

By August, Lodge was "bored silly." A few months later, he signaled Nixon that he wanted out—sensing that not only Hanoi but also the White House was treating the formal Paris talks as a sham. Since the summer, moreover, Nixon's national security adviser, Henry Kissinger, had maneuvered to open a back channel to Hanoi, further disillusioning Lodge. In November, he formally resigned, leaving his old Saigon sidekick Phil Habib temporarily in charge.[7]

Like the White House, Lodge thought the nominal Paris talks were a waste of time and that only a private, separate channel offered any hope to make progress. His preferred method, however, involved not Kissinger's trysts with Thuy (and later Le Duc Tho) but recruiting an outside mediator he thought was ideal for the job: D'Orlandi, now Rome's envoy to Greece. Before seeing Kissinger in January 1970, Lodge called to give him a heads-up:

L: When I see you I want to make a suggestion, but I wanted to tell it to you today so you'd have some time to think about it. You remember the Marigold Talks in 1966? Well, in 1968 I went to see [D'Orlandi]. LBJ [gave] me instructions not to continue with that line. [D'Orlandi] had contacts. Didn't want him to start again on his contacts in North Vietnam. In the meantime, the operation in Paris, which is foredoomed to failure because they are so public. [D'Orlandi] is that rare bird a talented and dependable go-between.

K: I thought you were going to make a racial comment and say "that rare bird—a talented and dependable Italian."

L: Well, that's true, too.

K: I met him, and share your opinion.

L: He's exceptional. You can't imagine anybody more heart and soul American. We've nothing to lose by trying this. There's no reason why we should be doomed by an error of LBJ's.[8]

Before seeing Kissinger, Lodge sent him a memo laying out his rationale. LBJ had blundered in March 1968, he wrote, by "deciding against using the highly and dependably secret D'Orlandi channel and deciding in favor of highly publicized direct talks." This, he felt, was actually LBJ's second mistake: His first was moving the December 1966 talks from Saigon—where he, D'Orlandi, and Lewandowski had handled them competently—to Warsaw. "Not only had D'Orlandi proven his usefulness then," Lodge wrote, "but I believe that Lewandowski had established a relationship in Hanoi which does not exist today. And I had a relationship with Lewandowski for which there is no counterpart today —to put it mildly.

"Passage of time convinces me," he continued, "that we had a better dialogue in the Marigold talks than we have ever had during the last twelve months in Paris—where, indeed, it cannot be truthfully said that we have ever had anything deserving of the name." He tended "more and more to the conclusion that direct talks are not the best way to an agreement, assuming that a well-qualified go-between is available." D'Orlandi, he stressed, superbly fit this description: He was "highly intelligent, thoroughly familiar with the issues, very dependable, a true and profoundly convinced pro-American," yet on "a thoroughly workable footing with the Communists," who trusted his discretion. "All the above has been proven and is not just conjecture. He is a known quantity."

Giving D'Orlandi the nod to reopen contacts with the DRV in Prague risked nothing, Lodge reasoned. If it failed, "no harm would be done, and the 'record' would show that President Nixon had made one more try for peace"; and if it succeeded in opening a new link to Hanoi, "so much the better." Lodge left the substance of a first message up to the White House—perhaps it could be that Nixon had "clearly won the battle for U.S. opinion" and would fight on if need be, but would offer a "generous settlement" if Hanoi compromised. The "crucial" thing was to supplement the Paris talks with a more productive track. And because he was now set to become Nixon's special envoy to the Vatican, Lodge noted that he could easily see D'Orlandi in Rome, to which the Italian returned periodically from Athens.[9]

Coveting his own back channel, Kissinger deflected Lodge's suggestion. "Making such a move now would confuse the North Vietnamese at a time when we are waiting for word about your Paris contact," his aide, Tony Lake, advised; and despite Lodge's assurance that the Italians could keep a secret, employing D'Orlandi might be "dangerous," given Marigold's well-known history and the risk that reporters might notice his or Lodge's "irregular" travels.[10] Nixon and Kissinger also disdained Fanfani (whom Kissinger termed "a slippery psychopath" to his boss), hardly enhancing their interest in using Rome.[11]

In late 1970, in semiretirement and with the Paris talks still deadlocked, Lodge made a last stab at convincing the White House to use D'Orlandi. Writing again to Kissinger, he explained that he had recently telephoned the Italian after hearing he had suffered a heart attack, "simply to ask after his health." During their talk, D'Orlandi said he had "recently received 'feelers' from the North Vietnamese." He did not want to say any more over the phone, but he invited Lodge to visit him in Greece so he could provide the "full details."

Having once received Kissinger's gentle brush-off, Lodge strained not to sound pushy. He stressed that he had told D'Orlandi such a trip would be "difficult" and was reporting his words simply for information, presuming that Washington had no present interest in another channel to Hanoi. Moreover, he added, Greece's military dictatorship (an international pariah) might well "blow up the news of my presence to make it look like a U.S. endorsement" were it to learn that he was in Athens.

Still, Lodge hardly wanted to foreclose a Kissingerian change of heart. The local U.S. embassy certainly *could* cloak a brief trip, he noted, and he was now (other than when he represented Washington to the pope) "a totally private citizen who has the perfect right to do some sightseeing in Greece if he wants to." Lodge ended by reaffirming his faith in D'Orlandi—"a very solid diplomat and his work is always of high quality"—and his belief that LBJ had erred by closing the Italian channel in early 1968.[12]

This time, Kissinger shut the door firmly. He replied bluntly that "we are not interested in working through another channel for Vietnam at this time" and, to avoid confusing Hanoi, did not want to explore "other avenues, no matter how tempting." Effectively vetoing the proposed trip, Kissinger advised that "we are on safer ground if you don't meet with D'Orlandi at this time."[13]

So ended, with a whimper, a last attempt to resuscitate Marigold, or its stepchild, as an operational component of U.S. efforts to achieve peace in Vietnam. But the battle to shape how the affair would be viewed by history, already influenced by the skirmishes in the Johnson administration's final two years, was just revving up.

"An Obscenity, It Really Was"

Departing government service freed some officials to put their stories on the record. The new LBJ Library at the University of Texas–Austin interviewed Johnson administration figures soon after they left office and, to encourage them to let their hair down, promised that the transcripts of these interviews would stay sealed for many years. The interviewer, Paige Mulhollan, pointedly asked about Marigold, often alluding to Kraslow and Loory and their haunting question: Had Washington blown a genuine chance for peace?

Absolutely not, most retorted. Dean Rusk called charges that the December 1966 raid had ruined a real opportunity "a pretext on the part of Hanoi, who did not want to talk. . . . I mean if there was any real interest on the part of Hanoi in peace and in these proposals, they would not have let these bombing incidents get in the way. This was simply a reflection of the lack of seriousness on their part."[14] With his usual self-assurance, Walt Rostow mocked Warsaw's labors. Unconvinced that the Poles had ever obtained a DRV pledge to talk on the basis of Lewandowski's ten points, he believed instead that they sought Lodge's commitment before approaching the North Vietnamese, who responded, "To hell with it." Rostow repeated a joke about a Polish marriage broker who, after much exertion, convinces a peasant to let his "lovely daughter" wed a prince—then sighs, "Ah, now for the Prince." "I've told this to Poles and they just laugh when I tell them the story because they know it's basically right," he said. "They never had Hanoi sewed up."[15] Warsaw, his aide Bill Jorden scoffed, "just had absolutely no charter from Hanoi to represent them."[16]

Some aides confessed regret over the Hanoi bombings—not because they ruined a real opening, but because they backfired politically. Nicholas Katzenbach, terming Marigold "phony," said Hanoi had used the attacks as a pretext to cancel the proposed contact, but he conceded that Washington had "badly handled" them.[17] Ben Read also doubted that the Poles could have produced the North Vietnamese, but he felt it would have been "wiser" to suspend raids near Hanoi as long as Marigold "was a live possibility, just to preclude having it being used as an excuse for failure." He called Kraslow and Loory biased, misled by the Poles, and driven by "a strong feeling that the United States government had goofed, and that feeling never departed them." Still, he admitted that their Marigold account was "depressingly accurate," despite a few errors. "And yet," he said, "we never saw the whites of their eyes in terms of the North Vietnamese. We don't have any proof to this day that they had actually started to Warsaw. . . . And I don't think we'll know until war's end and considerably after whether this was really a tragically missed opportunity or not."[18]

Bill Bundy also admitted that the administration had fumbled the bombings, "handing the other side an enormous public relations advantage" and leaving Washington "looking very sick indeed," a vulnerability that Hanoi and Warsaw happily exploited. Yet Bundy—still confusing Janusz and Bohdan Lewandowski[19] —vigorously denied that any peace prospect had been squandered. Noting Hanoi's denial (per Wilfred Burchett) that it had agreed to anything, he concluded that Rapacki never got his "customers" to sign on. "Well, I don't myself believe the

Polish thing was about to mature. This is a matter of refined examination, lots of things."[20] The Poles "played shell-games over and over again—the Russians never!"[21]

Harriman—who in early 1969 had invited Jerzy Michałowski to his home and grilled him about Warsaw's peace diplomacy[22]—had mixed sentiments. Though "satisfied that the Poles were acting in good faith," he too suspected that "they never had a firm commitment from Hanoi." He had "very little patience" for critics who bemoaned supposed missed opportunities, yet he agreed that Marigold (along with the Harold Wilson–Alexei Kosygin summit) came "closest" to fruition of all the efforts and may have yielded direct U.S.-DRV talks "if it had not been for the unfortunate bombing of Hanoi, but whether they would have come to anything or not it's very hard to say."[23] (On background to a reporter, Harriman "said that the North Vietnamese had a man picked for the Warsaw talks and that he either departed or was on the verge of it when our raids messed things up."[24])

The ex-officials who seemed most troubled by Marigold's memory were those most intimately linked with its birth and death: Chet Cooper and John Gronouski.

Shortly after leaving office, Gronouski spoke of writing up his Polish experiences, including his Vietnam talks, but cryptically said that they may "wind up being memoirs to my children."[25] He never did publicly air his views, so his 1969 oral history interview was his final pronouncement on Marigold. Released only more than three decades later, in response to the author's request, the transcript conveys his strong, if mixed, emotions.[26]

Essentially, Gronouski still adhered to the views he expressed to the Senate Foreign Relations Committee two years before, sharing the prevailing U.S. skepticism over whether Warsaw ever obtained a serious DRV commitment. Polish actions, he recalled, rapidly made him suspicious that "Hanoi never did say anything specific" about when it would open direct talks. "Each day I pressed [Rapacki] for the opportunity to sit down and talk to the Hanoi Ambassador, and each time the Hanoi Ambassador wasn't ready. . . . We were obviously being stalled."

Unlike some colleagues, however, Gronouski credited Rapacki's motives, at least in trying to extract enough U.S. concessions to achieve a breakthrough. He also believed that after his Christmas Eve gift (the 10-mile zone), Warsaw had done its best to sway Hanoi to enter talks. "My interpretation can be stated very simply," he summarized:

> One, that the Poles were trying to get something started again; that they certainly weren't on our side, but what they were trying to do I felt was to find the best possible bargain they could get out of us, as an agent of Hanoi; that Hanoi had always been very careful not to give them any authority to negotiate for Hanoi or to discuss this for Hanoi, but simply had given them what I call a hunting license to find

out what kind of a deal they could get out of us, and having found that out, to present that to Hanoi, and Hanoi then would make a judgment on whether they'd bite.[27]

The problem, he believed, was that "Hanoi just wouldn't bite. And in effect, we weren't put on by the Poles during this period of time; the Poles actually thought they were contributing. And they obviously had Russia's imprimatur on this. But they were probably as frustrated as we were in not getting anything out of Hanoi."

To this extent, Gronouski also felt the Hanoi bombings' "egregious error" was that they were a public relations debacle, not that they ruined a possibility for talks—a different view than that advanced by *The Secret Search for Peace in Vietnam*. He hailed Kraslow and Loory's "fantastic" reporting, yet he disputed their finding that the raids upended a real chance for peace; "history will bear this out," he predicted, "if the records are ever shown."

Yet Gronouski's belief that Hanoi was not ready to talk did not assuage his anger at Washington's handling of Marigold. He scoffed at the view that suspending the Hanoi raids risked exposure, perhaps alerting "Ky who would have blown his stack." Even if one had to "put Ky under lock and key," he felt, they should have been canceled, as "unobtrusively" as possible. Not doing so was a "bad error" that "undercut the credibility of our government and our President. . . . It made it very difficult to conduct a rational course of foreign policy around the world, and therefore had very long-lasting effects."

Cooper, despite a harshly self-critical tone, took an agnostic, ultimately skeptical view of Marigold.[28] In his interview, he confessed uncertainty as to whether Warsaw had ever secured Hanoi's go-ahead for the contact with the Americans, or was instead trying on its own (albeit with Moscow's knowledge and approval) to get talks going:

> I'm inclined to believe that basically Lewandowski came back from Hanoi [to] Saigon with no commitments from the North Vietnamese at all, but a kind of a thing that said, "This is interesting. See what you can work out, and if you can carry it off, we might play along with you." And I think that Lewandowski and the Poles, too, perhaps quite innocently or perhaps with malice, I don't know, overstated the North Vietnamese commitment. Maybe they wanted to; maybe they really believed in it. So it's conceivable that the whole thing in Warsaw was basically a holding operation for the North Vietnamese to have the Poles try to get the best—to see what they could get out of the Americans. . . . At the end of a certain point, if they thought they had the best possible terms they would walk in, and if they didn't feel they had the right terms they wouldn't; and that this . . . was a no-lose thing for them.[29]

However, Cooper acknowledged that a plausible case could be made that the North Vietnamese really were serious but that Washington sabotaged the talks. Polish and Soviet officials had repeatedly said so, "and we had a hell of a problem as a consequence of that because just an awful lot of people believed it, and who's to blame them? . . . What man in his right mind would want to bomb Hanoi at the moment that the North Vietnamese seemed ready to talk to us, especially after getting a warning?"[30]

Cooper, too, was "sore as hell" about the December 2 and 4 attacks, yet he was willing to write them off as "accidental," due to poor military and diplomatic co-ordination. What really riled him was the conscious decision to proceed with the December 13–14 raids, on fixed targets, despite Polish warnings that any further strikes could destroy the chance for talks. "Now those were really disgraceful," he said. "I frankly damn near picked up my marbles and just left. It was just an ob-scenity, it really was."[31]

✳ ✳ ✳

In late 1970, Cooper became the first official to tell the story publicly. *The Lost Crusade*, a Vietnam history-cum-memoir, recounted the descent into the South-east Asian maelstrom through the eyes of a midlevel aide who had not made the key decisions but had tried to implement them and closely observed their cata-strophic consequences. Ronald Steel, in the *New York Times*, called it a clear-eyed, unsentimental, brilliantly crafted account of policymaking gone horribly awry—yet one with "few harsh words and no villains" that never questioned the "first principles" that motivated the intervention.[32]

In this dispassionate spirit, Cooper titled his Marigold chapter "Tragedy of Errors" and toned down his language compared with what he said in his Lyndon B. Johnson Library interview.[33] Yet he left no doubt of his dismay at the disarray that prevented a rational probe of whether Marigold might have gotten some-where. The Hanoi raids were "just a piece of unfinished business" delayed by bad weather but then allowed when the clouds broke ("cruel acts of God"), carried out with knowledge of Marigold limited to "just a few people, most of whom were unaware of day-to-day bombing plans." If the DRV suspected U.S. officials of sending carefully crafted signals, it gave them "too much credit. The relationship between major bombing raids and American political decisions was by no means as intimate as the North Vietnamese, or even more sophisticated observers, might have assumed."

Cooper ultimately agreed with "even the most charitable among the 'Mari-golders'" that "at most the North Vietnamese had given Lewandowski a hunting license rather than any definite commitment when he was in Hanoi." Yet, even if that were so, it would not "excuse the slipshod, cavalier approach of the U.S. to the bombing of North Vietnam during the talks, especially in light of the Polish warnings."[34]

Although *The Lost Crusade* offered the most revealing account of Marigold yet by a participant—*too* revealing for McGeorge Bundy, who privately chided his ex-aide for excessive and premature candor[35]—it left much confusion to dispel about LBJ's role. Cooper fleetingly noted Johnson's determination to press ahead with the Hanoi strikes despite warnings from his aides to hold off until the situation clarified, yet emphasized a lack of coordination and excessive secrecy to explain them.[36] Those anticipating the ex-president's version eagerly awaited his memoirs. Assisted by a retinue of aides, he was reported to be hard at work at his ranch on a last testament, which would, above all else, explain the actions that had led his country into the Vietnam tar pit. But it was preempted by a publication that would have an even greater impact on how history would view his handling of the war.

Michałowski, Marigold, and the Pentagon Papers

On June 13, 1971, the *New York Times* began divulging the vast classified study of Vietnam War history commissioned in 1967 by a disillusioned McNamara. The newspaper, beneficiary of a leak to its reporter Neil Sheehan from a disgruntled former Pentagon consultant and gung-ho hawk, Daniel Ellsberg, presented evidence that blasted holes in the official justifications for U.S. military involvement in the conflict, bolstering charges that LBJ had hoodwinked Congress and the public about plans to escalate troop levels and the Tonkin Gulf incident. Nixon's Justice Department issued a restraining order against the *Times,* but new leaks quickly sprung up through other newspapers.

This secret chronicle of Vietnam policymaking emerged just as Michałowski—still bitter—ended his term. Poland's envoy to Washington was fond of America in many respects, occupying a post that should have been a capstone to a distinguished career. "Accomplished diplomat," read a brief U.S. bio, "has reputation of being pro-Western in outlook, . . . witty conversationalist, art collector."[37] Hardly a doctrinaire Communist, he flaunted his warm feelings for the West, to which he felt closely connected, a Janus-like identity symbolized by the two framed photos on his desk: King George VI and Ho Chi Minh.[38]

Yet Michałowski's Washington experience had not been pleasant. He was, in turn, stung by angry reactions to his early conversations about Vietnam peace failures; shaken by hard-line purges at home; harassed by hate mail from anti-communist émigrés; and so rattled by the inner-city crime around the Polish Embassy that, after several beatings and robberies, he erected a new fence around the compound on 16th Street, NW, and visited Washington's police chief to demand better protection. His wife, Mira, also had a lousy time, far preferring New York, where she thrived among the literary and cultural intelligentsia.

Moreover, dismal Polish-American relations, overshadowed by Vietnam, had cast a pall that was just beginning to lift. Frequently reduced to bemoaning the sorry state of bilateral ties, Michałowski mouthed Warsaw's line on various issues, yet U.S. officials sensed his discontent and his and Mira's "nervousness about their future."[39] "Personally, Michałowski is very charming," an aide advised Kissinger. "Being Jewish and in general on the liberal side, he has teetered on the brink of being purged at various times in his career."[40]

By early 1969, after a trip home that included a publicized chat with Gomułka, Michałowski felt "more self-confident" about his position, and U.S. officials concluded that the "danger" had passed.[41] Yet they continued to sense that he was mulling defection. In January 1971, after an intelligence alert to that effect, Secretary of State William Rogers approved contingency plans to grant the diplomat and his family asylum.[42] But he made no such request (though his sons would stay in the country to pursue their education and careers and would eventually acquire U.S. citizenship). One does not do such things, Mira later told their son, Piotr—implying that a sense of honor, dating from prewar days, precluded him from defecting despite private disillusionment.[43]

On June 22, Michałowski bade farewell to Rogers, for whom he had scant regard, even compared with Rusk, who had committed "grave errors" but "knew what he was about." The Pole could forgive his ignorance, given his foreign policy inexperience, but not his "lack of interest" and intellectual laziness. "Mr. Rogers," he told one American, "I could see as a Minister in the Netherlands or Denmark, but Secretary of State, never. He should stay with his golf and law."[44] He would not have been surprised to learn that Rogers was mainly a front man while Nixon entrusted his most vital foreign policy links (with Moscow, Beijing, Hanoi, etc.) to Kissinger, who, at that moment, behind Rogers' back, was packing his bags for the secret trip that would clinch the Sino-U.S. opening.

To Rogers, the Pole lamented that he was leaving just as bilateral ties finally seemed on the upswing, in sync with the U.S.-Soviet move toward détente. Otherwise, he seemed relieved, saying that he was "tired of his present work" and—perhaps sensing that his MSZ days were numbered—anticipated more freedom to teach, lecture, and write on foreign affairs. "Naturally, he would rely heavily on his experience here and particularly on his connection with events concerning Vietnam."

The Pentagon Papers were trickling out piecemeal—the Supreme Court had not yet cleared their publication—but Michałowski had read enough. Politely, Rogers thanked him for trying, at the United States' behest, to improve conditions for prisoners of war in North Vietnam. Far from mollified, the Pole "replied that he felt 'a bitter taste' after reading the newspaper articles about events in which he had been involved. He had assured his North Vietnamese contacts that the United States was sincere in its proposals and he now felt they had been right in their insistence to the contrary. He was afraid he had been 'a damn fool.'"

Oblivious to the tortured history behind Michałowski's comments, Rogers questioned "such cynical conclusions" and blandly wished the departing diplomat "every success for the future in his career."[45]

✱ ✱ ✱

Warsaw also noticed the Pentagon Papers. Foreign Minister Stefan Jędrychowski wondered if Poland, too, needed to gin up a postmortem of "Operacja Nogietek"

(Operation Marigold) using its own classified files to counter the U.S. version.[46] At his request, Asia Section head Romuald Spasowski—Lewandowski had gone to Cairo as ambassador—summarized Poland's involvement to date in public commentary on the affair (from the contacts with Kraslow and Loory to a Daniel Passent review of their book in *Polityka* that the MSZ instigated to "straighten out" errors) and expressed readiness to draft a report based on internal records of the December 1966 talks in Saigon, Hanoi, and Warsaw. However, he cautioned, the Vietnamese comrades (at whose request Poland had officially kept quiet) should be consulted before any release.[47] Spasowski was asked to draft a cable to Hanoi, but he advised holding off. U.S. indiscretions, he argued, should not force Poland's hand. An open leak might imperil future diplomacy; Warsaw had little to add to what was already revealed; and asking the DRV leaders to weigh in might put them, the Poles, or both in an awkward spot—though a flat refusal might be "difficult," the North Vietnamese might concur and yet insist that Poland tailor its account to Hanoi's present political or military aims, which in turn might exacerbate bilateral relations.[48]

Jędrychowski agreed. Given the "lack of enthusiasm," there was "no point in moving forward." Still, in case events later compelled Poland to issue a demarche, he directed Spasowski to draft a summary, "so we would be ready to do so immediately."[49]

LBJ's "Last Chance . . . with the History Books"

A day before leaving the White House, Johnson tried to lure a young aide to Texas to help with his main postpresidential project. "As soon as I get settled at home, I'm going to write my memoirs," he told Doris Kearns. "Those memoirs are the last chance I've got with the history books, and I've got to do it right. I've got to get my story out from beginning to end. We've got to go through my papers, and diaries, and ask hard questions to jog my memory. I want you all to be like vultures with me, picking out my eyes and my ears, tearing the memories and experience out of my guts putting all my insides into your sacks so you can help me write my story."

Yet, recalled the Harvard graduate student (who accepted LBJ's proposition on a part-time basis), "it soon became clear that he would rather be doing anything else"—aides trying to extract candid memories found him guarded, distracted, diffident; put before a tape recorder, "he froze; his language became artificial and he insisted on having sheaves of memos on his lap before he'd say a word." Straining to sound "presidential," the natural raconteur censored his salty language and vivid observations. The tooth-pulling yielded a "crashingly dull" narrative that resembled a circumspect commission report more than the voice of its uniquely boisterous nominal author.[50] A draft was reportedly done by early 1970, but "protracted revisions" were said to be so painful that when the Pentagon Papers began emerging the following June, "Mr. Johnson and his staff were either too weary or too distraught by late spring to go through the manuscript yet once again in order to accommodate the revelations."[51]

The Vantage Point: Perspectives of the Presidency, 1963–1969, which finally hit bookstores in late 1971, included a dismissive account of Marigold.[52] Unlike Rusk, LBJ was too polite to call the Poles "crooks," but his disdain shone through, anyway. The United States "never received through the Marigold exchanges anything that could be considered an authoritative statement direct from the North Vietnamese," he wrote. He termed the channel a "dry creek" exposed as a fraud when the DRV man failed to show up on December 6, 1966, in Warsaw—and touted Burchett's remarks to the *Washington Post* two years later as confirming this view. The Hanoi raids must have been an "excuse," because the meeting was not conditioned on a prior bombing halt. "The simple truth, I was convinced, was that the North Vietnamese were not ready to talk to us. The Poles had not only put the cart before the horse, when the time of reckoning came, they had no horse."

Johnson's account of Marigold—likely drafted by Rostow and/or Jorden[53]—confused more than edified the "history books." He again suggested that the Poles were not really in close touch with North Vietnam. And he threw a thicker blanket over his own authorization of continued strikes near Hanoi when the initiative hung in the balance, disregarding not merely Polish warnings but also the views of his own top aides—to which *The Vantage Point* did not refer, despite Cooper's prior revelation that, despite "strong objections" from McNamara, Katzenbach, and Tommy Thompson to further such raids, LBJ "would not be persuaded or diverted from his conviction that more pressure was the right prescription for Hanoi."[54] The only error the ex-president conceded was trying too hard, through too many channels, to convince the enemy of his "honest desire for peace," perhaps instead implying "that we wanted peace at any price." "Never once," he declared,

> was there a clear sign that Ho Chi Minh had a genuine interest in bargaining for peace. Never, through any channel or from any serious contact, did we receive any message that differed significantly from the tough line that Hanoi repeated over and over again: Stop all the bombing, get out of Vietnam, and accept our terms for peace. The North Vietnamese never gave the slightest sign that they were ready to consider reducing the Communists' half of the war or to negotiate seriously the terms of a fair peace settlement.[55]

In a *Washington Post* commentary, Cooper regretted that *The Vantage Point* failed to grapple with evidence and arguments in the Pentagon Papers (or his own book) and questioned its handling of Marigold and other initiatives. "Those of us who have found ourselves personally and emotionally involved in Vietnam during the period Mr. Johnson covers may, from another, lower vantage point, have seen the problem or parts of it very differently," he wrote. "How seriously, *really* seriously we conducted the 'peace probes' is an obvious case in point. To what extent did international and domestic public relations dominate the timing and style of the quest to the detriment of the objective we sought? To what extent did Johnson's Byzantine-like mode of making major decisions prosecuting the war and seeking a negotiated solution make it virtually impossible for responsible officials to pursue either course effectively?"[56]

Lyndon Johnson died in Texas on January 22, 1973—a day before Kissinger and Le Duc Tho signed the Paris Accords ending U.S. military involvement in Vietnam —so *The Vantage Point* indeed was his last word on Marigold, until he spoke posthumously through documents and tape recordings declassified decades later.

The Diplomatic Volumes

The Poles' fears notwithstanding, the initial Pentagon Papers leaks did not herald the imminent exposure of the classified Marigold record. Ellsberg felt that the hidden story of U.S. involvement in Vietnam should be made public, yet withheld the four (out of forty-seven) volumes of the study covering secret diplomacy. Because his aim was to end the war, he reasoned, he did not want to harm (or be accused of harming) any negotiating channels.[57]

Yet, with so much already in print and photocopies floating around, the still-classified diplomatic sections, too, soon began to seep out. In June 1972, Jack Anderson repeatedly alluded to them. Paraphrasing findings and spotlighting juicy quotations, he drew "painful lessons" from the secret record. Citing Marigold as an example of LBJ's "game of now-we-bomb-now-we don't," the muckraking columnist contended that his intensified bombing to buttress peace diplomacy had "repeatedly backfired"—yet Nixon (who had recently mined Haiphong Harbor and bombed Hanoi in response to North Vietnam's "Easter Offensive") seemed to be "using that same strategy."[58]

Anderson's disclosures prompted fresh government charges against Ellsberg and his confederate, Anthony J. Russo, who were already facing trial for conspiracy, espionage, and theft of government property for copying and divulging the classified Pentagon study; the Justice Department accused them of the new leaks, because only they and their lawyers had access to the still-secret diplomatic volumes as government exhibits in the case.[59]

The government's arguments did not impress Anderson, who in a gesture of contempt let the *Washington Post* see his copies of the volumes. On June 27, the paper bannered an exposé ("Papers Detail 4-Year Vietnam Diplomatic Stand-off"). In his lead article, Murrey Marder underlined a key point absent from *The Vantage Point*'s account of Marigold—that the December 1966 Hanoi bombings were "not merely a continuation of a pattern, but a greatly intensified series of attacks which had been prearranged and permitted to go ahead with no coordination with the diplomatic track."[60] Anderson, too, noted that LBJ had selectively used the secret record "to demonstrate how right and reasonable he had been" while omitting less flattering portions.[61] The *New York Times*, after also obtaining a set from Anderson, followed with its own splashy package.[62]

Despite their contingency planning, the Poles did not respond in kind. The leaks, though detailed, did not include extensive excerpts from classified Marigold files or spark any fresh criticism of Warsaw; to the contrary, Anderson effectively endorsed Polish arguments that LBJ's pressure tactics doomed the initiative. More important, after years "in the trough" (as Michałowski put it), bilateral relations had finally thawed. In early June, on his way home from his Moscow summit with Leonid Brezhnev, Nixon had stopped in Warsaw for a brief visit, ardently desired by the Poles. After his cordial conversations with President Edward Gierek (who had replaced Władysław Gomułka as the PZPR's first secretary) and Washington's approval of long-stalled measures to enhance economic ties, it hardly made sense for the Poles to harp on an old grievance (with a previous administration, no less).

The curtain parted a bit more in the spring of 1973—after Nixon's reelection, the Paris Accords ending U.S. military involvement in Vietnam, and the initial unraveling of the Watergate cover-up. Charged with stealing and leaking classified data, Ellsberg and Russo defended themselves, in part, by arguing that the information was already in the public domain. One witness called to back this case was Stuart H. Loory. In Los Angeles District Court, the journalist (now a TV news executive) gave alternately tedious and testy testimony over whether *The Secret Search for Peace in Vietnam*'s sagas of secret diplomacy, especially Marigold, meant suppressing the Pentagon Papers version amounted to locking the barn door after the horse had fled.[63] During the trial, reporters, lawyers, and anyone else at the courthouse could read uncensored copies of government exhibits, including the classified peace chronicles. Later that spring, the case was thrown out due to government misconduct, and the unpublished volumes went back under seal.

Only in the late 1970s, in response to Freedom of Information Act requests, did the government officially release a redacted version of the negotiation volumes of the Pentagon Papers, spawning the first serious scholarly attempts to assess Marigold on the basis of at least partial access to the declassified U.S. record.[64] Leslie H. Gelb published (with Richard K. Betts) an influential study of Vietnam policymaking drawing heavily on the Pentagon study he had overseen. Consistent with its analysis, *The Irony of Vietnam: The System Worked* called Marigold "promising" but also rapped Warsaw for having "blundered" and Washington for a lack of coordination by bombing Hanoi during the key phase, "succeeding neither in signaling nor in smashing."[65] In a study of the pitfalls of "coercive violence" in Vietnam, also informed by the Pentagon Papers, the political scientist Wallace J. Thies calculated in *When Governments Collide: Coercion and Diplomacy in the Vietnam Conflict, 1964–1968* that Marigold was likely the real deal and that LBJ had made a "disastrous" error by disregarding Polish warnings and failing to restrain the Hanoi bombings. North Vietnam, he judged, "likely . . . did agree to go through with the Warsaw talks, even though we have only Polish assurances in this respect. The Poles, after all, would only have looked foolish by stretching the truth on this matter, especially since the Italians (and very likely the Soviets) had been informed of the initiative from the start." "With the benefit of hindsight," he concluded, "it appears that the Marigold contact offered the best opportunity for the Johnson Administration to negotiate a settlement of the conflict."[66]

Arguing exactly the opposite, János Radványi, in *Delusion and Reality: Gambits, Hoaxes & Diplomatic One-Upmanship in Vietnam,* disparaged Marigold as an insincere Polish propaganda feint. Citing his authority as an ex-Communist diplomat and Eastern Bloc insider, he firmly insisted that no real chance for peace had existed.[67]

In 1983, George Herring, perhaps the Vietnam War's most eminent historian, rendered a cautiously hedged verdict. Assessing the negotiating volumes, he termed Marigold perhaps the "most intriguing" and "most controversial" of all Vietnam peace efforts, but he stressed the "mystery" and "confusion" still surrounding the affair and its central figure, Lewandowski—it was "not clear at the time and remains unclear today exactly what he had accomplished." In contrast to Thies' belief in Marigold's authenticity, he felt it "equally possible that the North Vietnamese were merely using the Poles to see what they might be able to get out of the United States or were offering vague responses simply to appear not to stand in the way of peace." Noting Radványi's claim that Lewandowski was a hard-line intelligence officer, Herring speculated that "the Russians may have had a hand in and directed [Marigold] behind the scenes." Yet he admitted that U.S. files "shed little light on the Soviet role or on Polish motives" and "leave unclear the central issue of whether Lewandowski was accurately representing the North Vietnamese."

His final word: "These questions may never be resolved satisfactorily."[68]

Memoirs, Published and Unpublished

Memoirs by U.S. participants in Marigold also sporadically appeared, most intoning the official view that it was much ado about very little. Rostow weighed in a year after his boss, and naturally sang the same tune. Without referring explicitly to the Poles, he wrote that in 1966–67, "the diplomatic networks were filled with suggestions emanating, or allegedly emanating, from Hanoi that a serious negotiating process was possible. In some cases, these hopes—expressed through third parties—were encouraged by Hanoi to create an environment of false hope and to try to erode the American negotiating position. In others, there was simply wishful thinking by third parties."[69]

In contrast to his private words to Kissinger, Lodge downgraded Marigold in his 1976 memoir *As It Was.* The Hanoi bombings, he wrote, gave Hanoi an "excuse" to terminate the initiative, and the Poles "ran away from the whole thing, using various pretexts." In light of its "transparently specious" excuses for delaying the proposed U.S.-DRV meeting, Lodge "surmised that the Polish Government had never been really authorized to deal for the Hanoi regime." Besides suggesting that Poland had inflated its mandate, he claimed that Rapacki "abandoned" and "broke off the talks" in Warsaw by December 5—when they had barely started—and Marigold had already "ceased" before the December 13–14 raids, ignoring the intense U.S.-Polish exchanges still under way. (Lodge's truncated account presumably reflected his departure from Saigon on December 12 and exclusion from subsequent cable traffic.)

"I was mystified by Hanoi's change of policy and today—ten years later—I still am," Lodge wrote. Gently, but more explicitly than at the time, he rued Washington's "inadequate" control of the air campaign, which "seemed to have been conducted on a largely military basis without enough regard for its political and diplomatic implications. . . . How much better it would have been had the bombings not occurred!"[70]

Rusk, in 1988 memoirs, still fumed at what he felt was a scurrilous Polish effort to snooker him and Washington into falsely believing that Warsaw had acted with a firm mandate from Hanoi. Declaring that he "doubted the authenticity of Marigold" all along, he termed Lewandowski's position "specious," because he "simply didn't reflect Hanoi's views," and—citing Radváyni—called him "a Polish intelligence agent acting on his own" and the entire initiative a "sham." Brushing off charges that the bombings ruined a promising approach, Rusk snorted that "there was nothing to collapse" in the first place.[71]

✳ ✳ ✳

Gronouski never wrote memoirs, remaining quiet about the episode he briefly hoped would mark the high point of his public life. Though his service as Johnson's man in Poland had ended unhappily, the association outlasted his presidency. In September 1969, Gronouski became the first dean of the LBJ School of Public Affairs at the University of Texas; in line with its namesake's wish to train practitioners, he helped shape a curriculum to prepare students to navigate the "'messiness' of public policy."[72] In the Jimmy Carter administration, he chaired the Board for International Broadcasting, which oversaw Radio Free Europe and Radio Liberty, the Cold War services set up to wean Eastern Europe from Soviet domination. Returning to academia, he taught at the LBJ School until retiring in 1989, and he died in 1996 at the age of seventy-six near his Green Bay home.

The *New York Times,* recalling the economist, public servant, and educator, noted Gronouski's "bridge building" in Poland, serving as "what amounted to President Johnson's personal envoy to Eastern Europe." But in a final insult, the paper failed to mention the aspect of the job he privately prized most—trying to end the Vietnam war—and how close he may have come in December 1966.[73]

✳ ✳ ✳

For more than a decade, the most important reconsideration of Marigold by a participant stayed hidden. Contrary to the surmise of some Americans who knew him, Michałowski went home when his term ended rather than apply for asylum; yet those who suspected that his diplomatic career was drawing to an unhappy end were not off base. By the time he returned to Warsaw in mid-1971, many old MSZ comrades were gone, and as the Rapacki crowd's most prominent survivor, he was ripe for removal. Dispirited with his work, at the age of sixty-two, he may have wanted to turn in a new direction—but he did not leave voluntarily: A belated victim of the 1968 purges, and "out of favor" with the Gierek regime, he was fired and expelled from the PZPR; the security services had never trusted him or Mira, compiling a fat file (1,600 pages!) on their private and social life in Warsaw, London, New York, and Washington. He was allowed to keep his apartment and pension but stripped of the perks he had long taken for granted: access to behind-the-curtain happenings, secret documents, fraternizing with fellow diplomats, confidential summaries of the Western press (now he had to rely on shortwave radio to catch the BBC or Voice of America, like ordinary Poles), and foreign travel—deprived of his diplomatic passport, and unable to go abroad for several years, he had to apply for a new one (in one humiliating incident, when his wife went to the Interior Ministry to seek new travel documents, an officer lectured her on proper behavior abroad and tried to recruit her as an informant). "He was suddenly thrown in with the hoi polloi, in their shoes instead of being one of the insiders, and I don't think he ever got used to that," his son Piotr recalled. "They taught him a lesson. . . . Once he was pushed aside like that, the light went out of him. . . . He was made into a nonperson."[74]

With his intellectual and professional oxygen having been abruptly severed, Michałowski started a new career as a translator of popular fiction and commentator on world events, reclaiming his "Stefan Wilkosz" pseudonym. Mira, besides her own prolific writing, had translated modern literary lions (she had hobnobbed with some of them in New York): Hemingway, Wilder, Nin, Stein, Plath, Doctorow, Vidal, Styron, and the like; by contrast, Jerzy rendered Polish versions of thrillers like *Six Days of the Condor, Day of the Jackal,* and *Shall We Tell the President?*

Yet Vietnam gnawed at him. Back in Washington, insisting that Warsaw had got a bum rap over Marigold, he had mused about one day writing a memoir to "clear Poland's and his own good name."[75] A decade later, he itched to rebut the U.S. accounts dribbling out; Lodge's "Saigon Reminiscence" especially irked him. Between foreign policy essays and an African travelogue—Michałowski (under his own name) melded closed MSZ files and his own memories to pen a detailed (128 single-spaced pages) manuscript, "Polish Secret Peace Initiatives in Vietnam." Naturally, it dwelt on Marigold and his mission to Hanoi a year before, vindicated Warsaw's actions, and cited U.S. sources to declare "that not only the Polish initiatives but all other attempts taken by the White House up to 1968 were insincere," concocted to deceive public opinion and probe Hanoi, not to seek peace. Until the Tet Offensive shattered illusions of victory, he concluded, the "war party" around LBJ had prevailed each time a political path seemed to open, persuading him to rely on force to ensure "American domination of South Vietnam." This pattern yielded the "fatal results" of deferring talks until Washington could enter into them from a position of strength.[76]

What made this postmortem so valuable was not Michałowski's analysis but his use of internal Polish files, which unveiled swaths of the story invisible in U.S. records, especially Warsaw's exchanges with other Communist actors. His report would have significantly contributed to history—if it had been published. For unknown reasons, however, the Foreign Ministry buried the manuscript. At one point, the MSZ called in Lewandowski to read it over to offer comments or corrections; he had nothing special to add, but when pressed, made some general comments, suggesting some historical context for non-Vietnam specialists. When the report did not appear, Lewandowski heard that the ministry and Michałowski had squabbled over royalty and copyright issues.[77] So whether for financial, legal, or political reasons, the report remained unknown to the outside world, but the author kept a personal copy.

The Three at the Center

What became of the men at the heart of Marigold? Like Lodge, Giovanni D'Orlandi had a last hurrah or two left. After his Killy peace probe ran adrift, his health stabilized enough to permit him to accept another foreign slot. Rather than send him back to Saigon, however, in November 1968 Fanfani named him Italy's ambassador to Greece, a less arduous post closer to urgent medical care.

D'Orlandi's Hellenic heritage stretched back to his Alexandria childhood (and Santorini-born mother), but this was no sentimental sinecure. Since "the colonels" had seized power in April 1967, Greece had seethed with intrigue and political passions that occasionally erupted into violence, and tension clouded Athens' ties with Rome's center-left government. D'Orlandi, reprising his unique role as refuge and lunch host in Saigon during coup attempts, soon established his embassy in Athens as a salon and haven for dissidents and critics (including the magistrate Christos Sartzetakis, portrayed in Costa Gavras' 1969 political thriller Z). D'Orlandi took the "resistance" under his wing on his own, not at Rome's prompting, and as a result drew the dictatorship's ire.

"What does the Italian ambassador have against us?" a minister exploded. "He is an agent against us! He is anti-Greek!" When his aide Paolo Janni related these remarks, his boss beamed at making the junta's enemies' list. Told he was also accused of belonging to a diplomatic cabal conspiring to undermine the regime, D'Orlandi rued that it was no longer a gang—his Australian colleague had left, leaving him the only member; besides, he could hardly be called anti-Greek because the national pastime was sitting in a café and griping about the government. D'Orlandi, Janni later wrote, stood "at the center of the battle (yes, the battle) to free a country that had given democracy—both the word and the practice—to the world from the whims of a rough military regime."[78]

The Italian's term was also noteworthy for personal reasons. He brought Colette to Athens, and the suave "Nino" and his Vietnamese companion became a hot item on the capital's elite social circuit. They married and in 1971 produced a daughter, Daniela, who would follow her father into the diplomatic corps.

Had Giovanni's health held out, he was said to be in line to become ambassador in Cairo (where Lewandowski, coincidentally, was *ending* his term as Poland's envoy). It did not. In June 1969, one person who had met him during Marigold raised an eyebrow at his health issues. Recalling their December 1966 encounter in Saigon, Bundy called D'Orlandi "a funny character, he's still living, although he was supposedly under a death sentence at that time."[79] D'Orlandi had a flair for the dramatic, yet his ailments were hardly psychosomatic. Each day, he took pills to combat his blood disorder, but the disease advanced. He died in Athens on September 25, 1973, a week shy of his fifty-sixth birthday, cutting short a remarkable diplomatic career and leaving behind a young bride, a two-year-old daughter, a handsome library—and a contested legacy.

While in Athens, D'Orlandi had flirted with publishing a memoir of his Vietnam experience, asking Janni to "put his papers in order" so they might appear in book form. The aide organized his diaries (which extended through his Greek posting) into an 800-page manuscript, but the Farnesina tried to censor it and, in the end, dissuaded D'Orlandi from going public.[80] But after his death, Colette jealously guarded his journals and, she said, repeatedly rejected Fanfani's entreaties to use them in edited form.[81]

With D'Orlandi's diary still hidden, a different Italian perspective emerged. In 1991, Mario Sica published a generally admiring portrait of his boss in Saigon and his and Fanfani's efforts. His narrative, which echoed D'Orlandi's critical view of Washington's handling of Marigold, largely relied on U.S. documentation, mostly from the Pentagon Papers; he later said that the Farnesina had let him examine but not cite or quote still-classified Italian telegrams (many of which he had decoded himself).[82] Sica also contacted Lewandowski, both in Warsaw and Athens, seeking his retrospective views; the Pole, still feeling bound by secrecy, provided general answers rather than any new documentation or details.[83]

The actual Italian record remained buried, until D'Orlandi's Marigold cables—still formally classified—were leaked to the present author in 2003. Two years later, Colette and Daniela allowed his Vietnam diary to be published by a Catholic Italian publisher (*30 Days*), with ex–prime minister Giulio Andreotti shepherding the project. Three decades after his death, Giovanni could finally fully reveal and explain his actions, and make his case for why Marigold had gone right and then so badly wrong, to history.

✳ ✳ ✳

In the late 1970s, after publishing two skimpy volumes of memoirs, Henry Cabot Lodge intended to write a substantial account of his Vietnam experiences. But he never completed it, and judging from the unfinished draft left in his papers at the Massachusetts Historical Society, this was not such a grievous loss. As a son recalled, he had a "terrible time" on it—his heart was not really in it, his stomach condition was worsening, and despite the Pentagon Papers, he still felt constrained by propriety, secrecy, and a lifetime of concealing rather than parading emotions or policy dissents.[84] Despite flickers of life, the manuscript—in the third person, with few traces of genuine introspection—was mostly a dry chronology, summarizing or excerpting one cable, memo, letter, or speech after another; its Marigold account rehashed the disjointed tale in *As It Was*.[85] Another episode also implied Lodge's reluctance to face a painful past. After he agreed to an oral history interview, an LBJ Library staff member flew to Boston, rented a car, and phoned to confirm their appointment. Instead, Lodge canceled it, saying that he was too busy. The interview was never rescheduled.[86]

In failing health, trying to enjoy retirement with Emily on their wooded estate on the shore of Salem Bay, Lodge was in no mood to rock the boat.[87] Discreet to the grave, he never grumbled to his family about the government's handling of Marigold, or further vented his feelings about the affair. He died in 1985.[88]

✴ ✴ ✴

Unlike D'Orlandi or Lodge, Janusz Lewandowski was still in his thirties, nearing the prime of his career, with decades of work ahead of him.[89] In early 1970, after three years in the MSZ's Asia Section, he received a new posting to Cairo, where a decade earlier he had been first secretary. Now he would go as ambassador, despite lingering rancor at the Interior Ministry, where officials even suspected him as a security risk. Just as his posting was proposed, the agency received a report from a Polish spy "prepared by us to infiltrate the American intelligence services" that the CIA had plotted to recruit Lewandowski in Saigon. The operation had gone so far as preparing to send a Polish double agent to South Vietnam, but was then "abandoned" for unclear reasons; the mole, code-named "Kordoński" (Cordon), believed that the CIA "cared very much about enlisting Lewandowski" and still hoped to do so.[90]

Alarmed, the Interior Ministry reexamined Lewandowski's past conduct—and accentuated the negative. An inspector who reviewed his files cast in a sinister light allegations that the MSW had ignored when it had approved his nomination as ICC commissioner four years before. As first secretary in Cairo, he had supposedly befriended a person "suspected for cooperation with one of the Western intelligence agencies" and targeting Poles in particular; in Tanganyika, he was accused of "wasteful management, abusing state funds for his private purposes" and unspecified "serious glitches" in his personal life; and in Vietnam, he was said to have reneged on vows to cooperate with the ministry, "actively interfered" with agents' work, and, as in Dar es Salaam, "created an atmosphere of antagonism among the employees." (When shown this report many years later, Lewandowski indignantly denied any impropriety.)

This record, Colonel Z. Zabawa warned, bolstered concerns that the diplomat might be susceptible to CIA blackmail: "These facts could have been used to some degree by the American intelligence in recruiting Lewandowski." His "frequent" visits to New York to attend UN sessions, as well as his Foreign Ministry work in Warsaw, "can become the basis for the American intelligence to become interested in his person," Zabawa added. He neither judged Lewandowski guilty nor urged his arrest, but urged further measures, including securing (verbally and in writing) a full list of his contacts with Americans (to ascertain which might have been intelligence approaches); warning him he was targeted for recruitment; and requesting that he apprise the MSW of any future provocations.[91]

The Interior Ministry's qualms, however, did not block Lewandowski from returning to Cairo. He arrived in October 1970, weeks after Nasser's death, in time to witness the rise of Anwar Sadat. Passing forty, the Pole also marked personal milestones. On April 15, 1970, he wed Wanda Brzozowski, an MSZ communications clerk fifteen years his junior. Unlike his first marriage, this one lasted, and made him a father twice over in Egypt; a son, Krzysztof, arrived in June 1971, and a daughter, Joanna, followed in May 1973.

Soon after he reached the Middle East, Lewandowski had a traumatic encounter with the region's violent radicalism. While he was accompanying the Polish head of state, Marian Spychalski, on an official visit to Pakistan, he was nearly felled in a terrorist assault during a welcoming ceremony at the Karachi airport. Spychalski was unhurt, but Deputy Foreign Minister Zygfryd Wolniak, with whom Lewandowski had traveled to Southeast Asia the previous year, was killed. Lewandowski had been chatting with him just a few moments before an airline cargo truck ploughed at full speed into a receiving line—but had fortuitously left to search for Wolniak's briefcase. The driver—who explained that he wished to "eliminate all enemies of Islam," including Polish "socialists" who "want to destroy Islam and Moslems"—was subsequently hanged by the Pakistani authorities.[92]

Although the Interior Ministry had approved Lewandowski's appointment as ambassador to Egypt, sharp yet muffled tensions between them persisted. In early 1973, an MSW agent working in Cairo sent superiors in Warsaw a cranky assessment of "the boss"—whom he termed a "cutthroat" careerist and a "spoiled child"—and what he described as the worsening "operational and political situation" at the embassy. Another, apparently more senior figure, who had worked as a "counselor" under Lewandowski, also criticized him to the secret police agency —yet, when asked to put his complaints in writing, refused to do so, citing doubts that they would be acted upon and fears of retribution given Lewandowski's "broad connections among influential people" and "well-known vengefulness." Again lacking the stomach (and evidence) for a full-blown confrontation, the

Interior Ministry in May 1973 issued a blandly positive internal report on Lewandowski that termed him an "exceptionally talented employee who continues to develop professionally"; noted that he had received "very good" ratings from the Communist Party; and, remarkably, stated that there was "no single controversial opinion in his files."[93]

The most dramatic event of Lewandowski's tenure in Cairo came in October 1973, when Egypt and Syria launched a surprise attack on Israel in a bid to regain lands lost six years before. From stray comments (Sadat aide Hafez Ismail told him that the present situation was untenable) and observations of troops heading east, the Pole suspected an imminent strike and asked Soviet ambassador Vladimir M. Vinogradov: "Don't you think something is in the air?" The veteran diplomat assured him nothing special was up—you know the Egyptians, they're always talking big; though Vinogradov told him the day after the war started that the Soviets were not forewarned, Lewandowski never trusted him again. When Sadat's forces crossed the Suez Canal, he felt lucky not to be trapped in the crossfire. Shortly before, he had gone to the Great Bitter Lake—a natural saltwater body midway through the waterway—to check on the skeleton crews of two Polish freighters stranded by the 1967 war; the MS *Djakarta* and MS *Boleslaw Bierut,* plus a dozen other ships, made up a "Yellow Fleet" (for the color of the sand carpeting their decks) that sailed, or was towed, only when the canal reopened in 1975.[94]

In 1974 Lewandowski returned to Warsaw, where the foreign minister, Stefan Olszowski, put him in charge of diplomatic protocol. The offer of a low-wattage slot after hot-spot service in Cairo and Saigon took him aback, but with two young children to raise, it at least offered a break from war zones in the third world. Moving into a modest apartment—where they still lived more than three decades later—Janusz and Wanda spent the next five years in the dour relative calm of Warsaw in the Gierek era, as Poland accumulated debt, its economy (like that of its Soviet neighbor) stagnated, and grumbling mounted.

By the time Poland exploded into outright defiance in the summer of 1980, with the Gdansk shipyard strike and the rise of the Solidarity free trade movement, Lewandowski had left again. In 1979, he became ambassador to Greece, which had shed its military dictatorship and restored civilian rule. From Athens, Lewandowski watched his own homeland's political and social upheaval, gaining firsthand glimpses only during brief trips home. When the Polish prime minister, General Wojciech Jaruzelski, under heavy Soviet pressure, declared martial law in December 1981 to crush Solidarity, Lewandowski faced a dilemma: Should he denounce the move and defect, or sit tight and await instructions?

With a news blackout in Poland—and coded communications down; a cipher clerk had suffered a heart attack—Lewandowski, like much of the world, learned about martial law from the radio and initially had trouble figuring out what was happening. Almost two decades earlier, as a young diplomat in Africa, he had been summoned by a mystified prime minister to explain the Cuban Missile Crisis. Now, amid rumors of resistance, violence, and a looming Soviet entry, Greek prime minister Andreas Papandreou summoned him to interpret the Polish confusion. In the dark, all he could do was plead for patience. "I said to him, 'We have to wait, we have to wait.'"

Though in office less than two months, Greece's first socialist prime minister (whose mother was Polish) had already warmed to Warsaw's envoy. If you have any problems, Papandreou told him, you are welcome here.

Lewandowski appreciated the offer, but repeated that he would have to wait and see. His red line was foreign intervention, he recalled: If Moscow invaded or Warsaw invited in Soviet troops, he would resign and go public. He grimly remembered the Kremlin's takeovers of Hungary and Czechoslovakia and had no illusions that the West would come to Poland's rescue, but he also feared that his compatriots might fight not only the Russians but also each other. We cannot survive another civil war, he told Papandreou.

Contrary to his own fears, General Jaruzelski crushed Solidarity without resorting to Soviet help—and Lewandowski stayed on the job. A U.S. diplomat had whispered that his embassy's doors were open if he wanted to seek asylum, but he declined to emulate Romuald Spasowski, now ambassador in Washington, who loudly defected to protest martial law.

Instead, Lewandowski cultivated ties with Papandreou, trying to preserve Poland's relations with the NATO country even as Washington called for sanctions and treating Warsaw as a pariah until it lifted martial law, released political prisoners, and restored Solidarity's legal status. As in Vietnam, he was caught up in a mediation effort—except instead of being the intermediary himself, he tried to convince the left-leaning Papandreou to be Jaruzelski's bridge to the Western countries that now shunned him.[95]

His arguments fell on receptive ears. Papandreou was as Americanized as any foreign leader, with a Harvard PhD in economics, Navy service in World War II, stints teaching at Berkeley and other universities, and even U.S. citizenship (which he later renounced). Yet he now saw the United States as an imperialist colossus and blamed the CIA for much mischief, including the 1967 coup that brought the colonels to power in Athens (despite Washington's pressuring them to release him and his elderly father), and he scorned Ronald Reagan's anti-Soviet policies.

Lewandowski's cultivation paid off handsomely. At Brezhnev's funeral in November 1982, Papandreou became the first NATO leader since martial law to shake Jaruzelski's hand (Reagan's delegate, Vice President George H. W. Bush, ignored him). Further riling Washington, he accepted Jaruzelski's invitation to visit Poland and agreed to lobby against anti-Warsaw sanctions.[96]

Privately, Lewandowski did not believe that Papandreou would really go, and it took two years—he insisted on some easing of martial law—but the Greek leader finally paid a state visit to Poland in late 1984. Still better (or worse, to Reagan, Margaret Thatcher, et al.), he hailed Jaruzelski as a "patriot" and criticized Solidarity for provoking martial law.[97]

Pleased, Jaruzelski invited Lewandowski to Warsaw to discuss the Greek leader's surprising warmth. In contrast to their prior talks, the general sent word that he wanted a long, informal evening chat. Over snacks and coffee, pleasantries (Jaruzelski praised his guest's Vietnam work) yielded to sharper exchanges. Resolving to be "absolutely frank," Lewandowski explained that Papandreou's sympathy reflected personal idiosyncrasies and annoyed many Greeks, who hated the military dictatorship.

What did *he* think about the situation in Poland? Jarzuelski asked, provocatively.

Lewandowski recalled answering bluntly: "Mr. Prime Minister, you cannot continue with military rule, because it is not good for the army, not good for the people, not good for the Polish image abroad, and it never is productive. . . . Wherever a military government has been established, it always fails." The impertinence startled Jaruzelski, but he did not argue. "I am feeling it, too," he said.

His Lewandowski's MSZ colleagues were aghast when they heard of the exchange—"My God, are you crazy?"—but Jaruzelski, impressed, asked Lewandowski to join his staff. As a career diplomat, Lewandowski was ambivalent; ideally, Jaruzelski would have named him UN ambassador, a prestigious post where he could follow in Michałowski's (and his namesake Bohdan's) footsteps. Yet, returning to Warsaw offered personal advantages; Krzystof and Joanna were entering their teens, and he preferred that they pursue higher education at home after attending a British school in Athens.

In the end, Jaruzelski "offered no choice," and Lewandowski accepted a post in the prime minister's office with the formal title of deputy head of the PZPR Central Committee's International Section; at the same time, unwilling to resign from the Foreign Service, he kept his status as an MSZ employee on "special assignment." For the Communist system in Poland's last half decade, almost to the end, he worked as a Jaruzelski political aide.

One assignment returned Lewandowski to Vietnam for the first time since the war. Hardly squeamish about consorting with Communist dictatorships (being one), the Socialist Republic of Vietnam—with the North and South now unified under Hanoi's control—invited Jaruzelski for a state visit. He could not go, but he sent Lewandowski to deliver a friendly reply. His trip overlapped one by the interior minister, General Czesław Kiszczak, leading to some amusing moments when they jointly met their Vietnamese hosts.

Receiving the Poles, Pham Van Dong—pushing eighty, but still hanging on as premier—warmly greeted Lewandowski, rising to hug and kiss him and then taking him aside to converse privately. Out of the corner of his eyes, Lewandowski saw the surprised expressions of Kiszczak and his delegation, who were unaware of his prior Vietnam history.

When they went to Saigon (now Ho Chi Minh City), the mayor threw a dinner for the Polish interior minister, but again, Lewandowski felt like the guest of honor. In his welcome, the city administrator, a Communist functionary, noted that when he was there as ICC commissioner, Lewandowski did not know them because they were underground, but they knew him very well, because he was their friend. The tribute grew so fulsome that Lewandowski feared Kiszczak might feel offended.

The mission also evoked Lewandowski's Marigold memories. Privately, Dong asked if he were going to write about those secret negotiations two decades before.

Mr. Prime Minister, he remembered answering, I am still bound by my oath of secrecy to you. Even if Marigold failed, I must still abide by my word.

If you want to write about it, go ahead, Dong told him: "I release you!" If he had any problems, he could speak with him and Giap.

Lewandowski appreciated the blessing, but he did not feel tempted. He was "very busy," did not relish digging through archives (his personal records were sparse), and still felt confused over the affair's denouement, which he sensed Warsaw had "very badly handled." So, unlike Michałowski, he was content to let the sleeping dogs lie.

Dong smiled as he bid Lewandowski farewell. "Good luck, my son," he said, leaving the Pole "very much touched."[98]

In early 1989—just before the regime and Solidarity agreed on the elections that propelled Poland toward noncommunist rule that summer—Lewandowski resumed his diplomatic career, going to Greece for another stint as ambassador. He hoped to renew his ties with Papandreou, but the prime minister soon lost a bid for reelection amid assorted scandals. Again, Lewandowski watched from Athens as Poland underwent a political crisis—this time bringing Solidarity to power.

A postcommunist foreign minister recalled Lewandowski in 1991 and told him that he was being replaced, not fired, but a personnel officer spoke of trouble finding a new position. Behind the sheepish excuses, Lewandowski sensed, was the view that his links with Jaruzelski and the PZPR had indelibly tainted him. Do not trouble yourself, he finally blurted. After more than thirty-five years in the Foreign Service, he had his pension; moreover, he felt that if the MSZ's leadership had lost confidence in him, he might as well leave: "If I'm not wanted, 'Goodbye.'" Only sixty, in good health, and with plenty of energy left, he retired and, by his own account, never again set foot in the Foreign Ministry.

"You know, I am proud man," he explained.

The Other Side(s) of the Story

The revolutions that swept the Soviet empire in Central and Eastern Europe in 1989, and dismantled the USSR itself within two years, not only ended the Cold War but also opened up new horizons for understanding it: Finally, historians could sift through long-closed Communist archives, and officials from the old order could tell their stories unshackled by censorship and party discipline. As fascinating revelations streamed out, I was lucky enough to have a front-row seat as the first director of the Woodrow Wilson Center's Cold War International History Project (CWIHP) in Washington, a new enterprise dedicated to assessing and disseminating the new evidence.

The first breakthrough in understanding Marigold's hidden Communist dimension, however, emerged not from Eastern Bloc archives but from the family of a participant haunted by its failure. Amid the rubble of the system for which he had worked for decades but which ultimately left him in the cold, Jerzy Michałowski died in Warsaw at the age of eighty-three, pleased to have outlived the Soviet experiment whose birth he had witnessed as a child in Kiev. His family had "begged" him to write memoirs, but he seemed uninterested. Yet, going through their father's papers, his sons found his unpublished Vietnam manuscript. Stefan faxed CWIHP a summary, explaining that the report "was brought to the United States shortly before his death in March of 1993."[99]

Intrigued, I compared the précis with the declassified U.S. record and quickly saw that Michałowski's version significantly amplified—and challenged—the story as then known. In 1996, I printed Stefan's summary in the *CWIHP Bulletin*, and a year later he kindly provided the full report. The Polish-Canadian historian Leszek Gluchowski translated it and managed to obtain from the MSZ archives some of the cables Michałowski cited.

This new Polish evidence made a strong prima facie case that LBJ had mishandled the matter, misjudging the extent to which Hanoi had authorized Warsaw to set up direct talks. Illuminating previously hidden Communist exchanges, it resolved what Herring had termed "the central issue of whether Lewandowski was accurately representing the North Vietnamese position."[100] However, discovering whether *Hanoi* (not just Warsaw) was serious clearly required still-inaccessible Vietnamese sources.

Coincidentally, a unique opportunity was arising to do just that. By the mid-1990s, Washington and Hanoi were finally preparing to normalize diplomatic ties, two decades after the last chopper lifted off from the U.S. Embassy's roof in Saigon. Since then, most Americans had tried to forget the war, historical exchanges between the two countries had focused narrowly on inquiries about soldiers who had been taken as prisoners of war or were missing in action, and—facing daunting obstacles of language, distance, and Communist secrecy—only a handful of hardy souls had seriously tried to discover what had taken place on the other side.[101]

Ironically, the event that led to a broader dialogue was McNamara's belated Vietnam memoir, *In Retrospect*, which confessed that the Johnson administration was "wrong, terribly wrong" to escalate the war—though he blamed errors and bad judgment, not ignoble intent. U.S. critics blasted McNamara (from both right and left), but Hanoi praised the American known as the war's "architect" for 'fessing up. In November 1995, Vietnam's government welcomed him (and a group

of scholars) to Hanoi to propose gathering former enemies for a history conference that would ask, among other questions, whether Washington or Hanoi had
"missed opportunities" to end or limit the war.

As CWIHP director, I found myself on that surreal expedition—"McNamara
in Hanoi" was as bizarre a notion as "Nixon in China." Eager to promote the delayed political and economic opening to the United States—and recalling the ex–
defense secretary's World Bank presidency—the Vietnamese authorities embraced a get-together of wartime enemies, which took place in June 1997. A team
of former U.S. officials headlined by McNamara and a Vietnamese delegation led
by ex–foreign minister Nguyen Co Thach gathered in Hanoi's Metropole Hotel,
the renovated French colonial palace that during the conflict had been known as
the Thong Nhat (Reunification) and had housed guests in considerably more austere conditions. For three days, in formal sessions and in hotel corridors, bars,
and restaurants, the ex-enemies swapped stories and arguments.

For me, a scholar at the table, the highlight came when a slight, bespectacled,
elderly Vietnamese man began softly relating his memories of a secret peace effort involving Poland. Many of those present found his remarks obscure, but I
snapped to alertness, recognizing Marigold. My excitement soon turned to confusion—for Nguyen Dinh Phuong's tale of secretly flying from Hanoi to Warsaw
was not only *absent* from U.S. *and* Polish sources but also utterly *contradicted* the
presumptive explanation of why direct contacts had failed to start on December
6, 1966. Though the Americans insisted that *they* were ready to talk but the North
Vietnamese were not, Phuong believed exactly the opposite—and vividly recalled
vainly waiting, with Do Phat Quang, all that day for Gronouski to show!

The conference moved on, but afterward I introduced myself, and during the
next two years sent Phuong copies of declassified U.S. Marigold documents, including Gronouski's cables. In June 1999, I returned to Hanoi and conducted an
interview that turned out to be the most moving, and ultimately depressing, experience I have ever had as a historian. Over several hours, in a sweltering conference room, Phuong recounted his experience, responded to questions, and provided a written account.[102]

Pondering the U.S. records, which he had not seen before, he began to consider the possibility that Gronouski, far from deliberately standing up Quang, had
fervently desired to meet him—but a misunderstanding had foiled a major step
toward peace. "It is pity, it is pity," he repeated, shaking his head slowly, his voice
thick with emotion.

Though frustrated by the lack of contemporaneous Vietnamese documentation, I believed that Phuong was telling the truth—and that the disparate Marigold evidence, U.S., Polish, Vietnamese, and more, when meticulously pieced
together, revealed a previously obscured portrait of a diplomatic disaster of grievous proportions. Trying to reconstruct what happened, I spent more than a decade ransacking archives from Austin to Kew Gardens to Warsaw to Rome to
Moscow and beyond and interviewing surviving participants.

One of the few who declined to talk was McNamara. Shortly after Marigold's collapse, he had told LBJ and Lodge, respectively, that it might have produced direct talks and "shortened the war by two years," but for the Hanoi bombings.[103] By the time he began speaking publicly about the war, however, he had forgotten or altered those views, and he never cited Marigold as a "missed opportunity."[104] Cooper, by contrast, reversed course in the opposite direction, confessing after hearing Phuong's story that "we were wrong" at the time in concluding that Hanoi was never serious about meeting Gronouski.[105]

But what transformed my book from a dissection of a diplomatic episode into a far more ambitious project was finding Janusz Lewandowski, living quietly in retirement in Warsaw.[106] Presuming that during Marigold he, like Lodge and D'Orlandi, had been a senior diplomat, probably in his fifties or sixties, and had already passed from the scene, I had not thought of seeking him out—until one day in June 2003. Rereading one of the myriad declassified documents clogging my basement, I noticed that Lewandowski was only thirty-five in 1966, meaning that he might still be alive! I emailed a Polish colleague, who found a local telephone number. I dialed it apprehensively, and to my relief a voice at the other end confirmed that yes, he was *that* Janusz Lewandowski, and was willing to talk with me; no one else had inquired. I flew to Warsaw a few days later.

We met on a Monday evening in the lobby of the Grand Hotel Orbis, less seedy since a recent face-lift but still a concrete reminder of the postwar rush to rebuild the city. Lewandowski appeared right on time, neatly attired in a gray suit, vest, and tie, his silver hair (matching his glasses' rims) carefully combed, his manner friendly if reserved, his English only slightly rusty. Within minutes it became clear that for Lewandowski, then seventy-two, Marigold still evoked strong, troubled memories and passionate views.

Day after day, we sat in the hotel's second-floor bar parsing the evidence—our table strewn with documents, books, and my tape-recorder, the air smoky from Lewandowski's Polish cigarettes, the two of us transported to wartime Saigon and Hanoi. In ensuing years, we would speak many times, in long-distance calls and more trips to Warsaw. His memories inspired me to write a tome that not only tackled Marigold but offered a unique "vantage point" on the Vietnam War, the perspective of a Communist diplomat in Saigon; opened vistas on other Cold War and American events; and told a compelling life story. At the center, however, was the attempt to alter the course of history, to end a war that had claimed so many lives, poisoned international and U.S. politics, wrecked LBJ's presidency, and shaken global culture in the 1960s and beyond.

"Looking back on your life and career," I asked Lewandowski, "what importance, what significance do you feel this story has for you?"

"I think that this was the most important operation I was engaged in," he replied. My God, he said, had he helped "stop this horrible conflict," he would have valued it forever. "I was disappointed when this failed, but I felt that I took part in something very important and I felt that I have done my best. Many times, . . . you think, if I have done something more, or something else—this came to my mind many times . . . [did I make] not enough efforts? But I think that I really can say with confidence that I have done what I *could* have done, what I can, I couldn't do anything more."

Lewandowski welcomed the January 1973 Paris Accords that ended American military involvement in Vietnam, but—as noted in the introduction—felt that he and his Marigold partners could have achieved that aim more than six years earlier, and at far lower human cost to both sides and political cost to the United States, "than this havoc" that had in fact occurred.

The Pole acknowledged that, realistically, if Hanoi and Washington had started talking in December 1966, they would not have quickly reached agreement "and the war [would] stop." However, he did think it likely that serious bargaining would have ensued with a clear outline of a solution, and in five or six months, "the whole business" would have moved to the negotiating table with a de facto cease-fire in place. "I did not expect it would happen overnight or over a week," he stressed, but it should at least have been possible to begin winding down the fighting, avoiding the Tet Offensive's carnage.[107]

What If? A "Counterfactual" Analysis

Can we give Lewandowski the last word? If Gronouski and Quang had met in Warsaw on December 6, 1966, or shortly thereafter, what difference would it have made? Even if Marigold had produced direct U.S.-DRV talks, would they have gone anywhere? Would Marigold really have ended the war significantly sooner?

Such questions bring us into the realm of "counterfactual history," which some historians disparage as inherently fanciful and pointless. "I believe that counterfactuals are a slippery business," one Vietnam chronicler observes warily, "and that history is too complex, with far too many variables in play, to be able to say with any degree of certainty how a particular situation would have turned out if a different path had been taken."[108] Yet historians do this kind of speculating all the time, without the label. Any criticism or praise of a decision or policy or action, for example, implies that an alternative, yielding a different chain of subsequent events that never, in fact, occurred, would have produced a better or worse outcome. Fredrik Logevall has provocatively tested "counterfactual history" in the specific context of the Vietnam War, addressing the endless debate over whether JFK would have escalated U.S. military involvement "if Oswald had missed." For maximum utility, he argues, this kind of analysis must obey clear rules and limits. Empirical evidence of prior behavior must be weighed carefully to ensure that alternate scenarios flow from the contemporary record; any deviations from reality must be plausible (e.g., options given serious contemporaneous consideration, contingent events that could have credibly gone differently); and chains of imagined consequences diminish in plausibility the longer they diverge, in time, from the actual record; conversely, alternative outcomes may be more compelling if immediately proximate to the branching event.[109]

With such considerations in mind, some conclusions can be confidently asserted. Resolving what Herring termed "the central issue of whether Lewandowski was accurately representing the North Vietnamese,"[110] the evidence presented here establishes that, contrary to U.S. suspicions and accusations (then and in retrospect), Hanoi *did* authorize the Poles to arrange the Warsaw meeting—and Lewandowski, far from freelancing, was closely coordinating with Rapacki, who in turn had secured green lights from Gomułka and Brezhnev. The evidence also shows that Hanoi was serious enough about the contact to make a strong personal commitment at the leadership level (i.e., Dong's pledge to Gomułka) and to send an authorized emissary carrying instructions halfway around the world. Therefore, *a U.S.-DRV meeting in Warsaw could and should have occurred* on December 6, 1966 or (as Dong allowed to Siedlecki) in the week thereafter, before the December 13 raids wiped out that possibility.

Why did it not? Though even now the evidence remains incomplete, the blame may be split among all three parties, in descending order of culpability: *the Americans,* for "bureaucratic blunders and gross management" (Herring) for letting the December 2 and 4 bombings of Hanoi occur uncoordinated with Marigold,[111] and then—and here the onus falls squarely on *Lyndon Johnson*—for approving further strikes despite ample, clear warnings from the Poles and his own top aides; *the Poles,* specifically *Rapacki,* for seeking an ideal arrangement for talks (i.e., pressuring Washington to drop the "important differences of interpretation" clause and forswear more bombings near Hanoi) instead of focusing on a first direct contact to "cross the Rubicon" (D'Orlandi); and *the North Vietnamese,* for neither informing the Poles when Quang received instructions nor consulting closely enough with them to preclude misunderstanding or miscommunication (as when Gronouski was expected but failed to show at the DRV Embassy).

Back to counterfactual history: Suppose Gronouski and Quang *had* met. So what? What would have happened? Gronouski would have carefully recited the script that Washington had sent him. On December 6 or 7, he would have read aloud the ten points and confirmed that they "broadly represent" U.S. policy, subject to "important differences of interpretation." In line with revised guidance, in response to Rapacki's plea, if they had met on December 8 or after, he would have confirmed that Lewandowski's summary "presents a general statement of the U.S. position on the basis of which we would be prepared to enter into direct discussions"—although some points needed "further elaboration" in direct talks, given "their complexity and the danger of varying interpretations."[112]

How would Quang have reacted? The DRV ambassador was instructed to say that Hanoi's Four Points remained the most "reasonable" basis for peace, but the only prerequisite for direct negotiations was for Washington to stop the bombing and all other acts of war against North Vietnam, Phong relates. Thach's guidance "envisaged several possibilities" for how to handle the first meeting: If the DRV diplomats judged the American's behavior "favorable"—if his "attitude, appearance, tone [were] polite"—they could keep talking, but if he seemed "arrogant," they should "cut off the discussion."[113]

In this case, one can confidently conjure Gronouski's demeanor: He passionately desired to promote peace in Vietnam, would have been overjoyed to meet Quang, and his enthusiasm and earnestness would have shone though—the personable politico far from an aloof, brusque, or imperious "Ugly American" scornful of his Asian Communist enemy. David Halberstam, who covered Gronouski in Poland for the *New York Times* (and was hardly shy about blasting U.S. officials), called him "a very, very decent man, . . . a kind of very good old-fashioned American of decency and honesty [who] couldn't have been nicer and straighter."[114] Zbigniew Brzezinski, who was then with the State Department's Policy Planning Staff, remembered him in similar terms—"a very straightforward guy, a straight shooter, not a diplomat."[115] He would have done his utmost to ensure a positive atmosphere, avoid gratuitous offense, and nurture the embryonic peace prospect. With high confidence, then, one can posit that the first Gronouski-Quang meeting would have gone well, characterized by correct, civil, and perhaps even cordial exchanges (as indeed happened in some other brief, lower-level U.S.-DRV encounters in Rangoon and Moscow).

Quang would have politely served his guest tea, conveyed the stop-the-bombing demand, and perhaps engaged in some innocuous banter, and yet he would probably have avoided substantive discussion of the ten points, reported the American's presentation to Hanoi, and awaited further instructions. Gronouski, also on a tight leash, would have promptly cabled his own account to Washington and eagerly anticipated hearing back.

What then? Would ongoing direct talks, or even formal negotiations, have ensued? From this point, counterfactual speculation gets much more tenuous. In this new context, the renewed demand for a complete halt to U.S. attacks on North Vietnam as a precondition for negotiations would likely have triggered an intense secret debate among LBJ's top advisers. Some hawks would have suspected a Communist trick; contended that Hanoi's willingness to accept the direct contact without an advance bombing halt (contrary to public pronouncements) and enter into talks without acceptance of the DRV's Four Points meant that the bombing was working, softening up the enemy; and urged more military pressure. Stopping the air campaign merely in exchange for an agreement to negotiate, they would claim, would prematurely relinquish America's trump card.[116]

Yet a successful Warsaw contact would have greatly bolstered those eager to get on a negotiating track. Entering into talks, even on the basis of the fuzzy ten points, appealed strongly to senior officials who were losing faith in escalation, especially the politically costly air strikes; desperately sought a tolerable exit route from Vietnam that could stem the hemorrhage of American blood and salvage LBJ's presidency; and were scaling back earlier ambitions ("pay any price, bear any burden") to assure Saigon a noncommunist future. We do not want to save face, Rusk had once told Rapacki, we want to save South Vietnam. Yet now, in view of the mounting cost, more officials were grudgingly ready to contemplate a less-than-perfect, less-than-ironclad settlement of the sort the ten points suggested, with the unsettling implications of a neutral South Vietnam, coalition rule in Saigon, and unclear disposition of PAVN forces below the 17th Parallel. Those who would have backed a bombing halt in exchange for Hanoi's entering into talks on the basis of the ten points would certainly have included McNamara, Katzenbach, and Thompson (the trio who strongly urged LBJ to cease further Hanoi raids during Marigold), and the relative doves Harriman and Cooper; even skeptics likes Rusk and Bundy would have conceded Hanoi's seriousness (and Warsaw's credibility) if Quang had actually received Gronouski.

Yet, that hardly guaranteed that LBJ would have paid Hanoi's price, a bombing halt, just to start direct talks—a year earlier, during the thirty-seven-day bombing pause, that swap might have sufficed, but now he wanted a more tangible quid pro quo. Most likely a bargaining process would have ensued, during which the air raids might have been significantly reduced but not halted altogether. To put the ball back in Hanoi's court, Washington would likely have directed Gronouski (or a more "seasoned" figure sent to replace him) to set up a new meeting with Quang to request a statement clarifying whether North Vietnam, too, formally accepted the ten points as a foundation for negotiations; only then would the bombing have stopped (though the sequence could have been masked through the Phase A/B device).

Such a message, in turn, would have forced Hanoi to put up or shut up, and perhaps reopened the stormy Politburo arguments of late November, before Dong told Lewandowski that he could arrange the U.S.-DRV rendezvous in Warsaw. Of course, the longer this process dragged out, the higher the likelihood that a contingent intervening event would have derailed it—a leak to the press or hard-line elements in either camp, or an especially egregious incident in the ongoing fighting, even without more Hanoi raids, might have caused one or both sides to harden terms, and shut Marigold down. One key variable, for instance, was the spate of Viet Cong attacks (attempted or carried out) around Saigon beginning on December 4, especially the furious assault on Tan Son Nhut days before Rusk landed there. If they were indeed payback for the December 2 and 4 bombings near Hanoi, as the NLF announced, then they presumably would not have happened; but if the timing was a coincidence, and they would have gone ahead in any case, they would have riled U.S. officials (particularly had they curbed attacks around the DRV capital) and perhaps inspired them—even after a successful Warsaw contact—to demand comparable restraint around Saigon as "reciprocity" for a bombing halt. That, of course, would have been a nonstarter and torpedoed the process right there.

But if contingent events did not interfere, Hanoi might well have taken the next logical step flowing from the secret decision it had already made to authorize the direct contact. On November 28, 1966, via Lewandowski, Dong had assured Gomułka (and through him, Moscow) that Hanoi would adopt a "positive attitude" if the United States acted in a forthcoming manner, for example, confirmed Lodge's statements. "A lot depends," he said, "on whether the Americans come to the meeting in Warsaw and what they say there."[117] Had Washington behaved "favorably" instead of furnishing grounds to accuse it of bad faith, the DRV could not have arbitrarily ditched the Warsaw channel without damaging ties with Poland and, behind it, the USSR. Besides, a Politburo majority evidently found Lodge's proposals intriguing enough to favor probing the U.S. stand and, if possible, forcing Washington to stop the bombing, which despite Hanoi's bravado inflicted enormous pain. Most important, North Vietnam could live with the ten points, which left hazy the status of PAVN forces in the South; implied an augmented NLF role in an open-ended political process to alter the Saigon regime; countenanced a neutral South Vietnam (long a proclaimed DRV goal, even as a stepping-stone to eventual unification under Communist control); and, above all, opened a path toward the removal of U.S. forces, easing a later renewed armed struggle, if necessary, to finish the job after they left. As Dong told Lewandowski, the North Vietnamese were "patient" and, "if the USA departs from South Vietnam there is no reason to hurry. They are ready to wait."[118]

A positive report from Warsaw should have strengthened pronegotiations figures, such as Dong, who had favored the contact in the first place, so it seems likely—barring untoward external events—that they would have prevailed again and that Hanoi, warily, would have authorized Quang to tell the Americans that the ten points were a valid basis for talks. This, in turn, should have triggered Washington's formal consent to halt the bombing, which would then have permitted ongoing direct discussions to start. These might have taken place in Warsaw or elsewhere (with an American more experienced in Vietnam issues and trusted by Washington than Gronouski); conducted under a flexible rubric, labeled formal negotiations or informal talks; and held behind closed doors yet probably publicly acknowledged once the bombing halted. Most important, they would have started a year and a half before they actually did, in far worse circumstances, in Paris in May 1968.

Of course, even if Marigold had led to ongoing direct talks, the war *might* not have ended a minute sooner, or with any less loss of life. Given the entrenched mutual enmity, distrust, and incomprehension, the inevitability of more bloodshed in some form (even a cease-fire hardly precluded nasty incidents), opposition by hard-liners on both sides to compromise, and above all the irreconcilable visions for (South) Vietnam's future, at best they would have been tense, difficult, and prone to breakdown.

Two issues, in particular, would have proven especially knotty if the parties had actually gotten down to brass tacks—and to "important differences of interpretation" of the ten points. For instance, point two contained the vital but vague U.S. concession that "the present status quo in South Vietnam must" (or "would") "be changed in order to take into account the interests of the parties presently opposing the United States in South Vietnam." Washington would grudgingly have tolerated the NLF's participation in South Vietnamese elections, but most U.S. officials (to say nothing of the Ky-Thieu regime) abhorred the idea of a coalition Saigon government (or powerful electoral commission) in which Communists held significant posts. Yet Hanoi would have pressed for nothing less.

Another likely stumbling block concerned North Vietnamese troops in the South, whose presence Hanoi steadfastly refused to acknowledge. The ten points only gingerly addressed this touchy topic: point three mandated a U.S. military pullout within six months of a settlement (per the Manila pledge), but the only explicit mention of a PAVN withdrawal was in point eight, which specified that Hanoi need not openly concede "that its armed forces are or were infiltrating into South Vietnam." Washington would have insisted that they leave—perhaps citing point nine's provision that it would not stomach Vietnam's unification "under military pressure"—and Hanoi would have just as stoutly denied its army's involvement in a homegrown insurgency against Saigon. Making it even harder to resolve, the issue engaged a basic divergence: U.S. officials branded the war an open-and-shut case of "international" aggression, requiring the DRV "invaders" to exit. Yet Hanoi, downgrading the 17th Parallel because Geneva only meant it as a temporary demarcation pending (never-held) 1956 national elections, considered all Vietnamese legitimate combatants in a civil war (and Americans the "foreign" aggressors).

The combatants' psychology and strategy posed an even tougher hurdle than their specific disputes. In both Washington and Hanoi, hawks who believed in military pressure but distrusted diplomacy would have latched onto any signs they could interpret to argue that force had caused their rival to blink, and more violence would further enhance their bargaining position. In this scenario— in which the Hanoi attacks did not occur, but the war otherwise continued as before—some U.S. aides (e.g., Rostow) would likely have cited North Vietnam's willingness to permit direct exchanges in Warsaw despite the ongoing air raids on its soil as evidence that Washington could safely disregard inconveniently intransigent DRV stands, for they might soften under duress. At the same time, the Vietnamese Communists, bitterly recalling Geneva (where they felt cheated after breaking the French at Dien Bien Phu), assuredly would have attributed any U.S. flexibility or concessions to their heroic armed struggle, not their enemy's goodwill, and felt a further erosion of American public tolerance for the war, like the ebbing French will a decade earlier, might be needed. With so much blood and treasure already invested and emotions running so high, few U.S. or DRV leaders admitted that their aggressive actions had at times boomeranged, causing their foe to harden stands or escalate, fearing to appear weak, rather than capitulate.

Yet there are strong countervailing reasons to argue that Marigold might have fundamentally altered subsequent events, not only in the Vietnam War but also in U.S. politics. Had the Warsaw contacts led within a year or so (i.e., by early

1968) to a peace deal—even a shaky one that later broke down—that would have neutralized the issue that fueled the revolt against LBJ's renomination within the Democratic Party, allowed him to refocus his presidency on domestic issues, and likely assured his reelection. (Robert F. Kennedy would have waited his turn, four years later, as he had planned.) True, even a "peace" based on the ten points would not have precluded Hanoi's resuming the armed struggle to unify the country under Communist control at a later date. But because the whole point would have been to renew hostilities, if necessary to assure the desired ultimate result, *after* a U.S. withdrawal, the dynamic could have resembled the complicated interweaving of military and diplomatic strategies that emerged in 1972–73: Nixon, with a successful reelection bid his overriding priority, pushed for a pact that would permit the extraction of troops and prisoners of war, while Hanoi was willing to defer a final victory. These overlapping interests permitted the porous Paris accords, which left North Vietnam poised to finish the job after U.S. forces left and a "decent interval" elapsed—but also allowed Nixon and Kissinger to reorient foreign policy along more rational lines, focusing on Moscow and Beijing and relegating Vietnam to the lower tier of concerns where it belonged. Similarly, one can imagine Hanoi letting LBJ remove U.S. forces under the terms of a Marigold-inspired peace settlement and win reelection, delaying plans for a nationwide uprising in the South, licking wounds, and amassing strength for a delayed showdown with Saigon, this time with the Americans gone and unlikely to return.

Even if the direct contacts had foundered, stalled, or collapsed, as was possible and even likely, the fact that they had actually started might have transformed the swirling domestic debate over Johnson's handling of the war. During 1967, and past the pivotal March 1968 New Hampshire primary, critics blasted LBJ for failing to start negotiations with Hanoi—because he had bungled real chances, or deliberately avoided them because he preferred to rely on force. For Johnson to be able to say that he had sat down with the North Vietnamese yet found them stubbornly intransigent, *forcing* him to continue the war, would have helped defuse dovish charges that he was uninterested in peace and stave off the internal rebellion that in fact compelled him to withdraw from the race. In this scenario, however, Hanoi would still have likely launched the Tet Offensive, hoping to force him back to the table in more favorable circumstances, with all that action's unfathomable ramifications for both U.S. politics and Vietnamese battlefields.

In Vietnam, the opening of talks and attendant cessation of bombing against the North would likely have changed the political and military landscape. For Washington, progress in the talks, or at least their continuation, might have vitiated the pressures that led to a steep escalation of the air war and a doubling of troop levels over the course of 1967. In Hanoi, a key test would have come quickly, behind closed doors. Would the VWP Politburo, and then the Central Committee, still have adopted the "fighting while talking, talking while fighting" strategy in January 1967? That resolution, it will be recalled, emerging from Politburo deliberations in late 1966, put more emphasis on the diplomatic struggle but recognized that the military and political fronts in South Vietnam remained paramount. If talks had already started, the leadership might well have put off such a clear definition of priorities until it saw where the contacts seemed headed—toward a deal that would let U.S. forces leave (in which case military pressure could be deferred), or into a long stalemate (perhaps impelling Hanoi to approve the talking-while-fighting strategy after all, bringing about a situation comparable to the war during the Paris negotiations).

Even the latter scenario, however, would have been an upgrade in one important sense. Marigold's collapse caused *both sides,* not just the Americans, to believe that the other had acted in bad faith. Vindicating skeptics and hard-liners in both Washington and Hanoi, it reinforced the taboo on direct substantive contacts and intensified mutual mistrust, making it harder to open talks than if Marigold had never occurred. Conversely, if direct exchanges in Warsaw had produced substantive discussions, and even if they had been futile in the short run, this would have created a precedent for further face-to-face discussions. In comparison with the barren seventeen months between Marigold's failure and the opening of the Paris talks, breaking the taboo in December 1966, it seems reasonable to suppose, might have fostered earlier, more frequent direct U.S.-DRV contacts, dealing—consonant with the ten points—with a broader range of issues than the endless quibbling over bombing halt terms. That alone could have shaved significant time, perhaps a year or two, off the grinding, excruciating process necessary to craft an accord.

At any rate, Marigold mattered. If it had enjoyed even a limited run, subsequent history could hardly have turned out any more disastrously than it actually did—and just might have allowed the Americans and North Vietnamese to meet on their invisible bridge, erected by Poles and Italians, and chart a course toward a quicker end to the war that was consuming them. The "lost chance" for peace was by no means a sure thing, but it genuinely existed, and if handled better had a reasonable shot at tangible, if now inscrutable, results. Instead, it was squandered. Perhaps this story, aside from clarifying a confusing aspect of Vietnam War (and Cold War) history, will inspire future bridge builders to emulate Janusz Lewandowski and Giovanni D'Orlandi, who labored valiantly and nearly succeeded in spanning a treacherous chasm between bitter enemies. Or perhaps it will serve as a cautionary tale for leaders seeking to avoid, limit, or escape future wars, suggesting the need to search more diligently and discerningly than Lyndon Johnson did to discover a less sanguinary and destructive path, however difficult it may be to envision.

Acknowledgments

Investigating Marigold expanded into a far longer and more labyrinthine odyssey than originally anticipated—one that was alternately intriguing, exciting, exhausting, exasperating, and exhilarating—and along the way I accumulated a mountain of debts. At the outset, let me apologize for inadvertent omissions: They don't call us absent-minded professors for nothing!

I would like to first thank the historical actors, and their families, who graciously submitted to my inquiries about events more than three decades old, and whose recollections invaluably supplemented the surviving written record.

On the Polish dimension of the story, Janusz Lewandowski consented to detailed interrogations during my five trips to Warsaw, and generously shared memories and photographs, and he and his wife, Wanda, offered kind hospitality when I visited their apartment. The sons of Jerzy Michałowski—Stefan, in Paris, and Piotr, in Ann Arbor—first roused my curiosity about Marigold, and stimulated this entire inquiry, by donating to the Cold War International History Project their late father's unpublished report on secret Polish peace diplomacy during the Vietnam War; later, they candidly discussed their family's experiences in both Poland and the United States, and provided additional files and photos. Daniel Passent, now a leading Polish political journalist, but in 1966 a reporter in Saigon (under cover as a translator for Poland's ICC delegation), and Jan Rowinski, a Polish diplomat in Beijing during the Cultural Revolution, helpfully related their experiences.

Regarding Italy's role, I applaud Colette D'Orlandi, the widow of Giovanni D'Orlandi, for allowing the publication of her late husband's detailed and candid journals from his years dealing with the Vietnam War (both as ambassador in Saigon and as an aide to Foreign Minister Amintore Fanfani in Rome). This publication is already enhancing scholarly and general comprehension of the war and Italian diplomacy, and it is hoped that Signora D'Orlandi will also assure that her late husband's other papers, including his diaries as Italy's ambassador to Greece, will be made available so that his unique perspective may deepen our understanding of important events. Ambassador D'Orlandi's top aide and peace co-conspirator in Saigon during Marigold, Mario Sica, who went on to become an ambassador himself, was a great help—not only by sharing his reminiscences during several interviews in Italy but also as a fellow historical detective swapping evidence and ideas via email.

For elucidating Hanoi's actions and perspectives, I thank two late North Vietnamese diplomats: Luu doan Huynh and Nguyen Dinh Phuong. I met them in Hanoi through the "critical oral history" project organized in the middle and late 1990s by James G. Blight and janet M. Lang, which brought together former North Vietnamese and U.S. enemies (most prominently Robert McNamara), and both gave interviews and answered many questions over the years. In particular, the uniquely energetic, informed, gregarious, and irreverent Mr. Huynh ("the Pepperpot," as janet memorably called him), the irreplaceable mentor to a generation of younger Vietnamese scholars and foreign Vietnam specialists, helped unveil the operations of the North Vietnamese Foreign Ministry; and Mr. Phuong recounted at length his previously unknown secret journey from Hanoi to Warsaw in December 1966.

Among American officials, I benefited from interviews with the late Chester L. Cooper (whom I met through the same McNamara project), and from additional information provided by his daughter, Susan; Nicholas Katzenbach, who welcomed me to his home, as did William Smyser; Bill Moyers (both in conversation and through email); Daniel I. Davidson; Thomas L. Hughes; Leslie H. Gelb; Herbert Kaiser; Daniel Ellsberg; the late Mary Gronouski; and Henry Cabot Lodge's two sons, Henry Sears Lodge and George Cabot Lodge (both answered questions over the phone, and George generously welcomed me to the family home in Beverly and lent the photo album that LBJ gave his father). For a Canadian perspective on the ICC (and Canadian-American interactions) in Vietnam in the 1960s, I thank J. Blair Seaborn, who served both as Ottawa's commissioner in Saigon and its special emissary to Hanoi.

As the "war of leaks" over Marigold also formed an important part of the story, I also want to thank several reporters who shared recollections and/or granted access to materials, above all Stuart H. Loory, who kindly allowed me to use materials in his papers at the American Heritage Center at the University of Wyoming related to the writing of *The Secret Search for Peace in Vietnam;* his *Los Angeles Times* colleague and coauthor, David Kraslow; Robert H. Estabrook, who initially broke the story for the *Washington Post;* the late David Halberstam, who covered Vietnam and Poland for the *New York Times;* Neil Sheehan; and Hedrick Smith.

Institutional support has been crucial to defray the considerable expenses required for research, travel, translation, and participation in relevant international conferences and projects. I would like to acknowledge in particular the support and comradeship in myriad forms over the past decade and a half of Tom Blanton and Malcolm Byrne, the director and deputy director of the National Security Archive; Christian Ostermann, the director of the Woodrow Wilson Center's Cold War International History Project; James G. Blight and janet M. Lang (formerly of the Thomas J. Watson Institute at Brown University, now at the Balsillie School of International Affairs at the University of Waterloo); Odd Arne Westad of the London School of Economics and Political Science; and David Wolff of the Slavic Research Center at Hokkaido University. I am also grateful for the support of various branches of my home institution, George Washington University, including the Institute of European, Russian, and Eurasian Studies and its directors (sequentially James Goldgeier, Hope Harrison, and Henry Hale); the History Department, especially chairs Tyler Anbinder, Bill Becker, Ed Berkowitz, and Muriel Atkin, and office manager Michael Weeks; the dean of the Elliott School of International Affairs, Michael E. Brown, and his predecessor, Harry Harding; and a University Fellowship Fund. I also want to express appreciation for the opportunity to focus on writing and research during George Washington University sabbaticals; a guest fellowship from the Norwegian Nobel Institute in Oslo; and a public policy scholarship from the Woodrow Wilson International Center for Scholars in Washington.

The most heartfelt compliment I ever heard used to describe a fellow historian was that he had an "iron ass"—that is, he was willing to suffer innumerable hours on the hard seats and benches of various archives to pore through mountains of materials in order to locate the scattered juicy bits needed for his investigation. I cannot claim the same anatomical credential, but while investigating Marigold I *did* spend uncounted hours in dozens of archives in many countries, and would like to thank in particular the staffs of those repositories who endured *repeated* visits from me over the years of research for this book: the National Security Archive (particularly Tom Blanton and Malcolm Byrne) and the Library of Congress in Washington; the Lyndon B. Johnson Presidential Library in Austin, particularly Claudia Anderson, Ted Gittinger, Regina Greenwell, and John Wilson; the National Archives II in College Park; the U.K. National Archives (formerly the Public Record Office) in Kew Gardens, England; the National Archives of Canada in Ottawa, particularly Paulette Dozois, who helped locate still-closed Department of External Affairs records; the Archive of the Ministry of Foreign Affairs (Archiwum Ministerstwa Spraw Zagranicznych) in Warsaw, particularly Henryk Szlajfer; the Massachusetts Historical Society and John F. Kennedy Presidential Library in Boston; the Mudd Library at Princeton University; the Archivio Storico del Senato in Rome, home of the Fanfani Papers; and the Foreign Ministry Archives (Arkhiv Vneshnei Politiki Rossiskoy Federatsii) and Russian State Archive of Contemporary History (Rossiskiy Gosudarstveniy Arkhiv

Noveyshey Istorii) in Moscow, especially Mikhail Prozumenschikov and Natalia Tomilina.

Among other archives that I visited and/or dealt with remotely, I wish to thank in particular the staffs of the Wisconsin Historical Society in Madison; the American Heritage Center at the University of Wyoming in Laramie; the Fondazione Gramsci in Rome (especially Silvio Pons); the Rare Book and Manuscript Library at Columbia University; the Nehru Memorial Museum and Library in New Delhi (especially Bhashyam Kasturi and Mridula and Aditya Mukherjee); the Charles E. Young Library at the University of California, Los Angeles; the National Defense University; the Hungarian National Archives (Magyar Orszagos Leveltar) in Budapest; the Czech National Archives in Prague; the Archive of Modern Acts (Archiwum Akt Nowych) and Institute of National Remembrance (Instytut Pamięci Narodowej) in Warsaw; the National Archives of Australia in Canberra (especially Carolyn Connor); the French Foreign Ministry archives in Nantes; the Italian Foreign Ministry archives in Rome; the Swedish National Archives in Stockholm (especially Markus Maijala); the National Archives in Washington; the U.S. Army Center of Military History at Fort McNair in Washington; the Folger Library at the University of Maine; the Nixon Presidential Library in Yorba Linda, California (especially Tim Naftali); the Vietnam Virtual Archive at Texas Tech in Lubbock; the Fort Frontenac Library, Kingston, Ontario (especially Serge Campion); and the United Nations Archive in New York City.

Many colleagues provided essential and exceptional assistance over the course of this project. Given the length of this book, I especially want to recognize three scholars who read the entire manuscript and gave helpful advice (and apologize to readers who wish I had listened better): William Burr, Mark Atwood Lawrence, and Fredrik Logevall. I also thank other colleagues who read individual chapters or listened to conference presentations (or other excited descriptions of the project) and gave valuable feedback: Larry Berman, Kai Bird, Tom Blanton, Malcolm Byrne, Charles Gati, Melvyn Leffler, Wallace Thies, Stein Tønnesson, and Odd Arne Westad; several editors also devoted time to the manuscript at various stages and gave useful responses, including Elisabeth Sifton, George Andreou, Chuck Grench, Niels Hooper, and Bob Loomis.

I particularly want to express my appreciation to several scholars for their aid in obtaining, deciphering, and/or understanding non-U.S. sources, or providing assistance during foreign visits. Leszek "Leo" Gluchowski translated the Michałowski Report and, after acquiring them from the Polish Foreign Ministry archives, the first batch of ciphered telegrams regarding Marigold; Malgorzata "Goshka" Gnoinska, as a research assistant, doctoral candidate at George Washington University, and now professor, interpreted reams of Polish-language materials; in Warsaw, Andrzej Paczkowski and Paweł Machcewicz expertly fielded my persistent inquiries and supplied additional documents, Wanda Jarzabek first put me in touch with Janusz Lewandowski, and Yvette Chin, Greg Domber, Mikołaj Morzycki-Markowski, and Doug Selvage also checked or obtained materials for me; Leopoldo Nuti helped me gain access to key Italian records and sources; Jim Blight and janet Lang gave me multiple opportunities to visit Hanoi, and Pierre Asselin, Mark Bradley, Bob Brigham, Bill Duiker, Lien T. Hang-Nguyen, the late Luu doan Huynh, Ngo Vinh Long, Merle Pribbenow, and Nguyen Vu Tung located or deciphered Vietnamese-language sources; the late Ilya Gaiduk, Vladimir Pechatnov, Mikhail Prozumenschikov, Sergey Radchenko, Svetlana Savranskaya, and Vladislav Zubok assisted with Russian sources; and polyglots Mark Kramer, Lorenz M. Luthi, Radchenko, Westad, and Wolff illuminated sources in various languages.

Besides those mentioned above, many other scholars also aided my efforts to tap non-U.S. and non-English-language materials. Concerning Italian sources, I also thank Alex Barrow, Giovanni Cubeddu, Ennio DiNolfo, Renata Moro, Fernando Orlandi, Isella O'Rourke, and Roberto Rotondo. For Canadian sources, I thank Paulette Dozois, Andrew Preston, and Ryan Touhey. For aid with Russian sources, I also thank Sergehy Kudryashov, Tigran Martirosyan, Richard Moss, Mari Olsen, and James Person. For aid with Chinese sources, I thank Chen Jian, Li Danhui, Qiang Zhai, Priscilla Roberts, and Shen Zhihua. Regarding Hungarian sources, I thank Csaba Bekes, Laszlo Borhi, Charles Gati, Balasz Szalontai, and Zoltan Szoke. For obtaining and/or translating Czechoslovak sources, I thank Kathleen Geaney, Guy Laron, and Oldrich Tuma. For obtaining and translating French sources, I thank Garret Martin, Yuko Torikata, Laurent Cesari, Pierre Journoud, and Maurice Vaisse. For locating, copying, and translating Dutch documents, I thank Debi Molnar, Rimko van der Maar, and Cees Wiebes. For East German sources, I thank Hope M. Harrison, Lorenz M. Luthi, Christian Ostermann, and Bernd Schaefer. For Danish documents, I thank Peer Henrik Hansen and Chris Larson. For help with Yugoslav/Serb sources, I thank Jovan Cavoski and Andrey Edemskiy. For Japanese documents and translations, I thank Hirata Masaki. For Romanian sources and translations, I thank Mircea Munteanu. I thank Steinar Andreassen for information on Norwegian sources, and Jordan Baev for aid on Bulgarian sources. For help obtaining British records (between my own visits), I thank Artemy Kalinovsky. For Swiss sources, I thank Lorenz M. Luthi. For aid with Swedish sources, I thank Fred Logevall. For Uzbek, Kyrgyz, and Mongolian sources, I thank Sergey Radchenko. Regarding Albanian records, I thank Ana Lalaj and Elidor Mehili (and the Woodrow Wilson Center for funding their translation). For providing materials from U.S. sources, I thank especially William Burr of the National Security Archive as well as Seth A. Center, R. E. G. Davies, David C. Geyer, Priscilla Roberts, and Andrew Schlessinger.

Over the years, I have profited greatly from the expertise and collegiality of many Vietnam War scholars, including David Anderson, Pierre Asselin, Larry Berman, Mark Bradley, Bob Brigham (and Monica Church), Chen Jian, Bill Duiker, Ilya Gaiduk, Lloyd Gardner, Ted Gittinger, Lien T. Hang-Nguyen, George Herring, Matthew Jones, Pierre Journoud, Jeffrey Kimball, Mark Lawrence, Fred

Logevall, David Milne, Ed Moise, Chris Mosher, Mari Olsen, John Prados, Andrew Preston, Sophie Quinn-Jones, Kent Sieg, Stein Tønnesson, Vu Tung, and Marilyn Young.

For their friendship, in addition to many of those mentioned above, I also want to thank Steve and Aileen Kantor, Marty and Susan Sherwin, Bob and Fran Elvin, Larry and Rebecca Grafstein, Scott Rosenberg and Dayna Macy, Bill Mc-Kibben and Sue Halpern, Mark Doctoroff, Mike Abramowitz, Alan Cooperman, Jeff Toobin and Amy McIntosh, Alexandra Korry, Joshua Cohen, Scott Orbach, David and Jane DeMillo, and Craig Keller.

For their skill in handling this gargantuan manuscript, I thank the Woodrow Wilson Center Press, and in particular its director, Joe Brinley, and managing editor, Yamile Kahn; the copy editor, Alfred Imhoff; the proofreader Stanley Thawley; the indexer, Enid Zafran; and the designer, Debra Naylor. And at Stanford University Press, I thank the deputy director, Alan Harvey; the director of scholarly publishing, Norris Pope; the director of sales and marketing, David Jackson; and the publicity manager, Mary Kate Maco.

✳ ✳ ✳

My family gave their unstinting love and support despite rising alarm as the years passed at my seemingly endless fascination with the Marigold story and determination to nail down every last detail, solve every lingering mystery, and stalk every last source. (My mother, in particular, would implore me to finish the book while there were any readers left who actually remembered the Vietnam War!) I thank my late grandparents, Ethel and Bill Ackerman and Ben and Anne Hershberg; my sisters Susan Carlacci and Ann Dugourd and their families (Cesare, Danielle, Alex, and Nicole; Fred, Chloe, and Dylan); Phyllis and Lewis Morrison and their clan (Lauri, Jeremy, David, and Amanda, whom we all miss); my wife's West Coast kin (Cynthia and Dave, Amanda and Phil, Molly, and Bridget); Ken Ackerman, my uncle and fellow author, for advice on the publishing business and much else; and my parents, David and Arline Hershberg—I hope they feel the final product was worth the wait (as they seemed to feel about their grandchildren!). As for my wife, Annie, no words can adequately express my love and appreciation, for sharing her life with me—and now with our son, Gabriel, and daughter, Vera. Now that this book is done, I pledge more time for driveway hockey and playing with our cat!

A Note on Sources

In addition to the abbreviations and archival information given below preceding the notes, supplementary information is presented here. Moreover, the author will make available online English translations of the non-U.S. documents used for this book; for further information, consult the Web sites of the Cold War International History Project (www.wilsoncenter.org/index.cfm?fuseaction=topics.home&topic_id=1409) and the National Security Archive (www.gwu.edu/~nsarchiv/).

American Sources

Essentially full sets of declassified State Department cables related to Marigold can be found in two locations: State Department files, in Record Group 59 (RG 59), at the National Archives II (NA II) in College Park, Maryland; and the National Security Files (NSF), at the Lyndon B. Johnson Presidential Library (LBJL) in Austin. To avoid cluttering the notes with long folder titles, the necessary folder information is presented here; the notes include box references. At the LBJL, cables and memorandums relating to Marigold's latter stages can be found in two chronological folders in box 147 of the National Security Files, Country Files, Vietnam (NSF:CO:VN): "Vietnam MARIGOLD [I] 10/16–12/15/66" and "Vietnam MARIGOLD [II], 12/16/66–6/2/67"—as well as an additional file of miscellaneous Marigold materials in box 148.

Because President Johnson was in Texas during much of Marigold's climactic phase, the cables at LBJ also include valuable cover notes added by Walt Rostow, the president's national security adviser, when they were relayed between Washington and the LBJ Ranch. In RG 59, NA II, the most important Marigold materials can be found in the "POL 27-14 VIET/MARIGOLD" folder, box 22, Formerly Top Secret Central Policy Files (FTSCPF), 1964–66 (as well as some records misfiled in the "POL 27-14 VIET/XYZ 11-1-65" folder in the same box); in the "POL 27-14 VIET/MARIGOLD 1/1/66" folder in box 3020, Central Foreign Policy Files (CFPF), 1964–66; in folder "POL 27-14 VIET/MARIGOLD," folders, boxes 2738–2739, CFPF, 1967–69; and in a compilation titled "Book 49: Vietnam Peace Feelers—Book of Peace, 1966," box 21, Briefing Books 1958–76, Lot 70D48.

The declassified documents in these repositories now offer a far more complete record of the American side of Marigold than that contained in the extensive chronology of the initiative, which includes only selected U.S. documents (full texts of some, excerpts of others), in the negotiating volumes of the Pentagon Papers (Part VI.C.2), or in the slightly sanitized version that was released under the Freedom of Information Act in the late 1970s and published in *The Secret Diplomacy of the Vietnam War: The Negotiating Volumes of the Pentagon Papers,* edited by George C. Herring (Austin: University of Texas Press, 1983), 209–370. This declassified U.S. documentation goes beyond—yet in key respects corroborates—the only serious English-language account of Marigold before this one, which was written shortly after the event by two *Los Angeles Times* journalists and based almost entirely on not-for-attribution interviews with officials: David Kraslow and Stuart H. Loory, *The Secret Search for Peace in Vietnam* (New York: Random House, 1968).

Polish Sources

At the Polish Foreign Ministry archives in Warsaw—the Archiwum Ministerstwa Spraw Zagranicznych (AMSZ)—ciphered telegrams are organized chronologically by post, so it is not generally necessary to give more specific locations; a researcher may simply request incoming or outgoing ciphergrams for a particular year from a specific diplomatic mission (e.g., Hanoi, Rome, Moscow, Washington). However, regarding Marigold, there is one important exception to this rule: For reasons that are not clear (which may have been related to the AMSZ's desire to have pertinent materials readily available for a possible rebuttal to U.S. leaks or a potential white paper), cables from various Polish diplomatic missions related to the secret initiative from mid-November 1966 until January 1967 were collected in a single dossier ostensibly containing only cables from Saigon: "Szyfrogramy from Saigon—1966, 6/77. w-173, t-858." Unfortunately, this dossier only contained *incoming* messages, and despite considerable efforts most outgoing messages from Warsaw (i.e., from Rapacki or Michałowski) relating to Marigold's climactic phase in November and December 1966 were not found.

Italian Sources

The highly classified coded telegrams concerning Marigold between Italy's embassy in Saigon (i.e., Ambassador Giovanni D'Orlandi) and Italy's Foreign Ministry in Rome (i.e., Foreign Minister Amintore Fanfani) can now be found in several locations. They presumably exist at the Historical Diplomatic Archives (Archivio Storico Diplomatico) at the Ministry of Foreign Affairs (the Ministero degli Affari Esteri) in the Palazzo della Farnesina in Rome. As of a few years ago, these files had not been formally opened to scholars, but I was fortunate to gain a copy of this "D'Orlandi dossier" through the intercession of friendly scholars.

More recently, these materials have been opened in the Fanfani papers at the Archivio Storico del Senato della Repubblica, Rome, where one may also consult Fanfani's handwritten diary; all of the Marigold-related telegrams can be found in the same archival location: busta 40, 17, "Segreto Vietnam," Senato della Repubblica, ASSR, Fondo Fanfani, Sezione 1, serie 1, s. serie 5. Unfortunately, photocopies or digital photographs are not allowed. That, fortunately, is not a problem with the published diaries of Ambassador D'Orlandi, who often (but not always) incorporated the texts of his secret telegrams into his journal entries; consult Giovanni D'Orlandi, *Diario Vietnamita, 1962–1968* (abbreviated in the endnotes as GD'O, *DV*), with an introduction by Giulio Andreotti and preface by Roberto Rotondo (Rome: 30Giorni, 2006). D'Orlandi's chief aide in Saigon published an Italian-language study of Marigold in 1991, but he was not permitted to quote from still-secret Italian documents (though he had encoded or decoded many of them himself): Mario Sica, *Marigold non fiorì: Il contributo italiano alla pace in Vietnam* (Florence: Ponte alle Grazie, 1991).

Vietnamese Sources

Despite repeated appeals from various scholars (including the author), Vietnam's government has refused to open the Foreign Ministry's archival files (especially the cable traffic between Hanoi and the North Vietnamese Embassy in Warsaw) that would permit the most accurate possible rendering of Hanoi's policy and actions regarding Marigold. In their absence, I have been forced to rely on non-Vietnamese (especially Polish) evidence, oral history testimony, and Vietnamese-language publications—some open, some intended for internal use—that quote, cite, or reproduce still-inaccessible contemporary party or state documents. Most important, in this respect, is the account of Hanoi's approach to negotiations before the Paris talks written by two former North Vietnamese diplomats and citing internal sources: Luu Van Loi and Nguyen Anh Vu, *Tiep xuc bi mat Viet Nam—Hoa Ky truoc Hoi nghi Pa-ri* [Secret interactions between Vietnam–United States before Paris negotiations] (Hanoi: Vien Quan He Quoc Te [Institute of International Relations], 1990; rev. ed., 2002). Scholars eagerly await the time that Hanoi will fully open its archives so authentic Vietnamese sources may speak for themselves—and some of the war's last lingering mysteries may finally be resolved.

✳ ✳ ✳

Descriptions of many conversations in the text are based on multiple, overlapping sources. (For example, all of the three-way "Marigold" talks in Saigon are based both on contemporaneous U.S., Polish, and Italian classified cables and on personal reflections ranging from D'Orlandi's diaries to Lodge's memoirs to Lewandowski's recollections in interviews.) To avoid encumbering the narrative, I have not separately and individually cited every quotation. In addition, in some cases where the meaning is not altered, minor typographical and punctuation errors in original documents have been corrected to avoid distraction. Any reader seeking further clarification, in addition to checking cited sources, is welcome to contact the author at jhershb@gwu.edu.

Notes

Abbreviations Used

(Positions given for individuals are at the time of the relevant Marigold events.)

AAN = Archiwum Akt Nowych [Archive of Modern Acts], Warsaw, Poland

ADEA = Australian Department of External Affairs

AE = Australian Embassy

AF = Amintore Fanfani, Italian foreign minister

AFD/AFP = Amintore Fanafani Diary/Papers, Archivio Storico del Senato della Repubblica, Rome

AMSZ = Archiwum Ministerstwa Spraw Zagranicznych (Archive of the Ministry of Foreign Affairs), Warsaw

AMZV = Archiv Ministerstvo Zaharanichnich Vetsi (Archive of the Ministry of Foreign Affairs), Prague

AR = Adam Rapacki, Polish foreign minister

ASS/EAPA = Subject Files of the Office of the Assistant Secretary of State for East Asian and Pacific Affairs, 1961-74, Lot File 85D240, RG 59, NA II

AVP RF = Arkhiv Vneshnei Politiki Rossiskoy Federatsii (Archive of Foreign Policy, Russian Federation), Moscow

BCG = British Consulate General (Hanoi)

BDM = Bill D. Moyers, White House press secretary (until January 1967)

BE = British Embassy

Book of Peace = "Book 49: Vietnam Peace Feelers—Book of Peace, 1966" in box 21, Briefing Books 1958-1976, Lot 70D48, RG 59, NA II

Candel = Canadian Delegation

CDEA = Canadian Department of External Affairs, Ottawa

CE = Canadian Embassy

CFPF = Central Foreign Policy Files, RG 59, NA II

CHC = Canadian High Commission

CHECO = Contemporary Historical Examination of Current Operations, as in *Project CHECO Report: Rolling Thunder, July 1965–December 1966*, HQ PACAF (Headquarters Pacific Air Forces, San Francisco), Directorate, Tactical Evaluation, CHECO Division, prepared by Wesley R.C. Melyan, Lee Bonetti, and S.E. Asia Team, n.d., originally classified Top Secret/NOFORN, accessed through The Virtual Vietnam Archive, Texas Tech University, record 98276, at http://star.vietnam.ttu.edu

Chubb's Folly = Self-published diary ("a day-to-day account of the trials and tribulations of a Canadian Army Officer serving in Vietnam during the period September 1966–September 1967 to include some comments and observations on people and events") of A. G. Chubb, *Chubb's Folly: There Be Dragons Here* (Saigon, 1966–67), courtesy of Fort Frontenac Library, Kingston, Ontario, Canada

CLC = Chester L. Cooper, State Department official, aide to W. Averell Harriman

CWIHP = Cold War International History Project, Woodrow Wilson International Center for Scholars, Washington

CWIHPB = Cold War International History Project Bulletin

CzE = Czechoslovak Embassy

CzFM = Czechoslovak Foreign Ministry

d. = delo (in Russian archives)

DDRS = Declassified Documents Reference System

DE = Dutch Embassy

Deptel = (State) Department telegram

DFMA = Dutch Foreign Ministry Archives, The Hague, Netherlands

DIA = Defense Intelligence Agency

DID = Daniel I. Davidson, State Department official, aide to W. Averell Harriman

DK = David Kraslow, *Los Angeles Times* journalist

DM = Debi Molnar (Dutch language translator)

DPQ = Do Phat Quang

DR = Dean Rusk, U.S. Secretary of State

DV = Giovanni D'Orlandi, *Diario Vietnamita, 1962–1968,* with an introduction by Giulio Andreotti and preface by Roberto Rotondo (Rome: 30Giorni, 2006).

Embtel = (U.S.) Embassy telegram

f. = fond (in Russian archives)

FAOHC = Foreign Affairs Oral History Collection of the Association for Diplomatic Studies and Training (Library of Congress Web site)

FCO = (British) Foreign and Colonial Office

FO = (British) Foreign Office

FOIA = Freedom of Information Act

FRUS = U.S. Department of State, *Foreign Relations of the United States* (Washington, D.C.: U.S. Government Printing Office, various years)

FTSCPF = Formerly Top Secret Central Policy Files, 1964–66, RG 59, NA II

GBP = George Ball Papers, Mudd Library, Princeton University

GD'O = Giovanni D'Orlandi, Italian ambassador to South Vietnam, 1962–67

GD'O dossier = A compilation of classified coded telegrams regarding Marigold from June 1966 to March 1967 between the Italian Embassy in Saigon (and Ambassador Giovanni D'Orlandi) and the Italian Foreign Ministry in Rome; obtained for the author from the *Ministero degli Affari Esteri* (MAE; Ministry of External Affairs) archives in Rome by Italian colleagues, they were translated for the author by Isella O'Rourke

Gibbons, IV = William Conrad Gibbons, *The U.S. Government and the Vietnam War: Executive Roles and Relationships, Part IV: July 1965–January 1968* (Princeton, N.J.: Princeton University Press, 1995)

GPP, IV = *The Pentagon Papers: The Defense Department History of United States Decisionmaking on Vietnam—The Senator Gravel Edition, Volume IV* (Boston: Beacon Press, 1971)

HA = Hungarian ambassador

HAK = Henry A. Kissinger, Harvard professor; from January 1969, assistant to the president for national security affairs

HCL = Henry Cabot Lodge Jr., U.S. ambassador, Saigon, 1963–64 and 1965–67

HCM = Ho Chi Minh, Democratic Republic of Vietnam president until his death in September 1969

HES = Harrison E. Salisbury, *New York Times* journalist

HES, RBML, CU = Harrison E. Salisbury Papers, Rare Book and Manuscript Library, Columbia University, New York City

HFM = Hungarian Foreign Minister
HQ PACAF = Headquarters, Pacific Air Force
HVL = Col. Ha Van Lau, PAVN liaison officer to the ICC
ICC/ICSC = International Control Commission / International Commission on Supervision and Control
IE = Italian Embassy
IE/S = Italian Embassy, Saigon
IFM = Italian Foreign Ministry
IO = Isella O'Rourke, scholar and Italian language translator
IPN = Instytut Pamięci Narodowej (Institute of National Remembrance), Warsaw
JAG = John A. Gronouski, U.S. ambassador to Poland
JAG SFRC = JAG testimony, Subcommittee on European Affairs, Committee on Foreign Relations, 10:40 a.m.–12:40 p.m., 15 May 1967, *Executive Sessions of the Senate Foreign Relations Committee together with Joint Sessions with the Senate Armed Services Committee (Historical Series)*, Vol. XIX, 90th Congress, 1st session, 1967, made public 2007 (Washington, D.C.: U.S. Government Printing Office, 2006), 471–504
JCS = U.S. Joint Chiefs of Staff
JCS-VN = Historical Division, Joint Secretariat, Joint Chiefs of Staff, 1 July 1970, *The History of the Joint Chiefs of Staff: The Joint Chiefs of Staff and the War in Vietnam, 1960–1968,* copy at National Security Archive, Washington
JFKL = John F. Kennedy Library, Boston
JL = Janusz Lewandowski, Polish commissioner, ICC, Saigon
JM = Jerzy Michałowski, Polish Foreign Ministry director-general (September 1967–June 1971: Polish ambassador to the United States)
JS = Jerzy Siedlecki, Polish ambassador to North Vietnam
l., ll. = listy (in Russian archives)
LAT = Los Angeles Times
LBJ = Lyndon B. Johnson
LBJL = Lyndon B. Johnson Library, Austin
LC = Library of Congress, Washington
LDT = Le Duc Tho, Lao Dong (Vietnamese Workers' Party) politburo member; negotiator in Paris negotiations opposite Henry Kissinger
LET = Llewellyn E. Thompson, State Department ambassador-at-large; from January 1967, U.S. ambassador to the Soviet Union
LG = Leszek Gluchowski, scholar and Polish language translator
LVL/NAV, *Before Paris* = Luu Van Loi and Nguyen Anh Vu, *Tiep xuc bi mat Viet Nam—Hoa Ky truoc Hoi nghi Pa-ri* [Secret interactions between Vietnam–United States before Paris negotiations] (Hanoi: Vien Quan He Quoc Te [Institute of International Relations], 1990; 2002 edition)
Marigold: A Chronology = "Marigold: A Chronology," a ninety-page, single-spaced chronology, top secret / nodis, n.d. [late spring 1967], folder "Vietnam MARIGOLD chronology," document #2a, NSF Country File-Vietnam, box 147, LBJL
MDR = Mandatory Declassification Review
memcon = memorandum of conversation
MG = Malgorzata Gnoinska, scholar and Polish language translator
ML, PU = Mudd Library, Princeton University
MOL = Magyar Orszagos Levaltar (Hungarian National Archives), Budapest
MP = Merle L. Pribbenow II, scholar and Vietnamese language translator
MR = Michałowski Report; Jerzy Michałowski, *Polskie tajne inicjatywy pokojowe w Wietnamie* [Polish secret peace initiatives in Vietnam], courtesy of Stefan Michałowski; translation by L. W. Gluchowski. N.B. Because the author relies on an unofficial translation rather than the Polish original, and as the report recounts events in strict chronology, page numbers are not given
MSW = Ministerstwa Spraw Wewnętrznych, Ministry of Internal Affairs, Poland
MSZ = Ministerstwo Spraw Zagranicznich (Polish Ministry of Foreign Affairs)
NA II = National Archives II, College Park, Maryland
NAA = National Archives of Australia, Canberra

NAC = National Archives of Canada, Ottawa
NC = Norman Cousins
NCT = Nguyen Co Thach
NDP = Nguyen Dinh Phuong
NDT = Nguyen Duy Trinh, DRV foreign minister
NK = Nicholas deB. Katzenbach, U.S. undersecretary of state from 3 October 1966
NLF = National Liberation Front
NPM = Nixon Presidential Materials
NSA = National Security Archive, Washington
NSC = National Security Council
NSF:CO = National Security Files, Country Files
NSF:CO:VN, National Security Files, Country Files, Vietnam
NSF:MtP:WR = National Security Files, Memos to President, Walt Rostow
NYT = *New York Times*
OH = Oral History
op. = opis (in Russian archives)
p. = papka (in Russian archives); also, occasionally elsewhere, "page," only as needed for clarity
PAVN = People's Army of (North) Vietnam
PDD = President's Daily Diary, LBJL
PE = Polish Embassy
PFM = Polish Foreign Ministry
POF = President's Office File (Office of the President File), LBJL
Poldel = Polish Delegation, ICC
PVD = Pham Van Dong, DRV premier
PVS = Phan Van Su, DRV ambassador to Czechoslovakia
PZPR = Polska Zjednoczona Partia Robotnicza (Polish United Workers' Party)
"Retrospective Accounts" = "Vietnam 6C 1961-1968 [1 of 3] Peace Initiatives + General Interna-
    tional Initiatives (Retrospective Accounts)" folder, box 94, NSF:CO:VN, LBJL
RG = Record Group
RGANI = Rossiskiy Gosudarstveniy Arkhiv Noveyshey Istorii (Russian State Archive of Contem-
    porary History), Moscow
RHE = Robert H. Estabrook, *Washington Post* journalist
RSM = Robert S. McNamara, U.S. secretary of defense
SAPMO-BArch = Stiftung der Parteien und Massenorganisationen der ehemaligen DDR im
    Bundesarchiv, Berlin
SDVW:NVPP = George C. Herring, ed., *The Secret Diplomacy of the Vietnam War: The Negotiating
    Volumes of the Pentagon Papers* (Austin: University of Texas Press, 1983)
SEAD = South-East Asia Department, U.K. Foreign Office
Secret Search = David Kraslow and Stuart H. Loory, *The Secret Search for Peace in Vietnam* (New
    York: Random House, 1968)
SHL = Stuart H. Loory, *Los Angeles Times* reporter
SHLP = Stuart H. Loory Papers, American Heritage Center, University of Wyoming, Laramie
SR = *Saturday Review*
sz. = *szyfrogram* (ciphergram; coded telegram)
Telcon = Telephone Conversation (or record of telephone conversation)
TNA = The National Archives (formerly Public Record Office), Kew Gardens, London
UNA = United Nations Archives, New York City
VCM = Victor C. Moore, Canadian Commissioner, ICC, Saigon
WAH = W. Averell Harriman, US ambassador-at-large
WAHP-LC = W. Averell Harriman Papers, Library of Congress
WAHP-NA = W. Averell Harriman Papers, Lot 71D461, RG 59, NA II
WHS = Wisconsin Historical Society, Madison
WP = *Washington Post*
WPB = William P. Bundy, assistant secretary of state for Far Eastern affairs
WWR = Walt W. Rostow, U.S. national security adviser

Introduction

1. Table of Comparative Military Casualties Vietnam, 6 Dec 1966, in White House Situation Room (McCafferty) to LBJ, CAP661186, rec'd LBJ Ranch Commcen 7:10 a.m. Tuesday 6 Dec 1966, box 38, NSF:CO:VN, LBJL. The tally of Viet Cong and North Vietnamese soldiers killed since 1961 was put, with absurd precision, at 158,346—a small fraction of the eventual figure, not including civilian casualties.
2. Alistair Horne, *Kissinger: 1973, The Crucial Year* (New York: Simon & Schuster, 2009), 35.
3. Arthur Schlesinger Jr., "The Diplomacy of Intervention and Extrication," *Washington Monthly,* March 1971, 59–64; the quotation is on 59.

Prologue

1. M. Sieradzki note, 29 Dec 1965, AMSZ, trans. MG.
2. PFM (AR) to PE/Hanoi (JS), sz. 12077, 29 Dec 1965, AMSZ, obt./trans. MG.
3. LBJ-McGeorge Bundy telcon, 27 May 1964, *FRUS, 1964–68, Vol. XXVII: Mainland Southeast Asia; Regional Affairs* (Washington, D.C.: U.S. Government Printing Office, 2000), doc. 53.
4. Doris Kearns Goodwin, *Lyndon Johnson and the American Dream* (New York: St. Martin's Press, 1976), 258.
5. *FRUS, 1964–68, Vol. II: Vietnam, January–June 1965* (Washington, D.C.: U.S. Government Printing Office, 1996), pp. 95–97.
6. Goodwin, *Lyndon Johnson,* 251–53.
7. On the escalation, see, e.g., Larry Berman, *Planning a Tragedy: The Americanization of the War in Vietnam* (New York: W. W. Norton, 1982); George McT. Kahin, *Intervention: How America Became Involved in Vietnam* (New York: Alfred A. Knopf, 1986); Fredrik Logevall, *Choosing War: The Lost Chance for Peace and the Escalation of War in Vietnam* (Berkeley: University of California Press, 1999); and Pierre Asselin, "Hanoi and Americanization of the War in Vietnam: New Evidence from Vietnam," *Pacific Historical Review* 74, no. 8 (Aug 2005): 427–39.
8. Dixie Bartholomew-Feis, *The OSS and Ho Chi Minh: Unexpected Allies in the War Against Japan* (Lawrence: University Press of Kansas, 2006); FDR to Cordell Hull, 24 Jan 1944, in *America in Vietnam: A Documentary History,* edited by W. A. Williams et al. (Garden City, N.Y.: Anchor/Doubleday, 1985), 30.
9. See, e.g., Archimedes Patti, *Why Viet Nam?* (Berkeley: University of California Press, 1975); Stein Tønneson, *The Vietnamese Revolution of 1945: Roosevelt, Ho Chi Minh and de Gaulle in a World at War* (London: PRIO/Sage Publications, 1991); David G. Marr, *Vietnam 1945: The Quest for Power* (Berkeley: University of California Press, 1995); Mark Philip Bradley, *Imagining Vietnam and America: The Making of Postcolonial Vietnam, 1919–1950* (Chapel Hill: University of North Carolina Press, 2000); and Mark Atwood Lawrence, *Assuming the Burden: Europe and the American Commitment to War in Vietnam* (Berkeley: University of California Press, 2005).
10. See, e.g., Lloyd C. Gardner, *Approaching Vietnam* (New York: W. W. Norton, 1988); John Prados, *Operation Vulture* (New York: I Books, 2004); and Fredrik Logevall, *Twilight War: The Fall of an Empire and the Making of America's Vietnam* (New York: Random House, 2012).
11. Chalmers M. Roberts, "The Day We Didn't Go to War," *Reporter* 11 (14 Sep 1954); George C. Herring and Richard H. Immerman, "'The Day We Didn't Go to War' Revisited," *American Historical Review* 71, no. 2 (Sep 1984): 343–63.
12. Dwight D. Eisenhower, *Mandate for Change, 1953–56* (Garden City, N.Y.: Doubleday, 1963), 372.
13. On this period, see, e.g., David L. Anderson, *Trapped by Success: The Eisenhower Administration and Vietnam, 1953–1961* (New York: Columbia University Press, 1991), and Ang Cheng Guan, *The Vietnam War from the Other Side: The Vietnamese Communists' Perspective* (New York: RoutledgeCurzon, 2002), 13–56.
14. WAH-Khiem memcon, 22 Jul 1962, Geneva, *FRUS, 1961–63, Vol. XXIV: Laos Crisis* (Washington, D.C.: U.S. Government Printing Office, 1994), 867–70; Rudy Abramson, *Spanning the*

Century: The Life of W. Averell Harriman, 1891–1986 (New York: William Morrow, 1992), 605–6; James G. Hershberg, "A Dialogue Aborted: The 1962 Geneva Encounter between Averell Harriman and North Vietnamese Foreign Minister Ung Van Khiem," in *The Failure of Peace? Indochina between the Two Geneva Accords (1954–1962),* edited by Christopher Goscha and Karine Laplante (Paris: Les Indes Savantes, 2009), 259–69.

15. Bernard B. Fall, "Master of the Red Jab," *Saturday Evening Post,* 24 Nov 1962.

16. For arguments that Hanoi but not Washington seriously considered Lao-style neutrality in South Vietnam (at least for a time before unification under communist control), see Logevall, *Choosing War,* chap. 1; and RSM, James G. Blight, and Robert K. Brigham with Thomas J. Biersteker and Col. Herbert Y. Schandler, *Argument Without End: In Search of Answers to the Vietnam Tragedy* (New York: PublicAffairs, 1999), chap. 4.

17. U. Alexis Johnson with Jef Olivarius McAllister, *The Right Hand of Power* (Englewood Cliffs, N.J.: Prentice Hall, 1984), 406.

18. Bothwell, "The Further Shore," *International Journal* 56, no. 1 (Winter 2000–1): 89–114 (quotation on 94).

19. See, e.g., Ramesh Chandra Thakur, *Peacekeeping in Vietnam: Canada, India, Poland, and the International Commission* (Edmonton: University of Alberta Press, 1984); Charles Taylor, *Snow Job: Canada, the United States, and Vietnam* (Toronto: House of Anansi Press, 1974), 3–41; and Douglas A. Ross, *In the Interests of Peace: Canada and Vietnam 1954–1973* (Toronto: University of Toronto Press, 1984). On India's approach to the ICC and relations with the two Vietnams (recognizing both de facto but not exchanging ambassadors), see, e.g., T. N. Kaul, speech to Norwegian Students Association, Oslo, 16 Apr 1966, Kaul Papers, Nehru Memorial Museum and Library, New Delhi; and K. R. Narayanan, "Consequences of Diplomatic Recognition of D.R.V.N.," 30 Sep 1969, subject file 253, P. N. Haksar Papers (installment III), courtesy D. Wolff, Nehru Memorial Museum and Library, New Delhi.

20. "Control Commission in Vietnam Remains Despite Lack of Effect," *NYT,* 6 Aug 1966.

21. MG, *Poland and Vietnam, 1963: New Evidence on Communist Diplomacy and the "Maneli Affair,"* CWIHP Working Paper 45 (Washington, D.C.: Woodrow Wilson International Center for Scholars, 2005); Mieczyslaw Maneli, *War of the Vanquished* (New York: Harper & Row, 1971).

22. William J. Duiker, *Ho Chi Minh: A Life* (New York: Hyperion, 2000), 548, 553–55; Bui Tin, *From Cadre to Exile: The Memoirs of a North Vietnamese Journalist* (Chiang Mai: Silkworm Books, 1995), 65. On Le Duan's rise to power and promotion of armed struggle in the South, I have benefited from the manuscript of Lien-Hang T. Nguyen's forthcoming book, an expansion of her Yale University PhD dissertation; hereafter, "Nguyen manuscript."

23. Seaborn: *SDVW:NVPP,* 4–44; Taylor, *Snow Job,* 47–85; Ross, *In the Interests of Peace,* 275–79; Andrew Preston, "Balancing War and Peace: Canadian Diplomacy and the Vietnam War, 1961–1965," *Diplomatic History* 27, no. 1 (Jan 2003): 73–111; Preston, "Missions Impossible: Canadian Secret Diplomacy and the Quest for Peace in Vietnam," in *The Search for Peace in Vietnam, 1964–1968,* edited by Lloyd C. Gardner and Ted Gittinger (College Station: Texas A&M University Press, 2004); "messenger boy": Seaborn telephone interview, 3 Aug 2007. HCL had suggested Seaborn for the job, having known him from his years as Ike's UN envoy.

24. On the Thant-Stevenson affair, see Mario Rossi, "U Thant and Vietnam: The Untold Story," *New York Review of Books,* 17 Nov 1966; DK and SHL, *The Secret Search for Peace in Vietnam* (New York: Random House, 1968), 91–109; Walter Johnson, "The U Thant-Stevenson Peace Initiatives in Vietnam, 1964–1965," *Diplomatic History* 1, no. 3 (Jul 1977): 285–95; and other references cited below.

25. Preston, "Balancing War and Peace," 104–5.

26. Wallace J. Thies, *When Governments Collide: Coercion and Diplomacy in the Vietnam Conflict, 1964–1968* (Berkeley: University of California Press, 1980), 421.

27. XYZ: *SDVW:NVPP,* 74–115.

28. Gibbons, IV, 80.

29. Paul Hendrickson, *The Living and the Dead: Robert McNamara and Five Lives of a Lost War* (New York: Alfred A. Knopf, 1996).

30. See, e.g., Gibbons, IV, 89–100; Robert Dallek, *Flawed Giant: Lyndon Johnson and his Times, 1961–1975* (Oxford: Oxford University Press, 1998), 284–92, 340 ff; HCL to Gen. Wheeler, 21 Dec 1965, reel 24, HCL II, MHS; re Bundy, see esp. Kai Bird, *The Color of Truth: McGeorge Bundy and William Bundy: Brothers in Arms* (New York: Simon & Schuster, 1998); Andrew Preston, *The War Council: McGeorge Bundy, the NSC, and Vietnam* (Cambridge, Mass.: Harvard University Press, 2006); and Gordon M. Goldstein, *Lessons in Disaster: McGeorge Bundy and the Path to War in Vietnam* (New York: Times Books, 2008). On BDM, see, e.g., Patrick Anderson, *The President's Men: White House Assistants of Franklin D. Roosevelt, Harry S. Truman, Dwight D. Eisenhower, John F. Kennedy, and Lyndon B. Johnson* (Garden City, N.Y.: Doubleday, 1968), 345; Robert F. Keeler, *Newsday: A Candid History of the Respectable Tabloid* (New York: William Morrow, 1990), 389. On RSM's deepening doubts about not only the bombing but the war as a whole, see esp. Benjamin T. Harrison and Christopher L. Mosher, "The Secret Diary of McNamara's Dove: The Long-Lost Story of John T. McNaughton's Opposition to the Vietnam War," *Diplomatic History* 35, no. 3 (June 2011): 505–34.
31. See, e.g., *FRUS, 1964–68, Vol. III: Vietnam June–December 1965* (Washington, D.C.: U.S. Government Printing Office, 1996), 585, 609, 653, and R. B. Smith, *An International History of the Vietnam War, Volume III: The Making of a Limited War, 1965–66* (London: Macmillan, 1991), 250–51.
32. On 7 Oct 1965 DR-Péter talk, see *FRUS, 1964–68*, 3:431–36. Péter and Hungary: James G. Hershberg, "Peace Probes and the Bombing Pause: Hungarian and Polish Diplomacy During the Vietnam War, December 1965–January 1966," *Journal of Cold War Studies* 5, no. 2 (Spring 2003): 32–67; and Zoltan Szoke, "Delusion or Reality? Secret Hungarian Diplomacy during the Vietnam War," *Journal of Cold War Studies* 12, no. 4 (Fall 2010): 119–80.
33. János Radványi, *Delusion and Reality: Gambits, Hoaxes, & Diplomatic One-Upmanship in Vietnam* (South Bend, Ind.: Gateway Editions, 1978), 68.
34. Bundy-Dobrynin memcon, 24 Nov 1965, *FRUS, 1964–68, Volume XIV: The Soviet Union* (Washington, D.C.: U.S. Government Printing Office, 2001), 356–57. WPB later called this message "very sober and realistic, . . . consistent with my belief that the Russians have never misled us; the Hungarians did, while we were not really fooled; the Poles have played shell-games over and over again—the Russians never!" WPB OH 3, 29 May 1969, 16, LBJL (all LBJL OHs conducted by Paige E. Mulhollan unless otherwise noted).
35. Bundy to LBJ, 27 Nov 1965, *FRUS, 1964–68*, 3:583, esp. n. 5.
36. LBJ meeting notes, 7 Dec 1965, ibid., 621.
37. Bundy to LBJ, 9 Dec 1965, with DR-LET-Dobrynin memcon, 8 Dec 1965, ibid., 624–30.
38. *NYT,* 25 Feb 1965.
39. Reedy comments, 24 Feb 1965, in *NYT,* 17 Nov 1965.
40. Eric Sevareid, "The Final Troubled Hours of Adlai Stevenson," *Look,* 30 Nov 1965.
41. U Thant, *View from the UN* (Garden City, N.Y.: Doubleday, 1978), 67.
42. Rio de Janeiro embtel, 18 Nov 1965, *FRUS, 1964–68,* 3:572–75.
43. *NYT,* 16 Nov 1965, 17 Nov 1965, and 27 Nov 1965.
44. After Sevareid's article, both the State Department and LBJ press secretary BDM secretly investigated the affair, concluding that no authentic DRV readiness to meet was ever established or communicated to LBJ but admitting that evidence remained spotty; "Chronology of U Thant Suggestion That DRV and U.S. Representatives Meet in Rangoon to Discuss Restoration of Peace in Vietnam," n.d., LBJL/DDRS; DK and SHL, *Secret Search,* 106–7. Only after the Soviet collapse did Moscow archives confirm Hanoi really approved the overture. In early August 1964, amid the Tonkin Gulf affair, Thant had met LBJ at the White House and secured his diffident OK to pursue a dialogue; LBJ-Thant memcons, 6 Aug 1964: *FRUS, 1964–68, Vol. I: Vietnam 1964* (Washington, D.C.: U.S. Government Printing Office, 1992), doc. 298, and UNA; U Thant, *View from the UN* , 63. Having met Khrushchev in late July, Thant used a Soviet diplomat (or KGB officer under cover) in the UN Secretariat to send a suitable "oral message" to HCM; ibid., 63–64. On 29 Aug 1964, in Hanoi, eight days after relaying the idea of direct talks to PVD, USSR chargé P.I. Privalov was told the North Vietnamese were "not against such a proposal but underlined that from their point of view the best solution was to

meet at a conference in Geneva or in a neutral country that both agree upon." Deputy Foreign Minister Hoang Van Tien treated the matter so warily that he banished everyone else from the room before providing the handwritten answer. Privalov's cables establish that Moscow and Thant had a concrete basis to declare that Hanoi would talk directly with Washington; Mari Olsen, *Soviet-Vietnam Relations and the Role of China, 1949–64: Changing Alliances* (London: Routledge, 2006), 133, 190 n. 84.

45. DK and SHL, *Secret Search*, 102.
46. DR as told to Richard Rusk, *As I Saw It,* edited by Daniel S. Papp (New York: W. W. Norton, 1990), 463.
47. On the La Pira affair, see DK and SHL, *Secret Search*, 126–36; Mario Sica, *Marigold non fiori: Il contributo italiano alla pace in Vietnam* (Florence: Ponte alle Grazie, 1991), 34–42; and Sica, "La Pira e la pace nel Vietnam, *Nuova Antogolia* n. 2258 (April–June 2011): 136–62.
48. AF to LBJ, 20 Nov 1965, *FRUS, 1964–68*, 3:576–77.
49. DR to LBJ, 20 Nov 1965, ibid., 578–79.
50. Moscow embtel 1691 (Guthrie), 22 Nov 1965, and Bundy to LBJ, 28 Nov 1965, *FRUS, 1964–68, Vol. XII: Western Europe* (Washington, D.C.: U.S. Government Printing Office, 2001), docs. 119–20; Rome airgram A-628, "Espresso Interview on Florentine Ex-Mayor Giorgio La Pira's Trip to Hanoi," 30 Nov 1965, POL 6 Biographic Data IT, box 2360, CFPF, 1964–66.
51. AF profile, March 1966, CIA Office of Central Reference, Biographic Register, 38th NATO Ministerial; Dec. 1966, CF-115, box 432, Conference Files, 1966–72, RG 59, NA II (also Italy—Memos vol. V 2/67-12/68, box 198, NSF:CO, LBJL) (hereafter CIA Fanfani profile); "small": Donald Grant, "Vietnam: The View from the United Nations," *The Progressive*, Apr 1966, 19; "bantam-size": *NYT*, 22 Sep 1965.
52. AF profile, n.d., PREM 13/1585, TNA.
53. Leopoldo Nuti, "The Center-Left Government in Italy and the Escalation of the Vietnam War," in *America, the Vietnam War, and the World: Comparative and International Perspectives,* edited by Andreas W. Daum, Lloyd C. Gardner, and Wilfried Mausbach (Washington, D.C.: German Historical Institute, 2003), 259–78.
54. See, e.g., AF to JFK, 26 Aug 1961, *FRUS, 1961–63, Vol. XIII: Western Europe and Canada* (Washington, D.C.: U.S. Government Printing Office, 1994), 818–19; and Italy-AF correspondence folders, box 121, NSF:CO, JFKL.
55. AF-DR memcon, NYC, 26 Sep 1965, *FRUS, 1964–68, Vol. XII*, doc. 117.
56. From 6 Sep 1965 entry, AFD, obt./trans. Mario Sica. Coincidentally, La Pira received HCM's invitation to visit Hanoi the very next day. [SHL,] La Pira interview notes, 2 Dec 1967, Interviews folder, box 15, SHLP.
57. *NYT*, 16 Dec 1965.
58. Richard Dudman, "New Peace Move from Hanoi Reportedly Rejected by U.S.," *St. Louis Post-Dispatch*, 18 Dec 1965; Deptel 9801 to American Embassy, Saigon, 17 Dec 1965, POL 15-1 Head of State, Executive Branch, IT 1/1/65, box 2365, CFPF, 1964–66; DK and SHL, *Secret Search*, 134–35.
59. *NYT*, 19 Dec 1965; articles in Vietnam Negotiations, box 13, Richard Dudman Papers, LC; 18 Dec 1965 entry, AFD.
60. On "inferiority," see Lorenz M. Luthi, *The Sino-Soviet Split: Cold War in the Communist World* (Princeton, N.J.: Princeton University Press, 2008), 329; Lien-Hang T. Nguyen, "The War Politburo: North Vietnam's Diplomatic Road to the Tet Offensive," *Journal of Vietnamese Studies* 1, nos. 1–2 (2006): 4–58, esp. 20–21; William J. Duiker, *U.S. Containment Policy and the Conflict in Indochina* (Stanford, Calif.: Stanford University Press, 1994), 356–58.
61. LVL/NAV, *Before Paris* (2002 ed.), 97–101, trans. MP.
62. Shown a translation of the LVL/NAV, *Before Paris* chapter on this conversation in early 2011, the academician who accompanied La Pira to Hanoi, Mario Primicerio (then a young mathematician), attested to its general accuracy but insisted that it understated the main point—that HCM had not insisted on a prior U.S. withdrawal as a precondition for entering talks with Washington—and was perhaps retroactively skewed to stress Hanoi's firmness. Mario Sica agreed that the North Vietnamese account "therefore presents La Pira in the same ludicrous

way as his vitriolic Italian critics: an incompetent amateur who indulged in wishful thinking." Sica email to the author, 4 Apr 2011.

63. AF vented his ire to Polish diplomats: Polish UN Mission, New York (Bohdan Lewandowski) to PFM (AR), sz. 15472, 20 Dec 1965, AMSZ, obt./trans. MG, and PE/Rome (Willmann) to PFM (Naszkowski), sz. 15399, 3 Dec 1966, AMSZ, trans. MG.

64. Rome embtel 1643 (Reinhardt), 28 Dec 1965, POL 15-1 Head of State. Executive Branch. IT 1/1/65, box 2365, CFPF, 1964-6; La Pira interviews: American Embassy, Rome, airgrams A-720, "La Pira in Hanoi–Diplomacy of the Absurd," 27 Dec 1965, and A-729, "La Pira Interview in *Il Borghese*," 29 Dec 1965, both ibid.; Airgram A-732, "La Pira Interview in *Il Borghese*," 30 Dec 1965, POL 1 General Policy. Background. IT 1/1/64, box 2358; A-756, "Gianna Preda and Giorgio La Pira Again," 10 Jan 1966, and A-766, "*Il Borghese* and La Pira; Chapter 3," 13 Jan 1966, both POL 15-1 IT 1966, box 2366; all CFPF, 1964-66.

65. Harold Wilson, *The Labour Government 1964–1970: A Personal Record* (Boston: Little, Brown, 1971), 186–88; "amateurs": *FRUS, 1964–68*, 3:658; "paragon": ibid., 644.

66. White House meeting notes, 18 Dec 1965, ibid., 660 (DR), 665 (Clifford).

67. RSM with Brian VanDeMark, *In Retrospect: The Tragedy and Lessons of Vietnam* (New York: Times Books, 1995), 230–31.

68. *FRUS, 1964–68*, 3:658.

69. LBJ-Sidey meeting notes, 8 Feb 1967, box 32, Marvin Watson OF, LBJL (reel 11, "Vietnam, the Media, and Public Support for the War" microfilm collection, LC).

70. Bundy notes, 11–12 Nov 1965, Gibbons, IV, 89.

71. Draft LBJ telegram to HCL, 18 Dec 1965, *FRUS, 1964–68*, 3:653.

72. WWR to LBJ, 23 Dec 1965, ibid., 698.

73. WPB, unpublished Vietnam ms., written 1969–72, chap. 33, 32, JFKL (copy courtesy Kai Bird).

74. Rusk unveiled the 14 points at a 29 Dec 1965 press conference: (1) The Geneva Agreements of 1954 and 1962 are an adequate basis for peace in Southeast Asia. (2) We would welcome a conference on Southeast Asia or on any part thereof. (3) We would welcome "negotiations without preconditions," as the 17 nations put it. (4) We would welcome unconditional discussions, as President Johnson put it. (5) A cessation of hostilities could be the first order of business at a conference or could be the subject of preliminary discussions. (6) Hanoi's Four Points could be discussed along with other points which others might wish to propose. (7) We want no U.S. bases in Southeast Asia. (8) We do not desire to retain U.S. troops in South Vietnam after peace is assured. (9) We support free elections in South Vietnam to give the South Vietnamese a government of their own choice. (10) The question of reunification of Vietnam should be determined by the Vietnamese through their own free decision. (11) The countries of Southeast Asia can be nonaligned or neutral if that be their opinion. (12) We would much prefer to use our resources for the economic reconstruction of Southeast Asia than in war. If there is peace, North Vietnam could participate in a regional effort to which we would be prepared to contribute at least 1 billion dollars. (13) The President has said: "The Viet Cong would not have difficulty being represented and having their views represented if for a moment Hanoi decides to cease the aggression. I do not think that would be an insurmountable problem." (14) We have said publicly and privately that we could stop the bombing of North Vietnam as a step toward peace although there has not been the slightest hint or suggestion from the other side as to what they would do if the bombing stopped.

75. DR-Radványi conversation, Washington, 23 Dec 1965, *FRUS, 1964–68*, 3:688–91.

76. RSM with VanDeMark, *In Retrospect*, 225–26.

77. DK and SHL, *Secret Search*, 137.

78. LBJ-Ball telcon, 10 p.m., 28 Dec 1965, *FRUS, 1964–68*, 3:733.

79. LBJ-WAH telcon, 10:36 a.m., 28 Dec 1965, ibid., 719–21.

80. WAH-DR telcon, 28 Dec 1965, ibid., 729–30.

81. MR.

82. On the Polish ICC role, see MG, "Poland and the Cold War in East and Southeast Asia, 1949–1965," PhD dissertation, George Washington University, 2009.

83. PVD-Cyrankiewicz memcon, Warsaw, 17 Jul 1961, Dept. II, Wietnam, z-49/64, w-4, AMSZ, trans. MG.

84. MR.
85. AR-Galbraith initiative: MG, "Poland and Vietnam, 1963," esp. 6-14, 43–54.
86. MR. JM, finding these ideas worth considering, sensed Galbraith's alarm at the risk of Chinese intervention in Vietnam, perhaps by sending "volunteers" as in Korea.
87. New Delhi embtel 2859 (Galbraith), 22 Jan 1963, India 1/20/63-1/25/63, box 109, NSF:CO, JFKL; John Kenneth Galbraith, *Ambassador's Journal: A Personal Account of the Kennedy Years* (Boston: Houghton Mifflin, 1969), 466; John Kenneth Galbraith, *A Life in Our Times: Memoirs* (Boston: Houghton Mifflin, 1981), 478.
88. JM-Gromyko talk, Moscow, 4 Feb 1963, in MR.
89. PE/Moscow (Jaszczuk) to PFM (AR), 13 Feb 1963, MG, "Poland and Vietnam, 1963," 46.
90. MR.
91. LBJ to HCL, 20 Mar 1964, *FRUS, 1964–68, Vol. I,* doc. 92.
92. MR; *FRUS, 1964–68, vol. XXVIII: Laos* (Washington, D.C.: U.S. Government Printing Office, 1998), 117–24, 134–40, 185–87, 191–96, 207–17.
93. DR-AR memcon, 10 Dec 1964, LBJL/DDRS.
94. Sergey Radchenko, *Two Suns in the Heavens: The Sino-Soviet Struggle for Supremacy, 1962–1967* (Washington, D.C., and Stanford, Calif.: Woodrow Wilson Center Press and Stanford University Press, 2009), 131–35.
95. Luthi, *Sino-Soviet Split,* chap. 10; Radchenko, *Two Suns,* 144–58; James G. Hershberg and Chen Jian, "Informing the Enemy: Sino-American 'Signaling' and the Vietnam War, 1965," in *Behind the Bamboo Curtain: China, Vietnam, and the Cold War,* edited by Priscilla Roberts (Washington, D.C. and Stanford, Calif.: Woodrow Wilson Center Press and Stanford University Press, 2006), 193–25.
96. Record of Polish-Soviet talks, 29–30 Oct 1965, in *Tajne dokumenty: Biura Politycznego PRL-ZSRR, 1956–1970,* edited by Andrzej Paczkowski (London: Aneks, 1998), doc. 27, trans. MG.
97. Record of Polish-Soviet talks, Warsaw, 6 Apr 1965, ibid., doc. 23, trans. MG.
98. Szoke, "Delusion or Reality?"; Hershberg, "Peace Probes."
99. See esp. PE/Rome (Willmann) to PFM (Rapacki), sz. 11517, 20 Sep 1965; PFM (Łobodycz) to PE/Rome, sz. 9274, 2 Oct 1965; and PE/Rome (Stefanski) to PFM (Łobodycz), 20 Oct 1965; all AMSZ, obt./trans. MG.
100. Memcon, 16 Nov 1965, Warsaw, PINTA (3) folder, box 548, WAHP-LC.
101. Paweł Machcewicz, *Rebellious Satellite: Poland 1956* (Washington, D.C., and Stanford, Calif.: Woodrow Wilson Center Press and Stanford University Press, 2009); Andrzej Paczkowski, *The Spring Will Be Ours: Poland and the Poles from Occupation to Freedom* (University Park: Pennsylvania State University Press, 2003), 269–86; LG articles in *CWIHPB* 5 (Spring 1995): 1, 38–49, and 10 (March 1998): 44–49; and A. Kemp-Welch, *Poland under Communism: A Cold War History* (New York: Cambridge University Press, 2008), chaps. 4–5.
102. Kemp-Welch, *Poland,* chap. 6.
103. David Halberstam, "Love, Life, and Selling Out in Poland," *Harper's,* Jul 1967, 78–89 (quotation 88); Halberstam, "Poland Has Seen The Future," *NYT,* 6 Feb 1966.
104. AR background: Piotr Wandycz, "Adam Rapacki and the Search for European Security," in *The Diplomats, 1939–1979,* edited by Gordon A. Craig and Francis L. Loewenheim (Princeton, N.J.: Princeton University Press, 1994), 289–317; Longin Pastusiak, *Adam Rapacki, 1909–1970* (Warsaw: Wydawnictwo Stonnictwa Demokratycznego, Listopad 1982), in MG dissertation.
105. "Polish Idea Man," *NYT,* 3 Feb 1958("facile"); "Builder at Warsaw," *NYT,* 6 Mar 1964; "Personality Notes for Luncheon by the Prime Minister for the Polish Foreign Minister" [c. February 1967], PREM 13/1699, TNA.
106. On the Rapacki Plan, see James R. Ozinga, *The Rapacki Plan* (Jefferson, N.C.: McFarland, 1989); Wandycz, "Adam Rapacki"; and Zoltán Maruzsa, "Denuclearization in Central Europe? The Rapacki Plan during the Cold War," available at www.coldwar.hu and first published in *Öt kontinens: Eötvös Loránd Tudományegyetem* (Budapest, 2008), 225–64.
107. Pastusiak, *Adam Rapacki,* 34, in MG dissertation.
108. Ozinga, *Rapacki Plan,* 77.

109. Abba Eban, *An Autobiography* (New York: Random House, 1977), 307; Abba Eban, *Personal Witness: Israel Through My Eyes* (New York: G. P. Putnam's Sons, 1992), 343.
110. "Polish Idea Man" ("exception"); "Builder at Warsaw."
111. "Polish Idea Man."
112. *NYT,* 11 Mar 1958; *WP,* 28 Apr and 26 Jun 1965; *NYT,* 29 Aug 1967; "Personality Notes for Luncheon by the Prime Minister for the Polish Foreign Minister," as above, circulated before AR's February 1967 visit to Britain, said he had had four heart attacks since 1958.
113. Wandycz, "Adam Rapacki," 296.
114. Henry Raymont, "Poles Try, But Fail to Calm Castro," *WP,* 9 Sep 1962; also documents from AMSZ; NSF:CO, JFKL; and Brazilian Foreign Ministry archives.
115. Ozinga, *Rapacki Plan,* 122–23.
116. Unless otherwise indicated, biographical data are from JM profile, Biographic Register, Office of Central Reference, CIA, 4 Jan 1967, POL 17-1 POL-US 1/1/67, box 2436, CFPF, 1967–69 (hereafter CIA JM profile); also "Confidential Biography, Jerzy Michałowski," with NK to LBJ, 26 Apr 1967, ibid.; JM bio, Walt Rostow Vol. 54 11–19 Dec 1967 [3 of 4], box 26, NSF:MtP:WR, LBJL, and DR to American Embassy, Vientiane, "Biographic Information," Instruction A-59, 5 May 1961, decimal file 742.521/5-561, RG 59, NA II, courtesy W. Burr; "Notatka Biograficzna, tow. Jerzego Michałowskiego," PZPR V/83, AAN; Piotr Michałowski telephone interviews, 12–13 Aug 2008; and Stefan Michałowski interview, Washington, 12 Dec 2010. Although Jerzy Michałowski's children do not use the customary diacritic on the "l" in the family surname, for simplicity's sake, the father's spelling is used throughout this book.
117. Piotr Michałowski, telephone interview, 12 Aug 2008.
118. Perhaps U.S. officials greased their path because they coveted Zlotowski's expertise, Piotr Michałowski speculated; Joliot's work on nuclear chain reactions was pertinent enough to be mentioned by Einstein in his famous August 1939 letter to FDR, which stimulated American action toward the atomic bomb.
119. Piotr and Stefan Michałowski, telephone interviews, 12 Aug 2008 and 12 Mar 2009; *WP,* 13 Sep 1967. The CIA JM profile and other sources said Mira was married to Kliszko before the war; Piotr denied this. Zlotowski bio: appendix to Gen. Izyador Modelski executive session testimony, HUAC, 31 Mar–1 Apr 1949, at http://www.archive.org/stream/documentarytesti1949 unit/documentarytesti1949unit_djvu.txt.
120. Piotr Michałowski, telephone interview, 12 Aug 2008.
121. "He screwed them and got away with it," his son recalled. Ibid., 13 Aug 2008.
122. American Embassy, Warsaw, airgram A-468, "High Government Official Evaluates President Kennedy's Administration," 9 Feb 1962, Poland-General-19/61-5/62, box 153, NSF:CO, JFKL; Stefan Wilkosz, "One Shot," *Polityka,* 30 Nov 1963, American Embassy, Warsaw, airgram A-459, 5 Dec 1963, at www.maryferrell.org.
123. David Halberstam telephone interview, New York, 28 Mar 2005.
124. American Embassy, Paris, airgram A-628, "Reports of Conversations in Paris with Polish Diplomat George Michałowski," 20 Oct 1966, POL 1 General Policy POL 1/1/64, box 2591, CFPF, 1964–66.
125. On "horse," see Richard E. Neustadt to McGeorge Bundy and WWR, "Subject: Conversation with Jerzy Michałowski," 17 May 1961, Poland-General-1/61-9/61, box 153, NSF:CO, JFKL; "front rank": DR to American Embassy, Vientiane, 5 May 1961, cited above.
126. Handwritten note from PVD to JM on PVD name card, 22 Jul 1964, courtesy of Stefan Michałowski.
127. Warsaw embtel 1412 (JAG), 9 Dec 1966, *SDVW:NVPP,* 295.
128. CIA JM profile; Polish intelligence: BU-01264/393 and 0586/2304, IPN. "One may say that from the beginning of his career Michałowski was closely surveilled by Polish special services which did not trust him (and especially his wife)," the historian Andrzej Paczkoswki concluded after reviewing JM's IPN files; email to the author, 17 Dec 2008.
129. David Halberstam, "Winter in Warsaw: Gray Skies and Slushy Streets," *NYT,* 12 Jan 1966.
130. WAH 29 Dec 1965 Warsaw talks: documents (esp. Warsaw embtels 1060, 1066, 1068–69, and 1073) in PINTA folders (2) and (3), box 548, WAHP-LC; MR; JAG OH-II, 10 Feb 1969, 1–6, and

WAH OH, 16 Jun 1969, 5–8, both LBJL; WAH, *America and Russia in a Changing World: A Half Century of Personal Observation* (Garden City, N.Y.: Doubleday, 1971), 117–19; *FRUS, 1964–68*, 3:737–38, 751–53, 756–57; Abramson, *Spanning*, 639–40.

131. WAH-Winiewicz memcon, 25 Oct 1965, Poland file, box 495, WAHP-LC.

132. Already admonished by AR, WAH probably did not appreciate it much when Washington, too, scolded him for using ultimatum-type language and suggested he use euphemisms in subsequent conversations (e.g., if necessary the US would "continue to carry out its commitment" to South Vietnam and counter DRV "escalation"): Deptel 15258 to American Embassy, Belgrade, 30 Dec 1965, PINTA (3) folder, box 548, WAHP-LC.

133. Gomułka-Kádár memcon, Budapest, 18–19 Jan 1966, KC PZPR, sygn. XI A/64, AAN, obt. D. Selvage, trans. MG.

134. The five points, which AR quickly transmitted to Hanoi, were (1) Washington had ordered the bombing pause to allow a "period of calm and tranquility" that would "facilitate entry onto a road of negotiations," and hoped the other side would "reciprocate with a parallel gesture." (2) Washington realized that Hanoi required "appropriate time" to consider the U.S. proposition, but would appreciate a response "at the earliest possible time," especially in view of domestic pressures on Johnson. (3) Though Washington did not recognize the NLF as a government, it took a "flexible" attitude toward ensuring that the NLF could make its views known during negotiations. (4) During talks "the U.S. side is ready to discuss the 4 points of the DRV as well as all other proposals coming from other parties including also South Vietnam." (5) The 14 points published on December 29 represents the U.S. "general attitude." Warsaw embtel 1073 (JAG), 30 Dec 1965, RG 59, NA II; PFM (AR) to PE/Hanoi (JS), sz. 12077, 29 Dec 1965, AMSZ, obt./trans. MG.

135. WAH-Gomułka memcon, 30 Dec 1965, PZPR 2596, AAN, 136–56, obt./trans. LG; JAG memcon, 30 Dec 1965, and Warsaw embtel 1075 (JAG), 30 Dec 1965, both PINTA (5) folder, WAHP-LC; JAG OH II, 10 Feb 1969, LBJL, 6–7; Gomułka-Kádár memcon, 19 Jan 1966; DK and SHL, *Secret Search*, 141–42; MR; WAH, *America and Russia in a Changing World*, 119–20.

136. Record of Polish-Soviet talks, Warsaw, 6 Apr 1965, cited above.

137. Gomułka-Kádár memcon, 19 Jan 1966.

138. JAG, WAH-Gomułka memcon, 30 Dec 1965, PINTA (5) folder, WAHP-LC.

139. MR. JAG recalled the quotation as "You are gangsters but we are willing to do business with gangsters to stop the war." [SHL,] JAG interview notes, Warsaw, 12 Dec 1967, box 41, SHLP.

140. JAG background: "Outspoken Postal Chief," *NYT*, 16 Feb 1965 ("bulky"); Deptel 12110 to American Embassy, Warsaw, 23 Aug 1965, and other documents in JAG personnel file, 1/1/65, box 184, CFPF, 1964–66, and JAG papers, WHS; JAG OH-I, 5 Feb 1969, LBJL; *NYT*, 10 Jan 1996 ("rumpled").

141. Herbert Kaiser telephone interview, Palo Alto, Calif., 31 Jul 2007. For mixed assessments of JAG by the diplomats who served with him in Warsaw, see FAOHC interviews with Richard Townsend Davies ("very shrewd and intelligent . . . but with no background at all, and a bit, I would say, at sea, as a result of that"); David M. Evans ("an extremely colorful figure, . . . pretty much of a clown, . . . very coarse manners . . . but . . . effective in one way, in that he was dynamic"); Robert C. Haney; Walter E. Jenkins Jr. ("a capable, intelligent person; . . . we hit it off"); S. Douglas Martin ("a night owl, . . . a character"); Gary L. Matthews ("a smashing success with the Poles"); David J. Fischer ("like many political appointees, he had dreams of grandeur"); Jack Mendelsohn ("a wonderful, sort of garrulous interesting guy who was a lot of fun to be around, . . . a good leader"); and John H. Trattner ("likable, irascible, and instinctively political" yet "didn't have much feel for diplomatic niceties").

142. On "build," see *FRUS, 1964–68*, 3:720; "favorite": Warsaw embtel 1068 (JAG), 30 Dec 1965, PINTA, Dec 1965–Jan 1966 (3), box 548, WAHP-LC.

143. JM interview notes, 22 Nov 1967, Interviews folder, box 15, SHLP.

144. "Outspoken Postal Chief" (WW II); JAG OH I, 5 Feb 1969, 26–30; *WP*, 7 Jun 1964.

145. Warsaw embtel 1078 (JAG), 30 Dec 1965, PINTA (3) folder, box 548; Belgrade embtel 965 (Elbrick), 31 Dec 1965, PINTA (11) folder, box 549; both WAHP-LC.

146. PFM (AR) to PE/Hanoi (JS), sz. 12077, 29 Dec 1965, AMSZ, obt./trans. MG.

147. LVL/NAV, *Before Paris,* chap. 11 ("Michałowski in Hanoi"), trans. Jason Hoai Tran; PE/Hanoi (JS) to PFM (AR), sz. 15800 ("lively"), 30 Dec 1965, and 15849 ("problems"), 31 Dec 1965, both AMSZ, obt./trans. MG.

148. Piotr Michałowski, telephone interview, 19 Sep 2003.

149. Besides Polish materials cited below, sources on JM's trip include V. V. Kuznetsov, "Reception for the Director-General of MID PPR comr. Ye. Michałowski," 15 Jan 1966, f. 0100, op. 59, d. 5, p. 525, ll. 1–6, AVP RF, obt./trans. L. Luthi; U Thant, "Note on Vietnam Situation," 7 Feb 1966, folder "Vietnam War (Confidential Papers), 1965–1966," and U Thant, "The Question of Vietnam," 15 Jan 1967, both DAG-1, 5.2.2.3.2, box 1, UNA; WAH-JM memcon, 26 Sep 1967, Sep 1967 folder, box FCL 33, WAHP-LC; and JM-WAH memcon, 19 Feb 1969, POL 27-14 Viet/Marigold 1969, box 2739, CFPF, 1967–69.

150. Piotr Michałowski, telephone interview, 19 Sep 2003.

151. PE/Moscow (Pszczółkowski) to PFM (AR), sz. 15848, 31 Dec 1965, AMSZ, obt./trans. LG; MR.

152. PZPR CC to CCP CC, 28 Dec 1965, Communist Party of Great Britain records, Labour History Archive, Manchester, courtesy S. Radchenko; Luthi, *Sino-Soviet Split,* 333.

153. Gomułka-Kádár memcon, 19 Jan 1966.

154. PE/Hanoi (JS) to PFM, sz. 15850 (Wierna), 31 Dec 1965, AMSZ, obt./trans. MG.

155. Quoted in MR.

156. On 2 Jan 1966 JM-Wang conversation, see PE/Beijing (Knothe/JM) to PFM (AR), sz. 13, 2 Jan 1966, AMSZ, Warsaw; obt./trans. LG; MR; JM-Kuznetsov memcon, 15 Jan 1966; "horse's hoof": JM-Kreisberg memcon, "ChiCom Attitude Towards North Vietnam," 7 May 1968, POL 27-14 VIET 5/1/68, box 2718, CFPF, 1967–69.

157. Liu Yanshun interview, Beijing, 25 Mar 2004; 24-course: JM-Kreisberg memcon, cited above.

158. Conversation with Jan Rowinski (then second secretary, Polish Embassy), Beijing, 24 Mar 2004; also Xiaoyuan Liu and Vojtech Mastny, eds., *China and Eastern Europe, 1960s–1980s* (Zurich: Zürcher Beiträge Nr. 72, 2004), 76.

159. *Renmin Ribao,* 3 Jan 1966, in MR.

160. MR.

161. On 4 Jan 1966 statement, see *SDVW:NVPP,* 131–33.

162. Thies, *When Governments Collide,* 117; Hershberg, "Peace Probes."

163. See Military History Institute of Vietnam, *Victory in Vietnam: The Official History of the People's Army of Vietnam, 1954–1975,* trans. MP (Lawrence: University Press of Kansas, 2002), 171–72; *History of the Communist Party of Vietnam* (Hanoi: Foreign Languages Publishing House, 1986), 180–85, and Duiker, *Ho Chi Minh,* 548–49, 667 n. 47.

164. Le Duan speech to Twelfth VWP CC Plenum, December 1965, "Advance Enthusiastically, Using All the Power of the People of both North and South to Defeat the American Imperialists and their Lackeys," *Van Dien Dang, Toan Tap, Tap 26, 1965* [Collected Party Documents, Volume 26, 1965], (Hanoi: Nha Xuat Ban Chinh Tri Quoc Gia, 2003), 593–94, trans. MP.

165. PE/Hanoi (JM) to PFM (AR), sz. 74, 4 Jan 1966, AMSZ, obt./trans. LG.

166. "Michałowski in Hanoi," 126–27.

167. JM's 4–5 Jan 1966 conversations with NDT: PE/Hanoi (JM) to PFM (AR), sz.s 74 (4 Jan 1966), 108 (5 Jan 1966), and 306 (9 Jan 1966), AMSZ, obt./trans. LG; MR.

168. JM-PVD 5 Jan 1966 conversation: PE/Hanoi (JM) to PFM (AR), sz. 159, 6 Jan 1966, AMSZ, obt./trans. LG; MR; "Michałowski in Hanoi," 127–34.

169. Thant, "Question of Vietnam," 15 Jan 1967; PE/Hanoi (JM) to PFM (AR), 6 Jan 1966, sz. 159, AMSZ, obt./trans. LG.

170. "Michałowski in Hanoi," 129–31.

171. JM-HCM 6 Jan 1966 talk: PE/Hanoi (JM) to PFM (AR), sz. 299, 6 Jan 1966, AMSZ, obt./trans. LG; MR; "Michałowski in Hanoi," 134–37.

172. See esp. Duiker, *Ho Chi Minh,* 548, 553–55.

173. "Michałowski in Hanoi," 134.

174. PE/Hanoi (JM) to PFM (AR), sz. 299, 6 Jan 1966, AMSZ, obt./trans. LG.

175. "Michałowski in Hanoi," 134–35.
176. Ibid., 136–37.
177. Thant, "Question of Viet-Nam," 15 Jan 1967, and JM-WAH memcon, 19 Feb 1969. JM's impression fits Duiker's view that HCM "was clearly beginning to show his age," citing reports that "he had difficulty breathing and experienced occasional lapses in mental acuity." Duiker, *Ho Chi Minh*, 554–55.
178. JM-Kuznetsov memcon, 15 Jan 1966.
179. American Embassy, Paris, airgram A-628, "Reports of Conversations in Paris with Polish Diplomat George Michałowski," 20 Oct 1966, cited above.
180. JM-Kuznetsov memcon, 15 Jan 1966.
181. JM-WAH memcon, 19 Feb 1969. PVD similarly impressed another Eastern European would-be mediator who visited Hanoi in late 1967. Romania's first deputy foreign minister told U.S. officials that PVD "made an outstanding impression, calm, reasonable, knowing what he was speaking about. A man you can have a dialogue with." WAH-Macovescu memcon, 5 Jan 1968, Romania 1964–68 folder, box FCL 16, WAHP-LC. A year later, JM called PVD "the real master of North Viet-Nam, . . . very much in control of the situation," though that description hardly fits his January 1966 visit, when PVD's supposedly more flexible approach lost out. Thant, "Question of Viet-Nam," 15 Jan 1967.
182. Honecker-Baranowski memcon, 6 Jan 1966, SAPMO-BArch,, obt./trans. C. Ostermann.
183. PE/Hanoi (JM) to PFM (AR), sz. 306, 9 Jan 1966, AMSZ; obt./trans. LG; MR.
184. Gomułka comments, 19 Jan 1966, Gomułka-Kádár talks.
185. PE/Hanoi (JM) to PFM (AR), sz. 209, 6 Jan 1966, AMSZ, obt./trans. LG.
186. PE/Hanoi (JM) to PFM (AR), sz. 311, 9 Jan 1966, ibid.; MR. Shelepin was in Hanoi 7–12 Jan 1966.
187. On "gay spirits" and "relishing," see Thant, "Question of Viet-Nam," 15 Jan 1967; "Polish cavalryman . . . changes of heart": JM-WAH memcon, 19 Feb 1969.
188. PE/Hanoi (JM) to PFM (AR), sz. 364, 11 Jan 1966, AMSZ, obt./trans. LG; MR.
189. Thant, "Note on Vietnam Situation," 7 Feb 1966, folder "Vietnam War (Confidential Papers), 1965–1966," DAG-1, 5.2.2.3.2, UNA.
190. Gomułka-Kádár talks, 19 Jan 1966. On DRV-NLF tensions see, e.g., Robert K. Brigham, *Guerrilla Diplomacy: The NLF's Foreign Relations and the Viet Nam War* (Ithaca, N.Y.: Cornell University Press, 1999).
191. Quoted from MR.
192. NC, *The Improbable Triumvirate: John F. Kennedy, Pope John, Nikita Khrushchev* (New York: W. W. Norton, 1972); Melvyn P. Leffler, *For the Soul of Mankind: The United States, the Soviet Union, and the Cold War* (New York: Hill and Wang, 2007), 160–61, 167–69, 184.
193. See chronologies (hereafter NC chrons) in folders 11–12, box 1222, NC Papers, Charles E. Young Research Library, UCLA; AR note re NC, 27 Dec 1965, AAN, trans. MG; and "Record of Mr. Norman Cousins' Contacts with the Poles," attached to WPB to WAH et al., "Subject: Attached Notes of Norman Cousins' Activities," 2 Feb 1966, Chron folder, Jan–Apr 1966 (pt. 2), box 3, ASS/EAPA (hereafter WPB NC chron); and NC, "How the U.S. Spurned Three Chances for Peace in Vietnam," *Look*, 29 Jul 1969, 45–48.
194. "Michałowski in Hanoi," 131; MR; and JM ciphergrams from Hanoi.
195. PE/Hanoi (JM) to PFM (AR), sz. 366, 11 Jan 1966, AMSZ, obt./trans. LG.
196. MR.
197. Le Duan: Thant, "The Question of Viet-Nam," 15 Jan 1967; LDT, "nationalists": WAH-JM memcon, 19 Feb 1969.
198. PE/Vientiane (JM) to PFM (AR), sz. 460, 13 Jan 1966, AMSZ, trans. MG.
199. WAH and JM in Vientiane on 13 Jan 1966: PE/Vientiane (JM) to PFM (AR), sz. 460, 13 Jan 1966, and PE/Vientiane (Wajda) to PFM (JM), sz. 542, 14 Jan 1966, both AMSZ, trans. MG; Vientiane embtel 752, 13 Jan 1966, *FRUS, 1964–68*, 28:438–41, and WAH-Souvanna memcon, PINTA (7), box 549, WAHP-LC; Vientiane (Mr. Warner) to FO, tel. 21, 14 Jan 1966, FO 371/186337, TNA ("bellicose"); Vietnamese speculation: "Michałowski in Hanoi," 137–38; DK and SHL, *Secret Search*, 149. WAH was mistakenly told (or misheard) that JM was headed *to*

Hanoi, but U.S. officials quickly established from ICC records that he had come *from* Hanoi en route to Bangkok.

200. See, e.g., *FRUS, 1964–68,* vol. 27, docs. 167 and 174, and materials in POL 27-14 CAMB 1/1/64, box 1971, CFPF, 1964–66.

201. PFM (Spasowski) to PE/Vientiane (Wajda for JM), sz. 292, 10 Jan 1966, and PE/Vientiane (JM) to PFM (Spasowski), sz. 377, 11 Jan 1966, both AMSZ, trans. MG.

202. PE/Vientiane (JM) to PFM (AR), sz. 459, 13 Jan 1966, ibid. JM later proposed reconvening Geneva but the idea went nowhere: Warsaw embtel 2220 (JAG), 17 Jun 1966, POL 27-14 CAMB 1/1/64, box 1971, CFPF, 1964–66.

203. On 15 Jan 1966 JM-Kuznetsov talk, see PE/Moscow (JM) to PFM (AR), sz. 586, 15 Jan 1966, AMSZ, obt./trans. LG, and JM-Kuznetsov memcon, 15 Jan 1966, *CWIHPB* 16 (Fall 2007–Winter 2008): 387–88.

204. JAG and "Ziggy Bonyarek [sp?]" interviews, Warsaw, 12 Dec 1967, Vietnam bombing pause 1966–67, box 41, SHLP; DK and SHL, *Secret Search,* 142; MR.

205. On 18 Jan 1966 AR-JAG talk, see MR, citing personal notes.

206. Daniel Schorr, "Red Poland Pursued a Big Role in Harriman's Hanoi Mission," *WP,* 26 Mar 1966; Warsaw embtels 1613 (JAG), 28 Mar 1966, Pinta Aftermath (1), box FCL 25, WAH, LC, and 2222 (JAG), 17 Jun 1966, POL 27-14 CAMB 1/1/64, box 1971, CFPF, 1964–66; conversation with Daniel Schorr, Miami, 22 Mar 2001; Daniel Schorr, *Staying Tuned: A Life in Journalism* (New York: Pocket Books, 2001), 186–87.

207. DK and SHL, *Secret Search,* 149; JAG OH II, 8.

208. On Shelepin, see Radchenko, *Two Suns,* 126.

209. Radványi, *Delusion and Reality,* 128; MR and JM cables contain no such Shcherbakov comment.

210. Ibid., 160–69, 276 nn. 12, 17; Ilya V. Gaiduk, "Peacemaking or Troubleshooting? The Soviet Role in Peace Initiatives during the Vietnam War," in *Search for Peace in Vietnam,* ed. Gardner and Gittinger, 268.

211. CIA Office of Current Intelligence, Intelligence Memorandum, "Communist Reaction to the US Peace Offensive," 20 Jan 1966, *FRUS, 1964–68,* 4:92–94; Ilya V. Gaiduk, *The Soviet Union and the Vietnam War* (Chicago: Ivan R. Dee, 1996), 84.

212. MR. In Hanoi, Shcherbakov affirmed that Shelepin would act "in a direction similar to ours." PE/Hanoi (JM) to PFM (AR), sz. 209, 6 Jan 1966, AMSZ; obt./trans. LG.

213. PE/Moscow (JM) to PFM (AR), sz. 586, 15 Jan 1966, ibid.

214. Luthi, *Sino-Soviet Split,* 333–35; Radchenko, *Two Suns,* 158.

215. A. Novotny-Brezhnev memcon, Moscow, 20 Jan 1966, Central State Archive, Prague, Czech Republic, in *Journal of Cold War Studies* 5, no. 3 (Summer 2003): 3–4, obt. O. Tůma, trans. M. Kramer.

216. PE/Moscow (JM) to PFM (AR), sz. 586, 15 Jan 1966, AMSZ, obt./trans. LG.

217. [GDR Foreign Minister] Winzer to Walter Ulbricht et al., 8 Mar 1966, SAPMO-BArch, DY 30/3667, pp. 197–204, Berlin, obt.. L. Luthi, trans. H. Harrison; also Luthi, *Sino-Soviet Split,* 333–34. Truong Chinh: Bui Tin, *From Cadre to Exile,* 29–31, 44; Duiker, *Ho Chi Minh,* 256, 428, 437–38, 440–41, 445–46, 477–79, 484–86, 507, 512, 536; and PE/Hanoi (JS) to PFM (Weirna), sz. 912, 22 Jan 1966, AMSZ trans. MG.

218. On other timid Soviet peace gestures at this juncture, see *FRUS, 1964–68,* 4:24 n. 3, 70–73, 117–21.

219. AR-Péter coordination: MR and PFM (AR) to PE/Hanoi (JS) sz. 424, 13 Jan 1966, AMSZ, trans. MG.

220. See, e.g., comments by a *Trybuna Ludu* correspondent to a Swiss diplomat in Beijing, in "Political Letter," 30 Aug 1966, E 2300-01, Aksession 1973/156, box 7, "1966 p.a. 21.31 Peking Politische Berichte," Bundesarchiv Bern, Switzerland, obt./trans. L. Luthi.

221. János Péter to HSWP Politboro, "Diplomatic Steps Concerning the Vietnam Conflict," 31 Jan 1966, Foreign Ministry records, XIX-J-1-j, box 111, MOL, obt. G. Cseh, trans. D. Evans (hereafter, Péter, "Diplomatic Steps"); Kádár-Gomułka memcon, 19 Jan 1966. Contributing to later confusion, Radványi, after defecting in May 1967, told U.S. officials that a secret AR-

Páter-Gromyko meeting occurred during the pause, but mistakenly dated it to late December 1965 and speculated that it had designated JM as the "Eastern Bloc's 'pause' representative." WPB, "Subject: Disclosure by János Radványi Concerning Vietnam Negotiations—Part I," 29 May 1967, box 2, NSF:Intelligence File, LBJL (hereafter "Radványi Disclosure").

222. Péter, "Diplomatic Steps." Gromyko's reported statement further contradicts Radványi's assertion that Shelepin made no effort to advocate negotiations or a political course.

223. Ibid.

224. They met at the funeral for Indian prime minister Lal Bahadur Shastri. *FRUS, 1964–68,* 14:367–69.

225. Péter, "Diplomatic Steps"; also report on meeting between Hungarian diplomat Karoly Erdelyi and Polish ambassador Kiljanczyk, Budapest, 24 Jan 1966, XOX-J-1-j, 112.doboz, IV-43-4/ E.K./1966, MOL, obt. C.Bekes, trans. A. Agoston.

226. MR; JAG OH II, 9, LBJL.

227. Ball to LBJ, "Possible Signal from Hanoi," 19 Jan 1966, *FRUS, 1964–68,* 4:91.

228. PFM (JM) to Polish UN Mission, New York (Wyzner), sz. 923, 27 Jan 1966, AMSZ, obt./trans. LG; MR.

229. NC's late January 1966 contacts with U.S. officials: NC chron, folder 11, box 1222, NC Papers, UCLA; WPB NC chron; and NC, "How the U.S. Spurned Three Chances for Peace in Vietnam," 47–48.

230. Polish UN Mission, New York (Wyzner) to PFM (JM), sz. 1122, 27 Jan 1966, AMSZ, obt./trans. LG.

231. NC, "How the U.S. Spurned Three Chances for Peace in Vietnam," 47.

232. Polish UN Mission, New York (Wyzner) to PFM (JM or Amb. Lewandowski), sz. 1173, 28 Jan 1966, AMSZ, obt./trans. LG.

233. NC, "How the U.S. Spurned Three Chances for Peace in Vietnam," 47.

234. Polish UN Mission, New York (Wyzner) to PFM, sz. 1173, 27 Jan 1966, as above.

235. DK and SHL, *Secret Search,* 151.

236. NSC minutes, 29 Jan 1966, 1:20–2:30 p.m., *FRUS, 1964–68,* 4:187.

237. PFM (AR) to Polish UN Mission, New York (Wyzner), sz. 995, 29 Jan 1966, AMSZ, obt./trans. LG.

238. On "adjudication," see PE/Hanoi (JM) to PFM (AR), sz. 159, 6 Jan 1966, ibid..

239. PFM (AR) to PE/Hanoi (JS), sz. 1038, and PFM (JM) to PE/Hanoi (JS), sz. 1040, both 30 Jan 1966, AMSZ, trans. MG.

240. MR.

241. Polish UN Mission, New York (Wyzner), to PFM (AR), sz. 1234, 29 Jan 1966, AMSZ, obt./ trans. LG.

242. PE/Hanoi (JS) to PFM (JM), sz. 1233, 30 Jan 1966, AMSZ, obt./trans. MG; PFM (JM) to Polish UN Mission, New York (Wyzner), sz. 1035, 30 Jan 1966, AMSZ, obt./trans. LG.

243. Polish UN Mission, New York (Wyzner), to PFM (JM), sz. 1246, noon, 30 Jan 1966, AMSZ, obt./trans. LG; according to WPB NC chron, NC spoke to Goldberg at 11:15 a.m. Sunday.

244. Polish UN Mission, New York (Wyzner), to PFM (JM), sz. 1247 (4:20 p.m., 30 Jan 1966), sz. 1249 (midnight, 30 Jan 1966), and sz. 1250 (1 a.m., 31 Jan 1966), all AMSZ, obt./trans. LG; MR.

245. DK and SHL, *Secret Search,* 152–53; "Points to Be Made to Mr. Cousins," Chron folder, Jan–Apr 1966 (pt. 2), box 3, ASS/EAPA; MR; also Rangoon embtel 394, 31 Jan 1966, *SDVW:NVPP,* 41–42. Speaking with WPB in May 1967, Radványi recalled that a Polish UN diplomat had told him "that Hanoi had in fact withdrawn a division from the South during the pause, but that the Pentagon had refused to admit this, and the Americans had missed the signal." WPB dismissed this as "an invention of the fertile Polish imagination" and more evidence that the Poles "were playing games with us throughout this period," with the "only honest Polish behavior" being their admission that JM had failed to achieve positive results. "Radványi Disclosure." Radványi was alluding to a talk in early February with Bohdan Lewandowski (just back from Warsaw) who said that in late January "the North Vietnamese troops fighting in South Vietnam suspended their activities" and U.S. analysts had evidence of a partial DRV

pullback. Radványi, "Subject: The Vietnam Issue," 18 Feb 1966, 112.doboz, XIX-J-l-j 1966, MOL, obt., C. Bekes, trans. A. Agoston.

246. On "subject," and "heartbreak," see WPB NC chronology; "shattering": NC, "How the U.S. Spurned."

247. JAG OH II, 10 Feb 1969, 10–13, LBJL.

248. *SDVW:NVPP*, 116–58 (quotation on 117); DK and SHL, *Secret Search*, 137–66; Thies, *When Governments Collide*, 112–22.

249. Due to this lack of evidence, the most important work on the war's international diplomacy, published in 1991, almost completely ignored these murky "efforts to make direct contact with Hanoi in the hope of evoking some kind of response which might lead to the prolongation of the bombing pause and then to secret negotiations." "We still have no details of the communication which took place with the Hungarian and Polish Governments," its author wrote. "It is not clear whether they acted as intermediaries with North Vietnam." Smith, *International History of the Vietnam War, Vol. III*, 253.

250. WPB to Gibbons, July 1993, in Gibbons, IV, 129 n. 51.

251. WAH to JAG, 25 Jan 1966, box 568, WAHP-LC.

252. WAH to McGeorge Bundy, 1 Feb 1966, box 568, WAHP-LC; WPB NC chron.

253. BDM comments, "Kennedy, Johnson, and Vietnam" conference, Saint Simons Island, Ga., 8–10 Apr 2005.

254. DR, *As I Saw It*, 466. LBJ, recalled an NSC aide, "was told by some of his friends that the pause was his greatest mistake, and that he was led down the garden path by the doves at home and the frauds abroad. So he took a very dim view of it." CLC OH-I, 9 July 1969, LBJL.

Chapter 1

1. BE/Saigon (Etherington-Smith) to FO (J. E. Cable), 30 Dec 1965, FO 371/186336, TNA.

2. [Szewczyk,] director, Human Resources Dept., MSZ, to Dept. 1, MSW, 3 Feb 1966, BU 0586/2162, IPN, obt. A. Paczkowski, trans. MG.

3. See, e.g., *FRUS, 1964–68*, 4:216–18; Gibbons, IV, 179–82, 230–32.

4. GPP, IV, 32–53, 58–68.

5. On public support, see Gibbons, IV, 167–68, 174–75, 335–36; UN proposal: *FRUS, 1964–68*, 4:189–92, 194–95, 260 n. 2; *NYT*, 2 Feb 1966.

6. *NYT*, 4 Feb 1966.

7. BE/Warsaw (G. L. Clutton) to FO, tels. 61 (2 Feb 1966), 65 (4 Feb 1966) and 66 (5 Feb 1966); and Clutton to A. J. de la Mare, FO, 17 Feb 1966; all FO 371/186338, TNA.

8. BE/Warsaw (Clutton) to FO, tel. 65, 4 Feb 1966, ibid.; and Clutton to de la Mare, FO, 24 Feb 1966, FO 371/186339, TNA.

9. BE/Warsaw (Clutton) to FO, tel. 61, 2 Feb 1966, FO 371/186338, TNA.

10. On Wendrowski-PVD talk, see PE/Hanoi (Wendrowski) to PFM (Spasowski), sz. 1495, 5 Feb 1966, AMSZ, obt./trans. MG; also BE/Saigon (Etherington-Smith) to FO, tel. 174, 8 Mar 1966, FO 371/186339, TNA.

11. On Wendrowski-Giap talk, see PE/Hanoi (Wendrowski) to PFM (Spasowski), sz. 1537, 6 Feb 1966, AMSZ, obt./trans. MG.

12. BE/Saigon (Etherington-Smith) to FO, tel. 174, 8 Mar 1966, FO 371/186339, and Etherington-Smith, BE/Saigon, to D.F Murray, SEAD, FO, 1 Apr 1966, in FO 371/186335, both TNA; also BE/Saigon (Etherington-Smith) to FO, tel. 169, 4 Mar 1966, ibid.

13. Lt.-Col. T. Walichnowski (MSW) to Szewczyk (director, Human Resources Department, MSZ), 5 Mar 1966, w. handwritten addendum, BU 0586/2162, IPN, obt. A. Paczkowski, trans. MG.

14. JL interview, Warsaw, 16 Jun 2003; JL telephone interview, 26 May 2004.

15. JL interviews, Warsaw, June 2003.

16. JL interviews, Warsaw, June/November 2003, and 20 Oct 2006; telephone interview, 26 May 2004.

17. JL telephone interview, 6 Dec 2004; Barbara Lewandowski description: classified intelligence "fiche" on JL which a U.S. Embassy officer in Saigon shared with a Dutch colleague. DE/Saigon (Derksen) to DFM, cable 85, tel. 8664, "Subject: Intelligence regarding the Polish ambassador," 2 Sep 1966, secret, Derksen cable file (1 July–31 December 1966), code 911, bloc 1965–74 (secret), DFMA, obt. R. van der Maar / trans. DM.

18. JL route: PFM (Szewczyk) to Poldel Saigon (Trela), sz. 4012, 2 Apr 1966, AMSZ, obt. Y. Chin; and PFM (Szewczyk) to PE/Phnom Penh (Milczek), sz. 3469, 6 Apr 1966, AMSZ, obt./trans. MG.

19. Herring commentary in *SDVW:NVPP*, 211, citing János Radványi, *Delusion and Reality: Gambits, Hoaxes, and Diplomatic One-Upmanship in Vietnam* (South Bend, Ind.: Gateway Editions, 1978), 194–95.

20. Unless otherwise noted, this account of JL's background derives from interviews with him in Warsaw, June and November 2003, October 2006, February 2008, and May 2011; telephone interviews on 6 Dec 2004 and 1 Oct 2007, and letter from JL to author, 4 Dec 2006; biographical data also in "special questionnaires" in JL MSW personnel files (BU 0586/2162 and BU 01930/202) in IPN, and JL brief biography, 24 Mar 1970, KC PZPR, Microfilm no. 2913, BP (Feb 1970–Dec 1970), 392–93, AAN, obt./trans. MG; U.S. intelligence "fiche" in DE/ Saigon (Derksen) to DFM, cable 85, ref. 8664, 2 Sep 1966, DFMA, obt. R. van der Maar, trans. DM; PFM (Szewczyk) to Poldel Saigon (Trela), sz. 2814, 19 Mar 1966, and sz. 3139, 28 Mar 1966, both AMSZ, obt. Y. Chin.

21. P. A. Wilkinson, BE/Saigon, to D. F. Murray, SEAD, FO, 5 Oct 1966 (10711/66), FO 371/186335, TNA; notes of interviews with W. R. Smyser, 4 Oct 1967, and Stanislaw Pawlak, 1 Nov 1967, both box 15, SHLP.

22. Passent telephone interviews, Warsaw, 29 Sep 2004 and 12 Oct 2004; JL to author, 4 Dec 2006. Inspired by such journalists as David Halberstam, R. W. Apple, and Neil Sheehan, Passent was eager to report on the war but could not get a South Vietnamese visa as a journalist because Warsaw and Saigon lacked normal ties. Instead, he finagled a post with Poland's ICC delegation through *Polityka* editor Mieczysław Rakowski, later Poland's last Communist prime minister. JL found Passent "very useful" and tried to extend his tour: Poldel Saigon (JL) to PFM (Szewczyk), sz. 9566, 20 July 1966, AMSZ, trans. MG. Passent published a book on the war (*Co Dzien Voina* (Warsaw: Czytelnik, 1968)), and after a career as a political commentator served Poland's postcommunist government as ambassador to Chile.

23. U.S. intelligence "fiche" in DE/ Saigon (Derksen) to DFM, cable 85, ref. 8664, 2 Sep 1966, DFMA, obt. R. van der Maar; also American Embassy, Warsaw, Airgram A-769, 29 Mar 1963, POL 6-1 POL, RG 59, NA II, obt. MG. The CIA in November 2004 rejected the author's FOIA request for its JL profile.

24. [SHL] JL interview notes, Warsaw, 13 Dec 1967, Interviews folder, box 15, SHLP.

25. JL brief biography, 24 Mar 1970, cited above.

26. This happened during the 1830–31 rising and Russo-Polish War; see Norman Davies, *God's Playground: A History of Poland, Volume II: 1795 to the Present* (New York: Columbia University Press, 1984), vol. 2, 315–33.

27. See, e.g., Davies, *God's Playground*, vol. 2, 369–73.

28. Janusz suspected his father spent time in the forests with Polish partisans, but this would have been an inconvenient biographical detail during the Communist era, and Józef never clarified the matter to his son before he died in 1985. JL interview, Warsaw, 4 Feb 2008.

29. JL interview, Warsaw, 4 Feb 2008.

30. Constantine Pleshakov, *There Is No Freedom without Bread!* (New York: Farrar Straus & Giroux, 2009), 42.

31. JL found the correct cemetery and his grandfather's name in a record book, but not the actual gravesite.

32. UN photograph, 5 Dec 1956, courtesy JL.

33. A vote on a motion approving a timetable to grant independence to the French Cameroons arose in a UN committee on which JL sat. Moscow opposed it, fearing pro-Western forces would sweep elections to form a postindependence government. Feeling Poland's advocacy of

decolonization made it hypocritical to delay independence, JL supported the motion. He feared his action might abruptly end his diplomatic career, especially after an angry Soviet protest, but AR backed him, saying, "They made the mistake, not you." JL interview, Warsaw, June 2003

34. On the Rapacki Plan, see Piotr Wandycz, "Adam Rapacki and the Search for European Security," in *The Diplomats, 1939–1979,* edited by Gordon A. Craig and Francis L. Loewenheim (Princeton, N.J.: Princeton University Press, 1994), 289–317.

35. JL to author, 4 Dec 2006.

36. "J." to AR, 31 Jan 1959, BU 0586/2162, IPN, obt. A. Paczkowski, trans. MG.

37. "Len," notes paraphrased from sz. 984, 28 May 1960, and "Len," JL profile, 1 Aug 1960, both BU 0586/2162, IPN, obt. A. Paczkowski, trans. MG.

38. U.S. intelligence "fiche" in DE/ Saigon (Derksen) to DFM, 2 Sep 1966, cited above.

39. Confusion also existed within the Polish Mission. When JL accompanied AR to New York in 1964–65, he and Bohdan occasionally received each other's mail. JL telephone interview, 1 Oct 2007.

40. JL interview, Warsaw, 21 June 2003; also JL letter to author, 4 Dec 2006.

41. WPB, "Radványi Disclosure."

42. Radványi, *Delusion and Reality,* 194–95, ix ("make-believe").

43. DE/Saigon (Derksen) to DFM, cable 85, tel. 8664, 2 Sep 1966, as above.

44. Passent telephone interview, Warsaw, 29 Sep 2004. Passent was not the only Pole working for JL whom the visiting "courier" tried to recruit; see chapter 13.

45. Radványi to WPB, 21 Jan 1974, folder 10 ("Radványi, János, 1972–1978"), box 3, WPB Papers, ML, PU. In the original, Radványi spelled JL's name "Lewandowsky."

46. NC clearly identifies which Lewandowski he spoke with in "How the U.S. Spurned Three Chances for Peace in Vietnam," *Look,* 29 Jul 1969, p. 46, and NC chrons. Bohdan's internal resume does not explicitly say he started out in intelligence work, but does not rule out such a beginning. Born in 1926, after working in a lumber mill during the last year of World War II, he began his government career at the age of twenty, before completing any higher education, in February 1945, receiving seven months of "practical training," allegedly at the Foreign Ministry, then was sent to Poland's embassy in Washington from 1946–48 as "chief of the chancellery section, consular secretary"—a description that could include code work. Transferred to the MSZ in Warsaw, he rose through the American Dept. (III) ranks from "clerical employee" to deputy director before going to the UN in 1960. Bohdan Lewandowski resume, n.d., KC PZPR 237-XXII-484, AAN, obt./trans. MG. In the 1970s, he was UN undersecretary-general under Kurt Waldheim.

47. Lt.-Col. T. Walichnowski (Head, Section III, Dept. I, MSW) to Citizen Szewczyk (Director, Human Resources Department, MSZ), 5 Mar 1966 (w. handwritten notation [by Deputy Director Milewski?]), BU 0586/2162, IPN, Warsaw, obt. A. Paczkowski, trans. MG.

48. Lt.-Col. T. Ziółkowski (Head, Section IV, Dept. I, MSW) to Col. T. Walichnowski (Head, Section III, Dept. I, MSW) 3/12/66, enc. Lt. W. Kikitiuk, "Note 'Edo' regarding [3/8/66] conversation with Janusz Lewandowski," 11 Mar 1966, BU 0586/2162, IPN, obt. A. Paczkowski, trans. MG.

49. Kikitiuk added that in light of his "whole conversation" with JL, the "operational conclusions" reached by Capt. Sołtysiak—the officer who dealt with him regarding the UN session—appeared "correct." I have not seen Sołtysiak's report, but the context implies that he, too, regarded JL as a less than enthusiastic informant who required careful and gradual cultivation.

50. Lt. Col. Wojciechowski (inspector, Section III, Dept. I, MSW), Note on 18 Mar 1966 meeting between JL and Capt. Bisztyga (deputy head, Section III, Dept. I, MSW) and Capt. Kiryczenko (MSW), 21 Mar 1966, BU 0586/2162, IPN, obt. A. Paczkowski, trans. MG.

51. *WP,* 21 Jun 2004.

52. William Fulbright, the SFRC chair, made the comment in a speech, then expressed regrets after protests. *NYT,* 6, 18 May 1966.

53. Frances Fitzgerald, *Fire in the Lake: The Vietnamese and the Americans in Vietnam* (Boston: Little, Brown, 1972), 272.

54. On a first arrival in Saigon at this juncture, see Ward Just, *To What End* (New York: PublicAffairs, 1968); and Jack Langguth, "Saigon Tries to Live in a Hurry," *NYT*, 8 Aug 1965.

55. Benjamin T. Harrison and Christopher L. Mosher, "The Secret Diary of McNamara's Dove: The Long-Lost Story of John T. McNaughton's Opposition to the Vietnam War," *Diplomatic History* 35, no. 3 (June 2011): 505–34; at 520–26.

56. On WWR, see David Milne, *America's Rasputin: Walt Rostow and the Vietnam War* (New York: Hill and Wang / Farrar, Straus & Giroux, 2008).

57. On the Buddhist crisis, see Robert J. Topmiller, *The Lotus Unleashed: The Buddhist Peace Movement in South Vietnam, 1964–1966* (Lexington: University Press of Kentucky, 2002); Gibbons, IV, chap. 7; *FRUS, 1964–68*, 4:277 ff.; Jeffrey J. Clark, *Advice and Support: The Final Years, 1965–1973 (The U.S. Army in Vietnam)* (Washington, D.C.: Center of Military History, 1988), chap. 7; and Fitzgerald, *Fire in the Lake,* chap. 8.

58. Poldel Saigon (JL) to PFM (Spasowski), sz. 4641, 13 Apr 1966, AMSZ, obt./trans. MG.

59. JL interview, Warsaw, 20 Oct 2006.

60. Seaborn telephone interview, 3 Aug 2007; *Chubb's Folly;* JL telephone interview, 1 Oct 2007.

61. Candel Saigon (VCM) to CDEA, tel. 302, 13 Apr 1966, "Vietnam—Views of POLCOM Lewandowski," file 20-22-VIETS-2-1, pt. 4, vol. 9397, NAC.

62. JL interviews, Warsaw, June 2003; U.S. Embassy, Saigon, Airgram A-88, "ICC Aircraft to Hanoi," 2 Aug 1967, POL 27-14 VIET 6/1/67, box 2716, CFPF, 1967–69; "Boeing 307 Stratoliner" at www.nasm/edu/nasm/aero/aircraft/boeing_307.htm.

63. JL interviews, Warsaw, June 2003.

64. Andrew Preston, "Balancing War and Peace: Canadian Foreign Policy and the Vietnam War, 1961–1965," *Diplomatic History* 27 (January 2003): 73–81; and Andrew Preston, "Missions Impossible: Canadian Secret Diplomacy and the Quest for Peace in Vietnam," in *The Search for Peace in Vietnam, 1964–1968,* edited by Lloyd C. Gardner and Ted Gittinger (College Station: Texas A&M University Press, 2004), 117-143; Robert Dallek, *Flawed Giant: Lyndon Johnson and His Times, 1961–1973* (New York: Oxford University Press, 1998), 258–60.

65. Ronning's March 1966 mission to Hanoi: records in file 20-22-VIET.S.-2-1-2, Pt. 2, vol. 9404, RG 25, NAC; *SDVW:NVPP,* 159–64, 169–86 (unsanitized copy in RSM Papers, LBJL); *FRUS, 1964–68*, 4:287–90; Chester Ronning, *A Memoir of China in Revolution: From the Boxer Rebellion to the People's Republic* (New York: Pantheon, 1974), 255–67; Ronning ("source CRO") interview, Ottawa, 4 Oct 1967, box 15, SHLP; DK and SHL, *Secret Search,* 155–56; Preston, "Missions Impossible," esp. pp. 131–34. AR rebuff: M. C. [Cadieux] to Martin, 2 Mar 1966, and CDEA to Candel Saigon, "Smallbridge Discussions in Hanoi," tel. Y-204, 2 Mar 1966, both file 20-22-VIET.S.-2-1-1, pt. 2, vol. 9404, RG 25, NAC. In Saigon en route to Hanoi, Ronning saw Wendrowski, who said the ICC might eventually play a "big role" in a Vietnam settlement but not "for many years." With the enemies so far apart, conditions for peace probes were not "ripe" so Warsaw could not join Canada's initiative. Candel Saigon to CDEA, "Smallbridge: Conversation with Polish Commissioner," tel. 161, 5 Mar 1966, ibid.

66. Brezhnev–Le Duan memcon, Moscow, 11 Apr 1966, quoted by Ilya V. Gaiduk, "Peacemaking or Troubleshooting? The Soviet Role in Peace Initiatives during the Vietnam War," in *Search for Peace in Vietnam,* ed. Gardner and Gittinger, 269. I thank S. Radchenko for translating the full record.

67. HVL description: Mary McCarthy, *The Seventeenth Degree* (New York: Harcourt Brace Jovanovich, 1967), 277.

68. PE/Hanoi (JL) to PFM (Spasowski), sz. 5088, 22 Apr 1966, AMSZ, obt./ trans. MG.

69. HVL background: conversations with Luu doan Huynh and Ngo Vinh Long, Philadelphia, 20–21 Jun 2005; Smyser interview notes, 4 Oct 1967, box 15, SHLP; HVL interview by MG, Hanoi, 19 Oct 2005, notes courtesy MG; Prince Andrei: McCarthy, *Seventeenth Degree,* 277.

70. JL interviews, Warsaw, June 2003. Asked about the origin of "Ludwik" or "Ludwig" (Polish documents used them interchangeably), HVL "smiled and said that he liked the nickname and that it was given to him by [one of JL's predecessors as Polish delegate to the ICC, Przemysław] Ogrodziński for security reasons." HVL interview by MG, Hanoi, 19 Oct 2005.

71. PVD said: "You know, fighting with the French was more difficult than with the Americans. Also, militarily, the French were much weaker, *but* the French knew us very well, and many of our people like the French also. Americans when they came to Vietnam they had no friends at all. With the French it was rather more difficult, the Americans are complete aliens, completely an alien element to Vietnamese society." JL interview, Warsaw, June 2003.

72. PE/Hanoi (JS) to PFM (JM), sz. 5182, 24 Apr 1966, AMSZ, obt./trans. MG.

73. Ibid.

74. JL interviews, Warsaw, Jun 2003 and May 2011.

75. JL interview, Warsaw, 11 Nov 2003.

76. JL interview, Warsaw, 20 Oct 2006.

77. PE/Hanoi (JS) to PFM (JM), sz. 5182, 24 Apr 1966, AMSZ, obt./trans. MG; "suitable": Poldel Saigon (JL) to PFM (Spasowski), sz. 5546, 30 Apr 1966, ibid.

78. JL interviews, Warsaw, Jun and Nov 2003, and 20 Oct 2006.

79. On Shcherbakov, see Ilya V. Gaiduk, *The Soviet Union and the Vietnam War* (Chicago: Ivan R. Dee, 1996), 15–16.

80. JL-Privalov memcon, 22 Apr 1966, RGANI, f. 5, trans. S. Savranskaya.

81. For sources on JS's background, I thank A. Paczkowski and MG. This sketch relies on JS resume, n.d., KC PZPR 237/XXII-484, 102, and AR, "Motion Regarding the Nomination for a Position of the Ambassador of the Polish People's Republic in Hanoi," 17 Jul 1962 ("devoted"), and JS personnel file, 8 Oct 1962, KC PZPR V-71, 452–53, both AAN, obt./trans. MG; MSW confidential 1978 publication, in Miroslaw Piotrowski, *Ludzie bezpieki* (Lublin: Klub Inteligencji Katolickiej, 1999), 382; Krzystof Szwagrzyk, ed., *Aparat Bezpieczeństwa w Polsce, Kadra Kierownicza, t. 1, 1944–1956* (Warsaw: Instytut Pamięci Narodowej, 2005), 71, 84.

82. Paweł Machcewicz, *Rebellious Satellite: Poland 1956* (Washington, D.C., and Stanford, Calif.: Woodrow Wilson Center Press and Stanford University Press, 2009); articles by Andrzej Paczkowski; 200,000: Pleshakov, *There Is No Freedom Without Bread!* 46.

83. A. Paczkowski email, 15 Sep 2007.

84. JS and DPRK: MG dissertation, cited above.

85. In November 1956, the intelligence activities formerly controlled by the MBP and the KGB-like Committee for Public Security were placed under the MSW.

86. MG, "Polish-DPRK Relations during the Cold War, 1949–1975" paper presented to international workshop on North Korea's Foreign Relations during the Cold War, Graduate School of North Korean Studies, Kyungnam University, Seoul, 11 May 2006.

87. Ibid.

88. JL interview, Warsaw, June 2003.

89. Candel Saigon to CDEA, tel. 343, 26 Apr 1966, FO 371/186292, TNA.

90. Poldel Saigon (JL) to PFM (Spasowski), sz. 5546, 30 Apr 1966, AMSZ, obt./trans. MG.

91. Poldel Saigon (JL) to PFM (Spasowski), sz. 5504, 30 Apr 1966, ibid.

92. DE/Saigon (Derksen) to DFM, cable 33++, ref. 4866, 27 Apr 1966, file 938, code 911, bloc 1965–74 (secret), DFMA, obt. R. van der Maar, trans. DM.

93. JL-Thieu conversation: JL interview, Warsaw, June 2003, and Poldel Saigon (JL) to PFM (Spasowski), sz. 5952, 7 May 1966, AMSZ, trans. MG. JL later sent Warsaw a sketch of Thieu, a "clever politician-opportunist" close to Catholic circles. In Communist fashion, he identified Thieu's class background—a "middle-class family of intelligentsia"—and noted that while his personal role in the coup against Diem was minor, his division's participation earned him a "place in the junta." Despite lacking significant public or army support, thereby precluding an "independent role," Thieu was reportedly trying to organize "a group against Ky." Poldel Saigon (JL) to PFM (Spasowski), sz. 6391, 17 May 1966, AMSZ, obt./trans. MG.

94. Shcherbakov-JL memcon, Hanoi, 1 Jun 1966, f. 5, op. 58, d. 264, ll. 75–77, RGANI, trans. S. Savranskaya.

95. U.S. officials endorsed Saigon's opposition to international supervision of the voting, particularly by the Commission, whose competence they scorned. "From point of view of our interests, we cannot think of [a] worse choice," Deputy Ambassador William J. Porter wrote Wash-

ington. "On basis past performance, ICC would probably be discussing election irregularities for the next century." Saigon embtel 4408 (Porter), 6 May 1966, Vietnam cables vol. 52 5/1-14/66 [1 of 2], box 31, NSF:CO:VN, LBJL.

96. MG, *Poland and Vietnam, 1963: New Evidence on Communist Diplomacy and the "Maneli Affair,"* CWIHP Working Paper 45 (Washington, D.C.: Woodrow Wilson International Center for Scholars, 2005).

97. GDO, *DV,* 576–77 (7 May 1966).

98. On ICC meetings during this period, see file 21-13-VIET-ICSC-8, Vol. 10128, RG 25, NAC.

99. See GD'O's extensive published diaries (GD'O, *DV*) as well as Mario Sica, *Marigold non fiorì: Il contributo italiano alla pace in Vietnam* (Florence: Ponte alle Grazie, 1991).

100. SHL, GD'O interview notes, Rome, 1 Dec 1967, box 15, SHLP.

101. GD'O suffered from "a type of slow moving leukemia" and received treatment from a U.S. Army doctor, HCL cabled. Saigon embtel 8583 (HCL), 16 Oct 1966, *FRUS, 1964–68,* 4:756; DK and SHL termed his ailment "a persistent parasitic infection that would progressively debilitate him." DK and SHL, *Secret Search,* 21.

102. GD'O background: interviews with Paolo Janni (who served with GD'O in Athens, 1971–74), Washington, 29 Sep 2006, and Colette D'Orlandi, Paris, 21 May 2008; *DV,* 19; Sica, *Marigold non fiorì,* xx.

103. Sica interviews, Trent, 13–14 Dec 2006.

104. Eddie Ortona (Italian ambassador to the United States), interview notes, 9 Nov 1967, interviews folder, box 15, SHLP.

105. JL interviews, Warsaw, June, 7 Nov 2003.

106. W. R. Smyser interview, Washington, 11 Jun 2004.

107. GD'O, *DV,* 576–77 (7 May 1966).

108. JL interview, Warsaw, 20 Oct 2006.

109. Mario Sica interview, Rome, 24 Feb 2006; Colette D'Orlandi interview, Paris, May 2008.

110. JL interviews, Warsaw, June 2003; SHL, GD'O interview notes, Rome, 4 Dec 1967, box 15, SHLP.

111. GD'O, *DV,* 576–77 (7 May 1966).

112. JL interviews, Warsaw, June 2003.

113. Sica, *Marigold non fiorì,* 43–49, 131.

114. Ibid., 48–49.

115. Ibid., 43–44; GD'O interview notes, 1 Dec 1967, box 15, SHLP; DK and SHL, *Secret Search,* 9.

116. Sica, *Marigold non fiorì,* 44–46.

117. Ibid., 46–47; GD'O interview notes, 1 Dec 1967, box 15, SHLP; DK and SHL, *Secret Search,* 9–10.

118. GD'O would champion the establishment of an orphanage in Saigon, which opened in October 1966, as a humanitarian, nonmilitary manifestation of Rome's support for South Vietnam.

119. GD'O diary, in Rotondo, "The Lost Paths to Peace," *30 Days* (Rome), June 2005.

120. GD'O diary, 29 May 1966, in ibid.

121. Sica, *Marigold non fiorì,* 48–49, trans. IO.

122. Poldel Saigon (JL) to PFM (Spasowski), sz. 6834, 27 May 1966, AMSZ, obt./trans. MG.

123. Poldel Saigon (JL) to PFM (Spasowski), sz. 6342, 13 May 1966, ibid.; "moon," own intelligence officer: JL interview, Warsaw, 7 Nov 2003; "weak" French: JL brief bio, 24 Mar 1970, cited above.

124. JL interview, Warsaw, 20 Oct 2006.

125. Ibid., 7 Nov 2003.

126. On "intelligent," see HCL to HAK, 3 Feb 1970, NPMP, NA II, obt. W. Burr; according to R. van der Maar, within the ministry, Derksen was accused of being insufficiently supportive of Washington on the war.

127. Poldel Saigon (JL) to PFM (Spasowski), sz. 5527, 30 Apr 1966, AMSZ, trans. MG; DE/Saigon (Derksen), cable 33+, 27 Apr 1966, ref. 4866, file 938, code 911, bloc 1965–74 (secret), DFMA, obt. R. van der Maar, trans. DM.

128. Saigon embtel 5097 (HCL), "Subj: Views of Polish ICC Commissioner," 29 May 1966, POL 27-14 VIET S 1/1/66, box 3018, CFPF, 1964-6.

129. JL telephone interview, 26 May 2004.

130. Poldel Saigon (JL) to PFM (Spasowski), sz. 6342, 13 May 1966, AMSZ, obt./trans. MG.

131. Poldel Saigon (JL) to PFM (Spasowski), sz. 7017, 30 May 1966, AMSZ, trans. MG.

132. Poldel Saigon (JL) to PFM (Spasowski), sz. 7444, 10 Jun 1966, ibid.

133. JL June 1966 talks with HVL and PVD: Poldel Saigon (JL) to PFM (Spasowski), sz. 7317, 6 Jun 1966, AMSZ, obt. author and MG, trans. MG.

134. 3 June 1966 ICC session: "Report on the Activities of the International Commission in Vietnam for the Month of June 1966," 3–7, file 21-13-VIET-ICSC-8, FP 7.2, vol. 10128, RG 25, NAC.

135. Poldel Saigon (JL) to PFM (Spasowski), sz. 7259, 6 Jun 1966, AMSZ, trans. MG.

136. Candel Saigon (VCM) to CDEA, "Visit to Hanoi, May 31–Jun 4," tel. 499, 15 Jun 1966, File 20-1-2 VIET.N Pt. 1.1, vol. 10061, RG 25, NAC.

137. Ibid.

138. Shcherbakov-JL memcon, Hanoi, 1 Jun 1966, f. 5, op. 58, d. 264, ll. 75–77, RGANI, Moscow, trans. A. Kalinovsky, S. Savranskaya.

139. Poldel Saigon (JL) to PFM (Spasowski), sz. 7317, 6 Jun 1966, AMSZ; JL interview, Warsaw, 7 Nov 2003. JL saw Shcherbakov before meeting PVD the next day, and left it up to Warsaw to decide whether to inform the Soviet about the conversation; it did so, sending a summary to relay to Shcherbakov two weeks later: PFM (Meller) to PE/Hanoi (JS), sz. 6469, 20 Jun 1966, AMSZ, trans. MG.

140. LBJ telcon with Senator Richard Russell, 27 May 1964, *FRUS, 1964–68, Vol. I,* doc. 52.

141. McGeorge Bundy to LBJ, 16 Feb 1966, *FRUS, 1964–68,* 4:231–35.

142. Saigon embtel 5776 (HCL), 26 Jun 1966, Vietnam NODIS-Vol 3 (B) 10-65-6/66, box 46, NSF:CO:VN, LBJL.

143. Bundy to LBJ, 16 Feb 1966, as above.

144. HCL background: William J. Miller, *Henry Cabot Lodge: A Biography* (New York: Heineman, 1967); Alden Hatch, *The Lodges of Massachusetts* (New York: Hawthorn Books, 1973); Anne E. Blair, *Lodge in Vietnam* (New Haven, Conn.: Yale University Press, 1995), 1–8. "Bostonian": Fitzgerald, *Fire in the Lake,* 267.

145. JFK comments, 30 Jul 1962, in Timothy Naftali, ed., *The Presidential Recordings: John F. Kennedy: The Great Crises, Volume One: July 30–August, 1962* (New York: W. W. Norton, 2001), 47–48.

146. *WP,* 27 Nov 1966; Just, *To What End,* 104.

147. Fitzgerald, *Fire in the Lake,* 268. Due to security concerns, Emily spent much of HCL's second term at the Oriental Hotel in Bangkok. Henry Sears Lodge interview, Beverly, Mass., 6 Jun 2007; Miller, *Lodge,* 383; Hatch, *Lodges of Massachusetts,* 306-07.

148. "Sometimes it was observed that Lodge was not in a very strong position; . . . even before Marigold, I had the sense that Henry Cabot Lodge was not participating in top strategy for Vietnam. . . . I think the president probably listened more to the group in Washington than to Lodge." JL interview, Warsaw, June 2003. Derksen comments in Poldel Saigon (JL) to PFM (Spasowski), sz. 5547, 30 Apr 1966, cited above. JL reported "persistently circulating" rumors among diplomats of "divergences" between HCL and LBJ due in part to LBJ's tendency to "blame [him] for political failures in Vietnam." Poldel Saigon (JL) to PFM (Spasowski), sz. 8201, 24 Jun 1966, AMSZ, trans. MG.

149. "It made no sense at all for the President to have as his ambassador a man whom he would not trust enough to make decisions about the presence or absence of his own wife!" McGeorge Bundy to WPB, 14 Nov 1969, box 88, McGeorge Bundy personal papers, JFKL.

150. C. L. Sulzberger, *An Age of Mediocrity: Memoirs and Diaries 1963–1972* (New York: Macmillan, 1973), 257 (21 Apr 1966); Special Annex to Komer Report, with Komer to Moyers and WWR, 19 Apr 1966, Vietnam Memos (C), Vol. 51, 4/9-30/66 [1 of 2], box 31, NSF:CO:VN, LBJL.

151. Saigon embtel 5316 (HCL), 6 Jun 1966, POL 27 VIET S Military Operations 6/6/66, box 3000, CFPF, 1964–66; "quickly": HCL, *As It Was: An Inside View of Politics and Power in the '50s and '60s* (New York: W. W. Norton, 1976), 171.

152. JL interview, Warsaw, June 2003.

153. Ibid., 7 Nov 2003.

154. HCL, *As It Was,* 171. HCL wrote that he "instantly reported" JL's words to LBJ and RSM, and this marked the "beginning of the 'Marigold' talks." In fact, the "Marigold" designation, and the first three-way HCL-JL-GD'O talks, did not begin until a month later. Moreover, his secret/limdis June 6 cable to the State Department reporting the talk with JL was directed routinely to "SecState" without any special instructions to bring it to the attention of LBJ, RSM, or any other officials. On HCL contacts with JL and VCM, see also HCL, "Viet-Nam Memoir," part four, VII-1-2, Reel 26, HCL II Papers, MHS.

155. Saigon embtel 5316 (HCL), 6 Jun 19/66, cited above.

156. Poldel Saigon (JL) to PFM (Spasowski), sz. 7444, 10 Jun 1966, AMSZ, trans. MG.

157. JL interview, Warsaw, June 2003; HCL interview notes, Washington, 12 Oct 1967, box 15, SHLP; DK and SHL, *Secret Search,* 10–11.

158. McNaughton diary, 85 (18 May 1966), courtesy C. Mosher.

159. Sulzberger, *Age of Mediocrity,* 251 (15 Apr 1966); also 107 (9 Sep 1964), in which HCL said losing Vietnam would vindicate China's hard line and embolden Moscow: "The Philippines, Malaya, and Thailand would go. Then there would be nothing to restrain Indonesia, and Australia fears it would be swallowed up. Our prestige in the whole underdeveloped world would be deeply wounded. The NATO countries would begin to lose their ability to honor their overseas commitments." HCL subscribed to the domino theory even before Eisenhower proclaimed it in April 1954; three years earlier, in rallying Americans to support the French military effort in Indochina, he had warned against letting Tonkin Province (where Hanoi is situated) fall to the Communists: "As it goes probably would go Siam, Burma, Malaya and probably India and everything up to the Suez Canal." Miller, *Lodge,* 219.

160. Sulzberger, *Age of Mediocrity,* 257 (21 Apr 1966).

161. HCL-VCM 8 Jun 1966 talk: Saigon embtel 5379 (HCL), 8 Jun 1966, "POL 27-14 VIET S 1/1/66," box 3018, CFPF, 1964–66; also HCL, *As It Was,* 171–72; and *SDVW:NVPP,* 192–93.

162. Candel Saigon (VCM) to CDEA, "Visit to Hanoi, May 31–Jun 4," tel. 499, 15 Jun 1966, as above.

163. In his 15 Jun 1966 cable, VCM merely mentioned that after JL had downplayed his talk with PVD, he had "subsequently heard at second hand" about the Pole's advocacy of the idea that Hanoi was ready to talk, but circumstantial evidence strongly suggests he heard this on June 8 from HCL.

164. WWR passed HCL's cable describing the 8 Jun 1966 talk with VCM to LBJ with the comment that it provided: "(1) Ronning's movements more precisely. (2) Evidence that the bombing hurts the North—but not enough. (3) One man's judgment on the need for secrecy and saving Hanoi's face." WWR to LBJ, 6/8/66, 1:45 p.m., Vietnam NODIS-Vol. 3 (B) 10-65-6/66, box 46, NSF:CO:VN, LBJL.

165. Paul Martin, *A Very Public Life, Volume II: So Many Worlds* (Toronto: Deneau, 1985), 440.

166. On U.S.-Canadian friction over Ronning, see ibid., 437–43; Ronning, *Memoir of China,* 258; Charles Taylor, *Snow Job: Canada, the United States, and Vietnam* (Toronto: House of Anansi Press, 1974), 3–41; Douglas A. Ross, *In the Interests of Peace: Canada and Vietnam 1954–1973* (Toronto: University of Toronto Press, 1984); Ramesh Chandra Thakur, *Peacekeeping in Vietnam: Canada, India, Poland, and the International Commission* (Edmonton: University of Alberta Press, 1984), 231–32, 349 n. 14; *SDVW:NVPP,* 184–89 ("teasing suggestion," 188); Preston, "Missions Impossible," 129–38; and documents in "Smallbridge" files in vols. 9403 and 9404, RG 25, NAC.

167. JAG delivered this proposition to PRC ambassador Wang Guoquan on 25 May 1966, and Undersecretary of State George Ball leaked it to the *NYT* a week later: U.S. Department of State, *FRUS, 1964–68, Vol. XXX: China* (Washington, D.C.: U.S. Government Printing Office, 1998), 310–11, 315; Ball-Reston/Finney telcon, 6:20 p.m., 2 Jun 1966, folder 2, box 160, GBP, ML, PU. The article appeared on June 3, just as Hanoi approved Ronning's trip. *SDVW:NVPP,* 191.

168. Candel Saigon (VCM) to CDEA, tel. 450 Emergency, 6 Jun 1966, file 20-22-VIET.S.-2-1-1, vol. 3, RG 25, NAC.

169. Saigon embtel 5437 (HCL), 10 Jun 1966, POL 27 VIET S Military Operations [6/10/66], box 3000, CFPF, 1964–66; also Gibbons, IV, 369 n. 56; HCL, *As It Was,* 172 ("fuzzy way"); HCL, "Viet-Nam Memoir," part four, VII-2, reel 26, HCLP,.

170. HCL to LBJ, 8 Jun 1966, *FRUS, 1964–68,* 4:412–16 (quotation 413).

171. Saigon embtel 5473 (HCL), 11 Jun 1966, POL 27 VIET S Military Operations 6/11/66, box 3000, CFPF, 1964–66.

172. Internal debate over POL strikes: *FRUS, 1964–68,* 4:331, 378–79, 411–12, 417–18, 437–44, 449–52 (Ball quotation on 452); Gibbons, IV, 360–77; Milne, *America's Rasputin,* chap. 6; David L. Stebenne, *Arthur J. Goldberg: New Deal Liberal* (New York: Oxford University Press, 1996), 358–63; and Jacob Van Staaveren, *Gradual Failure: The Air War Over North Vietnam, 1965–1966* (Washington, D.C.: Air Force History and Museum Programs, 2002), 279–89.

173. LBJ-Mansfield telcon, 10 Jun 1966, *FRUS, 1964–68,* 4:417–18.

174. Editorial note, ibid., 4:411–12.

175. DR cable (Brussels secto 87) to RSM, 8 Jun 1966, *SDVW:NVPP,* 192.

176. Ibid. Wilson likewise resisted LBJ's personal appeal for "solidarity" on Vietnam and plea not to use the phrase dissociation. LBJ to Wilson, 14 Jun 1966, *FRUS, 1964–68,* 4:426–28.

177. Ronning mission to Hanoi: file 20-22-VIET.S.-2-1-1, pt. 3, vol. 9404, RG 25, NAC; *SDVW:NVPP,* 197–206; Ronning, *China in Revolution,* 266–69 ("judgement" on 267); Ronning interview notes ("source CRO"), Ottawa, 5 Oct 1967, box 15, SHLP; Preston, "Missions Impossible," 135–38.

178. Ottawa embtel 1740 FLASH, 21 Jun 1966, and memcon, "Visit of Ambassador Ronning to Hanoi, June 14–17, 1966," *SDVW:NVPP,* 197–202.

179. Poldel Saigon (JL) to PFM (Spasowski), sz. 8198, 24 Jun 1966, AMSZ, obt./trans. LG.

180. JL interview, Warsaw, June 2003.

181. Poldel Saigon (JL) to PFM (Spasowski), sz. 8201, 24 Jun 1966, AMSZ, trans. MG.

182. PFM (Meller) to PE/Hanoi (JS), sz. 6415, 18 Jun 1966, trans. MG; Warsaw embtels 2183 (JAG), 11 Jun 1966, and 2220 (JAG), 17 Jun 1966, both POL 27-14 CAMB 1/1/64, box 1971, CFPF, 1964–66.

183. PFM (Meller) to PE/Hanoi (JS), sz. 6415, 18 Jun 1966MG.

184. JAG OH II, 10 Feb 1969, 14, LBJL.

185. Warsaw embtel 2222 (JAG), 17 Jun 1966, POL 27-14 CAMB 1/1/64, CFPF, 1964–66.

186. PFM (Meller) to PE/Hanoi (JS), sz. 6415, 18 Jun 1966MG.

187. DE/Saigon (Derksen) to DFM, cable 49, ref. 6595, "Subject: Washington and Contacts with Hanoi," 16 Jun 1966, file 938, code 911, bloc 1965–74 (secret), DFMA; obt. R. van der Maar, trans. DM. Exemplifying big-power cynicism, JL told Derksen he found "indisputable" proof in Hanoi that MiG fighters recently shot down over North Vietnam were Soviet, not Chinese, as Moscow and Washington both claimed.

188. Sica, *Marigold non fiorì,* 13.

189. Walston, for his part, loyally insisted that Washington was ready for talks and it was up to Hanoi to make the first move. BE/Saigon (Etherington Smith) to FO, tel. 511, 21 Jun 1966, FO 371/186339, TNA.

190. Poldel Saigon (JL) to PFM (Spasowski), sz. 8073, 22 Jun 1966, AMSZ, obt./trans. MG. JL had low regard for Walston's mission, viewing him as ill informed about both Vietnam and the ICC. JL interview, Warsaw, 20 Oct 2006.

191. Derksen quoted JL as saying that Hanoi had told Ronning that it was confused that Washington "had not taken advantage of recent riots in the South to install a representative government," since the Ky regime represented such a clear obstacle to Washington's efforts to achieve a political solution. JL, however, recognized that jettisoning Ky would be difficult for Johnson.

192. DE/Saigon (Derksen) to DFM, cable 55, ref. 6829, "Subject: Ronning's visit to Hanoi; a Polish tale," 23 Jun 1966, file 938, code 911, bloc 1965–74 (secret), DFMA, obt. Rimko van der Maar, trans. DM.

193. LBJ-RSM telcon, 7:59 a.m., 28 Jun 1966, *FRUS, 1964–68,* 4:458–60.

Chapter 2

1. DK and SHL, *Secret Search,* 17; Mario Sica interview, Rome, 24 Feb 2006.
2. *NYT,* 30 Jun 1966; *WP,* 30 Jun 1966; Jacob Van Staaveren, *Gradual Failure: The Air War over North Vietnam, 1965–1966* (Washington, D.C.: Air Force History and Museum Programs, 2002), 289–91; *Project CHECO Report: Rolling Thunder, July 1965–December 1966,* 56–65.
3. Ibid., 56.
4. *NYT,* 30 Jun 1966.
5. On the "big apple," see WPB OH 3, 29 May 1969, 33, LBJL; and *NYT,* 30 Jun 1966.
6. Van Staaveren, *Gradual Failure,* 291.
7. *NYT,* 30 Jun 1966.
8. PE/Hanoi (JS), to PFM (Meller), sz. 8419, 30 Jun 1966, AMSZ, trans. MG.
9. DK and SHL, *Secret Search,* 12–13.
10. *NYT,* 30 Jun and 1 Jul 1966.
11. HCL account of his 29 Jun 1966 talk with GD'O and reflections on reported proposals: Saigon embtels 5840 (HCL), 29 Jun 1966, and 5855 (HCL), 30 Jun 1966, *FRUS, 1964–68,* 4:467–72. Oddly, GD'O wrote in his diary that he told HCL of JL's proposals not on the evening of June 29 but at 10 am the next morning: GD'O, *DV,* 617–18 (30 Jun 1966).
12. GD'O reported his 27 Jun 1966 talk with JL in IE/S to IFM, tels. 212 (Noon), 213-215 (4 p.m.), 27 Jun 1966, GD'O dossier; and his 27 Jun 1966 diary entry, in "Bombs on Hanoi to Block Dialogue: Some Pages from Ambassador D'Orlandi's Diary," *30 Days in the Church and the World* (Rome), English edition, June 2005 (hereafter, "D'Orlandi diary"). GD'O's telegrams are also available in busta 40, 17. "Segreto Vietnam," sezione 1, serie 1, s. serie 5, AFP. Also see Mario Sica, *Marigold non fiorì: Il contributo italiano alla pace in Vietnam* (Florence: Ponte alle Grazie, 1991). Italian translations are, unless otherwise noted, by Isella O'Rourke.
13. A few days earlier, GD'O had recounted the talk with Sihanouk to HCL. The Cambodian, admitting this was "no time for negotiations with North Vietnam," had suggested Italy take some initiative, prompting GD'O to remark that Italy knew its limitations. Don't be so modest, Sihanouk told him. Saigon embtel 5762 (HCL), 25 Jun 1966, Vietnam-Memos (A) vol. 55, 6/66 [1 of 2], box 33, NSF:CO:VN, LBJL.
14. In fact, on returning to Paris from Hanoi in mid-July, Sainteny told U.S. diplomats that HCM and PVD did not "totally" reject negotiations, and that the latter even hinted, in Ho's presence, that the DRV might cease "infiltration" in reply to a bombing halt—a key U.S. demand. Hanoi, Sainteny speculated, would not attend a peace conference or engage in public negotiations, but act only through a "secret channel"—"an individual, not too well known, possibly here in Paris or in some other neutral capital." He reported that DRV leaders "were determined to fight to the bitter end in protection of North Vietnam" but might be more flexible regarding the South. Paris embtel 1022 (Bohlen), 21 Jul 1966, *FRUS, 1964–68,* 4:508–10. Later, Sainteny clarified that in his talks between "old enemies who are friends," HCM and PVD had not made any "formal commitment" to any particular action in response to a bombing halt but PVD gave his "personal assurance" that Hanoi would make an "important gesture." WAH-Sainteny memcon, Paris, 2 Dec 1966, box 569, WAHP-LC. Vietnamese sources say PVD told Sainteny that if Washington stopped bombing North Vietnam, "I promise you, we will do something to demonstrate our good will. . . . We do not oppose a negotiated settlement, but we do not want people to take us to a Munich." LVL/NAV, *Before Paris* (2002 edition), 150, trans. MP.
15. IE/S (GD'O) to IFM, tel. 215, 4 p.m., 27 Jun 1966, GD'O dossier.
16. Sica interviews, Rome, 24 Feb 2006, Trent, 14 Dec 2006. GD'O's exact words, Sica recalled, were "They're negotiating!" or "They are opening up!"
17. GD'O, *DV,* 617 (28 Jun 1966).
18. IFM (Marchiori) to IE/S (GD'O), tel. 29, 27 Jun 1966, GD'O dossier; Moro: 27 Jun 1966 entry, AFD.
19. HCL had wired DR personally to inform him of GD'O's "alarming condition"—"His spleen is tremendously swollen; he has fallen dead away two instances in a row and has had spasms

which have made it impossible for him to evacuate"—and request urgent help for this "whole-hearted and most helpful supporter of U.S. policies here." After securing permission for a C-54 to fly GD'O to Bangkok, where he could find comfortable onward travel to Rome to seek additional medical care, HCL accompanied his stretcher-bound friend to the Thai capital, and cabled ahead to colleagues in Rome to assure sympathetic attention until he could return to Saigon, in late February. See cables in POL-Political Aff. & Rel. IT-USS, box 2370, CFPF, 1964–66; GD'O, *DV,* 566 (10 Jan 1966); and HCL to Gen. Moore, 18 Jan 1966, reel 21, and Reinhardt to HCL, 24 Jan 1966, reel 22, both HCL II, MHS.

20. See *FRUS, 1961–1963, Vol. IV: Vietnam, August–December 1963* (Washington, D.C.: U. S. Government Printing Office, 1991), 125; and Ellen J. Hammer, *A Death in November* (New York: Oxford University Press, 1987), 228–29.

21. HCL to WAH, 3 Dec 1963, *FRUS, 1961–63,* 4:656. One scholar suggests that HCL, "troubled" by GD'O's closeness to Diem, doubted his ability to mediate: Andrew Preston, "Missions Impossible: Canadian Secret Diplomacy and the Quest for Peace in Vietnam," in *The Search for Peace in Vietnam, 1964–1968,* edited by Lloyd C. Gardner and Ted Gittinger (College Station: Texas A&M University Press, 2004), 119–20, 139 n. 11. HCL's stout endorsements of GD'O during and after Marigold suggest otherwise.

22. Saigon embtel 5840 (HCL), 29 Jun 1966, *SDVW:NVPP,* 237–39.

23. GD'O, *DV,* 617–18 (30 Jun 1966).

24. Saigon embtel 5855 (HCL), 30 Jun 1966, *SDVW:NVPP,* 240–42.

25. Saigon embtel (HCL), 1 Jul 1966, Vietnam NODIS—Vol. IV (B), 7/66-12/66, box 47, NSF:CO:VN, LBJL.

26. Deptel 4108 (to American Embassy, Saigon), 29 Jun 1966, *FRUS, 1964–68,* 4:470–71.

27. LBJ telcon with Federal Reserve Board chair William Martin, 9 a.m., 30 Jun 1966, ibid., 4:473.

28. Ball-WWR telcon, 30 Jun 1966, 1:15 p.m., folder 2, box 160, GBP, ML, PU.

29. Ball-WWR telcon, 1 Jul 1966, 10:55 a.m., ibid.

30. John T. McNaughton diary, 101 (1 Jul 1966 entry), courtesy Christopher L. Mosher.

31. Ibid., 102 (3 Jul 1966).

32. Ball memo, n.d., passed by White House Situation Room (Bromley Smith) to LBJ, CAP66425, 2 Jul 1966, Marigold—Incomplete, box 148, NSF:CO:VN, LBJL.

33. Canberra embtel secto 58, 30 Jun 1966, POL 27-14 VIET, box 2921, CFPF, 1964–66.

34. Ibid.

35. JL interview, Warsaw, 7 Nov 2003.

36. Saigon embtel 131 (HCL), 2 Jul 1966, *FRUS, 1964–68,* 4:483.

37. Herring in *SDVW:NVPP,* 211; Sica also depicted GD'O as receiving and conveying an initiative from JL, crediting the "Polish (and North Vietnamese) opening-up of June 27th" to their recognition of Italy's stature and close ties to Washington and the personalities of AF and GD'O. Sica, *Marigold non fiorì,* 43.

38. For the 2 Jun 1966 JL-PVD conversation, see chapter 1 of the present volume. (MR incorrectly dates the JL-PVD talk to 6 Jun.) The Polish evidence corrects considerable confusion over Marigold's genesis. Italian sources, for example, spread the notion that the contacts stemmed from a conversation JL had in late June with HCM. As early as 6 Jul 1966, Goldberg quoted Thant as revealing that AF had confided that JL "had had conversation with Ho Chi Minh on June 27 in which Ho presumably said that they would be prepared to engage in serious discussions with US, notwithstanding Chinese and Soviet objections, if bombings were suspended and if Viet Cong participated in talks"; U.S. Mission Geneva (Tubby), tel. 61, 6 Jul 1966, Book of Peace. Although this account obviously confuses the date of the alleged talk with HCM with the initial JL-GD'O conversation, it seems to reflect a genuine belief among some Italians that the Pole's statements reflected an audience with HCM. In 1991, Sica stated dramatically that at the outset of their June 27 meeting, JL "surprised" GD'O when, "suddenly lowering his voice," he asked if he "may speak freely" and said, "I have just returned from Hanoi where I met with Ho Chi Minh. I have been authorized by the North Vietnamese Politburo to test the

waters in view of the restoration of peace in Vietnam." Sica, *Marigold non fiorì*, 13. Apparently relying on such distorted accounts, one scholar asserted that the "origin of Lewandowski's initiative lay in a conversation he claimed to have had with Ho Chi Minh in late June 1966." Allan E. Goodman, *The Lost Peace* (Stanford, Calif.: Hoover Institution Press, 1978), 39. DR, in his memoirs, repeated the canard that JL "claimed to have met with Ho Chi Minh" before seeing HCL in July 1966; DR, *As I Saw It*, edited by Daniel S. Papp (New York: W. W. Norton, 1990), 466. It is unclear whether the tales of a JL-HCM encounter stemmed from overactive imaginations, warped memories, or deliberate disinformation (by JL, GD'O, or both). In any case, the present account establishes that JL did not rely on a conversation with HCM, was not "authorized" by the VWP Politburo, and had not—as U.S. officials also erroneously believed—"just returned from Hanoi" before seeing GD'O on June 27; see, e.g., *SDVW:NVPP*, 215, 217, 222, 237.

39. As noted, Rome had a special motive to foster peace in Vietnam, since sharper East/West tensions endangered efforts at domestic political cooperation between Moro's Christian Democrats (DC) and Pietro Nenni's socialist party (PSI), which harshly criticized U.S. military escalation and threatened to bolt the government if forced to back it openly. See Leopoldo Nuti, "Transatlantic Relations in the Era of Vietnam: Western Europe and the Escalation of the War, 1965–1968," paper presented at the conference "NATO, the Warsaw Pact and the Rise of Détente, 1965–1972," Dobbiaco, Italy, 26–28 Sep 2002; Leopoldo Nuti, "The Center-Left Government in Italy and the Escalation of the Vietnam War," in *America, the Vietnam War, and the World: Comparative and International Perspectives*, edited by Andreas W. Daum, Lloyd C. Gardner, and Wilfried Mausbach (Washington, D.C.: German Historical Institute, 2003); and CIA Fanfani profile.

40. JL interview, Warsaw, June 2003; "did not report": MR.

41. JL interviews, Warsaw, June 2003.

42. Ibid., June and November 2003.

43. Ibid., 7 Nov 2003.

44. GD'O, *DV*, 618 (30 Jun 1966).

45. Poldel Saigon (JL) to PFM (Spasowski), 1 Jul 1966, 3 p.m., sz. 8586, AMSZ, trans. MG.

46. DE/Saigon (Derksen) to DFM, "Subject: New Mediation Attempt in Vietnam War?" 4 Jul 1966, cable 60, ref. 7139, file 938, code 911, bloc 1965–74 (secret), DFMA, obt. R. van der Maar, trans. DM.

47. Poldel Saigon (JL) to PFM (Spasowski), 1 Jul 1966, 9 a.m., sz. 8541, AMSZ, trans. MG. JL judged that Washington's stepped-up bombing reflected a determination to achieve a "final military solution to the conflict in Vietnam" and a "conviction that regardless of the degree of escalation, there will not be any decisive reaction from the socialist camp." Poldel Saigon (JL) to PFM (Spasowski), sz. 8782, 7 Jul 1966, AMSZ, trans. MG.

48. Poldel Saigon (JL) to PFM (Spasowski), sz. 8585, 1 Jul 1966, AMSZ, obt./trans. LG.

49. Unless otherwise indicated, GD'O's account of his 1 Jul 1966 talk with JL is drawn from IE/S (GD'O) to IFM (Marchiori), tels. 226 and 228, 1 Jul 1966, GD'O dossier; GD'O, *DV*, 610 (1 Jul 1966); and Saigon embtel 131 (HCL), 2 Jul 1966, *FRUS, 1964–68*, 4:481–82.

50. Deptel 4108 to American Embassy, Saigon, 29 Jul 1966, *FRUS, 1964–68*, 4:470–71.

51. IE/S (GD'O) to IFM (Marchiori), tel. 222, 1 Jul 1966, GD'O dossier.

52. Polish record of Warsaw Pact summit, Bucharest, 5–7 Jul 1966, PZPR 2663, AAN, obt. LG, trans. MG.

53. PFM (Piotrowski) to PE/Moscow (Pszczółkowski), sz. 7126, 6 Jul 1966, AMSZ, obt. D. Selvage, trans. MG. The last sentence was crossed out, so it is not clear whether it was transmitted.

54. [SHL,] GD'O interview notes, Rome, 4 Dec 1967, box 15, SHLP.

55. Ibid., 1 Dec 1967.

56. Sica interview, Rome, 23 Feb 2006.

57. DE/Saigon (Van der Zwaal) to DFM, cable 47++, ref. 6295, "Subject: Vietnam," 6 Jun 1966, file 935, code 911, bloc 1965–74 (secret), DFMA, obt./trans. R. van der Maar.

58. DE/Saigon (Derksen) to DFM, cable 32++, ref. 803136, "Subject: Italy and Vietnam," 8 Mar 1967, file 939, ibid., obt. R. van der Maar, trans. DM.

59. This view jibes with DK and SHL, *Secret Search,* 13–14, with one important distinction. DK and SHL did not describe the real basis behind JL's position: his 2 Jun 1966 talk with PVD, which the Poles did not disclose.

60. [SHL,] GD'O interview notes, Rome, 1 Dec 1967, box 15, SHLP.

61. JL had another incentive to downplay his own role in his secret coded cables to Warsaw. The only three MSZ officials aware of his secret assignment to promote peace, he recalled, were AR, JM, and Winiewicz. Yet he was reporting to Spasowski and knew his cables would likely have wider internal distribution. JL, telephone interview, 6 Dec 2004

62. [SHL,] GD'O interview notes, Rome, 4 Dec 1967, box 15, SHLP.

63. Saigon embtel 131 (HCL), Saigon, 2 Jul 1966, *FRUS, 1964–68,* 4:482.

64. GD'O, *DV,* 619 (1 Jul 1966).

65. Ibid., 620 (2 Jul 1966).

66. IE/S (GD'O) to IFM (Marchiori), tel. 230, 3 Jul 1966, GD'O dossier.

67. GD'O, *DV,* 619 (1 Jul 1966).

68. *SDVW:NVPP,* 242–43.

69. Deptel 2619 (to U.S. Mission, Geneva), 7 Jul 1966, Book of Peace.

70. Deptel 1961 to American Embassy, Saigon, 6 Jul 1966, ibid. On LBJ's annoyance with Goldberg, see David L. Stebenne, *Arthur J. Goldberg: New Deal Liberal* (New York: Oxford University Press, 1996), 358–64.

71. Deptel 1773 to DR in Kyoto, 5 Jul 1966, *FRUS, 1964–68,* 4:484–85. Ball was somewhat reassured about Italy's role by a second visit from Fenoaltea that "cleared up [ambiguities] in a most favorable way." Ball-WWR telcon, 2 Jul 1966, 10 a.m., folder 2, box 160, GBP, ML, PU.

72. Ball-WWR telcon, 4 Jul 1966, 4:30 p.m., ibid.; *FRUS, 1964–68,* 4:484 nn. 1, 2.

73. Deptel 2673 (to American Embassy, Tokyo), 12 p.m., 7 Jul 1966, Book of Peace.

74. IFM (Marchiori) to IE/S (GD'O), tel. 41, 7 Jul 1966, GD'O dossier.

75. Deptel 2673 (to American Embassy, Tokyo), 7 Jul 1966, Book of Peace. On July 9, having already heard Thant's second-hand version, Goldberg received an account in Rome from Italian President Giuseppe Saragat. Rome embtel 145 (Reinhardt), 9 Jul 1966, ibid.; also *SDVW:NVPP,* 242–43, 245–47.

76. GD'O, *DV,* 623 (8 Jul 1966); IE/Saigon (GD'O) to IFM (Marchiori), tel. 244, 8 Jul 1966, GD'O dossier.

77. Ward Just, *To What End* (New York: PublicAffairs, 1968), 4.

78. HCL, *As It Was: An Inside View of Politics and Power in the '50s and '60s* (New York: W. W. Norton, 1976), 173 ff.

79. GD'O, *DV,* 623 (8 Jul 1966).

80. JL interviews, Warsaw, Jun 2003 and May 2011.

81. Sica interviews, Rome, 23–24 Feb 2006; Sica, *Marigold non fiorì,* 56 n. 9; Sica email to author, 21 Jun 2011.

82. Sica interview, Trent, 13 Dec 2006.

83. JL interview, Warsaw, 20 Oct 2006.

84. Sica interview, Rome, 24 Feb 2006.

85. IE/S (GD'O) to IFM (Marchiori), tel. 244, 8 Jul 1966, GD'O dossier. In his diary he wrote: "I consider my task to consist in making every effort to favor the agreement, while carefully avoiding any referee-like or fly in the ointment type of behavior on my part." GD'O, DV, 623 (8 Jul 1966).

86. This account of the 9 Jul 1966 HCL-JL-GD'O talk is based on all three participants' contemporaneous cables (they agreed not to prepare joint summaries or minutes but report to their governments separately): Saigon embtel 604 (HCL), 9 Jul 1966, Book of Peace and POL 27-14 VIET/XYZ 11-1-65, box 22, FTSCPF, 1964–66; Poldel Saigon (JL) to PFM (Spasowski), sz. 8935, 9 Jul 1966, AMSZ, obt./trans. LG; and IE/S (GD'O) to IFM (Marchiori), tels. 249 (7 pm), 250 (7:30 pm), 251 (8 pm), and 252 (8:30 pm), all 9 Jul 1966, GD'O dossier.

87. Sica interview, Rome, 24 Feb 2006; Colette D'Orlandi interview, Paris, 21 May 2008.

88. JL interviews, Warsaw, June 2003.

89. DK and SHL, *Secret Search,* 5, 8, 11.

90. IE/S (GD'O) to IFM (Marchiori), tel. 252, 8:30 p.m., 9 Jul 1966, GD'O dossier.

91. GD'O, *DV,* 624 (9 Jul 1966).

92. Ibid., 625 (9 Jul 1966).

93. Poldel Saigon (JL) to PFM (Spasowski), sz. 8935, 9 Jul 1966, AMSZ, obt./trans. LG.

94. JL interview, Warsaw, June 2003.

95. Saigon embtel 642 (HCL), 10 Jul 1966, Book of Peace.

96. PFM (JM) to PE/Hanoi (JS), sz. 242, 11 Jul 1966, AMSZ, trans. MG.

97. PE/Hanoi (JS) to PFM (JM), sz. 9070, 13 Jul 1966, ibid.

98. See notes on 740th (16 Jul 1966), 741st (21 Jul 1966), and 742nd (27 Jul 1966) meetings, "Report on the Activities of the International Commission in Vietnam for the Months of July–August 1966," file 21-13-VIET-ICSC-8, FP 6.3, vol. 10128, RG 25, NAC, and Poldel Saigon (JL) to PFM (Spasowski), sz. 9285, 17 Jul 1966, and 9647, 25 Jul 1966, AMSZ, trans. MG; HVL urging: Poldel Saigon (JL) to PFM (Spasowski), sz. 8521, 2 Jul 1966, ibid.

99. Ball-WWR telcon, 9 Jul 1966, 1:05 pm, folder 2, box 160, GBP, ML, PU.

100. Saigon embtel 958 (HCL), 14 Jul 1966, Book of Peace.

101. GD'O, *DV,* 627 (13 Jul 1966).

102. DR-WPB telcon, 15 Jul 1966, 4:29 p.m., box 56, DR Papers, RG 59, NA II.

103. Deptel 5454 (to American Embassy, Saigon), 11 Jul 1966, Vietnam cables, vol. 56 7/66, box 34, NSF:CO:VN, LBJL.

104. Saigon embtel 1350 (HCL), 19 Jul 1966, Vietnam memos (A), vol. 56 7/66, ibid.

105. WWR to LBJ, 16 Jul 1966, 1966, 9 p.m., Vietnam memos (B), vol. 67 7/66, ibid.

106. See Warsaw embtels 2334, 2335, and 2336 (JAG), all 30 Jun 1966, POL 27 VIET S Military Operations 6/30/66, box 3001, CFPF, 1964–66.

107. Warsaw embtel 023 (JAG), 4 Jul 1966, POL 27 VIET S, box 3002, CFPF, 1964–66.

108. See, e.g., *NYT,* 13 and 15 Jul 1966.

109. *NYT,* 17 Jul 1966.

110. Warsaw embtel 120 (JAG), 16 Jul 1966, Book of Peace.

111. PFM (AR) to PE/ Hanoi (JS), sz. 7485, 17 Jul 1966, AMSZ, trans. MG.

112. JL persuaded Rahman to resist U.S. pressure to have the ICC "meddle" in the affair. Poldel Saigon (JL) to PFM (Spasowski), sz. 9282, 16 Jul 1966, and 9647, 25 Jul 1966, ibid.

113. *NYT,* 16 Jul 1966.

114. Warsaw embtel 135 (JAG), 19 Jul 1966, Book of Peace.

115. See Paris embtel 1022 (Bohlen), 21 Jul 1966, *FRUS, 1964–68,* 4:509.

116. Warsaw embtel 286 (JAG), 4 Aug 1966, POL 27 VIET S 8/4/66, box 3005, CFPF, 1964–66.

117. See DR-Stoessel telcon, 3 p.m., 19 Jul 1966, box 56, DR Papers, RG 59, NA II.

118. Warsaw embtel 135 (JAG), 19 Jul 1966, Book of Peace.

119. On 22 Mar 1965, the NLF Central Committee issued a long, rather bombastic five-point statement "condemning the systematic war-seeking and aggressive policy of the U.S. imperialists in South Vietnam and enunciating the South Vietnamese people's unchanged viewpoint which is to resolutely kick out the U.S. imperialists in order to liberate the South, build an independent, democratic, and peaceful South Viet-Nam, and achieve national unification" as envisioned in the Geneva Accords. See *The Viet-Nam Reader,* edited by Marcus G. Raskin and Bernard B. Fall, rev. ed. (New York: Random House, 1967), 232–52; and *SDVW:NVPP,* 832.

120. PE/Hanoi (JS) to PFM (JM), sz. 9298, 18 Jul 1966, AMSZ, trans. MG.

121. PFM (JM) to PE/Hanoi (JS), sz. 7730, 21 Jul 1966, ibid.

122. PFM (JM) to Poldel Saigon (JL), sz. 7729, 21 Jul 1966, courtesy Stefan Michałowski, trans. MG; MR.

123. JL interview, Warsaw, June 2003.

124. GD'O, *DV,* 632–33 (19–21 Jul 1966).

125. IE/S (GD'O) to IFM, tel. 277, 12:30 p.m., 23 Jul 1966, GD'O dossier; GD'O, *DV,* 634 (23 Jul 1966).

126. Deptel 13554 (to American Embassy, Saigon), 22 Jul 1966, Book of Peace.

127. Saigon embtel 1695 (HCL), 23 Jul 1966, ibid.
128. WWR to LBJ, 23 Jul 1966, 12:15 p.m., Vietnam memos (B), vol. 56 7/66, box 34, NSF:CO:VN, LBJL.
129. GD'O, *DV,* 634 (23–24 Jul 1966).
130. This account relies on all three participants' contemporaneous cables: Saigon embtel 1785 (HCL), 24 Jul 1966, *FRUS, 1964–68,* 4:525–28; Poldel Saigon (JL) to PFM (JM), sz. 9646, 25 Jul 1966, AMSZ, obt./trans. LG; and IE/S (GD'O) to IFM (Marchiori), tels. 279 (8 p.m.), 280 (8:30 p.m.), 281–83 (9 p.m.), all 24 Jul 1966, GD'O dossier—and GD'O, *DV,* 634–36 (24 Jul 1966). JL told the MSZ that HCL had requested the meeting, even as HCL stressed that he had awaited a summons from GD'O.
131. Sica, *Marigold non fiorì,* 57.
132. According to JL, HCL made this request, whereas GD'O and HCL agree that it came from JL.
133. GD'O, *DV,* 636 (24 Jul 1966); IE/S (GD'O) to IFM (Marchiori), tels. 282–83, 9 p.m., 24 Jul 1966, GD'O dossier; "distressed": Saigon embtel 1788 (HCL), 24 Jul 1966, *FRUS, 1964–68,* 4:528–29.
134. WWR-DR telcon, 24 Jul 1966, 11:10 a.m., box 56, DR Papers, RG 59, NA II.
135. See, e.g., Roderick MacFarquhar, *The Origins of the Cultural Revolution, Volume 3: The Coming of the Cataclysm 1961–1966* (New York: Columbia University Press, 1997), 461.
136. Chinese sources indicate that HCM saw Mao and Zhou on June 10 and Zhou, Liu Shaoqi, and Deng Xiaoping on June 11: Pang Xianzhi and Jin Chongji et al., *Mao Zedong zhuan* (Beijing: Zhongyang wenxian, 2003), 1418; Liu Chongwen and Chen Shaoshou et al., *Liu Shaoqi nianpu,* vol. 2 (Beijing: Zhongyang wenxian, 1996), 638, 641–42; and Li Ping and Ma Zhisun et al., *Zhou Enlai nianpu,* vol. 3 (Beijing: Zhengyang wenxian, 1997), 37. I thank Chen Jian for these citations.
137. Roderick MacFarquhar and Michael Schoenhals, *Mao's Last Revolution* (Cambridge, Mass.: Harvard University Press, 2006), 38, 493 n. 27.
138. Copy of telegram from East German ambassador in Beijing, Bierbach, addendum to memorandum from Hegen to Ulbricht, Stoph, Honecker, Axen, 8 Jul 1966, SAPMO-BArch, Berlin, New York, 4182/1222, 129-131, obt./trans. L. Luthi.
139. Note on conversation with Soviet ambassador Shcherbakov, Hanoi, 28 Oct 1966, obt./trans. L. Luthi, *CWIHPB* 16, fall 2007/winter 2008, 392–93.
140. Two months before, in mid-April, Deng had apparently made a comparable threat, and not so subtly, to Le Duan, in the midst of a tirade accusing Hanoi of undue warmth toward Moscow and unfriendly incidents toward Chinese troops serving in Vietnam. Referring to unfriendly incidents involving some of the 100,000 Chinese military personnel in Vietnam, Deng asked Le Duan, "Are you suspicious that China helps Vietnam for our own [interests]? We hope that you can tell us directly if you want us to help. The problem will be easily solved. We will withdraw our military men at once. We have a lot of things to do in China. And the military men stationed along the border will be ordered back to the Mainland." Le Duan tried to smooth the problems over, disclaiming knowledge of anti-Chinese incidents and disavowing any concern among DRV leaders that China was "trying to take control over Vietnam" (while admitting that they would be "really concerned" were China not a socialist country). The Chinese forces stayed. See the record of the conversation between Zhou Enlai/Deng Xiaoping/Kang Sheng and Le Duan/NDT, Beijing, 13 Apr 1966, in *77 Conversations between Chinese and Foreign Leaders on the Wars in Indochina, 1964–1977,* CWIHP Working Paper 22, edited by Odd Arne Westad, Chen Jian, Stein Tønnesson, Nguyen Vu Tung, and James G. Hershberg (Washington, D.C.: Woodrow Wilson International Center for Scholars, 1998), 94–98.
141. Zhou Enlai–Enver Hoxha memcon, Tirana, 27 Jun 1966, *CWIHPB* 16 (Fall 2007–Winter 2008): 321.
142. PE/H (JS), to PFM (Meller), sz. 8419, 30 Jun 1966, AMSZ, trans. MG.
143. Sainteny paraphrased in HAK's memo of their 9 Sep 1966 conversation in Paris: POL 27 VIET S, CFPF, 1964–66. Sainteny also described Hanoi's hardening position in early July to WAH: Sainteny-WAH memcon, "Subject: VIETNAM," Paris, 2 Dec 1966, box 569, WAHP-LC.

Speaking to WAH the next day, the former Agence France-Presse reporter in Hanoi echoed Sainteny's interpretation—though without reference to the secret Marigold contacts in July— telling WAH that before the 29 Jun bombings, "certain elements in the North Vietnamese leadership had shown an interest" in talks, but "the bombings near the Vietnamese capital had hardened the North Vietnamese position; those who had favored negotiations before the bombings had lost their audience." WAH-Raffaelli memcon, Paris, 3 Dec 1966, box 554, ibid.

144. IE/S (GD'O) to IFM (Marchiori), telegram by hand no. 1, 3 Sep 1966, GD'O dossier.

145. The same interpretation—self-serving but plausible—could be put on Dobrynin's reaction when LET sounded him out a few days after the POL bombings started, but before Moscow learned of the "Italian initiative." On 2 Jul, LET, one of the few State Department officials in the know, without mentioning the Saigon contacts, probed Dobrynin about how to regard indirect hints of "some change of attitude on the part of Hanoi" about the possibility of entering talks. In reply, the envoy splashed cold water on U.S. hopes that inflicting more pain might push the enemy into surrender. "Dobrynin said that if in fact there was any change of attitude in Hanoi, he thought that our recent action in bombing POL storage near Hanoi and Haiphong would have had adverse effect and would have killed any possibility of progress," LET wrote. "He thought the effect of this bombing would be not only to increase the determination of Hanoi, but would also have a most adverse effect in the whole socialist camp, including his own country." LET-Dobrynin memcon, 2 Jul 1966, POL 27 VIET S 7/2/66, box 3002, CFPF, 1964–66.

146. "Chronology, the Air War in North Vietnam, 1965–1968," in GPP, IV, 5, 109; Van Staaveren, *Gradual Failure,* 294–97.

147. Poldel Saigon (JL) to PFM (Spasowski), sz. 9696, 26 Jul 1966, AMSZ, trans. MG.

Chapter 3

1. GD'O, *DV,* 642 (3 Aug 1966).

2. Tedeschi, "Fanfani Re-opens the Primicerio Channel,'" *Il Borghese,* 4 Aug 1966.

3. GD'O, *DV,* 642–43 (3 Aug 1966).

4. Mario Sica, *Marigold non fiorì: Il contributo italiano alla pace in Vietnam* (Florence: Ponte alle Grazie, 1991), 60, trans. IO.

5. Rome embtel 693 (Meloy), 4 Aug 1966, POL 27 VIET S 8/4/66, box 3005, CFPF, 1964–66; "consternation": Saigon embtel 3428 (HCL), 13 Aug 1966, Book of Peace.

6. For a detailed report on the leak inquiry, including a list of suspects, see "Rivelazioni del settimanale Il Borghese' in material di politica estera," n.d. [Aug 1966], in sezione i, serie 1, s. serie 5, busta 39, fasc. 14, AFP.

7. Sica, *Marigold non fiorì,* 59–60.

8. HCL to HAK, "Reactivation of D'Orlandi's Contacts with North Vietnam," w. Lake to HAK, "Your Appointment with Ambassador Cabot Lodge, 2:30 p.m., January 20, 1970," item 720, *U.S. Policy in the Vietnam War, Part II: 1969–1975* (Washington, D.C.: National Security Archive / Chadwyck-Healey, 2004).

9. Saigon embtel 3428 (HCL), 13 Aug 1966, Book of Peace.

10. PFM (JM) to Poldel Saigon (JL), sz. 8672, 19 Aug 1966, AMSZ, trans. MG.

11. Rome embtel 582 (Meloy), "Subject: Fanfani's Account of His Visits to Turkey and Poland," 29 Jul 1966, Italy July 1965–December 1966, box 13, lot file 69D277, RG 59, NA II. On AR's concern at this juncture over the prospect of Chinese intervention in response to escalated U.S. bombing, see also his conversation with visiting British envoy Lord Chalfont in BE/Warsaw (Clutton) to FO, tel. 410, 15 Jul 1966, FO 371/186339, TNA.

12. DE/Saigon (Derksen) to DFM, cable 75, ref. 8239, 15 Aug 1966, DFMA, obt. R. van der Maar, trans. DM (French phrase trans. G. Martin).

13. For the "segreto" Italian record of the AR-AF talks in Warsaw, see "Visit of the (Hon. Minister to Warsaw (25–27 July 1966)," Minutes of the Meetings, in "Visite di Stato / Visite Officiali: 1966 in Parte—Turchia Poland Romania, Secretaria Generale," Ministry of External Affairs archives, Rome; trans. IO.

14. Gaja comments in CE/Rome (Crean), to CDEA, 2 Aug 1966, tel. 971, "Fanfani Visit to Poland," file 20-22-VIETS-2, pt. 16, vol. 9396, RG 25, NAC.
15. From 26, 27, 29 Jul 1966 entries, AFD.
16. GD'O, *DV*, 640 (30 Jul 1966).
17. Ibid., 641–42 (1 and 3 Aug 1966).
18. PFM (JM) to Poldel Saigon (JL), sz. 8672, 19 Aug 1966, AMSZ; also see MR, trans. MG. AF sensed Polish unwillingness to risk another peace bid "in the absence of some possibility of success": Rome embtel 582 (Meloy), 29 Jul 1966, Italy July 1965-December 1966, box 13, lot file 69D277, RG 59, NA II.
19. PE/Rome (Willmann) to PFM (JM), sz. 10089, 4 Aug 1966, AMSZ, obt./trans. LG; "preaching": GD'O, *DV*, 643 (4 Aug 1966). Willmann's cable referred to a proposal for GD'O to see JM in Karlovy Vary, but GD'O told HCL in Saigon that the idea was to see both JM and AR there.
20. MR.
21. Saigon embtel 3428 (HCL), 13 Aug 1966, Book of Peace; also GD'O, *DV*, 647–48 (12 Aug 1966).
22. Saigon embtel 3563 (HCL), 15 Aug 1966, Book of Peace.
23. PFM (JM) to Poldel Saigon (JL), sz. 8672, 19 Aug 1966, AMSZ, trans. MG.
24. See BE/Saigon (Ford) to FO, tel. 711, 8 Sep 1966; Wilkinson, BE/Saigon, to Murray, SEAD, FO, 5 Oct 1966 (wing); Colvin, BCG/Hanoi, to Murray, 14 Oct 1966 ("brave"); et al., in FO 371/186335, TNA.
25. JL reports on Hanoi trip: PE/Hanoi (JL) to PFM (Spasowski), sz. 10837 and 10841, both 20 Aug 1966; sz. 10946, 23 Aug 1966; and sz. 10988, 24 Aug 1966; all AMSZ, trans. MG. As usual, JL passed to the DRV intelligence and analysis on the situation in the south. According to Prague's envoy, JL told authorities the CIA Saigon station intercepted communications between Hanoi and NLF and PAVN commanders, and local Polish embassy officials blamed recent military setbacks on Hanoi's "primitive coding system." CzE/Hanoi (Mucha) to CzFM, tel. 9168, 21 Sep 1966, AMZV, obt./trans. G. Laron.
26. GD'O related this JL quotation to HCL: Saigon embtel 5517 (HCL), 8 Sep 1966, *SDVW:NVPP*, 251.
27. H. B. Shepherd, BCG/Hanoi, to J. F. Ford, BE/Saigon, 23 Aug 1966, in FO 371/186289, TNA.
28. DE/Saigon (Derksen), cable 82++, ref. 8585, 8/31/66, code 911, bloc 1965-1974 (secret), DFMA, obt. R. van der Maar, trans. DM; JL told GD'O he had a "long meeting" with HCM: IE/S (GD'O) to IFM (Marchiori), telegram by hand no. 1, 3 Sep 1966, GD'O dossier, and GD'O, *DV*, 656 (3 Sep 1966). Some doubt persists; no JL cable mentioning a talk with HCM was found at AMSZ; in interviews JL recalled only meeting HCM briefly and suspected Derksen "exaggerated."
29. JL interviews, Warsaw, June 2003; NDT "short, stocky": Wilfred G. Burchett, *At the Barricades: Forty Years on the Cutting Edge of History* (New York: Times Books, 1981), 237. JL's firm impression of NDT as a hard-liner contradicted speculation by some seasoned Saigon observers. *Newsweek*'s François Sully in late 1967 placed him "toward the dovish, moderate side" of the DRV leadership. Sully to editors, "Subject: North Vietnam," 15 Dec 1967, Sully Papers, Joseph P. Healey Library, UMass-Boston
30. PE/Hanoi (JL) to PFM (Spasowski), sz. 10946, 23 Aug 1966, AMSZ, trans. MG.
31. JL interviews, Warsaw, June 2003.
32. PE/Hanoi (JL) to PFM (Spasowski), sz. 10946, 23 Aug 1966, as above.
33. JL instructions: PFM (JM) to Poldel Saigon (JL), sz. 8293, 8 Aug 1966; DRV re DMZ: Privalov-JL memcon, 22 Aug 1966, f. 079, op. 21, p. 51, d. 8, l. 88, AVPRF, trans. J. Person; 19 Aug 1966 ICC meeting: VCM, "Report on the Activities of the International Commission in Vietnam for the months of July–August 1966," 8, file 21-13-VIET-ICSC-8 FP 6.3, Vol. 10128, RG 25, NAC ("violent") and PE/Hanoi (JL) to PFM (Spasowski), sz. 10837, 20 Aug 1966, AMSZ, trans. MG; "livid": Saigon embtel 4141 (HCL), CINCPAC for POLAD, "Subject: ICC Actions on DMZ," 22 Aug 1966, DRV North Vietnam, Aug–Sept 1966, box 8, lot file 69D277, RG 59, NA II; "pique": Candel Saigon (VCM) to CDEA, tel. 748, "Vietnam: Prospects and the Commission," 26 Aug 1966, file 20-22-VIET-2-1, pt. 6, vol. 9397, RG 25, NAC; illness speculation: J.F. Ford, BE/Saigon, to R. A. Fyjis Walker, SEAD, FO, 31 Aug 1966, FO 371/186289, TNA.
34. JL telephone interview, Warsaw, 1 Oct 2007.

35. Privalov-JL memcon, 22 Aug 1966, ll. 81–88, trans. J. Person, S. Radchenko, cited above.
36. August 1966 Soviet-DRV talks in Moscow: HA/Moscow, to HFM, "Subject: Soviet-Vietnamese Talks about the Soviet Help," 21 Sep 1966, 64/1/1966/Sz.t., XIX-J-1-j. 1966, 107 doboz (Soviet relations), MOL, obt. C. Bekes, trans. A. Agoston; PE/Moscow (Paszkowski) to PFM (JM), sz. 10733, 18 Aug 1966, AMSZ, trans. MG; CPSU CC to PUWP CC, "Information," n.d., KC PZPR, XI A/81, 530–38, AAN, obt./trans. L. Luthi.
37. HA/Moscow, to HFM, "Subject: Soviet-Vietnamese Talks."
38. This exchange is drawn from CPSU CC to the PUWP CC, information report, n.d., cited above.
39. DRV deputy foreign minister Hoang Van Tien-Kuznetsov memcon, Moscow, 15 Aug 1966, f. 079, op. 21, p. 51, d. 5, l. 15, AVPRF, courtesy S. Radchenko.
40. On "stringent" and "frequently," see PE/Moscow (Paszkowski) to PFM (JM), sz. 10733, 18 Aug 1966, AMSZ, trans. MG; Geneva, 17th Parallel: CPSU CC to PUWP information report, n.d., cited above; "mouth": HA/Moscow, to HFM, "Subject: Soviet-Vietnamese Talks."
41. "When the Soviets asked about why they needed aluminum, they did not get a straight answer. The Soviets noted that it is beyond doubt that the Vietnamese asked for such items because the Chinese urged them to, and that the Chinese wanted to keep them for themselves."
42. HA/Moscow to HFM, "Subject: Soviet-Vietnamese Talks"; Ilya V. Gaiduk, *The Soviet Union and the Vietnam War* (Chicago: Ivan R. Dee, 1996), 69–72.
43. HA/Moscow to HFM, "Subject: Soviet-Vietnamese Talks."
44. On PRC-DRV friction, see Qiang Zhai, *China and the Vietnamese Wars, 1950–1975* (Chapel Hill: University of North Carolina Press, 2000), 152–55. Like the Soviets, the Chinese complained that during U.S. air attacks, local port authorities had refused permission for their ships to dock, leaving them exposed.
45. IE/S (GD'O) to IFM (Marchiori), telegram by hand no. 2, 3 Sep 1966, GD'O dossier.
46. Zhou Enlai–PVD talk, Beijing, 23 Aug 1966, in *77 Conversations between Chinese and Foreign Leaders on the Wars in Indochina, 1964–1977*, CWIHP Working Paper 22, edited by Odd Arne Westad, Chen Jian, Stein Tønnesson, Nguyen Vu Tung, and James G. Hershberg (Washington, D.C.: Woodrow Wilson International Center for Scholars, 1998), 98–99.
47. P. I. Privalov, memcon with Nguyen Van Vinh, 23 Aug 1966, f. 079, op. 21, p. 51, d. 8, l. 93, AVPRF, obt./trans. S. Radchenko; also f. 5, op. 58, d. 264, ll. 169–74, RGANI, trans. A. Kalinovsky.
48. On "welcoming," see Candel Saigon (VCM) to CDEA, tel. 748, "Vietnam: Prospects and the Commission," 26 Aug 1966, file 100-11-3 pt. 1 [pt. 2], vol. 9516, RG 25, NAC; ICC passenger manifests, file 100-11-5-2 pt. 1, vol. 9518, RG 25, NAC; CE/Phnom Penh to CDEA, "De Gaulle Visit: Contacts with Regional Communists," 1 Sep 1966, file 20-22-VIETS-2 pt. 17, vol. 9396, RG 25, NAC; Gibbons, IV, 393; *FRUS, 1964–68*, 4:627 n. 4; JL NLF contacts: JL interviews, Warsaw, June 2003.
49. On "nothing," see IE/S (GD'O) to IFM (Marchiori), telegram by hand no. 1 and no. 2, both 3 Sep 1966, GD'O dossier, and GD'O, *DV*, 656 (3 Sep 1966); "absolutely": DE/Saigon (Derksen), cable 82++, ref. 8585, 31 August 1966, code 911, bloc 1965–74 (secret), DFMA, obt. R. van der Maar, trans. DM; "profoundly": GD'O in Saigon embtel 5229 (HCL), 4 Sep 1966, POL 27-14 Viet/Marigold 1/1/66, box 3020, CFPF, 1964–66.
50. JAG OH-II, 10 Feb 1969, 1–15. LBJL.
51. From 25 Jul 1966 JAG-JM memcon, American Embassy, Warsaw, airgram A-91, 1 Aug 1966, POL 27 VIET S 8/1/66, box 3004, CFPF, 1964–66; also Warsaw embtel 185 (JAG), 26 Jul 1966, POL 27 VIET S 7/26/66, ibid.
52. From 25 Jul 1966 JAG-JM memcon, cited above; Warsaw embtel 198, 27 Jul 1966, POL 27 VIET S 7/27/66, ibid.
53. Warsaw embtel 298 (JAG), for LBJ and DR, 6 Aug 1966, POL 27 VIET S 8/5/66, box 3005, ibid.
54. WWR to LBJ, 6 Aug 1966–1 p.m., Poland–Memos Volume I 11/63-9/66, box 200, NSF:CO, LBJL.
55. Deptel 26097 to American Embassy, Warsaw (JAG), 11 Aug 1966, POL 27 VIET S 8/10/66, box 3005, CFPF, 1964–66.
56. WWR-DR telcon, 11 Aug 1966, 4:50 p.m., box 56, DR Papers, RG 59, NA II.

57. JAG saw LBJ on 18 May 1966 and at LBJ's request submitted a memo, copied to DR: JAG to LBJ, "Subject: Foreign Policy Recommendations," and JAG to DR, both 30 May 1966; and DR to JAG, 19 Aug 1966, all PER-Personnel Gronouski, John A. 1/1/65, box 184, CFPF, 1964–66.

58. Deptel 30272 (to American Embassy, Warsaw), 17 Aug 1966, POL 27-14 VIET S 1/1/66, box 3006, ibid.

59. Warsaw embtel 404 (JAG), 18 Aug 1966, POL 27-14 CAMB 1/1/64, box 1971, ibid. Goldberg eventually called on AR in New York and found him unenthusiastic about helping to bring about negotiations absent a bombing halt. USUN (Goldberg) tel. 1216, "Subj: Vietnam: Goldberg Conversation with Polish Formin," 4 Oct 1966, DDRS.

60. Warsaw embtels 404 (JAG), 18 Aug 1966, and 418 (Jenkins), 19 Aug 1966, both POL 27-14 CAMB 1/1/64, box 1971, CFPF, 1964–66.

61. Warsaw embtel 405 (JAG), 18 Aug 1966, POL 27 VIET S 8/17/66, box 3006, ibid. JAG added that he strongly favored Goldberg's proposed visit to Warsaw, *provided* he carried some fresh ideas on Vietnam (such as, hint hint, JAG's own proposal); otherwise, it would be "regarded as a pre-election propaganda ploy, not only in Poland and in other EE countries but in friendly and nonaligned countries as well."

62. Saigon embtel 4240 (HCL), 23 Aug 1966, POL 27-14 VIET/MARIGOLD 1/1/66, box 3020, ibid.

63. Deptel 36758 to American Embassy, Warsaw, 27 Aug 1966, Poland–Cables Volume I 11/63-9/66, box 200, NSF:CO, LBJL.

64. Gibbons, IV, 388–89; *FRUS, 1964–68,* 4:548 n. 1.

65. CLC biography: CLC interview, Washington, 8 Dec 2004; CLC OH I, 9 Jul 1976, 24–25; *WP,* 18 Aug 1966; CLC, *The Lost Crusade: America in Vietnam* (New York: Dodd, Mead, 1970); and CLC, *In the Shadows of History: Fifty Years behind the Scenes of Cold War Diplomacy* (Amherst, N.Y.: Prometheus Books, 2005).

66. CLC, *In the Shadows,* 238.

67. Notes of background interview with "~~chet cooper~~ cccc," 7 Nov 1967, Vietnam Bombing Pause, 1966–67, box 41, SHLP.

68. Memorandum of Meeting, Gov. Harriman's office, 4:30 p.m., 11 Aug 1966, Vietnam—General —Aug–Sept 1966, box 520, WAHP-LC. WAH found JAG's 25 Jul 1966 conversation with JM "extremely interesting," and his willingness to try this route may have been enhanced by a 10 Aug 1966 conversation an aide had with Harvard professor HAK and Pentagon official John McNaughton, who thought the JAG channel offered a chance to "make a real effort to redefine Hanoi's Four Points and send them back to Hanoi to see what the reaction is." Deptel 17437 to American Embassy, Warsaw, 28–29 Jul 1966, DDRS; and "Notes following Dinner—August 10," Vietnam—General—Aug–Sep 1966, box 520, WAH, LC.

69. PVD's original third point had stated: "The internal affairs of South Vietnam must be settled by the South Vietnamese people themselves in accordance with the program of the South Vietnam National Front for Liberation, without any foreign interference." In his 6 Aug 1966 cable (cited above), JAG had suggested the following reformulated point three: "The internal affairs of South Vietnam must be settled by the South Vietnamese people without outside interference, taking into account the program of their Government and all organized groups in South Vietnam whose aims are independence, democracy, peace and neutrality." The suggested third point forwarded by WAH and the Negotiations Committee to DR and LBJ on 29 Aug 1966 stated: "The internal affairs of South and North Vietnam must be settled respectively by the South and North Vietnamese people themselves in conformity with the principles of self-determination. Neither shall interfere in the affairs of the other nor shall there by any interference from any outside source." This repeated, verbatim, language for point three handed by U.S. ambassador to Burma Henry Byroade to the DRV chargé d'affaires in Rangoon on 18 Feb 1966. *FRUS, 1964–68,* 4:230.

70. Four Points reformulation: Negotiations Committee minutes, 18 Aug 1966, ibid., 584; CLC, *Lost Crusade,* 330–31; CLC OH-I, 26–27, LBJL; Negotiations Committee minutes and WAH to LBJ and DR, both 25 Aug 1966, Vietnam—General—Aug–Sep 1966, box 520, WAHP-LC; Gibbons, IV, 398–99, 402 n. 56; Thant in Moscow: *NYT,* 30 Jul and 31 Jul 1966; and Thant-Ball memcon, 2 Aug 1966, box 1, DAG-1, 5.2.2.3.2, UNA.

71. Deptel 36758 to American Embassy, Warsaw, 27 Aug 1966, Poland-Cables Volume I 11/63-9/66, box 200, NSF:CO, LBJL; "alive": Memorandum of Meeting, 4:30 p.m., Gov. Harriman's office, 25 Aug 1966, Vietnam—General—Aug–Sep 1966, box 520, WAHP-LC.

72. On 1 Sep 1966 JAG-Winiewicz conversation, see Warsaw embtel 523 (JAG), 5 Sep 1966, Poland-Cables Volume I 11/63-9/66, box 200, NSF:CO, LBJL. For a different account, see Winiewicz, urgent note, "From the Conversation with the Ambassador of the United States, 1st of This Month," Department III—1968, t. 10/75, AMSZ, trans. MG.

73. Though obviously a self-serving explanation of Warsaw's obstructive behavior, Winiewicz's words fit plausibly with JL's own account of building up his hard-line credentials in Hanoi as well as his report of HVL's warning to "unmask" U.S. peace efforts, in particular through the ICC.

74. Winiewicz's own report of this same conversation contained no evidence of a calculated overture. It claimed that JAG, not Winiewicz, had initiated the private talk, and depicted him as ardently seeking Poland's help and understanding. "I plead with you," he quoted JAG as saying. Not surprisingly, the Pole's record omitted the risqué comments about internal divisions between moderates and hard-liners in the Warsaw government, or between Communist powers, as well as the earnest vows of Polish help in seeking peace. Instead, it related, Winiewicz merely stated "with great certainty" the "thesis" that the United States faced inevitable defeat in Vietnam. When JAG asked for Polish aid in reaching a compromise over the Four Points and the NLF's role in negotiations—"He insisted that we do not dodge the assistance of seeking solutions facilitating Johnson's difficult decisions'"—Winiewicz noted vaguely that his answer accorded "with what we have continued to tell the Americans until now." Of course, given the nature of the Warsaw regime, one would hardly expect that Winiewicz would record the candid emissions that MSZ officials, including JM, periodically dispensed to Western associates as bona fides of their independence and integrity. See, e.g., JM comments to a U.S. journalist in Paris that fall, in which he reportedly complained about the "narrowness of vision" of Brezhnev and Kosygin, and recoiled at the idea that Washington retreat from the East Asian mainland and protect its interests by seapower. "You cannot withdraw," he said, horrified, since the Chinese "would be in there immediately." American Embassy, Paris, airgram A-628, 20 Oct 1966, POL 1 General Policy POL 1/1/64, box 2591, CFPF, 1964–66.

75. Deptel 44803 to American Embassy, Warsaw, 10 Sep 1966, POL 27 VIET S 9/9/66, box 3008, ibid.

76. On "prickly," see Candel Saigon (VCM) to CDEA, tel. 707, "Viet Nam: DZ and the Commission Generally," 16 Aug 1966, file 100-11-3 vol. 1 [pt. 2], Vol. 9516, RG 25, NAC; "convivial": Saigon embtel 4141 (HCL), CINCPAC for POLAD, "Subject: ICC Actions on DMZ," 22 Aug 1966, DRV North Vietnam, Aug–Sept 1966, box 8, lot file 69D277, RG 59, NA II.

77. Candel Saigon (VCM) to CDEA, tel. 1070, "Vietnam: Assessment by the FM," 25 Nov 1966, file 20-22-VIETS-2 pt. 18, vol. 9396, RG 25, NAC.

78. P. A. Wilkinson (BE/Saigon) to D. F. Murray, SEAD, FO, 5 Oct 1966 (10711/66), FO 371/186335, TNA.

79. Daniel Passent telephone interview, Warsaw, 29 Sep 2004.

80. "Policemen without Power," Newsweek, 5 Sep 1966, 35.

81. Chubb's Folly, 15 Sep 1966 entry.

82. Ibid., 11 Sep 1966 entry.

83. Ibid., 14 Sep 1966 entry.

84. Ibid.

85. Saigon embtel 26820 (HCL), 29 Sep 1966, box 3019, POL 27-14 VIET S 8/29/66, CFPF, 1964–66. On JL's determined resistance to proposals for strengthening the DMZ at this juncture, which "ended with some action by the Commission but not as much as Candel had sought," see "Report on the Activities of the International Commission in Vietnam for the Month of September 1966," 3–8, file 21-13-VIET-ICSC-8, FP 7.1, vol. 10128, RG 25, NAC.

86. Candel Saigon (VCM) to CDEA, tel. 933, "Vietnam: Commission Prospects," 20 Oct 1966, file 100-11-3, vol. 1 [pt. 2], vol. 9516, RG 25, NAC; "total quiescence": Candel Saigon (VCM) to CDEA, tel. 977, "Vietnam: DZ and Commission Prospects," 28 Oct 1966, same folder.

87. Saigon embtel 5965 (HCL), 14 Sep 1966, POL 27-14 Viet/Marigold 1/1/66, box 3020, CFPF, 1964–66.

88. PFM (JM) to Poldel Saigon (JL), sz. 8672, 19 Aug 1966, AMSZ, trans. MG.

89. On 3 Sep 1966 JL-GD'O talk, see Poldel Saigon (JL) to PFM (JM), sz. 11468, 3 Sep 1966, AMSZ, obt./trans. LG; IE/S (GD'O) to IFM (Marchiori), telegram by hand nos. 1 and 2, 3 Sep 1966, GD'O dossier, and GD'O, *DV,* 656–57 (3 Sep 1966); and Saigon embtel 5229 (HCL), 4 Sep 1966, POL 27-14 Viet/Marigold 1/1/66, box 3020, CFPF, 1964–66.

90. On JL's 20–21 Aug 1966 visit to Haiphong, also see PE/Hanoi (JL) to PFM (Spasowski), sz. 10988, 24 Aug 1966, AMSZ, trans. MG.

91. Poldel Saigon (JL) to PFM (JM), sz. 11468, 3 Sep 1966, AMSZ, obt./trans. LG. The notion of a U.S. landing in North Vietnam genuinely concerned GD'O, who had heard persistent, very weakly denied rumors of such an action from U.S. sources, though a general who came by his apartment for a whiskey did not confirm them. GD'O, *DV,* 653 (26 Aug 1966).

92. Ibid., 656.

93. IE/S (GD'O) to IFM (Marchiori), telegram by hand no. 3, 4 Sep 1966, GD'O dossier; Saigon embtel 5229 (HCL), 4 Sep 1966, POL 27-14 Viet/Marigold 1/1/66, box 3020, CFPF, 1964–66.

94. Saigon embtel 5229 (HCL), 4 Sep 1966, ibid.

95. GD'O, *DV,* 658 (4 Sep 1966).

96. On 5 Sep 1966 JL-GD'O talk, see IE/S (GD'O) to IFM (Marchiori), telegram by hand no. 4, 6 Sep 1966, GD'O dossier; GD'O, *DV,* 659 (5 Sep 1966); and Saigon embtel 5517 (HCL), 8 Sep 1966, *FRUS, 1964–68,*4:619–20.

97. GD'O, *DV,* 659, 661 (5 and 7 Sep 1966).

98. Deptel 41695 (to American Embassy, Saigon), 6 Sep 1966, *SDVW:NVPP,* 250; GD'O, *DV,* 660–61 (7 Sep 1966).

99. PFM (JM) to Poldel Saigon (JL), sz. 9280, 7 Sep 1966, AMSZ, trans. MG; MR. This hedged stance may have reflected internal MSZ divisions over the advisability of mediating in Vietnam. In a mid-September conversation with a visiting U.S. scholar, a ministry official described his colleagues as split, with a majority opposed on the "divergent grounds" that Washington "would get tired of the war and pull out" or, conversely, "was using negotiations as a smokescreen for escalation." Either way, "Poland could only compromise itself by mediation." HAK, "Conversation with Dobroscelski [Dobrosielski], member of the Policy Planning Staff of the Polish Foreign Ministry," 23 Sep 1966, HAK folder, box 481, WAHP-LC.

100. Saigon embtel 5517 (HCL), 8 Sep 1966, *FRUS, 1964–68,* 4:620.

101. Ibid., 4:619; also IE/S (GD'O) to IFM (Marchiori), telegram by hand no. 6, 7 Sep 1966, GD'O dossier.

102. Deptel 44917 to American Embassy, Saigon, 12 Sep 1966, *FRUS, 1964–68,* 4:621–22.

103. IE/S (GD'O) to IFM (Marchiori), telegram 6, [1]7 Sep 1966, GD'O dossier; GD'O delivered this assurance to JL at dinner on 16 Sep: IE/S (GD'O) to IFM (Marchiori), telegram by hand no. 7, 17 Sep 1966, GD dossier.

104. Saigon embtel 5965 (HCL), 14 Sep 1966, *SDVW:NVPP,* 252–53.

105. Saigon embtel 6280 (HCL), 18 Sep 1966, *FRUS, 1964–68,* 4:642–44; IE/S (GD'O) to IFM (Marchiori), telegram by hand no. 7, 17 Sep 1966, GD'O dossier.

106. McGeorge Bundy to LBJ, 7 Feb 1965, *FRUS, 1964–68,* 2:175.

107. Goldberg speech: Department of State *Bulletin* 55 (10 Oct 1966): 518–25; *NYT,* 23 Sep 1966.

108. "Editorial Note," *FRUS, 1964–68,* 4:658.

109. Saigon embtel 8583 (HCL), 16 Oct 1966, ibid., 754–56.

110. Saigon embtel 6280 (HCL), 18 Sep 1966, POL 27-14 Viet/Marigold 1/1/66, box 3020, CFPF, 1964–66.

111. 26 Sep 1966 HCL-GD'O talk: IE/S (GD'O) to IFM (Marchiori), telegram by hand no. 8, 26 Sep 1966, GD'O dossier; Saigon embtel 6990 (HCL), 27 Sep 1966, POL 27-14 Viet/Marigold 1/1/66, box 3020, CFPF, 1964–66.

112. Saigon embtel 7230 (HCL), 29 Sep 1966, ibid.; "fail": IE/S (GD'O) to IFM (Marchiori), telegram by hand no. 8, 26 Sep 1966, GD'O dossier.

113. Saigon embtel 7712 (HCL), 5 Oct 1966, *SDVW:NVPP,* 256.

114. Saigon embtel 8583 (HCL), 16 Oct 1966, ibid., 258–59.
115. Saigon embtel 8567 (HCL), 14 Oct 1966, ibid., 256–57.
116. Saigon embtel 7712 (HCL), 5 Oct 1966, and Saigon embtel 8567 (HCL), 14 Oct 1966, both in POL 27-14 Viet/Marigold 1/1/66, box 3020, CFPF, 1964–66; also Poldel Saigon (JL) to PFM (Spasowski), sz. 12696, 1 Oct 1966, and Poldel Saigon (JL) to PFM (Spasowski-Mikołaj), sz. 12978, 7 Oct 1966, both AMSZ, trans. MG. While dissuading Pignedoli from his mediation efforts, JL recalled intervening in Hanoi on the Vatican's behalf in the case of an elderly Catholic priest who had spent two decades in a DRV prison. When he next saw PVD, in late November, JL advocated this favorable gesture in light of the Pope's criticism of U.S. policy in Vietnam. PVD promised to look into the matter, and the priest was freed some months later. JL interview, Warsaw, 7 Nov 2003.
117. Saigon embtel 5965 (HCL), 14 Sep 1966, POL 27-14 Viet/Marigold 1/1/66, box 3020, CFPF, 1964–66.
118. Saigon embtel 8567 (HCL), 15 Oct 1966, ibid.
119. Draft telegram to Saigon, 14 Oct 1966; note from "HI" [Isham]; and deptel 66655 to American Embassy, Saigon, 14 Oct 1966, in ibid.; and Saigon embtel 8583 (HCL), 16 Oct 1966, *FRUS, 1964–68,* 4:754–56.
120. James G. Hershberg, "'A Half-Hearted Overture': Czechoslovakia, Kissinger, and Vietnam, Autumn 1966," in *The Search for Peace in Vietnam, 1964–1968,* edited by Lloyd C. Gardner and Ted Gittinger (College Station: Texas A&M University Press, 2004), 292–320.
121. DR-Péter 6 Oct 1966 conversation: secto 41, POL 27 VIET S, box 3010, CFPF, 1964–66. János Radványi later stated that Péter had invented the claim without any basis, an irresponsible act that helped convince him to defect. János Radványi, *Delusion and Reality: Gambits, Hoaxes, & Diplomatic One-Upmanship in Vietnam* (South Bend, Ind.: Gateway Editions, 1978), 214–29.
122. Memcon, "Rumanian Approach on Vietnam," 22 Oct 1966, *FRUS, 1964–68,* 4:767–69.
123. Mănescu made the comment to DR and Goldberg, who reported it to Thant. "Meeting with Ambassador Goldberg in the Secretary-General's Conference Room on Tuesday 8 November 1966 at 5:30 p.m.," Vietnam document C(25), Thant Papers, UNA.
124. Memorandum of Meeting, Gov. Harriman's office, 10 a.m., 29 Sep 1966, Vietnam, General, Aug–Sep 1966, box 520, WAHP-LC.
125. WAH to LBJ and DR, "Negotiations," 3 Oct 1966, *FRUS, 1964–68,* 4:691–92.
126. DR-AF memcon, 5 p.m., 19 Sep 1966, conference files, CF-83, box 422, RG 59, NA II.
127. "Marigold: A Chronology," 10–11; Rome embtel 1960 (Reinhardt), 12 Oct 1966, POL 27-14 Viet/Marigold 1/1/66, box 3020, CFPF, 1964–66.
128. Warsaw embtel 523 (JAG), 5 Sep 1966, Poland–cables vol. I 11/63-9/66, box 200, NSF:CO, LBJL.
129. LET to CLC, "Governor Harriman's Draft Memorandum to the Secretary Dated September 13, 1966," 13 Sep 1966, POL 27 VIET S 9/12/66, box 3008, CFPF, 1964–66.
130. Memo of meeting, Governor Harriman's office, 4 p.m., 15 Sep 1966, Vietnam, General, Aug–Sep 1966, box 520, WAH, LC.
131. Deptel tosec 38, DR-AR talk, 22 Sep 1966, POL 27 VIET S 9/22/66, box 3008, CFPF, 1964–66.
132. Warsaw embtel 716 (JAG), 23 Sep 1966, POL VIET S 9/23/66, box 3009, ibid.; also deptel 53886 (to USUN), 24 Sep 1966, ibid.; Brussels embtel 1348 (Knight), 22 Sep 1966, POL 27 VIET S 9/22/66, box 3008; and deptel 56271 (to American Embassy, Warsaw), 28 Sep 1966, POL VIET S 9/28/66, box 3009, all CFPF, 1964–66.
133. DR-AR memcon, "Viet Nam (Part I of II)," 23 Sep 1966, POL VIET S 9/23/66, box 3009, CFPF, 1964–66. Subsequent quotations from DR-AR talk are from this record unless otherwise indicated.
134. Polish Mission, UN to PFM (Naszkowski), sz. 12323, 24 Sep 1966 (conveying AR tel. 445, 23 Sep 1966), AMSZ, trans. MG.
135. USUN tel. no. 1018 (DR), "Secretary's Second Talk with Fanfani," 25 Sep 1966, POL 7 IT 1/1/66, box 2361, CFPF, 1964–66.
136. "Marigold: A Chronology," 10–11, citing DR to HCL cable, 29 Sep 1966.
137. McGeorge Bundy to WPB, "Subject: Conversation with Foreign Minister Adam Rapacki of Poland," 4 Oct 1966, Poland Memos Vol. II 10/66-5/68, box 201, NSF:CO, LBJL.

138. Polish UN Mission, New York (Winiewicz) to PFM (AR), sz. 13425, 19 Oct 1966, Dept. III–1966 27/74 W-2, AMSZ, trans. MG; WAH-Winiewicz memcon, 18 Oct 1966, POL 27 VIET S, CFPF, 1964–66.

139. DR-Gromyko memcon, 24 Sep 1966, *FRUS, 1964–68,* 4:662–68; quotation on 666.

140. DR-WWR telcon, 10:30 a.m., 25 Sep 1966, DR Papers, box 57, entry 5379, RG 59, NA II.

141. WAH to LBJ and DR, "Negotiations Committee," 30 Sep 1966, *FRUS, 1964–68,* 4:678–79.

142. LBJ-Gromyko memcon, 10 Oct 1966, ibid., 716–21.

143. WAH to LBJ and DR, 14 Oct 1966, ibid., 726–27; Gromyko comment cited by DR, ibid., 760.

144. Polish "Record of Conversation Conducted by the Party-Governmental Delegations of Socialist Countries in Moscow, October 21, 1966," AAN, obt. LG, trans. MG. Czech "Report on the Visit and Discussions in the USSR between 17 and 21 October 1966," obt. O. Tuma. See "A Detailed Report on the Statements of General Secretaries of Communist and Workers' Parties at a Meeting of 21 October 1966," f. 02 11, sv. 12, ar.j. 13, l. 29, b. 13, a-UV KSC, SUA, Prague; obt. O. Tuma, trans. F. Raska. This account uses both the Polish and Czech sources, particularly the more detailed Polish record—which, however, omits some of Gomułka's remarks.

145. Polish record, Moscow, 21 Oct 1966. Interestingly—and presciently, from a post–Cold War perspective—Gromyko acknowledged that despite the war, "Americans live comfortably. New industrial facilities are growing like mushrooms after the rain." Showing little confidence that a domestic antiwar movement could restrain U.S. policies, Gromyko reported that racial problems and inflation troubled LBJ far more than dissent over Vietnam.

146. The comments of the Communist leaders of the Eastern European countries most active in Vietnam diplomacy—Hungary and Poland—are worth noting.

America could not win militarily, Kádár said, nor could Hanoi, "at least not at any time soon." Hungary had "openly" urged the Vietnamese to negotiate, yet they firmly refused, presumably due to Chinese pressure; consequently, "our hands are tied." Validating cynical U.S. assessments, he said: "We also told them that the Americans are submitting statements of peace and at the same time they are continuing the aggression. Act, we advised them, similarly: Talk about peace and at the same time destroy the aggressors. Act like this, simultaneously."

Gomułka confessed uncertainty about the real situation on the ground in Vietnam, but made clear his preference that Hanoi abandon its focus on a military victory: "The Vietnamese comrades should publicly state that, at an appropriate time, they are willing to enter into negotiations with the United States of America on the condition that the bombing of the Democratic Republic of Vietnam is halted. Not only Vietnam is concerned here, but also a conflict between two world systems and this is serious. It is in our interest for the Vietnamese conflict to end in political victory for us. If the United States of America wins, this, conversely, will represent a major political blow to the international Communist movement."

147. Polish-Soviet talks, Moscow, 14 Oct 1966, in *Tajne dokumenty: Biura Politycznego PRL-ZSRR, 1956–1970,* edited by Andrzej Paczkowski (London: Aneks, 1998), 404–25, trans. MG.

148. Extracts from "An Appraisal of the Bombing of North Vietnam through 12 September 1966," CIA/DIA Report, in *FRUS, 1964–68,* 4:736. On the POL campaign's failure, see esp. Gibbons, IV, 379–85, 403; GPP, IV, 110ff; and Jacob Van Staaveren, *Gradual Failure: The Air War over North Vietnam, 1965–1966* (Washington, D.C.: Air Force History and Museum Programs, 2002), 299–307, 322–24.

149. "The Vietnamese Communists' Will to Persist," CIA Memorandum, 26 Aug 1966, in *Estimative Products on Vietnam, 1948–1975,* edited by National Intelligence Council (Washington, D.C.: U.S. Government Printing Office, 2005), 353–76 (summary and principal findings only); full text on enclosed CD-ROM and at www.cia..gov/nic; quotations: report 4–5, I-8; also see *FRUS, 1964–68,* 4:601–3. RSM commissioning of report: ibid., 601, 647; *Estimative Products on Vietnam, 1948–1975,* xxiv; and George W. Allen, *None So Blind: A Personal Account of the Intelligence Failure in Vietnam* (Chicago: Ivan R. Dee, 2001), 211–12.

150. "Vietnamese Communists' Will to Persist," in *FRUS, 1964–68,* 4:601.

151. "Vietnamese Communists' Will to Persist," annex I, I-36, I-9.

152. Allen, *None So Blind,* 213–17.

153. Pierre Asselin, *A Bitter Peace: Washington, Hanoi, and the Making of the Paris Agreement* (Chapel Hill: University of North Carolina Press, 2002), 11.
154. JL interviews, Warsaw, June 2003. CIA analysts also admired their enemy's handiwork and industriousness under fire. By devising "temporary expedients to keep traffic moving," the North Vietnamese, despite all the bombing they had sustained, were "presently in a better position to keep their lines of highway transportation open, by having developed a high degree of skill in repairing damaged structures and in building more alternate crossings in order to increase the options available for the routing of highway traffic." "Vietnamese Communists' Will to Persist," annex I, I-27, I-30.
155. WWR to LBJ, 19 Sep 1966, 1:20 p.m., *FRUS, 1964–68,* 4:647–48.
156. LBJ-RSM telcon, 5:39 p.m., 19 Sep 1966, Editorial Note, ibid., 649.
157. See, e.g., Frances Fitzgerald, *Fire in the Lake: The Vietnamese and the Americans in Vietnam* (Boston: Little, Brown, 1972), chap. 11.
158. RSM to LBJ, "Subject: Actions Recommended for Vietnam," 13 Oct 66, in *FRUS, 1964–68,* 4:727–38; also Van Staaveren, *Gradual Failure,* 305–7. Collecting gossip on RSM's visit to Saigon from diplomats and journalists, JL gathered that he faced a "difficult situation" on the battlefield, especially around the DMZ, and a "serious crisis" within the Saigon government. JL told Warsaw that RSM and Westmoreland had discussed further troop deployments to raise U.S. forces well above 500,000, and considered some form of offensive military action to break the stalemate. Poldel Saigon (JL) to PFM (Spasowski-JS-Ludwik-Mikolaj), sz. 13278, 14 Oct 1966, AMSZ, trans. MG. Much like RSM in his private memorandum to LBJ, JL also reported a growing conviction in Saigon that despite its escalating attacks Washington could not count on breaking its enemy's will or a decisive military success, and also remarked on the lack of coordination between military and civilian programs, exacerbated by pervasive corruption. In Saigon's "nervous" atmosphere, he even cited a rumor he suspected that U.S. Embassy officials deliberately (and implausibly) spread that Washington was considering using tactical nuclear weapons to cut infiltration routes from North Vietnam. Poldel Saigon (JL) to PFM (Spasowski), sz. 13148, 12 Oct 1966, ibid.
159. WAH-RSM 7 Oct 1966 memcon, Vietnam—General—Oct–Dec 1966, box 520, WAHP-LC.
160. *NYT,* 26 Oct 1966.
161. WAH memcon with LBJ, Manila, 26 Oct 1966, chron. file, Sep–Oct 1966, box 569, WAHP-LC. WAH had considered stopping in Poland, but dropped the idea after Winiewicz told him not to bother, given the lack of "fundamental changes" in U.S. policy. Polish UN Mission, New York (Winiewicz) to PFM (AR), sz. 13425, 19 Oct 1966, Dept.III–1966 27/74 W-2, AMSZ, trans. MG.

Chapter 4

1. "Villa Madama" at www.esteri.it; www.italycyberguide.com (Goethe); author's visit to Villa Madama and Roberto Massaro interview (Saint Peter's), 11 May 2005.
2. Cary Grant, *All About Cary: Autobiography,* chap. 9, at www.carygrant.org/allaboutcary.
3. Hitler did not sleep there, though, rejecting Villa Madama as "insufficiently magnificent" and staying instead at the more grandiose Palazzo Doria. The snub prompted the *NYT* to rue that Mussolini missed a golden opportunity to invite the "the leading artist of contemporary Germany, the best of all their past artists and undoubtedly the great German old master of the future" to redo Raphael's frescoes: "No doubt the distinguished visitor could have found a few free moments and would have been delighted to oblige." Hitler did dine at Villa Madama with Foreign Minister Galeazzo Ciano after a day of watching Italian military exercises. *NYT,* 6 Jan, 13 Jan, and 9 May 1938. On Nazi visitors, see *NYT,* 14 Jan 1937 (Goering) and 29 Oct 1938 (Ribbentrop).
4. Author's visit to Villa Madama, 11 May 2005; Massaro interview.
5. GD'O, *DV,* 694 (25 Oct 1966).
6. Ibid., 694 (28 Oct 1966).
7. CLC interview, Washington, 8 Dec 2004; CLC, *The Lost Crusade: America in Vietnam* (New York: Dodd, Mead, 1970), 322; CLC OH II, 17 Jul 1969, LBJL; CLC, *In the Shadows of History:*

Fifty Years Behind the Scenes of Cold War Diplomacy (Amherst, N.Y.: Prometheus Books, 2005), 243.

8. "Meeting with Amintore Fanfani, Minister of Foreign Affairs," Rome, 11/2/66, 10–11:30 [a.m.], chron file: 1–16 Nov 1966, box 569, and Manila Conference, Post-Trip I Italy, box 552, WAHP-LC; 2 Nov 1966 entry, AFD.

9. On 2 Nov 1966 Villa Madama lunch, see GD'O, *DV*, 697 (2 Nov 1966); 2 Nov 1966 entry, AFD; CLC, *Lost Crusade*, 322-3; CLC OH II, LBJL, 15–17, and U.S. memcon, AF lunch, Rome, 2 Nov 1966, chron file: 1–16 Nov 1966, box 569, and Manila Conference, Post-Trip I Italy, box 552, WAHP-LC.

10. CLC interview, Washington, 8 Dec 2004.

11. *FRUS, 1964–68*, 3:821.

12. From 2 Nov 1966 entry, AFD.

13. WAH notes, n.d., box 552 (552-11), WAHP-LC.

14. CLC interview, 8 Dec 2004. In a cable to LBJ and DR on his Rome talks, WAH said AF "claimed to have special knowledge that the Communists would prefer to negotiate directly with the United States" and "Hanoi would want to know the nature of a possible settlement before embarking on formal negotiations." AF therefore "suggested that it would be wise to attempt to work out an agreement with Hanoi in secret," which might yield a "fait accompli" that would help the DRV resist Chinese pressure to keep fighting. WAH clearly alluded to AF's endorsing of the Saigon channel, but edited out a paragraph in CLC's draft mentioning the Saigon channel and crediting GD'O with AF's suggestion. Presumably WAH judged it more politic to attribute the idea to AF and wiser to make the case for sending fresh proposals for JL after returning to Washington. Bonn embtel 5244 (McGhee), 5 Nov 1966, and CLC draft cable, 4 Nov 1966, both Manila Summit Conference, Post trip I, Italy, box 552, WAHP-LC.

15. CLC interview, Washington, 8 Dec 2004.

16. Memo of Meeting, 10 Nov 1966, 3 p.m., Washington, *FRUS, 1964–68*, 4:820–24; also CLC OH II, 18–20, 27.

17. ASPEN: *SDVW:NVPP*, 654–715; fully declassified copy, box 10, RSM Papers, LBJL; and Fredrik Logevall, "The ASPEN Channel and the Problem of the Bombing," in *The Search for Peace in Vietnam, 1964–1968*, edited by Lloyd C. Gardner and Ted Gittinger (College Station: Texas A&M University Press, 2004), 183–206.

18. DR-Nilsson 11 Nov 1966 talk: *FRUS, 1964–68*, 4:829–35; *SDVW:NVPP*, 655–61; Logevall, "ASPEN Channel," 190–91. DR would not have liked NDT's own summary of Petri's stand: "The Swedish Ambassador summarized the position of his country, which comes down to the following: the Americans' war in Vietnam goes against humanity, the bombing of the DRV must be stopped unconditionally, American forces must be pulled out of Vietnam, the NLF must participate in the negotiations." NDT-Gromyko memcon, Moscow, 12 Nov 1966, AVPRF, f. 079, op. 21, p. 51, d. 5, ll. 20–22, obt./trans. S. Radchenko.

19. Swedish aide-mémoire, sanitized in *SDVW:NVPP*, 656–57, but available in Pentagon Papers, vol. VI.C.4 [2 of 2], ASPEN pp. 2-3, box 10, RSM Papers, LBJL.

20. Logevall, "ASPEN Channel," 191.

21. LBJ approves RT-52: JCS-VN, pt. II, 36-17/18/19, NSA/FOIA; *FRUS, 1964–68*, 4:817–19 (also 599–600, 617–18; 740, 742, 756 n, 782, 809–16); *SDVW:NVPP*, 261–63; Wayne Thompson, *To Hanoi and Back: The U.S. Air Force and North Vietnam, 1966–1973* (Washington, D.C.: Smithsonian Institution Press, 2000), 41–43. LBJ-RSM rift: McNaughton diary, 131 (13 Nov 1966 entry), courtesy C. Mosher; also Benjamin T. Harrison and Christopher L. Mosher, "The Secret Diary of McNamara's Dove: The Long-Lost Story of John T. McNaughton's Opposition to the Vietnam War," *Diplomatic History* 35, no. 3 (June 2011): 505–34, at 528.

22. CLC, *Lost Crusade*, 334.

23. Deptel 83786 to Saigon, 13 Nov 1966, *FRUS, 1964–68*, 4:838–39.

24. GD'O, *DV*, 697 (2 Nov 1966), 698 (10 Nov 1966).

25. VCM and Rahman planned to attend, but JL thought it awkward to celebrate a state Warsaw considered illegitimate. Poldel Saigon (JL) to PFM (Spasowski), sz. 13564, 23 Oct 1966, and PFM (Spasowski) to Poldel Saigon (JL), sz. 11046, 26 Oct 1966, both AMSZ, trans. MG. JL later

reported that VCM, wanting to "show off," denounced him to an RVN official for violating protocol by missing the event. Poldel Saigon (JL) to PFM (Spasowski), sz. 14280, 7 Nov 1966, ibid. In its first such attack on Saigon's center, the Viet Cong shelled the National Day parade with mortar barrages that killed eight persons (including a U.S. Navy commander) and wounded more than thirty. When JL returned from Phnom Penh, Rahman (half-?)jokingly accused him of leaving town (and leaving his colleagues at risk) because he had been tipped off to the impending assault, which he denied. JL interview, Warsaw, 10 May 2011; *NYT,* 2 Nov 1966.

26. Washington and London told Warsaw that Sihanouk supported a larger ICC role in Cambodia, yet Hanoi insisted he had agreed to allow use of his country's territory to back the South Vietnamese insurgency. "Sihanouk is deeply convinced that the NLF will win," JL reported after speaking with PVD in April 1966. "He is at least smart enough that he does not volunteer to be a mediator." [PE/Hanoi (JS) to PFM (Wierna), sz. 5261, 24 Apr 1966, ibid.] Once, Sihanouk asked JL to intercede with Hanoi to curtail its violations of Cambodian sovereignty, which imperiled his neutral status. JL urged PVD and other DRV leaders to back Sihanouk, "the best man you can have there," especially since he hardly interfered with DRV activities; PVD disclaimed any long-term designs on Cambodian territory, only small temporary bases to support the HCM trail. JL interviews, June 2003.

27. DE/Saigon (Derksen) to DFM, tel. 111, "Subject: Hanoi, Liberation Front and the Vietnam Issue," 8 Nov 1966; DFMA, obt. R. van der Maar, trans. DM. The DRV Embassy organized and hosted JL's talks with NLF/DRV representatives. JL interview, Warsaw, Jun 2003.

28. Ibid.

29. Ibid. JL recalled more than one NLF rep at the meeting, not the single official reported in Derksen's cable.

30. DE/Saigon (Derksen) to DFM, "Subject: Hanoi."

31. IE/S (GD'O) to IFM, office memo 1, noon, 13 Nov 1966, GD'O dossier.

32. GD'O, *DV,* 702 (11 Nov 1966).

33. Ibid.; IE/S (GD'O) to IFM, office memo 1, noon, 13 Nov 1966.

34. JL related his plan to leave for Hanoi on 15 Nov 1966 (to return four days later) to Warsaw on November 9, which suggests he had already seen GD'O. Poldel Saigon (JL) to PFM (Spasowski), sz. 14397, 9 Nov 1966, AMSZ, trans. MG. But GD'O reports only reaching Saigon the next day; so, a mystery.

35. Poldel Saigon (JL) to PFM (JM), sz. 14596, 14 Nov 1966, AMSZ, obt./trans. LG; Saigon embtel 10741 (HCL), 13 Nov 1966, POL 27-14 Viet/XYZ 11-1-65, box 22, FTSCPF. At the 14 Nov 1966 meeting's outset, JL thanked HCL for being "so responsive to my request" to see him before leaving for Hanoi, HCL cabled. (Saigon embtel 10856, 14 Nov 1966, *FRUS, 1964–68,* 4:839–41.)

36. On 14 Nov 1966 three-way meeting, see Saigon embtel 10856 (HCL), 14 Nov 1966; Poldel Saigon (JL) to PFM (JM), sz. 14596, 14 Nov 1966, AMSZ, obt./trans. LG; IE/S (GD'O) to IFM (AF), office memos 2–5, all 6:45 p.m., 14 Nov 1966, GD'O dossier; GD'O, *DV,* 703–5 (14 Nov 1966).

37. JL interview, Warsaw, June 2003.

38. JL-GD'O meeting at Japanese Embassy: LVL/NAV, *Before Paris,* 165.

39. Deptel 84238 to Saigon, 14 Nov 1966, *FRUS, 1964–68,* 4:843–45.

40. On 15 Nov 1966 three-way talk, see Saigon embtel 10955 (HCL), 15 Nov 1966, POL 27-14 Viet/XYZ 11-1-65, box 22, FTSCPF; IE/S (GD'O) to IFM (AF), office memos 6–8, all noon, 15 Nov 1966, GD'O dossier; GD'O, *DV,* 705–6 (15 Nov 1966); Poldel Saigon (JL) to PFM (JM), sz. 14673, AMSZ, trans. MG/JL; MR; JL interviews, Warsaw, June 2003.

41. *SDVW:NVPP,* 265–66.

42. IE/S (GD'O) to IFM (AF), office memo 6, noon, 15 Nov 1966, GD'O dossier.

43. Ibid., office memo 8. In his own cable, HCL quoted JL as saying, "I thank you for your very serious and kind approach. I hope this unhappy, cruel war may be stopped as soon as possible."

44. GD'O, *DV,* 706.

45. Poldel Saigon (JL) to PFM (JM), sz. 14673, 16 Nov 1966, AMSZ, trans. MG and JL.

46. JL-Westmoreland talk: JL interview, Warsaw, June 2003; Westmoreland did not mention it in *A Soldier Reports* (Garden City, N.Y.: Doubleday, 1976), nor could the author find any reference to it in his papers at the U.S. Army Center of Military History, Fort McNair, Washington.

47. Poldel Saigon (JL) to PFM (Spasowski-JS-Ludwik-Mikolaj), sz. 13278, 14 Oct 1966, AMSZ, trans. MG.

48. MR.

49. Martin-AR memcons, Warsaw, 7–8 Nov 1966, file 20-22-VIETS-2-1 pt. 7, vol. 9398, RG 25, NAC.

50. PFM (JM) to Poldel Saigon (JL), sz. 11620, 12 Nov 1966, AMSZ, trans. MG.

51. [JM?], handwritten addendum dated "15.11" to Poldel Saigon (JL) to PFM (JM), sz. 14596, 14 Nov 1966, ibid.

52. As quoted in MR. JM does not precisely date or identify the author of the analysis, merely using the first person plural, but the context indicates that he is referring to himself and AR.

53. Ibid.

54. Brezhnev, when he met with AR in Sofia on 18 Nov 1966, said NDT had told him the DRV leadership was already debating HCL's proposals, and that he, Brezhnev, had received a "confirmation" of a message from JS relating to this. See MR and PE/Sofia (AR) to PFM (Naszkowski), sz. 14764, 18 Nov 1966, AMSZ, trans. MG.

55. On 18 Nov 1966 Brezhnev-AR talk, see PE/Sofia (AR) to PFM (Naszkowski), sz. 14764, 18 Nov 1966, AMSZ, trans. MG; and MR.

56. So JM claims in his report, Yet how could DRV leaders have already received (let alone discussed) HCL's proposals by 18 Nov, because JL did not convey them to Hanoi until 20 Nov (see below)? JL's cables describing his talks with HCL on 14–15 Nov were not decoded in Warsaw until the late afternoons of 15 and 17 Nov, respectively; conceivably, then, at least his first cable, including the U.S. proposals, could have been relayed to JS for DRV authorities. AR's cable merely reports that NDT "received the confirmation of JS's message. The leadership of the DRV discussed the totality of the situation. The negotiations were stopped without having undertaken any decisions."

57. The revelation that NDT canceled his Budapest trip to join other DRV leaders in Moscow for urgent Marigold-related consultations significantly expands the historical record. See James G. Hershberg, *Who Murdered Marigold? New Evidence on the Mysterious Failure of Poland's Secret Initiative to Start U.S.–North Vietnamese Peace Talks, 1966*, CWIHP Working Paper 27 (Washington, D.C.: Woodrow Wilson International Center for Scholars, 2000), 17 n. 66. In NDT's absence, Hanoi sent to Budapest interior minister (and ex–foreign minister) Ung Van Khiem; Nguyen Song Tung of the VWP CC Foreign Relations Department; and, in early December, Politburo member LDT; see János Radványi, *Delusion and Reality: Gambits, Hoaxes, and Diplomatic One-Upmanship in Vietnam* (South Bend, Ind.: Gateway Editions, 1978), 227; and HA/Hanoi (Imre Pehr) to HFM, "Subject: Comrade Le Duc Tho's Moscow Consultations," 19 Jan 1967, Vietnam Relations, 1967, Foreign Ministry records, Top Secret, box 93, 250-001223/1967, XIX-J-l-j, MOL, obt./trans. Z. Szoke.

59. On the 19 Nov 1966 AR-NDT talk, see AR, *pilna notatka* [urgent note], 21 Nov 1966, GM sygn. 1/77 w 16, t-39, *Tajne spec. znaczenia*, AMSZ, courtesy H. Szlajfer, trans. MG; MR; PE/Sofia (JM) to PFM (Malczyk), sz. 14796, 19 Nov 1966, AMSZ, trans. MG. U.S. aides had no idea of any link between AR's presence in Sofia (if they noticed it at all) and Vietnam diplomacy, nor of his talks with NDT and Brezhnev tied to Marigold; only scattered, vague allusions to these contacts emerged later. Hershberg, *Who Murdered Marigold?* 18 n. 68. The only previously published reference to AR's talks in Bulgaria with Brezhnev and NDT appeared in Henry Brandon, *Anatomy of Error* (Boston: Gambit, 1969), 74-5. Brandon was a well-connected Washington-based British journalist who apparently received inside information from Polish sources; in MR, JM lauded his account of Marigold as "more precise" than that of DK and SHL in *Secret Search*.

59. On the AR-Brezhnev 19 Nov 1966 conversation, see AR, *pilna notatka* [urgent note], Not. 447/Rap./66, 21 Nov 1966, GM sygn. 1/77 w 16, t-39, *Tajne spec. znaczenia*, AMSZ, courtesy H. Szlajfer, trans. MG.

60. PE/Moscow (Pszczółkowski) to PFM (Naszkowski), sz. 14885, 22 Nov 1966, AMSZ, obt. D. Selvage, trans. MG. Citing the Soviet record, Gaiduk also notes this 21 Nov 1966 Pszczółkowski briefing for Gromyko on the HCL-JL talks, indicating that Washington had implied a willing-

ness to cease bombing North Vietnam "provided there was reciprocity from Hanoi." Ilya V. Gaiduk, *The Soviet Union and the Vietnam War* (Chicago: Ivan R. Dee, 1996), 92, 270 n. 55.

61. Shcherbakov-PVD memcon, Hanoi, 2 Nov 1966, AVPRF, f. 079, op. 21, pap. 51, d. 8, p. 177, courtesy S. Radchenko.

62. NDT-Gromyko memcon, Moscow, 12 Nov 1966, ibid., d. 5, ll. 20-22, courtesy S. Radchenko.

63. PE/Hanoi (JS) to PFM (Wierna), sz. 14540, 13 Nov 1966, AMSZ, trans. MG.

64. The Poles heard these reports from a "rather authoritative" and "quite reliable" Vietnamese source (code named "W.D.") in late December 1966 or early January 1967. Reportedly distrustful of Mao's assurance, a majority of the VWP Politburo reportedly favored contacts with the United States in Rangoon rather than Warsaw, as the Chinese would have "greater opportunities to hinder the talks" in the Polish capital. PE/Hanoi (JS?) to PFM (Wierna), sz. 16274, 25 Dec 1966, AMSZ, obt./trans. LG; PE/Hanoi (JS) to PFM (AR), sz. 288, 8 Jan 1967, AMSZ, trans. MG; MR.

65. Mao–Le Duan memcon, 8 Nov 1966, information from Chinese source. A Chinese source indicates a Zhou–Le Duan talk in Beijing on 9 Nov 1966 at which Zhou discussed the Cultural Revolution. *Zhou Enlai Nianpu* [Zhou Enlai Chronology], vol. 3 (Beijing: Central Press of Historical Documents, 1997), 88.

66. Candel Saigon (VCM) to CDEA, tel. 798, "ICSC Aircraft—Future of Candel Hanoi," 13 Sep 1966, 100-11-3 vol. 1 [pt. 2], vol. 9516, RG 25, NAC.

67. Candel, ICC, Saigon (VCM) to CDEA, tel. 1035, "Viet Nam–Canadian Channel and ICSC Aircraft," 15 Nov 1966, ibid.

68. Poldel Saigon (JL) to PFM (Spasowski), sz. 14629, 16 Nov 1966, AMSZ, obt./trans. LG; PFM (Spasowski) to Poldel Saigon (JL), sz. 11806, 17 Nov 1966, AMSZ, trans. MG; JL interview, Warsaw, June 2003.

69. JL interview, Warsaw, June 2003.

70. Ibid. Largely due to "adverse weather," Rolling Thunder raids steeply decreased in Oct–Nov 1966 from a peak in Sep after the resumption of bombing in Feb after the thirty-seven-day pause. See Robert H. Wenzel to Benjamin H. Read, "Rolling Thunder Patterns in Late 1966," 28 Feb 1967, POL 27-14 Viet/Marigold 1967 folder, box 2739, CFPF, 1967–69.

71. PE/Hanoi (JL) to PFM (JM), sz. 14818, 20 Nov 1966, AMSZ, trans. MG.

72. JL interview, Warsaw, Jun 2003; NDP interview, Hanoi, 8 Jun 1999; and NDP, "The Marigold Drive," presented to author, 8 Jun 1999; LVL, NDP background: RSM, James G. Blight, and Robert K. Brigham with Thomas J. Biersteker and Col. Herbert Y. Schandler, *Argument Without End: In Search of Answers to the Vietnam Tragedy* (New York: PublicAffairs, 1999), xx–xxi.

73. LVL/NAV, *Before Paris,* 163–65, trans. MP (courtesy C. Goscha) and Lien-Hang T. Nguyen.

74. Ibid., 165–66; NDP, "Marigold Drive." JL's presentation (as supplied by LVL/NAV) bore a close, if not precise, resemblance to the "ten points" that JL later presented to HCL in Saigon; see chapter 5 of the present volume.

75. JL interviews, Warsaw, June 2003; NDP interview, Hanoi, 8 Jun 1999. JL reported that HVL felt the proposals merited "serious consideration" in PE/Hanoi (JL) to PFM (Naszkowski), sz. 14846, 21 Nov 1966, AMSZ, trans. MG. HVL confirmed he supported the Polish initiative when interviewed by MG in Hanoi on 19 Oct 2005.

76. PE/Hanoi (JL) to PFM (Naszkowski), sz. 14846, 21 Nov 1966.

77. JL interview, Warsaw, June 2003.

78. MR.

79. JL told VCM he had seen a "sphinx-like" Giap in Hanoi, but did not mention any contact in AMSZ ciphergrams. Candel Saigon (VCM) to CDEA, tel. 1116, 5 Dec 1966, file 20-22-VIETS-2-1, pt. 8, vol. 9398, RG 25, NAC.

80. This same week, in Moscow, NDT cautiously assessed Poland's ICC performance. At "his residence in the Lenin Hills," he told a Soviet official Hanoi favored keeping the ICC in existence—provided it "not take actions which could damage the interests of the DRV," which depended on socialist Poland's continuing to counteract Indian and Canadian pressure. He called the information JL and other Poles obtained in South Vietnam "of great interest."

Firyubin-NDT memcon, Moscow, 25 Nov 1966, AVPRF, f. 079, op. 21, p. 51, d. 5, l. 24, courtesy S. Radchenko.

81. JL-NCT talk: PE/Hanoi (JL), to PFM (JM), sz. 15134, 28 Nov 1966, AMSZ, trans. MG; MR ("declared"); JL interviews, Warsaw, June 2003. JL cabled his report of this talk on November 28, but agreed, on seeing the cable, that it must have occurred before November 25, since NCT would surely not have explicitly opposed a decision already made by the Politburo; MR dates it to November 22.

82. JL interviews, Warsaw, June 2003.

83. Ibid.

84. PE/Hanoi (JS) to PFM (Wierna), sz. 9579, 25 Jul 1966, AMSZ, trans. MG.

85. JL interviews, Warsaw, June 2003.

86. See enc. no. 1 to American Embassy, Saigon (Porter), to Department of State, airgram A-643, 19 May 1966, POL 2 Gen. Reports & Statistics VIET N 1/1/64, box 2922, CFPF, 1964–66.

87. Candel Saigon (VCM) to CDEA, tel 70, "Hanoi Visit—Other Discussions (1)," 17 Jan 1967, file 20-22-VIETS-2-1 pt. 10, vol. 9398, RG 25, NAC.

88. JL interviews, Warsaw, June 2003: "transmitted to Mikołaj": PE/Sofia (JM) to PFM (Malczyk), copies to JL, JS, and Naszkowski, sz. 14796, 19 Nov 1966, AMSZ, trans. MG.

89. Shcherbakov-PVD memcon, Hanoi, 21 Nov 1966, AVPRF, f. 079, op. 21, p. 51, d. 8, l. 191, trans. S. Radchenko. PVD also told Shcherbakov that JL had "stressed that the Americans and their Saigon puppets were in a fairly difficult situation" and "that our position has improved considerably" (ibid., l. 199). Presumably HVL relayed this assessment, which reflected JL's explanation for the comparatively forthcoming U.S. proposals.

90. JL-JS exchange: JL interviews, Warsaw, June 2003.

91. PE/Hanoi (JS) to PFM (Naszkowski), sz. 14867, 22 Nov 1966, AMSZ, trans. MG.

92. PFM (Naszkowski) to PE/Hanoi (JS), sz. 11939, 22 Nov 1966, ibid.

93. PE/Hanoi (JS) to PFM (Naszkowski), sz. 14929, 23 Nov 1966, ibid.

94. PE/Hanoi (JL) to PFM (Naszkowski), sz. 14846, 21 Nov 1966, ibid.; JL interview, Warsaw, June 2003.

95. WWR to LBJ, 9 Nov 1966, and LBJ-RSM telcon, 2:51 p.m., 9 Nov 1966, *FRUS, 1964–68,* 4:812–13, 816–17; also Thompson, *To Hanoi and Back,* 42. JCS Chair Gen. Earle G. Wheeler assured commanders that once Brown left Moscow, on or about November 25, clearance to attack deferred RT-52 targets—particularly the Haiphong cement and thermal power plant and the Thai Nguyen steel plant—should follow. "You can rely on me to press the matter," he promised. Gen. Wheeler, CJCS to Gen. Westmoreland, COMUSMACV, and Adm. Sharp, CINCPAC, JCS 6926 66, 11 Nov 1966, CMH 82-82 A + B, William C. Westmoreland [Eyes Only] Message File COMUSMACV 10/1–12/31/66, Westmoreland Papers, U.S. Army Center of Military History, Fort McNair, Washington, DC.

96. Brown in Moscow: records in FO 371/188928, TNA; deptel 91787 to American Embassy, London (Bruce), 27 Nov 1966, *FRUS, 1964–68,* 4:865–66.

97. JL-PVD 25 Nov 1966 talk: PE/Hanoi (JL) to PFM (JM) sz. 15023, 25 Nov 1966, AMSZ, obt. LG, trans. LG and JL; and JL interviews, Warsaw, June 2003.

98. JL on PVD appearance: Candel Saigon (VCM) to CDEA, tel. 1116, 5 Dec 1966, file 20-22-VIETS-2-1, pt. 8, vol. 9398, RG 25, NAC.

99. Vietnamese sources confirm this PVD statement: LVL/NAV, *Before Paris,* 166–67; in the 2002 edition, the authors footnote (p. 160) the notes of Nguyen Tu Huyen, chief of the Foreign Ministry's translation office.

100. On "animated," see IE/S (GD'O) to IFM (AF), office memo 10, noon, 1 Dec 1966, and "stormy": IE/S (GD'O) to IFM (AF), office memo 17, noon, 2 Dec 1966, both GD'O dossier.

101. PE/Moscow (Pszczółkowski) to PFM (AR), sz. 15106, 27 Nov 1966, AMSZ, trans. MG.

102. PE/Moscow (Pszczółkowski) to PFM (AR), sz. 15107, 27 Nov 1966, AMSZ, obt. D. Selvage, trans. MG. On 30 Nov 1966, Gromyko informed NDT (still in Moscow) about the exchanges with Brown, earning his praise for criticizing "the aggressor's accomplice." Gromyko-NDT memcon, Moscow, 30 Nov 1966, AVPRF, f. 079, op. 21, p. 51, l. 27, obt./trans. S. Radchenko.

103. Bucharest embtel 21555 (Davis), 23 Nov 1966, POL 7 VIET N 1/1/66, box 2923, CFPF, 1964–66.
104. PE/Moscow (Pszczółkowski) to PFM (AR), sz. 15107, 27 Nov 1966, AMSZ, cited above. Perhaps concealing such suspicions, Shcherbakov later told his Hungarian colleague that LDT's failure to see Brezhnev in Moscow in late November was due to "travel difficulties" which delayed his arrival. HA/Hanoi (Pehr) to HFM, "Subject: Comrade Le Duc Tho's Moscow Consultations," 19 Jan 1967, box 93, 250-001223/1967, XIX-J-l-j, Vietnam Relations, 1967, Foreign Ministry Documents, Top Secret, MOL, obt./trans. Z. Szoke.
105. GD'O, DV, 710 (23 Nov 1966).
106. Ibid. (26–27 Nov 1966).
107. On 28 Nov 1966 JL-PVD talk, see PE/Hanoi (JL) to PFM (AR), sz. 15133, 28 Nov 1966, AMSZ, obt. LG, trans. LG and JL; JL interviews, Warsaw, Jun 2003.
108. This cable has not been found but is inferred from JL's report to AR on the 28 Nov talk with PVD, which opened by stating that he "delivered according to Your instructions." JL agreed he must have received AR's instructions over the weekend in reply to his earlier cable reporting the 25 Nov talk with PVD.
109. JL interviews, Warsaw, June 2003. PVD's gesture may have been special but was not unique. A U.S. writer who met him in 1968 as part of a foreign delegation reported that after their talk spoke he "kissed us, each, with emotion when we said good-bye." Mary McCarthy, Hanoi (New York: Harcourt, Brace & World, 1968), 130.
110. Ibid.
111. SDVW:NVPP, 213.
112. P. H. Gore-Booth to T. Brimelow, 20 Mar 1967, FCO 15/646, TNA.
113. On the shifting VWP Politburo stance toward talks, see Lien-Hang T. Nguyen, "The War Politburo: North Vietnam's Diplomatic and Political Road to the Tet Offensive," Journal of Vietnamese Studies 1, nos. 1–2 (2006): 4–58 (esp. 19–25). On HCM at VWP Politburo on 23 Nov 1966, see William Duiker email to author, 13 Sep 2003, citing Ho Chi Minh bien nien tieu su [A chronological history of Ho Chi Minh].
114. PE/Hanoi (JS) to PFM (Wierna), sz. 15488, 6 Dec 1966, AMSZ, trans. MG.
115. PE/Hanoi (JS) to PFM (Wierna), sz. 14540, 13 Nov 1966, ibid.
116. Of course, JS's Vietnamese source might have told the Pole what he presumably wanted to hear; Hanoi had a vested interest in persuading Soviet Bloc officials that it took a more moderate and flexible stand on negotiations, as Moscow urged. Other diplomats in Hanoi, not only Communists, also spread rumors that the DRV merely awaited a suitable U.S. concession (such as a bombing halt or freeze on troop levels) to enter peace talks. But British observers based there—who lacked JS's "fraternal" ties but analyzed the regime more critically—were more skeptical. The outgoing chargé warned London against "wishful thinking" regarding Hanoi's willingness for talks, particularly if based on rumors "fostered, deliberately and perhaps cynically, by Eastern European sources who probably judge that the least unhopeful approach to a settlement lies in applying continued pressure on the U.S. government to make concessions." Around the same time JS reported a pro-negotiations faction in the leadership, the new U.K. representative questioned the diplomatic corps' optimism. Why, he asked, since the bombing campaign had clearly failed to break public morale or undermine the economy, should the DRV leadership feel compelled, "sooner rather than later," to negotiate? BE/Hanoi (H. B. Shepherd) to FO, "Mr. Shepherd's Valedictory Despatch," 5 Oct 1966, and BE/Hanoi (J. H. R. Colvin) to FO, "Conditions in Hanoi and the North Viet-Namese Attitude towards Negotiations," 15 Nov 1966, both FO 371/186289, TNA. Reading Colvin's uncertain analysis, an SEAD aide concluded "that the Hanoi diplomatic corps, even the Eastern Europeans, are almost as much in the dark as we are about the real motivations and intentions of the North Vietnamese; i.e., that the Eastern Europeans—and indeed the Soviet Union—have not yet 'got through' to the leaders in Hanoi. In fact, the dispatch does show how confusing the North Vietnamese position is even to those on the spot." D. F. Murray, "The North Vietnamese Attitude towards Negotiations," 7 Dec 1966 minute on Colvin's 15 Nov 1966 dispatch.
117. Le Duan extolled science and technology in "Saving the Country Is the Holy Task of All Our People," broadcast on Radio Hanoi, 29 December 1966, in FBIS, North Vietnam, 4 January

1967, jjj 10–jjj 16 (esp. jjj 15–jjj 16); Sophie Quinn-Judge, "The Ideological Debate in the DRV and the Significance of the Anti-Party Affair, 1967–68," *Cold War History* 5, no. 4 (November 2005): 479–500 (esp. 488–89).

118. On the Le Duan–LDT relationship, see esp. Nguyen manuscript (and the forthcoming book).

119. NDT 28 Jan 1967 interview: *SDVW,* 422–24.

120. VWP CC Resolution 13 (no. 155-NQ/TW), Hanoi, 27 Jan 1967: *Van Kien Dang, Toan Tap, 28, 1967* [Collected Party Documents, Vol. 28, 1967], chief ed. Tran Tinh (Hanoi: Nha Xuat Ban Chinh Tri Quoc Gia, 2003), 171–79, trans. MP; also [Institute of the History of the Communist Party of Vietnam,] *History of the Communist Party of Vietnam* (Hanoi: Foreign Languages Publishing House, 1986), 199–200 ("important, active, and innovatory"), and David W. P. Elliott, *The Vietnamese War: Revolution and Social Change in the Mekong Delta, 1930–1975* (Armonk, N.Y.: M. E. Sharpe, 2002), vol. 2, 1054–55 ("important, active, and positive").

121. "Politburo Resolution on Intensifying the Military Struggle and the Political Struggle in South Vietnam (October and November 1966)," no. 154-NQ/TW, Hanoi, 27 Jan 1967, *Van Kien Dang, Toan Tap, 28, 1967,* 141–70 (the quotation is on 150), trans. MP. I thank MP and Nguyen Vu Tung for help in locating and interpreting this source. For an alternate translation, see Tung, "Hanoi's Search for an Effective Strategy," in *The Vietnam War,* edited by Peter Lowe (New York: St. Martin's Press, 1998), 52, citing *"Party Documents* (vol. 11), p. 237."

122. Commenting on this document, an authority noted: "Politburo resolutions frequently exist in many forms, some shortened and some longer, as they are disseminated to various audiences and revised and reworded several times while they work their way up to the Central Committee. So I am certain that the above passages are simply a later rework of the originally approved November 1966 Politburo resolution." MP email to author, 22 Mar 2007.

123. JL interview, Warsaw, June 2003.

124. Ibid.

125. Kent to Helms, "Subject: The View from Hanoi," 30 Nov 1966, Walt Rostow vol. 16 [3 of 3] 1–13 Dec 1966, box 11 [2 of 2], NSF:MtP:WR, LBJL.

126. PE/Hanoi (JS) to PFM (JM), sz. 15205, 30 Nov 1966, AMSZ, trans. MG.

127. Ferenc Hidvégi, Hungarian chargé d'affaires, Hanoi, 153 / top. sec. / 1966, report on 29 Nov 1966 JL talk, 13 Dec 1966, Vietnamese Relations, 1966, Foreign Ministry Documents, Top Secret, 112. Doboz, IV-43-005238/1/1966, XiX-J-1-j, MOL, obt./trans. Z. Szoke; also CzE/Hanoi (Mucha) to CzFM, tel. 12180, 7 Dec 1966, AMZV, obt./trans. G. Laron.

128. Candel Saigon (VCM) to CDEA, tel. 1116, 5 Dec 1966, file 20-22-VIETS-2-1, pt. 8, vol. 9398, RG 25, NAC. On Rahman's own vain efforts in Hanoi to promote a "gradual de-escalation," see the Soviet record of his 26 Nov 1966 talk with Shcherbakov, AVPRF, f. 079, op. 21, p. 51, d. 8. Rahman was "apparently quite shaken by the self evident determination of the North to continue the war." *Chubb's Folly,* 30 Nov 1966 entry.

129. GD'O, *DV,* 707 (16 Nov 1966).

130. JL interview, Warsaw, June 2003.

Chapter 5

1. On 1 Dec 1966 JL-GD'O meeting, see GD'O, *DV,* 711–12 (1 Dec 1966), trans. IO; and IE/S (GD'O) to IFM (AF), office memos 10–11, both noon, 1 Dec 1966, GD'O dossier.

2. JL interview, June 2003.

3. HCL in Danang: Poldel Saigon (JL) to PFM (AR), sz. 15313, 9 a.m., 2 Dec 1966, AMSZ, obt./trans. LG; JL interview, Warsaw, June 2003; Saigon embtel 12711 (HCL), 7 Dec 1966, Vietnam NODIS Vol. IV (A) 7/66-12/66, NSF:CO:VN, box 47, LBJL; HCL to Lt. Gen. Walt, 3 Dec 1966, reel 24, HCLP , MHS.

4. GD'O, *DV,* 711 (30 Nov 1966).

5. IE/S (GD'O) to IFM (AF), office memos 10-11, both noon, 1 Dec 1966, GD'O dossier.

6. Saigon embtel 12247 (HCL), 1 Dec 1966, *FRUS, 1964–68,* 4:890–91.

7. On 1 Dec 1966 JL-HCL-GD'O meeting (unless otherwise noted), see Saigon embtels12247 (HCL), 1 Dec 1966, *FRUS, 1964–68,* 4:890–94, and 12323 (HCL), 1 Dec 1966, box 147, NSF:CO:VN,

LBJL; IE/S (GG'O) to IFM (AF), office memos 12-18, all noon, 2 Dec 1966, GD'O dossier; Poldel Saigon (JL) to PFM (AR), sz. 15313, 9 a.m., 2 Dec 1966, AMSZ, obt./trans. LG; JL interviews, Warsaw, June 2003; and GD'O, *DV,* pp. 713-6 (1 Dec 1966).

8. These were the ten points as reported by HCL in Saigon embtel 12247, 1 Dec 1966. For Italian and Polish versions—consistent save minor differences attributable to translation—see IE/S (GD'O) to IFM (AF), office memos 12–14, all noon, 2 Dec 1966, GD'O dossier; Poldel Saigon (JL) to PFM (AR), sz. 15398, 4 Dec 1966, AMSZ, trans. MG; and JL's own contemporaneous handwritten versions (in both Polish and English) of his presentation of the ten points to HCL, courtesy of JL. A comparison with the Vietnamese records of JL's 20 Nov 1966 presentations in Hanoi of his 14–15 Nov 1966 talks with HCL suggests they bore a close, if not exact, resemblance to the ten points he presented on 1 Dec 1966. LVL/NAV, *Before Paris,* 163–66, trans. MP (courtesy C. Goscha) and Lien-Hang T. Nguyen. The combination of U.S., Polish, Italian, and Vietnamese sources, then, suggests the "ten points" came into being through the following process: Before leaving Saigon on 18 Nov, JL prepared summaries of his 14–15 Nov talks with HCL, which he presented in Hanoi on 20 Nov; these documents contained language congruent to points 1 and 3–10 (albeit in different sequence); as a result of his talks with PVD on 25 and 28 Nov, JL added point 2, which also seemed consistent with U.S. statements; by the time he saw HCL in Saigon on 1 Dec, JL had distilled and reordered what he believed Hanoi and Washington could accept into the ten points.

9. IE/S (GD'O) to IFM (AF), office memo 16, noon, 2 Dec 1966, GD'O dossier.

10. Poldel Saigon (JL) to PFM (AR), sz. 15313, 2 Dec 1966, AMSZ.

11. Poldel Saigon (JL) to PFM (JM), sz. 15542, 7 Dec 1966, AMSZ, trans. MG.

12. JL interview, Warsaw, June 2003.

13. In his ciphergram 15313 reporting the 1 Dec 1966 meting with HCL and GD'O, JL assured AR that after recapitulating the U.S. stand he "presented the formulation as per Your [ciphergram] 12158." That message is missing from the AMSZ dossier containing ciphergrams to Saigon for Nov–Dec 1966, but MR reproduces the text.

14. JL interviews, Warsaw, June 2003.

15. Saigon embtel 12237 (HCL), 1 Dec 1966, cited above, and IE/S (GD'O) to IFM (AF), office memo 17, noon, 2 Dec 1966, GD'O dossier.

16. JL interview, Warsaw, June 2003.

17. Ibid.

18. IE/S (GD'O) to IFM (AF), office memo 18, noon, 2 Dec 1966, GD'O dossier.

19. GD'O diary, 1 Dec 1966.

20. DR-RSM telcons, 1:20 p.m. and 2:48 p.m., 1 Dec 1966, box 57, DR Papers, entry 5379, RG 59, NA II.

21. Deptel 94660 (to American Embassy, Saigon), 5:33 p.m., 1 Dec 1966, box 147, NSF:CO:VN, LBJL.

22. However, HCL did not exclude further probing or even a possible JL return trip to Hanoi to convey "any clarification or modification of the points which we would propose." Saigon embtel 12323 (HCL), rec'd 10:59 pm, 1 Dec 1966, POL 27-14 VIET/XYZ 11-1-65, box 22/22, FTSCPF.

23. NK, *Some of It Was Fun: Working with RFK and LBJ* (New York: W. W. Norton, 2008), 230–35.

24. WAH to NK, 4 Oct 1966, *FRUS, 1964–68,* 4:548 n. 1.

25. Ex-officials agreed that in cutting off CLC, WAH, and others from Marigold cables beginning 1 Dec 1966, DR likely acted to control policy rather than from security concerns. CLC, Hughes, NK interviews, April 2005.

26. Memo of meeting, Gov. Harriman's office, 4 p.m., 1 Dec 1966, Vietnam—General—Oct-Dec 1966, box 520, WAHP-LC. Subsequent quotations and descriptions of this meeting are from this document.

27. WAH's 29 Nov–14 Dec 1966 trip to England, France, Tunisia, Algeria, and Spain: boxes 553–54, 569, WAHP-LC. Though cut out of the latest Marigold cable traffic, and though WAH carefully avoided disclosing the channel himself, several of his contacts offered relevant perspectives, particularly two talks in Paris on 2 Dec. Stressing DRV distrust, Sainteny advised that, rather than publicized missions by special emissaries, "Vietnam can only be brought to

negotiate through secret discussions carried on by individuals in whom the Vietnamese have confidence and who they know also have the ear of the adversaries"—a description fitting Sainteny himself but also JL. "The Vietnamese like an aura of mystery, conspiracy and secrecy to surround their negotiations," he said. Separately, while urging Washington to do more to exploit intracommunist tensions (Sino-Vietnamese and Hanoi-NLF), Etienne Manac'h, the Quai d'Orsay Asian affairs director, proposed a formula almost identical to the still-secret Phase A/B concept to surmount the bombing stalemate.

28. Read "cut the squad" of Marigold-cleared officials (removing Isham) after mid-November, write DK and SHL, *Secret Search*, 44; LBJ himself ordered the "sharp reduction in the number of people permitted to read the relevant telegrams," notes CLC, *The Lost Crusade: America in Vietnam* (New York: Dodd, Mead, 1970), 335. However, documents suggest DR put this limit into effect on the afternoon of 1 Dec 1966; LBJ, in Texas, only received HCL's cable that night. Moreover, CLC considered Read "one of us" (i.e., comparatively dovish), so it is unlikely that he would unilaterally have excluded CLC and WAH (and others), who routinely handled sensitive matters, including Marigold; CLC interview, 10 Apr 2005. Hence, DR probably took the initiative to slash the roster; see also George C. Herring, *LBJ and Vietnam: A Different Kind of War* (Austin: University of Texas Press, 1994), 105–6.

29. NK interview, Princeton, N.J., 17 Apr 2005.

30. See *FRUS, 1964–68*, 4:843 n. 1.

31. CLC and DR: interviews with CLC, St. Simons Island, Ga., 10 Apr 2005, and NK, Princeton, N.J., 17 Apr 2005.

32. CLC interview, Saint Simons Island, Ga., 10 Apr 2005.

33. WWR to LBJ, 17 Nov 1966, *FRUS, 1964–68*, 4:853–56.

34. Memo of meeting, Gov. Harriman's office, 4 pm., 1 Dec 1966, cited above.

35. CLC interview, Saint Simons Island, Ga., 10 Apr 2005.

36. LBJ diary, 1 Dec 1966, box 9, PDD, LBJL.

37. WWR to LBJ, CAP661134, 1 Dec 1966, rec'd LBJ Ranch CommCen 8:08 p.m., and WWR to LBJ, CAP661136 (containing HCL cable), 1 Dec 1966, rec'd LBJ Ranch CommCen 11:45 p.m., both box 147, NSF:CO:VN, LBJL.

38. WWR to LBJ, 1 Dec 1966, CAP661134, cited above.

39. DR-WWR telcon, 9:02 a.m., 2 Dec 1966, box 57, DR Records, entry 5379, RG 59, NA II.

40. On the pre–December 2 poor weather, see *WP*, 28 Nov and 3 Dec 1966; *NYT*, 28 and 29 Nov 1966; 1 and 3 Dec 1966 ("monsoons"); Wayne Thompson, *To Hanoi and Back: The U.S. Air Force and North Vietnam, 1966–1973* (Washington, D.C.: Smithsonian Institution Press, 2000), 39, 43; a secret Air Force history of Rolling Thunder noted that Pacific Air Force commanders, worried about possible "excessive civilian casualties" in a strike on Van Dien, "stressed that extraordinary precautions should be taken to insure accuracy. The [Seventh Air Force] was directed to use only experienced, carefully prebriefed pilots and to attack only in weather permitting positive visual acquisition of target and delivery of ordnance. . . . Seven attempts to strike the target in November were canceled because of adverse weather." *Project CHECO Report: Rolling Thunder July 1965–December 1966*, 98.

41. *WP*, 3 Dec 1966; *NYT*, 3 Dec 1966; WH Situation Room (McCafferty) to LBJ, CAP661137 ("clouds", 194 planes), 2 Dec 1966, Vietnam cables (A), vol. 62 12/66, box 38, NSF:CO:VN, LBJL; *Project CHECO Report: Rolling Thunder July 1965–December 1966*, 99 (9 of 175 buildings); DK and SHL, *Secret Search*, 39.

42. PAVN liaison chief to the ICSC in Vietnam, 03100 [10 a.m., 3 Dec 1966], 597/QS/I/B, File 21-13-VIET-ICSC-8, FP 8.3, vol. 10129, RG 25, NAC, and *NYT*, 4 Dec 1966. JL cited a report from Polish military attaché Kurniwicz to GD'O: IE/Saigon (GD'O) to IFM (AF), office memo 35, 6:45 p.m., 8 Dec 1966, GD'O dossier; rumor (187 civilian casualties): Saigon embtel 13064 (HCL), 10 Dec 1966, box 147, NSF:CO:VN, LBJL. Sites reported hit on December 2 included a "Polish-Vietnamese Friendship" school 150–250 meters from a targeted auto-repair shop: PE/Hanoi (JS) to PFM (AR), sz. 15571, 8 Dec 1966, AMSZ, trans. MG. According to a secret AF history, 72 SAMs were fired on 2 Dec 1966, the most in a single day since the war began and believed responsible for downing five of eight AF and Navy jets lost (along with eleven pilots

and crew) that day, also the largest one-day tally. *Project CHECO Report*, 111; *WP*, 4 Dec 1966; *NYT*, 4 Dec 1966.

43. On the first attack since June 29 see *NYT*, 3 Dec 1966. Sources give slightly varying distances between Van Dien and Hanoi's center: 4 miles (Thompson, *To Hanoi and Back*, 43); 4.4 nautical miles (Robert H. Wenzel to Benjamin H. Read, "Allegations of Civilian Damage in Hanoi Resulting from June 1966 and December 1966 Strikes," 6 Dec 1967, POL 27-14 Viet/Marigold 1967, box 2739, CFPF, 1967–69); 4–5 miles (*WP*, 3 Dec 1966); 5 miles (*NYT*, 3 Dec 1966); 5 nautical miles (editorial note, *FRUS, 1964–68*, 4:897), 6.7 nautical miles (*SDVW:NVPP*, 274).; for Ha Gia, distances ranged from 14.5 miles (*NYT*, 3 Dec 1966) to 16 nautical miles (*SDVW:NVPP*, 274).

44. DK and SHL, *Secret Search*, 53–54.

45. Ibid., 43–54; Herring echoes this interpretation ("Bureaucratic blunders and gross mismanagement may have doomed that meeting") in *LBJ and Vietnam*, 105. DK and SHL incorrectly label Unger, the deputy assistant secretary of state for East Asian and Pacific affairs, the key person aware on 1 Dec 1966 of both the latest Marigold developments and "forthcoming target plans." Declassified documents give no indication Unger knew of the latest Marigold developments before 7 Dec, when he drafted a pertinent cable. It is unlikely, then, that he learned of HCL's 1 Dec cable in time to alert policymakers to the imminent Hanoi raids, even had he wished to do so.

46. DK and SHL, *Secret Search*, 3–5, 41; see also "from source 'nn' this day, deep background, no attribution," 13 Sep 1967, box 15, SHLP.

47. NK interview, Princeton, N.J., 17 Apr 2005.

48. NK OH II, 23 Nov 1968, II-15, LBJL.

49. NK interview, Princeton, N.J., 17 Apr 2005; NK appointments calendar, 1 Dec 1966, box 5, NK Papers, JFKL.

50. Read OH-I, 13 Jan 1969, I-10, LBJL.

51. Ibid.

52. CLC OH-II, 17 Jul 1969, 22–23, LBJL.

53. RSM note ("McN says:"), n.d., folder 10, box 50, Brandon Papers, LC.

54. DR OH-II, tape 1, 26 Sep 1969, 31, LBJL.

55. DR, *As I Saw It*, edited by Daniel S. Papp (New York: W. W. Norton, 1990), 468.

56. WWR to LBJ, 9 Nov 1966, *FRUS, 1964–68*, 4:812–13; also Gibbons, IV, 465–66.

57. LBJ-RSM telcon, 2:51 p.m., 9 Nov 1966, *FRUS, 1964–68*, 4:816–17.

58. WPB OH 4, 2 Jun 1969, 17–18, LBJL.

59. White House Situation Room (McCafferty) to LBJ, CAP661137, 2 Dec 1966, rec'd Washington 5:56 a.m., rec'd LBJ Ranch 6:55 a.m., Vietnam cables (A), vol. 62 12/66 folder, box 38, NSF: CO:VN, LBJL

60. DR-WWR telcon, 9:02 a.m., 2 Dec 1966, box 57, DR Records, entry 5379, RG 59, NA II.

61. Asked if JL had presented Phase A/B "fully and accurately" to Hanoi, HCL cabled that JL "merely . . . impli[ed] that he had given his presentation in accordance with your formulation." Deptel 94660 (to American Embassy, Saigon), 5:33 p.m., 1 Dec 1966, box 147, NSF:CO:VN, LBJL; Saigon embtel 12323 (HCL), rec'd 10:59 p.m., 1 Dec 1966, POL 27-14 VIET/XYZ 11-1-65, box 22, FTSCPF.

62. From "wjj" [William J. Jorden] to WWR, "Marigold," n.d. [1 or 2 Dec 1966], box 147, NSF: CO:VN, LBJL.

63. Agenda for 3 Dec 1966 DR-LBJ meeting: WWR to LBJ, 2 Dec 1966, Walt Rostow Vol. 16 [3 of 3] 1–13 Dec 1966, box 11 [2 of 2], NSF:MtP:WR, LBJL.

64. WPB to DR, 2 Dec 1966, POL 27-14 Viet/Marigold 1966, box 2739, CFPF, 1967–69.

65. WWR to LBJ, CAP661179, 5 Dec 1966, and deptel 98754 (to American Embassy, Warsaw), 7 Dec 1966, both box 147, NSF:CO:VN, LBJL; and NK interview, 17 Apr 2005.

66. On "tilted," see DR-WPB telcon, 26 Feb 1968, box 61, DR Papers, entry 5379, RG 59, NA II; on "concoction," see 4 Mar 1977 WPB interview by Wallace J. Thies, *When Governments Collide: Coercion and Diplomacy in the Vietnam Conflict, 1964–1968* (Berkeley: University of California Press, 1980), 146 n. 6; "wretched": WPB OH 4, 2 Jun 1969, 19, LBJL; "Metternich": WPB

interview notes, 2 Jan 1968, box 15, SHLP; "mish-mash": NK interview notes, 13 Nov 1967, box 15, SHLP (DK and SHL, *Secret Search*, 38, cites "American officials"); and "ballpark": CLC OH-II, 20, LBJL.

67. CLC, *Lost Crusade*, 337; CLC interview, Washington, 8 Dec 2005. Other officials echoed his assessment.

68. See draft cables to American Embassy, Saigon, and American Embassy, Warsaw, 2 Dec 1966, in Chron.-Jan. 1966, box 20, LET Papers, RG 59, NA II; notations indicate LET authored both.

69. Deptel 95709 (to American Embassy, Saigon), 2 Dec 1966, box 147, NSF:CO:VN, LBJL.

70. Jenkins was awarded undergraduate and master's degrees from Harvard University (in 1941 and 1948), served as an Army lieutenant-colonel during World War II, and taught political science at the University of Texas before joining the State Department in 1948. His subsequent career there included, in addition to posts in Washington, stints as a political officer in Taipei (1952–55) and Berlin (1955–57) and principal officer in Poznan, Poland (1961–63). He succeeded Albert W. Sherer as JAG's deputy chief of mission in July 1966. I thank the National Security Archive's M. Byrne and M. Klotzbach for locating this information from the 1973 and 1977 editions of the State Department's *Biographic Register;* also Jenkins interview by Charles Stuart Kennedy, 20 Feb 1991, FAOHC.

71. Deptel 95711 (to American Embassy, Warsaw), 2 Dec 1966, *FRUS, 1964–68*, 4:898–99. Had the initial contact led to ongoing talks, officials planned to send a more senior figure to Warsaw to oversee them—perhaps WAH. NK interview, Princeton, N.J., 17 Apr 2005.

72. NK interview, Princeton, NJ, 17 Apr 2005; NK-DR 8 p.m. night-cap: desk calendar, box 5, NK Papers, JFKL; desk calendar, box 3, DR Papers, LBJL; also NK, *Some of It Was Fun,* 215. Corroborating NK, another senior figure recalled that a DR drawback was "the extraordinary reserve with which he treated people, even those whom he knew quite well. . . . He would listen to what subordinates had to say and give no indication of his reaction, either in words or in expression on his round Buddha face. (He once told me he looked like a bartender.) He confided in no one. He carried his reserve to the point where it hurt him. Subordinates in the State Department felt alienated and were reluctant to approach him." Charles E. Bohlen, *Witness to History, 1929–1969* (New York: W. W. Norton, 1973), 527.

73. For Warsaw weather in December 1966, I thank MG for compiling reports from microfilmed editions of *Życie Warszawy* in the Biblioteka Narodowa in Warsaw, used in conjunction with daily *NYT* and *WP* weather tables.

74. Unlike HCL, who had cabled his report late Thursday evening, 1 Dec 1966, JL only sent his secret telegram (sz. 15313) at 9 a.m. Friday, 2 Dec, Saigon time; it reached Warsaw at 12:20 p.m. local time and was decoded later that afternoon.

75. Unfortunately, these cables were not located, but their existence (and numbers) may be inferred from later replies from Polish diplomats in Moscow, Saigon, and Hanoi.

76. MR. JM seems to rely on a contemporaneous document but does not quote, cite, or date it explicitly. He wrote, "Upon informing Pham Van Dong that we are waiting for Ambassador Gronouski to turn to us on 6 December in this matter, we asked for a reply to a series of questions." However, JM's statement seems incompatible with evidence Poland did not relay the U.S. statement (given by HCL to JL on 3 Dec 1966) agreeing to meet in Warsaw *on 6 Dec 1966* to PVD *until December 7* (see below). I thus infer from JS's report of his December 3 talk with PVD that he received these questions beforehand, rather than prior to his subsequent talk with PVD on December 7.

77. After becoming ambassador to Washington in September 1967, JM told France's envoy that "things had gone so far" in December 1966 that Poland's government "had already booked in Warsaw a pavilion house where the [U.S.-DRV] meeting could take place," and Canada's that "Polish authorities were sufficiently certain of their ground that they had started arranging accommodation for the [U.S.-DRV] discussions." A. E. Ritchie to E. Collins, 26 Sep 1967, file 20-22-VIETS-2-1, pt. 19, vol. 9400, RG 25, NAC; French ambassador in Washington (Charles Lucet) to Foreign Minister (Maurice Couve de Murville), telegrams 4832-4836, 9/26/67, Asie-Océanie, Conflit Vietnam, vol. 157, Ministère des Affaires Étrangères Français Archives, Paris, courtesy G. Martin.

78. PE/Hanoi (JS) to PFM (AR), with notations by JM, sz. 15353, 3 Dec 1966, AMSZ, trans. MG.

79. Saigon embtel 12434 (HCL), 3 Dec 1966, box 38, NSF:CO:VN, LBJL; HCL emotion: GD'O, *DV,* 719 (3 Dec 1966); timing: at 9:50 a.m. Saturday, JL cabled Warsaw that another meeting with HCL had been scheduled for that afternoon: Poldel Saigon (JL) to PFM (JM), sz. 15351, 3 Dec 1966, AMSZ, trans. MG.

80. On 3 Dec 1966 HCL-JL-GD'O meeting, see Saigon embtel 12428 (HCL), 3 Dec 1966, *FRUS, 1964–68,* 4:900–901; MR; Poldel Saigon (JL) to PFM (AR), sz. 15388, 11:30 p.m., 3 Dec 1966, AMSZ, obt./trans. LG; GD'O, *DV,* 719–21 (3 Dec 1966); IE/S (GD'O) to IFM (AF), office memos 19-24, all 6:45 p.m., 3 Dec 1966, GD'O dossier; and JL interviews, Warsaw, June 2003.

81. JL's cable otherwise accurately reporting the U.S. statement quoted it as saying that several points were the "subject *of* important differences of interpretation" [in English; emphasis added] rather than the correct wording, which was that some points were "subject *to* important differences of interpretation" (emphasis added). JL dismissed the discrepancy as unimportant. JL interview, Warsaw, June 2003 interview.

82. Ibid.

83. Ibid.

84. A summary of U.S. military activities that day noted that aside from "armed reconnaissance sorties" over North Vietnam "poor weather in the North caused some missions to be cancelled or diverted to other targets." "Situation Room Report for the President—Saturday December 3, 1966," CAP66154, box 38, NSF:CO:VN, LBJL.

85. JL interview, Warsaw, June 2003.

86. GD'O and HCL later described scotch as the libation of choice, "poured at all the meetings," while JL recalled wine as the only alcoholic beverage. Notes of interviews with HCL, 12 Oct 1967, and GD'O ("poured at all the meetings"), 1 Dec 1967, both box 15, SHLP; JL interview, Warsaw, June 2003.

87. HCL interview notes, 12 Oct 1967; DK and SH, *Secret Search,* 41.

88. Poldel Saigon (JL) to PFM (AR), sz. 15388, 3 Dec 1966, AMSZ, obt./trans. LG.

89. In a talk with LBJ on 19 Sep 1966, RSM was "more and more convinced that we ought definitely to plan on termination of the bombing in the north" after the November elections. *FRUS, 1964–68,* 4:649. RSM took Marigold seriously; as noted below, in early 1967 he told LBJ that a pronegotiations faction of the DRV leadership "was in the ascendancy during the latter part of last year and was prepared to start negotiations in December but was deterred from doing so by our bombing attacks [on Hanoi] of December 13 and 14," and in mid-1968 he told HCL that he had had "high hopes" for Marigold and "believed that these talks might have shortened the war by two years." RSM to LBJ, 9 Mar 1967, Mar 1967 [3 of 8], box 25, William Gibbons Papers, LBJL; Gibbons, IV, 496 n. 47; and HCL-RSM memcon, U.S. Embassy, Bonn / Bad Godesberg, 1 Jul 1968, reel 26, HCL Papers, MHS.

90. GD'O, *DV,* 720–21 (3 Dec 1966).

91. Jenkins interview, FAOHC, LC. After the first Marigold cable arrived, JAG later told SHL, a Marine guard (informed by a cipher clerk) awakened him with news of an urgent cable requiring his immediate attention, and he rushed to the embassy in the dead of night to read it; SHL and DK presented this as fact in their book: SHL, JAG interview notes, 12 Dec 1967, box 41, SHLP, *Secret Search,* 56–57. Given evidence presented below that JAG exaggerated the extent to which he was informed that weekend, his account must be treated with caution.

92. Just a few weeks before, he had drawn Washington's attention to a comment by Deputy Foreign Minister Winiewicz that "Poland's fingers were burned badly after Harriman's visit," but a bombing halt would "create [an] entirely different situation and Poland would do what it could to bring negotiations about." Warsaw embtel 1172 (JAG), 10 Nov 1966, POL 27 VIET S 11/10/66, box 3012, CFPF, 1964–66.

93. Jenkins interview, FAOHC, LC.

94. Warsaw embtel (JAG) 1359, 3 Dec 1966, rec'd 5:27 a.m., box 147, NSF:CO:VN, LBJL. Robert Haney, a public affairs officer with excellent French and prior Vietnamese experience, could translate, JAG noted.

95. Deptel 96255 (to American Embassy, Warsaw), 3 Dec 1966, sent 2:32 p.m., box 147, NSF:CO:VN, LBJL.

96. Tom Johnson, memo for Marie Fehmer and Mary Slater, and PDD, both 3 Dec 1966, box 9, PDD, LBJL.

97. See HCL-RSM memcon, 1 Jul 1968, reel 26, HCL Papers, MHS.

98. DR OH II, tape 1, 26 Sep 1969, 14, LBJL; on DR's skepticism toward Marigold, see *As I Saw It,* 466–68.

99. LBJ-DR telcon, 25 Dec 1966, *FRUS, 1964–68,* 4:973 n. 6.

100. WPB OH 4, 2 Jun 1969, 19–20, LBJL.

101. David Halberstam, *The Best and the Brightest* (New York: Ballantine Books, 1969), 65–66.

102. From 2 Dec 1966 entry, AFD, trans. IO.

103. On 3 Dec 1966 Willmann-AF talk, see PE/Rome (Willmann) to PFM (Naszkowski), sz. 15399, 3 Dec 1966, AMSZ, trans. MG. AF retreat: PE/Rome (Willmann) to PFM (Winiewicz), sz. 11065, 25 Aug 1966, ibid.

104. Saigon embtel 12400 (HCL), 4 Dec 1966, box 147, NSF:CO:VN, LBJL.

105. Candel Saigon (VCM) to CDEA, 5 Dec 1966, tel. 1114, "Vietnam: Military Indications and Mutual Deescalation," and Candel Saigon (VCM) to CDEA, 5 Dec 1966, tel. 1117, "Vietnam: Prospects," both in file 20-22-VIETS-2-1, pt. 8, vol. 9398, RG 25, NAC.

106. The account of the following exchange uses Saigon embtel 12392 (HCL), 4 Dec 1966, POL 27-14 Viet/Marigold 1/1/66, box 3020, CFPF, 1964–66, and Candel Saigon (VCM), 5 Dec 1966, tel. 1116, "Vietnam: Prospects," file 100-11-3, pt. 1 [pt. 2], vol. 9516, NAC, and file 20-22-VIETS-2-1, pt. 8, vol. 9398, NAC.

107. VCM's claim (per HCL's cable) that GD'O "rushed to see" JL after returning from Hanoi was in error: JL visited GD'O on December 1, not vice versa.

108. VCM did not name his source but said "the question" of JL's involvement in secret peace contacts "was raised with me informally on the Vietnamese side with the additional indications," beyond Rahman's suspicions, of secret meetings involving JL, HCL, and GD'O. Candel Saigon (VCM), 5 Dec 1966, tel. 1116, "Vietnam: Prospects." GD'O and perhaps HCL suspected that VCM had had JL tailed: GD'O, *DV,* 763 (19 Jan 1967).

109. GD'O, *DV,* 721 (4 Dec 1966).

110. On 4 Dec 1966 Saigon attacks, see *NYT,* 4 and 5 Dec 1966; *WP,* 4 and 5 Dec 1966; Poldel Saigon (JL) to PFM (Spasowski), sz. 15460, 5 Dec 1966, AMSZ, trans. MG.

111. *NYT,* 5 Dec 1966 (1,000-foot column, 500+ bombs); *Project CHECO Report: Rolling Thunder July 1965–December 1966,* 98 (20 sorties, 96 750-pound bombs, "smoke"); Thompson, *To Hanoi and Back,* 43; Ronald B. Frankum Jr., *Like Rolling Thunder: The Air War in Vietnam, 1964–1975* (Lanham, Md.: Rowman & Littlefield, 2005), 51; *WP,* 5 Dec 1966; *SDVW:NVPP,* 274; Yen Vien's distance from Hanoi's center is given as 5 nautical miles in Wenzel to Read, "Allegations of Civilian Damage in Hanoi Resulting from June 1966 and December 1966 Strikes," 6 Dec 1967, cited above.

112. *SDVW:NVPP,* 232.

113. HVL to Rahman, 2:10 p.m., 4 Dec 1966, File 21-13-VIET-ICSC-8, FP 8.3, Vol. 10129, RG 25, NAC.

114. On "recapitulation," see Poldel Saigon (JL) to PFM (AR), sz. 15398, 4 Dec 1966, AMSZ, trans. MG; on gunfire, see Poldel Saigon (JL) to PFM (Spasowski), sz. 15460, 5 Dec 1966, ibid.

115. JL interviews, Warsaw, June 2003.

116. *NYT,* 5 Dec 1966; *WP,* 5 Dec 1966.

117. As noted above, JL had agreed on 1 Dec 1966 that "must" could be changed to "would."

118. Saigon embtel 12399 (HCL), 4 Dec 1966, box 147, NSF:CO:VN, LBJL.

119. *WP,* 2 Dec 1966.

120. Saigon embtel 12399 (HCL), 4 Dec 1966, as above.

121. Saigon embtel 12400 (HCL), ibid.

122. Saigon embtel 12392 (HCL), 4 Dec 1966, POL 27-14 Viet/Marigold 1/1/66, box 3020, CFPF, 1964–66.

123. On 4 Dec 1966 JL-VCM meeting, see Candel Saigon (VCM) to CDEA, tel. 1116, "Vietnam: Prospects," 5 Dec 1966, file 20-22-VIETS-2-1, pt. 8, vol. 9398, RG 25, NAC.
124. JL interview, Warsaw, 20 Oct 2006.
125. Candel Saigon (VCM) to CDEA, tel. 1116, "Vietnam: Prospects," 5 Dec 1966, as above.
126. Appointment Calendar, 3–4 Dec 1966, box 3, DR Papers, LBJL; also DK and SHL, *Secret Search,* 66.
127. WWR to LBJ, 2:32 p.m., 4 Dec 1966, CAP 661168, with HCL cables 12392 (VCM's identity sanitized) and 12399, box 147, NSF:CO:VN, LBJL.
128. [SHL,] JAG interview notes, Warsaw, 11 Dec 1967, box 41, SHLP.
129. DK and SHL, *Secret Search,* 56–57.
130. JAG OH II, 10 Feb 1969, II-16, LBJL.
131. Poldel Saigon (JL) to PFM (AR), sz. 15388, 3 Dec 1966, AMSZ, obt./trans. LG.
132. MR.
133. *NYT,* 5 Dec 1966; *WP,* 5 Dec 1966.
134. JL interviews, Warsaw, Jun 2003.
135. JM note on Poldel Saigon (JL) to PFM (AR), sz. 15388, 3 Dec 1966, AMSZ, obt./trans. LG, and "Remark" on Poldel Saigon (JL) to PFM (AR), sz. 15517, 6 Dec 1966, AMSZ, trans. MG. The latter cable refers to instructions contained in sz. 12338, while the "Remark" alludes to sz. 12388—one of which is evidently a typographical error. Unfortunately, the original instructions were not found. They were presumably sent sometime Monday, December 5—after JL's 3 Dec 1966 cable was decoded in Warsaw late Sunday afternoon, and before JL saw HCL and GD'O on Tuesday. See also MR.
136. JL interview, Warsaw, June 2003.
137. Candel Saigon (VCM) to CDEA, tel. 1121, "Truce Arrangements," 6 Dec 1966, file 100-11-3, pt. 1 [pt. 2], vol. 9516, NAC.
138. See deptel 96255 (to American Embassy, Warsaw), 3 Dec 1966, sent 2:32 p.m., box 147, NSF:CO:VN, LBJL.
139. MR.
140. JAG OH-II, 10 Feb 1969, p. II-16, LBJL; "relieved": MR.
141. On 5 Dec 1966 JAG-AR meeting, see Warsaw embtel 1363 (JAG), 5 Dec 1966, *FRUS, 1964–68,* 4:902–4; *SDVW:NVPP,* 275–77; JAG OH II, 10 Feb 1969, 16–17; AR, urgent note nr 484/Rap./66, 7 Dec 1966, GM sygn. 1/77 w 16, t-39, *Tajne spec. znaczenia,* AMSZ;.and MR.
142. JAG OH-II, 10 Feb 1969, II-16.
143. IFM (AF) to IE/Saigon (GD'O), office memo, 5 Dec 1966 (rec'd 6 Dec 1966), GD'O dossier.
144. From 5 Dec 1966 entry, AFD diary, trans. IO.
145. WWR to LBJ, n.d. [5 Dec 1966], box 147, NSF:CO:VN, LBJL.
146. WWR to LBJ, CAP661179, 5 Dec 1966, ibid; Deptel 97016 to U.S. Embassy in Poland (JAG), 5 Dec 1966, 8:58 p.m., *FRUS, 1964–68,* 4:905.
147. WWR to LBJ, 5 Dec 1966, in box 11 [2 of 2], NSF:MtP:WR, LBJL.

Chapter 6

1. Quoted from MR.
2. Poldel Saigon (JL) to PFM (AR), sz. 15517, 6 Dec 1966, AMSZ, trans. MG.
3. Wilson's 7 Feb 1967 remark to Parliament actually alluded to the possibility of a JL-HCL misunderstanding.
4. Poldel Saigon (JL) to PFM (AR), sz. 15388, 3 Feb 1966, AMSZ, obt./trans. LG; JL interviews, Warsaw, June 2003. The extraordinarily long transmission time—more than eighteen hours—perhaps reflected what JM told JAG on 6 Dec were "technical difficulties of communicating with Hanoi"; Maneli noted that even "flash" Polish ICC communications from Saigon were sent to Warsaw via the Polish Embassy in Hanoi. Warsaw embtel 1376, 7 Dec 1966, box 147, NSF:CO:VN, LBJL; Mieczyslaw Maneli, *War of the Vanquished* (New York: Harper & Row, 1971), 142. GD'O rued JL's "less favorable situation regarding the speed of his communications

with Warsaw" compared to HCL's ability to obtain rapid replies from Washington. GD'O, *DV*, 711 (1 Dec 1966).

5. LVL/NAV, *Before Paris*, 167, trans. MP (courtesy C. Goscha) and Lien-Hang T. Nguyen.

6. However, there is no evidence the Poles actually sent any such cable.

7. Even if sent from Hanoi on Saturday or Sunday, the cable could not have reached DPQ by Monday morning. A former DRV Foreign Ministry aide said sending a cable from Hanoi to Warsaw required first dispatching it to the DRV Embassy in Moscow, which had to retransmit it to the Warsaw Embassy, where it had to be decoded and given to the ambassador. Any step could delay the process, although the ex-diplomat (who served in New Delhi, Moscow, Geneva, etc.) said cipher clerks worked over weekends. Luu doan Huynh interview, Washington, June 2005.

8. Xuan Ba, "The Man Who Interpreted Negotiators' Fighting Words," Vietnam News Service, 20 Jan 2003.

9. HAK, *Ending the Vietnam War* (New York: Simon & Schuster, 2002), 321.

10. NDP interview, Hanoi, 8 Jun 1999; and RSM, James G. Blight, and Robert K. Brigham with Thomas J. Biersteker and Col. Herbert Y. Schandler, *Argument Without End: In Search of Answers to the Vietnam Tragedy* (New York: PublicAffairs, 1999), xx–xxi.

11. As ambassador to Sweden, NDP was also accredited to other Scandinavian countries; however, he did not take up this post until long after Marigold; CLC, *In the Shadows of History: Fifty Years Behind the Scenes of Cold War Diplomacy* (Amherst, N.Y.: Prometheus Books, 2005), 246, mistakenly identifies him as "ambassador to Scandinavia" in December 1966. HVL recalls that when Marigold took place, NDP was "only an interpreter" rather than a substantive contributor to DRV diplomacy. HVL interview by MG, Hanoi, 19 Oct 2005.

12. LVL/NAV, *Before Paris*, 167, trans. MP (courtesy C. Goscha) and Lien-Hang T. Nguyen.

13. NDP's initial account came during a conference in Hanoi on 20–23 Jun 1997 (22 Jun afternoon session) organized by James G. Blight of Brown University's Thomas J. Watson Jr. Institute for International Studies together with the National Security Archive, the Institute for International Relations in Hanoi, and the CWIHP.

14. Kindly delivered to NDP in Hanoi in July 1998 by David Wolff.

15. The account presented below is, unless otherwise indicated, based on the author's interview with NDP, 8 Jun 1999, Hanoi; NDP, "The 'Marigold' Drive," a nine-page manuscript, n.d., presented to the author on that occasion; and a 4 Jan 2000 letter from NDP to the author, kindly delivered by Luu doan Huynh.

16. The conjunction of NDP's mission and the air raids seems consistent with Wilfred Burchett's rather hazy claim a year later to U.S. officials that the "North Vietnamese had agreed to talk at Warsaw last December and even had [an] official en route when U.S. resumed bombing Hanoi." Paris embtel 7540 (Wallner), 6 Dec 1967, Burchett folder, box 2, WAH Papers, lot 71D 461, RG 59, NA II; Burchett made no mention of such a claim in his own extensive English-language report of the conversation, enclosed with Tadeusz Mulicki, chief delegate, ICC Poldel, Cambodia, to Comrade JL, vice director, Dept. V, MSZ, 17 Jan 1968, D II Wietn.-0-22-1-71, AMSZ. U.S. officials and scholars have largely dismissed his assertion: "Burchett's claim, . . ." Thies wrote, "should be treated with skepticism, since he was obviously not an impartial observer." WPB (in a 4 Mar 1977 interview) said he knew of no evidence Hanoi actually sent an emissary to Warsaw. Wallace J. Thies, *When Governments Collide: Coercion and Diplomacy in the Vietnam Conflict, 1964–1968* (Berkeley: University of California Press, 1980), 340 n. 83.

17. They also, NDP recalled, made no reference to any problem with the "important differences of interpretation" clause that so bedeviled U.S.-Polish exchanges from 3 to 9 Dec 1966.

18. In a 4 Jan 2000 letter to the author, NDP clarified that NCT did not tell him the proposed date of the U.S.-DRV meeting and that he only learned of it from DPQ upon reaching Warsaw.

19. Aeroflot launched a Moscow-Hanoi route (via Karachi and Calcutta) on 5 Oct 1970: R.E.G. Davies, *Aeroflot: An Airline and Its Aircraft: An Illustrated History of the World's Largest Airline* (Rockville, Md.: Paladwr Press, 1992), 87. Aeroflot's absence of regular service to Hanoi as

of Dec 1966 (the closest stops were in Beijing and Rangoon) is confirmed by a winter 1966–67 timetable provided to the author by Davies.

20. Investigation virtually excluded the possibility that NDP started his journey to Moscow (and thence to Warsaw) by taking an ICC flight from Hanoi. The Dec 1966 ICC schedule indicated a 4 a.m. departure from Hanoi on Saturday, 3 Dec (after arriving from Vientiane at 7:10 p.m. Friday): MOVIET SAIGON to IC BUREAU, HANOI, 15 Nov 1966, in file 100-11-5-2, pt. 1 [part 2], vol. 9518, RG 25, NAC; passenger manifests and flight records for late Nov and early Dec 1966 were missing, so it was impossible to establish definitively whether they listed NDP as taking any flights during that period or whether the ICC flight on 3 Dec 1966 left Hanoi on schedule. Aeroflot only began service to Vientiane on 1 Oct 1970 and Phnom Penh on 12 Oct 1979: Davies, *Aeroflot*, 87. Nor did any other direct service apparently exist as of 1966 between either of those cities and Moscow; the only Soviet Bloc airline then flying directly between Eastern Europe and Indochina, Czechoslovak Airlines, offered weekly (Friday) service from Phnom Penh to Prague via Rangoon, Bombay, Bahrain, Cairo, and Belgrade: ČSA timetable, winter (1 Dec 1965–31 Mar 1966), courtesy Davies.

21. Interview with ex-DRV official, White Oak, Fla., December 1999; HES, *Behind the Lines: Hanoi, December 23, 1966–January 7, 1967* (New York: Harper & Row, 1967), 28–29.

22. NDP, personal communication to author relayed via email by Luu doan Huynh, 11 Mar 2004.

23. Conversations with Ilya V. Gaiduk, Santa Barbara, Calif., 30–31 Mar 2005.

24. For sleuthing to check flight schedules, I thank MG, who procured 1966–67 timetables (including 1 Nov 1966–31 Mar 1967) from the LOT library in Warsaw; Gina Gesmond and Carol Knight of OAG Worldwide, Chicago, who provided the reference to the *Official Airline Guide International Quick Reference Edition—December 1, 1966,* 988; and R.E.G. Davies, who shared LOT timetables from the winter of 1965–66 and for 1 April–31 Oct 1968.

25. Conversely, NDP did not recall Hanoi being bombed on the day of his departure, reinforcing his memory that he left the city on 3 Dec rather than 4 Dec. In a 4 Jan 2000 letter to the author, he wrote, "I don't think it happened on Sunday, because I left the ministry to go to NCT's house."

26. See BE/Warsaw (Brimelow) to FO, tel. 215, 7 Apr 1967, FCO 15/646, TNA.

27. Conversely, as we will see, JM's point, that the clause did not dissuade Hanoi from agreeing to the contact, had some basis.

28. JM-WAH memcon, 19 Feb 1969, POL 27-14 Viet/Marigold 1969, box 2739, CFPF, 1967–69.

29. MR.

30. Poldel Saigon (JL) to PFM (AR), sz. 15388, 3 Dec 1966, AMSZ, obt./trans. LG.

31. MR.

32. "Chronology of Events Regarding the Conversations J. Lewandowski-Lodge in the Year of 1966," n.d. [last entry 16 Dec 1966], AMSZ, trans. MG.

33. PE/Hanoi (JS) to PFM (AR), with notations by JM, sz. 15353, 3 Dec 1966, ibid.

34. DPQ, during the anti-French war, was Communist Party chief in Ben Tre Province in southern Vietnam; he then embarked on a diplomatic career, posted in the mid-1950s to Pyongyang and in the early 1960s to Moscow before becoming ambassador in Poland; email communication from Luu doan Huynh, 24 Aug 2005. A southerner from the Saigon area, DPQ served as first secretary at the DRV Embassy in Pyongyang until 1958, and then, after a stint as deputy director of the Foreign Ministry's Soviet Department, worked as counselor of the DRV Embassy in Moscow (1960–65). DPQ, the Polish Embassy in Moscow reported, carefully stuck to Hanoi's official line in fraternal contacts. PFM (Wierna) to PE/Moscow (Pszczółkowski), sz. 7476, 7 Aug 1965, and PE/Moscow (Pszczółkowski) to PFM (Morski), sz. 9837, 12 Aug 1965, both AMSZ, obt./trans. MG.

35. Suggesting Hanoi's confidence in DPQ, Communist archives disclose that, as early as June 1965, the DRV authorities had raised the possibility to Soviet comrades that direct U.S.-DRV discussions, when they eventually started in the context of a bombing halt, might occur in Warsaw at the ambassadorial level. Zoltan Szoke, "Delusion or Reality? Secret Hungarian Diplomacy during the Vietnam War," *Journal of Cold War Studies* 12, no. 4 (Fall 2010): 119–80.

36. On "effectuate," see Saigon embtel 12428 (HCL), 3 Dec 1966, in *FRUS, 1964–68,* 4:900; "entrusting": IE/S (GD'O) to IFM (AF), office memo 21, 6:45 p.m., 3 Dec 1966, GD'O dossier.

37. Warsaw embtel 1359 (JAG) and deptel 96235 (to American Embassy, Warsaw), both 3 Dec 1966, box 147, NSF:CO:VN, LBJL.

38. *FRUS, 1964–68,* 4:899, 900.

39. Moreover, NDP recalled that he and DPQ (unlike the Poles) did not consider the interpretation clause a bar to seeing the Americans—so its presence in the U.S. statement, had DPQ seen it on 5 Dec, should not have caused him to reject the planned contact. NDP interview, Hanoi, 8 Jun 1999.

40. PE/Hanoi (JS) to PFM (AR), sz. 15529, 7 Dec 1966, AMSZ, obt./trans. LG.

41. PE/Hanoi (JS) to PFM (AR), sz. 16329, 28 Dec 1966, AMSZ, trans. MG.

42. Evidently, Hanoi *never* informed Warsaw that it had sent an emissary, for if the Poles (JM in particular) had known this fact, they would surely have cited it as a powerful argument that North Vietnam was really serious about the initiative. Yet they never made such a claim—rather, the opposite. In Feb 1969, "Harriman asked [JM] whether the North Vietnamese delegation ever arrived in Warsaw. Michałowski said that it had not." JM-WAH memcon, 19 Feb 1969, cited above. Nor does MR mention a DRV emissary being sent to Warsaw in Dec 1966.

Chapter 7

1. Warsaw weather: *NYT* and *WP* summaries, 1–7 Dec 1966, and *Życie Warszawy* reports obtained by MG.

2. NDP interview, Hanoi, 8 Jun 1999; NDP, "The Marigold Drive," presented to author, 8 Jun 1999.

3. Besides describing this incident to the author in Warsaw in June 2003, JL mentioned it to GD'O two days later: The DRV authorities had telegraphed him the text of a bitter protest against the 4 Dec bombings "to be delivered to the civilized world," and he managed only "with great difficulty to dissuade Hanoi from publishing this protest (precisely on the 6th!)." IE/Saigon (GD'O) to IFM (AF), office memo 36, 8 Dec 1966, 6:45 p.m., GD'O dossier; and GD'O, *DV,* , 8 Dec 1966, in Rotondo, "The Lost Paths to Peace," *30 Days,* June 2005. For the statement Hanoi *did* publish, see *WP,* 5 Dec 1966.

4. On "squeezing," see JL interview, Warsaw, June 2003; on "encrypted": GD'O, *DV,* 721 (6 Dec 1966).

5. *NYT,* 7 Dec 1966, 2.

6. Saigon embtel 12601 (HCL), 6 Dec 1966, box 147, NSF:CO:VN, LBJL.

7. On 6 Dec 1966 HCL-JL-GD'O meeting, see ibid.; IE/Saigon (GD'O) to IFM (AF), office memos 29–32, all 6:45 p.m., 6 Dec 1966, GD'O dossier; GD'O, *DV,* 721–22 (6 Dec 1966); Poldel Saigon (JL) to PFM (AR), sz. 15517, 6 Dec 1966, AMSZ, trans. MG; JL interviews, Warsaw, June 2003.

8. JL received incongruous and likely coincidental support that day for his argument that the Hanoi attacks were diplomatically counterproductive and militarily pointless. The *Saigon Post,* an English-language daily put out by a close Ky associate (Bui Diem, later RVN ambassador to the United States), called raids on Hanoi "not worth the candle" and "urgently" urged Washington to rethink its bombing campaign. "Otherwise, instead of shortening Hanoi's resistance to coming to the conference table, we would only make its leaders more intransigent and give their acolytes in South Vietnam more reasons to believe in final victory. Indeed," the newspaper continued, "to lose eight modern jets and their valiant pilots for the poor (vehicle) depot of Viendien is like paying millions of dollars for a score of old rusty trucks ready for car cemeteries. What is worse is that such air raids also give the North Vietnamese the golden opportunities of training in air defense and some justification for the cause they pretend to be fighting for." *WP,* 7 Dec 1966.

9. IFM (AF) to IE/Saigon (GD'O), unnumbered office memo, 5 Dec 1966 (rec'd 6 Dec 1966), GD'O dossier.

10. GD'O, *DV,* 722 (6 Dec 1966).

11. JAG OH-II, 10 Feb 1969, 19, LBJL; re JAG's mindset, see also DK and SHL, *Secret Search*, 55–63; [SHL,] JAG interview notes, 11 Dec 1967, Vietnam Bombing Pause 1966–67, box 41, SHLP; JAG SFRC.

12. On 6 Dec 1966 JAG-AR meeting, see Warsaw embtel 1375 (JAG), 6 Dec 1966, box 147, NSF:CO:VN, LBJL, and *SDVW:NVPP*, 277–79; AR, urgent note nr 484/Rap./66, 7 Dec 1966, GM sygn. 1/77 w 16, t-39, *Tajne spec. znaczenia*, AMSZ, courtesy H. Szlajfer, trans. MG; and MR.

13. So JM told JAG that night: Warsaw embtel 1376 (JAG), 7 Dec 1966, box 147, NSF:CO:VN, LBJL. See also JM draft PFM cable to PE/Hanoi (JS), provided by Stefan Michałowski, discussed in the next chapter.

14. *WP*, 6 Dec 1966.

15. "Table of Comparative Military Casualties Vietnam," box 38, NSF:CO:VN, LBJL.

16. PDD, 6 Dec 1966, LBJL.

17. LBJ-RSM-JCS memcon, Austin, 6 Dec 1966, box 11 [2 of 2], NSF:MtP:WR, LBJL.

18. *Public Papers of the President: Lyndon Johnson—1966*, doc. 641; *WP*, 7 Dec 1966.

19. LBJ-RSM news conference, Austin, 6 Dec 1966: *PPOP:LBJ:1966*, doc. 642; *WP*, 7 Dec 1966.

20. LBJ-RSM telcon, 9 Nov 1966, in *FRUS*, 1964–68, 4:816–17.

21. The 6 Dec talk with RSM, the JCS, and other military officials mostly concerned weapons development issues relevant to the fiscal year 1967 budget, but at some point LBJ reportedly spoke for an hour with RSM, WWR, the JCS, and Vance "to discuss the bombing operations, including their effect on possible negotiations." Gibbons, IV, 495. Yet it is doubtful that Marigold would have been openly discussed at this stage with Vance and the JCS.

22. From 6 Dec 1966, PDD, LBJL.

23. NDP, "Marigold Drive"; NDP interview, Hanoi, 8 Jun 1999.

24. Warsaw embtel 1376 (JAG), 7 Dec 1966 (rec'd 8:25 a.m.), box 147, NSF:CO:VN, LBJL.

25. M. Dobrosielski note on conversation with Hilsman, 6 Dec 1966, Warsaw, AMSZ, trans. MG.

26. Bohlen memcon with Dobrosielski, 3 Mar 1961, Poland-General-1/61-9/61, box 153, NSF:CO, JFKL.

27. Dismissing most congressional critics (including Fulbright) as ineffective and unrealistic (because they only called for a bombing pause rather than an unconditional halt), Hilsman said only RFK (who had undergone "an unusually swift and positive political evolution" since his brother's death) could plausibly challenge LBJ's Vietnam policies.

28. [DK,] Hilsman telephone interview notes, 13 Dec 1967, Interviews folder, box 15, SHLP. Though the precise date of their conversation is not indicated, JM clearly referred to the 2 and 4 Dec (rather than 13–14) attacks, because Hilsman visited Poland from 4 to 8 Dec 1966: U.S. Embassy, Warsaw, airgram A-370 (JAG), JOINT WEEKA No. 49, p. 4, POL 2-1 POL 9/8/66, box 2592, CFPF, 1964–66.

29. Read OH-I, 13 Jan 1969, I-11, LBJL.

30. Deptel 97274 to American Embassy, Warsaw (JAG), sent 4:21 p.m., 6 Dec 1966, POL 27-14 Viet/Marigold, box 3020, CFPF, 1964–66.

31. Warsaw embtel 1375 (JAG), rec'd 6:15 p.m., 6 Dec 1966, box 147, NSF:CO:VN, LBJL.

32. *WP*, 7 Dec 1966.

33. NK interview, Princeton, N.J., 17 Apr 2005.

34. NK appointments calendar, 6 Dec 1966, box 5, NK Papers, JFKL.

35. Deptel 97930 to American Embassy, Warsaw (JAG), sent 12:03 a.m., 7 Dec 1966, box 147, NSF:CO:VN, LBJL.

36. NDP, letter to author, 4 Jan 2000.

37. LVL/NAV, *Before Paris* (2002 ed.), 167, trans. Lien-Hang Nguyen and MP. As noted above, the authors use internal DRV records at some points, but not on this episode, for which they might have relied on NDP as a primary source. If so, that would lend less credibility to NDP's account than an independent corroborative source, but would at least confirm that he was consistent, telling his story to Vietnamese colleagues, not merely to a foreign historian.

38. Luu Van Loi, *Fifty Years of Vietnamese Diplomacy 1945–1995 (Volume I: 1945–1975)* (Hanoi: Gioi Publishers, 2000), 174.

39. DR-Dobrynin memcon, "Subject: Viet-Nam—MARIGOLD," 5 Jan 1967, box 147, NSF:CO:VN, LBJL.

40. Warsaw embtel 1363 (JAG), 5 Dec 1966, in *FRUS, 1964–68*, 4:902–4.

41. A funny thing happened when JAG quoted AR's reading of HCL's December 3 statement to JL. Although the original statement read that the U.S. Embassy in Warsaw would be instructed to contact the DRV Embassy "on December 6"—U.S., Polish, and Italian sources confirm this—JAG cabled that AR had added the words "or as soon as possible thereafter" when he read the text. Because this extra phrase appears neither in Washington's instructions to HCL nor in JL's cable to AR, one may surmise that JAG himself inserted these words while reconstructing the conversation, most likely because the State Department instructions he had in fact received instructed him to arrange for an embassy officer to see the DRV ambassador "on December 6 or as soon thereafter as possible." Deptel 95711 (to American Embassy, Warsaw), 2 Dec 1966, in *FRUS, 1964–68*, 4:898–99. It seems unlikely, however, that this discrepancy reflected any meaningful JAG/AR divergence in understanding on the proposed contact's timing.

42. MR.

43. Saigon embtel 1695 (HCL), 23 Jul 1966, Book of Peace; also Saigon embtel 604 (HCL), 9 Jul 1966, cited above.

44. Saigon embtel 12399 (HCL), 4 Dec 1966, box 147, NSF:CO:VN, LBJL.

45. WWR to LBJ, 5 Dec 1966, box 11 [2 of 2], NSF:MtP:WR, LBJL.

46. HAK, "The Viet Nam Negotiations," *Foreign Affairs* 47, no. 2 (Jan. 1969): 211–34 (the quotation is on 217–18; emphases in the original). HAK reading still-classified Marigold record: Leslie H. Gelb interview, New York, 26 Jun 2003.

47. HAK, "Viet Nam Negotiations," 219.

Chapter 8

1. PVD-JS 7 Dec 1966 talk: PE/Hanoi (JS) to PFM (AR), sz. 15529, 3 p.m., 7 Dec 1966, AMSZ, obt. LG, trans. LG, JL, and MG; also MR. JS was fulfilling instructions in PFM (AR) to PE/Hanoi (JS), sz. 12419; I did not find this cable at AMSZ but on 12 Dec 2010 received from Stefan Michałowski JM's draft (apparently written late 4 Dec / early 5 Dec 1966) relating the 3 Dec 1966 JL-HCL talk, including the U.S. statement. Noting that HCL had asked MSZ's aid "to facilitate the contact," it directed JS to ask PVD five things: (1) "At what level of contact would be most appropriate? We think that sending someone especially for that purpose to Warsaw would make it difficult to keep the whole thing secret. We think that the best option would be to have Ambassador Gronouski who is the President's trusted person. At the same time, we can't exclude other American propositions." (2) "What time for a meeting would be most suitable for the DRV?" (3) "When will the DRV ambassador in Warsaw be informed about the issue and when will he receive appropriate instructions? We need to know this, because it will be necessary to discuss technical issues with him." (4) "We will secure a meeting place while guaranteeing its secrecy." (5) "In what other way can we assist our Vietnamese comrades regarding this contact?" There is no sign that PVD replied to these queries.

2. JL interview, Warsaw, June 2003.

3. PE/Hanoi (JS) to PFM (AR), sz. 16329, 28 Dec 1966, AMSZ, trans. MG.

4. PE/Hanoi (JS) to PFM (AR), sz. 15571, 8 Dec 1966, ibid.

5. Poldel Saigon (JL) to PFM (JM), sz. 15542, 7 Dec 1966, ibid.

6. JL interviews, Warsaw, June 2003.

7. WWR to LBJ, CAP661195, rec'd Washington Commcen 7:52 a.m., 7 Dec 1966, rec'd LBJ Ranch Commcen 10:18 a.m., 7 Dec 1966, box 147, NSF:CO:VN, LBJL.

8. Deptels 98753 and 09754 to American Embassy, Warsaw (JAG), 7 Dec 1966, both ibid.; 98753 noted that JAG would receive copies of the cables sent to HCL on 13–14 Nov 1966 for his meetings with JL.

9. *SDVW:NVPP*, 227–28.

10. John P. Roche OH, 16 Jul 1970, 69–70, LBJL; Saigon embtel 12953 (HCL), 9 Dec 1966, box 147, NSF:CO:VN, LBJL. After they spoke in Saigon, GD'O felt DR blamed AR's "hardening" posi-

tion on the Hanoi bombings on "firm Russian pressure": IE/Saigon (GD'O) to IFM, office memo 44, 10 Dec 1966, GD'O dossier.

11. Ilya V. Gaiduk, *The Soviet Union and the Vietnam War* (Chicago: Ivan R. Dee, 1996), 89–94.

12. *NYT*, 16 Nov and 27–30 Nov 1966, and 2 Dec 1966.

13. On 7 Dec 1966 Pszczółkowski-Brezhnev talk, see PE/Moscow (Pszczółkowski) to PFM (AR), sz. 15523, 7 Dec 1966, AMSZ, trans. MG; MR. Gromyko was out of town, with Kosygin in France.

14. Ibid.; MR quotes Brezhnev directly: "We could have helped, having the opportunity to apply pressure."

15. PE/Hanoi (JS) to PFM (Wierna), sz. 15488, 6 Dec 1966, AMSZ, trans. MG.

16. LBJ to Kosygin, 6 Dec 1966, *FRUS, 1964–68*, 4:906–8.

17. LET-Dobrynin memcon, part IV, 7 Dec 1966, Chron-Jan. 1966, box 20, LET Papers, RG 59, NA II; Gromyko later complained that LET referred to a "Polish initiative" as if to lessen Washington's role: PE/Moscow [Pszczółkowski] to PFM (AR), sz. 16134, 22 Dec 1966, AMSZ, trans. MG.

18. PE/Hanoi (JS) to PFM (AR), sz. 16329, 28 Dec 1966, ibid.; MR.

19. Henry Brandon, *Anatomy of Error* (Boston: Gambit, 1969), 77–8; MR. Brandon gives no sources, but likely spoke to JM. As Polish ambassador in Washington (1967–71)—overlapping Brandon's posting for *The Times* (London)—JM widely disseminated Warsaw's version of Marigold; Brandon's LC Papers failed to clarify the matter.

20. The reference to a "special representative" could have referred to later U.S.-DRV talks, since clearly DPQ (aided by NDP) would handle the first contact(s) with JAG.

21. JAG OH-II, 10 Feb 1969, 19, LBJL.

22. PE/Hanoi (JS) to PFM (AR), 7 Dec 1966, ciphered telegram 15529, AMSZ.

23. On 7 Dec 1966 AR-JAG talk, see Warsaw embtel 1394 (JAG), rec'd 4:31 p.m., 7 Dec 1966, *FRUS, 1964–68*, 4:912–13, AR, urgent note nr 490/Rap./66, GM sygn. 1/77 w 16, t-39, *Tajne spec. znaczenia*, AMSZ, courtesy H. Szlajfer, trans. MG; MR.

24. WWR to LBJ, CAP661207, sent to LBJ Ranch, 8:54 p.m., 7 Dec 1966, box 147, NSF:CO:VN, LBJL.

25. Deptel 98754 (NK) to American Embassy, Warsaw (JAG), sent 10:33 p.m., 7 Dec 1966, ibid.

26. RSM with Brian VanDeMark, *In Retrospect: The Tragedy and Lessons of Vietnam* (New York: Times Books, 1995), 249.

27. NK draft memo to LBJ, with insertions, n.d. [7 Dec 1966], "Department of State—Rusk," box 4/8, NK Papers, RG 59, NA II.

28. U.S. officials had learned two days earlier that Lennart Petri was due to reach Hanoi on December 12 and return to Beijing three days later: Stockholm embtel 681 (Parsons), 5 Dec 1966, POL 27-14 Viet/Aspen, CFPF, 1964–66. His visit was subsequently delayed until late January 1967: *SDVW:NVPP*, 663–71.

29. NK to LBJ, in CAP661211, 0622, 8 Dec 1966, from WH Situation Room (Brown) to Jacobsen for LBJ; also copy on State Department stationery, marked "sent to Ranch 1:22 AM, 8 Dec 66," CAP661211, Marigold," both box 147, NSF:CO:VN, LBJL.

30. "Proposed Message to Gronouski," n.d., with NK to LBJ, 8 Dec 1966, ibid.

31. The lineup of those arguing for and against suspending attacks on Hanoi during Marigold became a historical mystery akin to naming "hawks" and "doves" during the Cuban Missile Crisis. WPB correctly identified NK, RSM, and LET as having "strongly supported the recommendation that we in effect lay those authorizations [to hit Hanoi] aside and not do it again," but did not tie WWR to this advice. [WPB OH 4, 2 Jun 1969, 20, LBJL.] DK and SHL correctly put NK at the heart of opposition to further Hanoi strikes but note only that WWR backed LBJ's decision to continue the raids, without indicating he reversed an earlier stand. They also plausibly yet mistakenly identify CLC as opposing them before LBJ's decision; he later bitterly regretted the attacks but was not yet back into Marigold decisionmaking as of 8 Dec 8; DK and SHL, *Secret Search*, 63–65. JAG and HCL have been incorrectly named as urging LBJ at this juncture to avoid more Hanoi bombing; see George C. Herring, *LBJ and Vietnam: A Different Kind of War* (Austin: University of Texas Press, 1994), 106 (JAG, HCL); and Robert Dallek, *Flawed Giant: Lyndon Johnson and His Times, 1961–1973* (New York: Oxford University Press,

1998), 389 (HCL). JAG did so after the 13–14 Dec attacks; HCL sent no such advice from Saigon, and only in memoirs expressed keen regret over the 2 and 4 Dec attacks. HCL, *As It Was: An Inside View of Politics and Power in the '50s and '60s* (New York: W. W. Norton, 1976), 179–81.

32. WPB OH 4, 2 Jun 1969, 16–17, 19, LBJL.
33. See WPB comments at Negotiations Committee meeting, 16 Dec 1966, 5, box 569, WAHP-LC.
34. WPB OH 4, 2 Jun 1969, 20, LBJL.
35. Taipei embtel 1717, 8 Dec 1966, box 147, NSF:CO:VN, LBJL. LBJ saw DR's cable before responding to NK's memo later Thursday morning. WPB OH 4, 2 Jun 1969, 20, LBJL.
36. Read OH-I, 13 Jan 1969, I-11, LBJL.
37. On concealed presidential decisionmaking, see Fred I. Greenstein, *Hidden-Hand Presidency: Eisenhower as Leader* (New York: HarperCollins, 1982).
38. WPB OH 4, 2 Jun 1969, 20–21, LBJL; LBJ-WWR call timing: 8 Dec 1966, box 9, PDD, LBJL.
39. Wallace J. Thies, *When Governments Collide: Coercion and Diplomacy in the Vietnam Conflict, 1964–1968* (Berkeley: University of California Press, 1980), 354–55.
40. McNaughton diary, 11 Dec 1966, in Harrison and Mosher, "The Secret Diary of McNamara's Dove," 529.
41. LBJ, *The Vantage Point: Perspectives of the Presidency, 1963–1969* (New York: Holt, Rinehart & Winston, 1971), 251–52.
42. "Proposed Message to Gronouski," n.d., with NK to LBJ, 8 Dec 1966, box 147, NSF:CO:VN, LBJL. I thank LBJL staff for checking the handwriting on this document to confirm that LBJ or WWR did not write these words. R. Greenwell emails, 7 and 21 Nov 2005.
43. WWR to Jake Jacobsen for LBJ, CAP661214, ibid. The LBJ Ranch received this message, attaching the redrafted cable to JAG, at 10:50 a.m. on 8 Dec. For the sent cable, see deptel 98924 to American Embassy, Warsaw (JAG), 2:29 p.m., 8 Dec 1966, ibid. LBJ's decisive role in hardening the language in the cable to JAG, as described here, corroborates other accounts (while differing in particulars) pinning on LBJ the decision to continue the bombings. See, e.g., *SDVW:NVPP,* 838 n. 20; and DK and SHL, *Secret Search,* 63–65. DK and SHL say the key argument took place at the ranch on December 6 when LBJ, backed by WWR, overruled CLC and NK: "Thus, by December 6, the Administration appears to have decided (1) that Marigold had little chance of succeeding, and (2) that if it were going to succeed, the continued bombing of Hanoi would not hurt it." The present narrative depicts a process culminating in the same conclusion, but a few days later and accords with an internal JCS history indicating the decision was made on 8–9 Dec and does not mention a 6 Dec meeting: JCS-VN, part II, 36-9, and part III, 40-6, NSA.
44. NK interview, Princeton, NJ, 17 Apr 2005.
45. Poldel Saigon (JL) to PFM (Spasowski), sz. 15560, 8 Dec 1966, AMSZ, obt./trans. MG, and PFM (Spasowski) to Poldel Saigon (JL), sz. 12512, 8 Dec 1966, AMSZ, trans. MG, approving JL's request and instructing him to "urgently inform Ludwig [HVL] about our activity."
46. JL interviews, Warsaw, June 2003.
47. On 8 Dec 1966 GD'O-JL talk, see IE/S (GD'O) to IFM (AF), office memos 35-38, all 6:45 p.m., 8 Dec 1966, and office memos 39-41, all noon, 9 Dec 1966, GD'O dossier; GD'O, *DV,* 723–25 (8 Dec 1966).
48. JL had cabled the same morning that the PAVN liaison mission had reported to the ICC in Hanoi a *combined* figure of 66 dead and more than 50 injured for the 2 and 4 Dec bombings; Poldel Saigon (JL) to PFM (Spasowski), sz. 15560, 8 Dec 1966, AMSZ, obt./trans. MG.
49. GD'O, *DV,* 725 (8 Dec 1966).
50. Deptel 99476 to American Embassy, Warsaw (JAG), sent 7:23 p.m., 8 Dec 1966, in POL 27-14 Viet/Marigold, CFPF, 1964–66.
51. NDP interview, Hanoi, 8 Jun 1999, and NDP letter to author, 4 Jan 2000.
52. LBJ comments to Ball, 28 Dec 1966, *FRUS, 1964–68,* 3:733.
53. Thomas L. Hughes to DR, "Presenza: The Art and Objective of Italian Foreign Policy as Practiced by Amintore Fanfani," 7 Mar 1968, POL 1 IT 1/1/67, CFPF, 1967–69.
54. Andrzej Paczkowski, *The Spring Will Be Ours: Poland and the Poles from Occupation to Freedom* (University Park: Pennsylvania State University Press, 2003), 304–11.

55. AF comments in PE/Rome (Willmann) to PFM (Winiewicz), sz. 10099, 4 Aug 1966, and 11065, 25 Aug 1966, AMSZ, trans. MG.

56. *NYT,* 9 and 10 Dec 1966.

57. *NYT,* 9 Dec 1966; WWR to LBJ, 7 Dec 1966, CAP661209, DDRS.

58. *NYT,* 9 and 10 Dec 1966. DR was alternately quoted as saying, "There is no indication from the other side of interest in moving the problem to the conference table."

59. Poldel Saigon (JL) to PFM (Spasowski), sz. 15675, 15623, both 9 Dec 1966, AMSZ, obt./trans. MG.

60. Seeking to allay Polish skepticism regarding Italian discretion, AF reassured Willmann that he could preserve secrecy. Having obtained President Saragat's "general approval for action," he had not even informed Prime Minister Moro, and would act "only and exclusively" through the Saigon channel.

61. 9 Dec 1966 AF-Willmann talk: PE/Rome (Willmann) to PFM (AR), sz. 15648, 3 p.m., 9 Dec 1966, AMSZ, obt./trans. LG; MR; and IFM (AF) to IE/S (GD'O), office memo, noon, 9 Dec 1966, GD'O dossier; "demarche": Saigon embtel 12953 (HCL), 9 Dec 1966, box 147, NSF:CO:VN, LBJL.

62. IFM (AF) to IE/S (GD'O), office memo, noon, 9 Dec 1966, GD'O dossier.

63. On 9 Dec 1966 DR-GD'O talk, see Saigon embtel 12953 (HCL), 9 Dec 1966, box 147, NSF:CO:VN, LBJL; GD'O, *DV,* 726–27 (9 Dec 1966); IE/S (GD'O) to IFM (AF), office memos 42-44, all noon, 10 Dec 1966, GD'O dossier; and WPB OH 4, 2 Jun 1969, 20, LBJL.

64. WPB OH 4, 2 Jun 1969, 20, LBJL.

65. Poldel Saigon (JL) to PFM (JM), sz. 15698, 3:40 p.m., 10 Dec 1966, AMSZ, obt./trans. LG.

66. During a subsequent Italian peace probe (Killy) involving GD'O, WPB warned DR not to "play through this channel!" because GD'O "might give a misleading picture." Calling him "the man behind the 10 points" ("a ferociously tilted document"), WPB said GD'O "gave the wrong impressions on the MARIGOLD exercise": DR-WPB telcon, 7:10 p.m., 26 Feb 1968, box 61, DR Papers, entry 5379, RG 59, NA II.

67. William J. Miller, *Henry Cabot Lodge: A Biography* (New York: Heineman, 1967), 380.

68. Sica-Marine: GD'O, *DV,* 726 (9 Dec 1966); Sica interviews, Rome, 23–24 Feb 2005.

69. IFM (AF) to IE/S (GD'O), office memo, noon, 9 Dec 1966, GD'O dossier. GD'O wrote in his diary that he read the cable to DR, and told AF he had relayed "the news and requests as per the instructions issued to me by Y[our]. E[xcellency]." IE/S (GD'O) to IFM (AF), office memo 42, noon, 10 Dec 1966, ibid.

70. Saigon embtel 12953 notes only that GD'O related *Polish* criticism of the Hanoi raids. Perhaps HCL, DR, and/or WPB fudged the classified record to conceal that Rome had backed Warsaw on this touchy matter, on which LBJ had so emotional a view. In his LBJL OH, WPB falsely stated that "we cabled back what D'Orlandi had said" regarding his own view on the bombing.

71. WPB OH 4, 2 Jun 1969, 20, LBJL.

72. Saigon embtel 12953 (HCL), 9 Dec 1966, as above.

73. 9 Dec 1966 JAG-AR meeting: Warsaw embtels 1421 (JAG), 9 Dec 1966, and 1422 (JAG), 10 Dec 1966, both box 147, NSF, CO:VN, LBJL; *SDVW:NVPP,* 293–95; *FRUS, 1964–68,* 4:917–21; AR, urgent note nr 494/Rap./66, 12 Dec 1966, GM sygn. 1/77 w 16, t-39, *Tajne spec. znaczenia,* AMSZ, Warsaw, courtesy H. Szlajfer, trans. MG; and MR.

74. MR.

75. From 9 Dec 1966 entry, box 9, PDD, LBJL.

76. Ibid.; WWR note for PDD re meeting with LBJ, 9 Dec 1966, 4:30 p.m., box 11 [1 of 2], NSF:MtP:WR, NSF, LBJL; *FRUS, 1964–68,* 4:916.

77. Wheeler Washington to Sharp Hawaii & Westmoreland Saigon, JCS 7591-66, 101743Z, 10 Dec 1966, in COMUSMACV Eyes Only Message File, 1 Oct–31 Dec 1966, William C. Westmoreland Papers, U.S. Army Center of Military History, Fort McNair, Washington.

78. Carl Solberg, *Hubert Humphrey: A Biography* (New York: W. W. Norton, 1984; Borealis Books, 2003), 270–76; Dallek, *Flawed Giant,* 252–53.

79. On BDM background and early ties with LBJ, see Patrick Anderson, *The President's Men: White House Assistants of Franklin D. Roosevelt, Harry S. Truman, Dwight D. Eisenhower,*

John F. Kennedy, and Lyndon B. Johnson (Garden City, N.Y.: Doubleday, 1968), 321–52 ("cord" on 327); Patrick Anderson, "No. 2 Texan in the White House," *NYT Magazine,* 3 Apr 1966; Robert F. Keeler, *Newsday: A Candid History of the Respectable Tabloid* (New York: William Morrow, 1990), 385–88; "son": Joseph A. Califano Jr., *Inside: A Public and Private Life* (New York: PublicAffairs, 2004), 255.

80. Anderson, *President's Men,* 322–24.
81. Hopkins-BDM analogy: WWR OH-I, 21 Mar 1969, 32, LBJL.
82. *NYT,* 9 Jul 1965.
83. Keeler, *Newsday* , 389; Anderson, *President's Men,* 339–42; James C. Thomson Jr., OH I, 22 Jul 1971, LBJL, 26–27, 43; POL: BDM to LBJ, 30 Apr 1966, Moyers, Bill, 1966–67, box 8, POF, LBJL.
84. BDM email to author, 28 Nov 2010.
85. Keeler, *Newsday* , 390; BDM suspected DR: transcript, conference, "Kennedy, Johnson and Vietnam: The Impact of the Presidential Transition on the Course of the War, and Lessons for U.S. Foreign and Defense Policy," Saint Simons Island, Ga., 8–10 Apr 2005, 84.
86. Califano, *Inside,* 255.
87. BDM to LBJ, 6 June 1966, Moyers folder, box 8, POF, LBJL.
88. Dallek, *Flawed Giant,* 293–94; on "fatigue syndrome" and "conked out," see BDM to LBJ, 7 Mar 1966 and n.d. [1 September 1966], Moyers folder, box 8, POF, LBJL.
89. Harry McPherson OH III, 16 Jan 1969 by T. H. Baker, LBJL, 1–3.
90. BDM email to author, 28 Nov 2010.
91. Briefing reporters, BDM revealed LBJ's plans for upcoming trips to support Democrats campaigning for Congress; "irritated at Moyers' early release of plans he did not want made public," LBJ scotched the idea, leaving his press secretary "red-faced." Kathleen J. Turner, *Lyndon Johnson's Dual War: Vietnam and the Press* (Chicago: University of Chicago Press, 1985), 167.
92. Keeler, *Newsday,* 391; Guggenheim Papers, LC.
93. 26 Nov 1966 entry, box 9, PDD. LBJL.
94. Transcript of BDM interview, n.d., for *Vietnam: A Television History* (1983), 8–9, WGBH Educational Foundation records, Vietnam Project, Healey Library, University of Massachusetts–Boston.
95. NK and BDM spoke on the telephone on 7, 8, and 9 Dec. Though the substance is unknown, NK said that, given their relations, he probably discussed Marigold with BDM as it developed: NK desk calendar, box 5, NK Papers, JFKL, and NK interview, Princeton, N.J., 17 Apr 2005.
96. BDM to LBJ, 4:35 p.m., 7 Dec 1966, BDM Memos, Sept 1966–Feb 1967, box 12, Moyers OF, LBJL.
97. From 9 Dec 1966 entry, box 9, PDD, LBJL.
98. Ibid. The diary indicates BDM was with LBJ (and at least part of the time with Humphrey and Harry McPherson) from 5:33–7:10 pm.
99. BDM email to author, 28 Nov 2010.
100. BDM to LBJ, n.d. [not later than 9 Dec 1966], Moyers folder, box 8, POF, LBJL.
101. Draft letter, LBJ to BDM, n.d. [probably 9 Dec 1966], ibid.
102. From "mf" to LBJ, n.d. [probably 9 Dec 1966], ibid.
103. BDM telegram to *Time* magazine, 19 Dec 1966, ibid. The PDD indicates BDM saw LBJ at 10:45 a.m. on Saturday, 10 Dec, but does not show any meeting on 12 Dec.
104. BDM emails to author, 28 and 29 Nov 2010. BDM wrote that by late 1966 LBJ "knew I thought we should halt the bombing" but that his ultimate departure stemmed from "an accumulation of things, from my brother's death to the obsession with the war at the expense of domestic issues to my physical and emotional weariness, absence from my family, the closing of our options on many fronts, the press secretary job itself, my diminishing influence as the president turned increasingly to his war role."
105. On 10 Dec 1966 PVD-JS meeting, see PE/Hanoi (JS) to PFM (AR), sz. 15697, 7:30 p.m., and sz. 15700, 11:30 p.m., both 10 Dec 1966, AMSZ, obt./trans. LG; MR. JS, not entirely conversant himself with the A/B idea, promised to get back to PVD after checking with Warsaw: PE/Hanoi (JS) to PFM (JM), sz. 15717, 12 Dec 1966, AMSZ, trans. MG.

106. PE/Moscow (Pszczółkowski) to PFM (AR), sz. 15716, 12 Dec 1966, ibid.
107. That Friday night "was the most turbulent and the loudest since I arrived in Saigon [in July 1962] (with the sole exception of the night between All Saints' Day and All Souls' Day [i.e., 1–2 Nov] 1962)." Presumably he meant the night of the anti-Diem coup in 1963. GD'O, *DV,* 727–28 (10 Dec 1966).
108. GD'O-JL 10 Dec 1966 talk: ibid., 728 (10 Dec 1966); IE/S (GD'O) to IFM (AF), office memos 45–46, both 6:30 p.m., 10 Dec 1966, GD'O dossier; Poldel Saigon (JL) to PFM (JM), sz. 15698, 10 Dec 1966, AMSZ, obt./trans. LG.
109. The report JL cited may have stemmed from a December 8 raid by US F-105 fighters on a radar site 6 miles from Hanoi: *WP,* 10 Dec 1966.
110. JL interview, Warsaw, June 2003.
111. DR talks with Saigon leaders: Bangkok embtel 7466, 11 Dec 1966, *FRUS, 1964–68,* 4:925–28.
112. DR-GD'O 10 Dec 1966 talk: IE/S (GD'O) to IFM (AF), office memo 47, noon, 11 Dec 1966, GD'O dossier; GD'O, *DV,* 728–29 (10 Dec 1966). GD'O spent much of the evening talking with Westmoreland (not about Marigold). Confessing worry over the pope's call for an extended holiday truce (he opposed it) and expanded DRV use of Cambodia to infiltrate troops and matériel, the commander asked GD'O's view of the bombing campaign. GD'O said bluntly it should be suspended or drastically reduced, because the political cost was disproportionate to the military gain and risked provoking Soviet or Chinese intervention. He warned that even military success would not mean much unless matched by dramatic improvements in South Vietnam's political situation, and that Washington's assumption of a central combat role while demoting ARVN "has clearly made this war an American one" with all the peril that entailed.
113. Washington quickly relayed the data to JAG. Saigon embtel 13059 (HCL), 10 Dec 1966, 9:43 p.m.; WWR to LBJ, 11 Dec 1966, 12:35 p.m.; deptel 100700 to American Embassy, Warsaw (JAG), 11 Dec 1966; all box 147, NSF:CO:VN, LBJL.
114. WWR to LBJ, 10 Dec 1966, 8:55 a.m., ibid.
115. PE/Moscow (Pszczółkowski) to PFM (AR), sz. 15523, 7 Dec 1966, cited above.
116. Zinchuk–Kohler–Malcolm Toon memcon, "Vietnam," 11 a.m., 10 Dec 1966, CFPF, 1964–66; also WPB-Zinchuk memcon, 22 Dec 1966, box 147, NSF:CO:VN, LBJL.
117. Deptel 100624 to American Embassy, Saigon (HCL), 10 Dec 1966, sent 2.10 p.m., ibid.
118. Deptel 100627 to American Embassy, Warsaw (JAG), 10 Dec 1966, sent 2:30 p.m., ibid.
119. Ibid.
120. PE/Hanoi (JS) to PFM (AR), sz. 15700, 10 Dec 1966, was decoded at 7:45 p.m. Sunday.
121. Deptel 100624 to Saigon, 10 Dec 1966, box 147, as above. Since the cable was sent at 2:10 p.m. Washington time, it only reached Saigon well after midnight early Sunday morning.
122. *WP,* 14 Dec 1966; *NYT,* 14 Dec 1966; *Beverly* [Mass.] *Times,* 14 Dec 1966; George C. Lodge and Henry S. Lodge, telephone interviews, 12 and 14 Apr 2007; H. S. Lodge interview, Beverly, Mass., 6 Jun 2007.
123. GD'O, *DV,* 729 (12 Dec 1966).
124. JL to Maj. Gen. T.K. Theogaraj, MVC, acting chairman, ICSC, Saigon, 12 Dec 1966, file 100-10-1 pt. 6, vol. 9513, RG 25, NAC; "Report on the Activities of the International Commission in Vietnam for the Month of December 1966," 7, file 21-13-VIET-ICSC-8 FP 8.3, vol. 10129, ibid.
125. VCM to Wood, "Informal Meeting–December 12," 13 Dec 1966, file 100-10-2 vol. 1 [pt. 2], vol 9513, ibid.
126. PE/Hanoi (JS) to PFM (Sierna), sz. 15718, 12 Dec 1966, AMSZ, trans. MG.
127. Rome embtel 3181 (Reinhardt), 13 Dec 1966, RG 59, NA II; Rome embtel 3197 (Reinhardt), 13 Dec 1966 (quoting *L'Unità*), "Italy July 1965–December 1966" folder, box 13, Records of Negotiations about Vietnam, 1965–69, lot file 69D277, RG 59, NA II; communiqué: Oggi clandestine broadcast, 13 Dec 1966, *FBIS–North Vietnam,* 14 Dec 1966, JJJ 7.
128. "Delegazione Nord-Vietnam" folder, anno 1966, Paese Vietnam, Settore Estero, MF 537, FF 971–94, Busta 1454, Partito Comunista Italiano Papers, Fondazione Gramsci, Rome; trans. IO.

Unless otherwise noted, all quotations from DRV figures to the Partito Comunista Italiano delegation are from this source. The records include talks with Truong Chinh on 7 and 10 Dec and Xuan Thuy on 9 and 12 Dec, as well as a 9 Dec briefing by various figures on the international Communist situation.

129. PE/Hanoi (JS) to PFM (Wierna), sz. 15488, 6 Dec 1966, AMSZ, trans. MG.

130. *Nhan Dan* commentary, 12 Dec 1966, *FBIS Daily Report—12 December 1966—North Vietnam*, JJJ 7.

131. Sergey Radchenko, *Two Suns in the Heavens: The Sino-Soviet Struggle for Supremacy, 1962–1967* (Stanford, Calif., and Washington, D.C.: Stanford University Press and Woodrow Wilson Center Press, 2009), 182–88; *NYT*, 13 Dec 1966.

132. *NYT*, 14 Dec 1966, *WP*, 14 Dec 1966; on redeployment, see Radchenko, *Two Suns*, 189–90.

133. Brezhnev, "The Foreign Policy of the Soviet Union and the Efforts of the CSPU to Unite the Global Communist Movement," 12 Dec 1966, f. 2, op. 3, d. 45, l. 16, RGANI; obt./trans. G. Laron.

134. LBJ to Kosygin, 6 Dec 1966, *FRUS, 1964–68*, 4:906–8.

135. Brezhnev notes ("avtorski") for speech to CPSU CC Plenum, 12 Dec 1966, f. 2, op. 3, d. 45, l. 23, RGANI, obt./trans. S. Radchenko; it is not clear whether Brezhnev actually delivered these remarks, because he asked stenographers not to record all his comments and these do not appear in the edited version for closed circulation (Radchenko, emails to author, 16–17 Aug 2004).

136. DR-Chagla memcon, 12 Dec 1966, POL India-US 1966, box 2304, CFPF, 1964–66; also Brown-DR memcon ("categoric"), Paris, 14 Dec 1966, FO 371/190618, TNA.

137. Foreign Secretary C. S. Jha, Rusk-Chagla memcon, 12 Dec 1966, file 91, 18–23, M. C. Chagla Papers, Nehru Memorial Museum and Library, New Delhi.

138. Warsaw embtel 1429 (JAG), 12 Dec 1966, pol 27-14 Viet/Marigold, 12-3-66, box 22, FTSCPF, 1964–66.

139. 13 Dec 1966 JAG-AR talk: Warsaw embtel 1458 (JAG), 13 Dec 1966, rec'd 1:36 p.m., box 147, NSF:CO:VN, LBJL; AR, urgent note nr 498/Rap./66, 14 Dec 1966, GM sygn. 1/77 w 16, t-39, Tajne spec. znaczenia, AMSZ, courtesy H. Szlajfer, trans. MG; also *FRUS, 1964–68*, 4:933–35, and *SDVW:NVPP*, 296–97. MR wrongly implies that by this meeting, AR already knew of that day's raids on Hanoi; AR's conduct and own report confirm the contrary.

140. To associates, AR more candidly said he summoned JAG to, first, fill the time until Hanoi replied and deprive Washington of the pretext of a "futile waiting for a Warsaw contact"; second, to heap "entire blame" on the Americans for the delay in direct contacts and perhaps unsuccessful outcome; and third, to warn against more U.S. provocations, especially while Hanoi reconsidered the situation.

141. JCS-VN, Part III, 40–47.

142. NDP interview, Hanoi, 8 Jun 1999. Of course, DPQ could have received instructions from Hanoi of which NDP was not informed.

143. WPB OH 4, 2 Jun 1969, 20, LBJL.

144. DR OH-II, 26 Sep 1969, 31, LBJL.

145. Read OH-I, 13 Jan 1969, I-11, LBJL.

146. JAG OH-II, 10 Feb 1969, 18–19, LBJL.

147. "Of course if we had gotten started," he added, "I had an awful lot of problems because these were highly secret; I only had one man on my staff that could speak French effectively—... and if they really had gotten started, I'd probably have had to surreptitiously brought a couple of people over, a good French interpreter and someone from Washington who had been working day and night for months on this thing." Actually, the State Department would have *insisted* on taking over the talks had they started and sent WPB or a comparably trusted official to Warsaw to elbow JAG aside, however politely.

148. CLC, *The Lost Crusade: America in Vietnam* (New York: Dodd, Mead, 1970), 339.

149. CLC OH II, 24.

150. JL interviews, Warsaw, June 2003.

Chapter 9

1. On 13 Dec 1966 raids, see *Project CHECO Report,* 98–99; *NYT,* 14 and 16 Dec 1966; Gia Lam: "Observation Report," Hanoi, 1 November–15 December 1966," file 20-VIET-N-1-4 vol. 2, vol. 9001, RG 25, NAC; 850 mph: *WP,* 15 Dec 1966. Contradictory reports exist on the timing: a DRV Foreign Ministry briefing for diplomats and a PAVN complaint to the ICC said the attack began at 3 p.m., but an Italian Communist journalist with Berlinguer's delegation reported: "At 11 A.M. local time the criminal American aggressors carried out an atrocious terrorist bombardment in the center of Hanoi." HVL to Rahman, 608/QS/I/B, 8:30 p.m., 13 Dec 1966, file 21-13-VIET-ICSC-8 FP 8.3, vol. 10129, RG 25, NAC; P.I. Privalov memcon of ambassadors and DRV deputy foreign minister Hoang Van Loi, 9:30 p.m., 13 Dec 1966, f. 079, op. 21, p. 51, d. 8, ll. 209–10, AVPRF, trans. J. Person; *L'Unità* report in *NYT,* 15 Dec 1966.
2. *WP,* 15 Dec 1966.
3. Jacques Moalic dispatch, Agence France-Presse, 13 Dec 1966, FBIS, 14 Dec 1966—North Vietnam p. jjj 8; *NYT,* 14 and 15 Dec 1966. The raids happened early Wednesday, European time, but news reports did not reach there until late in the day, after AR and JAG met at 2 p.m. in Warsaw.
4. *Project CHECO Report,* 99. "Another flight crew stated that, due to poor weather, they had difficulty seeing the marshaling yards. They believed ordnance hit rolling stock on tracks but the impact of some bombs was not observed because of jinking after release."
5. See VWP Politburo Resolution 154-NQ/TW, 27 Jan 1967, "Resolution on Intensifying the Military Struggle and the Political Struggle in South Vietnam (October and November 1966)," *Van Kien Dang, Toan Tap, 28, 1967* [Collected Party Documents, Volume 28, 1967] (Hanoi: Nha Xuat Ban Chinh Tri Quoc Gia, 2003), 141–70, trans. MP.
6. HVL to Rahman, 608/QS/I/B, 8:30 p.m., 13 Dec 1966, as above.
7. Privalov memcon, ambassadors and Hoang Van Loi, 9:30 p.m., 13 Dec 1966, as above.
8. PE/Hanoi (JS) to PFM (Meller) sz. 15840, 14 Dec 1966, AMSZ, trans. MG.
9. PE/Hanoi (JS) to PFM (AR), sz. 15787, 11 p.m., 13 Dec 1966, ibid.
10. From 13 Dec 1966 entry, AFD; "pressure": PE/Rome (Willmann) to PFM (AR), sz. 16216, 23 Dec 1966, AMSZ, obt./trans. LG.
11. Gen. Wheeler, CJCS, to Gen. Westmoreland, COMUSMACV, and Adm. Sharp, CINCPAC, JCS 6926 66, 11 Nov 1966, and Sharp, Hawaii, to Westmoreland, Saigon; Beach, Harris, and Johnson, Hawaii; 12 Nov 1966, both CMH 82-82 A+B, Westmoreland [Eyes Only] Message File COMUSMACV 1 Oct–31 Dec 1966, Westmoreland Papers, US Army Center of Military History, Fort McNair, Washington.
12. *NYT,* 14 Dec 1966; Donnelley to DR, "Chronology of Public Statements on Air Strikes in the Hanoi Area," 19 Dec 1966, box 2, Christian OF, LBJL.
13. On 14 Dec 1966 PVD-JS talk, see PE/Hanoi (JS) to PFM (AR), sz. 15821, sent 3:15 p.m., 14 Dec 1966, AMSZ, trans. MG; also MR.
14. The chronology presented here corrects previous accounts asserting that Hanoi terminated Marigold after the bombings on both 13 and 14 Dec—when AR informed JAG of the decision. PVD told JS Wednesday morning that the DRV had decided to end the exchanges *before* that afternoon's raids.
15. On 14 Dec 1966 bombing, see *Project CHECO Report,* 98–99; *WP,* 15 Dec 1966; *NYT,* 15 Dec 1966; a DRV deputy foreign minister reported 11 groups of Navy planes (100 in all) and 9 groups of Air Force planes (about 60) took part, and 8 planes were shot down: PE/Hanoi (JS) to PFM (Meller), sz. 15840, 11:30 p.m., 14 Dec 1966, AMSZ, trans. MG; HVL to Rahman, 611/QS/I/B, 8 p.m., 14 Dec 1966, file 21-13-VIET-ICSC-8 FP 8.3, vol. 10129, RG 25, NAC; BCG/Hanoi to FO, tel. 257, 19 Dec 1966, FO 371/186354, TNA.
16. Hughes to DR, "Civilian Bomb Damage to North Vietnam," 30 Dec 1966, DDRS/LBJL.
17. Embassy damage: also HES, *Behind the Lines: Hanoi, December 23, 1966–January 7, 1967* (New York: Harper & Row, 1967), 69–71; and report (see below) by ICC reps who inspected the site on 15 Dec 1966. JS discovery: PE/Hanoi (JS) to PFM (Meller), sz. 15944, 16 Dec 1966, AMSZ, trans. MG. The CIA secretly reported that a small amount of shrapnel hit the Soviet Embassy,

but this was presumably false, because Moscow never protested such damage. Information Intelligence Cable, 18 Dec 1966, DDRS.

18. HES, *Behind the Lines*, 70; a Canadian officer in Saigon told U.S. officials the roof of Ottawa's Hanoi ICC delegation was "holed three times by flack": Saigon embtel 13647 (Porter), "Subject: ICC Visit December 15 to Damaged Sites Hanoi," 17 Dec 1966, box 38, NSF:CO:VN, LBJL.

19. PE/Hanoi (JS) to PFM (Meller) sz. 15840, 14 Dec 1966, AMSZ, trans. MG.

20. On 14 Dec 1966 ICC meeting, see Candel Saigon (VCM) to CDEA, tel. 1158, "Emergency Mtg of Commission," 14 Dec 1966, in FO 371/186335, TNA; also BE/Saigon (Wilkinson) to FO, tel. 955, 15 Dec 1966, ibid.; "Report on the Activities of the International Commission in Vietnam for the Month of December 1966," 3, file 21-13-VIET-ICSC FP 8.3, vol. 10129, RG 25, NAC; and Saigon embtel 13647 (Porter), 17 Dec 1966, box 38, NSF:CO:VN, LBJL.

21. Candel Saigon to CDEA, tel. 1159, "Emergency Mtg of Commission," 14 Dec 1966, FO 371/186335, TNA.

22. PFM (Spasowski) to Poldel Saigon (JL), sz. 12512, 8 Dec 1966, AMSZ, trans. MG.

23. GD'O, *DV*, 730 (14 Dec 1966).

24. D. F. Murray, "Vietnam: United States Air Attacks Near Hanoi," 9 Dec 1966, and P. H. Gore-Booth, "Viet-Nam," 23 Dec 1966, both FO 371/186354, TNA WPB: memo of meeting, Gov. Harriman's office, 3 p.m., 16 Dec 1966, box 569, WAHP-LC.

25. Paris embtel 9157 (DR), 14 Dec 1966, Conference Files, 1966-72, CF-109, box 431, RG 59, NA II.

26. Paris embtel 9261 (DR), 16 Dec 1966, *FRUS, 1964–68, Vol. XIII: Western Europe Region* (Washington, D.C.: U.S. Government Printing Office, 1995), doc. 229.

27. Brown-DR memcon, 14 Dec 1966, FO 371/190618, TNA; "deliver": Murray 9 Dec 1966 memo.

28. AR felt the ICC might *eventually* play a "positive role" but for the moment should avoid controversial issues and merely relay complaints and undertake any good offices job the parties asked. As for three-way talks, the most he imagined was a meeting, perhaps in Warsaw, on how the ICC "should adapt its activities to existing realities" by scaling back its original aims. Martin did not reject the idea but said Canada could not accept an overtly "non-activist policy." Gromyko dismissed his view that the ICC might effectively aid peace so long as U.S. "aggression" continued. Martin talks in Warsaw (7–8 Nov) and Moscow (9–12 Nov): file 20-22-VIETS-2-1 vols. 7 and 8, vol. 9398, RG 25, NAC. AR ("more in sorrow than in anger") and JM, echoing past claims to Westerners, said Warsaw's approach to Hanoi during LBJ's thirty-seven-day pause had yielded a positive response (HCM's letter, "diminished" military action in the South), but Washington ignored it and resumed bombing "with result that Poles found themselves in extremely awkward position vis-à-vis North Vietnamese." CE/Warsaw to CDEA, tel. 1457, "Vietnam: Polish Initiative During Bombing Pause," 8 Nov 1966, former top secret document, File 20-22-VIETS-2-1, RG 25, NAC, released to author. In Rome, Martin discussed Vietnam with Pope Paul VI and (separately) AF, who hid Italy's Marigold role; "we could expect no initiative from Eastern Europe at present time" as it "lined up firmly behind USSR on Vietnam problem," he said. CE/Rome to CDEA, tel. 1444, "Vietnam: Discussion between SSEA and FM Fanfani," 15 Nov 1966, File 20-22-VIETS-2-1 vol. 8, vol. 9398, RG 25, NAC.

29. On 25 Nov 1966 Martin-DR memcon, see CANDELNY to CDEA, tel. 2861, "SSEAS Conversation with Dean Rusk," 27 Nov 1966, File 20-VIET pt. 4, vol. 3096, ibid., and File #23, United States 1964-1968, vol. 226, Paul Martin Papers, Series 312, MG 32, NAC (courtesy R. Touhey); also CE/Washington to CDEA, tel. 3659, "SSEA-Rusk Mtg: Possible Utilization of ICC in Vietnam," 25 Nov 1966, and CDEA (Cadieux) to PERMISNY, tel. Y806 flash, "Vietnam-Commission Role in Getting Negotiations Going," 28 Nov 1966, both file 20-22-VIETS-2-1 vol. 8, Vol. 9398, RG 25, NAC.

30. Roger Fisher notes, 13 Nov 1966, New York dinner; and memo to Martin, "Vietnam," London, 16 Dec 1966, both ibid.

31. Paris embtel 9077 (DR), 14 Dec 1966, box 147, NSF:CO:VN, LBJL.

32. Paris embtel 9171 (DR), "Vietnam: Proposals for Commission Initiative," 15 Dec 1966, DDRS.

33. On "interconnection," see Paris embtel 9077 (DR), 14 Dec 1966, as above.

34. CDEA to CE/Washington, tel. Y134, "Vietnam," 1 Jan 1967, file 20-VIET, pt. 1, vol. 3097, RG 25, NAC.

35. Paris embtel 9077 (DR), 14 Dec 1966.
36. Deptel 102298 to American Embassy, Paris, 14 Dec 1966, 3:38 p.m., box 22, FTSCPF, 1964–66.
37. DK and SHL, *Secret Search,* 69; SHL, JAG interview notes, Warsaw, 11 Dec 1967, Vietnam Bombing Pause 1966–67, box 41, SHLP.
38. On 14 Dec 1966 JAG-AR talk, see Warsaw embtel 1471 (JAG), 15 Dec 1966, *FRUS, 1964–68,* 4:936–38; AR, urgent note nr. 501/Rap./66, 15 Dec 1966, GM sygn. 1/77 w 16, t-39, *Tajne spec. znaczenia,* AMSZ, courtesy H. Szlajfer; MR; "angry": JAG OH II, 20.
39. JS' ciphergram 15821 to AR was deciphered in Warsaw at 1 p.m. Wednesday.
40. MR; JAG's cable gave no indication that AR had exempted him from his ire at the U.S. government.
41. On "crushed," see DK and SHL, *Secret Search,* 71.
42. Warsaw embtel 1471 (JAG), 15 Dec 1966 (rec'd 12:30 a.m.), *FRUS, 1964–68,* 4:936–38, *SDVW:NVPP,* 302–4.
43. *NYT,* 15 Dec 1966; *WP,* 17 Dec 1966.
44. *NYT,* 15, 16, and 17 Dec 1966.
45. B. T. Gilmore (BE/Washington) to D. G. Waterstone, SEAD, FO, 16 Dec 1966, FO 371/186354, TNA.
46. Arthur M. Schlesinger Jr., *Journals: 1952–2000* (New York: Penguin, 2007), 257 (4 Jan 1967).
47. *NYT,* 15 and 16 Dec 1966; *WP,* 15 Dec 1966; BDM was "not a dove on Vietnam as such, but a man with solid connections to the less militant circles"; *NYT,* 18 Dec 1966.
48. *NYT,* 15 Dec 1966; *WP,* 15 Dec 1966.
49. BDM in deptel 102990 to American Embassy, London, 15 Dec 1966, POL 27 VIET S, box 3014, CFPF, 1964–66, and CE/Washington to CDEA, tel. 3811, "Vietnam Truces," 15 Dec 1966, file 20-22-VIETS-2 vol. 18, vol. 9396, RG 25, NAC.
50. On "young" and "serious," see *NYT,* 15 Dec 1966.
51. See, e.g., deptel 102958 to American embassies, Paris and London, 14 Dec 1966, 10:48 p.m., U.S. position, October 1966, box 11, Records of Negotiations about Vietnam, 1965–69, lot file 69D277, RG 59, NA II; WWR to LBJ, 3:30 p.m., 14 Dec 1966, box 12 [1 of 2], NSF: MtP:WR, LBJL.
52. Deptel 102298 to American Embassy, Paris, 14 Dec 1966, 3:38 pm, box 22, FTSCPF, 1964–66.
53. NK calendar, 14 Dec 1966, box 5, NK Papers, JFKL; LBJ diary, 14 Dec 1966, box 9, PDD, LBJL.
54. Succeeding quotations from deptel 102960 to American Embassy, Warsaw (JAG), 14 Dec 1966, 10:52 p.m., box 147, NSF:CO:VN, LBJL.
55. On the timing of messages, see the notations on relevant telegrams; on "difficulties," see Warsaw embtel 1475 (JAG), 15 December 1966, ibid.
56. *SDVW:NVPP,* 300.
57. Warsaw embtel 1459 (JAG), 13 Dec 1966, POL 27-14 Viet/Marigold 12-3-66, box 22, FTSCPF, 1964–66.
58. Deptel 102942 to American Embassy, Warsaw, 14 Dec 1966, 8:53 pm, ibid.
59. Candel Saigon (Wood) to CDEA, tel. 1172, "Bombing of Hanoi," 16 Dec 1966, in FO 371/186335, TNA; also BE/Saigon to FO, telno 960, 17 Dec 1966, ibid.
60. PE/Hanoi (JS) to PFM (JL), sz. 15890, 16 Dec 1966, AMSZ, obt./trans. LG.
61. Warsaw embtel 1475 (JAG), 15 Dec 1966 (rec'd 8:27 am), box 147, NSF:CO:VN, LBJL, and POL 24-14/MARIGOLD 12-15-66, box 22, FTSCPF, 1964–66; *SDVW:NVPP* oddly omits this key message.
62. On 15 Dec 1966 AR-DPQ conversation, see AR's handwritten report, 15 Dec 1966, D II Wietnamu—1971, 51/75, W-3, AMSZ, obt. W. Jarzabek, trans. MG. AR later told France's foreign minister that DPQ had endorsed JL's initiative when they met, but it is unclear whether he was alluding to the 15 Dec 1966 talk or an earlier one. AR–Couve de Murville talk, Paris, 26 Jan 1967, Commission des Archives Diplomatiques, Ministère des Étrangères, *Documents Diplomatiques Français,* 1967 tome I (1 Jan–1 Jul) (Brussels: P. I. E. Peter Lang, 2008), 156.
63. This account suggests that the Poles' apparent failure to coordinate closely with DPQ regarding the exchanges with JAG, instead exclusively relying on contacts in Hanoi between JS and PVD, may have been an error. During the crucial week of 6–13 Dec, when Marigold was in

limbo, closer Polish-DRV communication in Warsaw might have clarified DPQ's readiness to receive JAG and/or revealed the presence in Warsaw of a DRV representative specially sent from Hanoi to participate in talks with the Americans. AR's record of his 15 Dec talk with DPQ implies strongly that the DRV envoy did not on that occasion disclose NDP's presence in Warsaw, because the Poles would certainly have used this point in subsequent arguments that Hanoi was serious about entering direct talks.

64. NDP interview, Hanoi, 8 Jun 1999. NDP recalls receiving Hanoi's instructions on 15 or 16 Dec.

65. The Eighteenth Congress of the Parti Communiste Français took place 4–8 Jan 1967 in Lavallois near Paris.

66. Warsaw embtel 1487 (JAG), rec'd 9:24 p.m., 15 Dec 1966, POL 27-14 Viet/Marigold 12-15-66, box 22, FTSCPF, 1964–66; "Declaration of the Government of the Polish People's Republic" (Polish Press Agency–16 December 1966)," FO 371/186315, TNA. The resident *NYT* correspondent, Henry Kamn, observed that the formal declaration seemed a departure from Warsaw's custom of sending a diplomatic note to protest U.S. actions in Vietnam, even when a Polish ship had been struck in Haiphong Harbor. Though the statement did not reveal the still-secret diplomacy, anonymous "highly placed Poles" felt less constrained; in a comment that may have heightened U.S. suspicions that Warsaw was poised to leak accusations that Washington had killed Marigold, his article noted that "high Polish officials tell Western visitors that every peace initiative by the United States is followed by a step-up in military action." *NYT*, 16 Dec 1966.

67. DR, *As I Saw It*, edited by Daniel S. Papp (New York: W. W. Norton, 1990), 468.

68. Paris embtel 9131 (DR), 14 Dec 1966, *FRUS, 1964–68, Vol. XII: Western Europe* (Washington, D.C.: U.S. Government Printing Office, 2001), doc. 70.

69. Paris embtel 9261 (DR), 16 Dec 1966, *FRUS, 1964–68,* 13:516–17.

70. DR presentation: Paris embtel 9244 (DR), "Subject: NATO Ministerial Meeting Afternoon Session December 15 Continuation of Secretary's Remarks," 16 Dec 1966, DDRS; Candel, NATO-Paris to CDEA, tel. 2801, "NATO Ministerial Mtg-Rusk-Vietnam," 16 Dec 1966, file 20-22-VIETS-2 vol. 18, vol. 9396, RG 25, NAC; also *NYT*, 16 Dec 1966.

71. D. A. Campbell, minute on folder enc. text of DR's 15 Dec 1966 speech, FO 371/190617, TNA.

72. Paris embtel 9214 (DR), 1910Z, 15 Dec 1966, Vietnam, box 67, Rusk Papers, RG 59, NA II; n.d. copy in Vietnam MARIGOLD–Incomplete, box 148, NSF:CO:VN, LBJL. A notation on the LBJL copy indicates that it was not circulated within the State Department, which may explain its absence from the Pentagon Papers, departmental files, and the 1966 Vietnam *FRUS* volume. DR wrote erroneously in his memoirs that he sent this message from "the Far East" rather than Paris: *As I Saw It*, 468.

73. Don Cook to DK, 12 Jan 1968, U Thant–Stevenson 1964–68, box 39, SHLP.

74. McNaughton diary, 16 Dec 1966, quoted by Benjamin T. Harrison and Christopher L. Mosher, "The Secret Diary of McNamara's Dove: The Long-Lost Story of John T. McNaughton's Opposition to the Vietnam War," *Diplomatic History* 35, no. 3 (June 2011): 505–34, at 530.

75. Dobrynin later disclosed this exchange to DR; see deptel 143101 to American Embassy, Moscow, 24 Feb 1967, *SDVW:NVPP*, 493–95. NDT told JS that Brezhnev had approved of Hanoi's decision: PE/Hanoi (JS) to PFM (AR), sz. 15931, 16 Dec 1966, AMSZ, trans. MG.

76. Dobrynin-LET memcon, "Subject: Reply to President's Letter to Kosygin," 30 Dec 1966, NSF:CO:VN, box 147, LBJL.

77. In response, WWR insisted "that, as he knew, there was no plan to put pressure diplomatically on Hanoi at that stage and that subsequent events made clear that this was not the case." WWR-Dobrynin memcon, "Subject: Viet Nam," 27 Jan 1967, Pol 27-14 Viet/Marigold, box 2739, CFPF, 1967–69.

78. WAH-Dobrynin memcon, 19 Jan 1967, Chron File, Jan 1967, box 569, WAHP-LC; also remarks by Zinchuk to McNaughton, 3 Jan 1967, and Dobrynin to DR, 4 Jan 1967, cited below.

79. *NYT*, 16 Dec 1966.

80. PE/Moscow to PFM (AR), sz. 15901, 16 Dec 1966, AMSZ, trans. MG.

81. See record of Polish-Soviet talks, Lansk, 18 Jan 1967, in *Tajne dokumenty: Biura Politycznego PRL-ZSRR, 1956–1970,* edited by Andrzej Paczkowski (London: Aneks, 1998), 462–64, trans.

LG; also see Ilya V. Gaiduk, *The Soviet Union and the Vietnam War* (Chicago: Ivan R. Dee, 1996), 271 n. 62. Shcherbakov later paraphrased LDT's comments to his Hungarian colleague. Pressed to explain Hanoi's concept of combining negotiations and continued fighting, he had reportedly told the Soviets that entering talks "becomes possible when they will gain appropriate military superiority over the Americans, and when the Americans will prove by deeds that they sincerely want peace. For the time being, however, negotiations are out of the question as the Americans are increasing the aggression; they have even started to bomb downtown Hanoi." HA/Hanoi (Pehr) to HFM, "Subject: Comrade Le Duc Tho's Moscow Consultations," 19 Jan 1967, Vietnam Relations, 1967, Foreign Ministry records, Top Secret, box 93, 250-001223/1967, XIX-J-l-j, MOL, obt./trans. Z. Szoke. Partito Comunista Italiano (Italian Communist Party) records indirectly confirm that LDT took a more moderate stand than the public DRV position toward peace talks when he saw the Soviets in mid-December. On 20 Dec 1966, the same Partito Comunista Italiano delegation that had visited Hanoi stopped in Moscow and met with Suslov. Obviously alluding to the exchanges with LDT, Suslov noted that "in recent days, we have had fraternal and confidential talks" with the DRV. In general, he related, the content comported with what the Italians had heard—"they will not take any political initiatives due to the extent of the bombings" and oppose the Cultural Revolution but sought Soviet "understanding of their difficult position" regarding their ties with Beijing—but with one key exception: "With respect to the [Peace] Conference, they were not as flatly against it as you have indicated." "Meeting with Suslov in Moscow, 20/12/1966," "Delegazione Nord-Vietnam" folder, anno 1966, Paese Vietnam, Settore Estero, MF 537, FF 971-994, busta 1454, Partito Comunista Italiano Papers, Fondazione Gramsci, Rome; trans. IO.

82. *NYT,* 16 Dec 1966.

83. Ibid.; *WP,* 16 Dec 1966.

84. *WP,* 17 Dec 1966; Pentagon background briefing: Donnelley to DR, "Chronology of Public Statements on Air Strikes in the Hanoi Area," 19 Dec 1966, box 2, Christian OF, LBJL.

85. *WP,* 17 Dec 1966.

86. WWR forwarded Warsaw embtel 1471 to LBJ with a note marked "Thursday, Dec. 15, 1966, 9:50 a.m.," box 147, NSF:CO:VN, LBJL; and Warsaw embtel 1475 to LBJ with a note dated "Thurs., Dec. 15, 1966, 10:45 a.m.," box 12 [1 of 2], NSF:MtP:WR, LBJL.

87. Tape-recorded LBJ-DR telcon, 7:45 pm, 25 Dec 1966, LBJL.

88. Circumstantial evidence indicates LBJ initially provided this guidance after reading JAG's cable 1471 by calling WWR at 10:32 am; eight minutes later, WWR urgently telephoned NK, who in turn, after hanging up, immediately contacted Unger, already working on the response to JAG. NK also had a chance to gauge LBJ's reaction in an early afternoon off-the-record White House meeting attended by LBJ, WWR, and LET, among others. 15 Dec 1966 entries, NK desk calendar, JFKL, and LBJ diary, box 9, PDD, LBJL.

89. *SDVW:NVPP,* 232.

90. Deptel 103342 to American Embassy, Warsaw, 15 Dec 1966, 5:25 p.m., box 147, NSF:CO:VN, LBJL.

91. Deptel 103488, 6:22 p.m., 15 Dec 1966, and deptel 103586, 7:33 p.m., 15 Dec 1966, both POL 24-14/MARIGOLD, 12-15-66, box 22, FTSCPF, 1964–66.

92. See JCS 1471 (to CINCPAC), 15 Dec 1966, *SDVW:NVPP,* 306. Precisely when LBJ made this decision is not clear; he had a chance to relay it Thursday afternoon when he saw acting JCS chair Adm. David L. McDonald at the White House. McDonald, in turn, relayed the order to CINCPAC Hawaii, where Adm. Sharp oversaw aerial military operations. Thursday evening, Washington time (0210Z Friday), the Seventh Air Force sent a top secret message to the 355th Tactical Fighter Wing at Takhli airbase (where F-105s were based) in Thailand deleting Yen Vien from the target list. *Project CHECO,* 99, 144 n. 52.

93. *NYT,* 16 Dec 1966.

94. This and other telegrams re HES's Hanoi trip can be found in "Hanoi Messages, Photo Captions" folder, box 590, HES, RBML, CU.

95. HES, *Behind the Lines,* 5–9; HES, *A Time of Change: A Reporter's Tale of Our Time* (New York: Harper & Row, 1988), 118–21; HES OH-I, 26 Jun 1969, LBJL, 2–5.

96. In later accounts, HES contributed to confusion by describing the cable as coming "from Hanoi" rather than Phnom Penh and omitting its author's name—perhaps to avoid adding ammunition to critics who accused him of left-wing sympathies. Nor did Burchett clarify the matter in his own memoirs: Wilfred Burchett, *At The Barricades: Forty Years on the Cutting Edge of History,* introduction by HES (New York: Times Books, 1981), 235–37; and George Burchett and Nick Shimmin, eds., *Memoirs of a Rebel Journalist: The Autobiography of Wilfred Burchett* (Sydney: University of New South Wales Press, 2005), 572–73.

97. HES, *Behind the Lines,* 9.

98. Box 590, HES, RBML, CU.

99. JS-NDT talk: PE/Hanoi (JS) to PFM (AR), sz. 15931, 16 Dec 1966, AMSZ, trans. MG. AR's cable 12705, which JS relayed to NDT, has not been found; presumably Brezhnev indicated his view on 15 Dec when the DRV ambassador in Moscow delivered Hanoi's statement cutting off the Warsaw initiative.

100. See Capt. J. Krzuzanowski, Maj. P. Wilson, and R. Sethi, "IC Bureau Hanoi Statement and Report to IC Saigon Made on December 16, 1966," file 100-10-1 pt. 6, vol. 9513, RG 25, NAC, and Candel Saigon to CDEA, tel. 1184, 19 Dec 1966, FO 371/186335, TNA; all quotations here are from this source.

101. Besides the ICC report, see also BCG/Hanoi (Kelly) to FO, tel. 252A, 14 Dec 1966 (bamboo) and BCG/Hanoi (Colvin) to FO, tel. 257, 19 Dec 1966, both FO 371/186354, TNA.

102. PFM (Spasowski) to Poldel Saigon (JL), sz. 12913, 22 Dec 1966, AMSZ, trans. MG. In a crossed-out passage, Spasowski wrote that "Ludwig's suggestion [of] the press leak [is] dangerous and does not solve the matter."

103. Canadian sharing of the report's findings with British and U.S. colleagues: BE/Saigon to FO, tel 962, 19 Dec 1966 ("strict confidence"), and R. A. Fyjis-Walker, "Air Raid Damage at Hanoi," 20 Dec 1966, both FO 371/186335, TNA; and Saigon embtel 13647 (Porter), "Subject: ICC Visit December 15 to Damaged Sites Hanoi" (sanitized), 17 Dec 1966, box 38, NSF:CO:VN, LBJL; Canadian diplomats on December 20 officially passed the full text to U.S. officials in Washington, where it received DR's personal attention but did not alter official denials that American planes had dropped ordinance on Hanoi: CE/Washington to CDEA, tel. 3872, "Bombing of Hanoi," 21 Dec 1966, 20-VIET, pt. 1, vol. 3097, RG 25, NAC.

104. *NYT,* 16 Dec 1966.

105. DE/Saigon (Derksen), cable 122++, ref. 12626, 16 Dec 1966, code 911, bloc 1965–74 (secret), DFMA, obt. R. van der Maar, trans. DM. Polish sources do not mention this JL-Derksen conversation; JL denied that he improperly leaked information on Marigold to the Dutch diplomat. JL interview, Warsaw, June 2003.

106. Derksen found it "remarkable" that the *NYT* that very day editorialized that the Hanoi raids also bombed "any prospect of peace talks"—a comment he correctly attributed to "sheer coincidence."

107. GD'O diary, 16 Dec 1966, in Rotondo, "The Lost Paths to Peace," *30 Days,* June 2005.

108. JAG OH II, 20–22.

109. Warsaw embtel 1498 (JAG), 16 Dec 1966, box 147, NSF:CO:VN, LBJL.

110. Warsaw embtel 1488 (JAG), rec'd 1:47 am, 16 Dec 1966, POL 27-14 Viet/Marigold 12-15-66, box 22, FTSCPF, 1964–66.

111. Deptel 103576 to American Embassy, Paris, 15 Dec 1966, ibid.; "Marigold: A Chronology," 29. Although no U.S. record has surfaced of this private conversation, the Italian referred to it in IFM (AF) to IE/S (GD'O), office memo, 23 Dec 1966, GD'O dossier.

112. Paris embtel 9260 (DR), 16 Dec 1966, box 3014, CFPF, 1964–66.

113. Lewis to James B. Reston (*NYT* Washington bureau chief), 18 Dec 1966, RS 26/20/120, box 34, Reston Papers, University of Illinois at Urbana-Champaign Archives, Urbana.

114. Box 590, HES, RBML, CU.

115. See Mark Atwood Lawrence, "Mission Intolerable: Harrison Salisbury's Trip to Hanoi and the Limits of Dissent against the Vietnam War," *Pacific Historical Review* 75, no. 3 (Aug 2006): 429–59.

116. HES OH-I, 26 Jun 1969, 8-9, LBJL.

117. HES, *Time of Change,* 121.
118. Ibid., 143; HES OH-I, 26 June 1969, 7-8, LBJL. Circumstantial evidence to support the notion that DRV authorities had already decided to approve HES' visa in late November appears in a Soviet record of a 21 Nov 1966 conversation between PVD and the Soviet ambassador. During a discussion of propaganda efforts, Shcherbakov advised North Vietnam to "more widely use foreign correspondents, accredited in Hanoi, for acquainting them with American crimes," rather than introducing new restrictions on them. PVD responded that "the Vietnamese comrades have recently considered it necessary to receive many Western correspondents," but this must be done "with definite prudence." Shcherbakov-PVD memcon, 21 Nov 1966, f. 079, op. 21, p. 51, d. 8, AVPRF, trans. J. Person.
119. Box 590, HES, RBML, CU.
120. LBJ-RSM telcon, 9 Nov 1966, *FRUS, 1964–68,* 4:816–17.
121. Lady Bird Johnson, *A White House Diary* (New York: Holt, Rinehart & Winston, 1970), 462 (16 Dec 1966).
122. *NYT,* 16 Dec 1966.
123. Ibid.
124. London embtel 4953 (Bruce), 16 Dec 1966 (re conversation with Murray), United Kingdom Cables, vol. IX 8/66-1/67, box 210, NSF:CO, LBJL.
125. See memorandum of meeting, 3 p.m., 16 Dec 1966, box 569, WAHP-LC.
126. McNaughton diary, 16 Dec 1966, quoted by Harrison and Mosher, "Secret Diary," 530.
127. Ibid.
128. WAH Algerian contacts: documents in boxes 553–54, WAHP-LC, and also deptel 95040 to American Embassy, Algiers, 1 Dec 1966; Algiers embtel 1831 (Jernegan), 8 Dec 1966; Algiers embtels 1863 and 1866 (Jernegan), 10 Dec 1966; and deptel 100640, 10 Dec 1966, all DDRS.
129. Besides WAH, WPB, CLC, and Unger, others present included Sisco, Hughes, Monteagle Stearns, and the Pentagon's John McNaughton.
130. CLC memo for the record, 14 Dec 1966, WAHP-LC; CLC may have influenced Roberts (and therefore the *WP*) to echo administration claims that there had been neither policy shift nor military escalation, thereby taking a softer line than *NYT.* See Roberts, "LBJ Is Willing but Foe Rejects Extended Truce," *WP,* 15 Dec 1966.
131. CLC to NK et al. (Negotiations Committee), "Re 'A Package for Hanoi' (Rewrap No. 1)," 14 Dec 1966, box 520, WAHP-LC.
132. Robert N. Ginsburgh to WWR, "Subject: Continuation of Air Campaign Against North Vietnam," 16 Dec 1966, box 3, NSF:CO:VN, LBJL.
133. WWR notes of meeting with LBJ, 16 Dec 1966, *FRUS, 1964–68,* 948–52; unless otherwise noted, the account of this meeting relies on this source. See also LBJ diary, 16 Dec 1966, box 9, PDD, LBJL (according to which the meeting was also attended by Robert Komer, BDM, and the man who would soon replace BDM as LBJ's press secretary, George Christian).
134. After returning to Saigon in mid-January 1967, HCL disclosed to GD'O his lack of knowledge of the post–12 Dec 1966 Warsaw exchanges, also evident from the prematurely abbreviated Marigold account in his memoirs. IE/S (GD'O) to IFM (AF), office memo 81, 4:30 p.m., 19 Jan 1967, GD'O dossier; GD'O, *DV,* 762–63 (19 Jan 1967); and HCL, *As It Was,* 179–81.
135. On "scuttling," see deptel 104673 to American Embassy, Saigon, 17 Dec 1966, box 147, NSF:CO:VN, LBJL.
136. CLC noted WAH's "immense annoyance" to Wilson on 18 Jan 1967: PREM 13/1917, TNA.
137. *FRUS, 1964–68,* 4:950. WAH specifically noted that the Vietnamese Communists felt "twice fooled in negotiations"—their talks with the French in 1946 and at Geneva in 1954.
138. On "limelight," see State Department official in CE/Washington to CDEA, "Vietnam: Goldbergs Let to SecGen," 21 Dec 1966, file 20-VIET, pt. 1, vol. 3097, RG 25, NAC; "bad light": Canadian UN Mission, New York (Ignatieff), to CDEA, tel. 3353, "Vietnam: Commission Initiative: Talk with Goldberg," 22 Dec 1966, file 100-11-3 vol. 1 [part 2], vol. 9516, RG 25, NAC; failure to convince LBJ on extended truce: Goldberg in Thant, "The Question of Vietnam," 19 Dec 1966, "Vietnam War (Confidential Papers), 1965–1966," DAG-1, 5.2.2.3.2, box 1, UNA. When Goldberg in early 1967 discussed resigning, he stressed disagreement on Vietnam policy and

"was especially critical" of the 13–14 Dec bombings, DR told LBJ: Gibbons, IV, 496; Goldberg unhappiness: David L. Stebenne, *Arthur J. Goldberg: New Deal Liberal* (New York: Oxford University Press, 1996), chap. 11; James A. Wechsler (*New York Post*), memo of conversation with Goldberg, 19 Dec 1966, box 2, Wechsler Papers, WHS.

139. WH press release, 16 Dec 1966, re HCL press conference, West Lobby, White House, 6:45 pm; also *WP*, 17 Dec 1966. HCL also repeated the official line that the Hanoi bombings did not constitute an escalation.

140. Deptel 104408 to American Embassy, Warsaw, 7:43 pm, 16 Dec 1966, POL 24-14//MARI-GOLD, 12-15-66, box 22, FTSCPF, 1964–66; White House dinner from 7:45 to 8:25 pm: PDD, LBJL.

141. 17 Dec 1966 GD'O-JL talk: IE/S (GD'O) to IFM (AF), office memos 48-51, all 4 p.m., 18 Dec 1966, GD'O dossier; GD'O, *DV*, 732 (17 Dec 1966); and Poldel Saigon (JL) to PFM (JM), sz. 16120, 4:20 p.m., 21 Dec 1966, AMSZ, obt./trans. LG. G'DO gave Habib a detailed account the next day: Saigon embtel 13618 (Porter), 18 Dec 1966, box 22, FTSCPF, 1964–66.

142. See Saigon embtel 13640 (Porter), 17 Dec 1966 (sanitized), box 147, NSF:CO:VN, LBJL, ex-cerpted in *SDVW:NVPP*, 307; the full version of LBJL copy was released September 2005 through author's MDR, case NLF 04-212 appeal.

143. R. A. Fyjis-Walker, "United States Air Attacks near Hanoi," 17 Dec 1966, FO 371/186354, TNA.

144. Deptel 104673 to American Embassy, Saigon, 17 Dec 1966, box 147, NSF:CO:VN, LBJL.

145. Leonard C. Meeker to DR, "Saigon and Hanoi as 'Open Cities,'" 17 Dec 1966, and Sisco to DR (through NK), "'Open Cities': Variations on a Theme," 17 Dec 1966, both POL 27 VIET S, box 3014, CFPF, 1964–66.

146. NK note on Sisco to DR, "'Open Cities': Variations on a Theme," 17 Dec 1966.

147. On 18 Dec 1966 GD'O-Habib talk, see Saigon embtel 13618 (Porter), 18 Dec 1966, POL 27-14/MARIGOLD 12/15/66, box 22, FTSCPF, 1964–66; IE/S (GD'O) to IFM (AF), office memos 52-54, all noon, 18 Dec 1966, GD'O dossier; GD'O, *DV*, 732–33 (18 Dec 1966).

148. Saigon embtel 13618 (Porter), 18 Dec 1966, POL 27-14/MARIGOLD 12/15/66, box 22, FTSCPF, 1964–66.

149. On "business," see BE/Washington to FO, tel. 3456, 20 Dec 1966, PREM 13/2837, TNA, cour-tesy A. Kalinovsky; on "atmosphere," see WWR to LBJ (enc. DR to LBJ and draft Goldberg to Thant), CAP661246, rec'd LBJ Ranch 1:25 p.m., 18 Dec 1966, DDRS/LBJL.

150. See deptel 104408 to American Embassy, Warsaw, sent 7:43 p.m., 16 Dec 1966, POL 27-14/MARIGOLD 12/15/66, box 22, FTSCPF, 1964–66.

Chapter 10

1. Warsaw embtel 1506 (JAG), rec'd 5:56 a.m., 19 Dec 1966, and deptel 104776 to American Em-bassy, Warsaw, sent 7:34 a.m., 19 Dec 1966, POL 27-14 Viet/Marigold, box 22, FTSCPF; "trou-blesome": "Marigold: A Chronology," 31.

2. Quotations from 19 Dec 1966 JAG-AR conversation, other than from JAG's oral presentation, are from Warsaw embtel 1513 (JAG), 19 Dec 1966, *FRUS, 1964–68*, 4:958–61; AR, urgent note 509/Rap./66, 20 Dec 1966, GM sygn. 1/77 w 16, t-39, *Tajne spec. znaczenia*, AMSZ, courtesy H. Szlajfer; and MR.

3. For the full text, see Warsaw embtel 1508 (JAG), 19 Dec 1966, *FRUS, 1964–68*, 4:952–57. The Pentagon Papers summarized its objectives as "(1) keeping the door open for talks to develop" and "(2) letting the record show our persistent efforts to move forward, while refuting Polish contentions that our actions and statements blocked the opening of conversations." *SDVW:NVPP*, 299.

4. JAG OH II, 21.

5. MR. In his own internal report, AR did not mention pounding the table, merely stating: "At this point, I sharply interrupted Gronouski." AR, *pilna notatka* [urgent note], 20 Dec 1966, GM sygn. 1/77 w 16, t-39, *Tajne spec. znaczenia*, AMSZ, courtesy H. Szlajfer, trans. MG.

6. JM-WAH memcon, 19 Feb 1969, POL 27-14 Viet/Marigold 1969, box 2739, CFPF, 1967–69.

7. Saigon embtel 22598 (HCL), 10 Apr 1967, POL 27-14 MARIGOLD 1967, ibid.

8. JAG believed it was only "because of [their] pretty good personal relationship" that he was able to "calm [AR] down" and finish the meeting. JAG OH II, 21.

9. JM handwritten draft account, courtesy of Stefan Michałowski.

10. Poldel Saigon (JL) to PFM (Spasowski), sz. 15985, 19 Dec 1966, AMSZ, obt./trans. MG.

11. London embtel 5016 (Bruce), "Subj: British Reaction to Bombing Near Hanoi," 20 Dec 1966, United Kingdom cables, vol. IX 8/66-1/67, box 210, NSF:CO, LBJL.

12. London embtel 5010 (Bruce), 19 Dec 1966, deptel 105399 to American Embassy London, 19 Dec 1966, and DR-Sir Patrick Dean memcon, 20 Dec 1966, all POL 27 VIET S, box 3014, CFPF, 1964–66; BE/Washington to FO, tel. 3456, 20 Dec 1966, PREM 13/2837, TNA; Brown to DR, 30 Dec 1966, United Kingdom cables, vol. IX 8/66-1/67, box 210, NSF:CO, LBJL.

13. Thant, 19 Dec 1966 entry, "The Question of Viet-Nam," folder "Vietnam War (Confidential Papers), 1965–1966," DAG-1, 5.2.2.3.2, UNA.

14. USUN 3340 (Goldberg), 20 Dec 1966, United Nations, vol. 6, 12/1/66 [2 of 2], box 68, NSF: Agency, LBJL.

15. Dixon Donnelley to DR, 19 Dec 1966, Department of State–Rusk, box 4, NK Papers, RG 59, NA II.

16. DR-WPB telcon, 4:28 p.m., 19 Dec 1966, box 57, DR Papers, RG 59, NA II. Ottawa agreed the Viet Cong actions in Saigon were deplorable but thought it "very difficult to tie these actions to the issue of bombing attacks against the North." Memcon, "Canadian Position Re Alleged Bombing of Hanoi," 19 Dec 1966, POL 27 VIET S, box 3014, CFPF, 1964–66.

17. Donnelley to Sylvester, "Subject: Secretary's Backgrounder," 19 Dec 1966, Department of State–Rusk folder, box 4, NK Papers; DR desk calendar, LBJL.

18. CE/Washington (Ritchie) to CDEA, tel. 3850, "Vietnam: Proposals for Commission Initiative," 19 Dec 1966, file 100-11-3, vol. 1 [pt. 2], vol. 9516, RG 25, NAC (also tel. 3857, 20 Dec 1966, same folder); deptel 105380, 19 Dec 1966, Vietnam NARCISSUS, box 142, NSF:CO:VN, LBJL.

19. Martin to Chagla: M.C. [Marcel Cadieux] memo to Martin, "Vietnam—Commission Initiative"; and CDEA to CHC/Delhi, tel. Y-859, "Vietnam: Commission Initiative," all 19 Dec 1966, file 20-22-VIETS-2-1 vol. 8, vol. 9398, RG 25, NAC.

20. Far East Division chief Klaus Goldschlag in Ottawa embtel 1023 (Butterworth), 20 Dec 1966, POL 27 VIET S, box 3014, CFPF, 1964–66.

21. See PE/Rome (Willmann) to PFM (AR), sz. 16028, sz. 16053, and sz. 16054, all 20 Dec 1966, AMSZ, trans. MG.

22. PE/Rome (Willmann) to PFM (Kliszko-AR), sz. 16058, 20 Dec 1966. Polish documents establish that the leak occurred on the 20 Dec, contradicting AR's statement to AF (via Willmann), that the Poles gave the pope the "whole story" on Marigold on the 19 Dec. IFM (AF) to IE/S (GD'O), office memo, 9:50 p.m., 27 Dec 1966, GD'O dossier, and Rome embtel 3409 (Reinhardt), 28 Dec 1966, SDVW:NVPP, 310, 318–20.

23. PE/Rome (Willmann) to PFM (AR), sz. 16112, 21 Dec 1966, AMSZ, trans. MG.

24. Ibid.

25. Positive reaction: WP, 20 Dec 1966; NYT, 20, 21, and 22 Dec 1966.

26. DR-Martin telcon, 12:24 p.m., 21 Dec 1966, box 57, DR Papers, entry 5379, RG 59, NA II; CDEA (Martin) to Canadian UN Mission, New York, tel. Y869 Flash, "Vietnam—Commission Initiative," 22 Dec 1966, file 100-11-3 vol. 1 [pt. 2], vol. 9516, RG 25, NAC ; "flickerings": Ottawa embtel 1027 (Butterworth), 21 Dec 1966, POL 27 VIET S, box 3014, CFPF, 1964–66; also CHC/Delhi (Michener) to CDEA, tel. 2788, 21 Dec 1966 and CHC/Delhi (Michener) to CDEA, tel. 2820 flash, "Vietnam: Commission Initiative," 23 Dec 1966, file 100-11-3 vol. 1 [pt. 2], vol. 9516, RG 25, NAC.

27. WWR to Jake Jacobsen for LBJ, 20 Dec 1966, forwarding Warsaw embtel 1513, 19 Dec 1966, box 147, NSF:CO:VN, LBJL.

28. Deptel 105909 (to American Embassy, Warsaw), 20 Dec 1966, LBJL/DDRS; also FRUS, 1964–68, 4:961 n. 3.

29. WPB draft paper, "1967 and Beyond in Vietnam," Washington, 21 Dec 1966, ibid., 962–66; WPB's citation of "recent intelligence" alluded to the 30 Nov 1966 CIA report described above.

30. Foreshadowing later debates about a "decent interval" strategy, WPB calculated that Washington could not accept "major early risks" of an outright Communist victory—which "would in itself virtually doom the Administration to defeat [in 1968] and might well set off a wave of isolationist revulsion against all of our now-promising efforts in the rest of East Asia"—but might have to accept an accord that elevated odds of an eventual Communist takeover to 30 percent from 20 percent.

31. Memo of meeting, Gov. Harriman's Office, 4 p.m., 21 Dec 1966, and WAH to DR, "Subject: A Package Deal for Hanoi (Attached)," 22 Dec 1966, in boxes 520, 569, WAHP-LC.

32. 20–21 Dec 1966 entries, box 9, PDD, LBJL; NK desk calendar, NK Papers, JFKL.

33. RSM-DR telcon, 11:17 a.m., 22 Dec 1966, box 57, DR records, entry 5379, RG 59, NA II.

34. White House to DR, LBJ, WH6326 from LBJ Ranch, NK and RSM for DR, 1:32 p.m., 21 Dec 1966, POL 27-14 Viet/Marigold, box 22, FTSCPF.

35. Goldberg later told GD'O he had been assigned to go to Warsaw should the 10-mile zone around Hanoi lead to direct U.S.-DRV talks. IE/Saigon (GD'O) to IFM (AF), office memo 110, 4 Mar 1967, GD'O dossier.

36. Deptel 106358 to American Embassy, Warsaw, 21 Dec 1966, POL 27-14 Viet/Marigold, box 22, FTSCPF.

37. CE/Washington to CDEA, "Bombing of Hanoi," 21 Dec 1966, File 20-VIET, pt. 1, vol. 3097, RG 25, NAC. Queried at DR's request, CDEA officials explained that though there was no provision explicitly mandating the ICC to inspect bomb damage, it would have been "legalistic" to refuse a request from one of the parties. Ottawa embtel 1019 (Butterworth), 19 Dec 1966, POL 27 VIET S, box 3014, CFPF, 1964–66.

38. PE/Hanoi (JS) to PFM, sz. 16062, 21 Dec 1966, AMSZ, trans. MG.

39. JS-NDT 21 Dec 1966 meeting: PE/Hanoi (JS) to PFM (AR), sz. 16085, 21 Dec 1966, and sz. 16124, 22 Dec 1966, both ibid.; MR.

40. JL-GD'O 21 Dec 1966 dinner: Poldel Saigon (JL) to PFM (JM), sz. 16120, 21 Dec 1966, AMSZ, obt./trans. LG; GD'O, *DV,* 734 (20 Dec 1966); JL denials: Saigon embtel 14015 (Porter), 22 Dec 1966, POL 27-14 Viet/Marigold, box 22, FTSCPF.

41. Saigon embtel 14015 (Porter), 22 Dec 1966, ibid.

42. JAG OH II, 22.

43. Telephone interview with Herbert and Joy Kaiser, Palo Alto, Calif., 31 Jul 2007.

44. Warsaw embtel 1529 (JAG) and deptel 106150 to American Embassy, Warsaw, both 21 Dec 1966, POL 27-14 Viet/Marigold, box 22, FTSCPF.

45. Warsaw embtel 1535 (JAG), 21 Dec 1966, *FRUS, 1964–68,* 4:966–67; AR, urgent note 515/Rap./66, 22 Dec 1966, GM sygn. 1/77 w 16, t-39, *Tajne spec. znaczenia,* AMSZ, courtesy H. Szlajfer, trans. MG.

46. 22 Dec 1966 JAG-AR conversation: Warsaw embtel 1536 (JAG), rec'd 9:12 p.m., 21 Dec 1966, and Warsaw embtel 1537 (JAG), 22 Dec 1966, both in POL 27-14 Viet/Marigold, box 22, FTSCPF; AR, urgent note 515/Rap./66, 22 Dec 1966, GM sygn. 1/77 w 16, t-39, *Tajne spec. znaczenia,* AMSZ, courtesy H. Szlajfer, trans. MG; and MR.

47. Handwritten comment on A. J. de la Mare, "Vietnam: the 'Martin Plan,'" 22 Dec 1966, FCO 15/282, TNA.

48. PE/New Delhi (Ogrodziński) to PFM (JM), sz. 16132, 22 Dec 1966, AMSZ, trans. MG.

49. MR.

50. PE/Moscow to PFM (AR), sz. 16134, 22 Dec 1966, AMSZ, trans. MG.

51. *WP,* 23 Dec 1966; JAG's routing: deptel 106813 to American consul, Frankfurt, 21 Dec 1966, and American consul, Frankfurt 3850, 22 Dec 1966, both PER-Personnel Gronouski, John A. 1/1/65, box 184, CFPF, 1964–66; DK and SHL, *Secret Search,* 72.

52. WWR-DR telcon, 10:40 a.m., 22 Dec 1966, box 57, DR records, entry 5379, RG 59, NA II.

53. DR-RSM telcon, 11:17 a.m., 22 Dec 1966, ibid.

54. WPB-Zinchuk memcon, "Subject: NODIS/MARIGOLD," 1–2:30 p.m., 22 Dec 1966, box 147, NSF:CO:VN, LBJL.

55. Unless otherwise noted, the account of JAG's consultations in Washington relies on JAG OH-II, 23–25; also DR appointment book, 22–23 Dec 1966, box 3, DR Papers, LBJL.

56. DR via WWR to LBJ, CAP661300, 23 Dec 1966, rec'd Washington Comcenter 11:03 am, rec'd LBJ Ranch Comcenter 11:50 a.m., Vietnam MARIGOLD—Incomplete, box 148, NSF:CO:VN, LBJL.

57. WWR noted Zinchuk's influence when he passed LBJ a record of WPB's talk with him: WWR to LBJ, 3:30 p.m., 23 Dec 1966, box 148, NSF:CO:VN, LBJL.

58. WWR to LBJ, draft, 23 Dec 1966, box 147, NSF:CO:VN, LBJL; NK request: DR-WWR telcon, 10:40 a.m., 22 Dec 1966, box 57, DR records, entry 5379, RG 59, NA II.

59. CLC, *The Lost Crusade: America in Vietnam* (New York: Dodd, Mead, 1970), 340.

60. WWR addendum to CAP661300, 23 Dec 1966.

61. CAP661291, WWR to LBJ, 22 Dec 1966, enclosing Warsaw embtel 1537, box 147, NSF:CO:VN, LBJL.

62. Tape recording of RSM-LBJ telcon, 1:01 p.m., 23 Dec 1966, LBJL; also *FRUS, 1964–68*, 4:968 n. 1.

63. McNaughton diary, 146 (24 Dec 1966), courtesy C. Mosher.

64. JCS telegram 2135, 23 Dec 1966, 4:08 p.m., in *FRUS, 1964–68*, 4:968 n. 1.

65. Sharp to Wheeler, 24 Dec 1966, ibid., 969–70.

66. DR via WWR to LBJ, CAP661300, 23 Dec 1966, as above.

67. On the debt package that JAG promoted in Washington, see Francis M. Bator to LBJ, 26 Dec 1966, in *FRUS, 1964–68, Volume XVII: Eastern Europe* (Washington, D.C.: U.S. Government Printing Office, 1996), 347–49; and *NYT*, 30 Dec 1966.

68. JAG OH II, 27.

69. Deptel 10780 (to American Embassy, Warsaw), 23 Dec 1966, 3:43 p.m., POL 24-14/MARIGOLD, box 22, FTSCPF. JAG told AR that he personally witnessed RSM's order. MR.

70. Deptel 107911 (to American Embassy, Warsaw), 23 Dec 1966, 4:21 p.m., in *FRUS, 1964–68*, 4:968–69.

71. Tape recording of LBJ-DR telcon, 7:45 p.m., 25 Dec 1966, LBJL.

72. "Christmas Present": CLC, *Lost Crusade*, 340; JAG routing: deptel 10780 to American Embassy, Warsaw (JAG to Jenkins), 23 Dec 1966, 3:43 p.m., POL 24-14/Marigold, box 22, FTSCPF; "high hopes": Warsaw embtel 1596 (JAG), 30 Dec 1966, CAP661394, Vietnam MARIGOLD—Incomplete, box 148, NSF:CO:VN, LBJL.

73. CDEA (Martin) to Canadian UN Mission, New York, tel. Y869 Flash, "Vietnam—Commission Initiative," 22 Dec 1966, and Canadian UN Mission, New York, to CDEA, tel. 3361, "Vietnam: Commission Initiative," 23 Dec 66, both file 100-11-3 vol. 1 [pt. 2], vol. 9516, RG 25, NAC; USUN cables 3394 (Goldberg), 22 Dec 1966, and 3403 (Goldberg), 23 Dec 1966, both Vietnam NARCISSUS, box 142, NSF:CO:VN, LBJL.

74. George Ignatieff, *The Making of a Peacemonger* (Toronto: University of Toronto Press, 1985), 226–27.

75. Canadian UN Mission, New York (Ignatieff), to CDEA, tel. 3353, "Vietnam: Commission Initiative: Talk with Goldberg," and tel. 3354, "Vietnam: Commission Initiative: Talk with U Thant," both 22 Dec 1966, file 100-11-3 vol. 1 [pt. 2], vol. 9516, RG 25, NAC; 22 Dec 1966 entry, U Thant, "The Question of Viet-Nam," 15 Jan 1967, in "Vietnam War (Confidential Papers), 1965–1966," DAG-1, 5.2.2.3.2, box 1, UNA.

76. On the 23 Dec 1966 Thant-Tomorowicz talk, see Polish UN Mission, New York (Tomorowicz), to PFM (AR), sz. 16224, 23 Dec 1966, AMSZ, obt./trans. LG; and 23 Dec 1966 entry, Thant, "Question of Viet-Nam."

77. Canadian UN Mission, New York (Cox), to CDEA, tel. 3363 flash, "Saigon—Vietnam Commission Initiative," 23 Dec 66, file 20-22-VIETS-2-1 vol. 9, vol. 9398, RG 25, NAC.

78. 22 Dec 1966 entry, AFD, trans. IO.

79. Ibid., 22 and 23 Dec 1966 entries.

80. AF-Willmann 23 Dec 1966 talk: 23 Dec 1966 entry, ibid.; IFM (AF) to IE/Saigon (GD'O), office memo, 23 Dec 1966, GD'O dossier; PE/Rome (Willmann) to PFM (AR), sz. 16216, 7 p.m., 23 Dec 1966, AMSZ, obt./trans. LG.

81. IFM (AF) to IE/S (GD'O), office memo, 23 Dec 1966, GD'O dossier.

82. MR.

83. Ibid.

84. PFM (Spasowski) to Poldel Saigon (JL), sz. 12913, 22 Dec 1966, AMSZ, trans. MG.

85. CDEA to CE/Warsaw, tel. Y875 Immed, "Vietnam—Commission Initiative," 23 Dec 1966, file 100-11-3, vol. 1, [part 2], vol. 9516, RG 25, NAC.

86. On the 23 Dec 1966 informal ICC meeting, see "Report on the Activities of the International Commission in Vietnam for the Month of December 1966," file 21-13-VIET-ICSC-8 FP 8.3, vol. 10129, ibid., and Poldel Saigon (JL) to PFM (Spasowski), sz. 16222, 23 Dec 1966, AMSZ, obt./trans. MG; JL's goals for meeting in Hanoi: Poldel Saigon (JL) to PFM (Spasowski), sz. 15941, 16 Dec 1966, ibid.

87. PE/Hanoi (JS) to PFM (AR), sz. 16143, 22 Dec 1966, AMSZ, trans. MG.

88. PE/Hanoi (JS) to PFM (Meller), sz. 16213, 23 Dec 1966, ibid.

89. On the trip to Hanoi, see HES, *Behind the Lines: Hanoi, December 23, 1966–January 7, 1967* (New York: Harper & Row, 1967), 12–39; HES, *A Time of Change: A Reporter's Tale of Our Time* (New York: Harper & Row, 1988), 126–30; and George Burchett and Nick Shimmin, eds., *Memoirs of a Rebel Journalist: The Autobiography of Wilfred Burchett* (Sydney: University of New South Wales Press, 2005), 573 (HES does not mention his presence on the same ICC flight).

90. Unfortunately, JM's report does not give the precise timing or method of the message's delivery, and AR's ciphergram 13014, which prompted JS's meeting, has not been located, so I am inferring from circumstantial evidence that this was the message he delivered.

91. PE/Hanoi (JS) to PFM (AR), sz. 16273, 25 Dec 1966, AMSZ, trans. MG.

92. HES, *Behind the Lines*, 40–75; HES, *Time of Change*, 131–35; anonymous typed account of Christmas Eve party in box 168, HES, RBML, CU.

93. IFM (AF) to IE/S (GD'O), unnumbered office memo, sent 23 Dec 1966, rec'd 4:30 p.m., 24 Dec 1966, GD'O dossier; GD'O, *DV,* 737–38 (24 Dec 1966).

94. IE/Saigon (GD'O) to IFM (AF), 24 Dec 1966, unnumbered office note (4:30 p.m.) and office note 55 (4:50 p.m.), both AFP, trans. A. Barrow.

95. GD'O-Habib, 24 Dec 1966: Saigon embtel 14206 (Porter), 24 Dec 1966, POL 27-14 Viet/Marigold 12-15-66, box 22, FTSCPF; IE/S (GD'O) to IFM (AF), office memo 56, noon, 26 Dec 1966, GD'O dossier; GD'O, *DV,* 738–39 (26 Dec 1966).

96. Ibid., 737–38 (24 Dec 1966).

97. Deptel 107817 (to American embassies in Warsaw, Vienna, and London), 23 Dec 1966, PER-Personnel Gronouski, John A. 1/1/65, box 184, CFPF, 1964–66.

98. Warsaw embtel 1554 (JAG), 25 Dec 1966, , box 147, NSF:CO:VN, LBJL.

99. Deptel 107911 (to American Embassy, Warsaw), 23 Dec 1966, in *FRUS, 1964–68,* 4:968–69.

100. AR hinted to JAG that after hearing Hanoi's response, Warsaw "might make proposals to both sides"—a possible allusion to the suggested scenario for an extended bombing halt leading to direct talks that the PZPR Politburo had *already* secretly transmitted to the Vietnamese Communist leadership.

101. On the 24 Dec 1966 JAG-AR meeting, see Warsaw embtel 1553 (JAG), 24 Dec 1966, box 147, NSF:CO:VN, LBJL, and Warsaw embtel 1555 (JAG), 24 Dec 1966, in *FRUS, 1964–68,* 4:971–73; AR urgent note nr. 522/Rap./66, 27 Dec 1966, GM sygn. 1/77 w 16, t-39, *Tajne spec. znaczenia,* AMSZ, courtesy H. Szlajfer; MR; JAG OH II, 25–26, 28; JAG SFRC ; DK and SHL, *Secret Search,* 73.

Chapter 11

1. GD'O, *DV,* 738 (25 Dec 1966).

2. JL interview, Warsaw, 20 Oct 2006.

3. Vung Tau trip: JL interview, Warsaw, 20 Oct 2006; Poldel Saigon (JL) to PFM (Spasowski), sz. 16394, 29 Dec 1966, AMSZ, obt./trans. MG.

4. JL interview, Warsaw, June 2003.

5. Observations: Poldel Saigon (JL) to PFM (Spasowski), sz. 16394, 29 Dec 1966, AMSZ, obt./trans. MG.

6. MR; it is unclear whether JS personally saw PVD or gave another official the message for him.

7. PE/Hanoi (JS) to PFM (Wierna), sz, 16274, 25 Dec 1966, AMSZ, trans. LG.

8. On "shattered," see HES, "U.S. Raids Batter 2 Towns; Supply Route Is Little Hurt," *NYT,* 27 Dec 1966; shelters: HES, *Behind the Lines: Hanoi, December 23, 1966–January 7, 1967* (New York: Harper & Row, 1967), 43; Hanoi, Beijing radio: *WP,* 26 Dec 1966; PE/Hanoi (JS) to PFM (JL), sz. 16275, 26 Dec 1966, and Poldel Saigon (JL) to PFM (Spasowski), sz, 16304, 27 Dec 1966, both AMSZ, trans. MG.

9. HES, "A Visitor to Hanoi Inspects Damage Laid to U.S. Raids," *NYT,* 25 Dec 1966.

10. HES, *A Time of Change: A Reporter's Tale of Our Time* (New York: Harper & Row / Cornelia & Michael Bessie, 1988), 130–31.

11. WWR to LBJ, 25 Dec 1966, CAP661328, enc. Warsaw embtels 1554 and 1555 and Saigon embtel 14206, Vietnam MARIGOLD—Incomplete, box 148, NSF:CO:VN, LBJL.

12. In his cable describing the Christmas Eve talk with AR, JAG noted that he had said "there are two sides to the picture, and in Washington there are those who have real questions about drastic actions around Saigon during the critical phase of discussions in the first half of December." LBJ at first thought his envoy had referred to "drastic actions around *Hanoi*" and criticized U.S. actions when in fact he was dutifully implementing a directive to emphasize Viet Cong attacks around Saigon. LBJ only realized his error when he read the passage to DR.

13. Tape recording of LBJ-DR telcon, 7:45 p.m., 25 December 1966, LBJL; also *FRUS, 1964–68,* 4:973 n. 6.

14. HES, "Hanoi During an Air Alert: Waitresses Take Up Rifles," *NYT,* 28 Dec 1966; also Poldel Saigon (JL) to PFM (Spasowski), sz. 16304, 27 Dec 1966, AMSZ, trans. MG. At least, HES *reported* observing "pretty waitresses with rifles rushing to take up battle stations": after visiting Hanoi a few weeks later, VCM claimed it never happened. To back his description of HES as "a twister, at least one given to poetic license to a degree which excludes him from the short list of honest reporters," VCM cited Canadian NCO eyewitnesses at the Thong Nhat as stating that, during the Christmas air alert, "Salisbury was not at the hotel, that the ladies did not go to the shelter, and that they sat it out and continued their conversation throughout the alert in the hearing of the CDNs." Candel Saigon (VCM) to CDEA, tel. 99, "Vietnam: Foreign Correspondents in Hanoi," 21 Jan 1967, file 20-22-VIETS-2-1 pt. 10, vol. 9398, RG 25, NAC.

15. WWR-DR telcon, 10:05 a.m., 27 Dec 1966, box 57, DR Papers, RG 59, NA II; "throats": Patrick Dean to Paul Gore-Booth, 29 Dec 1966, PREM 13/1917, TNA; snow: *WP,* 25 and 26 Dec 1966.

16. Deptel 108773 to American Embassy, Rome (info Saigon and Warsaw), 27 Dec 1966, POL 27-14 Viet/Marigold 12-15-66, box 22, FTSCPF.

17. *FRUS, 1964–1968, Volume V: Vietnam 1967* (Washington, D.C.: U.S. Government Printing Office, 2002), 38.

18. Telephone interview with Joy Kaiser, Palo Alto, Calif., 31 Jul 2007.

19. Mary Gronouski telephone interview, 25 Nov 2003.

20. DK and SHL, *Secret Search,* 73.

21. Warsaw embtel 1567 (JAG), 27 Dec 1966, box 147, NSF:CO:VN, LBJ; *WP,* 27 Dec 1966.

22. MR.

23. Warsaw embtel 1567 (JAG), 27 Dec 1966.

24. Deptel 108664 (to American Embassy, Warsaw), 27 Dec 1966, POL 24-14/MARIGOLD, box 22, FTSCPF.

25. MR; DK and SHL, *Secret Search,* 73; JAG OH II, 26.

26. Spellman visit, GD'O reaction: GD'O, *DV,* 739 (26 Dec 1966); *NYT,* 24–27 and 29 Dec 1966.

27. IE/S (GD'O) to IFM (AF), office memo 57, noon, 26 Dec 1966, GD'O dossier; GD'O, *DV,* 739 (26 Dec 1966).

28. JL interview, Warsaw, 20 Oct 2006; also Poldel Saigon (JL) to PFM (Spasowski), sz. 16394, 29 Dec 1966, AMSZ, obt./trans. MG.

29. Peter Arnett, *Live from the Battlefield* (New York: Simon & Schuster, 1994), 145.

30. JL interview, Warsaw, 20 Oct 2006.

31. IE/S (GD'O) to IFM (AF), office memo 58, 5:30 pm, 27 Dec 1966, GD'O dossier.

32. IE/S (GD'O) to IFM (AF), office memo 59, 6:15 p.m., 27 Dec 1966, ibid.; GD'O, *DV,* 739–40 (27 Dec 1966).

33. PE/Rome (Willmann) to PFM (AR), sz. 16299, 27 Dec 1966, AMSZ, trans. MG.

34. From 27 Dec 1966 entry, AFD, diary, trans. IO; "subtle game": IFM (AF) to IE/Saigon (GD'O), office memo, rec'd 4:30 p.m., 28 Dec 1966, GD'O dossier.

35. PE/Rome (Willmann) to PFM (AR), sz. 16318, 27 Dec 1966, AMSZ, trans. MG.

36. HES, "U.S. Raids Batter 2 Towns; Supply Route Is Little Hurt," *NYT,* 27 Dec 1966; Neil Sheehan, "Washington Concedes Bombs Hit Civilian Areas in North Vietnam," *NYT,* 27 Dec 1966; also HES, "No Military Targets, Nam Dinh Insists," *NYT,* 31 Dec 1966, and HES, *Time of Change,* 138–42. For a Pentagon critique of Salisbury's reporting, see Phil G. Goulding, *Confirm or Deny* (New York: Harper & Row, 1970), 52–92.

37. NDP also apparently quotes from the original Vietnamese record in his own account to the author.

38. NDT-JS 28 Dec 1966 meeting: PE/Hanoi (JS) to PFM (AR), sz. 16329, 28 Dec 1966, AMSZ, trans. MG; also LVL/NAV, *Before Paris* (2002 edition), 160–61, trans. MP (courtesy C. Goscha); and NDP, "The Marigold Drive," presented to author, 8 Jun 1999, 4.

39. NDP, "Marigold Drive," 4.

40. The excerpt in LVL/NAV, *Before Paris,* stops here, so the remainder is based on JS's cable.

41. NDP, "Marigold Drive," 4.

42. On 28 Dec 1966 GD'O-Porter talk, see GD'O, *DV,* 740 (28 Dec 1966); IE/Saigon (GD'O) to IFM (AF), office memo 62, 11:30 a.m., 29 Dec 1966, GD'O dossier.

43. IFM (AF) to IE/Saigon (GD'O), office memo, rec'd 4:30 p.m., 28 Dec 1966, GD'O dossier; GD'O, *DV,* 741.

44. On 28 Dec 1966 GD'O-Habib talk, see GD'O, *DV,* 741 (28 Dec 1966); IE/Saigon (GD'O) to IFM (AF), office memo 61, 11:30 a.m., 29 Dec 1966, GD'O dossier.

45. IFM (AF) to IE/S (GD'O), office memo 1, sent 11 p.m., 28 Dec 1966, GD'O dossier.

46. GD'O, *DV,* 742 (29 Dec 1966).

47. On 28 Dec 1966 ICC meeting, see Candel Saigon to CDEA, "753rd Mtg of Commission—Bombing of Hanoi," tels. 1211, 1212, and 1213, 28 Dec 1966, FCO 15/283, TNA; Poldel Saigon (JL) to PFM (Spasowski), sz. 16345, 28 Dec 1966, AMSZ, obt./trans. MG.

48. VCM to Wood, "Commission Meetings," 30 Dec 1966, file 100-10-1 pt. 6, vol. 9513, RG 25, NAC.

49. Poldel Saigon (JL) to PFM (Spasowski), sz. 16345, 28 Dec 1966, cited above.

50. On 29 Dec 1966 ICC meeting, see "Report on the Activities of the International Commission in Vietnam for the Month of December 1966," file 21-13-VIET-ICSC-8 FP 8.3, vol. 10129, RG 25, NAC; Poldel Saigon (JL) to PFM (Spasowski-Ludwik-Mikołaj), sz. 16398, 29 Dec 1966, AMSZ, obt./trans. MG.

51. On 28 Dec 1966 Meloy-AF talk, see Rome embtel 3409 (Reinhardt), 28 Dec 1966, POL 27-14 Viet/Marigold, box 22, FTSCPF; IFM (AF) to IE/S (GD'O), office memo 1, 11 p.m., 28 Dec 1966, GD'O dossier.

52. *NYT,* 26 and 28–29 Dec 1966.

53. PE/Rome (Willmann) to PFM (Kliszko-AR), sz. 16319, 28 Dec 1966, AMSZ, trans. MG.

54. PE/Moscow (Pszczółkowski) to PFM (JM), sz. 16331, 28 Dec 1966, ibid.

55. 28 Dec 1966 Thant-Ignatieff talk: Canadian UN delegation, New York (Ignatieff) to CDEA, tel. 3368 Flash, "Vietnam. Commission Initiative: Discussion with SecGen," 28 Dec 1966, 20-22-VIETS-2-1, top secret dossier, RG 25, NAC; for locating and declassifying this and other top secret documents, I thank P. Dozois and her NAC and CDEA colleagues.

56. CE/Warsaw (Berlis) to CDEA, tel. 1689, "Vietnam—Commission Initiative," 28 Dec 1966, and CDEA to CHC/Delhi, tel. Y877 Immed, "Vietnam—Commission Initiative," 28 Dec 1966, both file 100-11-3 vol. 1 [pt. 2], vol. 9516, RG 25, NAC.

57. Thant's statement contradicted Tomorowicz's report, noted above, that the UN leader had agreed with Poland that the proposed New Delhi meeting, unless adequately prepared, could do more harm than good.

58. HES, "Hanoi During an Air Alert"; HES, "New Capital City Planned by Hanoi," *NYT,* 29 Dec 1966; 28 Dec 1966 telegram from Daniel: HES, *Time of Change,* 142, copy in box 590, HES, RBML, CU, and in same file, 29 Dec 1966 cable from Topping suggesting that in view of the "considerable controversy" his articles were raising, HES "make special effort to cite best attribution available especially on statements likely [to] be challenged." See also Mark Atwood Lawrence, "Mission Intolerable: Harrison Salisbury's Trip to Hanoi and the Limits of Dissent against the Vietnam War," *Pacific Historical Review* 75, no. 3 (Aug 2006): 429–59 (quotation on 452–53).

59. MR.

60. Record of Polish-Soviet talks, Warsaw, 28 Dec 1966, in *Tajne dokumenty: Biura Politycznego PRL-ZSRR, 1956–1970,* edited by Andrzej Paczkowski (London: Aneks, 1998), doc. 29, trans. MG. It is difficult to reconcile Andropov's comment here with Brezhnev's statements to Gomułka a few weeks later (noted above) that the DRV was "practically begging" for Soviet aid in opening peace contacts with the Americans.

61. PZPR Politburo protocol 34, 28 Dec 1966, AAN, trans. MG.

62. CE/Warsaw (Berlis) to CDEA, tel. 1689, "Vietnam—Commission Initiative," 28 Dec 1966, file 100-11-3 vol. 1 [pt. 2], vol. 9516, RG 25, NAC,

63. MR.

64. Deptel 109639 to American Embassy, Warsaw (JAG), 28 Dec 1966, POL 27-14 Viet/Marigold, box 22, FTSCPF.

65. Warsaw embtel 1583 (JAG), 29 Dec 1966, ibid.

66. Deptel 110170 to American Embassy, Warsaw, 29 Dec 1966, ibid.

67. CDEA to CHC/Delhi, tel. Y877, 28 Dec 1966, 100-11-3 vol. 1 [pt. 2], vol. 9516, RG 25, NAC.

68. M.C. [Candieux] memo for Martin, "Vietnam," 29 Dec 1966, file 20-22-VIETS-2-1, top secret dossier, ibid.

69. Candel Saigon to CDEA, "753rd Mtg of Commission—Bombing of Hanoi," tel. 1211, 28 Dec 1966, FCO 15/283, TNA.

70. CDEA to Candel Saigon, tel no. Y884, 29 Dec 1966, cited in Candel Saigon (VCM) to CDEA, "755 Mtg of Commission: Bombing in Hanoi Area," tel. 1230, 31 Dec 1966, ibid.

71. *NYT,* 29 Dec 1966.

72. IE/Saigon (GD'O) to IFM (AF), office memo 63, 11 a.m., 30 Dec 1966, GD'O dossier.

73. GD'O, *DV,* 742–43 (30 Dec 1966); IE/Saigon (GD'O) to IFM (AF), office memo 65, 11 a.m., 31 Dec 1966, GD'O dossier.

74. Candel Saigon (VCM) to CDEA, tel. 1231, "Vietnam: Commission Initiative," 31 Dec 1966, file 20-22-VIETS-2-1, pt. 8, vol. 9398, RG 25, NAC.

75. This was, of course, more than a week since JAG initially raised the notion to AR at their post-midnight meeting early on 22 Dec, and more than five days since he had returned from Washington to Warsaw on Christmas Eve with news of the unilateral U.S. bombing halt within a 10-mile radius of central Hanoi.

76. Poldel Saigon (JL) to PFM (JM), sz. 16447, 9 p.m., 30 Dec 1966, AMSZ, trans. MG.

77. Warsaw embtel 1587 (JAG), 30 Dec 1966, POL 27-14 Viet/Marigold 12-15-66, box 22, FTSCPF.

78. 30 Dec 1966 JAG-AR meeting: Warsaw embtel 1596 (JAG), 30 Dec 1966, box 147, NSF:CO:VN, LBJL; AR, urgent note 532/Rap./66, 31 Dec 1966, GM sygn. 1/77 w 16, t-39, *Tajne spec. znaczenia,* AMSZ, courtesy H. Szlajfer; JM report; JAG OH II, p. 26 ("horribly crestfallen").

79. MR.

80. Ibid.

81. D. F. Murray, "The Martin Plan,'" 30 Dec 1966, FCO 15/282, TNA.

82. British public reaction to Salisbury articles: *NYT,* 29–30 Dec 1966.

83. See Brown to DR, 30 Dec 1960; Brown to Dean re telcon with DR; and DR-Dean memcon, 2–5 p.m., 30 Dec 1966, United Kingdom Cables, vol. IX 8/66-1/67, box 210, NSF:CO, LBJL; DR-Brown telcon, 1:36 p.m., 30 Dec 1966, box 57, DR Papers, entry 5379, RG 59, NA II; "Dawe from Andrews," 30 Dec 1966, PREM 13/1917, *NYT,* 31 Dec 1966.

84. *NYT,* 1 Jan 1967.

85. Canadian UN delegation, New York (Ignatieff) to CDEA, tel. 3379 Immed, "Vietnam: Commission Initiative: Discussion with SecGen," 30 Dec 1966, 20-22-VIETS-2-1, top secret dossier, RG 25, NAC, declassified at author's request.

86. French UN Representative, New York (Seydoux) to Foreign Minister Couve de Murville, tels. 4363–69, 30 Dec 1966, Commission des Archives Diplomatiques, Ministère des Étrangères, *Documents Diplomatiques Français,* 1966 tome 2 (1 Jun–31 Dec) (Brussels: P. I. E. Peter Lang, 2006), 1080–81, trans. G. Martin.

87. Canadian UN delegation, New York (Ignatieff) to CDEA, tel. 3368 Flash, "Vietnam. Commission Initiative: Discussion with SecGen," 28 Dec 1966, 20-22-VIETS-2-1, top secret dossier, RG 25, NAC.

88. See draft Thant letter to Goldberg, 30 Dec 1966, USUN 3445, 30 Dec 1966, LBJL/DDRS.

89. HES, "Hanoi Propaganda Stresses Tradition: War against Odds," *NYT,* 30 Dec 1966; Hanson W. Baldwin, "Bombing of the North," *NYT,* 30 Dec 1966.

90. DR-Sulzberger telcon, 9:55 p.m., 30 Dec 1966, box 57, DR Papers, RG 59, NA II. Sulzberger had taken on the job prematurely at age forty, three years before, when the family's anointed choice, his brother-in-law Orvil Dryfoos, suddenly succumbed to a heart attack. David Halberstam, *The Powers That Be* (New York: Alfred A. Knopf, 1979), 620–21.

91. DR-Daniel telcon, 10:17 p.m., 30 Dec 1966, box 57, DR Papers, RG 59, NA II.

92. Lawrence, "Mission Intolerable," passim; "Behind Enemy Lines," *Newsweek,* 9 Jan 1967; Halberstam, *Powers That Be,* 744–45; Goulding, *Confirm or Deny,* 52–92.

93. Warsaw embtel 1587 (JAG), rec'd 6:49 a.m., 30 Dec 1966, POL 27-14 Viet/Marigold 12/15-66, box 22, FTSCPF.

94. Dobrynin-LET memcon, "Reply to President's Letter to Kosygin," 30 Dec 1966, *FRUS, 1964– 68,* 4:981–82.

95. DR, LET, and Dobrynin memcon, "Viet-Nam and Other Matters," 30 Dec 1966, box 147, NSF:CO:VN, LBJL, and folder 1, box 2, LET Papers, RG 59, NA II.

96. See Brown to DR, 30 Dec 1960; Brown to Dean re telcon with DR; and DR-Dean memcon, 2–5 p.m., 30 Dec 1966, cited above; DR-Brown telcon, 1:36 p.m., 30 Dec 1966, cited above.

97. See Dean to Gore-Booth, 28, 29, and 30 Dec 1966; C.M. MacLehose to A. M. Palliser, 3 Jan 1967; and A. J. de la Mare, "Vietnam," 2 Jan 1967; all PREM 13/1917, TNA.

98. Thomas L. Hughes to DR, "Subject: Civilian Bomb Damage in North Vietnam," 30 Dec 1966, box 38, NSF:CO:VN, LBJL.

99. WWR-DR telcon, 5:10 p.m., 30 Dec 1966, box 57, DR Papers, entry 5379, RG 59, NA II.

100. Tape recording of DR-LBJ telcon, 3:14 p.m., 30 Dec 1966, LBJL.

101. WWR to LBJ, CAP661394, 30 Dec 1966, enc. Warsaw embtel 1596, in *FRUS, 1964–68,* 4:983.

102. Note by "Mary S," 7:30 p.m., 30 Dec 1966, box 148, NSF:CO:VN, LBJL.

103. VCM suspected that Rahman had planned to oppose the resolution but did not want to cast the only no vote and thereby deviate from New Delhi's careful balancing act by seeming more sympathetic to Saigon than Ottawa.

104. On 31 Dec 1966 ICC meeting, see Candel Saigon (VCM) to CDEA, "755 Mtg of Commission: Bombing in Hanoi Area," tel. 1230, 31 Dec 1966, FCO 15/283, TNA; Summary of Decisions Taken at the 755th Formal Meeting of the ICSC in Vietnam, 10 a.m., 31 Dec 1966, file 100-10-1 pt. 6, vol. 9513, RG 25, NAC; Poldel Saigon (JL) to PFM (Spasowski), sz, 20, 31 Dec 1966, AMSZ, trans. MG. Warsaw's instructions and expectations: PFM (Korolczyk) to Poldel Saigon (JL), sz. 13146, 30 Dec 1966, ibid.

105. *WP,* 18 Aug and 17 and 18 Sep 1966; *WP,* 19 Mar 1967; www.dinhdoclap.gov.vn. Not all foreign visitors scoffed. The former head of the Tennessee Valley Authority and U.S. Atomic Energy Commission, who visited Saigon in February 1967, after seeing Ky in the palace called it "one of the most beautiful public buildings I have ever seen: indeed, I think the most beautiful. Not because of its grandeur, though there is something of that. But the design is that of an open space through which air and light flow almost as if visible. Instead of marble (as in Tehran, for example) there is a happy combination of all kinds of materials—here the deep dark brown wood of the twin stairways leading up to the Prime Minister's office; there a wall of small matched blocks of limestone. The feeling of being in a beautiful park. And only two sentries in special uniforms, standing at attention with short bayonets attached, in contrast to the flocks of guards and little fortresses of sandbags spread all over the city." David E. Lilienthal, *The Journals of David E. Lilienthal, Volume VI: Creativity and Conflict, 1964-1967* (New York: Harper & Row, 1976), 377.

106. "Address to be Delivered by the Dean of the Diplomatic and Consular Corps, Ambassador of Italy, to His Excellency the Chairman of the National Leadership Committee," Saigon, 31 Dec 1966, file 22-13 vol. 1 [pt. 2], vol. 9502, RG 25, NAC.
107. Candel Saigon (VCM) to CDEA, tel. 227, "Vietnam and Commission and Indian Relations," 18 Feb 1967, series A1838, 3020/9/4 (North Vietnam–ICC), NAA.
108. On the 31 Dec 1966 reception, see Candel Saigon (VCM) to CDEA, tel. 1229, 31 Dec 1966, file 20-22-VIETS-2-1, pt. 8, vol. 9398, RG 25, NAC; Poldel Saigon (JL) to PFM (Spasowski), sz. 16479, 31 Dec 1966, AMSZ, obt./trans. MG; Rahman statement: file 22-13 volume 1 [pt. 2], vol. 9502, RG 25, NAC.
109. Poldel Saigon (JL) to PFM (Spasowski), sz. 16232, 24 Dec 1966, and PFM (Spasowski; approved by JM) to Poldel Saigon (JL), sz. 13003, 24 Dec 1966, both AMSZ, obt./trans. MG.
110. TVD may have sought the Viet Minh's agreement to oppose partition, but PVD "confined the discussion to generalities." For the most part, TVD was "left to wander disconsolately on the fringes of the Conference." Donald Lancaster, *The Emancipation of French Indochina* (Oxford: Oxford University Press, 1961), 333–34.
111. TVD also attempted to send a similar message to PVD via VCM when he visited Hanoi in early January. Seeing VCM before his departure, TVD also recalled his Geneva encounter with PVD and asked VCM to relay that he "accepts Pham Van Dong is a patriot (in his own way) and that Mr. Dong must accept that Dr Do is also a patriot." VCM should assure PVD he had "no reason for suspicion" regarding Saigon's support for a U.S. troop withdrawal after a settlement, and pass along TVD's belief that to save the Vietnamese people from more suffering, they and their governments should reach "a modus vivendi" essentially enshrining the status quo. VCM only saw HVL and NDT in Hanoi, so he only passed the message along in a general way. Candel Saigon (VCM) to CDEA, tel. 12, "Vietnam-Foreign Minister Dr Do and Hanoi," 5 Jan 1967, and Candel Saigon (VCM) to CDEA, tel. 60, "Vietnam: Hanoi Visit," 14 Jan 1967, both file 20-22-VIETS-2-1 vol. 9, Vol. 9398, RG 25, NAC.
112. JL interview, Warsaw, June 2003.
113. Candel Saigon (VCM) to CDEA, tel. 1229, 31 Dec 1966, file 20-22-VIETS-2-1, pt. 8, vol. 9398, RG 25, NAC.
114. Poldel Saigon (JL) to PFM (JM), sz. 162, 4 Jan 1967, AMSZ, obt./trans. LG.
115. JL interview, Warsaw, June 2003.
116. GD'O, *DV*, 743 (31 Dec 1966). Porter had already discussed the British proposal with TVD, who in turn had already consulted Thieu. TVD assured Porter that Saigon would respond positively, because it had no objection in principle to a meeting with the DRV authorities, but "he anticipates flat Hanoi rejection in any case." Saigon embtel 14678 (Porter), 31 Dec 1966, box 47, NSF:CO:VN, LBJL. Checking his sarcasm, when he talked with the Crown's ambassador in Saigon, Porter diplomatically lavished "handsome and sincere" praise on Brown's initiative and "went out of his way to say how much he welcomed it and how much he admired its timing." P. A. Wilkinson, BE/Saigon, to A. J. de la Mare, FO, 10 Jan 1967, FCO 15/580, TNA.
117. Saigon embtel 14702 (Porter), 31 Dec 1966, box 147, NSF:CO:VN, LBJL.
118. GD'O, *DV*, 743 (31 Dec 1966).
119. IE/Saigon (GD'O) to IFM (AF), office memos 66 and 67, 11 a.m., 1 Jan 1967, GD'O dossier.
120. PE/Moscow (Pszczółkowski) to PFM (AR), ciphergram 16449, 31 Dec 1966, AMSZ, trans. MG; *NYT*, 31 Dec 1966.
121. From 31 Dec 1966 entry, AFD diary, trans. IO.
122. HES, "No Military Targets, Nam Dinh Insists" and "Problems of Coverage," both *NYT*, 31 Dec 1966.
123. DR telcons with Sisco (8:06 p.m.), WWR (8:15 p.m.), Goldberg (8:15 p.m., 10:15 p.m.), and WPB (8:34 p.m.), 30 Dec 1966, and Sisco (9:30 a.m.), WWR (9:50 a.m.), and Goldberg (10:18 a.m.), 31 Dec 1966, box 57, DR Papers, RG 59, NA II; deptel 111082 to LBJ Ranch (DR to LBJ), 31 Dec 1966, LBJL/DDRS.
124. Polish UN Mission, New York (Tomorowicz) to PFM (AR), sz. 6, 31 Dec 1966, AMSZ, trans. MG.
125. *NYT*, 1 Jan 1967.

126. Ibid.; *WP*, 1 Jan 1967 ("gloves").
127. *NYT*, 2 Jan 1967; *WP*, 2 Jan 1967.
128. Tape recording of LBJ-Goldberg telcon, 8:23 a.m., 31 Dec 1966, LBJL; also *FRUS, 1964–68,* 4:986–87.
129. *NYT*, 1 Jan 1967.
130. DK and SHL, *Secret Search,* 74.
131. WWR to LBJ, 8:45 a.m.., 4 Jan 1967, enc. deptel 111909 (to American Embassy, Tokyo), 3 Jan 1967, in Walt W. Rostow vol. 18 [1 of 2], 1–14 Jan 1967, box 12 [1 of 2], NSF:MtP:WR, LBJL. WPB likely shared DR's theory, as he drafted the cable expressing departmental "concern" over the Japanese envoy's misstatement.
132. Deptel 111909 to Tokyo, 3 Jan 1967, cited above, summarized a Japanese report of Japanese-DRV conversations in Moscow since the previous summer.
133. [SHL,] HCL interview notes, 12 Oct 1967, box 15, SHLP ("copped out"); HCL to Read, "Subject: Press Contact," 13 Oct 1967, Vietnam 6C 1961–68 [1 of 3] Peace Initiatives & General International Initiatives (Retrospective Accounts), box 94, NSF:CO:VN, LBJL ("better keep fighting").
134. In his unpublished "Viet-Nam Memoir," HCL wrote that JAG related this explanation "months" after Marigold's collapse during a conversation in Washington (probably in May 1967). Reel 26, HCI II, MHS, VII-17.
135. *WP*, 1 Jan 1967.
136. PZPR-VWP inter-Politburo message, described in chapter 10; cited in MR.
137. See "Politburo Resolution on Intensifying the Military Struggle and the Political Struggle in South Vietnam (October and November 1966)," no. 154–NQ/TW, Hanoi, 27 Jan 1967, in *Van Kien Dang, Toan Tap, 28, 1967* [Collected Party Documents, Vol. 28, 1967], chief ed. Tran Tinh (Hanoi: Nha Xuat Ban Chinh Tri Quoc Gia, 2003), 141–70 (quotation on 145), trans. MP.
138. CE/Washington to CDEA, 9 Jan 1967, tel. 79, file 100-11-3, pt. 2, vol. 9510, RG 25, NAC.

Chapter 12

1. GD'O, *DV,* 745 (1 Jan 1967).
2. Herbert Y. Schandler, *The Unmaking of a President: Lyndon Johnson and Vietnam* (Princeton, N.J.: Princeton University Press, 1977), chap. 2; Gibbons, IV, chaps. 13–15, 17.
3. Official U.S. casualty figures in Vietnam for 1966: 6,053 deaths (5,008 killed in action, 1,045 additional nonhostile) and 29,992 wounded; and for 1967: 11,058 deaths (9,378 killed in action, 1,680 nonhostile) and 56,013 wounded. On intensifying ground operations and the Vietnamese civilian toll, see Gibbons, IV, 540–47.
4. Lady Bird Johnson, *A White House Diary* (New York: Holt, Rinehart & Winston, 1970), 469 (5 Jan 1967).
5. *NYT*, 9 Jan 1967.
6. WWR to LBJ, 3 Jan 1967, *FRUS, 1964–1968, Vol. V: Vietnam 1967* (Washington, D.C.: U.S. Government Printing Office, 2002), 14.
7. Sean Wilentz, "The Legacy of '67," *Rolling Stone,* 12–26 July 2007, 28ff; Barry Miles, *Hippie* (New York: Sterling, 2005), 184–91.
8. Telcon with assistant secretary for European affairs John Leddy, 1 Jan 1967, 11:16 a.m., box 57, DR Papers, RG 59, NA II.
9. Telcon, Martin to DR, 1 Jan 1967, 11:25 a.m., ibid.
10. CDEA (Martin) to CE/Washington (Ritchie), tels. Y885 Flash and Y134 Flash, 1 Jan 1967, file 20-VIET, pt 1, vol. 3097, RG 25, NAC (declassified at author's request); on "fit," see Paul Martin, *A Very Public Life, Volume II: So Many Worlds* (Toronto: Deneau, 1985), 446 n. 19.
11. DR-Ritchie 2 Jan 1967 talk: DR-Ritchie memcon, 2 Jan 1967, attached to DR to LBJ, 3 Jan 1967, POL 27-14 Viet/Marigold, box 2739, CFPF, 1967–69; CE/Washington (Ritchie) to CDEA, "Vietnam: Polish-USA Talks," tel. 2, 2 Jan 1967, file 20-VIET, pt. 1, RG 25, NAC (declassified at author's request).
12. The draft account stated: "On December 13, Rapacki told Gronouski that Hanoi was now unwilling to have the contact in Warsaw take place, and that it must be postponed." In the mar-

gin alongside this sentence, Read scrawled: "This was not so! See reports!" Nevertheless, the language remained unchanged when the account was circulated to the Canadians, the pope, the British, et al.

13. DR to LBJ, "Subject: Necessary Actions in Connection with the MARIGOLD Project," 3 Jan 1967, *FRUS, 1964–68,* 5:10–13. Notations on subsequent cables suggest WPB drafted the account.

14. USUN 3458 (Goldberg), "Subject: Marigold," 3 Jan 1967, 27-14 Viet/Marigold 1967, box 2739, CFPF, 1967–69; U Thant, "The Question of Viet-Nam," 3 Jan 1967, in "Vietnam War (Confidential Papers), 1965–1966," DAG-1, 5.2.2.3.2, box 1, UNA; DR-Goldberg telcons, 4:15 and 4:19 p.m., 3 Jan 1967, box 57, DR Papers, entry 5379, RG 59, NA II.

15. Reinhardt conveyed the account on January 8; in response, the pope mentioned the Polish approach but said Warsaw had not provided detailed information, and—noting public "confusion" caused by HES' "uncritical reporting"—said Washington needed to do more to convince the world it was defending South Vietnam from aggression. Rome embtel 3531 (Reinhardt), in "Marigold: A Chronology," 56–57.

16. Candel UN, New York (Ignatieff), to CDEA, tel. 14, "Vietnam: Polish/USA Talks," 5 Jan 1967, file 20-22-VIETS-2-1, formerly top secret records declassified at author's request, RG 25, NAC; USUN 3465, 4 Jan 1967, POL 27-14 Viet/Marigold, box 2739, CFPF, 1967–69.

17. On 4 Jan 1967 Ritchie-WPB meeting, see CE/Washington (Ritchie) to CDEA, "Vietnam: Polish-USA Talks," tel. 32, and "Points to Be in the Possession of Mr. Moore during His Visit to Hanoi," 4 Jan 1967, 20-VIET, pt. 1, vol. 3097, RG 25, NAC; WPB, memo for the record, "Subject: Disclosure of MARIGOLD to the British and Canadians," 5 Jan 1967, POL 27-14 Viet/Marigold, box 2739, CFPF, 1967–69.

18. Martin, *Very Public Life,* 447.

19. CDEA to Candel Saigon for VCM in Hanoi, tel. Y-70, "Vietnam: Contacts in Hanoi," 9 Jan 1967, file 20-22-VIETS-2-1, formerly top secret records declassified at author's request, RG 25, NAC. In a separate message sent the same day (tel. Y-71), Martin also notified VCM that the U.S. bombing prohibition within 10 miles of central Hanoi remained in force for an "indefinite period."

20. *WP,* 7 Jan 1967; Ritchie-WPB 7 Jan 1967 talk in "Marigold: A Chronology," 58.

21. D. F. Murray, "Vietnam: Canadian Activities in Hanoi," 12 Jan 1967, FCO 15/282, TNA.

22. Candel Hanoi (VCM) to CDEA, unnumbered flash tel., "Vietnam: Visit Adieu à Hanoi," 10 Jan 1967, file 20-22-VIETS-2-1, formerly top secret records declassified at author's request, RG 25, NAC.

23. VCM-NDT memcon, Hanoi, 12 Jan 1967, file 20-22-VIETS-2-1 pt. 10, vol. 9398, RG 25, NAC. VCM relayed the Phase A/B idea even though Martin's telegram describing WPB's message only reached him on the eve of his departure from Hanoi, making "very valuable reading" on the trip back to Saigon. Candel Saigon to CDEA, tel. 35 flash, "Vietnam: Contacts in Hanoi," 10 Jan 1967, and Candel Saigon (VCM) to CDEA, tel. 67, "Vietnam: Visit to Hanoi and Other Contacts There," 17 Jan 1967, both file 20-22-VIETS-2-1, formerly top secret records declassified at author's request, RG 25, NAC.

24. Candel Saigon (VCM) to CDEA, tel. 64, "Vietnam: Conversations with Ha Van Lau Ngueyn Trinh," 16 Jan 1967, FCO 15/282, TNA.

25. Candel Saigon (VCM) to CDEA, tel. 60, "Vietnam: Hanoi Visit," 14 Jan 1967, file 20-22-VIETS-2-1 pt. 9, vol. 9398, RG 25, NAC.

26. Candel Saigon (VCM) to CDEA, tel. 67, "Vietnam: Visit to Hanoi and Other Contacts There," 17 Jan 1967, as above.

27. Martin, *Very Public Life,* 447.

28. Ibid., 452–55. On Martin and Pearson, see Charles Taylor, *Snow Job: Canada, the United States, and Vietnam* (Toronto: House of Anansi Press, 1974), 3–41; Douglas A. Ross, *In the Interests of Peace: Canada and Vietnam 1954–1973* (Toronto: University of Toronto Press, 1984); conversation with Liberal Party senator Jerry S. Grafstein, 14 Oct 2007, New York; and Andrew Preston, "Balancing War and Peace: Canadian Foreign Policy and the Vietnam War, 1961–1965," *Diplomatic History* 27 (January 2003): 73–81.

29. Brown-AF memcon, 3 Jan 1967, PREM 13/1917, TNA.

30. BCG/Hanoi (Colvin) to FO, tel. 4, 2 Jan 1967, and FO to BE/Washington, tel. 45, 3 Jan 1967, ibid.

31. DR-Stewart 3 Jan 1967 talk: BE/Washington (Stewart) to FO, tels. 15 and 16, 3 Jan 1967, ibid.; WPB memo, "Subject: Disclosure of MARIGOLD to the British and Canadians," 5 Jan 1967, as above; "embarrassed": Stewart to MacLehose, 4 Jan 1967, FCO 15/646, TNA.

32. WPB-Stewart 4 January 1967 talk: Stewart to MacLehose, 4 Jan 1967, as above; WPB memo for the record, "Subject: Disclosure of MARIGOLD to the British and Canadians," 5 Jan 1967.

33. Stewart to MacLehose, 4 Jan 1967, as above.

34. George Brown, *In My Way* (New York: St. Martin's Press, 1971), 143.

35. FO to BE/Rome (Permanent Under Secretary to Brown), tel. 31, 4 Jan 1967, PREM 13/1917, TNA.

36. Brown to DR, enc. Stewart to DR, 4 Jan 1967, Vietnam, box 67, DR Papers, entry 5380, RG 59, NA II.

37. A. M. Palliser to prime minister, "Vietnam," 4 January 1967, PREM 13/1912, TNA.

38. Harold Wilson, *The Labour Government 1964–1970: A Personal Record* (Boston: Little, Brown, 1971), 345; Sylvia Ellis, *Britain, America, and the Vietnam War* (Westport, Conn.: Praeger, 2004), 48–52.

39. Wilson-Bruce memcon, 10 Jan 1967, PREM 13/1917, TNA; "second-class citizen": Bruce diaries, 10 Jan 1967, Bruce Papers, Virginia Historical Society, Richmond, courtesy P. Roberts; Bruce to DR, 10 Jan 1967, in "Marigold: A Chronology," 61. CLC with U.S. Embassy in London from 1955 to 1958: CLC, *In the Shadows of History: Fifty Years Behind the Scenes of Cold War Diplomacy* (Amherst, N.Y.: Prometheus Books, 2005), chaps. 7–8.

40. Wilson to LBJ, 12 Jan 1967, POL 27-14 Viet/Marigold, box 2739, CFPF, 1967–69; drafts: PREM 13/1917, TNA. The cryptic wire initially aroused confusion, because Bruce's letter to DR about the talk with Wilson had not yet arrived.

41. DR to Brown, in deptel 112632 to American Embassy, London, 4 Jan 1967, box 147, NSF:CO:VN, LBJL; MacLehose to Dean, 11 Jan 1967, and MacLehose to Palliser, 11 Jan 1967, both PREM 13/1917, TNA. Dean passed the reprimand to WPB. See also Murray, "Secret Exchanges with the North Vietnamese," 5 Jan 1967, FCO 15/646, TNA.

42. Dean to MacLehose, 15 Jan 1967, FO 800/977, TNA; Deptel 118905 to American Embassy, London, 15 Jan 1967, box 147, NSF:CO:VN, LBJL.

43. WWR to LBJ, 16 Jan 1967, *FRUS, 1964–68,* 5:35.

44. LBJ comment on WWR to LBJ, 16 Jan 1967—11:10 a.m., box 147, NSF:CO:VN, LBJL.

45. CLC went to Paris on a vain mission to prompt another Sainteny visit to Hanoi to sound out DRV leaders; he was willing, but de Gaulle vetoed the idea.

46. CLC, *In the Shadows of History,* 248–50; London embtel 5707 (Kaiser), CLC for DR, 19 Jan 1967, POL 27-14 Viet/Marigold, box 2739, CFPF, 1967–69; Brown-CLC talks, 11 a.m. and 5 p.m., 18 Jan 1967, FO 800/977, TNA; Wilson-CLC talk, 6 p.m., 18 Jan 1967, PREM 13/1917, TNA. CLC omitted the crack about LBJ's "psychotic" state from his own cable.

47. London embtel 5694 (Bruce), CLC for DR, 18 Jan 1967, box 147, NSF:CO:VN, LBJL.

48. Saigon embtel 15204 (Porter), 9 Jan 1967, ibid; *SDVW:NVPP,* pp. 328-9, 332.

49. DR to LBJ, "Subject: Necessary Actions in Connection with the MARIGOLD Project," 3 Jan 1967, *FRUS, 1964–68,* 5:12.

50. McNaughton-Zinchuk 3 Jan 1967 memcon, box 147, NSF:CO:VN, LBJL.

51. DR-Dobrynin 4 Jan 1967 memcon, "Subject: Viet-Nam—MARIGOLD," ibid.

52. CE/Washington (Ritchie) to CDEA, tel. 71, "Vietnam: Polish-USA Talks," 7 Jan 1967, 20-VIET pt. 1, vol. 3097, RG 25, NAC; also CE/Washington to CDEA, tel. 83, "Vietnam: Polish-USA Talks," 9 Jan 1967, ibid.

53. Warsaw embtel 1631 (JAG), 4 Jan 1967, box 147, NSF:CO:VN, LBJL.

54. JAG-JM 5 Jan 1967 talk: Warsaw embtel 1646 (JAG), 6 Jan 1967, ibid.; JM, urgent note, 6 Jan 1967, GM sygn. 1/77 w 16, t-39, *Tajne spec. znaczenia,* AMSZ, courtesy H. Szlajfer, trans. MG.

55. PE/Rome (Willmann) to PFM (AR), sz. 104, 3 January 1967, AMSZ, trans. MG; IFM (AF) to IE/S (GD'O), office memo 2, 2:45 p.m., 3 Jan 1967 (rec'd 12:45 p.m., 4 Jan 1967), GD'O dossier.

56. IE/S (GD'O) to IFM (AF), office memos 70-71, both 6:30 p.m., 5 Jan 1967, ibid.; "curiously naive": Saigon embtel 14921 (Porter), 5 Jan 1967, POL 27-14 Viet/Marigold, box 2739, CFPF, 1967–69.

57. JL-GD'O 6 Jan 1967 talk: GD'O, *DV,* 749–50.
58. JL suspected the nearly simultaneous releases of the fishermen and contractors was no coincidence but "a triangular transaction between the US, the PRC and the NLF." Poldel Saigon (JL) to PFM (Spasowski), sz. 421, 11 Jan 1967, AMSZ, obt./trans. MG.
59. GD'O, *DV,* 750 (6 Jan 1967).
60. Memorandum of meeting, 5 Jan 1967, *FRUS, 1964–68,* 5:25.
61. Deptel 114370 (to American Embassy, Warsaw), 6 Jan 1967, ibid., 27–28.
62. JAG OH II, 27.
63. Deptel 114278 (to American Embassy, Rome), 6 Jan 1967, and Rome embtel 3571 (Reinhardt), 10 Jan 1967, box 2739, CFPF, 1967–69; and IFM (AF) to IE/S (GD'O), office memo 3, 9:30 p.m., 9 Jan 1967, GD'O dossier.
64. GD'O-JL 11 Jan 1967 talk: IE/S (GD'O) to IFM (AF), office memos 77–78, both 11:30 a.m., 12 Jan 1967, GD'O dossier; GD'O, *DV,* 758–59 (11 Jan 1967).
65. Besides Fall's writings, see Dorothy Fall, *Bernard Fall: Memories of a Soldier-Scholar* (Washington, D.C.: Potomac Books, 2006).
66. On "foreboding," see Bernard Fall, *Last Reflections on a War* (New York: Schocken Books, 1972), preface, 12; and Michael E. Ruane, "A Triangle Comes Full Circle," *WP,* 17 Nov 2007.
67. Poldel Saigon (JL) to PFM (Spasowski), sz. 232, 6 Jan 1967, AMSZ, obt./trans. MG.
68. JL interview, Warsaw, 20 Oct 2006.
69. Poldel Saigon (JL) to PFM (Spasowski), sz. 667, 17 Jan 1967, AMSZ, trans. MG.
70. Murray, "The 'Martin Plan,'" 5 Jan 1967, FCO 15/282, TNA.
71. USUN 3468 (Goldberg), 4 Jan 1967, POL 27-14 Viet/Narcissus, box 2739, CFPF, 1967–69.
72. CHC/Delhi (Michener) to CDEA, tel. 13, "Vietnam Commission Initiative," 5 Jan 1967, file 20-22-VIETS-2-1 pt. 9, vol. 9398, RG 25, NAC.
73. CHC/Delhi (Michener) to CDEA, tel. 29 flash, "Vietnam Commission Initiative," 7 Jan 1967, FCO 15/282, TNA.
74. See, e.g., Nirvana folder, box 2739, CFPF, 1967–69; and Mark A. Lawrence, "The Limits of Peacemaking: India and the Vietnam War, 1962–1968," in *The Search for Peace in Vietnam, 1964–1968,* edited by Lloyd C. Gardner and Ted Gittinger (College Station: Texas A&M University Press, 2004), 231–59 (esp. 231–32, 251–55).
75. *NYT,* 6 Jan 1967.
76. CHC/Delhi (Michener) to CDEA, tel. 29 flash, "Vietnam Commission Initiative," 7 Jan 1967, FCO 15/282, TNA.
77. CE/Washington to CDEA, tel. 79, "Vietnam: Commission Initiative," 9 Jan 1967, file 100-11-3 pt. 2, Vol. 9516, RG 25, NAC; CLC, memo for record, 10 Jan 1967, POL 27-14 Viet/Marigold, box 2739, CFPF, 1967–69.
78. PFM (JM) to PE/New Delhi (Ogrodzińksi), sz. 158, 6 Jan 1967, AMSZ, obt./trans. MG.
79. PE/New Delhi (Ogrodziński) to PFM (JM), sz. 260, 7 Jan 1967, ibid.
80. PFM (Naszkowski) to PE/New Delhi (Ogrodzińksi), sz. 215, 7 Jan 1967, and sz. 227, 9 Jan 1967, AMSZ, ibid.
81. PE/Hanoi (JS) to PFM (JM), sz. 29, 2 Jan 1967, AMSZ, trans. MG.
82. PE/New Delhi (Ogrodziński) to PFM (JM), sz. 286, 8 Jan 1967, and sz. 302, 9 Jan 1967, AMSZ, obt./trans. MG.
83. PFM (Naszkowski) to PE/New Delhi (Ogrodzińksi), sz. 215, 7 Jan 1967, and 227, 9 Jan 1967, as above.
84. PE/New Delhi (Ogrodziński) to PFM (JM), sz. 349, 10 Jan 1967, AMSZ, obt./trans. MG.
85. CE/Delhi (Michener) to CDEA, tel. 70, "Vietnam: Commission Initiative," 12 Jan 1967, file 100-11-3 pt. 2, vol. 9516, RG 25, NAC and file 20-22-VIETS-2-1 pt. 9, vol. 9398, RG 25, NAC; also PE/New Delhi (Ogrodziński) to PFM (JM), sz. 496, 13 Jan 1967, AMSZ, obt./trans. MG.
86. CHC/Delhi (Michener) to CDEA, tel. 70, "Vietnam: Commission Initiative," 12 Jan 1967.
87. Ottawa embtel 1130 (Butterworth), 13 Jan 1967, Vietnam NARCISSUS, box 142, NSF:CO:VN, LBJL.
88. WPB to S/S (DR), 12 Jan 1967 (enc. CHC/Delhi (Michener) to CDEA, tel. 70, 12 Jan 1967), ibid.

89. *NYT,* 14 Jan 1967; *WP,* 14 Jan 1967; Warren Unna, "India Detects Hopeful Shift in Hanoi's Stand," *WP,* 31 Jan 1967. On U.S. annoyance, see Goldberg's comments to Bunche, 13 Jan 1967, in "Question of Vietnam," by Thant; Polish annoyance: PFM (Naszkowski) to PE/New Delhi (Ogrodziński), sz. 363, 12 Jan 1967, AMSZ, obt./trans. MG.

90. Record of CLC and Bruce meeting with Wilson and Brown, 10 Downing St., London, 10 a.m., 4 Feb 1967, PREM 13/1917, TNA. Wilson incorrectly implies that CLC's allusion to a potential US-DRV meeting "under a palm tree" referred to a plan for a specific meeting during the Tet truce; see Wilson, *Labour Government,* 346.

91. See deptel 95040 to American Embassy, Algiers (Jernegan), 1 Dec 1966, and deptel 95515 to American Embassy, Algiers (Jernegan), 2 Dec 1966, LBJL/DDRS. WAH and NLF: WAH to LBJ and DR, 6 Jan 1967, box 569, WAHP-LC

92. Bouteflika would become Algeria's president in 1999.

93. WAH Algerian contacts: documents in boxes 553–54, WAHP-LC; Algiers embtel 1831 (Jernegan), 8 Dec 1966 (DRV/NLF rejection of talks); Algiers embtels 1863 and 1866 (Jernegan), 10 Dec 1966; deptel 100640, 10 Dec 1966; and WAH, "Memorandum on Algeria," 12 Dec 1966, all LBJL/DDRS; record of negotiations group meeting, 16 Dec 1966, box 569, WAHP-LC; "better job": White House meeting, 16 Dec 1966, *FRUS, 1964–68,* 4:950.

94. Unless otherwise noted, this account of the 21 Dec 1966 Jernegan-Wychowaniec talk relies on Algiers embtel 1978 (Jernegan), 21 Dec 1966, POL 27 VIET S 12/20/66, box 3014, CFPF, 1964–66.

95. Algiers embtel 1831 (Jernegan), 8 Dec 1966, LBJL/DDRS.

96. PE/Algiers (Wychowaniec) to PFM (Spasowski), sz. 16186, 22 Dec 1966, AMSZ, obt./trans. MG.

97. Algiers embtel 1978 (Jernegan), 21 Dec 1966, POL 27 VIET S 12/20/66, box 3014, CFPF, 1964–66.

98. Memo of meeting, 5 Jan 1967, *FRUS, 1964–68,* 5:24–25; WAH to LBJ and DR, 6 Jan 1967, box 569, WAHP-LC.

99. PE/Algiers (Wychowaniec) to PFM (JM), sz. 61, 5 Jan 1967, AMSZ, obt./trans. LG.

100. Wychowaniec noted his conversation with Soviet ambassador Pegov to Jernegan: Algiers embtel 2161 (Jernegan), 11 Jan 1967, 27-14 Viet/Primrose, box 2741, CFPF, 1967–69.

101. Warsaw embtel 1646 (JAG), 6 Jan 1967, box 147, NSF:CO:VN, LBJL.

102. PE/Algiers (Wychowaniec) to PFM (AR), sz. 381, 11 Jan 1967, AMSZ, obt./trans. LG. In this cable, Wychowaniec indicated that on 7 Jan 1967, he met Tran Noi Nam as instructed in PFM (AR) to PE/Algiers, sz, 188 (not found).

103. Algiers embtel 2161 (Jernegan), 11 Jan 1967, 27-14 Viet/Primrose, box 2741, CFPF, 1967–69; "calmly": PE/Algiers (Wychowaniec) to PFM (AR), sz. 611, 16 Jan 1967, AMSZ, trans. MG. Wychowaniec relayed Nam's gossip about Bouteflika and the Chinese to Jernegan in the same terms he reported it to Warsaw. On the Maneli affair, see MG, "Poland and Vietnam, 1963."

104. WAH to LBJ and DR, "Subject: 'Negotiations Committee'," 14 Jan 1967, chron file, Jan. 1967, box 569, WAHP-LC.

105. Deptel 121565 to American Embassy, Algiers (drafted by WPB), 19 Jan 1967, PRIMROSE, box 142, NSF:CO:VN, LBJL; Warsaw embtel 1596 (JAG), 30 Dec 1966, box 147, NSF:CO:VN, LBJL.

106. See Algiers embtel 2264 (Jernegan), 21 Jan 1967, PRIMROSE, box 142, NSF:CO:VN, LBJL, and Algiers embtels 2246 (Hoffacker) and 2244 (Hoffacker), both 20 Jan 1967, ibid.

107. See the documents in ibid.

108. Algiers embtel 2381 (Jernegan), 31 Jan 1967, ibid.

109. See esp. deptel 129573 to American Embassy, Algiers, 1 Feb 1967, and deptel 131713, 4 Feb 1967, ibid. Nor did JM's unexpected arrival in Algiers in early February arouse any interest in bringing the Poles back into play.

110. See documents in Primrose folders in box 2741, CFPF, 1967–69, and box 142, NSF:CO:VN, LBJL.

111. JM letter to Nason, 12 Nov 1966, JM cables to Nason, 16 and 30 Dec 1966, Nason cables to JM, 19 and 30 Dec 1966, all "Centennial Celebration" folder, "President's Office subject files—John

Nason presidency, 1962–70" (series POF5, box 5), Carleton College archives, Gould Library, Northfield, Minn. I thank E. Hillemann for helping to locate these materials.

112. Warsaw embtel 1646 (JAG), 6 Jan 1967.

113. CE/Washington to CDEA, tel. 83, "Vietnam: Polish-USA Talks," 9 Jan 1967, file 20-22-VIETS-2-1, formerly top secret records declassified at author's request, RG 25, NAC.

114. Canadian hints: A. E. R. [Ritchie] to Beaulne and Shenstone, 7 Jan 1967, 20-VIET, pt. 1, Vol. 3097, ibid.

115. Hughes interview, Washington, 1 Jun 2007.

116. JM, Carleton presentation: "The United States in Foreign Eyes," *The Voice of the Carleton Alumni,* March 1967, 17–20, enc. w. Hughes to DR, 20 Apr 1967, POL 17-1 POL-US 1/1/67, box 2436, CFPF, 1967–69.

117. Young did not so indicate in the six-page, single-spaced record of their conversation which he circulated to U.S. officials, but mentioned cryptically that JM *also* made unspecified "disclosures," which he "asked me never to repeat to anyone." Young recorded these points in a "private memorandum for my own files," but the author was unable to locate it in Young's Papers at Harvard's Houghton Library; through the Asia Society; or in contacts with his son, Stephen B. Young. Considering his candor to NC, whom he saw immediately afterward , JM likely also dished to Young.

118. Kenneth T. Young, memo for the record, 10 Jan 1967 conversation with George [*sic.*] Michałowski, "Vietnam and China," 19 Jan 1967, POL 27-14 VIET 1/1/67, box 2715, and box 2739, both CFPF, 1967–69.

119. 10 Jan 1967 JM-NC talk: NC's memcon with "Mr. X," 10 Jan 1967, folder 7, box 1221, and folder 5, box 1222, NC Papers, Young Research Library, UCLA. JM quotations are in NC's paraphrase.

120. See memo of NC conversations with Thant (New York, 25 Jan 1967), Humphrey (Washington, 3 Feb 1967), DR (telephone call, 1 Apr 1967), and John P. Roche, Jorden, WAH, and Fulbright (Washington, 6 April 1967), folder 7, box 1221, NC Papers, Young Library, UCLA; NC, "Vietnam and the Fourth Group," *Saturday Review,* 1 April 1967, 22; and WWR to LBJ, CAP67306, 18 April 1967, and other documents in Norman Cousins Activities, box 191, NSF:CO:VN, LBJL. LBJ authorized: John P. Roche, "The Difference in 'News Leaks,'" *WP,* 6 Jul 1972.

121. JM-Thant 15 Jan 1967 talk: Polish UN Mission, New York (Tomorowicz/JM) to PFM (AR), sz. 578, 14 [*sic;* 15] Jan 1967, AMSZ, trans. MG; Thant, 15 Jan 1967, "Question of Vietnam."

122. After JM left New York, FBI director J. Edgar Hoover circulated raw (and inaccurate) intelligence quoting a confidential source as saying the true aim of his trip was to relay Thant a DRV offer to stop infiltration in exchange for a bombing halt. WWR passed LBJ the "interesting FBI report," predicting that were there anything to it Thant would shortly contact them. He didn't: Thant later told Goldberg about his talk with JM, but related nothing of the sort. FBI Director to LBJ, DR, et al., "Jerzy Michałowski, Internal Security—Poland; Foreign Political Matters—Poland—North Vietnam," 10:30 p.m., 17 Jan 1967, folder 5 ("Vietnam Negotiations, Misc., 1968"), box 11, Assistant Secretary of State for East Asia and Pacific Affairs (WPB) Papers, entry 5408, lot file 85D249, RG 59, NA II; WWR to LBJ, 8:30 a.m., 18 Jan 1967, United Nations, vol. 6 12/1/66 [1 of 2], box 68, NSF:Agency File, LBJL; US UN 3805 (Goldberg), 31 Jan 1967, POL 27-14 Viet/Marigold, box 2739, CFPF, 1967–69; UN record of Thant-Goldberg meeting, 31 Jan 1967, DAG-1, 5.2.2.3.2, box 1, Rest. Strictly Confidential, UNA.

123. Polish UN Mission, New York (Tomorowicz) to PFM (Milnikiel), sz. 371, 10 Jan 1967, and to PFM (AR), sz, 530, 14 Jan 1967; and Polish UN Mission, New York (Tomorowicz/JM) to PFM (AR), sz. 578, 14 [15] Jan 1967; all AMSZ, trans. MG.

124. Polish UN Mission, New York (Tomorowicz/JM) to PFM (AR), sz. 578, 14 [15] Jan 1967. Indian awareness in Warsaw: CE/Warsaw (Berlis) to CDEA, tel. 15, "Vietnam: Polish-USA Talks," 5 Jan 1967, file 20-22-VIETS-2-1, formerly top secret records declassified at author's request, RG 25, NAC, and Warsaw embtel 1701 (JAG), 12 Jan 1967, box 147, NSF:CO:VN, LBJL.

125. PE/Ottawa (Stradowski) to PFM (JM), sz. 691, 17 Jan 1967, AMSZ, obt./trans. MG.

126. Hence, en passant, AR's rejection of Martin's appeal to attend the New Delhi meeting.

127. On 16 Jan 1967 JM-Canadian meeting, see CDEA to CE/Warsaw, tel. Y-95, "Vietnam," 20 Jan 1967, file 20-22-VIETS-2-1 pt. 10, vol. 9398, RG 25, NAC; Polish UN Mission, New York (Tomorowicz) to PFM (AR), sz. 617, 16 January 1967, AMSZ, trans. MG.

128. CE/Washington to CDEA, tel. 287, "Vietnam: Contacts with Poles," 24 Jan 1967, 20-VIET pt. 1, vol. 3097, RG 25, NAC; JRB to WPB, WPB to DR, both 23 Jan 1967, POL 27/14 Viet/Marigold 1967, box 2739, CFPF, 1967–69.

129. JM letter to Nason, 3 Mar 1967, "Centennial Celebration" folder, "President's Office subject files—John Nason presidency, 1962–70" (series POF5, box 5), Carleton College Archives.

130. DK and SHL, *Secret Search,* 75.

131. HCL-LBJ 11 Jan 1967 talk: Gibbons, IV, 575–76; *FRUS, 1964–68,* 5:32–33.

132. Deptels 112005 (4 Jan 1967), 114483 (6 Jan 1967), and 117678 (12 Jan 1967), all to American Embassy, Rome, Lodge, Henry Cabot Per 1/1/67, box 178, CFPF, 1967–69.

133. On 15 Jan 1967 AF-HCL talk, see "Marigold: A Chronology," p. 62; IFM (AF) to IE/S (GD'O), office memo 4, 11:10 p.m., 16 Jan 1967, GD'O dossier.

134. On 16 Jan 1967 Pope-HCL talk, see Rome embtel 3678 (Reinhardt), 17 Jan 1967, Vietnam: January–March 1967, box 6, NSF:Rostow, LBJL.

135. GD'O, *DV,* 761 (16 Jan 1967).

136. Ibid., 761–62 (17 Jan 1967).

137. On 19 Jan 1967 GD'O-HCL lunch, see ibid., 762–63 (19 Jan 1967); IE/S (GD'O) to IFM (AF), office memos 81–83, all 4:30 p.m., 19 Jan 1967, GD'O dossier; Saigon embtel 16017 (HCL), 19 Jan 1967, POL 27-14 Viet/Marigold, box 2739, CFPF, 1967–69.

138. AF-Rostow conversation: IFM (AF) to IE/S (GD'O), office memo 5, 20 Jan 1967, GD'O dossier.

139. GD'O, *DV,* 766 (21 Jan 1967), trans. IO.

140. Rome embtel 3787 (Reinhardt). 20 Jan 1967, box 147, NSF:CO:VN, LBJL; "Marigold: A Chronology," 66, 68–69.

141. Rome embtel 3812 (Reinhardt), 24 Jan 1967, *FRUS, 1964–68,* 5:60–61.

142. From 16 Jan 1967 entry, AFD, obt./trans. Mario Sica.

143. From 17 Jan 1967 entry, ibid.

144. From 20 and 23 Jan 1967 entries, ibid.

145. From 24 Jan 1967 entry, ibid.

146. IE/S (GD'O) to IFM (AF), office memo 89, 11:30 a.m., 24 Jan 1967, GD'O dossier.

147. WWR to LBJ, 19 Jan 1967, *FRUS, 1964–68,* 5:50–51.

148. DR-WPB telcon, 11 a.m., 21 Jan 1967, box 58, DR Papers, entry 5379, RG 59, NA II.

149. Dobrynin-LET memcon, 30 Dec 1966, *FRUS, 1964–68,* 4:981–82. On "Sunflower," see esp. *SDVW:NVPP,* 371–516, and documents in boxes 255–56, NSF:CO:VN, LBJL.

150. The actual quotation, which HES omitted from his published report of his 2 Jan 1967 interview with PVD in the *NYT* on January 8, went: "If the US really wants a settlement, the first thing is to have good will. Of course we know what we should do if the US shows good will. If they stop the whole war, we know what we should do. If they stop doing harm to the North, we know what we should do." See DR to LBJ, "Subject: Highlights of Harrison Salisbury Private Report to Me," 14 Jan 1967, Vietnam MARIGOLD—Incomplete, box 148, NSF:CO:VN, LBJL; HES-PVD 3 Jan 1967 interview notes comparison and 13 Jan 1967 HES-DR memcon, in Rostow, vol. 19 [2 of 2] January 15–31, 1967, box 12 [2 of 2], NSF:MtP:WR, LBJL.

151. WAH to LBJ, 24 Jan 1967, and other documents in Vietnam, General, Jan–March 1967, box 520, WAHP-LC.

152. WWR to LBJ, 3 Jan 1967, *FRUS, 1964–68,* 5:15.

153. From 6 Feb 1967 diary entry, folder 3, box 7, Brandon Papers, LC.

154. Polish record of Polish-Soviet talks, 18 Jan 1967, in *Tajne dokumenty: Biura Politycznego PRL-ZSRR, 1956–1970,* edited by Andrzej Paczkowski (London: Aneks, 1998), 462–64, trans. LG.

155. See *SDVW:NVPP,* 227–28.

156. The Poles here appear to rely on JS' report that Mao Zedong had told Le Duan in November that he did not oppose negotiations and it was up to the Vietnamese to decide: PE/Hanoi (JS) to PFM (Wierna), sz. 16274, 25 Dec 1966, obt./trans. LG, and PE/Hanoi (JS) to PFM (AR), sz. 288, 8 Jan 1967, both AMSZ, trans. MG.

157. Record of Polish-Soviet talks, 18 Jan 1967, cited above.

158. Gromyko memorandum, 13 Jan 1967, quoted by Anatoly Dobrynin, *In Confidence: Moscow's Ambassador to America's Six Cold War Presidents (1962–1986)* (New York: Times Books / Random House, 1995), 156–58, 640–42.

159. On Sino-Soviet acrimony in Jan–Feb 1967, see esp. Sergey Radchenko, *Two Suns in the Heavens: The Sino-Soviet Struggle for Supremacy, 1962–1967* (Stanford, Calif., and Washington, D.C.: Stanford University Press and Woodrow Wilson Center Press, 2009), 188–95.

160. *NYT,* 26 29 Jan 1967.

161. See, e.g., *NYT,* 28, 29 Jan 1967, and 4, 8 Feb 1967; and *Newsweek,* 20 Feb 1967.

162. *NYT,* 4, 8 Feb 1967; "bacchanalia": Radchenko, *Two Suns in the Heavens,* 189.

163. *NYT,* 3 Feb 1967.

164. NDT interview: *SDVW:NVPP,* 422–24; Wilfred G. Burchett, *At the Barricades: Forty Years on the Cutting Edge of History* (New York: Times Books, 1981), 237–40; George Burchett and Nick Shimmin, eds., *Memoirs of a Rebel Journalist: The Autobiography of Wilfred Burchett* (Sydney: University of New South Wales Press, 2005), 580–83.

165. Chalmers M. Roberts, "U.S. Experts See 'Signals' from Hanoi Indicating Desire for Starting Talks," *WP,* 31 Jan 1967.

166. New Zealand Embassy, Washington, to New Zealand Foreign Ministry, Wellington, tel. 90, 2 Feb 1967, series A1838, item 3020/11/161/2, NAA.

167. Moscow embtel 3231 (Thompson), 28 Jan 1967, in *SDVW:NVPP,* 421–22.

168. *NYT,* 1, 3, 4 Feb 1967; *WP,* 5 Feb 1967.

169. For these reasons, CLC told the British that the White House and State Department considered NDT's remarks "very significant." CLC-Brown talks, 4 Feb 1967, FO 800/977, PRO/TNA.

170. PE/Hanoi (JS) to PFM (AR), sz. 288, 8 Jan 1967, AMSZ, trans. MG.

171. Ibid.

172. "Politburo Resolution on Intensifying the Military Struggle and the Political Struggle in South Vietnam (October and November 1966)," No. 154—NQ/TW, Hanoi, 27 Jan 1967, and VWP CC 13th Plenum Resolution (No. 155—NQ/TW), "On intensifying the diplomatic struggle and taking the offensive against the enemy in support of our people's resistance war against the Americans to save the nation," Hanoi, 27 Jan 1967, in *Van Kien Dang, Toan Tap, 28, 1967* [Collected Party Documents, Vol. 28, 1967], trans. MP (Hanoi: Nha Xuat Ban Chinh Tri Quoc Gia, 2003), 141–70, 171–79.

173. NDT report to VWP CC, "Intensifying diplomatic activities to seize the political initiative and employ our fighting while talking, talking while fighting strategy," 23 Jan 1967, ibid., 116–40.

174. "Uncle Huong" [VWP Politburo], Secret Cable No. 00 [on the Diplomatic Struggle] to COS-VN and Region V, 23 Jan 1967, ibid., 84–87.

175. Ibid., 85.

176. NDT report to VWP CC, 23 Jan 1967, 118 ("lobbying") and 127 ("package deal").

177. VWP CC Resolution No. 155—NQ/TW, 27 Jan 1967, 173; NDT report to VWP CC, 23 Jan 1967, 125; "strategic impasse": David W. P. Elliott, *The Vietnamese War: Revolution and Social Change in the Mekong Delta, 1930–1975,* vol. 2 (Armonk, N.Y.: M. E. Sharpe, 2002), 1048.

178. NDT report to VWP CC, 23 Jan 1967, 127–28.

179. Quoted by Lien-Hang T. Nguyen, "The War Politburo: North Vietnam's Diplomatic and Political Road to the Tet Offensive," *Journal of Vietnamese Studies* 1, nos. 1–2 (2006): 4–58, at 24.

180. Tet planning: MP, "General Vo Nguyen Giap and the Mysterious Evolution of the Plan for the 1968 Tet Offensive," *Journal of Vietnamese Studies* 3, no. 2 (2008): 1–33; Elliott, *Vietnamese War,* vol. 2, 1036–1125; Ang Cheng Guan, "Decision-making Leading to the Tet Offensive (1968): The Vietnamese Communist Perspective," *Journal of Contemporary History* 33, no. 3 (1998): 341–53; Nguyen, "War Politburo," 4–58. Noting contradictory impulses toward diplomacy and protracted guerrilla struggle, on the one hand, and a decisive spontaneous uprising, Hang perceives "schizophrenic shifts in VWP policy" in early 1967.

181. Moscow embtel 3218, 27 Jan 1967, and deptel 128175, 31 Jan 1967, *SDVW:NVPP,* 419–20, 424–25.

182. PE/Hanoi to PFM (Meller), sz. 1102, 27 Jan 1967 (vice minister Thien), and PE/Hanoi (Badowski) to PFM (Meller), sz. 1159, 29 Jan 1967 (Burchett/Shcherbakov), both AMSZ, trans. MG.

183. Poldel Saigon (JL) to PFM (JM), sz. 1166, 29 Jan 1967, ibid.

184. On 26 Jan 1967 JL-GD'O talk, see Poldel Saigon (JL) to PFM (JM), sz. 1239, 31 Jan 1967, ibid.; and GD'O, *DV,* 768–69 (26 Jan 1967).

185. JL interview, Warsaw, 21 Jun 2003.

186. VCM-HVL memcon, Hanoi, 7 Jan 1967, file 20-22-VIETS-2-1 pt. 9, Vol. 9398, RG 25, NAC.

187. Poldel Saigon (JL) to PFM (Spasowski), sz. 623, 16 Jan 1967, AMSZ, trans. MG.

188. PFM (Spasowski) to Poldel Saigon (JL), sz. 562, 19 Jan 1967, AMSZ, obt./trans. MG.

189. On 27 Jan 1967 ICC meeting, see Candel Saigon (VCM) to CDEA, tel. 135, "756th Mtg of Commission," 27 Jan 1967, FCO 15/283, TNA; Poldel Saigon (JL) to PFM (Spasowski), sz. 1123, 27 Jan 1967, AMSZ, trans. MG.

190. Canadian diplomat quoted in deptel 132375 to American Embassy, Saigon, "Subj: ICC Citations of NVN," 6 Feb 1967, POL 27 VIET S 2-2-67, box 2775, CFPF, 1967–69.

191. *Chubb's Folly,* 27 Jan 1967 entry.

192. GD'O, *DV,* 771 (27 Jan 1967).

193. JL telephone interview, 1 Oct 2007.

194. *Chubb's Folly,* 27 Jan 1967 entry; CDEA to Candel Saigon, tel. Y139, "756 Mtg," 31 Jan 1967, FCO 15/283, TNA.

195. Candel Saigon to CDEA, tel. 172, "Cancellation of ICC Flt to Hanoi Jan 27," 6 Feb 1967, file 20-22-VIETS-2-1, pt. 10, vol. 9398, RG 25, NAC.

196. PFM (Spasowski) to Poldel Saigon (JL), sz. 978, 1 Feb 1967, AMSZ, obt./trans. MG.

Chapter 13

1. HES, *A Time of Change: A Reporter's Tale of Our Time* (New York: Harper & Row / Cornelia & Michael Bessie, 1988), 121.

2. AR-Couve de Murville memcon, 26 Jan 1967, and AR–de Gaulle memcon, 27 Jan 1967, Commission des Archives Diplomatiques, Ministère des Affaires Étrangères, *Documents Diplomatiques Français, 1967,* tome I (1 Jan–1 Jul) (Brussels: P. I. E. Peter Lang, 2008), 155–60, 162–70, trans. G. Martin. After hearing AR's story, de Gaulle—declaring Vietnam "first a moral [issue], then a political one"—delivered a typically Olympian pronouncement: "Deep down, . . . the Americans are a people who have never suffered. They have never been invaded, they never experienced a revolution. They had the civil war, but that happened more than one hundred years ago. They never lived through an invasion or bombings. They suffered casualties during the war, but low in comparison to their population. They spent a lot of money but, their losses were moderate compared to their riches. They do not have the same psychology as you, as we, and naturally as poor Vietnam. . . . We spent a long time in Indochina, we made war in Indochina. We are convinced that the Americans, with their great means, will not win in Indochina. It is a war without victories, a war that is not like others. We told this to the Americans, but they chose to get involved for ideological reasons and also because they wanted to take our place. So they invented Diem, then another, then Ky. They took our place. As much if not more than us, they found themselves in a dead end and could not get out. That is their problem. It is a pity for Vietnam. We have kept a lot of affection for North Vietnam, South Vietnam, Cambodia, Laos. They, they have kept a bit of affection for us. We suffer to see them suffer. But we can't prevent the Americans from persisting, we can only tell them to leave. It is only slowly that the world and the United States themselves will understand that it is pointless and that thus it is bad to get involved. But it will take time." De Gaulle–AR memcon, 27 Jan 1967, Cabinet du Ministre, Couve de Murville, vol. 386, Ministère des Affaires Étrangères Français archives, Paris, obt./trans. G. Martin.

3. Arthur M. Schlesinger Jr., *Robert Kennedy and His Times* (Boston: Houghton Mifflin, 1978; 2002 ed.), 733–34.

4. Dudy memcon with RFK, 27 Jan 1966, AMZV, Prague, obt./trans. O. Tuma; also PE/Washington (JM) to PFM (Milnikiel), sz. 14834, 1 Dec 1967, AMSZ.

5. RFK-LBJ rivalry: Jeff Shesol, *Mutual Contempt: Lyndon Johnson, Robert F. Kennedy, and the Feud That Defined a Decade* (New York: W. W. Norton, 1997).

6. *WP,* 29 Jan 1967; *NYT,* 5 Feb 1967.

7. RFK–de Gaulle memcon, Paris, 31 Jan 1967, *Documents Diplomatiques Français 1967,* I:189.

8. PE/Rome (Willmann) to PFM (Naszkowski), sz. 15399, 3 Dec 1966, AMSZ, trans. MG.

9. RFK-AF memcon, Rome, 10:30 am, 3 Feb 1967, "Background Materials—RFK Trips: Europe, 1967" folder, box W-62, Arthur M. Schlesinger Jr. Papers, JFKL; also Schlesinger, *Robert Kennedy and His Times,* 764–76. U.S. officials later learned from "Italian sources" that AF had "described [to RFK] contacts mentioned in Estabrook's Washington Post article." Rome embtel 4127 (Reinhardt), 9 Feb 1967, Italy vol. V, box 197, NSF:CO, LBJL.

10. RHE, "Polish Peace Move Failure Laid to Hanoi Area Bombing," *WP,* 2 Feb 1967.

11. Sisco to Read, "Viet Nam," 21 Jan 1967, box 147, NSF:CO:VN, LBJL.

12. Saigon embtel 16677 (HCL), 27 Jan 1967, *SDVW: NVPP,* 341.

13. Draius Jhabvala, "Hanoi Agreed to Peace Talks Last Fall but Was Rebuffed," *Boston Globe,* 2 Feb 1967, in Candel UN to CDEA, tel. 225, "Vietnam," 2 Feb 1967, file 20-22-VIETS-2-1 pt. 10, vol. 9398, RG 25, NAC.

14. USUN 3904 (Goldberg), "Vietnam Negotiations," 4 Feb 1967, United Nations, vol. 6, 12/1/66 [2 of 2], box 68, NSF:Agency, LBJL.

15. RHE, "Canadians See Hanoi Willing to Negotiate," *WP,* 22 Jan 1967.

16. RHE, *Never Dull: From Washington Editor and Foreign Correspondent to Country Publisher* (Lanham, Md.: Hamilton Books, 2005), chaps. 1–12 (esp. 94–95, 108–9); RHE dedicated his memoirs to Wiggins, "whose career exemplified the journalistic principles and values I have tried to uphold." See also Katharine Graham, *Personal History* (New York: Random House, 1997), 208, 285 ("harmony," "turned on"); Chalmers M. Roberts, *In the Shadow of Power: The Story of The Washington Post* (Cabin John, Md.: Seven Locks Press, 1989), 306–7, 322, 324, 327, 359; and David Halberstam, *The Powers That Be* (New York: Alfred A. Knopf, 1979), 525.

17. RHE, *Never Dull,* chaps. 13–22; Ben Bradlee, *A Good Life: Newspapering and Other Adventures* (New York: Simon & Schuster, 1995), 274–89; *WP,* 15 Nov 1964.

18. RHE, *Never Dull,* 170.

19. Ibid., chaps. 23–24.

20. USUN 3251 (Goldberg), 16 Dec 1966, POL 27 VIET S, box 3014, CFPF, 1964–66; also US UN 2927 (Goldberg), 5 Dec 1966, United Nations vol. 6 12/1/66 [2 of 2], box 68, NSF:Agency, LBJL.

21. RHE, *Never Dull,* chap. 25–26.

22. DR-Goldberg telcon, 10:38 a.m., 2 Feb 1967, box 58, DR Papers, entry 5379, RG 59, NA II.

23. Candel UN, NY, to CDEA, tel. 226, "Vietnam: Polish-USA Talks," 2 Feb 1967, file 20-22-VIETS-2-1, pt. 10, vol. 9398, RG 25, NAC.

24. DR-Christian telcon, 10:56 a.m., 2 Feb 1967, box 58, DR Papers, entry 5379, RG 59, NA II.

25. WWR to LBJ, 3 Feb 1967, 11:30 a.m., Rostow vol. 20 [4 of 4] Feb. 1–11, 1967, box 13, NSF:MtP:WR, LBJL.

26. Candel UN (Ignatieff) to CDEA, tel. 228, "Vietnam," 2 Feb 1967, file 20-22-VIETS-2-1 pt. 10, vol. 9398, RG 25, NAC.

27. Goldberg-Tomorowicz 3 Feb 1967 talk: USUN 3908 (Goldberg), 6 Feb 1967, United Nations, vol. 6, 12/1/66 [2 of 2], box 68, NSF:Agency, LBJL; Polish UN Mission, New York (Tomorowicz), to PFM (Winiewicz), sz. 1452, 4 Feb 1967, AMSZ, trans. MG. Tomorowicz informed Warsaw that Goldberg had "insinuated, even though he did not say this clearly, that he thought that the December intensification of the bombings [was] harmful and regrettable." Goldberg reportedly said the events placed him "in difficult situations several times and he supposedly had a clash with McNamara with whom he is friends. He talks to the president personally about Vietnam, but 'he is not the only adviser.'" Not surprisingly, Goldberg did not report such sentiments to Washington, though senior officials sensed his unhappiness and desire to "leave his post with appropriate dignity." WWR to LBJ, 10:15 a.m., 31 Jan 1967, Rostow Memos [2 of 3], box 7, NSF: Name File, LBJL.

28. RHE, "'66 Hanoi Approval On Talks Reported," *WP,* 4 Feb 1967.

29. *WP,* 20 Nov 2000.

30. DR-Wiggins telcon, 2:45 p.m., 4 Feb 1967, box 58, DR Papers, entry 5379, RG 59, NA II.

31. They did so even without recognizing a telltale trace of Polish DNA: RHE's February 4 story incorrectly dated the three-way meetings in Saigon at GD'O's as having occurred on December 2 and 3—instead of December 1 and 3—a minor error apparently reflecting confusion in Warsaw caused by the fact that JL sent his report of the December 1 meeting only the following

morning yet still wrote, "Today I met with L at O's." Poldel Saigon (JL) to PFM (AR), sz. 15313, 9 a.m., 2 Dec 1966, AMSZ, trans. MG.

32. Michael Stewart, BE/Washington, to A. J. de la Mare, FO, "Vietnam: Possibilities of a Settlement," 4 Feb 1967, FCO 15/646, TNA.

33. *FRUS, 1964–68,* 5:98–99.

34. USUN 3847 (Goldberg), 2 Feb 1967, POL 27-14 Viet/Marigold, box 2739, CFPF, 1967–69; also USUN 3904 (Goldberg), "Vietnam Negotiations," 4 Feb 1967, ibid. An "irritated" Goldberg told Seydoux that the *WP* story was leaked by Tomorowicz "and to a certain extent" Thant and the Canadians ("thus confirming that the news was not without basis," the French ambassador noted): French UN Mission (Seydoux) tels. 241–44, 4 Feb1967, Vietnam folder, box 160, UN, Archives Diplomatiques Français, Nantes, trans. G. Martin.

35. Warsaw embtel 1939 (JAG), 8 Feb 1967, box 147, NSF:CO:VN, LBJL; Martin "miffed": Warsaw embtel 1701 (JAG), 12 Jan 1967, ibid.

36. Polish UN Mission, New York (Tomorowicz), to PFM (Winiewicz), sz. 1327, 2 Feb 1967, AMSZ, trans. MG.

37. Polish UN Mission, New York (Tomorowicz), to PFM (Winiewicz), sz. 1430, 4 Feb 1967, ibid.

38. Polish UN Mission, New York (Tomorowicz), to PFM (AR), sz. 1691, 10 Feb 1967, ibid.

39. RHE telephone interviews ("bungled"; "dropped"), 15, 17 Nov 2003 and 19 Jul and 20 Nov 2007; "blighted arrangement": RHE, *Never Dull,* 213; also RHE, "Journalists and Policymakers: A 1950s and 1960s Retrospective," *SHAFR Newsletter,* December 1992, 15. The Dane's identification confirms a report by an RHE colleague that his stories, while "primarily of Polish inspiration," were also "encouraged" by an unnamed NATO ally. Paul Ward, "Thant Is Drawn into Viet Debate," *Baltimore Sun,* 10 May 1967.

40. Polish record of Krag's 4 Jan 1967 talks: Dept. III, 8/75 w-1, AMSZ. For Danish records re Krag's visit to Warsaw, see files 5.D.49ᶜ (Krag trip to Poland) and 169 D 1ᵉ pk.XXVI/1967 (South Vietnam), Danish Foreign Ministry (*Undenrigsministeriet*) archives, Copenhagen. I thank C. Larsen for finding these records. See also Warsaw embtel 1939 (JAG), 8 Feb 1967, cited above, and *NYT,* 7 Jan 1967.

41. Danish DFM-Goldberg: USUN 3847, 2 Feb 1967, cited above.

42. RHE memo of off-the-record conversation with Thant, 30 Jan 1967, "RHE Memorandums" 1967, MCHC71-034, box 15, RHE Papers, WHS.

43. RHE, *Never Dull,* 213, implies this sequence, though it conflates the February 2 and 4 stories.

44. RHE telephone interviews, 19 Jul and 20 Nov 2007.

45. RHE memo of off-the-record conversation with Thant, 30 Jan 1967, cited above.

46. When RHE described an earlier talk with Duhaček, US UN officers "were struck by his exceptionally glowing report on reliability this particular source." USUN 3251 (Goldberg), 16 Dec 1966, POL 27 VIET S, box 3014, CFPF, 1964–66. I thank J. Cavoski for data on Duhaček's intelligence affiliation.

47. RHE memo of lunch with Duhaček, 1 Feb 1967, "RHE Memorandums" 1967, MCHC71-034, box 15, RHE Papers, WHS.

48. RHE implied this sequence when he wrote a fellow journalist that his second, more detailed February 4 story "came from a Western ambassadorial source here after some detective work on my part to find out who knew the background." RHE to SHL, 11 Jul 1968, box 37, SHLP.

49. Ibid.; RHE telephone interviews, 19 Jul 2007, 15 and 17 Nov 2003; Gornicki: RHE, *Never Dull,* 215; also RHE, "U.S. Secrecy Cuts Credibility at U.N.," *WP,* 15 May 1967.

50. Deptel 131714 (to American Embassy, Moscow), 4 Feb 1967, SUNFLOWER, box 255, NSF:CO:VN, LBJL. State had heard at multiple remove—a *St. Louis Post-Dispatch* reporter told a U.S. UN official of a conversation with a Polish source who in turn cited a cable from Warsaw—that Hanoi was "furious" over the *WP* leak and now "in [a] very embarrassing position vis-à-vis Peking for having agreed to secret talks with us without informing Chinese." USUN 3904 (Goldberg), 4 Feb 1967, POL 27-14 Viet/Marigold 1967, box 2739, CFPF, 1967–69.

51. Moscow embtel 3375 (LET), 6 Feb 1967, *FRUS, 1964–68,* 5:84.

52. Moscow embtel 3387 (LET), 7 Feb 1967, POL 27-14 Viet/Marigold, box 2739, CFPF, 1967–69; PE/Moscow (Pszczółkowski,) to PFM (Wierna), sz. 1562, 8 Feb 1967, AMSZ.

53. Deptel 131715 to American Embassy, Saigon, 4 Feb 1967, and Saigon embtel 17482 (HCL), 7 Feb 1967, LBJL/DDRS; *SDVW:NVPP,* p. 351

54. Deptel 106089, 20 Dec 1966, POL 27 VIET S 12/20/66, box 3014, CFPF, 1964–66. The growing Australian contingent in February 1967 numbered 4,500: Theodore H. Draper, "Vietnam: How Not to Negotiate," *New York Review of Books,* 4 May 1967.

55. CLC, *The Lost Crusade: America in Vietnam* (New York: Dodd, Mead, 1970), 341; CLC, *In the Shadows of History: Fifty Years Behind the Scenes of Cold War Diplomacy* (Amherst, N.Y.: Prometheus Books, 2005), 248; Ignatieff: CLC OH II, 30. CLC said Furlonger's outburst was "the first hint we had that the Poles had breached the understanding about keeping the talks secret" but U.S. officials already knew about Warsaw's disclosure to the pope.

56. WPB-DR telcon, 10:43 a.m., 14 Jan 1967, box 57, DR Papers, entry 5379, RG 59, NA II.

57. Deptel 132347 (to American embassies in Canberra and Wellington), 6 Feb 1967, LBJL/DDRS; Inward cablegrams, AE/Washington (Waller) to ADEA (Minister), nos. 453-4, 4 Feb 1967, Series A6364, WH1967/02, NAA.

58. Inward cablegram 538, AE/Washington (Waller) to ADEA (Minister), 11 Feb 1967, Series A1838, TS696/8/8/1 part 2, NAA.

59. Outward cablegram 481, ADEA (Minister) to AE/Washington (Waller), 21 Feb 1967, ibid.

60. WWR: *NYT,* 5 Feb 1967; *WP,* 5 Feb 1967; State: depcircular 131690, 4 Feb 1967, POL 27 VIET S 2/2/67, box 2775, CFPF, 1967–69.

61. GD'O, *DV,* 774 (4 Feb 1967).

62. Ibid.

63. Ibid., 775–76 (6 Feb 1967); *WP,* 6 Feb 1967.

64. GD'O, *DV,* 776 (8 Feb 1967).

65. *NYT, WP,* 8 Feb 1967.

66. London embtel 6384 (Bruce), 8 Feb 1967, POL 27 VIET S 2-2-67, box 2775, CFPF, 1967–69; "nurture": Danish Embassy/Washington (P. Fergo), 13 Feb 1967, document UM/Bil. 169.D.Ie, Danish Foreign Ministry archives, Copenhagen, obt./trans. C. Larsen.

67. Handwritten changes altered "President greatly disturbed" to "We are greatly distressed." See "Personal for Michael Palliser from Walt Rostow, (via private wire to London), 2/8/67," and CAP67039, WWR to Palliser, 8 Feb 1967, both SUNFLOWER PLUS (1 of 2), box 256, NSF:CO:VN, LBJL. British reactions: PREM 13/1917, TNA.

68. RHE, "Thant Knew of Dec. Bid For Viet Peace Parley," *WP,* 9 Feb 1967.

69. For memcons of the 31 Jan 1967 RFK-Manac'h talk, see Rostow vol. 20 [2 of 4] February 1–11, 1967, box 13, NSF:MtP:WR, LBJL (Dean quote), and RFK Trips-Europe, 1967, box W-62, Arthur M. Schlesinger Jr. Papers, JFKL; and *Documents Diplomatiques Français 1967,* I:190–97.

70. LBJ-RFK episode: DK and SHL, *Secret Search,* 200–204; Schlesinger, *Robert Kennedy and His Times,* 767–69; Shesol, *Mutual Contempt,* 363–67; NK, *Some of It Was Fun: Working with RFK and LBJ* (New York: W. W. Norton, 2008), 261–63; WWR to LBJ, "SUBJECT: Hanoi 'Proposal' Through Senator Kennedy," 6 Feb 1967, *FRUS, 1964–68,* 5:88–89; *Newsweek,* 20 Feb 1967, 31–32; gossip (from Newbold Noyes): WWR to LBJ, 14 Feb 1967, Rostow vol. 21 [4 of 4] Feb. 12–28, 1967, box 13, NSF:MtP:WR, LBJL; NK to LBJ, 14 Feb 1967, in Gibbons, IV, 551; WWR-LBJ tel-con, 15 Feb 1967, *FRUS, 1964–68,* 5:176; RFK related AF complaint: "bk" interview notes, 6 Nov 1967, "Interviews" folder, box 15, SHLP.

71. WWR to LBJ, "News Media Contacts," 7 Feb 1967, 6:30 p.m., Walt W. Rostow vol. 20 [2 of 4], February 1–11, 1967, box 13, NSF:MtP:WR, LBJL.

72. WWR to LBJ, 7 Feb 1967, 4:45 p.m., ibid.

73. WWR to LBJ, 8 Feb 1967, 7 p.m., Vietnam: January–March 1967, box 6, NSF:Rostow, LBJL (also box 13, NSF:MtP:WR, LBJ); Alsop in *WP,* 10 Feb 1967.

74. Halberstam, *Powers That Be,* 756–61, 809; Roberts, *Shadow of Power,* 374–75, 384–86, 391, 394–95; Graham, *Personal History,* 397–402, 410.

75. "Rumors of Peace," *WP,* 8 Feb 1967; also see "Signs and Signals," *WP,* 11 Feb 1967.

76. LBJ-Sidey meeting notes, 8 Feb 1967, box 32, Marvin Watson OF, LBJL (reel 11, "Vietnam, the Media, and Public Support for the War" microfilm collection, LC).

77. Robert E. Kintner to LBJ, 10 Feb 1967, 4:30 p.m. Friday, Kintner Memos, box 5, NSF:Name File, LBJL.

78. See WWR to LBJ, 9 pm, 12 Feb 1967, Rostow vol. 21 [4 of 4] Feb. 12–28, 1967, box 13, NSF: MtP:WR, LBJL, and chronologies of Marigold and Sunflower in boxes 147–48 and 255–56, NSF:CO:VN, LBJL.

79. Candel Saigon to CDEA, tel. 182, "DRVN Attitude towards ICC," 9 Feb 1967, A1838, 3020/9/4, NAA.

80. PE/Hanoi (JL) to PFM (Spasowski), sz. 1480, 6 Feb 1967, AMSZ, trans. MG.

81. JL-PVD conversation: PE/Hanoi (JL) to PFM (JM), sz. 1567, 7 Feb 1967, AMSZ, trans. MG.

82. JL telephone interview, 1 Oct 2007.

83. IE/S (GD'O) to IFM (AF), office memo 102, 16 Feb 1967, GD'O dossier.

84. Poldel Saigon (JL) to PFM (JM), sz. 1167, 29 Jan 1967, AMSZ, trans. MG.

85. PE/Hanoi (JL) to PFM (JM), sz. 1567, 7 Feb 1967, cited above; "smiling broadly": JL interview, Warsaw, June 2003.

86. Ibid.

87. French General Representative, Hanoi (Simon de Quirelle), tels. 62–66, 8 Feb 1967, Vietnam folder, box 160, UN, Archives Diplomatiques Français, Nantes, trans. G. Martin.

88. Incident at party: JL interviews, Warsaw, June 2003 and 4 Feb 2008; PE/Hanoi (JL) to PFM (Spasowski), sz. 1566, 7 Feb 1967, AMSZ, trans. MG; CzE/Hanoi (Posvic) to CzFM, tel. 1371, 7 Feb 1967, AMZV, Prague, obt./trans. G. Laron.

89. *WP*, 31 Jan 1967; Candel Saigon to CDEA, tel. 203, "DRVN Attitude towards ICC," 15 Feb 1967, series A1838, 3020/9/4 (North Vietnam–I.C.C.), NAA.

90. Candel Saigon to CDEA, tel. 182, "DRVN Attitude towards ICC," 9 Feb 1967, ibid.

91. JL telephone interview, 1 Oct 2007.

92. *NYT*, 9 Feb and 11 Feb 1967; editorial note, *FRUS, 1964–68*, 5:96–97.

93. Wilson-Kosygin talks: see esp. boxes 255–56, NSF:CO:VN, LBJL; *FRUS, 1964–68*, 5:90–170; PREM 13/1917, 13/1918, and 13/1840, TNA; John Dumbrell and Sylvia Ellis, "British Involvement in Vietnam Peace Initiatives, 1966–1967: Marigolds, Sunflowers, and 'Kosygin Week,'" *Diplomatic History* 27:1 (January 2003): 113–49; Sylvia Ellis, *Britain, America, and the Vietnam War* (Westport, Conn.: Praeger, 2004), 214–47; and Sergey Radchenko, *Two Suns in the Heavens: The Sino-Soviet Struggle for Supremacy, 1962–1967* (Stanford, Calif., and Washington, D.C.: Stanford University Press and Woodrow Wilson Center Press, 2009), 195–98.

94. See, e.g., deptel 141591 (to American Embassy, Moscow), 3 Feb 1966, *SDVW:NVPP*, 429.

95. Anatoly Dobrynin, *In Confidence: Moscow's Ambassador to America's Six Cold War Presidents (1962–1986)* (New York: Times Books / Random House, 1995), 155.

96. London embtel 6315 (Bruce), 6 Feb 1967, SUNFLOWER, box 255, NSF:CO:VN, LBJL; also London embtel 6406 (Bruce), 9 Feb 1967, SUNFLOWER PLUS (2 of 2), box 256, ibid. Kosygin's anti-Chinese comments, relayed by British officials to CLC and Bruce, were censored from "Sunflower" documents when first declassified in the late 1970s; compare versions in *SDVW:NVPP* and boxes 255-6, NSF:CO:VN, LBJL.

97. WWR to LBJ, 3 Jan 1967, and WWR to DR, 6 January 1967, *FRUS, 1964–68*, 5:14–15, 28; Gibbons, IV, 512. WWR claimed Dobrynin's implicit endorsement for his favored method of communicating with Hanoi. In late January, the Soviet purportedly told him that "only a direct, bilateral, secret" U.S.-DRV discussion "could be effective," and "too many intermediaries" had tried to make themselves "important." WWR-Dobrynin memcon, "Subject: Viet Nam," 27 January 1967, POL 27-14 Viet/Marigold, box 2739, CFPF, 1967–69.

98. USUN 3848, 2 Feb 1967, Walt W. Rostow vol. 20 [3 of 4], February 1-11, 1967, box 13, NSF:MtP:WR, LBJL.

99. WWR to LBJ, n.d. [4 Feb 1967], ibid.

100. See LBJ to HCM, [7 Feb 1967], *FRUS, 1964-68*, 5:91-3.

101. LBJ to Wilson, in deptel 132481, 7 Feb 1967, POL 27-14 VIET 2/1/67, box 2715, CFPF, 1967–69; also *FRUS, 1964-68*, 5:91n5.

102. PE/Ottawa (Stradowski) to PFM (Milnikiel), sz. 1570, 7 Feb 1967, AMSZ, obt./trans. MG;

CDEA to CE/Warsaw, tel. Y-165, "Vietnam" 9 Feb 1967, file 20–22-VIETS-2-1 pt. 11, vol. 9398, RG 25, NAC.

103. Deptel 134661, 10 Feb 1967, POL 27 VIET S 2/9/67, box 2779, CFPF, 1967–69.

104. Chagla's contact with the DRV consul-general: Australian High Commissioner, New Delhi, to Secretary, ADEA, Canberra, "North Vietnamese Attitude Towards the I.C.C.," 7 Mar 1967, series A1838, 3020/9/4 (North Vietnam–I.C.C.), NAA.

105. PE / New Delhi (Mrozek) to PFM (Spasowski), sz. 1607, 9 Feb 1967, AMSZ, obt./trans. MG.

106. Candel Saigon to CDEA, tel. 187 flash, "Vietnam Peace Appeal," 12 Feb 1967, FCO 15/282, TNA.

107. Poldel Saigon (JL) to PFM(Spasowski), sz. 1751, 12 Feb 1967, AMSZ, trans. MG.

108. Polish rejection: PFM (Spasowski) to PE / New Delhi (Mrozek), sz. 1377, 13 Feb 1967; PFM (Spasowski) to Poldel Saigon (JL), sz. 1380, 13 Feb 1967; and PFM (Naszkowski) to PE/Hanoi (Badowski), sz. 1428, 14 Feb 1967, all AMSZ, obt./trans. MG.

109. IFM (AF) to IE/Saigon (GD'O), office memo 8, 9 Feb 1967, GD'O dossier.

110. GD'O, DV, p. 777 (9 Feb 1967).

111. IE/Saigon (GD'O) to IFM (AF), office memo 95, 10 Feb 1967, GD'O dossier.

112. GD'O, DV, 782 (13 Feb 1967).

113. IFM (AF) to IE/Saigon (GD'O), office memo 9, 12 Feb 1967, GD'O dossier; PE/Rome (Stefański) to PFM (AR), sz. 1749, 13 Feb 1967, AMSZ; Rome embtel 4183 (Reinhardt), 12 Feb 1967, POL 27 VIET S 2/12/67, box 2776, CFPF, 1967–69; also box 2715, ibid.

114. DR-WPB telcon, 3:08 p.m., 12 Feb 1967, box 58, DR Papers, entry 5379, RG 59, NA II.

115. DR to LBJ, "SUBJECT: Resumption of Operations against North Viet-Nam Over the Next Two Days," 11 Feb 1967, FRUS, 1964–68, 5:128–30; "hell of a situation": Wilson to LBJ, 12 Feb 1967, ibid., 139.

116. "Gallant": LBJ to Wilson, [13] Feb 1967, ibid., 160–61; PVD: Ilya V. Gaiduk, The Soviet Union and the Vietnam War (Chicago: Ivan R. Dee, 1996), 105–6; intercept: London embtel 6500 (Kaiser), 13 Feb 1967, SUNFLOWER PLUS (1 of 2), box 256, NSF:CO:VN, LBJL; "hopeless": Moscow embtel 3562 (LET), 18 Feb 1967, FRUS, 1964–68, 5:186–91 (quotation on 191).

117. Deptel 136252 (to American Embassy, Buenos Aires), 13 Feb 1967, 7:12 p.m., POL 27-14 Viet/Marigold, box 2739, CFPF, 1967–69.

118. GD'O-HCL 14 Feb 1967 talk: IE/S (GD'O) to IFM (AF), office memos. 98-9 (6:30 p.m., 14 Feb 1967) and 100 (noon, 16 Feb 1967), all GD'O dossier; GD'O, DV, 783 (14 Feb 1967); Saigon embtel 17948 (HCL), 14 Feb 1967, POL 27-14 Viet/Marigold 1967, box 2739, CFPF, 1967–69.

119. Deptel 137000 (to American Embassy, Saigon), 14 Feb 1967, ibid.

120. GD'O, DV, pp. 783–84 (15 Feb 1967).

121. GD'O-JL 15 Feb 1967 talk: IE/S (D'Orlandi) to IFM (AF), office memos. 100–101 (noon), 102–5 (12:30 p.m.), 106 (12:45 p.m.), all 16 Feb 1967, GD'O dossier; French alternative: also DE/Saigon (Derksen) to DFM, "Subject: Senator Kennedy and the Vietnam issue," tel. 22+, 17 Feb 1967, DFMA, obt. R. van der Maar, trans. DM.

122. HCM to LBJ, 15 Feb 1967, FRUS, 1964–68, 5:173–74.

123. WWR to LBJ, 10:15 a.m., 15 Feb 1967, ibid., 5:172.

124. Saigon embtels 18329 (HCL), 18 Feb 1967, and 18535 (HCL), 20 Feb 1967, POL 27-14 Viet/Marigold, box 2739, CFPF, 1967–69.

125. JL telephone interview, 1 Oct 2007; also JL interviews, Warsaw, June 2003.

126. JL interview, Warsaw, 10 May 2011.

127. Ibid.

128. Bog[two letters illegible]cki (MSW informant/agent, Polish ICC Delegation, Saigon), handwritten report, 20 Apr 1967, BU 0586/2162, IPN, obt. A. Paczkowski, trans. MG. Col. Iwanciów himself was affiliated with the general staff's intelligence (II) bureau: see Iwanción IPN file (BU 0243/20), courtesy A. Packowski (email to author, July 2011).

129. JL to Rahman, 14 Feb 1967, in Candel Saigon to CDEA, tel. 219, "756th Mtg Question of Referring Resln to Cochairmen," 17 Feb 1967, FCO 15/283, TNA; also Candel Saigon to CDEA, tel 218, 17 Feb 1967; "net . . . hat": deptel 132375 to American Embassy, Saigon, 6 Feb 1967, POL 27 VIET S 2-2-67, box 2775, CFPF, 1967–69.

130. Candel Saigon (VCM) to CDEA, tel. 225, "DRVN Attitude to ICSC," 18 Feb 1967, FCO 15/283, TNA.

131. Ibid.

132. Poldel Saigon (JL) to PFM (JM-Szewczyk), sz. 2072, 20 Feb 1967, AMSZ, trans. MG.

133. Candel Saigon to CDEA, tel. 212, "DRVN Attitude to ICC," 17 Feb 1967, file 20-1-VIET.N pt. 1.1, vol. 10061, RG 25, NAC.

134. Candel Saigon (VCM) to CDEA, tel. 232, "Vietnam Prospects: Polish Comments," 20 Feb 1967, file 20-22-VIETS-2-1 pt. 11, vol. 9398, ibid.

135. Candel Saigon (VCM) to CDEA, tel. 225, "DRVN Attitude to ICSC," 18 Feb 1967, FCO 15/283, TNA/PRO.

136. Poldel Saigon (JL) to PFM (Spasowski), sz. 1123, 27 Jan 1967, AMSZ, trans. MG; deptel 132375 to American Embassy, Saigon, "Subj: ICC Citations of NVN," 6 Feb 1967, POL 27 VIET S 2-2-67, box 2775, CFPF, 1967–69; WWR to LBJ, 17 Feb 1967, Rostow vol. 21 [3 of 4] Feb. 12–28, 1967, box 13, NSF:MtP:WR, LBJL

137. Candel Saigon (VCM) to CDEA, tel. 225, "DRVN Attitude to ICSC," 18 Feb 1967, FCO 15/283, TNA.

138. Candel Saigon (VCM) to CDEA, tel. 232, "Vietnam Prospects: Polish Comments," 20 Feb 1967, file 20-22-VIETS-2-1 pt. 11, vol. 9398, RG 25, NAC.

139. Poldel Saigon (JL) to PFM (Klasa), sz. 2433, 27 Feb 1967, AMSZ, trans. MG.

140. Saigon embtel 18243 (HCL), 17 Feb 1967, and WWR to LBJ, 18 Feb 1967, 9:30 a.m., both in Rostow vol. 21 [3 of 4], Feb. 12–28, 1967, box 13, NSF:MtP:WR, LBJL; Candel Saigon (VCM) to CDEA, tel. 235, "Vietnam Propsects [*sic*]: Cabot Lodge," 21 Feb 1967, file 20-22-VIETS-2-1 pt. 11, vol. 9398, RG 25, NAC.

141. Gibbons, IV, 557–70; 17 Feb 1967 meeting notes, *FRUS, 1964–68,* 5:182-5.

142. McNaughton diary, 22 Jan 1967, quoted by Benjamin T. Harrison and Christopher L. Mosher, "The Secret Diary of McNamara's Dove: The Long-Lost Story of John T. Mc-Naughton's Opposition to the Vietnam War," *Diplomatic History* 35, no. 3 (June 2011): 505–34, at 530.

143. Gibbons, IV, 575–79; *FRUS, 1964–68,* 5:192–93, 226–27.

144. Polish aid: Polish UN Mission, New York (Tomorowicz), to PFM (Winiewicz), sz. 1118, 27 Jan 1967, AMSZ, trans. MG; NDT: PE/Hanoi (JS) to PFM (JM), sz. 46, 2 Jan 1967, AMSZ, trans. MG. JL told GD'O that "Polish intercession had made the meeting possible": GD'O, *DV,* p. 805 (8 Mar 1967).

145. Thant-HVL 2 Mar 1967 meeting in Rangoon and aftermath: U Thant, *View from the UN* (Garden City, N.Y.: Doubleday, 1978), 72–77. Reflecting their positive appraisal of Thant both as UN head and as an "Asian statesman," Warsaw rejected Hanoi's entreaty (via DPQ) to strongly denounce Thant and his latest proposals: "We are not going to do it, we don't think it right." PFM (JM) to Podel Saigon (JL), sz. 3569, 10 Apr 1967, AMSZ, trans. MG.

146. AF-Thant meeting: IFM (AF) to IE/Saigon (GD'O), office memo 10, 5 Mar 1967, GD'O dossier; also Rome embtel 4572 (Reinhardt), 6 Mar 1967, POL 27 VIET S 3-2-67, box 2777, CFPF, 1967–69.

147. *NYT,* 8 Mar 1967.

148. Transcript of Goldberg press conference, White House, 12:45 p.m., 8 Mar 1967, White House Press Secretary.

149. Schlesinger, *Robert Kennedy and His Times,* 769–74; Gibbons, IV, 593–94.

150. WWR to LBJ, 3:55 p.m., 17 Feb 1967, United Nations, vol. 6 12/1/66 [1 of 2], box 68, NSF:Agency, LBJL.

151. DR to LBJ, 8 Mar 1967, NSF:MtP:WR, LBJL, in Gibbons, IV, 496; also David L. Stebenne, *Arthur J. Goldberg: New Deal Liberal* (New York: Oxford University Press, 1996), 370–71.

152. RSM to LBJ, 9 Mar 1967, copy in March 1967 [3 of 8], box 25, Gibbons Papers, LBJL.

153. WWR to LBJ, 10 March 1967, *FRUS, 1964–68,* 5:241–43.

154. Lunch Meeting with President, 7 Mar 1967, "Meetings with the President January thru June 1967" folder, box 1, NSF:WWR, LBJL; also Gibbons, IV, 570.

155. WWR to LBJ, 8 Mar 1967, 12:15 p.m., w/att. drafts, Vietnam: January–March 1967, box 6, NSF:WWR, LBJL. Both drafts describe Marigold, but neither names the "intermediaries who claimed to be in direct contact with Hanoi." Also WWR to LBJ, 10:45 a.m., 6 Mar 1967, Sunflower Plus (1 of 2), box 256, NSF:CO:VN, LBJL.

156. WWR to LBJ, 2:15 p.m., 4 Apr 1967, Walt W. Rostow vol. 25 [4 of 4] April 1–15, 1967, box 15, NSF:MtP:WR, LBJL; "Two Years, 45 Peace Feelers: Ho Keeps Saying No," *US News & World Report,* 10 Apr 1967, 42.
157. Moose to WWR, 13 Mar 1967, and Moose to Christian and Johnson, 22 Mar 1967, "Retrospective Accounts."
158. Gomułka's comments to Hungary's Kadar, Budapest, 8–9 Mar 1967, and Bulgaria's Zhivkov, Sofia, 4 Apr 1967, AAN, trans. MG.
159. Paris embtel 15626 (Farley), 6 Apr 1967, POLISH TRACK (V) "Open Cities," Jan. 1967, box 16, Records of Negotiations about Vietnam, 1965–69, lot file 69D277, RG 59, NA II.
160. President Saragat and Prime Minister Ochab memcon, Rome, 7 April 1967, Visite Di Stato/ Visite Officiali: 1967—II Parte, Ministry of External Affairs archives, Rome, trans. IO; also Rome embtel 5363 (Reinhardt), 12 Apr 1967, POLISH TRACK (V) "Open Cities," Jan. 1967 folder, cited above.
161. Paris embtel 16578 (Cleveland), 19 Apr 1967, ibid.
162. Candel UN to CDEA, tel. 1835, 22 Jun 1967, file 21-13-VIET-ICSC pt. 3, vol. 11089, RG 25, NAC.
163. RHE, "U.S. Seeks Escalation, Reds Hold," 17 Apr 1967, *WP.* Tomorowicz did not aid his original stories in February, RHE later wrote SHL, but "several weeks later he did tell me certain details which I subsequently reported." RHE to SHL, 11 Jul 1968, box 37, SHLP, and M71-034, box 13, RHE papers, WHS. In a 20 Nov 2007 telephone interview, RHE did not recall the story's source but agreed circumstantial evidence suggested Tomorowicz.
164. CLC, *Lost Crusade,* 368.
165. Polish UN Mission, New York (Tomorowicz), to PFM (Winiewicz), sz. 1430, 4 Feb 1967, AMSZ, trans. MG.
166. Burchett AP dispatch, 7 Feb 1967, in "Red Writer Gives Hanoi's Views," *WP,* 8 Feb 1967.
167. Burchett to HES, 8 Feb 1967, box 399, HES, RBML, CU.
168. HES to Burchett, 15 Feb 1967, ibid.; HES memcons with Thant, 18 Jan and 16 Mar 1967, box 590, ibid.
169. USUN 4083 (Goldberg), for DR and WPB, 22 Feb 1967 (enc. Hudson draft article, "The Nearest to Negotiations Yet"), United Nations, vol. 6 12/1/66 [2 of 2], box 68, NSF:Agency, LBJL; "very well-informed": Hudson letter, *NYT,* 12 May 1967.
170. Deptel 142154 to USUN, 22 Feb 1967, POL 27-14 Viet/Marigold, box 2739, CFPF, 1967–69.
171. USUN 4119 (Buffum), 24 Feb 1967, ibid.
172. DR-WPB telcon, 24 Feb 1967, 8:08 p.m., box 58, entry 5379, DR Papers, RG 59, NA II.
173. Hudson, "The Nearest to Negotiations Yet," *War/Peace Report,* March 1967, 3–4. In an earlier draft, he had also listed, then dismissed, two other "theoretically possible" explanations for the bombings, that the damage was caused by pilot error or mistake or falling antiaircraft missiles.
174. Rome Reuters dispatch, 2021Z, 7 Mar 1967; *Il Messagero* (Rome), 8 Mar 1967, in "Some Comments From Italy and Poland," *War/Peace Report,* March 1967, 4. Hudson circulated an advance draft dated 28 Feb 1967, copy in box 590, HES, RBML, CU.
175. Hudson to HES, 9 Mar 1967, in ibid.
176. HES to Burchett, 20 Mar 1967 and Burchett to HES, 3 Mar 1967, box 399, ibid.
177. Deptel 139631 (to American Embassy, Moscow), 17 Feb 1967, SUNFLOWER PLUS (1 of 2), box 256, NSF:CO:VN, LBJL.
178. IFM (AF) to IE/Saigon (GD'O), office memo 10, 5 Mar 1967, GD'O dossier.
179. Goldberg-GD'O 3 Mar 1967 talk: USUN 4238 (Goldberg), 6 Mar 1967, 27-14 Viet/Marigold, box 2739, CFPF, 1967–69; IE/S (GD'O) to IFM (AF), office memos 108-10, 4 Mar 1967, GD'O dossier; GD'O, *DV,* 798–800 (2–3 Mar 1967).
180. Poldel Saigon (JL) to PFM (JM), sz. 2773, 6 Mar 1967, AMSZ, trans. MG.
181. Dier CV: file 22-13 vol 1 [pt. 2], vol. 9502, RG 25, NA.
182. Dier-Goldberg conversation: Candel Saigon (Dier) to CDEA, tel. 294, "Conversation with Goldberg," 7 Mar 1967, file 20-22-VIETS-2-1 pt. 12, vol. 9398, RG 25, NAC; also USUN 4237 (Buffum), 6 Mar 1967, United Nations. vol. 6 12/1/66 [2 of 2], box 68, NSF:Agency, LBJL; "dove": Candel UN (Ignatieff) to CDEA, tel. 395, "Vietnam: Dier's Talk with Goldberg," 21 Feb 1967, file 20-22-VIETS-2-1 pt. 11, vol. 9398, RG 25, NAC.

183. USUN 4390 (Goldberg), 15 Mar 1967, POL 27-14 Viet/Marigold 1967, box 2739, CFPF, 1967–69.
184. On "responsibility," see "Record of a Meeting at 10 Downing Street at 10.40 p.m. on Saturday, February 11," PREM 13/1918, TNA; "grasp": *NYT,* 15 Feb 1967, p. 1; "historic opportunity": Wilson, *A Personal Record,* p. 365.
185. Brown-AR memcon, 3 p.m., 22 Feb 1967, PREM 13/1918, TNA, and Wilson-AR memcon, 24 Feb 1967, FCO 15/645, TNA; Polish notes: Dept. III, 8/75 w-4, AMSZ. After his London talks, AR reported internally that Wilson mouthed U.S. arguments that Hanoi's refusal to stop infiltration had doomed recent peace efforts but "did not hide his disappointment with Johnson's policy" and assessed that U.K. efforts to moderate U.S. policy had "minimal" significance. PFM (Meller) to PE/Hanoi (Wasilewski), sz. 2281, 7 Mar 1967, AMSZ, trans. MG.
186. Wilson-WWR memcon, London, 5:30 p.m., 24 Feb 1967, PREM 13/1918, TNA, and FO, "The Kosygin Visit: A Study in Anglo-American Relations," February 1967, FCO 15/634, TNA, and other documents in FCO 15/633 and PREM 13/2458. U.S. perspectives: boxes 255-6, NSF:CO: VN, LBJL.
187. Not trusting WWR to give LBJ a "full and accurate" picture of his "very serious anxieties," Wilson insisted on writing him directly, and having Dean take up the matter personally with him. PM Personal Minute, 15 Mar 1967, FCO 15/633, TNA, and documents in PREM 13/2458. Over the demurrals of DR, WWR, and CLC that he should "not go into too much detail" lest he "provoke a strong reaction," Dean reviewed the Kosygin affair at length with LBJ, accompanied only by WWR. The Americans stoutly denied responsibility for any communications "breakdown" or "failure," but the British derived satisfaction from WWR's admission that Washington had altered its Phase A/B formulation during Kosygin's visit due to enhanced DRV infiltration—precisely the topic about which Wilson had desired more timely information. BE/Washington (Dean) to Wilson, 10 Apr 1967, PREM 13/2458.
188. H. W. King, BE/Warsaw, to H.F.T. Smith, Northern Dept., FO, 2 Mar 1967, FCO/645; and Murray, "Vietnam: The Lewandowski Affair," 14 Mar 1967, w. minutes by de la Mare, 15 Mar 1967, et al., FCO 15/646, all TNA.
189. London embtel 6998 (Kaiser), 1 Mar 1967, SUNFLOWER PLUS (1 of 2), box 256, NSF:CO:VN, LBJL.
190. Deptel 158246 (NK) to American Embassy, London, 19 Mar 1967, *SDVW:NVPP,* 127–29.
191. London embtel 7602, 21 Mar 1967, SUNFLOWER (2 of 2), box 255, NSF:CO:VN, LBJL.
192. CLC memo for the record, 4 Apr 1967, SUNFLOWER Double Plus, box 256, ibid.
193. P. H. Gore-Booth to T. Brimelow, 20 Mar 1967, FCO 15/646, TNA, and U.S. memos, same file.
194. Brimelow-JM memcon, Warsaw, 10-11:20 a.m., 4 Apr 1967, BE/Warsaw (Brimelow) to FO, 4 Apr 1967, tel 203, and Brimelow to Gore-Booth, FO, "Viet Nam: The November–December Talks," 5 Apr 1967, all FCO 15/646, TNA.
195. There was one puzzling apparent discrepancy. After speaking with him at a reception two days after their long talk, Brimelow quoted JM as stating that the "North Vietnamese had known from 3 December that the Americans had reservations about Lewandowski's ten points" but had "nonetheless instructed their Ambassador in Warsaw to prepare for talks with the United States Ambassador." BE/Warsaw (Brimelow) to FO, tel. 215, 7 Apr 1967, ibid. This assertion contradicts Polish and U.S. records indicating that Warsaw did not convey the "interpretation clause" to Hanoi until December 6, so Hanoi could hardly have known about it three days earlier. Moreover, as noted above, MR suggests that as of December 5 JM believed DPQ had *not* been "instructed" about the proposed meeting with JAG. JM likely misspoke or was misquoted.
196. Murray, "Vietnam: The Lewandowski Affair," 14 Apr 1967, in ibid.
197. Handwritten comments on ibid.
198. MacLehose to Palliser, 17 Apr 1967; also MacLehose to Palliser, 18 May 1967, both ibid.
199. Washington regarded JM's account as following "traditional [Polish] lines." "Marigold: A Chronology," 89.
200. Murray, "Vietnam."
201. MacLehose to Palliser, 18 May 1967, PREM 13/1912, TNA.
202. See Murray, "Vietnam," 14 and 27 Apr 1967, and handwritten comments on both; Palliser to MacLehose, 17 Apr 1967; and Palliser to MacLehose, 29 Apr 1967, all FCO 15/646, TNA.

203. MacLehose to Palliser, 18 May 1967, ibid. The FO found four main reasons why the initiative collapsed: (1) the Poles "appear to have given the impression throughout their discussions with the Americans that they had greater influence with, and a firmer mandate from, the North Vietnamese than ever was the case"; (2) HCL was "ill-advised" to let JL to go to Hanoi in mid-November "without ensuring that the latter had in his pocket a document which had already received American endorsement"; (3) Washington should have clarified the "reservations" they had in mind; and (4) the Hanoi bombings may have been the "prime reason" why Hanoi broke off the talks, but if so it "tends to confirm that they were far less committed to negotiations with the Americans than the Poles were apparently making out." Murray, "Vietnam."
204. Palliser, May 19 handwritten note on MacLehose to Palliser, 18 May 1967, PREM 13/1912, TNA.
205. See Wilson handwritten note on MacLehose to Palliser, 18 May 1967, and Palliser to Mac-Lehose, 22 May 1967, FCO 15/646, TNA. When Wilson had a chance to speak face to face with LBJ in early June, however, he could not resist stressing (despite being urged against doing so by Brown) the "possible grave consequences" of the Anglo-American "shambles" during the Kosygin visit, speculating that Administration "hawks" had forced a stiffening of US policy in February; but he made scant mention of the Polish affair. Wilson-LBJ memcon, Washington, 2 June 1967, and Palliser to MacLehose, 21 April 1967, both in PREM 13/1919, TNA.
206. Hightower interview notes, 29 Jan 1968, Interviews folder, box 15, SHLP; see also Hightower notebooks, Hightower papers (MCHC71-047), WHS.
207. DR-Hightower telcon, 5 May 1967, 1:40 p.m., box 58, entry 5379, DR Papers, RG 59, NA II. DR had already seen the reporter four days earlier: May 1967 Appointment Book, box 4, DR Papers, LBJL.
208. WP reporters Marder, Roberts, and Phillip Geyelin conducted background interviews with Foy Kohler, WPB, Unger, and Sisco (to whom Roberts posed the quoted query): Donnelly to DR/Read, 11 May 1967, Rostow vol. 27 [1 of 4] May 1-15, 1967, box 16 [1 of 2], NSF:MtP:WR, LBJL; DR: May 1967 appointment book, box 4, DR Papers, LBJL. Before receiving the WP reporters, DR called WWR, who confirmed DR's supposition that they were "pretty well informed on MARIGOLD." DR-WWR telcon, 3:03 p.m., 6 May 1967, box 58, DR Papers, entry 5379, RG 59, NA II. After Hightower scooped the WP reporters on the Polish angle, they omitted it from their final article: WP, 21 May 1967.
209. DR-WWR telcon, 6 May 1967, 3:40 p.m., cited above. Hightower saw DR at 3 p.m., May 1967 Appointment Book, box 4, DR Papers, LBJL.
210. John P. Roche to LBJ, 2 May 1967, Roche Memos, Jan–Oct 1967, box 7, NSF:Name File, LBJL (reel 6, "Vietnam, the Media, and Public Support for the War" microfilm collection). Roche cited Stewart Alsop as an example of a "responsible journalist" who was "very interested in doing a study of 'non-facts' about negotiations."
211. CE/Washington (Ritchie) to CDEA, tel. 1752, "Vietnam: USA Thinking," 10 May 1967, file 20-22-VIETS-2-1 pt. 15, vol. 9399, RG 25, NAC.
212. Deptel 190899 to American Embassy, Warsaw, 9 May 1967, box 147, NSF:CO:VN, LBJL; DK and SHL, Secret Search, 79–80.
213. RHE, "U.S. Secrecy Cuts Credibility at U.N.," WP, 15 May 1967; the original article did not name the source of this comment, but RHE's internal version to WP foreign editor Foisie noted: "FYI high State Department official quoted was Rusk in a remark to me at Scarsdale last Sunday." See original in box 15, RHE papers, M71-034, WHS.
214. Instead of using Hightower's piece, the Post put on an inside page a much shorter story distributed by AP's wire service rival, UPI, essentially outlining the same information. WP, 9 May 1967.
215. On "suggest," see Hightower interview notes, 29 Jan 1968, Interviews folder, box 15, SHLP; Hudson letter, NYT, 12 May 1967, 46.
216. RHE, "U.S. Secrecy Cuts Credibility at U.N.," WP, 15 May 1967.
217. Paul Ward, "Thant Is Drawn Into Viet Debate," Baltimore Sun, 10 May 1967; Candel UN to CDEA, tel. 1225, "Vietnam: USA," 10 May 1967, file 20-22-VIETS-2-1 pt. 15, vol. 9399, RG 25, NAC.

218. DK and SHL, *Secret Search,* 79.
219. *L'Unità,* "Before the State Department Publishes Its Secret Documents, We Shall Reveal Now the United States Prevented Negotiations to Put an End to the Conflict in Vietnam," 9 May 1967; *NYT,* 10 May 1967.
220. *WP, NYT,* 12 May 1967; Mario Sica, *Marigold non fiorì: Il contributo italiano alla pace in Vietnam* (Florence: Ponte alle Grazie, 1991) 87–90; CE/Rome to CDEA, tel. 408, "Vietnam: Italian Attitude," 12 May 1967, and CE/Rome (Crean) to CDEA, tel. 411, "Vietnam: Italian Attitude," 12 May 1967, both file 20-22-VIETS-2-1 pt. 15, vol. 9399, RG 25, NAC. AF indiscretions to Willmann and RFK are described above; for his comments to the Libyan foreign minister, that through his efforts peace was "very near, but negotiations were cut off after 'escalation of war by United States,'" see Tripoli embtel 3826 (Newsom), 15 May 1967, Italy folder, box 15, Records of Negotiations about Viet Nam, 1965–69, lot file 69D277, RG 59, NA II.
221. Polish UN Mission, New York (Tomorowicz), to PFM (AR), sz. 176, 9 May 1967, AMSZ, trans. MG.
222. JAG-JM and JAG-Winiewicz 9 May 1967 talks: Warsaw embtel 2700 (JAG), 9 May 1967, POL 27-14 Viet/Marigold 1967, box 2739, CFPF, 1967–69; PFM (Sieradzki) to Polish UN Mission, New York (Tomorowicz), and PE/Washington (Szewczyk), sz. 55761, 11 May 1967, AMSZ, trans. MG.
223. Deptel 190899 to American Embassy, Warsaw, 9 May 1967, box 147, NSF:CO:VN, LBJL.
224. JM-Kaiser 10 May 1967 talk: Warsaw embtel 2727 (Jenkins), 10 May 1967, POL 27-14 Viet/Marigold 1967, box 2739, CFPF, 1967–69; JM, "Urgent Note," and PFM (Sieradzki) to Polish UN Mission, New York (Tomorowicz), and PE/Washington (Szewczyk), sz. 55761, 11 May 1967, both AMSZ, trans. MG.
225. CE/Washington (Ritchie) to CDEA, tel. 1752, "Vietnam: USA Thinking," 10 May 1967, file 20-22-VIETS-2-1 pt. 15, vol. 9399, RG 25, NAC.
226. When shown a wire service summary that had appeared in a Swedish newspaper, a DRV diplomat in Warsaw (DPQ's deputy, Hoang Hoan Nghinh) denounced the story as "an old American trick to spread rumors on fast-moving contacts with North Vietnam in various places in the world in order to give the impression of a general American desire for peace and North Vietnamese 'intransigence' on the negotiations question" and "further proof that USA once again sought to mislead world opinion and wanted through the newly publicized claims to denigrate North Vietnam." Report by J.-C.Oberg, 10 May 1967, Utrikesdpartementet HP1 XV/ spec. vol. 1220, Foreign Ministry records, Swedish National Archives, Stockholm, trans. F. Logevall.
227. PE/Hanoi (JL) to PFM (JM), sz. 6156, 15 May 1967, AMSZ, trans. MG.
228. PE/Hanoi (Wasilewski) to PFM (JM), sz. 6326, 18 May 1967, ibid.
229. PFM (Meller) to PE/Hanoi (Wasilewski), sz. 5208, 19 May 1967, AMSZ, trans. MG.
230. See internal JM chronologies (7 pp. and 22 pp.), 1 Jun 1967, GM sygn. 1/77 w 16, t-39, *Tajne spec. znaczenia,* AMSZ, courtesy H. Szlaijfer.
231. WWR to LBJ, 4 p.m., 11 May 1967, Rostow vol. 27 [2 of 4] May 1-15, 1967, box 16 [1 of 2], NSF: MtP:WR, LBJL.
232. JAG saw LBJ from 12:55-1:30 p.m., 18 May 1967 entry, box 11, PDD, LBJL. No record of this JAG-LBJ discussion has been found, but LBJ's continuing disdain toward any Polish role in Vietnam diplomacy resurfaced in April 1968 when he angrily rejected Warsaw as a site for US-DRV negotiations; see below.
233. On Fulbright and LBJ, see Gibbons, IV, passim, esp. chap. 6; Robert Dallek, *Flawed Giant: Lyndon Johnson and His Times, 1961–1973* (New York: Oxford University Press, 1998), esp. 288–89, 349–51, 357–58, 369–71, 538 ("easier"); Robert D. Schulzinger, *A Time for War: The United States and Vietnam, 1941–1975* (New York: Oxford University Press, 1997), pp. 218-26 ("hoodwinked," 218); Randall B. Woods, *LBJ: Architect of American Ambition* (New York: Free Press, 2006), esp. 633, 717, 719–20, 727, 766–67; Robert Mann, *A Grand Delusion: America's Descent into Vietnam* (New York: Basic Books, 2001), 487–97; and Halberstam, *Powers That Be,* 688–706.
234. 11 Jan 1967, SFRC executive session transcript in Gibbons, IV, 580.

235. LBJ meeting with Sens. Mansfield and Dirksen, 17 Jan 1967, *FRUS, 1964–68*, 5:42.

236. LBJ-Fulbright telephone transcript, 20 January 1967, *FRUS, 1964–68*, 5:54.

237. In early May 1967, Fulbright sniped at the administration's "Madison Avenue gimcrackery," and LBJ groused to Christian: "This man is doing everything he can to create problems for the President who is doing everything he can to make the best of a difficult situation. Less caustic carping and more constructive criticism would be welcome." Gibbons, IV, 674, 680–81.

238. Memcon, NK, Fulbright, WAH, WPB, Jorden, Baggs, Ashmore, Isham, 4 Feb 1967, POL 27-14 VIET 1/1/67, box 2715, CFPF, 1967–69; Mann, *Grand Delusion*, 528–29.

239. Fulbright to DR, 17 Feb 1967 (also 9 Mar 1967), and DR to Fulbright, 14 Mar 1967, folder 3, box 44, subseries 17. Vietnam (General Materials), 1965–74, Fulbright Papers, University of Arkansas Libraries, Fayetteville.

240. RWPB-DR telcon, 15 May 1967, 9:44 a.m., box 58, DR Papers, entry 5379, RG 59, NA II.

241. DR saw JAG from 9:48–9:54 a.m. (WPB present from 9:50 a.m.), 15 May 1967, May 1967 Appointment Book, box 4, DR Papers, LBJL.

242. Quotations from JAG's testimony: JAG SFRC, esp. 487 ff.

243. Other senators present were Democrats Sparkman, Claiborne Pell, and Stuart Symington, and Republicans Hickenlooper, John Sherman Cooper, and Karl E. Mundt.

244. See Discussion Regarding the Secretary of State's Testimony, 16 May 1967, and DR testimony, 23 May 1967, SFRC 1967 *Executive Sessions*, 505–19, 539–86.

245. Six months later, the SFRC chair confirmed to a reporter that only JAG had testified to the committee regarding Marigold: Fulbright telephone interview notes, 8 Nov 1967, Interviews folder, box 15, SHLP. In April 1968—his curiosity perhaps piqued by a lengthy conversation with JM, now Polish ambassador in Washington—Fulbright formally asked DR for further information on Marigold, but it does not appear this request led to any substantial inquiry. PE/Washington (JM) to PFM (AR), sz. 1690, 12 Feb 1968, AMSZ, trans. MG; Fulbright to DR, 24 Apr 1968, copy in HCL Papers II, reel 20, MHS.

246. May 1967 Appointments Book, box 4, DR Papers, LBJL.

247. Perhaps hoping to get back into LBJ's good graces, a few months later JAG gave a speech at the University of Wisconsin lambasting "academic intellectuals" for dogmatic and myopic opposition to the president's Vietnam policies (e.g., not backing his "bridge building" to Eastern Europe). An aide passed the speech to LBJ, and WWR gushed to JAG that it was "first class" and "lucid and mature"; conversely, Arthur M. Schlesinger Jr. termed "nonsense" his charge of "conformity" and sloganeering among intellectual antiwar critics. JAG, "The Intellectual and American Foreign Policy," 8 Aug 1967, speech file, box 37; Harry C. McPherson Jr. to Jack Scanlon, 16 Aug 1967, WWR to JAG, 23 Aug 1967, and Schlesinger to JAG, 3 Sep 1967, correspondence file, box 36; all JAG papers, WHS.

248. On Radványi's defection, see János Radványi, *Delusion and Reality: Gambits, Hoaxes, and Diplomatic One-Upmanship in Vietnam* (South Bend, Ind.: Gateway Editions, 1978), 229–82; draft [WWR?] handwritten letter to President, 17 [*sic;* 16] May 1967, box 2, "Radanyi, Janos" [*sic*] folder, NSF:Intelligence File, LBJL; 16 May 1967 entry, May 1967 Appointment Book, box 4, DR Papers, LBJL; memcons, Leslie C. Tihany and Radványi, 16 May 1967, 6:25 p.m. ("like a dog"), and 16 and 20 May 1967 ("con artist"), box 2182, CFPF, 1967–69, courtesy Z. Szoke; *NYT, WP,* AP, and *Time* coverage; Zoltan Szoke, "Delusion or Reality? Secret Hungarian Diplomacy during the Vietnam War," *Journal of Cold War Studies* 12, no. 4 (Fall 2010): 119–80.

249. *NYT,* 19 May 1967.

250. WPB, Memorandum for the Record, Subject: Disclosure by János Radványi Concerning Vietnam Negotiations—Part I, 29 May 1967, box 2, NSF:Intelligence File, LBJL.

251. WPB to DR, "Subject: First Full Interview with Radványi," 1 Jun 1967, POL 27 VIET S 6/1/67, box 2783, CFPF, 1967–69.

252. CE/Washington (Ritchie) to CDEA, tel. 2068, "Vietnam," 1 Jun 1967, file 20-22-VIETS-2-1 pt. 10, vol. 9399, RG 25, NAC; AE/Washington (Waller) to ADEA, tel. 342, 19 Jun 1967, File 3020/11/161/2 Pt. 20, North Vietnam—Relations with USA & Policy Aspects of the Vietnam War Settlement, series A1838, NAA.

253. WPB to J. Blair Seaborn (head, CDEA Far Eastern Division), in Seaborn to R. E. Collins, 13 Sep 1967, file 20-22-VIETS-2-1 pt. 18, vol. 9399, RG 25, NAC.
254. WPB to RSM, 3 July 1967, "Subject: Thoughts on Vietnam," Jul 1967, box FCL 33, WAHP-LC.
255. WAH memcon with Yoshiguro Sato (Japanese Embassy 2d sec.), 10 Jul 1967, box 520, ibid.
256. LBJ-Wilson memcon, 2 Jun 1967, PREM 13/1919, TNA.
257. State Department transcript, DR background briefing to National Foreign Policy Conference for Editors and Broadcasters, 22 May 1967, pp. A-25, A-26, B-1, "Vietnam—Unclassified (2 of 2)" folder, box 2, Christian OF, LBJL. DR used the same shtick a month later in "background only" remarks to educators when one raised reports of "unexplored peace initiatives": "No. Really, what happens on these matters is basically this: There are an awful lot of candidates for the Nobel Peace Prize running around the world these days. (Laughter and applause.) And thank heaven—please, I'm not being cynical about that effort. We must always have people trying to do what they can in the interest of peace. But, you know, much of the time they don't understand what they hear. And if the ladies will forgive me, they frequently come out of Hanoi or some other contact eight-months pregnant (laughter); and then we find that there's nothing in it. (Laughter and applause). Now, I realize that the photographers in Washington tell me I look like the neighborhood bartender (laughter), but I can assure you that I'm not the village idiot (laughter); and we would not be doing our job if we were not following up day and night every clue, every allusion, every hint through any channel anywhere that would help open this thing to a peaceful settlement. You, at least, ought to carry a presumption that maybe what I just said is correct. (Applause.)" DR comments to National Foreign Policy Conference for Educators, 19 Jun 1967, in Carl Marcy to Sen. Fulbright, "Subj: Peace to Break Out in Rangoon!" 11 Jul 1967, "CM Chrons—July, Aug & Sept 1967," box 8, Carl Marcy Papers, RG 46, NA, Washington. A few weeks after that, he told the Lions International in Chicago: "There have been a good many upside-down comments on peace moves. . . . We have tried unremittingly to bring the other side to the negotiating table. We have made many proposals ourselves and have supported the initiatives of many other governments and individuals. Hanoi has said 'no' to all of them." State Department press release, 6 Jul 1967.
258. Arthur M. Schlesinger Jr., "Remarks on United States Foreign Policy," 8 Mar 1967, in *The Politics of Hope and The Bitter Heritage: American Liberalism in the 1960s*, by Arthur M. Schlesinger Jr. (Princeton, N.J.: Princeton University Press, 2008), 373–85; also *NYT, WP*, 9 Mar 1967.
259. Arthur M. Schlesinger Jr., *Journals: 1952–2000* (New York: Penguin Press, 2007), 260 (27 Apr 1967).
260. Theodore Draper, "Vietnam: How Not to Negotiate," *New York Review of Books*, 4 May 1967.
261. From 17 May 1967 Harris Survey, cited by Gibbons, IV, 686, 692.

Chapter 14

1. DE/Saigon (Derksen) to DFM, "Subject: Italy and Vietnam," tel. 32++, 9 Mar 1967, DFMA, obt. R. van der Maar, trans. DM; also GD'O, *DV,* 779–80 (10 Feb 1967).
2. BE/Saigon (Wilkinson) to FO, tel. 472, 22 Jun 1967, FCO 15/484, TNA.
3. Poldel Saigon (JL) to PFM (JM), sz. 2773, 6 Mar 1967, AMSZ, trans. MG.
4. GD'O, *DV,* 800 (4 Mar 1967).
5. Ibid., 802 (7 Mar 1967).
6. Ibid., 805–6 (8 Mar 1967).
7. Ibid., 809–10 (10 Mar 1967);IE/S (GD'O) to IFM (AF), office memos 119-120, 12 Mar 1967.
8. AF to DR, 14 Mar 1967, Political Aff. + Rel. IT-US, box 2238, CFPF, 1967–69.
9. DR-WWR telcon, 3:02 p.m., 16 Mar 1967, and DR-Unger telcon, 9:19 a.m., 17 Mar 1967, box 58, DR Papers, RG 59, NA II.
10. Poldel Saigon (JL) to PFM (JM), sz. 3107, 13 Mar 1967, trans. MG.
11. Saigon embtel 20590 (HCL), 17 Mar 1967, POL 27-14 Viet/Marigold, box 2739, CFPF, 1967–69; JL interviews, Warsaw, June 2003 and October 2006.
12. GD'O, *DV,* 810 (10 Mar 1967).

13. Ibid., 810–11 (12 Mar 1967).

14. Ibid., 809, 811 (10 and 12 Mar 1967).

15. Ibid., 813 (15 Mar 1967), trans. IO.

16. Ibid., 814 (16 Mar 1967).

17. Candel Saigon to CDEA, tel. 401, "758 Formal Mtg," 8 Apr 1967, FCO 15/253, TNA.

18. *Chubb's Folly,* 6 Apr 1967 entry.

19. Ibid., 19 Apr 1967 entry; also Candel Saigon to CDEA, tel. 462, "759th Formal Mtg," 20 Apr 1967, FCO 15/253, TNA.

20. *Chubb's Folly,* 20 Apr 1967 entry.

21. Ibid., 16–17 Apr 1967 entries.

22. Ibid., 23 Apr 1967 entry.

23. BCG/Hanoi (Colvin) to D. F. Murray, FO, 4 Apr 1967, FCO 15/253, TNA.

24. Candel Saigon (Wood) to CDEA, tel. 273, "Possible Appeal by ICC," 1 Mar 1967, ibid.

25. Maj. J. J. Donahue to Senior Political Adviser, "Items for IC Meeting Requested by Polish Delegation," 29 Mar 1967, file 100-10-1 pt. 6, vol. 9513, RG 25, NAC.

26. Saigon embtel 22496 (HCL), "Subj: Hanoi-ICC Relations," 8 Apr 1967, POL 27-14 VIET 4/1/67, box 2715, CFPF, 1967–69.

27. "He sounds like a real light weight, real Chairman and all that, but nothing else. If the Poles send a replacement of the same order it will be an indication of the future of this organization." *Chubb's Folly,* 20 Apr 1967 entry.

28. Ibid., 26 April 1967 entry.

29. GD'O, *DV,* 814–15 (6 Apr 1967); Rome embtel 5266, 7 Apr 1967, POL 27-14 Viet/Marigold 1967, box 2739, CFPF, 1967–69.

30. On 8 Apr 1967 JL-HCL talk, see Saigon embtel 22598, 10 Apr 1967, ibid.; Poldel Saigon (JL) to PFM (Kulaga), sz. 4471, 10 Apr 1967, AMSZ, trans. MG.

31. Deptel 179156 (to American Embassy, Saigon), 20 Apr 1967, and deptel 180271 (to American Embassy, Rome), 21 Apr 1967, both in POL 27-14 MARIGOLD 1967, box 2739, CFPF, 1967–69.

32. Poldel Saigon (JL) to PFM (JM), sz. 4470, 10 Apr 1967, AMSZ, trans. MG; JL interview, Warsaw, Jun 2003.

33. PFM (Klasa) to Poldel Saigon (JL), sz. 3645, 12 Apr 1967; PFM (Kulaga) to Poldel Saigon (JL), sz. 3760, 14 Apr 1967; and PFM (JM) to Poldel Saigon (JL), sz. 4039, 20 Apr 1967, all AMSZ, trans. MG; JL interview, 19 Jun 2003.

34. JL interviews, Warsaw, 19 Jun 2003 and 4 Feb 2008.

35. Saigon embtel 23719 (HCL), 22 Apr 1967, POL 27-14 MARIGOLD 1967, box 2739, CFPF, 1967–69. HCL told DR he had "a theory as to why [JL] is so much more friendly, which I will tell you when we meet."

36. HCL, "Viet-Nam Memoir," pt. one: 4 (pp. 1-2), reel 26, HCL, MHS; Gibbons, IV, 541.

37. HCL second-term regret: Poldel Saigon (JL) to PFM (Kulaga), sz. 4471, 10 Apr 1967; interviews with H. S. Lodge, Beverly, Mass., June 2007, and JL, Warsaw, June 2003; "fade-out" and "Oh, my!": *NYT,* 25 Apr 1967.

38. Dier-PVD 28 Apr 1967 talk: Candel Saigon (Dier) to CDEA, tel. 521, "Interview with NVN Prime Minister," 4 May 1967, file 20-22-VIETS-2-1 pt. 15, vol. 9399, RG 25, NAC; Bunker-Dier 5 May 1967 talk: Saigon airgram A-645, 7 May 1967, POL 27 VIET S 5/5/67, box 2782, CFPF, 1967–69; also ("au contraire") CAS Debriefing of Canadian Major Peter Downe, 5 May 1967, Saigon airgram A-642, 6 May 1967, ibid.

39. PFM (JM) to PE/Hanoi (Wasilewski for JL), sz. 4439, and PFM (JM) to Poldel Saigon (JL), sz. 4450, both 2 May 1967; PE/Hanoi (JL) to PFM (JM), sz. no. 5543, 3 May 1967, all AMSZ, trans. MG.

40. PE/Hanoi (JL) to PFM (JM), sz. 5850, 10 May 1967, ibid.; surge: *FRUS, 1964–68,* 5:333; Gibbons, IV, 568.

41. LBJ to HCM, 6 Apr 1967, in *FRUS, 1964–68,* 5:302–3; and Gibbons, IV, 521.

42. Gibbons, IV, 521.

43. PE/Hanoi (JL) to PFM (JM), sz. 5579, 4 May 1967, AMSZ, trans. MG.

44. Poldel Saigon (JL) to PFM (Kulaga), sz. 5188, 24 Apr 1967, ibid.

45. PFM (JM) to PE/Hanoi (Wasilewski for JL), sz. 4607, 4–5 May 1967, AMSZ, obt./trans. MG.
46. JL-PVD talk: PE/Hanoi (JL) to PFM (JM), sz. 5761, 8 May 1967, AMSZ, trans. MG.
47. From 6 May 1967 entry, cited in "Diplomatic Folder, against Americans 1968, North American Affairs, Policy Guidelines," in Bo Ngoai Giao [Ministry of Foreign Affairs], *Dai su ky chuyen de: Dau tranh ngoai giao va van dong quoc te trong nhung chiev chong My cuu nuoc, 1954–1975* [Important account of a special subject: The diplomatic struggle and international activities of the Anti-American resistance and national salvation, 1954–1975] (Hanoi: Internal Foreign Ministry Publication, 1987), vol. 3, 133, trans. Lien-Hang Thi Nguyen.
48. PE/Hanoi (JL) to PFM (JM), sz. 5761, 8 May 1967, AMSZ, trans. MG.
49. On 7 May 1967 party, see PE/Hanoi (JL) to PFM (JM), sz. 5759, 8 May 1967, ibid.; Lt. Col. J. W. Sheen, [Canadian] Permanent Representative, Hanoi Detachment, to Sr. Political Advisor [W. M. Wood], "Subject: Polish Delegation Cocktail Party," 9 May 1967, file 20 Viet-N-2-1 pt. 2, vol. 10067, RG 25, NAC.
50. PE/Hanoi (Wasilewski) to PFM (Wierna), sz. 5807, 9 May 1967, AMSZ, trans. MG.
51. JL interview, Warsaw, 19 Jun 2003.
52. From 13 Apr 1967 entry, General Westmoreland's History Notes, 10–30 Apr 1967, #15 history file: 27 Mar–30 Apr 1967, CMH 126-82, Westmoreland Papers, U.S. Army Center of Military History, Fort McNair, Washington.
53. JL interview, Warsaw, 19 Jun 2003; Muzeum Wojska Polskiego receipt, 10 Apr 1968, courtesy JL. The revolver belonged to U.S. Air Force Major Jack William Bomar, whose EB66C "Sky-warrior" electronic warfare plane was shot down on 4 Feb 1967. When Bomar was kept in solitary confinement in the notorious "Hanoi Hilton," he used a cup held against a wall to communicate with a fellow American prisoner held in an adjacent cell—who turned out to be the future senator and presidential candidate John McCain. Bomar was released along with other U.S. prisoners of war after the Paris accords were concluded in 1973, and died in 2009. "POW Who Communicated by code with McCain Dies," *Arizona Republic,* 28 May 2009.
54. Nguyen manuscript; MP, "General Vo Nguyen Giap and the Mysterious Evolution of the Plan for the 1968 Tet Offensive"; Nguyen, "The War Politburo"; and Quinn-Judge, "The Ideological Debate in the DRV and the Significance of the Anti-Party Affair."
55. PE/Hanoi (JL) to PFM (JM), sz. 5778, 8 May 1967, AMSZ, trans. MG.
56. JL-NDT talk: PE/Hanoi (JL) to PFM (JM), sz. 5862, 10 May 1967, ibid.
57. Gomułka-NDT memcon, 21 Apr 1967, East Berlin, PZPR 2602, AAN, obt. LG, trans. MG.
58. PE/Hanoi (JL) to PFM (JM), sz. 5850, 10 May 1967, and PFM (JM) to PE/Hanoi (Wasilewski for JL), sz. 4791, 10 May 1967, both AMSZ, trans. MG.
59. JL 9 May 1967 briefing: CzE/Hanoi (Mucha) to CzFM, tel. 5085, 13 May 1967, AMZV, obt./trans. G. Laron.
60. U.S. soldiers also learned this lesson. A GI who leaned his M-16 and rested his chin on a dike during a night patrol to set up an ambush soon found his "chin, neck and upper chest were suddenly on fire." "After a single encounter, the red ants were the ones you'd never forget. Their color is striking, but it's their pincers that make them memorable." See "Bugs!!!" at http://www.i-kirk.info/tales/vn4c03.html.
61. On the Haiphong trip, see JL interviews, Warsaw, 20 Oct 2006 and 10 May 2011.
62. PFM (AR) to PE/Hanoi (Wasilewski for JL), sz. 4873, 11 May 1967, and PE/Hanoi (JL) to PFM (JM), sz. 6070, 13 May 1967, both AMSZ, trans. MG.
63. PE/Hanoi (JL) to PFM (JM), sz. 6070, 13 May 1967, ibid.; "Diplomatic Defeat for Ho," *Newsweek,* 15 May 1967, 13. In Saigon, Chubb also noted the disclosure and wondered who had leaked the secret resolution, which of course was widely known in diplomatic circles. "It will also be most interesting to see the reaction of the North, who will surely be livid and I would think very prone to do something about it; like asking Canada and India to withdraw. If, however, they do not do so it will be apparent that they have been running some sort of bluff for some unexplained reason." *Chubb's Folly,* 9 May 1967 entry.
64. Ibid., 23 May 1967 entry.
65. It featured a "decent" menu "including Dalat lamb, which made a pleasant change." Ibid., 24 May 1967 entry.

66. JL-Diers 25 May 1967 talk: Candel Saigon (Dier) to CDEA, tel. 616, "Talk with Polish Commissioner," 25 May 1967, file 100-11-3, pt. 2, vol. 9516, and file 20-22-VIETS-2-1, pt. 15, vol. 9399, both RG 25, NAC. Chubb, too, had observed "the simply ghastly clouds on the international skyline. The world is rushing to ultimate destruction and where the fault lies, I, for one, am not prepared to say. I do feel that we are heading for a cataclysmic showdown, almost certainly in my own lifetime and as an individual feel just as helpless as our fathers as World War I and World War II came to pass." *Chubb's Folly,* 12 May 1967 entry.

67. Candel Saigon (Dier) to CDEA, tel. 616, 25 May 1967.

68. *Chubb's Folly,* 26 May 1967 entry.

69. Ibid., 28 May 1967 entry; Candel Saigon to CDEA, tel. 643, "Polcoms Views," 31 May 1967, file 20-22-VIETS-2-1, pt. 15, vol. 9399, RG 25, NAC.

70. Candel Saigon (Dier) to CDEA, tel. 616, "Talk with Polish Commissioner," 25 May 1967, ibid.

71. Bog[two letters illegible]cki, handwritten report, 20 April 1967, BU 0586/2162, IPN, obt. A. Paczkowski, trans. MG.

72. Comments on ibid.

73. See above and Rome embtel 6506, 6 Jun 1967, *SDVW:NVPP,* 370.

74. JL left at 5:30 a.m., according to Poldel Saigon (Kowalski) to PFM (Szewczyk-Wilski), sz. 6937, 31 May 1967, AMSZ, trans. MG.

75. JL route: PE/Hanoi (JL) to PFM (JM), sz. 6070, 13 May 1967; PFM (Szewczyk) to Poldel Saigon (JL), sz. 5104, 17 May 1967; Poldel Saigon (JL) to PFM (Szewczyk), sz. 6419, 19 May 1967; PFM (JM-Szewczyk) to Poldel Saigon (JL), sz. 5324, 22 May 1967; Poldel Saigon (JL) to PFM (JM), sz. 6634, 24 May 1967; FM (Szewczyk) to Poldel Saigon (JL), sz. 5496, 26 May 1967; and PFM (Wilski) to PE/Beirut (Wójcik), sz. 5435, 26 May 1967, all ibid.

76. On JL in Beirut and onward, see JL interviews, Warsaw, Jun 2003, 4 Feb 2008, and 10 May 2011; and JL telephone interview, 1 Oct 2007.

77. JL interview, Warsaw, Jun 2003; also PE/Beirut (Wójcik) to PFM (Wilski), sz. 7207, 5 Jun 1967 and PFM (Szewczyk) to PE/Beirut (Wójcik), sz. 5877, 6 Jun 1967, AMSZ.

78. JL interview, Warsaw, Jun 2003; also PE/Beirut (Wójcik) to PFM (Wilski), sz. 7272, 6 Jun 1967, AMSZ.

79. PE/Beirut (Wójcik) to PFM (Wilski), sz. 7503, 10 Jun 1967, AMSZ.

80. On "right-hand man," see Warsaw embtel 1293 (JAG), 24 Nov 1966, POL 27 VIET S 11/23/66, CFPF, 1964–66.

Chapter 15

1. For the *Los Angeles Times* background, see David Halberstam, *The Powers That Be* (New York: Alfred A. Knopf, 1979), 135–75, 360–420, 479–93, 547–64; and Marshall Berges, *The Life and Times of Los Angeles: A Newspaper, a Family and a City* (New York: Atheneum, 1984).

2. John Corry, "The Los Angeles Times," *Harper's,* December 1969, 75.

3. Halberstam, *Powers That Be,* 407.

4. Robert J. Donovan, *Boxing the Kangaroo: A Reporter's Memoir* (Columbia: University of Missouri Press, 2000), 125–27.

5. Robert E. Kintner to LBJ, 9 Feb 1967, LO folder, box 147, confidential file: name file, LBJL; Kathleen J. Turner, *Lyndon Johnson's Dual War: Vietnam and the Press* (Chicago: University of Chicago Press, 1985), 175.

6. He would return to Moscow two decades later as CNN bureau chief.

7. SHL email to author, 1 Apr 2011.

8. Ibid.; Christian to LBJ, 3 p.m., 19 Apr 1967, Chron April 1967 folder, and Christian to SHL, 12 May 1967, and Christian to LBJ, 16 May 1967, both Chron May 1967 folder, all box 5, Christian OF, LBJL; LBJ-SHL memcon, 1 May 1967, Notes on Meetings—President—1967, box 1, ibid.; SHL, "President Searches for Understanding," *LAT,* 7 May 1967; SHL telephone interview, 8 Jul 2003.

9. DK and Robert Boyd, *A Certain Evil* (Boston: Little, Brown, 1965).

10. SHL, "The Secret Search for Peace in Vietnam," unpublished manuscript, n.d., "Vietnam Bombing Pause 1966–67" folder, box 41, SHLP (hereafter SHL, "Secret Search"). Also nine-question memo [DK, May 1967?], "37 Day Pause (Vietnam) 1965–68" folder, box 39, SHLP.

11. Bill McGaffin, of the *Chicago Daily News,* was the other. Benjamin C. Bradlee, *Conversations with Kennedy* (New York: W. W. Norton, 1975), 136.

12. Anonymous memo, 16 May 1967, 37 Day Pause (Vietnam) 1965–68, box 39, SHLP.

13. SHL (with Tom Lambert, Ted Sell, and DK), "U.S. Can't Find New Third Party for Viet Negotiations," *LAT,* 21 May 1967.

14. Sell memo, "Re: Bombing," 16 May 1967, 37 Day Pause (Vietnam) 1965–68, box 39, SHLP.

15. On "heartbroken," conversation with BDM, Saint Simons Island, Ga., 8 Apr 2005; "any good": Arthur M. Schlesinger Jr., *Journals: 1952–2000* (New York: Penguin Press, 2007), 257 (4 Jan 1967).

16. BDM email to author, 28 Nov 2010.

17. See Moyers, Bill 1966–67, box 8, POF, LBJL, esp. BDM to LBJ, 18 Jul 1967 (relating a "campaign" by "Arthur Schlesinger, Dick Goodwin, Blair Clark, and others" to convince RSM to resign in protest against the war) and Judith Moyers to Lady Bird Johnson, 6 May 1968 (trying to patch up the rift between their husbands); also Patrick Anderson, *The President's Men: White House Assistants of Franklin D. Roosevelt, Harry S. Truman, Dwight D. Eisenhower, John F. Kennedy, and Lyndon B. Johnson* (Garden City, N.Y.: Doubleday, 1968), 349. Soon after BDM left, LBJ "was very angry that he had shot his mouth off" (after the columnist Jimmy Breslin reported his cocktail party comments): Stewart (BE/Washington) to MacLehose (FO), 2 Feb 1967, FCO 15/598, TNA. BDM claimed Breslin "really distorted and butchered what I had said": BDM to WWR, 6 Feb 1967, Walt W. Rostow vol. 20 [3 of 4] February 1–11, 1967, box 13, NSF:MtP:WR, LBJL.

18. Notes "from ~~bill moyers~~ source M," "about July or August" 1967, Interviews folder, box 15, SHLP; DK and SHL, *Secret Search,* 54.

19. SHL, "Secret Search."

20. SHL telephone interview, 8 Jul 2003 ("a book"); DK telephone interview, 9 Jul 2003; SHL, "Secret Search" ("massive test").

21. Luther A. Huston, "Kraslow-Loory peace mission rates prize," *Editor & Publisher,* 15 Mar 1969, 52, 54; SHL, "Secret Search"; also Corry, "Los Angeles Times," 76.

22. SHL telephone interview, 8 Jul 2003 ("presumption"); DK telephone interview, 9 Jul 2003; SHL, "Secret Search" ("gamble").

23. Unidentified source interview notes, 29 Aug 1967, Interviews folder, box 15, SHLP.

24. Notes "from source 'n' this day, deep background, no attribution," 13 Sep 1967, ibid.

25. Arthur M. Schlesinger Jr., *Robert Kennedy and His Times* (Boston: Houghton Mifflin, 1978; 2002 ed.), 777.

26. "BK" interview notes, 19 Sep 1967, Interviews folder, box 15, SHLP; DK telephone interviews, 17 May, 9 Jul 2003; SHL telephone interview, 8 Jul 2003.

27. WWR interview notes, 20 Sep 1967, Interviews folder, box 15, SHLP; Christian to LBJ, 7:30 p.m., 19 Sep 1967, Chron September 1967 folder, box 6, Christian OF, LBJL

28. NC, "Is the National Honor Being Bombed?" *SR,* 9 Sep 1967, 22.

29. NC and WPB accounts of 19 Sep 1967 phone call: WPB folder, box 316, NC Papers, Young Library, UCLA, and Chron Files, September–October 1967 (folder 2), box 4, ASS/EAPA. U.S. aides still cited Radványi's statements as "their most conclusive evidence they had to support their suspicion that the Poles had got themselves out on a limb": WPB in Seaborn to Collins, 13 Sep 1967, file 20-22-VIETS-2-1 pt. 18, vol. 9399, RG 25, NAC.

30. NC, "The Tragic Trap" *SR,* 21 Oct 1967, 24, 55; WPB to NC, w. att., 23 Oct 1967, et al. in NC and WPB folders in previous footnote; and correction in *SR,* 25 Nov 1967.

31. NC interview notes, 27 Sep 1967, Interviews folder, box 15, SHLP.

32. Fernand Rouillmon, 27 Sep 1967, and Martin, 28 Sep 1967, interview notes, both ibid.

33. James G. Hershberg, "'A Half-Hearted Overture': Czechoslovakia, Kissinger, and Vietnam, Autumn 1966," in *The Search for Peace in Vietnam, 1964–1968,* edited by Lloyd C. Gardner

and Ted Gittinger (College Station: Texas A&M University Press, 2004), 292–320; Robert K. Brigham and George C. Herring, "The Pennsylvania Peace Initiative: June–October, 1967," in ibid., 59–72; *SDVW:NVPP*, 521–22, 716–71; Hershberg talk on HAK, Sainteny, and Vietnam, SHAFR annual meeting, 23 June 2007, Chantilly, Va.

34. *SDVW:NVPP*, esp. 726, 756; *FRUS, 1964–68*, 5:837.

35. Gelb interview, New York, 26 Jun 2003.

36. "kiss": [HAK] interview notes, 2 Oct 1967, Interviews folder, box 15, SHLP.

37. DK telephone interview, 17 May 2003.

38. Ibid., 9 Jul 2003.

39. Warsaw embtel 2700, 9 May 1967, POL 27-14 MARIGOLD 1967, box 2739, CFPF, 1967-9.

40. JM-LBJ 12 Sep 1967 talk: "Subject: President's Conversation with new Polish Ambassador" (pt. 3 on Vietnam), 12:23–12:28 p.m., 12 Sep 1967, POL 17-1 POL-US 1/1/67, box 2436, CFPF, 1967–69; PE/Washington (JM) to PFM (AR), sz. 11586, 12 Sep 1967, AMSZ, trans. MG; MR.

41. JM draft letter to E. Ernest Goldstein, 28 Mar 1990, courtesy of Stefan Michałowski; LBJ contacts with foreigners: David Kaiser, *American Tragedy: Kennedy, Johnson, and the Origins of the Vietnam War* (Cambridge, Mass.: Harvard University Press, 2000), 286—87, 427; Fredrik Logevall, *Choosing War: The Lost Chance for Peace and the Escalation of War in Vietnam* (Berkeley: University of California Press, 1999), 79.

42. Nathaniel Davis to WWR, 21 Sep 1967, Poland-Memos vol. II 10/66-5/68, box 201, NSF:CO, LBJL.

43. *FRUS, 1964–68*, 5:778.

44. WAH-JM memcon, 26 Sep 1967, folder: September 1967, box FCL 33, WAHP-LC.

45. A. E. Ritchie to Ralph Collins, 26 Sep 1967, File 20-22-VIETS-2-1 pt. 19, vol. 9400, RG 25, NAC; Tomorowicz made similar arguments to Canadian diplomats: Candel UN, NYC to CDEA, tel. 2506, 23 Sep 1967, file 20-22-VIETS-2-1 pt. 18, vol. 9399, ibid.

46. French Embassy, Washington (Lucet) to Foreign Minister (Couve de Murville), tel. 4832-4836, 26 Sep 1967, in Asie-Océanie, Conflit Vietnam, vol. 157, Ministère des Affaires Étrangères Français archives, Paris, obt./trans. G. Martin.

47. Hughes to DR, 20 Apr 1967, POL 17-1 POL-US 1/1/67, box 2436, CFPF, 1967-69.

48. Brzezinski to WWR, 2 Oct 1967, "Subject: Alleged Breakdown of the December Talks on Vietnam," Vietnam MARIGOLD—Incomplete, box 148, NSF:CO:VN, LBJL. Brzezinski, who later became Jimmy Carter's national security adviser, was so convinced that the Soviets rather enjoyed the American predicament and therefore were "actually trying to prolong the war" rather than end it that he felt "no hesitation" about end-running DR and WAH by "phoning up people in the White House and bootlegging memos to the White House," once taking his concern directly to LBJ. Some Poles, such as AR and JM, may have wished to be helpful, he believed, but the Kremlin did not—and it ultimately called the tune. Brzezinski OH, 12 Nov 1971, 6–7, LBJL; Brzezinski telephone interview, 1 Apr 2011.

49. Habib through DR to NK, "Possible Discussion of Marigold at Meeting with Ambassador Michałowski, October 11, 12:00 Noon—Information Memorandum," 11 Oct 1967, POL 27-14 MARIGOLD 1967, box 2739, CFPF, 1967–69. JM purveyed his views not only to LBJ and WAH but also Deputy Assistant Secretary for European Affairs Walter Stoessel, Assistant Secretary for Economic Affairs Anthony M. Soloman, and Undersecretary for Political Affairs Eugene Rostow.

50. JM-NK talk: memcon, "Polish Views on Viet-Nam Peace Negotiations," 11 Oct 1967, ibid.

51. Probably alluding to JM's talk with NK, WPB told Ritchie he had "called him in and spoken to him 'as strongly as one can with a country with which you wish to maintain friendly relations'" that his contacts with reporters hurt US-Polish ties and might endanger any potential future Polish role as a Vietnam "go-between." Ritchie to Collins, 16 Oct 1967, file 20-22-VIETS-2-1 pt. 19, vol. 9400, RG 25, NAC.

52. Nathaniel Davis, memo for the record, "Subject: Luncheon Conversation with Polish Ambassador," 26 Apr 1968, POL POL-US, box 2436, CFPF, 1967–69.

53. Ashmore/Baggs interview notes, 25 Sep 1967, Interviews folder, box 15, SHLP.

54. "CRO" (4-5 Oct 1967) and J. B. Seaborn (5 Oct 1967) interview notes, ibid.

55. Seaborn to R. E. Collins, "Vietnam Negotiations," 10 Oct 1967, file 20-22-VIETS-2-1 pt. 19, vol. 9400, RG 25, NAC.

56. SHL to Martin, 3 Oct 1967, ibid.; Martin to SHL, 24 Oct 1967, file 20-22-VIETS-2-1 pt. 20, RG 25, NAC.

57. Interview notes with Ken Kerst, 4 Oct 1967; Dick Smyser, 4 Oct 1967; "source his" [Isham], 11 Oct 1967; "targeting procedure," 19 Oct 1967; "bm" [Bill Marsh?], 31 Oct 1967; Jim Rosenthal, 3 November 1967; and Chuck Floweree, 13 Nov 1967; all Interviews folder, box 15, SHLP.

58. Charles C. Floweree to Habib, "Subject: Conversation with *Los Angeles Times* Reporters," 15 Nov 1967, "Retrospective Accounts."

59. "source R" interview notes, 3 Oct 1967, Interviews folder, box 15, SHLP.

60. WAH interview notes, 7 Oct 1967, Vietnam Bombing Pause 1966–67, box 41, SHLP; WAH memcon with SHL, 11 am, 7 Oct 1967, "Memcons 'L'" folder, box 587, WAHP-LC.

61. HCL to Read, "Subject: Press Contact," 12 Oct 1967, reel 19, HCL, MHS; HCL interview notes, 12 Oct 1967, Interviews folder, box 15, SHLP.

62. WPB "backgrounder" notes, 16 Oct 1967, ibid.

63. Ortona interview notes, 9 Nov 1967, ibid.

64. Pawlak interview notes, 1 Nov 1967, ibid.

65. JM conversation notes, 2 Nov 1967, ibid.

66. Packers: *SDVW:NVPP,* 772–815.

67. Gomułka–Le Duan memcon, Moscow, 6 Nov 1967, AAN, obt. LG, trans. MG.

68. Draft note [PUWP Politburo?] to AR, n.d. [Nov. 1967], ibid.

69. Handwritten sz., PFM (AR) to PE/Washington (JM), 5 Nov 1967, AMSZ, trans. MG.

70. "agency" interview notes, 9 Nov 1967, Interviews folder, box 15, SHLP; "probably Kraslow": in "Secret Search," SHL termed DK "one of the few newsmen in Washington who could pick up the telephone and call, say, Richard Helms, the CIA director, and have Helms come to the phone."

71. *Secret Search,* p. 44, prudishly sanitized Helms' quotation (attributed to "one frequent White House visitor"), altering "while he's sitting on the can" to "in the bathtub."

72. The CIA station chief in Warsaw (1965-7) was not even aware of the "Marigold" cryptonym and recalled being far more absorbed with running agents and operations against Polish party and military targets. David W. Forden telephone interview, Williamsburg, VA, 8 Feb 2008.

73. CLC-DK/SHL talk, 7 Nov 1967: CLC, "Conversation with David Kraslow and Stuart Loory of the *Los Angeles Times,*" 8 Nov 1967, Cooper, Chester 1965-1968 (3), box 451, WAHP-LC; "chet cooper cccc" interview notes, 7 Nov 1967, Vietnam Bombing Pause 1966–67, box 41, SHLP; DK termed CLC "very very circumspect" though SHL called him "consistently our best source": DK telephone interview, 17 May 2003, SHL telephone interview, 8 Jul 2003.

74. Holbrooke would serve in senior State Department posts under presidents Carter, Clinton, and Obama.

75. NK-DK/SHL talk, 13 Nov 1967: NK interview notes, 13 Nov 1967, Interviews folder, box 15, SHLP; Holbrooke, "Subject: Conversation with David Kraslow and Stuart Loory of the *Los Angeles Times,*" 15 Nov 1967, "Retrospective Accounts."

76. NK interview notes, 13 Nov [1967], Interviews folder, box 15, SHLP.

77. From "dick holbrook[e] phone conversation: assumed off the record," 16 Nov 1967, ibid.

78. DR-JM 18 Nov 1967 talk: PE/Washington (JM) to PFM (Rapacki), sz. 14260, 20 Nov 1967, AMSZ, trans. MG; memcon, "Subject: Viet-Nam: Polish Ambassador's Views," 18 Nov 1967, Poland Memos Vol. II 10/66-5/68, box 201, NSF:CO, LBJL; memcon, "Polish Ambassador's Call on the Secretary for a *Tour d'Horizon,*" 18 Nov 1967, POL POL-US 1/1/67, box 2435, CFPF, 1967–69.

79. PE/Washington (JM) to PFM (Naszkowski), sz. 11103, 1 Sep 1967, AMSZ.

80. Oslo embtel 2033 (Tibbetts), 14 Nov 1967, *SDVW:NVPP,* 645. AR had earlier told the Dutch that Washington "sabotaged" the December 1966 effort: Polish Track (V) 'Open Cities' Jan. 1967, box 16, Records of Negotiations about Vietnam, 1965–69, lot file 69D277, RG 59, NA II

81. Memo for the record, "Vietnam," 21 Sep 1967, FO 800/958, TNA.

82. See Alsop, Joseph—Article, box 5, NSF:Rostow, LBJL, esp. Read to WWR, 16 Nov 1967, and WWR to LBJ, 5:10 p.m., 17 Nov 1967; Robert W. Merry, *Taking on the World: Joseph and Stewart Alsop—Guardians of the American Century* (New York: Viking Penguin, 2006), 434–35.

83. WPB to DR, "Subject: Attached Draft Outline of a Major Publication on the Search for Peace," 20 Nov 1967, enc. "The Search for Peace in Southeast Asia," in 1965–67 Summaries, box 9, ASS/EAPA.

84. Clifford conversation notes, 14 Nov 1967; Bunker interview notes, 15 Nov 1967; Fulbright interview notes, 16 Nov 1967; Toon interview notes, 20 Nov 1967; Clark Clifford interview notes ("strictly," "tall," "smooth"), 20 Nov 1967; all Interviews folder, box 15, SHLP.

85. Fulbright interview notes, 16 Nov [1967], ibid.

86. See notes dated "Nov 20" and "11-20," ibid.; SHL telephone interview, 9 Jul 2003.

87. MR.

88. JM interview notes, 22 Nov 1967, Interviews folder, box 15, SHLP.

89. PE/Washington (JM) to PFM (AR), sz. 14475, 23 Nov 1967, and PE/Washington (JM) to PFM (Frackiewicz), sz. 14477, 23 Nov 1967; both AMSZ, trans. MG.

90. PFM (Wolniak) to PFM (JM), sz. 11772, 25 Nov 1967; and PE/Washington (JM) to PFM (Wolniak), sz. 14626 ("strengthen"), 27 Nov 1967, both ibid.

91. See RSM to LBJ, 1 Nov 1967, *FRUS, 1964–68,* 5:943–50.

92. RSM interview notes, 24 Nov 1967, Interviews folder, box 15, SHLP.

93. Read to WWR, "Subject: Kraslow and Loory's Book on Viet-Nam," 20 Nov 1967, "Retrospective Accounts" and Vietnam: July–December 1967 folder, box 6, NSF:Rostow, LBJL.

94. November 28, 1967—1:40 p.m. Rusk, McNamara, Wheeler, Helms, Rostow, Christian, T. Johnson, box 1, Tom Johnson's Notes of Meetings, LBJL.

95. "If the Pentagon Papers showed the top level of the American government to be liars, as they surely did, then they also showed reporters like Chal Roberts to have been at least partial collaborators in a shell game performed on the American people." Halberstam, *Powers That Be,* 804; also 745.

96. GD'O, *DV,* 845–46 (23, 30 Nov 1967).

97. SHL-GD'O 1 Dec 1967 talk: GD'O interview notes, 1 Dec 1967, Interviews folder, box 15, SHLP; GD'O, *DV,* 846 (1 Dec 1967).

98. See the account of "Killy" in chapter 16.

99. La Pira interview notes, 2 Dec [1967], Interviews folder, box 15, SHLP.

100. SHL-GD'O 4 Dec 1967 talk: GD'O interview notes, 4 Dec 1967, ibid.; GD'O, *DV,* 847 (4 Dec 1967); GD'O to AF, telegramma in partenza, 5 Dec 1967, N. 00015, AFP.

101. Rome embtel 4458 (Reinhardt), 27 Feb 1968, POL 27-14 Viet/Marigold 1968, box 2739, CFPF, 1967–69.

102. GD'O, *DV,* 847–48 (4 Dec 1967).

103. Notes of interviews with Tran Thanh (DRV cultural attaché, Prague), 7 Dec 1967, and Pham Van Chuong (Liberation Press Agency of South Vietnam correspondent), 9 Dec 1967, both Vietnam Bombing Pause 1966–67, box 41, SHLP.

104. Beam and Jan Petranek interview notes, both 8 Dec 1967, Interviews folder, box 15, SHLP.

105. Bruce interview notes, 27, 29 Nov 1967, ibid.; Bruce to DR, memo, "Re: Deptel 82448 and David Kraslow," 10 Dec 1967, "Retrospective Accounts."

106. London embtel 4649 (Bruce), 8 Dec 1967, POL 27-14 VIET 9/15/67, box 2716, CFPF, 1967–69.

107. Murray (w. Robin Haydon) interview notes, 28 Nov 1967, Interviews folder, box 15, SHLP.

108. William Brubeck (political counselor, U.S. embassy) interview notes, 27 Nov 1967; "Konopotski (sp?)" (Polish press attaché), 27 Nov 1967, Yuri Pavlov (2nd secretary, Soviet Embassy), 28 Nov 1967; Henry James (Wilson press secretary), 1 Dec 1967; all ibid.

109. Wallner to Read, 11 Dec 1967, enc. Dean-DK memcon, Paris, 4 Dec 1967, "Retrospective Accounts."

110. Dean-DK memcon, 4 Dec 1967, "Retrospective Accounts"; Dean interview notes, 4 Dec 1967, Interviews folder, box 15, SHLP.

111. Dean interview notes, 6 Dec 1967, ibid.

112. Laughlin Campbell (CIA station chief, Paris) interview notes, 4–5 Dec 1967, ibid.

113. Marcovich telcon notes, 5 Dec 1967, and interview, 6 Dec 1967, both Vietnam Bombing Pause 1966–67, box 41, SHLP.

114. Marcovich to HAK, 6 Dec 1967; Read memo for the record, 11 Dec 1967; both "Retrospective Accounts."

115. DK to Huynh Tieng, questions for Bo; Huynh Tieng interview notes; both 7 Dec 1967, Interviews folder, box 15, SHLP.

116. Burchett-Isham/Dean 5 Dec 1967 talk: Paris embtel 7540, 6 Dec 1967, Matilda folder, box 141, NSF:CO:VN, LBJL; Burchett memcon ("tall"): D II Wietn-0-22-1-71, AMSZ; Wilfred G. Burchett, *Grasshoppers & Elephants* (New York: Urizen Books, 1977), 126–27 ("tall"); George Burchett and Nick Shimmin, eds., *Memoirs of a Rebel Journalist: The Autobiography of Wilfred Burchett* (Sydney: University of New South Wales Press, 2005), 605–6.

117. Paris embtel 7540, 6 Dec 1967.

118. HES, memcon with Burchett, Paris, 8 Dec 1967, box 590, HES, RBML, CU.

119. Burchett memcon; Burchett, *Memoirs*, 606.

120. Leslie Fielding (BE/Paris) to R.A. Fyjis-Walker, FO, 12 Dec 1967, FCO 15/584, TNA.

121. Chalmers M. Roberts, "Part of the Record of a Peace Effort," *WP*, 8 Dec 1967 (also *International Herald Tribune*, 9–10 Dec 1967); Fielding (BE/Paris) to Fyjis-Walker, 12 Dec 1967, FCO 15/584, TNA.

122. PE/Washington (JM) to PFM (AR), sz. 15137, 8 Dec 1967, AMSZ, trans. MG.

123. GD'O, *DV,* 848 (10–11, 16 Dec 1967).

124. Marcovich to HAK, 15 Dec 1967, Vietnam-Pennsylvania, box 140, NSF:CO:VN, LBJL.

125. Read telephone conversation notes, 11 Dec 1967, Interviews folder, box 15, SHLP.

126. SHL-JAG talks, 11-13 Dec 1967: [SHL,] JAG interview notes, 11–13 Dec 1967, Vietnam Bombing Pause 1966–67, box 41, SHLP; Warsaw embtel 1578 (JAG), 12 Dec 1967, Poland, Volume 2, 10/66-5/68, box 201, NSF:CO, LBJL and POL 27-14 VIET 9/15/67, box 2716, CFPF, 1967–69; JAG OH II, 10 Feb 1969, 30–32 ("stupid"), LBJL.

127. Brimelow interview notes, 11–12 Dec 1967, Interviews folder, box 15, SHLP.

128. M. Sieradzki, note from conversation with JAG, Warsaw, 12 Dec 1967, Dept. II—Vietnam, AMSZ, trans. MG; also Warsaw embtel 4344 (JAG), 12 Dec 1967, cited above.

129. JL interviews, Warsaw, June 2003.

130. Ibid.

131. JL interview notes, 13 Dec 1967, Interviews folder, box 15, SHLP.

132. James C. Thomson Jr. OH-I, 22 Jul 1971, 11–12, LBJL

133. JL interview, Warsaw, June 2003.

134. SHL telephone interview, 8 Jul 2003.

135. JL interviews, Warsaw, June 2003, 4 Feb 2008.

136. PFM (Sieradzki) to PE/Washington (JM), sz. 12496, 18 Dec 1967; also PFM (Winiewicz) to PE/Rome (Chabasinski), sz. 12444, 15 Dec 1967, both AMSZ, trans. MG.

137. GD'O interview notes, 15 Dec 1967, Interviews folder, box 15, SHLP.

138. Aubrac interview notes, 15 Dec 1967, ibid.; "face went white": SHL, "Secret Search."

139. Read telcon notes, 11 Dec 1967, Interviews folder, box 15, SHLP.

140. Read OH I, 13 Jan 1969, 8–9, LBJL.

141. WWR [phone?] conversation notes, 18 Dec 1967, Interviews folder, box 15, SHLP. No "Poppycock" file surfaced, though DK/SHL believed one existed under that name: *Secret Search,* 27 n. 2.

142. Isham phone conversation notes, 19 Dec 1967, Interviews folder, box 15, SHLP.

143. Habib phone conversation notes, 2 Jan 1968, ibid.

144. CLC, memo for the record, "Subject: David Kraslow of the *Los Angeles Times*," 18 Dec 1967, "<u>Chron</u>-Memcon" folder, box 5, WAHP-NA.

145. HAK telephone talk notes, 20 Dec 1967, Interviews folder, box 15, SHLP.

146. W.A.K.L [Lake] memcon, Princeton, NJ, 3 Jan 1968, "Retrospective Accounts"; also will a.k. lake interview notes, 3 Jan 1968, Interviews folder, box 15, SHLP. Lake was later an NSC aide to HAK and national security adviser to Clinton.

147. DR buzz to NK, 10:20 a.m., 22 Dec 1967, box 60, DR Papers, entry 5379, RG 59, NA II.

148. Read OH I, 13 Jan 1969, 9, LBJL.

149. WPB interview notes, 2 Jan 1968, Interviews folder, box 15, SHLP.
150. WWR-DK/SHL talk, 4 Jan 1968: DK telephone interview, 17 May 2003; WWR, memo for the record, "Subject: Conversation with Kraslow and Loory of the *Los Angeles Times* on Vietnam —January 4, 1968," 11 Jan 1968, Vietnam: January–February 1968 folder, box 6, NSF:Rostow, LBJL; WWR interview notes, 4 Jan 1968, Interviews folder, box 15, SHLP.
151. Goodwin (26 Dec 1967) and Thomson (27 Dec 1967) interview notes, both ibid.
152. U Soe Tin interview notes, 26 Dec 1967, Vietnam Bombing Pause 1966–67, box 41, SHLP.
153. NK interview notes, 30 Dec 1967, ibid.
154. SHL phone interview, 8 Jul 2003; Thant interview notes, 3 Jan 1968, Interviews folder, box 15, SHLP.
155. Hightower interview notes, 29 Jan 1968, ibid.
156. SHL, "Secret Search"; SHL-Loomis correspondence, SHLP.
157. Draft Viet-Nam history, n.d., in "EA/VN 1968 History (folder 1)," box 13, ASS/EAPA; WPB to Edmund A. Gullion, 13 Sep 1968, "Chron Files, June–December 1968 (folder 2)," box 6, ibid., replying to Gullion to WPB, 10 Sep 1967. The ex–State Department official, involved in the "XYZ" contacts, had urged the administration to "make public in simple form the long record of its efforts to stop hostilities."
158. "Our Efforts to Seek a Peaceful Settlement of the Vietnam Conflict," taken by WAH to 20 Feb 1968 meeting with LBJ; 19 Feb 1968 DID draft; both Vietnam General, Jan–Mar 1968, box 521, WAHP-LC.
159. WPB to WWR, 14 Dec 1967, Chron File, Nov–Dec 67 (folder 2), box 5, ASS/EAPA.
160. WPB to DR, "Subject: Life Project on Negotiations and Other Matters," 20 Feb 1968, Chron File, Jan–Mar 1968 (folder 1), ibid.; note on contacts with McCullough, 19, 21 Feb 1968, WPB Press Contacts, 1965–68, box 10, ibid. McCullough: Jason Felch and Marlena Telvick, "Unsung Hero," *American Journalism Review,* June–July 2004.
161. "A Study in Intransigence," Editorial, *Life,* 22 Mar 1968, 21; Frank McCulloch, "Peace Feelers: This Frail Dance of the Seven Veils," *Life,* 22 Mar 1968, 32–38; János Radványi, "A Bizarre Adventure in Make-Believe Diplomacy," *Life,* 22 Mar 1968, 60–68, 71–72, 74. Summarizing Marigold, McCulloch echoed the administration line by implying JL instigated the affair on his own—in Hanoi he "sounded out the North Vietnamese about a 10-point program for peace Lewandowski himself had drafted" (no mention of HCL relating U.S. proposals). He also wrote incorrectly that Washington had ordered the 10-mile zone around Hanoi promptly after hearing from JL that North Vietnam was interested in direct talks but then ended its "restraint" by bombing the capital on December 13 because "word had already reached Washington that Hanoi was not interested."
162. WWR interview notes, 4 Jan 1968, as above.
163. SHL, "Secret Search."

Chapter 16

1. AF to DR message, delivered 3 Feb 1968, KILLY-DD's background, box 1, WAHP-NA. Ortona, attuned to U.S. doubt about Rome's discretion, stressed that he decoded, translated, and transcribed it himself.
2. R. W. Duemling to WPB, "Subject: Message from Fanfani to Secretary," 3 Feb 1968, ibid.
3. GD'O, *DV,* 815–28 (19 Jun–7 Jul 1967), trans. by IO unless otherwise noted; TVD request: BE/Saigon (Wilkinson) to FO, tel. 472, 22 Jun 1967, FCO 15/484, TNA; Rome embtels 6845 and 6981 (both Reinhardt), 19 and 24 Jun 1967, both Italy vol. V, box 197, NSF:CO, LBJL.
4. GD'O, *DV,* 828 (7 Jul 1967); also 7 Jul 1967 entry, AFD, courtesy M. Sica.
5. GD'O, *DV,* 831–32 (18 Jul 1967).
6. Ibid., 832 (20 Jul 1967).
7. From 6 Jun 1967 entry, AFD, courtesy M. Sica.
8. Mario Sica, *Marigold non fiorì: Il contributo italiano alla pace in Vietnam* (Florence: Ponte alle Grazie, 1991), 92–94, citing Carlo Galluzzi, *La svolta: Gli Anni Cruciali del Partido Comunista Italiano* (Milano: Sperling & Kupfer, 1983). Galluzzi recalled clearing the start of an Italy-

North Vietnam dialogue with senior DRV figure Xuan Thuy in a meeting near Paris, but perhaps in error since Xuan Thuy only came to Paris for the opening of U.S.-DRV talks in May 1968; he may have conflated this with a later meeting with Thuy or else actually saw Paris-based DRV representative Mai Van Bo (which is what Sica believes after reviewing the evidence; email to author, 23 Mar 2011).

9. GD'O, *DV,* 833 (31 July and 4 Aug 1967).
10. Sica, *Marigold non fiorì,* 92, citing Galluzzi, *La svolta.*
11. GD'O, *DV,* 833 (2 Aug 1967).
12. Ibid., 834 (5, 16, and 22 Aug 1967).
13. Ibid., 834 (22 Aug 1967).
14. Ibid., 834–35 (23 Aug 1967).
15. Ibid., 835–36 (24 Aug 1967).
16. GD'O-PVS talk: ibid., 836–39 (25 Aug 1967); also GD'O to AF, tel. 00012, 26 Aug 1967, AFP, and Rome embtel 4429 (Reinhardt), 24 Feb 1968, POL 27-14 Viet/Killy folder, box 2738, CFPF, 1967–69.
17. GD'O, *DV,* 839 (25 Aug 1967).
18. Ibid. (26 and 28 Aug 1967).
19. From 18 Sep 1967 entry, AFD, obt./trans. M. Sica.
20. GD'O, *DV,* 841 (3 Oct 1967), trans. A. Barrow.
21. Ibid. (29 Sep 1967), trans. A. Barrow.
22. 20 Oct 1967 entry, AFD, obt./trans. M. Sica.
23. GD'O to AF, 20 Oct 1967, in AFD, obt./trans. M. Sica; AF statement (in French), 18 Oct 1967, given to PCI for delivery to DRV, in 1966 Vietnam Estero 546-1015, PCI archives, Fondazione Istituto Gramsci, Rome.
24. GD'O, *DV,* 842 (30 Oct 1967), trans. A. Barrow.
25. Ibid., 843–44 (6 Nov 1967); 8 Nov 1967 entry, AFD, obt./trans. M. Sica; Rome embtel 4429, 24 Feb 1968, as above.
26. GD'O, *DV,* 851–53 (19 and 23 Jan 1968), trans. A. Barrow; 26 Jan 1968, AFD, obt./trans. M. Sica.
27. Herring in *SDVW:NVPP,* 525.
28. GD'O, *DV,* 854 (25 Jan 1968), trans. A. Barrow; also entries for 1, 2, and 3 Feb 1968.
29. See above and 3 Feb 1968 entry, AFD, obt./trans. M. Sica.
30. GD'O, *DV,* 855 (3, 4 Feb 1968), trans. A. Barrow; Colette to Capri: Colette D'Orlandi interview, Paris, 21 May 2008; AF's comments ("showed") were recalled the next day by PVS in records cited below.
31. PVS-AF/GD'O 5 Feb 1968 talks: translated verbatim Italian notes, KILLY folder, box 10, WAHP-NA; GD'O on Su visit: *DV,* 855–66 (4–6 Feb 1968); 5 Feb 1968 entry, AFD, obt./trans. M. Sica.
32. Rome embtel 4418 (Reinhardt), 23 Feb 1968, POL 27-14 Viet/Killy, box 2738, CFPF, 1967–69. Unless otherwise indicated, all subsequent U.S. cables on "Killy" between the State Department and the U.S. Embassy in Rome may be found in this folder.
33. PVS-AF/GD'O meeting, 10 a.m.–1 p.m., 5 Feb 1968: Italian record, KILLY, box 10, WAHP-NA.
34. GD'O, *DV,* 861–62 (5 Feb 1968).
35. PVS-AF/GD'O meeting, 6 p.m., 5 Feb 1968: Italian record, KILLY, box 10, WAHP-NA.
36. Ortona translation of AF cable read to DR on 7 Feb 1968, KILLY-DD's background, box 1, ibid.
37. Rome embtel 4292 (Reinhardt), "Subject: GOI Reveals Hanoi Peace Approach," 14 Feb 1968, ibid.; *NYT,* 15 Feb 1968; *WP,* 15 Feb 1968; 14 Feb 1968 entry, AFD, obt./trans. M. Sica; GD'O, *DV,* 867 (14 Feb 1968 .
38. PE/Rome (Chabiński) to PFM, 18 Feb 1968, in PE/Rome to PFM (Winiewicz), sz. 1960, 19 Feb 1968, AMSZ, trans. MG. Neither AF nor GD'O mentioned a deliberate leak in their diaries. However, the day before the *Paese Sera* dropped its bombshell, GD'O noted that the United States' delay in responding to AF was "worrisome in light of" possible "discretions," especially given a report from Galluzzi that Czechoslovak diplomats and intelligence agents had taken a "lively interest" in Su's trip to Rome (although they did not know what he did there). GD'O, *DV,* 866–67 (9, 13 Feb 1968), trans. A. Barrow.

39. *NYT,* 15 Feb 1968.
40. GD'O, *DV,* 686 (15 Feb 1968), trans. A. Barrow.
41. WPB to DR, "Subject: Message from Italian Foreign Minister Fanfani on Contacts with North Vietnamese," 12 Feb 1968, w. proposed DR to AF message, KILLY-DD's background, box 1, WAHP-NA; see also Ortona to AF, office note from Italian Embassy, Washington, sent 10:15 p.m., 14 Feb 1968, AFP, trans. A. Barrow.
42. [Isham,] "Comments on the Fanfani Message," Killy-DD's background, box 1, WAHP-NA.
43. AF message to DR transmitted by Ortona on 16 Feb 1968, in ibid.; deptel 117384 to American Embassy, Rome/Saigon, 17 Feb 1968.
44. Ortona to AF, 14 Feb 1968, as above.
45. *WP,* 16 Feb 1968; Isham to WPB, [16?] Feb 1968, KILLY-DD's background, box 1, WAHP-NA; deptel 117384 to American Embassy, Rome/Saigon, 17 Feb 1968, as above.
46. Deptel 117364 to American Embassy, Rome/Saigon, 17 Feb 1968.
47. From 18 Feb 1968 entry, AFD, obt./trans. M. Sica; GD'O, *DV,* 876 (18, 19 Feb 1968).
48. DID telephone interview, 25 Apr 2008.
49. Rome embtel 4418 (Reinhardt), 23 Feb 1968.
50. Rome embtel 4422 (Reinhardt), 24 Feb 1968; DID's 21–24 Feb 1968 talks: telegrams in this folder and KILLY folder, box 139, NSF:CO:VN, LBJL, 21-22 entries, AFD, obt./trans. M. Sica; and GD'O, *DV,* 878–93 ("marathon," 889).
51. DID telephone interview, 25 Apr 2008.
52. Rome embtel 4441 (Reinhardt), 26 Feb 1968.
53. DR call to WPB, 12:48 p.m., 26 Feb 1968, box 61, DR Papers, entry 5379, RG 59, NA II.
54. DR call to WPB, 7:10 p.m., ibid. The negative impact of WPB's (and Isham's) memory of GD'O's part in the Polish affair belies the Pentagon Papers' assertion, in its analysis of KILLY, that Italy's "role in MARIGOLD had been respected by both sides." *SDVW:NVPP,* 532.
55. Deptel 120937 to American Embassy, Rome, 27 Feb 1968, KILLY, box 139, NSF:CO:VN, LBJL.
56. Rome embtel 6201 (Reinhardt), 27 Feb 1968; GD'O, *DV,* 892 (27 Feb 1968); DID telephone interview, 25 Apr 2008.
57. DID, notes of DID/Meloy-AF/GD'O talk, 1:15 p.m., 28 Feb 1968, KILLY, box 10, WAHP-NA; also Rome embtel 4508 (Reinhardt), 28 Feb 1968; and GD'O, *DV,* 892–95 (28 Feb 1968).
58. From 28 Feb 1968 entry, AFD, obt./trans. M. Sica.
59. GD'O, *DV,* 895–97 (1 Mar 1968); Rome embtels 4590 (Meloy), 4 Mar 1968, and 4634 (Meloy), 5 Mar 1968 ("absolutely").
60. GD'O, *DV,* 897 (2 Mar 1968); "pointless": Leopoldo Nuti, "The Center-Left Government in Italy and the Escalation of the Vietnam War," in *America, the Vietnam War, and the World: Comparative and International Perspectives,* edited by Andreas W. Daum, Lloyd C. Gardner, and Wilfried Mausbach (Washington, D.C.: German Historical Institute, 2003), 276.
61. DID, notes of DID/Meloy-GD'O conversation, 11 a.m., 4 Mar 1968, KILLY folder, box 10, WAHP-NA; DID interview, Washington, 7 May 2008; also Rome embtel 4590, 4 Mar 1968, and GD'O, *DV,* 898–900 (4–5 Mar 1968).
62. Rome embtel 4603 (Meloy), 4 Mar 1968.
63. GD'O, *DV,* 900–901 (6 Mar 1968).
64. DID recalled an anecdote that epitomized WAH's outlier status. One day soon after DID joined his staff, they were in the seventh-floor elevator when DR entered. In an "uncharacteristically bitter" remark, WAH said DR should know his assistant—"After all, he and I are the only two people in this building working for peace." DID telephone interview, 25 Apr 2008.
65. DID interview, Washington, 7 May 2008.
66. WWR to LBJ, 8:10 p.m., 4 Mar 1968, KILLY folder, box 139, NSF:CO:VN, LBJL. WWR also distrusted DID, once accusing him of "gilding the lily" in a cable regarding peace prospects, provoking WPB to demand that he apologize: DID interview, Washington, 7 May 2008.
67. HAK-HCL telcon, 9:55 a.m., 12 Jan 1970, NPM, NA II, courtesy W. Burr; HCL, "Reactivation of D'Orlandi's Contacts with North Vietnam," attached to Lake to HAK, "Subject: Your Appointment with Ambassador Cabot Lodge, 2:30 p.m., January 20, 1970," 20 Jan 1970, LODGE Henry Cabot, Vol. I thru 20 Apr 70 [1 of 2], box 823, NSC Files-Name Files, NPM, NA II. LBJ

was also cold to reviving Marigold's Polish dimension. In mid-March, NC urged him to send Humphrey to Warsaw so the Poles could set up a secret talk with a DRV rep (presumably DPQ) after a bombing halt of as little as three or four days. LBJ deflected the idea, insisting that Hanoi was "not interested in negotiating until after our election." LBJ-NC memcon, 15 Mar 1968, box 32, Marvin Watson OF, LBJL (reel 11, "Vietnam, the Media, and Public Support for the War," LC).

68. From 11 Mar 1968, AFD, obt./trans. M. Sica.
69. Rome embtel 4584 (Meloy), 15 Mar 1968.
70. HCL-GD'O-AF 15 March 1968 talk: Rome embtel 4878 (Meloy), 16 March 1968; GD'O, *DV,* 902–3 (14 [*sic*] Mar 1968); 15, 18 Mar 1968 entries, AFD, obt./trans. M. Sica.
71. Rome embtel 4878 (Meloy), 16 Mar 1968.
72. Hughes to DR, "Subject: Evaluation of Hanoi Intentions and Statements in KILLY," 22 Mar 1968, POL 27-14 Viet/Killy, box 2738, CFPF, 1967–69.
73. Wallace J. Thies, *When Governments Collide: Coercion and Diplomacy in the Vietnam Conflict, 1964–1968* (Berkeley: University of California Press, 1980), 208.
74. Deptel 134985 to American Embassy, Rome, 22 March 1968; 23 Mar 1968 entry, AFD, obt./trans. M. Sica; GD'O, *DV,* 904 (23 Mar 1968).
75. Ibid. (28 Mar 1968).
76. Nuti, "Center-Left Government," 276.
77. "His" [Isham] interview notes, 1 Feb 1968; DID interview notes, 9 Feb 1968; WPB telcon notes, 12 Feb 1968; and notes "from his" [Isham], 21 Feb 1968, all Interviews folder, box 15, SHLP; DID memo to WPB, 15 Feb 1968, Marigold, box 2, WAHP-NA; Isham to WPB, "SUBJECT: Stuart Loory's Request for Comment on Alleged Polish Ten Points," 20 Feb 1968, [General Subjects], box 7, ibid.
78. GD'O to SHL, 10 Mar 1968, "Ashmore-London 1967" folder, box 17, SHLP.
79. SHL identified NK as a key Washington figure (along with WWR and Fulbright) with whom DK "was on intimate terms." SHL, "The Secret Search."
80. "Nick" interview notes, 22 Mar 1968, Vietnam Bombing Pause 1966–67, box 41, SHLP.
81. SHL telephone interview, 8 Jul 2003; SHL, "The Secret Search."
82. Ibid.
83. CLC predicted the morning after LBJ's speech that Hanoi would "probably" reject his offer, judging his exit from the presidential race a sign of weakness ("under pressure of doves and that Bobby is now a shoe-in") and sticking to the demand for a total bombing halt. CLC handwritten note to WAH, 8:30 a.m., 1 Apr 1968, Vietnam General 1968-1969 folder, box 521, WAHP-LC.
84. From Prague, via Galluzzi, Su sent word to AF that "for the time being a meeting is not appropriate, since a direct contact has been established between Hanoi and Washington," even though he politely added that the "very useful" Rome channel should be preserved "for any further possibility." 6 Apr 1968 entry, AFD, obt./trans. M. Sica.
85. DK and SHL's "The Secret Search for Peace" series included "Unheralded Emissaries Opened Way to Hanoi," *LAT,* 4 Apr 1968; "Wilson Switch at U.S. Behest Blamed for Lost Opportunity," *LAT,* 5 Apr 1968; "Italian, Pole Developed 'Marigold' Initiative," *LAT,* 7 Apr 1968; "Poorly Timed Bombing Hurt Good Chance for Talks in '66," *LAT,* 8 Apr 1968; "Flash Telegram Set '66 Scene for Talks That Never Came," *LAT,* 9 April 1968; and "Polish Envoy Runs Into Great Wall of China," *LAT,* 10 Apr 1968.
86. CM (Marcy) to Senator (Fulbright), 17 Apr 1968, CM Chrons—Apr, May, and Jun 1968, box 9, Carl Marcy Papers, RG 46, NA.
87. J. E. Killick, BE/Washington, to A. M. Palliser, 8 May 1968; Palliser to Killick, 13 May 1968, both FCO 15/633, TNA. In Rome, AF and GD'O discussed the *LAT* series and agreed that DK and SHL had the makings of a "very interesting book." They agreed that it reflected extensive leaking by U.S. officials with a "clear taste of electoral maneuvers" against LBJ, which, combined with Poland's leak to the Vatican, left Italy as the only one of the three main actors that had not revealed its side of the story; AF asked GD'O to organize his journal for possible publication should it prove necessary. GD'O, *DV,* 915 (12, 17 Apr 1968).

88. *FRUS, 1964–68,* vol. VI: *Vietnam, January–August 1968,* 557–58 n. 7, 563 n. 2.

89. Hughes to DR, INR Intelligence Notes no. 270, 12 Apr 1968, ibid., 572 n. 5. Cyrus R. Vance, who would serve as WAH's deputy in Paris (and later as Carter's secretary of state), told WAH that he "would have liked" Warsaw and thought it a "fine" choice: Vance-WAH telcon, 11 Apr 1968, ibid., 566.

90. LBJ-WAH telcon, 11 Apr 1968, ibid., 564–65.

91. LBJ, *The Vantage Point: Perspectives of the Presidency, 1963–1969* (New York: Holt, Rinehart & Winston, 1971), 502.

92. See, e.g., *FRUS, 1964–68,* 6:614.

93. LBJ, *Vantage Point,* 502.

94. See, e.g., Andrzej Paczkowski, *The Spring Will Be Ours: Poland and the Poles from Occupation to Freedom* (University Park: Pennsylvania State University Press, 2003); Norman Davies, *God's Playground: A History of Poland, Volume II: 1795 to the Present* (New York: Columbia University Press, 1984), 588–89; Rafal Pankowski, "When 'Zionist' Meant 'Jew': Revisiting the 1968 Events in Poland," *Z Word,* February 2008, available at www.z-word.com; CIA Intelligence Report, "The Struggle in the Polish Leadership and the Revolt of the Apparat (Reference Title: ESAU XVII/69)," 5 Sep 1969, available at www.cia.gov; and A. Kemp-Welch, *Poland under Communism: A Cold War History* (New York: Cambridge University Press, 2008), chap. 7. On Moczar, see Halberstam, "Poland Has Seen The Future," *NYT,* 6 Feb 1966.

95. CIA, "Struggle in the Polish Leadership," 30–31. Perhaps some enemies remembered AR's cordial reception for visiting Israeli diplomats in 1966—despite the Soviet Bloc's official coldness to the Jewish state—when he vowed (a year before Warsaw broke ties during the June 1967 war) that Poland would "maintain steadfast links with Israel based on 'memories of a common struggle and a common agony.'" Abba Eban, *Personal Witness: Israel Through My Eyes* (New York: G. P. Putnam's Sons, 1992), 343; Abba Eban, *An Autobiography* (New York: Random House, 1977), 307.

96. Piotr Wandycz, "Adam Rapacki and the Search for European Security," in *The Diplomats, 1939–1979,* edited by Gordon A. Craig and Francis L. Loewenheim (Princeton, N.J.: Princeton University Press, 1994), 294, 313 n. 14. "This was a man of real integrity trying to do best he could under circumstances," recalled the U.S. Embassy's political officer at the time; Herbert Kaiser, telephone interview, 31 Jul 2007.

97. John Darnton, "Waking Up, Getting Out," *NYT,* 30 Mar 1986; also "Government Shuffle," *Time,* 3 Jan 1969.

98. CIA, "Struggle in the Polish Leadership," 31.

99. JL interview, Warsaw, 4 Feb 2008.

100. Ibid.; Naszkowski biography: KC PZPR V-85, 542–43, AAN, obt./trans. MG.

101. JL interviews, Warsaw, 21 Jun 2003 and 4 Feb 2008.

102. Ibid., 10 May 2011; 14–15 Jul 1968 Warsaw meeting transcript, quoted by Jaromír Navrátil, ed., *The Prague Spring 1968: A National Security Archive Documents Reader* (Budapest: Central European University Press, 1998), 212–33, and esp. 213–15.

103. American Embassy, Warsaw (Jenkins/JAG), Airgram A-596, "The War between the 'Boors and the Jews' for Power in Poland," 15 Apr 1968, POL 15 POL 1/1/67, box 2433, CFPF, 1967–69.

104. American Embassy, Warsaw, airgram A-956, 14 Oct 1968, POL 17 POL 1/1/67, box 2434, ibid.

105. JM-Bohlen memcon ("unpleasant"), "Subject: Courtesy Call by Polish Ambassador," 8 May 1968, POL 17 POL-US 1/1/68, box 2436, and JM-Stoessel-JAG memcon ("fuss"), "Subject: U.S.-Polish Bilateral Relations," 28 May 1968, POL POL-US 1/1/67, box 2435; Warsaw embtel 656 ("targets"), 11 March 1969, POL 17 POL-US 1/1/67, box 2436; all ibid. During the purge, JM was included on a list of MSZ employees who did not meet "established criteria" set by a party commission: list dated 29 May 1968, forwarded on Kliszko's instructions to PZPR Secretariat, 11 Jul 1968, KC PZPR XI/561, AAN, pp. 1-3, courtesy MG.

106. Nathaniel Davis, memo for record, "Subject: Luncheon Conversation with Polish Ambassador," 26 Apr 1968, POL 17 POL-US 1/1/68, box 2436, ibid.

107. See documents in POL 17 POL-US 1/1/67 and POL 17 POL-US 1/1/68, both ibid.

108. JM–Doyle V. Martin memcon, "Current Ferment in Poland," 29 Apr 1968, POL 2-1 POL 1/1/68. box 2431, ibid.
109. JM-Stoessel-JAG memcon, "Subject: U.S.-Polish Bilateral Relations," 28 May 1968, POL POL-US 1/1/67, box 2435, ibid.
110. DID interview, Washington, 7 May 2008; DID telephone interview, 25 Apr 2008.
111. Warsaw embtel 3538 (Jenkins), 11 Jun 1968, POL 7 POL 1/1/68, box 2432, CFPF, 1967–69.
112. JL–David J. Fischer memcon, "Subject: Polish-U.S. Relations, European Security," 8 Nov 1969, POL POL-US 1/1/69, box 2435, ibid.
113. Piotr Michałowski, telephone interview, 12 Aug 2008.
114. Stefan Michałowski, telephone interview, 12 Mar 2009.
115. JM-Davis memcon, 17 Sep 1968, *FRUS, 1964–68*, 17: doc. 137.
116. Warsaw embtel 2798 (JAG) and deptel 146335 to American Embassy, Warsaw, both 12 Apr 1968, POL 27-14 Viet/Crocodile 4/1/68, box 2736; Warsaw embtel 2813 (Jenkins) and deptel 147585 to Amerian Embassy, Warsaw, both 16 Apr 1968, and Warsaw embtel 2836 (Jenkins), 18 Apr 1968, POL 27-14 Viet/Crocodile 4/16/68, box 2737; all CFPF, 1967–69.
117. Warsaw embtel 2833 (Jenkins), 17 Apr 1968, and other cables in POL 27-14 Viet/Crocodile 4/16/68 and 4/20/68, ibid.; telegram from Swedish Embassy, Warsaw (Petri), 19 Apr 1968, Beskickningsarkivet i Warzawa, serie F 1D:54 och E 2:2, National Archives, Stockholm, obt. Markus Maijala (National Archives), trans. F. Logevall.
118. Davis memo, "Subject: Luncheon Conversation with Polish Ambassador," 26 Apr 1968, POL 17 POL-US 1/1/68, box 2436, CFPF, 1967–69; PE/Washington (JM) to PFM (Winiewicz), sz. 4898, 24 Apr 1968, AMSZ, trans. MG.
119. Rome embtels 5480 and 5503, both 18 Apr 1968, and WPB, memo for record re AF message to DR, 19 Apr 1968, all POL 27-14 Viet/Crocodile, box 2737, CFPF, 1967–69.
120. Deptel 150456 to American Embassy, Warsaw, 20 Apr 1968, and Warsaw embtel 2916 (JAG), 24 Apr 1968; also WPB to DR, "Subject: Next Steps on a Location for Contacts," 22 Apr 1968, all ibid.
121. DR-Clifford telcon, 10:20 a.m., 27 Apr 1968, POL 27-14 Viet/Crocodile 4/20/68, ibid.
122. JAG OH-II, 32–33; Warsaw embtels 2959 and 2980 (JAG), 29 and 30 Apr 1968, and deptel 155242 to American Embassy, Warsaw, 30 Apr 1968, POL 27-14 Viet/Crocodile, box 2737, CFPF, 1967–69. It is not clear why JAG would expect approval, given DR's firm cable informing him Warsaw was now unacceptable. Perhaps he recalled that the previous summer, when the Swiss ambassador relayed a "nibble" of DPQ interest in talking with JAG, State had promptly authorized him to "convey our strong interest" in an "exploratory conversation" (it did not happen). Deptel 9112 to American Embassy, Warsaw, 19 Jul 1967, Poland-Cables vol. II 10/66-5/68, box 201, NSF:CO, LBJL.
123. Roberts, "Tracing Peace Feelers," *WP*, 20 Jul 1968.
124. David Schoenbrun, "Behind the Credibility Gap," *NYT*, 7 Jul 1968; Fremont-Smith, "'Marigold' and Other Embarrassments," *NYT*, 5 Aug 1968.
125. Williams to DK, 17 Jul 1968, "Secret Search 1967–70" folder, box 37, SHLP; Huston, "Kraslow-Loory peace mission rates prize," *Editor & Publisher*, 15 Mar 1969, 54. DK and SHK were finalists along with five other contenders for the Pulitzer Prize in the international affairs reporting category won by their *LAT* colleague William Tuohy for his coverage of the Vietnam War. Report of the international reporting jury, Pulitzer Prizes for 1969, Historical Files, Pulitzer Prize Office, Columbia University; DK telephone interview, 27 May 2011. Besides the Polk, for their inquest into Vietnam peace efforts, DK and SHL received the Raymond Clapper Memorial Award for distinguished Washington reporting and the Dumont Award for "excellence in international reporting" from the University of California, Los Angeles.
126. David [?], FO, to A. M. Palliser, 21 Aug 1968, PREM 13/2458, TNA.
127. DK and SHL, *Secret Search*, 240.
128. Gelb interview, New York, 26 Jun 2003.
129. The Pentagon Papers assessed Warsaw's principal aims as (1) "ending the violence in Vietnam"; (2) "doing so on terms relatively favorable to the Communist side"; (3) "building a case" to use against Washington as pressure during the contact and to embarrass it should the effort fail and be exposed, as actually happened; and (4) prestige. *SDVW:NVPP*, 217, 220.

130. CIA, "The Attitudes of North Vietnamese Leaders toward Fighting and Negotiating (Reference Title: ESAU XXXVII)," 25 Mar 1968, 21–22, www.foia.cia.gov/CPE/ESAU/esau-36.pdf.
131. "Operation MARIGOLD," n.d., Vietnam: Marigold Peace Approach 1968, Vietnam/Southeast Asia Collection, box 1, NSA/FOIA. Another Pentagon study more warily concluded that the "question remains" whether different U.S. tactics might have yielded direct contacts in December 1966. It acknowledged that critics blamed Marigold's failure on the Hanoi raids, yet noted "equally valid speculation . . . that Hanoi only agreed to talk in the first place on the basis of a false and misleading presentation by Lewandowski" and then, on learning Washington still demanded "compensating military deescalation" for stopping the bombing, used the bombings as a pretext to cancel the Warsaw meeting. JCS-VN, part III, 40-8.
132. JAG OH-III, 14 Feb 1969, 30–32, LBJL; *WP*, 1 Jun 1968.
133. JAG OH-II, 30.
134. HCL-RSM memcon, 1 Jul 1968, reel 26, HCL Papers, MHS; RSM to LBJ, 9 March 1967, box 8, WWR Papers, LBJL, copy in box 25, Gibbons Papers, LBJL.
135. RHE, "Ho Rejected '66 Proposal, Writer Says," *WP*, 5 Dec 1968.
136. From 23 Dec 1968 diary entry, folder 6, box 7, Brandon Papers, LC.
137. WAH memcon with Dobrynin, 27 Dec 1967, box FCL-8, WAHP-LC.
138. MR and JM, "Polish Secret Peace Initiatives in Vietnam," *CWIHPB*, nos. 6–7 (Winter 1995–96): 259; also PE/Washington (JM) to PFM (Winiewicz), sz. 500, 14 Jan 1969, AMSZ, trans. MG.

Epilogue

1. On "hopeful" and "Gobelin," see "A Harsh Beginning in Paris," *Time*, 31 Jan 1969.
2. JL-HCL 10 Mar 1969 talk: JL interview, Warsaw, 21 Jun 2003; PE/Delhi (Wolniak) to PFM (Jedrychowski), sz. 2776, 14 Mar 1969, AMSZ, obt./trans. MG; Paris embtel 343 (HCL), 10 Mar 1969, Paris cables—Paris meetings/NODIS—Paris meetings/NODIS—plus-vol. III [1 of 2], box 187, NSF, NPM.
3. PE/Delhi (Wolniak) to PFM (Jedrychowski), sz. 2776, 14 Mar 1969. "We will naturally share this conversation with Hanoi, but rather in a careful manner, and this is because it contains too many optimistic assessments of the military operations in the South," Deputy Minister Zygfryd Wolniak wrote. JL's month-long Asian trip with Wolniak included his first Hanoi visit since May 1967; American Embassy, Warsaw (Andrews), airgram A-210, 18 Apr 1969, POL 7 POL 1/1/69, box 2432, CFPF, 1967–69.
4. JL interview, Warsaw, 21 Jun 2003.
5. Paris embtel 3436 (HCL), 10 Mar 1969, cited above.
6. HAK, *Ending the Vietnam War* (New York: Simon & Schuster, 2002), 73.
7. HCL frustration: Kent Sieg, "The Lodge Peace Mission of 1969 and Nixon's Vietnam Policy," *Diplomacy and Statecraft* 7, no. 1 (March 1996): 175–96; "bored": C. L. Sulzberger, *An Age of Mediocrity: Memoirs and Diaries 1963–1972* (New York: Macmillan, 1973), 565 (1 Aug 1969). David Bruce later replaced HCL as delegation head.
8. HAK-HCL telcon, 9:55 a.m., 12 Jan 1970, NPM, NA II (courtesy W. Burr).
9. HCL to HAK, "Reactivation of D'Orlandi's Contacts with North Vietnam," [20 Jan 1970], Lodge, Henry Cabot, vol. I thru 20 Apr 70 [1 of 2], box 823, NSC:Name File, NPM, NA II. In another Marigold spinoff, HCL also suggested HAK use J. J. Derksen—the Dutch diplomat he had known in Saigon, now posted to Beijing—as an intermediary in seeking improved U.S.-Chinese relations. Vouching for Derksen's intelligence, discretion, and reliability, HCL noted his intention to preserve secrecy by communicating only orally ("nothing in writing") to the Netherlands' prime minister (cutting out the Dutch foreign minister and Foreign Ministry entirely) and added, "From our experiences with D'Orlandi, at the time of the Marigold talks in 1966, I believe this is a satisfactory arrangement and that we would be completely protected against the Russians knowing about whatever Derksen will do." After meeting with him and HCL, HAK tried to use Derksen to signal the Chinese and Zhou Enlai in particular, indicating White House interest in moving beyond the Warsaw ambassadorial talks to a more produc-

tive dialogue, but the channel fizzled out. HAK to Nixon, "Subject: Henry Cabot Lodge's Discussion with Mr. J. J. Derksen, Netherlands Minister Accredited to Communist China," [4 or 5 Feb 1970], *FRUS, 1969–1976, Volume XVIII: China, 1969–1972* (Washington, D.C.: U.S. Government Printing Office, 2006), doc. 66; and HCL to HAK, 3 Feb 1970, NPM, NA II, courtesy W. Burr.

10. Lake to HAK, "Your Appointment with Ambassador Cabot Lodge, 2:30 p.m., January 20, 1970," 20 Jan 1970, "Lodge, Henry Cabot, vol. I thru 20 Apr 70 [1 of 2]" folder, box 823, NSC: Name file, NPM, NA II.

11. HAK-Nixon telcon, 7 p.m., 25 Feb 1970, NPM, courtesy W. Burr. HAK called AF "wildly ambitious" and "a total fraud" and Nixon said he "never thought much of him." HAK-Nixon telcon, 18 Feb 1971, ibid.

12. HCL to HAK, 19 Nov 1970, reel 9, HCL II, MHS.

13. HAK to HCL, 3 Dec 1970, reel 9, ibid.; Sieg, "The Lodge Peace Mission of 1969 and Nixon's Vietnam Policy," 191.

14. DR OH-II, 26 Sep 1969, 30–32, LBJL.

15. WWR OH-I, 21 Mar 1969, 49–50, LBJL.

16. Jorden OH-I, 22 Mar 1969, 30, LBJL.

17. NK OH-II, 23 Nov 1968, 16–17, LBJL.

18. Read OH-I, 13 Jan 1969, 8–11, LBJL.

19. WPB OH 4, 2 Jun 1969, 18, LBJL.

20. Ibid., 21; RHE, "Ho Rejected '66 Proposal, Writer Says," *WP*, 5 Dec 1968.

21. WPB OH 3, 29 May 1969, 16, LBJL.

22. WAH-JM memcon, 19 Feb 1969, POL 27-14 Viet/Marigold 1969, box 2739, CFPF, 1967–69. According to JM, WAH blamed "Saigon generals" for torpedoing Marigold by "exploiting" LBJ's prior consent to bomb Hanoi, and DR viewed Polish efforts as "dishonest" because Warsaw preferred to see Washington tied down in Vietnam. PE/Washington (JM) to PFM (Winiewicz), sz. 1540, 11 Feb 1969, AMSZ, trans. MG.

23. WAH OH, 16 Jun 1969, 22–23, 27–28, LBJL.

24. Notes of lunch with WAH, 8 Feb 1969, folder 6, box 94, Hedrick Smith Papers, LC.

25. *WP*, 15 Jun 1969, 236.

26. JAG OH-II, 10 Feb 1969, 15–32, LBJL.

27. Ibid., 28.

28. See esp. CLC OH II, 17 Jul 1969, 15–31, LBJL.

29. Ibid., 25.

30. Ibid., 26–27.

31. Ibid., 22–24.

32. Ronald Steel, "Why Vietnam Went Wrong—A Version without Villains," *NYT*, 8 Nov 1970.

33. CLC, *The Lost Crusade: America in Vietnam* (New York: Dodd, Mead, 1970), esp. 322–42.

34. Ibid., 337–38, 341–42.

35. McGeorge Bundy to CLC, 1 Dec 1969, courtesy Susan Cooper. "I still take the old-fashioned view that people who have worked on staffs ought not to draw on what they saw confidentially for public purposes," wrote Bundy, who steadfastly refused to pen his own Vietnam memoir for several decades, then died in 1996 while working on one. "I believe that a President in office should be free from the thought that staff officers are going to second-guess him five years later in public."

36. CLC, *Lost Crusade*, 342.

37. JM bio, Walt Rostow vol. 54 11–19 Dec, 1967 [3 of 4], box 26, NSF:MtP:WR, LBJL.

38. Dinners, photographs: Thomas L. Hughes conversation, Washington, 9 Sep 2008.

39. Sonnenfeldt to HAK, "Subject: Your Meeting with Ambassador Michałowski, Monday, March 22," 18 Mar 1971, Poland vol. I 1969–71, box 698, NSC:CO:Europe, NPM, NA II.

40. Helmut Sonnenfeldt to HAK, "Subject: Your Schedule Meeting with Polish Ambassador Michałowski, ~~Friday, December 12 at 6:00 p.m.~~ Tuesday, February 2 at 4:30 p.m.," 11 Dec 1969, ibid.

41. Warsaw embtel 786 (Stoessel), 21 Mar 1969, and deptel 101569 to American Embassy, London, 20 Jun 1969, both POL 17 POL-US 1/1/67, box 2436, CFPF, 1967–69.

42. Theodore L. Eliot Jr. to HAK, "Subject: Possible Defection of Polish Ambassador," 16 Jan 1971, Poland vol. I 1969–71, box 698, NSC:CO:Europe, NPM, NA II. In doing so, Rogers brushed aside likely criticism from "some Members of Congress and certain less responsible publications" (which had spread charges that "Madam Michałowski" had spied against the U.S. Embassy in Warsaw and while in the United States during World War II).

43. Piotr Michałowski, telephone interviews, 12–13 Aug 2008; interview with Stefan Michałowski, Washington, 12 Dec 2010.

44. JM-Fischer memcon, 8 Nov 1969, POL POL-US 1/1/69, box 2435, CFPF, 1967–69.

45. JM-Rogers memcon, "Farewell Call of Polish Ambassador," 22 Jun 1971, POL 17 POL-US, CFPF, courtesy D. Geyer.

46. Jedrychowski, note to deputy FM Czyrek re [PE/Washington] sz. 5710, 22 Jun 1971, Sygn. D II 28/79 wh, AMSZ, courtesy H. Szlajfer, trans. MG.

47. R. Spasowski, note on Polish mediation DRV-USA, 1966, 29 Jun 1971, ibid.; Daniel Passent, "Operacja Nogietek," *Polityka*, 20–27 Dec 1969.

48. Spasowski to Jedrychowski, note on matter of publication regarding our mediation DRV-U.S.A., 5 Jul 1971, ibid.

49. Jedrychowski 7 July handwritten note on Spasowski to Jedrychowski, 5 Jul 1971, cited above.

50. Doris Kearns Goodwin, *Lyndon Johnson and the American Dream* (New York: St. Martin's Press, 1976), xiii–xv, 353–55.

51. CLC, "Through a Texas Window, Reflections on the Presidency," *WP*, 8 Nov 1971; *NYT*, 14 May 1971.

52. LBJ, *The Vantage Point: Perspectives of the Presidency, 1963–1969* (New York: Holt, Rinehart & Winston, 1971), 251–52.

53. Jorden OH-IV by Ted Gittinger, 7 Nov 1985, 18, LBJL. After reading an early draft of the memoirs, McGeorge Bundy sent LBJ a private critique. At one point, after complaining that "some of the draftsmen do not seem to have soaked themselves enough in the factual materials," Bundy wrote that "I am sorry to say that in my own conversations with Walt it seemed to me that he had not taken the time to do the necessary homework. Moreover, Walt has always had a reputation among historians as a man who reaches his conclusions first and searches the evidence later, and I fear that this tendency becomes still stronger in most of us when we are dealing with things that relate to our own public activities. For this reason I believe that Walt is simply not a reliable judge of the accuracy of discussions of matters in which he was closely involved, and in a measure the same point applies to Bill Jorden, who was also heavily engaged in the active conduct of the Vietnamese matter. Obviously the same thing would be true of many of the rest of us, with due allowances for variations in the degrees of detachment and objectivity." In his reply, LBJ somewhat testily defended his aides' objectivity, remarking that he was "not happy" to read Bundy's comments on WWR and Jorden and "like[d] even less the implication that they are here working with me in order to prove me right in all I did. I just don't think you know them very well." McGeorge Bundy memo to LBJ, 9 Apr 1970, and LBJ to Bundy, 24 Apr 1970, both in box 48, McGeorge Bundy personal papers, JFKL.

54. CLC, *Lost Crusade*, 339.

55. LBJ, *Vantage Point*, 250.

56. CLC, "Through a Texas Window."

57. *SDVW:NVPP*, vii–xxvi; Tom Wells, *Wild Man: The Life and Times of Daniel Ellsberg* (New York: Palgrave, 2001), 399.

58. Jack Anderson, "3 Hanoi Lessons Still Unlearned," *WP*, 26 Jun 1972; Anderson's other two lessons: Hanoi's leaders had kept their eyes on the prize, "control of all Vietnam," and were "prepared to outwait and outlast all enemies." For other allusions to the diplomatic volumes, see Jack Anderson's *WP* columns of 9, 10, 11, 14, 16, and 27 Jun 1972.

59. *NYT*, 23 Jun 1972; *WP*, 23 and 28 Jun 1972.

60. *WP*, 27 Jun 1972.

61. Jack Anderson, "The Government Secrecy Syndrome," *WP*, 27 Jun 1972.

62. *NYT*, 28 Jun 1972.

63. *NYT*, 30 Mar 1973; SHL testimony, 29–30 Mar 1973, copy in box 12, SHLP.

64. Lacking access to the diplomatic volumes, and frustrated by State Department rebuffs of his FOIA requests, Allen E. Goodman briefly reviewed Marigold in a 1978 study of Vietnam peace efforts. He noted LBJ's belief that "he had been had by Lewandowski" and U.S. contentions that the Hanoi raids offered the DRV and Poland a "pretext" to break off the contact. However, he also wrote that Marigold convinced both Washington and Hanoi "that the other was insincere about negotiations in the first place." Allan E. Goodman, *The Lost Peace* (Stanford, Calif.: Hoover Institution Press, 1978), 3, 38–45.

65. Leslie H. Gelb with Richard K. Betts, *The Irony of Vietnam: The System Worked* (Washington, D.C.: Brookings Institution Press, 1979), 151–53.

66. Wallace J. Thies, *When Governments Collide: Coercion and Diplomacy in the Vietnam Conflict, 1964–1968* (Berkeley: University of California Press, 1980), 148 n. 11, 149; "disastrous": 340, 355, 368; "hindsight": 341.

67. János Radványi, *Delusion and Reality: Gambits, Hoaxes, and Diplomatic One-Upmanship in Vietnam* (South Bend, Ind.: Gateway Editions, 1978), 194–95.

68. Herring in *SDVW:NVPP,* 211–13.

69. WWR, *The Diffusion of Power, 1957–1972* (New York: Macmillan, 1972), 515.

70. HCL, *As It Was: An Inside View of Politics and Power in the '50s and '60s* (New York: W. W. Norton, 1976), 172–81. HCL also omitted the 14–15 Nov 1966 three-way meetings before JL's trip to Hanoi, falsely stating that the trilateral session on 1 Dec 1966 (at which JL presented the 10 points) occurred "more than four months after our last meeting" (p. 177).

71. DR, *As I Saw It,* edited by Daniel S. Papp (New York: W. W. Norton, 1990), 467–68.

72. LBJ School of Public Affairs Web site; *NYT,* 30 May 1971.

73. Robert McG. Thomas Jr., "John Gronouski, 76, Kennedy-Era Postal Chief," *NYT,* 10 Jan 1996.

74. Piotr Michałowski, telephone interviews, 12–13 Aug 2008; JM (prepared by Stefan Michałowski), "Polish Secret Peace Initiatives in Vietnam," *CWIHPB* 6–7 (Winter 1995–96): 241, 258–59; JM files, BU-01264/393 and 0586/2304, IPN; A. Paczkowski email to author, 17 Dec 2008.

75. Helmut Sonnenfeldt to HAK, "Subject: Lunch with Polish Ambassador Michałowski, November 23," 27 Nov 1970, Poland vol. I, box 648, NSC:CO:Europe, NPM, NA II.

76. MR; JM proposed the report in 1981: JM memo, "Polish Secret Peace Initiatives in Indochina," 22 Aug 1981, courtesy of Stefan Michałowski, trans. MG.

77. JL interviews, Warsaw, 21 Jun 2003, 20 Oct 2006.

78. Paolo Janni (counselor, Italian Embassy, Athens, 1971–4) interview, Washington, 29 Sep 2006; Janni, "D'Orlandi and 'Operation Marigold,'" *US Italia Weekly* (New York), 4 Jun 2006, 1, 2.

79. WPB OH 4, 2 Jun 1969, 20, LBJL.

80. Janni interview; Janni, "D'Orlandi and 'Operation Marigold,'" 1, 2.

81. Colette D'Orlandi interview, Paris, 21 May 2008.

82. Mario Sica, *Marigold non fiorì: Il contributo italiano alla pace in Vietnam* (Florence: Ponte alle Grazie, 1991); Sica interviews, Rome, 24 Feb 2006, and Trent, 14 Dec 2006.

83. JL interview, Warsaw, 21 Jun 2003.

84. Henry Sears Lodge interview, Beverly, Mass., 6 Jun 2007.

85. HCL, "Viet-Nam Memoir," chap. 7, reel 26, HCL, MHS. Adding one point to his earlier, published account, HCL cited JAG's theory that Marigold ultimately collapsed when HES' *NYT* articles "persuaded Hanoi that it had a pretty strong hand after all and did not need to talk peace."

86. Ted Gittinger, LBJL, email to author, 8 Mar 2004.

87. Occasionally, HCL flirted with mild heresy. Looking back at the Vietnam disaster, in a draft article (apparently never published), he judged that "the most salient lesson to be learned" was that America must more carefully estimate the cost, and whether it was willing to pay it, before entering a war. More startling, the grizzled Cold Warrior and true believer in the domino theory now cautiously embraced the notion that Washington had fundamentally misconstrued the conflict all along as an "orthodox military struggle" against ideological Communism. HCL now judged FDR correct in backing Vietnamese independence from French colonial rule after World War II; had that policy not been reversed after his death, "we might have avoided much grief and developed an efficient working relationship with Ho Chi Minh," a

potential Asian Tito. HCL, "Some Lessons of Vietnam," fourth draft, 17 Mar 1977, box 38, Vietnam folder, HCL, MHS.

88. Telephone interviews with G. C. Lodge, 12 Apr 2007, and H. S. Lodge, 14 Apr 2007; H. S. Lodge interview, Beverley, Mass., 6 Jun 2007.

89. Unless otherwise noted, this account of JL's career relies on interviews in Warsaw in June and November 2003; October 2006; February 2008; and May 2011 telephone interviews; and biographical materials in his MSW files (BU 01930/202 and BU 0586/2162, IPN).

90. Fr. Krawczyk, "Information from the 'Kordoński' Source from 9 February 1970," 5 Mar 1970, and Col. Z. Zabawa (Senior Inspector, Dept. I, Section III, MSW), note re Lewandowski, 21 Mar 1970, both BU 0586/2162, IPN, obt. A. Paczkowski, trans. MG.

91. Col. Zabawa, note re Lewandowski, 21 Mar 1970. Zabawa cited no evidence to support his charge of JL's financial malfeasance in Dar es Salaam. Responding to this allegation, JL suspected that it arose from a technical requirement by the local Barclay's Bank branch in Dar es Salaam that resulted in his temporarily depositing official funds in his personal account before an embassy account was set up—an incident he clarified at the time to MSZ superiors. Regarding the episode in Cairo, JL explained that this stemmed from lessons in Arabic (not English, as the MSW memo states) that he was taking from an Armenian teacher, who suddenly cut off his work with the embassy and complained to JL that he was being pressured to engage in espionage activities; JL recalled asking an embassy security officer to lay off the tutor but now infers that this also cast suspicion on him. JL interview, Warsaw, 10 May 2011.

92. JL interview, Warsaw, 10 May 2011; NYT, 2, 3, and 4 Nov 1970, 11 May 1971, and 13 Jun 1971.

93. See documents in JL's MSW file, esp. information from MSW employee, Cairo, to Sławkowski, 18 Mar 1973; [signature illegible], inspector of Section III, Dept. 1, MSW, memcon with Stanislaw Pawliszewski ("a former counselor" at Poland's embassy in Cairo, now in the MSZ American Affairs Department), 9 May 1973; and Section II, MSW "Official Note" re JL, 10 May 1973; all BU 0586/2162, IPN, obt. A. Paczkowski, trans. MG.

94. JL interview, Warsaw, 4 Feb 2008; Vinogradov claim: PE/Cairo (JL) to PFM, 7 Oct 1973, AMSZ.

95. NYT, 17 Nov 1982.

96. NYT, 16 Nov 1982; NYT, 17 Nov 1982.

97. NYT, 26 Oct 1984.

98. It was their last meeting; PVD retired in 1987 after thirty-two years as prime minister; he died in 2000 at the age of ninety-four.

99. JM, "Polish Secret Peace Initiatives in Vietnam."

100. SDVW:NVPP, 213.

101. In 1990, two ex–DRV Foreign Ministry aides using closed files had published a Vietnamese-language account of pre-Paris initiatives (including Marigold) to open U.S.-DRV talks; however, it was intended for internal circulation and only slowly seeped out to foreign scholars. LVL/NAV, Before Paris.

102. NDP interview, Hanoi, 8 Jun 1999; NDP, "The 'Marigold' Drive." NDP died in 2010.

103. RSM to LBJ, 9 Mar 1967, and HCL, memo of talk with RSM, 1 July 1968, both cited above.

104. RSM omitted Marigold from the "missed opportunities"; see RSM, James G. Blight, and Robert K. Brigham with Thomas J. Biersteker and Col. Herbert Y. Schandler, Argument Without End: In Search of Answers to the Vietnam Tragedy (New York: PublicAffairs, 1999).

105. CLC, In the Shadows of History: Fifty Years Behind the Scenes of Cold War Diplomacy (Amherst, N.Y.: Prometheus Books, 2005), 247–48. CLC died in 2005.

106. JL saw his children become successful adults as they navigated Poland's postcommunist transition. Like Daniela D'Orlandi, Krysztof followed his father into the diplomatic corps, working on Southeastern Europe, and was posted to the Polish embassies in Athens, where he had learned Greek as a child, and Ankara. In 2006, JL proudly displayed a cellphone photograph of Joanna, in her early thirties, a Motorola employee, and five years later he and Wanda eagerly anticipated their first grandchild.

107. Eight years later—just past his eightieth birthday, weakened by a bout with cancer yet still clear-minded and resolute, and living quietly with Wanda in their apartment in southern Warsaw decorated with Asian, African, and Middle Eastern souvenirs of his diplomatic ca-

reer—JL still adhered to these views, convinced that a great opportunity had been wasted. JL interviews, Warsaw, 10–11 May 2011.

108. MP, "General Vo Nguyen Giap and the Mysterious Evolution of the Plan for the 1968 Tet Offensive," 24.

109. Logevall, "Vietnam and the Question of What Might Have Been," in *Kennedy: The New Frontier Revisited,* edited by Mark J. White (New York: New York University Press, 1998), 19–62; Fredrik Logevall, *Choosing War: The Lost Chance for Peace and the Escalation of War in Vietnam* (Berkeley: University of California Press, 1999), 395–413.

110. Herring in *SDVW:NVPP,* 213.

111. Herring, *LBJ and Vietnam,* 105–6.

112. Deptel 98754 (Katzenbach) to American Embassy, Warsaw (JAG), 7 Dec 1966, box 147, NSF:CO:VN, LBJL.

113. NDP interview, Hanoi, 8 Jun 1999; NDP, "The 'Marigold' Drive."

114. Halberstam telephone interview, New York, 28 Mar 2005.

115. Brzezinski telephone interview, Washington, 1 Apr 2011.

116. Certainly the Joint Chiefs of Staff and Westmoreland would have advanced such arguments, but they were out of the Marigold loop and it is not clear when they would have been cut in.

117. PE/Hanoi (JL) to PFM (AR), sz. 15133, 28 Nov 1966, AMSZ, trans. LG.

118. PE/Hanoi (JL) to PFM (JM), sz. 15023, 25 Nov 1966, ibid.

Selected Bibliography

Government and Communist Party Archives and Collections

Note: Archives and collections researched only by mail, email, and/or with the help of colleagues are indicated by an asterisk.

Archiwum Akt Nowych [Archive of Modern Acts], Warsaw.
Archiv Ministerstvo Zaharanichnich Vetsi [Archive of the Ministry of Foreign Affairs], Prague.*
Archivio Storico Diplomatico, Ministero degli Affari Esteri [Ministry of Foreign Affairs], Rome.
Archiwum Ministerstwa Spraw Zagranicznych [Archive of the Ministry of Foreign Affairs], Warsaw.
Arkhiv Vneshnei Politiki Rossiskoy Federatsii [Archive of Foreign Policy, Russian Federation], Moscow.
Centre des Archives Diplomatiques, Nantes, France.
Communist Party of Italy records, Fondazione Gramsci, Rome.
Declassified Documents Reference Service.
Dutch Ministry of Foreign Affairs archives, The Hague.*
Instytut Pamięci Narodowej [IPN; Institute of National Remembrance], Warsaw.*
Japanese Foreign Ministry archives, Tokyo.*
Lyndon B. Johnson Library, Austin (National Security Files, oral histories, tape recordings, and other collections).
John F. Kennedy Library, Boston (National Security Files and other collections).
Library and Archives Canada, Ottawa.
Magyar Orszagos Levaltar [Hungarian National Archives], Budapest.
Ministère des Affaires Étrangères Français [Ministry of Foreign Affairs of France] archives, Paris.
Národní Archiv [Czech National Archives], Prague.
National Archives of Australia, Canberra.*
Richard M. Nixon Presidential Materials, College Park, Maryland (National Security Files and other collections).
Riksarkivet [Swedish National Archives], Stockholm.*
Rossiskiy Gosudarstveniy Arkhiv Noveyshey Istorii [Russian State Archive of Contemporary History], Moscow.

Stiftung der Parteien und Massenorganisationen der ehemaligen DDR im Bundesarchiv [SAPMO-BArch], Berlin.*
Undenrigsministeriet [Danish Foreign Ministry] archives, Copenhagen.*
United Nations Archives, New York City.
U.S. National Archives, Washington.
U.S. National Archives II, College Park, Maryland (mostly Record Group 59, State Department records).

Collections of Private and Personal Papers

Note: Collections researched only by mail, email, and/or with the help of colleagues are indicated by an asterisk.

Associated Press Archives, New York City.*
George W. Ball Papers, Seeley G. Mudd Library, Princeton University, Princeton, N.J.
Francis M. Bator Papers, Lyndon B. Johnson Library, Austin.
Henry Brandon Papers, Library of Congress, Washington.
George Brown Papers, The U.K. National Archives, Kew Gardens, London.
David K. E. Bruce Papers, Virginia Historical Society, Richmond.*
Ralph J. Bunche Papers, Charles E. Young Research Library, University of California, Los Angeles.*
McGeorge Bundy Papers, John F. Kennedy Library, Boston.
William P. Bundy Papers, Seeley G. Mudd Library, Princeton University, Princeton, N.J.
M. C. Chagla Papers, Nehru Memorial Museum and Library, New Delhi.
George Christian Office Files, Lyndon B. Johnson Library, Austin.
Clark Clifford Papers, Library of Congress, Washington.
Chester L. Cooper Papers, courtesy of Susan Cooper.
Norman Cousins Papers, Charles E. Young Research Library, University of California, Los Angeles.*
Richard Dudman Papers, Library of Congress, Washington.
Robert H. Estabrook Papers, John F. Kennedy Library, Boston.
Robert H. Estabrook Papers, Wisconsin Historical Society, Madison.
Bernard B. Fall Papers, John F. Kennedy Library, Boston.
Amintore Fanfani Papers and Diaries, Archivio Storico del Senato della Repubblica, Rome.
Foreign Affairs Oral History Collection of the Association for Diplomatic Studies and Training. Library of Congress Web site.
J. Williams Fulbright Papers, University of Arkansas Libraries, Fayetteville.
John Kenneth Galbraith Papers, John F. Kennedy Library, Boston.
Arthur M. Goldberg Papers, Library of Congress, Washington.
John A. Gronouski Papers, Wisconsin Historical Society, Madison.
W. Averell Harriman Papers, Library of Congress, Washington.
Alden Hatch Papers, Smathers Library, University of Florida, Gainesville.*
John M. Hightower Papers, Wisconsin Historical Society, Madison.
Nicholas Katzenbach Papers, John F. Kennedy Library, Boston.
T. N. Kaul Papers, Nehru Memorial Museum and Library, New Delhi.
Robert F. Kennedy Papers, John F. Kennedy Library, Boston.
Robert E. Kintner Office Files, Lyndon B. Johnson Library, Austin.
Henry Cabot Lodge Jr. Papers, Massachusetts Historical Society, Boston.
Stuart H. Loory Papers, American Heritage Center, University of Wyoming, Laramie.
Carl Marcy Papers, U.S. National Archives, Washington.
Paul Martin Papers, National Archives of Canada, Ottawa.
Robert S. McNamara Papers, Lyndon B. Johnson Library, Austin.
Jerzy Michałowski Papers, courtesy of Stefan Michałowski.
Bill D. Moyers Office Files, Lyndon B. Johnson Library, Austin.
National Security Archive, Washington (various collections).
Pulitzer Prize Committee Archives, Columbia University, New York City.*

James B. Reston Papers, University of Illinois, Urbana-Champaign.*
Walt W. Rostow Papers, Lyndon B. Johnson Library, Austin.
Dean Rusk Papers, Lyndon B. Johnson Library, Austin.
Harrison E. Salisbury Papers, Rare Book and Manuscript Library, Columbia University, New York City.
Arthur M. Schlesinger Jr. Papers, John F. Kennedy Library, Boston.
David Schoenbrun Papers, Wisconsin Historical Society, Madison.
Neil Sheehan Papers, Library of Congress, Washington.
Hedrick Smith Papers, Library of Congress, Washington.
François Sully Papers, Joseph B. Healey Library, University of Massachusetts, Boston.
James A. Wechsler Papers, Wisconsin Historical Center, Madison.
William C. Westmoreland Papers, Center for Military History, Fort McNair, National Defense University, Washington.
J. Russell Wiggins Papers, Folger Library, University of Maine, Orono.*
Kenneth T. Young Papers, Houghton Library, Harvard University, Cambridge, Massachusetts.*

Interviews

Note: Conversations conducted only by telephone are indicated by an asterisk.

Francis M. Bator, 2007.*
Zbigniew Brzezinski, 2011.*
Chester L. Cooper, Hanoi, 1997; Washington, December 2004 and December 2005; Saint Simons Island, Georgia, April 2005.
Daniel I. Davidson, Washington, May 2008; and telephone interviews, 2008.
Colette D'Orlandi, Paris, May 2008.
Daniel Ellsberg, 2003.*
Robert H. Estabrook, 2003 and 2007.*
David W. Forden, February 2008.*
Leslie H. Gelb, New York City, June 2003.
Jerry S. Grafstein, New York City, October 2007.
Mary Gronouski, 2003.*
David Halberstam, 2005.*
Thomas L. Hughes, Washington, June 2007.
Paolo Janni, Washington, September 2006.
Herbert and Joy Kaiser, 2007.*
Nicholas Katzenbach, Princeton, N.J., April 2005.
David Kraslow, 2003 and 2011.*
Janusz Lewandowski, Warsaw, June and November 2003; October 2006; February 2008; and May 2011; and various telephone interviews, 2003–11.
George Cabot Lodge, 2007.*
Henry Sears Lodge, Beverly, Massachusetts, June 2007.
Stuart H. Loory, Warsaw, May 2011; and telephone interviews, 2003 and 2011.
Luu doan Huynh, Hanoi, 1995, 1997 1999; Washington, 2005; Philadelphia, 2005; and Paris, 2008.
Piotr Michałowski, 2003 and 2008.*
Stefan Michałowski, Washington, December 2010; and telephone interviews, 2009.
Bill Moyers, Saint Simons Island, Georgia, April 2005.
Nguyen Dinh Phuong, Hanoi, June 1999.
Daniel Passent, 2004.*
Blair Seaborn, 2007 and 2011.*
Neil Sheehan, 2005.*
Mario Sica, Rome, February 2006; and Trento, December 2006.
W. R. Smyser, Washington, June 2004.

Published Works

Note: Rather than list every book I consulted on the Vietnam War and the Cold War, I have only listed works which were particularly useful in exploring the diplomatic and other aspects covered in the present work.

Compilations of Documents and Official Reports

Commission des Archives Diplomatiques, Ministère des Étrangères. *Documents Diplomatiques Français,* 1966 tome II (1 juin–31 décembre). Brussels: P. I. E. Peter Lang, 2006.

——. *Documents Diplomatiques Français,* 1967 tome I (1 janvier–1 juillet). Brussels: P. I. E. Peter Lang, 2008.

Herring, George C., ed. *The Secret Diplomacy of the Vietnam War: The Negotiating Volumes of the Pentagon Papers,* Austin: University of Texas Press, 1983.

Joint Chiefs of Staff. *The History of the Joint Chiefs of Staff: The Joint Chiefs of Staff and the War in Vietnam, 1960–1968.* Joint Secretariat, Historical Division, 1970. Copy in National Security Archive, Washington, D.C.

Michałowski, Jerzy. *Polskie tajne inicjatywy pokojowe w Wietnamie* [Polish secret peace initiatives in Vietnam], courtesy of Stefan Michałowski; translation by L. W. Gluchowski.

Paczkowski, Andrzej, ed. *Tajne dokumenty: Biura Politycznego PRL-ZSRR, 1956–1970.* London: Aneks, 1998.

The Pentagon Papers: The Defense Department History of United States Decisionmaking on Vietnam —The Senator Gravel Edition, vol. IV. Boston: Beacon Press, 1971.

Project CHECO Report: Rolling Thunder, July 1965–December 1966. Headquarters Pacific Air Forces, San Francisco, Directorate, Tactical Evaluation, CHECO Division. Prepared by Wesley R. C. Melyan, Lee Bonetti, and S.E. Asia Team, n.d. Originally classified Top Secret/NOFORN, accessed through Virtual Vietnam Archive, Texas Tech University, record 98276, at http://star .vietnam.ttu.edu.

Senate Foreign Relations Committee. *Executive Sessions of the Senate Foreign Relations Committee together with Joint Sessions with the Senate Armed Services Committee (Historical Series),* vol. XIX, 90th Congress, 1st Session, 1967, made public 2007 Washington, D.C.: U.S. Government Printing Office, 2006.

Tran Tinh, chief ed. *Van Kien Dang, Toan Tap, 28, 1967* [Collected Party Documents, Vol. 28, 1967]. Hanoi: Nha Xuat Ban Chinh Tri Quoc Gia, 2003.

U.S. Department of State. *Foreign Relations of the United States.* Washington, D.C.: U.S. Government Printing Office, various years and volumes.

Westad, Odd Arne, Chen Jian, Stein Tønnesson, Nguyen Vu Tung, and James G. Hershberg, eds. *77 Conversations between Chinese and Foreign Leaders on the Wars in Indochina, 1964–1977.* Cold War International History Project Working Paper 22. Washington, D.C.: Woodrow Wilson International Center for Scholars, 1998.

Memoirs and Personal Recollections of Officials

Brown, George. *In My Way* (New York: St. Martin's Press, 1971),

Chubb, A. G. *Chubb's Folly: There Be Dragons Here.* Saigon, 1966–67. Self-published diary ("a day-to-day account of the trials and tribulations of a Canadian Army Officer serving in Vietnam during the period September 1966–September 1967 to include some comments and observations on people and events"), courtesy of Fort Frontenac Library, Kingston, Ontario.

Cooper, Chester L. *In the Shadows of History: Fifty Years behind the Scenes of Cold War Diplomacy.* Amherst, N.Y.: Prometheus Books, 2005.

———. *The Lost Crusade: America in Vietnam.* New York: Dodd, Mead, 1970.

D'Orlandi, Giovanni. *Diario Vietnamita, 1962–1968,* with an introduction by Giulio Andreotti and preface by Roberto Rotondo. Rome: 30Giorni, 2006.

Johnson, Lyndon B. *The Vantage Point: Perspectives of the Presidency, 1963–1969.* New York: Holt, Rinehart & Winston, 1971.

Katzenbach, Nicholas. *Some of It Was Fun: Working with RFK and LBJ.* New York: W. W. Norton, 2008.

Kissinger, Henry A. *Ending the Vietnam War* (New York: Simon & Schuster, 2003)

———. *White House Years.* Boston: Little, Brown, 1979.

Lodge, Henry Cabot. *As It Was: An Inside View of Politics and Power in the '50s and '60s.* New York: W. W. Norton, 1976.

Maneli, Mieczyslaw. *War of the Vanquished.* New York: Harper & Row, 1971.

Martin, Paul. *A Very Public Life; Volume II: So Many Worlds.* Toronto: Deneau, 1985.

McNamara, Robert S., with Brian VanDeMark. *In Retrospect: The Tragedy and Lessons of Vietnam.* New York: Times Books, 1995.

Ronning, Chester. *A Memoir of China in Revolution: From the Boxer Rebellion to the People's Republic.* New York: Pantheon, 1974.

Rusk, Dean. *As I Saw It,* edited by Daniel S. Papp. New York: W. W. Norton, 1990.

Secondary Accounts

Bator, Francis M. "No Good Choices: LBJ and Vietnam/Great Society Connection." *Diplomatic History* 32, no. 3 (June 2008): 355–59.

Brandon, Henry. *Anatomy of Error.* Boston: Gambit, 1969.

Brigham, Robert K., and George C. Herring. "The PENNSYLVANIA Peace Initiative, June–October, 1967." In *The Search for Peace in Vietnam, 1964–1968,* edited by Lloyd C. Gardner and Ted Gittinger. College Station: Texas A&M University Press, 2004.

Burchett, George, and Nick Shimmin, eds. *Memoirs of a Rebel Journalist: The Autobiography of Wilfred Burchett.* Sydney: University of New South Wales Press, 2005.

Burchett, Wilfred G. *At the Barricades: Forty Years on the Cutting Edge of History.* New York: Times Books, 1981.

Cousins, Norman. "How the U.S. Spurned Three Chances for Peace in Vietnam." *Look,* July 29, 1969, 45–48.

Dallek, Robert. *Flawed Giant: Lyndon Johnson and His Times, 1961–1973.* New York: Oxford University Press, 1998.

Duiker, William J. *Ho Chi Minh: A Life.* New York: Hyperion, 2000.

Ellis, Sylvia. *Britain, America, and the Vietnam War.* Westport, Conn.: Praeger, 2004.

Estabrook, Robert H. *Never Dull: From Washington Editor and Foreign Correspondent to Country Publisher.* Lanham, Md.: Hamilton Books, 2005.

Fitzgerald, Frances. *Fire in the Lake: The Vietnamese and the Americans in Vietnam.* Boston: Little, Brown, 1972.

Gaiduk, Ilya V. "Peacemaking or Troubleshooting: The Soviet Role in Peace Initiatives during the Vietnam War." In *The Search for Peace in Vietnam, 1964–1968,* edited by Lloyd C. Gardner and Ted Gittinger. College Station: Texas A&M University Press, 2004.

———. *The Soviet Union and the Vietnam War.* Chicago: Ivan R. Dee, 1996.

Gardner, Lloyd C., and Ted Gittinger, eds. *The Search for Peace in Vietnam, 1964–1968.* College Station: Texas A&M University Press, 2004.

Gibbons, William Conrad. *The U.S. Government and the Vietnam War: Executive Roles and Relationships, Part IV: July 1965–January 1968.* Princeton, N.J.: Princeton University Press, 1995.

Gnoinska, Malgorzata. "Poland and the Cold War in East and Southeast Asia, 1949–1965." PhD dissertation, George Washington University, 2009.

———. *Poland and Vietnam, 1963: New Evidence on Communist Diplomacy and the "Maneli Affair."* Cold War International History Project Working Paper 45. Washington, D.C.: Woodrow Wilson International Center for Scholars, 2005.

Goodman, Allan E. *The Lost Peace.* Stanford, Calif.: Hoover Institution Press, 1978.

Goodwin, Doris Kearns. *Lyndon Johnson and the American Dream.* New York: St. Martin's Press, 1976.

Halberstam, David. *The Best and the Brightest.* New York: Random House, 1972.

———. *The Powers That Be.* New York: Alfred A. Knopf, 1979.

Hatch, Alden. *The Lodges of Massachusetts*. New York: Hawthorn Books, 1973.

Herring, George C. *America's Longest War: The United States and Vietnam 1950–1975*, 4th ed. New York: McGraw-Hill, 2001.

———. *LBJ and Vietnam: A Different Kind of War*. Austin: University of Texas Press, 1994.

Hershberg, James G. "'A Half-Hearted Overture': Czechoslovakia, Kissinger, and Vietnam, Autumn, 1966." In *The Search for Peace in Vietnam, 1964–1968*, edited by Lloyd C. Gardner and Ted Gittinger. College Station: Texas A&M University Press, 2004.

———. "Peace Probes and the Bombing Pause: Hungarian and Polish Diplomacy during the Vietnam War, December 1965–January 1966." *Journal of Cold War Studies* 5, no. 2 (Spring 2003): 32–67.

———. *Who Murdered "Marigold"? New Evidence on the Mysterious Failure of Poland's Secret Initiative to Start U.S.-North Vietnamese Peace Talks, 1966*. Cold War International History Project Working Paper 27. Washington, D.C.: Woodrow Wilson International Center for Scholars, 2000.

Jian, Chen. *Mao's China and the Cold War*. Chapel Hill: University of North Carolina Press, 2001.

Kraslow, David, and Stuart H. Loory. *The Secret Search for Peace in Vietnam*. New York: Random House, 1968.

Lawrence, Mark Atwood. "Mission Intolerable: Harrison Salisbury's Trip to Hanoi and the Limits of Dissent against the Vietnam War." *Pacific Historical Review* 75, no. 3 (August 2006): 429–59.

———. *The Vietnam War: A Concise International History*. New York: Oxford University Press, 2010.

Logevall, Fredrik. "The ASPEN Channel and the Problem of the Bombing." In *The Search for Peace in Vietnam, 1964–1968*, edited by Lloyd C. Gardner and Ted Gittinger. College Station: Texas A&M University Press, 2004.

———. *Choosing War: The Lost Chance for Peace and the Escalation of War in Vietnam*. Berkeley: University of California Press, 1999.

———. "Vietnam and the Question of What Might Have Been." In *Kennedy: The New Frontier Revisited*, edited by Mark J. White. New York: New York University Press, 1998.

Luthi, Lorenz M. *The Sino-Soviet Split: Cold War in the Communist World*. Princeton, N.J.: Princeton University Press, 2008.

Luu Van Loi. *Fifty Years of Vietnamese Diplomacy 1945–1995 (Volume I: 1945–1975)*. Hanoi: Gioi Publishers, 2000.

Luu Van Loi and Nguyen Anh Vu. *Tiep xuc bi mat Viet Nam–Hoa Ky truoc Hoi nghi Pa-ri* [Secret Interactions between Vietnam–U.S. Before Paris Negotiations]. Hanoi: Vien Quan He Quoc Te [Institute of International Relations], 2002; orig. pub. 1990.

Maraniss, David. *They Marched into Sunlight: War and Peace Vietnam and America October 1967*. New York: Simon & Schuster, 2003.

McNamara, Robert S.. James G. Blight, and Robert K. Brigham, with Thomas J. Biersteker and Herbert Y. Schandler. *Argument Without End: In Search of Answers to the Vietnam Tragedy*. New York: PublicAffairs, 1999.

Michałowski, Jerzy, prepared by Stefan Michałowski. "Polish Secret Peace Initiatives in Vietnam." *Cold War International History Project Bulletin*, nos. 6–7 (Winter 1995–96): 241, 258–59.

Miller, William J. *Henry Cabot Lodge: A Biography*. New York: Heineman, 1967.

Nguyen, Lien-Hang T. "The War Politburo: North Vietnam's Diplomatic Road to the Tet Offensive." *Journal of Vietnamese Studies* 1, nos. 1–2 (2006): 4–58.

Nuti, Leopoldo. "The Center-Left Government in Italy and the Escalation of the Vietnam War." In *America, the Vietnam War, and the World: Comparative and International Perspectives*, edited by Andreas W. Daum, Lloyd C. Gardner, and Wilfried Mausbach. Washington, D.C.: German Historical Institute, 2003.

Olsen, Mari. *Soviet-Vietnam Relations and the Role of China, 1949–64: Changing Alliances*. London: Routledge, 2006.

Prados, John. *Vietnam: The History of an Unwinnable War 1945–1975*. Lawrence: University Press of Kansas, 2009.

Preston, Andrew. "Balancing War and Peace: Canadian Diplomacy and the Vietnam War, 1961–1965." *Diplomatic History* 27, no. 1 (January 2003): 73–111.

———. "Missions Impossible: Canadian Secret Diplomacy and the Quest for Peace in Vietnam." In *The Search for Peace in Vietnam, 1964–1968,* edited by Lloyd C. Gardner and Ted Gittinger. College Station: Texas A&M University Press, 2004.

———. *The War Council: McGeorge Bundy, the NSC, and Vietnam.* Cambridge, Mass.: Harvard University Press, 2006.

Pribbenow, Merle L., II. "General Vo Nguyen Giap and the Mysterious Evolution of the Plan for the 1968 Tet Offensive." *Journal of Vietnamese Studies* 3 (Summer 2008): 1–33.

Quinn-Judge, Sophie. "The Ideological Debate in the DRV and the Significance of the Anti-Party Affair, 1967–68." *Cold War History* 5, no. 4 (November 2005): 479–500.

Radchenko, Sergey. *Two Suns in the Heavens: The Sino-Soviet Struggle for Supremacy, 1962–1967.* Washington, D.C., and Stanford, Calif.: Woodrow Wilson Center Press and Stanford University Press, 2009.

Radványi, János. *Delusion and Reality: Gambits, Hoaxes, & Diplomatic One-Upmanship in Vietnam.* South Bend, Ind.: Gateway Editions, 1978.

Roberts, Priscilla, ed. *Behind the Bamboo Curtain: China, Vietnam, and the Cold War.* Washington, D.C., and Stanford, Calif.: Woodrow Wilson Center Press and Stanford University Press, 2006.

Ross, Douglas A. *In the Interests of Peace: Canada and Vietnam 1954–1973.* Toronto: University of Toronto Press, 1981.

Salisbury, Harrison E. *Behind the Lines: Hanoi, December 23, 1966–January 7, 1967.* New York: Harper & Row, 1967.

———. *A Time of Change: A Reporter's Tale of Our Time.* New York: Harper & Row, 1988.

Sica, Mario. *Marigold non fiorì: Il contributo italiano alla pace in Vietnam.* Florence: Ponte alle Grazie, 1991.

Smith, R. B. *An International History of the Vietnam War, Volume III: The Making of a Limited War, 1965–66.* London: Macmillan, 1991.

Staaveren, Jacob Van. *Gradual Failure: The Air War Over North Vietnam, 1965–1966.* Washington, D.C.: Air Force History and Museum Programs, 2002.

Steininger, Rolf. "'The Americans Are in a Hopeless Position': Great Britain and the War in Vietnam." *Diplomacy and Statecraft* 7 (1996): 404–35.

Szoke, Zoltan. "Delusion or Reality? Secret Hungarian Diplomacy during the Vietnam War." *Journal of Cold War Studies* 12, no. 4 (Fall 2010): 119–80.

Taylor, Charles. *Snow Job: Canada, the United States, and Vietnam (1954 to 1973).* Toronto: House of Anansi Press, 1974.

Thakur, Ramesh Chandra. *Peacekeeping in Vietnam: Canada, India, Poland, and the International Commission.* Edmonton: University of Alberta Press, 1984.

Thies, Wallace J. *When Governments Collide: Coercion and Diplomacy in the Vietnam Conflict, 1964–1968.* Berkeley: University of California Press, 1980.

Zhai, Qiang. *China and the Vietnamese Wars, 1950–1975.* Chapel Hill: University of North Carolina Press, 2000.

About the Author

James G. Hershberg is Associate Professor of History and International Affairs at George Washington University and former Director of the Cold War International History Project at the Woodrow Wilson International Center for Scholars. His first book, *James B. Conant: Harvard to Hiroshima and the Making of the Nuclear Age* (Alfred A. Knopf, 1993; Stanford University Press, 1995), was awarded the Bernath Prize by the Society for Historians of American Foreign Relations, and his articles on Cold War and nuclear history have appeared in diverse scholarly and popular publications. He lives in Washington, D.C., with his wife, Annie; son, Gabriel; and daughter, Vera.

Index

(continued from p. ii)

Economic Cold War
America's Embargo against China and the Sino-Soviet Alliance, 1949–1963
By Shu Guang Zhang

Brothers in Arms
The Rise and Fall of the Sino-Soviet Alliance, 1945–1963
Edited by Odd Arne Westad